Elements of Econometrics

Macmillan Series in Economics
Lawrence R. Klein, Consulting Editor

Jan Kmenta

Professor of Economics
Michigan State University

Elements of Econometrics

Macmillan Publishing Co., Inc.
NEW YORK
Collier Macmillan Publishers
LONDON

Printed in the United States of America

MACMILLAN PUBLISHING CO., INC.
866 Third Avenue, New York, New York 10022

Collier Macmillan Canada, Ltd.

Library of Congress catalog card number: 70–97762

PRINTING 18 YEAR 456

ISBN 0-02-365060-5

To Joan

Preface

This book has been written for economists—that is, for people who should understand and may want to use modern econometric techniques—rather than for prospective econometricians who plan to participate in the development and refinement of methods. The contents are designed to cover a one-year course in introductory econometrics offered to first-year economics graduate students in many universities. However, the book may also serve as a text for a course in economic or business statistics for advanced undergraduates, or as a reference book for economists of all specializations who want to keep up with current applied economic research.

Both students and teachers of economics face an increasing need for familiarity with quantitative methods in order to understand current economic literature and to be effective in their own research efforts. I have tried to cover most of the statistical and econometric methods that modern economists might need. In my opinion there appears to be a need for a book which will give the economist as much econometrics as possible without making excessive demands on his mathematical skills. I have found, from my experience with the graduate students at the University of Wisconsin and at Michigan State University, that it is perfectly possible to start at a low level of statistical knowledge and to move rather rapidly to quite sophisticated econometric topics. This, of course, requires a lot of effort on the part of the students as well as on the part of the teacher. I have been fortunate to have had students who were strongly motivated and who derived a lot of pleasure out of being able to do things which only two weeks earlier appeared to be beyond reach. As for the work of the teacher, I think that it is his obligation to emphasize at all times complete understanding rather than a cookbook type of learning, and to spare no effort at making everything as clear as possible. This is the spirit in which this book has been written.

Every textbook writer owes it to his readers to spell out the technical background which he thinks is necessary if the book is to be reasonably well understood. In my case, I have assumed what is coming to be the usual standard for an entering economics graduate student, namely a knowledge of intermediate economic theory, of college algebra and basic calculus, and of some basic descriptive statistics. Because the book is carefully planned to develop the foundations of statistics in a gradual way, these prerequisites will be sufficient for all the material covered in the text except for the last two chapters which require some matrix algebra. A convenient survey of what is needed is provided in Appendix B.

As suggested earlier, the basic philosophy underlying this book is to make everything as simple and clear as possible. All methods are explained and discussed within the simplest framework, and generalizations are presented as logical extensions of the simple cases. This, of course, reduces to a minimum the use of mathematics and particularly of matrix algebra. It represents a conscious and laborious effort on my part. Throughout the book I have tried to present all relevant work from econometric literature in the simplest and clearest form while, at the same time, hopefully avoiding the danger of over-simplification. I hope that this will make the subject aesthetically pleasing, more accessible, and will make the application of it easier. While every attempt has been made to preserve a relatively high degree of rigor, every conflict between rigor and clarity of exposition or understanding was resolved in favor of the latter.

The book consists of two parts. Part One, which contains six chapters, covers the elements of the theory of statistics, while Part Two contains seven chapters on various topics of regression analysis and simultaneous equation problems. The first part should provide the students with a good understanding of the process of scientific generalization from incomplete information. The emphasis is on explaining the basic ideas rather than on presenting formulas and rules to be applied. In line with this, more than usual attention is paid to hypothesis testing and parameter estimation. Part One is a prerequisite for Part Two, but it might also be used as a self-contained unit. Part Two of the book contains a thorough exposition of all basic econometric methods, and includes some of the most recent developments in several areas. While many topics represent standard parts of econometrics texts, several other topics are treated much more extensively than is usually the case. In particular, a great deal of attention is given to models involving binary variables, to nonlinear and distributed lag models, to restricted estimation, and to generalized linear regression.

Since the book has already exceeded its originally intended length by a fair amount, there are a few topics which are not included. One of these is spectral analysis which, while providing an interesting new technique, has not yet been closely integrated with economic theory, and is fairly unwieldy for a non-specialist to manipulate. Further, a discussion of the Bayesian approach to statistics would constitute another worthwhile topic (some of my friends would say *the* worthwhile topic), but to do it justice would require considerable space. A third topic regretfully left out is econometric model simulation. The economist who is interested in these topics may consult more specialized texts. The aim of the present book is to provide him with the basic tools which would make such consultation more easy and more efficient.

There are several direct and less direct acknowledgments that should be made in connection with this book. My long-standing thanks are due to Arthur Goldberger whose excellence in teaching and devotion to research—and clarity in both—have inspired much of the spirit of my work. Several of the topics that I treat in the book have been developed by Arnold Zellner. I owe him thanks not only on this count, but mainly because he has been always most gracious in discussing problems in econometrics and in giving me the benefit of his exceptional insights. I have also received editorial help and encouragement from Lawrence Klein who kindly read the entire manuscript and offered many useful comments and suggestions. Unfortunately, I was not able to incorporate all of them into the book because of limitations of time and space, but the book would undoubtedly have been improved if all of the suggestions were followed up. Indirect but nevertheless important help has been given to me by Robert Basmann and Karl Brunner who made me painfully aware of many methodological shortcomings, and by James Ramsey whose technical knowledge and imaginative insights have been made constantly available to me. Specific thanks are due to Roy Gilbert for aiding me with the computer, to Jeffrey Roth for verifying the examples, and to William Ruble for his assistance with the simultaneous equation programs. Mrs. Elisabeth Belfer of The Macmillan Company deserves special commendation for her painstaking assistance at the proofreading stage. Of course, the largest thanks go to my wife who has served as a most patient proofreader as well as a caretaker of all family affairs that would otherwise intrude upon my work.

Finally, I would like to express my appreciation and indebtedness to Arnold Zellner and Martin Geisel for permission to cite unpublished work, and to J. Zubrzycki for permission to use the data in the examples of Section 9–2. In addition, I am indebted to the Literary Executor of the late Sir Ronald Fisher, F.R.S., and to Oliver & Boyd Ltd., Edinburgh, for their permission to reprint Table D–2 from their book *Statistical Methods for Research Workers*; to Professor E. S. Pearson and the *Biometrika* trustees for permission to reproduce the material in Tables D–3, D–4, and D–5; and to the Rand Corporation for permission to reproduce the material in Table D–6 from their book *A Million Random Digits and One Hundred Thousand Deviates*. The publication of the material in Table D–5 was also authorized by Professor J. Durbin and Professor G. S. Watson.

East Lansing J. K.

Contents

Part ONE
Basic Statistical Theory

Part TWO Basic Econometric Theory

Part ONE

Basic Statistical Theory

1 Introduction to Statistical Inference

Until the early part of the nineteenth century, statistics was understood to be concerned with characteristics of the state, particularly those related to political and military institutions. Descriptions of these characteristics were at first mainly in verbal terms, but they gradually became more and more numerical. The change to an increasingly more quantitative character was accompanied by an extension to fields other than those concerned with the affairs of the state. Later advances in probability led to the development of the theory of statistics that permits scientific generalization from incomplete information—in other words, statistical inference.

As a result of this historical development, the subject known as "statistics" consists of two parts, descriptive statistics and statistical inference. Descriptive statistics deals with the collection, organization, and presentation of data, while statistical inference deals with generalizations from a part to the whole. Statistical inference, like any other science, is concerned with the development of methods (statistical theory) as well as with their use (statistical application).

In econometrics we are mainly concerned with statistical inference. Descriptive statistics is relevant only to the extent that measures developed by descriptive statisticians for the purpose of summarizing various characteristics of the data—averages, measures of dispersion, etc.—are also used in statistical inference. The basic difference lies in the fact that in the field of descriptive statistics these measures represent ends in themselves, whereas in statistical inference they are only means in the process of inquiry.

1–1 Basic Concepts of Statistical Inference

Before explaining the nature of statistical inference more specifically, we must introduce a few basic concepts. The most crucial ones are those of a population and of a sample.

A *population* can be defined as the totality of all possible observations on measurements or outcomes. Examples are incomes of all people in a certain country in a specific period of time, national income of a country over a number of periods of time, and all outcomes of repeatedly tossing a coin. A population may be either finite or infinite. A *finite population* is one in which the number of all possible observations is less than infinity. However, the distinction between finite and infinite populations is more subtle than may at first appear. For instance, a series of national income figures for the United States for a number of years, e.g., 1948–1967, represents a finite collection of twenty observations and thus might seem to be a finite population. But this would be a very narrow interpretation of historical events, since it would imply that the twenty measurements of national income were the only possible ones, i.e., that there is only one course that history might have taken. Now there are obviously not many people who would take such an extremely fatalistic view of the world; most people would admit that it was not impossible for some other, even if only slightly different, values of national income to have occurred. This latter view underlies virtually all policy-oriented research in economics and econometrics and will be used throughout this book. Thus a population of national incomes in a given time interval includes not only the actual history represented by the values that were in fact observed but also the potential history consisting of all the values that might have occurred but did not. The population so defined is obviously an infinite one. Similarly, the population of all possible outcomes of coin tosses is also infinite, since the tossing process can generate an infinite number of outcomes, in this case "heads" and "tails." Most of the populations with which we deal in econometrics are infinite.

Related to the concept of a population is the concept of a *sample*, which is a set of measurements or outcomes selected from the population. The selection can be done by the investigator, in which case we can speak of a sampling experiment, or it may happen independently either by design of others or by nature. In the latter case, the investigator is a mere observer, and this situation is particularly frequent in econometrics. While samples from infinite populations can themselves be infinite, the relevance of such samples is at best only a theoretical one. In practice we deal only with finite samples and, regrettably, quite often only very small ones. Since samples are obtained by a selection from a given population, the principle of selection clearly plays an important part in determining the composition of the sample. In econometrics our attention is confined to samples drawn in accordance with some specified chance mechanism. Such samples are called *probability samples*. An important type of probability sample is the *random sample*. In finite populations, the principle of selecting a random sample is that of giving every individual in the population an equal chance of being chosen. In the case of infinite populations, a sample is random if each observation (of a measurement or an outcome) is independent of every other observation. The meaning of *independence* will be given in a rigorous way later; at present it is sufficient to note that two events (which can be either measured or counted) are independent if the occurrence of one in no way influences the occurrence of the other.

Both populations and samples can be described by stating their characteristics. Numerical characteristics of a population are called *parameters*; the characteristics of a sample, given in the form of some summary measure, are called *statistics* (a plural of the word "statistic"). Such characteristics may be, for instance, central tendency of measurements (e.g., the mean or the mode), their dispersion (e.g., standard deviation), or, in the case of qualitative phenomena, the proportion of observations of a given kind. Obviously, the parameters of an infinite population are never observed; the parameters of a finite population could be observed in theory but may be impossible to observe in practice.

From our discussion so far it should be clear that statistics deals with phenomena that can be either measured or counted. With respect to a phenomenon that can be measured, we speak of a *variable*, meaning a homogeneous quantity that can assume different values at different points of observation. If a phenomenon can only be counted but not measured (each observation representing one count), we speak of an *attribute*. Thus an attribute is the presence or absence of a given characteristic. An outcome of an event such as the birth of a child leads to an observation of an attribute of sex (i.e., "male" or "not male"); an outcome of a toss of a die may be classified as a presence or an absence of "1," of "2," and so on. In a way the concept of attribute is redundant because we can, and often do, simply assign the value of 1 to the presence, and 0 to the absence, of a given characteristic. In this case we equate "attribute" with the concept of a *qualitative* or *binary variable*. Another and more colorful name, "dummy variable," has also been used.

The definition of a *variable*, and indeed the name itself, stresses the possibility of variation at different points of observation. On the other hand, a quantity that cannot vary from one observation to another is called a *constant*. (Note that a parameter is also a constant since it does not vary from observation to observation.) If the quantity in question is a variable and not a constant, one may wish to ask about the general source of variation. In particular, it is important to distinguish between those variations that can and those that cannot be fully controlled or manipulated. In the case of a variation that cannot be fully controlled, its existence is due to chance. An obvious example of an uncontrolled variation would be the outcomes of tossing a coin (in the absence of cheating, of course), but many other less obvious instances exist. In fact, as we shall elaborate at length in the rest of this book, most economic variables are always to some extent determined by chance. The variables whose values cannot be fully controlled or determined prior to observation are called *random* or *stochastic variables*; their chief characteristic is that they assume different values (or fall into different value intervals) with some probability other than one. In contrast, a *nonrandom* or *nonstochastic* or *fixed variable* is one that is fully controllable or at least fully predictable. A constant may be regarded as a special case of a fixed variable.

Another important classification of variables is that which distinguishes between continuous and discrete variables. A *continuous variable* is a variable that can assume any value on the numerical axis or a part of it. Typical examples are time and temperature, but income, expenditure, and similar variables can all be classified as continuous. In fact, most economic variables are continuous or at least approximately so. The last qualification is added to take care of such possible objections as those pointing out that money values of less than a dollar (or possibly a cent) are, in fact, not observable. In contrast to a continuous variable, a *discrete variable* is one that can assume only some specific values on the numerical axis. These values are usually (but not always) separated by intervals of equal length. Examples are a number of children in a family, a number of dots on a die after a toss, or any binary variable.

Table 1–1

Number of Children (= Variable)	Number of Families (= Absolute Frequency)	Proportion of Families (= Relative Frequency)
0	4	0.0625
1	12	0.1875
2	20	0.3125
3	16	0.2500
4	8	0.1250
5 and over	4	0.0625
Totals	64	1.0000

The final concept to be introduced at this stage is that of a *distribution.* In the case of a sample we have a frequency distribution, while in the case of a population we speak of a probability distribution. A *frequency distribution* represents an organization of data so as to give the number of observations for each value of the variable (in the case of a discrete variable) or for each interval of values of the variable (in the case of a continuous variable). The number of observations in each class (represented by a point in the case of a discrete variable or by an interval in the case of a continuous variable) is called *absolute frequency.* This can be distinguished from *relative frequency*, which gives the proportion of observations rather than their number for each class. As an example, consider a sample of 64 families being observed with respect to the number of children. The results might be those given in Table 1–1. Another example, this time related to a continuous variable, is given by family income distribution in the United States in 1962 (Table 1–2). Here, absolute frequencies are not shown, and the relative frequencies are stated in percentages rather than in simple proportions. Sample data in the form of a time series, such as national income figures for a number of years, could also be presented in the form of a frequency distribution, although this is usually not done. The fact that different observations are made at different points of time is relevant only to the extent that the population from which the sample was drawn may have changed through time.

In a population the concept corresponding to a sample frequency distribution is known as a *probability distribution.* Consider, for instance, the population of

United States families classified by income received in 1962 as shown in Table 1–2. It is fairly clear that to state that 12.7% of all families received an income of less than \$2000 is equivalent to stating that the probability of selecting (at random) a family with an income of less than \$2000 is 0.127. If the population is infinite, the probabilities can be represented by *limits* of relative frequencies

Table 1–2

Income After Taxes (= Variable)	Percent Consumer Units* (= Relative Frequency)
Under \$2,000	12.7
\$2,000 to \$4,999	31.9
\$5,000 to \$9,999	39.7
\$10,000 and over	15.7
Total	100.0

Source: *Statistical Abstract of the United States, 1965*, p. 341.

* Includes families and unattached individuals (total number = 57,890,000).

(this will be explained more rigorously in Chapter 3). Picturing, then, the probability distribution of one variable as a counterpart of the frequency distribution in a sample, we can see that it is possible to deal with more than one variable at a time. For example, a distribution giving the probability of death at various ages confines itself to one variable—it is an *univariate distribution.* If, however, we tabulate these probabilities separately for each sex, we are considering two variables and have a *bivariate distribution.* A further classification by other characteristics could produce a *multivariate distribution.*

1–2 The Nature of Statistical Inference

Having introduced, however briefly, some of the most important concepts of statistical theory, we are now in a position to describe the nature of statistical inference. As indicated earlier, statistical inference is concerned with generalizations about the population on the basis of information provided by a sample. Such a procedure is, of course, frequent in everyday life: we make generalizations about the temperature of our soup on the basis of the first spoonful, or about the life expectancy of a pair of tennis shoes on the basis of past experience. This is precisely what is done in statistical inference, except that we go about it in a somewhat more scientific way. What makes the application of statistical inference scientific is that we take into account the way in which the sample was selected, and that we express our generalization in specific probability terms. For example, instead of saying that tennis shoes last five years, we specify a range and state the level of probability associated with it.

To sum up, we use a sample to make a judgment about the population from which the sample comes. If the population is infinite, then it can never be observed as a whole and any judgment about it can only come from a sample. But even if the population is a finite one, there may be a good reason for observing only a sample since making observations (as in the case of tasting soup or measuring the lifetime of light bulbs) is destructive or, at best, expensive. Now, in general we are not interested in knowing everything about a population but are concerned with only *some* of its characteristics, which, it may be recalled, we call parameters. The purpose of sampling, and the business of statistical inference, is to make judgments about population parameters on the basis of sample statistics. These judgments are, in fact, guesses endowed with a specific degree of reliability and they can be of two types, one concerned with estimation of a parameter and the other with testing some hypothesis about it. Estimation is done with the help of an *estimator*, which is a formula describing a procedure of guessing the value of a given population parameter; a specific value of an estimator is called an *estimate*. Judgments in the form of *hypothesis testing* involve an a priori assumption about the value of a parameter. If the sample information provides evidence against the hypothesis, we reject it; otherwise, we keep it. The evidence provided by the observations in the sample is, for the purpose of hypothesis testing, summarized in the form of a *test statistic*; this is then used in arriving at a verdict concerning the hypothesis.

A sample provides evidence about the population from which it was drawn. This evidence can be summarized in the form of an estimator when the problem is one of estimation, or in the form of a test statistic when the problem is one of hypothesis testing. In either case we follow some formula into which we substitute the values observed in our sample. The values thus obtained for an estimator and for a test statistic are closely related, as they ought to be, since they draw upon the same source of information, i.e., the sample. In any case, the value of an estimator or of a test statistic represents a guess concerning the relevant population parameter. Now it is obvious that different samples would lead to different guesses. Some will be closer to the truth (e.g., to the true value of the parameter) than others. In reality we have, of course, usually just one sample and therefore only one guess. But it is obviously important for us to know what the guesses might have been had we had different samples. If all possible samples lead to guesses that are always near the truth, any single guess is obviously quite reliable. On the other hand, if all possible samples lead to widely differing guesses, only some of the guesses can be near the truth and no single guess can be trusted much. The third extreme case is one where all possible guesses are similar to each other but far from the true value of the parameter.

1–3 Sampling Distributions

The preceding paragraph suggests that the way to know the reliability of a guess is by knowing the behavior of all guesses that could be made on the basis of all possible samples. We can envision drawing one sample after another, from each sample calculating the value of our guess (say, an estimate of a certain population parameter), and arranging these guesses in the form of a distribution. If we had an infinite number of such samples, the resulting distribution would be called a *sampling distribution.* Consider, for example, the problem of estimating the mean family income in the United States in a given year on the basis of a sample of, say, 100 families. One possibility is to calculate the mean family income in our sample and use it as our estimate of the population mean. Of course, we could use the mode, or the median, or some other measure as our estimator. Suppose we estimate the population mean by using the sample mean. Then we wish to know how reliable this estimator is. One way to find this out would be by drawing an infinite number of such samples, calculating the value of the sample mean from each sample, and arranging these values in the form of a distribution. Note that although the population of all families in the United States is a finite one, the number of samples that we can draw from this population is infinite as long as we allow each family to be included in any sample. Such sampling is called *sampling with replacement.* By studying the resulting sampling distribution, we would know all about the possible behavior of our guess. If we, in fact, knew the characteristics of the population beforehand, then this exercise would serve the function of extending our knowledge about the relationship between the sample and the population mean; this knowledge could then be used in other cases when we are limited to only one sample.

If each family contained in the sample is selected at random, we do not know beforehand what its income is going to be. Thus, in this case family income is a random variable. Furthermore, the *mean* income observed in a sample is also a random variable. This means that the sampling distribution of sample mean (based on an infinite number of samples) is really a probability distribution. This distribution could be either discrete or continuous depending upon whether the population variable is a discrete or a continuous; in our example the sampling distribution is continuous since income is a continuous variable. Of course, the idea is quite general: *a sampling distribution is a probability distribution of an estimator or of a test statistic.*

It is quite obvious that samples of different sizes give different amounts of information about the population from which they are drawn. Therefore, estimators that use all information contained in a sample and are based on samples of different sizes will display different degrees of reliability. To avoid the effects of changed sample size upon the quality of an estimator, any given sampling distribution always refers to samples of the same size. The effects of changing the sample size are best studied by comparing different sampling distributions.

Suppose we are dealing with a population of all possible values of a variable X (e.g., family incomes in a given year) and are interested in estimating a parameter θ (e.g., the mean family income). To estimate this parameter, we use a sample statistic $\hat{\theta}$. In usual terminology, $\hat{\theta}$ is an estimator of θ, while a specific value of $\hat{\theta}$ (obtained from a specific sample) is called an estimate of θ. Incidentally, a common notation is to use plain Greek letters to describe population parameters and to use Greek letters with hats, tildes, etc., to describe estimators. Then if X is a continuous variable (as in the case of family income), the sampling distribution of $\hat{\theta}$ may look something like the distribution in Figure 1–1. As pointed out earlier, this is really a probability distribution; since we do not intend to define and describe probability distributions until Chapter 3, we are not in a position to discuss sampling distributions with any degree of rigor. However, we may gain a better understanding of the concept of a sampling distribution if we view it for the time being simply as a relative frequency distribution compiled from an infinite number of observations, i.e., samples in this case. In Figure 1–1 the relative frequencies of $\hat{\theta}$ are measured along the $f(\hat{\theta})$ axis.

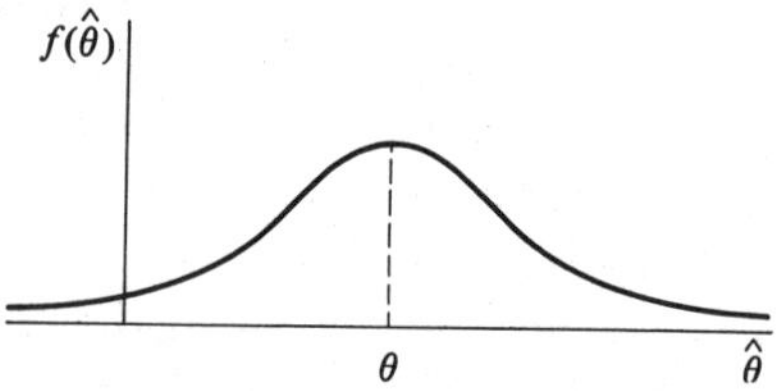

Figure 1–1

A reasonable and generally useful way of judging the quality of a guess is to evaluate the quality of the procedure that produced the guess. Suppose, for example, that a man, who has spent a lot of time learning about horse racing, goes to a race track with his wife, who is completely ignorant of such matters, and in the first race the wife wins her bet whereas the man does not. Then we do not necessarily conclude that the wife's guesses are better in general and that we should bet on the same horse that she does in the next race. Such a conclusion could be reached only after more evidence (i.e., more observations) was gathered and the wife's "system" led to bigger gains (or smaller losses) than that of her husband. Of course, if only one bet—that on the first race, say—was allowed, then there is no question that the wife's guess was better, since it led to a win while her husband lost, but this is obviously a special case of little general interest. In general, the result of any specific act of guessing is considered of little relevance; what is relevant is how often a guessing procedure leads to bad results and how often it leads to good ones. In other words, we need to know about the results of a large number of guesses, each based on the same guessing procedure. This is precisely the information conveyed by a sampling distribution. To compare the quality of guesses we compare the results of the guessing procedures from which these guesses were derived, which means that we compare their sampling distributions.

1–4 Properties of Sampling Distributions

The preceding discussion brings us to the question of what is a good guessing procedure, i.e., a good estimator. Or, to put it slightly differently, we want to know which are the specific features of a sampling distribution that enable us to pass a judgment on a particular estimator. We shall deal with this question quite thoroughly in Chapter 6, but some observations can be made right now. We may start with the simplest case, which is that of a perfect estimator. A perfect estimator is one that is never wrong, i.e., one whose sampling distribution is concentrated entirely in one point, the point that happens to be the true value of the parameter to be estimated. Needless to say, perfect estimators are very rare. One case under which we can have a perfect estimator is that of no variation in the population. In our example on sampling the temperature of a bowl of soup by a spoonful, our guessing would be perfect if the temperature were the same everywhere in the bowl and we used the temperature of the spoonful as an estimate. Normally this would be achieved by a thorough mixing before tasting. In the example on family income, we would have a perfect estimator if all families had the same income and we used the mean of a sample as an estimate of the population mean. Another case that may produce perfect estimation is when the sample is of infinite size. But it should be noted that the existence of either of the two cases does not by itself guarantee perfect estimation results; if a part or all of the sample information is ignored or wrongly used, we may still make mistakes. For instance, if our estimator of mean family income were not the sample mean but the sample mean increased by, say, 10% (perhaps in the belief that people tend to underestimate their incomes), when there was no need for it (people were, in fact, honest about their incomes), then our estimator would not be perfect regardless of the lack of variation in the population or regardless of sample size.

Almost invariably estimators are not perfect but are such that only a small proportion of an estimator's values is at or near the true value of the parameter. This means that we have to be satisfied by lesser achievements; these can be summarized by stating some properties of an estimator that are commonly considered desirable. At this stage we shall only mention the basic idea behind three of these properties; an elaborate and extended discussion will be left for another chapter. Perhaps the best-known desirable property of an estimator is that of *unbiasedness*. An unbiased estimator is one that has a sampling distribution with a mean equal to the parameter to be estimated. A perfect estimator gives a perfect guess every time; an unbiased estimator gives a perfect result only on the average. An unbiased estimator will lead to estimates that are sometimes higher and sometimes lower than the true value of the parameter, but the amount of overstating and understating "averages out" when an infinite number of estimates is made. If the sampling distribution is symmetric, then the fact that an estimator is unbiased implies that half of all possible estimates are higher and half are lower than the value of the parameter. Such a situation (in the case of a continuous estimator) is depicted by Figure 1–1. It should be emphasized that unbiasedness tells us nothing about the distance between the estimates and the value of the parameter, only that all the (positive and negative) distances add up to zero. It is quite possible that an unbiased estimator will never produce an estimate that is, in fact, equal to the value of the parameter. Consider our example on estimating the mean family income by using the mean of a sample. Let us accept the proposition—which we shall prove later—that the sample mean is an unbiased estimator of the population mean. Suppose the population mean family income is \$6573.46; obviously, the probability that a sample mean would be *precisely* the same figure is negligible.

A further important desirable property of an estimator is *efficiency*, a property concerned with the distances of the values of an estimator from the value of the

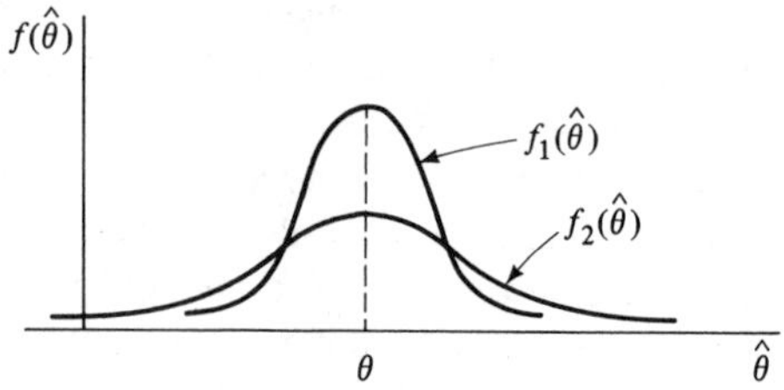

Figure 1–2

parameter. Unfortunately, there is no generally accepted definition of efficiency that would cover all cases. There is, however, a generally accepted definition if we restrict our consideration to unbiased estimators only; in this case, an efficient estimator is one that has the smallest dispersion, i.e., one whose sampling distribution has the smallest variance. In Figure 1–2 we depict two estimators, $\hat{\theta}_1$ with sampling distribution $f_1(\hat{\theta})$ and $\hat{\theta}_2$ with sampling distribution $f_2(\hat{\theta})$. Both estimators are unbiased, but $\hat{\theta}_2$ is obviously more dispersed than $\hat{\theta}_1$ and is, therefore, less efficient. If we could find no other unbiased estimator that would

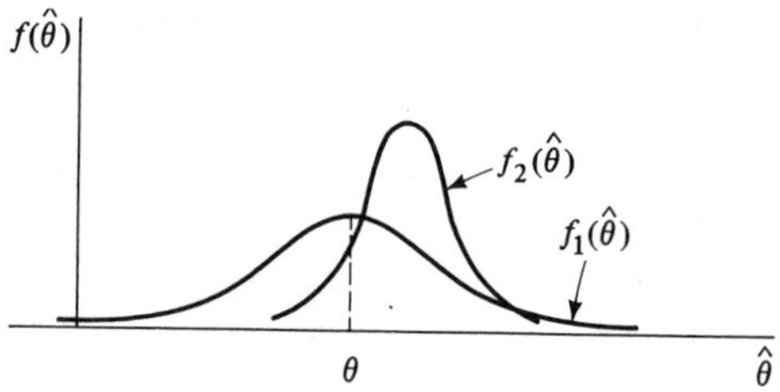

Figure 1–3

have a smaller variance than $\hat{\theta}_1$, then $\hat{\theta}_1$ would be an efficient estimator among the family of all unbiased estimators. If we do not wish to be restricted only to unbiased estimators, then the concept of efficiency becomes ambiguous since in that case it is necessary to consider the trade-off between bias and variance. Figure 1–3 demonstrates a case in point: the estimator $\hat{\theta}_1$ is unbiased but has a large variance, whereas $\hat{\theta}_2$ is biased but has a small variance. We cannot say which of the two estimators is more efficient unless we assign relative weights (i.e., prices) to bias and to variance. It is worth noting, though, that minimum variance by itself is not a desirable property; if it were, we could simply use some constant (which has, by definition, zero variance) regardless of sample evidence. The sampling distribution of such an "estimator" would be concentrated entirely in one point and yet obviously the estimator would be useless.

Another desirable property is *consistency*. This property relates to changes in the sampling distribution as sample sizes are increased. An estimator is said to be consistent if its sampling distribution tends to become concentrated on the true value of the parameter as sample size increases to infinity. Figure 1–4

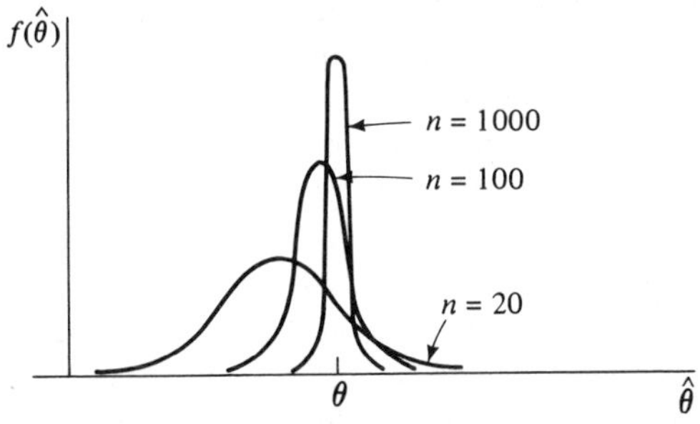

Figure 1–4

shows the sampling distributions of a consistent estimator for different sample sizes. As we move from a smaller sample size to a larger one, two things happen: (a) the bias becomes smaller, and (b) the estimates become less dispersed. Consistency is an important property because it guarantees that our estimates improve with sample size. If it is at all possible to increase sample size, then we can buy greater reliability by spending more on sampling. Even observations from national income accounts can be made more numerous by having data for shorter periods of time.

Estimating a parameter from a sample can be compared to our shooting at a target with a rifle. In this parallel, the bull's-eye represents the true value of the parameter, each shot represents a particular estimate (sample), the rifle is our estimator (i.e., estimation formula), and the distance from the target reflects our sample size. In reality we normally have only one sample and thus can make only one estimate; that is—in our parallel—we are allowed only one shot. However, the quality of any shot before it is made is clearly judged by the quality of the rifle. The rifle can be judged either by its actual performance, i.e., by making a large number of shots, or by examining its construction, the type of material used, etc. The former corresponds to empirical and the latter to theoretical derivation of properties of an estimator. An unbiased rifle is one that produces shots that are randomly scattered around the bull's-eye. If we compare all unbiased rifles, then the one whose shots are most heavily concentrated around the bull's-eye can be considered efficient. Finally, a rifle may be considered consistent if the probability of a shot falling within some (small) distance from the bull's-eye increases when the distance between the shooter and the target is decreased. Note that the quality of a rifle is judged by its repeated performance (actual or expected) and not by a single shot. Given just one shot, it may happen that an inaccurate rifle may hit the bull's-eye while an obviously superior and highly accurate rifle may not. Obviously, this would not affect our judgment of the respective qualities of the two rifles unless it tended to happen repeatedly.

So far we have not considered the question of constructing an estimator. As pointed out earlier, an estimator is a formula for generating estimates. Consider, for instance, sample mean as an estimator of population mean. Here the formula requires that we take all values of the variable observed in our sample, add them up, and divide them by the number of observations. A specific sample will lead to a specific estimate. In this case we have chosen the sample mean for an estimator of population mean more or less because it appears intuitively plausible. This, indeed, is one way of obtaining estimators—namely, by invoking some plausible idea and trying it out—which, in this context, means finding the properties of such estimators. Another way is to construct an estimator by design, to develop a formula so as to satisfy certain conditions that ensure at least some of the desirable properties. Or, finally, we may use some principles that, although not directly guaranteeing desirable properties, nevertheless appear promising on some other grounds. We shall discuss this in detail in Section 6–2.

1–5 Derivation of Sampling Distributions

The main purpose of the preceding discussion was to explain the crucial importance of sampling distributions in statistical inference. The next problem is to derive the sampling distributions of given estimators. In general, this can be done either experimentally or theoretically. The *experimental derivation* is based upon simulation: we create a specific population (which is, therefore, completely known to us) and actually draw from it a large number of random samples. These samples enable us to construct an approximate sampling distribution of the estimator we are examining. While the result is only specific in the sense that it applies solely to the specific population (characterized by specific parameters) with which we are experimenting, we usually hope to be able to generalize our results at least within a certain range. Such generalizations can be tested by further experiments on populations with different parameter values. The *theoretical derivation* of sampling distributions uses probability theory; instead of physically drawing a large number of samples as in the experimental approach, we can find what would happen without actually doing it. Thus, theory may save us a lot of work, which is a great advantage. Another advantage is that theory is more precise: while in experiments we can never produce an infinite number of samples, in theory the concept of infinity may be handled quite easily. And last but not least, in contrast to the experimental method, the results of theoretical derivation are quite general, at least within some well-defined boundaries. Theoretical derivation of sampling distribution is thus clearly superior to the experimental derivation. Its only drawback is that we may not always be able to manage it. The problem is sometimes so complicated that our knowledge is simply insufficient to deal with it. This has been particularly the case with estimation problems in modern econometrics, as will be demonstrated in the discussion of simultaneous economic relations.

The experimental approach will be used in the next chapter to derive the sampling distributions of two common estimators. Our reason for doing so is not, in this case, the difficulty of implementing the laws of probability. Rather, our intention is to familiarize the student with the concept of sampling distribution as much as possible. By first giving the theory a physical content provided by our experiments, we hope to make the idea much clearer. The theoretical approach to the same problem will also be demonstrated and compared with the experimental approach; however, we will need to introduce the basic tools provided by probability theory before attempting a theoretical derivation.

EXERCISES

In the exposition of the basic principles of statistical inference, we assume that the reader has a working knowledge of basic algebra. The short questions in Exercises 1–1 through 1–8 are designed to check the validity of this assumption.

1–1. Sketch the graphs of the following functions:

a. $y = x + 1.$ **b.** $y = \sqrt{x}.$ **c.** $\log y = \frac{1}{2} \log x.$

1–2. Solve for x and y:

$$ax + by = b^2 \quad \text{and} \quad x + y = a.$$

1–3. Simplify the following expressions:

a. $\dfrac{x^5}{x^2}.$ **b.** $\sqrt[3]{x^6}.$ **c.** $\dfrac{(x/y) - (y/x)}{(x - y)/(x + y)}.$

1–4. What is $\sum_{i=1}^{5} x_i$ if

a. $x_i = i.$ **b.** $x_i = 1 + 2i.$ **c.** $x_i = 2^{i-1}.$

1–5. Solve the following equation: $x^2 - 5x + 6 = 0.$

1–6. Find the maximum value of y given that:

$$y = 1 + 2x - x^2.$$

1–7. Derive the first and second derivatives of y for:

a. $y = (x + a)^2.$ **b.** $y = \sqrt{x}.$ **c.** $y = \dfrac{a - x}{b - x}.$

1–8. Let $x > 0$ and $y > 0$. Prove that

$$(x/y + y/x) \geq 2.$$

In our exposition we also assume that the reader is familiar with the basic concepts of descriptive statistics. Exercises 1–9 through 1–12 provide practice in this respect. (Note that an outline of basic algebra of summations is given in Appendix A.)

1–9. The sum of ten numbers $x_1, x_2, \ldots, x_{10}$ is 60, and the sum of their squares is 396. Find the following:

a. The arithmetic mean $\bar{x}$.

b. The standard deviation of x, say, s (using 10 as the denominator).

c. $\sum_{i=1}^{10} (x_i - \bar{x})/s$. **d.** $\sum_{i=1}^{10} 2(x_i - 5)$.

e. The arithmetic mean of z_i, where $z_i = x_i - (x_i - \bar{x})/s$.

1–10. Draw a rough sketch of each of the frequency distributions characterized as follows:

a. The frequency is the same for all values of the variables.
b. The variable assumes the same value at each observation.
c. The distance between the upper quartile and the median is twice as long as the distance between the lower quartile and the median.
d. The value of the standard deviation is zero.
e. The value of the arithmetic mean is smaller than that of the mode.

1–11. Suppose we wish to determine the mean age in a specified population of individuals. Suppose further that in the census one quarter of the individuals underestimate their ages by one year, one half give their correct ages, and one quarter overestimate their ages by two years. Determine the relationship between the true mean age and the mean age obtained from the census.

1–12. The percentage frequency distributions of industrial workers by the amount of monthly wages in the Soviet Union in the years 1929 and 1934, that is, before and after the wage reform of 1931–1933, are given in Table 1–3.[1] A claim was made that

> "the wages of the lower-paid groups increased most and of the medium-paid groups the least. Although the difference between the wages of the lower-paid workers and the wages of the medium-paid workers lessened somewhat, the gap between the wages of the medium- and higher-paid workers increased."[1]

Check whether the data support this claim.

[1] A. Aganbegian, "Methods of Analyzing and Calculating the Distribution of Workers and Employees by the Amount of Wages," *Problems of Economics*, Vol. 3, October 1960, p. 24.

Table 1–3

Monthly Wages, Rubles	March 1929	October 1934
Under 30	2.3	0.0
30 to 49	15.2	0.8
50 to 69	23.6	2.6
70 to 89	21.1	7.9
90 to 109	15.0	12.7
110 to 129	9.4	14.3
130 to 149	5.8	13.3
150 to 169	1.8	10.6
170 to 199	4.1	11.9
200 to 249	1.3	12.0
250 to 299	0.4	6.6
300 and over	0.0	7.3
	100.0	100.0

2 Experimental Derivation of Sampling Distributions

Sampling distribution of an estimator can be viewed as a relative frequency distribution of the values of the estimator obtained from an infinite number of random samples, each sample being of the same size and drawn from the same population. We can do this experimentally as follows. First we create our own population with certain given characteristics, i.e., parameters. Next we choose the parameter to be estimated and the formula for its estimation from the information provided by the sample. Then we draw a large number of random samples of equal size and from each sample calculate the value of the estimator. Finally, we analyze the results in the form of a relative frequency distribution. This will be an approximation of the sampling distribution of the given estimator. We say "an approximation" because we have only a finite, although large, number of samples, while a proper sampling distribution is based upon an infinite number of samples.

The problem of creating or simulating a population is generally a very simple one. For one thing, some populations do not need to exist physically before we start drawing samples. An example would be the population of all possible outcomes of some chance mechanism such as the population of all outcomes of a toss of a coin. Suppose we wish to estimate the probability of getting a head and use as an estimator the proportion of heads in, say, 30 tosses. Then we may take a coin with known probability of getting a head (e.g., an unbiased coin for which the probability of getting a head is one half), toss it 30 times, and record the result. By repeating this a large number of times we should be able to construct a reasonable approximation of the sampling distribution of the proportion of heads in samples of size 30. In the case of other populations, it may be necessary to have a physical representation of each unit before drawing samples. Thus, for instance, the population of United States families may be represented by cards bearing relevant information, one card for each family. A random sample of families would then be given by a random sample of cards.

In this chapter we consider experimental derivation of sampling distributions in two simple cases. In case A we consider sampling of attributes. In particular, we would like to estimate the proportion of people (objects, outcomes, etc.) possessing a certain attribute and to use the proportion found in the sample as our estimator. Then our task is to derive the sampling distribution of this estimator. To make the case more concrete, we may envision it as a problem of estimating the proportion of coffee-drinkers in a given population. In case B we shall be concerned with sampling of a (nonbinary) variable. Here we will wish to derive the sampling distribution of sample mean as an estimator of population mean. As an illustrative interpretation, we may think of a variable describing the number of dental appointments for each adult per year, and consider the problem of estimating the mean number of dental appointments per person in the population.

The mechanical aspects of the sampling experiment to be carried out are the same in both cases. We have a container with a large number of differently marked marbles representing units of the population. The container is shaken, and a number of marbles equal to the desired sample size are selected at random. The result is recorded and the marbles are put back into the container. This is repeated a large number of times. Since after each drawing the marbles are returned into the container and shaken before another drawing is made, each sample has the same chance of being chosen. A slight complication arises, however, because our population is finite (although large) and the marbles are not returned until *after* the whole sample has been collected. This means that the second marble has a slightly higher chance of being picked up than the first one, the third marble has a greater chance than the second one, and so on, since, as the number of marbles in the container decreases, the chance for each remaining marble to be selected increases. But if the population is large, the change in the probabilities is so small that it can be disregarded.

It should be noted that simulating a population by using marbles, or any other objects, to represent units of population is possible only if the variable is not continuous. If the population consisted of all possible values within a certain interval, we could not represent it by a collection of discrete objects. For such cases we would have to use some other ways of simulation. A device that would go a long way toward achieving a reasonable simulation for variables with a finite range of values is a dial with a needle freely rotating around its center. Other methods, particularly those relying on electronic computers, are also available. In the cases discussed here this problem does not arise since we do not use a continuous variable.

2-1 Sampling Distribution of Sample Proportion of Successes

Let us consider the proportion of successes (e.g., coffee-drinkers) in the sample as an estimator of the proportion of successes in the population. We wish to derive the sampling distribution of this estimator by repeated sampling. Our population is a container with a large number of marbles that are identical in every respect except for color. In this particular population, 70% of all marbles are red and 30% are white. We may envision that the red balls represent successes (coffee-drinkers) and the white ones failures. We conduct two experiments with this population. In the first experiment we draw 100 samples of size 4, and in the second experiment 100 samples of size 16. Note that in each experiment we use 100 samples as our approximation of an infinite number of samples, and thus our results will contain errors of approximation. These errors could be decreased by making the number of samples larger if one should so desire. For our purposes the degree of approximation given by 100 samples is sufficient. In describing the results we shall use the following notation:

π = proportion of successes in the population;

$\hat{\pi}$ = proportion of successes in the sample (an estimator of π);

f = relative frequency;

n = size of sample.

In our experiments, $\hat{\pi}$ will assume 100 values, one for each sample. Note that in our population $\pi = 0.7$.

EXPERIMENT A.1: 100 samples of size 4. Here $n = 4$, so that each sample may give only 1 of 5 possible results (no success, one success, etc.). These results are described in Table 2–1 and Figure 2–1. The last column of Table 2–1 gives the

Table 2–1

Successes		Frequency	
Number	Proportion: $\hat{\pi}$	Absolute	Relative: f
0	0.00	1	0.01
1	0.25	6	0.06
2	0.50	28	0.28
3	0.75	42	0.42
4	1.00	23	0.23
		100	1.00

frequencies that approximate the sampling distribution in question. The main characteristics of this sampling distribution are

$$\text{Mean} = \sum_{i=0}^{4} f_i \hat{\pi}_i = 0.01 \times 0 + 0.06 \times 0.25 + 0.28 \times 0.50 + 0.42 \times 0.75 + 0.23 \times 1.00 = 0.700.$$

$$\text{Standard deviation} = \sqrt{\sum_{i=0}^{4} f_i(\hat{\pi}_i - 0.7)^2} = 0.2233.$$

(Note that here $\hat{\pi}_0 = 0$, $\hat{\pi}_1 = 0.25$, $\hat{\pi}_2 = 0.50$, etc., and f_0, f_1, f_2, etc., are the corresponding relative frequencies.) An examination of the derived sampling distribution shows that had we used the sample proportion of successes from sample size 4 as our estimate of the proportion of successes in the population, we would have made a serious underestimate 35% of the time (0.01 + 0.06 + 0.28 = 0.35) and a serious overestimate 23% of the time, and we would have been quite close to the true value 42% of the time. These percentages are, of course, only approximate since our experience is limited to 100 samples.

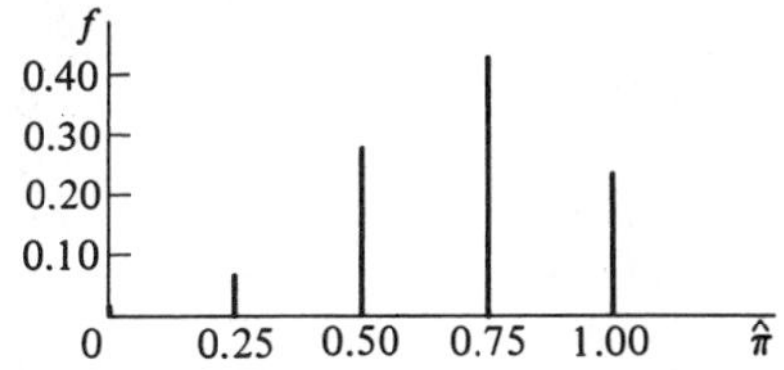

Figure 2-1

EXPERIMENT A.2: 100 samples of size 16. Here $n = 16$, so that there are 17 different possible results. These are presented in Table 2-2 and Figure 2-2. The main characteristics of the sampling distribution in this case are

$$\text{Mean} = \sum_{i=0}^{16} f_i \hat{\pi}_i = 0.7006.$$

$$\text{Standard deviation} = \sqrt{\sum_{i=0}^{16} f_i(\hat{\pi}_i - 0.7006)^2} = 0.1191.$$

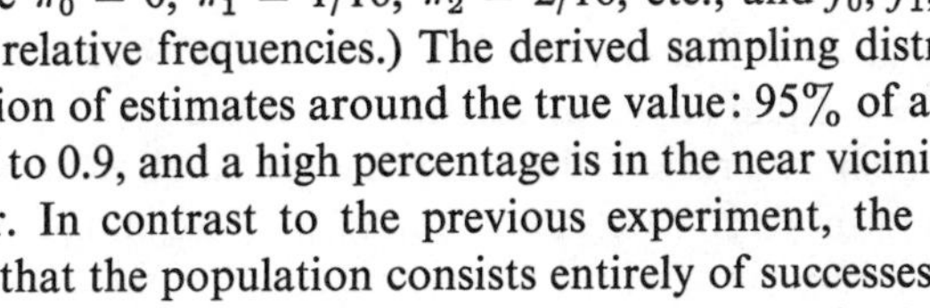

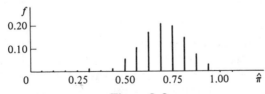

Figure 2-2

(Note that here $\hat{\pi}_0 = 0$, $\hat{\pi}_1 = 1/16$, $\hat{\pi}_2 = 2/16$, etc., and f_0, f_1, f_2, etc., are the corresponding relative frequencies.) The derived sampling distribution shows a fair concentration of estimates around the true value: 95% of all estimates lie in the interval 0.5 to 0.9, and a high percentage is in the near vicinity of the population parameter. In contrast to the previous experiment, the sample evidence never suggests that the population consists entirely of successes or of failures.

The main results of our experiments can be summarized in the following points: (i) in both experiments the mean of the sampling distribution is found to be virtually equal to the value of the population parameter; (ii) the dispersion of the sampling distribution for samples size 16 is less than that for samples size 4, the standard deviation of the former being about one half of that of the latter; and (iii) the sampling distribution for samples size 16 is considerably more symmetric than that for samples size 4.

Table 2–2

Successes		Frequency	
Number	Proportion: $\hat{\pi}$	Absolute	Relative: f
0	0.0000	0	0.00
1	0.0625	0	0.00
2	0.1250	0	0.00
3	0.1875	0	0.00
4	0.2500	0	0.00
5	0.3125	1	0.01
6	0.3750	0	0.00
7	0.4375	1	0.01
8	0.5000	5	0.05
9	0.5625	10	0.10
10	0.6250	17	0.17
11	0.6875	21	0.21
12	0.7500	20	0.20
13	0.8125	15	0.15
14	0.8750	7	0.07
15	0.9375	3	0.03
16	1.0000	0	0.00
		100	1.00

These results have been obtained by repeated sampling from a dichotomous population (i.e., a population containing only two types of individuals) with a proportion of successes equal to 0.7. Only two sampling distributions, those corresponding to samples size 4 and size 16, have been derived. But even given this specific character of our experiments, the results clearly inspire certain generalizations about the sampling distribution of the proportion of successes observed in a sample ($\hat{\pi}$) as an estimator of the proportion of successes in the population (π). These generalizations are

1. $\hat{\pi}$ is an *unbiased estimator* of π (i.e., the mean of the sampling distribution of $\hat{\pi}$ is equal to the population parameter π).
2. As sample size increases, the sampling distribution of $\hat{\pi}$ becomes increasingly more concentrated around π. This implies that $\hat{\pi}$ is a *consistent estimator* of π.
3. Sampling distribution of $\hat{\pi}$ based on larger samples tends to be more symmetric than that based on small samples.

The fourth generalization is less obvious and involves a greater degree of uncertainty than the first three. It arises in connection with generalization 2; since dispersion (or, conversely, concentration) is measured by standard deviation, we would expect some relationship between the change in sample size and the change in the standard deviation. Noting that as sample size is increased fourfold, the standard deviation is halved, we may suspect that the proposition given below also holds:

4. The standard deviation of the sampling distribution of $\hat{\pi}$ decreases with the square root of the sample size.

This final generalization appears to be more risky than the previous three. For one thing, the standard deviation for samples size 16 is only roughly equal to one half of that for sample size 4; for another thing, we only have two sample sizes (i.e., one ratio) from which we generalize. The first difficulty could be remedied by using more than 100 samples and thus sharpening the accuracy, the second by conducting further experiments.

It may have been noticed that our sampling experiment does not allow any generalizations about the efficiency of $\hat{\pi}$. While it would certainly be interesting to see whether any other unbiased estimator has a smaller variance than $\hat{\pi}$, the answer cannot be extracted from our experiments since we considered only one estimator and thus are not able to make comparisons. But even if we did consider several alternative estimators rather than just one, sampling experiments would at best settle the question of efficiency within the small class of estimators actually considered and not with respect to all (unbiased) estimators as desired.

We hope the foregoing generalizations hold for all values of the population parameter π and all sample sizes n. Whether they do or do not will be found when we derive the sampling distribution theoretically in Chapter 4.

2–2 Sampling Distribution of Sample Mean

Let us now consider the problem of deriving the sampling distribution of sample mean as an estimator of the population mean. The population we are simulating is that of, say, all adults in a given geographical region, each being characterized by the number of dental appointments in a given year. Our variable X then represents the number of dental appointments by an adult in a year. To simplify the construction of the population we will postulate that X can only assume the values 0, 1, 2, . . . , 9, and that each of these values can be observed with equal probability. Such a distribution of values is called a *discrete uniform distribution*. This population is simulated by a container with a large number of marbles that are identical in every respect except for a numeral embossed in the surface. The numerals are 0, 1, 2, . . . , 9, and the container includes an equal number of marbles of each denomination. A more elaborate description of the population is given in Table 2–3.

As in case A, we will again conduct two sampling experiments. In the first experiment, we will draw 100 samples of size 5 and derive the sampling distribution of sample mean. To get some idea about its efficiency we will also derive the sampling distribution of an alternative estimator, namely sample median. Thus each sample will be used for producing two estimates of the population mean.

Table 2–3

Value of X	Relative Frequency in the Population
0	0.1
1	0.1
2	0.1
3	0.1
4	0.1
5	0.1
6	0.1
7	0.1
8	0.1
9	0.1
	1.0

Population mean: $\mu = 4.5$.
Population standard deviation: $\sigma = 2.8723$.

In the second experiment, we will draw 100 samples of size 10 and derive the distribution of sample mean. As in the experiments in connection with case A, we will again be satisfied with approximating infinity by a mere 100 samples. In describing the results, the following notation will be used:

μ = population mean;

σ = population standard deviation;

$\bar{X}$ = sample mean;

$\tilde{X}$ = sample median;

f = relative frequency;

n = size of sample.

Experiment B.1 100 samples of size 5. Let us first consider the sampling distribution of sample mean, which is the focal point of our interest. Obviously, even though the variable (and thus individual observations) can assume only integer values 0 to 9, sample means will, in general, not be integers. Thus the sampling distribution will be a frequency distribution with classes defined by intervals and not by points. We may, of course, choose a single value such as the center of each interval to represent each class. The distribution obtained as a result of our experiment is shown in Table 2–4 and illustrated by Figure 2–3.

Table 2–4

Value of Sample Mean: $\bar{X}$		Frequency	
Interval	Midpoint	Absolute	Relative: f
0.5 to 1.499	1	1	0.01
1.5 to 2.499	2	5	0.05
2.5 to 3.499	3	12	0.12
3.5 to 4.499	4	31	0.31
4.5 to 5.499	5	28	0.28
5.5 to 6.499	6	15	0.15
6.5 to 7.499	7	5	0.05
7.5 to 8.499	8	3	0.03
8.5 to 9.499	9	0	0.00
		100	1.00

The main characteristics of this distribution are

$$\text{Mean} = \sum_{i=1}^{9} f_i \bar{x}_i = 4.60.$$

$$\text{Standard deviation} = \sqrt{\sum_{i=1}^{9} f_i(\bar{x}_i - 4.60)^2} = 1.3638.$$

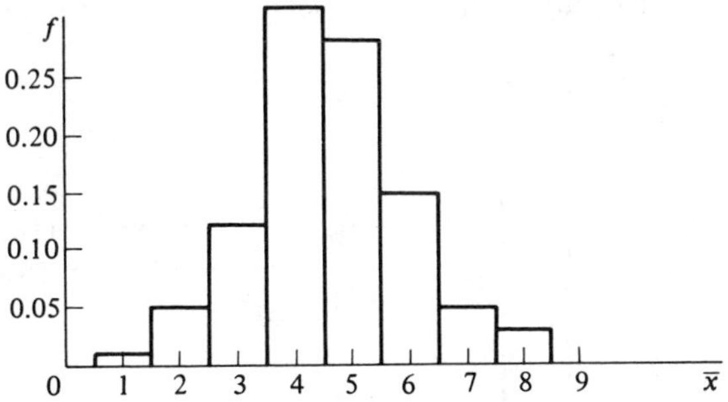

Figure 2–3

The results indicate that 59% of the estimated values (0.31 + 0.28 = 0.59) fall within ±1 of the true value of 4.5, while 86% of the estimates lie within ±2 of 4.5.

Next we present the derived sampling distribution of sample median. Since the sample size is an odd number, sample median will always be an integer. The distribution is given in Table 2–5. The main characteristics of this distribution are

$$\text{Mean} = \sum_{i=0}^{9} f_i \tilde{x}_i = 4.68.$$

$$\text{Standard deviation} = \sqrt{\sum_{i=0}^{9} f_i(\tilde{x}_i - 4.68)^2} = 1.8758.$$

Table 2–5

Value of Sample Median: $\tilde{X}$	Frequency	
	Absolute	Relative: f
0	1	0.01
1	4	0.04
2	4	0.04
3	19	0.19
4	23	0.23
5	14	0.14
6	17	0.17
7	11	0.11
8	5	0.05
9	2	0.02
	100	1.00

The distribution is shown graphically in Figure 2–4. To facilitate a comparison with the sampling distribution of sample mean, we reproduce the distribution of

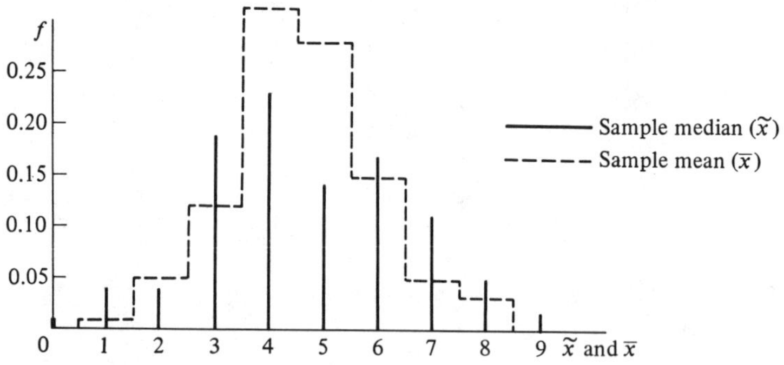

Figure 2–4

Figure 2–3 on the same diagram with dotted lines. It is obvious at first sight that the two distributions are quite different, that of $\tilde{X}$ being much less regular and considerably more dispersed than that of $\bar{X}$.

EXPERIMENT B.2 100 samples of size 10. The results of this experiment are summarized in Table 2–6 and Figure 2–5. The main characteristics of this distribution are

$$\text{Mean} = \sum_{i=2}^{7} f_i \bar{x}_i = 4.57.$$

$$\text{Standard deviation} = \sqrt{\sum_{i=2}^{7} f_i(\bar{x}_i - 4.57)^2} = 1.0416.$$

Table 2–6

Value of Sample Mean: $\bar{X}$		Frequency	
Interval	Midpoint	Absolute	Relative: f
0.5 to 1.499	1	0	0.00
1.5 to 2.499	2	1	0.01
2.5 to 3.499	3	14	0.14
3.5 to 4.499	4	34	0.34
4.5 to 5.499	5	32	0.32
5.5 to 6.499	6	16	0.16
6.5 to 7.499	7	3	0.03
7.5 to 8.499	8	0	0.00
8.5 to 9.499	9	0	0.00
		100	1.00

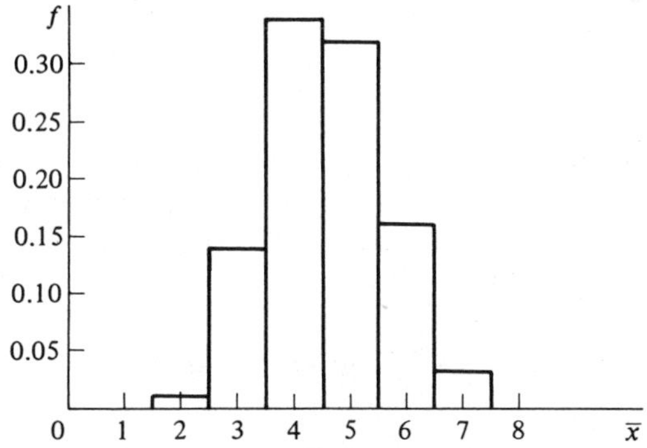

Figure 2–5

The results of our sampling experiments in case B can be summarized as follows: (i) the mean of the sampling distribution of sample mean is approximately equal to the population mean for both sample sizes examined; (ii) the dispersion of the sampling distribution of sample mean for samples size 10 is less than that for samples size 5, the variance of the latter (1.3638^2) being almost twice as large as that of the former (1.0416^2); and (iii) the mean of the sampling distribution of sample median is also approximately equal to the population mean, but its variation is greater than that of the sample mean in samples of equal size.

These results, although based on a specific case, obviously inspire some generalizations:

1. Sample mean $\bar{X}$ is an *unbiased estimator* of the population mean μ.
2. As sample size increases, the sampling distribution of $\bar{X}$ becomes increasingly more concentrated around the population mean; thus $\bar{X}$ is a *consistent estimator* of μ.
3. Sample median $\tilde{X}$ is an unbiased estimator of μ, but its variance is greater than that of $\bar{X}$; thus $\tilde{X}$ is an inefficient estimator of μ.

These generalizations follow quite obviously from the main findings of our experiments. The next generalization is less obvious and somewhat more risky.

4. The standard deviation of the sampling distribution of $\bar{X}$ decreases with the square root of sample size.

Generalization 4 is borne out by our experiment only very roughly; it means that we consider $1.3638 \div 1.0416 = 1.3093$ as "approximately equal" to $\sqrt{2} = 1.4142$.

These four generalizations will be considered again when we discuss theoretical derivations of sampling distributions. For the time being we will hold them only tentatively and hope to be able to confirm or refute them later. Before we do that, we have to master the basic tools of probability theory, and this is the subject of Chapter 3.

EXERCISES

2–1. Using 100 samples, construct experimental sampling distributions of the proportion of heads for samples of 4 and of 16 tosses of a coin. Calculate the mean and the standard deviation of both distributions, and compare the results with those presented under case A of this chapter.

2–2. Consider a population consisting of equal proportions of numbers 1, 2, and 3.

a. Construct all possible samples of size 3, noting that the relative frequency of each sample is the same. Describe the resulting distribution of sample mean and of sample median. Calculate the means and the standard deviations of the two distributions. (HINT: There are 27 different samples of size 3 that can be drawn from this population.)

b. Do the same for samples of size 4. Compare the ratio of the standard deviation of the mean to the standard deviation of the median with the corresponding ratio obtained in **a** above.

2–3. Call getting two heads and a tail in tossing three coins of equal denominations a "success." Make 10 such tosses and record the number of successes. Repeat this 100 times, each time making 10 tosses and recording the number of successes.

a. Present the resulting sampling distribution.

b. Calculate the mean and the standard deviation of the proportion of successes.

2–4. Using the table of random normal deviates provided in Appendix D, construct an empirical sampling distribution of sample mean for samples of size 5 drawn from a normal population.

3 Probability and Probability Distributions

In spite of the fact that probability is a concept which is frequently used in many branches of science as well as in everyday life, the term itself is very difficult to define and is surrounded by controversy. We will mention the main points of view and illustrate the nature of the difficulties. According to the so-called *classical* view, the probability of a favorable outcome is given by the ratio f/n where n is the number of all possible mutually exclusive and equally likely outcomes and f is the number of those outcomes which are taken as favorable. Two outcomes are mutually exclusive if the occurrence of one rules out the occurrence of the other; for example, the appearance of a head when tossing a coin rules out the appearance of a tail in the same toss. Furthermore, outcomes are "equally likely" if it is expected a priori that each outcome would occur with equal frequency in the long run. Thus the probability of getting a 3 when tossing a fair six-sided die is 1/6 since there are six possible outcomes and, assuming that the die is fair, they are all equally likely. As another example, consider the probability of getting two heads as a result of tossing two unbiased coins. The possible outcomes are

1st Coin	2nd Coin
H	H
H	T
T	H
T	T

Thus there are four (not three!) possible and equally likely outcomes, and the probability of getting two heads is then 1/4. Note that this definition of probability may easily be adapted to continuous cases as well. Consider, for example, a clock dial without the clock and with only one freely rotating hand. Here there is an infinite number of points at which the hand may stop after being rotated. Since a point has no dimension and, in particular, no length, the probability that the hand stops at any specific point is zero. However, any interval (unlike a point) has a nonzero length, and thus the probability that the hand will stop within any interval is positive and can be determined. The probability definition given above is rephrased in terms of length (volume, etc.) instead of numbers; for example, in our illustration the probability that the hand stops between the 10th and the 12th minute is 1/30.

There are two major difficulties associated with the use of the classical definition of probability. The first arises from the crucial dependence of the definition on the assumption that all outcomes are equally likely. If we were asked what is the probability of throwing a head when the coin is biased in an unspecified way, we would not be able to answer. The second difficulty is similar. There exist some events for which it is impossible—with our present knowledge—to derive prior probabilities. Examples are given by mortality tables, labor force participation rates, income changes, and many others. Both of these difficulties are due to the fact that the classical definition relies on prior analysis. In fact, probabilities determined by using the classical definition are sometimes called "prior probabilities" to emphasize their theoretical nature.

The difficulties associated with the classical view of probability are avoided if we adopt the *objectivistic* or *frequency* concept of probability. This view of probability represents a newer development in probability theory; it defines probabilities as the limits of relative frequencies as the number of observations approaches infinity. The relative frequencies in a large number of trials can be used as approximations of probabilities. Thus, if we were to toss an unbiased coin a large number of times, we would notice that the proportion (i.e., relative frequency) of heads tends to become stable and close to 1/2. In this objectivistic view, probabilities are considered as empirically determined; thus they are sometimes labeled "positive probabilities." The difficulty with this view is its dependence on observations; since infinity can never be observed, empirically determined probabilities are necessarily only approximations of the limiting values. Another difficulty is that in some cases the relative frequency may not approach a limiting value.

A third approach to defining probability is one which considers probability as the *degree of rational belief*. This definition covers frequently made or implied probability statements which cannot be justified by the use of either classical or frequency definitions of probability. We are here referring to cases in which it is impossible to count (or measure) favorable or also all possible outcomes. Examples are such statements as "I am almost certain that I will fail the examination tomorrow" or "It is quite probable that we will never know the full truth about the death of President Kennedy." In none of these examples is it possible to use well-defined theory for the development of prior probabilities or to conceive of natural repetitions to obtain probabilities *a posteriori*.

The diversity of views on probability may appear somewhat bewildering, but, fortunately, it causes relatively little difficulty in practice. In part, this is because quite often the specific probability given to an event is the same from all viewpoints. For example, if a respectable person produces a normal-looking coin, the probability of getting a head would be considered as 1/2 regardless of which definition of probability one uses. In cases of disagreement (or where the classical definition fails to give an answer) one can use the frequency interpretation of probability, which is precisely what we shall do.

3–1 Sets and Sample Spaces

The elements of probability theory can be developed rather conveniently with the help of simple *set theory*. This seems desirable also because the language of set theory has acquired great popularity in modern statistics and to some extent in economics as well. A *set* is a collection of definite and well-distinguished objects (members, elements). For example, a set may be three numbers 1, 2, and 3; then we write

$$S = \{1, 2, 3\}.$$

But note that a set for five numbers 1, 2, 2, 3, 3 is also

$$S = \{1, 2, 3\}$$

since only three of the five numbers are well distinguished. Also note that the order in which the elements are listed does not matter. A set can be specified either by listing all its elements, or by giving a rule which would enable us to decide whether any given object does or does not belong to it. Thus we can conceive of a rule to define a set of all families in the United States at a given time instead of having a full list. A *null*, or an *empty set*, is one with no elements in it; we write

$$S = \varnothing .$$

If element a belongs to the set S, we write

$$a \in S;$$

if it does not, then

$$a \notin S.$$

If every element in S_1 is an element of S, then S_1 is a *subset* of S. This is expressed by

$$S_1 \subseteq S.$$

For example, if $S_1 = \{1\}$ and $S = \{1, 2, 3\}$, then $S_1 \subseteq S$. S_1 is a *proper subset* of of S if S contains at least one element not in S_1; this can be written as

$$S_1 \subset S.$$

If $S_1 = \{1\}$ and $S = \{1, 2, 3\}$, then S_1 is a proper subset of S. As an example of the logic and set construction consider the statement

$$\varnothing \subseteq S.$$

This must be true because if it were not true then $\varnothing$ would have at least one element not in S; but $\varnothing$ has no elements, thus the statement must hold. Further, if $S \neq \varnothing$, then S contains at least one element not in $\varnothing$, so $\varnothing$ must be a proper subset of S, i.e., $\varnothing \subset S$.

Let us now define two concepts that are of particular relevance to probability theory. The first of these is the *union of sets*. The union of two sets S_1 and S_2 is defined as the set of elements that belong either to S_1 or to S_2, or to both. If we denote by S the set that is the union of S_1 and S_2, then we can write

$$S = S_1 \cup S_2.$$

For example, if $S_1 = \{a, b, c, 2\}$ and $S_2 = \{1, 2, 3\}$, then $S = S_1 \cup S_2 = \{a, b, c, 1, 2, 3\}$. A diagrammatic representation of the concept is given in Figure 3–1. The other concept of importance in probability theory is that of

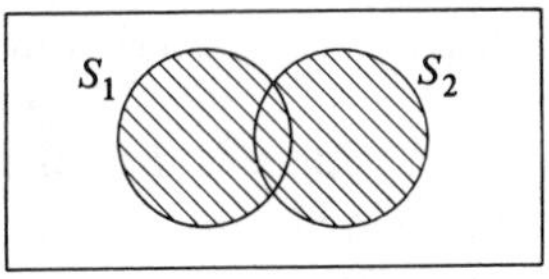

Figure 3–1

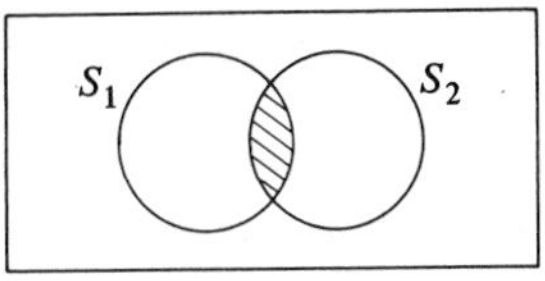

Figure 3–2

intersection of sets. The intersection of two sets S_1 and S_2 is the set of elements that belong to both S_1 and S_2. If such a set is denoted by S, then we have

$$S = S_1 \cap S_2.$$

For example, if $S_1 = \{a, b, c, 2\}$ and $S_2 = \{1, 2, 3\}$, then $S = S_1 \cap S_2 = \{2\}$. Figure 3–2 illustrates this concept diagrammatically.

The algebra of sets is based upon a few basic postulates or laws. These postulates include, among others, the so-called *commutative* and *associative laws*. Consider the sets $S_1, S_2, S_3, \ldots$, all of which are subsets of some set S. Then the commutative law states:

$$S_1 \cup S_2 = S_2 \cup S_1.$$

$$S_1 \cap S_2 = S_2 \cap S_1.$$

The associative law gives the following:

$$(S_1 \cup S_2) \cup S_3 = S_1 \cup (S_2 \cup S_3),$$

$$(S_1 \cap S_2) \cap S_3 = S_1 \cap (S_2 \cap S_3).$$

These laws allow us to extend the definitions of the union and of the intersection of sets to cover more than two sets.

The most important set in probability and sampling theory is called *sample space*. This is a set whose elements represent all possible well-distinguished outcomes of an experiment (where the experiment may either have been conducted by design or have happened naturally). Thus the sample space corresponding to the experiment of tossing a coin consists of two elements, viz. $\{H, T\}$, the sample space corresponding to the experiment of tossing a die consists of six elements, viz. $\{1, 2, 3, 4, 5, 6\}$; and so on. A sample space that consists of a finite number of elements (or an infinite number but with elements that can be counted) is called a *discrete sample space*. Any other sample space is a *continuous* one. It should be noted that the sample space corresponding to an experiment need not be unique. That is, two or more different sample spaces may refer to the same experiment. Suppose, for example, that the experiment consists of tossing two coins. One sample space corresponding to this experiment is

{no head, one head, two heads},

and another is

{head on both coins, tail on both coins, head on first coin and tail on second coin, tail on first coin and head on second coin}.

The difference between the first and the second sample space is that one element of the first sample space (one head) is further subdivided into two elements in the second set. In general, it is desirable to use sample spaces whose elements cannot be further subdivided. Finally, in connection with discrete sample spaces, note that an *event* is simply a subset of the sample space.

3–2 Permutations and Combinations

A discrete sample space can be defined, and its elements counted, by making out a complete list. Alternatively, we may develop counting formulas that will simplify this task, particularly where there is a larger number of elements involved. These counting formulas refer to the number of *permutations* and *combinations* of various outcomes; they will be of particular use in the theoretical derivation of sampling distributions when we deal with attributes.

Let us consider permutations first. By a *permutation* we mean an arrangement of objects in a definite order. We are concerned with finding the number of permutations that can be formed using the elements of a given set. Consider, for example, the set $\{A, B, C\}$. In this set there are three types of permutations possible: those consisting of one element, those consisting of two elements, and those consisting of three elements. The complete enumeration is as follows:

1. Possible permutations of *one* element: A, B, C (i.e., three in number).
2. Possible permutations of *two* elements: AB, BA, AC, CA, BC, CB (i.e., six in number).
3. Possible permutations of *three* elements: $ABC, BAC, ACB, CAB, BCA, CBA$ (i.e., six in number).

Next consider the general case of a set with n elements $\{A, B, \ldots, Z\}$.

1. Possible permutations of *one* element: $A, B, \ldots, Z$. There are obviously n of these.
2. Possible permutations of *two* elements: $AB, BA, AC, CA, \ldots, AZ,$

$ZA, BC, CB, \ldots, YZ, ZY$. The construction of these two-element permutations can be shown explicitly as follows:

$$\left.\begin{array}{c} B \\ A \longleftrightarrow C \\ \vdots \\ Z \end{array}\right\} \quad \text{i.e., } 2 \times (n-1)$$

$$\left.\begin{array}{c} C \\ B \longleftrightarrow D \\ \vdots \\ Z \end{array}\right\} \quad \text{i.e., } 2 \times (n-2)$$

$$\begin{array}{ll} Y \longleftrightarrow Z\} & \text{i.e., } 2 \times [n-(n-1)] \\ Z \qquad \} & \text{i.e., } 2 \times (n-n). \end{array}$$

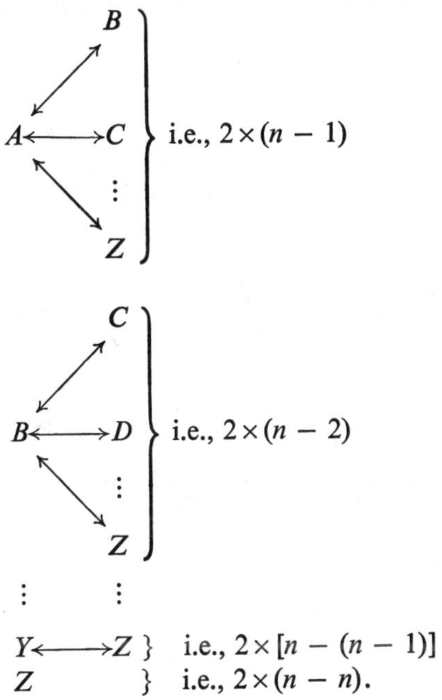

(The two-way arrows indicate that the associations go both ways; e.g., $A \leftrightarrow B$ stands for AB *as well as* BA.) The sum total of these permutations is

$$2[(n-1) + (n-2) + \cdots + 2 + 1]$$

$$= 2\left[\left(\frac{n-1}{2}\right)n\right] = n(n-1).$$

This result could also be obtained by noting that in the case of two-element permutations each of the n elements gets associated with the remaining $(n-1)$ elements. Since there are altogether n elements, the total must be $n(n-1)$.

3. Possible permutations of *three* elements: $ABC, BAC, ADC, DAC,$ $\ldots, AZX, ZAX, BCA, CBA, \ldots, YZX, ZYX$. That is, each of the $n(n-1)$ permutations obtained in 2 gets associated with the remaining $(n-2)$ elements of the set. The sum total is, therefore, $n(n-1)(n-2)$.

This could be continued but the answers should be quite obvious by now. They can be summarized in Table 3–1. Let us denote by $_nP_r$ the number of permutations of r distinct elements selected from a set of n elements. Then from the formula for permutations of r elements, listed in Table 3–1, we have

$$_nP_r = n(n-1)(n-2)\cdots(n-r+1).$$

Table 3–1

Number of Elements	Number of Permutations
1	n
2	$n(n-1)$
3	$n(n-1)(n-2)$
$\vdots$	$\vdots$
r	$n(n-1)(n-2)\cdots(n-r+1)$
$\vdots$	$\vdots$
$(n-1)$	$n(n-1)(n-2)\cdots 2$
n	$n(n-1)(n-2)\cdots 2\times 1$

This expression can be simplified by using the so-called factorial notation. A *factorial* of a number n is denoted by $n!$ and defined as

$$n! = n(n-1)(n-2)\cdots 3\times 2\times 1,$$

where n can be any positive integer. We also define

$$0! = 1.$$

When we use these symbols, the formula for the number of permutations becomes

(3.1) $$_nP_r = \frac{n!}{(n-r)!}.$$

The following points are worth noting:

1. $_nP_0 = 1$, i.e., there is only one way in which an empty set can be arranged.
2. Suppose we have n objects of which k objects are exactly the same. Then

(3.2) $$_nP_n^{(k)} = \frac{n!}{k!}.$$

For example, consider the number of permutations of the four letters in the word POOH:

POOH	HPOO	OPHO	
POHO	HOPO	OPOH	
PHOO	HOOP	OHPO	Total = 12.
		OHOP	
		OOHP	
		OOPH	

$$_4P_4^{(2)} = \frac{4!}{2!} = \frac{4\times 3\times 2\times 1}{2\times 1} = 12.$$

This result can be extended to the case of n objects of which k are of one kind (and all are exactly the same), ℓ are of another kind, etc. Then

$$(3.3) \qquad {}_nP_n^{(k,\ell,\ldots)} = \frac{n!}{k!\,\ell!\cdots}.$$

3. If one set of objects can be arranged in m_1 ways and another set of objects in m_2 ways, then the total number of permutations is $m_1 \times m_2$. This is sometimes known as the *multiplication principle.*

As an example of the multiplication principle, consider the number of permutations given by the outcomes of tossing two coins. Here m_1 is the number of permutations given by the possible outcomes of tossing the first coin (H and T) and is equal to 2, and m_2 refers to the outcomes of tossing the second coin and is also equal to 2. Thus, the total number of permutations is $2 \times 2 = 4$. This can be easily verified: the possible outcomes of tossing two coins are HH, HT, TH, TT, i.e., four in number. As another example, consider the number of permutations given by the outcomes of tossing two six-sided dice. In this case, $m_1 = 6$ and $m_2 = 6$, so that the total number is 36.

All permutations that involve the same elements represent a given combination. More precisely, a *combination* is a subset of r elements selected, without regard to their order, from a set of n different elements. It is assumed that $n \geq r$. Consider the set $\{A, B, C\}$. From the elements of this set we can form combinations of one, two, or three elements. These are as follows.

1. Combinations of *one* element: $\{A\}$, $\{B\}$, $\{C\}$ (i.e., three in number).
2. Combinations of *two* elements: $\{A, B\}$, $\{A, C\}$, $\{B, C\}$ (i.e., three in number).
3. Combinations of *three* elements: $\{A, B, C\}$ (i.e., *one* in number).

Next consider the general case of n elements $\{A, B, C, \ldots, Z\}$.

1. Combinations of *one* element: $\{A\}$, $\{B\}$, $\ldots$, $\{Z\}$. These are n in number.
2. Combinations of *two* elements: $\{A, B\}$, $\{A, C\}$, $\ldots$, $\{X, Z\}$. These can be depicted as follows:

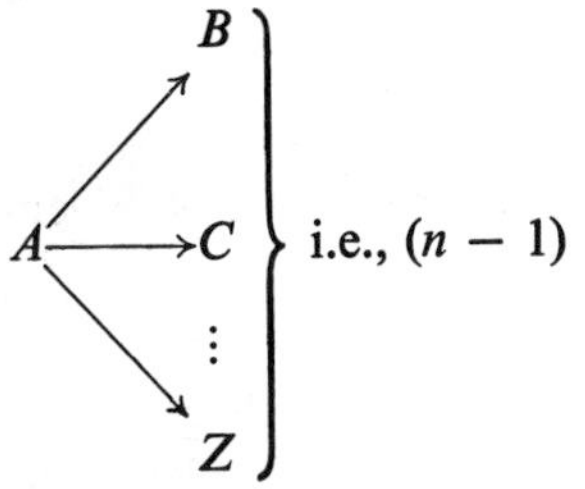

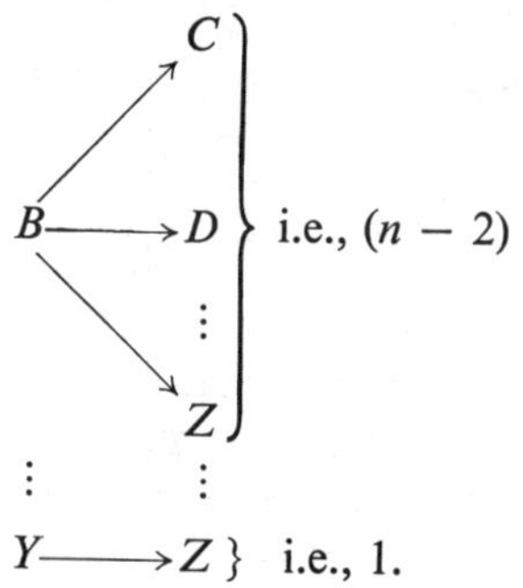

The total is

$$(n - 1) + (n - 2) + \cdots + 1 = \frac{1}{2}n(n - 1) = \frac{1}{2}{}_nP_2.$$

This result could also be obtained by noting that any two-letter combination leads to two permutations. Thus all we have to do to get the total number of two-letter combinations is to divide the total number of two-letter permutations by two.

3. Combinations of *three* elements: $\{A, B, C\}, \{A, B, D\}, \ldots, \{X, Y, Z\}$. Since any three-letter combination leads to $3! = 6$ permutations, the total number of three-letter combinations is

$$\frac{1}{6}{}_nP_3 = \frac{n(n - 1)(n - 2)}{3!}.$$

This could be continued for any number of elements; the results are summarized in Table 3–2. The number of combinations of r distinct elements

Table 3–2

Number of Elements	Number of Combinations
1	n
2	$\frac{n(n-1)}{2}$
3	$\frac{n(n-1)(n-2)}{3!}$
⋮	
r	$\frac{n(n-1)\cdots(n-r+1)}{r!}$
⋮	⋮
$(n - 1)$	n
n	1

selected without regard to order from a set of n elements is usually denoted by $\binom{n}{r}$. From Table 3–2 we obviously have

$$\binom{n}{r} = \frac{n!}{(n - r)!r!}. \tag{3.4}$$

Note that

$$\binom{n}{0} = 1,$$

$$\binom{n}{n} = 1,$$

$$\binom{n}{r} = \binom{n}{n-r}.$$

A well-known use of the formula for the number of combinations is the determination of *binomial coefficients*. Consider the following algebraic expansions:

$$(a+b)^0 = 1,$$
$$(a+b)^1 = a + b,$$
$$(a+b)^2 = a^2 + 2ab + b^2,$$
$$(a+b)^3 = a^3 + 3a^2b + 3ab^2 + b^3,$$
$$(a+b)^4 = a^4 + 4a^3b + 6a^2b^2 + 4ab^3 + b^4,$$

and so on.

The numerical coefficients in the foregoing expansions are known as the binomial coefficients. Note that they are, in fact, given by the formula for the number of combinations, since the expansions could equivalently be written as

$$(a+b)^0 = 1,$$
$$(a+b)^1 = \binom{1}{0}a + \binom{1}{1}b,$$
$$(a+b)^2 = \binom{2}{0}a^2 + \binom{2}{1}ab + \binom{2}{2}b^2,$$
$$(a+b)^3 = \binom{3}{0}a^3 + \binom{3}{1}a^2b + \binom{3}{2}ab^2 + \binom{3}{3}b^3,$$
$$(a+b)^4 = \binom{4}{0}a^4 + \binom{4}{1}a^3b + \binom{4}{2}a^2b^2 + \binom{4}{3}ab^3 + \binom{4}{4}b^4,$$

and so on.

Generalizing we have

$$(a+b)^n = \binom{n}{0}a^n + \binom{n}{1}a^{n-1}b + \binom{n}{2}a^{n-2}b^2 + \cdots + \binom{n}{n}b^n \quad (3.5)$$
$$= \sum_{r=0}^{n} \binom{n}{r} a^{n-r}b^r.$$

An easy way of calculating the binomial coefficients is by using what is known

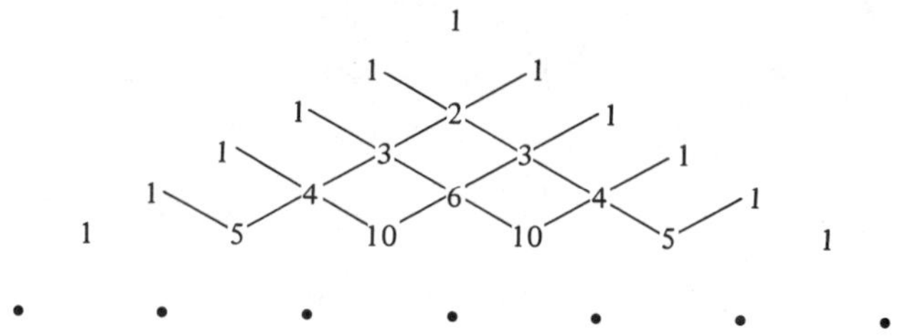

Figure 3–3

as *Pascal's triangle* (Figure 3–3). Each row begins and ends with a 1; each other number is a sum of the two neighboring numbers in the row immediately above.

The binomial formula (3.5) facilitates the determination of the total number of subsets that can be formed from a set of n distinct elements. The first subset is the null set, then there are n subsets of one element each, $n(n - 1)/2$ subsets of two elements, and so on. The total number is given by the sum

$$\binom{n}{0} + \binom{n}{1} + \binom{n}{2} + \cdots + \binom{n}{n}.$$

These are the binomial coefficients for the expansion with $a = 1$ and $b = 1$, i.e.,

$$(1 + 1)^n = \binom{n}{0} + \binom{n}{1} + \binom{n}{2} + \cdots + \binom{n}{n}.$$

But, obviously,

$$(1 + 1)^n = 2^n.$$

Thus we have found that *a set of n elements has* 2^n *subsets.*

3–3 Basic Theorems of Probability Theory

Let us now consider the basic theorems of probability theory. Let $A, B, C, \ldots$ be events represented by subsets of a discrete sample space S and let $P(A)$, $P(B)$, $P(C), \ldots$ be their respective probabilities. We postulate that

$$0 \leq P(A) \leq 1 \quad \text{for each subset } A \text{ of } S, \qquad \text{and} \qquad P(S) = 1.$$

Theorem 1 *If $\bar{A}$ is an event "not A," then* $P(\bar{A}) = 1 - P(A)$.

This, we hope, needs no elaboration. If the probability that it will rain is 0.40, then it is quite obvious that the probability that it will not rain is 0.60. Theorem 1 is represented by Figure 3–4.

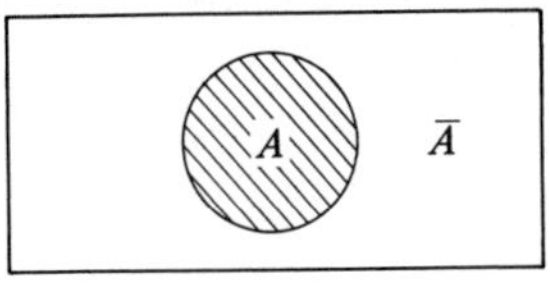

Figure 3–4

Before we proceed any further, we ought to digress in order to clarify the meaning of conditional statements of the form "if . . . , then . . ." and similar, which are frequently used in the language of theorems and proofs. Such a clarification requires that we distinguish between different types of conditions; in particular, we have to distinguish between a "necessary," a "sufficient," and a "necessary and sufficient" condition. This distinction will be illustrated by reference to two nonidentical propositions P_1 and P_2. First, take a *sufficient* condition: if P_1 is true, then P_2 is true. This is sometimes expressed as "P_1 implies P_2." Here P_1 is a sufficient condition for P_2. For instance, P_1 may be "being a mother" and P_2 "being a woman," since motherhood is obviously a sufficient condition for womanhood. Or, as another example, P_1 may be a statement "today is Tuesday" and P_2 a statement "tomorrow is Wednesday." Next, consider a *necessary* condition: if P_1 is not true, then P_2 is not true, or alternatively, P_2 is true *only if* P_1 is true. Here P_1 is a necessary condition for P_2. For instance, "being a woman" is a necessary condition for "being a mother." Note that a sufficient condition may or may not be a necessary one; similarly, a necessary condition may or may not be sufficient. An example of a sufficient but not necessary condition is "being a mother" as a condition for "being a woman," since it is possible to be a woman without being a mother. If we reverse these propositions and put "being a woman" as a condition of "being a mother," we have an example of a necessary but not sufficient condition since being a woman is not enough for being a mother. The last example illustrates a universal property of a sufficiency relation: *if* P_1 *is sufficient* for P_2, *then* P_2 *is necessary for* P_1. Finally, we have the case of a *necessary and sufficient condition*: if P_1, then P_2, and if P_2, then P_1. This condition is described by an "if and only if" statement. For example, "if and only if today is Tuesday, then tomorrow is Wednesday." That is, the truth of "today is Tuesday" is not only sufficient but also necessary for the truth of "tomorrow is Wednesday."

In our discussion the most frequently used conditional statement will be "if P_1, then P_2." This means that P_1 is a sufficient, but may or may not be a necessary, condition for P_2. The fact that this statement omits the clause "and only if" should not be interpreted to mean that P_1 is not a necessary condition for P_2. The omission of this clause is simply an indication that, for our purposes, the fact that P_1 is or is not a necessary condition for P_2 does not matter and thus is of no interest. Only when the condition of necessity is relevant to subsequent arguments shall we insert the "only if" qualification in the statement. With this remark we finish our digression and return to the discussion of basic theorems in probability.

Theorem 2 (*Addition Theorem*) $P(A \cup B) = P(A) + P(B) - P(A \cap B)$

This theorem states that the probability of either A or B or of both is equal to the probability of A *plus* the probability of B *minus* the probability of both A and B occurring simultaneously. It is illustrated by Figure 3–5. Because A and B overlap, the term $P(A \cap B)$ has to be deducted from the sum $P(A) + P(B)$; otherwise it would be counted twice.

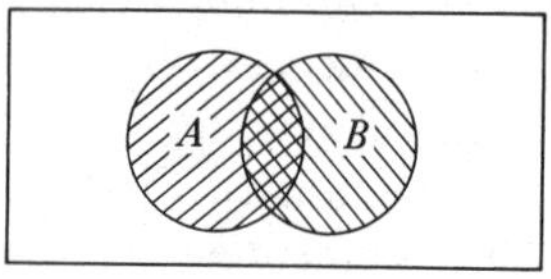

Figure 3–5

EXAMPLE 1 Consider the probability that a card drawn at random from a pack of 52 cards is either a spade or a face card. Let A = spade and B = face card. Note that

$$P(A) = \frac{13}{52} \quad \text{(since there are 13 spades in a pack),}$$

$$P(B) = \frac{12}{52} \quad \text{(since there are 12 face cards in a pack),}$$

$$P(A \cap B) = \frac{3}{52} \quad \text{(since there are 3 face cards in a suit of spades).}$$

Then

$$P(A \cup B) = \frac{13}{52} + \frac{12}{52} - \frac{3}{52} = \frac{22}{52}.$$

EXAMPLE 2 What is the probability that a toss of a six-sided die will result in a "1" or "2"?

$$\begin{aligned} P(\text{“1”} \cup \text{“2”}) &= P(\text{“1”}) + P(\text{“2”}) - P(\text{“1”} \cap \text{“2”}) \\ &= \frac{1}{6} + \frac{1}{6} - 0 \\ &= \frac{1}{3}. \end{aligned}$$

The second example brings us to the theorem that deals with the probability of mutually exclusive events already mentioned in connection with the classical definition of probability. In the language of set theory, events (i.e., subsets of the sample space) are mutually exclusive if and only if their interaction is an empty set. The theorem is as follows:

Theorem 3 *If A and B are mutually exclusive, then* $P(A \cup B) = P(A) + P(B)$.

This theorem is illustrated by Figure 3–6. It can be extended to any number of mutually exclusive events. In particular, if $A, B, C, \ldots, Z$ are all mutually exclusive, then

$$P(A \cup B \cup C \cup \ldots \cup Z) = P(A) + P(B) + P(C) + \cdots + P(Z).$$

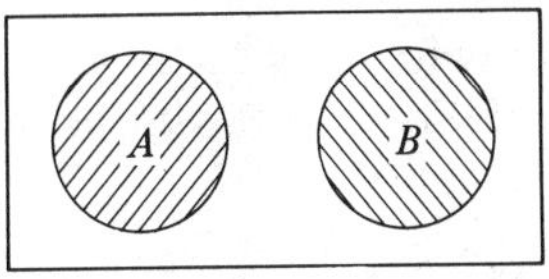

Figure 3–6

Let us now examine events that are not mutually exclusive. Consider, for example, the situation where we randomly select a person from a certain population and record two characteristics, smoking habit (S or $\bar{S}$) and sex (M or F). The two characteristics are obviously not mutually exclusive, at least not in a modern society. The sample space for this experiment is $\{(MS), (FS), (M\bar{S}), (F\bar{S})\}$, where MS represents "male smoker," etc. If the population is a finite one, the distribution may be described by absolute frequencies as follows:

		Smoking Habit S	Smoking Habit $\bar{S}$	Totals
Sex	M	a	b	$a + b$
	F	c	d	$c + d$
Totals		$a + c$	$b + d$	N

where $N = a + b + c + d$ is the population total. In terms of probabilities this distribution would be

		Smoking Habit S	Smoking Habit $\bar{S}$	
Sex	M	$P(M \cap S)$	$P(M \cap \bar{S})$	$P(M)$
	F	$P(F \cap S)$	$P(F \cap \bar{S})$	$P(F)$
		$P(S)$	$P(\bar{S})$	1

The probabilities in the body of the table, represented by intersections of sets, are called *joint probabilities*. For example, $P(M \cap S)$ is the probability that a person selected at random will be both a male and a smoker, i.e., has the two joint characteristics. The probabilities that appear in the last row and in the last column of the table are known as *marginal probabilities*. Thus, $P(M)$ gives the probability of drawing a male regardless of his smoking habits, $P(S)$ gives the probability of selecting a smoker regardless of sex, and so on. Let us see how the addition theorem given earlier works in this situation:

$$P(M \cup S) = P(M) + P(S) - P(M \cap S) = \frac{a+b}{N} + \frac{a+c}{N} - \frac{a}{N}$$

$$= \frac{a+b+c}{N} = 1 - \frac{d}{N} = 1 - P(F \cap \bar{S}).$$

That is, the probability of drawing either a male or a smoker or both is simply equal to 1 *minus* the probability of drawing a female nonsmoker (the only category not covered by $M \cup S$). Similarly,

$$P(M \cup \bar{S}) = 1 - P(F \cap S),$$

$$P(F \cup S) = 1 - P(M \cap \bar{S}),$$

$$P(F \cup \bar{S}) = 1 - P(M \cap S).$$

Suppose now that we wish to know the probability that a person of *given* sex is a smoker (nonsmoker), or that a person of *given* smoking habits is a male (female). Such probabilities are known as *conditional probabilities*, and we write them as $P(S|M)$, which we read "probability of S, given M," etc. For instance, $P(S|M)$ means that we have a male and want to know the probability that he is a smoker. This probability, in a finite population, is obviously given by the total number of male smokers divided by the total number of males. Thus we have

$$P(S|M) = \frac{a}{a+b}.$$

Similarly,

$$P(\bar{S}|M) = \frac{b}{a+b},$$

$$P(S|F) = \frac{c}{c+d},$$

$$P(\bar{S}|F) = \frac{d}{c+d},$$

$$P(M|S) = \frac{a}{a+c},$$

$$P(F|S) = \frac{c}{a+c},$$

$$P(M|\bar{S}) = \frac{b}{b+d},$$

$$P(F|\bar{S}) = \frac{d}{b+d}.$$

Note that

$$P(S|M) + P(\bar{S}|M) = 1,$$

$$P(S|F) + P(\bar{S}|F) = 1,$$

and so on.

In terms of probabilities we can write

$$P(S|M) = \frac{P(S \cap M)}{P(M)},$$

$$P(\bar{S}|M) = \frac{P(\bar{S} \cap M)}{P(M)},$$

and so on.

This applies whether the population is finite or infinite.

This discussion leads to an important theorem:

Theorem 4 (*Conditional Probability*) *If A and B are subsets of a discrete sample space and $P(B) \neq 0$, then $P(A|B) = P(A \cap B)/P(B)$.*

That is, the conditional probability of A, given B, is equal to the joint probability of A and B divided by the (nonzero) marginal probability of B.

The following points should be noted in connection with this theorem on conditional probability:

1. $A|B$ is *not* a set.
2. $P(A|B)$ and $P(B|A)$ are not necessarily the same. In fact, they are equal to each other if and only if $P(A) = P(B) \neq 0$.
3. By writing $P(A|B)$ we do not imply any temporal ordering between A and B. It does not matter whether B occurred prior to, simultaneously with, or after A.
4. Since the conditional probability theorem could also be written in the form $P(A \cap B) = P(A|B)[P(B)]$, it sometimes is called the *multiplication theorem*.

Example 1

$$P(\text{face card}|\text{spade}) = \frac{3/52}{13/52} = \frac{3}{13}$$

and

$$P(\text{spade}|\text{face card}) = \frac{3/52}{12/52} = \frac{3}{12}.$$

Example 2 Suppose we toss an unbiased coin twice. What is the probability that the outcome of the second toss is a head, given that the outcome of the first toss was a head? Let H_i stand for "head in the ith toss." Then

$$P(H_2|H_1) = \frac{P(H_1 \cap H_2)}{P(H_1)} = \frac{1/4}{1/2} = \frac{1}{2}.$$

Let us consider the second example more closely. The results show that the probability of getting a head in the second toss, given that we obtained a head in the first toss, is 1/2. But 1/2 is precisely the probability of getting a head in *any* toss, regardless of what happened in the first toss. Indeed, we should be very surprised if we got any other answer since the coin obviously has no memory. Therefore, what happened to it in the first toss is irrelevant for determining what is going to happen to it in the second toss. Such events for which the occurrence of one event in no way affects the probability of occurrence of the other event are called *independent events*. Thus, if A is independent of B, we must have

$$P(A|B) = P(A). \tag{3.6}$$

That is, the conditional probability of A, given B, is equal to the marginal probability of A. By using the development of $P(A|B)$ given by *Theorem 4* (under the assumption that $P(B) \neq 0$, we obtain

$$\frac{P(A \cap B)}{P(B)} = P(A). \tag{3.7}$$

If we now also assume that $P(A) \neq 0$, we can rewrite (3.7) as

$$\frac{P(A \cap B)}{P(A)} = P(B). \tag{3.8}$$

But the left-hand side of (3.8) is nothing else than $P(B|A)$, so that we have

$$P(B|A) = P(B). \tag{3.9}$$

That is, if A is independent of B, then B is independent of A. Equations (3.7) and (3.8) lead to the following important theorem:

Theorem 5 (*Independence*) *If $P(A) \neq 0$ and $P(B) \neq 0$, then A and B are independent if and only if $P(A \cap B) = P(A) \times P(B)$.*

In other words, A and B are independent if and only if their joint probability is equal to the product of their respective marginal probabilities. The theorem can be extended to any number of events. In particular, $A, B, C, \ldots, Z$, each occurring with nonzero probability, are independent if and only if

$$P(A \cap B \cap C \cdots \cap Z) = P(A) \times P(B) \times P(C) \times \cdots \times P(Z).$$

Example 1 Suppose we toss two six-sided dice. What is the probability that one die will show an even and the other an odd number? Let E = even number and O = odd number. Then $P(E) = 1/2$, $P(O) = 1/2$. $P(E \cap O) = 1/2 \times 1/2 = 1/4$.

Example 2 What is the probability of getting three heads in three tosses of an unbiased coin?

$$P(H_1 \cap H_2 \cap H_3) = P(H_1) \times P(H_2) \times P(H_3) = \frac{1}{2} \times \frac{1}{2} \times \frac{1}{2} = \frac{1}{8}.$$

EXAMPLE 3 Suppose smoking habits are independent of sex, i.e., $P(M \cap S) = P(M) \times P(S)$. Does this necessarily imply that $P(F \cap \bar{S}) = P(F) \times P(\bar{S})$?
We have

	S	$\bar{S}$	
M	$P(M)P(S)$	$P(M \cap \bar{S})$	$P(M)$
F	$P(F \cap S)$	$P(F \cap \bar{S})$	$P(F)$
	$P(S)$	$P(\bar{S})$	1

Now,

$$P(F \cap S) = P(S) - P(M)P(S) = P(S)[1 - P(M)] = P(S)P(F)$$

and

$$P(F \cap \bar{S}) = P(F) - P(F \cap S) = P(F) - P(F)P(S)$$
$$= P(F)[1 - P(S)] = P(F)P(\bar{S}).$$

The answer, then, is yes.

Those not well versed in probability theory often tend to confuse the applicability of the addition theorem for mutually exclusive events with the applicability of the multiplication theorem for independent events. The confusion is due to the failure of distinguishing $P(A \cup B)$ (i.e., probability that *either A or B or both A and B* will occur) from $P(A \cap B)$ (i.e., probability that *both A* and *B* will occur) (see Figure 3–7). Now if A and B are mutually exclusive, then

Figure 3–7

(3.10) $$P(A \cap B) = 0,$$

as implied by *Theorem 3* and illustrated by Figure 3–6. For A and B to be independent we require that

(3.11) $$P(A \cap B) = P(A) \times P(B)$$

But Equations (3.10) and (3.11) can hold simultaneously only if either $P(A)$ or $P(B)$ (or both) is equal to zero. But according to our *Theorem 5* this is ruled out. Thus, mutually exclusive events cannot be independent at the same time. This should be obvious even by much less formal reasoning. If A and B are mutually exclusive, then the occurrence of one prevents the occurrence of the other, i.e., the occurrence of A makes the probability of occurrence of B zero. However, we described independent events as those for which the occurrence of one in *no way* affects the probability of the other, and this is clearly not the case when two events are mutually exclusive. By the same reasoning it is also quite clear that independent events cannot be mutually exclusive.

3–4 Discrete Random Variables and Probability Functions

Suppose we carry out an experiment that consists of tossing two coins. The sample space associated with this experiment can be described by $S = \{TT, TH, HT, HH\}$. Each element of this sample space is associated with a given number of heads (or tails). Thus we have

Elements of Sample Space	Number of Heads
TT	0
TH	1
HT	1
HH	2

Alternatively, we could present this association as follows:

Number of Heads	Elements of Sample Space
0	TT
1	TH, HT
2	HH

The principle of associating the elements of a sample space with some numerical characteristic can obviously be applied quite generally to any sample space. This numerical characteristic is called a *discrete random* (or *stochastic*) *variable*. Thus a discrete random variable is a variable whose values are associated with the elements of a sample space. A common notation is to denote a random variable by a capital letter (e.g., X) and its values by small letters (e.g., x); if the values follow some ordering (e.g., a sequence of observations), the order is indicated by a subscript (e.g., x_1, x_2, etc.). In our example we associated the number of heads with the elements of the sample space, but we could have equally well chosen the proportion, rather than the number, of heads as the numerical characteristic. Obviously, either the number or the proportion of heads is a random variable.

Since a sample space consists of elements that refer to outcomes of an experiment, each element can be associated with a certain probability value. In addition, since each value of a discrete random variable is associated with (one or more) elements of the sample space, it follows that each value can be associated with a certain probability. That is, a discrete random variable can be described as a variable that assumes different values with given probabilities. In our example of tossing two coins, each element of the sample space consists of two independent events. If the coins are unbiased, we have

$$P(T \cap T) = P(T)P(T) = \frac{1}{4}$$

$$P(T \cap H) = P(T)P(H) = \frac{1}{4}$$

$$P(H \cap T) = P(H)P(T) = \frac{1}{4}$$

$$P(H \cap H) = P(H)P(H) = \frac{1}{4}$$

Let x be the number of heads and $f(x)$ the probability of getting that number. Then we can write

Elements of Sample Space	Number of Heads: x	Probability of x: $f(x)$
TT	0	1/4
TH	1	1/4
HT	1	1/4
HH	2	1/4
		1

An alternative way of presenting the above information is simply

x	$f(x)$
0	1/4
1	1/2
2	1/4
	1

The above distribution is known as a probability function. The idea can easily be generalized to give the following definition:

If X is a discrete random variable with values $x_1, x_2, \ldots, x_n$ and with associated probabilities $f(x_1), f(x_2), \ldots, f(x_n)$, then the set of pairs,

$$\begin{matrix} x_1 & f(x_1) \\ x_2 & f(x_2) \\ \vdots & \\ x_n & f(x_n) \end{matrix}$$

is called the probability function (or distribution) of X.

As an example, consider the experiment of tossing two six-sided dice. Let the random variable in this case be the total number of dots observed. Its values then are 2, 3, . . ., 12. The sample space corresponding to this experiment can be considered to consist of all possible permutations of the two sets of numbers from 1 to 6. By the multiplication principle there will be $6 \times 6 = 36$ such permutations, each occurring with equal probability (assuming that the dice are not loaded). The resulting probability distribution for the total number of dots observed is given in Table 3–3.

Table 3–3

x	Elements of Sample Space	$f(x)$
2	11	1/36
3	12, 21	2/36
4	13, 31, 22	3/36
5	14, 41, 23, 32	4/36
6	15, 51, 24, 42, 33	5/36
7	16, 61, 25, 52, 34, 43	6/36
8	26, 62, 35, 53, 44	5/36
9	36, 63, 45, 54	4/36
10	46, 64, 55	3/36
11	56, 65	2/36
12	66	1/36
		1

When X assumes any given value, say x_i, this represents an event, and $f(x_i)$ represents the probability of this event. Since X can assume only one value at a time, the probability that the value of X is x_i *or* x_j $(x_i \neq x_j)$ is the probability of two mutually exclusive events; by Theorem 3 this is equal to $f(x_i) + f(x_j)$. For example, the probability that the total number of dots obtained by a toss of two dice is either 4 or 8 is equal to $3/36 + 5/36 = 2/9$. And, of course, the probability that X will assume any value *other than* x_i is equal to $1 - f(x_i)$ by Theorem 1.

For some problems, we need to find the probability that X will assume a value *less than or equal to* a given number. Such probabilities are called *cumulative probabilities* and are usually denoted by $F(x)$. If $x_1, x_2, \ldots, x_n$ are values of X given in increasing order of magnitude, that is, if $x_1 < x_2 < \cdots < x_n$, then the cumulative probability of x_k is given by

$$F(x_k) = f(x_1) + f(x_2) + \cdots + f(x_k) = \sum_{i=1}^{k} f(x_i). \tag{3.12}$$

Since the values outside the range of X (i.e., values smaller than x_1 or larger than x_n) occur only with probability equal to zero, we may equally well write

$$F(x_k) = \sum_{i=-\infty}^{k} f(x_i). \tag{3.13}$$

A distribution that gives the cumulative probabilities $F(x)$ for every value of X is known as the *cumulative distribution* of X. For the experiment of tossing two six-sided dice the cumulative distribution is given in Table 3–4. The probability

Table 3–4

x	$F(x)$
2	1/36
3	3/36
4	6/36
5	10/36
6	15/36
7	21/36
8	26/36
9	30/36
10	33/36
11	35/36
12	1

function and the cumulative distribution for this experiment are illustrated diagrammatically by Figure 3–8. The following points related to the cumulative probabilities should be noted:

1. If x_n is the largest value of X, then $F(x_n) = 1$.
2. $F(-\infty) = 0$, $F(\infty) = 1$.
3. $F(x_i) - F(x_{i-1}) = f(x_i) \qquad (x_i > x_{i-1} > x_{i-2} > \cdots)$.

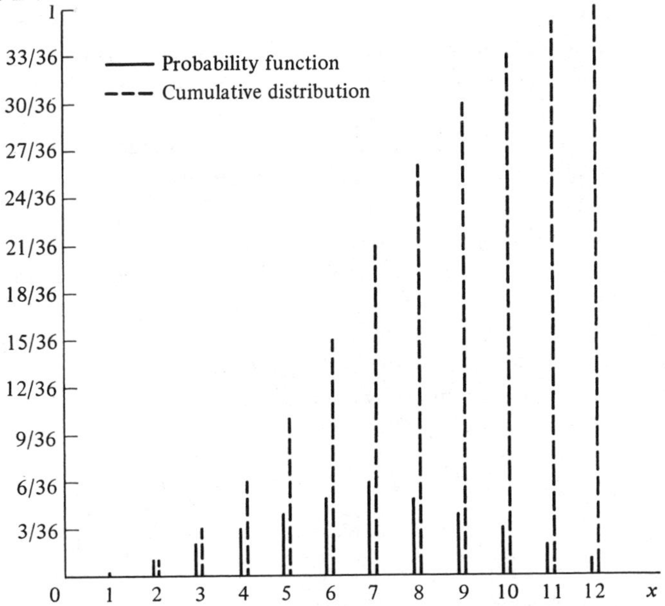

Figure 3–8

So far we have concerned ourselves with only one random variable and its probability distribution. Such distributions may be termed *univariate* distributions. To extend our scope, we can consider a sample space which involves more than one random variable at a time. The corresponding probability distribution is then called a *multivariate* distribution; the case involving only two random variables is a special case known as the *bivariate* distribution. As an example, we might consider the experiment of drawing a card from a pack of 52 cards. Each card is distinguished by two characteristics, denomination and suit. Let X be the denomination with values 1 (for ace), 2, 3, . . . 10, 11 (for Jack), 12 (for Queen), and 13 (for King), and let Y be the suit with values 1 (for Hearts), 2 (for Diamonds), 3 (for Spades), and 4 (for Clubs). The bivariate probability distribution corresponding to this experiment is as follows:

		Values of X						
		1	2	3	. . .	12	13	$f(y)$
Values of Y	1	1/52	1/52	1/52	. . .	1/52	1/52	13/52
	2	1/52	1/52	1/52	. . .	1/52	1/52	13/52
	3	1/52	1/52	1/52	. . .	1/52	1/52	13/52
	4	1/52	1/52	1/52	. . .	1/52	1/52	13/52
	$f(x)$	4/52	4/52	4/52	. . .	4/52	4/52	1

The probability that X assumes a given value x and Y assumes a given value y is called the *joint probability* of x and y and is written as $f(x, y)$. For instance, the probability of drawing a Queen of Hearts is $f(12, 1) = 1/52$. The probability that X will assume a given value x *whatever the value of* Y is called the *marginal probability* of x; the distribution of these probabilities is called the *marginal distribution of* X and, in our example, is given in the bottom row. Similarly, the *marginal distribution of* Y consists of probabilities of different values of Y regardless of the values assumed by X; in our example this distribution is shown in the last right-hand column. Thus, for example, the probability of drawing a Queen (whatever suit) is 4/52, and the probability of drawing a Heart (whatever denomination) is 13/52. Marginal probability distributions are, in fact, univariate distributions and are denoted in the same way, that is, $f(x)$, $f(y)$, etc. Note that the probabilities of the marginal distribution of one variable are given by adding up the corresponding probabilities over *all* values of the other variable. Thus in the bivariate case we can write

$$f(x_i) = \sum_{j=1}^{\infty} f(x_i, y_j) = f(x_i, y_1) + f(x_i, y_2) + \cdots \tag{3.14}$$

and

$$f(y_i) = \sum_{j=1}^{\infty} f(x_j, y_i) = f(x_1, y_i) + f(x_2, y_i) + \cdots. \tag{3.15}$$

Finally, the probability that X is equal to x, *given* that Y is equal to y, is known as the *conditional probability of* x, *given* y, and is denoted by $f(x|y)$. Similarly, the *conditional probability of* y, *given* x, is denoted $f(y|x)$. By applying Theorem 4 we get

$$f(x|y) = \frac{f(x,y)}{f(y)}. \tag{3.16}$$

Using our example of drawing a card from a pack, we see that the probability of drawing, say, a Queen, *given* that the card is a Heart, is

$$f(12|1) = \frac{1/52}{13/52} = \frac{1}{13}$$

and the probability that the card is a Heart, *given* that its denomination is Queen, is

$$f(1|12) = \frac{1/52}{4/52} = \frac{1}{4}.$$

When we consider multivariate distributions, the question of dependence or independence becomes relevant. Earlier we defined independence as the condition under which the conditional probability of an event is equal to its marginal probability. Thus X and Y are independent if and only if, for all values of X and Y,

$$f(x|y) = f(x) \qquad [f(y) \neq 0]$$

and

$$f(y|x) = f(y) \qquad [f(x) \neq 0].$$

This means that for each variable the conditional and the marginal distributions are precisely the same. A further implication given by Theorem 5 is that X and Y are independent if and only if

$$f(x,y) = f(x)f(y) \tag{3.17}$$

for all values of X and Y. This can be generalized to any number of random variables. In particular, discrete random variables $X, Y, Z, \ldots$ are considered to be independent if and only if

$$f(x,y,z,\ldots) = f(x)f(y)f(z)\ldots \tag{3.18}$$

for all values of X, Y, Z, ...

Consider, for example, the experiment of tossing two six-sided dice *twice*. Let X be the variable with values given by the number of dots in the first toss, and Y the variable with values given by the number of dots in the second toss. Obviously, the probabilities of various outcomes of the second toss are completely unaffected by the outcome of the first toss, and vice versa, so that X and Y are independent. Note that the (marginal) distribution of X is precisely the same as that of Y and can be found in Table 3-3. From this we find that the probability of throwing 7 twice is $(6/36)\times(6/36) = 1/36$, the probability of throwing 4 followed by 8 is $(3/36)\times(5/36) = 5/432$, and so on.

With the exception of the various examples, our discussion of probability functions in this section has been quite general. It is obvious that different experimental situations may lead to different probability distributions. When describing these distributions, it is not always necessary to write out the whole distribution as we have done in our examples; frequently we may find an algebraic formula for $f(x)$ (or even for the multivariate case) that will provide a complete description of the distribution in question. Some of the distributions are very common in the sense that they describe the probabilities of many experimental situations encountered in practice. One of the most common probability distributions, and the simplest one, is the so-called *uniform distribution.* In this distribution the probability that X will assume any of a number of specific values is the same; i.e., $f(x)$ is a constant for all values of X. This distribution describes the probabilities of various outcomes of a toss of a die, of pulling a card of a given suit from a pack, of winning in a lottery, and many others. Another extremely common distribution is the so-called *binomial distribution*, which is especially important in statistical inference and will be discussed in detail in Section 4–1.

3–5 Continuous Random Variables and Probability Functions

In the discrete case the elements of sample space are represented by points that are separated by finite distances. To each point we can ascribe a numerical value and to each value we can ascribe a given probability. However, there are many experiments for which the sample space does not consist of countable points but covers an entire interval (or collection of intervals). The random variable associated with the outcomes of such experiments is called a *continuous random variable.* An example of such an experiment is that of observing a freely rotating hand on a clock dial. The random variable in this case may be the time (say in hours) indicated by the hand when stopped at random. There is obviously an infinite number of points between 0 and 12 at which the hand may stop, so that the probability that the hand stops at any particular *point* is zero. On the other hand, the probability that the hand stops within an *interval* around any particular point is nonzero and can be found.

The probabilities associated with the clock-dial experiment for all intervals are shown graphically by Figure 3–9. The probabilities that the value of X will

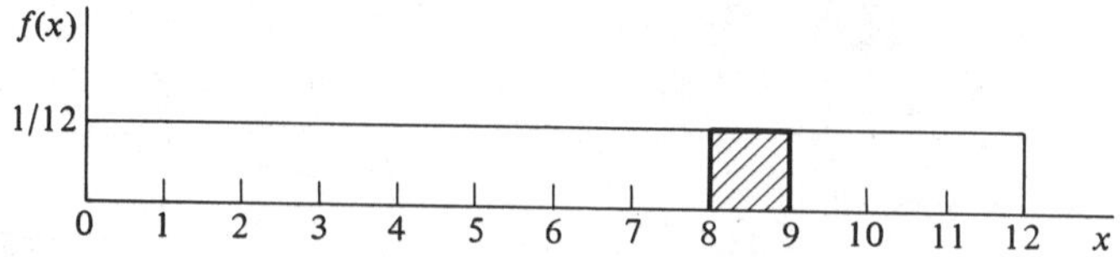

Figure 3–9

fall within any interval are given by the corresponding area under the curve (in this case a straight line). For example, the shaded area in Figure 3–9 gives the probability that x will fall between 8 and 9, which is 1/12. This idea can be generalized to apply to other experiments involving continuous variables. Thus the *probability distribution for a continuous variable X (called the probability density function) is represented by a curve, and the probability that X assumes a value in the interval from a to b* ($a < b$) *is given by the area under this curve bounded by a and b*. Most probability distributions that we will encounter will be continuous.

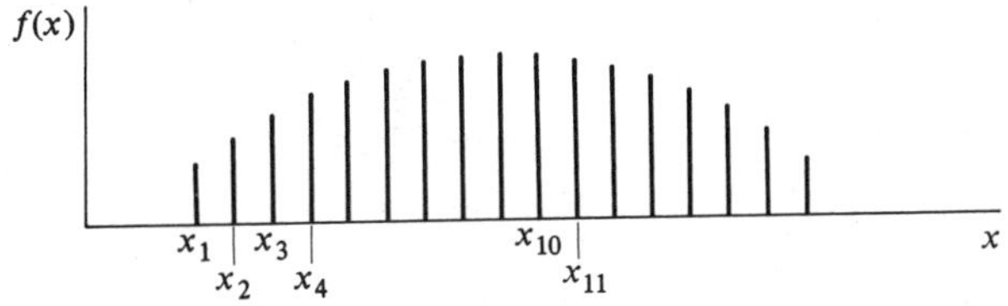

Figure 3–10

To develop the idea of the probability density function further, we can contrast it with the probability function of a discrete variable. Suppose we have a discrete random variable that can assume values $x_1, x_2, \ldots, x_n$, and the values are in ascending order of magnitude. Suppose that the probability function of this variable is given by Figure 3–10. Now the probability that, e.g., X will assume a value greater than x_3 but smaller than or equal to x_{10} is as follows:

$$P(x_3 < x \leq x_{10}) = f(x_4) + f(x_5) + \cdots + f(x_{10}) = \sum_{i=4}^{10} f(x_i).$$

Alternatively we could write

$$P(x_3 < x \leq x_{10}) = F(x_{10}) - F(x_3),$$

where $F(x)$ represents a cumulative distribution function. Suppose we now have a continuous random variable with probability density given by Figure 3–11. Then the probability that X will assume a value in the interval from x_3 to x_{10} is given by the shaded area under the curve. Now, areas under a curve are determined by integrals so that, given that the algebraic formula describing the

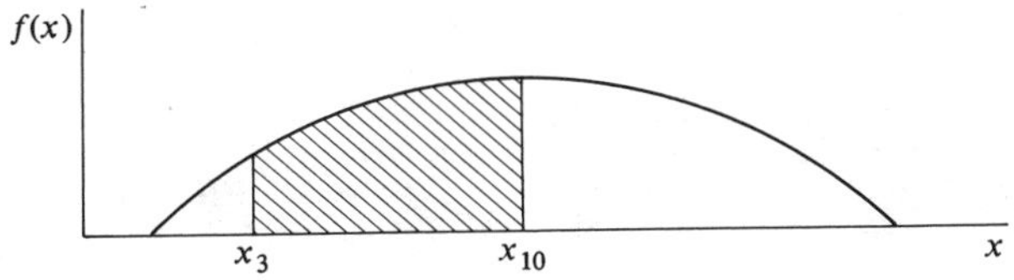

Figure 3–11

density function in Figure 3–11 is $f(x)$, the area under the curve between x_3 and x_{10} is given by the appropriate integral. Thus we have

$$P(x_3 < x < x_{10}) = \int_{x_3}^{x_{10}} f(x)dx.$$

(Since the probability that $x = x_{10}$ is zero, $P(x_3 < x < x_{10})$ and $P(x_3 < x \leq x_{10})$ are equivalent.) The integration from x_3 to x_{10} in the case of the continuous variable is analogous to the summation of probabilities in the discrete case. In general, *if X is a continuous random variable, then the probability that it assumes a value in the interval from a to b is determined by the following*:

(3.19) $$P(a < x < b) = \int_a^b f(x)dx,$$

where f(x) is the relevant probability density function. As it turns out, we will have very little need for actual enumeration of integrals, but they do provide a convenient conceptual framework for considering probability densities.

Since the probability that X will assume *any* value is 1 (i.e., it is a certainty),

(3.20) $$P(-\infty < x < +\infty) = \int_{-\infty}^{+\infty} f(x)dx = 1.$$

Furthermore, the probability that X will assume any value less than or equal to some specific x is

(3.21) $$F(x) = \int_{-\infty}^{x} f(x)dx.$$

As in the discrete case, $F(x)$ is called the *cumulative probability of x*. Note that

1. $F(-\infty) = 0$ and $F(+\infty) = 1$.
2. For $a < b$,

$$F(b) - F(a) = \int_{-\infty}^{b} f(x)dx - \int_{-\infty}^{a} f(x)dx = \int_a^b f(x)dx = P(a < x < b).$$

(In other words, the difference between two cumulative probabilities is equal to simple probability.)

A diagrammatic representation of cumulative probability is given in Figure 3–12.

As in the case of discrete variables, continuous sample spaces may involve more than one variable at a time. The corresponding probability distribution is

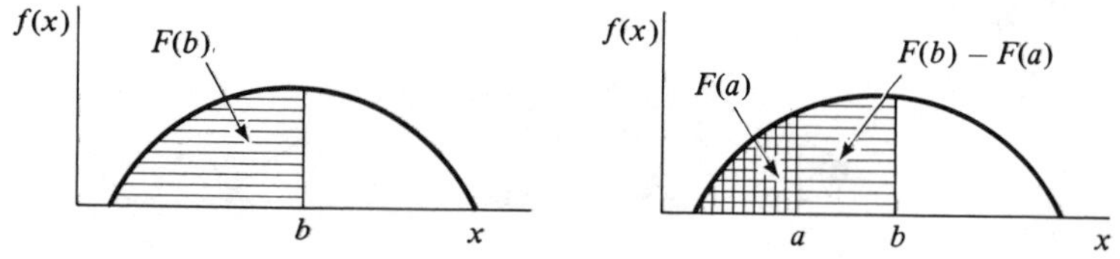

Figure 3–12

called *multivariate probability density*. It gives the *joint probability* that each of the variables involved will fall within specified intervals; if the variables are, e.g., X, Y, Z, then the *joint probability density* would be $f(x, y, z)$. In an analogy with the discrete case, we define *marginal density* of X as the probability density of X whatever the values of the remaining variables. Note that the marginal density of one variable is given by integrating the joint distribution over all values of the other variable, namely,

$$f(x) = \int_{-\infty}^{+\infty} f(x,y)dy \qquad \text{and} \qquad f(y) = \int_{-\infty}^{+\infty} f(x,y)dx.$$

Also, as in the discrete case, the continuous random variables X, Y, Z, . . . are *independent* if and only if

$$f(x, y, z, \ldots) = f(x)f(y)f(z)\ldots. \tag{3.22}$$

Some continuous distributions are of special importance because they are frequently encountered in practice. The *continuous uniform distribution*, used in connection with our clock-dial example and depicted by Figure 3–9, is one such distribution. Another one is the so-called *normal distribution*, which is extremely common and will be discussed at length in Section 4–2. Other distributions will be introduced as the occasion arises.

3–6 Mathematical Expectation

Probability distributions, like ordinary frequency distributions, display various characteristics. These characteristics, of which the best known are the mean and the variance, are defined in terms of so-called *expected values* or *mathematical expectations*. An explanation of these terms can best be carried out by analogy to an ordinary frequency distribution. Suppose, for instance, that we have a sample of 64 families classified by the number of children as shown in Table 3–5. Here n represents absolute frequencies and f represents

Table 3–5

Number of children: x	Number of families: n	Proportion of families: f
0	4	0.06250
1	12	0.18750
2	20	0.31250
3	16	0.25000
4	8	0.12500
5	2	0.03125
6	2	0.03125
	64	1.00000

relative frequencies. There are seven different values of X, $x_1 = 0$, $x_2 = 1, \ldots$, $x_7 = 6$, associated with various frequencies. Let us now determine the average number of children per family. Although several different types of averages exist, most people would in this case probably choose the arithmetic mean—the total number of children in the sample divided by the total number of families. This is given by

$$\bar{x} = \frac{\sum_{i=1}^{7} n_i x_i}{\sum_{i=1}^{7} n_i} = \frac{1}{64}(4 \times 0 + 12 \times 1 + \cdots + 2 \times 6) = 2.40625.$$

The same result would be obtained by using relative frequencies:

$$\bar{x} = \sum_{i=1}^{7} f_i x_i = (0.06250 \times 0 + 0.18750 \times 1 + \cdots + 0.03125 \times 6)$$

$$= 2.40625.$$

That is, the arithmetic mean of a frequency distribution is, in fact, a weighted mean of the different values of the variable with weights given by the respective relative frequencies. Consider now a *discrete random variable* X with the following probability function:

x	$f(x)$
x_1	$f(x_1)$
x_2	$f(x_2)$
$\vdots$	$\vdots$
x_n	$f(x_n)$

where n is some finite number. Then the *expected value* or the *mathematical expectation* of X is

(3.23) $$E(X) = \sum_{i=1}^{n} x_i f(x_i).$$

We can see that $E(X)$ is nothing else but a weighted average of the different values of X with weights given by the respective probabilities. This is the reason why $E(X)$ is identified with the population mean μ; that is,

(3.24) $$\mu = E(X).$$

The analogy between the mean of an ordinary frequency distribution and the expected value of a discrete random variable X should be clear from our exposition.

The term *expected value* is used to emphasize the relation between the population mean and one's anticipation about the outcome of an experiment. Suppose, for instance, that we are asked to toss a six-sided die and are told that we will receive as many dollars as the number of dots shown. The question is how much do we expect to receive before actually throwing the die. If our expectation is formed in accordance with the rule given by (3.23), the answer is

$$E(X) = 1 \times \frac{1}{6} + 2 \times \frac{1}{6} + \cdots + 6 \times \frac{1}{6} = 3.5.$$

While we cannot actually get (and therefore do not "expect" in the colloquial sense of the word) \$3.50, this figure represents a summary of the possible results. If the tosses were repeated an infinite number of times, the average return per toss would be precisely \$3.50.

The *expected value of a continuous variable* is defined in a very similar fashion. As we mentioned earlier, we may view a continuous variable as a limiting case of a discrete variable, where the values that the variable can assume get more and more numerous and closer and closer to each other. Therefore, if X is a continuous random variable with probability density $f(x)$, its expected value (or mathematical expectation) is

$$E(X) = \int_{-\infty}^{+\infty} x f(x) dx. \tag{3.25}$$

The integration is carried out from $-\infty$ to $+\infty$ to make sure that all possible values of X are covered.

It should be noted that there are some probability distributions for which the *expected value of the variable does not exist*; that is, $E(X)$ might be equal to infinity. A classical example is given by the following probability function:

x	$f(x)$
2	1/2
4	1/4
8	1/8
16	1/16
⋮	⋮

This is a perfectly legitimate probability function since $f(x) \geq 0$ for every x and

$$\sum_{i=1}^{\infty} f(x_i) = \frac{1}{2} + \frac{1}{4} + \frac{1}{8} + \cdots = 1.$$

In fact, $f(x)$ can be interpreted as representing the probability of getting 1 head in 1 toss of an unbiased coin, 2 heads in 2 tosses, 3 heads in 3 tosses, and so on in an ascending order. The expected value of X is[1]

[1] This case is known as the *St. Petersburg paradox*. Suppose somebody asks us to toss a coin and offers to pay us \$2 if we get a head in the first toss but not in the second; \$4 if we get a head in the first and the second toss but not in the third; \$8 if we get a head in the first, second, and third toss but not in the fourth; and so on. How much is the value of this game to us? According to our calculations, the expected value (i.e., the expected gain in this case) is infinity, but it is unlikely that anybody would be willing to pay that amount (or even, say, a mere million dollars) for the privilege of playing this game. This is the paradoxical aspect of the situation.

$$E(X) = 2\times\frac{1}{2} + 4\times\frac{1}{4} + 8\times\frac{1}{8} + \cdots = 1 + 1 + 1 + \cdots = \infty.$$

Fortunately, distributions of this sort are not very frequent. In what follows we shall assume that we are dealing with distributions for which expected values exist. When this is not the case, we shall make the point of emphasizing it.

The concept of mathematical expectation can easily be extended to apply to problems other than simple determination of the mean value of X. In particular, if X is a random variable and $g(X)$ is a single-valued function of this variable, then,

$$(3.26) \qquad Eg(X) = \begin{cases} \sum_{i=1}^{\infty} g(x_i)f(x_i) & (X \text{ discrete}) \\ \int_{-\infty}^{+\infty} g(x)f(x)dx & (X \text{ continuous}). \end{cases}$$

As an example, we shall prove the following theorem.

Theorem 6 *If X is a random variable and a and b are constants, then*

$$E(aX + b) = aE(X) + b.$$

Proof: (a) X is discrete:

$$\begin{aligned} E(aX + b) &= \sum_{i=1}^{n} (ax_i + b)f(x_i) \\ &= \sum_i ax_i f(x_i) + \sum_i bf(x_i) \\ &= a\sum_i x_i f(x_i) + b\sum_i f(x_i) \\ &= aE(X) + b. \end{aligned}$$

(b) X is continuous:

$$\begin{aligned} E(aX + b) &= \int_{-\infty}^{+\infty} (ax + b)f(x)dx \\ &= \int axf(x)dx + \int bf(x)dx \\ &= aE(X) + b. \end{aligned}$$

A direct application of (3.26) enables us to determine special characteristics of a probability distribution called *moments*. These represent a family of parameters which characterize a distribution. Two kinds of moments can be distinguished: moments about the origin (i.e., zero) and moments about the mean (i.e., μ). *Moments about the origin* are defined by

$$(3.27) \qquad \mu_r' = E(X^r) = \begin{cases} \sum_i x_i^r f(x_i) & (X \text{ discrete}) \\ \int_{-\infty}^{+\infty} x^r f(x)dx & (X \text{ continuous}) \end{cases}$$

for $r = 0, 1, 2, \ldots$. That is, substitution of different values for r will lead to moments of different order. In particular,

$$\mu_0' = 1,$$

$$\mu_1' = E(X) = \mu.$$

Thus the *mean is the first moment about the origin.* Moments about the origin of order higher than one are less commonly used and have no special names. *Moments about the mean* are defined by

$$(3.28) \qquad \mu_r = E[(X - \mu)^r] = \begin{cases} \sum_i (x_i - \mu)^r f(x_i) & (X \text{ discrete}) \\ \int_{-\infty}^{+\infty} (x - \mu)^r f(x) dx & (X \text{ continuous}) \end{cases}$$

for $r = 0, 1, 2, \ldots$. Note that

$$\mu_0 = 1,$$

$$\mu_1 = E(X - \mu) = E(X) - \mu = 0,$$

$$\mu_2 = E(X - \mu)^2 = \text{Var}(X).$$

Thus the *variance is the second moment about the mean.* Its square root is called the *standard deviation* of the distribution.

The most important characteristics of a distribution are noted below.

1. The *mean* $\mu = E(X)$ is a measure of central tendency of a distribution. Its chief distinction is the fact that in the population the deviations of all the values of X from μ average out to zero. This is true whether the variable is discrete or continuous. In particular, we see that in the discrete case we have:

$$\sum_i (x_i - \mu) f(x_i) = \sum_i x_i f(x_i) - \mu = E(X) - \mu = 0.$$

If the distribution is symmetric, then the mean lies in its center.

2. The *variance* σ^2 or Var(X), frequently presented as

$$(3.29) \qquad \text{Var}(X) = E[X - E(X)]^2,$$

is a measure of the spread or dispersion of a distribution. It is, in fact, the mean of the squared deviations of X from μ since, by the definition of mathematical expectation,

$$\sigma^2 = \begin{cases} \sum_i (x_i - \mu)^2 f(x_i) & (X \text{ discrete}) \\ \int_{-\infty}^{+\infty} (X - \mu)^2 f(x) dx & (X \text{ continuous}). \end{cases}$$

Variance, of course, can never be negative. If all values of X are highly concentrated, the point of concentration must be the mean (or at least its neighborhood) and the variance will be very small. In the extreme case where all values of X are the same (i.e., X is a constant), the variance will be equal to zero. Note that an alternative way of determining the variance can be developed as follows:

(3.30)
$$\sigma^2 = E(X - \mu)^2 = E(X^2 - 2\mu X + \mu^2)$$
$$= E(X^2) - 2\mu E(X) + \mu^2 = E(X^2) - \mu^2,$$

since μ is a constant. Further, we have an important theorem:

Theorem 7 *If X is a random variable and a and b are constants, then*

$$Var(aX + b) = a^2 Var(X).$$

Proof:

$$\text{Var}(aX + b) = E[(aX + b) - E(aX + b)]^2$$

by the definition of a variance. Now,

$$E(aX + b) = aE(X) + b$$

by Theorem 6, where $E(X) = \mu$ by definition. Therefore,

$$\text{Var}(aX + b) = E[aX + b - (a\mu + b)]^2 = E[aX - a\mu]^2$$
$$= E[a^2(X - \mu)^2] = a^2E[(X - \mu)^2] = a^2\text{Var}(X).$$

Sometimes it is more convenient to use the *standard deviation* of X, which is simply

$$\sigma = \sqrt{\text{Var}(X)}.$$

3. A *measure of skewness* (departure from symmetry) is given by

(3.31)
$$\mu_3 = E(X - \mu)^3.$$

If the distribution is symmetric, μ_3 will be equal to zero. If the distribution is skewed to the left (i.e., its left tail is elongated), μ_3 will be negative, and if the distribution is skewed to the right, μ_3 will be positive. In Figure 3–13, the first distribution, $f_1(x)$, is skewed to the left, the second, $f_2(x)$, is symmetric, and the

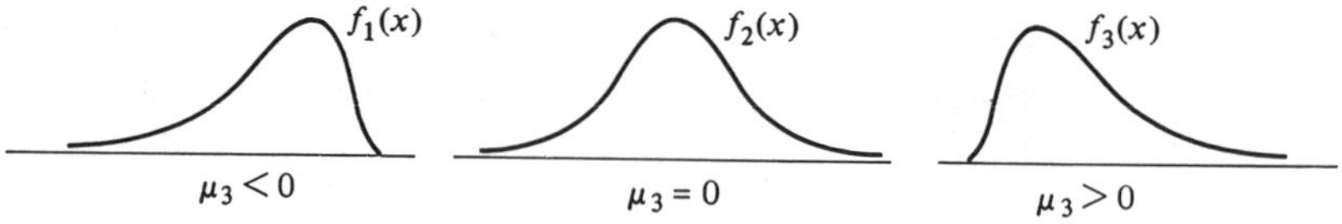

Figure 3–13

third, $f_3(x)$, is skewed to the right. For many purposes it is preferable to use a slightly different measure of skewness, called α_3, which is defined as

(3.32)
$$\alpha_3 = \frac{\mu_3}{\sigma^3}.$$

The denominator in this expression functions as a scale factor so that comparisons of different distributions with respect to skewness are not distorted by the differences in dispersion. Since $\sigma^3 = [\text{Var}(X)]^{3/2}$ is always positive, the sign of α_3 is fully determined by the sign of μ_3.

So far we have considered only univariate probability distributions, but there is no difficulty in extending the concept of mathematical expectation to distributions involving more than one random variable. Suppose we have two random variables X and Y with a joint distribution $f(x,y)$. We wish to determine the expected value of some single-valued function of X and Y, say $g(X, Y)$. Then,

$$(3.33) \qquad E[g(X, Y)] = \begin{cases} \sum_{i=1}^{\infty} \sum_{j=1}^{\infty} g(x_i, y_j) f(x_i, y_j) & (X \text{ and } Y \text{ discrete}) \\ \int_{-\infty}^{+\infty} \int_{-\infty}^{+\infty} g(x,y) f(x,y) dx dy & (X \text{ and } Y \text{ continuous}). \end{cases}$$

This can be generalized for any number of random variables. Some functions of random variables are of special interest; these are given in the following theorems, which are very important in econometric theory. We shall prove them for two discrete random variables, but the extension to other cases is quite straightforward.

Theorem 8 *The expected value of a sum of random variables is equal to the sum of their expected values, i.e.,* $E(X + Y + Z + \cdots) = E(X) + E(Y) + E(Z) + \cdots$.

Proof:

$$\begin{aligned} E(X + Y) &= \sum_i \sum_j (x_i + y_j) f(x_i y_j) = \sum_i \sum_j x_i f(x_i, y_j) + \sum_i \sum_j y_j f(x_i, y_j) \\ &= \sum_i x_i \sum_j f(x_i, y_j) + \sum_j y_j \sum_i f(x_i, y_j) = \sum_i x_i f(x_i) + \sum_j y_j f(y_j) \\ &= E(X) + E(Y). \end{aligned}$$

Theorem 9 *The expected value of a linear combination of random variables is equal to the linear combination of their expected values, i.e.,*

$$E(aX + bY + cZ + \cdots) = aE(X) + bE(Y) + cE(Z) + \cdots,$$

where $a, b, c, \ldots$ *are any constants.*

Proof:

$$\begin{aligned} E(aX + bY) &= \sum_i \sum_j (ax_i + by_i) f(x_i, y_j) \\ &= \sum_i \sum_j ax_i f(x_i, y_j) + \sum_i \sum_j by_j f(x_i, y_j) \\ &= a \sum_i x_i \sum_j f(x_i, y_j) + b \sum_j y_j \sum_i f(x_i, y_j) \\ &= aE(X) + bE(Y). \end{aligned}$$

Theorem 10 *If X and Y are two independent random variables, then the expected value of their product is equal to the product of their expected values, i.e.,* $E(XY) = E(X)E(Y)$.

Proof:

$$E(XY) = \sum_i \sum_j x_i y_j f(x_i, y_j).$$

But if X and Y are independent,

$$f(x_i, y_j) = f(x_i)f(y_j).$$

Therefore,

$$E(XY) = \sum_i \sum_j x_i y_j f(x_i)f(y_j) = \sum_i x_i f(x_i) \sum_j y_j f(y_j) = E(X)E(Y).$$

It is important to note the difference in the expected value of a sum and the expected value of a product. The expected value of a sum is *always* equal to the sum of expected values, whereas the expected value of a product is equal to the product of the expected values *only* if the variables are uncorrelated.

The last theorem on expected values that we intend to present requires the definition of a *covariance* between two random variables, say X and Y. This is usually denoted by $\text{Cov}(X, Y)$ (or sometimes σ_{XY}) and is defined as

$$\text{Cov}(X, Y) = E[X - E(X)][Y - E(Y)]. \tag{3.34}$$

The sign of the covariance depends on the direction of association between X and Y. If there is a positive association—that is, if small values of X tend to be associated with small values of Y and large values of X with large values of Y—then the covariance will be *positive*. If, on the other hand, there is a negative association—that is, if small values of X tend to be associated with large values of Y and large values of X with small values of Y—the covariance will be *negative*. (Here by "small" we mean values less than the mean and by "large," values greater than the mean.) That is, if there is a positive association, then $[x - E(X)]$ and $[y - E(Y)]$ will tend to be of the same sign; therefore, their product will tend to be positive and this will make for a positive covariance. But if there is a negative association, $[x - E(X)]$ and $[y - E(Y)]$ will tend to be of opposite signs; therefore, their product will tend to be negative, and this will be reflected in the sign of the covariance. An illustration is given by Figure 3–14.

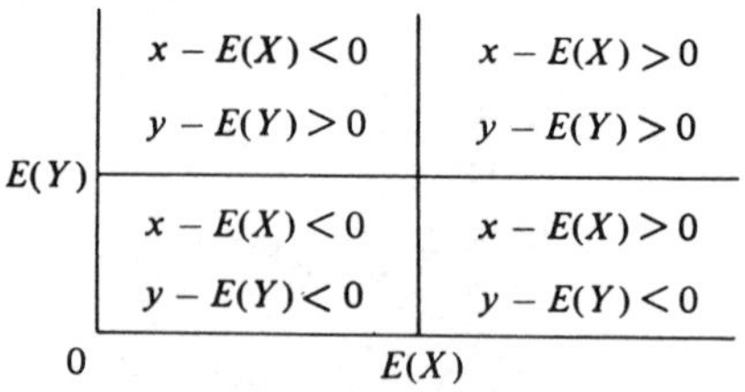

Figure 3–14

With this introduction we can now present the following theorem:

Theorem 11 *If X and Y are two independent random variables, then*

$$Cov(X, Y) = 0.$$

Proof:

$$\begin{aligned}\text{Cov}(X, Y) &= E[X - E(X)][Y - E(Y)] \\ &= E[XY - YE(X) - XE(Y) + E(X)E(Y)] \\ &= E(XY) - E(X)E(Y).\end{aligned}$$

But if X and Y are independent, then, by Theorem 10,

$$E(XY) = E(X)E(Y);$$

therefore $$\text{Cov}(X, Y) = E(X)E(Y) - E(X)E(Y) = 0.$$

It is important to note that while independence necessarily implies zero covariance, the *converse is not true.* It is not very difficult to find cases for which $\text{Cov}(X, Y) = 0$ and yet X and Y are not independent. As an example consider the following distribution:

		Values of Y 0	1	$f(x)$
Values of X	1	0	1/3	1/3
	2	1/3	0	1/3
	3	0	1/3	1/3
	$f(y)$	1/3	2/3	1

X and Y are obviously not independent since the conditional and the marginal distributions are quite different. Now,

$$\text{Cov}(X, Y) = E[X - E(X)][Y - E(Y)] = E(XY) - E(X)E(Y).$$

But $$E(XY) = \sum_i \sum_j x_i y_j f(x_i, y_j) = 1\times 1\times\frac{1}{3} + 2\times 0\times\frac{1}{3} + 3\times 1\times\frac{1}{3} = \frac{4}{3}.$$

Further, $$E(X) = 1\times\frac{1}{3} + 2\times\frac{1}{3} + 3\times\frac{1}{3} = 2$$

and $$E(Y) = 0\times\frac{1}{3} + 1\times\frac{2}{3} = \frac{2}{3}.$$

Therefore, $$\text{Cov}(X, Y) = \frac{4}{3} - 2\times\frac{2}{3} = 0.$$

The variables that have zero covariance are called *uncorrelated*. The point of the preceding discussion was to show that independence is a sufficient but not necessary condition for zero covariance. In a broad sense, the difference between independence and noncorrelation lies in the fact that independence rules out any kind of relationship, whereas noncorrelation rules out only *linear* relations between variables.

As a final point we note that, in analogy to the concept of conditional probability, we have *conditional expectation* of, say, Y given X, which is defined as

$$(3.35)\qquad E(Y|X) = \begin{cases} \sum_i y_i f(y_i|x_i) & (Y \text{ discrete}) \\ \int_{-\infty}^{+\infty} y f(y|x) dy & (Y \text{ continuous}). \end{cases}$$

That is, the conditional expectation of Y given X is equal to the mean of the conditional distribution of Y given X. In terms of the example just given, the conditional expectation of Y given that the value of X is 1 is

$$E(Y|x = 1) = 0 \times \frac{0}{1/3} + 1 \times \frac{1/3}{1/3} = 1.$$

Also

$$E(Y|x = 2) = 0 \times \frac{1/3}{1/3} + 1 \times \frac{0}{1/3} = 0$$

and

$$E(Y|x = 3) = 0 \times \frac{0}{1/3} + 1 \times \frac{1/3}{1/3} = 1,$$

while the unconditional mean of Y is

$$E(Y) = 0 \times \frac{1}{3} + 1 \times \frac{2}{3} = \frac{2}{3}.$$

The concept of the conditional expectation can be generalized to any single-valued function of Y, say $g(Y)$. Then, we have

$$(3.36)\qquad E[g(Y)|X] = \begin{cases} \sum_i g(y_i) f(y_i|x_i) & (Y \text{ discrete}) \\ \int_{-\infty}^{+\infty} g(y) f(y|x) dy & (Y \text{ continuous}). \end{cases}$$

There is one important difference between an unconditional and a conditional expectation: while $E[g(Y)]$ is always a constant, $E[g(Y)|X]$ is not necessarily a constant but may be a function of X.

In the rest of this book, operations involving expected values will be quite frequent. This is because we are very much concerned with the derivation of the properties of sampling distributions, and, as pointed out earlier, sampling distributions are nothing but probability distributions of estimators or test statistics. Expected values are very convenient means of describing the characteristics of these distributions.

EXERCISES

3–1. List the elements of the sample spaces corresponding to the following experiments:

a. Drawing (with replacement) two balls from an urn containing 7 white and 3 red balls.

b. Flipping a coin and, providing a head appears, rolling a six-sided dice (if a tail appears, the experiment is stopped).

c. Drawing cards from a pack of 52 cards until a face card is obtained.

3–2. In how many different ways can three men and three women sit around a dinner table if **(a)** the seating arrangement is not restricted in any way; **(b)** each woman is to be between two men; **(c)** the arrangement is to be the same as in **(b)** but the hostess insists on sitting on the chair nearest to the kitchen?

3–3. How many different samples of size 20 can be drawn (with replacement) from a population of 30 objects?

3–4. The following questions will require probability calculations with a six-sided die. Determine the probability of **(a)** getting an even number or a number in excess of 3; **(b)** getting a 4 followed by a 5; **(c)** not getting a 4 in either of two rolls; **(d)** getting a 4 at least once in two rolls; **(e)** not getting two 7's in two rolls.

3–5. Consider the following set of equally likely outcomes:

$$S = \{1, 2, \ldots, n\}$$

where n is a multiple of six. Define

$$S_1 = \{1, 3, \ldots, (n-1)\}.$$
$$S_2 = \{2, 4, \ldots, n\}.$$
$$S_3 = \{3, 6, \ldots, n\}.$$

Find the following probabilities:

a. $P(n)$, $P(S_1)$, $P(S_2)$, and $P(S_3)$.

b. $P(S_1 \cap S_3)$.

c. $P(S_2 \cap S_3)$.

d. $P(S_1 \cup S_2)$.

e. $P(S_1 \cup S_3)$.

f. $P(S_2 \cup S_3)$.

g. $P[S_1(S_2 \cap S_3)]$.

3–6. Let S_1 and S_2 be subsets of the sample space S. Given $P(S_1)$, $P(S_2)$, and $P(S_1 \cap S_2)$, find

a. $P(\bar{S}_1 \cup \bar{S}_2)$.

b. $P(\bar{S}_1 \cap \bar{S}_2)$.

c. $P(\bar{S}_1 \cap S_2)$.

d. $P(\bar{S}_1 \cup S_2)$.

3–7. Three boys are asked to guess which of three jars contains a cookie. If the guess of the first is correct, he will get the cookie. If the guess is incorrect, the empty jar will be removed and the next boy will have his turn at guessing. If his guess is correct, he will get the cookie, otherwise the cookie will go to the third boy. Is there any advantage in being the first, second, or third boy? Give reasons.

3–8. In Michigan, the automobile license plates show two letters followed by four numbers. How many different license plates can be made in this way?

3–9. Show that $\sum_{i=0}^{n} \binom{a}{i}\binom{b}{n-i} = \binom{a+b}{n}$, $\quad a, b > n$.

3–10. The records for a certain large city show the following distribution of applicants for unskilled jobs by the duration of their unemployment:

Duration of unemployment (weeks)	0	1	2	3	4	5	6	7	8	9–12
Proportion of applicants	0.25	0.20	0.15	0.10	0.10	0.05	0.04	0.03	0.02	0.06

a. What is the expected duration of unemployment of an applicant?

b. Calculate the value of the standard deviation and of the α_3-measure of skewness of this distribution.

3–11. If X is a random variable with mean μ and variance σ^2, and if Z is defined as $Z = X - (X - \mu)/\sigma$, find $E(Z)$ and $\text{Var}(Z)$.

3–12. If X is a random variable with mean μ and b is a constant different from μ, prove that $E(X - \mu)^2 < E(X - b)^2$.

3–13. If X and Y are two random variables and a and b are constants, prove that

a. $\text{Var}(X + a) = \text{Var}(X)$.

b. $\text{Var}(Y + b) = \text{Var}(Y)$.

c. $\text{Cov}[(X + a), (Y + b)] = \text{Cov}(X, Y)$.

3–14. Consider a sample of identically and independently distributed variables $X_1, X_2, \ldots, X_n$, each having a mean μ and variance σ^2. Find, for $i = 1, 2, \ldots, n$ and $i \neq j$:

a. $E(X_i\bar{X})$.

b. $E(X_i^2)$.

c. $E(\bar{X}^2)$.

d. $E[X_i(X_i - \bar{X})]$.

e. $E[\bar{X}(X_i - \bar{X})]$.

f. $E[X_i(X_j - \bar{X})]$.

g. $\text{Var}(X_i - \bar{X})$.

h. $\text{Cov}(X_i, \bar{X})$.

i. $\text{Cov}[(X_i - \bar{X}), \bar{X}]$.

j. $\text{Cov}[(X_i - \bar{X}), (X_j - \bar{X})]$.

3–15. Consider three random variables X, Y, and Z. Prove that **(a)** the fact that X is uncorrelated with Y and Y is uncorrelated with Z does not imply that X is uncorrelated with Z; **(b)** the fact that X is independent of Y and Y is independent of Z does not imply that X is independent of Z.

3–16. Prove that

$$\mu_r = \mu'_r + (-1)^1\binom{r}{1}\mu'_{r-1}\mu + \cdots + (-1)^i\binom{r}{i}\mu'_{r-i}\mu^i + \cdots + (-1)^{r-1}(r-1)\mu^r$$

for $r = 1, 2, 3, \ldots$.
(If the proof for the general case is too difficult, give a proof for $r = 1, 2$, and 3.)

3–17. The joint distribution of X and Y is as follows:

		X				
		−2	−1	0	1	2
Y	10	.09	.15	.27	.25	.04
	20	.01	.05	.08	.05	.01

a. Find the marginal distributions of X and Y.

b. Find the conditional distribution of X given $y = 20$.

c. Are X and Y uncorrelated?

d. Are X and Y independent?

3–18. A company has to decide between two investment projects. Project A will yield a \$20,000 profit if it is successful or a loss of \$2,000 if it is unsuccessful, whereas Project B will yield \$25,000 profit if it is successful or \$5,000 loss if it is not. The probability of a project being successful is thought to be the same for both projects. Find this probability given that, on the basis of expected profit, the two projects were judged to be equivalent.

4 Theoretical Derivation of Sampling Distributions

The purpose of the discussion on probability and probability distributions in Chapter 3 was to provide tools for theoretical derivation of the sampling distributions of estimators and test statistics, and also to facilitate our understanding of the process and results of estimation or hypotheses testing. In this chapter we come to the point where we shall *use* probability theory to derive various sampling distributions. As explained in Section 1–5, sampling distributions can be derived either experimentally or theoretically. In the experimental approach we construct our population from which we draw a large number of samples. Each sample then provides us with one value of the estimator or test statistic with which we are concerned. The resulting frequency distribution is our approximation of the probability distribution that we would have obtained had the number of samples been not just large but infinite. The experimental approach has two major disadvantages. The first is that we have to be satisfied with approximations of sampling distributions instead of their exact forms, and the second is that the results are, strictly speaking, applicable only to the specific population underlying the experiment. Theoretically derived sampling distributions are free from both of these difficulties and are, therefore, clearly superior to those that are experimentally derived. The one drawback in using the theoretical approach is that it may not always work—in the sense that our mathematical knowledge and skill may not be sufficient to lead to results. This happens particularly frequently with respect to estimators of a system of economic relations, as we shall see in Chapter 13.

In this chapter we shall limit ourselves to the derivation of the sampling distribution of sample proportion of successes and of sample mean. Both of these distributions were already derived experimentally for specific populations in Chapter 2, and can be derived mathematically for any population without much difficulty. Other sampling distributions will be discussed later as the occasion arises.

4–1 Sampling Distribution of Sample Proportion of Successes: Binomial Distribution

Consider a population in which every unit can be classified as either possessing or not possessing a given attribute. This population may or may not be infinite.

If it is not infinite, then we assume that, when we draw a sample, every unit drawn is replaced before another unit is drawn (i.e., we have sampling with replacement). This means that there is no limit to sample size. A unit that possesses the given attribute will be called a *success*; that which does not, a *failure*. As a concrete example, we may envision that we are dealing with the adult population of the United States at a given point of time and that the attribute of interest is whether a person is a coffee-drinker or a non-coffee-drinker. Drawing a coffee-drinker is considered a success, a non-coffee-drinker a failure. In accordance with Section 2–1 let us use the following notation:

π = proportion (or limit of relative frequency) of successes in the population;

ρ = proportion (or limit of relative frequency) of failures in the population;

n = size of sample;

$\hat{\pi}$ = proportion of successes in the sample;

X = number of successes in the sample.

Note that if we make a single random drawing, the probability of success is π and of failure ρ. Let S stand for "success," and F for "failure." Then we have

$$P(S) = \pi$$

and

$$P(F) = \rho \quad \text{or} \quad P(F) = 1 - \pi,$$

since F is "not S."

Let us now derive the sampling distributions of X and $\hat{\pi}$ for samples of various sizes. Since there is a one-to-one correspondence between X and $\hat{\pi}$ given by the fact that

$$\hat{\pi} = \frac{X}{n} \quad \text{or} \quad X = n\hat{\pi},$$

knowledge of the distribution of X gives a complete knowledge of the distribution of $\hat{\pi}$, and vice versa. We will give a full description of sampling distributions for each sample size, using X as the random variable; however, we will determine the main distributional characteristics for both X as well as $\hat{\pi}$. In presenting each distribution, we will determine the values of X, their probability, and the values of $xf(x)$ and $x^2f(x)$ which are needed for calculating the mean and the variance.

Sampling Distribution for Samples Size 1

Number of Successes: x		Probability: $f(x)$	$xf(x)$	$x^2f(x)$
0		$P(F) = \rho$	0	0
1		$P(S) = \pi$	π	π
	Sum	$\rho + \pi = 1$	π	π

Mean and variance of X:

$$E(X) = \sum_i x_i f(x_i) = \pi,$$

$$\text{Var}(X) = E(X^2) - [E(X)]^2 = \sum_i x_i^2 f(x_i) - \left[\sum_i x_i f(x_i)\right]^2$$

$$= \pi - \pi^2 = \pi(1 - \pi) = \pi\rho,$$

Mean and variance of $\hat{\pi}$:

$$E(\hat{\pi}) = E\left(\frac{X}{n}\right) = E(X) = \pi,$$

$$\text{Var}(\hat{\pi}) = \text{Var}\left(\frac{X}{n}\right) = \text{Var}(X) = \pi\rho.$$

Sampling Distribution for Samples Size 2

Number of Successes: x	Probability: $f(x)$	$xf(x)$	$x^2f(x)$
0	$P(F)P(F) = \rho^2$	0	0
1	$P(S)P(F) + P(F)P(S) = 2\pi\rho$	$2\pi\rho$	$2\pi\rho$
2	$P(S)P(S) = \pi^2$	$2\pi^2$	$4\pi^2$
Sum	$(\rho + \pi)^2 = 1$	$2\pi(\rho + \pi)$	$2\pi(\rho + 2\pi)$

Note that the "no success" can be obtained only if both the first and second observations are failures. Since drawings are random, the outcomes of the first and the second drawings are independent, therefore the probability of two failures is equal to the product $P(F)P(F)$. The same applies to the probability of two successes. However, "one success and one failure" can be obtained in two ways, either success followed by failure or failure followed by success. The two are mutually exclusive so that the probability of one failure and one success is $P(S)P(F) + P(F)P(S)$, as shown.

Mean and variance of X:

$$E(X) = 2\pi(\rho + \pi) = 2\pi,$$

$$\text{Var}(X) = 2\pi(\rho + 2\pi) - [2\pi]^2 = 2\pi\rho + 4\pi^2 - 4\pi^2 = 2\pi\rho.$$

Mean and variance of $\hat{\pi}$:

$$E(\hat{\pi}) = E\left(\frac{X}{2}\right) = \pi,$$

$$\text{Var}(\hat{\pi}) = \text{Var}\left(\frac{X}{2}\right) = \frac{1}{4}\text{Var}(X) \quad \text{(by Theorem 7)}$$

$$= \frac{\pi\rho}{2}.$$

Sampling Distribution for Samples Size 3

Number of Successes: x	Probability: $f(x)$	$xf(x)$	$x^2f(x)$
0	$P(F)P(F)P(F) = \rho^3$	0	0
1	$P(S)P(F)P(F) + P(F)P(S)P(F) + P(F)P(F)P(S) = 3\pi\rho^2$	$3\rho^2\pi$	$3\rho^2\pi$
2	$P(S)P(S)P(F) + P(S)P(F)P(S) + P(F)P(S)P(S) = 3\pi^2\rho$	$6\rho\pi^2$	$12\rho\pi^2$
3	$P(S)P(S)P(S) = \pi^3$	$3\pi^3$	$9\pi^3$
	Sum $(\rho + \pi)^3 = 1$		

Mean and variance of X:

$$E(X) = 3\rho^2\pi + 6\rho\pi^2 + 3\pi^3 = 3\pi(\rho^2 + 2\rho\pi + \pi^2) = 3\pi(\rho + \pi)^2 = 3\pi.$$

$$\begin{aligned}\text{Var}(X) &= 3\rho^2\pi + 12\rho\pi^2 + 9\pi^3 - (3\pi)^2 = 3\rho^2\pi + 12\rho\pi^2 + 9\pi^2(\pi - 1)\\ &= 3\rho^2\pi + 12\rho\pi^2 - 9\rho\pi^2 = 3\rho\pi(\rho + 4\pi - 3\pi) = 3\rho\pi.\end{aligned}$$

Mean and variance of $\hat{\pi}$:

$$E(\hat{\pi}) = E\left(\frac{X}{3}\right) = \pi.$$

$$\text{Var}(\hat{\pi}) = \text{Var}\left(\frac{X}{3}\right) = \frac{1}{9}\,\text{Var}(X) = \frac{\pi\rho}{3}.$$

We could continue this for larger and larger sample sizes, but the results are already obvious: the probabilities of drawing 0, 1, 2, . . . , n successes in a sample size n are given by the respective terms of $(\rho + \pi)^n$, the so-called *binomial*

Table 4–1

	$f(x)$					
x	Size 1	Size 2	Size 3	Size 4	. . .	Size n
0	ρ	ρ^2	ρ^3	ρ^4		ρ^n
1	π	$2\rho\pi$	$3\rho^2\pi$	$4\rho^3\pi$		$\binom{n}{1}\rho^{n-1}\pi$
2		π^2	$3\rho\pi^2$	$6\rho^2\pi^2$		$\binom{n}{2}\rho^{n-2}\pi^2$
3			π^3	$4\rho\pi^3$		$\binom{n}{3}\rho^{n-3}\pi^3$
4				π^4		$\binom{n}{4}\rho^{n-4}\pi^4$
⋮						⋮
$n - 1$						$\binom{n}{n-1}\rho\pi^{n-1}$
n						π^n

expansion. Table 4–1 summarizes the distributions of X for various sample sizes. Note that the first element in the last column could also be written as

$$\rho^n = \binom{n}{0}\rho^n\pi^0,$$

and the last element in the same column as

$$\pi^n = \binom{n}{n}\rho^0\pi^n.$$

Thus the probability of getting x successes in a sample size n is

$$f(x) = \binom{n}{x}\rho^{n-x}\pi^x. \tag{4.1}$$

Similarly, the probability of obtaining $\hat{\pi}$ proportion of successes in a sample size n is

$$f(\hat{\pi}) = \binom{n}{n\hat{\pi}}\rho^{n(1-\hat{\pi})}\pi^{n\hat{\pi}}. \tag{4.2}$$

These probabilities can be interpreted as limits of relative frequencies, i.e., the frequencies that would be obtained if an infinite number of samples of each size were taken. The distributions defined by these probabilities are, therefore, the true and exact sampling distributions: (4.1) defines the sampling distribution of the number of successes, and (4.2) the sampling distribution of the proportion of successes.

The calculation of the individual probabilities of the binomial distribution becomes quite laborious unless the sample size is very small. Some work can be saved by using *Pascal's triangle* (Figure 3–3), which gives the values of

$$\binom{n}{1},\ \binom{n}{2},\ \binom{n}{3},\ \text{and so on,}$$

for any n. But we can save ourselves all the calculating work involved if we use the tables of *binomial probabilities* which give the probabilities for different values of n and π.[1] For large values of n, the binomial distribution can be reasonably well approximated by the so-called *normal distribution* (unless π is very small and $n\pi$ remains constant as $n \to \infty$). This will be discussed in detail in Section 4–2.

Let us now derive the basic characteristics of the sampling distribution of X and of $\hat{\pi}$. In particular, we are interested in the mean, the variance, and the skewness of these distributions. The mean and the variance for samples size 1, 2, and 3 are summarized in Table 4–2. The generalization to sample size n is quite straightforward. Its validity could be proved without much difficulty, but the

[1] These are available in quite a few statistical texts or handbooks, including John E. Freund, *Mathematical Statistics* (Englewood Cliffs, N.J.: Prentice-Hall, 1962).

Table 4–2

Sample Size	Mean: Number of Successes: x	Mean: Proportion of Successes: $\hat{\pi}$	Variance: Number of Successes: x	Variance: Proportion of Successes: $\hat{\pi}$
1	π	π	$\pi\rho$	$\pi\rho$
2	2π	π	$2\pi\rho$	$\pi\rho/2$
3	3π	π	$3\pi\rho$	$\pi\rho/3$
⋮	⋮	⋮	⋮	⋮
n	$n\pi$	π	$n\pi\rho$	$\pi\rho/n$

proof would involve a fair amount of tedious algebra and therefore will not be given here. As for the measure of skewness, we can use α_3 given as

$$\alpha_3 = \frac{\mu_3}{(\mu_2)^{3/2}},$$

where μ_2 is the variance and μ_3 is the third moment around the mean. Then it can be shown that, for the distribution of X as well as for that of $\hat{\pi}$, the expression for α_3 is

$$\alpha_3 = \frac{2\rho - 1}{\sqrt{n\pi\rho}}. \tag{4.3}$$

The basic characteristics of the two sampling distributions are summarized in Table 4–3.

Table 4–3

Characteristic	Distribution of X	Distribution of $\hat{\pi}$
Mean	$n\pi$	π
Variance	$n\pi\rho$	$\pi\rho/n$
α_3 (skewness)	$(2\rho - 1)/\sqrt{n\pi\rho}$	$(2\rho - 1)/\sqrt{n\pi\rho}$

Since now we have a complete knowledge of the sampling distribution of $\hat{\pi}$ for *any* specific population parameter π and for *any* sample size n, we can draw definite conclusions about the *properties* of $\hat{\pi}$ (proportion of successes in the sample) as an estimator of π (proportion of successes or the probability of success in the population). The main conclusions are

1. The mean of the sampling distribution of $\hat{\pi}$ is equal to the population parameter π. That is, *$\hat{\pi}$ is an unbiased estimator of π.*

2. Since the standard deviation of the sampling distribution of $\hat{\pi}$ is

$$\sigma_{\hat{\pi}} = \sqrt{\frac{\pi\rho}{n}}, \tag{4.4}$$

the distribution becomes more and more concentrated as the sample size is increased. This, together with conclusion 1, implies that $\hat{\pi}$ *is a consistent estimator of* π.

3. Given the formula for $\sigma_{\hat{\pi}}$ it follows that *the dispersion of the sampling distribution of* $\hat{\pi}$ (as measured by its standard deviation) *decreases with the square root of sample size.* This can be seen as follows. Consider two samples, the first of size n and the second of size $2n$. Then using the appropriate formula of Table 4–3, we have

$$\frac{\sigma_{\hat{\pi}}\text{ (2nd sample)}}{\sigma_{\hat{\pi}}\text{ (1st sample)}} = \frac{\sqrt{\pi\rho/2n}}{\sqrt{\pi\rho/n}} = \frac{1}{\sqrt{2}};$$

i.e.,
$$\sigma_{\hat{\pi}}\text{ (2nd sample)} = \frac{\sigma_{\hat{\pi}}\text{ (1st sample)}}{\sqrt{2}}.$$

In other words, as the sample size is increased k times, the standard deviation of the sampling distribution decreases $\sqrt{k}$ times.

4. For any given sample size, the sampling distribution of $\hat{\pi}$ is *most dispersed* when the population parameter π is equal to 1/2, and is *least dispersed* when π is 0 or 1. This follows from the fact that $0 \leq \pi \leq 1$ and

$$\sigma_{\hat{\pi}} = \sqrt{\frac{\pi\rho}{n}} = \sqrt{\frac{\pi(1-\pi)}{n}}$$

is at maximum when $\pi = 1/2$ and at minimum when $\pi = 0$ or 1. In fact, the largest value which $\sigma_{\hat{\pi}}$ can have is $1/(2\sqrt{n})$ and the smallest is 0.

5. *The skewness (asymmetry) of the sampling distribution of* $\hat{\pi}$ *decreases with the square root of sample size.* This clearly follows from (4.3) above.

6. For any *given* sample size, the sampling distribution of $\hat{\pi}$ is *least skewed* when π is equal to 1/2, and is *most skewed* when π is 0 or 1. This can be seen from (4.3) again: α_3 is zero when $\pi = 1/2$ and its departure from zero is greatest when π is either 0 or 1.

These conclusions have been reached with the help of probability theory and apply quite universally. In Section 2–1 we tried to derive the sampling distribution of $\hat{\pi}$ from a sampling experiment related to a population with $\pi = 0.70$. The experiment consisted of drawing 100 samples of size 4 and 100 samples of size 16. It enabled us to construct frequency distributions (one for each sample size), which were supposed to approximate the true sampling distributions. The results led to generalizations about the sampling distribution of $\hat{\pi}$ for any π and any sample size. Now we are in a position, first, to check the results to see how well the experimentally derived distributions fit the theoretical ones and, second, to verify or refute the validity of the generalizations.

Let us first compare the experimental and the theoretical distributions and their characteristics.

Sampling Distribution for Samples Size 4 (Table 4–4). The results for the experimentally determined probabilities are the relative frequencies of Table 2–1.

Table 4–4

Proportion of Successes: $\hat{\pi}$	Experimental $f(\hat{\pi})$	Theoretical $f(\hat{\pi})$
0.00	0.01	0.01
0.25	0.06	0.07
0.50	0.28	0.26
0.75	0.42	0.41
1.00	0.23	0.24
Mean	0.7	0.7
Standard deviation	0.2233	0.2291

The theoretical probabilities were derived from Freund,[2] rounded off to two decimal places. They could be calculated as follows:

$$f(0) = \left(\frac{4!}{4!0!}\right)(0.3)^4(0.7)^0 = (0.3)^4 = 0.0081 \approx 0.01,$$

$$f\left(\frac{1}{4}\right) = \left(\frac{4!}{3!1!}\right)(0.3)^3(0.7)^1 = 4 \times (0.3)^3 \times (0.7) = 0.0756 \approx 0.07,$$

and so on.

Sampling Distribution for Sample Size 16 (Table 4–5). The results for the experimentally determined probabilities have been taken from Table 2–2. The theoretical probabilities are from the same source as those for Table 4–4, again rounded off to two decimal places.

It is clear that the experimental results describe the sampling distributions quite closely; the errors are quite small and are unlikely to be of practical importance. Thus, in this case, distributions based on 100 samples come quite close to those that would result from an infinite number of samples. Furthermore, the generalizations made on the basis of experimental results—namely unbiasedness, consistency, relative change in the standard deviation, and decrease in skewness

[2] *Ibid.*, Table 1.

—all proved to be correct. However, the experimental results compare unfavorably with the theoretical ones in two respects. In the first place, the experimental results fail to give us any formulas for variance, measure of skewness, and, of course, the individual probabilities. In the second place, and this is much more important, there is no guarantee at all that the generalizations deduced from the experimental distributions are, in fact, valid. The conclusions are not proved, only suggested by the results of isolated experiments.

Table 4–5

Proportion of Successes: $\hat{\pi}$	Experimental $f(\hat{\pi})$	Theoretical $f(\hat{\pi})$
0	0	0
1/16	0	0.00
2/16	0	0.00
3/16	0	0.00
4/16	0	0.00
5/16	0.01	0.00
6/16	0	0.01
7/16	0.01	0.02
8/16	0.05	0.05
9/16	0.10	0.10
10/16	0.17	0.17
11/16	0.21	0.21
12/16	0.20	0.20
13/16	0.15	0.15
14/16	0.07	0.07
15/16	0.03	0.02
1	0	0.00
Mean	0.7006	0.7
Standard deviation	0.1191	0.1146

4–2 Normal Distribution as the Limiting Case of Binomial Distribution

One of the findings of Section 4–1 was that the binomial distribution tends to be increasingly more symmetric as n (size of sample) increases, regardless of the value of π. Even the distributions with π close to zero (or to unity), which for small n are very skewed, tend to become symmetric when n is somewhat larger. This point is demonstrated by Figure 4–1 which shows the binomial probabilities for $\pi = 0.10$ for various values of n. Note also that as n increases, the points become more numerous and the connecting lines become smoother.

In this section, we shall carry the previous point still farther by asserting that *as n approaches infinity, the binomial distribution approaches the so-called normal distribution.*[3] Normal distribution is a continuous distribution with probability density

$$f(x) = \frac{1}{\sqrt{2\pi\sigma^2}} e^{-(1/2)[(x-\mu)/\sigma]^2}, \tag{4.5}$$

where σ = standard deviation of X,

μ = mean of X,

$\pi = 3.14159\ldots$ (not to be confused with π, the population parameter),

$e = 2.71828\ldots.$

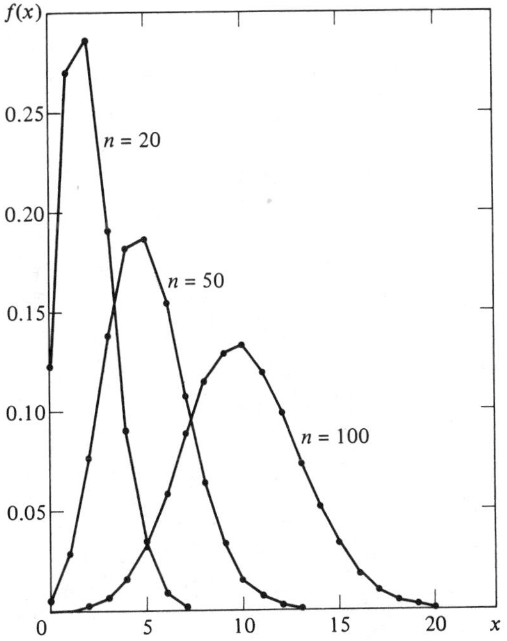

Figure 4–1

Graphical representation of a normal distribution is given in Figure 4–2. This shows that the distribution is symmetric around its mean μ, and that it extends from $-\infty$ to $+\infty$. Other properties are discussed on pages 82–83.

The fact that the binomial distribution approaches normal as $n \to \infty$ means, in effect, that for a large n we can use normal distribution as an approximation to

[3] The proof can be found in many statistical texts. A relatively simple proof is presented in G. Udny Yule and M. G. Kendall, *An Introduction to the Theory of Statistics* (London: Charles Griffin, 1950), pp. 177–181.

the binomial distribution. Thus, if X is the number of successes in the sample and if n is large, we can write

$$f(x) = \frac{1}{\sqrt{2\pi}} \frac{1}{\sqrt{n\pi\rho}} e^{-(1/2)[(x-n\pi)/\sqrt{n\pi\rho}]^2} \tag{4.6}$$

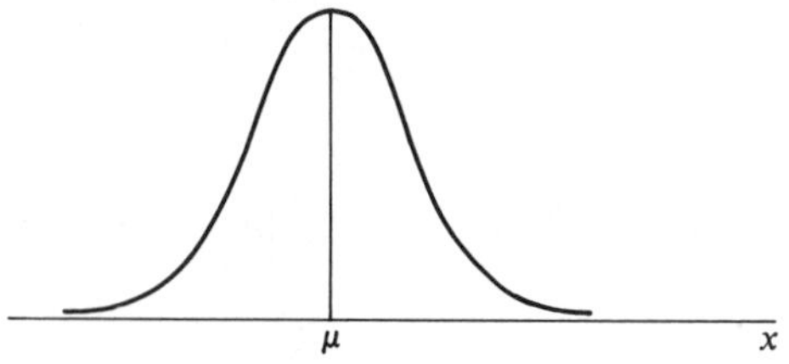

Figure 4–2

since the mean of X is $n\pi$ and the variance is $n\pi\rho$. Similarly, when n is large the probability function of the proportion of successes in the sample ($\hat{\pi}$) can be represented by

$$f(\hat{\pi}) = \frac{1}{\sqrt{2\pi}} \frac{\sqrt{n}}{\sqrt{\pi\rho}} e^{-(1/2)[(\hat{\pi}-\pi)\sqrt{n}/\sqrt{\pi\rho}]^2}, \tag{4.7}$$

since the mean of $\hat{\pi}$ is π and its variance is $\pi\rho/n$. How good these approximations are depends on n and π. If π is not too far from 1/2, the correspondence between the binomial and the normal curve is surprisingly close even for low values of n. In general, in most practical situations one can use the normal distribution as a reasonable approximation of the binomial distribution without much hesitation as long as $n \geq 30$.

When using the normal distribution formula to approximate a binomial distribution, we must take into account the fact that we are trying to approximate a *discrete* distribution by a *continuous* one. This can be done by representing the point values of the discrete variable by neighboring intervals. For example, if $n = 20$ the points and the corresponding intervals would be as shown in Table 4–6. Since the normal distribution extends, in fact, from $-\infty$

Table 4–6

x (Discrete)	x (Continuous Approximation)	$\hat{\pi}$ (Discrete)	$\hat{\pi}$ (Continuous Approximation)
0	$-\frac{1}{2}$ to $\frac{1}{2}$	0	$-1/40$ to $1/40$
1	$\frac{1}{2}$ to $1\frac{1}{2}$	1/20	1/40 to 3/40
2	$1\frac{1}{2}$ to $2\frac{1}{2}$	2/20	3/40 to 5/40
3	$2\frac{1}{2}$ to $3\frac{1}{2}$	3/20	5/40 to 7/40
⋮	⋮	⋮	⋮
20	$19\frac{1}{2}$ to $20\frac{1}{2}$	1	39/40 to 41/40

to $+\infty$, we may start the first intervals at $-\infty$ and end the last intervals at $+\infty$ instead of the lower and upper limits shown.

The reconciliation between the discrete binomial and the continuous normal distribution becomes easier as the sample size gets larger. This can be seen particularly clearly with respect to the distribution of $\hat{\pi}$. As n gets larger, the intervals corresponding to each value of $\hat{\pi}$ become shorter. As an example, consider the intervals corresponding to the point $\hat{\pi} = 0.1$ for various sample sizes:

n	Interval
10	0.05 to 0.15
20	0.075 to 0.125
50	0.090 to 0.110
100	0.095 to 0.105
1000	0.0995 to 0.1005
	etc.

Note that, e.g., for $n = 1{,}000$, we replace the probability of $\hat{\pi}$ being equal to 0.1 by the probability that $\hat{\pi}$ is within 0.1 ± 0.0005, which is certainly not too rough. If we represent the binomial probabilities of $\hat{\pi}$ by rectangles with base equal to the appropriate interval and heights equal to $nf(\hat{\pi})$ (to make the total *area* equal to unity), we can see how the broken curve gets smoother as n gets larger. This is illustrated by Figure 4–3 for π equal to 0.1.

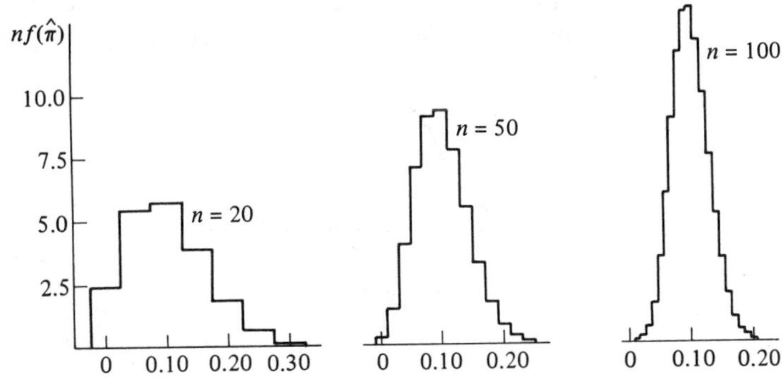

Figure 4–3

In asserting that binomial distribution converges to normal as n approaches infinity, we took it for granted that the population parameter π (and therefore ρ) is fixed, and that it is different from 0 or 1. If π is *not* fixed but decreases as $n \to \infty$ (so that $n\pi$ remains constant), the limiting form of the binomial disbution is not normal but becomes what is known as the *Poisson distribution*. This distribution became famous because it fitted extremely well the frequency of deaths from the kick of a horse in the Prussian army corps in the last quarter of the nineteenth century. As it is, the Poisson distribution has little relevance to us since our attention is confined to populations with a fixed proportion (probability) of successes. As for the cases in which π is equal to zero or one (i.e., the cases in which the population consists *entirely* of failures or of successes), the proportion of successes ($\hat{\pi}$) is the same in each sample and is equal to π. This means that the sampling distributions are concentrated on one point regardless of sample size, and thus the question of convergence to normal distribution does not arise.

Normal distribution is extremely important in econometrics, not only because it represents the limiting form of the binomial distribution, but because it applies to many other situations as well. This will become apparent in the subsequent section and in further discussions throughout the book. For that reason, it will be useful to consider the normal distribution in greater detail. First, let us describe its *main features*.

1. The distribution is *continuous* and *symmetric* around its mean μ. This has the following implications: (a) the mean, the median and the mode are all equal; and (b) the mean divides the area under the normal curve into exact halves.
2. The range of the distribution extends from $-\infty$ to $+\infty$, i.e., the distribution is *unbounded*.
3. The maximum height of the normal curve is attained at the point $x = \mu$, and the points of inflection (i.e., the points where the distribution starts flattening out) occur at $x = \mu \pm \sigma$. This means that the standard deviation measures the distance from the center of the distribution to a point of inflection, as illustrated in Figure 4–4.

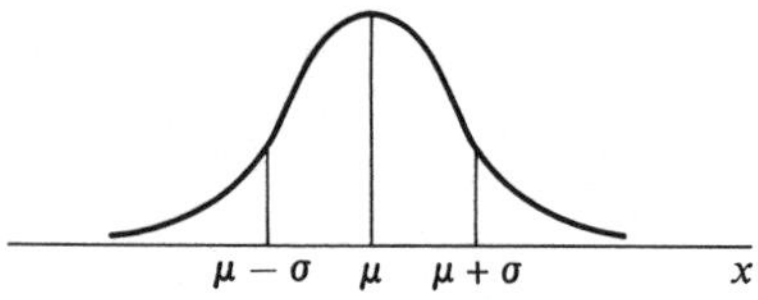

Figure 4–4

4. Normal distribution is *fully specified by two parameters, mean and variance*. This means that if we know μ and σ^2 of a normal distribution, we know all there is to know about it. Note that the binomial distribution is also fully specified by only two parameters, π and n. Figure 4–5 shows various comparisons of two normal distributions. Case (a) represents two normal distributions with different means but equal variances. In case (b) the means are equal but the variances are different, and in (c) both means and variances differ.

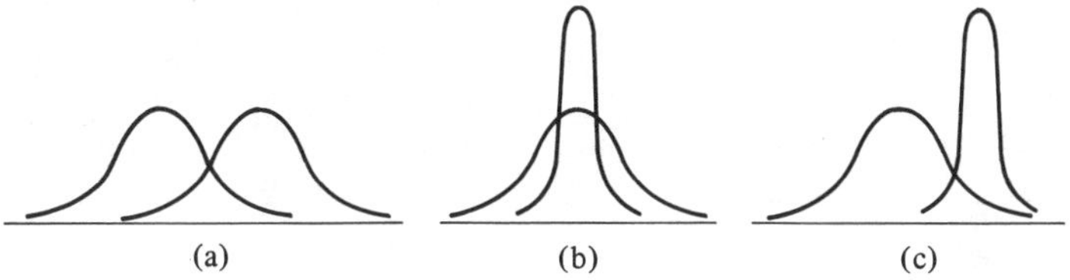

Figure 4–5

5. The last feature to be mentioned will be found particularly useful in later work. We present it here in the form of a theorem:

Theorem 12: *If $X, Y, Z, \ldots,$ are normally and independently distributed random variables and $a, b, c, \ldots,$ are constants, then the linear combination $aX + bY + cZ + \cdots$ is also normally distributed.*

The proof of this theorem can be found in many texts on mathematical statistics.[4]

Having stated the main properties of the normal distribution, we still have to face the problem of how to operate with it. In particular, we would like to be able to calculate different probabilities for a variable which is normally distributed. This was, at least in principle, no problem in the case of the binomial distribution since the terms of binomial expansion are determined by a straightforward formula. In the case of a normal distribution, however, the probability density formula is quite formidable. Fortunately, we do not have to use the formula; the probabilities, given by the corresponding areas under the curve, can be obtained from tabulated results. Of course, different normal distributions lead to different probabilities but since the differences can only be due to differences in means and variances, this presents no difficulty. If we know the areas under one specific normal curve, we can derive the areas under any other normal curve simply by allowing for the difference in the mean and the variance. The one specific distribution for which areas (corresponding to relatively narrow intervals) have been tabulated is a normal distribution with mean $\mu = 0$ and variance $\sigma^2 = 1$, called *standard normal distribution* (sometimes also called *unit normal distribution*).

The problem of determining the probabilities for a normally distributed variable X can be then stated as follows: given that we know (a) μ and σ^2 of X, and (b) the areas under the standard normal curve, how do we determine the probability that x will lie within some interval bordered by, say, x_1 and x_2?

To develop the solution, let us introduce the following notation:

Z = a normally distributed variable with mean zero and variance equal to unity (i.e., a "standard normal variable");

$P(x_1 < x < x_2)$ = probability that X will lie between x_1 and x_2 $(x_1 < x_2)$;

$P(z_1 < z < z_2)$ = probability that Z will lie between z_1 and z_2 $(z_1 < z_2)$.

[4] See, for example, R. L. Anderson and T. A. Bancroft, *Statistical Theory in Research* (New York: McGraw-Hill, 1952), pp. 63–64.

We will proceed in two steps: first we determine the relationship between X and Z, and then we examine the relationship between corresponding areas under the two curves.

Since X is normally distributed, a linear function of X will also be normal (see Theorem 12). Such a linear function can be represented generally as

$$aX + b,$$

where a and b are some constants. If we find a and b such that they would make the mean of $(aX + b)$ zero and its variance unity, we will have a standard normal variable. That is, we require that

$$E(aX + b) = 0 \qquad \text{and} \qquad \text{Var}(aX + b) = 1.$$

This can be written as

$$a\mu + b = 0 \quad \text{(by Theorem 6)}$$

and

$$a^2\sigma^2 = 1 \quad \text{(by Theorem 7)}.$$

Solving for a and b we obtain

$$a = \frac{1}{\sigma} \qquad \text{and} \qquad b = -\frac{\mu}{\sigma}.$$

Thus we have

$$aX + b = \frac{X - \mu}{\sigma}.$$

Since $(X - \mu)/\sigma$ has mean zero and variance equal to one, it is a standard normal variable, i.e.,

$$\frac{X - \mu}{\sigma} = Z. \tag{4.8}$$

Thus any normal variable with mean μ and variance σ^2 can be transformed into a standard normal variable by expressing it in terms of deviations from its mean, each deviation being divided by σ.

Let us consider $P(x_1 < x < x_2)$, where $x_1 < x_2$, which is a probability statement about X. We wish to find an exactly equivalent probability statement about Z. Now

$$\frac{X - \mu}{\sigma} = Z \qquad \text{implies} \qquad X = \sigma Z + \mu.$$

Therefore, we can write

$$x_1 = \sigma z_1 + \mu \qquad \text{and} \qquad x_2 = \sigma z_2 + \mu.$$

Consequently, by substitution we have

$$P(x_1 < x < x_2) = P(\sigma z_1 + \mu < \sigma z + \mu < \sigma z_2 + \mu).$$

After canceling out all the common positive terms in the right-hand-side inequality, this becomes

$$P(x_1 < x < x_2) = P(z_1 < z < z_2), \tag{4.9}$$

where $$z_1 = \frac{x_1 - \mu}{\sigma} \quad \text{and} \quad z_2 = \frac{x_2 - \mu}{\sigma}.$$

Thus we have found that the probability that x lies between x_1 and x_2 is equal to the probability that a standard normal variable lies between $(x_1 - \mu)/\sigma$ and $(x_2 - \mu)/\sigma$.

As an example, consider a normally distributed variable X which has a mean of 5 and standard deviation of 2. The problem is to find the probability $P(2 < x < 3)$. To do that we have to find an equivalent probability statement in terms of the standard normal variable Z. Here the lower limit $x_1 = 2$ and the upper limit $x_2 = 3$. Since

$$z_1 = \frac{x_1 - \mu}{\sigma},$$

we have $$z_1 = \frac{2 - 5}{2} = -\frac{3}{2}.$$

Similarly, $$z_2 = \frac{x_2 - \mu}{\sigma} = \frac{3 - 5}{2} = -1.$$

Therefore, $P(2 < x < 3) = P(-3/2 < z < -1)$. This is shown graphically in Figure 4–6. The two shaded areas under the two curves are exactly the same.

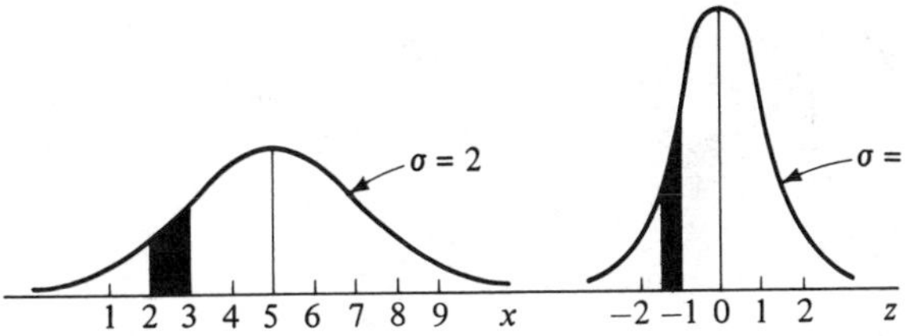

Figure 4–6

After these preliminaries, all that is left to do is to learn how to use the table of areas under the standard normal distributions. Such a table can be found in practically every text on introductory statistics. The most common tabular presentation is that of giving the probabilities that Z will lie between 0 and a positive number z_0 (rounded off to two decimal places) as shown in Figure 4–7.

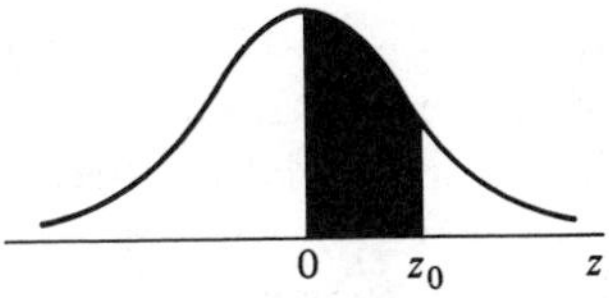

Figure 4–7

The table given in Appendix D of this book is of that form. The probabilities shown refer to only one half of the distribution. Since the distribution is perfectly symmetric this is, of course, sufficient. The largest probability (area) shown could

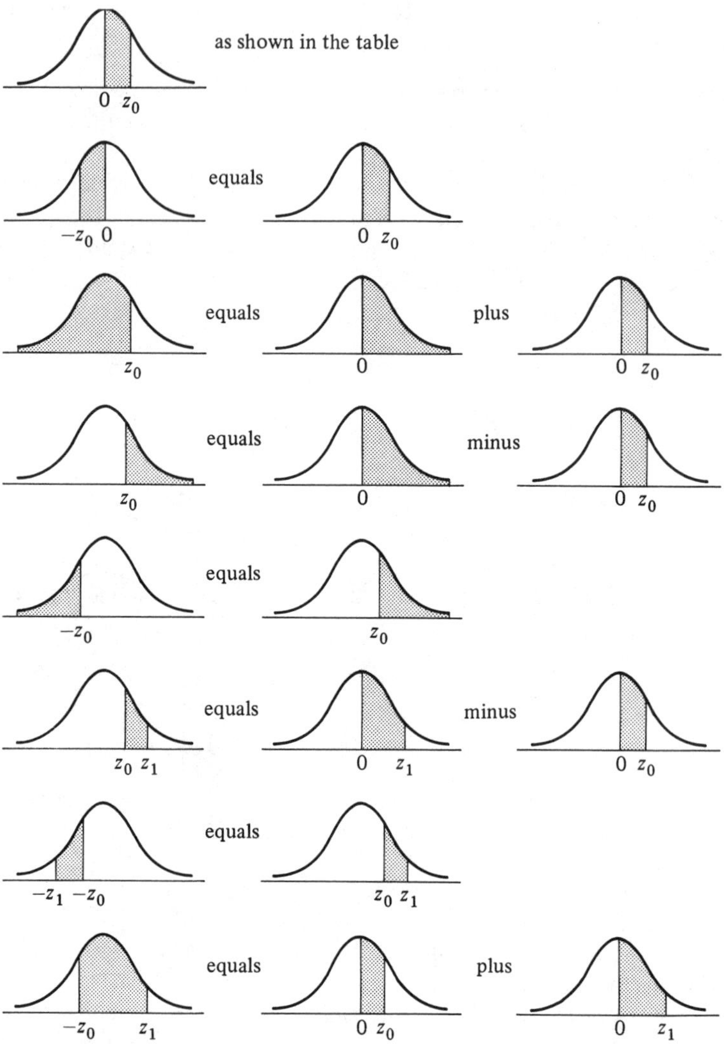

Figure 4–8

then be 0.5 at the point where $z = +\infty$. However, since the tail of the distribution tapers off fairly rapidly, the probability that z lies between 0 and 3 is already very close to 0.5 (in fact, it is 0.4987); therefore, most tables stop there. (Some tables give probabilities that z lies between $-\infty$ and a positive number. In these tables the *lowest* probability shown is 0.5 and the highest is close to 1.) The use of the table for solving various problems is indicated in Figure 4–8.

Note that $z_0 > 0$ and $z_1 > z_0$.

Let us now consider two examples on the use of the table areas under the standard normal curve. The first example will provide us with information that will prove useful in later work. The second example is concerned with the relationship between the binomial and the normal distribution in a specific case which is of interest to us.

EXAMPLE 1 If X is a random normal variable with mean μ and variance σ^2, find the following:

(a) $P(\mu - \sigma < x < \mu + \sigma)$,
(b) $P(\mu - 2\sigma < x < \mu + 2\sigma)$,
(c) $P(\mu - 3\sigma < x < \mu + 3\sigma)$,
(d) the two values of X which cut off the central 95 per cent of the area under the curve.
(e) the two values of X which cut off the central 99 per cent of the area under the curve.

The answers are found as follows.

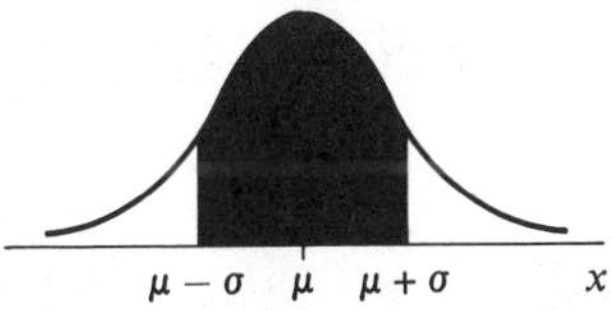

Figure 4–9

For (a). We wish to determine the area shown in Figure 4–9. The corresponding lower and upper limits in terms of the standard normal variable are as follows:

$$z_1 = \frac{x_1 - \mu}{\sigma} = \frac{(\mu - \sigma) - \mu}{\sigma} = -1$$

and

$$z_2 = \frac{x_2 - \mu}{\sigma} = \frac{(\mu + \sigma) - \mu}{\sigma} = +1.$$

Then

$$P(-1 < z < +1) = P(0 < z < +1) + P(0 < z < +1) = 0.3413 + 0.3413 = 0.6826.$$

That is, *the probability that x lies within one standard deviation in either direction from its mean is* 68.26%.

For (b)

$$P(\mu - 2\sigma < x < \mu + 2\sigma) = P\left(\left[\frac{(\mu - 2\sigma) - \mu}{\sigma}\right] < z < \left[\frac{(\mu + 2\sigma) - \mu}{\sigma}\right]\right)$$

$$= P(-2 < z < +2) = 0.4772 + 0.4772 = 0.9544.$$

That is, *the probability that x lies within two standard deviations in either direction from its mean is* 95.44%.

For (*c*)

$$P(\mu - 3\sigma < x < \mu + 3\sigma) = P\left(\left[\frac{(\mu - 3\sigma) - \mu}{\sigma}\right] < z < \left[\frac{(\mu + 3\sigma) - \mu}{\sigma}\right]\right)$$

$$= P(-3 < z < +3) = 0.4987 + 0.4987 = 0.9974.$$

That is, *the probability that x lies within three standard deviations in either direction from its mean is* 99.74%. In other words, practically all values of X are confined to an interval of six standard derivations; the midpoint of this interval is, of course, the mean.

The previous problems were all cases in which we knew the values of X and determined the areas under the curve bounded by these values. The two problems that follow are of just the opposite kind: this time we know the area and want to find the boundary values of X.

For (*d*). Here we have $P(x_1 < x < x_2) = 0.95$, and the interval x_1 to x_2 is centered around the mean. Our problem is to find x_1 and x_2. We solve it by first finding the corresponding boundaries of the standard normal distribution. Given the probability statement for X, the corresponding probability statement for the standard normal variable Z is $P(z_1 < z < z_2) = 0.95$, and the interval z_1 to z_2 is centered around 0 (Figure 4–10). Because of the centering around zero we have

$$P(0 < z < z_2) = P(z_1 < z < 0) = \frac{0.95}{2} = 0.475.$$

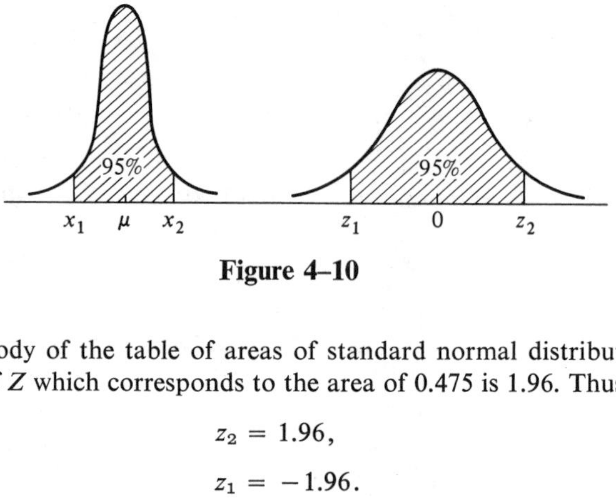

Figure 4–10

Searching the body of the table of areas of standard normal distribution, we find that the value of Z which corresponds to the area of 0.475 is 1.96. Thus,

$$z_2 = 1.96,$$

$$z_1 = -1.96.$$

Therefore $$\frac{x_2 - \mu}{\sigma} = 1.96,$$

$$\frac{x_1 - \mu}{\sigma} = -1.96.$$

This gives $$x_2 = \mu + 1.96\,\sigma$$

and $$x_1 = \mu - 1.96\,\sigma.$$

That is, *the interval* $\mu \pm 1.96\sigma$ *contains the central* 95% *of all values of* X.

For (*e*)

$$P(x_1 < x < x_2) = 0.99,$$

$$P(z_1 < z < z_2) = 0.99,$$

$$P(0 < z < z_2) = 0.495.$$

The value of Z corresponding to the area of 0.495 is 2.57. Thus,

$$z_2 = 2.57,$$

$$z_1 = -2.57,$$

and therefore $$x_2 = \mu + 2.57\,\sigma$$

and $$x_1 = \mu - 2.57\,\sigma.$$

That is, *the interval* $\mu \pm 2.57\sigma$ *contains the central* 99% *of all values of X.*

EXAMPLE 2 Consider the distribution of sample proportion $\hat{\pi}$ for samples of size 16 coming from a population with a proportion of successes $\pi = 0.7$. This is the binomial distribution which was derived earlier; it is given in the last column of Table 4–5 (and reproduced in the last column of Table 4–7). We are supposed to find a normal approximation of this distribution. The solution is as follows. First, we have to replace the points $\hat{\pi}$ of the discrete binomial distribution by intervals that would pertain to the corresponding normal distribution. This was explained and described at the beginning of this section. The next step is to obtain the normal probabilities corresponding to each interval. Since in this case the binomial distribution of $\hat{\pi}$ has a mean of 0.7 and standard deviation of 0.11464, the approximating normal distribution must be characterized by these parametric values. To find the probabilities we have to make a transformation to the standard normal variable given by

$$z = \frac{\hat{\pi} - 0.7}{0.11464} = 8.72872\hat{\pi} - 6.11010.$$

This will enable us to state the intervals in terms of z rather than $\hat{\pi}$, and to find the corresponding probabilities from the table of areas of the standard normal distribution. The results are presented in Table 4–7. It is obvious that the normal approximation to the binomial distribution is extremely close in spite of the fact the size of the sample is only 16.

In our discussion about the normal distribution, we started with the assertion that normal distribution is the limiting form of binomial distribution. It should be pointed out that this is only one way in which the normal distribution may be deduced and that there are other lines of reasoning which would lead to it.[5] Of these the most important one is that in which the derivation is based on the behavior of random errors. For instance, consider the problem of measuring the length of an object. Under ordinary circumstances each measurement may be subject to an error. Now let us suppose that any error is the result of some infinitely large number of small causes, each producing a small deviation.

[5] For a compact survey, see C. R. Rao, *Linear Statistical Inference and Its Applications* (New York: Wiley, 1965), pp. 126ff.

If we then assume that all of these small deviations are equal and that positive deviations are just as likely as negative deviations, then it can be shown that the *errors are normally distributed* about zero, i.e., that the measurements are normally distributed about the "true" value. The basis of this derivation can, of course, be interpreted quite generally. In particular, the term "error" can

Table 4–7

$\hat{\pi}$ (Discrete Values)	$\hat{\pi}$ (Intervals)	z (Intervals)	$F(\hat{\pi})$ (Cumulative Normal Approximation)*	$f(\hat{\pi})$ (Normal Approximation)†	$f(\hat{\pi})$ (Binomial Distribution)
0	−1/32 to 1/32	$-\infty$ to −5.84	0.0000	0.0000 (0.00)	0.00
1/16	1/32 to 3/32	−5.84 to −5.29	0.0000	0.0000 (0.00)	0.00
2/16	3/32 to 5/32	−5.29 to −4.75	0.0000	0.0000 (0.00)	0.00
3/16	5/32 to 7/32	−4.75 to −4.20	0.0000	0.0000 (0.00)	0.00
4/16	7/32 to 9/32	−4.20 to −3.66	0.0000	0.0000 (0.00)	0.00
5/16	9/32 to 11/32	−3.66 to −3.11	0.0009	0.0009 (0.00)	0.00
6/16	11/32 to 13/32	−3.11 to −2.57	0.0050	0.0041 (0.00)	0.01
7/16	13/32 to 15/32	−2.57 to −2.02	0.0217	0.0167 (0.02)	0.02
8/16	15/32 to 17/32	−2.02 to −1.48	0.0694	0.0477 (0.05)	0.05
9/16	17/32 to 19/32	−1.48 to −0.93	0.1762	0.1068 (0.11)	0.10
10/16	19/32 to 21/32	−0.93 to −0.38	0.3520	0.1758 (0.17)	0.17
11/16	21/32 to 23/32	−0.38 to 0.16	0.5636	0.2116 (0.21)	0.21
12/16	23/32 to 25/32	0.16 to 0.71	0.7611	0.1975 (0.20)	0.20
13/16	25/32 to 27/32	0.71 to 1.25	0.8944	0.1333 (0.13)	0.15
14/16	27/32 to 29/32	1.25 to 1.80	0.9641	0.0697 (0.07)	0.07
15/16	29/32 to 31/32	1.80 to 2.34	0.9904	0.0263 (0.03)	0.02
1	31/32 to 33/32	2.34 to $+\infty$	1.0000	0.0096 (0.01)	0.00

* $F(\hat{\pi})$ is represented by the area from $-\infty$ to the upper limit of each interval.

† $f(\hat{\pi})$ is given by the area corresponding to each interval. The figures in brackets are the probabilities rounded off to two decimal places.

be taken to mean any deviation from some systematic behavior, and this is the interpretation which underlies most theoretical developments in modern econometrics. This will become obvious as soon as we start discussing regression models. For now we ought to mention that the extensive use of the normal distribution has led to the following abbreviated notation:

$X \sim N(\mu, \sigma^2)$ means that X is a normally distributed random variable with mean μ and variance σ^2. Therefore, $X \sim N(0, 1)$ stands for standard normal variable. This notation will be followed hereafter.

4–3 Sampling Distribution of Sample Mean

In the case of the sampling distribution of sample proportion discussed in Section 4–1, we dealt with sampling from a dichotomous population. Every observation was classified as a failure or a success, and we considered the proportion of successes in the sample as an estimator of the probability of success in the population. As mentioned earlier, the labeling of observations as failure or success could be replaced by numerical values, namely 0 for failure and 1 for success. Thus instead of dealing with attributes we would be dealing with a *binary variable.* Suppose we call this variable Y and observe the following values in a sample of six observations:

$$y_1 = 0,$$

$$y_2 = 1,$$

$$y_3 = 0,$$

$$y_4 = 0,$$

$$y_5 = 1,$$

$$y_6 = 0.$$

Then the observed proportion of successes is

$$\hat{\pi} = \frac{0 + 1 + 0 + 0 + 1 + 0}{6} = \frac{2}{6} = \frac{1}{n}\sum_{i=1}^{6} y_i = \bar{y}.$$

That is, the proportion of successes in the sample is nothing else but the sample mean of Y. Further, we know that the probability of success in the population is the limit of the relative frequency of successes as the number of observations approaches infinity. Since the limit of relative frequency of y is the probability of y—which we labeled $f(y)$—and since observing a success means that $y = 1$, it follows that

$$\pi = P(\text{success}) = P(y = 1) = f(1),$$

or

$$\pi = 1 \times f(1).$$

This may as well be written as

$$\pi = 0 \times f(0) + 1 \times f(1),$$

since zero times any number is zero. But writing the expression for π in this form shows that π is, in fact, equal to the weighted average of the different values of Y (i.e., 0 and 1) with the weights given by the respective probabilities. This is precisely the definition of the mathematical expectation of Y as stated in (3.23). Therefore, we have

$$\pi = E(Y) = \mu_Y.$$

In other words, the probability of success in the population is the population mean of Y. Therefore, the sampling distribution of sample proportion (as an estimator of the probability of success) can be viewed as a sampling distribution of sample mean (as an estimator of population mean) when the variable is a binary one.

At this stage we are interested in the problem of deriving the sampling distribution of sample mean in cases in which the variable can assume more than two values and have any kind of distribution. In general, we expect that different distributions of the variable in the population (i.e., "parent" distributions) lead to different forms of sampling distributions of sample mean. For example, there is no apparent reason why the distribution of sample mean for samples drawn from a highly skewed population should have the same form as that for samples drawn from a symmetric population. However, we cannot and do not want to discuss every conceivable form of parent distribution individually. For our purpose, it is sufficient if we limit ourselves to a detailed discussion of only two distributions—a discrete uniform and a normal distribution—and consider all the other distributions in general terms. The discrete uniform distribution is of special interest to us because it was used as the basis of our sampling experiment in Section 2–2; it also provides a convenient background for illustrating a way of deriving theoretical sampling distributions. The normal distribution will be discussed because many inference statements in econometrics depend heavily on the assumption of normality in the parent population.

First, we take up the problem of deriving the sampling distribution of sample mean when the variable of interest (say, X) has a *discrete uniform distribution.* This means that X can assume a finite number of different values, each with equal probability. The case of a binary variable represents a special case; we already know that this case leads to a binomial distribution of sample mean (see Section 4–1). Here our concern is with a more general problem. We will start by specifying the parental distribution as that which was used in our sampling experiment in Section 2–2. There, it may be recalled, we let X take on values $0, 1, 2, \ldots, 9$, each with probability of $1/10$. As worked out earlier, the main characteristics of this distribution are:

Mean: $$E(X) = 4.5$$

Variance: $$\text{Var}(X) = 2.8723^2 = 8.25.$$

Later on we shall generalize this case to allow for any number of different values of X.

Let us then derive the sampling distribution of $\bar{X}$ as an estimator of $\mu = 4.5$. In this we will follow the procedure of Section 4–1 by "building up" the probabilities of individual values of the estimator and by calculating the main characteristics of the resulting distribution. As before, we will do this for different sample sizes and try to discover the pattern that would allow us to develop a general formula to apply to any sample size.

Sampling Distribution of $\bar{X}$ for Sample Size 1. In this case $\bar{X}$ can assume 10 different values: $0, 1, 2, \ldots, 9$, the same as the variable X. The probability of each of these values is $1/10$, as shown in Table 4–8 and Figure 4–11.

Table 4–8

$\bar{x}$	$f(\bar{x})$	$\bar{x}f(\bar{x})$	$\bar{x}^2f(\bar{x})$
0	$P(0) = 1/10$	0	0
1	$P(1) = 1/10$	1/10	1/10
2	$P(2) = 1/10$	2/10	4/10
3	$P(3) = 1/10$	3/10	9/10
4	$P(4) = 1/10$	4/10	16/10
5	$P(5) = 1/10$	5/10	25/10
6	$P(6) = 1/10$	6/10	36/10
7	$P(7) = 1/10$	7/10	49/10
8	$P(8) = 1/10$	8/10	64/10
9	$P(9) = 1/10$	9/10	81/10
	Sum 1	45/10	285/10

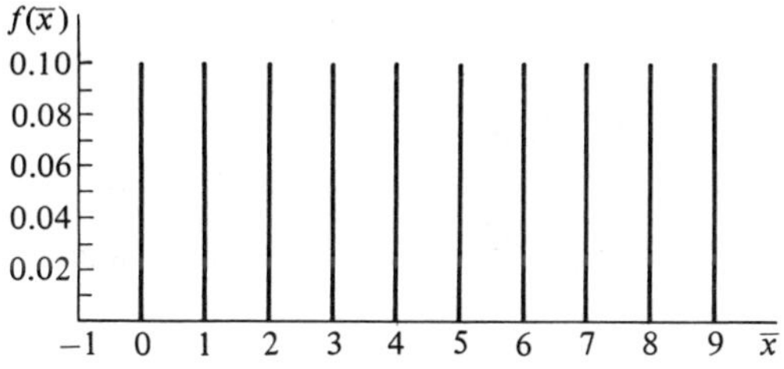

Figure 4–11

Mean and variance of $\bar{X}$:

$$E(\bar{X}) = \sum_i \bar{x}_i f(\bar{x}_i) = 4.5,$$

$$\text{Var}(\bar{X}) = E(\bar{X}^2) - [E(\bar{X})]^2 = \sum_i \bar{x}_i^2 f(\bar{x}_i) - \Big[\sum_i \bar{x}_i f(\bar{x}_i)\Big]^2 = 28.5 - 4.5^2 = 8.25.$$

The mean and variance of $\bar{X}$ in this case are, of course, the same as those of X in the population.

Sampling Distribution of $\bar{X}$ for Sample Size 2. Here the possible values of $\bar{X}$ are 0, 1/2, 2/2, . . ., 18/2. That is, there are 19 different values that $\bar{X}$ can assume. The probability distribution is given in Table 4–9. The complete enumeration of various probabilities in Table 4–9 can be replaced by combinatorial formulas as developed in Section 3–2. In particular, we can write:

$$P(0, 0) = \binom{1}{1} \Big/ 10^2$$

$$P(0, 1) + P(1, 0) = \binom{2}{1} \Big/ 10^2$$

$$P(0, 2) + P(2, 0) + P(1, 1) = \binom{3}{1} \Big/ 10^2$$

$$P(0,3) + P(3,0) + P(1,2) + P(2,1) = \binom{4}{1} \Big/ 10^2$$

$$\vdots$$

$$P(0,9) + P(9,0) + P(8,1) + P(1,8) + P(2,7) + P(7,2) + P(3,6) + P(6,3) + P(4,5) + P(5,4) = \binom{10}{1} \Big/ 10^2$$

$$P(1,9) + P(9,1) + P(2,8) + P(8,2) + P(3,7) + P(7,3) + P(4,6) + P(6,4) + P(5,5) = \left[\binom{11}{1} - 2\right] \Big/ 10^2$$

$$\vdots$$

$$P(8,9) + P(9,8) = \left[\binom{18}{1} - 16\right] \Big/ 10^2$$

$$P(9,9) = \left[\binom{19}{1} - 18\right] \Big/ 10^2.$$

The resulting distribution has a "triangular" form, as shown in Figure 4–12.

Table 4–9

$\bar{x}$	$f(\bar{x})$		$\bar{x}f(\bar{x})$	$\bar{x}^2 f(\bar{x})$
0	$P(0,0)$	$= 1/10^2$	0.00	0.000
1/2	$P(0,1) + P(1,0)$	$= 2/10^2$	0.01	0.005
2/2	$P(0,2) + P(2,0) + P(1,1)$	$= 3/10^2$	0.03	0.030
3/2	$P(0,3) + P(3,0) + P(1,2) + P(2,1)$	$= 4/10^2$	0.06	0.090
4/2	...	$= 5/10^2$	0.10	0.200
5/2	...	$= 6/10^2$	0.15	0.375
6/2	...	$= 7/10^2$	0.21	0.630
7/2	...	$= 8/10^2$	0.28	0.980
8/2	...	$= 9/10^2$	0.36	1.440
9/2	$P(0,9) + P(9,0) + P(1,8) + P(8,1) + P(2,7) + P(7,2) + P(3,6) + P(6,3) + P(4,5) + P(5,4)$	$= 10/10^2$	0.45	2.025
10/2	$P(1,9) + P(9,1) + P(2,8) + P(8,2) + P(3,7) + P(7,3) + P(4,6) + P(6,4) + P(5,5)$	$= 9/10^2$	0.45	2.250
⋮	⋮	⋮	⋮	⋮
17/2	$P(8,9) + P(9,8)$	$= 2/10^2$	0.17	1.445
18/2	$P(9,9)$	$= 1/10^2$	0.09	0.810
	Sum	1	4.50	24.375

Mean and variance of $\bar{X}$:

$$E(\bar{X}) = 4.5,$$

$$\mathrm{Var}(\bar{X}) = 24.375 - 4.5^2 = 24.375 - 20.25 = 4.125.$$

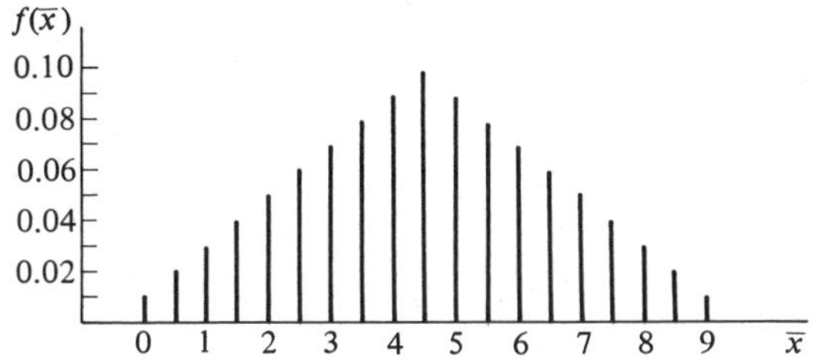

Figure 4-12

Sampling Distribution of $\bar{X}$ for Sample Size 3. The possible values of $\bar{X}$ in this case are 0, 1/3, 2/3, . . ., 27/3. The corresponding probabilities are derived in Table 4-10. The distribution is perfectly symmetric around the point 4.5. Its graphical representation is given in Figure 4-13.

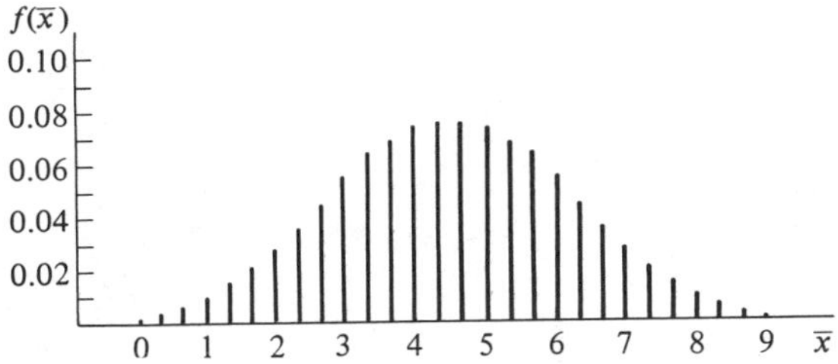

Figure 4-13

Mean and variance of $\bar{X}$:

$$E(\bar{X}) = 4.5,$$

$$\mathrm{Var}(\bar{X}) = 23.00 - 4.5^2 = 2.75.$$

By now it should be clear how to go about constructing the sampling distributions, and there is no need for us to continue in detail. Instead, let us present the distribution for various sample sizes in a summary form. We hope this will inspire a generalization that would enable us to determine the probability of *any* given value of $\bar{X}$ for *any* sample size from one formula.

Table 4-11 has been set up in a way which would make the presentation as concise as possible without a loss of clarity. Since the values of $\bar{X}$ are always of the form $0/n$, $1/n$, $2/n$, . . ., $9n/n$, each one of them depends on the sample size n. To avoid having to present a different column of values of $\bar{X}$ for each sample

Table 4–10

$\bar{x}$	$f(\bar{x})$			$\bar{x}f(\bar{x})$	$\bar{x}^2 f(\bar{x})$
0	$P(0,0,0)$	$= \binom{2}{2}\Big/10^3$	$= 1/10^3$	0.000	0.000 000
1/3	$P(0,0,1) + P(0,1,0)$ $+ P(1,0,0)$	$= \binom{3}{2}\Big/10^3$	$= 3/10^3$	0.001	0.000 333
2/3	...	$= \binom{4}{2}\Big/10^3$	$= 6/10^3$	0.004	0.002 667
3/3	...	$= \binom{5}{2}\Big/10^3$	$= 10/10^3$	0.010	0.010 000
4/3	...	$= \binom{6}{2}\Big/10^3$	$= 15/10^3$	0.020	0.026 667
5/3	...	$= \binom{7}{2}\Big/10^3$	$= 21/10^3$	0.035	0.058 333
6/3	...	$= \binom{8}{2}\Big/10^3$	$= 28/10^3$	0.056	0.112 000
7/3	...	$= \binom{9}{2}\Big/10^3$	$= 36/10^3$	0.084	0.196 000
8/3	...	$= \binom{10}{2}\Big/10^3$	$= 45/10^3$	0.120	0.320 000
9/3	...	$= \binom{11}{2}\Big/10^3$	$= 55/10^3$	0.165	0.495 000
10/3	...	$= \left[\binom{12}{2} - 3\right]\Big/10^3$	$= 63/10^3$	0.210	0.700 000
11/3	...	$= \left[\binom{13}{2} - 9\right]\Big/10^3$	$= 69/10^3$	0.253	0.927 667
12/3	...	$= \left[\binom{14}{2} - 18\right]\Big/10^3$	$= 73/10^3$	0.292	1.168 000
13/3	...	$= \left[\binom{15}{2} - 30\right]\Big/10^3$	$= 75/10^3$	0.325	1.408 333
14/3	...	$= \left[\binom{16}{2} - 45\right]\Big/10^3$	$= 75/10^3$	0.350	1.633 333
15/3	...	$= \left[\binom{17}{2} - 63\right]\Big/10^3$	$= 73/10^3$	0.365	1.825 000
⋮		⋮	⋮	⋮	⋮
26/3		$= \left[\binom{28}{2} - 375\right]\Big/10^3$	$= 3/10^3$	0.026	0.225 333
27/3		$= \left[\binom{29}{2} - 405\right]\Big/10^3$	$= 1/10^3$	0.009	0.081 000
		Sum	1	4.500	23.000 000

Table 4–11

$n\bar{x}$	$10^n f(\bar{x})$				
	$n=1$	$n=2$	$n=3$	$n=4$	$n=5$
0	1	$\binom{1}{1} = 1$	$\binom{2}{2} = 1$	$\binom{3}{3} = 1$	$\binom{4}{4} = 1$
1	1	$\binom{2}{1} = 2$	$\binom{3}{2} = 3$	$\binom{4}{3} = 4$	$\binom{5}{4} = 5$
2	1	$\binom{3}{1} = 3$	$\binom{4}{2} = 6$	$\binom{5}{3} = 10$	$\binom{6}{4} = 15$
⋮	⋮	⋮	⋮	⋮	⋮
8	1	$\binom{9}{1} = 9$	$\binom{10}{2} = 45$	$\binom{11}{3} = 165$	$\binom{12}{4} = 495$
9	1	$\binom{10}{1} = 10$	$\binom{11}{2} = 55$	$\binom{12}{3} = 220$	$\binom{13}{4} = 715$
10		$\binom{11}{1} - 2 = 9$	$\binom{12}{2} - 3 = 63$	$\binom{13}{3} - 4 = 282$	$\binom{14}{4} - 5 = 996$
11		$\binom{12}{1} - 4 = 8$	$\binom{13}{2} - 9 = 69$	$\binom{14}{3} - 16 = 348$	$\binom{15}{4} - 25 = 1{,}340$
12		$\binom{13}{1} - 6 = 7$	$\binom{14}{2} - 18 = 73$	$\binom{15}{3} - 40 = 415$	$\binom{16}{4} - 75 = 1{,}745$
⋮		⋮	⋮	⋮	⋮
18		$\binom{19}{1} - 18 = 1$	$\binom{20}{2} - 135 = 55$	$\binom{21}{3} - 660 = 670$	$\binom{22}{4} - 2{,}475 = 4{,}840$
19			$\binom{21}{2} - 165 = 45$	$\binom{22}{3} - 880 = 660$	$\binom{23}{4} - 3{,}575 = 5{,}280$
20			$\binom{22}{2} - 195 = 36$	$\binom{23}{3} - 1{,}138 = 633$	$\binom{24}{4} - 4{,}995 = 5{,}631$
21			$\binom{23}{2} - 225 = 28$	$\binom{24}{3} - 1{,}432 = 592$	$\binom{25}{4} - 6{,}775 = 5{,}875$
22			$\binom{24}{2} - 255 = 21$	$\binom{25}{3} - 1{,}760 = 540$	$\binom{26}{4} - 8{,}950 = 6{,}000$
⋮			⋮	⋮	⋮
28				$\binom{31}{3} - 3{,}330 = 165$	$\binom{32}{4} - 31{,}625 = 4{,}335$
29				$\binom{32}{3} - 4{,}840 = 120$	$\binom{33}{4} - 37{,}125 = 3{,}795$
30				$\binom{33}{3} - 5{,}240 = 84$	$\binom{34}{4} - 43{,}130 = 3{,}246$
31				$\binom{34}{3} - 5{,}928 = 56$	$\binom{35}{4} - 49{,}650 = 2{,}710$
32				$\binom{35}{3} - 6{,}510 = 35$	$\binom{36}{4} - 56{,}700 = 2{,}205$
⋮				⋮	⋮
$\sum_i \bar{x}_i f(\bar{x}_i)$	4.5	4.50	4.500	4.5000	4.5000
$\sum_i \bar{x}_i^2 f(\bar{x}_i)$	28.5	24.375	23.000	22.3125	21.9000

size, we use only the numerators 0, 1, 2, ... These are pure numbers independent of sample size in every respect other than the determination of the last one. They are, of course, nothing else but $n\bar{x}$ as shown in the heading of the first column. In writing out the actual numbers in this column, we confine ourselves only to those which center around the "breaking-off" points given by multiples of 10. The individual probabilities themselves are fractions with 10^n for denominator. To avoid repeated rewriting of this denominator, we present only the numerators; this accounts for the label "$10^n f(\bar{x})$" instead of the usual $f(\bar{x})$. In other respects the table is quite conventional.

The best way of analyzing the probability coefficients given in the main body of Table 4–11 is by considering them in groups of 10 at a time. The reason for this is the fact that there are 10 different values of X in the population so that the pattern of probabilities of $\bar{x}$ changes after each 10th, 20th, etc., coefficient. The thresholds separating the groups are represented in the table by horizontal dotted lines. Let us begin by considering the first 10 coefficients where the pattern is the simplest. For sample size 1, all of the coefficients are the same and are equal to 1. To make the notation consistent with that of the other columns, we may as well write out these coefficients as

$$\binom{0}{0}, \binom{1}{0}, \binom{2}{0}, \ldots, \binom{9}{0},$$

since each one is equal to unity anyway (see Section 3–2). Then a simple inspection of the table shows that, for the values of $n\bar{x}$ from 0 to 9, the probabilities are

$$f(\bar{x}) = \binom{n\bar{x} + n - 1}{n - 1} \Big/ 10^n.$$

For example, the probability that $\bar{x}$ of sample size 5 will be equal to 1 is

$$\binom{5 + 5 - 1}{5 - 1} \Big/ 10^5 = 0.00126.$$

The formula for the first 10 coefficients applies to the second group of coefficients only after a certain modification has been made. This modification consists of deducting a number which we shall call a correction factor c_1. That is, for $n\bar{x}$ from 10 to 19, we have

$$f(\bar{x}) = \left[\binom{n\bar{x} + n - 1}{n - 1} - c_1\right] \Big/ 10^n.$$

The problem is to discover a formula for c_1. Note that c_1 is in every case a multiple of the corresponding sample size. Dividing each value of c_1 by the sample size n we find the following sequences:

$n\bar{x}$	$n = 2$	$n = 3$	$n = 4$	$n = 5$
10	1	1	1	1
11	2	3	4	5
12	3	6	10	15
13	4	10	20	35
⋮	⋮	⋮	⋮	⋮

Now it appears that these sequences are simply the probability coefficients given ten places earlier. That is,

$$c_1 = n\binom{n\bar{x} - 10 + n - 1}{n - 1},$$

and, therefore, the probabilities of different values of $\bar{X}$ for $n\bar{x}$ from 10 to 19 are:

$$f(\bar{x}) = \left[\binom{n\bar{x} + n - 1}{n - 1} - n\binom{n\bar{x} - 10 + n - 1}{n - 1}\right] \Big/ 10^n.$$

For example, the probability that $\bar{x}$ of sample size 4 will be equal to 4.5 is

$$\left[\binom{18 + 4 - 1}{4 - 1} - 4\binom{18 - 10 + 4 - 1}{4 - 1}\right] \Big/ 10^4 = \left[\binom{21}{3} - 4\binom{11}{3}\right] \Big/ 10^4$$
$$= 0.0670.$$

Applying the formula developed for the second group of coefficients to determine the coefficients in the third group reveals that a further correction is necessary. Consider, for instance, the coefficient for $n\bar{x} = 20$ in sample size 3. This coefficient is equal to

$$\binom{22}{2} - 195 = 36.$$

But the application of the formula of the preceding paragraph gives

$$\binom{22}{2} - 3\binom{12}{2} = 33 \neq 36.$$

Thus we need another correction factor to be called c_2. Then, for $n\bar{x}$ from 20 to 29, we have

$$f(\bar{x}) = \left[\binom{n\bar{x} + n - 1}{n - 1} - n\binom{n\bar{x} - 10 + n - 1}{n - 1} + c_2\right] \Big/ 10^n.$$

The values of c_2 are

$n\bar{x}$	$n = 3$	$n = 4$	$n = 5$
20	3	6	10
21	9	24	50
22	18	60	150
23	30	120	350
⋮	⋮	⋮	⋮

Note that all the values in the column "$n = 3$" are multiples of 3, those in the column "$n = 4$" multiples of 6, and those in the column "$n = 5$" multiples of 10. The relationship of these common factors to the respective sample sizes can be identified, after some reflection, as follows: $3 = \binom{3}{2}$, $6 = \binom{4}{2}$, and $10 = \binom{5}{2}$. In general, the common factor is equal to $\binom{n}{2}$. After dividing each column by the respective common factor we get

$n\bar{x}$	$n = 3$	$n = 4$	$n = 5$
20	1	1	1
21	3	4	5
22	6	10	15
23	10	20	35
⋮	⋮	⋮	⋮

These sequences are simply the probability coefficients given twenty places earlier. Therefore, the formula for the probabilities of different values of $\bar{X}$ for $n\bar{x}$ ranging from 20 to 29 is

$$f(\bar{x}) = \left[\binom{n\bar{x} + n - 1}{n - 1} - n\binom{n\bar{x} - 10 + n - 1}{n - 1} + \binom{n}{2}\binom{n\bar{x} - 20 + n - 1}{n - 1}\right] \Big/ 10^n.$$

As an example consider the probability that $\bar{x}$ of sample size 4 will be equal to 6. This is

$$\left[\binom{24 + 4 - 1}{4 - 1} - 4\binom{24 - 10 + 4 - 1}{4 - 1} + 6\binom{24 - 20 + 4 - 1}{4 - 1}\right] \Big/ 10^4 = 0.0415.$$

We could continue this further but by now the pattern is quite clear. To calculate the probability of *any* value of $\bar{X}$ for *any* sample size n, we simply extend the preceding formula for $f(\bar{x})$ by adding further correction factors of the same type. In general, the probability distribution of $\bar{X}$ will then be

$$(4.10)\quad f(\bar{x}) = \frac{1}{10^n}\left[\binom{n\bar{x} + n - 1}{n - 1} - \binom{n}{1}\binom{n\bar{x} - 10 + n - 1}{n - 1} + \binom{n}{2}\binom{n\bar{x} - 20 + n - 1}{n - 1} - \binom{n}{3}\binom{n\bar{x} - 30 + n - 1}{n - 1} + \cdots\right].$$

The sum in (4.10) is to be continued as long as $(n\bar{x} - 10)$, $(n\bar{x} - 20)$, . . . remain positive or zero, i.e., until 10, 20, 30, . . . remain less or equal to $n\bar{x}$.

Equation (4.10) gives us the sampling distribution of $\bar{X}$ for samples drawn from a discrete uniform population with values of X equal to 0, 1, 2, . . ., 9. It is a simple matter to modify the formula to apply to a situation where X can assume, with equal probability, any one of k different values which are separated by equal distances. All that is needed to make this generalization is to replace 10, 20, 30, . . . in formula (4.10) by k, $2k$, $3k$, . . . to get

$$(4.11)\quad f(\bar{x}) = \frac{1}{k^n}\left[\binom{n\bar{x}+n-1}{n-1} - \binom{n}{1}\binom{n\bar{x}-k+n-1}{n-1} + \binom{n}{2}\binom{n\bar{x}-2k+n-1}{n-1} - \binom{n}{3}\binom{n\bar{x}-3k+n-1}{n-1} + \cdots\right].$$

Let us now determine the basic characteristics of the sampling distributions given by (4.10) and (4.11). With respect to the former, the values of the means and variances obtained earlier for sample sizes 1, 2, 3, 4, and 5 are summarized in Table 4–12. (The variances for sample sizes 1, 2, and 3 were calculated earlier;

Table 4–12

Sample Size	Mean	Variance
1	4.5	8.25
2	4.5	4.125
3	4.5	2.75
4	4.5	2.0625
5	4.5	1.65

those for sample sizes 4 and 5 can be obtained from the bottom line of Table 4–11 by deducting 4.5^2.) The most obvious feature of Table 4–12 is the fact that the value of the mean is equal to the population mean for all sample sizes examined. As far as the variance is concerned, note that its value for sample size 1 is exactly equal to the population variance and that the remaining values decrease in proportion to sample size, i.e., that

$$4.125 = \frac{8.25}{2},$$

$$2.75 = \frac{8.25}{3},$$

$$2.0625 = \frac{8.25}{4},$$

$$1.65 = \frac{8.25}{5}.$$

Finally, since we found all the sampling distributions to be exactly symmetric, the third moment μ_3 (and, therefore, also α_3) must be equal to zero. These results can easily be generalized to apply to any sample size n. Then we have

$$E(\bar{X}) = \mu,$$

$$\sigma_{\bar{x}}^2 = \frac{\sigma_x^2}{n},$$

$$\alpha_3 = 0,$$

where $\quad \sigma_{\bar{x}}^2 = \mathrm{Var}(\bar{X}) \quad$ and $\quad \sigma_x^2 = \mathrm{Var}(X)$.

It can be shown that these generalizations are perfectly valid and, furthermore, that they apply not only to the distribution (4.10) but also to its generalized version given by (4.11). (The proof concerning the mean and the variance will be given toward the end of this section; the proof concerning α_3 is left to the reader.)

Now we are in a position to make definite statements about the properties of sample mean as an estimator of the population mean for samples from a *discrete uniform population* with equally spaced values of X. The following conclusions can be made:

1. *$\bar{X}$ is an unbiased estimator of μ.*
2. *The variance of $\bar{X}$ is equal to the variance of X divided by sample size.* Thus, as the sample size increases, the distribution of $\bar{X}$ becomes more and more concentrated.
3. Conclusions 1 and 2 together imply that *$\bar{X}$ is a consistent estimator of μ.*
4. *The distribution of $\bar{X}$ is perfectly symmetric.*

These properties of $\bar{X}$ have been deduced from the theoretically derived sampling distribution. In Section 2–2 we tried to find these properties by conducting a sampling experiment on a discrete uniform population with values of X equal to 0, 1, 2, . . ., 9. The experiment consisted of drawing 100 samples of size 5 and 100 samples of size 10. For sample size 5, we constructed frequency distributions of sample mean and of sample median, and for sample size 10 of sample mean alone. The frequency distributions obtained in this way were assumed to approximate the true sampling distributions of these estimators. The results enabled us to make some tentative conclusions concerning the properties of these estimators. With respect to sample mean we are now in a position to check the experimental results by comparing them with the theoretically derived ones.

First, let us look at the sampling distribution of sample mean for sample size 5. The experimental results for this case are given in Table 2–4. They are reproduced in Table 4–13, alongside the theoretical results obtained from Table 4–11, and presented in a comparable form.

Next we compare the experimental and the theoretical results for sample size 10. The experimental results are given in Table 2–6; the theoretical results have been calculated by using formula (4.10) and the derived expressions for $E(\bar{X})$ and $\sigma_{\bar{x}}$. The distributions are presented in a comparable form in Table 4–14. The theoretical distribution is, of course, perfectly symmetric, although this is not immediately apparent from Table 4–14 because of the way the interval limits are spaced.

Tables 4–13 and 4–14 show that the experimentally derived frequency distributions give a reasonable approximation of the true sampling distributions. The tentative conclusions about $\bar{X}$ as an estimator of the population mean—namely unbiasedness, consistency, and reduction of variance proportional to sample size—all proved to be correct. However, the experimental results did not give us any formulas for the variance and were not clear enough to suggest symmetry. The theoretical results are not only more accurate, but they are also considerably more explicit and more general.

Table 4-13

	Sample Size 5	
Interval: $\bar{x}$	Experimental $f(\bar{x})$	Theoretical $f(\bar{x})$
0.5 to 1.499	0.01	0.01
1.5 to 2.499	0.05	0.05
2.5 to 3.499	0.12	0.16
3.5 to 4.499	0.31	0.28
4.5 to 5.499	0.28	0.28
5.5 to 6.499	0.15	0.16
6.5 to 7.499	0.05	0.05
7.5 to 8.499	0.03	0.01
8.5 to 9.499	0.00	0.00
Mean	4.60	4.5
Standard deviation	1.3638	1.2845

Table 4-14

	Sample Size 10	
Interval: $\bar{x}$	Experimental $f(\bar{x})$	Theoretical $f(\bar{x})$
0.5 to 1.499	0.00	0.00
1.5 to 2.499	0.01	0.01
2.5 to 3.499	0.14	0.11
3.5 to 4.499	0.34	0.35
4.5 to 5.499	0.32	0.37
5.5 to 6.499	0.16	0.14
6.5 to 7.499	0.03	0.02
7.5 to 8.499	0.00	0.00
8.5 to 9.499	0.00	0.00
Mean	4.57	4.5
Standard deviation	1.0416	0.9829

So far we have dealt with sampling from a discrete uniform population. Let us now turn to sampling from *normal populations.* In particular, our task now is to find the sampling distribution of sample mean given that the variable X, whose values make up the sample, is distributed normally with mean μ and variance σ^2, i.e., given that $X \sim N(\mu, \sigma^2)$. Note that we made a slight change in notation: instead of σ_x^2 we use σ^2 to describe the population variance. Now we know that

$$\bar{X} = \frac{1}{n}\sum_{i=1}^{n} X_i = \frac{1}{n}(X_1 + X_2 + \cdots + X_n) = \frac{1}{n}X_1 + \frac{1}{n}X_2 + \cdots + \frac{1}{n}X_n.$$

The n observations $X_1, X_2, \ldots, X_n$ can be viewed as n variables, each having the same distribution, mean, and variance as X. That is, X_1 stands for all possible values of X that can be obtained when drawing the first observation, X_2 for all possible values of X that can be obtained when drawing the second observation, and so on. This way of looking at the sample—which is, of course, perfectly legitimate—makes the subsequent analysis simpler and neater. Since n (and, therefore, $1/n$) is, for a given sample size, a constant, it follows that $\bar{X}$ can be regarded as a linear combination of n independent normal variables $X_1, X_2, \ldots, X_n$. But we know, by Theorem 12 of this chapter, that a linear combination of normally distributed independent random variables is also normally distributed. This saves us all the work of deriving the form of the sampling distribution of $\bar{X}$ because the theorem clearly implies that *if X (and therefore $X_1, X_2, \ldots, X_n$) is normal, then $\bar{X}$ is also normal, whatever the sample size.*

Having obtained this result, our task is reduced to determining the mean and the variance of the sampling distribution of $\bar{X}$. As emphasized in Section 4–2, the knowledge of the mean and the variance of a normal distribution is sufficient for its complete identification. Fortunately, the derivation of these two parameters turns out to be relatively simple. Let us start with the mean:

$$E(\bar{X}) = E\frac{1}{n}\sum_{i=1}^{n} X_i.$$

Since $1/n$ is a constant, we can, according to Theorem 6, write this as

$$E(\bar{X}) = \frac{1}{n}E\sum_{i} X_i.$$

But, by Theorem 8, the expectation of a sum is equal to the sum of expectations so that

$$E(\bar{X}) = \frac{1}{n}\sum_{i} E(X_i) = \frac{1}{n}[E(X_1) + E(X_2) + \cdots + E(X_n)].$$

Now each of $X_1, X_2, \ldots, X_n$ has the same mean as X, i.e., μ. Therefore,

$$E(\bar{X}) = \frac{1}{n}[\mu + \mu + \cdots + \mu] = \frac{n\mu}{n} = \mu.$$

That is, the mean of the sampling distribution of $\bar{X}$ is equal to the population mean μ. Next we derive the variance of $\bar{X}$ denoted by $\sigma_{\bar{x}}^2$. We have

$$\sigma_{\bar{x}}^2 = \text{Var}(\bar{X}) = \text{Var}\left[\frac{1}{n}\sum_{i=1} X_i\right] = \frac{1}{n^2}\text{Var}\left[\sum_{i} X_i\right] \quad \text{(by Theorem 7)}$$

Since $X_1, X_2, \ldots, X_n$ are, by assumption of random sampling, independent of each other, we can use the following theorem.

Theorem 13 *The variance of a sum of independent random variables is equal to the sum of their variances.*

Proof: Let $X_1, X_2, \ldots, X_n$ be a set of independent random variables. Then

$$\begin{aligned}\text{Var}\left[\sum_{i=1}^{n} X_i\right] &= E[(X_1 + X_2 + \cdots + X_n) - E(X_1 + X_2 + \cdots + X_n)]^2 \\ &= E\{[X_1 - E(X_1)] + [X_2 - E(X_2)] + \cdots + [X_n - E(X_n)]\}^2 \\ &= \sum_i E[X_i - E(X_i)]^2 + 2\sum_{i<j} E[X_i - E(X_i)][X_j - E(X_j)].\end{aligned}$$

But since the variables are independent of each other, their covariances are all equal to zero and we have

$$\text{Var}\left[\sum_{i=1}^{n} X_i\right] = \sum_{i=1}^{n} \text{Var}(X_i).$$

Thus for the variance of $\bar{X}$ we can write

$$\sigma_{\bar{x}}^2 = \frac{1}{n^2}[\text{Var}(X_1) + \text{Var}(X_2) + \cdots + \text{Var}(X_n)].$$

Now each of $X_1, X_2, \ldots, X_n$ has the same variance as X, i.e., σ^2. Therefore,

$$\sigma_{\bar{x}}^2 = \frac{1}{n^2}[\sigma^2 + \sigma^2 + \cdots + \sigma^2] = \frac{\sigma^2}{n}.$$

That is, the variance of the sampling distribution of $\bar{X}$ is equal to the population variance divided by sample size. These results can be summarized as follows:

If $X \sim N(\mu, \sigma^2)$, then $\bar{X} \sim N(\mu, \sigma^2/n)$.

This result is very important and will be used frequently throughout the rest of the book.

The preceding result implies certain properties of $\bar{X}$ as an estimator of the mean (μ) of a normal population.

1. Since $E(\bar{X}) = \mu$, *$\bar{X}$ is an unbiased estimator of μ.*
2. Since $\sigma_{\bar{x}}^2 = \sigma^2/n$, the distribution of $\bar{X}$ becomes more and more concentrated as the sample size n increases.
3. The preceding two properties imply that *$\bar{X}$ is a consistent estimator of μ.*
4. Since the distribution of $\bar{X}$ is normal, it is perfectly symmetric.

These properties are the same as those of $\bar{X}$ as an estimator of the mean of a discrete uniform population, although the sampling distributions themselves are somewhat different.

Another interesting implication of the result concerns the relationship between the variance of the sampling distribution of $\bar{X}$ and the variance of X in the population. Note that the dispersion of $\bar{X}$ depends only on two things, the size of the sample and the dispersion of the variable X in the population. For a given sample size, the smaller the population variance happens to be, the less dispersed (that is, the more reliable) are our guesses about the population mean. We use the term "happens to be" to emphasize the fact that the size of the population variance, unlike that of the sample, is not under our control—not even in theory. Thus, if we were to estimate the mean of some normally distributed variable such as, e.g., annual family expenditure of families in a given income bracket, we would obtain a more reliable estimate from a population with similar tastes, values, etc., than from a less conformist population. (The relationship between the variance of $\bar{X}$ and that of X was found to be the same in the case of a discrete uniform parent population as in the case of a normal parent. However, the former case is less interesting in practice, and thus we made no comment about it at the time.)

We have now completed a detailed derivation of the sampling distribution of sample mean for two parent populations—a discrete uniform population and a normal population. The latter is of considerable practical importance but, even so, cases of sampling from nonnormal populations (and from nonuniform populations) arise quite often in econometric work. However, we cannot conceivably pay individual attention to all remaining distributions, nor do we have any useful criterion for singling out some in preference to others. Therefore, we shall deal with the rest of the distributions only in a summary form, while trying to come to as many conclusions of general applicability as possible. Fortunately, we can go quite some way in this direction by establishing results which are independent of the form of the parent distribution of X.

One feature of the sampling distribution of $\bar{X}$, which in no way depends on the form of the distribution of X in the population, has already been obtained in connection with sampling from a normal population. This concerns the mean and the variance of $\bar{X}$. Suppose that the variable X has *any* distribution with mean μ and variance σ^2, and that $X_1, X_2, \ldots, X_n$ are regarded as n variables, each having exactly the same mean and variance as X. Then the mean of $\bar{X}$ is given by

$$E(\bar{X}) = E\frac{1}{n}(X_1 + X_2 + \cdots + X_n) = \mu,$$

and the variance of $\bar{X}$ is

$$\mathrm{Var}(\bar{X}) = \mathrm{Var}\left[\frac{1}{n}(X_1 + X_2 + \cdots + X_n)\right] = \frac{\sigma^2}{n}\cdot$$

These results are summarized in the following theorem.

Theorem 14 *If X is a variable with mean μ and variance σ^2 then, whatever the distribution of X, the sampling distribution of $\bar{X}$ has the same mean μ and variance equal to σ^2/n.*

Another feature of the sampling distribution of $\bar{X}$ which is independent of the distribution of X is described in the next theorem. This theorem, generally referred to as the *central limit theorem*, is one of the most important propositions in the theory of statistics. Its proof can be found in many texts on mathematical statistics and will not be developed here.[6]

Theorem 15 (*Central Limit Theorem*). *If X has any distribution with mean μ and variance σ^2, then the distribution of $\bar{X}$ approaches the normal distribution with mean μ and variance σ^2/n as sample size n increases.*

This is quite a remarkable result. Its clear implication is that, for large samples, the distribution of $\bar{X}$ can be approximated by a normal distribution whatever the parent distribution of X. It is this implication which gives the central limit theorem practical importance.

As an application of the central limit theorem, we may try to use normal distribution to approximate the sampling distribution of $\bar{X}$ based on samples from a discrete uniform population. In particular, let the parent distribution of X be such that X takes on only the values 0, 1, 2, . . ., 9. This is the same parent distribution as that which served as a basis for our sampling experiment described in Section 2–2. In this experiment, we constructed distributions of $\bar{X}$ from 100 samples of size 5 and 100 samples of size 10. The exact formula for the distribution of $\bar{X}$ was derived in the first part of the present section so that we know precisely what the true distribution of $\bar{X}$ is. Let us now try to use normal distribution (with mean $\mu = 4.5$ and variance $\sigma^2/n = 8.25/n$) as an approximation of the true distribution of $\bar{X}$. Although the approximation is presumed to be reasonable only for large samples and samples of size 5 or 10 obviously cannot be considered large, it may be instructive to see how it works in small samples.

First, let us try the sampling distribution of $\bar{X}$ for sample size 5. In this case, the mean and the standard deviation of the distribution are

$$E(\bar{X}) = 4.5$$

$$\sigma_{\bar{x}} = \sqrt{\frac{8.25}{5}} = 1.2845.$$

Therefore, the standard normal variable Z—which we need in order to use the normal probability table—is

$$z = \frac{\bar{x} - \mu}{\sigma_{\bar{x}}} = \frac{\bar{x} - 4.5}{1.2845} = 0.7785\bar{x} - 3.5033.$$

[6] The exact formulation of the central limit theorem varies from text to text. We shall follow that of R. L. Anderson and T. A. Bancroft, *Statistical Theory in Research* (New York: McGraw-Hill, 1952), p. 71, which makes the theorem easier to understand than some other formulations. It ought to be emphasized, though, that the validity of the theorem is restricted by the assumption that the variables X_i are mutually independent and that they are drawn from the same population with constant parameters.

In constructing the normal distribution we shall follow the procedure of Section 4–2 as illustrated in Table 4–7. The results are given in Table 4–15,

Table 4–15

		Sample Size 5			
Interval: $\bar{x}$	Interval: z	$f(z)$ (Cumulative Normal)	$f(\bar{x})$ (Normal Approx.)	$f(\bar{x})$ (Theoretical)	$f(\bar{x})$ (Experimental)
0.5 to 1.499	$-\infty$ to -2.33	0.010	0.01	0.01	0.01
1.5 to 2.499	-2.33 to -1.56	0.059	0.05	0.05	0.05
2.5 to 3.499	-1.56 to -0.78	0.218	0.16	0.16	0.12
3.5 to 4.499	-0.78 to 0.00	0.500	0.28	0.28	0.31
4.5 to 5.499	0.00 to 0.78	0.782	0.28	0.28	0.28
5.5 to 6.499	0.78 to 1.56	0.941	0.16	0.16	0.15
6.5 to 7.499	1.56 to 2.33	0.990	0.05	0.05	0.05
7.5 to 8.499	2.33 to 3.11	0.999	0.01	0.01	0.03
8.5 to 9.499	3.11 to ∞	1.000	0.00	0.00	0.00

together with the experimental and the theoretical probabilities reproduced from Table 4–13. The results given by the normal approximation are very good. In fact, it turns out that the fitted normal distribution is exactly the same—at least up to two decimal places—as the exact, theoretically determined distribution of $\bar{X}$.

Next, let us consider the sampling distribution for sample size 10. The mean and the standard deviation of this distribution are

$$E(\bar{X}) = 4.5,$$

$$\sigma_{\bar{x}} = \sqrt{\frac{8.25}{10}} = 0.9083.$$

The corresponding standard normal variable then is

$$z = \frac{\bar{x} - 4.5}{0.9083} = 1.1010\bar{x} - 4.9549.$$

The calculations are presented in Table 4–16; the columns giving the theoretical and the experimental probabilities are taken from Table 4–14. The results again indicate that normal distribution provides a very good approximation to the sampling distribution of $\bar{X}$. The fit in this case appears slightly worse than in Table 4–15 because, with sample size given by an even number, the theoretical distribution has only one peak at 4.5; when the sample size is odd, the theoretical distribution has two equal peaks, one just below and just above 4.5. With the interval limits as specified, the distributions based on even sample size have a spurious appearance of asymmetry.

The preceding results indicate that normal distribution may provide a reasonable approximation to the sampling distribution of $\bar{X}$ even when the sample size is small, but this is not true in general. The specific feature of the preceding case that made the normal approximation come out so well was the symmetry of the parent distribution and, consequently, of the distribution of $\bar{X}$ for any sample

Table 4–16

	Sample Size 10				
Interval: $\bar{x}$	Interval: z	$f(z)$ (Cumulative Normal)	$f(\bar{x})$ (Normal Approx.)	$f(\bar{x})$ (Theoretical)	$f(\bar{x})$ (Experimental)
0.5 to 1.499	$-\infty$ to -3.30	0.001	0.00	0.00	0.00
1.5 to 2.499	-3.30 to -2.20	0.014	0.02	0.01	0.01
2.5 to 3.499	-2.20 to -1.10	0.136	0.12	0.11	0.14
3.5 to 4.499	-1.10 to 0.00	0.500	0.36	0.35	0.34
4.5 to 5.499	0.00 to 1.10	0.864	0.36	0.37	0.32
5.5 to 6.499	1.10 to 2.20	0.986	0.12	0.14	0.16
6.5 to 7.499	2.20 to 3.30	0.999	0.02	0.02	0.03
7.5 to 8.499	3.30 to 4.40	1.000	0.00	0.00	0.00
8.5 to 9.499	4.40 to ∞	1.000	0.00	0.00	0.00

size. In cases where the parent distribution is highly skewed, it would take a large sample size before one could feel reasonably satisfied with using normal distribution for $\bar{X}$. And this, in fact, is all that one can legitimately expect from the central limit theorem.

Our discussion on sampling distribution of sample mean may best be closed by highlighting the most important results. We started by deriving the sampling distribution of $\bar{X}$ for samples drawn from a *discrete uniform population*. The resulting distribution of $\bar{X}$ turned out to be perfectly symmetric and capable of being closely approximated by a normal distribution, whatever sample size. Next, we found that the distribution of $\bar{X}$ for samples from a *normal population* is itself exactly normal for every sample size. Finally, by invoking the central limit theorem, we concluded that the distribution of $\bar{X}$ of a large sample will be approximately normal whatever the parent population. All these results bring out the importance of a normal distribution in statistical inference. In dealing with large samples we can *always* rely on normal distribution to describe the sampling distribution of $\bar{X}$. (Strictly speaking, the central limit theorem does not hold in the case in which the population variance is not finite. The statement in the text is based on the assumption that such cases are excluded from our discussion. Also, note the qualifying remarks made in footnote 6 on page 107.) If the parent population is not normal, the description will be approximate; if it is normal, the description will be exact. In dealing with small samples, normal distribution will give a perfect description of the distribution of $\bar{X}$ if the parent population is normal, and an approximate description if the parent population is nonnormal but symmetric. Only in the case of small samples and a skewed parent population would it be inadvisable to approximate the distribution of $\bar{X}$ by a normal distribution. Finally, concerning the properties of the sample mean as an estimator of the population mean, we found that, whatever the parent population, the distribution of $\bar{X}$ has a mean equal to the population mean and variance equal to the population variance divided by sample size. Thus $\bar{X}$ is an unbiased and consistent estimator of the population mean.

EXERCISES

4–1. In a certain city, 20% of all consumers are users of Brand D soap. What are the probabilities that in an elevator containing 10 people there will be 0, 1, 2, . . ., 10 users of Brand D soap?

4–2. How many times would we have to toss a coin in order that the probability will be at least 0.95 that the proportion of heads will lie between 0.40 and 0.60?

4–3. Given that the mean number of successes in n trials is 8 with standard deviation equal to 2, find n and π.

4–4. Consider a discrete uniform population with $X = 0, 1, \ldots, 5$. Derive the sampling distribution of the range (i.e., the difference between the largest and the smallest observation) for samples of size 4.

4–5. Consider a continuous uniform population with $0 < x < 1$. What is the probability that the mean of 20 observations will lie between 0.4 and 0.6?

4–6. A population consists of 10 balls of which 5 are white and 5 are red. Construct the sampling distribution of the proportion of white balls in a sample of 5 balls which are drawn *without replacement*.

4–7. A company operating in a certain city has been charged with making excessive profits. As evidence, it has been stated that the company's rate of profit last year was 22% while the national average for the industry was 16%. In defense, the officials of the company claimed that the profits in their industry are highly variable and that substantial deviations from the average are not infrequent. They pointed out that, while the mean rate of profit for the industry was 16%, the standard deviation was as large as 4%. Assuming that profits are normally distributed, what is the probability of making a profit of 22% or higher by pure chance?

4–8. If $X \sim N(8, 16)$, find each of the following:

a. $P(6 < X < 10)$. **b.** $P(10 < X < 12)$. **c.** $P(X < 0)$. **d.** $P(X > 20)$.

e. The two values of X which cut off the central 50% of the area under the curve.

4–9. Let Y = income and X = log Y. A frequently made claim is that the distribution of X is approximately normal. Check this claim by fitting a normal curve to the distribution of X obtained from the data in Table 4–17.

Table 4–17 Income of Families and Unattached Individuals, United States, 1962

Income	Percentage Frequency
Under $2,000	12.0
$2,000 to $2,999	8.5
$3,000 to $3,999	9.8
$4,000 to $4,999	10.2
$5,000 to $5,999	10.2
$6,000 to $7,499	14.1
$7,500 to $9,999	15.7
$10,000 to $14,999	12.3
$15,000 and over	7.2

Source: *Statistical Abstract of the United States, 1965* (U.S. Department of Commerce), p. 341.

5 Tests of Hypotheses

At the beginning of this text we stated that there are essentially two kinds of statistical inference: estimation and tests of hypotheses. Both are concerned with making judgments about some unknown aspect of a given population on the basis of sample information. The unknown aspect may be the value of one or more of the population parameters or, less frequently, the functional form of the population. Whether a problem is one of estimation or one of hypothesis testing is determined by the type of question that is being asked. In the case of estimation, we ask a question about the value of a particular parameter. In hypothesis testing the question is preceded by a statement concerning the population; the question then is whether this statement is true or false. In other respects the two cases are quite similar. In either case we arrive at an answer by combining our prior knowledge and assumptions about the population with the evidence provided by the sample. In either case we make considerable use of the concept of a sampling distribution developed in the previous sections. Finally, whatever the type of question, the answer is always tentative. However, there are some differences in approach which warrant separate discussion. Accordingly, we shall devote this chapter to the problem of testing hypotheses and the next to that of estimation.

5–1 Design and Evaluation of Tests

A hypothesis is defined as an assumption about the population. Typically, we make more than one such assumption, but not all of them are to be tested. Those assumptions that are not intended to be exposed to a test are called the *maintained hypothesis*. They consist of all the assumptions that we are willing to make and to believe in. Of course, we are never absolutely certain that these assumptions are valid; if we were, they would cease to be assumptions and would become facts. The usual situation in this respect is one in which we believe that the assumptions in question very likely hold at least approximately so that the maintained hypothesis is very nearly correct. The remaining assumptions that are to be tested are called the *testable hypothesis*. Usually the testable hypothesis consists of a statement that a certain population parameter is equal to a given value. In statistical theory this hypothesis is called the *null hypothesis* since it implies that there is no difference between the *true* value of the population parameter and that which is being hypothesized.

As an example, consider the statement that "economists and psychologists spend an equal average amount on tipping during their annual conventions." This can be interpreted as a testable hypothesis stating that the population means of the two professional groups are equal. One would normally test this by drawing a random sample of economists and a random sample of psychologists, and by comparing the respective sample means (in a manner to be discussed presently). The maintained hypothesis in this case might consist of the following assumptions.

1. If there is a difference in average tipping behavior, it depends entirely on the profession of the tipper; other factors such as income, sex, and age are of no relevance.
2. In each group the amount spent on tipping is normally distributed with the same variance.
3. There is no definite prior presumption that either of the two population means is greater than the other.

The first of these assumptions implies that no factors other than difference in profession have to be taken into account when the test is carried out. The second assumption is needed in order to determine the sampling distribution of the test statistic. The final assumption determines the alternative to the null hypothesis. In this case the alternative hypothesis is that the means are *not* the same. The specification of the alternative hypothesis is needed when setting up the test.

The idea of an alternative hypothesis is quite important and requires elaboration. Since the null hypothesis is a testable proposition, there must exist a counterproposition to it, otherwise there would be no need for a test. The counterproposition is called the *alternative hypothesis*. Suppose the null hypothesis states that the population mean μ is equal to some value, say, μ_0. Usually we denote the null hypothesis by H_0 and the alternative by H_A. Then the alternative hypothesis may be, for instance, the proposition that μ is equal to some *other* value, say, μ_A. That is, we would have

$$H_0: \quad \mu = \mu_0,$$
$$H_A: \quad \mu = \mu_A.$$

If this is the case, the implication is that μ can be equal to either μ_0 or μ_A, but nothing else. Obviously such a case is very rare since it means that we know really quite a lot about the population mean a priori; the only thing that we are not certain about is which of the two values it has. More frequently, our prior knowledge concerning the population mean (or any other population parameter) is much less. If we know absolutely nothing about μ, then the alternative hypothesis would be that μ is *not* equal to μ_0, as described by

$$H_0: \quad \mu = \mu_0,$$
$$H_A: \quad \mu \neq \mu_0.$$

Sometimes we are reasonably certain that μ is greater (or smaller) than μ_0. Then we would have

$$H_0: \quad \mu = \mu_0,$$

$$H_A: \quad \mu > \mu_0 \qquad (\text{or } H_A: \quad \mu < \mu_0).$$

Hypotheses of a general form such as $\mu \neq \mu_0$, $\mu > \mu_0$, or $\mu < \mu_0$ are called *composite hypotheses*, whereas specific claims such as $\mu = \mu_0$ are called *simple hypotheses*.

Since specific claims are easier to disprove than vague claims, it is desirable—and it has been the common practice—to formulate problems of hypotheses testing so that the null hypothesis is stated as specifically as possible. Thus, if—as very frequently is the case—we have two rival hypotheses, one simple and one composite, we choose the simple one as the null hypothesis to be tested. This means that we often introduce the null hypothesis as that proposition which we actually wish to disprove. A good example of this is a test of a new drug. There is an obvious presumption that the new drug will do better, say in terms of mean percentage of recoveries, than the old drug or therapy used, otherwise there would be no point in testing. Yet the null hypothesis for this case will be the proposition that the new drug leads to the same mean percentage of recoveries as the old drug; the alternative hypothesis will be that the mean percentage is higher for the new drug.

The decision as to which of the two rival hypotheses is to be regarded as the null hypothesis has some implications which ought to be taken into account. According to established methodology, a null hypothesis is a proposition which is considered valid unless evidence throws serious doubt on it. In this respect a statistical test is like a trial in a court of law. A man on trial is considered innocent unless the evidence suggests *beyond reasonable doubt* that he is guilty. Similarly, a null hypothesis is regarded as valid unless the evidence suggests—also beyond reasonable doubt—that it is not true. (However, while in court the definition of "reasonable doubt" is presumably the same from case to case, in statistical tests it may vary depending upon the cost of making an incorrect verdict.) Furthermore, just as in court it is up to the prosecution to prove the accused guilty, so in statistical testing it is up to the statistician to prove the null hypothesis incorrect. Of course, in neither case is the word "prove" to be taken in an absolute sense since a "shadow" of a doubt always exists; only God knows whether a man is really guilty or a null hypothesis is really incorrect. Finally, there is also a similarity in procedure. In court all evidence and other information relevant to the case are produced and weighed in accordance with the rules set by law, and a verdict of "guilty" or "not guilty" is reached. Similarly, when a statistical test is conducted, all evidence and prior information is used in accordance with predetermined rules, and a conclusion of "reject" or "do not reject" the null hypothesis is obtained. Interestingly enough, just as a court pronounces a verdict as "not guilty" rather than "innocent," so the conclusion of a statistical test is "do not reject" rather than "accept."

The parallel between a trial in a court and a statistical test stops abruptly when it comes to the application of the Fifth Amendment of the United States Constitution. Unlike a man on trial who is not to "be subject for the same offense to be twice put in jeopardy of life or limb," a null hypothesis is *always* open to a test. In fact, while a null hypothesis is viewed as valid unless thrown into serious evidence, such a view is always held only tentatively. In this respect, a null hypothesis is like a titleholder who is forever open to challenge. In fact, one can visualize the course of science as a process of establishing hypotheses and then busily collecting evidence to bring about their downfall. Only the sturdiest hypotheses withstand the repeated attacks and become worthy of our faith, at least until the next attack comes along.

So far we have not mentioned the question concerning the source of hypotheses. In principle, this question has a simple answer: economic hypotheses are drawn from economic theory. In practice, however, the matter is much less simple. In the first place, economic theory is rarely sufficiently precise and detailed to lead to hypotheses suitable for application of statistical tests. For instance, one would be hard put to find in economic literature a theoretical development which would lead to a proposition specifying a definite value of the government expenditure multiplier as well as spelling all the assumptions that would be embraced by the maintained hypothesis. Economic theory typically specifies only the interrelationships between different economic variables, usually described in quite general terms. The econometrician, then, must specify the mathematical form of those relationships and spell out the maintained hypothesis more completely and in greater detail. The null hypothesis usually states that the postulated relationship does *not* exist, which normally means that the value of one or more of the parameters is equal to zero, while the alternative hypothesis states that the relationship does exist. The second difficulty with economic theory as a source of hypotheses is that frequently the variables involved are difficult to define, or to measure, or both. This, unfortunately, applies not only to such notoriously difficult concepts as capital, but also to less obviously troublesome concepts such as income or consumption. Finally, there are many problems for which economic theory is not at all well developed, and thus it offers little help in leading to relevant hypotheses. In these situations the researcher usually resorts to ad hoc theorizing, that is, to setting up maintained and testable hypotheses by using his common sense and whatever inspiration he can get from theory. Most of the applied econometric work that has been done so far is of this kind, or at least predominantly so. All these difficulties in setting up economic hypotheses to some extent account for the greater concentration on problems of estimation rather than on problems of hypothesis testing in past econometric research.

Setting up the null hypothesis and its alternative represents the first step in dealing with a problem involving hypothesis testing. The next step consists of devising a criterion that would enable us to decide whether the null hypothesis is or is not to be rejected on the basis of evidence. This criterion or rule is in principle the same regardless of the problem: it defines a test statistic and a boundary for dividing the sample space into a region of rejection and a region of nonrejection. The test statistic is simply a formula telling us how to confront the null hypothesis with the evidence. It is a random variable whose value varies from sample to sample. The *region of rejection*, sometimes called the *critical region*, is a subset of the sample space such that if the value of the test statistic falls in it, the null hypothesis is rejected. Similarly, the *region of nonrejection*, usually called the *acceptance region*, is a subset of the sample space such that if the value of the test statistic falls in it, the null hypothesis is not rejected. The boundary between the rejection and the acceptance regions is determined by prior information concerning the distribution of the test statistic, by the specification of the alternative hypothesis, and by considerations of the costs of arriving at an incorrect conclusion. An important feature of the boundary is the fact that it does not depend on sample information; in fact, its determination comes logically prior to drawing the sample.

Test Criterion

The procedure of devising a criterion for rejecting the null hypothesis can be conveniently explained with reference to a standard textbook problem of hypothesis testing. Consider a null hypothesis which states that the mean of some variable X is equal to μ_0. Suppose that our maintained hypothesis consists of the following assumptions: (1) X is normally distributed; (2) the variance of X is σ^2 and is *known*. Since the maintained hypothesis tells us nothing about μ (for instance, that μ is restricted to positive values or some such information), the alternative hypothesis is then simply that μ is not equal to μ_0. Thus we can write

$$H_0: \quad \mu = \mu_0,$$

$$H_A: \quad \mu \neq \mu_0.$$

Let us now develop a suitable test statistic. The information that we will receive from the sample will obviously tell us *something* about the population mean; the question is how this information should be used. Our discussion in Section 4–3 indicated that sample mean has some desirable properties as an estimator of the population mean. This suggests that we may use the sample mean to summarize the sample evidence about the population mean. Then an obvious criterion for rejecting or not rejecting the null hypothesis will be as follows: if the value of $\bar{X}$ is very different from μ_0, reject the null hypothesis; if it is not very different, do not reject it.

The foregoing criterion is clearly useless for defining the critical and the acceptance region unless we state precisely which values of $\bar{X}$ are to be regarded as "very different" from μ_0 and which are not. To decide that, we have to consider the sampling distribution of $\bar{X}$. If X is normal and has, in fact, mean μ_0 and variance σ^2, then $\bar{X}$ will be normal with mean μ_0 and variance σ^2/n (where n is the sample size). Of course, since the normal distribution extends from $-\infty$ to $+\infty$, *any* value of $\bar{X}$ can be observed whatever the population mean. However, if the true mean is μ_0, then the values of $\bar{X}$ in intervals close to μ_0 will occur with greater probability than those in intervals (of the same length) farther away from μ_0. It is natural then to regard as "very different from μ_0" those values of $\bar{X}$ which—if μ_0 were the true mean—would occur by chance only very rarely. By "very rarely" we mean, at least for the time being, "with probability 0.01."

At this stage we have to introduce the alternative hypothesis which states that $\mu \neq \mu_0$. This, in fact, means that if the null hypothesis does not hold, the true mean may be on either side of μ_0. Therefore, values of $\bar{X}$ that are very much larger than μ_0 *as well as* values that are very much smaller would constitute evidence against the null hypothesis. (If the alternative hypothesis were, for example, that $\mu > \mu_0$, then only those values of $\bar{X}$ that are very much *larger* than μ_0 would represent evidence against the null hypothesis.) That is, the boundaries between the critical and the acceptance regions must be such that we would reject the null hypothesis if the value of $\bar{X}$ turned out to be *either* so low *or* so high compared to μ_0 that its occurrence by chance would be very unlikely. Since we decided to call an event very unlikely (i.e., very rare) if it occurs with probability of only 0.01, this probability must be "shared" equally by excessively low and excessively high values of $\bar{X}$. In other words, the boundaries are to be set in such a way that the probability of $\bar{x}$ being that excessively low is 0.005 and the probability of $\bar{x}$ being that excessively high is also 0.005. Then, by the Addition Theorem (Theorem 2), the probability that $\bar{x}$ will be either excessively high or excessively low compared to μ_0 will be $0.005 + 0.005 = 0.01$, as required.

Let us denote that value below which $\bar{x}$ would be considered excessively low by μ_L, and that value above which $\bar{x}$ would be considered excessively high by μ_H. These points are marked off on the sampling distribution of $\bar{X}$ shown in Figure 5–1. We have

$$P(\bar{x} < \mu_L) = 0.005,$$

$$P(\bar{x} > \mu_H) = 0.005;$$

therefore $$P(\mu_L \leq \bar{x} \leq \mu_H) = 0.99.$$

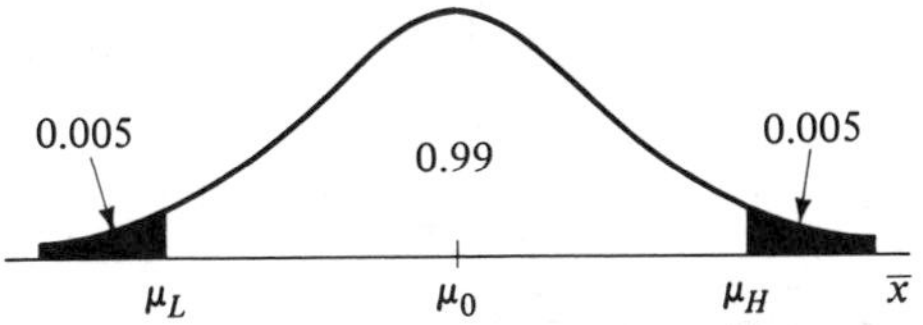

Figure 5–1

We could actually consider $\bar{X}$ as an appropriate test statistic and the interval from μ_L to μ_H as the acceptance region, but this is not very practical since we do not know the location of μ_L and μ_H. We can, however, very easily determine the location of their counterparts in a standard normal distribution for which probabilities are tabulated. How this can be done was described in detail in Section 4–2.

Given that $\bar{X} \sim N(\mu_0, \sigma^2/n)$, the corresponding standard normal variable will be

$$(5.1) \qquad Z = \frac{\bar{X} - \mu_0}{\sqrt{\sigma^2/n}} = \frac{(\bar{X} - \mu_0)\sqrt{n}}{\sigma}.$$

This will be our *test statistic.*

Now we wish to find those values on the z scale which correspond to μ_L and μ_H on the $\bar{x}$ scale. These values of Z, which we will call z_L and z_H, can be found by noting that they have to cut off on each end 0.005 of the area under the curve, as

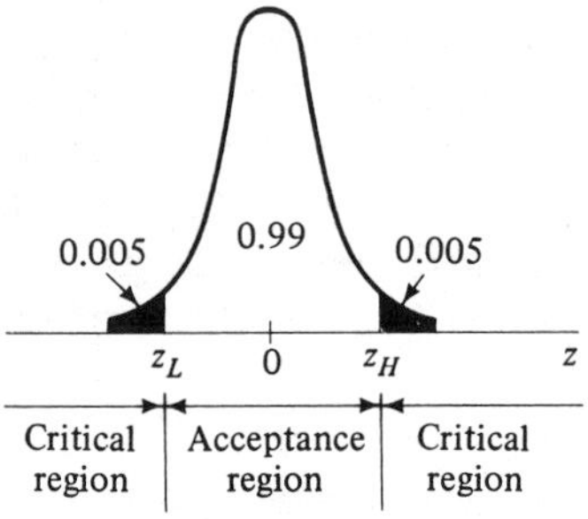

Figure 5–2

shown in Figure 5–2. That is, we have to find from the normal probability tables the value of z_L such that

$$P(z < z_L) = 0.005,$$

or, which amounts to exactly the same,

$$P(z \geq z_L) = 0.995.$$

Similarly, we have to find z_H such that

$$P(z > z_H) = 0.005,$$

or, equivalently,

$$P(z \leq z_H) = 0.995.$$

By consulting the normal probability tables we get

$$z_L = -2.575$$

$$z_H = +2.575$$

This completes our task. The interval from -2.575 to $+2.575$ represents the acceptance region, and the intervals from $-\infty$ to -2.575 and from $+2.575$ to $+\infty$ our critical region. (Since the probability of getting a value of Z equal to z_L or z_H is zero, it is of little practical importance whether the acceptance region does or does not include the boundary values.) The criterion for rejecting or not rejecting the null hypothesis is then as follows:

$$\textit{reject if} \quad \frac{(\bar{x} - \mu_0)\sqrt{n}}{\sigma} < -2.575 \quad \textit{or if} \quad \frac{(\bar{x} - \mu_0)\sqrt{n}}{\sigma} > +2.575;$$

$$\textit{do not reject if} \quad -2.575 \leq \frac{(\bar{x} - \mu_0)\sqrt{n}}{\sigma} \leq +2.575.$$

This division between the critical and the acceptance regions is contingent upon our decision to consider as "very different" from μ_0 only those values of $\bar{X}$ which would occur by chance with probability of 0.01. In other words, if we drew an infinite number of samples from the population with mean μ_0, only 1% of the time would we get a value of $\bar{X}$ that would lead to an incorrect rejection of the null hypothesis. This probability is known as the *significance level* of the test. Of course, there is nothing sacrosanct about the figure of 1% which we chose; in absence of any information, some other figure may just as well have been chosen. Had we chosen a higher percentage, the acceptance region would have been narrower and the critical region wider. As it happens, 1% is one of the "popular" levels of significance but that is all that can be said for it at this stage. We shall discuss the possibility for a more rational choice of the level of significance before the end of the present section, but first let us consider a numerical example of the test procedure that we have just developed.

EXAMPLE Psychological studies indicate that in the population at large intelligence —as measured by IQ—is normally distributed with mean of 100 and standard deviation of 16. Suppose we want to test whether a given subpopulation—for instance, all people who are left-handed—is characterized by a different mean. As our maintained hypothesis, we assume that intelligence among the left-handed is normally distributed with the same standard deviation as that of the population at large, i.e., 16. Let us call the mean IQ among left-handed persons μ. The null and the alternative hypotheses will be

$$H_0: \quad \mu = 100,$$

$$H_A: \quad \mu \neq 100.$$

Our test statistic will then be

$$\frac{(\bar{X} - 100)\sqrt{n}}{16}.$$

As the appropriate level of significance we choose 5%, which happens to be the other "popular" level. That is, if the value of $\bar{X}$ should be so different from the hypothesized mean of 100 that it would occur by pure chance only 5% of the time, we will consider the null hypothesis as unlikely and reject it. Now, to find the boundaries of the acceptance region, we have to locate those values of the standard normal variable which cut off 2.5% of total area at each end of the distribution, as shown in Figure 5-3. From the normal probability tables we find

$$z_L = -1.96,$$

$$z_H = +1.96.$$

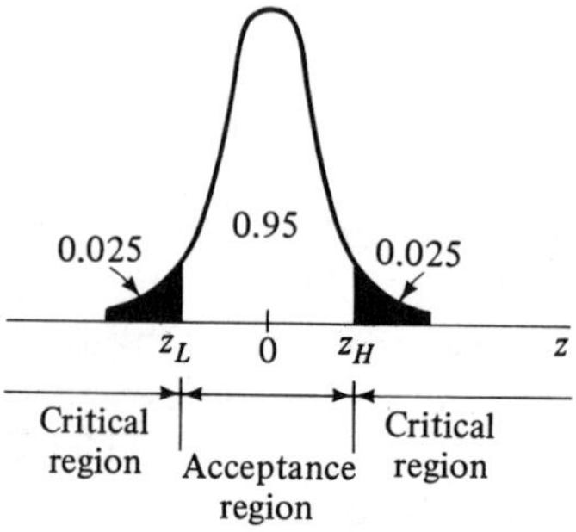

Figure 5-3

Therefore our criterion is:

do not reject H_0 *if* $-1.96 \leq \frac{(\bar{x} - 100)\sqrt{n}}{16} \leq +1.96;$

otherwise reject it.

At this stage we can draw a sample and calculate the value of $\bar{X}$ and of the test statistic. Suppose the sample consists of 400 observations of left-handed persons, and the mean IQ is 99. Then the value of our test statistic will be

$$\frac{(99 - 100)\sqrt{400}}{16} = -1.25.$$

This obviously falls into the acceptance region so that the sample gives no evidence against the null hypothesis. In other words, there is no evidence that the mean IQ of left-handed persons is any different from that of the population at large. This completes the answer to the problem.

Thus far we have made no assumptions that would help us in formulating the alternative hypothesis. Therefore the alternative hypothesis had to be of the form $\mu \neq \mu_0$. Consequently, the rejection region covered both tail ends of the distribution of the test statistic. A test with this kind of rejection region is called a *two-tail test*. However, sometimes we are able to make assumptions that permit a somewhat less general specification of the alternative hypothesis. In particular, sometimes we are reasonably certain that the only alternative to the claim that $\mu = \mu_0$ is the claim that μ is greater (or smaller) than μ_0. For instance, it has been claimed that the marginal propensity to save (MPS) of "profit makers" is higher than that of the labor force at large. In this case the null hypothesis would be that the two propensities are equal, and the alternative hypothesis would be the claim that the MPS of the profit makers is higher. In such cases the values of $\bar{X}$ (and therefore of the test statistic) that would be regarded as evidence against the null hypothesis would all be concentrated at just one end of the distribution. A test of this kind is called a *one-tail test*.

To illustrate the point, consider again a variable $X \sim N(\mu, \sigma^2)$ where σ^2 is known. Suppose the null and the alternative hypotheses are given as follows:

$$H_0: \quad \mu = \mu_0,$$

$$H_A: \quad \mu > \mu_0.$$

As our test statistic we use

$$Z = \frac{(\bar{X} - \mu_0)\sqrt{n}}{\sigma},$$

as given by (5.1). Suppose now that we wish to carry out the test at 1% level of significance. That is, we will reject the null hypothesis if the value of $\bar{X}$ is so much greater than μ_0 that it would occur by chance with probability of only 0.01. In this case the acceptance and the critical regions will be as shown in Figure 5–4.

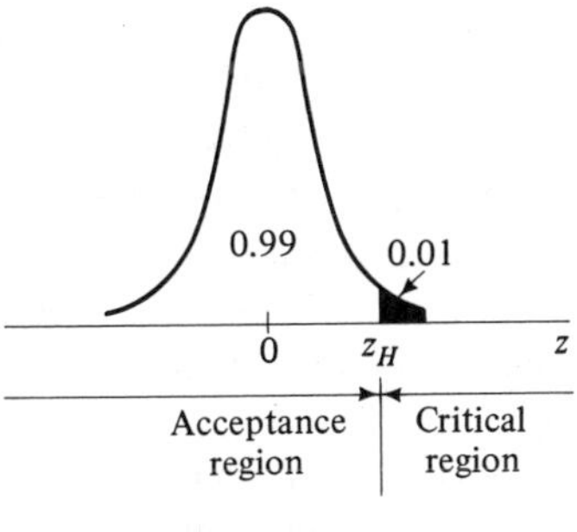

Figure 5–4

The value of z_H, which can be looked up in the normal probability tables, is 2.327. Therefore, the criterion for rejecting H_0 in this case is

$$\textit{reject if} \quad \frac{(\bar{x} - \mu_0)\sqrt{n}}{\sigma} > 2.327;$$

do not reject otherwise.

If the chosen level of significance were 5% instead of 1%, the criterion would be

$$\textit{reject if} \quad \frac{(\bar{x} - \mu_0)\sqrt{n}}{\sigma} > 1.645;$$

do not reject otherwise.

Types of Error

The criterion for rejecting or not rejecting the null hypothesis on the basis of sample evidence is not a guarantee of arriving at a correct conclusion. Let us now consider in detail the kinds of errors that could be made. Suppose we have a problem of testing a hypothesis about the population mean, as in the preceding discussion. The solution of the problem consists essentially of two basic steps: setting up the boundaries between the acceptance and the critical regions and obtaining the sample value of the test statistic. Two outcomes are possible: either the value of the test statistic falls in the acceptance region or it does not. Let us take the second outcome first. In this case the value of the test statistic is such that, if the null hypothesis were in fact true, the probability of this happening by chance would be very small, e.g., 5% or 1%. This means that if the test were repeated an infinite number of times and if the null hypothesis were in fact true, we would *incorrectly reject* the null hypothesis 5% or 1% (or whatever the level of significance) of the time. Such an error is called *Error Type I.* Earlier we compared statistical testing to a trial in a court of law where the innocence of the accused (our null hypothesis) is challenged by the claim of guilt by the prosecution (our alternative hypothesis). Using this parallel, the Error Type I would be represented by the error of convicting an innocent man. In statistical testing the probability of committing this error is given precisely by the chosen level of significance. Consider now the second possible outcome of the test, that is, the case where the value of the test statistic falls inside the acceptance region. In this case we do not reject the null hypothesis, i.e., we keep on believing it to be true. However, the possibility that we came to an incorrect conclusion, namely that the null hypothesis is in fact false, cannot be ruled out. An error of this sort is called *Error Type II.* In terms of the parallel with the court trial, the Error Type II would mean letting a guilty man go. In statistical testing the exact probability of this kind of error is usually unknown.

The general idea behind the two types of error can be clearly illustrated by the —unfortunately not very common—case of testing a simple null hypothesis against a *simple* alternative. Suppose the hypotheses are

$$H_0: \quad \mu = \mu_0,$$

$$H_A: \quad \mu = \mu_A,$$

where μ_0 and μ_A are given numbers and $\mu_A > \mu_0$. As before, we assume X to be normal with a known variance σ^2. Thus the two hypotheses can be identified with two competing populations, both normal with the same variance σ^2 but distinguished by their means. Each population generates—for a given sample size n—its own sampling distribution of $\bar{X}$. To carry out the test we have to establish the boundary between the critical and the acceptance region. This will depend, as we have seen, on the chosen level of significance and on the alternative hypothesis. The level of significance can be chosen a priori as, say, 5%. Since the alternative hypothesis is that $\mu = \mu_A$ and since $\mu_A > \mu_0$, only high values of $\bar{X}$ relative to μ_0 would constitute evidence against H_0. That is, the appropriate test is a one-tail test with the critical region concentrated at the right-hand tail of the distribution. With these considerations in mind, we can determine the boundary between the acceptance and the critical region for the distribution of the test statistic

$$Z = \frac{(\bar{X} - \mu_0)\sqrt{n}}{\sigma}.$$

For the 5% level of significance with the critical region concentrated at the right tail of the distribution, the boundary value z_H is equal to 1.645. Therefore the acceptance region will be

$$z \leq 1.645.$$

If the true mean is μ_0, then the probability that a value of $\bar{X}$ falls inside the acceptance region is 0.95. To determine the probability of Error Type II, we have to find the probability that a value of $\bar{X}$ falls inside the acceptance region if the true mean is *not* μ_0 but μ_A. This can be found as follows. First we note that

$$P(z > 1.645) = 0.05$$

can be written as

$$P\left[\frac{(\bar{x} - \mu_0)\sqrt{n}}{\sigma} > 1.645\right] = 0.05.$$

Consider the inequality inside the square bracket. By multiplying both sides by $\sigma/\sqrt{n}$, we get

$$(\bar{x} - \mu_0) > 1.645\left[\frac{\sigma}{\sqrt{n}}\right].$$

Adding μ_0 to both sides gives

$$\bar{x} > \mu_0 + 1.645\left[\frac{\sigma}{\sqrt{n}}\right].$$

Thus we can write

$$P\left[\bar{x} > \mu_0 + 1.645\left(\frac{\sigma}{\sqrt{n}}\right)\right] = 0.05,$$

which is a probability statement about $\bar{X}$ rather than Z. Thus the boundary between the acceptance and the critical region on the $\bar{x}$ axis is given by $[\mu_0 + 1.645(\sigma/\sqrt{n})]$. Since μ_0, σ, and n are known, the boundary will be a known number. Figure 5–5 shows the two distributions with the boundaries marked off.

Now let us consider the sampling distribution of $\bar{X}$ for samples from the population with mean μ_A. This distribution will be normal with mean equal to the population mean (i.e., μ_A) and variance σ^2/n. Thus the only way in which this distribution differs from the distribution of $\bar{X}$ from the population with mean μ_0

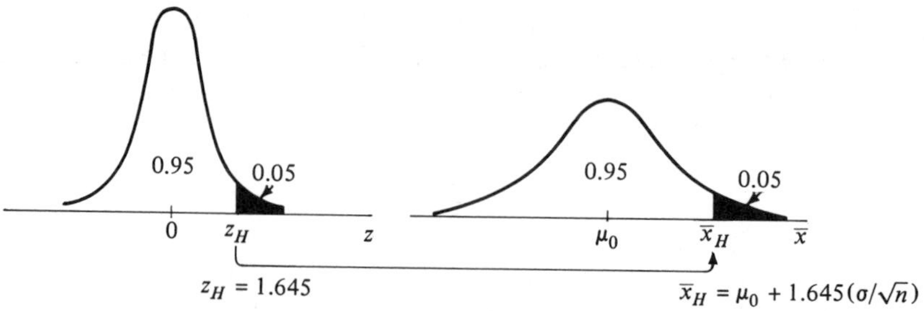

Figure 5–5

is with respect to the mean. The two distributions of $\bar{X}$ are compared in Figure 5–6, which shows clearly the probabilities of the two types of error involved in hypothesis testing. Recall that Error Type I is committed any time we reject H_0 when it is, in fact, the correct hypothesis. This happens whenever $\bar{x}$ falls to the right of the boundary point $\bar{x}_H$. Note that if H_0 is correct, then $\bar{X}$ follows distribution 1 in Figure 5–6. Therefore the probability of Error Type I is given by the chosen level of significance (0.05) and corresponds to the blackened area. The Error Type II occurs whenever we do not reject H_0 when it is in fact false. This happens whenever $\bar{x}$ falls to the left of $\bar{x}_H$. In the present case if H_0 should be false, i.e., if μ_0 were not the true mean, then the only other possibility is that the

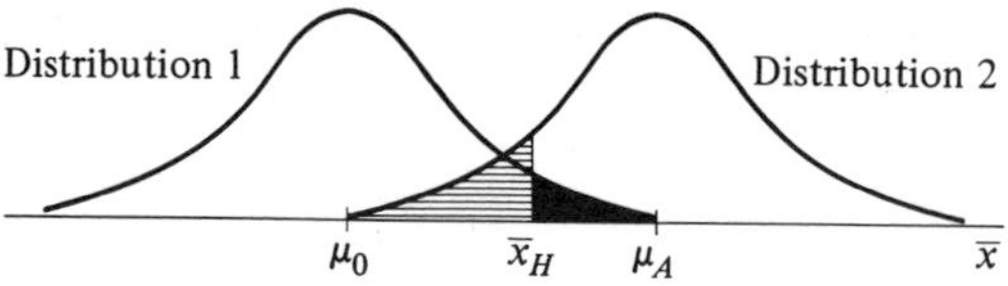

Figure 5–6

true mean is μ_A. But if μ_A should be the true mean, the sample mean $\bar{X}$ would follow distribution 2, and the probability of making Error Type II is given by the striped area in Figure 5–6. In reality we do not know which is the true mean and therefore do not know which is the true distribution of $\bar{X}$. If the true distribution of $\bar{X}$ is "1," then our test will lead to an incorrect conclusion 5% (or whatever the chosen level of significance) of the time. If the true distribution of $\bar{X}$ is "2," then our test will produce incorrect results with a probability given by the striped area to the left of $\bar{x}_H$.

The preceding discussion, although restricted to the case of a simple alternative hypothesis, brings out an important facet of hypothesis testing which remains equally relevant in tests involving composite alternatives. This is the fact that *by decreasing the probability of one type of error we increase the probability of the other type of error*. For instance, we can make the probability of Error Type I (rejecting H_0 when in fact it is true) as small as we like by setting a very low level of significance. In terms of Figure 5–6, this amounts to shifting the boundary point $\bar{x}_H$ farther to the right. But by doing this we would obviously increase the striped area, which represents the probability of Error Type II (not rejecting H_0 when in fact it is false). Similarly, we can reduce the probability of Error Type II by increasing the level of significance, i.e., by shifting $\bar{x}_H$ to the left, but this would increase the probability of Error Type I. By reference to our comparison of statistical testing with trials before a court of law, we could obviously diminish the probability of convicting an innocent man by letting almost everybody go, but this would clearly increase the probability of not convicting a guilty man. Similarly, we could reduce the probability of letting a guilty man go free by requiring less stringent evidence for conviction, but this would increase the probability of convicting an innocent man. In statistical testing, the only way in which we could reduce the probabilities of both kinds of error at the same time is by increasing the sample size (assuming that the test statistic used is the best that can be devised).

EXAMPLE A manufacturer produces two types of tires, one type with a life expectancy of 25,000 miles and the other with a life expectancy of 30,000 miles. The variation in durability around the expected lifetime is the same for both types of tires, the standard deviation being 3,000 miles. The distribution can be assumed to be normal. The two types of tires are indistinguishable except for markings. At the time of inventory taking, it is discovered that there is a forgotten case with 100 tires that do not have any markings. The examining engineer thinks that the tires are of the less durable kind but recommends a test. The test is to be performed on a sample of 4 tires. What should be the appropriate test criterion?

First, we specify the null and the alternative hypotheses as follows:

$$H_0: \quad \mu = 25{,}000,$$

$$H_A: \quad \mu = 30{,}000.$$

Next, we set up the boundary between the acceptance and the critical regions. This will depend on the chosen level of significance. We shall consider 1%, 5%, and 10% levels of significance and determine the corresponding probabilities of Error Type II. Because μ_0 (=25,000) < μ_A (=30,000), we shall use the upper-tail critical region in every case.

1. If the level of significance is 1%, the boundary point on the z scale (for the standard normal distribution) will be the point which cuts off the top 1% of the area. From the normal probability tables, we find that this is given by

$$z_H = 2.327.$$

To determine the probability of Error Type II we have to find the corresponding point on the $\bar{x}$ scale, $\bar{x}_H$. From the previous discussion, we know that

$$\bar{x}_H = \mu_0 + 2.327 \frac{\sigma}{\sqrt{n}}.$$

Substituting, we get

$$\bar{x}_H = 25{,}000 + 2.327\left[\frac{3000}{\sqrt{4}}\right] = 28{,}490.5.$$

Now we have to determine the probability that $\bar{x} < 28{,}490.5$ *given* that the mean of $\bar{X}$, $E(\bar{X})$, is 30,000. To do that we have to make the appropriate transformation to standard normal variable. We can write

$$P[\bar{x} < 28{,}490.5 \mid E(\bar{X}) = 30{,}000] = P\left[z < \frac{(28{,}490.5 - 30{,}000)\sqrt{4})}{3000}\right]$$

$$= P[z < -1.0063].$$

But from the normal probability tables we find

$$P[z < -1.0063] = 0.1571.$$

This is the probability of making Error Type II.

2. If the chosen level of significance is 5%, then

$$z_H = 1.645,$$

and

$$\bar{x}_H = 25{,}000 + 1.645\left[\frac{3000}{\sqrt{4}}\right] = 27{,}467.5.$$

The probability that $\bar{x} < 27{,}467.5$ *given* that the mean of $\bar{X}$ is 30,000 is

$$P[\bar{x} < 27{,}467.5 \mid E(\bar{X}) = 30{,}000] = P\left[z < \frac{(27{,}467.5 - 30{,}000)\sqrt{4}}{3000}\right]$$

$$= P[z < -1.6883] = 0.0457.$$

3. Finally, if the level of significance is 10%, then

$$z_H = 1.280,$$

and

$$\bar{x}_H = 25{,}000 + 1.280\left[\frac{3000}{\sqrt{4}}\right] = 26{,}920.$$

Consequently

$$P[\bar{x} < 26{,}920 \mid E(\bar{X}) = 30{,}000] = P\left[z < \frac{(26{,}920 - 30{,}000)\sqrt{4}}{3000}\right]$$

$$= P[z < -2.0533] = 0.0200.$$

In summary, the results are

Boundary		Probability of	
z scale	$\bar{x}$ scale	Error Type I	Error Type II
2.327	28,490.5	0.01	0.1571
1.645	27,467.5	0.05	0.0457
1.280	26,920.0	0.10	0.0200

These results show that, as expected, the two probabilities are inversely related. The question then is which pair of probabilities should be considered as the optimal choice. The answer depends on the cost of making each of the two kinds of error. If the error of rejecting the null hypothesis which is in fact true (Error Type I) is costly relative to the error of not rejecting the null hypothesis which is in fact false (Error Type II), it will be rational to set the probability of the first kind of error low. If, on the other hand, the cost of making Error Type I is low relative to the cost of making Error Type II, it will pay to make the probability of the first kind of error high (thus making the probability of the second type of error low).

A concrete illustration of this point can be given by extending the information in the given example. Suppose the manufacturer sells the less durable tires for \$10 and the more durable ones for \$12. Suppose further that the more durable tires carries a "money-back" guarantee if the tire should wear out before 25,000 miles, and that there is no guarantee attached to the less durable tire. Given this information, we can estimate the cost of either type of error.

Cost of Error Type I If the hypothesis that $\mu = 25{,}000$ is rejected, the manufacturer will sell the tires for the higher price. This will represent a gain of $100 \times (\$12 - \$10) = \$200$. On the other hand, if the true mean actually is 25,000 miles, one half of all tires (in the population) will have a lifetime of less than that. Thus in a shipment of 100 tires the expected number of returns will be 50, and the corresponding outlay will be $50 \times \$12 = \$600$. Therefore, the total cost of making Error Type I is $\$600 - \$200 = \$400$.

Cost of Error Type II If the hypothesis that the mean is 25,000 miles is *not* rejected while, in fact, the mean is 30,000 miles, the tires will be sold for \$1000 instead of \$1200. The latter figure, however, has to be adjusted downward because the guarantee does represent a de facto reduction in price. If the mean is 30,000 miles, then 4.78% of the tires will not last for 25,000 miles. This is the result of the fact that

$$P\left[z < \frac{25{,}000 - 30{,}000}{3000}\right] = 0.0478.$$

Therefore in a shipment of 100 tires of the more durable kind the expected number of returns will be 4.78. The cost of the guarantee is then $4.78 \times \$12 = \$57.36$. Thus the expected revenue from selling 100 better quality tires is $\$1200 - \$57.36 = \$1142.36$. The total net cost of making Error Type II then is $\$1142.36 - \$1000 = \$142.36$.

With the additional information on the problem on hand, we find that Error Type I is costlier than Error Type II. Thus it will be rational to set the probability of Error Type I lower than that of Error Type II. Just how much lower can be determined by comparing the expected losses for each level of significance. "Expected loss" is defined as the amount of loss multiplied by the probability of its occurrence. For example, if the loss is \$400 and the probability of its occurrence is 0.01, the expected loss is \$4.00. The calculations of the expected losses in our example are

Error Type I		Error Type II	
Probability	Expected Loss	Probability	Expected Loss
0.01	\$4.00	0.1571	\$22.36
0.05	\$20.00	0.0457	\$6.51
0.10	\$40.00	0.0200	\$2.85

Assuming that the manufacturer gets no utility from gambling as such, the rational choice will be one which gives equal expected loss for each type of error. From the above figures it appears that this would be realized somewhere between the 1% and

5% levels of significance. Carrying out the calculations for levels in this interval leads to the following:

Error Type I		Error Type II	
Probability	Expected Loss	Probability	Expected Loss
0.02	\$8.00	0.1006	\$14.32
0.03	\$12.00	0.0732	\$10.42
0.04	\$16.00	0.0567	\$8.07

It appears, then, that the optimum of significance lies between 2% and 3%. If the level of significance is set at 2.75%, then the expected loss from Error Type I will be approximately the same as that from Error Type II (about \$11.00). This then would be optimal level of significance in our example.

The preceding example illustrates the relevance of considering the cost implications of different decisions in setting up statistical tests. Modern statistical theory puts a great emphasis on this and develops a formal apparatus for incorporating loss and risk functions in the determination of a proper test criterion. Unfortunately very little of this is of use or relevance in econometric research since prior (or even posterior) ideas about losses due to incorrect conclusions are either completely nonexistent or are so vague that they offer no guidance at all. For instance, consider the question whether liquid assets do or do not affect consumption expenditure. The econometrician will specify the relevant maintained and testable hypothesis and calculate the value of the appropriate test statistic, but he has absolutely no idea as to what is the cost—to him, to the profession, to the society—of drawing an incorrect conclusion. Consequently, it has been a standard practice in econometrics to use the traditional approach of classical statistics, namely, to fix the level of significance at 1% or 5% and to use a test statistic that would make the probability of Error Type II as small as possible. If the value of the test statistic is such that it falls in the critical region given by the 5% significance level, it is said to be *significant*; if the value of the test statistic falls in the critical region given by the 1% significance level, it is said to be *highly significant*. However, there is nothing superior about these two significance levels other than that they are widely used. And it is only this popularity which stifles the competition from other levels of significance.

Power of a Test

The classification of errors into the two types was explained with reference to the case of a simple null hypotheses and a simple alternative. The idea can easily be extended to the more common case of testing a null hypothesis against a composite alternative. Suppose we have

$$H_0: \quad \mu = \mu_0,$$

$$H_A: \quad \mu \neq \mu_0.$$

As before, the probability of Error Type I (rejecting H_0 when it is true) is given by the level of significance. However, the probability of Error Type II (not rejecting H_0 when it is false) is now no longer a single number for a given level of significance but depends on the value of μ. For values of μ close to μ_0 the probability of Error Type II will be high compared to the probability of this error for values of μ farther away from μ_0. If, for example, the null hypothesis states that the mean is equal to 10, then the probability of *not* rejecting H_0 is obviously greater if the true mean is 15 than if it is 20. This is illustrated by Figure 5–7, where the probability of Error Type II is shown by the striped area.

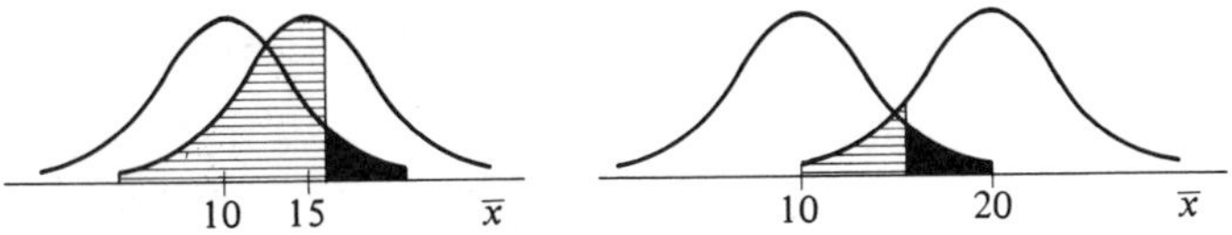

Figure 5–7

Obviously, we can determine the probability of Error Type II for any value of μ. The smaller this probability, the better is the test in discriminating between true and false hypotheses. In the illustration given in Figure 5–7, the test will discriminate more clearly between the null hypothesis and the alternative hypothesis if the alternative mean is 20 than if it is 15. In the common terminology of statistics, the lower the probability of not rejecting H_0 when it is false, the more *powerful* is the test. That is, the *power of a test* is measured by the *probability of rejecting H_0 when it is false*. Since the probability of Error Type II is the probability of *not* rejecting H_0 when it is false, the power of a test is equal to

$$1 - P(\text{Error Type II}).$$

Furthermore, since for composite alternatives the probability of Error Type II depends on the value of μ, the power of a test is likewise dependent on μ. If we plot the probabilities of rejecting H_0 when it is false on the vertical axis against the values of μ on the horizontal axis, we get what is known as the *power function* of a test.

EXAMPLE Consider the following statement of hypotheses concerning the mean of a variable $X \sim N(\mu, 81)$

$$H_0: \quad \mu = 10,$$
$$H_A: \quad \mu \neq 10.$$

Suppose the test statistic is based on sample size 9 and the chosen level of significance is 5%. The appropriate test is then a two-tail one with the acceptance region given by

$$-1.96 \leq \frac{(\bar{x} - 10)\sqrt{9}}{\sqrt{81}} \leq 1.96$$

or

$$-1.96 \leq \frac{\bar{x} - 10}{3} \leq 1.96.$$

On the $\bar{x}$ scale, the equivalent acceptance region is

$$4.12 \leq \bar{x} \leq 15.88.$$

To find the power function we have to calculate [1 − P(Error Type II)] for the acceptance region for various values of μ. Let us start with some very small value of μ, say −10. Then

$$P[\text{Error Type II}] = P[4.12 \leq \bar{x} \leq 15.88 \mid \mu = -10]$$

$$= P\left[\frac{4.12 - (-10)}{3} \leq z \leq \frac{15.88 - (-10)}{3}\right]$$

$$= P(4.707 \leq z \leq 8.627) = 0.0000,$$

where, as before, z is the value of a standard normal variable. The value of the power function therefore is $1 - 0.0000 = 1.0000$. Carrying out these calculations for other values of μ leads to the following results:

μ	Power	μ	Power
−10	1.0000	10	0.0500
−5	0.9988	12	0.1022
0	0.9152	14	0.2659
2	0.7602	16	0.5159
4	0.5159	18	0.7602
6	0.2659	20	0.9152
8	0.1022	25	0.9988

A graphical representation of this power function is shown in Figure 5–8. The graph confirms our previous contention that the power of a test increases as μ gets farther away from μ_0 in the direction (or directions) specified by the alternative hypothesis.

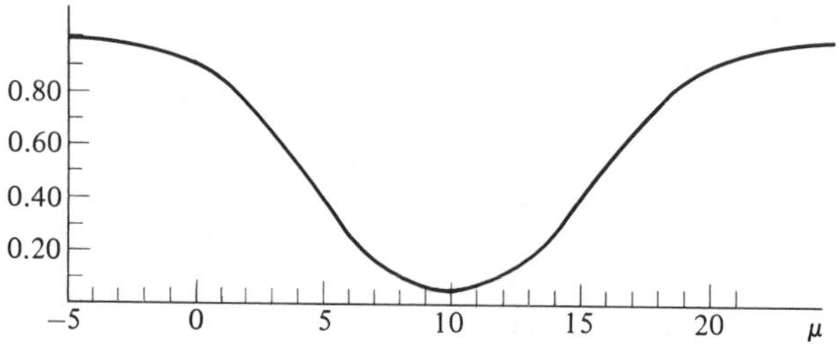

Figure 5–8

In our case we see that if the true value of μ were −5 or +25, we would correctly reject the false hypothesis virtually every time. If the true value of μ were equal to 0 or +20, we would correctly reject the false hypothesis 91.5% of the time. Note that if the true mean were almost equal to +10, we would correctly reject the false hypothesis only about 5% of the time.

The power function in Figure 5-8 has a shape which is typical for symmetric two-tail tests concerning the mean of a normal population. A one-tail test leads to quite a different curve, which we shall not present here. The interested reader can do the calculations and plotting for himself, or he can consult almost any standard test on statistical inference. We only wish to point out that the power function is another way of demonstrating some weaknesses of statistical testing. An ideal power function—which, needless to say, does not exist—would be one that would show a value of 1 for all values of μ (or whatever the relevant parameter) specified by the alternative hypothesis, and a value of 0 for the value of μ specified by the null hypothesis.

Quality of a Test

What is the best test we can design, given the size of the sample and given all the prior information that is available? We can answer this question by noting the choices that are open to us when we are setting up the test criterion. In general, there are three areas of choice that are relevant:

1. Choice of the level of significance.
2. Choice of the location of the acceptance region.
3. Choice of test statistic.

We have already found that a rational choice can be made in the first area *providing* we have a way of assessing the losses due to an incorrect conclusion. Otherwise—and this is normally the case in econometric research—we have no firm basis for the choice of the level of significance other than tradition.

The second area of choice concerns the location of the acceptance region on the z or the $\bar{x}$ axis. Suppose the problem involves the hypotheses

$$H_0: \quad \mu = \mu_0$$

$$H_A: \quad \mu \neq \mu_0$$

and the chosen level of significance is 5%. Previously, in a problem of this kind, we chose a two-tail test and located the acceptance region symmetrically around 0 on the z axis or, equivalently, around μ_0 on the $\bar{x}$ axis. The acceptance region then covered the central 95% of the area, leaving 2.5% of the area at each tail to be taken up by the critical region. Obviously, we could have the same 5% level of significance—and therefore the same probability of Error Type I—with the acceptance region located in a different position. For instance, we could locate the acceptance region in such a way that it would cut off 1% of the area at the lower tail and 4% of the area at the upper tail. The number of possibilities is clearly infinite. Previously we justified our choice of the symmetric acceptance region largely on intuitive grounds; now we are in a position to make a stronger case for such a choice. Since any acceptance region that preserves the same level of significance automatically preserves the same probability of Error Type I, the argument in favor of the symmetric acceptance region can only run in terms of probabilities of Error Type II. But because the problem involves a composite alternative hypothesis, different values of μ embraced by the alternative hypothesis will be associated with different probabilities of Error Type II. Therefore, we have to compare the *power functions* of tests based on differently located acceptance regions, not just individual probability values. Suppose we compare the power function of a test with a symmetric acceptance region with the power function of a test with an asymmetric acceptance region, such as one which cuts off 1% of the area at the lower tail and 4% of the area at the upper tail. Then, as can be easily confirmed by carrying out the necessary calculations, the symmetric test turns out to be more powerful for values of μ smaller than μ_0. Since the power function measures the capability of a test to discriminate between a true and a false hypothesis, the comparison shows that the symmetric test discriminates better than the asymmetric test (with a smaller lower and a larger upper tail) when $\mu < \mu_0$ and worse when $\mu > \mu_0$. If there is no reason why we should want to be able to discriminate between hypotheses more effectively when μ is on one side of μ_0 than when it is on the other, then a symmetric test is clearly more appropriate than an asymmetric one. If there *is* a reason, it must be included in the prior information relevant to testing and the acceptance region would be then located accordingly. Normally the choice of a symmetric acceptance region (when H_A is $\mu \neq \mu_0$) is the most reasonable one that can be specified. Incidentally, it is interesting to note that this acceptance region is shorter than any other one based on the same test statistic and the same level of significance. By similar reasoning we can also establish that, for problems involving alternative hypothesis of the kind $\mu > \mu_0$ or $\mu < \mu_0$, the most reasonable test is a one-tail test as previously described.

This leaves only the third area of choice, that involving the test statistic. For the problem of testing a hypothesis concerning the population mean of a normal population—the only problem specifically considered in this section—we used as the test statistic the standard normal variable Z constructed as

$$Z = \frac{\bar{X} - \mu_0}{\sigma_{\bar{x}}},$$

where μ_0 is the population mean postulated by the null hypothesis and $\sigma_{\bar{x}} = \sigma/\sqrt{n}$. The use of $\bar{X}$ was justified on the grounds that it is an unbiased and consistent estimate of μ and thus represents a reasonable summary of the sample evidence about the population mean. For, say, a two-tail test with 5% level of significance, the acceptance region for the Z statistic is

$$-1.96 \leq z \leq 1.96;$$

and for $\bar{X}$,

$$\mu_0 - 1.96\sigma_{\bar{x}} \leq \bar{x} \leq \mu_0 + 1.96\sigma_{\bar{x}}.$$

Let us now demonstrate why the desirable properties of an estimator (unbiasedness, etc.) are also desirable when it comes to hypothesis testing. Consider a test statistic similar to Z but one in which instead of $\bar{X}$ we use an unspecified estimator of μ to be called $\hat{\mu}$. The variance of this estimator, which is also unspecified, is $\sigma_{\hat{\mu}}^2$. The only restriction that we place on $\hat{\mu}$ is that it should be normally distributed (at least approximately) so that we can make the transformation to the standard normal variable. The latter will then be given by

$$Z^* = \frac{\hat{\mu} - E(\hat{\mu})}{\sigma_{\hat{\mu}}}.$$

Now in the form in which it is given, Z^* does not involve μ_0 and therefore does not fulfil the basic function of a test statistic, namely confronting the null hypothesis with sample evidence. However, we can introduce μ_0 into the formula quite easily by writing

$$Z^* = \frac{\hat{\mu} - E(\hat{\mu})}{\sigma_{\hat{\mu}}} + \frac{\mu_0}{\sigma_{\hat{\mu}}} - \frac{\mu_0}{\sigma_{\hat{\mu}}} = \frac{(\hat{\mu} - \mu_0) - [E(\hat{\mu}) - \mu_0]}{\sigma_{\hat{\mu}}}.$$

If the null hypothesis is valid and μ_0 is the true mean, $[E(\hat{\mu}) - \mu_0]$ represents the bias and will be equal to zero only if $\hat{\mu}$ is an unbiased estimator of μ. The acceptance region for a two-tail test with 5% level of significance will be

$$-1.96 \leq \frac{(\hat{\mu} - \mu_0) - [E(\hat{\mu}) - \mu_0]}{\sigma_{\hat{\mu}}} \leq 1.96.$$

The equivalent acceptance region on the $\hat{\mu}$ axis will be

$$\mu_0 - 1.96\sigma_{\hat{\mu}} + [E(\hat{\mu}) - \mu_0] \leq \hat{\mu} \leq \mu_0 + 1.96\sigma_{\hat{\mu}} + [E(\hat{\mu}) - \mu_0].$$

The first property of $\hat{\mu}$ which we shall consider is *unbiasedness*. Suppose $\hat{\mu}$ is a biased estimator of μ. The obvious consequence of this is the fact that the above acceptance region is not symmetric around μ_0. For instance, if $\mu_0 = 10$, $E[\hat{\mu}) = 5$, and $\sigma_{\hat{\mu}} = 3$, the acceptance region will be

$$10 - 1.96 \times 3 + (5 - 10) \leq \hat{\mu} \leq 10 + 1.96 \times 3 + (5 - 10),$$

that is,

$$-0.88 \leq \hat{\mu} \leq 10.88,$$

which is clearly not symmetric around 10. If such an asymmetric acceptance region were to be used, then the power function of the test would be shifted so that its lowest value would be at the point $E(\hat{\mu})$ and not at μ_0. Unless there is a special reason why we would wish to have the capacity for discriminating between true and false hypotheses so unevenly distributed, a test like this is hardly appropriate. Of course, if the extent of the bias of $\hat{\mu}$ is not known, then we cannot specify the boundary between the acceptance and the critical region as we did above and thus cannot carry out the test. But even more troublesome is the situation when the estimator *is* biased but we are not aware of it. Then we would clearly be using an acceptance region which is incorrect for the chosen level of significance, and our conclusion would be correspondingly distorted. All this applies equally to one-tail tests and points to the desirability of using an unbiased estimator of μ in constructing the test statistic.

Next let us consider *consistency*. Earlier we described an estimator as consistent if its distribution tends to become more and more concentrated around the true value of the parameter as sample size increases. Except for some special cases (i.e., estimators which do not have a finite mean or variance or both), this means that as sample size increases both the bias (if any) and the variance of the distribution will decrease and, in the limit, will approach zero. Therefore, the larger the sample size, the narrower is the acceptance region on the $\hat{\mu}$ scale, and the more powerful is the test. This is illustrated in Figure 5–9. Here μ_0 is the value

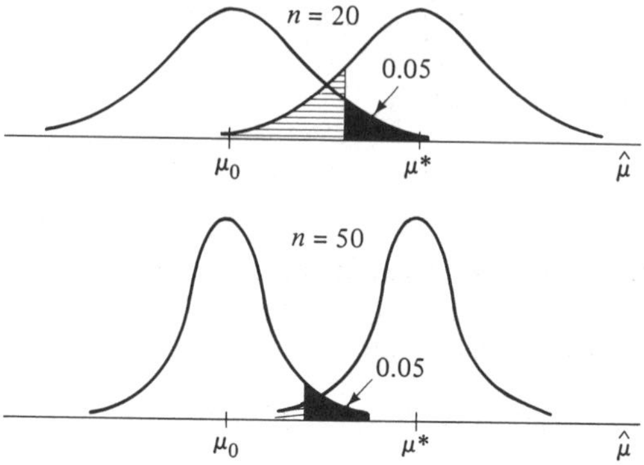

Figure 5–9

of the mean postulated by the null hypothesis, and μ^* is one of the values of the mean postulated by the alternative hypothesis. The blackened area represents the probability of Error Type I and the striped area the probability of Error Type II. The diagram illustrates how, for the same level of significance, the increase in sample size reduces the probability of Error Type II or, equivalently, increases the power of the test. If the variance of the distribution did not decrease with an increase in sample size—i.e., if the estimator were not consistent—then an increase in sample size would not reduce the probability of Error Type II. This would be obviously undesirable since it would mean that the additional cost involved in increasing the size of the sample would result in no additional information about the population mean.

The last property that we shall mention in this context is *efficiency*. If we have two estimators of the population mean, both unbiased and normally distributed but characterized by different variances, then the estimator with the larger variance is not efficient. The acceptance region of this estimator—measured on the $\hat{\mu}$ axis—will be wider than that of the other estimator and the corresponding power of the test will be lower. A demonstration is given in Figure 5–10. In the diagram, $\hat{\mu}_{\mathrm{I}}$ is more efficient compared with $\hat{\mu}_{\mathrm{II}}$. If we were to compare the power functions of the two tests corresponding to these two estimators, we would find that the values of the power function related to μ_{I} are always higher than those of the power function related to μ_{II}. Thus, efficiency is obviously a highly desirable feature in setting up a statistic.

The preceding discussion about an optimal design of a test indicates that, for most problems in econometrics, the only way of getting the best design is by using the best estimator in constructing the appropriate test statistic. Normally, we have no information that would allow us to make a rational choice of the level of significance or of the location of the acceptance region. Thus, for given prior information and for a given sample size, the only avenue of search is that for the best estimator. As we shall see, for some problems the search is already completed; that is, the best estimator has already been found.[1] Unfortunately,

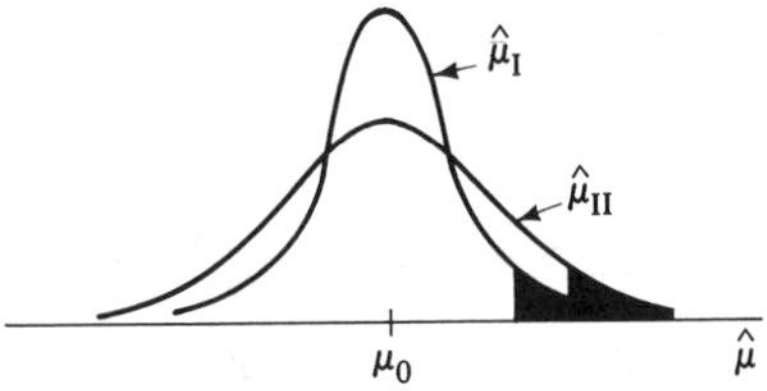

Figure 5-10

this is true only for simple problems—such as estimating the mean of a normal population—but for many problems in econometrics the search still goes on. This, at least in part, is the reason for the heavy concentration of pure econometric research on problems of estimation.

Concluding Remarks

This brings us to the end of the section on design and evaluation of statistical tests. The reader may recall that the discussion started with the division of hypotheses into maintained hypotheses on one hand and testable hypotheses on the other. There is a question about this division that has never been asked, namely why *any* hypothesis should be considered as maintained, that is, beyond challenge. It would appear more reasonable to test all the assumptions involved rather than just some. This certainly would be safer than relying upon our prior beliefs that make up the maintained hypothesis. The difficulty with doing this, however, lies in the fact that our *factual* knowledge of the population is very meager, so that without assumptions the only source of information would be the sample. As a result, the scope for making errors would be greater and, thus, the power of the test would be weakened. Consider, for instance, the problem of testing a hypothesis about the mean of a normal population with known variance—a problem considered throughout this section. A part of the maintained hypothesis is the assumption that the population variance is known. If this assumption is not made, the variance of the distribution of sample mean is not known and we cannot construct the test statistic given by (5.1). We can, of course, estimate the population variance from sample data. But using an estimate rather than the actual value of the variance increases the degree of uncertainty concerning the population and, predictably, results in a wider acceptance region. We still can choose whatever level of significance we desire but, with a wider

[1] There is, however, also the question of whether we use *all* prior information as effectively as possible. Some prior knowledge (e.g., the numerical results of previous estimations) is typically not used at all unless one adopts the Bayesian approach to statistical inference.

acceptance region, the power of the test will be diminished (a detailed explanation of this test is given in Section 5–2). Thus, by replacing an assumption with a sample estimate, we lose some information and pay for it by having a less powerful test. Of course, if we have *no idea* about the value of the population variance, then we have no choice. On the other hand, by relying on the assumptions contained in the maintained hypothesis, we get results that are strictly conditional on these assumptions and do not hold without them. This elementary fact seems to be frequently forgotten in applied econometric research.

5–2 Distribution of Selected Test Statistics

In Section 5–1 we illustrated the ideas underlying the test of statistical hypotheses by considering the problem of testing a hypothesis about the mean of a normal population with known variance σ^2. As the test statistic we suggested

$$Z = \frac{(\bar{X} - \mu_0)}{\sigma_{\bar{x}}},$$

where μ_0 is the mean postulated by the null hypothesis, and $\sigma_{\bar{x}}$ is the standard deviation of the distribution of $\bar{X}$ given by $\sigma/\sqrt{n}$. If $\bar{X}$ is the best estimator of the population mean that can be found, then Z is the best test statistic that can be devised. As we shall see in Chapter 6, $\bar{X}$ is—except for special circumstances—the best estimator of the population mean so that we cannot, in general, improve on Z.

Test for the Difference Between Two Means

A test procedure similar to the one just described can be employed in the problem involving *two independent samples* from two normal populations with known variances. The question may arise whether there is any difference between the two population means. Suppose the mean of the first population is μ_1 and the mean of the second population is μ_2. Then the null hypothesis is

$$H_0: \quad \mu_1 = \mu_2,$$

and the alternative hypothesis is

$$H_A: \quad \mu_1 \neq \mu_2 \qquad (\text{or } \mu_1 > \mu_2).$$

As the sample summary of evidence about the population means, we can use the respective sample means, say $\bar{X}_1$ and $\bar{X}_2$. If the null hypothesis is true, then $(\mu_1 - \mu_2) = 0$; therefore, the value of $(\bar{X}_1 - \bar{X}_2)$ would seldom be very different from zero. Consequently, sample values of $(\bar{X}_1 - \bar{X}_2)$ which *are* very different from zero could be considered as evidence against the null hypothesis. If we determine the distribution of $(\bar{X}_1 - \bar{X}_2)$, we can specify the appropriate acceptance and critical region. Now, since both $\bar{X}_1$ and $\bar{X}_2$ come from normal populations, their difference must also be normally distributed. The mean of this distribution is

$$E(\bar{X}_1 - \bar{X}_2) = E(\bar{X}_1) - E(\bar{X}_2) = \mu_1 - \mu_2,$$

which, if the null hypothesis is true, is equal to zero. Thus the only thing to determine is the variance. Since $\bar{X}_1$ and $\bar{X}_2$ are means of two independent samples, their covariance is zero and we have

$$\text{Var}(\bar{X}_1 - \bar{X}_2) = \text{Var}(\bar{X}_1) + \text{Var}(\bar{X}_2) = \frac{\sigma_1^2}{n_1} + \frac{\sigma_2^2}{n_2},$$

where σ_1^2 and σ_2^2 are the variances of the two normal populations from which the samples were drawn, and n_1 and n_2 are the respective sample sizes. When the two population means are the same as postulated by the null hypothesis,

$$(\bar{X}_1 - \bar{X}_2) \sim N\left[0, \frac{\sigma_1^2}{n_1} + \frac{\sigma_2^2}{n_2}\right].$$

The corresponding standard normal variable then is

$$Z_{(\bar{x}_1 - \bar{x}_2)} = \frac{\bar{X}_1 - \bar{X}_2}{\sigma_{(\bar{x}_1 - \bar{x}_2)}} = \frac{\bar{X}_1 - \bar{X}_2}{\sqrt{\sigma_1^2/n_1 + \sigma_2^2/n_2}}. \tag{5.2}$$

This is the appropriate test statistic for which we can define the acceptance and the critical region with the help of normal probability tables.

Estimation of σ^2

In both tests considered so far, we have assumed that the population variance is always known. Usually this is not the case and the variance has to be estimated from the sample. But if we use an *estimate* of the population variance rather than its actual value, the tests concerning the population mean have to be modified. Before developing the necessary modification, we shall discuss the problem of estimating the population variance of $X \sim N(\mu, \sigma^2)$. As a possible candidate we may consider the sample variance, which we shall call $\hat{\sigma}^2$ and which is defined as follows:

$$\hat{\sigma}^2 = \frac{1}{n}\sum_{i=1}^{n}(X_i - \bar{X})^2. \tag{5.3}$$

Different samples will, of course, lead to different values of $\hat{\sigma}^2$. We are interested to know whether $\hat{\sigma}^2$ has any desirable properties and what its distribution is.

We may start by examining $\hat{\sigma}^2$ for biasedness. This we can do by taking the mathematical expectation of $\hat{\sigma}^2$ and by checking whether it is equal to σ^2 or not. If it is, then $\hat{\sigma}^2$ is unbiased. We have

$$E(\hat{\sigma}^2) = E\frac{1}{n}\sum_i(X_i - \bar{X})^2 = \frac{1}{n}\sum_i E(X_i - \bar{X})^2.$$

As it is, we do not know $E(X_i - \bar{X})^2$. However, we know that

$$E(X_i - \mu)^2 = \text{Var}(X_i) = \sigma^2,$$

since X_i has exactly the same distribution as X and, therefore, the same variance. Also, we know that

$$E(\bar{X} - \mu)^2 = \text{Var}(\bar{X}) = \frac{\sigma^2}{n}$$

by Theorem 13 (Section 4–3). Therefore, we will rewrite the expression for $E(\hat{\sigma}^2)$ by simultaneously adding and deducting μ:

$$E(\hat{\sigma}^2) = \frac{1}{n}\sum_i E[(X_i - \mu) - (\bar{X} - \mu)]^2$$

$$= \frac{1}{n}\sum_i [E(X_i - \mu)^2 + E(\bar{X} - \mu)^2 - 2E(X_i - \mu)(\bar{X} - \mu)]$$

$$= \frac{1}{n}\sum_i E(X_i - \mu)^2 + \frac{1}{n}\sum_i E(\bar{X} - \mu)^2 - \frac{2}{n}\sum_i E(X_i - \mu)(\bar{X} - \mu)$$

$$= \frac{1}{n}\sum_i \sigma^2 + \frac{1}{n}\sum_i \frac{\sigma^2}{n} - 2E(\bar{X} - \mu)\frac{1}{n}\sum_i (X_i - \mu)$$

$$= \sigma^2 + \frac{\sigma^2}{n} - 2E(\bar{X} - \mu)^2 = \sigma^2 + \frac{\sigma^2}{n} - 2\frac{\sigma^2}{n}.$$

That is,

$$E(\hat{\sigma}^2) = \left[\frac{n-1}{n}\right]\sigma^2, \tag{5.4}$$

which is not equal to σ^2. This means that $\hat{\sigma}^2$ is a *biased* estimator of σ^2.

This result, although negative, is nevertheless helpful since it suggests an easy way of finding an unbiased estimator of $\hat{\sigma}^2$. By multiplying both sides of (5.4) by $n/(n - 1)$ we obtain

$$\left[\frac{n}{n-1}\right] E(\hat{\sigma}^2) = \sigma^2,$$

which can be written as

$$E\left[\frac{n}{n-1}\right]\hat{\sigma}^2 = \sigma^2,$$

or

$$E\left[\frac{n}{n-1}\right]\frac{1}{n}\sum_i (X_i - \bar{X})^2 = \sigma^2,$$

that is,

$$E\frac{1}{n-1}\sum_i (X_i - \bar{X})^2 = \sigma^2, \tag{5.5}$$

so that an estimator of σ^2, which we shall call s^2 and which is defined as

$$s^2 = \frac{1}{n-1}\sum_i (X_i - \bar{X})^2, \tag{5.6}$$

is an *unbiased* estimator of σ^2.

Because of the property of unbiasedness, we shall use s^2 as our preferred estimator of σ^2. Its distribution, which we shall not derive or present here, is a special case of the so-called gamma distribution.[2] The exact shape of the distribution of s^2 depends on two parameters, the population variance σ^2 and the sample size n. The distribution is always skewed to the right for small sample sizes and becomes more and more symmetric as the sample size increases. The mean of the distribution is, as shown, equal to σ^2 and its variance is given[3] by

$$\text{Var}(s^2) = \frac{2\,\sigma^4}{n-1}. \tag{5.7}$$

Since s^2 is unbiased and since its variance approaches zero as $n \to \infty$, s^2 is a *consistent* estimator of σ^2. Another feature of s^2 that is worth a passing reference is the fact that s^2 is independent of $\bar{X}$ in the sense that the joint distribution of s^2 and $\bar{X}$ is equal to the product of their respective marginal distributions. That is,

$$f(s^2, \bar{x}) = f(s^2)f(\bar{x}).$$

The Chi-Square Distribution

To determine the probability that s^2 lies within any specific interval, we would have to find the areas under the corresponding gamma curve. This curve would be different for each different combination of σ^2 and n, and the determination of the appropriate area would be quite complicated. This problem has already been encountered in connection with the normal distribution, which also differs from one combination of parameter values—in this case μ and σ^2—to another, and for which the mathematical formula is also highly complicated. In the case of the normal distribution, the problem was solved by transforming a normal variable to one with mean 0 and variance 1 (a "standard normal variable") for which the probabilities are tabulated. In the case of s^2, the solution is similar. The transformation in this case is to a variable called *chi-square*, which is defined as

$$\chi^2 = \frac{(n-1)s^2}{\sigma^2}, \tag{5.8}$$

and for which probabilities are calculated. However, unlike the standard normal distribution, the distribution of χ^2 changes its shape with sample size. For small samples the distribution is skewed to the right, but it becomes more and more symmetric as the sample size increases. No value of χ^2 is, of course, negative. Because of the dependence of the chi-square distribution on sample size, we usually use an identifying subscript. For instance, (5.8) would normally be written as

$$\chi^2_{n-1} = \frac{(n-1)s^2}{\sigma^2}. \tag{5.8a}$$

[2] See, e.g., John E. Freund, *Mathematical Statistics* (Englewood Cliffs, N.J.: Prentice-Hall, 1962), pp. 127–28. For the special case of s^2 we have, in Freund's notation, $\alpha = (n-1)/2$ and $\beta = 2\sigma^2/(n-1)$.

[3] *Ibid.*, p. 147. Note that the mean of s^2 is equal to σ^2 regardless of the form of the parent distribution of X but the variance formula (5.7) hinges on the assumption of normality of X.

An equivalent way of writing (5.8a) is

$$\chi^2_{n-1} = \frac{\sum_{i=1}^{n} (X_i - \bar{X})^2}{\sigma^2}. \tag{5.8b}$$

The subscript of χ^2, which is equal to the sample size reduced by 1, is called the number of *degrees of freedom* and is often designated by ν instead of $(n - 1)$. The terms "degrees of freedom" refers to the number of independent squares in the numerator of the chi-square statistics, i.e., in

$$\sum_{i=1}^{n} (X_i - \bar{X})^2.$$

The total number of squares in this expression is n, but only $(n - 1)$ of them are independent since after calculating any first $(n - 1)$ squares, the value of the nth square will be automatically determined. The reason for this is the presence of $\bar{X}$ and one of the well-known features of $\bar{X}$ is that

$$\sum_i (X_i - \bar{X}) = 0.$$

This represents a restriction that must be fulfilled. For example, suppose we have three squares of which the values of the first two are

$$(x_1 - \bar{x})^2 = 2^2,$$

$$(x_2 - \bar{x})^2 = 4^2.$$

If the third square were independent of the first two, its value could be any number, say 5^2. But that cannot be because in that case we would have

$$\sum_i (x_i - \bar{x}) = 2 + 4 + 5,$$

which adds up to 11 and not to 0 as required. In fact, with the first two squares being 2^2 and 4^2, the third square can only be equal to $(-6)^2 = 36$ because only then we get $2 + 4 - 6 = 0$. This explanation of the determination of the number of degrees of freedom in the present context is relatively straightforward; in other cases the issue is more clouded. For that reason most basic statistical texts do not dwell too much upon the subject and suggest that the reader may think of the degrees of freedom as simply a name given to a parameter.

From the knowledge of the probability distribution of χ^2 we can determine the probabilities for the sampling distribution of s^2. This can be seen as follows. If a and b are any constants such that $0 \leq a \leq b$, then

$$P(a \leq \chi^2_{n-1} \leq b) = P\left[a \leq \frac{(n-1)s^2}{\sigma^2} \leq b\right]$$

$$= P\left[a\left(\frac{\sigma^2}{n-1}\right) \leq s^2 \leq b\left(\frac{\sigma^2}{n-1}\right)\right],$$

so that a probability statement about χ^2 can readily be translated into an equivalent probability statement about s^2. Finally, it may be noted that the mean and the variance of the chi-square distribution are

$$E(\chi^2_{n-1}) = n - 1$$

and

$$\text{Var}(\chi^2_{n-1}) = 2(n - 1),$$

and its modal value is $(n - 3)$. A graph of the chi-square distribution for various degrees of freedom ν is given in Figure 5–11.

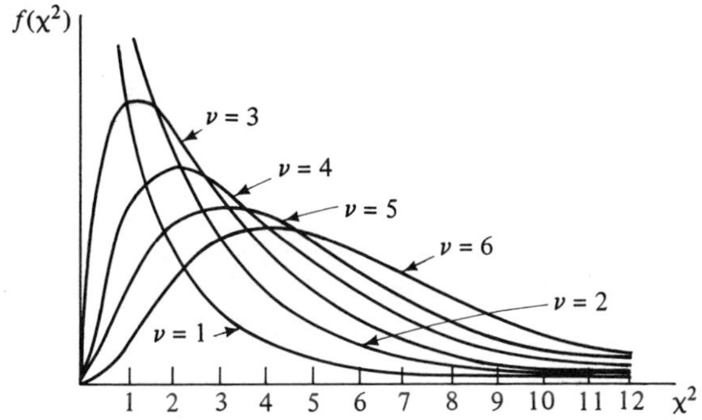

Figure 5–11

The nature of the chi-square distribution can be made clearer by comparing it with the normal distribution. The normal distribution appears in statistics for two principal reasons. First, it is a distribution of some importance on its own right, in the sense that it provides a description of many parent populations. It is not very difficult to find variables which refer to natural or social phenomena and which are—or can be assumed to be—normally distributed. Examples are intelligence, physical height of persons, errors of measurement or behavior, successes in a large number of observations, and many others. The second reason for the use of the normal distribution is the fact that it describes some important sampling distributions, in particular that of sample mean. Thus the normal distribution can serve as a description of a parent population or of a sampling distribution. The chi-square distribution, on the other hand, serves only as a description of certain sampling distributions, one of which is the distribution of the statistic (5.8).[4] There are no noted parent populations whose distributions could be described by the chi-square distribution.

[4] Apart from describing the distribution of (5.8), the chi-square distribution also describes the distribution of a certain statistic used in testing for independence in contingency tables and for "goodness of fit" of frequency distributions. The test for independence in contingency tables will be discussed in connection with binary variables in Chapter 11; the goodness-of-fit test is described at the end of this section.

The *t* Distribution

Having settled the problem of estimating the population variance, we may return to the original problem of testing a hypothesis about the population mean of a normally distributed variable with unknown variance. To recapitulate, we know that if

$$X \sim N(\mu, \sigma^2),$$

then

$$\bar{X} \sim N\left[\mu, \frac{\sigma^2}{n}\right].$$

Further, if the null hypothesis is given as

$$H_0: \quad \mu = \mu_0,$$

then the appropriate test statistic is

$$\frac{(\bar{X} - \mu_0)\sqrt{n}}{\sigma} \sim N(0, 1),$$

providing σ is known. When, as presently supposed, the value of σ is not known, we may replace it by its estimate obtained from

$$s = \sqrt{\frac{1}{n-1}\sum_i (X_i - \bar{X})^2},$$

which follows directly from (5.6). The test statistic then would be

$$\frac{(\bar{X} - \mu_0)\sqrt{n}}{s}.$$

The problem is to find its distribution. Note that by dividing the numerator and the denominator by σ and rearranging the result we get

$$\frac{(\bar{X} - \mu_0)\sqrt{n}/\sigma}{\sqrt{(n-1)s^2/(n-1)\sigma^2}}.$$

The numerator is the standard normal variable Z, and in the denominator $(n - 1)s^2/\sigma^2 = \chi_{n-1}$, as we saw from (5.8a). That is, we have

$$\frac{Z \sim N(0, 1)}{\sqrt{\chi^2_{n-1}/(n-1)}}.$$

This variable has a distribution known as the *t distribution*. Because of the presence of the chi-square variable in the denominator, the shape of this distribution depends on the size of the sample. Therefore, we usually use an identifying subscript and write

$$\frac{(\bar{X} - \mu_0)\sqrt{n}}{s} \sim t_{n-1}. \tag{5.9}$$

Here $(n - 1)$ is referred to as the number of the degrees of freedom. The number of the degrees of freedom is, of course, derived from the chi-square variable in the denominator. But unlike the chi-square distribution, the t distribution is *always* symmetric; its mean is equal to zero and its variance is $(n - 1)/(n - 3)$, which is close to unity when n is large. As the sample size increases, the t distribution approaches the standard normal distribution. The probabilities for different sample sizes are available in tabulated form (see Appendix D).

To carry out a test of a hypothesis that the population mean is equal to a given value, we have to specify the boundary between the acceptance and the critical region for the test statistic (5.9). This will depend on the form of the alternative hypothesis, on the desired level of significance, and on the number of degrees of freedom. Suppose we wish to test

$$H_0: \quad \mu = \mu_0$$
$$H_A: \quad \mu \neq \mu_0.$$

The desired level of significance is some number α. Then the acceptance region is defined as

$$-t_{n-1,\alpha/2} \leq \frac{(\bar{X} - \mu_0)\sqrt{n}}{s} \leq t_{n-1,\alpha/2}.$$

Here $t_{n-1,\alpha/2}$ stands for the value of the t statistic with $(n - 1)$ degrees of freedom which cuts off $\alpha/2$ of the area of the distribution at each tail end. This value can be looked up in the table of probabilities of the t distribution. The table is arranged in such a way that each row corresponds to a different number of the degrees of freedom, and each column corresponds to a different area at the tail end of the distribution. For instance, in the row labeled "14" and column "0.05," the value shown is 1.761. This means that a value of the t statistic—calculated from a sample of size 15—that would exceed 1.761 (or, alternatively, one that would be less than -1.761) would occur with a probability of 0.05. That is, the values of the test statistic are shown in the main body of the table, and the probabilities are given on the margin. This is a different arrangement from that of the normal probability tables where the order is just the reverse. The table of the t values gives, in fact, a description of many different distributions (as many as there are rows) and is therefore much less detailed than the normal probability table.

Consider now the two-tail test mentioned above. If the desired level of significance is 5%, then $\alpha/2$ is 0.025, and the appropriate column in the t table would be headed by this number. Which is the appropriate row would depend on the size of the sample. Some selected values are

Sample Size (n)	Degrees of Freedom (ν)	Value of $t_{n-1,0.025}$
5	4	2.776
10	9	2.262
20	19	2.093
30	29	2.045
∞		1.960

Note that the values of t get smaller as n gets larger, and that they approach 1.960, the value that would be assumed by a standard normal variable at the same level of significance. In comparison to the tests in which the population variance is known and therefore does not have to be estimated, the acceptance region based on the t distribution is always wider. This can be seen by noting that in each column of the t table all values are larger than the value in the bottom row which corresponds to standard normal variable. The consequence of having a wider acceptance region is a higher probability of Error Type II and, therefore, a less powerful test.

The test outlined above is a two-tail test. The procedure in the case of a one-tail test is very similar. Instead of giving a general description, we shall illustrate it by a numerical example.

EXAMPLE A worker handling a certain product takes, on the average, 7 minutes to complete his task. An efficiency expert suggests a slightly different way of handling the product and decides to take a sample to see if there is any saving of time. The null and the alternative hypotheses then are

$$H_0: \quad \mu = 7 \text{ min. (or 420 sec.)}$$

$$H_A: \quad \mu < 7 \text{ min.}$$

The level of significance is to be the traditional 5% and the size of the sample 16. Assuming that the parent population is normal, the appropriate test statistic is t of (5.9) with 15 degrees of freedom. The boundary on the t distribution can be looked up in the t table in row "15" and column "0.05." The resulting test criterion is

$$\textit{do not reject if} \quad \frac{(\bar{X} - 420)\sqrt{16}}{s} \geq -1.753;$$

reject otherwise.

Note that $\bar{x}$ and s are to be measured in seconds. The recorded observations are

6 min. 26 sec.	6 min. 0 sec.	7 min. 30 sec.	6 min. 4 sec.
6 min. 38 sec.	7 min. 0 sec.	7 min. 8 sec.	6 min. 42 sec.
6 min. 48 sec.	7 min. 12 sec.	7 min. 20 sec.	7 min. 6 sec.
6 min. 58 sec.	6 min. 46 sec.	6 min. 22 sec.	6 min. 48 sec.

The following results are obtained:

$$\bar{x} = 6{,}528/16 = 408 \text{ (i.e., 6 min. 48 sec.)}$$

$$s = \sqrt{9872/15} = 25.65.$$

Therefore, the value of the test statistic is

$$\frac{(408 - 420)\sqrt{16}}{25.65} = -1.871.$$

This falls outside the acceptance region and thus the "7 minute" hypothesis has to be rejected at the 5% level of significance.

Tests Concerning the Mean of a Nonnormal Population

The preceding discussion involved a test concerning the population of a normally distributed variable with unknown variance. A similar procedure can be devised to deal with the problem concerning the difference between two means of two normal populations and involving two independent samples. This test will not be described because it can be found in any introductory text on mathematical statistics. A test which we will mention here, though, is the test concerning the value of the mean of a variable which is *not necessarily normally distributed* (but has a finite variance). Thus, *if the sample is large*, we can invoke the central limit theorem (our Theorem 15) which states that whatever the distribution of X, the distribution of $\bar{X}$ in large samples will be approximately normal. Given this, and given the fact that for large n the t distribution is approximately normal, it follows that

$$\frac{(\bar{X} - \mu_0)\sqrt{n}}{s} \qquad (n \geq 30)$$

has a distribution which can be approximated by the standard normal distribution. Therefore, in this situation we can use the test described in Section 5–1. If the sample size is small and the parent distribution is not known, we can resort to so-called *distribution-free* or *nonparametric* tests, which are described in many texts.

Tests Concerning σ^2

Let us now consider some tests concerning the population variance. Suppose we wish to test the null hypothesis that the variance of a normal population has a specified value against the alternative claim that it has a different value. That is,

$$H_0: \quad \sigma^2 = \sigma_0^2,$$

$$H_A: \quad \sigma^2 \neq \sigma_0^2.$$

This hypothesis can be tested by taking a sample estimate of σ^2 as defined by (5.6), namely,

$$s^2 = \frac{1}{n-1} \sum_{i=1}^{n} (X_i - \bar{X})^2,$$

and by setting up the acceptance and the critical region for the distribution of s^2. We use, as our test statistic, a transformation of s^2 given as

$$\chi^2_{n-1} = \frac{(n-1)s^2}{\sigma_0^2},$$

where $(n - 1)$ is the number of *degrees of freedom*. The properties of this distribution were discussed earlier. If the chosen level of significance is α, then the acceptance region for a two-tail test is

$$\chi^2_{n-1,1-\alpha/2} \leq \frac{(n-1)s^2}{\sigma_0^2} \leq \chi^2_{n-1,\alpha/2},$$

where the subscripts $1 - \alpha/2$ and $\alpha/2$ refer to the area to the *right* of the particular boundary value of χ^2. The table of the chi-square probabilities is arranged in the same way as the table of the t distribution. The rows refer to different degrees of freedom, the columns to different probabilities, and the entries in the main body of the table are the corresponding values of χ^2. For instance, in the row labeled "4" and the column "0.975" the value shown is 0.484. The row refers to the chi-square distribution for samples of size 5, and the value 0.484 is that value of the chi-square variable which would be exceeded with a probability of 0.975. In other words, 0.484 is the lower limit of an interval which extends to $+\infty$, and 0.975 is the probability that a value of χ^2_4 would fall in that interval. Some selected values of χ^2 for a two-tailed test with 5% level of significance are given below.

Sample Size (n)	Degrees of Freedom (ν)	Values of $\chi^2_{n-1,\,0.975}$	Values of $\chi^2_{n-1,\,0.025}$
5	4	0.484	11.143
10	9	2.700	19.023
20	19	8.907	32.852
30	29	16.047	45.722
1001	1000	914	1090

For large n we can determine the chi-square probabilities by using the fact that $[\sqrt{2\chi^2} - \sqrt{2(n-1)}]$ has a distribution which can be approximated by the standard normal distribution. For instance, when $(n - 1) = 1000$, then

$$\sqrt{2 \times 914} - \sqrt{2 \times 1000} = -1.966$$

and

$$\sqrt{2 \times 1090} - \sqrt{2 \times 1000} = +1.969$$

which is almost the same as the corresponding values -1.960 and $+1.960$ of a standard normal variable. Our explanation of the above test procedure referred to a two-tail test but can be easily adapted to a one-tail test for H_A: $\sigma^2 > \sigma_0^2$ or $\sigma^2 < \sigma_0^2$; this will be left to the reader.

EXAMPLE Consider the previous example dealing with the time taken by a worker to perform a certain task. Suppose the variance of this variable, which is assumed to be normally distributed, is claimed to be 30^2 seconds. The efficiency expert contends that the new method of handling the product which he suggested will also change the previous variation in the time. The null and the alternative hypotheses will then be

$$H_0: \quad \sigma^2 = 900,$$

$$H_A: \quad \sigma^2 \neq 900.$$

The null hypothesis is to be tested at the 5% level of significance by using the 16 observations given in the previous example. The acceptance region is defined as

$$6.262 \leq \frac{(n-1)s^2}{900} \leq 27.488,$$

where the boundary values are taken from the chi-square table. From the observations the value of the test statistic is

$$\frac{9872}{900} = 10.97,$$

which falls inside the acceptance region. Thus the sample provides no evidence against the null hypothesis.

The F Distribution

Another test concerning the population variance and one which is widely used involves the hypothesis that two normal populations have the same variance. The most common alternative hypothesis is the claim that one of the variances is larger than the other.[5] That is,

$$H_0: \quad \sigma_1^2 = \sigma_2^2,$$

$$H_A: \quad \sigma_1^2 > \sigma_2^2,$$

where we regard as the *first* population the one which may, according to H_A, have the larger variance. The null hypothesis can be tested by drawing a sample from each of the two populations and calculating the estimates s_1^2 and s_2^2 of the respective variances. The samples are assumed to be independently drawn and to be of size n_1 and n_2 respectively. As the appropriate test statistic, we may consider the ratio s_1^2/s_2^2. If the null hypothesis is true, this ratio would differ from unity only because the sample estimates differ from the respective parameters. In any case, we would expect s_1^2/s_2^2 to approach unity as both sample sizes get larger unless the null hypothesis were false.

To carry out the test we have to set up the boundary between the acceptance and the critical regions, and for that we have to know the sampling distribution of s_1^2/s_2^2. Let us divide the numerator by σ_1^2 and the denominator by σ_2^2; if the null hypothesis is true, the ratio will be unaffected. Thus we can write

$$\frac{s_1^2/\sigma_1^2}{s_2^2/\sigma_2^2},$$

which is equivalent to

$$\frac{(n_1 - 1)s_1^2/(n_1 - 1)\sigma_1^2}{(n_2 - 1)s_2^2/(n_2 - 1)\sigma_2^2} = \frac{\chi^2_{n_1-1}/(n_1 - 1)}{\chi^2_{n_2-1}/(n_2 - 1)}$$

by (5.8a). Since the two samples are independent of each other, the numerator and the denominator of the preceding expression are likewise independent. We mention this because the distribution of a ratio of two independent chi-square variables, each divided by its respective number of degrees of freedom, is the well-known *F distribution.* This distribution is asymmetric and depends on two

[5] A two-sided alternative $\sigma_1^2 \neq \sigma_2^2$ could, of course, also be considered, but it happens to be much less common so it will not be discussed here.

parameters, the number of the degrees of freedom in the numerator and the number of degrees of freedom in the denominator. These two numbers are usually given as subscripts of F to ensure proper identification. Thus we write

$$\frac{s_1^2}{s_2^2} \sim F_{n_1-1,\, n_2-1}. \tag{5.10}$$

The values for the F distribution are available in tabulated form. Usually there are two tables, one for 5% and one for 1% level of significance. Each table gives the boundary value of F for a one-tail test. The rows in each table refer to the number of degrees of freedom in the denominator and the columns to the number of degrees of freedom in the numerator. For example, in the table for the 5% level of significance, the entry in the row labeled "10" and column labeled "15" is 2.85. This means that when we have two independent samples, one of size 16 and the other of size 11, the probability that the ratio (s_1^2/s_2^2) would exceed 2.85 is 0.05. That is, the value 2.85 stands for the lower limit of an interval which extends to $+\infty$, and the probability that a value of (s_1^2/s_2^2) would fall within this interval is 0.05.

These tests concerning population variances are strictly true only for normal parent populations. There are some indications, however, that the results apply to a large extent also to other types of parent populations, providing they do not differ from the normal population too markedly.[6] But if there are good reasons to suspect that the parent population is highly skewed or U-shaped, then the tests cannot be applied with much confidence.

Goodness-of-Fit Test

The *goodness-of-fit* test is applicable to problems of deciding whether a sample frequency distribution is compatible with some given theoretical distribution. It would be used, for instance, to test the assumption that some variable is normally distributed. In general, the null hypothesis is the proposition that a certain variable has a specified probability distribution, while the alternative hypothesis states that the proposition is not true. To test the null hypothesis, we use the frequency distribution obtained in the sample as the evidence concerning the form of the distribution in the population. The test statistic commonly used in this case is

$$\sum_{i=1}^{m} \frac{(f_i - e_i)^2}{e_i},$$

where f_i is the sample frequency in the ith interval, e_i is the frequency expected in the theoretical (hypothesized) distribution, and m is the number of intervals. It can be shown that this test statistic has a distribution which for *large samples* can be approximated by the *chi-square distribution*. In particular, if the sample is large, then

$$\sum_{i=1}^{m} \frac{(f_i - e_i)^2}{e_i} \sim \chi^2_{m-k-1}, \tag{5.11}$$

[6] For a discussion on this topic see, e.g., G. Udny Yule and M. G. Kendall, *An Introduction to the Theory of Statistics* (London: Griffin, 1950), p. 486.

where the subscript $(m - k - 1)$ refers to the number of degrees of freedom. The sample frequencies f_i are observed, and the theoretical frequencies e_i can be calculated by using the distribution formula specified by the null hypothesis. This formula will involve some unknown parameters which have to be replaced by their respective sample estimates. For instance, if the null hypothesis specifies that the population distribution is normal, it will be necessary to estimate the mean and the variance of this distribution from the sample. (Actually, if (5.11) is to hold, the estimates must be of a certain kind. Specifically, the estimates should be of "maximum likelihood" type—a term that will be explained in Section 6–2. At this stage it is sufficient to note that $\bar{X}$ *is* a maximum likelihood estimate, and s^2 is approximately so in large samples.) The number of the degrees of freedom is determined as follows:

m = number of intervals;

k = number of parameters that had to be replaced by sample estimates.

For the test to be reasonably satisfactory, it is required that $m \geq 5$ and $e_i \geq 5$ for each i.

If the null hypothesis is true, f_i can be considered as a sample estimate of e_i, and the expression in (5.11) will differ from zero only because we observe a sample rather than the entire population. Therefore, if we observe a sample for which the value of the test statistic (5.11) is large, we consider it as evidence against the null hypothesis. To carry out the test we have to determine the boundary between the acceptance and the critical region. This depends on the number of degrees of freedom and the chosen level of significance and can be looked up in the chi-square table. Note that since the statistic (5.11) cannot be negative, evidence against the null hypothesis can only take the form of very large values (and not very small ones) so that the appropriate test is a *one-tail* test.

EXAMPLE Economists are often interested in the distribution of personal incomes. Let us consider the hypothesis that family incomes are normally distributed. To test this hypothesis we may use the data in Table 5–1. These data may be considered as a sample from a population that includes all possible incomes that *could* have been received during 1962 in the United States. The statistic to be used for the test is

$$\sum_{i=1}^{9} \frac{(f_i - e_i)^2}{e_i} = \left[\frac{\sum f_i}{100}\right] \sum_i \frac{(p_i - \pi_i)^2}{\pi_i},$$

where p_i = observed percentage frequencies, and π_i = expected percentage frequencies. The expected frequencies have to be calculated by fitting a normal distribution to the observed data. To do that we have to estimate *two* parameters—the mean and the variance—from the sample. For this purpose we shall use the sample mean and the sample variance whose values are

$$\bar{x} = 6507 \quad \text{and} \quad \hat{\sigma}^2 = 4920^2.$$

Table 5-1

Interval	Midpoint*	Percent of Families†
Under $2,000	1,130	12.7
$2,000 to $2,999	2,560	9.4
$3,000 to $3,999	3,490	10.8
$4,000 to $4,999	4,510	11.7
$5,000 to $5,999	5,480	11.4
$6,000 to $7,499	6,690	14.4
$7,500 to $9,999	8,570	13.9
$10,000 to $14,999	11,960	10.5
$15,000 and over	22,780	5.2
Total		100.0
Total number	57,890,000	

* Midpoints were calculated by dividing total income (after tax) in each income class by the number of recipient families in that class.

† Includes unattached individuals.

Source: *Statistical Abstract of the United States, 1965*, U.S. Department of Commerce, Table 467.

To obtain the frequencies of the normal distribution with the above mean and variance, we shall follow the procedure described in Section 4–2 and illustrated in Table 4–7. First, we form the standard normal variable

$$Z = \frac{X - 6507}{4920}$$

(where X = income), and recalculate the interval limits in terms of this variable. Then we find the normal probabilities for each income class from the table of areas under the normal curve. The results are presented in the Table 5–2. Using these results, we find that

$$\sum_{i=1}^{9} \frac{(f_i - e_i)^2}{e_i} = 9{,}454{,}950.$$

The tabulated value of chi-square with $9 - 2 - 1 = 6$ degrees of freedom at 1% level of significance is 16.812. Values smaller than that would fall into the acceptance region and values that are larger into the critical region. Since in our case the value of the test statistic far exceeds the boundary value of 16.812, the null hypothesis is to be rejected. That is, the data do not appear to be consistent with the proposition that family incomes are normally distributed.

Conclusion

This brings us to the end of the present section containing the description of several basic tests. There was a twofold purpose to it. First, we wanted to illustrate the development of test procedures in general so that the reader could see in concrete terms the kind of problems involved and the method of handling them. Actually, the specific problems and related tests given in this section are *not* very frequently encountered in enconometrics. This is because the statistical models used are too simple to satisfy the usual demands of economic theory. In particular, the concentration on one variable to the exclusion of all other factors does not do justice to the complexity of economic relations. There is, however, one common feature between the simple tests discussed in this section and the tests applicable to more complex situations. This common feature is the use of distributions described on the preceding pages: the normal, the chi-square, the t and the F distributions. This was the second and the more important purpose of this section. The discussion of the simple tests enabled us to introduce these distributions in a natural way, and gave us an opportunity to highlight their main characteristics and to relate them to each other. For this reason this section is really indispensable for a complete understanding of econometric methods.

Table 5–2

Intervals		Cumulative Normal Probabilities	Normal Probabilities	
x	z		$f(z)$	Percent
Under 2,000	$-\infty$ to -0.92	0.1788	0.1788	17.9
2,000 to 2,999	-0.92 to -0.71	0.2388	0.0600	6.0
3,000 to 3,999	-0.71 to -0.51	0.3050	0.0662	6.6
4,000 to 4,999	-0.51 to -0.31	0.3783	0.0733	7.3
5,000 to 5,999	-0.31 to -0.11	0.4562	0.0779	7.8
6,000 to 7,499	-0.11 to 0.20	0.5793	0.1231	12.3
7,500 to 9,999	0.20 to 0.71	0.7612	0.1819	18.2
10,000 to 14,999	0.71 to 1.73	0.9582	0.1970	19.7
15,000 and over	1.73 to $+\infty$	1.0000	0.0418	4.2
			1.0000	100.0

EXERCISES

5–1. Let $X \sim N(\mu, 81)$. The null and the alternative hypotheses are

$$H_0: \quad \mu = 10,$$

$$H_A: \quad \mu > 10.$$

The test statistic is to be based on a sample of size 9, and the chosen level of significance is to be 5%. Draw a diagram of the power function for this test.

5–2. In conducting a survey of food prices, two samples of prices of a given food item were collected. Sample I came from a congested city area, and Sample II was obtained in the suburbs. The results were as follows:

	Sample I	Sample II
n	14	18
$\sum_{i=1}^{n} p_i$	12.60	14.96
$\frac{1}{n}\sum_{i=1}^{n} p_i^2$	1.68	1.96

where p_i = price recorded in the ith store. Test the hypothesis that there is no difference between the mean price of the particular food item in the two areas. (Use 5% level of significance.)

5–3. When allocating federal subsidies to localities, a certain town was classified as a high-income area. The mayor objected and produced evidence, based on a random sample of 25 families, that the average family income in his town was \$7145. A nationwide survey of towns of similar size showed that the average family income is \$6500, with standard deviation of \$920. Are the sample results produced by the mayor consistent with his claim that the town in question is no more prosperous than other similar towns in the nation?

5–4. Let Y = income and X = log Y. Using the data on income distribution in the United States given in Table 5–1, test the hypothesis that X is normally distributed.

5–5. A claim is made that the cyclical fluctuations in the demand for teenage workers are greater than those in the demand for married males. Test this claim by reference to Table 5–3.

Table 5–3 Unemployment in the United States

	Unemployment Rate, %	
	Married Men	Teenagers 14–19 years
1949	3.4	12.2
1950	4.6	11.3
1951	1.5	7.7
1952	1.4	8.0
1953	1.7	7.1
1954	4.0	11.4
1955	2.6	10.2
1956	2.3	10.4
1957	2.8	10.8
1958	5.1	14.4
1959	3.6	13.2
1960	3.7	13.6
1961	4.6	15.2

Source: *Economic Report of the President, 1965* (Washington, D.C.: U.S. Government Printing Office, 1965), p. 217.

5–6. Design and carry out an experiment, involving the chi-square test, designed to test the randomness of the last digits of the entries in the table of normal deviates in Appendix D.

5–7. The owner of a pizza restaurant wants to start a delivery service for which he needs a van. The choice is eventually confined to two makes, A and B. Van A costs $300 more than van B, but its average mileage is claimed to be 24 miles per gallon, which compares favorably with the 20 miles per gallon expected of B. The restaurant owner is allowed to use each van for four days before making a final commitment. What should be the appropriate test criterion, given that the expected productive life of each van is 50,000 miles and that the cost of gasoline is 40¢ per gallon?

6 Estimation

In the introductory chapter we described briefly the traditional division of the problems of statistical inference into problems of hypothesis testing and problems of estimation. The similarity between the two types of problems lies in the fact that they are both concerned with questions concerning the value of some unknown population parameter or parameters. The difference is that in estimation, unlike in hypothesis testing, we make no prior claims whose credibility would be disputed. In hypothesis testing, the initial ingredients are prior information (in the form of a maintained hypothesis) and a claim concerning the value of the parameter in question. In estimation we also start with prior information (in the form of a model), but we have an open mind as to the value of the parameter. (Prior specification about the possible *range* of the parameter—e.g., a specification that the parameter must be positive—is considered to be a part of the model.) As mentioned earlier, estimation problems have received more attention by the econometricians than problems of hypothesis testing. Thus estimation theory for various types of economic models is quite well developed, although, of course, many difficulties still remain.

The theory of estimation can be divided into two parts, point estimation and interval estimation. In *point estimation* the aim is to use the prior and the sample information for the purpose of calculating a value which would be, in some sense, our best guess as to the actual value of the parameter of interest. In *interval estimation* the same information is used for the purpose of producing an interval which would contain the true value of the parameter with some given level of probability. Since an interval is fully characterized by its limits, estimating an interval is equivalent to estimating its limits. The interval itself is usually called a *confidence interval.* Confidence intervals can also be viewed as possible measures of the precision of a point estimator. This view will be adopted in our discussion of confidence intervals in Section 6–3 at the end of the present chapter.

The problem of point estimation is that of producing an estimate that would represent our best guess about the value of the parameter. To solve this problem we have to do two things: first, we have to specify what we mean by "best guess" and, second, we have to devise estimators that would meet this criterion or at least come close. In other words, we have to specify what we want, and provide a formula that would tell us how to get it or at least how to come close to getting it. The first part of the problem—the definition of the best guess—amounts to specifying various properties of an estimator that can be considered desirable. Since an estimator is a random variable whose value varies from sample to sample, its properties are, in fact, the properties of its sampling distribution. These properties will be discussed in Section 6–1. The second part of the problem involves devising estimators that would have at least some of the desirable properties. This will be the subject of Section 6–2. The last section will be, as mentioned earlier, devoted to a discussion of confidence intervals.

6–1 Properties of Estimators

Let us consider some random variable X whose distribution is characterized, among others, by some parameter θ which we would like to estimate. Thus the parent population consists of all possible values of X, and θ is one of the parametric characteristics of this population. X may be continuous or discrete, or even an attribute (i.e., a binary variable). An example would be family income—which is a continuous variable—and its mean. This specification constitutes a relatively simple estimation problem; a more complicated problem would involve a joint estimation of several parameters related to several variables. As it is, the simple estimation problem is perfectly sufficient for the purpose of describing various properties of estimators and for outlining the basic estimation methods. The more complicated estimation problems, which are typical in econometrics, will be considered in the following chapters.

To estimate a population parameter we combine the prior information that we may have with the information provided by the sample. The prior information is really nothing else but what, in the context of hypothesis testing, was called the "maintained hypothesis." In the context of estimation we usually use the term *model* but the term *maintained hypothesis* is also perfectly acceptable. Such prior information concerns the population of X; it may consist of assumptions about the form of the distributions, the value of some parameters other than θ, or some specification (e.g., range) concerning θ itself. The information provided by the sample is given by the sample observations $X_1, X_2, \ldots, X_n$. The way of utilizing the information to obtain an estimate of θ is prescribed by the estimation formula called the *estimator*. There may be, and generally is, more than one such formula to choose from. In this chapter we will, for the most part, consider only problems with a minimum of prior information. Problems involving more elaborate models will be discussed in the rest of the book.

An estimator of parameter θ, which is one of the characteristics of the distribution of X, may be called $\hat{\theta}$. Since $\hat{\theta}$ is constructed by substituting sample observations of X into a formula, we may write

$$\hat{\theta} = \hat{\theta}(x_1, x_2, \ldots, x_n),$$

which is read "$\hat{\theta}$ is a function of $x_1, x_2, \ldots, x_n$." (If not *all* sample observations are to be used, the expression will be modified accordingly.) This function can be of any form *except* for the restriction that it must not involve any unknown parameters including, of course, θ itself. The basic characteristics of the distribution of $\hat{\theta}$ are its mean $E(\hat{\theta})$ and the variance,

$$\text{Var}(\hat{\theta}) = E[\hat{\theta} - E(\hat{\theta})]^2 = E(\hat{\theta}^2) - [E(\hat{\theta})]^2.$$

The standard deviation of $\hat{\theta}$, defined as $\sqrt{\text{Var}(\hat{\theta})}$, is known as the *standard error* of $\hat{\theta}$. Of special importance are also the following concepts:

$$\text{Sampling error} = \hat{\theta} - \theta,$$

$$\text{Bias} = E(\hat{\theta}) - \theta,$$

$$\text{Mean square error} = E(\hat{\theta} - \theta)^2.$$

Sampling error is simply the difference between the value of the estimator and the true value of the parameter to be estimated. The extent of the sampling error does, of course, vary from sample to sample. *Bias* is the difference between the mean of the sampling distribution of a given estimator and the true value of the parameter. This value is, for any given estimator, a fixed value which may or may not be equal to zero. Finally, the *mean square error* is a concept related to the dispersion of the distribution of an estimator, and, thus, is similar to the concept of the variance. The difference between the variance of an estimator and its mean square error is that while the variance measures the dispersion of the distribution *around the mean*, the mean square error measures the dispersion *around the true value of the parameter*. If the mean of the distribution coincides with the true value of the parameter, then the variance and the mean square error are identical, otherwise they differ.

The relationship between the mean square error (MSE) and the variance can be shown explicitly as follows:

$$\begin{aligned}\text{MSE}(\hat{\theta}) &= E(\hat{\theta} - \theta)^2 = E[\hat{\theta} - E(\hat{\theta}) + E(\hat{\theta}) - \theta]^2 \\ &= E\{[\hat{\theta} - E(\hat{\theta})] + [E(\hat{\theta}) - \theta]\}^2 \\ &= E[\hat{\theta} - E(\hat{\theta})]^2 + E[E(\hat{\theta}) - \theta]^2 + 2E[\hat{\theta} - E(\hat{\theta})][E(\hat{\theta}) - \theta].\end{aligned}$$

Consider the last term,

$$2E[\hat{\theta} - E(\hat{\theta})][E(\hat{\theta}) - \theta] = 2\{[E(\hat{\theta})]^2 - [E(\hat{\theta})]^2 - \theta E(\hat{\theta}) + \theta E(\hat{\theta})\} = 0.$$

Taking this into account and noting that the expected value of a constant is simply the constant itself, we can write

$$\text{MSE}(\hat{\theta}) = E[\hat{\theta} - E(\hat{\theta})]^2 + [E(\hat{\theta}) - \theta]^2 = \text{variance } \textit{plus} \text{ squared bias}.$$

That is, the value of the mean square error can never be smaller than that of the variance, and the difference between the two is precisely equal to the squared bias.

Let us now turn to the description of some of the properties of estimators which are commonly considered to be desirable. These can be divided into two groups depending upon the size of sample. *Finite sample* or *small sample properties* refer to the properties of the sampling distribution of an estimator based on any fixed sample size. Finite sample properties may characterize estimates calculated from any number of observations; they are frequently called small sample properties because they may apply *even* if the samples are small. On the other hand, *asymptotic* or *large sample properties* are restricted to sampling distributions based on samples whose size approaches infinity. These properties, when they apply, are assumed to hold only approximately when the sample size is large, and possibly not at all when the samples are small. This will be discussed more fully when we come to the actual description of various asymptotic properties, but first we shall concern ourselves with finite samples.

Small Sample Properties

The first property that we shall mention is *unbiasedness.* This property of an estimator is more widely known among empirical research workers than any other. We already explained the meaning of unbiasedness in Section 1–4, where we stated that an unbiased estimator is one whose mean is equal to the value of the population parameter to be estimated. Now, after having discussed the meaning and terminology of mathematical expectation, we can define unbiasedness in a precise and technical way as follows:

(6.1) *$\hat{\theta}$ is an unbiased estimator of θ if $E(\hat{\theta}) = \theta$.*

An illustration of an unbiased estimator is given in Figure 6–1; since the

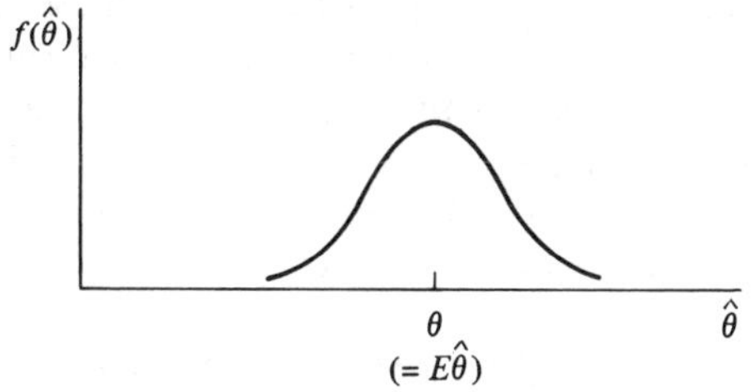

Figure 6–1

distribution shown is a symmetric one, the mean is at the center of the distribution, and it is equal to the value of the parameter. An example of an unbiased estimator is the sample mean as an estimator of the population mean, since

$$E(\bar{X}) = E\frac{1}{n}\sum_{i=1}^{n} X_i = \frac{1}{n}\sum E(X_i) = \mu.$$

(Note that $E(X_i)$ is the mean of X_i, which is μ.)

It should be emphasized that unbiasedness by itself is not a very comforting property since it implies nothing about the *dispersion* of the distribution of the estimator. An estimator which is unbiased, but one which has a large variance, will frequently lead to estimates that are quite far off the mark. On the other hand, an estimator which has a very small variance but is biased—and the extent of the bias is not known—is even less useful. This can be seen by taking the extreme case of an estimator with zero variance. Such an estimator is not hard to construct since any constant, which has zero variance by definition, qualifies. Thus if we decide that our estimate of θ will always be the number 5, then the sampling distribution of this "estimator" will be entirely concentrated at the point $\hat{\theta} = 5$. Such an estimator makes obviously very little sense since it pays no attention to the evidence provided by the sample and thus disregards all the information from this source. In light of this argument, it would seem desirable that an estimator should minimize the mean square error. Indeed, it can be shown that such an estimator would be an optimal one in the case where the loss of using an estimate in place of the true value of the parameter increases with the distance of $\hat{\theta}$ from θ. Unfortunately, in practice the formula for an estimator that would give the minimum value of mean square error very frequently includes the true value of the parameter to be estimated. This obviously makes the formula quite useless; it would be like a recipe for a cake that starts with "take a cake . . . ." Our definition of an estimator specifically excluded such formulas as not being worthy of the name "estimator."

The preceding discussion provides a background to the introduction of the concept of *efficiency* in estimation. As mentioned in Section 1–4, there is a lack of general agreement as to the most appropriate definition of this concept in statistical literature. Some authors equate efficiency with minimum mean square error in spite of the difficulty just mentioned; others define efficiency only in the context of asymptotic rather than finite sample properties, and others consider an estimator to be efficient if (and only if) it is unbiased and at the same time has a minimum variance. This last view of efficiency is becoming quite common among the econometricians and we will adopt it here. Accordingly, we make the formal definition of efficiency as follows:

(6.2) $\hat{\theta}$ *is an efficient estimator of* θ *if the following conditions are satisfied:*

(a) $\hat{\theta}$ *is unbiased;*

(b) $Var(\hat{\theta}) \leq Var(\tilde{\theta})$, *where* $\tilde{\theta}$ *is any other unbiased estimator of* θ.

An efficient estimator thus defined is also sometimes called "minimum variance unbiased estimator" or "best unbiased estimator." Note that, by our definition, an estimator which is even slightly biased cannot be called efficient no matter how small its variance is. A diagrammatic illustration of efficiency is given in Figure 6–2. Here are shown the distributions of three estimators of θ, namely, $\hat{\theta}_a$, $\hat{\theta}_b$, and $\hat{\theta}_c$. Of these, $\hat{\theta}_a$ has the smallest variance but is not efficient because it is biased. Furthermore, $\hat{\theta}_b$ and $\hat{\theta}_c$ are both unbiased, but $\hat{\theta}_c$ has a larger variance than $\hat{\theta}_b$ so that $\hat{\theta}_c$ is also not efficient. That leaves $\hat{\theta}_b$, which is efficient *providing* there is no other unbiased estimator which would have a smaller variance than $\hat{\theta}_b$.

The last remark brings us to considering one practical aspect of efficiency, and that is the problem of ascertaining whether a given estimator is or is not efficient. We have not worried about this kind of a problem in connection with unbiasedness since there the problem is, at least in principle, quite trivial. All we have to do to check whether an estimator is or is not unbiased is to determine its mathematical expectation, i.e., the mean of its sampling distribution. In connection with efficiency, and in particular with the condition of minimum

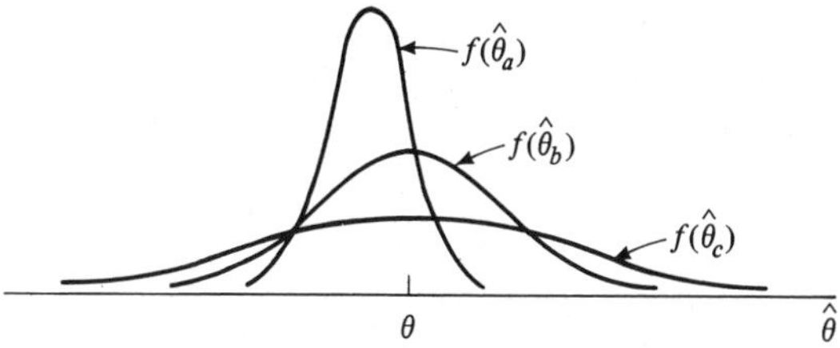

Figure 6–2

variance, the problem is potentially very complex. Since we have to make a statement about the variance of *all* unbiased estimators, of which there may be an infinite number, it may be hard to claim that a particular estimator is efficient. One way of avoiding this difficulty is by lowering our standards and, instead of proclaiming a given unbiased estimator as better—in the sense of having a smaller variance—or at least as good as any other unbiased estimator, we may be satisfied with the claim that the estimator in question is better than some other unbiased estimator. Thus, in comparing two unbiased estimators, we could concern ourselves merely with their *relative efficiency* and declare that estimator which has a smaller variance as more efficient than the other estimator. A case in point is the comparison of sample mean and sample median as estimators of population mean. As we saw in Section 2–2, both estimators are unbiased, but the variance of sample mean is smaller than the variance of sample median. Then we can say that sample mean is a more efficient estimator of the population mean relative to sample median.

Fortunately, in quite a few cases there is no need for us to confine ourselves to comparing the variances of a small number of estimators since we can make a definite statement concerning efficiency in an absolute sense. The reason is the existence of the following theorem, which is known as the *Cramer-Rao inequality*.

Theorem 16 *Let X be a random variable with a probability distribution $f(x)$ characterized by parameters $\theta_1, \theta_2, \ldots, \theta_k$. Let $\hat{\theta}_i$ be any unbiased estimator of θ_i derived from a sample $X_1, X_2, \ldots, X_n$. Define $L = \log f(x_1, x_2, \ldots, x_n)$; L is known* *as the logarithmic likelihood function of a given sample. Form the following matrix:*

$$\begin{bmatrix} -E\left[\frac{\partial^2 L}{\partial \theta_1^2}\right] & -E\left[\frac{\partial^2 L}{\partial \theta_1 \partial \theta_2}\right] & \cdots & -E\left[\frac{\partial^2 L}{\partial \theta_1 \partial \theta_k}\right] \\ -E\left[\frac{\partial^2 L}{\partial \theta_2 \partial \theta_1}\right] & -E\left[\frac{\partial^2 L}{\partial \theta_2^2}\right] & \cdots & -E\left[\frac{\partial^2 L}{\partial \theta_2 \partial \theta_k}\right] \\ \vdots & \vdots & & \vdots \\ -E\left[\frac{\partial^2 L}{\partial \theta_k \partial \theta_1}\right] & -E\left[\frac{\partial^2 L}{\partial \theta_k \partial \theta_2}\right] & \cdots & -E\left[\frac{\partial^2 L}{\partial \theta_k^2}\right] \end{bmatrix}$$

The matrix is called the information matrix. Consider now the inverse of the information matrix, and call the element in the ith row and the ith column of this inverse matrix I^{ii}. Then the Cramer-Rao inequality is

$$\text{Var}(\hat{\theta}_i) \geq I^{ii}.$$

This theorem enables us to construct a lower limit (greater than zero) for the variance of *any* unbiased estimator providing we can specify the functional form of the parent distribution.[1] The lower limit specified in the theorem is called the *Cramer-Rao lower bound.* If we can find an unbiased estimator whose variance is equal to the Cramer-Rao lower bound, then we know that no other unbiased estimator can have a smaller variance and the estimator under consideration is efficient. For example, we know that the variance of sample mean $\bar{X}$ is equal to (σ^2/n). Now if the parent population is normal, then it can be shown that (σ^2/n) is, in fact, equal to the Cramer-Rao lower bound for unbiased estimators of the population mean. Therefore $\bar{X}$ is an efficient estimator of the mean of a normal population. It should be noted, though, that the use of the Cramer-Rao inequality need not always work to our satisfaction, because the lower bound need not be *attainable* by any unbiased estimator. For instance, in the case of estimating the variance of a normal population the Cramer-Rao lower bound for an unbiased estimator is $(2\sigma^4/n)$ but there is *no* unbiased estimator of σ^2 that would have a variance as low as that.[2]

The preceding discussion indicates that determining efficiency is not without difficulties. At best we have to be able to specify the form of the parent distribution and hope that there is an unbiased estimator with variance equal to the Cramer-Rao lower bound. If we do not know the form of the parent distribution or if the Cramer-Rao lower bound happens to be unattainable, then we have little hope of establishing that a given estimator is or is not efficient. For this reason we may be willing to abandon the idea of looking for an estimator with minimum variance among *all* unbiased estimators and may confine our attention

[1] This inequality holds under very general conditions. Full details are given in, e.g., C. R. Rao, *Linear Statistical Inference and Its Applications* (New York: Wiley, 1965), pp. 265 ff.

[2] *Ibid.*, p. 268.

to a smaller class of unbiased estimators. In fact, it turns out that the problem of finding an unbiased estimator with minimum variance may be quite simple if we confine ourselves to the estimators which are *linear* functions of the sample observations. This has led to the definition of a more specialized concept of efficiency as described below.

(6.3) *$\hat{\theta}$ is a best linear unbiased estimator (or BLUE) of θ if the following three conditions are satisfied:*

(a) *$\hat{\theta}$ is a linear function of the sample observations;*
(b) *$\hat{\theta}$ is unbiased;*
(c) *$Var(\hat{\theta}) \leq Var(\tilde{\theta})$, where $\tilde{\theta}$ is any other linear unbiased estimator of θ.*

The condition of linearity means that, for a sample $X_1, X_2 \ldots, X_n$, the estimator has to be of the form $a_1X_1 + a_2X_2 + \cdots + a_nX_n$ where $a_1, a_2, \ldots, a_n$ are some constants. Thus, for instance, $\bar{X}$ is a linear estimator since

$$\bar{X} = \frac{1}{n}\sum_{i=1}^{n} X_i = \frac{1}{n}X_1 + \frac{1}{n}X_2 + \cdots + \frac{1}{n}X_n.$$

It should be noted that the fact that we are limiting ourselves to the class of linear estimators may not be too restrictive since many functions may be reasonably well approximated by a linear function over a wide range of values. In general, one of the following situations may prevail:

1. The efficient estimator is itself linear in the sample observations. In this case the BLUE and the efficient estimator are identical. Thus, for example, since $\bar{X}$ is an efficient estimator of the mean of a normal population, μ, and since $\bar{X}$ is linear in the sample observations, $\bar{X}$ is also the BLUE of μ.
2. The efficient estimator is *approximately* linear. In this case the BLUE is not efficient, but its variance is likely to be close to that of the efficient estimator.
3. The efficient estimator is highly nonlinear. In this case the variance of the efficient estimator may be quite considerably smaller than that of BLUE. This case, it is to be hoped, occurs infrequently.

Another finite sample property of an estimator which is sometimes mentioned is *sufficiency*. An estimator is said to be sufficient if it utilizes all the information about the parameter that is contained in the sample. Since the value of every observation tells us something about the population, an estimator, to be sufficient, must be based on the values of all sample observations. Thus, for instance, sample median is not a sufficient estimator since it uses only the ranking and not the values of sample observations. Note that there is nothing desirable about sufficiency as such; we obviously do not care whether an estimation formula does or does not utilize all the sample observations as long as it produces good estimates of the parameter in question. The real relevance of sufficiency lies in the fact that sufficiency is a necessary condition for efficiency.[3] That is, an estimator cannot be efficient—as defined in (6.2)—unless it makes use of all the sample information. This is the important aspect of sufficiency and the reason for mentioning it.

The three properties—unbiasedness, efficiency, and best linear unbiasedness—represent all the desirable small sample properties of estimators that are important and commonly mentioned in econometric work. They are all defined in terms of means and variances and thus cannot be determined for those estimators whose means or variances do not exist. For instance, let us consider unbiasedness. If $\hat{\theta}$ is an estimator of θ whose distribution is continuous and described by $f(\hat{\theta})$, then, for $\hat{\theta}$ to be unbiased, we would require that

$$E(\hat{\theta}) = \theta.$$

But, by definition,

$$E(\hat{\theta}) = \int_{-\infty}^{+\infty} \hat{\theta} f(\hat{\theta}) d\hat{\theta}.$$

Now, the above integral represents nothing else but the area under the curve $\hat{\theta} f(\hat{\theta})$ measured from $-\infty$ to $+\infty$, and one cannot exclude the possibility that this area is infinite. If this happens, we say that the integral is *divergent* and that the mean of the distribution *does not exist*. We mention this since we will come across estimators whose mean or variance may not exist, and the reader should be clear as to what it means.

Asymptotic Properties

Let us now turn to the asymptotic properties of estimators. As mentioned earlier, these properties relate to the distribution of an estimator when the sample size is large and approaches infinity. In general, the distribution of a given estimator based on one sample size is different from the distribution of this estimator based on a different sample size. The distributions may differ not only with respect to the mean or variance but even with respect to the mathematical form. Take, for example, the distribution of the mean of samples from a discrete uniform population discussed at the beginning of Section 4–3. We found that for samples of size 1, the distribution was uniform, i.e., rectangular in shape; for samples of size 2, the distribution was triangular (see Figure 4–12), and for samples of size 5 and 10 the distribution was close to being normal. The process of change in the distribution of sample mean for samples from *any* population is described by the Central Limit Theorem (i.e., Theorem 15 in Section 4–3). This theorem states, in essence, that as the sample size increases, the distribution of sample mean approaches the normal distribution. Then we say that normal distribution is the *asymptotic* (or *limiting*) *distribution* of sample mean. In general, if the distribution of an estimator tends to become more and more similar in form to some specific distribution as the sample size increases,

[3] See, e.g., A. M. Mood and F. A. Graybill, *Introduction to the Theory of Statistics* (New York: McGraw-Hill, 1963), p. 176.

then such a specific distribution is called the *asymptotic distribution* of the estimator in question.

The use of the term "asymptotic" should not lead the reader into thinking that the asymptotic distribution is necessarily the final form that the distribution of an estimator takes as the sample size approaches infinity. In fact, what typically happens to the distribution of an estimator as the sample size approaches infinity is that it collapses on one point—hopefully that representing the true value of the parameter. (A distribution which is entirely concentrated at one point is called a *degenerate* distribution.) Again take the distribution of sample mean as an example. We know (by Theorem 14 of Section 4-3) that for *every* sample size the mean of this distribution is equal to the population mean and its variance is equal to (σ^2/n), where σ^2 is the population variance and n is the sample size. Now, clearly, as the sample size approaches infinity, (σ^2/n) approaches zero, and the distribution will collapse on the population mean. A graphical representation of such a distribution would show a straight vertical line of height equal to 1. This is obviously *not* the normal distribution which, as we know by the Central Limit Theorem, represents the asymptotic distribution of sample mean. What is meant by the asymptotic distribution is not the ultimate form of the distribution, which may be degenerate, but the form that the distribution tends to put on in the last part of its journey to the final collapse (if this occurs). As for the distribution of sample mean, as the sample size increases, the distribution will have a smaller and smaller variance, but it also will look more and more like a normal distribution. Just before the distribution collapses, it will be indistinguishable from a normal distribution, although one with an extremely small variance.

Having discussed the meaning of "asymptotic distribution," we can now turn to the problem of how to determine its existence and its form. In many cases this is relatively simple. First, some estimators have a distribution which is of the same form regardless of the sample size, and this form is known. If that is the case, then the estimators will also have that form when the sample size is large and approaches infinity. The asymptotic distribution of these estimators is therefore the same as the finite sample distribution. An example is sample mean as an estimator of the mean of a *normal* population. The distribution of sample mean in this case is normal for *every* sample size, with mean equal to the population mean and variance equal to (σ^2/n). Therefore, the asymptotic distribution of sample mean is also normal with mean μ and variance (σ^2/n). Second, some estimators have a distribution which, although not necessarily always of the same form, is known for every sample size. The asymptotic distribution of these estimators is the distribution based on a sample size which tends to infinity. This case is exemplified by the distribution of sample proportion of successes. As we found in Section 4-2, this distribution is binomial but converges to a normal distribution as n approaches infinity. Thus the asymptotic distribution of sample proportion of successes is normal. Third, for some estimators the distribution is not necessarily known for every sample size, but it is known for $n \to \infty$. An example of such an estimator is sample mean as an estimator of the mean of a nonnormal population. We know, by the Central Limit Theorem, that this distribution tends to become normal as $n \to \infty$. The three categories of estimators just enumerated cover most of the problems that are encountered in estimation problems in economics. Furthermore, in practice many asymptotic distributions are normal, which is convenient since the normal distribution is so well known.

Asymptotic distributions, like other distributions, may be characterized by their moments. Of these the most important are the mean, known as the *asymptotic mean*, and the variance, known as the *asymptotic variance*. The asymptotic mean may be found by determining the limiting value (as $n \to \infty$) of the finite sample mean. Consider an estimator $\hat{\theta}$. By definition, the mean of this estimator is equal to its mathematical expectation, i.e., $E(\hat{\theta})$. Its *asymptotic mean* is equal to $\lim_{n \to \infty} E(\hat{\theta})$ providing, of course, that the mean of $\hat{\theta}$ exists. The asymptotic variance, however, is *not* equal to $\lim_{n \to \infty} \text{Var}(\hat{\theta})$. The reason is that in the case of estimators whose variance decreases with an increase in n, the variance will approach zero as $n \to \infty$. This will happen when the distribution collapses on a point. But, as we explained, the asymptotic distribution is *not* the same as the collapsed (degenerate) distribution, and its variance is *not* zero. For example, consider the distribution of sample mean. The asymptotic distribution of sample mean is normal and its variance is (σ^2/n). But $\lim_{n \to \infty}(\sigma^2/n) = 0$, which is not the variance of a normal distribution. The term "asymptotic variance" is thus somewhat misleading; it is, strictly speaking, just an abbreviation for the term "variance of the asymptotic distribution." The following formula for asymptotic variance may often be used[4]

$$\text{Asymptotic Var}(\hat{\theta}) = \frac{1}{n} \lim_{n \to \infty} E[\sqrt{n}(\hat{\theta} - \lim_{n \to \infty} E\hat{\theta})]^2.$$

In what follows we shall describe three so-called asymptotic properties of an estimator which are considered desirable: asymptotic unbiasedness, consistency and asymptotic efficiency. Two of these, asymptotic unbiasedness and asymptotic efficiency, are defined in terms of specific features of the asymptotic distribution of an estimator as just described, while the remaining property, consistency, is defined as a feature of the "collapsed" (i.e., degenerate) distribution given when $n \to \infty$.

Let us begin with the *asymptotic unbiasedness*.

(6.4) *$\hat{\theta}$ is an asymptotically unbiased estimator of θ if $\lim_{n \to \infty} E(\hat{\theta}) = \theta$.*

This definition simply states that an estimator is asymptotically unbiased if it becomes unbiased as the sample size approaches infinity. Note that if an estimator is unbiased, it is also asymptotically unbiased, but the reverse is not necessarily true. Unbiasedness implies asymptotic unbiasedness because if an estimator is unbiased, its expectation is equal to the true value of the parameter

[4] See A. S. Goldberger, *Econometric Theory* (New York: Wiley, 1964), p. 116.

for *every* sample size, including one close to infinity. A common example of a biased but asymptotically unbiased estimator is the sample variance:

$$\hat{\sigma}^2 = \frac{1}{n}\sum_{i=1}^{n}(X_i - \bar{X})^2$$

and, by (5.4),

$$\lim_{n\to\infty} E(\hat{\sigma}^2) = \lim_{n\to\infty}\left[\frac{n-1}{n}\right]\sigma^2 = \sigma^2,$$

since $(n - 1)/n$ approaches unity as $n \to \infty$.

The next desirable property to consider is *consistency*. As mentioned above, this property is defined in reference to the "collapsed" distribution of an estimator when $n \to \infty$. The point on which the distribution of an estimator, say, $\hat{\theta}$, collapses is called the *probability limit of* $\hat{\theta}$, frequently abbreviated as plim $\hat{\theta}$. More formally, let θ^* be some point which may or may not be equal to θ. Then the statement

$$\text{plim } \hat{\theta} = \theta^*$$

is equivalent to the statement

$$\lim_{n\to\infty} P(\theta^* - \varepsilon \leq \hat{\theta} \leq \theta^* + \varepsilon) = 1$$

where ε is any arbitrarily small positive number. Now, an estimator is considered to be consistent if it collapses on the point of the true value of the parameter. Specifically,

(6.5) *$\hat{\theta}$ is a consistent estimator of θ if plim $\hat{\theta} = \theta$.*

A way of finding whether an estimator is consistent is to trace the behavior of the bias and of the variance of an estimator as the sample sizes approach infinity. If the increase in sample size is accompanied by a reduction in bias (if there is one) as well as in variance, and if this continues until both the bias and the variance approach zero when $n \to \infty$, then the estimator in question is consistent. This is depicted in Figure 1–4. Since the sum of squared bias and variance is equal to the mean square error, the disappearance of the bias and the variance as $n \to \infty$ is equivalent to the disappearance of the mean square error. Thus we can state the following:

(6.6) *If $\hat{\theta}$ is an estimator of θ and if $\lim_{n\to\infty} MSE(\hat{\theta}) = 0$, then $\hat{\theta}$ is a consistent estimator of θ.*

The condition described by (6.6) is, in general, a sufficient but not necessary condition for consistency. That is, it is possible to find estimators whose mean square error does *not* approach zero when $n \to \infty$, and yet they are consistent. Such a situation may arise when the asymptotic distribution of an estimator is such that its mean or variance does not exist. This complicates the problem of determining whether an estimator is consistent or not. Fortunately, estimators with nonexisting asymptotic means or variances are not frequent.

EXAMPLE Following is an example[5] of a consistent estimator whose mean square error does not approach zero when $n \to \infty$. Let $\hat{\alpha}$ be an estimator of α, and let the probability distribution of $\hat{\alpha}$ be

$\hat{\alpha}$	$f(\hat{\alpha})$
α	$1 - \frac{1}{n}$
n	$\frac{1}{n}$

That is, $\hat{\alpha}$ can assume only two different values, α and n. Clearly, $\hat{\alpha}$ is consistent since as $n \to \infty$, the probability that $\hat{\alpha}$ is equal to α will approach unity. But

$$\begin{aligned} \lim_{n\to\infty} \text{MSE}(\hat{\alpha}) &= \lim_{n\to\infty} E(\hat{\alpha} - \alpha)^2 \\ &= \lim_{n\to\infty}\left[(\alpha - \alpha)^2\left(1 - \frac{1}{n}\right) + (n - \alpha)^2\left(\frac{1}{n}\right)\right] = \infty. \end{aligned}$$

If we expressly exclude such estimators from consideration and confine ourselves to estimators with finite asymptotic means and variances, then condition (6.6) represents a necessary, as well as a sufficient, condition for consistency. Some authors refer to this somewhat more limited concept as the *square-error consistency*.[6] Since the fact that the mean square error of an estimator approaches zero as $n \to \infty$ implies that bias also goes to zero, an estimator which is square error consistent is necessarily asymptotically unbiased. The reverse is not true since asymptotic unbiasedness *alone* is not sufficient for square error consistency.

An important feature of consistent estimators is the fact that any continuous function of a consistent estimator is itself a consistent estimator. This is established by the following theorem:

Theorem 17 (*Slutsky Theorem*) *If plim $\hat{\theta} = \theta$ and $g(\hat{\theta})$ is a continuous function of $\hat{\theta}$, then plim $g(\hat{\theta}) = g(\theta)$.*

The proof of this theorem is given elsewhere.[7] This property of consistent estimators, sometimes also described as "consistency carries over," is very convenient, and we shall make good use of it later on. It means, for instance, that if $\hat{\theta}$ is a consistent estimator of θ, then $(1/\hat{\theta})$ is a consistent estimator of $(1/\theta)$, $\log \hat{\theta}$ is a consistent estimator of $\log \theta$, etc. Note carefully that the same does not, in general, apply to unbiasedness. That is to say, unlike consistency, unbiasedness *does not* "carry over." In particular, the fact that $\hat{\theta}$ is an unbiased estimator of θ does not imply that $(1/\hat{\theta})$ is an unbiased estimator of $(1/\theta)$, or that $\log \hat{\theta}$ is an unbiased estimator of $\log \theta$, and so on.

[5] This example was suggested to me by Professor Phoebus Dhrymes.

[6] See, e.g., Mood and Graybill, *op. cit.*, p. 173.

[7] See S. S. Wilks, *Mathematical Statistics* (New York: Wiley, 1962), pp. 102–103.

The last desirable property that we shall mention is *asymptotic efficiency*, which is related to the dispersion of the asymptotic distribution of an estimator. Asymptotic efficiency is defined only for those estimators whose asymptotic mean and variance exist (i.e., are equal to some finite numbers). In fact, it is a property which gives us a criterion of choice within the family of estimators which are square error consistent (and therefore asymptotically unbiased). Given that the distribution of consistent estimators collapses on the true value of the parameter when $n \to \infty$, preference should be given to those estimators which approach this point in the fastest possible way. These will be the estimators whose asymptotic distributions have the smallest variance. This is because asymptotic distribution represents the last stage before the distribution completely collapses, and estimators with the smallest variance are closer to collapsing than the other consistent estimators.

The above considerations lead to the following definition of asymptotic efficiency:

(6.7) *$\hat{\theta}$ is an asymptotically efficient estimator of θ if all of the following conditions are satisfied:*

(a) *$\hat{\theta}$ has an asymptotic distribution with finite mean and finite variance.*

(b) *$\hat{\theta}$ is consistent.*

(c) *No other consistent estimator of θ has a smaller asymptotic variance than $\hat{\theta}$.*

The first two conditions taken together state that an estimator must be square error consistent to qualify for asymptotic efficiency. Whether this is or is not satisfied can be established simply by determining the limiting value (as $n \to \infty$) of the mean square error. The estimator in question is or is not square error consistent depending upon whether the limiting value of its mean square error is or is not equal to zero. To establish whether a consistent estimator satisfies the third condition of asymptotic efficiency is more difficult, very much like the problem of establishing efficiency in the finite sample case. As in the case of finite sample efficiency, the question of the smallest asymptotic variance can be settled only for those estimators for which we know the distributional form of the parent population. For such estimators we can establish asymptotic efficiency by comparing their asymptotic variance with the Cramer-Rao lower bound (as defined in Theorem 16); if the two are equal, then the estimator in question is asymptotically efficient. Thus both efficiency and asymptotic efficiency are established by reference to the Cramer-Rao lower bound—in the case of efficiency by comparing it with ordinary (finite sample) variance and in the case of asymptotic efficiency by comparing it with asymptotic variance. Since an estimator which is efficient is efficient for *any* sample size no matter how large, it follows that efficiency implies asymptotic efficiency. The reverse, however, is not true.

Concluding Remarks

This brings us toward the end of our discussion of desirable properties of an estimator. These properties can be listed as follows:

Finite (Small) Sample Properties	Asymptotic (Large) Sample Properties
Unbiasedness	Asymptotic unbiasedness
Efficiency	Consistency
BLUE	Asymptotic efficiency

In our early discussion of estimation in Section 1–4, we compared estimation of a parameter to shooting at a target with a rifle. The bull's-eye can be taken to represent the true value of the parameter, the rifle the estimator, and each shot a particular estimate (calculated from a particular sample). The distance from the target is inversely related to the size of sample. In this parallel desirable properties of an estimator are described in terms of various qualities of a rifle. An unbiased rifle is one whose shots are scattered around the bull's-eye as the center, whereas the shots from a biased rifle are centered around some other point. If we compare all unbiased rifles, then that rifle whose shots are, on the whole, closest to the bull's-eye is regarded as efficient. If we know what kind of bullet is being used, we can determine the minimum possible scatter of the shots; this corresponds to the Cramer-Rao lower bound. With respect to the BLUE property, the comparison is restricted to rifles of a particular and relatively simple construction. A BLUE rifle is unbiased and produces shots which are closer to the bull's-eye than the shots from any other unbiased rifle of the same construction. Coming now to the asymptotic properties we must consider the effect of decreasing the distance from the target. Asymptotic unbiasedness means that the shots tend to become centered around the bull's-eye as the distance from the target decreases. Consistency means that the probability of hitting the bull's-eye, or being within some small distance from it, increases with a decrease in distance. Square error consistency (which implies consistency) can be viewed as the tendency for the shots to become centered around the bull's-eye and to be less and less scattered as the distance is decreased. Finally, a rifle can be considered as asymptotically efficient if it is square error consistent, and if its shots are closer to the bull's eye than those from other consistent rifles when the distance from the target is nearly negligible.

The discussion about desirable properties of estimators presented in this section is quite crucial since it provides a basis for much of the work in econometrics. We shall close it by giving an example on the determination of various properties of three estimators of the mean of a normal population.

EXAMPLE Let X be a normally distributed variable with mean μ and variance σ^2.

Consider the problem of estimating μ from a random sample of observations on $X_1, X_2, \ldots, X_n$. Three estimators are proposed:

$$\bar{X} = \frac{1}{n}\sum_{i=1}^{n} X_i,$$

$$\hat{\mu} = \frac{1}{n+1}\sum_{i=1}^{n} X_i,$$

$$\tilde{\mu} = \frac{1}{2}X_1 + \frac{1}{2n}\sum_{i=2}^{n} X_i.$$

What are the desirable properties (if any) of each of these estimators?

1. *Unbiasedness*

$$E(\bar{X}) = E\left[\frac{1}{n}\sum_{i=1}^{n} X_i\right] = \frac{1}{n}\sum_{i=1}^{n} E(X_i) = \mu;$$

i.e., $\bar{X}$ is unbiased.

$$E(\hat{\mu}) = E\left[\frac{1}{n+1}\sum_{i=1}^{n} X_i\right] = \left[\frac{n}{n+1}\right]\mu;$$

i.e., $\hat{\mu}$ is biased.

$$E(\tilde{\mu}) = E\left[\frac{1}{2}X_1 + \frac{1}{2n}\sum_{i=2}^{n} X_i\right] = \frac{1}{2}E(X_1) + \frac{1}{2n}\sum_{i=2}^{n} E(X_i)$$

$$= \frac{1}{2}\mu + \left[\frac{n-1}{2n}\right]\mu = \left[\frac{2n-1}{2n}\right]\mu;$$

i.e., $\tilde{\mu}$ is biased.

2. *Efficiency.* Since $\hat{\mu}$ and $\tilde{\mu}$ are biased, only $\bar{X}$ qualifies as a candidate for efficiency. We know that the variance of $\bar{X}$ is (σ^2/n). We know further that the sample comes from a normal population. Therefore we can determine the Cramer-Rao lower bound for the variance of an unbiased estimator of μ. It can be shown that this is also equal to (σ^2/n), from which it follows that $\bar{X}$ is an efficient estimator of μ.

3. *BLUE.* Here again only $\bar{X}$ qualifies as a candidate since the other two estimators are biased. $\bar{X}$ also satisfies the condition of linearity since

$$\bar{X} = \frac{1}{n}\sum_{i=1}^{n} X_i = \frac{1}{n}X_1 + \frac{1}{n}X_2 + \cdots + \frac{1}{n}X_n.$$

Finally, since $\bar{X}$ is efficient, it has the smallest variance among *all* unbiased estimators. Therefore $\bar{X}$ must also have the smallest variance among those unbiased estimators which are linear in observations. Consequently $\bar{X}$ is BLUE. (A full derivation of the BLUE property of $\bar{X}$ independent of the form of the parent distribution is given in Section 6–2.)

4. *Asymptotic unbiasedness*

$$\lim_{n\to\infty} E(\bar{X}) = \lim_{n\to\infty} \mu = \mu;$$

i.e., $\bar{X}$ is asymptotically unbiased.

$$\lim_{n\to\infty} E(\hat{\mu}) = \lim_{n\to\infty}\left[\frac{n}{n+1}\right]\mu = \mu;$$

i.e., $\hat{\mu}$ is asymptotically unbiased.

$$\lim_{n\to\infty} E(\tilde{\mu}) = \lim_{n\to\infty}\left[\frac{2n-1}{2n}\right]\mu = \mu;$$

i.e., $\tilde{\mu}$ is asymptotically unbiased.

5. *Consistency*

$$\text{MSE}(\bar{X}) = \text{Var}(\bar{X}) = \frac{\sigma^2}{n},$$

$$\lim_{n\to\infty} \text{MSE}(\bar{X}) = 0;$$

i.e., $\bar{X}$ is consistent.

$$\text{MSE}(\hat{\mu}) = \text{Var}(\hat{\mu}) + (\text{Bias of } \hat{\mu})^2 = \text{Var}\left[\frac{1}{n+1}\sum_{i=1}^{n} X_i\right] + \left[\left(\frac{n}{n+1}\right)\mu - \mu\right]^2$$

$$= \left[\frac{1}{n+1}\right]^2 \sum_{i=1}^{n} \text{Var}(X_i) + \left[\frac{-1}{n+1}\right]^2 \mu^2 = \frac{n\sigma^2 + \mu^2}{(n+1)^2},$$

$$\lim_{n\to\infty} \text{MSE}(\hat{\mu}) = 0;$$

i.e., $\hat{\mu}$ is consistent.

$$\text{MSE}(\tilde{\mu}) = \text{Var}(\tilde{\mu}) + (\text{Bias of } \tilde{\mu})^2$$

$$= \text{Var}\left[\frac{1}{2}X_1 + \frac{1}{2n}\sum_{i=2}^{n} X_i\right] + \left[\left(\frac{2n-1}{2n}\right)\mu - \mu\right]^2$$

$$= \frac{1}{4}\text{Var}(X_1) + \left[\frac{1}{2n}\right]^2 \sum_{i=2}^{n} \text{Var}(X_i) + \left[\frac{-1}{2n}\right]^2 \mu^2$$

$$= \frac{(n^2 + n - 1)\sigma^2 + \mu^2}{4n^2},$$

$$\lim_{n\to\infty} \text{MSE}(\tilde{\mu}) = \frac{\sigma^2}{4}.$$

Since $\lim_{n\to\infty}$ MSE$(\tilde{\mu})$ is not equal to zero, $\tilde{\mu}$ is not square error consistent. In fact, it can be shown that $\tilde{\mu}$ is not consistent in the general sense either, but the proof is beyond the scope of the book.

6. *Asymptotic efficiency.* $\bar{X}$ and $\hat{\mu}$ satisfy the condition of square error consistency and thus qualify as candidates for asymptotic efficiency; $\tilde{\mu}$ does not qualify. Now, since $\bar{X}$ is efficient for *any* sample size, it is also efficient when the sample size increases toward infinity. Thus $\bar{X}$ is asymptotically efficient as well. Note that since $\text{Var}(\bar{X}) = (\sigma^2/n)$ for any n, (σ^2/n) is also the asymptotic variance of $\bar{X}$. Concerning $\hat{\mu}$, we have

$$\text{Var}(\hat{\mu}) = \frac{n\sigma^2}{(n+1)^2} = \left[\frac{n}{n+1}\right]^2 \frac{\sigma^2}{n}.$$

In large samples $n/(n + 1)$ will be close to unity so that the asymptotic variance of $\hat{\mu}$ will be (σ^2/n). Since this is the same as the asymptotic variance of $\bar{X}$, and since $\bar{X}$ is asymptotically efficient, it follows that $\hat{\mu}$ is also asymptotically efficient.

The above results are summarized in Table 6–1. The general conclusion then is that $\bar{X}$ is the superior estimator in small samples, but in large samples $\bar{X}$ and $\hat{\mu}$ are equally good. The third estimator, $\tilde{\mu}$, has none of the desirable properties except for asymptotic unbiasedness.

Table 6–1

	Estimator		
Properties	$\bar{X}$	$\hat{\mu}$	$\tilde{\mu}$
Finite sample			
Unbiasedness	Yes	No	No
Efficiency	Yes	No	No
BLUE	Yes	No	No
Asymptotic properties			
Unbiasedness	Yes	Yes	Yes
Consistency	Yes	Yes	No
Efficiency	Yes	Yes	No

6–2 Methods of Estimation

Having defined the desirable properties of estimators, we come to the problem of devising estimation formulas that would generate estimates with all or at least some of these desirable properties. At the outset of Section 6–1, we defined an estimator as an estimation formula which does not involve any unknown parameters. Estimators can originate in several ways. One possible way is to invoke some more or less intuitively plausible principle, use this principle to derive a formula, and then check whether the resulting estimator possesses any of the desirable properties. The estimators are given names that indicate the nature of the principle used in deriving the formula. The *method of moments*, the *least squares method*, and the *maximum likelihood method*, all lead to estimators of this kind. Another way of devising estimators is to construct an estimation formula in such a way that the desirable properties are built into it in the process of construction. The so-called *BLUE method*, which leads to best linear unbiased estimators, is the most notable representative of this category.

Method of Moments

The *method of moments* is probably the oldest estimation method known in statistics. It is based on a very simple principle which states that one should estimate a moment of the population distribution by the corresponding moment of the sample. Thus the population mean is to be estimated by the sample mean, the population variance by the sample variance, and so on. As for the properties of the moments estimators, it can be shown that, under very general conditions, these estimators are square error consistent (and therefore generally consistent) and asymptotically normal.[8] They may, of course, have other desirable properties as well, but this need not be so. For instance, the sample mean as an estimator of the population mean has other desirable properties in addition to consistency. The method of moments is not applicable when the population moments do not exist, and may be difficult to apply when dealing with more complicated problems of estimation.

Least Squares Estimation

Another method of estimation which has long been used is the *method of least squares*. This method is suitable for estimating moments about zero of a population distribution. The underlying principle is somewhat more involved than in the case of the method of moments. Consider a random variable X and its rth moment about zero:

$$E(X^r) = \mu'_r,$$

where $r = 0, 1, 2, \ldots$. The sample to be used is given by $X_1, X_2, \ldots, X_n$. To derive the least squares estimator of μ'_r we form the following sum:

$$\sum_{i=1}^{n} [X_i^r - \mu'_r]^2.$$

As the least squares estimator we select that value of μ'_r which makes the above sum as small as possible. For instance, to find the least squares estimator of the population mean $\mu(=\mu'_1)$, we find that value of μ which minimizes the sum

$$\sum_{i=1}^{n} [X_i - \mu]^2.$$

Note that since X_i^r is the ith observation on X^r and $E(X_i^r) = \mu'_r$ is the mean of X_i^r, the expression to be minimized is, in fact, equal to the sum of squared deviations of the observed values from their mean. The least squares estimator of this mean is that value which makes the sum as small as possible.

To derive the least squares estimation formula we have to solve the problem of minimizing a function with respect to a given "variable"—in our case with respect to μ'_r. It is well known from elementary calculus, that a necessary condition for the occurrence of a minimum (or a maximum) is that the first derivative of the function to be minimized be equal to zero. That is, we have to differentiate the sum of squares with respect to μ'_r, set this derivative equal to zero, and solve the resulting equation for μ'_r. The solution then satisfies the necessary condition for the occurrence of a minimum or a maximum. However, it can be easily shown that what we are getting is really a minimum and not a maximum so that the solution does, in fact, represent the least squares estimator of μ'_r.

We may illustrate the derivation of the least squares estimation formula by

[8] See, e.g., Mood and Graybill, *op. cit.*, p. 187.

considering the problem of estimating population mean. Here the sum to be minimized is

$$\sum_{i=1}^{n} (X_i - \mu)^2.$$

Differentiating with respect to μ we get

$$\frac{d\sum_i (X_i - \mu)^2}{d\mu} = \sum_i \left[\frac{d(X_i - \mu)^2}{d\mu}\right] = \sum_i 2(X_i - \mu)(-1) = -2\sum_i (X_i - \mu).$$

Equating this to zero and putting a "hat" on μ to indicate that it is only the estimator of μ (rather than its true value) which satisfies this equation, we obtain

$$-2\sum_i (X_i - \hat{\mu}) = 0,$$

$$\left(\sum_i X_i\right) - n\hat{\mu} = 0,$$

$$\hat{\mu} = \frac{1}{n}\sum_i X_i = \bar{X}.$$

Thus we find that the least squares estimator of the population mean is given by the sample mean, i.e., is equal to the moments estimator. As another example, let us derive the least squares estimator of $E(X^2) = \mu_2'$. In this case we minimize the sum

$$\sum_{i=1}^{n} (X_i^2 - \mu_2')^2.$$

Differentiating with respect to μ_2' gives

$$\frac{d\sum_i (X_i^2 - \mu_2')^2}{d(\mu_2')} = -2\sum_i (X_i^2 - \mu_2').$$

Equating this to zero, we have

$$-2\sum_i (X_i^2 - \hat{\mu}_2') = 0,$$

$$\left(\sum_i X_i^2\right) - n\hat{\mu}_2' = 0,$$

$$\hat{\mu}_2' = \frac{1}{n}\sum_i X_i^2,$$

which is the same as the moments estimator of μ_2'.

The properties of least squares estimators have to be established in each case. In the two examples given in the preceding paragraph, least squares estimators were the same as moments estimators and, therefore, we are justified in claiming that they are consistent. This need not be the case with more complicated models.

Indeed, a large part of modern econometrics owes its existence to the discovery that in many economic models, least squares estimators are, in fact, inconsistent.

Maximum Likelihood Estimation

The third method of estimation is the *maximum likelihood method.* This method is based on the relatively simple idea that different populations generate different samples, and that any given sample is more likely to have come from some populations than from others. To illustrate this idea, let us consider the case of normal populations and a given sample of n observations. The sample observations are points on the numerical axis scattered around their mean. Suppose the observed sample mean is equal to 5. The question is: To which population does this sample most likely belong? In general, any normal population is a candidate. Since normal populations are fully characterized by a mean and a variance, they differ only with respect to these two parameters. Let us, for the time being, consider populations with the same variance. Of these the one with mean 5 will, of course, generate samples with mean equal to or near 5 more frequently than a population with mean 6, a population with mean 6 will generate such samples more frequently than a population with mean 7, and so on. Similar statements could be made by considering populations with means less than 5.

The foregoing argument is shown graphically in Figure 6–3. The points $x_1, x_2, \ldots, x_{10}$ represent some 10 specific sample observations. Strictly speaking, these observations could have come from any normal population whatsoever, since the range of a normal population extends from $-\infty$ to $+\infty$ (three such populations are shown in the diagram). However, if the true population is either

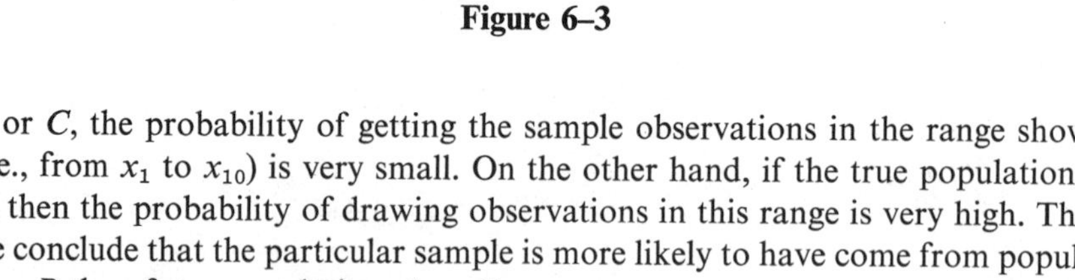

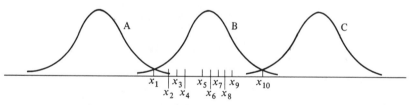

Figure 6–3

A or C, the probability of getting the sample observations in the range shown (i.e., from x_1 to x_{10}) is very small. On the other hand, if the true population is B, then the probability of drawing observations in this range is very high. Thus we conclude that the particular sample is more likely to have come from population B than from population A or C.

In the example just given we have not considered populations that would differ with respect to the variance as well as the mean. Such an extension makes the explanation of the likelihood principle somewhat more complicated but leads to the same conclusion. A given sample may have come from a population characterized by *any* mean and *any* variance, but some populations would generate such a sample more frequently than others. Just as a sample with mean 5 is more likely to have come from a population with mean 5 than from a population with the same variance but with mean 6 or 7, so a sample with a large variance is more likely to have come from a population with a large variance than from a population with a small variance. All that is required is that we consider combinations of specific mean and variance in the population in relation to combinations of specific mean and variance in the sample.

With these introductory remarks in mind we may now define *maximum likelihood estimators*:

If a random variable X has a probability distribution $f(x)$ characterized by parameters $\theta_1, \theta_2, \ldots, \theta_k$ and if we observe a sample $x_1, x_2, \ldots, x_n$, then the maximum likelihood estimators of $\theta_1, \theta_2, \ldots, \theta_k$ are those values of these parameters that would generate the observed sample most often.

In other words, the maximum likelihood estimators of $\theta_1, \theta_2, \ldots, \theta_k$ are those values for which the probability (or probability density) of the given set of sample values is at maximum. That is, to find the maximum likelihood estimators of $\theta_1, \theta_2, \ldots, \theta_k$ we have to find those values which maximize $f(x_1, x_2, \ldots, x_n)$.

Let us take a simple example to illustrate the concept of the maximum likelihood estimator (MLE). Suppose X is a binary variable which assumes a value of 1 with probability π and a value of 0 with probability $(1 - \pi)$. That is,

$$f(0) = 1 - \pi,$$

$$f(1) = \pi.$$

This means that the distribution of X is characterized by a single parameter π, which can be viewed as the proportion of successes (or a probability of success) in the population. Suppose a random sample—drawn by sampling with replacement—consists of the following three observations:

$$\{1, 1, 0\}.$$

Our problem is to find the MLE of π. From the description of the population, it is obvious that π cannot be less than 0 or more than 1. To find which population would generate the given sample {1, 1, 0} most often, we can simply consider various values of π between 0 and 1, and for these values determine the probability of drawing our sample. Let us start with $\pi = 0$. If this is the case, there are no "successes" in the population, and it would be impossible to observe two 1's. Thus for $\pi = 0$, the probability of drawing our sample is 0. Consider now $\pi = 1/10$. In this case the probability of drawing a 1 is 1/10 and the probability of drawing a 0 is 9/10. Therefore, the probability of drawing our sample in this case is

$$f(1, 1, 0) = f(1)f(1)f(0) = \frac{1}{10} \times \frac{1}{10} \times \frac{9}{10} = \frac{9}{1000},$$

since the sample observations are independent. (Recall that in the case of independence the joint probability is equal to the product of simple—i.e., marginal—probabilities.) Thus for $\pi = 1/10$ the probability of observing our sample is 9/1000. Similarly, we can calculate the probability of drawing {1, 1, 0} for other values of π. The results are:

π	$f(1, 1, 0)$
0	0
1/10	0.009
2/10	0.032
3/10	0.063
4/10	0.096
5/10	0.125
6/10	0.144
7/10	0.147
8/10	0.128
9/10	0.081
1	0.000

The function $f(1, 1, 0)$ is the *likelihood function* for the sample {1, 1, 0}. In our calculations we selected values of π at intervals of one tenth. Obviously, we could have selected shorter intervals since the likelihood function is continuous. Figure 6–4, which is based on the preceding calculations, reveals that the likelihood function for our sample is maximized when π is about 0.7. That is, a

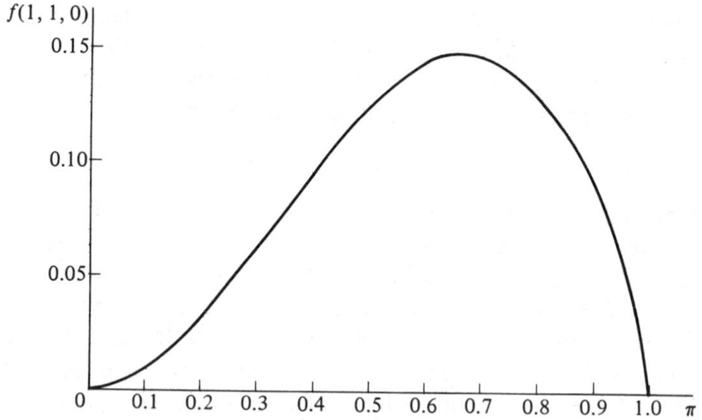

Figure 6–4

population with $\pi = 0.7$ would generate samples {1, 1, 0} more frequently than any other population. Thus the MLE of π is 0.7 (see also Example 1 on page 179).

The concept of a *likelihood function* is crucial for the derivation of maximum likelihood estimates and thus deserves a more general explanation. A likelihood function, usually denoted by ℓ, is a name given to the formula of the joint probability distribution of the sample. The reader may recall our discussion in Sections 3–4 and 3–5 of a joint probability distribution of random variables $X, Y, Z, \ldots,$ described as $f(x, y, z, \ldots)$. It was stated that if $X, Y, Z,$ are independent, then we have

$$f(x, y, z, \ldots) = f(x)f(y)f(z)\ldots.$$

Now consider a random variable X with probability distribution $f(x)$ characterized by some parameters $\theta_1, \theta_2, \ldots, \theta_k$. A random sample $X_1, X_2, \ldots, X_n$ represents a set of n independent random variables, each having exactly the same probability distribution as X. Then the likelihood function ℓ is defined by the formula of the joint probability distribution of the sample, i.e.,

$$\ell = f(x_1, x_2, \ldots, x_n). \tag{6.8a}$$

Since the sample observations are independent, we can also write

$$\ell = f(x_1)f(x_2)\ldots f(x_n). \tag{6.8b}$$

While the formula for the joint probability distribution of the sample is exactly the same as that for the likelihood function, the interpretation of the formula is different. In the case of the joint probability distribution the parameters $\theta_1, \theta_2, \ldots, \theta_k$ are considered as fixed and the X's (representing the sample observations) as variable. In the case of the likelihood function the values of the parameters can vary but the X's are fixed numbers as observed in a particular sample. The maximum likelihood estimates are found by maximizing the likelihood function with respect to the parameters.

Obtaining the maximum likelihood estimators involves specifying the likelihood function and finding those values of the parameters which give this function its maximum value. As mentioned in connection with the least squares method, a necessary condition for a function to be at a maximum (or a minimum) is that at this point its first derivative is equal to zero. If there is only one unknown parameter in the likelihood function, then there is only one first derivative for which this applies. In general, however, the number of the unknown parameters in the likelihood function is more than one and we have to resort to partial derivatives. In this case it is required that the partial derivative of ℓ with respect to *each* of the unknown parameters is to be equal to zero. That is, if the unknown parameters are $\theta_1, \theta_2, \ldots, \theta_k$, the equations given by the necessary conditions for the occurrence of a maximum (or a minimum) are:

$$\frac{\partial \ell}{\partial \theta_1} = 0, \quad \frac{\partial \ell}{\partial \theta_2} = 0, \quad \ldots, \quad \frac{\partial \ell}{\partial \theta_k} = 0. \tag{6.9a}$$

Thus we have k equations to solve for the values of the k unknown parameters. These equations are sometimes referred to as the first-order conditions for the occurrence of a maximum (or a minimum). These conditions guarantee that, for the values of $\theta_1, \theta_2, \ldots, \theta_k$ obtained by solving the above equations, we obtain *either* a maximum *or* a minimum value of ℓ. To be sure that the solution of (6.9a) gives, in fact, a maximum value of ℓ, certain second-order conditions have to be fulfilled. A description of these conditions is beyond the scope of our discussion, but it is not very difficult to show that they are fulfilled in the cases with which we shall be dealing.[9] However, an easy way of ascertaining that we do *not* have a minimum (rather than a maximum) is by calculating the value of ℓ corresponding to the solution of (6.9a) and then calculating the value of ℓ for slightly different values of $\theta_1, \theta_2, \ldots, \theta_k$. If the second result gives a smaller number than the first, the first result obviously could *not* have been a minimum.

A final point to be made in connection with the maximization procedure concerns the form of the first-order conditions. In practice these conditions are usually stated somewhat differently than as given in (6.9a). The development of the alternative formulation is based on the fact that the *logarithm* of ℓ is a "monotonic transformation" of ℓ. This means that whenever ℓ is increasing, its logarithm is also increasing, and whenever ℓ is falling, its logarithm is also falling. Therefore, the point corresponding to the maximum of ℓ is also the point which corresponds to the maximum of the logarithm of ℓ. Since ℓ, being a formula for a joint probability distribution, can never be negative, there is no problem about obtaining its logarithm. A sketch illustrating the monotonicity of the logarithmic transformation in the case of one unknown parameter (θ) is given in Figure 6–5. The point $\hat{\theta}$ clearly corresponds to a maximum on both

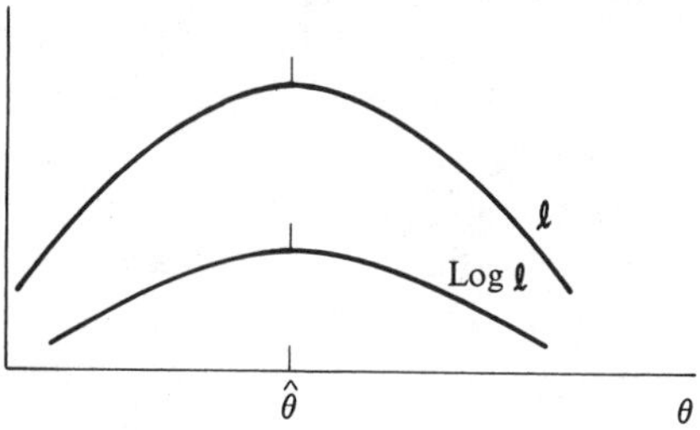

Figure 6–5

the ℓ function as well as the log ℓ function. Therefore, it does not matter whether we maximize ℓ or log ℓ. Since in practice the solution of the first-order conditions turns out to be easier when working with log ℓ than with ℓ, we put

$$L = \log_e \ell,$$

and restate the first-order conditions as

$$\text{(6.9b)} \qquad \frac{\partial L}{\partial \theta_1} = 0, \quad \frac{\partial L}{\partial \theta_2} = 0, \quad \ldots, \quad \frac{\partial L}{\partial \theta_k} = 0.$$

We shall illustrate the derivation of MLE's by presenting two examples. The

[9] A simple description of the second-order conditions can be found in, e.g., T. Yamane, *Mathematics for Economists* (Englewood Cliffs, N.J.: Prentice-Hall, 1962), pp. 344–345.

first of these relates to the problem of estimating the proportion of "successes" in the population and provides a theoretical generalization of the graphical solution given in Figure 6–4. The second example deals with the standard problem of deriving the MLE of the mean of a normal population.

EXAMPLE 1 Suppose X is a binary variable which assumes a value of 1 with probability π and a value of 0 with probability $(1 - \pi)$. Observing a "1" can be considered as a "success," and observing a "0" a "failure." Thus we have

$$f(0) = 1 - \pi,$$

$$f(1) = \pi.$$

Note that the probability distribution of X can be described by

$$f(x) = (1 - \pi)^{1-x}\pi^{x}.$$

We can check the appropriateness of this by substituting the values 0 and 1 for x. We get

$$f(0) = (1 - \pi)^{1-0}\pi^{0} = (1 - \pi)^{1} = (1 - \pi)$$

and

$$f(1) = (1 - \pi)^{1-1}\pi^{1} = \pi^{1} = \pi,$$

which agrees with the earlier specification. Also note that

$$E(X) = 0 \times (1 - \pi) + 1 \times \pi = \pi,$$

so that π can be interpreted as the mean of X. Now suppose we draw a random sample of n values $\{x_1, x_2, \ldots, x_n\}$. Our problem is to find the MLE of π. To this end we first derive the likelihood function:

$$\begin{aligned}
\ell &= f(x_1)f(x_2)\ldots f(x_n)\\
&= [(1 - \pi)^{1-x_1}\pi^{x_1}][(1 - \pi)^{1-x_2}\pi^{x_2}]\ldots[(1 - \pi)^{1-x_n}\pi^{x_n}]\\
&= (1 - \pi)^{(1-x_1)+(1-x_2)+\cdots+(1-x_n)}\pi^{x_1+x_2+\cdots+x_n}\\
&= (1 - \pi)^{n-\sum x_i}\pi^{\sum x_i}.
\end{aligned}$$

The logarithm of this function is

$$L = (n - \sum x_i)\log(1 - \pi) + (\sum x_i)\log \pi.$$

The only unknown parameter involved in L is π. Differentiating L with respect to π gives

$$\frac{dL}{d\pi} = (n - \sum x_i)\left[\frac{1}{1 - \pi}\right](-1) + (\sum x_i)\left[\frac{1}{\pi}\right].$$

Equating this to zero and putting a "triangle" on π to indicate that we are solving for an estimator of π and not for π itself, we obtain

$$\frac{(\sum x_i) - n}{1 - \hat{\pi}} + \frac{\sum x_i}{\hat{\pi}} = 0.$$

For a $\hat{\pi}$ not equal to 0 or 1 we can multiply both sides of the equation by $\hat{\pi}(1 - \hat{\pi})$ to get

$$[(\sum x_i) - n]\hat{\pi} + (\sum x_i)(1 - \hat{\pi}) = 0,$$

which gives

$$\hat{\pi} = \frac{1}{n} \sum x_i.$$

Since $\sum x_i$ is the number of "successes" and n is the number of all observations in the sample, the MLE of π is simply the proportion of successes found in the sample. In the specific case considered earlier, in which the sample was $\{1, 1, 0\}$, the MLE of π is

$$\hat{\pi} = \frac{2}{3} \approx 0.7.$$

EXAMPLE 2 Consider a normally distributed random variable X with mean μ and variance σ^2, i.e., $X \sim N(\mu, \sigma^2)$. We observe a random sample $\{x_1, x_2, \ldots, x_n\}$. Find the MLE of μ. Now the normal density function is defined as

$$f(x) = (2\pi\sigma^2)^{-1/2} e^{-(1/2)[(x-\mu)/\sigma]^2}$$

where $\pi = 3.14159$. Its logarithm is

$$\log f(x) = -\frac{1}{2} \log (2\pi\sigma^2) - \frac{1}{2}\left[\frac{x-\mu}{\sigma}\right]^2$$

since $\log_e e = 1$. The likelihood function is

$$\ell = f(x_1)f(x_2)\ldots f(x_n),$$

and its logarithm is

$$L = \sum_{i=1}^{n} \log f(x_i).$$

Substituting for $\log f(x_i)$ gives

$$L = \sum_i \left[-\frac{1}{2} \log (2\pi\sigma^2) - \frac{1}{2}\left(\frac{x_i - \mu}{\sigma}\right)^2\right] = -\frac{n}{2} \log (2\pi\sigma^2) - \frac{1}{2\sigma^2} \sum_i (x_i - \mu)^2.$$

There are two unknown parameters involved in L: μ and σ^2. Differentiating with respect to each of them gives

$$\frac{\partial L}{\partial \mu} = -\frac{1}{2\sigma^2} \sum_i 2(x_i - \mu)(-1),$$

$$\frac{\partial L}{\partial(\sigma^2)} = -\frac{n}{2}\frac{1}{\sigma^2} + \frac{1}{2\sigma^4} \sum_i (x_i - \mu)^2.$$

Equating these to zero, we get

$$\text{(6.10a)} \qquad \frac{1}{\hat{\sigma}^2} \sum_i (x_i - \hat{\mu}) = 0,$$

$$\text{(6.10b)} \qquad -\frac{n}{2}\frac{1}{\hat{\sigma}^2} + \frac{1}{2\hat{\sigma}^4} \sum_i (x_i - \hat{\mu})^2 = 0.$$

For $\hat{\sigma}^2$ different from zero the first equation reduces to

$$\sum_i (x_i - \hat{\mu}) = 0,$$

giving

$$\hat{\mu} = \frac{1}{n} \sum_i x_i .$$

Thus the maximum likelihood estimator of the mean of a normal population is equal to the sample mean. It should be noted that the two equations (6.10a) and (6.10b) can also be solved for $\hat{\sigma}^2$, which is the MLE of σ^2. Multiplying the second equation by $2\hat{\sigma}^4$ leads to

$$-n\hat{\sigma}^2 + \sum_i (x_i - \hat{\mu})^2 = 0.$$

Substituting $\bar{x}$ for $\hat{\mu}$ and solving for $\hat{\sigma}^2$ gives

$$\hat{\sigma}^2 = \frac{1}{n} \sum_i (x_i - \bar{x})^2 .$$

That is, the maximum likelihood estimator of the variance of a normal population is simply equal to the sample variance. As shown earlier, the sample variance is a *biased* estimator of the population variance. In fact, by equation (5.4) we see that

$$E(\hat{\sigma}^2) = \left[\frac{n-1}{n}\right]\sigma^2 .$$

We mention this to illustrate the fact that a maximum likelihood estimator need not always be unbiased.

Knowledge of the likelihood function enables us to determine not only the MLE's of μ and σ^2 but also the Cramer-Rao lower bounds for the variances of the unbiased estimators of μ and σ^2. These are obtained by substituting into the formula for the information matrix given in Theorem 16 (Section 6–1) as follows:

$$\begin{bmatrix} -E\dfrac{\partial^2 L}{\partial \mu^2} & -E\dfrac{\partial^2 L}{\partial \mu \partial(\sigma^2)} \\ -E\dfrac{\partial^2 L}{\partial \mu \partial(\sigma^2)} & -E\dfrac{\partial^2 L}{\partial(\sigma^2)^2} \end{bmatrix}^{-1} = \begin{bmatrix} \dfrac{n}{\sigma^2} & 0 \\ 0 & \dfrac{n}{2\sigma^4} \end{bmatrix}^{-1} = \begin{bmatrix} \dfrac{\sigma^2}{n} & 0 \\ 0 & \dfrac{2\sigma^4}{n} \end{bmatrix}$$

The Cramer-Rao lower bound for an unbiased estimator of the mean of a normal population is given by the element in the upper left corner of the last matrix, i.e., it is equal to (σ^2/n).

The maximum likelihood principle is based on the intuitively appealing idea of choosing those parameters from which the actually observed sample is most likely to have come. However, this intuitive appeal by itself is of little value unless the resulting estimators have some desirable properties. This, in fact, is the case. It can be shown[10] that, under quite general conditions, maximum likelihood estimators are

1. Consistent as well as squared-error consistent.
2. Asymptotically efficient.

[10] See, e.g., Wilks, *op. cit.*, pp. 358–365. The general conditions under which the MLE's have the stated properties are not very restrictive. The one condition which may sometimes cause problems and which is frequently neglected is the requirement that the number of parameters in the likelihood function be finite; see E. Malinvaud, *Statistical Methods of Econometrics* (Chicago: Rand McNally, 1966), p. 339.

Another convenient feature of the MLE's is that their asymptotic distribution is normal, and that a formula for determining their asymptotic variances is readily available. In particular, the asymptotic variances of the MLE's are given by the diagonal elements of the inverse of the information matrix; that is, they are equal to the Cramer-Rao lower bounds. In finite samples we use as estimates of the asymptotic variances the diagonal elements of

$$\begin{bmatrix} -\dfrac{\partial^2 L}{\partial \theta_1^2} & -\dfrac{\partial^2 L}{\partial \theta_1 \partial \theta_2} & \cdots & -\dfrac{\partial^2 L}{\partial \theta_1 \partial \theta_k} \\ -\dfrac{\partial^2 L}{\partial \theta_2 \partial \theta_1} & -\dfrac{\partial^2 L}{\partial \theta_2^2} & \cdots & -\dfrac{\partial^2 L}{\partial \theta_2 \partial \theta_k} \\ \vdots & & & \\ -\dfrac{\partial^2 L}{\partial \theta_k \partial \theta_1} & -\dfrac{\partial^2 L}{\partial \theta_k \partial \theta_2} & \cdots & -\dfrac{\partial^2 L}{\partial \theta_k^2} \end{bmatrix}^{-1}$$

evaluated at θ_i = MLE of θ_i $(i = 1, 2, \ldots, k)$. While all these properties are only asymptotic, in many situations this is frequently all that we can hope for.

Best Linear Unbiased Estimation

The last method of estimation to be discussed at this stage is the *best linear unbiased estimation method.* This method, unlike the preceding ones, leads to an estimation formula which guarantees certain desirable properties by definition. Let $\tilde{\theta}$ be a best linear unbiased estimator (BLUE) of some parameter θ. Then the formula for $\tilde{\theta}$ must satisfy the following conditions:

1. $\tilde{\theta}$ is a linear function of the sample observations;
2. $E(\tilde{\theta}) = \theta$;
3. $\text{Var}(\tilde{\theta}) \leq \text{Var}(\theta^*)$, where θ^* is any other linear unbiased estimator of θ.

In addition, the formula for $\tilde{\theta}$ must not involve θ or any other unknown parameter, otherwise $\tilde{\theta}$ would not qualify as an estimator. To devise a best linear unbiased estimator, we have to find that linear function of the sample observations which satisfies conditions 2 and 3. We shall show how to go about finding such a function by deriving the BLUE of the population mean.

Suppose a random variable X comes from a population with mean μ and variance σ^2. The sample observations are $X_1, X_2, \ldots, X_n$. We wish to find the BLUE of μ, say, $\tilde{\mu}$. To do that we consider each of the three conditions in turn.

1. *Linearity.* Since $\tilde{\mu}$ is to be a linear combination of the sample observations, we can write

$$\tilde{\mu} = \sum_{i=1}^{n} a_i X_i, \tag{6.11}$$

where $a_1, a_2, \ldots, a_n$ are constants to be determined. Thus the whole problem of finding the BLUE of μ is really a problem of specifying $a_1, a_2, \ldots, a_n$ in such a way that the conditions 2 and 3 are satisfied.

2. *Unbiasedness.* For $\tilde{\mu}$ to be unbiased we require that

$$E(\tilde{\mu}) = \mu.$$

Now,

$$E(\tilde{\mu}) = E\Big[\sum_i a_i X_i\Big] = \sum_i a_i E(X_i) = \sum_i a_i \mu = \mu \sum_i a_i.$$

That is, for $E(\tilde{\mu})$ to be equal to μ we require that $\sum_i a_i = 1$. The condition then is that the constants $a_1, a_2, \ldots, a_n$ add up to unity.

3. *Minimum variance.* Finally, we require that, among all estimators of μ which satisfy the above conditions, $\tilde{\mu}$ is the one with the smallest variance. We have

$$\begin{aligned}\mathrm{Var}(\tilde{\mu}) &= \mathrm{Var}\Big[\sum_i a_i X_i\Big] = E\Big[\sum_i a_i X_i - E\Big(\sum a_i X_i\Big)\Big]^2 \\ &= E\Big[\sum_i a_i X_i - \mu \sum_i a_i\Big]^2 = E\Big[\sum_i a_i (X_i - \mu)\Big]^2 \\ &= E\Big[\sum_i a_i^2 (X_i - \mu)^2\Big] + E\Big[\sum_i \sum_j a_i a_j (X_i - \mu)(X_j - \mu)\Big] \\ &= \sum_i a_i^2 E(X_i - \mu)^2 + \sum_i \sum_j a_i a_j E(X_i - \mu)(X_j - \mu) \qquad (i \neq j).\end{aligned}$$

But

$$E(X_i - \mu)^2 = \mathrm{Var}(X_i) = \sigma^2,$$

and since X_i and X_j are independent,

$$E(X_i - \mu)(X_j - \mu) = \mathrm{Cov}(X_i, X_j) = 0.$$

Therefore

$$\mathrm{Var}(\tilde{\mu}) = \sum_i a_i^2 \sigma^2 = \sigma^2 \sum_i a_i^2. \tag{6.12}$$

This means that we have to find $a_1, a_2, \ldots, a_n$ such that $\sum a_i = 1$ (by condition 2) and at the same time $\sigma^2 \sum a_i^2$ is as small as possible. That is, our problem is to minimize $\sigma^2 \sum a_i^2$ subject to the condition that $\sum a_i = 1$. This is a problem of minimizing a function subject to a constraint, and it can be solved with the help of the *Lagrange multiplier method.*[11]

Very briefly, the Lagrange multiplier method works as follows. Suppose we wish to find those values of $z_1, z_2, \ldots, z_m$ which would minimize (maximize) a function $F(z_1, z_2, \ldots, z_m)$ subject to the condition that $G(z_1, z_2, \ldots, z_m) = 0$. The function G is the constraint expressed in such a way that all terms are transferred to the left-hand side of the equation. Then we form a new function, say H, defined as

$$H = F(z_1, z_2, \ldots, z_m) - \lambda G(z_1, z_2, \ldots, z_m). \tag{6.13}$$

[11] See, e.g., Yamane, *op. cit.*, pp. 116–120.

Here λ is the Lagrange multiplier. Its value is to be determined, along with the values of $z_1, z_2, \ldots, z_m$ that minimize (maximize) F subject to the condition G. To obtain the required solution we differentiate H with respect to $z_1, z_2, \ldots, z_m$ and λ and put each of the derivatives equal to zero. This gives us $(m + 1)$ equations to be solved for the $(m + 1)$ unknowns. The solution represents the first-order (necessary) conditions; the second-order conditions, which determine whether the solution is a minimum or a maximum, are given elsewhere.[12] A well-known application of the Lagrange multiplier method in economics arises in connection with the problem of utility maximization subject to the budget constraint.[13]

Let us turn now to the specific problem of minimizing $\sigma^2 \sum a_i^2$ subject to $\sum a_i = 1$. In this problem the function F to be minimized is

$$F(a_1, a_2, \ldots, a_n) = \sigma^2 \sum_i a_i^2,$$

and the constraint G is

$$G(a_1, a_2, \ldots, a_n) = \sum_i a_i - 1.$$

Following the Lagrange multiplier method, we form

$$H = \sigma^2 \sum_i a_i^2 - \lambda\Big[\sum_i a_i - 1\Big].$$

The first-order conditions are

(6.14a) $$\frac{\partial H}{\partial a_1} = 0, \quad \frac{\partial H}{\partial a_2} = 0, \ldots, \quad \frac{\partial H}{\partial a_n} = 0, \quad \frac{\partial H}{\partial \lambda} = 0$$

or, explicitly,

(6.14b) $$\begin{aligned} 2a_1\sigma^2 - \lambda &= 0, \\ 2a_2\sigma^2 - \lambda &= 0, \\ &\vdots \\ 2a_n\sigma^2 - \lambda &= 0, \\ -\Big[\sum_i a_i - 1\Big] &= 0. \end{aligned}$$

This gives us $(n + 1)$ equations to be solved for the unknowns $a_1, a_2, \ldots, a_n$ and λ. From the first n equations we get

$$a_1 = \frac{\lambda}{2\sigma^2}, \quad a_2 = \frac{\lambda}{2\sigma^2}, \quad \ldots, \quad a_n = \frac{\lambda}{2\sigma^2}.$$

Substituting into the last equation gives

$$-\left[\frac{n\lambda}{2\sigma^2} - 1\right] = 0,$$

[12] See, e.g., *ibid.*, pp. 345–348.

[13] See, e.g., M. Friedman, *Price Theory* (Chicago: Aldine, 1962), p. 40.

or

$$\lambda = \frac{2\sigma^2}{n}.$$

Therefore,

$$a_1 = \frac{1}{n}, \quad a_2 = \frac{1}{n}, \quad \ldots \quad a_n = \frac{1}{n}.$$

These are then the constants that make $\tilde{\mu}$ unbiased and minimize its variance. Substituting for $a_1, a_2, \ldots, a_n$ into the formula for $\tilde{\mu}$ given by (6.11) leads to

$$\tilde{\mu} = \sum_i \frac{1}{n} X_i = \frac{1}{n} \sum_i X_i = \bar{X}.$$

In other words, the BLUE of the population mean is given by the sample mean. Further, substituting for a_i into the formula for the variance of $\tilde{\mu}$ given by (6.12), we get

$$\text{Var}(\tilde{\mu}) = \sigma^2 \sum_i \left(\frac{1}{n}\right)^2 = \sigma^2 n \left(\frac{1}{n}\right)^2 = \frac{\sigma^2}{n},$$

which is a well-known expression for the variance of the sample mean.

The best linear unbiased estimator can be considered as a special case of a *linear-minimum-weighted-square-error estimator* (LMWSEE), say, θ^*, obtained by minimizing

$$[w \text{ Var}(\theta^*) + (1 - w)(\text{Bias of } \theta^*)^2],$$

where w is some preassigned weight such that $0 < w < 1$. By selecting $w \to 0$ we get the BLUE. As it happens, many values of w are "outlawed" because they lead to formulas involving unknown parameters. As an example, consider a LMWSEE of the population mean when $w = 1/2$. This estimator is

$$\mu^* = \sum_i a_i X_i,$$

where the constants $a_1, a_2, \ldots, a_n$ are to be determined so as to minimize

$$\frac{1}{2} [\text{Var}(\mu^*) + (\text{Bias of } \mu^*)^2].$$

That is, setting $w = 1/2$ implies that we wish to minimize the *mean square error* of μ^*. The resulting formula is

$$\mu^* = \left[\frac{n\mu^2}{n\mu^2 + \sigma^2}\right] \bar{X},$$

which clearly indicates that μ^* does not qualify as an estimator since μ^2 and σ^2 are unknown. However, since for any value of μ^2 and σ^2 other than zero

$$\frac{n\mu^2}{n\mu^2 + \sigma^2} < 1,$$

hence the absolute value of the linear-minimum-mean-square-error estimator of μ is less than that of $\bar{X}$, though of course we do not know how much less.

Conclusion

This brings us to the end of our present discussion on methods of estimation. We have confined our attention to four basic methods; additional methods will be developed in the following chapters. The methods discussed do, however, provide the backbone of most if not all of the other estimation methods. The usefulness of the four methods has been illustrated by applying them to the problem of estimating the population mean. By each of the four methods we have obtained exactly the same estimator, namely, the sample mean. This result is rather reassuring since we know from Section 6–1 that sample mean as an estimator of the population mean has all the optimal properties.

6–3 Confidence Intervals

Now we take up the question of the precision of an estimator. Suppose we are interested in a population parameter θ for which there is an estimator $\hat{\theta}$. Suppose further that $\hat{\theta}$ possesses all the optimal properties of an estimator and incorporates all our knowledge concerning the relevant population. Since this knowledge is not complete, we shall be making an error by using $\hat{\theta}$ in place of the true parameter θ. The question then arises as to the size of this error. It is in this context that we speak of the precision of an estimator. That is, having obtained the best estimator that can be constructed given our limited knowledge, we may want to ask how well we can expect this estimator to perform.

The answer is obviously connected with the dispersion of the sampling distribution of the estimator. If this dispersion is small, a large proportion of estimates will lie within a close range from the true value of the parameter; if the dispersion is large, the same proportion of estimates will lie within a wider range. Thus the degree of precision of an estimator could be measured by the standard deviation of its sampling distribution, i.e., by its standard error. In most cases in practice this is not known but can be estimated from the sample along with the value of the estimator itself. Indeed, it is becoming an almost standard practice in econometrics to present not only the value of the estimator but also the calculated standard error. The latter is usually presented in parentheses below the value of the estimator, i.e.,

$$\underset{(s_{\hat{\theta}})}{\hat{\theta}}.$$

A more systematic and explicit method of indicating the precision of an estimator exists in the case in which we know the form of the sampling distribution of the estimator. We are then able to construct so-called *confidence intervals* for the population parameter. The idea of confidence intervals can best be explained by reference to our discussion on hypothesis testing in Section 5–1, using as an illustration the problem of estimating the mean of a normal population. In this case we use as an estimator the sample mean $\bar{X}$, which has all the optimal properties. We know that if the normal population in question has mean

μ and variance σ^2, the distribution of the sample mean will be normal with mean μ and variance (σ^2/n), i.e., $\bar{X} \sim N(\mu, \sigma^2/n)$. Therefore,

$$\frac{\bar{X} - \mu}{\sqrt{\sigma^2/n}} \sim N(0, 1),$$

where $N(0, 1)$ is the standard normal distribution whose areas have been calculated and tabulated (see Appendix D). With this knowledge we are able to make certain probability statements that, in turn, lead to the construction of confidence intervals for μ.

The reader may recall that in the case of a variable with standard normal distribution, 95% of all values fall within -1.96 and $+1.96$. That is, we can write

$$P\left(-1.96 \leq \frac{\bar{X} - \mu}{\sqrt{\sigma^2/n}} \leq +1.96\right) = 0.95. \tag{6.15}$$

This statement implies that 95% of all samples drawn from a normal population with mean μ and variance σ^2 will have $\bar{X}$ such that

$$-1.96 \leq \frac{\bar{X} - \mu}{\sqrt{\sigma^2/n}} \leq +1.96 \tag{6.16}$$

will be true. Multiplying this inequality by $\sqrt{\sigma^2/n}$ throughout, we get

$$-1.96\sqrt{\sigma^2/n} \leq (\bar{X} - \mu) \leq +1.96\sqrt{\sigma^2/n}.$$

Deducting $\bar{X}$ from all sides gives

$$-1.96\sqrt{\sigma^2/n} - \bar{X} \leq (-\mu) \leq +1.96\sqrt{\sigma^2/n} - \bar{X}.$$

Finally, multiplying throughout by -1 and switching the sides around leads to

$$\bar{X} - 1.96\sqrt{\sigma^2/n} \leq \mu \leq \bar{X} + 1.96\sqrt{\sigma^2/n}. \tag{6.17}$$

The expression in (6.17) is called the *95% confidence interval* for the population mean μ. The probability that this interval covers the true mean μ is equal to 0.95. This means that if we drew an infinite number of samples from the specified population, and if, for each sample, we computed the interval according to (6.17), then 95% of those intervals would contain the true mean μ. The measure "95%" represents the degree of our confidence that the interval—constructed on the basis of a given sample—will contain the true population mean. Note that we cannot say that "the probability that μ will lie within the stated interval is 0.95" because μ is a fixed number, not a random variable. The only probability statement that can be made about μ is that μ will assume its true value with probability 1 and all other values with probability 0. However, the end points of the interval—and therefore the interval itself—are random.

In setting up a confidence interval we can, of course, choose any level of confidence we like. However, we should realize that the higher the level of confidence, the wider the corresponding confidence interval and, therefore, the less useful is the information about the precision of the estimator. This can be seen by taking an extreme case, namely, that in which the confidence level is 100%. In this case the corresponding confidence interval, derived from a normally distributed estimator, is from $-\infty$ to $+\infty$, which obviously conveys no information about the precision of the estimator. On the other hand, narrower confidence intervals will be associated with lower levels of confidence. The problem here is very much like that of the level of significance in the context of hypothesis testing. A common solution in both cases is to use those levels which are most frequently used by others. In connection with hypothesis testing, we pointed out that there are two customarily employed levels of significance, 5% and 1%. Similarly, in connection with confidence intervals the two customary levels of confidence are 95% and 99%. For the mean of a normal population—with $\bar{X}$ as an estimator—the 95% confidence interval was given in (6.17); the 99% confidence interval is

$$\bar{X} - 2.57\sqrt{\sigma^2/n} \leq \mu \leq \bar{X} + 2.57\sqrt{\sigma^2/n}. \tag{6.18}$$

In constructing this interval we have made use of the fact that in the case of the standard normal distribution 99% of all values fall within -2.57 and $+2.57$.

The confidence interval (6.17) has been derived from a probability statement about the standard normal distribution. In particular, we have used the boundary points -1.96 and $+1.96$ that contain 95% of the total area. These boundary points are not unique since we can find other boundaries that also contain 95% of the area, for instance, -2.10 and $+1.85$, or -2.20 and $+1.80$, among others. The difference is that the interval from -1.96 to $+1.96$ contains the *central* portion of the area since it cuts off 2.5% of the area at each end of the distribution, whereas all the other intervals are asymmetric. The fact that the interval from -1.96 to $+1.96$ is symmetric implies that it is the *shortest* of all intervals that contain 95% of the area. This, in turn, means that the resulting 95% confidence interval is shorter than any other interval of the same level of confidence. The same conclusion can be drawn with respect to the 99% confidence interval (6.18). Obviously, given the level of confidence, a shorter interval is more desirable than a longer one.

EXAMPLE As a numerical example consider the following problem. Suppose we wish to construct a 95% confidence interval for the mean of $X \sim N(\mu, 16)$, having drawn a sample of 400 observations and obtained $\bar{x} = 99$. Then the 95% confidence interval is

$$99 - 1.96\sqrt{16/400} \leq \mu \leq 99 + 1.96\sqrt{16/400}$$

or

$$98.61 \leq \mu \leq 99.39.$$

That is, the probability that the interval from 98.61 to 99.39 will contain the true mean is 0.95. Note that the 99% confidence interval in this case is

$$99 - 2.57\sqrt{16/400} \leq \mu \leq 99 + 2.57\sqrt{16/400}$$

or

$$98.36 \leq \mu \leq 99.64.$$

The reader has probably noticed the similarity between confidence intervals for the population mean and acceptance regions of a test about the population mean. Let us consider this in explicit terms. Suppose, for instance, that we are dealing with a variable $X \sim N(\mu, \sigma^2)$ and that we wish to test the null hypothesis

$$H_0: \quad \mu = \mu_0$$

against the alternative,

$$H_A: \quad \mu \neq \mu_0.$$

Then the acceptance region corresponding to a 5% level of significance is

$$-1.96 \leq \frac{\bar{X} - \mu_0}{\sqrt{\sigma^2/n}} \leq +1.96.$$

This can be rewritten as

$$\bar{X} - 1.96\sqrt{\sigma^2/n} \leq \mu_0 \leq \bar{X} + 1.96\sqrt{\sigma^2/n}.$$

Now compare this with the 95% confidence interval for the population mean μ given by (6.17):

$$\bar{X} - 1.96\sqrt{\sigma^2/n} \leq \mu \leq \bar{X} + 1.96\sqrt{\sigma^2/n}.$$

The implication is that the 95% confidence interval is simply an interval that contains all those hypotheses about the population mean (i.e., all μ_0's) that would be accepted in a two-tail test at the 5% level of significance. A similar case could be made out for a 99% confidence interval and a two-tail test at the 1% level of significance. The difference between the acceptance regions and the confidence intervals is implied by the difference between hypothesis testing and estimation: in one case we make statements about the population and check whether or not they are contradicted by sample evidence; in the other case we regard the population as a blank that is to be filled by the sample.

So far we have assumed that the construction of confidence intervals involves estimators with optimal properties. In discussing confidence intervals for the mean of a normal population, the estimator was represented by the sample mean that satisfies this condition. Now we shall concern ourselves with the desirability of these optimal properties in confidence interval construction. First, if the estimator in question should be biased and the extent of the bias were not known, then the stated level of confidence would be incorrect. This can be easily demonstrated by replacing $\bar{X}$ in (6.17) or (6.18) by $(\bar{X} + B)$, where B is the bias and the value of B is not known. It is obvious that the interval involving $(\bar{X} + B)$ is associated with a different probability statement than the interval involving only $\bar{X}$ (unless, of course, $B = 0$), and thus the two intervals are characterized by different levels of confidence. Second, if the estimator is unbiased but not efficient, then the confidence interval is wider than otherwise. This follows from the fact that the variance of an inefficient estimator is larger than that of the efficient one and this "pushes" the end points of a confidence interval farther apart. Finally, squared-error consistency guarantees that as the sample size increases, the confidence interval narrows down and, at the limit, completely collapses at the point of the true value of the parameter.

In our discussion about confidence intervals, we have used as an illustration the problem of constructing confidence intervals for the mean of a normal population with *known* variance. In practical applications we rarely know the population variance but rather have to estimate it from the sample. An unbiased estimator of σ^2 was derived earlier and presented by (5.6) as

$$s^2 = \frac{1}{n-1}\sum_{i=1}^{n}(X_i - \bar{X})^2.$$

Furthermore, we know by (5.9) that if

$$\frac{(\bar{X} - \mu)}{\sqrt{\sigma^2/n}} \sim N(0, 1),$$

then

$$\frac{(\bar{X} - \mu)}{\sqrt{s^2/n}} \sim t_{n-1},$$

where t_{n-1} represents the t distribution with $(n - 1)$ degrees of freedom. This enables us to make the following probability statement:

$$P\left[-t_{n-1,\,\alpha/2} \leq \frac{\bar{X} - \mu}{\sqrt{s^2/n}} \leq +t_{n-1,\,\alpha/2}\right] = 1 - \alpha, \tag{6.19}$$

where $t_{n-1,\,\alpha/2}$ stands for the value of the t statistic with $(n - 1)$ degrees of freedom that cuts off $\alpha/2$ of the area of the t distribution at each tail end. The term $(1 - \alpha)$ represents the area between the points $-t_{n-1,\,\alpha/2}$ and $+t_{n-1,\,\alpha/2}$. From (6.19) we can construct a confidence interval for μ at any level of confidence. For instance, the 95% confidence interval for μ is

$$\bar{X} - t_{n-1,\,0.025}\sqrt{s^2/n} \leq \mu \leq \bar{X} + t_{n-1,\,0.025}\sqrt{s^2/n}. \tag{6.20}$$

EXAMPLE As a numerical example, consider the problem of constructing the 95% confidence interval for the mean μ of $X \sim N(\mu, \sigma^2)$, given that $\bar{X} = 20$, $s^2 = 100$, and $n = 25$. In this case the value of $t_{24,0.025}$ is 2.064 so that the 95% confidence interval for μ is

$$20 - 2.064\sqrt{100/25} \leq \mu \leq 20 + 2.064\sqrt{100/25}$$

or

$$15.872 \leq \mu \leq 24.128.$$

In a similar way we could construct intervals corresponding to 99% level of confidence, or any other level we might desire.

The idea of a confidence interval, developed above with respect to the mean of a normal population, can be used quite generally in connection with any parameter for which we have an estimator with known sampling distribution. For instance, we could construct a confidence interval for the variance of a normal population since we know that $[(n-1)s^2/\sigma^2]$ has the chi-square distribution with $(n-1)$ degrees of freedom. In our discussion we have viewed confidence intervals as a certain means of formally measuring the precision of an estimator. An alternative and more traditional view is to regard confidence intervals as more or less a separate subject treated under the heading of "interval estimation," to be distinguished from "point estimation," which is the subject of our Sections 6–1 and 6–2. We do not follow this traditional view since the connection between "point estimation" and "interval estimation" is so intimate as to make the separation rather artificial.

EXERCISES

6–1. Let $X \sim N(\mu, \sigma^2)$. Consider two independent random samples of observations on X. The samples are of size n_1 and n_2 with means $\bar{X}_1$ and $\bar{X}_2$, respectively. Two estimators of the population mean are proposed:

$$\hat{\mu} = \frac{1}{2}(\bar{X}_1 + \bar{X}_2),$$

$$\tilde{\mu} = \frac{n_1\bar{X}_1 + n_2\bar{X}_2}{n_1 + n_2}.$$

Compare the properties of these estimators.

6–2. Let $X \sim N(\mu, \sigma^2)$. Consider the following estimator of the population mean obtained from a random sample of n observations on X:

$$\bar{\mu} = \bar{X} + \frac{a}{n},$$

where a is a finite constant.

a. What are the asymptotic mean and the asymptotic variance of $\bar{\mu}$?

b. Prove that $\bar{\mu}$ is consistent and asymptotically efficient.

6–3. Let X be the number of successes in a sample of size n. The observations are assumed to be independent. Two estimators of the population proportion of successes, π, are

$$\hat{\pi} = \frac{X}{n},$$

$$\tilde{\pi} = \frac{(X+1)}{(n+1)}.$$

Examine the properties of these estimators.

6–4. A k-sided die has sides marked 1, 2, . . ., k. The die is tossed, and the uppermost number shown is 9. On the basis of this observation, obtain the maximum likelihood estimate of k and draw the likelihood function.

6–5. Let X be a random variable with mean μ and variance σ^2. Find a linear estimator of μ, say $\mathring{\mu}$, such that

$$\frac{\mathrm{Var}(\mathring{\mu})}{\sigma^2} + \frac{(\text{Bias of } \mathring{\mu})^2}{\mu^2}$$

is at minimum.

6–6. Let $X \sim N(\mu, \sigma^2)$. Consider the following two estimators of σ^2:

$$\hat{\sigma}^2 = \frac{1}{n} \sum_{i=1}^{n} (X_i - \bar{X})^2,$$

$$s^2 = \frac{1}{n-1} \sum_{i=1}^{n} (X_i - \bar{X})^2.$$

Show that

a. $\mathrm{Var}(\hat{\sigma}^2) < \mathrm{Var}(s^2)$;

b. $\mathrm{MSE}(\hat{\sigma}^2) < \mathrm{MSE}(s^2)$;

c. Both estimators are consistent.

[HINT: $\mathrm{Var}(\hat{\sigma}^2) = 2\sigma^4(n-1)/n^2$.]

6–7. Following are 20 observations drawn from a normal population:

0.464	0.137	2.455	−0.323
0.060	−2.526	−0.531	−0.194
1.486	−0.354	−0.634	0.697
1.022	−0.472	1.279	3.521
1.394	−0.555	0.046	0.321

a. Find the 95% confidence interval for the population mean.

b. Plot the likelihood function for the population mean and the ML estimate of μ.

[NOTE: Since the ML estimate of μ does not depend on σ^2, for the purpose of graphing we can set its value to be some convenient number, e.g., unity.]

6–8. The Air Conditioning Maintenance and Repair Company contemplates opening a branch in Belair Hills. You have been engaged to conduct a sample survey to estimate the percentage of homes with air conditioning in this community. The conditions of the contract between you and A.C.M.R. are as follows:

1. The required confidence limits for the population proportion are 95%.
2. The sample used as a basis for the estimate must be strictly random and must contain at least 30 families.
3. You will get paid \$500, *less* \$10 for each percentage unit of the estimated interval for the population proportion; for example, if you should find that, with 95% confidence, the population proportion lies between 0.4 and 0.6, you will receive \$500 − \$10 (60 − 40) = \$300.

In the preliminary investigation you have found out that the cost of obtaining sample information is \$2 per family included in the sample. The results of the interviews with the families included in your sample can be obtained by using the "census" of Belair Hills presented in Table 6–2. There are 250 families, each occupying a house;

houses with air conditioning are marked by a tick. [NOTE: The large-sample 95% confidence interval for the proportion of successes in a finite population is given as

$$\hat{\pi} \pm 1.96\sqrt{\frac{\hat{\pi}(1-\hat{\pi})}{n}}\sqrt{\frac{N-n}{N-1}},$$

where n = sample size, and N = population size.]

a. Draw a full report to A.C.M.R. in which you describe the technique used in selecting the sample and the method of estimation, and present the results.

b. Produce a bill to A.C.M.R.

c. Work out your *net* remuneration for the work carried out.

d. Show an extract from a letter to a friend, whom you wish to entice into partnership, in which you describe how cleverly you applied the profit-maximization principle in connection with the job for A.C.M.R.

Table 6–2 Complete Listing of Families in Belair Hills

Family No.	Family No.	Family No.	Family No.	Family No.	Family No.	Family No.	Family No.
1 √	33	65	96	127	158	189	220
2	34 √	66 √	97 √	128 √	159 √	190	221
3 √	35	67	98	129 √	160 √	191	222
4 √	36 √	68	99	130 √	161	192 √	223
5	37 √	69 √	100	131	162	193	224
6 √	38	70 √	101	132	163	194	225 √
7	39 √	71 √	102 √	133	164 √	195 √	226
8	40 √	72	103	134	165 √	196	227 √
9 √	41 √	73	104	135	166 √	197 √	228 √
10	42	74 √	105	136	167 √	198	229 √
11 √	43	75	106	137 √	168 √	199 √	230
12 √	44	76	107 √	138	169 √	200	231 √
13 √	45	77 √	108	139	170 √	201	232 √
14	46 √	78 √	109 √	140	171 √	202	233 √
15 √	47	79 √	110	141	172	203	234
16	48 √	80	111 √	142	173	204 √	235
17	49	81	112 √	143	174 √	205	236
18	50	82	113	144	175	206 √	237 √
19 √	51	83 √	114 √	145 √	176	207 √	238
20 √	52	84	115	146	177	208	239
21	53	85 √	116 √	147 √	178 √	209 √	240
22	54	86 √	117 √	148 √	179	210	241
23 √	55	87	118	149	180	211	242 √
24 √	56 √	88	119 √	150 √	181	212	243
25 √	57	89	120	151	182	213	244
26 √	58 √	90	121 √	152	183 √	214	245
27 √	59 √	91	122 √	153 √	184	215 √	246 √
28 √	60	92 √	123 √	154	185	216 √	247
29 √	61 √	93 √	124	155 √	186	217 √	248
30 √	62	94 √	125	156	187	218	249 √
31	63	95 √	126	157	188	219	250 √
32 √	64 √						

Part TWO

Basic Econometric Theory

7 Simple Regression

Economic theory is mainly concerned with relations among variables. Demand and supply relations, cost functions, production functions, and many others are familiar to every student who has taken a course in economics. In fact, the entire body of economic theory can be regarded as a collection of relations among variables.[1] As pointed out in Chapter 1, econometrics is concerned with testing the theoretical propositions embodied in these relations, and with estimating the parameters involved. In the chapters of Part Two we will discuss various methods that can be used in performing this task and the problems encountered in the process. In the present chapter we will discuss the simplest case of a linear relation involving only two measurable variables; the subsequent chapters will contain increasingly more complicated cases.

7-1 Relations Between Variables

An appropriate way to start our discussion is by defining the new concepts with which we will be working. We define a *relation* between variables X and Y as a set of all values of X and Y which are characterized by a given equation. For example, if the characterizing equation is given by

$$y = \alpha + \beta x,$$

where α and β are some constants, then the relation between X and Y is the set $\{x,y\}$ consisting of all possible values of X and Y that satisfy the equation. Typically, the form of the characterizing equation gives the name to the corresponding relation: a linear equation describes a linear relation, an exponential equation describes an exponential relation, and so on. The concept of a relation is closely associated with the concepts of a domain and of a range. If a relation between X and Y is characterized by an equation $y = f(x)$, then the *domain* of this relation is the set of all possible values of X, and the *range* is the set of all possible corresponding values of Y. In practice, relations are usually described

[1] See, e.g., Paul A. Samuelson, *Foundations of Economic Analysis* (Cambridge, Mass.: Harvard University Press, 1947).

simply by stating the appropriate characterizing equation, while the domain and the range are implied but unstated.

All relations can be classified as either deterministic or stochastic. A relation between X and Y is *deterministic* if each element of the domain is paired off with *just one* element of the range. That is, a relationship between X and Y characterized as $y = f(x)$ is a deterministic relation if for each value of X there is only one corresponding value of Y. However, the *variables* X and Y may both be nonstochastic (i.e., they may assume values that are fully controllable or predictable), or they may both be stochastic. This means that a relation may be deterministic (i.e., nonstochastic) even if both variables involved are stochastic; however, if both variables are stochastic while the relation is deterministic, the conditional distribution of Y given X is degenerate (see page 163). On the other hand, a relation between X and Y is said to be *stochastic* if for each value of X there is a whole probability distribution of values of Y. Thus, for any given value of X the variable Y may, in this case, assume some specific value—or fall within some specific interval—with a probability smaller than one and greater than zero.

To illustrate the distinction between a deterministic and a stochastic relation, suppose we conduct a series of experiments in class to determine the demand for Mackintosh apples at different prices. Let q_t = quantity of apples sold at time t, and let p_t = price in cents. The apples are offered for sale at a given price every time the class meets during the term. The results at the end of the term may be as follows:

p_t	q_t
25	1
20	3
15	5
10	7
5	9
0	11

These results can be summarized in the form of a "demand equation" as

$$q_t = 11 - 0.4p_t.$$

The relation between price and quantity then is such that *any time* the apples were offered at 25 cents apiece, only one apple was sold. Any time the price was 20 cents, three apples were sold, and so on. This is a deterministic relation, since for each price there is always only one corresponding quantity of apples sold. Now consider a different set of results (Table 7–1). The "demand equation" must now be rewritten as

$$q_t = 11 - 0.4p_t + \varepsilon_t,$$

Table 7-1

p_t	q_t
25	0 apples 25% of the time 1 apple 50% of the time 2 apples 25% of the time
20	2 apples 25% of the time 3 apples 50% of the time 4 apples 25% of the time
⋮	⋮
0	10 apples 25% of the time 11 apples 50% of the time 12 apples 25% of the time

where ε_t is a random variable having the following probability distribution, whatever the specified price:

ε_t	$f(\varepsilon_t)$
−1	0.25
0	0.50
+1	0.25
	1.00

This variable is commonly called a *random disturbance* since it "disturbs" an otherwise deterministic relation (an alternative expression for ε_t is "a random error term"). The last relation is a stochastic one since, because of the presence of the disturbance, there are several quantities demanded for each price, each quantity occurring with a given probability. A diagrammatic representation of the two relations is shown in Figure 7-1.

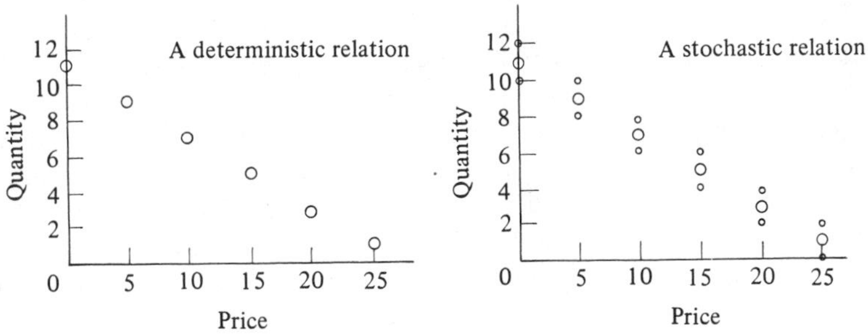

Figure 7-1

Let us now consider the question of dependence between two variables involved in a relation. First, consider a deterministic relation characterized by

$$y = f(x).$$

Then, if $f(x)$ is not constant over all values of X (that is, if $f(x)$ is not constant over all elements of the domain), we say that *Y is dependent on X in the functional sense.* In other words, Y is considered to depend on X if, at least for some values of X, a change in X implies a change in Y. If, in a two-dimensional diagram, the values of Y are measured along the vertical and those of X along the horizontal axis, then Y is dependent on X if all points do not lie on a straight horizontal line. With respect to a *stochastic relation*, we say that *Y is dependent on X in the functional sense* if the probability distribution of Y is not the same for all values of X. A typical case of dependence of Y on X arises when the mean of Y changes as X assumes different values. However, Y would be considered as dependent on X even if the mean of Y remained constant for all values of X, as long as some other characteristic of the distribution of Y would change with X. For instance, if the variance of Y were to increase with increases in X, this alone would make Y dependent on X according to our definition.

It is interesting to note that, in the numerical example on the stochastic demand curve given above, the mean quantity demanded changes with price while the variance remains unchanged. In particular, we have

p_t	$E(q_t)$	$\text{Var}(q_t)$
25	1	0.5
20	3	0.5
15	5	0.5
10	7	0.5
5	9	0.5
0	11	0.5

In a more general case of dependence both the mean and the variance of Y may change in response to changes in X.

In economic theory all relations are, as a rule, stated in a deterministic form. This is not because economists would believe in a complete absence of chance when it comes to economic relations, but because they consider the stochastic disturbances to be of less importance than the systematic influences. The introduction of stochastic disturbances into the economic relations would greatly complicate the task of the theorist. However, the stress on the need for *testing* economic theories, which is frequently encountered in economic writings, implies a belief in the existence of stochastic factors. If the theoretical relations were, in fact, deterministic, the question of statistical testing would not arise; all that we would have to do to determine the values of the unknown parameters would be to carry out precise measurements rather than tests. To illustrate this, we may consider a theory that Y is linearly dependent on X. If the relation between Y and X were, in fact, deterministic, we would simply measure two pairs of values of X and Y. If the line connecting these two points were horizontal, the theory would be rejected; in all other cases the theory would be verified. The intercept and the slope of the line could be simply read off the graph. If, however, the relation between X and Y were stochastic, our observations of the values of the two variables would have to be considered as a sample. The sample would then be used to test a proposition about the population, and the slope and the intercept would have to be estimated.

7-2 The Regression Model

In econometrics we deal exclusively with stochastic relations. The simplest form of stochastic relation between two variables X and Y is called a *simple linear regression model.* This model is formally described as

$$Y_i = \alpha + \beta X_i + \varepsilon_i, \tag{7.1}$$

where Y is called the "dependent variable," X the "explanatory variable," and ε the "stochastic disturbance," and α and β are the "regression parameters," which are unknown. The subscript i refers to the ith observation. The values of the variables X and Y are observable, but those of ε are not. Observations on X and Y can be made over time, in which case we speak of having "time-series data," or they can be made over individuals, groups of individuals, objects, or geographical areas, in which case we speak of having "cross-section data." Thus the subscript i may refer to the ith point or period of time, or to the ith individual, object, etc. Of course, data of both kinds can be combined to obtain "pooled time-series and cross-section data"; for example, we may have data on consumption expenditure and income of N individual households for T periods of time. In this case it would be convenient to use a double subscript. However, data of this kind are not very common. Typically, aggregate relations such as aggregate consumption functions, market demand relations, or aggregate production functions are estimated from time-series data, while microrelations such as household expenditure functions or firm production functions are estimated from cross-section data obtained from sample surveys. The origin of the data is not explicitly taken into account in the development of estimators of the regression parameters. But, as we shall see, the properties of these estimators depend on certain assumptions concerning the observations, and some of these assumptions are more likely to be violated when the data are of one kind than another. In this respect the type of data used in estimation is of relevance.

The stochastic nature of the regression model implies that for every value of X there is a whole probability distribution of values of Y. This means that the value of Y can never be forecast exactly. The uncertainty concerning Y arises because of the presence of the stochastic disturbance ε which, being random, imparts randomness to Y. Consider, for example, a production function of a firm. Suppose that output depends in some specified way on the quantity of labor input in accordance with the engineer's blueprint. Such a production function may apply in the short run when the quantities of other inputs are fixed. But, in general, the same quantity of labor will lead to different quantities of output because of variations in weather, human performance, frequency of machine breakdowns, and many other factors. Output, which is the dependent variable in this case, will depend not only on the quantity of labor input, which is the explanatory variable, but also on a large number of random causes, which we summarize in the form of the stochastic disturbance. The probability distribution of Y and its characteristics are then determined by the values of X and by the probability distribution of ε. If the "blueprint" relation between output and labor were completely and correctly specified, then we could measure the value of ε from the observations on X and Y after each production run. In reality this is almost never the case. In fact, we consider ourselves lucky when we know even the mathematical form of the relation without knowing the parameters. Typically, the mathematical form of the relation has to be assumed and the values of the parameters are estimated from observations on X and Y. Using the estimated values of the parameters, we can then "estimate" the values of the stochastic disturbance for each pair of values of X and Y.

It should be clear now that the full specification of the regression model includes not only the form of the regression equation as given in (7.1) but also a specification of the probability distribution of the disturbance and a statement indicating how the values of the explanatory variable are determined. This information is given by what we shall call the *basic assumptions*. These assumptions, which are taken to apply to *all* observations, are as follows:

(7.2) *Normality:* ε_i is normally distributed.

(7.3) *Zero mean:* $E(\varepsilon_i) = 0.$

(7.4) *Homoskedasticity:* $E(\varepsilon_i^2) = \sigma^2.$

(7.5) *Nonautoregression:* $E(\varepsilon_i \varepsilon_j) = 0 \quad (i \neq j).$

(7.6) *Nonstochastic X:* X_i is a nonstochastic variable with values fixed in repeated samples and such that, for *any* sample size,

$$\frac{1}{n}\sum_{i=1}^{n}(X_i - \bar{X})^2$$

is a finite number different from zero.

The full specification of the simple linear regression model then consists of the regression equation (7.1) and the five basic assumptions (7.2) through (7.6).[2] This represents the so-called "classical normal linear regression model," which provides a point of departure for most of the work in econometric theory.

[2] Strictly speaking, there is one further assumption, which is made only implicitly, namely, that there exists no other regression model with a disturbance that would be correlated with ε_i of (7.1). The relevance of this assumption will become quite clear when we discuss "seemingly unrelated regressions."

Let us now examine the meaning of the various assumptions. The first two assumptions state that, for each value of X_i, the disturbance is normally distributed around zero. The implications are that ε_i is continuous and ranges from $-\infty$ to $+\infty$, that it is symmetrically distributed around its mean, and that its distribution is fully determined by two parameters, the mean and the variance. The rationalization of normality relies on the same argument as that which applies to the behavior of random errors of measurement and which was mentioned at the end of Section 4–2. In particular, we may consider each value of the stochastic disturbance as the result of a large number of small causes, each cause producing a small deviation of the dependent variable from what it would be if the relation were deterministic. Under these circumstances the analogy with the behavior of errors of measurement may be valid and the assumptions of normality and zero mean appropriate. The third assumption concerning homoskedasticity means that every disturbance has the same variance σ^2 whose value is unknown. This assumption rules out, for example, the possibility that the dispersion of the disturbances would be greater for higher than for lower values of X_i. In terms of our production functions example, the assumption of homoskedasticity implies that the variation in output is the same whether the quantity of labor is 20, 100, or any other number of units. The fourth assumption requires that the disturbances be nonautoregressive. Under this assumption the fact that, say, output is higher than expected today should not lead to a higher (or lower) than expected output tomorrow. Note that assumptions (7.3) and (7.5) together imply that the disturbances are uncorrelated, and assumptions (7.2), (7.3), and (7.5) together imply that the disturbances are independent in the probability sense.[3] The final assumption, which states that the explanatory variable is to be nonstochastic, is quite straightforward. This assumption confines us to considering those situations in which the values of X_i are either controllable or fully predictable. The additional statement that the values of X_i are "fixed in repeated samples" indicates that the set of values of X is taken to be the same from sample to sample. Finally, the requirement that $(1/n) \sum (X_i - \bar{X})^2$ be a finite number different from zero means that the values of X in the sample must not all be equal to the same number, and that they cannot grow or decline without limit as the sample size increases.

The assumptions underlying the classical normal linear regression model are used in deriving estimators of the regression parameters. Since the disturbance is assumed to be normally distributed with a mean equal to zero, the only thing that is not known about this distribution is its variance σ^2. Thus the model described by (7.1) through (7.6) involves altogether three unknown parameters, the regression parameters α and β and the variance of the disturbance σ^2. It should be emphasized, however, that we do not ignore the possibility that any one or more of the basic assumptions may not be fulfilled. In fact, Chapter 8 is devoted to precisely this question. There we shall examine what happens to the properties of the estimators developed in the present chapter when various

[3] For normally distributed random variables, uncorrelatedness implies independence. See, e.g., A. S. Goldberger, *Econometric Theory* (New York: Wiley, 1964), pp. 107–108.

assumptions are violated. We shall also try to develop alternative estimators appropriate to the situation on hand whenever necessary.

Having made a complete specification of the regression model as described by the regression equation and the five basic assumptions, we may take a closer look at some of its basic features. In particular, let us turn to the probability distribution of the dependent variable Y_i. First, the mean of Y_i can be obtained by taking the mathematical expectation of both sides of equation (7.1). We get

$$(7.7) \qquad E(Y_i) = E(\alpha + \beta X_i + \varepsilon_i) = \alpha + \beta X_i.$$

This follows from the specification that α and β are parameters, X_i is nonstochastic (i.e., some given number), and the mean of ε_i is 0 by (7.3). Furthermore, the variance of Y_i is

$$(7.8) \qquad \begin{aligned} \operatorname{Var}(Y_i) &= E[Y_i - E(Y_i)]^2 = E[(\alpha + \beta X_i + \varepsilon_i) - (\alpha + \beta X_i)]^2 \\ &= E(\varepsilon_i^2) = \sigma^2. \end{aligned}$$

In this derivation we first used the general definition of a variance, then substituted for Y_i from (7.1) and for $E(Y_i)$ from (7.7), and finally made use of the assumption of homoskedasticity given by (7.4). Concerning the distribution of Y_i, we can see from equation (7.1) that Y_i is merely a linear function of ε_i. Since ε_i is normally distributed, it follows by Theorem 12 that Y_i is also normally distributed. Therefore, we can assert that Y_i is a normally distributed variable with mean $(\alpha + \beta X_i)$ and variance σ^2, i.e., that $Y_i \sim N(\alpha + \beta X_i, \sigma^2)$. This is illustrated graphically by Figure 7–2. Note that the means of the distributions all lie on a straight line, and that each distribution has exactly the same variance.

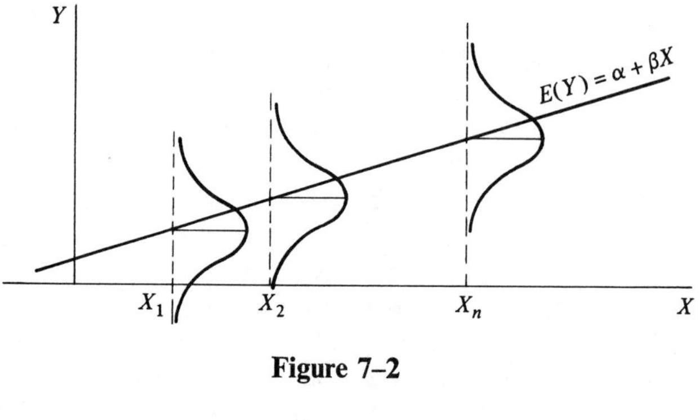

Figure 7–2

Equation (7.7), which gives the mean value of Y for each value of X, is known as the *population regression line*. The intercept of this line, α, measures the mean value of Y corresponding to zero value of X. The slope of the line, β, measures the change in the mean value of Y corresponding to a unit change in the value of X. If, for instance, Y represents aggregate consumption and X aggregate income, then α measures the subsistence level of consumption and β represents the marginal propensity to consume. Since the values of these parameters are not known, the population regression line is not known. When the values of α and β are estimated, we obtain a *sample regression line* that serves as an estimate of the population regression line. If α and β are estimated by $\hat{\alpha}$ and $\hat{\beta}$ respectively, then the sample regression line is given by

$$\hat{Y}_i = \hat{\alpha} + \hat{\beta}X_i, \tag{7.9}$$

where $\hat{Y}_i$ is the fitted value of Y_i. Most, if not all, of the observed values of Y_i will not lie exactly on the sample regression line so that the values of Y_i and $\hat{Y}_i$ will differ. This difference is called a *residual* and is designated by e_i. Thus we have to distinguish the following:

$$Y_i = \alpha + \beta X_i + \varepsilon_i \quad \text{(population);}$$

$$Y_i = \hat{\alpha} + \hat{\beta}X_i + e_i \quad \text{(sample).}$$

Note that, in general, e_i is different from ε_i because $\hat{\alpha}$ and $\hat{\beta}$ differ from the true values of α and β. In fact, one can view the residuals e_i as "estimates" of the disturbances ε_i. (Alternatively, we might say that the distribution of e_i is used to estimate the parameters of the distribution of ε_i.) This is illustrated in Figure 7–3. In Section 7–3 we will develop a procedure for estimating the regression parameters and, therefore, the population regression line.

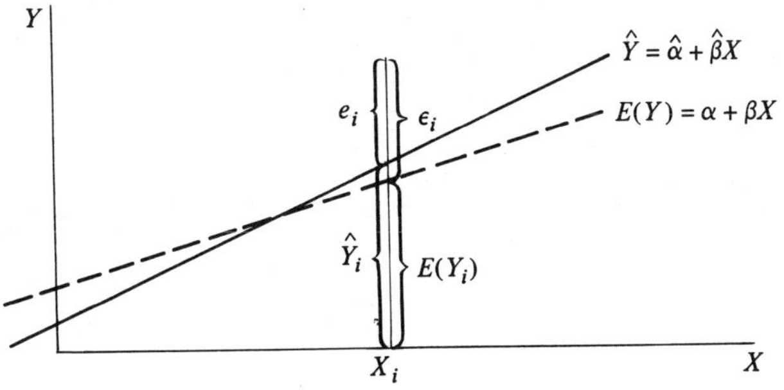

Figure 7–3

7–3 Estimation of the Regression Parameters

The problem of estimating the parameters of the regression model can be viewed as one of estimating the parameters of the probability distribution of the dependent variable Y_i. As we have shown, under the assumptions of the model, Y_i is normally distributed with the mean $E(Y_i) = \alpha + \beta X_i$ and variance $\text{Var}(Y_i) = \sigma^2$. The problem of estimating the regression parameters α and β is thus equivalent to the problem of estimating the mean of Y_i. This can be solved by a number of different estimation methods as described in Section 6–2.

We shall try three such methods—least squares, best linear unbiased estimation, and maximum likelihood—and compare the resulting estimators and their properties. The object is to obtain an estimator that will have as many desirable properties as possible. Such an estimator can then be used to test hypotheses about the regression model and to make predictions.

Least Squares Estimation

Let us begin with the derivation of the *least squares estimators* of α and β. The principle of least squares estimation involves minimizing the sum of squared deviations of the observed values from their mean. That is, we have to find the value of the mean that makes the required sum as small as possible. In our case we have to minimize the sum S given by

$$S = \sum_{i=1}^{n} [Y_i - E(Y_i)]^2,$$

or

$$S = \sum_{i=1}^{n} [Y_i - \alpha - \beta X_i]^2.$$

To find the values of α and β that minimize this sum we have to differentiate S with respect to α and β. This gives

$$\frac{\partial S}{\partial \alpha} = \sum_i \frac{\partial (Y_i - \alpha - \beta X_i)^2}{\partial \alpha} = \sum_i 2(Y_i - \alpha - \beta X_i)(-1)$$

$$= -2 \sum_i (Y_i - \alpha - \beta X_i),$$

and

$$\frac{\partial S}{\partial \beta} = \sum_i \frac{\partial (Y_i - \alpha - \beta X_i)^2}{\partial \beta} = \sum_i 2(Y_i - \alpha - \beta X_i)(-X_i)$$

$$= -2 \sum_i X_i(Y_i - \alpha - \beta X_i).$$

Equating each of these derivatives to zero and putting a "hat" on α and β to indicate that the resulting equations are satisfied by the least squares estimators of α and β, not by their true values, we obtain

$$-2 \sum_i (Y_i - \hat{\alpha} - \hat{\beta} X_i) = 0,$$

$$-2 \sum_i X_i(Y_i - \hat{\alpha} - \hat{\beta} X_i) = 0;$$

or, equivalently,

$$\sum Y_i = \hat{\alpha} n + \hat{\beta}\left(\sum X_i\right), \tag{7.10}$$

$$\sum X_i Y_i = \hat{\alpha}\left(\sum X_i\right) + \hat{\beta}\left(\sum X_i^2\right). \tag{7.11}$$

These equations are generally known as the "least squares normal equations."[4] Since we can write

$$Y_i = \hat{\alpha} + \hat{\beta}X_i + e_i,$$

where e_i represents the "least squares residuals," the least squares normal equations can be presented more simply as

$$\sum e_i = 0, \tag{7.10a}$$

$$\sum X_i e_i = 0. \tag{7.11a}$$

Equations (7.10) and (7.11) can be solved for $\hat{\alpha}$ and $\hat{\beta}$. The solution for $\hat{\beta}$ is

$$\hat{\beta} = \frac{n(\sum X_i Y_i) - (\sum X_i)(\sum Y_i)}{n(\sum X_i^2) - (\sum X_i)^2}. \tag{7.12}$$

This expression can be written in a somewhat different way. Note that

$$\begin{aligned} (7.13)\quad n\sum (X_i - \bar{X})(Y_i - \bar{Y}) &= n\left(\sum X_i Y_i\right) - n\bar{X}\left(\sum Y_i\right) - n\bar{Y}\left(\sum X_i\right) + n^2\bar{X}\bar{Y} \\ &= n\left(\sum X_i Y_i\right) - \left(\sum X_i\right)\left(\sum Y_i\right) - \left(\sum X_i\right)\left(\sum Y_i\right) + \left(\sum X_i\right)\left(\sum Y_i\right) \\ &= n\left(\sum X_i Y_i\right) - \left(\sum X_i\right)\left(\sum Y_i\right), \end{aligned}$$

which is the numerator of the expression for $\hat{\beta}$. Also

$$\begin{aligned} (7.14)\quad n\sum (X_i - \bar{X})^2 &= n\left(\sum X_i^2\right) - 2n\bar{X}\left(\sum X_i\right) + n^2\bar{X}^2 \\ &= n\left(\sum X_i^2\right) - 2\left(\sum X_i\right)^2 + \left(\sum X_i\right)^2 \\ &= n\left(\sum X_i^2\right) - \left(\sum X_i\right)^2, \end{aligned}$$

which is the denominator of the expression for $\hat{\beta}$. Therefore, we can write

$$\hat{\beta} = \frac{\sum (X_i - \bar{X})(Y_i - \bar{Y})}{\sum (X_i - \bar{X})^2},$$

since the n in the numerator and the denominator cancel out. A further simplification can be achieved by introducing new notation for the deviations of X_i and Y_i from their respective sample means. In particular, let

$$x_i' = X_i - \bar{X} \quad \text{and} \quad y_i' = Y_i - \bar{Y}.$$

[4] The following rule may be found useful in memorizing. In the regression equation, $Y_i = \alpha + \beta X_i + \varepsilon_i$, the multiplier of α is 1 and the multiplier of β is X_i. The first least squares normal equation is obtained by multiplying both sides of the regression equation by 1, adding all observations, and omitting the last term involving ε_i. The second equation is obtained by multiplying both sides of the regression equation by X_i, adding all observations, and omitting the last term involving ε_i. This rule can be extended to regression equations with any number of explanatory variables.

Of course, this implies that $\sum x_i' = 0$ and $\sum y_i' = 0$. The expression for the least squares estimator of $\hat{\beta}$ then simplifies to

(7.12a)
$$\hat{\beta} = \frac{\sum x_i' y_i'}{\sum x_i'^2}.$$

Once $\hat{\beta}$ is determined, the solution for $\hat{\alpha}$ can be obtained quite easily from equation (7.10). This leads to

(7.15)
$$\hat{\alpha} = \frac{1}{n}\left(\sum Y_i\right) - \hat{\beta}\frac{1}{n}\left(\sum X_i\right) = \bar{Y} - \hat{\beta}\bar{X},$$

which means that the sample regression line

$$\hat{Y}_i = \hat{\alpha} + \hat{\beta}X_i$$

passes through the point $(\bar{X}, \bar{Y})$. The value of $\hat{\alpha}$ measures the intercept, and the value of $\hat{\beta}$ the slope of the sample regression line. The sampling properties of these estimators will be discussed at the end of this section.

EXAMPLE As a numerical example, consider the data in Table 7–2 on prices and quantities of oranges sold in a supermarket on twelve consecutive days. Let X_i be the price charged and Y_i the quantity sold on the ith day. Let us further postulate that the demand function is of the form

Table 7–2

Price, ¢/lb	Quantity, lb
100	55
90	70
80	90
70	100
70	90
70	105
70	80
65	110
60	125
60	115
55	130
50	130

$$Y_i = \alpha + \beta X_i + \varepsilon_i$$

and such that the basic assumptions of the classical normal regression model are satisfied. We wish to obtain the least squares estimate of α and β. Carrying out the appropriate calculations we get

$$\bar{X} = 70, \qquad \sum x_i' y_i' = -3550,$$

$$\bar{Y} = 100, \qquad \sum x_i'^2 = 2250.$$

(We also note for future reference that $\sum y_i'^2 = 6300$.) The least squares estimates then are

$$\hat{\beta} = \frac{-3550}{2250} = -1.578,$$

$$\hat{\alpha} = 100 - (-1.578) \times 70 = 210.460,$$

so that the estimated sample regression line is

$$\hat{Y}_i = 210.460 - 1.578X_i.$$

This is our estimated demand curve. Since the function is linear, the price elasticity of demand is different at different prices. At the point of average price (i.e., when $X_i = 70$), the price elasticity η is estimated as

$$\hat{\eta}_{X_i=\bar{X}} = (-1.578) \times \frac{70}{100} = -1.105,$$

indicating that the demand is estimated to be slightly elastic at this point.

Best Linear Unbiased Estimation

Let us now turn to the derivation of the *best linear unbiased estimators* (BLUE) of α and β. The BLU estimation method requires that the estimator be a linear combination of sample observations, that it be unbiased, and that its variance be smaller than that of any other linear unbiased estimator. We shall use this method to derive the BLUE of β, say, $\tilde{\beta}$, first. By the condition of linearity we have

$$\tilde{\beta} = \sum_i a_i Y_i, \tag{7.16}$$

where a_i ($i = 1, 2, \ldots, n$) are some constants to be determined. Now

$$E(\tilde{\beta}) = E\left(\sum a_i Y_i\right) = \sum a_i E(Y_i) = \sum a_i(\alpha + \beta X_i) = \alpha\left(\sum a_i\right) + \beta\left(\sum a_i X_i\right).$$

This means that for $\tilde{\beta}$ to be unbiased we require that

$$\sum a_i = 0 \qquad \text{and} \qquad \sum a_i X_i = 1.$$

Finally, we require that $\tilde{\beta}$ have a smaller variance than any other estimator that satisfies the above conditions. The variance of $\tilde{\beta}$ is given as

$$\operatorname{Var}(\tilde{\beta}) = \operatorname{Var}\left(\sum_i a_i Y_i\right) = E\left[\left(\sum a_i Y_i\right) - E\left(\sum a_i Y_i\right)\right]^2$$

$$= E\left[\sum a_i(Y_i - EY_i)\right]^2 = E\left[\sum a_i \varepsilon_i\right]^2.$$

This expression for the sum of squares can be developed further. For example, consider the square of the sum of three numbers called c_1, c_2, and c_3. We have

$$(c_1 + c_2 + c_3)^2 = c_1^2 + c_2^2 + c_3^2 + 2c_1c_2 + 2c_1c_3 + 2c_2c_3.$$

That is, a square of a sum is equal to the sum of squares plus two times the sum of cross products, where the cross products include all possible pairs for which the first subscript is smaller than the second one. We can, in fact, write

$$\Big(\sum_i c_i\Big)^2 = \sum_i c_i^2 + 2\sum_{i<j} c_i c_j.$$

This result, which is of general interest, can be extended to any number of terms. Thus we obtain

$$\text{(7.17)} \qquad \begin{aligned} \operatorname{Var}(\tilde{\beta}) &= E\sum_i (a_i\varepsilon_i)^2 + 2E\sum_{i<j}(a_i\varepsilon_i)(a_j\varepsilon_j) \\ &= \sum_i a_i^2 E(\varepsilon_i^2) + 2\sum_{i<j} a_i a_j E(\varepsilon_i\varepsilon_j) = \sigma^2\sum_i a_i^2 \end{aligned}$$

by the assumptions of homoskedasticity and nonautoregression.

The problem now is to find $a_1, a_2, \ldots, a_n$ such that $\sum a_i = 0$, $\sum_i a_i X_i = 1$, and, at the same time, $\sigma^2 \sum a_i^2$ is as small as possible. That is, we have to minimize

$$\sigma^2 \sum a_i^2$$

subject to the conditions

$$\sum a_i = 0 \qquad \text{and} \qquad \Big(\sum a_i X_i\Big) - 1 = 0.$$

This is a problem of constrained minimization, which can be solved with the help of *Lagrange multiplier method.* The method for the case of one constraint was outlined earlier in describing the derivation of best linear unbiased estimators (Section 6–2). An extension to the case of two or more constraints can be made by simple analogy.[5] In the problem at hand we form a new function

$$H = \sigma^2\sum_i a_i^2 - \lambda_1\Big(\sum_i a_i\Big) - \lambda_2\Big[\Big(\sum_i a_i X_i\Big) - 1\Big],$$

which consists of the function to be minimized, the two constraints imposed, and two Lagrange multipliers, λ_1 and λ_2. To obtain the required solution we differentiate H with respect to $a_1, a_2, \ldots, a_n, \lambda_1$, and λ_2, and put each of the derivatives equal to zero. That is,

$$\text{(7.18a)} \qquad \frac{\partial H}{\partial a_1} = 0, \quad \frac{\partial H}{\partial a_2} = 0, \ldots, \frac{\partial H}{\partial a_n} = 0, \quad \frac{\partial H}{\partial \lambda_1} = 0, \quad \frac{\partial H}{\partial \lambda_2} = 0,$$

or, explicitly,

$$\text{(7.18b)} \qquad \begin{aligned} 2a_1\sigma^2 - \lambda_1 - \lambda_2 X_1 &= 0 \\ 2a_2\sigma^2 - \lambda_1 - \lambda_2 X_2 &= 0 \\ &\vdots \\ 2a_n\sigma^2 - \lambda_1 - \lambda_2 X_n &= 0 \\ -\sum_i a_i &= 0 \\ -\Big(\sum_i a_i X_i\Big) + 1 &= 0. \end{aligned}$$

[5] See, e.g., T. Yamane, *Mathematics for Economists* (Englewood Cliffs, N.J.: Prentice-Hall, 1962), pp. 119–120.

This gives us $(n + 2)$ equations to be solved for the unknown $a_1, a_2, \ldots, a_n, \lambda_1$, and λ_2. The first n equations can be rewritten as

(7.19)
$$\begin{aligned} a_1 &= \frac{1}{2\sigma^2}(\lambda_1 + \lambda_2 X_1) \\ a_2 &= \frac{1}{2\sigma^2}(\lambda_1 + \lambda_2 X_2) \\ &\vdots \\ a_n &= \frac{1}{2\sigma^2}(\lambda_1 + \lambda_2 X_n). \end{aligned}$$

By summing up these equations we get

(7.20)
$$\sum_i a_i = \frac{1}{2\sigma^2}\left(\lambda_1 n + \lambda_2 \sum_i X_i\right).$$

Furthermore, multiplying the first equation of (7.19) by X_1, the second by X_2, the third by X_3, and so on, and then summing up over all n equations leads to

(7.21)
$$\sum_i a_i X_i = \frac{1}{2\sigma^2}\left[\lambda_1\left(\sum_i X_i\right) + \lambda_2\left(\sum_i X_i^2\right)\right].$$

Substituting for $\sum a_i$ and $\sum a_i X_i$ from (7.20) and (7.21) into the last two equations of (7.18b) then gives

$$-\frac{1}{2\sigma^2}\left(\lambda_1 n + \lambda_2 \sum_i X_i\right) = 0,$$

$$-\frac{1}{2\sigma^2}\left[\lambda_1\left(\sum_i X_i\right) + \lambda_2\left(\sum_i X_i^2\right)\right] = -1.$$

Thus we have obtained two equations in two unknowns, λ_1 and λ_2. The reader can easily verify that the solution is

$$\lambda_1 = \frac{-2\sigma^2 \sum X_i}{n(\sum X_i^2) - (\sum X_i)^2},$$

$$\lambda_2 = \frac{2n\sigma^2}{n(\sum X_i^2) - (\sum X_i)^2}.$$

These expressions for λ_1 and λ_2 can be substituted into (7.19) to obtain the solution for $a_1, a_2, \ldots, a_n$. This is

(7.22)
$$a_i = \frac{-(\sum X_i) + nX_i}{n(\sum X_i^2) - (\sum X_i)^2} \qquad (i = 1, 2, \ldots, n).$$

These are then the constants that make $\tilde{\beta}$ an unbiased estimator and minimize its variance.[6] Substituting for a_i into the formula for $\tilde{\beta}$ given by (7.16) leads to

[6] It can be shown that the second-order conditions for the existence of a minimum are also fulfilled. For an elaboration see, e.g., Yamane, *op. cit.*, pp. 345–348.

$$\tilde{\beta} = \sum_i \left[\frac{-(\sum X_i) + nX_i}{n(\sum X_i^2) - (\sum X_i)^2}\right] Y_i = \sum_i \left[\frac{-Y_i(\sum X_i) + nX_iY_i}{n(\sum X_i^2) - (\sum X_i)^2}\right]$$

$$= \frac{-(\sum Y_i)(\sum X_i) + n(\sum X_iY_i)}{n(\sum X_i^2) - (\sum X_i)^2}.$$

This is precisely the same result as that obtained for the least squares estimator of β. By (7.12) we have

$$\tilde{\beta} = \hat{\beta} = \frac{\sum x_i'y_i'}{\sum x_i'^2},$$

utilizing the abbreviated notation of (7.12a).

The application of the BLUE principle leads not only to the derivation of the formula for the estimator in question, but also to the determination of its variance. The formula for the variance of $\tilde{\beta}$ given by (7.17) is

$$\text{Var}(\tilde{\beta}) = \sigma^2 \sum a_i^2.$$

To eliminate the term $\sum a_i^2$ we use the result given in (7.22). Multiplying both sides of (7.22) by a_i and summing over all observations we get

$$\sum a_i^2 = \frac{-(\sum X_i)(\sum a_i) + n(\sum a_iX_i)}{n(\sum X_i^2) - (\sum X_i)^2}.$$

But from the last two equations in (7.18b) we know that

$$\sum a_i = 0 \quad \text{and} \quad \sum a_iX_i = 1.$$

This means that, in fact,

$$\sum a_i^2 = \frac{n}{n(\sum X_i^2) - (\sum X_i)^2},$$

so that

$$\text{(7.23)} \qquad \text{Var}(\tilde{\beta}) = \frac{n\sigma^2}{n(\sum X_i^2) - (\sum X_i)^2} = \frac{\sigma^2}{\sum x_i'^2},$$

after using the result of (7.14). This then is the variance of the BLUE (and, equivalently, of the LSE) of β.[7]

Having obtained the BLUE of β we are left with the task of finding the BLUE

[7] It should be noted that $\tilde{\beta}$ is not, in general, a linear estimator of β *with the minimum mean square error*. The formula for the linear combination of sample observations that gives the minimum MSE is

$$\left(\frac{\beta^2}{(\sigma^2/\sum x_i'^2) + \beta^2}\right)\hat{\beta}.$$

While this expression does not qualify as an estimator (since it involves unknown parameters), it shows that—for β and σ^2 different from zero—the value of the linear minimum MSE estimator of β is less than $\hat{\beta}$ by some unknown amount ($\hat{\beta} > 0$).

of α, the intercept of the regression line. The derivation of this estimator—to be called $\tilde{\alpha}$—proceeds in exactly the same steps as the derivation of $\tilde{\beta}$ and, therefore, will not be presented here. As in the case of $\tilde{\beta}$, the process of determining the BLUE of α leads not only to the formula for the estimator itself, but also to the formula for its variance. The results are as follows:

$$\tilde{\alpha} = \bar{Y} - \tilde{\beta}\bar{X}, \tag{7.24}$$

$$\mathrm{Var}(\tilde{\alpha}) = \frac{\sigma^2(\sum X_i^2)}{n(\sum x_i'^2)} = \frac{\sigma^2(\sum x_i'^2 + n\bar{X}^2)}{n(\sum x_i'^2)} = \sigma^2\left[\frac{1}{n} + \frac{\bar{X}^2}{\sum x_i'^2}\right]. \tag{7.25}$$

By noting that $\tilde{\beta}$ and $\hat{\beta}$ are the same, and by comparing (7.24) with (7.15), we can see that the BLUE of α is the same as the least squares estimator of α. The interpretation of the formula for its variance will be discussed in the next section.

Maximum Likelihood Estimation

The last method to be applied is the *maximum likelihood method.* As explained in Section 6–2, the maximum likelihood estimators (MLE's) of the parameters of a given population are considered to be those values of the parameters which would generate the observed sample most often. To find these estimators we have to determine the likelihood function for the observations in the sample and then maximize it with respect to the unknown parameters. In the case of our regression model, the sample consists of observations on the n variables Y_1, $Y_2, \ldots Y_n$. These variables are normally distributed with means $(\alpha + \beta X_1)$, $(\alpha + \beta X_2), \ldots, (\alpha + \beta X_n)$ and with a common variance equal to σ^2. Let us denote these observations by $y_1, y_2, \ldots, y_n$. Then the likelihood function is

$$\ell = f(y_1, y_2, \ldots, y_n).$$

We shall now establish that the observations are mutually independent (in the probability sense) so that their joint probability distribution can be expressed as a product of individual (marginal) distributions.

We may start by pointing out that if the disturbances of the regression model are normally distributed, nonautoregressive, and have zero mean, they must be independent. Thus our only problem is to show that the mutual independence of the disturbances implies mutual independence of the Y's. This can be established with the help of the following theorem.

Theorem 18 (*Change of Variable*). *If a random variable X has a probability density $f(x)$, and if a variable Z is a function of X such that there is a one-to-one correspondence between X and Z, then the probability density of Z is $f(z) = |dx/dz| f(x)$, $dx/dz \neq 0$.*

Here $|dx/dz|$ stands for the absolute value of the derivative of x with respect to z. The proof of this theorem can be found elsewhere.[8] Its importance lies in

[8] See, e.g., John E. Freund, *Mathematical Statistics* (Englewood Cliffs, N.J.: Prentice-Hall, 1962), pp. 132–133.

the fact that, under general conditions, it enables us to determine the distribution of one variable from the knowledge of the distribution of a related variable. In the context of our regression model the known distribution is that of ε_i, and the distribution to be determined is that of Y_i. Since we have

$$Y_i = \alpha + \beta X_i + \varepsilon_i,$$

there is obviously a one-to-one correspondence between Y_i and ε_i. Therefore, we can write

$$f(y_i) = \left|\frac{d\varepsilon_i}{dY_i}\right| f(\varepsilon_i).$$

But

$$\varepsilon_i = Y_i - \alpha - \beta X_i,$$

so that

$$\frac{d\varepsilon_i}{dY_i} = 1.$$

Consequently, we have

$$f(y_i) = f(\varepsilon_i).$$

Further, since the Y's are normal and uncorrelated, they are independent.

Armed with this result, we can present the likelihood function as

$$\ell = f(y_1)f(y_2)\ldots f(y_n).$$

Since the values of the parameters which maximize ℓ are the same as those which maximize its logarithm, we can operate with $L = \log \ell$ instead of operating with ℓ itself. Thus we wish to maximize

$$L = \sum_{i=1}^{n} \log f(y_i).$$

Now, since Y_i is normally distributed with mean $(\alpha + \beta X_i)$ and variance σ^2 we have, from the formula for normal distribution,

$$\log f(y_i) = -\frac{1}{2}\log(2\pi\sigma^2) - \frac{1}{2}\left[\frac{Y_i - \alpha - \beta X_i}{\sigma}\right]^2,$$

where $\pi = 3.14159\ldots$. (In writing out the formula, we use a capital letter for the values of the variables Y_i and X_i in order to conform to the notation customarily used in a simple regression model in other texts.) Therefore,

$$(7.26) \qquad L = -\frac{n}{2}\log(2\pi) - \frac{n}{2}\log\sigma^2 - \frac{1}{2\sigma^2}\sum_i (Y_i - \alpha - \beta X_i)^2.$$

There are three unknown parameters in L, namely, α, β, and σ^2. Differentiating with respect to each of them, we obtain

$$\frac{\partial L}{\partial \alpha} = -\frac{1}{2\sigma^2}\sum_i 2(Y_i - \alpha - \beta X_i)(-1),$$

$$\frac{\partial L}{\partial \beta} = -\frac{1}{2\sigma^2}\sum_i 2(Y_i - \alpha - \beta X_i)(-X_i),$$

$$\frac{\partial L}{\partial \sigma^2} = -\frac{n}{2\sigma^2} + \frac{1}{2\sigma^4}\sum_i (Y_i - \alpha - \beta X_i)^2.$$

Equating these to zero and putting a "triangle" on the parameters to be estimated leads to

$$\frac{1}{2\hat{\sigma}^2}\sum_i (Y_i - \hat{\alpha} - \hat{\beta}X_i) = 0,$$

$$\frac{1}{2\hat{\sigma}^2}\sum_i X_i(Y_i - \hat{\alpha} - \hat{\beta}X_i) = 0,$$

$$-\frac{n}{2\hat{\sigma}^2} + \frac{1}{2\hat{\sigma}^4}\sum (Y_i - \hat{\alpha} - \hat{\beta}X_i)^2 = 0.$$

A simple manipulation of the first two equations gives

$$\sum Y_i = \hat{\alpha}n + \hat{\beta}(\sum X_i),$$

$$\sum X_i Y_i = \hat{\alpha}(\sum X_i) + \hat{\beta}(\sum X_i^2).$$

These equations are precisely the same as the least squares normal equations given by (7.10) and (7.11) above. This means that *the maximum likelihood estimators of* α *and* β *are the same as the least squares estimators.* The third equation gives the maximum likelihood estimator of σ^2, which is

(7.27) $$\hat{\sigma}^2 = \frac{1}{n}\sum_i (Y_i - \hat{\alpha} - \hat{\beta}X_i)^2;$$

or, since $\hat{\alpha}$ and $\hat{\beta}$ are equal to the least squares estimators,

(7.27a) $$\hat{\sigma}^2 = \frac{1}{n}\sum_i e_i^2,$$

where, in accordance with the earlier notation, the terms e_i represent least squares residuals. Since $\sum e_i = 0$, it follows from (7.27a) that the MLE of the variance of the disturbances is equal to the sample variance of the least squares residuals.

Conclusion

In summary, we find then that each of the three estimation methods leads to the same estimates of the regression parameters. In other words, under the assumption of the classical normal linear regression model, the least squares estimators of the regression parameters are equivalent to the best linear unbiased and the maximum likelihood estimators. However, while the least squares method provided us only with the formulas for the estimators of α and β, the BLU estimation method supplied us also with the formulas for their variances, and the ML estimation method gave us a formula for an estimator of σ^2. Both of these subsidiary results are very useful.

Let us now consider the properties of the least squares estimators of α and β.

Beginning with the finite sample properties, we see immediately that the least squares estimators are *unbiased* because they are BLUE. We can also show that they are *efficient*. The Cramer-Rao lower bounds for unbiased estimators of α and β are given by the first two diagonal elements of the following matrix:

$$\begin{bmatrix} -E\left(\frac{\partial^2 L}{\partial \alpha^2}\right) & -E\left(\frac{\partial^2 L}{\partial \alpha \partial \beta}\right) & -E\left(\frac{\partial^2 L}{\partial \alpha \partial \sigma^2}\right) \\ -E\left(\frac{\partial^2 L}{\partial \beta \partial \alpha}\right) & -E\left(\frac{\partial^2 L}{\partial \beta^2}\right) & -E\left(\frac{\partial^2 L}{\partial \beta \partial \sigma^2}\right) \\ -E\left(\frac{\partial^2 L}{\partial \sigma^2 \partial \alpha}\right) & -E\left(\frac{\partial^2 L}{\partial \sigma^2 \partial \beta}\right) & -E\left(\frac{\partial^2 L}{\partial (\sigma^2)^2}\right) \end{bmatrix}^{-1} = \begin{bmatrix} \frac{n}{\sigma^2} & \frac{\sum X_i}{\sigma^2} & 0 \\ \frac{\sum X_i}{\sigma^2} & \frac{\sum X_i^2}{\sigma^2} & 0 \\ 0 & 0 & \frac{n}{2\sigma^4} \end{bmatrix}^{-1}$$

$$= \begin{bmatrix} \frac{\sigma^2 \sum X_i^2}{n(\sum x_i'^2)} & \frac{-\bar{X}\sigma^2}{\sum x_i'^2} & 0 \\ \frac{-\bar{X}\sigma^2}{\sum x_i'^2} & \frac{\sigma^2}{\sum x_i'^2} & 0 \\ 0 & 0 & \frac{2\sigma^4}{n} \end{bmatrix}$$

Comparison of the first two diagonal elements with the formulas (7.25) and (7.23) of the text shows that these elements are, indeed, equal to the variances of the regression parameters.

Finally, the least squares estimators have all the desirable asymptotic properties since they are the same as the maximum likelihood estimators, and the latter are known to be *asymptotically unbiased*, *consistent*, and *asymptotically efficient*. Therefore, the least squares estimators of the regression parameters of the classical normal linear regression model have all the desirable finite sample *and* asymptotic properties. In Section 7–4 we shall be concerned with other features of these estimators and discuss further questions of statistical inference in the context of our regression model.

7–4 Further Results of Statistical Inference

In Section 7–3 we derived the least squares estimators of the regression parameters and established their desirable properties. We shall now consider other features of these estimators, and show how the regression model can be used for testing hypotheses about the regression parameters and for prediction.

Distribution of $\hat{\alpha}$ and $\hat{\beta}$

The distribution of the least squares estimators $\hat{\alpha}$ and $\hat{\beta}$ is easy to deduce from the results so far obtained. First, since these estimators are unbiased, their means are equal to the true values of α and β, respectively. Second, from the derivation of the BLUE properties we know what their variances are. Finally, since both $\hat{\alpha}$ and $\hat{\beta}$ are linear combinations of independent normal variables $Y_1, Y_2, \ldots, Y_n$, they must themselves be normally distributed (see Theorem 12). That is, we can write

(7.28)
$$\hat{\alpha} \sim N\left[\alpha, \sigma^2\left(\frac{1}{n} + \frac{\bar{X}^2}{\sum x_i'^2}\right)\right]$$
$$\hat{\beta} \sim N\left[\beta, \frac{\sigma^2}{\sum x_i'^2}\right],$$

using the variance formulas (7.23) and (7.25).

Let us now consider the variances of $\hat{\alpha}$ and $\hat{\beta}$ in greater detail. By examining the formulas we can observe the following:

1. The larger the variance of the disturbance (σ^2), the larger the variances of $\hat{\alpha}$ and $\hat{\beta}$.
2. The more dispersed the values of the explanatory variable X, the smaller the variances of $\hat{\alpha}$ and $\hat{\beta}$.
3. If all the values of X were the same, i.e., if $X_1 = X_2 = \cdots = X_n$, both variances would be infinitely large.
4. The variance of $\hat{\alpha}$ is smallest when $\bar{X} = 0$ $(\sum x_i'^2 \neq 0)$.

The first point is obvious; it means that the greater the dispersion of the disturbance around the population regression line, the greater the dispersion of our "guesses" concerning the value of the regression parameters. If all disturbances were completely concentrated at their means—that is, if all disturbances were equal to zero—our "guesses" as to the values of the regression parameters would always be perfect (as long as we observed at least two different values of the dependent variable, of course). The second point is based on the fact that the larger the dispersion of the X's, the larger $\sum x_i'^2$. In fact, if we have an absolutely free choice of selecting a given number of values of X within some interval—say, from a to b $(0 < a < b)$—then *the optimal choice would be to choose one half of the X's equal to* a *and the other half equal to* b. Such a choice would maximize $\sum x_i'^2$. The third point follows from the fact that if all values of the explanatory variable were the same, the value of $\sum x_i'^2$ would be zero, and any finite number divided by zero is equal to infinity. Another way of making the same point is to state that if all observed values of Y were to lie along a vertical line (as they would do if they all corresponded to the same value of X), we could not make any inference about either the slope or the intercept of the regression line. The final point is somewhat less important in practice since it refers only to the variance of $\hat{\alpha}$. If the range of X includes negative as well as positive values, $\text{Var}(\hat{\alpha})$ would be smallest if the values of X were selected so as to make $\bar{X}$ equal to zero. In this case $\text{Var}(\hat{\alpha})$ would be equal to σ^2/n, which is its lowest attainable value.

EXAMPLE To illustrate the gain in efficiency that can be achieved by a judicious choice of the values of the explanatory variable, we use the example given in Section 7.3, which involved estimating the demand for oranges. The values of X (=price of oranges) were given as follows: 100, 90, 80, 70, 70, 70, 70, 65, 60, 60, 55, and 50. For these twelve values we found that $\bar{X} = 70$ and $\sum x_i'^2 = 2250$. The variances of the least squares estimators in this case are

$$\text{Var}(\hat{\alpha}) = \sigma^2\left[\frac{1}{n} + \frac{\bar{X}^2}{\sum x_i'^2}\right] = \sigma^2\left[\frac{1}{12} + \frac{70^2}{2250}\right] = 2.261111\sigma^2.$$

$$\text{Var}(\hat{\beta}) = \frac{\sigma^2}{\sum x_i'^2} = \frac{\sigma^2}{2250} = 0.000444\sigma^2.$$

Suppose now that instead of the above values we had $X_1 = X_2 = \cdots = X_6 = 100$ and $X_6 = X_7 = \cdots = X_{12} = 50$. Then we would have $\bar{X} = 75$ and $\sum x_i'^2 = 7500$. The resulting variances would then be

$$\text{Var}(\hat{\alpha}) = \sigma^2\left[\frac{1}{12} + \frac{75^2}{7500}\right] = 0.833333\sigma^2.$$

$$\text{Var}(\hat{\beta}) = \frac{\sigma^2}{7500} = 0.000133\sigma^2.$$

Comparing the variances for these two cases we get

$$\frac{\text{Var}(\hat{\alpha})_{\text{case I}}}{\text{Var}(\hat{\alpha})_{\text{case II}}} = \frac{2.261111\sigma^2}{0.833333\sigma^2} = 2.713.$$

$$\frac{\text{Var}(\hat{\beta})_{\text{case I}}}{\text{Var}(\hat{\beta})_{\text{case II}}} = \frac{0.000444\sigma^2}{0.000133\sigma^2} = 3.338.$$

That is, the variance of $\hat{\alpha}$ in the first case is more than $2\frac{1}{2}$ times, and that of $\hat{\beta}$ $3\frac{1}{3}$ times, as large as the corresponding variance in the second case.

It is clear that the gain in efficiency resulting from an optimal choice of the values of X can be quite considerable. In practice the difficulty is, of course, that the econometrician usually has no choice in the matter because the sampling has been done by somebody else and the econometrician gets only the completed sample results.[9]

Covariance of $\hat{\alpha}$ and $\hat{\beta}$

A question that is of some interest concerns the relationship between $\hat{\alpha}$ and $\hat{\beta}$. By using $\hat{\alpha}$ instead of α and $\hat{\beta}$ instead of β, we are committing sampling errors, and it is of some relevance to know whether these two sampling errors can be expected to be of the same sign or not. That is, we wish to find the sign of

$$E(\hat{\alpha} - \alpha)(\hat{\beta} - \beta),$$

which is, by definition, the covariance of $\hat{\alpha}$ and $\hat{\beta}$. Now, by (7.15) we have

$$\hat{\alpha} = \bar{Y} - \hat{\beta}\bar{X}.$$

[9] It is to be noted, though, that the optimality of the sampling design which "piles up" the values of X at each end of the range is crucially dependent on the linearity of the model. Such a sampling design would be poor for models in which linearity were not to be assumed but to be tested for.

The regression model is, as stated earlier,

$$Y_i = \alpha + \beta X_i + \varepsilon_i.$$

Adding all sample observations and dividing by n we get

$$\bar{Y} = \alpha + \beta\bar{X} + \bar{\varepsilon} \quad \text{or} \quad \alpha = \bar{Y} - \beta\bar{X} - \bar{\varepsilon}, \tag{7.29}$$

so that

$$\hat{\alpha} - \alpha = (\bar{Y} - \hat{\beta}\bar{X}) - (\bar{Y} - \beta\bar{X} - \bar{\varepsilon}) = -(\hat{\beta} - \beta)\bar{X} + \bar{\varepsilon}. \tag{7.30}$$

Further, by (7.12a) we have

$$\hat{\beta} = \frac{\sum x_i'y_i'}{\sum x_i'^2};$$

but by deducting (7.29) from (7.1), we get

$$(Y_i - \bar{Y}) = \beta(X_i - \bar{X}) + (\varepsilon_i - \bar{\varepsilon}), \tag{7.31}$$

or, using the abbreviated notation for deviations from sample means,

$$y_i' = \beta x_i' + \varepsilon_i'. \tag{7.31a}$$

Substituting this into the formula for $\hat{\beta}$ gives

$$\hat{\beta} = \frac{\sum x_i'(\beta x_i' + \varepsilon_i')}{\sum x_i'^2} = \beta + \frac{\sum x_i'\varepsilon_i'}{\sum x_i'^2},$$

so that

$$\hat{\beta} - \beta = \frac{\sum x_i'\varepsilon_i'}{\sum x_i'^2} = \frac{\sum x_i'(\varepsilon_i - \bar{\varepsilon})}{\sum x_i'^2} \tag{7.32}$$

$$= \frac{\sum x_i'\varepsilon_i - \bar{\varepsilon}\sum x_i'}{\sum x_i'^2} = \frac{\sum x_i'\varepsilon_i}{\sum x_i'^2},$$

which is the sampling error of $\hat{\beta}$. Thus, combining (7.30) and (7.32), we obtain

$$E(\hat{\alpha} - \alpha)(\hat{\beta} - \beta) = E[-(\hat{\beta} - \beta)\bar{X} + \bar{\varepsilon}](\hat{\beta} - \beta)$$

$$= -\bar{X}E(\hat{\beta} - \beta)^2 + E\bar{\varepsilon}\left[\frac{\sum x_i'\varepsilon_i}{\sum x_i'^2}\right].$$

Let us consider the last term:

$$E\bar{\varepsilon}\left[\frac{\sum x_i'\varepsilon_i}{\sum x_i'^2}\right] = E\left[\frac{\sum x_i'\varepsilon_i\bar{\varepsilon}}{\sum x_i'^2}\right] = \frac{\sum x_i'E\varepsilon_i(1/n)(\varepsilon_1 + \varepsilon_2 + \cdots + \varepsilon_i + \cdots + \varepsilon_n)}{\sum x_i'^2}$$

$$= \frac{(1/n)\sum x_i'(E\varepsilon_i\varepsilon_1 + E\varepsilon_i\varepsilon_2 + \cdots + E\varepsilon_i^2 + \cdots + E\varepsilon_i\varepsilon_n)}{\sum x_i'^2}$$

$$= \frac{(1/n)\sum x_i'(0 + 0 + \cdots + \sigma^2 + \cdots + 0)}{\sum x_i'^2} = \frac{(1/n)\sigma^2\sum x_i'}{\sum x_i'^2} = 0$$

because $\sum x_i' = 0$. Therefore,

$$(7.33)\quad E(\hat{\alpha} - \alpha)(\hat{\beta} - \beta) = -\bar{X}E(\hat{\beta} - \beta)^2 = -\bar{X}\text{Var}(\hat{\beta}) = -\bar{X}\left[\frac{\sigma^2}{\sum x_i'^2}\right],$$

by (7.23). This, then, is the covariance of $\hat{\alpha}$ and $\hat{\beta}$. From this result we can see that, *as long as $\bar{X}$ is positive*, the sampling errors of $\hat{\alpha}$ and $\hat{\beta}$ can be expected to be of opposite sign. In this case an overstatement of the true value of α can be expected to be associated with an understatement of the true value of β, and vice versa.

Method of Semi-averages

As a matter of interest we may compare the sample regression line fitted by the method of least squares with that fitted by some other method. One such method which has been used in practical applications is the so-called *method of semi-averages*. This method calls for arranging the observations so that the values of X proceed in order of magnitude, dividing them into two equal (or approximately equal) parts, and calculating the average values of X and Y for each part separately. This gives us two points, one for each part. The estimated regression line is the line passing through these two points. For simplicity, we assume that the number of observations is even. Let $\bar{X}_A$ and $\bar{Y}_A$ be the sample means of the first $n/2$ values of X and Y, and $\bar{X}_B$ and $\bar{Y}_B$ the sample means of the last $n/2$ values of X and Y. Further, let a and b be the "semi-average" estimators of α and β, respectively. Then a and b can be calculated from

$$\bar{Y}_A = a + b\bar{X}_A$$
$$\bar{Y}_B = a + b\bar{X}_B,$$

since the estimated regression line is required to pass through the points $(\bar{X}_A, \bar{Y}_A)$ and $(\bar{X}_B, \bar{Y}_B)$. The solution is

$$b = \frac{\bar{Y}_A - \bar{Y}_B}{\bar{X}_A - \bar{X}_B} \quad \text{and} \quad a = \bar{Y}_A - b\bar{X}_A.$$

Let us find the mean and the variance of b. Since

$$Y_i = \alpha + \beta X_i + \varepsilon_i,$$

we have

$$\bar{Y}_A = \alpha + \beta\bar{X}_A + \bar{\varepsilon}_A,$$
$$\bar{Y}_B = \alpha + \beta\bar{X}_B + \bar{\varepsilon}_B,$$

where $\bar{\varepsilon}_A$ and $\bar{\varepsilon}_B$ are the (unobserved) sample means of the regression disturbance for the first and the second half of the observations, respectively. Therefore,

$$\bar{Y}_A - \bar{Y}_B = \beta(\bar{X}_A - \bar{X}_B) + (\bar{\varepsilon}_A - \bar{\varepsilon}_B).$$

Then, we get

$$E(b) = E\left[\frac{\bar{Y}_A - \bar{Y}_B}{\bar{X}_A - \bar{X}_B}\right] = \frac{E[\beta(\bar{X}_A - \bar{X}_B) + (\bar{\varepsilon}_A - \bar{\varepsilon}_B)]}{\bar{X}_A - \bar{X}_B} = \frac{\beta(\bar{X}_A - \bar{X}_B)}{\bar{X}_A - \bar{X}_B} = \beta,$$

so that b is an unbiased estimator of β. Further,

$$\mathrm{Var}(b) = E\left[\frac{\bar{Y}_A - \bar{Y}_B}{\bar{X}_A - \bar{X}_B} - E\left(\frac{\bar{Y}_A - \bar{Y}_B}{\bar{X}_A - \bar{Y}_B}\right)\right]^2 = E\left[\frac{\beta(\bar{X}_A - \bar{X}_B) + (\bar{\varepsilon}_A - \bar{\varepsilon}_B)}{\bar{X}_A - \bar{X}_B} - \beta\right]^2$$

$$= E\left[\frac{\bar{\varepsilon}_A - \bar{\varepsilon}_B}{\bar{X}_A - \bar{X}_B}\right]^2 = \frac{E(\bar{\varepsilon}_A)^2 + E(\bar{\varepsilon}_B)^2 - 2E(\bar{\varepsilon}_A\bar{\varepsilon}_B)}{(\bar{X}_A - \bar{X}_B)^2}.$$

But by the basic assumptions about ε_i we have

$$E(\bar{\varepsilon}_A)^2 = E\left[\frac{1}{n/2}(\varepsilon_1 + \varepsilon_2 + \cdots + \varepsilon_{n/2})\right]^2$$

$$= \left[\frac{1}{n/2}\right]^2\left[E(\varepsilon_1^2) + E(\varepsilon_2^2) + \cdots + E(\varepsilon_{n/2}^2)\right]$$

$$= \left[\frac{1}{n/2}\right]^2(\sigma^2 + \sigma^2 + \cdots + \sigma^2) = \left[\frac{1}{n/2}\right]^2(n/2)\sigma^2 = \frac{\sigma^2}{n/2},$$

and, similarly,

$$E(\bar{\varepsilon}_B)^2 = \frac{\sigma^2}{n/2}.$$

Finally,

$$E(\bar{\varepsilon}_A\bar{\varepsilon}_B) = E\left[\frac{1}{n/2}(\varepsilon_1 + \varepsilon_2 + \cdots + \varepsilon_{n/2})\right]\left[\frac{1}{n/2}(\varepsilon_{n/2+1} + \varepsilon_{n/2+2} + \cdots + \varepsilon_n)\right] = 0,$$

by the assumption of nonautoregression. Therefore, we get

$$\mathrm{Var}(b) = \frac{\sigma^2/(n/2) + \sigma^2/(n/2)}{(\bar{X}_A - \bar{X}_B)^2} = \frac{4\sigma^2}{n(\bar{X}_A - \bar{X}_B)^2}.$$

We have, of course,

$$\mathrm{Var}(b) \geq \mathrm{Var}(\hat{\beta}),$$

where $\hat{\beta}$ is the least squares estimator of β.

EXAMPLE We shall demonstrate the advantage of the least squares method over the method of semi-averages by using the example of the demand for oranges. There are 12 observations which can be divided into two groups with 6 observations in each. The results are

$$\bar{X}_A = 60 \qquad \bar{Y}_A = 115$$

$$\bar{X}_B = 80 \qquad \bar{Y}_B = 85$$

This gives

$$b = \frac{115 - 85}{60 - 80} = -1.5$$

$$a = 115 - (-1.5) \times 60 = 205.$$

The regression line estimated by the method of semi-averages then is

$$\hat{\hat{Y}}_i = 205 - 1.5X_i.$$

The variance of b is

$$\text{Var}(b) = \frac{4\sigma^2}{12(60 - 80)^2} = \frac{\sigma^2}{1200}.$$

Comparing $\text{Var}(b)$ with $\text{Var}(\hat{\beta})$ we get

$$\frac{\text{Var}(b)}{\text{Var}(\hat{\beta})} = \frac{\sigma^2/1200}{\sigma^2/2250} = 1.875.$$

Thus we see that the method of semi-averages leads to an estimate of the regression slope with variance 87.5% larger than the variance of the corresponding least squares estimate. In other words, if our "guesses" about the slope of the population regression line in the present instance were formed by using the method of semi-averages, they would be considerably more dispersed about the true value than the "guesses" based on the least squares formula.

Estimation of Var($\hat{\alpha}$) and Var($\hat{\beta}$)

Under the assumptions of the classical normal linear regression model, the least squares estimators of α and β have all the desirable properties of an estimator. But whether or not they are really useful depends on the size of their variances. If their variances were to be very large, the fact that no other unbiased estimator can have a smaller variance is of little consolation. With large variances our guesses about the true values of the parameters are likely to be far off the mark. In Section 7–3 we developed formulas for the variances of $\hat{\alpha}$ and $\hat{\beta}$, but these formulas involve an unknown parameter σ^2 so that their evaluation is impossible. However, σ^2 can be estimated; in fact, we have already derived an estimation formula for it in connection with the maximum likelihood estimators in Section 7–3 above. The estimator of σ^2 was a "by-product" of getting the maximum likelihood estimators of α and β. The formula, given by (7.27), is

$$\hat{\sigma}^2 = \frac{1}{n}\sum_i (Y_i - \hat{\alpha} - \hat{\beta}X_i)^2.$$

Since this is a maximum likelihood estimator of σ^2, it has all the desirable asymptotic properties, but its small sample properties remain to be established. In particular, we may want to check whether $\hat{\sigma}^2$ is or is not an unbiased estimator of σ^2. To do this we rewrite the expression for $\hat{\sigma}^2$ in a somewhat different form. First, substituting for Y_i gives

$$\hat{\sigma}^2 = \frac{1}{n}\sum (\alpha + \beta X_i + \varepsilon_i - \hat{\alpha} - \hat{\beta}X_i)^2 = \frac{1}{n}\sum [-(\hat{\alpha} - \alpha) - (\hat{\beta} - \beta)X_i + \varepsilon_i]^2.$$

Next, substituting for $(\hat{\alpha} - \alpha)$ from (7.30) we get

$$\hat{\sigma}^2 = \frac{1}{n} \sum [(\hat{\beta} - \beta)\bar{X} - \bar{\varepsilon} - (\hat{\beta} - \beta)X_i + \varepsilon_i]^2$$

$$= \frac{1}{n} \sum [-(\hat{\beta} - \beta)x_i' + \varepsilon_i']^2$$

$$= \frac{1}{n} \sum [(\hat{\beta} - \beta)^2 x_i'^2 + \varepsilon_i'^2 - 2(\hat{\beta} - \beta)\, \varepsilon_i' x_i']$$

$$= \frac{1}{n} (\hat{\beta} - \beta)^2 \sum x_i'^2 + \frac{1}{n} \sum \varepsilon_i'^2 - \frac{2}{n} (\hat{\beta} - \beta) \sum \varepsilon_i' x_i'.$$

But from (7.32) we have

$$\sum x_i' \varepsilon_i' = (\hat{\beta} - \beta) \sum x_i'^2,$$

so that we can write

$$\hat{\sigma}^2 = -\frac{1}{n} (\hat{\beta} - \beta)^2 \sum x_i'^2 + \frac{1}{n} \sum \varepsilon_i'^2.$$

Taking mathematical expectation onboth sides, we obtain

$$E(\hat{\sigma}^2) = -\frac{1}{n} \sum x_i'^2 E(\hat{\beta} - \beta)^2 + \frac{1}{n} \sum E(\varepsilon_i'^2).$$

Now $$E(\hat{\beta} - \beta)^2 = \text{Var}(\hat{\beta}) = \frac{\sigma^2}{\sum x_i'^2},$$

and

$$E(\varepsilon_i'^2) = E(\varepsilon_i - \bar{\varepsilon})^2 = E(\varepsilon_i^2) + E(\bar{\varepsilon}^2) - 2E(\varepsilon_i \bar{\varepsilon})$$

$$= \sigma^2 + \frac{\sigma^2}{n} - 2E\varepsilon_i(\varepsilon_1 + \varepsilon_2 + \cdots + \varepsilon_i + \cdots + \varepsilon_n)/n$$

$$= \sigma^2 + \frac{\sigma^2}{n} - 2[E(\varepsilon_i\varepsilon_1) + E(\varepsilon_i\varepsilon_2) + \cdots + E(\varepsilon_i^2) + \cdots + E(\varepsilon_i\varepsilon_n)]/n$$

$$= \sigma^2 + \frac{\sigma^2}{n} - 2(0 + 0 + \cdots + \sigma^2 + \cdots + 0)/n$$

$$= \sigma^2 + \frac{\sigma^2}{n} - \frac{2\sigma^2}{n} = \left[\frac{n-1}{n}\right]\sigma^2.$$

We use these results to get

$$E(\hat{\sigma}^2) = -\frac{1}{n}\left(\sum x_i'^2\right)\left[\frac{\sigma^2}{\sum x_i'^2}\right] + \frac{1}{n}\sum\left[\frac{n-1}{n}\right]\sigma^2 \tag{7.34}$$

$$= -\frac{\sigma^2}{n} + \left[\frac{n-1}{n}\right]\sigma^2 = \left[\frac{n-2}{n}\right]\sigma^2.$$

That is, $\hat{\hat{\sigma}}^2$ is a *biased* estimator of σ^2. However, given the result in (7.34) it is easy to devise an unbiased estimator of σ^2. Multiplying both sides of (7.34) by $n/(n-2)$ gives

$$\left[\frac{n}{n-2}\right]E(\hat{\hat{\sigma}}^2) = \sigma^2,$$

or

$$E\left[\frac{n}{n-2}\right]\frac{1}{n}\sum(Y_i - \hat{\alpha} - \hat{\beta}X_i)^2 = \sigma^2,$$

which reduces to

$$E\left[\frac{1}{n-2}\right]\sum(Y_i - \hat{\alpha} - \hat{\beta}X_i)^2 = \sigma^2.$$

Thus an unbiased estimator of σ^2, say, s^2, is given by

$$s^2 = \frac{1}{n-2}\sum(Y_i - \hat{\alpha} - \hat{\beta}X_i)^2 = \frac{1}{n-2}\sum e_i^2. \tag{7.35}$$

Since asymptotically there is no difference between $1/(n-2)$ and $1/n$, s^2 is asymptotically equal to $\hat{\hat{\sigma}}^2$ and, therefore, has the same optimal asymptotic properties.

For the purpose of computing the value of s^2, the formula (7.35) can be simplified so that we avoid the need for calculating individual e_i's, the deviations of the observed values from the sample regression line. By substituting for $\hat{\alpha}$ we obtain

$$s^2 = \frac{1}{n-2}\sum[Y_i - (\bar{Y} - \hat{\beta}\bar{X}) - \hat{\beta}X_i]^2 = \frac{1}{n-2}\sum(y_i' - \hat{\beta}x_i')^2$$

$$= \frac{1}{n-2}\left[\sum y_i'^2 + \hat{\beta}^2\sum x_i'^2 - 2\hat{\beta}\sum x_i'y_i'\right];$$

but from (7.12a) we have

$$\hat{\beta}\sum x_i'^2 = \sum x_i'y_i',$$

so that

$$\hat{\beta}^2\sum x_i'^2 = \hat{\beta}\sum x_i'y_i'.$$

Using this result leads to

$$s^2 = \frac{1}{n-2}\left[\sum y_i'^2 - \hat{\beta}\sum x_i'y_i'\right], \tag{7.36}$$

which is much easier to compute than the result given by (7.35).

By using s^2 as the estimator of σ^2, we can obtain estimators of $\text{Var}(\hat{\alpha})$ and $\text{Var}(\hat{\beta})$; these estimators will be unbiased and will have optimal asymptotic properties. Following the customary notation, we denote the estimator of $\text{Var}(\hat{\alpha})$ by $s_{\hat{\alpha}}^2$ and the estimator of $\text{Var}(\hat{\beta})$ by $s_{\hat{\beta}}^2$. The appropriate formulas are

$$s_{\hat{\alpha}}^2 = s^2\left[\frac{1}{n} + \frac{\bar{X}^2}{\sum x_i'^2}\right]$$

(7.37)

$$s_{\hat{\beta}}^2 = \frac{s^2}{\sum x_i'^2}.$$

The square roots of these estimators, $s_{\hat{\alpha}}$ and $s_{\hat{\beta}}$, represent the estimated standard errors of $\hat{\alpha}$ and $\hat{\beta}$. They are used extensively as measures of precision of $\hat{\alpha}$ and $\hat{\beta}$. (In referring to $s_{\hat{\alpha}}$ and $s_{\hat{\beta}}$ research workers frequently use the term "standard errors" instead of "estimated standard errors." Since the true standard errors are hardly ever known, the omission of the word "estimated" usually creates no confusion.)

Confidence Intervals for α. and β.

A more formal indication of the precision of $\hat{\alpha}$ and $\hat{\beta}$ can be achieved by constructing the confidence intervals for α and β. Let us begin with β. Since

$$\hat{\beta} \sim N(\beta, \sigma_{\hat{\beta}}^2),$$

where $\sigma_{\hat{\beta}}^2 = \text{Var}(\hat{\beta})$, it follows that

$$\frac{\hat{\beta} - \beta}{\sigma_{\hat{\beta}}} \sim N(0, 1).$$

Furthermore, we know from (5.8b) that

$$\frac{\sum (Y_i - \hat{\alpha} - \hat{\beta}x_i)^2}{\sigma^2} \sim \chi_{n-2}^2.$$

In this case the number of the degrees of freedom of the chi-square distribution is $(n - 2)$, since two degrees of freedom got "used up" for calculating $\hat{\alpha}$ and $\hat{\beta}$. Note that we can write

$$\frac{\sum (Y_i - \hat{\alpha} - \hat{\beta}X_i)^2}{\sigma^2} = \frac{(n-2)s^2}{\sigma^2} = \frac{(n-2)s^2/(\sum x_i'^2)}{\sigma^2/(\sum x_i'^2)} = \frac{(n-2)s_{\hat{\beta}}^2}{\sigma_{\hat{\beta}}^2}.$$

Thus we have

$$\frac{(n-2)s_{\hat{\beta}}^2}{\sigma_{\hat{\beta}}^2} \sim \chi_{n-2}^2.$$

Therefore,

$$\frac{(\hat{\beta} - \beta)/\sigma_{\hat{\beta}}}{\sqrt{(n-2)s_{\hat{\beta}}^2/(n-2)\sigma_{\hat{\beta}}^2}} = \frac{\hat{\beta} - \beta}{s_{\hat{\beta}}}$$

is a ratio in which the numerator is a standard normal variable and the denominator an independent $[\chi^2_{n-2}/(n-2)]^{1/2}$ variable. As explained in Section 5–2, such a ratio has a t distribution with $(n-2)$ degrees of freedom. That is,

$$\frac{\hat{\beta}-\beta}{s_{\hat{\beta}}} \sim t_{n-2}. \tag{7.38}$$

By a similar deduction we also get

$$\frac{\hat{\alpha}-\alpha}{s_{\hat{\alpha}}} \sim t_{n-2}. \tag{7.39}$$

These results enable us to make the following probability statements:

$$P\left[-t_{n-2,\lambda/2} \leq \frac{\hat{\alpha}-\alpha}{s_{\hat{\alpha}}} \leq +t_{n-2,\lambda/2}\right] = 1-\lambda,$$

$$P\left[-t_{n-2,\lambda/2} \leq \frac{\hat{\beta}-\beta}{s_{\hat{\beta}}} \leq +t_{n-2,\lambda/2}\right] = 1-\lambda,$$

where $t_{n-2,\lambda/2}$ stands for the value of the t statistic with $(n-2)$ degrees of freedom, which cuts off $\lambda/2$ of the area of the t distribution at each tail end. This value can be looked up in the t table for whatever λ we desire. The term $(1-\lambda)$ represents the area of the distribution between the points $-t_{n-2,\lambda/2}$ and $+t_{n-2,\lambda/2}$. From these probability statements we can construct the confidence intervals for α and β as

$$\begin{aligned} \hat{\alpha} - t_{n-2,\lambda/2}s_{\hat{\alpha}} &\leq \alpha \leq \hat{\alpha} + t_{n-2,\lambda/2}s_{\hat{\alpha}} \\ \hat{\beta} - t_{n-2,\lambda/2}s_{\hat{\beta}} &\leq \beta \leq \hat{\beta} + t_{n-2,\lambda/2}s_{\hat{\beta}}. \end{aligned} \tag{7.40}$$

The probability that the specified confidence interval covers the true value of the regression parameter is $(1-\lambda)$. This is referred to as the "level of confidence." As mentioned in Section 6–3, the most commonly used levels are 95% and 99%.

EXAMPLE As a numerical example, let us construct the 95% confidence intervals for α and β for the function describing the demand for oranges from the data given in Section 7–3. To do that we have to calculate the estimates of the standard errors of $\hat{\alpha}$ and $\hat{\beta}$ using the formulas (7.36) and (7.37). From the data given for this example, we already calculated

$$\begin{aligned} \bar{X} &= 70, \\ \bar{Y} &= 100, \\ \sum x_i' y_i' &= -3550, \\ \sum x_i'^2 &= 2250, \end{aligned}$$

which led to

$$\begin{aligned} \hat{\alpha} &= 210.460, \\ \hat{\beta} &= -1.578. \end{aligned}$$

In addition we have

$$\sum y_i'^2 = 6300.$$

Substituting into (7.36) gives

$$s^2 = \frac{1}{12 - 2}[6300 - (-1.578)(-3550)] = 69.8.$$

Further substitution into (7.37) leads to

$$s_{\hat{\alpha}}^2 = 69.8\left[\frac{1}{12} + \frac{70^2}{2250}\right] = 157.825555$$

and

$$s_{\hat{\beta}}^2 = \frac{69.8}{2250} = 0.031022.$$

The resulting estimates of the standard errors of $\hat{\alpha}$ and $\hat{\beta}$ are

$$s_{\hat{\alpha}} = 12.563,$$

$$s_{\hat{\beta}} = 0.176.$$

The last piece of information needed for the construction of the confidence intervals is the appropriate t value. Since we had 12 observations, we have 10 degrees of freedom. Furthermore, since the desired level of confidence is 95%, we want to find the value of t that cuts off 0.025 of the area at the tail end of the distribution. Thus we look up the row labeled "10" and the column labeled "0.025" in the t table. The corresponding entry is 2.228. Therefore, the 95% confidence intervals for α and β are

$$210.460 - 2.228 \times 12.563 \leq \alpha \leq 210.460 + 2.228 \times 12.563$$

$$182.470 \leq \alpha \leq 238.450,$$

and

$$-1.578 - 2.228 \times 0.176 \leq \beta \leq -1.578 + 2.228 \times 0.176$$

$$-1.970 \leq \beta \leq -1.186.$$

Confidence Interval for $E(Y_i)$

We may extend the use of confidence intervals and consider the precision of the entire sample regression line as a representation of the population regression line. The population regression line is given by $E(Y_i) = \alpha + \beta X_i$ and is defined for *any* value of X_i within some range. Its estimator is the sample regression line $\hat{Y}_i = \hat{\alpha} + \hat{\beta}X_i$. Since $E(\hat{Y}_i) = \alpha + \beta X_i$, $\hat{Y}_i$ is an unbiased estimator of $E(Y_i)$. Other desirable properties of $\hat{Y}_i$ as an estimator of $E(Y_i)$ can also be established; heuristically, we may argue that since $\hat{\alpha}$ and $\hat{\beta}$ are the best estimators of α and β we can devise, $(\hat{\alpha} + \hat{\beta}X_i)$ is the best estimator of $(\alpha + \beta X_i)$. To determine the confidence interval for any given point on the population regression line $E(Y_i)$, we have to find the variance of its estimator $\hat{Y}_i$. Let us call this variance $\sigma^2_{\hat{Y}_i}$. It can be determined as follows:

$$\begin{aligned}\sigma^2_{\hat{Y}_i} &= E[\hat{Y}_i - E(\hat{Y}_i)]^2 = E[(\hat{\alpha} + \hat{\beta}X_i) - (\alpha + \beta X_i)]^2\\ &= E[(\hat{\alpha} - \alpha) + (\hat{\beta} - \beta)X_i]^2\\ &= E(\hat{\alpha} - \alpha)^2 + E(\hat{\beta} - \beta)^2 X_i^2 + 2E(\hat{\alpha} - \alpha)(\hat{\beta} - \beta)X_i\\ &= \text{Var}(\hat{\alpha}) + X_i^2\text{Var}(\hat{\beta}) + 2X_i\text{Cov}(\hat{\alpha},\hat{\beta})\\ &= \sigma^2\left[\frac{1}{n} + \frac{\bar{X}^2}{\sum x_i'^2}\right] + X_i^2\left[\frac{\sigma^2}{\sum x_i'^2}\right] - 2X_i\bar{X}\left[\frac{\sigma^2}{\sum x_i'^2}\right].\end{aligned}$$

The last result has been obtained by substitution from (7.23), (7.25), and (7.33). Further manipulation gives

$$\text{(7.41)}\qquad \begin{aligned}\sigma^2_{\hat{Y}_i} &= \frac{\sigma^2}{\sum x_i'^2}\left[\frac{\sum x_i'^2}{n} + \bar{X}^2 + X_i^2 - 2X_i\bar{X}\right]\\ &= \frac{\sigma^2}{\sum x_i'^2}\left[\frac{\sum x_i'^2}{n} + (X_i - \bar{X})^2\right] = \sigma^2\left[\frac{1}{n} + \frac{(X_i - \bar{X})^2}{\sum x_i'^2}\right].\end{aligned}$$

Having determined the mean and the variance of $\hat{Y}_i$, we should consider its distribution. This turns out to be quite simple: since $(\hat{\alpha} + \hat{\beta}X_i)$ is a linear combination of normally and independently distributed random variables $\varepsilon_1, \varepsilon_2, \ldots, \varepsilon_n$, it will also be normally distributed. Thus we have

$$\hat{Y}_i \sim N\left[\alpha + \beta X_i,\ \sigma^2\left(\frac{1}{n} + \frac{(X_i - \bar{X})^2}{\sum x_i'^2}\right)\right];$$

and, therefore,

$$\frac{\hat{Y}_i - (\alpha + \beta X_i)}{\sigma_{\hat{Y}_i}} \sim N(0,1).$$

In general, the expression for $\sigma^2_{\hat{Y}_i}$ given by (7.41) cannot be evaluated because it involves an unknown parameter σ^2. However, we can replace σ^2 by its unbiased, consistent, and asymptotically efficient estimator s^2 given by formula (7.35). This will lead to an estimator of $\sigma^2_{\hat{Y}_i}$, say $s^2_{\hat{Y}_i}$, which has the same desirable properties and which is defined as

$$\text{(7.42)}\qquad s^2_{\hat{Y}_i} = s^2\left[\frac{1}{n} + \frac{(X_i - \bar{X})^2}{\sum x_i'^2}\right].$$

Then we have

$$\frac{\hat{Y}_i - (\alpha + \beta X_i)}{s_{\hat{Y}_i}} \sim t_{n-2},$$

and the confidence interval for $(\alpha + \beta X_i)$ will be

$$\hat{Y}_i - t_{n-2,\lambda/2}s_{\hat{Y}_i} \leq (\alpha + \beta X_i) \leq \hat{Y}_i + t_{n-2,\lambda/2}s_{\hat{Y}_i},$$

where $(1 - \lambda)$ is the chosen level of confidence. Since this confidence interval can be calculated for any value of X_i within the applicable domain, we can construct confidence intervals for *any* point on the population regression line. This enables us to construct a *confidence band* for the population regression line as a whole.

EXAMPLE For an illustration we can use the example of Section 7–3 on the demand for oranges. We will construct the 95% confidence band for the population demand curve. We note that the estimated sample regression line was

$$\hat{Y}_i = 210.460 - 1.578X_i.$$

The estimate of the variance of $\hat{Y}_i$ is

$$s^2_{\hat{Y}_i} = 69.8\left[\frac{1}{12} + \frac{(X_i - 70)^2}{2250}\right],$$

and the value of the t statistic is 2.228 as before. These are all the necessary ingredients for the calculation of the confidence band. Table 7–3 shows the results of these calculations. The last two columns represent the intervals that, we expect, will contain the corresponding population values. Note that the narrowest interval is the one

Table 7–3

				95% Confidence Interval	
X_i	$\hat{Y}_i$	$s_{\hat{Y}_i}$	$2.228s_{\hat{Y}_i}$	Lower Limit	Upper Limit
0	210.46	12.57	28.01	182.45	238.47
10	194.66	10.84	24.15	170.51	218.81
20	178.88	9.14	20.36	158.52	199.24
30	163.10	7.45	16.60	146.50	179.70
40	147.32	5.81	12.94	134.38	160.26
50	131.54	4.27	9.51	122.03	141.05
60	115.76	2.98	6.64	109.12	122.40
70	99.98	2.41	5.37	94.61	105.35
80	84.20	2.98	6.64	77.56	90.84
90	68.42	4.27	9.51	58.91	77.93
100	52.64	5.81	12.94	39.70	65.58
110	36.86	7.45	16.60	20.26	53.46
120	21.08	9.14	20.36	0.72	41.44

that corresponds to $X_i = 70$, i.e., to $\bar{X}$. The intervals get wider as we move farther away from $\bar{X}$. By connecting the appropriate points we get the lower and the upper boundaries of the confidence band for the population regression line, as illustrated in Figure 7–4.

Decomposition of the Sample Variation of *Y*

Certain concepts connected with the problem of decomposing the sample variation of the values of the dependent variable[10] can be used to supplement

[10] By "variation of the dependent variable" we mean the changes in Y from one sample observation to another. This is to be distinguished from the "variance of Y_i," which refers to the dispersion of the values of Y_i corresponding to one fixed value of X, say X_i. In the case of the sample variation of Y, the values of X may change from observation to observation.

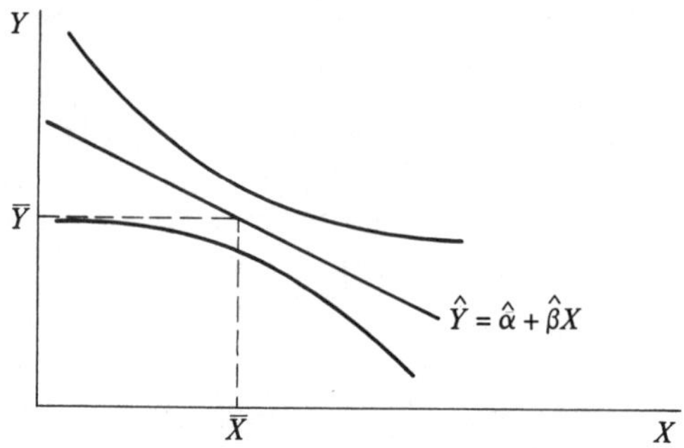

Figure 7–4

the estimation results we have derived. As an illustration, consider the variation of Y as shown in Figure 7–5. Here the values of Y observed in a given sample have been plotted against the corresponding values of X. Such a graph is generally known as a "scatter diagram." In Figure 7–5 we give 10 observations on Y

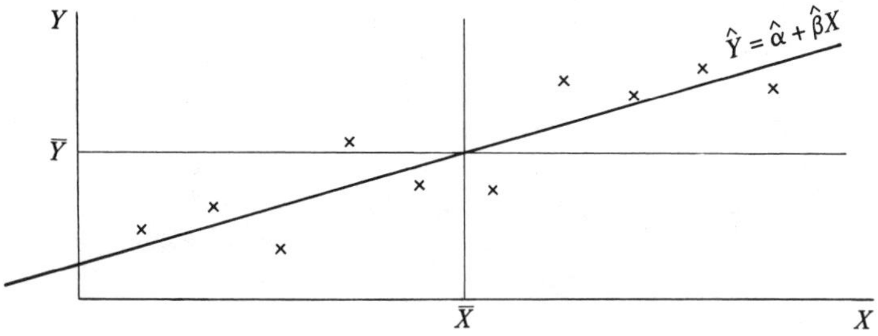

Figure 7–5

corresponding to 10 different values of X. The question that now arises is why the values of Y differ from observation to observation. The answer, in accordance with the hypothesized regression model, is that the variation in Y is partly due to changes in X—which lead to changes in the expected value of Y—and partly due to the effect of the random disturbance. The next question, then, is how much of the observed variation in Y can be attributed to the variation in X and now much to the random effect of the disturbance. This question can be answered with the help of certain measures that we develop below.

First of all, let us define the term "sample variation of Y." If there were no variation, all the values of Y, when plotted against X, would lie on a horizontal line. Since if all values of Y were the same, they would all be equal to their sample mean, the horizontal line would be the one corresponding to $\bar{Y}$ in Figure 7–5. Now, in reality, the observed values of Y will be scattered around this line so that the variation of Y could be measured by the distances of the observed values of Y from $\bar{Y}$. A convenient summary measure of these distances is the sum of their squared values, usually called the "total sum of squares," abbreviated to SST. That is, we define

$$\text{SST} = \sum_i (Y_i - \bar{Y})^2 = \sum_i y_i'^2.$$

Our aim is to decompose this sum of squares into two parts, one designed to account for the variations of Y which can be ascribed to the variations of X, and the other presumed to account for the variations in Y which can be ascribed to random causes.

Let us now return to Figure 7–5 and the sample observations shown therein. Suppose a sample regression line has been obtained by the method of least squares and drawn in the scatter diagram as shown. Since, as the name of the estimation method implies, the line is such that the sum of squares of deviations from it is a minimum, it is sometimes called the "line of the best fit." Consider now a specific observation, say Y_i, which corresponds to the value of X equal to X_i. We are interested in the vertical distance of (X_i, Y_i) from $\bar{Y}$. From Figure 7–6,

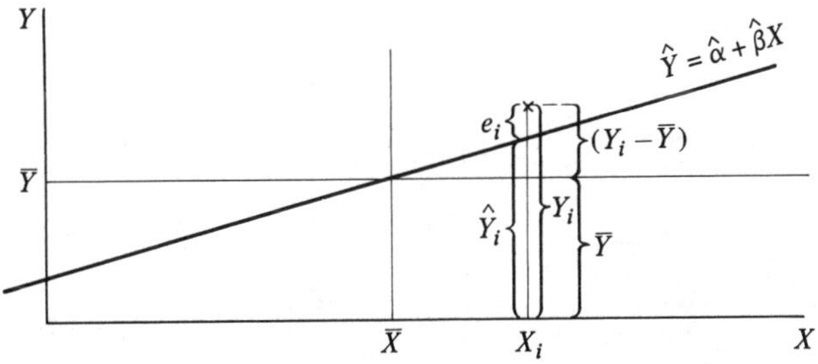

Figure 7–6

we can see that this distance can be divided into two parts, one represented by the distance of the observed point from the sample regression line, and the other by the distance of the sample regression line from $\bar{Y}$. That is, we have

$$Y_i = \hat{Y}_i + e_i,$$

where $\hat{Y}_i$ is the point on the sample regression line corresponding to X_i. Deducting $\bar{Y}$ from both sides we obtain

$$\underset{\substack{\text{Total}\\\text{distance}\\\text{from } \bar{Y}}}{(Y_i - \bar{Y})} = \underset{\substack{\text{Distance}\\\text{of the}\\\text{regression}\\\text{line from } \bar{Y}}}{(\hat{Y}_i - \bar{Y})} + \underset{\text{Residual}}{e_i}.$$

This analysis applies to a single observation. Since we want a summary measure for *all* sample observations, we square both sides of this equality and sum over all sample observations. This gives

$$\sum_i (Y_i - \bar{Y})^2 = \sum_i [(\hat{Y}_i - \bar{Y}) + e_i]^2$$
$$= \sum_i (\hat{Y}_i - \bar{Y})^2 + \sum_i e_i^2 + 2\sum_i (\hat{Y}_i - \bar{Y})\, e_i.$$

Consider the last term on the right-hand side. Substituting for $\hat{Y}_i$ we get

$$2\sum_i (\hat{Y}_i - \bar{Y})e_i = 2\sum_i (\hat{\alpha} + \hat{\beta}X_i - \bar{Y})e_i$$
$$= \hat{\alpha}\sum_i e_i + \hat{\beta}\sum_i X_i e_i - \bar{Y}\sum_i e_i.$$

But by (7.10a) and (7.11a) we know that $\sum_i e_i = 0$ and $\sum_i X_i e_i = 0$, so we conclude that

$$2\sum_i (\hat{Y}_i - \bar{Y})e_i = 0.$$

Therefore,

(7.43) $$\sum_i (Y_i - \bar{Y})^2 = \sum_i (\hat{Y}_i - \bar{Y})^2 + \sum_i e_i^2.$$

Total sum of squares (SST)	Regression sum of squares (SSR)	Error sum of squares (SSE)

The term SSR can be further developed as follows:

(7.44) $$\text{SSR} = \sum (\hat{Y}_i - \bar{Y})^2 = \sum (\hat{\alpha} + \hat{\beta}X_i - \bar{Y})^2$$
$$= \sum [(\bar{Y} - \hat{\beta}\bar{X}) + \hat{\beta}X_i - \bar{Y}]^2$$
$$= \sum [\hat{\beta}(X_i - \bar{X})]^2$$
$$= \hat{\beta}^2 \sum (X_i - \bar{X})^2 = \hat{\beta}^2 \sum x_i'^2.$$

Thus we have found that the sample variation of Y (SST) can be decomposed into two parts, one describing the variation of the fitted values of Y and the other describing the variation of the regression residuals. That is, SSR represents the estimated effect of X on the variation of Y, and SSE the estimated effect of the random disturbance.

The decomposition of the sample variation of Y leads to a measure of the "goodness of fit," which is known as the *coefficient of determination* and denoted by R^2. This is simply the proportion of the variation of Y that can be attributed to the variation of X. Since

$$\text{SST} = \text{SSR} + \text{SSE},$$

dividing through by SST gives

$$1 = \frac{\text{SSR}}{\text{SST}} + \frac{\text{SSE}}{\text{SST}}.$$

The coefficient of determination is defined as

$$R^2 = \frac{\text{SSR}}{\text{SST}} = \frac{\hat{\beta}^2 \sum x_i'^2}{\sum y_i'^2}, \tag{7.45}$$

or

$$R^2 = 1 - \frac{\text{SSE}}{\text{SST}} = 1 - \frac{\sum e_i^2}{\sum y_i'^2}. \tag{7.45a}$$

R^2 is a measure commonly used to describe how well the sample regression line fits the observed data. Note that R^2 cannot be negative or greater than one, i.e.,

$$0 \leq R^2 \leq 1.$$

A zero value of R^2 indicates the poorest, and a unit value the best fit that can be attained.

A necessary but not sufficient condition for R^2 to be zero is that the sample regression line be horizontal—that is, that $\hat{\beta}$ be equal to zero. Note that the sample regression line can be horizontal for several different reasons. This is illustrated in Figure 7–7. In case (*a*) the observations are scattered randomly

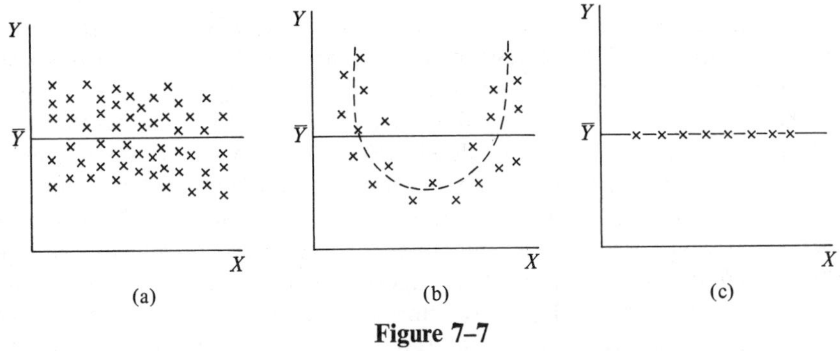

Figure 7–7

around $\bar{Y}$. In case (*b*) the observations are scattered around a curve such that the best-fitting straight line is a horizontal one. In this case there *is* a relationship between X and Y, but the relationship is highly nonlinear so that a straight line gives a very poor fit. Finally, in case (*c*) all observed values of Y are the same regardless of X. This is an exceptional case. With all values of Y being constant there is *no* variation to be explained, and thus the question of decomposition of variation is irrelevant. The value of R^2 in this case is indeterminate.

Two final points about decomposing the sample variation of Y should be noted.

First, nowhere in the discussion have we alluded to problems of statistical inference. This omission was deliberate since our purpose was only to provide certain information about the sample. Second, the decomposition of SST as developed above is crucially dependent on the use of the method of least squares to obtain the sample regression line. If we used an estimation method that would lead to a different sample regression line, the decomposition of SST into SSR and SSE would not have been possible. As for R^2, however, we can generalize the formula (7.45a) to apply to *any* estimation method by defining R^2 as

$$(7.45b) \qquad R^2 = 1 - \frac{\text{Sum of Squares of Residuals}}{\text{SST}}.$$

Here the residuals are represented by the deviations from the sample regression line regardless of the method of estimation that is used. But if the sample regression line is different from the one that would be obtained by the least squares method, R^2 can no longer be interpreted as a measure of the proportion of variation of Y attributable to sample regression. In this case, R^2 would be used purely as a measure of the goodness of fit.

If R^2 is regarded as a descriptive statistic, we might ask about the value of the information that it conveys. Suppose, in particular, we find a very low value of R^2 for a given sample. This means that the sample regression line fits the observations rather poorly. One possible explanation is that X is a poor explanatory variable in the sense that variation in X leaves Y unaffected. This is a proposition about the population regression line—a proposition that states that the population regression line is horizontal—and consequently can be tested by reference to the sample. We shall explain how this can be done presently. The validity of the test depends on the validity of the maintained hypothesis—that is, on the correct specification of the regression equation and on the validity of the basic assumptions. In particular, correct specification of the regression equation implies that no other explanatory variable enters into the model and that the effect of X_i on $E(Y_i)$ is a linear one. If we do not reject the hypothesis that the population regression line is horizontal, we are, in fact, claiming that Y is influenced *only* by the random disturbance ε. Another possible explanation of a low value of R^2 is that while X is the relevant explanatory variable, its influence on Y is weak compared to the influence of the random disturbance. This, indeed, seems to be the case for relationships describing household behavior that have been estimated from cross-section data. For example, a typical value of R^2 for various household behavior functions from the University of Michigan's Survey Research Center data (about 3000 observations) is close to 0.20. This would indicate that 80% of the sample behavioral variation from household to household can be accounted for by factors other than the explanatory variable or variables. A third possible explanation of a low value of R^2 is that the regression equation is misspecified. In practice, this is frequently the conclusion that the research worker reaches in this case. The value of R^2 tends to be taken as an indicator of the "correctness" of the specification of the model. This is obviously a purely operational criterion that has no foundation in statistical inference. We shall say more about it when we come to the discussion of specification errors. In any case, it is customary to state the value of R^2 along with the results of the estimation procedure when presenting the regression results.

EXAMPLE The decomposition of SST and the calculation of R^2 can be illustrated with the example of demand for oranges introduced in Section 7–3. From the previous calculations we have:

$$\sum y_i'^2 = 6300,$$

$$\sum x_i'^2 = 2250,$$

$$\hat{\beta} = -1.578.$$

Thus,

$$\text{SST} = \sum y_i'^2 = 6300,$$

$$\text{SSR} = \hat{\beta}^2 \sum x_i'^2 = 5602,$$

$$\text{SSE} = \text{SST} - \text{SSR} = 698.$$

That is,

$$\underset{(\text{SST})}{6300} = \underset{(\text{SSR})}{5602} + \underset{(\text{SSE})}{698}.$$

The coefficient of determination is

$$R^2 = \frac{\text{SSR}}{\text{SST}} = \frac{5602}{6300} = 0.889.$$

This means that 88.9% of the sample variation of Y can be attributed to the variation of the fitted values of Y, i.e., to $\hat{Y}$. The value of R^2 indicates that the sample regression line fits the observations quite well. This is shown graphically in Figure 7–8.

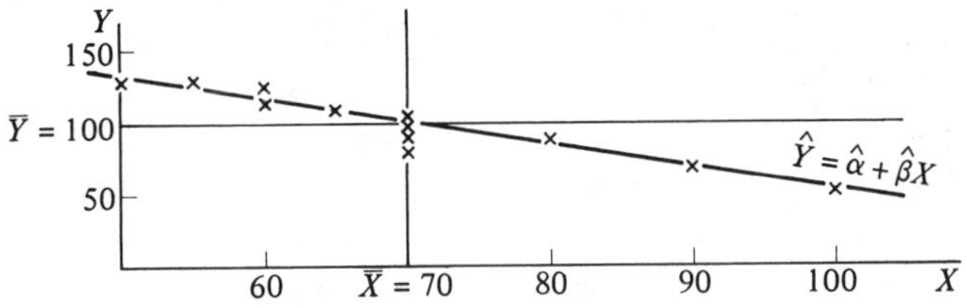

Figure 7–8

Tests of Hypotheses

Let us now turn to the problem of using the regression model for the purpose of *testing hypotheses*. The most common type of hypothesis which is tested with the help of the regression model is that there is no relationship between the explanatory variable X and the dependent variable Y. This hypothesis can be given a more precise interpretation if we first specify the ingredients of the associated maintained hypothesis; that is, if we state all the assumptions about the population that we are willing to make. These assumptions are all those underlying the classical normal linear regression model as specified by statements (7.1) through (7.6). Under this maintained hypothesis the relationship between X and Y is given by the linear dependence of the mean value of Y_i on X_i, i.e., by $E(Y_i) = \alpha + \beta X_i$. Thus the statement that "there is no relationship between X and Y" is to be interpreted as meaning that the mean value of Y_i is *not* linearly dependent on X_i—that is, that the population regression line is horizontal. But this is simply another way of saying that β is equal to zero. Therefore, the *null hypothesis* of no relationship between X and Y is

$$H_0: \quad \beta = 0.$$

If we have no prior knowledge about the values of the regression parameters, the alternative hypothesis would be

$$H_A: \quad \beta \neq 0.$$

If we know a priori that β cannot be positive or negative, the alternative hypothesis would be modified accordingly. To test H_0 we have to develop a test statistic and determine the acceptance and the critical regions. The test statistic can be derived from the least squares estimator of β, which has all the optimal properties under the given assumptions. We can simply utilize the fact that

$$\frac{\hat{\beta} - \beta}{s_{\hat{\beta}}} \sim t_{n-2},$$

as given by (7.38). Under the null hypothesis, β equals zero and thus the appropriate test statistic is

$$\frac{\hat{\beta}}{s_{\hat{\beta}}}$$

which has a t distribution with $(n - 2)$ degrees of freedom. The boundary between the acceptance and the critical region can be determined from the table of the t distribution for any given level of significance and for any number of degrees of freedom. For a two-tail test with λ level of significance and $(n - 2)$ degrees of freedom the acceptance region is defined by

$$(7.46) \qquad -t_{n-2,\,\lambda/2} \leq \frac{\hat{\beta}}{s_{\hat{\beta}}} \leq +t_{n-2,\,\lambda/2}.$$

EXAMPLE As an example, consider the demand for oranges estimated by a linear regression model from the data given in Section 7–3. The null hypothesis of no relationship between X (price) and Y (quantity demanded) is tantamount to the claim that the demand for oranges is not influenced by price. We have

$$H_0: \quad \beta = 0.$$

For the alternative hypothesis, we take

$$H_A: \quad \beta \neq 0.$$

We wish to test H_0 at 1% level of significance. Since the t distribution extends from $-\infty$ to $+\infty$, *any* value of $\hat{\beta}/s_{\hat{\beta}}$ is consistent with the null hypothesis. But if H_0 is true, values of $\hat{\beta}/s_{\hat{\beta}}$ which are "far" from zero are not very likely. Our decision to use 1% level of significance means that if the deviation of $\hat{\beta}/s_{\hat{\beta}}$ from zero is so great as to occur by chance only 1% of the time, we shall reject H_0. Since we have 12 observations, the appropriate value of the t statistic for a two-tail test is the value corresponding to $t_{10,0.005}$. From the table of the t distribution, we find that this is equal to 3.169. The acceptance region for our test then is

$$-3.169 \leq \frac{\hat{\beta}}{s_{\hat{\beta}}} \leq +3.169.$$

From the previous calculations we have

$$\hat{\beta} = -1.578 \qquad \text{and} \qquad s_{\hat{\beta}} = 0.176,$$

so that

$$\frac{\hat{\beta}}{s_{\hat{\beta}}} = -8.965,$$

which clearly lies outside the acceptance region. Therefore, the hypothesis of no relationship between X and Y is to be rejected. Actually, in a case like this we would probably want to use a one-sided alternative hypothesis since positive values of β (that is, an upward-sloping demand curve) can be ruled out on theoretical grounds. Thus a "sharper" test would be one with the alternative hypothesis stated as

$$H_A: \quad \beta < 0,$$

and the acceptance region given by

$$-t_{n-2,\lambda} \leq \frac{\hat{\beta}}{s_{\hat{\beta}}},$$

or

$$-2.764 \leq \frac{\hat{\beta}}{s_{\hat{\beta}}}.$$

Since -8.965 lies outside this region, the verdict of rejecting H_0 is unchanged.

It should be noted that the hypothesis of no relationship between X and Y can also be tested by using a different test than the t test. If the null hypothesis is true, then the variation of Y from observation to observation will not be affected by changes in X but must be explained by the random disturbance alone. This means that the "sum of squares due to regression" (SSR) departs from zero only because we are observing a sample and not the entire population. Indeed, from the formula (7.44) we have

$$\text{SSR} = \hat{\beta}^2 \sum_i x_i'^2.$$

If $\beta = 0$, the value of SSR in the population would also be zero. Furthermore, since by (7.43) we have

$$\text{SST} = \text{SSR} + \text{SSE},$$

the corollary of a zero value of SSR is that SST and SSE are equal. Thus, if there is no relationship between X and Y, the ratio SSR/SSE would be different from zero only because of sampling. Now it can be shown[11] that under the null hypothesis the statistic

$$\frac{\text{SSR}/1}{\text{SSE}/(n-2)}$$

is a ratio of two independent chi-square variables, each divided by its respective number of degrees of freedom. This means that this ratio has an F distribution (see page 147), i.e., that

$$\frac{\text{SSR}/1}{\text{SSE}/(n-2)} \sim F_{1,n-2}. \tag{7.47}$$

The acceptance region for the null hypothesis of no relationship between X and Y would then be

$$\frac{\text{SSR}/1}{\text{SSE}/(n-2)} \leq F_{1,n-2}^{(\lambda)}, \tag{7.48}$$

where $F_{1,n-2}^{(\lambda)}$ is the value of the F statistic with 1 and $(n-2)$ degrees of freedom that corresponds to a level of significance λ. The test (7.48) is equivalent to the two-tail t test (7.46) in the sense that both tests give the same answer as long as the level of significance and the sample data are the same. The difference, as we shall see, is that the F test can be readily generalized to apply to a regression model with more than one explanatory variable, whereas the t test can only be applied to a single regression coefficient.

EXAMPLE For the numerical example given in the preceding paragraph we have

$$\text{SSR} = 5602,$$

$$\text{SSE} = 698,$$

so that

$$\frac{\text{SSR}/1}{\text{SSE}/(n-2)} = \frac{5602}{698/10} = 80.26.$$

Since the value of the F statistic with 1 and 10 degrees of freedom at 1% level of significance is 10.0, the null hypothesis is obviously to be rejected.

In addition to testing a hypothesis about the existence of a relationship between X and Y, we can carry out tests for any specific values of the regression coefficients. For example, a hypothesis that α is equal to zero is, in fact, a hypothesis that the population regression line passes through the origin. The appropriate test statistic would be

$$\frac{\hat{\alpha}}{s_{\hat{\alpha}}}$$

[11] See, e.g., R. L. Anderson and T. A. Bancroft, *Statistical Theory in Research* (New York: McGraw-Hill, 1952), pp. 158–160.

which has a t distribution with $(n - 2)$ degrees of freedom. Or we may wish to test the hypothesis that the regression slope β is equal to some value β_0. In this case the test statistic would be

$$\frac{\hat{\beta} - \beta_0}{s_{\hat{\beta}}} \sim t_{n-2}.$$

Prediction

Apart from estimation and hypotheses testing, the regression model can also be used for prediction. In particular, we are frequently interested in "*forecasting*" the value of Y for a given value of X. For example, the manager of a supermarket may be interested to know what quantity of oranges he can expect to sell when he sets the price at a certain level. To be specific, suppose the given value of the explanatory variable is X_0 so that our task is to predict the value of Y_0. Since Y_0 is a *random* variable with values scattered around the point on the population regression line corresponding to X_0, we will never know its value prior to the experiment, not even if we knew all the population parameters. If the population parameters *were known*, our predictor of Y_0 would be its mean,

$$E(Y_0) = \alpha + \beta X_0,$$

which defines a point on the population regression line. This is the best predictor of Y_0 in the sense that the variance of Y_0 around $E(Y_0)$ is smaller than around any other point. The values of Y_0 will be normally distributed with variance equal to σ^2. This follows from the presence of the random disturbance ε in the regression equation. In reality, $E(Y_0)$ is not known and has to be estimated. The estimator is the corresponding point on the sample regression line,

$$\hat{Y}_0 = \hat{\alpha} + \hat{\beta} X_0,$$

since $\hat{\alpha}$ and $\hat{\beta}$ are the best estimators of α and β that we can devise under given assumptions. Now, the actual value of Y_0 will differ from the predicted value $\hat{Y}_0$ for the following two reasons:

1. The value of Y_0 will not be equal to $E(Y_0)$—i.e., will not lie on the population regression line—because of the random disturbance ε_0.
2. The sample regression will not be the same as the population regression line because of the sampling error.

Formally, we may write

$$Y_0 - \hat{Y}_0 = [Y_0 - E(Y_0)] + [E(Y_0) - \hat{Y}_0].$$

The first type of error is inherent in the mechanism by which the values of the dependent variable are generated, and there is nothing that we can do to diminish it. However, the second type of error would be reduced if we increased the precision of estimating the population regression line by increasing the sample size.

The difference between the actual value of Y_0 and the predicted value Y_0 is known as the *forecast error*. We note that

$$Y_0 - \hat{Y}_0 = (\alpha + \beta X_0 + \varepsilon_0) - (\hat{\alpha} + \hat{\beta} X_0)$$

is a linear combination of normally and independently distributed random variables $\varepsilon_0, \varepsilon_1, \varepsilon_2 \ldots, \varepsilon_n$. Therefore, the forecast error is also a normally distributed random variable. Thus its distribution is fully determined by its mean and its variance. The mean can be simply determined as follows:

$$\begin{aligned} E(Y_0 - \hat{Y}_0) &= E(\alpha + \beta X_0 + \varepsilon_0 - \hat{\alpha} - \hat{\beta} X_0) \\ &= \alpha + \beta X_0 + E(\varepsilon_0) - E(\hat{\alpha}) - E(\hat{\beta}) X_0 = 0. \end{aligned}$$

The variance of the forecast error is

$$\begin{aligned} E[(Y_0 - \hat{Y}_0) - E(Y_0 - \hat{Y}_0)]^2 &= E(Y_0 - \hat{Y}_0)^2 \\ &= E\{[Y_0 - E(Y_0)] + [E(Y_0) - \hat{Y}_0]\}^2 \\ &= E[Y_0 - E(Y_0)]^2 + E[E(Y_0) - \hat{Y}_0]^2 \\ &\quad + 2E[Y_0 - E(Y_0)][E(Y_0) - \hat{Y}_0]. \end{aligned}$$

Taking the last term on the right-hand side,

$$\begin{aligned} 2E[Y_0 - E(Y_0)][E(Y_0) - \hat{Y}_0] &= 2E(\varepsilon_0)[E(Y_0) - \hat{Y}_0] \\ &= 2E(\varepsilon_0)(\alpha + \beta X_0 - \hat{\alpha} - \hat{\beta} X_0) \\ &= 2E(\varepsilon_0)[-(\hat{\alpha} - \alpha) - (\hat{\beta} - \beta) X_0] \\ &= 0, \end{aligned}$$

since $(\hat{\alpha} - \alpha)$ and $(\hat{\beta} - \beta)$ each depend only on the sample disturbances ε_1, $\varepsilon_2, \ldots, \varepsilon_n$, and these are independent of ε_0. Thus

$$E(Y_0 - \hat{Y}_0)^2 = E[Y_0 - E(Y_0)]^2 + E[E(Y_0) - \hat{Y}_0]^2 \tag{7.49}$$

Total variance of the forecast error (σ_F^2)	Variance due to random disturbance (σ^2)	Variance due to sampling error ($\sigma_{\hat{Y}_0}^2$)

or

$$\sigma_F^2 = \sigma^2 + \sigma_{\hat{Y}_0}^2.$$

That is, the variance of the forecast error consists of two parts, one equal to the variance of the disturbance and the other to the variance of the predictor $\hat{Y}_0$ around its mean $E(Y_0)$. The variance of the disturbance is beyond our control, but the variance of the predictor can be diminished by increasing the size of the sample used for estimating the population regression line.

By using the expression for $\sigma_{\hat{Y}_0}^2$ given by (7.41) above, we obtain the following formula for the variance of the forecast error:

$$\sigma_F^2 = \sigma^2 + \sigma^2\left[\frac{1}{n} + \frac{(X_0 - \bar{X})^2}{\sum x_i'^2}\right] = \sigma^2\left[1 + \frac{1}{n} + \frac{(X_0 - \bar{X})^2}{\sum x_i'^2}\right]. \tag{7.50}$$

This means that the variance of the forecast error will be the smaller:

1. The larger the sample size n.
2. The greater the dispersion of the explanatory variable in the sample (i.e., the larger $\sum x_i'^2$).
3. The smaller the distance between X_0 and the sample mean $\bar{X}$.

The first two conclusions are quite straightforward; they reflect the fact that the better the estimate of the population regression line, the smaller the variance of the forecast error. The third conclusion is more interesting; it means that our forecast will be better for values of X which are close to $\bar{X}$ than for those which lie farther away from $\bar{X}$. This is consistent with the intuitively plausible contention that we are better able to forecast within our range of experience than outside of it. In this case the range of our "experience" is represented by the sample values of the explanatory variable X, and the central point of this range is $\bar{X}$. The farther away we venture with our forecasting, the less reliable the forecast.

In general, the expression for σ_F^2 given by (7.50) will not be known and must be estimated. This can be done simply by replacing σ^2 by its estimator s^2, which will give an unbiased, consistent, and asymptotically efficient estimator of σ_F^2, say, s_F^2, defined as

$$s_F^2 = s^2\left[1 + \frac{1}{n} + \frac{(X_0 - \bar{X})^2}{\sum x_i'^2}\right]. \tag{7.51}$$

In summary, we have found that the forecast error $(Y_0 - \hat{Y}_0)$ is normally distributed, has zero mean, and its variance is σ_F^2. That is,

$$(Y_0 - \hat{Y}_0) \sim N(0, \sigma_F^2);$$

and, therefore

$$\frac{Y_0 - \hat{Y}_0}{\sigma_F} \sim N(0, 1).$$

Replacing σ_F with s_F gives

$$\frac{Y_0 - \hat{Y}_0}{s_F} \sim t_{n-2}.$$

The last result enables us to make definite probability statements about our forecast. In particular, we can set up an interval that will contain the actual value of Y_0 with a given probability. Let this level of probability be $(1 - \lambda)$, where λ is any given number between 0 and 1 that we care to choose. Then we can write

$$P\left[-t_{n-2,\lambda/2} \leq \frac{Y_0 - \hat{Y}_0}{s_F} \leq +t_{n-2,\lambda/2}\right] = 1 - \lambda.$$

The corresponding confidence interval for Y_0 is

$$\hat{Y}_0 - t_{n-2,\lambda/2}s_F \leq Y_0 \leq \hat{Y}_0 + t_{n-2,\lambda/2}s_F.$$

This interval is symmetric around the predictor $\hat{Y}_0$, and can be expected to contain the actual value of Y_0 with a probability $(1 - \lambda)$.

EXAMPLE Suppose we wish to predict the demand for oranges at a price of 110¢ per pound, using the previously estimated demand curve. The predicted quantity demanded will be

$$\hat{Y}_0 = 210.460 - 1.578 \times 110 = 36.88,$$

with standard error

$$s_F = \sqrt{69.9\left[1 + \frac{1}{12} + \frac{(110 - 70)^2}{2250}\right]} = 11.20.$$

The 95% confidence interval for Y_0 is $36.88 \pm 2.228 \times 11.20$ or from 12 to 62 pounds.

Presentation of Regression Results

One last note to be added before we close this chapter concerns the presentation of the results of the regression analysis. Whatever the purpose, operating on sample data will involve estimating the regression coefficients and the standard errors of these estimators. These results are usually supplemented by R^2, the coefficient of determination, which indicates how well the sample regression line fits the observations. It has become customary to present all these results by writing out the estimated regression equation with the estimated standard errors in parentheses under the respective coefficients. This is followed by the value of R^2. That is, we write

$$\underset{}{\hat{Y}_i} = \underset{(s_{\hat{\alpha}})}{\hat{\alpha}} + \underset{(s_{\hat{\beta}})}{\hat{\beta}} X_i, \qquad R^2 = \cdots.$$

In the case of our example on the demand for oranges, we have

$$\hat{Y}_i = \underset{(12.563)}{210.460} - \underset{(0.176)}{1.578} X_i, \qquad R^2 = 0.889.$$

The "hat" on $\hat{Y}_i$ indicates that the equation holds only for the fitted values of the dependent variable, not for the actually observed values. Alternatively, we can write

$$Y_i = \underset{(s_{\hat{\alpha}})}{\hat{\alpha}} + \underset{(s_{\hat{\beta}})}{\hat{\beta}} X_i + e_i, \qquad R^2 = \cdots,$$

where e_i represents the least squares residuals. But note that writing $Y_i = \hat{\alpha} + \hat{\beta} X_i$ is incorrect. Some researchers present the ratios of the estimated coefficients to their estimated standard errors in place of the estimated standard errors themselves, which is an acceptable alternative.

EXERCISES

All problems in this set of exercises refer to a simple linear regression model,

$$Y_i = \alpha + \beta X_i + \varepsilon_i,$$

for which assumptions (7.2) through (7.6) are all satisfied.

7–1. Derive the best linear unbiased estimator of α and its variance.

7–2. Consider any two regression disturbances ε_t and ε_s $(t \neq s)$. By our assumptions, these disturbances have the same variance and are mutually independent. Can the same be asserted about the respective least squares residuals e_t and e_s?

7–3. Using the method of semi-averages and the data on the demand for oranges given in the text, we estimated the regression line as

$$\hat{\hat{Y}}_i = 205 - 1.5X_i.$$

Calculate the value of R^2.

7–4. Which of the assumptions (7.2) through (7.6) are *necessary* for the least squares estimator of β to be **(a)** unbiased; **(b)** best linear unbiased; **(c)** consistent?

7–5. Suppose Y_i = log value of production per worker, X_i = log wage rate, and the subscript i refers to the ith firm. The parameter β may be interpreted as a measure of the elasticity of substitution between labor and capital. The least squares results for industry A are

$$Y_i = -0.4 + \underset{(0.1)}{1.0}X_i + e_i \qquad (n = 52).$$

For industry B the results are

$$Y_i = -0.3 + \underset{(0.1)}{0.8}X_i + e_i \qquad (n = 50).$$

The two samples can be considered to be independent.

a. Show that $R_A^2 = 2/3$ and $R_B^2 = 4/7$.

b. Test the hypothesis that both industries are characterized by the same elasticity of substitution, i.e., that $\beta_A = \beta_B$.

7–6. Suppose we have calculated the values of $\hat{\alpha}$, $\hat{\beta}$, $s_{\hat{\alpha}}$, $s_{\hat{\beta}}$, and R^2 on the basis of a sample of n observations. Suppose now that we add another observation to our sample and recalculate these five values. Compare the recalculated values with the original ones—stating whether we get an increase, a decrease, no change, or an uncertain result—given the following situations:

a. $X_{n+1} = \frac{1}{n}\sum_{i=1}^{n} X_i.$

b. $X_{n+1} = \max\{X_1, X_2, \ldots, X_n\}.$

c. $X_{n+1} = 0.$

7–7. Suppose the explanatory variable X can only assume the values 0 and 1. The sample consists of n_1 observations for which $X = 0$, and n_2 observations for which $X = 1$. Let $\bar{Y}_1$ be the mean value of Y for the n_1 observations for which $X = 0$, and $\bar{Y}_2$ be the mean value of Y for the n_2 observations for which $X = 1$. Find $\hat{\alpha}$, $\hat{\beta}$, $\text{Var}(\hat{\alpha})$, and $\text{Var}(\hat{\beta})$.

7–8. Three alternative models, designed to explain the changes in aggregate expenditure of food in the United States, have been suggested:

$$\text{Model A:} \qquad Y_t = \alpha + \beta X_t + \varepsilon_{1t}$$

$$\text{Model B:} \qquad Y_t = \gamma + \delta Z_t + \varepsilon_{2t}$$

$$\text{Model C:} \quad \log Y_t = \alpha^* + \beta^* \log X_t + \varepsilon_{3t},$$

where Y = personal expenditure on food (excluding alcoholic beverages), X = personal disposable income, Z = total personal consumption expenditure, and t = time in years. On the basis of the data in Table 7–4,

a. Estimate the three regression equations by the method of least squares.

b. For each model obtain an estimate (given by a single numerical value) of the income elasticity of demand for food defined as

$$\frac{dQ}{dX}\frac{X}{Q},$$

where Q is the quantity of food consumed, i.e., value divided by price.

c. Examine the results obtained in **a** to see whether they help in the choice between the three models.

7–9. The least squares regression equation estimated from 22 observations is

$$Y_i = 10 + 5X_i + e_i, \qquad R^2 = 0.8.$$

Carry out the test for the existence of a relationship between X and Y by using (**a**) the t test; (**b**) the F test.

7–10. Two research workers, working independently of each other, estimated the coefficients of

$$Y_i = \alpha + \beta X_i + \varepsilon_i$$

by the method of least squares. When they found out about each other's work, they decided to pool their results to obtain one joint estimate of β. Two possible ways of doing this were considered:

1. Taking a simple arithmetic mean of their two estimates.
2. Combining their two samples and obtaining a new estimate of β.

Do the two procedures differ? If so, which one would lead to a better estimate of β?

7–11. One test for the existence of a relationship between X and Y is carried out by constructing a t statistic $\hat{\beta}/s_{\hat{\beta}}$. Show that this is exactly equal to

$$[R^2(n-2)/(1-R^2)]^{1/2}.$$

7–12. The true relationship between X and Y in the population is given by

$$Y_i = 2 + 3X_i + \varepsilon_i.$$

Table 7–4

Year	Personal Consumption Expenditure* Total	Food	Personal Disposable Income*
1929	79.0	19.5	83.1
1930	71.0	18.0	74.4
1931	61.3	14.7	63.8
1932	49.3	11.4	48.7
1933	46.4	10.9	45.7
1934	51.9	12.2	52.0
1935	56.3	13.6	58.3
1936	62.6	15.2	66.2
1937	67.3	16.4	71.0
1938	64.6	15.6	65.7
1939	67.6	15.7	70.4
1940	71.9	16.7	76.1
1946	147.1	40.7	160.6
1947	165.4	45.8	170.1
1948	178.3	48.2	189.3
1949	181.2	46.4	189.7
1950	195.0	47.4	207.7
1951	209.8	53.4	227.5
1952	219.8	55.8	238.7
1953	232.6	56.6	252.5
1954	238.0	57.7	256.9
1955	256.9	59.2	274.4
1956	269.9	62.2	292.9
1957	285.2	65.2	308.8
1958	293.2	67.4	317.9
1959	313.5	68.1	337.1
1960	328.2	69.7	349.9
1961	337.3	71.0	364.7
1962	356.8	73.9	384.6
1963	375.0	76.0	402.5
1964	399.2	80.0	431.8

Source: *Economic Report of the President*, January, 1965, Tables B–7 and B–9.
* In billions of dollars.

Suppose the values of X in the sample of 10 observations are 1, 2, . . ., 10. The values of the disturbances are drawn at random from a normal population with zero mean and unit variance:

$$\varepsilon_1 = 0.464 \qquad \varepsilon_6 = 0.906$$
$$\varepsilon_2 = 0.060 \qquad \varepsilon_7 = -1.501$$
$$\varepsilon_3 = 1.486 \qquad \varepsilon_8 = -0.690$$
$$\varepsilon_4 = 1.022 \qquad \varepsilon_9 = 0.179$$
$$\varepsilon_5 = 1.394 \qquad \varepsilon_{10} = -1.372$$

a. Present the 10 observed values of X and Y.

b. Use the least squares formulas to estimate the regression coefficients and their standard errors, and compare the results with the true values.

c. Carry out a test for the existence of a relationship between X and Y.

d. Obtain the predicted value of Y—and its 95% confidence limits—for $X = 12$.

8 Violations of Basic Assumptions

In Chapter 7 we have developed a so-called classical normal linear regression model and showed how this model can be used for estimation, hypothesis testing, and prediction. In deriving the results we have made use of certain assumptions, which we termed *basic assumptions*, concerning the stochastic disturbance ε_i and the explanatory variable X_i. The first four assumptions involving the stochastic disturbance are normality, zero mean, homoskedasticity, and nonautoregression. The fifth assumption concerns the explanatory variable, which is assumed to be nonstochastic and such that its sample variance is a finite number, whatever the sample size. Given these assumptions, we have been able to show that the least squares estimators of the regression parameters have all the desirable properties. The main objective of the present chapter is to find how the properties of the least squares estimators are affected when any one of the basic assumptions is violated. Furthermore, if and when we find that the consequences of such a violation are serious, we shall try to develop alternative methods of estimation which would give more satisfactory results.

Perhaps we should start with a warning. While all the results pertaining to the classical normal linear regression model discussed in the preceding chapter are well established, the problems arising in situations in which the basic assumptions do not hold have not been always satisfactorily resolved. In fact, it is the preoccupation with these problems that distinguishes an econometrician from a statistician. The main reason for this is that some of the basic assumptions are likely to be violated because of the particular nature of economic relationships. The resulting problems of estimation and hypotheses testing are thus of special relevance to economics. Many of the results to be presented here are relatively new. Some of the unresolved problems are the subject of current research and hopefully will be solved in the near future; others may stay unresolved for a long time.

Of the five basic assumptions the first two assumptions, normality and zero mean of the disturbance, do not require an extended discussion. If the assumption that the disturbance is normally distributed is dropped, the least squares estimators of the regression coefficients are still BLUE, since this property is independent of the form of the parent population. This means that even without the assumption of normality the least squares estimators are unbiased and have the smallest variance among all linear unbiased estimators of the respective parameters. However, they can no longer be claimed to be efficient because, without the specification of the distributional form, the Cramer–Rao lower bound of their variances is not known. Also, the least squares estimators are no longer maximum likelihood estimators since the likelihood function, based on the assumption of normality, no longer applies. With respect to the asymptotic properties, least squares estimators are consistent and asymptotically unbiased regardless of the distribution of the disturbance. Further, it is also known that the distribution of the least squares estimators of the regression coefficients approaches normality as $n \to \infty$. This statement can be proved with the help of the central limit theorem.[1] The implication of this is that the least squares estimators have *asymptotically* the same distribution as the maximum likelihood estimators based on the assumption of normality; therefore, they have the same asymptotic mean and variance. To sum up, when the assumption of normality of the disturbance is dropped, the least squares of the regression coefficients retain most of their desirable properties and the formulas for the variances of these estimators remain unchanged. The confidence intervals and the tests of significance for α and β do, however, depend crucially on the assumption of normality. Without the assumption of normality the least squares estimators are not normally distributed in small samples; strictly speaking, therefore, the confidence limits and the tests described in Section 7–4 no longer apply. Fortunately, if the distribution of the disturbance is not very radically different from normal, the quoted confidence limits and tests of significance are not too badly affected and can be used as reasonable approximations.[2]

The second assumption—zero mean of the regression disturbance—is made in accordance with the specification that the population regression line is

$$E(Y_i) = \alpha + \beta X_i.$$

If the mean of the disturbance is not zero but, say, μ_i, we have

$$E(Y_i) = \alpha + \beta X_i + \mu_i.$$

The implications of this depend on the nature of μ_i. In particular, we have to distinguish between the case where μ_i has the same value for all observations and the case where μ_i may vary. In the first case we can write $\mu_i = \mu$, and the true population regression line is

$$E(Y_i) = \alpha + \mu + \beta X_i$$

or

$$E(Y_i) = \alpha^* + \beta X_i.$$

It is clear, then, that while the least squares estimator of β is unaffected, the least squares formula for estimating the intercept gives an estimation of α^* and not of

[1] E. Malinvaud, *Statistical Methods of Econometrics* (Chicago: Rand McNally, 1966), pp. 195–197.

[2] *Ibid.*, pp. 251–254.

α. There is *no* way in which we can estimate α and μ separately and get unbiased or at least consistent estimates. In the second case where μ_i is not a constant, the intercept becomes $(\alpha + \mu_i)$; that is, it may vary from observation to observation. This means that the mean value of the dependent variable, $E(Y_i)$, changes not only because of changes in X_i but also for other reasons; in other words, the relationship between X_i and Y_i has not been correctly specified. This and other kinds of specification errors will be examined in detail in Chapter 10.

After this preliminary discussion we are left with the remaining three assumptions. It may be noted that when the disturbance is not homoskedastic, it is called "heteroskedastic"; this case will be discussed in Section 8-1. Sections 8-2 and 8-3 will deal with autoregressive disturbances and with stochastic explanatory variables.

8-1 Heteroskedasticity

By the assumption (7.4) of the classical normal linear regression model, we have

$$E(\varepsilon_i^2) = \sigma^2 \quad \text{for all } i.$$

Since the mean of ε_i is assumed to be zero, we can write

$$\text{Var}(\varepsilon_i) = \sigma^2.$$

This feature of the regression disturbance is known as homoskedasticity. It implies that the variance of the disturbance is constant for all observations. This assumption may not be too troublesome for models involving observations on aggregates over time, since the values of the explanatory variable are typically of a similar order of magnitude at all points of observation, and the same is true of the values of the dependent variable. For example, in an aggregate consumption function the level of consumption in recent years is of a similar order of magnitude as the level of consumption twenty years ago, and the same is true of income. Unless there are some special circumstances, the assumption of homoskedasticity in aggregate models seems plausible. However, when we are dealing with microeconomic data, the observations may involve substantial differences in magnitude, as, for example, in the case of data on income and expenditure of individual families. Here, the assumption of homoskedasticity is not very plausible on a priori grounds since we would expect less variation in consumption for low-income families than for high-income families. At low levels of income the average level of consumption is low, and variation around this level is restricted: consumption cannot fall too far below the average level because this might mean starvation, and it cannot rise too far above the average because the asset and the credit position does not allow it. These constraints are likely to be less binding at higher income levels. Empirical evidence suggests that these prior considerations are in accord with actual behavior.[3] The appropriate model in this and other similar cases is then one with *heteroskedastic* disturbances.

[3] See S. J. Prais, and H. S. Houthakker, *The Analysis of Family Budgets* (Cambridge, England: The University Press, 1955).

Properties of Least Squares Estimators

If the regression disturbance is heteroskedastic, we have

$$E(\varepsilon_i^2) = \sigma_i^2.$$

This implies that the variance of the disturbance may vary from observation to observation, and we want to know how this behavior of the variance affects the properties of the least squares estimators of the regression coefficients. First, we consider the property of unbiasedness. The least squares estimator of β is

$$\hat{\beta} = \frac{\sum x_i' y_i'}{\sum x_i'^2} = \beta + \frac{\sum x_i' \varepsilon_i}{\sum x_i'^2},$$

as given by (7.32). Then

$$E(\hat{\beta}) = \beta + E\left[\frac{\sum x_i'\varepsilon_i}{\sum x_i'^2}\right] = \beta.$$

Similarly, $$\hat{\alpha} = \bar{Y} - \hat{\beta}\bar{X} = (\alpha + \beta\bar{X} + \bar{\varepsilon}) - \hat{\beta}\bar{X},$$

and $$E(\hat{\alpha}) = \alpha + \beta\bar{X} + E(\bar{\varepsilon}) - E(\hat{\beta})\bar{X} = \alpha.$$

That is, the least squares estimators are *unbiased* even under the conditions of heteroskedasticity.

Next, let us see whether the least squares estimators are still best linear unbiased estimators (BLUE). We can check this by deriving the BLUE formulas for the heteroskedastic case and by comparing them with the least squares formulas. If there is a difference, the least squares estimators are not BLUE. Beginning with the BLUE of β, say $\tilde{\beta}$, we have

$$\tilde{\beta} = \sum_i a_i Y_i$$

by the condition of linearity. Here, a_i ($i = 1, 2, \ldots, n$) are constants to be determined. Furthermore,

$$E(\tilde{\beta}) = E\Big(\sum_i a_i Y_i\Big) = \sum_i a_i(\alpha + \beta X_i) = \alpha\Big(\sum_i a_i\Big) + \beta\Big(\sum_i a_i X_i\Big).$$

For $\tilde{\beta}$ to be unbiased we require, as in the case of homoskedasticity, that

$$\sum_i a_i = 0 \qquad \text{and} \qquad \sum_i a_i X_i = 1.$$

The variance of $\tilde{\beta}$ is given as

$$\begin{aligned}\operatorname{Var}(\tilde{\beta}) &= E\Big[\sum_i a_i Y_i - E\Big(\sum_i a_i Y_i\Big)\Big]^2 = E\Big[\sum_i a_i(Y_i - EY_i)\Big]^2 \\ &= E\Big[\sum_i a_i\varepsilon_i\Big]^2 = E\sum_i a_i^2\varepsilon_i^2 + 2E\sum_{i<j} a_i\varepsilon_i a_j\varepsilon_j,\end{aligned}$$

recalling the result in (7.17). Since $E(\varepsilon_i^2) = \sigma_i^2$ and $E(\varepsilon_i\varepsilon_j) = 0$ $(i < j)$, we obtain

$$\operatorname{Var}(\tilde{\beta}) = \sum_i a_i^2\sigma_i^2.$$

Now we have to find $a_1, a_2, \ldots, a_n$ such that the preceding expression is as small as possible and, at the same time, the conditions $\sum a_i = 0$ and $\sum a_i X_i = 1$ are met. Using the Lagrange multiplier method, we form a function,

$$H = \sum_i a_i^2 \sigma_i^2 - \lambda_1 \Big(\sum_i a_i\Big) - \lambda_2 \Big(\sum_i a_i X_i - 1\Big),$$

which is to be minimized with respect to $a_1, a_2, \ldots, a_n$, λ_1 and λ_2. Differentiating H and putting the resulting first derivatives equal to zero, we get

$$\begin{aligned}
2a_1\sigma_1^2 - \lambda_1 - \lambda_2 X_1 &= 0,\\
2a_2\sigma_2^2 - \lambda_1 - \lambda_2 X_2 &= 0,\\
&\vdots\\
2a_n\sigma_n^2 - \lambda_1 - \lambda_2 X_n &= 0,\\
-\sum_i a_i &= 0,\\
-\Big(\sum_i a_i X_i\Big) + 1 &= 0.
\end{aligned}$$

This gives $(n + 2)$ equations for the unknowns $a_1, a_2, \ldots, a_n$, λ_1 and λ_2. Let us now introduce a more convenient notation by writing

$$\frac{1}{\sigma_i^2} = w_i.$$

Then, the first n of the above equations can be written as

$$\begin{aligned}
a_1 &= \tfrac{1}{2}(\lambda_1 w_1 + \lambda_2 w_1 X_1),\\
a_2 &= \tfrac{1}{2}(\lambda_1 w_2 + \lambda_2 w_2 X_2),\\
&\vdots\\
a_n &= \tfrac{1}{2}(\lambda_1 w_n + \lambda_2 w_n X_n).
\end{aligned}$$

Adding we get

$$\sum_i a_i = \tfrac{1}{2}\Big(\lambda_1 \sum_i w_i + \lambda_2 \sum w_i X_i\Big).$$

Further, by multiplying the first equation by X_1, the second equation by X_2, the third equation by X_3, and so on, and then adding, we obtain

$$\sum_i a_i X_i = \tfrac{1}{2}\Big(\lambda_1 \sum w_i X_i + \lambda_2 \sum w_i X_i^2\Big).$$

Substituting zero for $\sum_i a_i$ and unity for $\sum_i a_i X_i$ gives

$$\begin{aligned}
0 &= \tfrac{1}{2}\Big(\lambda_1 \sum_i w_i + \lambda_2 \sum_i w_i X_i\Big),\\
1 &= \tfrac{1}{2}\Big(\lambda_1 \sum_i w_i X_i + \lambda_2 \sum_i w_i X_i^2\Big).
\end{aligned}$$

The solution for λ_1 and λ_2 is

$$\lambda_1 = \frac{-2 \sum w_i X_i}{(\sum w_i)(\sum w_i X_i^2) - (\sum w_i X_i)^2},$$

$$\lambda_2 = \frac{2 \sum w_i}{(\sum w_i)(\sum w_i X_i^2) - (\sum w_i X_i)^2}.$$

These expressions can be substituted into the solutions for $a_1, a_2, \ldots, a_n$,

$$a_i = \tfrac{1}{2}(\lambda_1 w_i + \lambda_2 w_i X_i) \qquad (i = 1, 2, \ldots, n),$$

to give

$$a_i = \frac{-w_i(\sum w_i X_i) + w_i X_i(\sum w_i)}{(\sum w_i)(\sum w_i X_i^2) - (\sum w_i X_i)^2}.$$

These are the constants that minimize the variance of $\tilde{\beta}$ and, at the same time, make it an unbiased estimator. Substitution for a_i into $\tilde{\beta} = \sum a_i Y_i$ leads to

$$\tilde{\beta} = \frac{(\sum w_i)(\sum w_i X_i Y_i) - (\sum w_i X_i)(\sum w_i Y_i)}{(\sum w_i)(\sum w_i X_i^2) - (\sum w_i X_i)^2}, \tag{8.1}$$

which is obviously a different formula than that for the least squares estimator of β. The variance of $\tilde{\beta}$ is

$$\text{Var}(\tilde{\beta}) = \sum_i a_i^2 \sigma_i^2 = \frac{(\sum w_i)}{(\sum w_i)(\sum w_i X_i^2) - (\sum w_i X_i)^2}. \tag{8.2}$$

In a similar way we can derive the best linear unbiased estimator of α and its variance when the disturbance is heteroskedastic. This is

$$\tilde{\alpha} = \frac{\sum w_i Y_i}{\sum w_i} - \tilde{\beta}\left[\frac{\sum w_i X_i}{\sum w_i}\right], \tag{8.3}$$

which again is different from the least squares estimator of α. The variance of $\tilde{\alpha}$ is

$$\text{Var}(\tilde{\alpha}) = \frac{\sum w_i X_i^2}{(\sum w_i)(\sum w_i X_i^2) - (\sum w_i X_i)^2}. \tag{8.4}$$

Given these results, we have to conclude that the least squares estimators of the regression coefficients are not BLUE when the assumption of homoskedasticity does not hold. This means that the least squares estimators do not have the smallest variance in a class of unbiased estimators and, therefore, that they are not efficient.

Turning to the asymptotic properties, we can check whether the least squares estimators are consistent under heteroskedasticity by establishing their probability limits as defined in Section 6–1. We have

$$\text{plim}\, \hat{\beta} = \text{plim}\left[\frac{\sum x_i' y_i'}{\sum x_i'^2}\right] = \beta + \text{plim}\left[\frac{\sum x_i' \varepsilon_i}{\sum x_i'^2}\right]$$

$$= \beta + \frac{\text{plim}(\sum x_i' \varepsilon_i / n)}{\text{plim}(\sum x_i'^2 / n)}$$

by the use of the Slutsky Theorem (Theorem 17 of Section 6–1). In the last term on the right-hand side, the numerator is equal to zero because $(\sum x_i'\varepsilon_i/n)$ is a consistent estimator of the "covariance" of X_i and ε_i which is zero, and the denominator is a finite number different from zero by assumption (7.6). Therefore,

$$\text{plim}\, \hat{\beta} = \beta,$$

indicating that $\hat{\beta}$ is a consistent estimator of β. Similarly,

$$\begin{aligned}\text{plim}\, \hat{\alpha} &= \text{plim}\,(\bar{Y} - \hat{\beta}\bar{X}) = \text{plim}\,(\alpha + \beta\bar{X} + \bar{\varepsilon} - \hat{\beta}\bar{X})\\ &= \alpha + \beta\bar{X} + \text{plim}\,(\bar{\varepsilon}) - \text{plim}\,(\hat{\beta}\bar{X}) = \alpha.\end{aligned}$$

That is, the least squares estimators of the regression coefficients are *consistent* even if the disturbance is not *homoskedastic*.

To find whether the least squares estimators are asymptotically efficient under the condition of heteroskedasticity, we derive the appropriate maximum likelihood estimators which are known to be asymptotically efficient. Then, we will check whether the variances of the maximum likelihood estimators are asymptotically equivalent to those of the least squares estimators. If they are not, the least squares estimators are not asymptotically efficient. Setting up the likelihood function as in (7.26) but allowing for heteroskedasticity, we get

$$L = -\frac{n}{2}\log(2\pi) - \frac{1}{2}\sum_{i=1}^{n}\log\sigma_i^2 - \frac{1}{2}\sum_{i=1}^{n}\left[\frac{Y_i - \alpha - \beta X_i}{\sigma_i}\right]^2. \tag{8.5}$$

The first derivatives of L with respect to α and β are

$$\frac{\partial L}{\partial \alpha} = \sum_i \left[\frac{Y_i - \alpha - \beta X_i)}{\sigma_i^2}\right],$$

$$\frac{\partial L}{\partial \beta} = \sum_i \left[\frac{X_i(Y_i - \alpha - \beta X_i)}{\sigma_i^2}\right].$$

Putting these derivatives equal to zero and solving for the estimators of α and β leads to the formulas (8.1) and (8.3) for the best linear unbiased estimators. Consequently, the variances of the maximum likelihood estimators are also the same as those of the best linear unbiased estimators. These are given by formulas (8.2) and (8.4). We should compare these variances with those of the least squares estimators. The variance of the least squares estimator of β under heteroskedasticity is

$$\begin{aligned}\text{Var}(\hat{\beta}) &= E(\hat{\beta} - \beta)^2 = E\left[\frac{\sum x_i'\varepsilon_i}{\sum x_i'^2}\right]^2 \\ &= E\left[\frac{\sum x_i'^2\varepsilon_i^2}{(\sum x_i'^2)^2}\right] + 2E\sum_{i<j}\left[\frac{x_i'\varepsilon_i x_j'\varepsilon_j}{\sum x_i'^2}\right] \\ &= \frac{\sum x_i'^2\sigma_i^2}{(\sum x_i'^2)^2} = \frac{\sum(x_i'^2/w_i)}{(\sum x_i'^2)^2}.\end{aligned} \tag{8.6}$$

This variance obviously differs from the variance of $\tilde{\beta}$ given by (8.2), *whatever the sample size*. A similar conclusion can be reached with respect to the variance of the least squares estimator of α. Therefore, since the variances of the least squares estimators are not asymptotically equivalent to the variances of the maximum likelihood estimators, the least squares estimators are *not* asymptotically efficient when the disturbance is not homoskedastic.

Properties of the Estimated Variances of the Least Squares Estimators

We have found that under heteroskedasticity the least squares estimators of the regression coefficients are unbiased and consistent but not efficient or asymptotically efficient. Thus, if the disturbance is heteroskedastic and we do not know it (or know it but disregard it) and use the least squares formulas, the resulting estimators will still have some desirable properties. But when we come to using these estimators for testing hypotheses or constructing confidence intervals, we require not only that the estimators themselves be unbiased, but also that their estimated variances be unbiased. Otherwise, the tests are invalid and the constructed confidence intervals incorrect. Therefore, the next question concerns the biasedness or unbiasedness of the estimated variances obtained from the conventional formulas for the least squares estimators. For the least squares estimator of the regression slope, $\hat{\beta}$, the conventional formula for calculating the variance is given by (7.37) as

$$s_{\hat{\beta}}^2 = \frac{s^2}{\sum x_i'^2},$$

where $s^2 = [\sum (Y_i - \hat{\alpha} - \hat{\beta}X_i)^2]/(n - 2)$. Under homoskedasticity, this is an unbiased estimator of the variance of $\hat{\beta}$. We wish to know whether the property of unbiasedness of $s_{\hat{\beta}}^2$ is preserved when the assumption of homoskedasticity does not hold. To answer this we have to find the mathematical expectation of s^2. We have

$$E(s^2) = E\left[\frac{1}{n-2}\right] \sum_i [\alpha + \beta X_i + \varepsilon_i - \hat{\alpha} - \hat{\beta}X_i]^2$$

$$= \frac{1}{n-2} \sum_i E[-(\hat{\alpha} - \alpha) - (\hat{\beta} - \beta)X_i + \varepsilon_i]^2.$$

Substituting for $(\hat{\alpha} - \alpha)$ from (7.30) we get

$$E(s^2) = \frac{1}{n-2} \sum_i E[-(\hat{\beta} - \beta)x_i' + \varepsilon_i']^2$$

$$= \frac{1}{n-2} \left[E(\hat{\beta} - \beta)^2 \sum_i x_i'^2 + E \sum_i \varepsilon_i'^2 - 2E(\hat{\beta} - \beta) \sum x_i'\varepsilon_i'\right].$$

Now, under heteroskedasticity

$$E(\hat{\beta} - \beta)^2 = \frac{\sum x_i'^2 \sigma_i^2}{(\sum x_i'^2)^2}$$

by (8.6). Further,

$$E(\varepsilon_i'^2) = E(\varepsilon_i^2) + E(\bar{\varepsilon})^2 - 2E(\varepsilon_i\bar{\varepsilon}) = E(\varepsilon_i^2) + \frac{1}{n^2}E\Big[\sum_i \varepsilon_i^2 + 2\sum_{i<j}\varepsilon_i\varepsilon_j\Big]$$

$$- \frac{2}{n}E\varepsilon_i(\varepsilon_1 + \varepsilon_2 + \cdots + \varepsilon_i + \cdots + \varepsilon_n)$$

$$= \sigma_i^2 + \frac{\sum \sigma_i^2}{n^2} - \frac{2\sigma_i^2}{n} = \left[\frac{n-2}{n}\right]\sigma_i^2 + \frac{\sum \sigma_i^2}{n^2}.$$

Finally,

$$E(\hat{\beta} - \beta)\sum x_i'\varepsilon_i' = E\left[\frac{\sum x_i'\varepsilon_i'}{\sum x_i'^2}\right]\left(\sum x_i'\varepsilon_i'\right) = E\left[\frac{\sum x_i'\varepsilon_i'}{\sum x_i'^2}\right]^2\left(\sum x_i'^2\right)$$

$$= [\mathrm{Var}(\hat{\beta})]\left(\sum x_i'^2\right) = \left[\frac{\sum x_i'^2\sigma_i^2}{(\sum x_i'^2)^2}\right]\left(\sum x_i'^2\right).$$

Substituting these results into the expression for $E(s^2)$, we obtain

$$(8.7)\qquad E(s^2) = \frac{1}{n-2}\left\{\left[\frac{\sum x_i'^2\sigma_i^2}{(\sum x_i'^2)^2}\right]\left(\sum x_i'^2\right) + \sum\left[\sigma_i^2 + \frac{\sum \sigma_i^2}{n^2} - \frac{2\sigma_i^2}{n}\right]\right.$$

$$\left. -2\left[\frac{\sum x_i'^2\sigma_i^2}{(\sum x_i'^2)^2}\right]\left(\sum x_i'^2\right)\right\}$$

$$= \frac{1}{n-2}\left[-\frac{\sum x_i'^2\sigma_i^2}{\sum x_i'^2} + \sum \sigma_i^2 + \frac{\sum \sigma_i^2}{n} - \frac{2\sum \sigma_i^2}{n}\right]$$

$$= \frac{-n(\sum x_i'^2\sigma_i^2) + (n-1)(\sum x_i'^2)(\sum \sigma_i^2)}{n(n-2)(\sum x_i'^2)}$$

and

$$(8.8)\qquad E(s_{\hat{\beta}}^2) = \frac{E(s^2)}{\sum x_i'^2} = \frac{-n(\sum x_i'^2\sigma_i^2) + (n-1)(\sum x_i'^2)(\sum \sigma_i^2)}{n(n-2)(\sum x_i'^2)^2}.$$

Since this expression is *not* the same as the expression for the variance of $\hat{\beta}$ given by (8.6), we have to conclude that the conventionally calculated variance of $\hat{\beta}$ is *biased* when the disturbance is heteroskedastic. A similar conclusion can be reached with respect to $\hat{\alpha}$.

The consequence of the preceding result is that if we use the least squares estimators of the regression coefficients when the assumption of homoskedasticity is not satisfied, the confidence limits and the tests of significance developed in Chapter 7 *do not apply*. This means that if we proceed with our regression analysis under the false belief that the disturbance is homoskedastic, our inferences about the population coefficients are incorrect—that is, the calculated confidence intervals and acceptance regions will be wrong. It would be interesting to know the direction of error in this case because then we would be able to say whether the incorrect confidence intervals and acceptance regions are likely to be wider or narrower than the correct ones. We can find the answer by determining the direction of the bias of the calculated variance. If the bias is positive, the incorrect intervals and acceptance regions will be wider than the correct ones; if the bias is negative, they will be narrower. The bias is given by

$$(8.9) \qquad E(s_{\hat{\beta}}^2) - \mathrm{Var}(\hat{\beta}) = \frac{-n(\sum x_i'^2\sigma_i^2) + (n-1)(\sum x_i'^2)(\sum \sigma_i^2)}{n(n-2)(\sum x_i'^2)^2} - \frac{\sum x_i'^2\sigma_i^2}{(\sum x_i'^2)^2}$$

$$= \frac{-n(n-1)(\sum x_i'^2\sigma_i^2) + (n-1)(\sum x_i'^2)(\sum \sigma_i^2)}{n(n-2)(\sum x_i'^2)^2}.$$

The direction of the bias depends on the sign of this expression. Since for $n > 2$ the denominator is always positive, it is only the sign of the numerator which is decisive. The latter depends on the direction of the association between $x_i'^2$ and σ_i^2. It can be shown—by setting $\sigma_i^2 = a + bx_i'^2$ $(b > 0)$ and making the appropriate substitution in (8.9)—that when $x_i'^2$ and σ_i^2 are *positively* associated, the bias is negative. In cases like this, a reliance on the conventionally calculated standard errors will tend to lead to confidence intervals and acceptance regions that are narrower than the correct ones. This means that the estimators will then be presented as having a greater precision than is justified by the chosen level of confidence, and that the probability of rejecting the null hypothesis will be higher than indicated by the stated level of significance.

Assumptions Concerning σ_i^2

Having examined the properties of the least squares estimators of the regression coefficients under the conditions of heteroskedasticity, we come to considering alternative methods of estimation. The reader will recall that we already developed estimation formulas for the heteroskedastic case earlier in the present section. These formulas, given by (8.1) and (8.3), satisfy both the BLUE and the maximum likelihood principles. At this point, we may note an alternative and simpler way of deriving these formulas. The regression equation is

$$Y_i = \alpha + \beta X_i + \varepsilon_i,$$

where, in the case of heteroskedasticity, $\varepsilon_i \sim N(0, \sigma_i^2)$. Now, let us write

$$\varepsilon_i = \frac{u_i}{\sigma\sqrt{w_i}},$$

where $u_i \sim N(0, \sigma^2)$ and w_i are nonstochastic quantities. Then,

$$\sigma_i^2 = \frac{E(u_i^2)}{\sigma^2 w_i} = \frac{\sigma^2}{\sigma^2 w_i} = \frac{1}{w_i}.$$

The regression equation can then be written as

$$Y_i = \alpha + \beta X_i + \frac{u_i}{\sigma\sqrt{w_i}}.$$

Multiplying both sides of this equation by $\sigma\sqrt{w_i}$, we get

$$(8.10) \qquad (Y_i\sigma\sqrt{w_i}) = \alpha(\sigma\sqrt{w_i}) + \beta(X_i\sigma\sqrt{w_i}) + u_i.$$

Equation (8.10) may be viewed as a regression equation in which the dependent variable is $(Y_i\sigma\sqrt{w_i})$ and which includes two explanatory variables $(\sigma\sqrt{w_i})$ and $(X_i\sigma\sqrt{w_i})$. Note that these variables can be measured only if $\sigma\sqrt{w_i}$ are known, and that the intercept of the regression equation is zero. The purpose of the transformation leading to (8.10) is to make the regression equation satisfy the condition of homoskedasticity, since the new disturbance u_i has a constant variance. By applying the least squares principle, we obtain the following "least squares normal equations" (see fn. 4, page 207)

$$\sum_i (w_i Y_i) = \tilde{\alpha} \sum_i (w_i) + \tilde{\beta} \sum_i (w_i X_i) \tag{8.11}$$

$$\sum_i (w_i X_i Y_i) = \tilde{\alpha} \sum_i (w_i X_i) + \tilde{\beta} \sum_i (w_i X_i^2)$$

because the term σ^2 cancels out. By solving these equations for $\tilde{\alpha}$ and $\tilde{\beta}$ we obtain the formulas (8.1) and (8.3). We may note in passing that these formulas are sometimes called "weighted least squares" formulas since the sample observations are, in fact, given differential weights.

The difficulty with estimation formulas (8.1) and (8.3) is that they involve the terms σ_i^2 (or their reciprocals w_i), which are generally unknown. Thus the expressions do not qualify as estimators since they cannot be evaluated. In many cases this difficulty can be overcome either by making certain assumptions about σ_i^2 or by estimating σ_i^2 from the sample. We will first discuss the situations in which we are able to bring in additional information about σ_i^2. The information is frequently in the form of an assumption stating that σ_i^2 is associated with some variable, say Z_i. For instance, in the case of the microconsumption function the variance of the disturbance is often assumed to be positively associated with the level of income. In this case the place of Z_i would be taken by the explanatory variable of the regression equation, X_i (income). An alternative, though similar, assumption would be that the variance of the disturbance is positively associated with the mean level of consumption, in which case the place of Z_i would be taken by $E(Y_i)$. Or the changes in the variance of the disturbance may be thought to be associated with changes in some "outside" variable, for instance the size of the family. Using Z_i just gives us a way of formulating the assumption about σ_i^2 in a fairly general manner. However, to make the assumption operational, we have to specify the form of the association. One form that is very convenient and may be quite plausible is

$$\sigma_i^2 = \sigma^2 Z_i^\delta, \tag{8.12}$$

which involves two parameters, σ^2 and δ. Of particular importance is the parameter δ, which measures the strength of heteroskedasticity: the lower its magnitude, the smaller the differences between individual variances. When $\delta = 0$, the model is homoskedastic.

The two parameters in (8.12) may both be unknown, in which case they have to be estimated along with the regression coefficients α and β, or the value of at least one of them may be specified a priori. For example, the value of δ is sometimes assumed to be 2 since this makes the standard deviation of the disturbance proportional to Z_i. We shall first discuss the estimation problem in general, and then consider some special cases. The complete regression model for this kind of heteroskedastic condition then is

$$Y_i = \alpha + \beta X_i + \varepsilon_i,$$

$$\varepsilon_i \sim N(0, \sigma_i^2),$$

$$\sigma_i^2 = \sigma^2 Z_i^\delta \qquad (\sigma > 0;\ Z_i > 0).$$

The disturbance ε_i is, of course, assumed to be nonautoregressive, and X_i and Z_i are considered to be nonstochastic. Then we can obtain the maximum likelihood estimators of α, β, σ^2, and δ by a simple substitution for σ_i^2 in the likelihood function (8.5), which then becomes

$$L = -\frac{n}{2}\log 2\pi - \frac{1}{2}\sum_{i=1}^{n}(\log\sigma^2 + \delta\log Z_i) - \frac{1}{2}\sum_{i=1}^{n}\left[\frac{Y_i - \alpha - \beta X_i}{\sigma Z_i^{\delta/2}}\right]^2. \tag{8.13}$$

The first derivatives of L are

$$\frac{\partial L}{\partial \alpha} = \frac{1}{\sigma^2}\sum_i\left[\frac{Y_i - \alpha - \beta X_i}{Z_i^\delta}\right] \tag{8.14}$$

$$\frac{\partial L}{\partial \beta} = \frac{1}{\sigma^2}\sum_i\left[\frac{(Y_i - \alpha - \beta X_i)X_i}{Z_i^\delta}\right]$$

$$\frac{\partial L}{\partial \sigma^2} = -\frac{n}{2\sigma^2} + \frac{1}{2\sigma^4}\sum_i\left[\frac{Y_i - \alpha - \beta X_i}{Z_i^{\delta/2}}\right]^2$$

$$\frac{\partial L}{\partial \delta} = -\frac{1}{2}\sum_i \log Z_i + \frac{1}{2\sigma^2}\sum_i\left[\frac{(Y_i - \alpha - \beta X_i)^2\log Z_i}{Z_i^\delta}\right].$$

By putting each of these derivatives equal to zero, we obtain four equations to be solved for the four unknown values of α, β, σ^2, and δ. However, these equations are highly nonlinear and their solution may be quite troublesome.

Let us now consider some special cases of (8.12) that have been used in practical applications.

Case A: $\delta = 2$ *and* $Z_i = X_i$. In this case, $\sigma_i^2 = \sigma^2 X_i^2$; that is, the variance of the disturbance is assumed to be proportional to the squared value of the explanatory variable. The likelihood function (8.13) now contains only three unknown parameters, α, β, and σ^2. We can substitute for δ and Z_i in the first three expressions of (8.14), put each of these expressions equal to zero, and solve for the three unknowns. It is easily seen that the solution is exactly the same as that given by (8.1) and (8.3) except that w_i is replaced by $1/(\sigma^2 X_i^2)$. That is, we have

$$(8.15)\qquad \hat{\beta}_A = \frac{[\sum (1/X_i^2)][\sum (Y_i/X_i)] - [\sum (1/X_i)][\sum (Y_i/X_i^2)]}{n \sum (1/X_i^2) - [\sum (1/X_i)]^2};$$

$$(8.16)\qquad \hat{\alpha}_A = \frac{\sum (Y_i/X_i^2)}{\sum (1/X_i^2)} - \hat{\beta}_A \left[\frac{\sum (1/X_i)}{\sum (1/X_i^2)}\right],$$

where the subscript A indicates that the estimators have been derived for the specification of Case A. If the specification of the model is correct, these estimators are BLUE, consistent, and asymptotically efficient. The estimator of σ^2 is

$$(8.17)\qquad \hat{\sigma}_A^2 = \frac{1}{n} \sum_i \left[\left(\frac{Y_i}{X_i}\right) - \hat{\alpha}_A\left(\frac{1}{X_i}\right) - \hat{\beta}_A\right]^2$$

$$= \frac{1}{n}\left[\sum_i \left(\frac{Y_i}{X_i}\right)^2 - \hat{\alpha}_A \sum \left(\frac{Y_i}{X_i^2}\right) - \hat{\beta}_A \sum \left(\frac{Y_i}{X_i}\right)\right].$$

This estimator is consistent and asymptotically efficient but not unbiased. An unbiased estimator of σ^2, say, s_A^2, is

$$(8.18)\qquad s_A^2 = \left[\frac{n}{n-2}\right] \hat{\sigma}_A^2.$$

The variances of $\hat{\alpha}_A$ and $\hat{\beta}_A$ are given by (8.2) and (8.4), after w_i is replaced by $1/(\sigma^2 X_i^2)$. Unbiased estimators of these variances can be obtained by replacing σ^2 by s_A^2. This gives

$$(8.19)\qquad s_{\hat{\beta}_A}^2 = \frac{s_A^2 \sum (1/X_i^2)}{n \sum (1/X_i^2) - [\sum (1/X_i)]^2}$$

and

$$(8.20)\qquad s_{\hat{\alpha}_A}^2 = \frac{n s_A^2}{n \sum (1/X_i^2) - [\sum (1/X_i)]^2}.$$

Example Consider the following sample data on annual expenditures for clothing and on income, collected from a sample of 20 families.

Income, \$	Number of Families	Clothing Expenditures, \$
2000	8	160, 160, 180, 200, 210, 220, 230, 250
4000	7	200, 220, 230, 300, 310, 340, 350
6000	5	300, 300, 400, 450, 540

These observations are shown graphically in Figure 8–1. The relationship between expenditure on clothing and income is hypothesized to be

$$Y_i = \alpha + \beta X_i + \varepsilon_i,$$

where Y = expenditure on clothing, X = income, ε = random disturbance, and the subscript i refers to the ith family. The explanatory variable X_i is considered to be nonstochastic, and the disturbance ε_i is assumed to be a normally distributed, nonautoregressive random variable with zero mean and variance σ_i^2. The ordinary least squares estimators of the regression coefficients are

$$\hat{\beta} = \frac{\sum y_i' x_i'}{\sum x_i'^2} = \frac{2{,}425{,}000}{50{,}200{,}000} = 0.0483,$$

$$\hat{\alpha} = \bar{Y} - \hat{\beta}\bar{X} = 277.5 - 0.0483 \times 3700 = 98.79,$$

and the coefficient of determination is

$$R^2 = \frac{\hat{\beta} \sum x_i' y_i'}{\sum y_i'^2} = \frac{0.0483 \times 2{,}425{,}000}{190{,}975} = 0.6133.$$

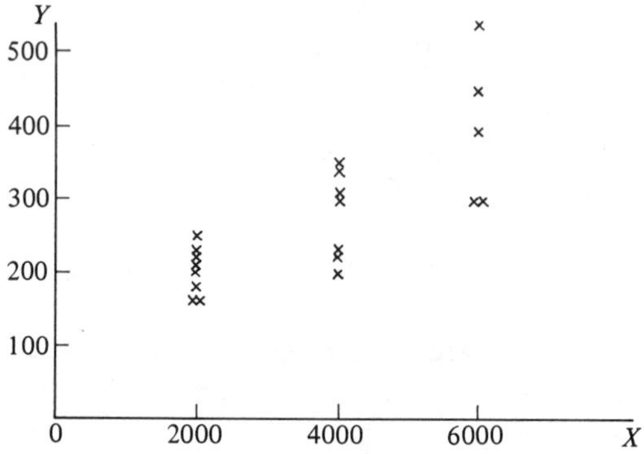

Figure 8–1

Given that the model is a heteroskedastic one, the least squares estimators are unbiased but not efficient or asymptotically efficient. Their conventionally calculated standard errors are biased and, therefore, are not presented. Note that the above value of R^2 is the maximum value for the given sample since the least squares regression line gives the best fit of any line by definition.

Now, if we assume that

$$\sigma_i^2 = \sigma^2 X_i^2,$$

we can obtain efficient estimators of the regression coefficients by using formulas (8.15) and (8.16). These call for the following quantities calculated from the sample data:

$$\sum_i \left[\frac{1}{X_i}\right] = \frac{8}{2000} + \frac{7}{4000} + \frac{5}{6000} = 0.006583;$$

$$\sum_i \left[\frac{1}{X_i}\right]^2 = \frac{8}{2000^2} + \frac{7}{4000^2} + \frac{5}{6000^2} = 0.000002567;$$

$$\sum_i \left[\frac{Y_i}{X_i}\right] = \frac{160}{2000} + \frac{160}{2000} + \cdots + \frac{540}{6000} = 1.624167;$$

$$\sum \left[\frac{Y_i}{X_i^2}\right] = \frac{160}{2000^2} + \frac{160}{2000^2} + \cdots + \frac{540}{6000^2} = 0.000579630.$$

Also we note that

$$\sum_i \left[\frac{Y_i}{X_i}\right]^2 = 0.141388.$$

Substitution then gives

$$\hat{\beta}_A = 0.0451 \qquad \text{and} \qquad \hat{\alpha}_A = 109.82.$$

Further, using formulas (8.19) and (8.20) we obtain estimates of the standard errors of $\hat{\alpha}_A$ and $\hat{\beta}_A$:

$$s^2_{\hat{\beta}_A} = 0.00017932, \qquad s_{\hat{\beta}_A} = 0.0134,$$

$$s^2_{\hat{\alpha}_A} = 1{,}391.7020, \qquad s_{\hat{\alpha}_A} = 37.30$$

Finally, $$R^2 = 1 - \frac{\sum (Y_i - \hat{\alpha}_A - \hat{\beta}_A X_i)^2}{\sum y_i'^2} = 1 - \frac{74{,}364}{190{,}975} = 0.6106.$$

These results can be summarized as follows:

$$Y_i = \underset{(37.30)}{109.82} + \underset{(0.0134)}{0.0451} X_i + e_i, \qquad R^2 = 0.6106.$$

As expected, the value of R^2 is lower than that for the least squares regression, but the difference is very small. Note that the implied estimate of the average income elasticity of demand for clothing is

$$\hat{\eta}_{\text{INC}} = \hat{\beta}_A\left[\frac{\bar{X}}{\bar{Y}}\right] = 0.6013,$$

which suggests that the demand for clothing is income-inelastic.

Case B: $\delta = 2$ and $Z_i = E(Y_i)$. In this case it is assumed that the variance of the disturbance is proportional to the squared mean of Y_i. That is, we assume that

$$\sigma_i^2 = \sigma^2[E(Y_i)]^2 = \sigma^2(\alpha + \beta X_i)^2$$

The likelihood function (8.13) in this case becomes

$$L = -\frac{n}{2}\log(2\pi) - \frac{n}{2}\log\sigma^2 - \sum_i \log(\alpha + \beta X_i) - \frac{1}{2\sigma^2}\sum_i \left[\frac{Y_i - \alpha - \beta X_i}{(\alpha + \beta X_i)}\right]^2. \tag{8.21}$$

This function, as in Case A, involves only three unknown parameters, α, β, and σ^2. We could take the first derivatives of L with respect to each of the three parameters, put each of them equal to zero, and solve for the three unknown values.[4] However, the resulting equations are highly nonlinear and their solution

[4] Note that it would be incorrect simply to substitute for Z_i (and for δ) in the expressions for the first derivatives given in (8.14) because these were derived on the understanding that Z_i does not involve any of the unknown parameters. This is not true when, as in the present case, $Z_i = \alpha + \beta X_i$.

is difficult. We can simplify the problem by replacing $E(Y_i)$ with $\hat{Y}_i$, which represents the values of Y calculated from the least squares regression. That is, we take the standard deviation of the disturbance to be proportional to the distance of the least squares regression line from the horizontal axis. Since $\hat{Y}_i$ is a consistent estimator of $E(Y_i)$, we can write

$$\sigma_i = \sigma E(Y_i)$$

as

$$\sigma_i = \sigma \operatorname{plim} \hat{Y}_i,$$

so that putting

$$\sigma_i = \sigma \hat{Y}_i$$

does not damage the consistency of the resulting estimators of the regression coefficients. Strictly speaking, these estimators are not *exactly* maximum likelihood estimators but serve as their approximations.

By allowing ourselves the foregoing simplification, we can use formulas (8.1) and (8.3) for estimating α and β, providing we replace w_i by $1/(\sigma^2 \hat{Y}_i^2)$. Then we obtain

$$\hat{\beta}_B = \frac{\sum (1/\hat{Y}^2) \sum (XY/\hat{Y}^2) - \sum (X/\hat{Y}^2) \sum (Y/\hat{Y}^2)}{\sum (1/\hat{Y}^2) \sum (X^2/\hat{Y}^2) - [\sum (X/\hat{Y}^2)]^2}, \tag{8.22}$$

and

$$\hat{\alpha}_B = \frac{\sum (Y/\hat{Y}^2)}{\sum (1/\hat{Y}^2)} - \hat{\beta}_B \left[\frac{\sum (X/\hat{Y}^2)}{\sum (1/\hat{Y}^2)}\right], \tag{8.23}$$

where the subscript B indicates that the estimators apply to the specification of Case B. If the specification of the model is correct, these estimators approximate the maximum likelihood estimators which are known to be consistent and asymptotically efficient. The estimator of σ^2 is

$$s_B^2 = \frac{1}{n-2}\left[\sum_i \left(\frac{Y_i^2}{\hat{Y}_i^2}\right) - \hat{\alpha}_B \sum \left(\frac{Y_i}{\hat{Y}_i^2}\right) - \hat{\beta}_B \sum \left(\frac{X_i Y_i}{\hat{Y}_i^2}\right)\right]. \tag{8.24}$$

Finally, the estimators of the standard errors of $\hat{\alpha}_B$ and $\hat{\beta}_B$ are given by

$$s_{\hat{\beta}_B}^2 = \frac{s_B^2 \sum (1/\hat{Y}_i^2)}{\sum (1/\hat{Y}_i^2) \sum (X_i^2/\hat{Y}_i^2) - [\sum (X_i/\hat{Y}_i^2)]^2} \tag{8.25}$$

and

$$s_{\hat{\alpha}_B}^2 = \frac{s_B^2 \sum (X_i^2/\hat{Y}_i^2)}{\sum (1/\hat{Y}_i^2) \sum (X_i^2/\hat{Y}_i^2) - [\sum (Y_i/\hat{Y}_i^2)]^2}. \tag{8.26}$$

EXAMPLE In the example on the relationship between family expenditure on clothing and income given in connection with Case A, we assumed that $\sigma_i = \sigma X_i$. Let us change this assumption to $\sigma_i = \sigma E(Y_i)$ in accordance with Case B. In carrying out the calculations we shall approximate $E(Y_i)$ by $\hat{Y}_i$, previously determined to be

$$\hat{Y}_i = 98.79 + 0.0483 X_i.$$

The following quantities have been calculated from the sample data:

$$\sum_i \left[\frac{1}{\hat{Y}_i^2}\right] = 0.000322729,$$

$$\sum_i \left[\frac{X_i}{\hat{Y}_i^2}\right] = 0.946107,$$

$$\sum_i \left[\frac{X_i^2}{\hat{Y}_i^2}\right] = 3{,}271.421,$$

$$\sum_i \left[\frac{Y_i}{\hat{Y}_i^2}\right] = 0.077417,$$

$$\sum \left[\frac{Y_i^2}{\hat{Y}_i^2}\right] = 20.503404,$$

$$\sum \left[\frac{X_i Y_i}{\hat{Y}_i^2}\right] = 250.091731.$$

By making the appropriate substitutions into formulas (8.22) through (8.26) we get

$$\overset{\triangle}{\beta}_B = 0.0465,$$

$$\overset{\triangle}{\alpha}_B = 103.56,$$

and

$$s^2_{\overset{\triangle}{\beta}_B} = 0.00009558, \qquad s_{\overset{\triangle}{\beta}_B} = 0.0098,$$

$$s^2_{\overset{\triangle}{\alpha}_B} = 968.9202, \qquad s_{\overset{\triangle}{\alpha}_B} = 31.13.$$

Finally,

$$R^2 = 1 - \frac{\sum (Y_i - \overset{\triangle}{\alpha}_B - \overset{\triangle}{\beta}_B X_i)^2}{\sum y_i'^2} = 1 - \frac{74{,}063}{190{,}975} = 0.6122.$$

In summary, the results for Case B are

$$\underset{}{Y_i = \underset{(31.13)}{103.56} + \underset{(0.0098)}{0.0465} X_i + e_i}, \qquad R^2 = 0.6122.$$

Case C: $Z_i = X_i$. This case is more general than the previous two cases since we do not make any prior specification concerning the value of δ. The assumption about the nature of heteroskedasticity in this case is

$$\sigma_i^2 = \sigma^2 X_i^\delta,$$

or

$$\log \sigma_i = \log \sigma + \frac{\delta}{2} \log X_i.$$

The likelihood function (8.13) then involves *four* unknown parameters, α, β, σ^2, and δ. As mentioned earlier, δ measures the strength of heteroskedasticity in the sense that the smaller the value of δ, the smaller the difference between the individual variances of the disturbance. In Case C, unlike Cases A and B, we are letting the data tell us what this strength seems to be, rather than specifying it a priori. The only prior specification that we make is that the standard deviation of the disturbance is related to the explanatory variable—and that this relationship is log-linear. The price that we pay for a greater generality in the present case is the higher degree of complexity of estimation.

The problem of obtaining maximum likelihood estimates of the regression coefficients, although more complicated than in the previous two cases, is manageable if we use an electronic computer. A relatively simple way of handling it is as follows. By putting each of the first three derivatives of (8.14) equal to zero, substituting X_i for Z_i, and rearranging terms we obtain the following three equations:

$$\text{(8.27)} \qquad \sum_i \left[\frac{Y_i}{X_i^{\delta}}\right] = \hat{\alpha} \sum_i \left[\frac{1}{X_i^{\delta}}\right] + \hat{\beta} \sum_i \left[\frac{X_i}{X_i^{\delta}}\right],$$

$$\text{(8.28)} \qquad \sum_i \left[\frac{X_i Y_i}{X_i^{\delta}}\right] = \hat{\alpha} \sum_i \left[\frac{X_i}{X_i^{\delta}}\right] + \hat{\beta} \sum_i \left[\frac{X_i^2}{X_i^{\delta}}\right].$$

$$\text{(8.29)} \qquad \hat{\sigma}^2 = \frac{1}{n}\left[\sum_i \left(\frac{Y_i^2}{X_i^{\delta}}\right) - \hat{\alpha} \sum_i \left(\frac{Y_i}{X_i^{\delta}}\right) - \hat{\beta} \sum \left(\frac{X_i Y_i}{X_i^{\delta}}\right)\right].$$

If δ were known, equations (8.27) through (8.29) could be solved for $\hat{\alpha}$, $\hat{\beta}$, and $\hat{\sigma}^2$. Therefore, by selecting different values of δ we obtain different estimates of the remaining three parameters. In this way we can obtain estimates of α, β, and σ^2 for $\delta = 0$, $\delta = 0.1$, $\delta = 0.2$, and so on until we come to values of δ that are clearly unreasonable (in most practical situations this would be perhaps 5.0 or 6.0). For each value of δ—and the corresponding values of $\hat{\alpha}$, $\hat{\beta}$, and $\hat{\sigma}^2$—we also calculate the value of L as given by (8.13). Then, of all the solutions, we select the one that gives the largest value of L. This solution will maximize the likelihood function as desired. The standard errors of $\hat{\alpha}$ and $\hat{\beta}$ can be estimated by using formulas (8.2) and (8.4), after replacing w_i by $(1/\hat{\sigma}^2 X_i^{\hat{\delta}})$. The variance of $\hat{\delta}$ can be estimated by $s_{\hat{\delta}}^2 = 2/[\sum_i (\log_e X_i)^2]$, where $\log_e X_i = 2.302585 \log_{10} X_i$. This formula represents the asymptotic variance of $\hat{\delta}$ as defined on page 182. Incidentally, if the precision of one decimal place for $\hat{\delta}$ is not sufficient, we can choose finer intervals for the successive values of δ in the vicinity of the solution.

Estimation of σ_i^2

When no assumptions about the nature of heteroskedasticity are made, we have to rely entirely on the sample information and estimate the variances of the disturbance from the data. Since for each specific value of X the value of the variance of the disturbance may be different, we need several observations on the dependent variable for each X_i. If we had only one observation for each value of X, we could obviously find no information about the dispersion of *all* potential observations. Suppose, therefore, that there are m different values of X in the sample, and that for each X_i we have n_i observations on the dependent variable.

Then the regression equation can be written as

$$Y_{ij} = \alpha + \beta X_i + \varepsilon_{ij} \qquad (i = 1, 2, \ldots, m; j = 1, 2, \ldots, n_i),$$

$$n = \sum_{i=1}^{m} n_i,$$

$$X_i \neq X_j \qquad (i \neq j).$$

To illustrate the new subscript notation, we use the data on family expenditure on clothing and income on page 259. There we have

$$m = 3,$$
$$n_1 = 8,$$
$$n_2 = 7,$$
$$n_3 = 5,$$
$$n = 20.$$

Also, for example, $Y_{25} = 310$ is the value of the dependent variable for the fifth family in the \$4000 income bracket. In general, there are $(m + 2)$ parameters to be estimated: $\alpha, \beta, \sigma_1^2, \sigma_2^2, \ldots, \sigma_m^2$. The appropriate likelihood function is given by

$$(8.30) \qquad L = -\frac{n}{2}\log(2\pi) - \frac{1}{2}\sum_{i=1}^{m} n_i \log \sigma_i^2 - \frac{1}{2}\sum_{i=1}^{m}\sum_{j=1}^{n_i}\left[\frac{Y_{ij} - \alpha - \beta X_i}{\sigma_i}\right]^2.$$

By differentiating L with respect to the unknown parameters, and by putting the resulting derivatives equal to zero, we would obtain $(m + 2)$ equations that could be solved for the $(m + 2)$ values of the parameters. However, the solution is quite difficult to compute.

One way of overcoming the computational difficulty is to use an iterative procedure, as follows.

1. Obtain ordinary least squares estimates of α and β, to be called $\hat{\alpha}$ and $\hat{\beta}$. Use these to get "first round" estimates of σ_i^2, say $\hat{\sigma}_i^2$, given as

$$\hat{\sigma}_i^2 = \frac{1}{n_i}\sum_{j=1}^{n_i}(Y_{ij} - \hat{\alpha} - \hat{\beta}X_i)^2.$$

2. In formulas (8.1) and (8.3), replace w_i with $1/\hat{\sigma}_i^2$, and obtain new estimates of α and β, say $\hat{\hat{\alpha}}$ and $\hat{\hat{\beta}}$. Use these to obtain "second round" estimates of σ_i^2, say $\hat{\hat{\sigma}}_i^2$, given as

$$\hat{\hat{\sigma}}_i^2 = \frac{1}{n_i}\sum_{j=1}^{n_i}(Y_{ij} - \hat{\hat{\alpha}} - \hat{\hat{\beta}}X_i)^2.$$

3. In formulas (8.1) and (8.3), replace w_i by $1/\hat{\hat{\sigma}}_i^2$, and obtain a new set of estimates of α and β. Use these estimates to obtain "third round" estimates of σ_i^2.

This is to be continued until the values of the estimates converge, that is, until the differences between successive sets of estimates are negligible.[5] The standard errors of the estimated regression coefficients can be estimated by putting $w_i = 1/\tilde{\sigma}_i^2$ (where $\tilde{\sigma}_i^2$ is the "final round" estimate of σ_i^2) in formulas (8.2) and (8.4).

This iterative procedure is obviously quite laborious. A simple alternative is to estimate σ_i^2 by

(8.31) $$s_i^2 = \frac{1}{n_i} \sum_{j=1}^{n_i} (Y_{ij} - \bar{Y}_i)^2,$$

where $$\bar{Y}_i = \frac{1}{n_i} \sum_{j=1}^{n_i} Y_{ij}.$$

It is easy to show that s_i^2 is a consistent estimator of σ_i^2. By replacing w_i with $1/s_i^2$ in (8.1) and (8.3), we obtain estimates of the regression coefficients; and by making the same substitution in (8.2) and (8.4), we obtain their estimated standard errors. The price that we are paying for this simplification is that the resulting estimates are not exactly equal to the maximum likelihood estimates, but only asymptotically so.

EXAMPLE Returning to the data on family expenditure on clothing and income, we can consider estimating the variances of the disturbance from the data rather than making any assumptions about them. Using (8.31) we obtain

$$s_1^2 = 935.94,$$
$$s_2^2 = 3183.67,$$
$$s_3^2 = 8416.00.$$

Formulas (8.1) through (8.4) require the following quantities:

$$\sum_{i=1}^{m} \sum_{j=1}^{n_i} w_i = \sum_{i=1}^{m} n_i w_i = \frac{n_1}{s_1^2} + \frac{n_2}{s_2^2} + \frac{n_3}{s_3^2} = 0.011340725;$$

$$\sum_{i=1}^{m} \sum_{j=1}^{n_i} w_i X_i Y_{ij} = \sum_{i=1}^{m} w_i X_i \sum_{j=1}^{n_i} Y_{ij} = \frac{X_1}{s_1^2} \sum_{j=1}^{8} Y_{1j} + \frac{X_2}{s_2^2} \sum_{j=1}^{7} Y_{2j} + \frac{X_3}{s_3^2} \sum_{j=1}^{5} Y_{3j}$$
$$= 7{,}309.240;$$

$$\sum_{i=1}^{m} \sum_{j=1}^{n_i} w_i X_i = \sum_{i=1}^{m} n_i w_i X_i = \frac{n_1 X_1}{s_1^2} + \frac{n_2 X_2}{s_2^2} + \frac{n_3 X_3}{s_3^2} = 29.455270;$$

$$\sum_{i=1}^{m} \sum_{j=1}^{n_i} w_i Y_{ij} = \sum_{i=1}^{m} w_i \sum_{j=1}^{n_i} Y_{ij} = \frac{1}{s_1^2} \sum_{j=1}^{8} Y_{1j} + \frac{1}{s_2^2} \sum_{j=1}^{7} Y_{2j} + \frac{1}{s_3^2} \sum_{j=1}^{5} Y_{3j}$$
$$= 2.569218;$$

$$\sum_{i=1}^{m} \sum_{j=1}^{n_i} w_i X_i^2 = \sum_{i=1}^{m} n_i w_i X_i^2 = \frac{n_1 X_1^2}{s_1^2} + \frac{n_2 X_2^2}{s_2^2} + \frac{n_3 X_3^2}{s_3^2} = 90{,}758.660.$$

[5] The correctness of this procedure rests on two assertions; namely, (a) that the procedure always leads to convergence and (b) that the final values of the estimates coincide with the values of the maximum likelihood estimators. While the author is not aware of the existence of a formal proof of these assertions, they did appear to hold in every case that has been tried.

Then, the estimates of the regression coefficients are

$$\tilde{\beta} = 0.0446 \quad \text{and} \quad \tilde{\alpha} = 110.63,$$

and

$$s^2_{\tilde{\beta}} = 0.00007015, \qquad s_{\tilde{\beta}} = 0.0084;$$

$$s^2_{\tilde{\alpha}} = 561.4306, \qquad s_{\tilde{\alpha}} = 23.69.$$

Finally, $$R^2 = 1 - \frac{\sum_i \sum_j (Y_{ij} - \tilde{\alpha} - \tilde{\beta} X_i)^2}{\sum_i \sum_j (Y_{ij} - \bar{Y})^2} = 1 - \frac{74{,}591}{190{,}975} = 0.6094.$$

In summary, the results are

$$Y_{ij} = \underset{(23.69)}{110.63} + \underset{(0.0084)}{0.0446} X_i + e_{ij}, \qquad R^2 = 0.6094.$$

These results are similar to those obtained in Case A and Case B under various assumptions concerning σ_i^2.

Tests for Homoskedasticity

Up to this point, our discussion has been concerned with the implications of heteroskedasticity in a linear regression model. We have examined the effects of heteroskedasticity on the properties of ordinary least squares estimators and their conventionally calculated standard errors, and we have discussed various alternative estimators designed for heteroskedastic models. However, if we do not know whether the model under investigation is or is not homoskedastic, and if we are unwilling to make an assumption about it, we may not be able to decide which estimation procedure to use. In such cases we have to resort to the information provided by the sample, and carry out a test. Specifically, we may want to test the null hypothesis,

$$H_0\colon \quad \sigma_1^2 = \sigma_2^2 = \cdots = \sigma_m^2 \qquad (m \leq n),$$

where m is the number of different values of the explanatory variable. The nature of the test will depend upon the specification of the maintained hypothesis. If the maintained hypothesis is

$$\sigma_i^2 = \sigma^2 Z_i^{\delta} \qquad (i = 1, 2, \ldots, m),$$

where Z_i is some known nonstochastic variable (e.g., X_i), then the null hypothesis may be stated as

$$H_0\colon \quad \delta = 0.$$

This is because if $\delta = 0$, then $\sigma_i^2 = \sigma^2$, and this means homoskedasticity. We have already discussed the problem of obtaining a maximum likelihood estimator of δ and its estimated standard error. In large samples this estimator will be normally distributed (at least approximately) so that the test of H_0 is rather simple. At the 5% level of significance, the acceptance region for H_0 will be

$$-1.96 \leq \frac{\hat{\delta}}{s_{\hat{\delta}}} \leq +1.96,$$

where $\hat{\delta}$ is the maximum likelihood estimator of δ, and $s_{\hat{\delta}}$ its estimated standard error.

A test of the homoskedasticity hypothesis when no specification is made concerning the nature of heteroskedasticity, can be carried out if we have several observations on the dependent variable for each specific value of the explanatory variable. If this is the case, we can form the following test statistic:

$$\hat{\lambda} = \frac{-4.60517 \log M}{1 + N}, \tag{8.32}$$

where

$$\log M = \left\{\sum_i \left[\frac{n_i - 1}{2}\right] \log \left[\frac{n_i s_i^2}{n_i - 1}\right]\right\} - \left\{\sum_i \left[\frac{n_i - 1}{2}\right]\right\}\left\{\log \left[\frac{\sum n_i s_i^2}{\sum (n_i - 1)}\right]\right\},$$

$$N = \frac{1}{3(m-1)}\left\{\sum_i \left[\frac{1}{n_i}\right] - \frac{1}{n}\right\} \qquad (i = 1, 2, \ldots, m),$$

and s_i^2 is defined as in (8.31). This test statistic is approximately distributed as chi-square distribution with $(m - 1)$ degrees of freedom.[6] The acceptance region for H_0 at the 5% level of significance then is

$$\hat{\lambda} \leq \chi^2_{m-1,\,0.05}.$$

EXAMPLE In our example on family expenditure and income we have three different values of X so that the test statistic $\hat{\lambda}$ will have a chi-square distribution with two degrees of freedom. The 5% acceptance region for the hypothesis of homoskedasticity then is

$$\hat{\lambda} \leq 5.991,$$

where the value 5.991 has been taken from the chi-square table. By substitution from the sample data we obtain

$$\begin{aligned}\log M &= \frac{7}{2}\log\left[\frac{8\times 935.94}{7}\right] + \frac{6}{2}\log\left[\frac{7\times 3183.67}{6}\right] + \frac{4}{2}\log\left[\frac{5\times 8416}{4}\right] \\ &\quad - \left[\frac{7}{2} + \frac{6}{2} + \frac{4}{2}\right]\left\{\log\left[\frac{8\times 935.94 + 7\times 3183.67 + 5\times 8416}{7 + 6 + 4}\right]\right\} \\ &= -1.46505\end{aligned}$$

$$N = \frac{1}{3\times 2}\left[\frac{1}{8} + \frac{1}{7} + \frac{1}{5} - \frac{1}{20}\right] = 0.06964.$$

[6] See Paul G. Hoel, *Introduction to Mathematical Statistics*, 2nd ed. (New York: Wiley, 1955), p. 195. Note that in our definition (8.32) we use *common* logarithms. A modification of (8.32) to deal with the case in which we observe only one value of Y for each specific value of X is suggested in J. B. Ramsey, "Tests for Specification Errors in Classical Linear Least-squares Regression Analysis," *Journal of the Royal Statistical Society*, Series B, Vol. 31, 1969, pp. 350–371. Some special tests can also be found in S. M. Goldfeld and R. E. Quandt, "Some Tests for Homoscedasticity," *Journal of the American Statistical Association*, Vol. 60, September, 1965, pp. 539–547.

Therefore,

$$\hat{\lambda} = \frac{(-4.60517) \times (-1.46505)}{1.06964} = 6.305.$$

Since the value of $\hat{\lambda}$ lies outside the acceptance region, we reject the hypothesis of homoskedasticity at the 5% level of significance. The evidence suggests that the variance of the disturbance is not constant.

8–2 Autoregressive Disturbances

By the assumption (7.5) of the classical normal linear regression model, we have

$$E(\varepsilon_i \varepsilon_j) = 0 \quad \text{for all } i \neq j.$$

Since the mean of ε_i and of ε_j is assumed to be zero, we can write

$$\text{Cov}(\varepsilon_i, \varepsilon_j) = E[\varepsilon_i - E(\varepsilon_i)][\varepsilon_j - E(\varepsilon_j)] = E(\varepsilon_i \varepsilon_j) = 0.$$

This feature of the regression disturbances is known as nonautoregression; some authors refer to it as the absence of serial correlation. It implies that the disturbance occurring at one point of observation is not correlated with any other disturbance. This means that when observations are made over time, the effect of the disturbance occurring at one period does not carry over into another period. For instance, in a study of the relationship between output and inputs of a firm or industry from monthly observations, nonautoregression of the disturbance implies that the effect of machine breakdown is strictly temporary in the sense that only the current month's output is affected. In the case of cross-sectional observations such as those on income and expenditure of different families, the assumption of nonautoregression means that if the expenditure behavior of one family is "disturbed"—for example, by the visit of a relative—this does not affect the expenditure behavior of any other family.

Our present task is to consider the plausibility of the assumption of nonautoregression, to examine the consequences of its violation on the properties of the least squares estimators, and to develop alternative methods of estimation if needed. In Section 8–1 we argued that the assumption of homoskedasticity is frequently reasonable in the case of models describing the behavior of aggregates over time, but that its plausibility is questionable when microeconomic relations are estimated from cross-sectional data. Here, in connection with the assumption of nonautoregression, the argument is just the reverse. The usual contention is that the assumption of nonautoregression is more frequently violated in the case of relations estimated from time series data than in the case of relations estimated from cross-sectional data. This contention relies largely on the interpretation of the disturbance as a summary of a large number of random and independent factors that enter into the relationship under study, but which are not measurable. Then, one would suspect that the effect of these factors operating in one period would, in part, carry over to the following periods. This seems more likely than that the effect would carry over from one family, firm, or other similar unit to another—assuming, of course, that the units are selected at random from a large population.

Autoregression of the disturbances can be compared with the sound effect of tapping a musical string: while the sound is loudest at the time of impact, it does not stop immediately but lingers on for a time until it finally dies off. This may also be the characteristic of the disturbance, since its effect may linger for some time after its occurrence. But while the effect of one disturbance lingers on, other disturbances take place, as if the musical string were tapped over and over, sometimes harder than at other times. The shorter the time between the tappings, the greater the likelihood that the preceding sound can still be heard. Similarly, the shorter the periods of individual observations, the greater the likelihood of encountering autoregressive disturbances. Thus we would be more suspicious of the presence of autoregression when dealing with monthly or quarterly observations than when the data are given at annual intervals.

The presumption that relationships estimated from observations over time involve autoregressive disturbances is so common that, in any discussion of autoregression in the literature, the variables are given a subscript t (for "time") rather than the subscript i that is used in the general case. We shall follow this custom in our discussion. Thus, if the disturbances are autoregressive, we have

$$E(\varepsilon_t \varepsilon_{t-s}) \neq 0 \qquad (t > s).$$

This expression implies that the disturbance occurring at time t is related to the disturbance occurring at time $(t - s)$. The consequences of autoregression for estimation are difficult to trace unless its nature is specified more precisely. Most of the work in this context has been done on the assumption that

$$E(\varepsilon_t \varepsilon_{t-s}) = \rho^s \sigma^2 \qquad (s < t) \tag{8.33}$$

or

$$\text{Cov}(\varepsilon_t, \varepsilon_{t-s}) = \rho^s \sigma^2,$$

where ρ is a parameter whose value is less than $+1$ and more than -1, and σ^2 is the variance of ε_t as before.[7] The successive covariances of the disturbances are

$$\begin{aligned}
\text{Cov}(\varepsilon_t, \varepsilon_{t-1}) &= \rho\sigma^2, \\
\text{Cov}(\varepsilon_t, \varepsilon_{t-2}) &= \rho^2\sigma^2, \\
\text{Cov}(\varepsilon_t, \varepsilon_{t-3}) &= \rho^3\sigma^2, \\
&\ \vdots \\
\text{Cov}(\varepsilon_t, \varepsilon_1) &= \rho^{t-1}\sigma^2.
\end{aligned}$$

If the value of ρ is equal to some number between 0 and 1, ρ^2 will be smaller than ρ, ρ^3 will be smaller than ρ^2, and so on. This means that the greater the number of periods between two disturbances, the smaller their covariance. If ρ is

[7] To suppose that $|\rho| = 1$ would mean that the covariances do not diminish as s increases; it would also mean that the variance of the disturbance would grow infinitely large (see (8.37)). In most economic contexts this is implausible.

equal to zero, each covariance will be equal to zero, so that the assumption of nonautoregression is preserved. If ρ lies between -1 and 0, the values of $\rho, \rho^2, \rho^3, \ldots$ will decrease in absolute magnitude, but they will alternate in sign. The same will be true of the respective covariances.

Generation of the Disturbances

The question that has to be answered now concerns the manner in which the disturbances are generated so that they are related to each other as specified by (8.33). In the case where all the basic assumptions hold, each disturbance represents an independent random drawing from a normal population with zero mean and variance σ^2. When the disturbances are autoregressive, the drawings are no longer independent. Specifically, we shall postulate that the disturbances are generated in accordance with the following scheme:

$$\varepsilon_t = \rho\varepsilon_{t-1} + u_t \qquad (t = 1, 2, \ldots), \tag{8.34}$$

where u_t is a normally and independently distributed random variable with mean zero and a variance σ_u^2 that is assumed to be independent of ε_{t-1}. That is,

$$\begin{aligned} u_t &\sim N(0, \sigma_u^2) && \text{for all } t, \\ E(u_t u_s) &= 0 && \text{for all } t \neq s. \\ E(u_t \varepsilon_{t-1}) &= 0 && \text{for all } t. \end{aligned} \tag{8.35}$$

A relationship such as (8.34) is known as a *first-order autoregressive scheme.* It implies that each current disturbance is equal to a "portion" of the preceding disturbance *plus* a random effect represented by u_t. By a successive substitution for $\varepsilon_{t-1}, \varepsilon_{t-2}, \ldots, \varepsilon_1$, we obtain

$$\begin{aligned} \varepsilon_t &= \rho\varepsilon_{t-1} + u_t \\ &= \rho(\rho\varepsilon_{t-2} + u_{t-1}) + u_t \\ &= \rho^2\varepsilon_{t-2} + \rho u_{t-1} + u_t \\ &= \rho^2(\rho\varepsilon_{t-3} + u_{t-2}) + \rho u_{t-1} + u_t \\ &= \rho^3\varepsilon_{t-3} + \rho^2 u_{t-2} + \rho u_{t-1} + u_t \\ &\;\;\vdots \\ &= \rho^t\varepsilon_0 + \rho^{t-1}u_1 + \rho^{t-2}u_2 + \cdots + \rho^2 u_{t-2} + \rho u_{t-1} + u_t. \end{aligned}$$

This means that each disturbance ε_t is generated as a linear function of the random effects $u_1, u_2, \ldots, u_t$ and the "initial disturbance" ε_0. We have already specified how the u's are generated; to complete the description of ε_t we have to make an additional specification concerning the initial value of ε_0. For reasons that will become clear later, we assume that ε_0 is a normally distributed random variable with mean zero and variance $\sigma_u^2/(1 - \rho^2)$. That is,

$$\varepsilon_0 \sim N\left[0, \frac{\sigma_u^2}{1 - \rho^2}\right]. \tag{8.36}$$

Let us now demonstrate that the first-order autoregressive scheme as specified by (8.34) through (8.36) does, in fact, lead to the covariances between successive disturbances as stated in (8.33) and, at the same time, does not conflict with the assumptions of normality, zero mean, and homoskedasticity of the ε's. First, since ε_t is a linear combination of $\varepsilon_0, u_1, u_2, \ldots, u_t$, all of which are normal and independent of each other, ε_t itself must be normal. Furthermore, we have

$$E(\varepsilon_t) = \rho^t E(\varepsilon_0) + \rho^{t-1}E(u_1) + \cdots + \rho E(u_{t-1}) + E(u_t) = 0,$$

so that the assumption of zero mean of ε_t is also preserved. Next, we note that

$$\begin{aligned}(8.37)\qquad \text{Var}(\varepsilon_t) &= (\rho^t)^2\text{Var}(\varepsilon_0) + (\rho^{t-1})^2\text{Var}(u_1) + (\rho^{t-2})^2\text{Var}(u_2) + \cdots \\ &= \rho^{2t}\left[\frac{\sigma_u^2}{1-\rho^2}\right] + \rho^{2(t-1)}\sigma_u^2 + \cdots + \rho^2\sigma_u^2 + \sigma_u^2 \\ &= \rho^{2t}\left[\frac{\sigma_u^2}{1-\rho^2}\right] + \sigma_u^2[\rho^{2(t-1)} + \rho^{2(t-2)} + \cdots + \rho^2 + 1] \\ &= \sigma_u^2\left[\frac{\rho^{2t}}{1-\rho^2} + \frac{1-\rho^{2t}}{1-\rho^2}\right] = \frac{\sigma_u^2}{1-\rho^2}.\end{aligned}$$

Since σ_u^2 is constant through time, $\text{Var}(\varepsilon_t)$ will also be constant, so that the assumption of homoskedasticity also holds. Note that this result has been obtained by making use of (8.36). Finally, from (8.34) we have

$$\begin{aligned}\varepsilon_t &= \rho\varepsilon_{t-1} + u_t \\ &= \rho^2\varepsilon_{t-2} + \rho u_{t-1} + u_t \\ &\;\vdots \\ &= \rho^s\varepsilon_{t-s} + \rho^{s-1}u_{t-s+1} + \cdots + \rho u_{t-1} + u_t.\end{aligned}$$

Multiplying both sides of the above expression by ε_{t-s} and taking mathematical expectations, we obtain

$$\begin{aligned}E(\varepsilon_t\varepsilon_{t-s}) &= \rho^s E(\varepsilon_{t-s}^2) + \rho^{s-1}E(\varepsilon_{t-s}u_{t-s+1}) + \cdots + \rho E(\varepsilon_{t-s}u_{t-1}) + E(\varepsilon_{t-s}u_t) \\ &= \rho^s\text{Var}(\varepsilon_{t-s}) = \rho^s\sigma^2,\end{aligned}$$

which is the same as the specification (8.33). Therefore, the generating mechanism (8.34) through (8.36) does give the correlation between the disturbances as specified earlier, and does not in any way conflict with the remaining basic assumptions.

The preceding remarks make it clear that the relationships between disturbances are crucially dependent on the value of the parameter ρ. This dependence is particularly emphasized by the following interpretation of ρ. In (8.33), the covariance between any two successive disturbances, say ε_t and ε_{t-1}, is given by

$$\text{Cov}(\varepsilon_t, \varepsilon_{t-1}) = \rho\sigma^2.$$

Therefore,

$$\rho = \frac{\text{Cov}(\varepsilon_t, \varepsilon_{t-1})}{\sigma^2},$$

which, since $\sigma^2 = \text{Var}(\varepsilon_t) = \text{Var}(\varepsilon_{t-1})$, can be written as

$$\rho = \frac{\text{Cov}(\varepsilon_t, \varepsilon_{t-1})}{\sqrt{\text{Var}(\varepsilon_t)}\sqrt{\text{Var}(\varepsilon_{t-1})}}.$$

Now, an expression in which the covariance of two variables is divided by the product of the standard deviations of these variables is known as the *coefficient of correlation* between the two variables. This coefficient measures the degree of the relationship between two random variables and its values range from -1 to $+1$. Positive values of the coefficient reflect the existence of a positive relationship, and negative values the presence of a negative relationship. The coefficient of correlation whose value is close to $+1$ or to -1 indicates a high degree of relationship between the variables, and the coefficient whose value is close to zero indicates a low degree of relationship. This means that ρ is, in fact, the coefficient of correlation between ε_t and ε_{t-1}, ρ^2 is the coefficient of correlation between ε_t and ε_{t-2}, ρ^3 is the coefficient of correlation between ε_t and ε_{t-3}, and so on. Note that $\rho = +1$ or $\rho = -1$ is ruled out by the maintained hypothesis specified in connection with (8.33). *When ρ is equal to zero*, we have

$$\varepsilon_t = u_t,$$

$$\text{Var}(\varepsilon_t) = \sigma_u^2,$$

$$\text{Var}(\varepsilon_0) = \sigma_u^2.$$

and since u_t is a normally and independently distributed variable with zero mean and constant variance, *all* the basic assumptions concerning ε hold.

Properties of the Least Squares Estimators

Let us now examine the properties of the least squares estimators of α and β in

$$Y_t = \alpha + \beta X_t + \varepsilon_t,$$

when the disturbance ε_t is autoregressive. The least squares estimator of β is

$$\hat{\beta} = \frac{\sum x_t' y_t'}{\sum x_t'^2} = \beta + \frac{\sum x_t' \varepsilon_t}{\sum x_t'^2},$$

as given by (7.32). Then,

$$E(\hat{\beta}) = \beta + \frac{\sum x_t' E(\varepsilon_t)}{\sum x_t'^2} = \beta.$$

The least squares estimator of α is

$$\hat{\alpha} = \bar{Y} - \hat{\beta}\bar{X} = (\alpha + \beta\bar{X} + \bar{\varepsilon}) - \hat{\beta}\bar{X};$$

and $$E(\hat{\alpha}) = \alpha + \beta\bar{X} + E(\bar{\varepsilon}) - E(\hat{\beta})\bar{X} = \alpha.$$

This means that the least squares estimators are *unbiased* even when the disturbances are autoregressive.

Next, we determine whether the least squares estimators are still best linear unbiased estimators (BLUE) by deriving the BLUE formulas for the autoregressive case and by comparing them with the least squares formulas. If the two sets of formulas differ, then the least squares estimators are not BLUE. Let us start by considering the BLUE of β. By the condition of linearity, we have

$$\tilde{\beta} = \sum_{t=1}^{n} a_t Y_t,$$

where a_t $(t = 1, 2, \ldots, n)$ are constants to be determined. Further,

$$E(\tilde{\beta}) = E\Big(\sum_t a_t Y_t\Big) = \sum_t a_t(\alpha + \beta X_t) = \alpha\Big(\sum_t a_t\Big) + \beta\Big(\sum_t a_t X_t\Big).$$

By the condition of unbiasedness, we require that

$$\sum a_t = 0 \qquad \text{and} \qquad \sum a_t X_t = 1.$$

The variance of $\tilde{\beta}$ is given as

$$\begin{aligned}\text{Var}(\tilde{\beta}) &= E\Big[\sum_t a_t Y_t - E\Big(\sum_t a_t Y_t\Big)\Big]^2 = E\Big[\sum_t a_t \varepsilon_t\Big]^2 \\ &= E\sum_t a_t^2 \varepsilon_t^2 + 2E\sum_{s<t} a_t \varepsilon_t a_{t-s} \varepsilon_{t-s} \\ &= \sigma^2 \sum_i a_t^2 + 2\sigma^2 \sum_{s<t} a_t a_{t-s} \rho^s.\end{aligned}$$

To minimize $\text{Var}(\tilde{\beta})$ subject to the conditions that $\sum a_t = 0$ and that $\sum a_t X_t = 1$, we use the Lagrange multiplier technique and form a function H as follows:

$$H = \sigma^2 \sum_t a_t^2 + 2\sigma^2 \sum_{s<t} a_t a_{t-s} \rho^s - \lambda_1\Big(\sum_t a_t\Big) - \lambda_2\Big(\sum_t a_t X_t - 1\Big).$$

This function is to be minimized with respect to $a_1, a_2, \ldots, a_n$, λ_1 and λ_2. Differentiating and putting each of the derivatives equal to zero, we obtain

$$\begin{aligned}2a_1\sigma^2 + 2\sigma^2(a_2\rho + a_3\rho^2 + \cdots + a_n\rho^{n-1}) - \lambda_1 - \lambda_2 X_1 &= 0 \\ 2a_2\sigma^2 + 2\sigma^2(a_1\rho + a_3\rho + \cdots + a_n\rho^{n-2}) - \lambda_1 - \lambda_2 X_2 &= 0 \\ &\vdots \\ 2a_n\sigma^2 + 2\sigma^2(a_1\rho^{n-1} + a_2\rho^{n-2} + \cdots + a_{n-1}\rho) - \lambda_1 - \lambda_2 X_n &= 0 \\ -\sum_t a_t &= 0 \\ -\sum_t a_t X_t + 1 &= 0\end{aligned}$$

These $(n + 2)$ equations can be solved for the $(n + 2)$ unknown values of $a_1, a_2, \ldots, a_n$, λ_1 and λ_2. The solution is algebraically rather cumbersome and will not be developed here;[8] but just by looking at the equations, it is obvious that the solution for $a_1, a_2, \ldots, a_n$ will involve the parameter ρ. This means that the formula for the BLUE of β will also involve ρ, and thus will differ from the formula for the least squares estimator of β. In fact, it can be shown[9] that the BLUE of β is given by

$$(8.38)\quad \tilde{\beta} = \frac{(1-\rho^2)x_1'y_1' + \sum (x_t' - \rho x_{t-1}')(y_t' - \rho y_{t-1}')[1+(1+\rho)/(n-1)(1-\rho)]}{(1-\rho^2)x_1'^2 + \sum (x_t' - \rho x_{t-1}')^2\,[1+(1+\rho)/(n-1)(1-\rho)]}$$

$$= \frac{\sum(x_t' - \rho x_{t-1}')(y_t' - \rho y_{t-1}')}{\sum(x_t' - \rho x_{t-1}')^2} + \tilde{\delta}_{\beta},$$

where the subscript t runs from $t = 2$ to $t = n$, and $\tilde{\delta}$ is a correction factor that, for most practical purposes, can be disregarded. Other results are

$$(8.39)\quad \operatorname{Var}(\tilde{\beta}) = \frac{\sigma_u^2}{\sum (x_t' - \rho x_{t-1}')^2} + \tilde{\delta}_{\operatorname{Var}(\tilde{\beta})},$$

$$(8.40)\quad \tilde{\alpha} = \frac{1}{1-\rho}\left\{\frac{1}{n-1}\sum (Y_t - \rho Y_{t-1}) - (\tilde{\beta} - \tilde{\delta}_{\beta})\left[\frac{1}{n-1}\sum (X_t - \rho X_{t-1})\right]\right\} + \tilde{\delta}_{\tilde{\alpha}},$$

and

$$(8.41)\quad \operatorname{Var}(\tilde{\alpha}) = \frac{\sigma_u^2}{(1-\rho)^2}\left\{\frac{1}{n-1} + \frac{[\sum (X_t - \rho X_{t-1})/(n-1)]^2}{\sum (x_t' - \rho x_{t-1}')^2}\right\} + \tilde{\delta}_{\operatorname{Var}(\tilde{\alpha})},$$

where in each expression, as in (8.38), the subscript t runs from $t = 2$ to $t = n$, and $\tilde{\delta}$ represents a correction factor which may be disregarded in practice. These results are clearly different from those given by the least squares formulas. Thus, we have to conclude that the least squares estimators are *not* BLUE when the disturbances are autoregressive. This implies that in this case the least squares estimators are *not efficient* estimators. (Intuitively, the loss of efficiency can be explained as a result of the fact that the dependence among the disturbances reduces the *effective* number of independent pieces of information in the sample.) It may be noted that when $\rho = 0$, formulas (8.38) through (8.41)—including the correction factors—reduce to the least squares formulas; if the correction factors are disregarded, these formulas are the same as those obtained by the least squares method *after* discarding the first observation.

Let us now turn to the asymptotic properties of the least squares estimators of the regression coefficients under autoregression in the disturbances. With respect to consistency, we may check whether the variances of these estimators approach zero as the sample size grows to infinity. Since the least squares estimators are

[8] The interested reader may consult, e.g., J. Johnston, *Econometric Methods* (New York: McGraw-Hill, 1963), pp. 179–187.

[9] *Ibid.*

unbiased, this is a sufficient condition for consistency. Starting with the variance of $\hat{\beta}$, the least squares estimator of β, we have

$$(8.42)\quad \mathrm{Var}(\hat{\beta}) = E(\hat{\beta} - \beta)^2 = E\left[\frac{\sum x_t'\varepsilon_t}{\sum x_t'^2}\right]^2$$

$$= \frac{1}{(\sum x_t'^2)^2} E\Big[\sum_t x_t'^2 \varepsilon_t^2 + 2 \sum_{s<t} x_t'\varepsilon_t x_{t-s}'\varepsilon_{t-s}\Big]$$

$$= \frac{\sigma^2}{(\sum x_t'^2)^2}\Big[\sum_t x_t'^2 + 2 \sum_{s<t} x_t' x_{t-s}' \rho^s\Big]$$

$$= \frac{\sigma^2}{\sum x_t'^2} + \frac{2\sigma^2}{(\sum x_t'^2)^2}\Big[\rho \sum_{t=2}^{n} x_t' x_{t-1}' + \rho^2 \sum_{t=3}^{n} x_t' x_{t-2}' + \cdots\Big].$$

To simplify notation, we introduce the coefficient of correlation between X_t and X_{t-s}, say, r_s, which we define as

$$r_s = \frac{(1/n)\sum x_t' x_{t-s}'}{\sqrt{(1/n)\sum x_t'^2}\,\sqrt{(1/n)\sum x_{t-s}'^2}} = \frac{\sum x_t' x_{t-s}'}{\sqrt{\sum x_t'^2}\,\sqrt{\sum x_{t-s}'^2}},$$

where $s = 1, 2, \ldots, n-1$; $t = s+1, s+2, \ldots, n$; and $s < t$. It can easily be shown that the maximum value of r_s^2 (like that of any squared coefficient of correlation) is unity. Then we can write $\mathrm{Var}(\hat{\beta})$ as

$$(8.42a)\quad \mathrm{Var}(\hat{\beta}) = \frac{\sigma^2}{\sum x_t'^2}$$

$$+ \frac{2\sigma^2}{(\sum x_t'^2)^2}\left[\rho r_1 \sqrt{\sum x_t'^2}\sqrt{\sum x_{t-1}'^2} + \rho^2 r_2 \sqrt{\sum x_t'^2}\sqrt{\sum x_{t-2}'^2} + \cdots\right]$$

$$= \frac{(\sigma^2/n)}{(1/n)\sum x_t'^2} + \frac{2(\sigma^2/n)}{[(1/n)\sum x_t'^2]^2}\left[\rho r_1 \sqrt{\frac{1}{n}\sum x_t'^2}\sqrt{\frac{1}{n}\sum x_{t-1}'^2}\right.$$

$$\left. + \rho^2 r_2 \sqrt{\frac{1}{n}\sum x_t'^2}\sqrt{\frac{1}{n}\sum x_{t-2}'^2} + \cdots\right].$$

As n approaches infinity, the terms

$$\frac{1}{n}\sum x_t'^2,\quad \frac{1}{n}\sum x_{t-1}'^2,\quad \frac{1}{n}\sum x_{t-2}'^2,\quad \ldots,$$

will all approach the same finite positive number, say, m_{xx}, and the terms $r_1, r_2, r_3, \ldots$, will approach some numbers with an absolute value less than or equal to one, say, $r_1^*, r_2^*, r_3^*, \ldots$. Therefore, we have

$$\lim_{n\to\infty} \mathrm{Var}(\hat{\beta}) = \frac{\lim(\sigma^2/n)}{m_{xx}} + \frac{2\lim(\sigma^2/n)}{m_{xx}}[\rho r_1^* + \rho^2 r_2^* + \cdots]$$

$$= \frac{\lim(\sigma^2/n)}{m_{xx}}[1 + 2\rho r_1^* + 2\rho^2 r_2^* + \cdots].$$

Now, since ρ lies between -1 and $+1$ and $r_1^*,\ r_2^*,\ \ldots,$ are each less than one in absolute value, the sum of the infinite series

$$[1 + 2\rho r_1^* + 2\rho^2 r_2^* + \cdots]$$

will be a finite number.

Thus, since $\lim_{n\to\infty}(\sigma^2/n) = 0,$

$$\lim_{n\to\infty} \operatorname{Var}(\hat{\beta}) = 0.$$

By using a similar argument we can also show that

$$\lim_{n\to\infty} \operatorname{Var}(\hat{\alpha}) = 0.$$

This means that the least squares estimators of the regression coefficients are *consistent* even when the regression disturbances are autoregressive.

The last property that is of interest to us is asymptotic efficiency. This can be examined by comparing the asymptotic variances of the least squares estimators with the asymptotic variances of the best linear unbiased estimators (or, rather, their approximations) given by (8.38) and (8.40). Using the formula for the asymptotic variance of an estimator given in Section 6–1, we can determine the asymptotic variance of the least squares estimator of β as follows:

$$\begin{aligned}
\text{Asympt. Var}(\hat{\beta}) &= \frac{1}{n}\lim_{n\to\infty} En\left[\frac{\sum x_t'\varepsilon_t}{\sum x_t'^2}\right]^2 \\
&= \frac{1}{n}\lim_{n\to\infty} \frac{n}{(\sum x_t'^2)^2}\Big[\sigma^2 \sum_t x_t'^2 + 2\sigma^2 \sum_{s<t} x_t'x_{t-s}'\rho^s\Big] \\
&= \frac{\sigma^2}{n}\left[\frac{m_{xx} + 2\rho r_1^* m_{xx} + 2\rho^2 r_2^* m_{xx} + \cdots}{m_{xx}^2}\right] \\
&= \frac{\sigma^2}{nm_{xx}}[1 + 2\rho r_1^* + 2\rho^2 r_2^* + \cdots].
\end{aligned}$$

As an alternative estimator of β, consider $\tilde{\tilde{\beta}}$ defined as

(8.43) $$\tilde{\tilde{\beta}} = \tilde{\beta} - \delta_{\beta},$$

where $\tilde{\beta}$ is the best linear unbiased estimator given in (8.38), and δ is the correction factor, which is considered to be unimportant. The variance of $\tilde{\tilde{\beta}}$ is

(8.44) $$\operatorname{Var}(\tilde{\tilde{\beta}}) = \operatorname{Var}(\tilde{\beta}) - \delta_{\operatorname{Var}(\tilde{\beta})},$$

as defined in (8.39). The asymptotic variance of $\tilde{\tilde{\beta}}$ then is

$$\begin{aligned}
\text{Asympt. Var}(\tilde{\tilde{\beta}}) &= \frac{1}{n}\lim_{n\to\infty} n\left[\frac{\sigma^2(1-\rho^2)}{\sum (x_t' - \rho x_{t-1}')^2}\right] = \frac{1}{n}\left[\frac{\sigma^2(1-\rho^2)}{m_{xx} - 2\rho r_1^* m_{xx} + \rho^2 m_{xx}}\right] \\
&= \frac{\sigma^2}{nm_{xx}}\left[\frac{1-\rho^2}{1 - 2\rho r_1^* + \rho^2}\right]
\end{aligned}$$

The asymptotic variances of $\hat{\beta}$ and $\tilde{\tilde{\beta}}$ can be compared by forming the ratio

$$\frac{\text{Asympt. Var}(\hat{\beta})}{\text{Asympt. Var}(\tilde{\tilde{\beta}})} = \frac{(\sigma^2/nm_{xx})[1 + 2\rho r_1^* + 2\rho^2 r_2^* + \cdots]}{(\sigma^2/nm_{xx})[(1 - \rho^2)/(1 - 2\rho r_1^* + \rho^2)]}$$

$$= \frac{1 + 2\rho r_1^* + 2\rho^2 r_2^* + \cdots}{[(1 - \rho^2)/(1 - 2\rho r_1^* + \rho^2)]}.$$

If this ratio is greater than one, then $\hat{\beta}$ cannot be considered to be asymptotically efficient. (Strictly speaking, this statement is true only if ρ is known or can be consistently estimated; otherwise $\tilde{\tilde{\beta}}$ would not qualify as an estimator. The problem of developing a consistent estimator of ρ will be discussed in the latter part of the present section.) Suppose we evaluate the above ratio for $1 > \rho > 0$ and $r_2^* = r_1^{*2}$, $r_3^* = r_1^{*3}, \ldots$. That is, we consider a situation in which the disturbances are positively autocorrelated, and the coefficients of correlation between X_t and X_{t-1}, X_t and X_{t-2}, etc., follow a geometrical progression. Such situations are thought to be quite common with economic time series.[10] With this specification we obtain

$$\frac{\text{Asympt. Var}(\hat{\beta})}{\text{Asympt. Var}(\tilde{\tilde{\beta}})} = \frac{1 + 2\rho r_1^* + 2\rho^2 r_1^{*2} + \cdots}{[(1 - \rho^2)/(1 - 2\rho r_1^* + \rho^2)]}$$

$$= \frac{1 - \rho r_1^* - 2\rho^2 r_1^{*2} + \rho^2 + \rho^3 r_1^*}{1 - \rho r_1^* - \rho^2 + \rho^3 r_1^*}.$$

This expression will be greater than or equal to one if

$$1 - \rho r_1^* - 2\rho^2 r_1^{*2} + \rho^2 + \rho^3 r_1^* \geq 1 - \rho r_1^* - \rho^2 + \rho^3 r_1^*$$

or

$$-2\rho^2 r_1^{*2} + \rho^2 \geq -\rho^2;$$

that is, if

$$2\rho^2(1 - r_1^{*2}) \geq 0.$$

This condition will always be satisfied. For example, when $\rho = 0.6$ and $r_1^* = 0.8$, $r_2^* = 0.64$, $r_3^* = 0.512$, etc., the ratio of the two asymptotic variances is equal to 1.78, i.e., the asymptotic variance of $\hat{\beta}$ is 78 percent larger than that of $\tilde{\tilde{\beta}}$. A similar result can be obtained with respect to $\hat{\alpha}$. Thus we have to conclude that the least squares estimators of the regression coefficients are *not asymptotically efficient* when the disturbances are autoregressive.

Properties of the Estimated Variances of the Least Squares Estimators

To sum up, we have established that when the disturbances are autoregressive, the least squares estimators of the regression coefficients are unbiased and consistent, but they are not efficient or asymptotically efficient. Thus, if we use

[10] See E. Ames and S. Reiter, "Distributions of Correlation Coefficients in Economic Time Series," *Journal of the American Statistical Association*, Vol. 56, September 1961, pp. 637–656. The authors consider 100 annual series of 25 observations selected at random from the abstract of statistics of the United States. They find that, on the average, the first five autocorrelation coefficients were 0.84, 0.71, 0.60, 0.53 and 0.45.

the least squares formulas when the disturbances are autoregressive, the resulting estimators will still have some desirable properties. However, if we want to use these estimators for the purpose of testing hypotheses or constructing confidence intervals, we require unbiasedness not only of the estimators themselves, but also of their estimated variances. The question then is whether the conventional formulas for estimating the variances of the least squares estimators do, in fact, guarantee unbiasedness even under autoregression in the disturbances. We note that the conventional least squares formula for estimating the variance of $\hat{\beta}$ is

$$s_{\hat{\beta}}^2 = \frac{s^2}{\sum x_t'^2},$$

where s^2 is an estimator of σ^2 defined as the sum of squares of the least squares residuals divided by $(n - 2)$. Since $\sum x_t'^2$ is nonstochastic, we only have to concern ourselves with s^2. For that, we have

$$s^2 = \frac{1}{n-2}\sum_t (y_t' - \hat{\beta}x_t')^2 = \frac{1}{n-2}\sum_t (\beta x_t' + \varepsilon_t' - \hat{\beta}x_t')^2$$

$$= \frac{1}{n-2}\sum_t [-(\hat{\beta} - \beta)x_t' + \varepsilon_t']^2$$

$$= \frac{1}{n-2}\Big[(\hat{\beta} - \beta)^2 \sum_t x_t'^2 + \sum_t \varepsilon_t'^2 - 2(\hat{\beta} - \beta)\sum_t x_t'\varepsilon_t'\Big]$$

$$= \frac{1}{n-2}\Big[\sum_t \varepsilon_t'^2 - (\hat{\beta} - \beta)^2 \sum_t x_t'^2\Big]$$

and

$$E(s^2) = \frac{1}{n-2}\Big[\sum_t E(\varepsilon_t'^2) - \Big(\sum_t x_t'^2\Big)\text{Var}(\hat{\beta})\Big].$$

Now we know what $\text{Var}(\hat{\beta})$ is from (8.42) so that our only problem is to find $E(\varepsilon_t'^2)$. We have

$$E(\varepsilon_t'^2) = E(\varepsilon_t - \bar{\varepsilon})^2 = E(\varepsilon_t^2) + E\left[\frac{1}{n}\sum_t \varepsilon_t\right]^2 - 2E\left[\varepsilon_t \frac{1}{n}\sum_t \varepsilon_t\right]$$

$$= \sigma^2 + \frac{\sigma^2}{n} + \frac{2}{n^2}E\Big[\sum_{s<t} \varepsilon_{t-s}\varepsilon_t\Big]$$

$$- \frac{2}{n}E[\varepsilon_t(\varepsilon_1 + \varepsilon_2 + \cdots + \varepsilon_t + \cdots + \varepsilon_n)]$$

$$= \sigma^2 + \frac{\sigma^2}{n} + \frac{2}{n^2}[E(\varepsilon_1\varepsilon_2) + E(\varepsilon_1\varepsilon_3) + \cdots + E(\varepsilon_1\varepsilon_n) + E(\varepsilon_2\varepsilon_3)$$

$$+ E(\varepsilon_2\varepsilon_4) + \cdots + E(\varepsilon_2\varepsilon_n) + E(\varepsilon_3\varepsilon_4) + \cdots + E(\varepsilon_{n-1}\varepsilon_n)]$$

$$- \frac{2}{n}[E(\varepsilon_t\varepsilon_1) + E(\varepsilon_t\varepsilon_2) + \cdots + E(\varepsilon_t^2) + \cdots + E(\varepsilon_t\varepsilon_n)]$$

$$= \frac{(n+1)\sigma^2}{n} + \frac{2\sigma^2}{n^2}[(n-1)\rho + (n-2)\rho^2 + \cdots + \rho^{n-1}]$$

$$- \frac{2\sigma^2}{n}[\rho^{t-1} + \rho^{t-2} + \cdots + \rho + 1 + \rho + \cdots + \rho^{n-t}].$$

Then

$$\sum_t E(\varepsilon_t'^2) = (n+1)\sigma^2 + \frac{2\sigma^2}{n}[(n-1)\rho + (n-2)\rho^2 + \cdots + \rho^{n-1}]$$

$$- \frac{2\sigma^2}{n}\sum_t [\rho^{t-1} + \rho^{t-2} + \cdots + \rho + 1 + \rho + \cdots + \rho^{n-t}].$$

Consider the last summation:

$$\sum_t [\rho^{t-1} + \rho^{t-2} + \cdots + \rho + 1 + \rho + \cdots + \rho^{n-t}]$$

$$= (1 + \rho + \rho^2 + \cdots + \rho^{n-1})$$
$$+ (\rho + 1 + \rho + \cdots + \rho^{n-2})$$
$$+ (\rho^2 + \rho + 1 + \cdots + \rho^{n-3})$$
$$\vdots$$
$$+ (\rho^{n-1} + \rho^{n-2} + \rho^{n-3} + \cdots + 1)$$
$$= n + 2(n-1)\rho + 2(n-2)\rho^2 + \cdots + 4\rho^{n-2} + 2\rho^{n-1}.$$

Therefore,

$$\sum_t E(\varepsilon_t'^2) = (n+1)\sigma^2 + \frac{2\sigma^2}{n}\{[(n-1)\rho + (n-2)\rho^2 + \cdots + \rho^{n-1}]$$

$$- [n + 2(n-1)\rho + 2(n-2)\rho^2 + \cdots + 4\rho^{n-2} + 2\rho^{n-1}]\}$$

$$= (n+1)\sigma^2 - \frac{2\sigma^2}{n}A,$$

where $A = n + (n-1)\rho + (n-2)\rho^2 + \cdots + 2\rho^{n-2} + \rho^{n-1}.$

Now, since

$$A - \rho A = n + (n-1)\rho + (n-2)\rho^2 + \cdots + 2\rho^{n-2} + \rho^{n-1}$$

$$- n\rho - (n-1)\rho^2 - \cdots - 3\rho^{n-2} - 2\rho^{n-1} - \rho^n$$

$$= n - \rho - \rho^2 - \cdots - \rho^{n-1} - \rho^{n-2} - \rho^n = n - \frac{\rho(1-\rho^n)}{(1-\rho)}$$

$$= \frac{n(1-\rho) - \rho(1-\rho^n)}{(1-\rho)},$$

we have

$$A = \frac{n(1-\rho) - \rho(1-\rho^n)}{(1-\rho)^2}$$

and

$$\sum_t E(\varepsilon_t'^2) = (n+1)\sigma^2 - \frac{2\sigma^2}{n}\left[\frac{n(1-\rho) - \rho(1-\rho^n)}{(1-\rho)^2}\right]$$

$$= (n-1)\sigma^2 - \frac{2\sigma^2}{n}\left[\frac{n\rho(1-\rho) - \rho(1-\rho^n)}{(1-\rho)^2}\right].$$

Substituting this result and the expression for $\mathrm{Var}(\hat{\beta})$ into $E(s^2)$, we obtain

$$(8.45)\quad E(s^2) = \frac{1}{n-2}\left\{(n-1)\sigma^2 - \frac{2\sigma^2}{n}\left[\frac{n\rho(1-\rho) - \rho(1-\rho^n)}{(1-\rho)^2}\right]\right\}$$

$$- \frac{1}{n-2}\sum_t x_t'^2\left\{\frac{\sigma^2}{\sum x_t'^2} + \frac{2\sigma^2}{(\sum x'^2)^2}\left[\rho\sum_{t=2}^{n} x_t'x_{t-1}'\right.\right.$$

$$\left.\left. + \rho^2\sum_{t=3}^{n} x_t'x_{t-2}' + \cdots\right]\right\}$$

$$= \sigma^2 - \frac{2\sigma^2}{n-2}\left[\frac{n\rho(1-\rho) - \rho(1-\rho^n)}{n(1-\rho)^2}\right.$$

$$\left. + \frac{\rho\sum x_t'x_{t-1}' + \rho^2\sum x_t'x_{t-2}' + \cdots}{\sum x_t'^2}\right],$$

so that

$$(8.46)\quad E(s_{\hat{\beta}}^2) = \frac{\sigma^2}{\sum x_t'^2} - \frac{2\sigma^2}{(n-2)\sum x_t'^2}\left[\frac{n\rho(1-\rho) - \rho(1-\rho^n)}{n(1-\rho)^2}\right.$$

$$\left. + \frac{\rho\sum x_t'x_{t-1}' + \rho^2\sum x_t'x_{t-2}' + \cdots}{\sum x_t'^2}\right].$$

Since the expression for $E(s_{\hat{\beta}}^2)$ differs from that for $\mathrm{Var}(\hat{\beta})$ given by (8.42), we conclude that the conventionally calculated variance of $\hat{\beta}$ is *biased* when the disturbances are autoregressive. A similar result can be obtained with respect to $\hat{\alpha}$.

The preceding result implies that when the disturbances are autoregressive, the conventional formulas for carrying out tests of significance or constructing confidence intervals with respect to the regression coefficients lead to incorrect statements. That is, the calculated acceptance regions or confidence intervals will be either narrower or wider than the correct ones, depending on whether the bias in estimating the variance is negative or positive. Therefore, let us see whether we can determine the direction of the bias. By deducting (8.42) from

(8.46) we obtain an expression for the bias in estimating the variance of $\hat{\beta}$ as given by

$$(8.47)\qquad E(s_{\hat{\beta}}^2) - \text{Var}(\hat{\beta}) = \frac{-2\sigma^2}{\sum x_t'^2}\left\{\left[\frac{n\rho(1-\rho) - \rho(1-\rho^n)}{n(n-2)(1-\rho)^2}\right] + \frac{(n-1)}{(n-2)\sum x_t'^2}\left[\rho \sum_{t=2}^{n} x_t'x_{t-1}' + \rho^2 \sum_{t=3}^{n} x_t'x_{t-2}' + \cdots\right]\right\}.$$

From this it can be seen that when $\rho > 0$ and X_t is positively correlated with $X_{t-1}, X_{t-2}, \ldots$, the bias is negative. As pointed out earlier, such a situation is fairly common with economic time series. Thus, if the disturbances are autoregressive and we persist in using the conventional least squares formulas, the calculated acceptance regions or confidence intervals will be often *narrower* than they should be for the specified level of significance or confidence. To obtain an idea about the extent of the bias, take, for example, the case when $\rho = 0.6$ and $r_1 = 0.8$, $r_2 = (0.8)^2$, $r_3 = (0.8)^3$, etc. Assuming that $\sum x_t'^2, \sum x_{t-1}'^2, \sum x_{t-2}'^2, \ldots$ are all approximately equal, the biases in estimating $\text{Var}(\hat{\beta})$ for various sample sizes would be as given in Table 8–1. These results indicate that the extent of the bias may be quite substantial.

Table 8–1

Sample Size	$E(s_{\hat{\beta}}^2)$	$\text{Var}(\hat{\beta})$	Bias	$\dfrac{E(s_{\hat{\beta}}^2)}{\text{Var}(\hat{\beta})}$
20	$0.752\left[\frac{\sigma^2}{\sum x_t'^2}\right]$	$2.846\left[\frac{\sigma^2}{\sum x_t'^2}\right]$	$-2.094\left[\frac{\sigma^2}{\sum x_t'^2}\right]$	0.264
50	$0.902\left[\frac{\sigma^2}{\sum x_t'^2}\right]$	$2.846\left[\frac{\sigma^2}{\sum x_t'^2}\right]$	$-1.944\left[\frac{\sigma^2}{\sum x_t'^2}\right]$	0.317
100	$0.951\left[\frac{\sigma^2}{\sum x_t'^2}\right]$	$2.846\left[\frac{\sigma^2}{\sum x_t'^2}\right]$	$-1.895\left[\frac{\sigma^2}{\sum x_t'^2}\right]$	0.334

BLU and Maximum Likelihood Estimations

The preceding discussion has enabled us to uncover the shortcomings of the least squares estimators of the regression coefficients in the case when the disturbance does not satisfy the assumption of nonautoregression. Now we shall turn to the problem of developing alternative estimators that would not suffer from these shortcomings. In the process we shall confine ourselves to the case in which the disturbance ε_t follows a first-order autoregressive scheme as described by (8.34) and (8.35). The reader will recall that we have already developed the formulas for the best linear unbiased estimators for the autoregressive model. These estimators, which we labeled $\tilde{\alpha}$ and $\tilde{\beta}$, and their variances are given by (8.38) through (8.41). If we disregard the correction factors appended to each formula, the resulting expressions are simpler, though, of course, no longer *exactly* BLUE. If $\tilde{\tilde{\alpha}}$ and $\tilde{\tilde{\beta}}$ are used to represent $\tilde{\alpha}$ and $\tilde{\beta}$ *minus* the respective correction factors, we have

$$\tilde{\tilde{\beta}} = \frac{\sum(y'_t - \rho y'_{t-1})(x'_t - \rho x'_{t-1})}{\sum(x'_t - \rho x'_{t-1})^2}, \tag{8.48}$$

$$\mathrm{Var}(\tilde{\tilde{\beta}}) = \frac{\sigma_u^2}{\sum(x'_t - \rho x'_{t-1})^2}, \tag{8.49}$$

$$\tilde{\tilde{\alpha}} = \frac{1}{1-\rho}[(\bar{Y} - \rho\bar{Y}_{-1}) - \tilde{\tilde{\beta}}(\bar{X} - \rho\bar{X}_{-1})], \tag{8.50}$$

and

$$\mathrm{Var}(\tilde{\tilde{\alpha}}) = \frac{\sigma_u^2}{(1-\rho)^2}\left[\frac{1}{n-1} + \frac{(\bar{X} - \rho\bar{X}_{-1})^2}{\sum(x'_t - \rho x'_{t-1})^2}\right], \tag{8.51}$$

where the subscript t runs from $t = 2$ to $t = n$, and

$$\bar{Y} = \frac{1}{n-1}\sum_t Y_t,$$

$$\bar{Y}_{-1} = \frac{1}{n-1}\sum_t Y_{t-1},$$

$$\bar{X} = \frac{1}{n-1}\sum_t X_t,$$

$$\bar{X}_{-1} = \frac{1}{n-1}\sum_t X_{t-1}.$$

Before considering the feasibility and the usefulness of these estimators, we may note an alternative and simpler way of deriving them. The value of the dependent variable in period t is determined by

$$Y_t = \alpha + \beta X_t + \varepsilon_t,$$

and that in period $t - 1$ by

$$Y_{t-1} = \alpha + \beta X_{t-1} + \varepsilon_{t-1}.$$

Multiplying the latter by ρ and subtracting the result from the former, we obtain

$$Y_t - \rho Y_{t-1} = \alpha(1-\rho) + \beta(X_t - \rho X_{t-1}) + (\varepsilon_t - \rho\varepsilon_{t-1}).$$

But since, by (8.34),

$$\varepsilon_t - \rho\varepsilon_{t-1} = u_t,$$

we can write

$$Y_t - \rho Y_{t-1} = \alpha(1-\rho) + \beta(X_t - \rho X_{t-1}) + u_t \qquad (t = 2, 3, \ldots, n). \tag{8.52}$$

Equation (8.52) may be viewed as a regression equation in which the dependent variable is $(Y_t - \rho Y_{t-1})$ and the explanatory variable is $(X_t - \rho X_{t-1})$. Both of these variables can be measured if ρ is a known quantity. Since u_t is a normally and independently distributed random variable with mean zero and a constant variance, and $(X_t - \rho X_{t-1})$ is nonstochastic and bounded, all the basic assumptions of the classical normal linear regression model are satisfied. Therefore, least squares estimators of (8.52) would have all the desirable properties except for the fact that, by using as variables $(Y_t - \rho Y_{t-1})$ instead of Y_t and $(X_t - \rho X_{t-1})$ instead of X_t, we lose one observation. This loss implies that these estimators are not exactly BLUE, a fact that has already been noted.

The difficulty with the estimation formulas (8.48) and (8.50) is that they involve the parameter ρ whose value is rarely known. If ρ is not known, these formulas cannot be evaluated, and, consequently, $\tilde{\tilde{\alpha}}$ and $\tilde{\tilde{\beta}}$ do not qualify as estimators. This difficulty can be overcome by estimating ρ (along with α and β) from the sample observations. Several estimation methods are available and will be discussed. First, let us consider maximum likelihood estimation of (8.52). Since

$$u_t = (Y_t - \rho Y_{t-1}) - \alpha(1 - \rho) - \beta(X_t - \rho X_{t-1}) \qquad (t = 2, 3, \ldots, n),$$

the logarithmic likelihood function for $Y_2, Y_3, \ldots, Y_n$ is

$$(8.53) \quad L = -\frac{n-1}{2}\log(2\pi) - \frac{n-1}{2}\log\sigma_u^2 - \frac{1}{2\sigma_u^2}\sum_{t=2}^{n}[(Y_t - \rho Y_{t-1}) - \alpha(1-\rho) - \beta(X_t - \rho X_{t-1})]^2.$$

Note that

$$f(y_2, y_3, \ldots, y_n) = \left|\frac{\partial u}{\partial Y}\right| f(u_2, u_3, \ldots, u_n),$$

where $|\partial u/\partial Y|$ is the absolute value of the determinant

$$\begin{vmatrix} \dfrac{\partial u_2}{\partial Y_2} & \dfrac{\partial u_2}{\partial Y_3} & \cdots & \dfrac{\partial u_2}{\partial Y_n} \\ \dfrac{\partial u_3}{\partial Y_2} & \dfrac{\partial u_3}{\partial Y_3} & \cdots & \dfrac{\partial u_3}{\partial Y_n} \\ \vdots & \vdots & & \vdots \\ \dfrac{\partial u_n}{\partial Y_2} & \dfrac{\partial u_n}{\partial Y_3} & \cdots & \dfrac{\partial u_n}{\partial Y_n} \end{vmatrix}.$$

This is an extension of Theorem 18 (the "change-of-variable" theorem) from one variable to several variables. The determinant is known as the *Jacobian* of the transformation from $u_2, u_3, \ldots, u_n$ to $Y_2, Y_3, \ldots, Y_n$. It has been set up as *conditional* upon a given value of Y_1, i.e., as if Y_1 were a constant. This enabled us to ignore $\partial u_2/\partial Y_1$. It is easy to show that $|\partial u/\partial Y| = 1$ so that $f(u_2, u_3, \ldots, u_n) = f(y_2, y_3, \ldots, y_n)$.

By differentiating L with respect to α, β, ρ, and σ_u^2 and putting each derivative equal to zero, we obtain four equations to solve for the values of the four unknown parameters. However, these equations are highly nonlinear and their solution is rather difficult. A relatively simple way of handling this problem is available if we utilize the fact that *if* ρ were known, the maximum likelihood estimators of α and β would be equal to $\tilde{\tilde{\alpha}}$ and $\tilde{\tilde{\beta}}$ as given by (8.48) and (8.50), and the maximum likelihood estimator of σ_u^2, say, $\tilde{\tilde{\sigma}}_u^2$, would be

$$(8.54)\qquad \tilde{\tilde{\sigma}}_u^2 = \frac{1}{n-1}\sum_{t=2}^{n}[(Y_t - \rho Y_{t-1}) - \tilde{\tilde{\alpha}}(1-\rho) - \tilde{\tilde{\beta}}(X_t - \rho X_{t-1})]^2.$$

This means that different values of ρ lead to different values of $\tilde{\tilde{\alpha}}$, $\tilde{\tilde{\beta}}$, and $\tilde{\tilde{\sigma}}_u^2$. Thus we can obtain different solutions for, say, $\rho = -0.95, -0.90, -0.85, \ldots, +0.85, +0.90, +0.95$, and then select that value of ρ—as well as the corresponding values of $\tilde{\tilde{\alpha}}$ and $\tilde{\tilde{\beta}}$—that leads to the smallest value of $\tilde{\tilde{\sigma}}_u^2$. This solution will maximize the likelihood function L as required. The estimators obtained in this way will be called $\hat{\alpha}$, $\hat{\beta}$, $\hat{\rho}$, and $\hat{\sigma}_u^2$. The estimated standard errors of $\hat{\alpha}$ and $\hat{\beta}$ can be obtained by using formulas (8.49) and (8.51), after replacing ρ by $\hat{\rho}$ and σ_u^2 by $\hat{\sigma}_u^2$. The variance of $\hat{\rho}$ can be estimated by

$$(8.55)\qquad s_{\hat{\rho}}^2 = \frac{1-\hat{\rho}^2}{n}.$$

Formula (8.55) represents estimated asymptotic variance as defined in Section 6–1.

Under quite general conditions, maximum likelihood estimators are known to possess optimal properties in large samples. These optimal properties are assured by general theorems on maximum likelihood estimation. However, in the present case there is some question whether the general theorems apply because $Y_2, Y_3, \ldots, Y_n$ are not independent, i.e.,

$$f(y_2, y_3, \ldots, y_n) \neq f(y_2)f(y_3)\cdots f(y_n).$$

This means that the likelihood function is not the product of independent identical distributions.[11] Nevertheless, it can be shown that the maximum likelihood estimators of (8.52) are consistent and asymptotically equivalent to best-linear-unbiased estimators.[12] An indication of the small sample properties of the maximum likelihood estimators will be given on page 293.

EXAMPLE Friedman and Meiselman[13] estimated an equation representing a simple form of the quantity theory of money:

$$C_t = \alpha + \beta M_t + \varepsilon_t$$

[11] This point is particularly emphasized in C. Hildreth and J. Y. Lu, "Demand Relations with Autocorrelated Disturbances," *Technical Bulletin 276*, Michigan State University Agricultural Experiment Station, November 1960, p. 14.

[12] Consistency has been proved; *ibid.*, Appendix B. Asymptotic equivalence to BLUE has been demonstrated in Malinvaud, *op. cit.*, pp. 440–441.

[13] Milton Friedman and David Meiselman, "The Relative Stability of Monetary Velocity and the Investment Multiplier in the United States, 1897–1958," in Commission on Money and Credit, *Stabilization Policies* (Englewood Cliffs, N.J.: Prentice-Hall, 1963).

where C = consumer expenditure and M = stock of money, both measured in billions of current dollars. We shall re-estimate this relation using the quarterly data in Table 8–2 and assuming that the disturbance follows a first-order autoregressive scheme.

Table 8–2

Year and Quarter		Consumer Expenditure*	Money Stock*	Year and Quarter		Consumer Expenditure*	Money Stock*
1952	I	214.6	159.3	1954	III	238.7	173.9
	II	217.7	161.2		IV	243.2	176.1
	III	219.6	162.8				
	IV	227.2	164.6	1955	I	249.4	178.0
					II	254.3	179.1
1953	I	230.9	165.9		III	260.9	180.2
	II	233.3	167.9		IV	263.3	181.2
	III	234.1	168.3				
	IV	232.3	169.7	1956	I	265.6	181.6
					II	268.2	182.5
1954	I	233.7	170.5		III	270.4	183.3
	II	236.5	171.6		IV	275.6	184.3

Source: Milton Friedman and David Meiselman, "The Relative Stability of Monetary Velocity and the Investment Multiplier in the United States, 1897–1958," in Commission on Money and Credit, *Stabilization Policies* (Englewood Cliffs, N.J.: Prentice-Hall, 1963), p. 266.

* In billions of dollars.

Following the procedure for obtaining the maximum likelihood estimates of α and β, we calculate the values of $\tilde{\tilde{\sigma}}_u^2$—or, rather, $(n - 1)\tilde{\tilde{\sigma}}_u^2$—for different values of ρ. The computer results are given in Table 8–3. We can see that the value of ρ that gives the smallest $\tilde{\tilde{\sigma}}_u^2$ is 0.85. The corresponding least squares estimates of the coefficients and their estimated standard errors are

$$(C_t - 0.85C_{t-1}) = \underset{(13.926)}{-38.256} + \underset{(0.512)}{2.859}(M_t - 0.85M_{t-1}) + \hat{u}_t, \qquad R^2 = 0.647.$$

Table 8–3

ρ	$(n-1)\tilde{\tilde{\sigma}}_u^2$	ρ	$(n-1)\tilde{\tilde{\sigma}}_u^2$	ρ	$(n-1)\tilde{\tilde{\sigma}}_u^2$
−0.95	919.30	−0.05	302.75	0.75	85.26
−0.90	874.77	0.00	279.99	0.80	82.71
−0.85	831.45	0.05	258.44	**0.85**	**82.14**
⋮	⋮	0.10	238.10	0.90	84.48
		⋮	⋮	0.95	88.67
−0.10	326.73				

From these results we obtain:

$$\hat{\beta} = 2.859, \qquad \text{and} \qquad s_{\hat{\beta}} = 0.512,$$

$$\hat{\alpha} = \frac{-38.256}{1-0.85} = -255.040, \qquad \text{and} \qquad s_{\hat{\alpha}} = \frac{13.926}{1-0.85} = 92.840.$$

$$\hat{\rho} = 0.85, \qquad \text{and} \qquad s_{\hat{\rho}} = 0.178.$$

To obtain an idea of how well the estimated regression line fits the sample observations, we also calculate the value of R^2. From formula (7.45b)

$$R^2 = 1 - \frac{\text{SSE}}{\text{SST}},$$

where

$$\text{SSE} = \sum_{t=2}^{20} (C_t - \hat{\alpha} - \hat{\beta}M_t)^2 \approx \sum_{t=2}^{20} (c_t' - \hat{\beta}m_t')^2$$

$$= \sum_{t=2}^{20} c_t'^2 - 2\hat{\beta} \sum_{t=2}^{20} c_t'm_t' + \hat{\beta}^2 \sum_{t=2}^{20} m_t'^2,$$

and

$$\text{SST} = \sum_{t=2}^{20} c_t'^2.$$

In the following calculations we let the summations extend from $t = 2$ to $t = n$ because the values of these summations are available as by-products of the least squares estimation with $\rho = 0$. In this case we get

$$\sum_{t=2}^{20} c_t'^2 = 5{,}803.63,$$

$$\sum_{t=2}^{20} m_t'^2 = 1{,}013.07,$$

and

$$\sum_{t=2}^{20} c_t'm_t' = 2.335 \times 1{,}013.07 = 2{,}365.52,$$

so that

$$R^2 = 0.904.$$

The complete result then is

$$C_t = \underset{(92.840)}{-255.040} + \underset{(0.512)}{2.859}\, M_t + e_t, \qquad R^2 = 0.904.$$

Iterative and Two-Stage Estimation

An alternative estimation procedure for estimating regression equations with autoregressive disturbances is an *iterative method*,[14] which consists of the

[14] See D. Cochrane and G. H. Orcutt, "Application of Least Squares Regressions to Relationships Containing Autocorrelated Error Terms," *Journal of the American Statistical Association*, Vol. 44, March 1949, pp. 32–61.

following steps:

1. Obtain ordinary least squares estimates of

$$Y_t = \alpha + \beta X_t + \varepsilon_t,$$

and calculate the residuals $\hat{\varepsilon}_1, \hat{\varepsilon}_2, \ldots, \hat{\varepsilon}_n$. Use these to get the "first round" estimate of ρ, say, $\hat{\rho}$, given as

$$\hat{\rho} = \frac{\sum \hat{\varepsilon}_t \hat{\varepsilon}_{t-1}}{\sum \hat{\varepsilon}_{t-1}^2} \qquad (t = 2, 3, \ldots, n).$$

2. Construct new variables $(Y_t - \hat{\rho} Y_{t-1})$ and $(X_t - \hat{\rho} X_{t-1})$, and obtain ordinary least squares estimates of

$$(Y_t - \hat{\rho} Y_{t-1}) = \alpha^* + \beta(X_t - \hat{\rho} X_{t-1}) + u_t^*,$$

where $\alpha^* = \alpha(1 - \hat{\rho})$. These "second round" estimates, which may be called $\hat{\hat{\alpha}}$ and $\hat{\hat{\beta}}$, lead to "second round" residuals $\hat{\hat{\varepsilon}}_1, \hat{\hat{\varepsilon}}_2, \ldots, \hat{\hat{\varepsilon}}_n$ (calculated as $\hat{\hat{\varepsilon}}_t = Y_t - \hat{\hat{\alpha}} - \hat{\hat{\beta}} X_t$). The latter then are used to obtain a new estimate of ρ:

$$\hat{\hat{\rho}} = \frac{\sum \hat{\hat{\varepsilon}}_t \hat{\hat{\varepsilon}}_{t-1}}{\sum \hat{\hat{\varepsilon}}_{t-1}^2} \qquad (t = 2, 3, \ldots, n).$$

3. Construct new variables $(Y_t - \hat{\hat{\rho}} Y_{t-1})$ and $(X_t - \hat{\hat{\rho}} X_{t-1})$, and then proceed as in Step 2.

The steps are to be followed until the values of the estimators converge. It can be shown that the procedure is convergent and that, in fact, the "final round" estimates of α and β coincide with the values of the maximum likelihood estimators described above.[15] Thus the only difference between the maximum likelihood estimators developed above and the iterative estimators suggested by Orcutt and others is in the computational design.

The iterative procedure can be reduced to a *two-stage procedure* by stopping after obtaining the "second round" estimates of $\hat{\hat{\alpha}}$ and $\hat{\hat{\beta}}$, based on the "first round" value of ρ. The two-stage estimators will have the same asymptotic properties as the maximum likelihood estimators; some evidence concerning their small sample properties is presented on page 293. The estimates of the standard errors of $\hat{\hat{\alpha}}$ and $\hat{\hat{\beta}}$ can be obtained by using the formulas (8.49) and (8.51), with ρ replaced by $\hat{\rho}$.

EXAMPLE We can use the "quantity theory" relation and the data of the previous example to illustrate the two-stage estimation procedure. The "first round" estimate of ρ is

$$\hat{\rho} = 0.827.$$

[15] See J. D. Sargan, "Wages and Prices in the United Kingdom: A Study in Econometric Methodology," in P. E. Hart, G. Mills, and J. K. Whitaker (eds.), *Econometric Analysis for National Economic Planning* (London: Butterworths, 1964).

Note that this value is numerically very close to the maximum likelihood estimate of ρ of the previous example. The least squares estimates of the regression coefficients based on transformed data are

$$(C_t - 0.827C_{t-1}) = \underset{(13.760)}{-42.290} + \underset{(0.442)}{2.805}(M_t - 0.827M_{t-1}) + e_t, \qquad R^2 = 0.703.$$

This leads to the following estimates for the untransformed observations:

$$C_t = \underset{(79.537)}{-244.450} + \underset{(0.442)}{2.805}M_t + e_t, \qquad R^2 = 0.912.$$

These results are very similar to those obtained earlier by the maximum likelihood method.

Durbin's Method

A different estimation method has been suggested by Durbin.[16] Like the preceding method, *Durbin's procedure* consists of two steps. First, we rewrite (8.52) as

$$Y_t = \alpha(1 - \rho) + \rho Y_{t-1} + \beta X_t - \beta\rho X_{t-1} + u_t$$

or

$$Y_t = \alpha^* + \rho Y_{t-1} + \beta X_t + \gamma X_{t-1} + u_t.$$

This expression can be treated as a regression equation with three explanatory variables, X_t, X_{t-1} and Y_{t-1}, and estimated by the ordinary least squares method (as described in Chapter 10). The resulting estimator of ρ, say, $\tilde{\rho}$, is to be used to construct new variables $(Y_t - \tilde{\rho}Y_{t-1})$ and $(X_t - \tilde{\rho}X_{t-1})$. In the second step, we estimate

$$(Y_t - \tilde{\rho}Y_{t-1}) = \alpha^* + \beta(X_t - \tilde{\rho}X_{t-1}) + u_t^*,$$

where $\alpha^* = \alpha(1 - \tilde{\rho})$. The estimators of α and β that we get will have the same *asymptotic* properties as the maximum likelihood estimators described earlier.

The Use of First Differences

In earlier applied studies, research workers frequently attempted to deal with the problem of autoregression in disturbances by using the *method of first differences*. This method calls for transforming the original data on Y and X into first differences $(Y_t - Y_{t-1})$ and $(X_t - X_{t-1})$, and for setting up the regression equation as

$$(Y_t - Y_{t-1}) = \alpha^{**} + \beta(X_t - X_{t-1}) + v_t. \tag{8.56}$$

α^{**} and β are then estimated by the method of least squares. Note that since

$$Y_t = \alpha + \beta X_t + \varepsilon_t$$

and

$$Y_{t-1} = \alpha + \beta X_{t-1} + \varepsilon_{t-1},$$

it follows that $\alpha^{**} = 0$ and $v_t = \varepsilon_t - \varepsilon_{t-1}$. The rationale of the method of first differences is the belief that the true value of ρ is close to unity. Since $\alpha^{**} = 0$,

[16] J. Durbin, "Estimation of Parameters in Time-Series Regression Models," *Journal of the Royal Statistical Society*, Series B, Vol. 22, January 1960, pp. 139–153.

one does not expect that its estimate in (8.56) would be significantly different from zero. The implication is that α cannot be estimated by this method. We note in passing that a result giving the estimate of α^{**} as significantly different from zero has often been rationalized by the claim that the original model had been misspecified and that, in addition to X_t, it should have included a trend as an explanatory variable. If that were the case and the trend were measured by the "time variable" t, we would have

$$Y_t = \alpha + \beta X_t + \delta t + \varepsilon_t,$$

$$Y_{t-1} = \alpha + \beta X_{t-1} + \delta(t-1) + \varepsilon_{t-1},$$

and
$$Y_t - Y_{t-1} = \beta(X_t - X_{t-1}) + \delta + (\varepsilon_t - \varepsilon_{t-1}),$$

so that the intercept in (8.56) would measure the coefficient of the trend variable.

Let us consider the properties of the estimator of β when using the method of first differences. We assume, as before, that ε_t follows a first-order autoregressive scheme as described by (8.34) through (8.36). Now the disturbance in (8.56) is

$$v_t = \varepsilon_t - \varepsilon_{t-1},$$

so that

$$E(v_t) = 0,$$

$$E(v_t^2) = E(\varepsilon_t^2 + \varepsilon_{t-1}^2 - 2\varepsilon_t\varepsilon_{t-1}) = \sigma^2 + \sigma^2 - 2\rho\sigma^2 = 2\sigma^2(1-\rho)$$

$$= \frac{2\sigma_u^2(1-\rho)}{(1-\rho^2)} = \frac{2\sigma_u^2}{(1+\rho)},$$

$$E(v_t v_{t-1}) = E(\varepsilon_t - \varepsilon_{t-1})(\varepsilon_{t-1} - \varepsilon_{t-2})$$

$$= E(\varepsilon_t\varepsilon_{t-1} - \varepsilon_{t-1}^2 - \varepsilon_t\varepsilon_{t-2} + \varepsilon_{t-1}\varepsilon_{t-2}) = \rho\sigma^2 - \sigma^2 - \rho^2\sigma^2 + \rho\sigma^2$$

$$= -\sigma^2(1-\rho)^2 = \frac{-\sigma_u^2(1-\rho)}{(1+\rho)}.$$

It follows, then, that the disturbance in (8.56) has zero mean and a constant variance but is still autoregressive, although, of course, the extent of autoregression would be small if ρ were close to unity.

The least squares estimator of β based on first differences, say $\bar{\beta}$, is

(8.57)
$$\bar{\beta} = \frac{\sum (y_t' - y_{t-1}')(x_t' - x_{t-1}')}{\sum (x_t' - x_{t-1}')^2}$$

$$= \beta + \frac{\sum z_t'(\varepsilon_t - \varepsilon_{t-1})}{\sum z_t'^2} \qquad (t = 2, 3, \ldots, n)$$

where
$$z_t' = x_t' - x_{t-1}'.$$

Now
$$E(\bar{\beta}) = \beta,$$

so that $\bar{\beta}$ is unbiased. Further,

$$\operatorname{Var}(\bar{\beta}) = E\left[\frac{\sum z_t'(\varepsilon_t - \varepsilon_{t-1})}{\sum z_t'^2}\right]^2 = \frac{1}{(\sum z_t'^2)^2}\Big[E\sum_t z_t'^2(\varepsilon_t^2 - 2\varepsilon_t\varepsilon_{t-1} + \varepsilon_{t-1}^2)$$

$$+ 2E\sum_{s<t} z_t'z_{t-s}'(\varepsilon_t\varepsilon_{t-s} - \varepsilon_{t-1}\varepsilon_{t-s} - \varepsilon_t\varepsilon_{t-s-1} + \varepsilon_{t-1}\varepsilon_{t-s-1})\Big]$$

$$= \frac{2\sigma^2}{(\sum z_t'^2)^2}\Big[(1-\rho)\sum_t z_t'^2 + \sum_{s<t} z_t'z_{t-s}'\rho^{s-1}(2\rho - 1 - \rho^2)\Big]$$

$$= \frac{2\sigma^2(1-\rho)}{\sum z_t'^2}\left\{1 - \frac{(1-\rho)}{\sum z_t'^2}\left[\sum_{t=3}^{n} z_t'z_{t-1}' + \rho\sum_{t=4}^{n} z_t'z_{t-2}' + \cdots\right]\right\}.$$

The estimator $\bar{\beta}$ is based on the assumption that $\rho \to 1$, while the ordinary least squares estimator $\hat{\beta}$ can be considered as based on the assumption that $\rho = 0$. Thus it may be interesting to compare the variances of these two estimators for different values of ρ. We shall restrict the comparison to the situations characterized as follows.

1. The samples are large enough so that, for all practical purposes,

$$\sum_t x_t'^2 = \sum_t x_{t-1}'^2 = \sum_t x_{t-2}'^2 = \cdots.$$

2. $0 \leq \rho < 1$.
3. $r_s = r^s \quad (s = 1, 2, \ldots)$, where

$$r_s = \frac{\sum x_t'x_{t-s}'}{\sqrt{\sum x_t'^2}\sqrt{\sum x_{t-s}'^2}} = \frac{\sum x_t'x_{t-s}'}{\sum x_t'^2} \quad \text{(using 1 above).}$$

With these simplifications we have

$$\sum z_t'^2 = \sum x_t'^2 - 2\sum x_t'x_{t-1}' + \sum x_{t-1}'^2 = 2(1-r)\sum x_t'^2,$$

$$\sum z_t'z_{t-1}' = \sum x_t'x_{t-1}' - \sum x_{t-1}'^2 - \sum x_t'x_{t-2}' + \sum x_{t-1}'x_{t-2}' = -(1-r)^2\sum x_t'^2,$$

$$\sum z_t'z_{t-2}' = -r(1-r)^2\sum x_t'^2,$$

$$\sum z_t'z_{t-3}' = -r^2(1-r)^2\sum x_t'^2,$$

$$\vdots$$

so that

$$\operatorname{Var}(\bar{\beta}) = \frac{2\sigma^2(1-\rho)}{2(1-r)\sum x_t'^2}\left\{1 + \frac{(1-\rho)(1-r)^2\sum x_t'^2}{2(1-r)\sum x_t'^2}[1 + \rho r + \rho^2r^2 + \cdots]\right\}$$

$$= \frac{\sigma^2(1-\rho)}{\sum x_t'^2}\left[\frac{1}{1-r} + \frac{(1-\rho)}{2(1-\rho r)}\right].$$

The variance of the ordinary least squares estimator of β is given by (8.42). With the above simplification this becomes

$$\text{Var}(\hat{\beta}) = \frac{\sigma^2}{\sum x_t'^2}[1 + 2\rho r + 2\rho^2 r^2 + \cdots] = \frac{\sigma^2}{\sum x_t'^2}\left[\frac{1+\rho r}{1-\rho r}\right].$$

To facilitate the comparison, we evaluate these variances for selected values of ρ and r. The results of the calculations are shown in Table 8–4, with λ representing $\sigma^2/\sum x_t'^2$. As anticipated, $\text{Var}(\bar{\beta})$ is relatively small when ρ is close to

Table 8–4

Value of ρ	$r = 0.4$		$r = 0.8$	
	$\text{Var}(\bar{\beta})$	$\text{Var}(\hat{\beta})$	$\text{Var}(\bar{\beta})$	$\text{Var}(\hat{\beta})$
0.0	2.17λ	1.00λ	5.50λ	1.00λ
0.3	1.44λ	1.27λ	3.82λ	1.63λ
0.6	0.77λ	1.63λ	2.15λ	2.85λ
0.9	0.17λ	2.12λ	0.52λ	6.14λ

unity, and relatively large when ρ is small. However, it should be emphasized that the *estimator* of the variance of $\bar{\beta}$, like that of the variance of $\hat{\beta}$, is biased. Therefore, the use of $\bar{\beta}$ for testing hypotheses or constructing confidence intervals is inappropriate.[17] For this reason, the use of the method of first differences is not recommended unless it is really believed that ρ is very close to unity.

Small Sample Properties of Alternative Estimators

The small sample properties of the alternative estimators of the regression coefficients in models with autoregressive disturbances are generally unknown because the determination of the sampling distributions of these estimators is very complicated. Nevertheless, we can get some idea about the small-sample behavior of these estimators by deriving their sampling distributions *experimentally*. This can, of course, be done only for specific models and specific populations of the disturbances. The experimental derivation of sampling distributions for the case of discrete variables was discussed in Section 2–2. In the case of normally distributed disturbances, the variables are continuous, but the principle of experimental sampling remains the same. Sampling experiments of this sort have become known as *Monte Carlo experiments* because of their similarity to games of chance. We now describe one such experiment, which was designed for the purpose of comparing several estimators of the regression coefficients in a model with an autoregressive disturbance.

[17] The reader can determine the bias in estimating the variance of $\bar{\beta}$ by the conventional formula as an exercise. It may also be interesting to note that if ρ is positive, the values of $\bar{\beta}$ and $\hat{\beta}$ contain between them the value of $\tilde{\beta}$ that would be obtained if ρ were known. See Malinvaud, *op. cit.*, pp. 444–445.

Consider the population regression equation

$$Y_t = 10 + 2X_t + \varepsilon_t \qquad (t = 1, 2, \ldots)$$

with

$$\varepsilon_t = 0.8\varepsilon_{t-1} + u_t,$$

where

$$u_t \sim N(0, 0.36),$$

$$E(u_t\varepsilon_{t-1}) = 0,$$

and

$$\varepsilon_0 \sim N(0, 1).$$

Therefore,

$$E(\varepsilon_t) = 0,$$

$$\text{Var}(\varepsilon_t) = 1,$$

$$\rho = 0.8.$$

The values of X, which were selected more or less arbitrarily, are

$$\begin{array}{lll} X_1 = 2, & X_6 = 1, & X_{11} = X_1, \\ X_2 = 0, & X_7 = 4, & X_{12} = X_2, \\ X_3 = 1, & X_8 = 9, & \vdots \qquad \vdots \\ X_4 = 3, & X_9 = 4, & X_{99} = X_9, \\ X_5 = 9, & X_{10} = 3, & X_{100} = X_{10}. \end{array}$$

The experiment consists of drawing 100 samples of size 10, 20, and 100. The random drawings for the disturbances were obtained from the table *One Million Random Digits and One Hundred Thousand Deviates* (published by the Rand Corporation, Santa Monica, Calif., 1950). From each sample we calculated the values of the ordinary least squares (OLS), maximum likelihood (ML), and two-stage (TS) estimators of the regression coefficients. After 100 samples of a given size were drawn, we obtained the mean and the standard deviation for each of the estimators. The results of estimating the regression slope—whose true value is 2—are presented in Table 8–5. From these results it

Table 8–5

	Estimator					
	OLS		ML		TS	
Sample Size	Mean	S.D.	Mean	S.D.	Mean	S.D.
10	2.0070	0.1029	2.0079	0.0634	2.0058	0.0754
20	2.0008	0.0634	1.9995	0.0402	1.9997	0.0412
100	2.0001	0.0201	1.9990	0.0136	1.9990	0.0136

Source: J. Kmenta and R. F. Gilbert, "Estimation of Seemingly Unrelated Regressions with Autoregressive Disturbances," Michigan State University Econometrics Workshop Paper No. 6805, December 1968, p. 18.

is apparent that all three estimators are unbiased, and that the OLS estimator is inefficient relative to the ML and TS estimators. The latter two have identical standard deviations in large samples and nearly the same standard deviations in samples size 20, but in samples size 10 the ML estimator is more efficient. Although generalizations from particular experiments are somewhat hazardous, the results nevertheless offer some evidence concerning the small sample behavior of the estimators considered.

Tests for the Absence of Autoregression

Thus far in this section we have been concerned with the implications of the presence of autoregressive disturbances in a linear regression model. We have examined the properties of the ordinary least squares estimators of the regression coefficients and, having uncovered their shortcomings, we discussed various alternative estimation methods. However, if we do not know—or are not willing to assume—that the model is or is not autoregressive, we may not be able to decide which estimation method to use. In such a case we have to turn to the sample for information. In particular, we may want to test the hypothesis of no autoregression,

$$H_0: \quad \rho = 0,$$

against a one-sided or a two-sided alternative. The usual alternative hypothesis in economic relations is that of positive autoregression, i.e.,

$$H_A: \quad \rho > 0.$$

One test for the presence of autoregression follows, at least implicitly, from our discussion of the maximum likelihood estimation. Since, when using the maximum likelihood method, we estimate the value of ρ along with the values of the regression coefficients, we may simply test whether the estimated value of ρ is significantly different from zero. In large samples the maximum likelihood estimator of ρ is approximately normally distributed with estimated variance given by (8.55) as

$$s_{\hat{\rho}}^2 = \frac{1 - \hat{\rho}^2}{n}.$$

This can be used in smaller samples as an approximation.

EXAMPLE In illustrating maximum likelihood estimation under autoregression, we used the "quantity theory" equation of Friedman and Meiselman. The maximum likelihood estimate of ρ was found to be 0.85. Its estimated large-sample standard error is

$$\sqrt{\frac{1 - 0.85^2}{20}} = 0.118.$$

If we use a 5% test against the one-sided alternative of positive autoregression, the acceptance region for the null hypothesis is

$$\frac{\hat{\rho}}{s_{\hat{\rho}}} < 1.645.$$

In our case, we have

$$\frac{\hat{\rho}}{s_{\hat{\rho}}} = \frac{0.85}{0.118} = 7.20.$$

Since this lies clearly outside the acceptance region, the hypothesis of no autoregression has to be rejected.

An alternative test, which has been widely used in econometric applications, is known as the *Durbin-Watson test.* To apply this test we calculate the value of a statistic d given by

$$d = \frac{\sum_{t=2}^{n} (e_t - e_{t-1})^2}{\sum_{t=1}^{n} e_t^2},$$

where the e's represent the ordinary least squares residuals. If the alternative hypothesis is that of positive autoregression, the decision rules are:

1. Reject if $d < d_L$.
2. Do not reject if $d > d_U$.
3. The test is inconclusive if $d_L \leq d \leq d_U$.

The values of d_L (for "lower limit") and d_U (for "upper limit") are given in the table provided by Durbin and Watson and reproduced in Appendix D.[18] These values vary with the number of observations and the number of explanatory variables in the regression equation. If the alternative hypothesis is a two-sided one, the decision rules for the Durbin-Watson test are:

1. Reject if $d < d_L$, or if $d > 4 - d_L$.
2. Do not reject if $d_U < d < 4 - d_U$.
3. The test is inconclusive if $d_L \leq d \leq d_U$, or if $4 - d_U \leq d \leq 4 - d_L$.

A diagrammatic representation of the test is shown in Figure 8–2. Incidentally, it should be noted that the Durbin-Watson test is not applicable to regression equations in which the place of the explanatory variable is taken by the lagged value of the dependent variable.

[18] A table that is free of the inconclusive region, but is based on certain assumptions concerning the explanatory variable or variables, is given in H. Theil and A. L. Nagar, "Testing the Independence of Regression Disturbances," *Journal of the American Statistical Association*, Vol. 56, December 1961, pp. 793–806.

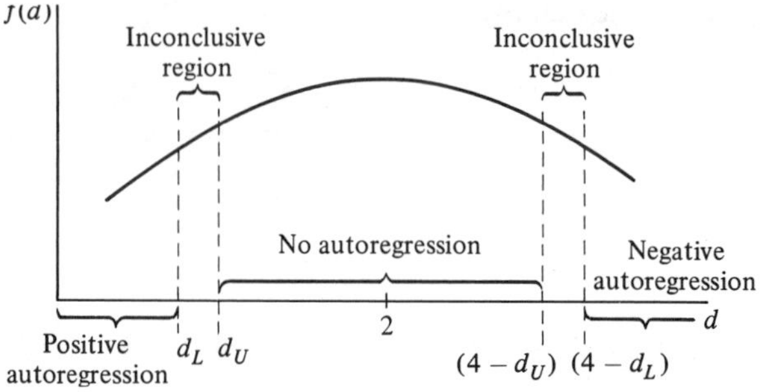

Figure 8–2

EXAMPLE Consider again estimation of the "quantity theory" equation. Suppose we wish to test the hypothesis

$$H_0: \quad \rho = 0$$

against

$$H_A: \quad \rho > 0$$

at the 5% level of significance, using the Durbin-Watson test. From the table, the appropriate values of d_L and d_U for twenty observations and one explanatory variable are

$$d_L = 1.20, \qquad \text{and} \qquad d_U = 1.41.$$

This means that we will reject H_0 if $d < 1.20$, and not reject H_0 if $d > 1.41$. The calculated value of the d statistic is

$$d = 0.321,$$

so that the hypothesis of no autoregression ($\rho = 0$) has to be rejected under this test as well.

As mentioned earlier, the Durbin-Watson test has been widely used in econometric applications. In fact, in most studies concerned with estimating regression equations from time-series data, the value of the d statistic is presented along with the other estimates. The question then is what action, if any, is to be taken in response to a particular outcome of the test. If no autoregression is indicated, we can retain the least squares estimates without fearing a loss of efficiency and a bias of the estimated standard errors. However, if the test indicates autoregression, then we have some reason to be concerned. One response is to re-estimate the equation, using one of the estimation methods designed for this situation (e.g., maximum likelihood or the two-stage procedure). Alternatively, we may take a second look at the specification of the regression model, since the autoregression of the disturbance may simply reflect the presence of some unexplained systematic influence on the dependent variable. A fairly commonly adopted ad hoc way of searching for this influence is to plot the residuals and then to try finding a variable whose peaks and troughs resemble those of the plotted residuals. Finally, if the result of the test is inconclusive, we may or may not respond. There is some evidence[19] that when the explanatory variable evolves gradually without any sharp, short, regular fluctuations, the appropriate boundary region is nearer d_U.

8-3 Stochastic Explanatory Variable

Assumption (7.6) of the classical normal linear regression model consists of the following:

1. X is nonstochastic.
2. Values of X are fixed in repeated samples.
3. $(1/n) \sum_i (X_i - \bar{X})^2$ is equal to a finite, nonzero number for any sample size.

In this section we shall be concerned mainly with 1; 2 and 3 deserve only a brief mention. To start with, the requirement that the values of X are fixed in repeated samples is only of theoretical interest since, in reality, we rarely draw or observe more than one sample for a given set of values of X. The purpose of this requirement is to set the framework for the sampling distributions of the various estimators that we discuss. It really amounts to saying that *if* we drew an infinite number of samples of one size (i.e., an infinite number of sets of values of $Y_1, Y_2, \ldots, Y_n$) for a fixed set of values of X (i.e., *one* set of values of $X_1, X_2, \ldots, X_n$), then the sampling distributions and properties of the estimators would be as we asserted. Thus we avoid the complications that would arise if the values of X were to change from sample to sample. Note that the values of X can be considered to be held fixed from sample to sample even if X is a stochastic variable (as long as holding X fixed does not make Y fixed as well).

By the assumption that for any sample size $\sum_i (X_i - \bar{X})^2/n$ is a finite number different from zero, it is required that the values of X in the sample are not all the same, and that they do not grow or decline without limit. The first requirement—that not all values of X are the same—is crucial, since otherwise the determination of the least squares regression coefficients would become impossible, as pointed out in Section 7-4. If the values of X are not all the same but the differences between them are very small, $\sum (X_i - \bar{X})^2$ will be small, and the variances of the estimators are likely to be very large. This, in turn, implies that in the tests of significance the probability of Error Type II (accepting H_0 when it is false) is high, and that the confidence intervals for the population parameters are wide. This is what the researchers mean when, in commenting on their regression results, they say: "Unfortunately, there was very little variation in the explanatory variable." As to the second requirement, the restriction that the values of X should be bounded is less crucial. It is

[19] See *ibid.*; also Malinvaud, *op. cit.*, p. 425.

utilized mainly in proving desirable asymptotic properties, but it is *not* a necessary condition for consistency in all cases.

As an example of a case where the values of the explanatory variable are not bounded, consider the equation for a "linear trend" given as

$$Y_t = \alpha + \beta t + \varepsilon_t \qquad (t = 1, 2, \ldots, n),$$

where t measures time in terms of specified periods. Assume that all the basic assumptions about the disturbance ε_t hold. Then, obviously, as n increases to infinity, so do the values of t. In fact,

$$\begin{aligned}\frac{1}{n}\sum_{t=1}^{n}(t-\bar{t})^2 &= \frac{1}{n}\sum_t t^2 - \left[\frac{1}{n}\sum_t t\right]^2\\ &= \frac{1}{n}[1^2 + 2^2 + \cdots + n^2] - \frac{1}{n^2}[1 + 2 + \cdots + n]^2\\ &= \frac{1}{n}\left[\frac{n}{6}(n+1)(2n+1)\right] - \frac{1}{n^2}\left[\frac{n}{2}(1+n)\right] = \frac{n^2-1}{12}.\end{aligned}$$

The small sample properties of the least squares estimators are not affected by this. As for consistency, we have

$$\mathrm{Var}(\hat{\beta}) = \frac{\sigma^2}{\sum(t-\bar{t})^2} = \frac{\sigma^2/n}{\sum(t-\bar{t})^2/n} = \frac{12\sigma^2}{n(n^2-1)},$$

so that

$$\lim_{n\to\infty}\mathrm{Var}(\hat{\beta}) = 0.$$

This implies that $\hat{\beta}$ is a consistent estimator of β.

The foregoing discussion leaves only the requirement of a nonstochastic explanatory variable to be considered. Let us now deal with the problem of estimating the coefficients of a regression equation when this is violated, i.e., when X is a stochastic variable. In this case the values of X are not fixed; instead, different values of X—or intervals of values of X—occur with certain probabilities. Regressions with stochastic explanatory variables are common, if not predominant, in econometrics. In many economic relations the values of the explanatory variable are determined, along with those of the dependent variable, as a result of some probability mechanism rather than being controlled by the experimenter or other persons or institutions. If X is stochastic, the important thing is whether it is or is not independent of the disturbance ε, and if dependent, what is the nature of the dependence. We shall distinguish between three possibilities:

1. X and ε are independent.
2. X and ε are contemporaneously uncorrelated.
3. X and ε are *not* independent *or* contemporaneously uncorrelated.

In each case we shall be concerned with the properties of the least squares estimators of the regression coefficients, given that all the basic assumptions about the disturbance term hold. We shall also make the assumption that the variance of X is a finite number different from zero.

Let us start with the case where X and ε are *independent*. As an example, consider the relationship

$$Y_i = \alpha + \beta X_i + \varepsilon_i,$$

with X_i and Y_i defined as follows:

$$Y_i = \log\left[\frac{V}{PL}\right]_i,$$

$$X_i = \log\left[\frac{W}{P}\right]_i,$$

where V = value added in production, L = labor input, P = price of product, W = money wage rate, and the subscript i refers to the ith region. The observations are made for a particular industry and a given period of time. The coefficient β represents the elasticity of substitution between labor and capital.[20] Here X is a stochastic variable which can be assumed to be independent of ε. The least squares estimator of β is

$$\hat{\beta} = \beta + \frac{\sum x_i'\varepsilon_i}{\sum x_i'^2}$$

and

$$E(\hat{\beta}) = \beta + E\left[\frac{\sum x_i'}{\sum x_i'^2}\right]E(\varepsilon_i) = \beta.$$

This result follows from the assumptions that X and ε are independent and that $E(\varepsilon_i) = 0$, using Theorem 10 of Section 3–6. Similarly,

$$E(\hat{\alpha}) = E(\bar{Y} - \hat{\beta}\bar{X}) = E(\alpha + \beta\bar{X} + \bar{\varepsilon} - \hat{\beta}\bar{X})$$

$$= \alpha + \beta E(\bar{X}) + E(\bar{\varepsilon}) - E\left[\beta + \frac{\sum x_i'\varepsilon_i}{\sum x_i'^2}\right]\bar{X} = \alpha,$$

so that $\hat{\alpha}$ and $\hat{\beta}$ retain their property of unbiasedness.

Since X is a stochastic variable, $\hat{\alpha}$ and $\hat{\beta}$ are no longer linear functions of $Y_1, Y_2, \ldots, Y_n$; that is, they can no longer be described as equal to $\sum_i a_i Y_i$ where $a_1, a_2, \ldots, a_n$ are *constants*. Therefore, in the strictest sense, $\hat{\alpha}$ and $\hat{\beta}$ cannot be considered as best-*linear*-unbiased estimators. However, it is not difficult to see that $\hat{\alpha}$ and $\hat{\beta}$ are efficient if we consider their variances as being conditional on a given set of values of $X_1, X_2, \ldots, X_n$. We may think of the population of all pairs of values of X and Y as an enormous card file with each card representing a specific pair. Then we can specify one set of values of $X_1, X_2, \ldots, X_n$ and have the sorting machine pull out all the cards with these values of X. This

[20] See K. J. Arrow et al., "Capital-Labor Substitution and Economic Efficiency," *Review of Economics and Statistics*, Vol. 43, August 1961, p. 238, eq. (8a).

subset of cards represents a population from which samples can be drawn. Each such sample can be used to estimate the regression coefficients. If we drew an infinite number of these samples, we could construct sampling distributions for these estimators and determine their properties. Obviously, the properties of the estimators determined in this way would be conditional on the chosen values $X_1, X_2, \ldots, X_n$. This means that these values can be treated *as if* they were fixed numbers, which in fact they are *after* we pull out all the appropriate cards from the original file. Now we know that for a fixed set of values $X_1, X_2, \ldots, X_n$, the least squares estimators of the regression coefficients are efficient. We also know that this is true for *any* fixed set of values of X. Therefore, since the least squares estimators of the regression coefficients are unconditionally unbiased, and since for *each* set of values of $X_1, X_2, \ldots, X_n$ they are efficient, it follows that they are *efficient* unconditionally, too.

It is easy to show that the least squares estimators of the regression coefficients also retain their desirable asymptotic properties when X is stochastic but independent of ε. One way is by relying upon the maximum likelihood principle. The probability distribution for a single observation, say the ith, is given by $f(x_i, \varepsilon_i)$. For n independent observations, we have

$$f(x_1, \varepsilon_1) f(x_2, \varepsilon_2) \ldots f(x_n, \varepsilon_n),$$

which, since X and ε are independent, can be written as

$$f(x_1) f(x_2) \ldots f(x_n) f(\varepsilon_1) f(\varepsilon_2) \ldots f(\varepsilon_n).$$

The probability transformation from the ε's, which are not observable, to the Y's is

$$f(y_i) = \left|\frac{\partial \varepsilon_i}{\partial Y_i}\right| f(\varepsilon_i) = f(\varepsilon_i),$$

so that the logarithmic likelihood function becomes

$$\begin{aligned} L &= \log [f(x_1) f(x_2) \ldots f(x_n)] + \log [f(\varepsilon_1) f(\varepsilon_2) \ldots f(\varepsilon_n)] \\ &= \sum_i \log f(x_i) - \frac{n}{2} \log (2\pi) - \frac{n}{2} \log \sigma^2 - \frac{1}{2\sigma^2} \sum_i (Y_i - \alpha - \beta X_i)^2. \end{aligned}$$

As long as the distribution of X does not involve any of the parameters α, β, or σ^2, maximizing the likelihood function with respect to these parameters will not be affected by the presence of the term $\sum \log f(x_i)$. The resulting estimators of α and β will then be the same as the least squares estimators. Thus, the least squares estimators of the regression coefficients are consistent, asymptotically efficient, and asymptotically normal whether X is nonstochastic or stochastic, provided X and ε are independent.

As a final point, consider the variances of the least squares estimators of α and β. For $\hat{\beta}$ we have

$$\operatorname{Var}(\hat{\beta}) = E\left[\frac{\sum x_i' \varepsilon_i}{\sum x_i'^2}\right]^2 = E\left[\frac{\sum x_i'^2 \varepsilon_i^2}{(\sum x_i'^2)^2}\right] + 2E\left[\frac{\sum\limits_{i<j} x_i' x_j' \varepsilon_i \varepsilon_j}{(\sum x_i'^2)^2}\right] = \sigma^2 E\left[\frac{1}{\sum x_i'^2}\right].$$

Similarly, we can show that

$$\mathrm{Var}(\hat{\alpha}) = \sigma^2 E\left[\frac{1}{n} + \frac{\bar{X}^2}{\sum x_i'^2}\right].$$

That is, the variances of $\hat{\alpha}$ and $\hat{\beta}$ are the same as when X is nonstochastic, *except* that the terms involving X are replaced by their mathematical expectations. The formulas for unbiased estimators of $\mathrm{Var}(\hat{\alpha})$ and $\mathrm{Var}(\hat{\beta})$ are given by (7.37). Also, the classical procedures for interval estimation and hypothesis testing developed in Chapter 7 remain valid when X is stochastic but independent of ε. Thus, *relaxing the assumption that X is nonstochastic and replacing it by the assumption that X is stochastic but independent of ε does not change the desirable properties and feasibility of least squares estimation.*

Now we come to the second possibility concerning the explanatory variable, namely, the case where X and ε are *contemporaneously uncorrelated.* That is, we assume that

$$\mathrm{Cov}(X_1, \varepsilon_1) = \mathrm{Cov}(X_2, \varepsilon_2) = \cdots = \mathrm{Cov}(X_n, \varepsilon_n) = 0.$$

Note that we do not assume that X and ε are contemporaneously independent, which would be a stronger requirement. As an example, consider the following highly simplified model of income determination:

$$C_t = \gamma_0 + \gamma_1 Y_t + \varepsilon_{1t} \qquad \text{(consumption function)},$$

$$I_t = \delta_0 + \delta_1 Y_{t-1} + \varepsilon_{2t} \qquad \text{(investment function)},$$

$$Y_t = C_t + I_t \qquad \text{(income identity)},$$

where C = consumption, Y = income, I = investment, and ε_{1t} and ε_{2t} are random disturbances that satisfy the basic assumptions. The three-equation model can be reduced to one equation by solving for Y_t to get

$$Y_t = (\gamma_0 + \gamma_1 Y_t + \varepsilon_{1t}) + (\delta_0 + \delta_1 Y_{t-1} + \varepsilon_{2t}).$$

This can be written as

$$(8.58) \qquad Y_t = \alpha + \beta Y_{t-1} + \varepsilon_t,$$

where

$$\alpha = \frac{\gamma_0 + \delta_0}{1 - \gamma_1},$$

$$\beta = \frac{\delta_1}{1 - \gamma_1},$$

and

$$\varepsilon_t = \frac{\varepsilon_{1t} + \varepsilon_{2t}}{1 - \gamma_1}.$$

In (8.58) the explanatory variable is represented by the lagged value of the dependent variable. A model of this kind is generally known as a "model autoregressive in variables." In our case, we shall confine it to the situations where $-1 < \beta < 1$. By carrying out successive substitutions we can express Y_t as

$$Y_t = \alpha(1 + \beta + \beta^2 + \cdots + \beta^{t-1}) + \beta^t Y_0 + \varepsilon_t + \beta\varepsilon_{t-1} + \beta^2\varepsilon_{t-2} + \cdots + \beta^{t-1}\varepsilon_1 .$$

As $t \to \infty$, Y_t becomes

$$Y_t = \frac{\alpha}{1-\beta} + \varepsilon_t + \beta\varepsilon_{t-1} + \beta^2\varepsilon_{t-2} + \cdots;$$

that is, in the long run Y_t "settles down" to random fluctuations around a fixed level. Note that in (8.58) the explanatory variable Y_{t-1} is *not* correlated with the current disturbance ε_t since Y_{t-1} depends on $Y_0, \varepsilon_1, \varepsilon_2, \ldots, \varepsilon_{t-1}$ but not on ε_t.

Consider now the least squares estimator of β in (8.58). We have

$$\hat{\beta} = \beta + \frac{\sum y'_{t-1}\varepsilon_t}{\sum y'^2_{t-1}}.$$

Now y'_{t-1} and ε_t are not independent since

$$y'_{t-1} = Y_{t-1} - \frac{1}{n}(Y_0 + Y_1 + \cdots + Y_t + \cdots + Y_{n-1});$$

that is, y'_{t-1} involves Y_t, which is *not* independent of ε_t. This means that we cannot separate out ε_t when taking mathematical expectation of $\hat{\beta}$ as we could in case of independence. Thus $\hat{\beta}$ cannot be said to be unbiased. However, the probability limit of $\hat{\beta}$ is

$$\text{plim}\,\hat{\beta} = \beta + \frac{\text{plim}\,(\sum y'_{t-1}\varepsilon_t)/n}{\text{plim}\,(\sum y'^2_{t-1})/n} = \beta,$$

since $(\sum y'_{t-1}\varepsilon_t)/n$ is a consistent estimator of the population covariance of Y_{t-1} and ε_t, which is zero, and $(\sum y'^2_{t-1})/n$ is a consistent estimator of the variance of Y_{t-1}, which is a finite number different from zero. Thus $\hat{\beta}$ is a consistent estimator of β. Similarly, $\hat{\alpha}$ can be shown to be a consistent estimator of α. Asymptotic efficiency and asymptotic normality of the least squares estimators of α and β are more difficult to prove, but they also have been established.[21] The conclusion then is that *when the explanatory variable and the disturbance are contemporaneously uncorrelated* (*as in the model which is autoregressive in variables*), *the classical results of least squares estimation established in Chapter 7 hold only asymptotically.*

The last possibility concerning the explanatory variable is the case where X and ε are *neither independent nor contemporaneously uncorrelated.* In this case,

$$\text{plim}\,\hat{\beta} = \beta + \frac{\text{plim}\,(\sum x'_t\varepsilon_t)/n}{\text{plim}\,(\sum x'^2_t)/n} \neq \beta$$

and

$$\text{plim}\,\hat{\alpha} \neq \alpha,$$

[21] For details and relevant references see Malinvaud, *op. cit.*, pp. 452–453.

so that the least squares estimators of the regression coefficients are not even consistent. An intuitive explanation for this is that the least squares estimation method is designed in such a way that the total variation of Y (SST) can always be divided into two parts, one representing the variation due to the explanatory variable (SSR) and the other representing the variation due to other factors. But when the explanatory variable and the disturbance are correlated, such a division is not valid since it does not allow for the *joint* effect of X and ε on Y.

EXAMPLE As an example of a situation in which the explanatory variable and the disturbance are contemporaneously correlated, consider a market demand equation given by

$$Q_t = \alpha + \beta P_t + \varepsilon_t \qquad (\alpha > 0, \beta < 0),$$

where Q = quantity and P = price of a given commodity. If the market is in equilibrium, the quantity of the commodity sold in the market and the equilibrium price are determined by the intersection of the demand and the supply functions. Suppose the supply function is

$$Q_t = \gamma + \delta P_t + \eta_t \qquad (\gamma > 0, \delta > 0),$$

where $\eta_t \sim N(0, \sigma_\eta^2)$ is a stochastic disturbance which is nonautoregressive and independent of ε_t. The demand and the supply equations can be solved for the equilibrium quantity and price to give

$$Q_t = \frac{\alpha\delta - \beta\gamma}{\delta - \beta} + \frac{\delta\varepsilon_t - \beta\eta_t}{\delta - \beta},$$

$$P_t = \frac{\alpha - \gamma}{\delta - \beta} + \frac{\varepsilon_t - \eta_t}{\delta - \beta}.$$

From the last result we can see that P_t and ε_t are correlated; in particular,

$$\mathrm{Cov}(P_t, \varepsilon_t) = E[P_t - E(P_t)][\varepsilon_t - E(\varepsilon_t)] = E\left[\frac{\varepsilon_t - \eta_t}{\delta - \beta}\right]\varepsilon_t = \frac{\sigma^2}{\delta - \beta}.$$

The least squares estimator of the slope of the demand equation is

$$\hat{\beta} = \beta + \frac{\sum p_t'\varepsilon_t'}{\sum p_t'^2},$$

where

$$p_t' = P_t - \bar{P} = \frac{\varepsilon_t' - \eta_t'}{\delta - \beta}.$$

Substitution for p_t' into $\hat{\beta}$ gives

$$\hat{\beta} = \beta + \frac{\left[\frac{1}{\delta - \beta}\right]\sum \varepsilon_t'(\varepsilon_t' - \eta_t')}{\left[\frac{1}{\delta - \beta}\right]^2 \sum (\varepsilon_t' - \eta_t')^2} = \beta + \frac{(\delta - \beta)\left[\frac{1}{n}\sum \varepsilon_t'^2 - \frac{1}{n}\sum \varepsilon_t'\eta_t'\right]}{\frac{1}{n}\sum \varepsilon_t'^2 + \frac{1}{n}\sum \eta_t'^2 - \frac{2}{n}\sum \varepsilon_t'\eta_t'}.$$

Therefore,

$$\operatorname{plim} \hat{\beta} = \beta + \frac{(\delta - \beta)\sigma^2}{\sigma^2 + \sigma_\eta^2},$$

which proves that the least squares estimator of β is inconsistent. This example illustrates the so-called "simultaneous equation problem," which occurs when estimating certain economic relationships.

Regression equations in which the explanatory variable and the disturbance are correlated are rather common in econometrics, most notoriously in the area of simultaneous equation models, illustrated by the preceding example. However, the problem arises also in connection with some single equation models, such as the "distributed lag" model or the "errors-in-variables" model, which will be discussed in the following chapters. In each case the breakdown of the least squares estimation method has led to development of alternative methods of estimation that provide us with consistent estimates. These methods will be discussed in connection with the models for which they were developed or to which they were found to be applicable.

EXERCISES

8–1. Derive the formulas (8.3) and (8.4).

8–2. Prove that if $x_i'^2$ and σ_i^2 are positively associated, the bias in (8.9) is negative.

8–3. Consider the following model:

$$Y_i = \alpha + \varepsilon_i,$$

where

$$\varepsilon_i \sim N(0, \sigma^2 X_i),$$

$$E(\varepsilon_i \varepsilon_j) = 0 \qquad (i \neq j),$$

and X_i is nonstochastic. Find the best linear unbiased estimator of α and its variance.

8–4. Using the data in Table 8–6 on income (X) and expenditure (Y) of a sample of households, estimate the regression equation

$$Y_i = \alpha + \beta X_i + \varepsilon_i$$

for the following heteroskedastic models:

a. $\text{Var}(\varepsilon_i) = \sigma^2 X_i^2$. **b.** $\text{Var}(\varepsilon_i) = \sigma^2 [E(Y_i)]^2$. **c.** $\text{Var}(\varepsilon_i) = \sigma_i^2$.

Table 8–6

	Y										
X	14	19	21	23	25	27	29	31	33	35	Total
18	74	13	7	1							95
23	6	4	2	7	4						23
25	2	3	2	2	4						13
27	1	1	2	3	3	2					12
29	2		1	3	2		6				14
31	2		2	1			1	2	1		9
33				2			1	1	3		7
35		1		1					2		4
37					1	1		1		1	4

8–5. Prove the validity of the formula (8.38).

8–6. Prove that formulas (8.38) through (8.41) reduce to the least squares formulas when $\rho = 0$.

8–7. Prove that the conventional least squares formula for estimating the variance of the estimator in (8.57) leads to biased results.

8–8. One representation of the aggregate consumption function for the United States economy is:

$$C_t = \alpha + \beta Y_t + \varepsilon_t,$$

where C = personal consumption expenditure in constant prices, Y = personal disposable income in constant prices, and t = time in years.

a. Assume that all the basic assumptions of the simple regression model are satisfied. Estimate the relationship from the data in Table 8–7, following the computational design given in Appendix C.

b. On the basis of the results obtained in **a**, carry out the Durbin-Watson test for the presence of autoregression among the disturbances.

c. Assume that the disturbance follows a first-order autoregressive scheme and obtain asymptotically efficient estimates of the regression coefficients and their estimated standard errors.

Table 8–7

Year	Personal Consumption Expenditure*		Personal Disposable Income* in Current Prices†
	In Current Prices (1)	In Constant 1954 Prices (2)	(3)
1948	178.3	199.3	189.3
1949	181.2	204.3	189.7
1950	195.0	216.8	207.7
1951	209.8	218.5	227.5
1952	219.8	224.2	238.7
1953	232.6	235.1	252.5
1954	238.0	238.0	256.9
1955	256.9	256.0	274.4
1956	269.9	264.3	292.9
1957	285.2	271.2	308.8
1958	293.2	273.2	317.9
1959	313.5	288.9	337.1
1960	328.2	298.1	349.9
1961	337.3	303.8	364.7
1962	356.8	318.5	384.6
1963	375.0	330.6	402.5
1964	399.3	347.5	431.8

Sources: 1948–1960: *Business Statistics*, 1963 ed. (U.S. Department of Commerce); 1961–1964: *Statistical Abstract of the United States*, 1965 (U.S. Department of Commerce).

* In billions of dollars.

† To obtain "real" personal disposable income, deflate by the price deflator given implicitly by columns (1) and (2).

8–9. Derive the formula given in (8.55).

8–10. An aggregate food consumption function is specified as

$$Y_t = \alpha + \beta Z_t + \varepsilon_t,$$

where Y = personal expenditure on food, and Z = total personal consumption expenditure. The data for the United States for the years 1929–1964 are given in Exercise **7–8** (Table 7–4). Conduct a test for the absence of positive autoregression of the disturbances by

a. Using the Durbin-Watson test.

b. Using the maximum likelihood large-sample test.

9 Estimation with Deficient Data

In Chapter 8 we dealt with the problem of estimating the coefficients of a linear regression equation when one of the basic assumptions of the classical normal linear regression model does not hold. The discussion in the present chapter deals with the estimation problem in situations where the sample data are in some respect deficient. The particular deficiencies that we discuss are:

1. Presence of errors of measurement.
2. Grouped data.
3. Missing observations.

These deficiencies, which are likely to be encountered in empirical work, give rise to estimation problems that deserve our special attention.

9–1 Errors of Measurement

Up to this point, we have always taken for granted that the values of the variables in the regression model are measured without error. This presumption has been implicit in our entire discussion, and all of our formulas are based on it. Here we are investigating what happens to the estimators of the regression coefficients when this is not true and what can be done to cope with such a situation. In doing so, we restrict ourselves to cases in which the errors of measurement can be assumed to be random and to have specific probability characteristics. This fairly standard way of treating errors of measurement in the statistical and econometric literature corresponds to a wide variety of situations encountered in real life.

Let us start by considering the problem of errors of measurement in the context of the classical normal linear regression model of Chapter 7. As before, the regression equation is

$$Y_i = \alpha + \beta X_i + \varepsilon_i .$$

We also retain all the basic assumptions (7.2) through (7.6). Suppose, now, that our observations on Y and X contain errors, so that instead of Y_i and X_i we observe Y_i^* and X_i^*, which are given as

$$Y_i^* = Y_i + v_i,$$

$$X_i^* = X_i + w_i,$$

where v_i and w_i represent the errors in measuring the ith value of Y and of X. The behavioral characteristics of the errors are assumed to be as follows:

$$v_i \sim N(0, \sigma_v^2), \tag{9.1}$$

$$w_i \sim N(0, \sigma_w^2);$$

$$E(v_i v_j) = 0 \qquad (i \neq j), \tag{9.2}$$

$$E(w_i w_j) = 0 \qquad (i \neq j);$$

$$E(v_i w_i) = 0, \tag{9.3}$$

$$E(v_i \varepsilon_i) = 0,$$

$$E(w_i \varepsilon_i) = 0.$$

Assumption (9.1) states that each error is a random normal variable with zero mean and a constant variance. Assumption (9.2) rules out situations in which the errors are autoregressive; together with (9.1), this assumption implies that errors made at one point of observation are independent of errors made at other points of observation. Assumption (9.3) states how the errors are related—or, rather, unrelated—to each other. Assumptions (9.1) through (9.3) and the basic assumptions about the disturbance ε jointly imply that the errors of measurement are independent of each other, of the disturbance in the regression equation and, for a nonstochastic X, of the true values of X and Y.

Let us now consider the problem of estimating the regression coefficients from data on Y^* and X^*. Since

$$Y_i = Y_i^* - v_i$$

and

$$X_i = X_i^* - w_i,$$

the regression equation can be rewritten as

$$(Y_i^* - v_i) = \alpha + \beta(X_i^* - w_i) + \varepsilon_i$$

or

$$Y_i^* = \alpha + \beta X_i^* + \varepsilon_i^*, \tag{9.4}$$

where

$$\varepsilon_i^* = \varepsilon_i + v_i - \beta w_i.$$

Now, when the regression model is written in the form (9.4) where the dependent and the explanatory variables are observable, the explanatory variable X_i^* is contemporaneously correlated with the disturbance ε_i^*. In particular,

$$\text{Cov}(X_i^*, \varepsilon_i^*) = E[X_i^* - E(X_i^*)]\varepsilon_i^* = E[w_i(\varepsilon_i + v_i - \beta w_i)] = -\beta\sigma_w^2.$$

This means that the least squares estimator of β is *inconsistent*. The same is true of the least squares estimator of α.

Instrumental Variables Estimation

Equation (9.4) is sometimes referred to as a model with *errors in variables and errors in equation*. An attempt to estimate this model by using the maximum likelihood method breaks down in the sense that the resulting estimators are not consistent.[1] One method known to give consistent estimates in this case is the *method of instrumental variables*. This method is available whenever we can find a new variable Z_i such that

1. $\text{plim}\left(\sum z_i' \varepsilon_i^{*\prime}\right)/n = 0.$
2. $\text{plim}\left(\sum z_i' x_i^{*\prime}\right)/n$ is a finite number different from zero.

Here, in accordance with the previously adopted notation, we define

$$z_i' = Z_i - \bar{Z},$$
$$x_i^{*\prime} = X_i^* - \bar{X}^*.$$

The first condition will be satisfied if Z_i is uncorrelated with ε_i, v_i, and w_i. The second condition will be satisfied if Z_i and X_i^* are correlated with each other. An additional condition, which is not necessary for consistency but helps to reduce the asymptotic variance of the instrumental variables estimator, is that the plim $(\sum z_i' x_i^{*\prime})/n$ is as large as possible—that is, that the degree of correlation between Z_i and X_i^* is high. The variable Z_i, which is called an "instrumental variable," may be either stochastic or nonstochastic. Finally, it does not matter whether Z_i is or is not measured without error as long as the specified conditions are satisfied with respect to the observable values of Z. The estimators of α and β, say, $\alpha^\dagger$ and $\beta^\dagger$, are then defined as follows:

$$\beta^\dagger = \frac{\sum y_i^{*\prime} z_i'}{\sum x_i^{*\prime} z_i'}, \tag{9.5a}$$

$$\alpha^\dagger = \bar{Y}^* - \beta^\dagger \bar{X}_i^*, \tag{9.5b}$$

where

$$y_i^{*\prime} = Y_i^* - \bar{Y}^*.$$

For reasons of computational convenience we usually measure the values of the instrumental variable in such units that $\bar{Z}$ is equal to $\bar{X}^*$. This can be easily achieved by multiplying each value of the instrumental variable by the factor $(\bar{X}^*/\bar{Z}^*)$, where $\bar{Z}^*$ is the sample mean of the values of the instrumental variable

[1] See J. Johnston, *Econometric Methods* (New York: McGraw-Hill, 1963), pp. 151–152. The breakdown of the maximum likelihood method occurs because the likelihood function includes the "true" values of the explanatory variable, which are not known and therefore have to be treated as unknown parameters. This means that as the sample size increases, so does the number of unknown parameters. In this case the likelihood function does not have a maximum.

measured in terms of original units. Such a transformation leaves unaffected the correlations between Z and ε^* and between Z and X^*.

The idea behind the method of instrumental variables can be explained by reference to the least squares "normal equations" given by (7.10) and (7.11). For the regression equation (9.4) the least squares normal equations are:

$$\sum Y_i^* = \hat{\alpha} n + \hat{\beta} \sum X_i^*,$$

$$\sum Y_i^* X_i^* = \hat{\alpha} \sum X_i^* + \hat{\beta} \sum X_i^{*2}.$$

A rule for obtaining these equations is as follows. To obtain the first normal equation, multiply both sides of (9.4) by the multiplier of α (which is 1), add all observations, and omit the last term involving the disturbance. To obtain the second normal equation, multiply both sides of (9.4) by the multiplier of β (which is X_i^*), add all observations, and omit the last term involving the disturbance. In obtaining the normal equations for the instrumental variables estimators, we proceed in a similar way. The first normal equation is obtained in exactly the same way as the first normal equation in the least squares method. The second normal equation is obtained by multiplying both sides of (9.4) by Z_i instead of X_i^* as in the case of least squares. The result is:

$$\sum Y_i^* = \alpha^\dagger n + \beta^\dagger \sum X_i^*,$$

$$\sum Y_i^* Z_i = \alpha^\dagger \sum Z_i + \beta^\dagger \sum X_i^* Z_i.$$

This leads to the formulas for instrumental variables estimators as given by (9.5a) and (9.5b).

Note that in the case of a regression equation in which the explanatory variable X_i is independent of the disturbance ε_i, a suitable instrumental variable would be X_i itself since, in this case, X_i is uncorrelated with ε_i and at the same time is (perfectly) correlated with itself; therefore, conditions 1 and 2 are satisfied. Thus, an ordinary least squares estimator may be thought of as an instrumental variables estimator with $Z_i = X_i$.

Let us now demonstrate that the instrumental variables estimators are consistent. With respect to $\beta^\dagger$, we have

$$\beta^\dagger = \frac{\sum y_i^{*\prime} z_i'}{\sum x_i^{*\prime} z_i'} = \beta + \frac{\sum \varepsilon_i^{*\prime} z_i'}{\sum x_i^{*\prime} z_i'},$$

and

$$\text{plim}\, \beta^\dagger = \beta + \frac{\text{plim}\,(\sum \varepsilon_i^{*\prime} z_i')/n}{\text{plim}\,(\sum x_i^{*\prime} z_i')/n} = \beta$$

by making use of the conditions that Z_i is supposed to satisfy. Similarly,

$$\text{plim}\, \alpha^\dagger = \text{plim}\,(\bar{Y}^* - \beta^\dagger \bar{X}^*) = \text{plim}\,(\alpha + \beta \bar{X}^* + \bar{\varepsilon}^* - \beta^\dagger \bar{X}^*) = \alpha.$$

This shows that $\alpha^\dagger$ and $\beta^\dagger$ are consistent. Note that we cannot prove that $\beta^\dagger$ is unbiased, because in the last term of

$$\beta^\dagger = \beta + \frac{\sum \varepsilon_i^{*\prime} z_i'}{\sum x_i^{*\prime} z_i'}$$

we cannot separate z_i' from the rest (even if Z_i is nonstochastic) when taking the mathematical expectation.

The asymptotic variances of the instrumental variables estimators can be derived from the appropriate formulas.[2] The results are:

$$\text{(9.6a)} \qquad \text{Asympt. Var}(\beta^\dagger) = \text{plim} \frac{\sigma_{\varepsilon^*}^2 \sum z_i'^2}{(\sum x_i^{*\prime} z_i')^2},$$

$$\text{(9.6b)} \qquad \text{Asympt. Var}(\alpha^\dagger) = \text{plim}\, \sigma_{\varepsilon^*}^2 \left[\frac{1}{n} + \frac{\bar{X}^{*2} \sum z_i'^2}{(\sum x_i^{*\prime} z_i')^2}\right],$$

where $$\sigma_{\varepsilon^*}^2 = \text{Var}(\varepsilon_i^*) = \sigma^2 + \sigma_v^2 + \beta^2 \sigma_w^2.$$

In these derivations we have made use of the fact that Z is measured in such a way that $\bar{Z} = \bar{X}^*$. Since $\sigma_{\varepsilon^*}^2$ is not known, it has to be estimated. A consistent estimator of $\sigma_{\varepsilon^*}^2$, say, s^{*2}, is given by

$$\text{(9.7)} \qquad s^{*2} = \frac{1}{n-2} \sum_i (Y_i^* - \alpha^\dagger - \beta^\dagger X_i^*)^2,$$

i.e., by dividing the sum of squared residuals by $(n - 2)$. This enables us to obtain estimators of the asymptotic variances of $\alpha^\dagger$ and $\beta^\dagger$ as

$$\text{(9.8a)} \qquad s_{\beta^\dagger}^2 = \frac{s^{*2} \sum z_i'^2}{(\sum x_i^{*\prime} z_i')^2},$$

$$\text{(9.8b)} \qquad s_{\alpha^\dagger}^2 = s^{*2} \left[\frac{1}{n} + \frac{\bar{X}^{*2} \sum z_i'^2}{(\sum x_i^{*\prime} z_i')^2}\right].$$

Although these estimators refer to asymptotic variances, they have been used in finite samples as approximations. It can be shown that the results (9.5), (9.7), and (9.8) also apply when the "true" explanatory variable X is stochastic but independent of ε^*.

The choice of the instrumental variable is limited only by the requirement that it should be uncorrelated with ε^* and correlated with X^*. There can be, and in general there will be, many variables that may qualify as instruments. We will try to choose the one that has the highest correlation with X^*, since this will give smaller asymptotic variances of the estimators than otherwise. For instance, when the data are in the form of a time series, a suitable choice may be that of $Z_t = X_{t-1}^*$, i.e., the lagged value of the explanatory variable. If ε_t^* is nonautoregressive, X_{t-1}^* would be uncorrelated with ε_t^* and, at the same time, probably highly correlated with X_t^*. However, we can never be sure that we may not do better by choosing a different instrumental variable from the one we had selected. Therefore, we cannot assert that our particular instrumental variables estimator has the minimum asymptotic variance, i.e., that it is asymptotically efficient. Thus the only desirable property of instrumental variables estimators is consistency. This limitation, combined with the arbitrariness in the choice of

[2] For details see A. S. Goldberger, *Econometric Theory* (New York: Wiley, 1964), pp. 285–286.

instrumental variables and the difficulty of checking that the chosen variable is indeed uncorrelated with ε^*, makes the method somewhat unattractive. Unfortunately, when it comes to models with errors in variables and errors in equation, we have no better method available to us—at least in the context of classical sampling theory. In previous econometric work, the tendency has been to avoid the issue by assuming that the errors of measurement are so small that they can be safely neglected.

EXAMPLE In a well-known paper on capital-labor substitution,[3] the authors estimate the following relationship:

$$Y_i = \alpha + \beta X_i + \varepsilon_i,$$

with X_i and Y_i defined as

$$X_i = \log (W/P)_i,$$

$$Y_i = \log (V/PL)_i,$$

where W = money wage rate, P = price of product, V = value added in production, L = labor input, and the subscript i refers to the ith country. The observations are made for a particular industry and a given year. In their estimation, the authors used the method of least squares. Since it is quite likely that the observations on X and Y contain errors of measurement, we may re-estimate the relationship by using the method of instrumental variables. We shall confine our attention to the *furniture manufacturing industry* (group 260), which is one of two industries for which price data are given in the paper. As the instrumental variable we shall use $\log (W/P)_i$ for the knitting-mill products (group 232), with an appropriate adjustment so that $\bar{Z} = \bar{X}$. This instrumental variable is very likely to satisfy the two requirements for consistency: the wage rate in knitting mills is unlikely to be related to the disturbance (and errors of measurement) in the furniture manufacturing industry, but is likely to be related to the wage rate in that industry. The relevant data are given in Table 9–1. The price variable is expressed as an index, with the value for the United States equal to 1. If the errors of measurement are negligible, i.e., if $X_i^* = X_i$ and $Y_i^* = Y_i$, then least squares estimates are appropriate. These are

$$\underset{}{Y_i} = \underset{(0.0996)}{-2.2877} + \underset{(0.0331)}{0.8401}X_i + e_i, \qquad R^2 = 0.986.$$

If, on the other hand, there are serious errors of measurement present, estimates obtained by the method of instrumental variables would be preferable since they are consistent. The regression equation estimated by this method is

$$Y_i^* = \underset{(0.1025)}{-2.2978} + \underset{(0.0342)}{0.8435}X_i^* + e_i^*, \qquad R^2 = 0.985.$$

The results obtained by the method of instrumental variables are very similar to those obtained by the least squares method.

[3] K. J. Arrow, et al., "Capital-Labor Substitution and Economic Efficiency," *Review of Economics and Statistics*, Vol. 43, August 1961, pp. 225–250.

Table 9–1

Country	Furniture Manufacturing Industry					Knitting Mill Products			
	L/V	P	W ($)	$\log(V/PL) = Y^*$	$\log(W/P) = X^*$	P	W ($)	$\log(W/P) = Z^*$	$Z^*\bar{X}^*/\bar{Z}^* = Z$
United States	0.1706	1.0000	3515	0.7680	3.5459	1.0000	2698	3.4310	3.4241
Canada	0.2385	1.5470	2668	0.4330	3.2367	1.4891	2260	3.1812	3.1748
New Zealand	0.3678	0.9482	1834	0.4575	3.2865	1.0346	1548	3.1750	3.1686
Australia	0.3857	0.8195	1713	0.5002	3.3202	0.7358	1487	3.3055	3.2989
Denmark	0.5040	0.8941	1288	0.3462	3.1585	0.7713	1169	3.1806	3.1742
Norway	0.5228	0.9437	1342	0.3068	3.1529	0.8990	1021	3.0553	3.0492
United Kingdom	0.6291	0.6646	1078	0.3787	3.2101	0.6030	802	3.1238	3.1175
Colombia	0.7200	1.8260	738	−0.1188	2.6066	2.2570	845	2.5733	2.5681
Brazil	0.9415	1.4590	448	−0.1379	2.4872	0.9720	364	2.5734	2.5682
Mexico	0.9017	1.7580	471	−0.2001	2.4280	1.2458	546	2.6417	2.6364
Argentina	1.0863	2.2300	464	−0.3845	2.3182	1.3901	523	2.5755	2.5703

Generalized Errors-in-Equation Model

When describing Equation (9.4), we referred to it as a model with "errors in variables and errors in equation." The term *errors in variables* is used to describe the measurement errors v_i and w_i, while the term *errors in equation* refers to the stochastic disturbance ε_i. Thus a regression model in which the variables are measured without errors may be called a model with "errors in equation." Let us now consider a model in which measurement errors occur only with respect to the dependent variable. That is, let

$$w_i = 0 \quad \text{for all } i.$$

Then, a substitution of

$$Y_i = Y_i^* - v_i$$

into the regression equation

$$Y_i = \alpha + \beta X_i + \varepsilon_i$$

gives

(9.9) $$Y_i^* = \alpha + \beta X_i + \eta_i,$$

where $$\eta_i = \varepsilon_i + v_i.$$

Since ε_i and v_i are assumed to be normal and independent of each other, we have

$$\eta_i \sim N(0, \sigma_\eta^2),$$

where $$\sigma_\eta^2 = \sigma^2 + \sigma_v^2.$$

Equation (9.9) can be described as a *generalized errors-in-equation model.* Since η_i can be viewed as a random variable that behaves precisely like ε_i, equation (9.9) is formally equivalent to the regression equation (7.1) of the classical normal linear regression model. This means that the least squares estimators of the regression coefficients have the desirable properties. However, there are two differences between η_i and ε_i that are worth noting:

A. The variance of ε_i reflects the behavioral characteristics of the factors that influence the dependent variable in addition to the systematic influence of the explanatory variable. As a rule, this variance cannot be altered by the observer. On the other hand, the variance of the measurement error v_i—and therefore the variance of η_i—can be reduced by improving the methods of measurement.

B. Since, in fact, the methods of measuring economic variables have been improving over the last decades, the variance of v_i—and therefore the variance of η_i—may have been diminishing over time. Thus if v_i is not negligible, η_i may be heteroskedastic when the observations are in the form of time series.

These differences, however, do not create any estimating problems serious enough to warrant extended discussion.

Suppose now that, instead of the dependent variable, the explanatory variable is measured with errors. That is, we consider a situation where

$$v_i = 0 \quad \text{for all } i.$$

Then, we have

$$X_i = X_i^* - w_i,$$

which can be substituted into the regression equation,

$$Y_i = \alpha + \beta X_i + \varepsilon_i$$

to get

$$Y_i = \alpha + \beta X_i^* + \zeta_i, \tag{9.10}$$

where

$$\zeta_i = \varepsilon_i - \beta w_i.$$

Here X_i^* and ζ_i are contemporaneously correlated. In fact,

$$\text{Cov}(X_i^*, \zeta_i) = E[X_i^* - E(X_i^*)][\zeta_i - E(\zeta_i)] = E(w_i\zeta_i) = -\beta\sigma_w^2 \neq 0,$$

so that the least squares estimators of α and β in (9.10) are *inconsistent*. Consistent estimators can be obtained by using the method of instrumental variables described earlier.

Errors-in-Variables Model

Finally, we come to a model that is used quite frequently in the natural sciences but very rarely in modern econometrics. We consider it here partly for the sake of completeness and partly because it has an important application in connection with the so-called "permanent income hypothesis." The model is generally known as a model with *errors in variables*. The presumption underlying this model is that the relationship between the dependent and the explanatory variable is a deterministic one, and that the only reason why sample points do not all lie on a straight line is that we do not have exact measurements on X and Y. In our terminology, the errors-in-variables model is characterized by the assumption that

$$\varepsilon_i = 0 \quad \text{for all } i.$$

This model is not generally used in econometrics because it is commonly believed that a stochastic disturbance is an essential part of economic relations. One exception is the formulation of the "permanent income" hypothesis by Friedman[4] who postulated a deterministic relation between "permanent consumption" and "permanent income." In this case our measurements of actual consumption and actual income are erroneous, since they contain "transient components," which can be viewed as errors of measurement. There are also

[4] Milton Friedman, *A Theory of Consumption Function* (Princeton: Princeton University Press, 1957).

other cases in which the errors of measurement may reasonably be expected to be substantial, while the regression disturbance may be considered relatively unimportant. International statistics, for example, are often highly inaccurate. In such cases we may prefer to use the errors-in-variables model, on the assumption that the inaccuracies due to the neglect of the regression disturbance are not serious.

Suppose, then, that the relationship between X and Y is

$$Y_i = \alpha + \beta X_i, \tag{9.11}$$

where X_i may be stochastic or nonstochastic. If X_i is stochastic, we assume it to be independent of v_i and w_i. Since we do not measure X_i and Y_i but only X_i^* and Y_i^*, we have to substitute

$$Y_i = Y_i^* - v_i \qquad \text{and} \qquad X_i = X_i^* - w_i,$$

to get

$$Y_i^* = \alpha + \beta X_i^* + \xi_i, \tag{9.12}$$

where

$$\xi_i = v_i - \beta w_i.$$

Since X_i^* and ξ_i are obviously correlated, least squares estimators of α and β are *inconsistent*. To obtain consistent estimators, we can use the method of instrumental variables providing we can find an instrument that would satisfy the conditions of being uncorrelated with ξ_i while being correlated with X_i^*.

Method of Group Averages

An alternative way of estimating (9.12) is by the *method of group averages*, which, in its simplest form, requires ordering the observed pairs (X_i^*, Y_i^*) by the magnitude of the X_i^*'s so that

$$X_1^* \leq X_2^* \leq \cdots \leq X_n^*.$$

The pairs are then divided into three groups of approximately equal size. The group-averages estimators of the regression coefficients are

$$\beta^{\dagger\dagger} = \frac{\bar{Y}_3^* - \bar{Y}_1^*}{\bar{X}_3^* - \bar{X}_1^*}, \tag{9.13a}$$

$$\alpha^{\dagger\dagger} = \bar{Y}^* - \beta^{\dagger\dagger}\bar{X}^*, \tag{9.13b}$$

where $\bar{Y}_1^*$ and $\bar{Y}_3^*$ are the calculated means of Y of the first and the third group, respectively, and $\bar{X}_1^*$ and $\bar{X}_3^*$ are the corresponding means of X. The group-averages estimators are consistent providing the grouping is such that, had we grouped the data by the unobserved X's rather than by the observed X^*'s, no pairs in the first group would have to be re-allocated to the third group and vice versa. It is interesting to note that the method of group averages can be viewed as a special case of the method of instrumental variables. If the three groups of observations are of equal size, and if the values of the instrumental variable Z_i are such that

$$\begin{aligned} Z_i &= -1 \quad \text{if } i \text{ belongs to the 1st group,} \\ &= 0 \quad \text{if } i \text{ belongs to the 2nd group,} \\ &= 1 \quad \text{if } i \text{ belongs to the 3rd group,} \end{aligned}$$

we find that (9.5a) and (9.5b) are equivalent to (9.13a) and (9.13b), respectively. We can then utilize formulas (9.8a) and (9.8b) to estimate the variances of $\alpha^{\dagger\dagger}$ and $\beta^{\dagger\dagger}$.

EXAMPLE Let us calculate the group-averages estimates for the relationship between $\log(V/PL)$ and $\log(W/P)$ discussed in the previous example. From the data in Table 9–1, we see that there are eleven observations; we shall use four observations for the first and third groups, leaving three observations unused. The calculations are

$$\bar{X}_1^* = \frac{1}{4}(2.3182 + 2.4280 + 2.4872 + 2.6066) = 2.4600,$$

$$\bar{X}_3^* = \frac{1}{4}(3.2367 + 3.2865 + 3.3202 + 3.5459) = 3.3473,$$

$$\bar{Y}_1^* = \frac{1}{4}(-0.3845 - 0.2001 - 0.1379 - 0.1188) = -0.2103,$$

$$\bar{Y}_3^* = \frac{1}{4}(0.4330 + 0.4575 + 0.5002 + 0.7680) = 0.5397.$$

Then,

$$\beta^{\dagger\dagger} = \frac{0.5397 - (-0.2103)}{3.3473 - 2.4600} = 0.8453$$

$$\alpha^{\dagger\dagger} = \frac{1}{11}(2.3491 - 0.8453 \times 32.7508) = -2.3031.$$

The estimated relationship would then be

$$Y_i^* = -2.3031 + 0.8453X_i^* + \xi_i,$$

which is numerically quite similar to the result obtained previously.

Weighted Regression

Another way to obtain consistent estimators of the coefficients of the errors-in-variables model is available if we can make a prior assumption about the ratio of the error variances. In particular, let

$$\frac{\sigma_w^2}{\sigma_v^2} = \lambda,$$

where λ is known. For example, at times we may reasonably expect that the errors in measuring X have about the same dispersion as the errors in measuring

Y. In such a case, we may be willing to assume that $\lambda = 1$. Let us now develop consistent estimators of α and β for a given λ. These estimators are frequently called *weighted regression estimators*. We may start by considering the least squares estimator of β, which is

$$\hat{\beta} = \frac{\sum y_i^{*\prime} x_i^{*\prime}}{\sum x_i^{*\prime 2}}.$$

Since

$$y_i^{*\prime} = y_i' + v_i' = \beta x_i' + v_i',$$

and

$$x_i^{*\prime} = x_i' + w_i',$$

we can write $\hat{\beta}$ as

$$\hat{\beta} = \frac{\sum (\beta x_i' + v_i')(x_i' + w_i')}{\sum (x_i' + w_i')^2} = \frac{\beta \sum x_i'^2 + \sum x_i' v_i' + \beta \sum x_i' w_i' + \sum v_i' w_i'}{\sum x_i'^2 + 2 \sum x_i' w_i' + \sum w_i'^2}.$$

The probability limit of $\hat{\beta}$ is

$$\text{(9.14)} \qquad \text{plim}\, \hat{\beta} = \frac{\beta \sigma_x^2}{\sigma_x^2 + \sigma_w^2},$$

where the term σ_x^2 is used for the variance of X if X is stochastic, or for $\lim (\sum x_i'^2)/n$ if X is nonstochastic. In deriving (9.14) we have made use of the assumptions of independence between v_i, w_i, and X_i. Formula (9.14) indicates that the cause of inconsistency of $\hat{\beta}$ is the presence of the term σ_w^2 in the denominator. If that term were not there, σ_x^2 in the numerator would cancel against the σ_x^2 in the denominator and the estimator would be consistent. This suggests that a consistent estimator of β would be given by

$$\text{(9.15)} \qquad \tilde{\beta} = \frac{(\sum y_i^{*\prime} x_i^{*\prime})/n}{(\sum x_i^{*\prime 2})/n - \tilde{\sigma}_w^2},$$

where $\tilde{\sigma}_w^2$ is a consistent estimator of σ_w^2. The problem thus reduces to finding an expression for a consistent estimator of σ_w^2 in terms of X^*, Y^*, and $\tilde{\beta}$. By substituting this expression into (9.15), we could solve for $\tilde{\beta}$, which then would be consistent.

If λ is known, we have

$$\sigma_w^2 = \lambda \sigma_v^2,$$

which can be written as

$$\begin{aligned}
\text{plim}\, \frac{1}{n} \sum w_i'^2 &= \lambda\, \text{plim}\, \frac{1}{n} \sum v_i'^2 = \lambda\, \text{plim}\, \frac{1}{n} \sum (y_i^{*\prime} - y_i')^2 \\
&= \lambda\, \text{plim}\, \frac{1}{n} \sum (y_i^{*\prime} - \beta x_i')^2 \\
&= \lambda \left[\text{plim}\, \frac{1}{n} \sum y_i^{*\prime 2} - 2\beta\, \text{plim}\, \frac{1}{n} \sum y_i^{*\prime} x_i' + \beta^2\, \text{plim}\, \frac{1}{n} \sum x_i'^2 \right]
\end{aligned}$$

Now, we need to get rid of x_i', which is not observable. Substituting $x_i' = x_i^{*\prime} - w_i'$, we get

$$\text{plim}\,\frac{1}{n}\sum y_i^{*\prime}x_i' = \text{plim}\,\frac{1}{n}\sum y_i^{*\prime}(x_i^{*\prime} - w_i') = \text{plim}\,\frac{1}{n}\sum y_i^{*\prime}x_i^{*\prime}$$

and

$$\text{plim}\,\frac{1}{n}\sum x_i'^2 = \text{plim}\,\frac{1}{n}\sum (x_i^{*\prime} - w_i')^2 = \text{plim}\,\frac{1}{n}\sum x_i^{*\prime 2} - \text{plim}\sum\frac{1}{n}w_i'^2.$$

At this stage, we shall introduce the following abbreviated notation:

$$\frac{1}{n}\sum y_i^{*\prime 2} = m_{yy}^*,$$

$$\frac{1}{n}\sum x_i^{*\prime 2} = m_{xx}^*,$$

$$\frac{1}{n}\sum x_i^{*\prime}y_i^{*\prime} = m_{xy}^*.$$

Using this notation, and replacing the probability limits by their sample counterparts, we get

$$\tilde{\sigma}_w^2 = \lambda[m_{yy}^* - 2\tilde{\beta}m_{xy}^* + \tilde{\beta}^2(m_{xx}^* - \tilde{\sigma}_w^2)].$$

Solving this expression for $\tilde{\sigma}_w^2$, we obtain

$$\tilde{\sigma}_w^2 = \frac{\lambda}{1 + \lambda\tilde{\beta}^2}[m_{yy}^* - 2\tilde{\beta}m_{xy}^* + \tilde{\beta}^2 m_{xx}^*]. \tag{9.16}$$

This is the desired expression for $\tilde{\sigma}_w^2$ in terms of the observable quantities, m_{yy}^*, m_{xy}^*, and m_{xx}^* and in terms of $\tilde{\beta}$. A substitution for $\tilde{\sigma}_w^2$ from (9.16) into (9.15) gives

$$\tilde{\beta} = \frac{m_{xy}^*}{m_{xx}^* - [\lambda/(1 + \lambda\tilde{\beta}^2)](m_{yy}^* - 2\tilde{\beta}m_{xy}^* + \tilde{\beta}^2 m_{xx}^*)},$$

which can be expressed as a quadratic equation,

$$\tilde{\beta}^2\lambda m_{xy}^* + \tilde{\beta}(m_{xx}^* - \lambda m_{yy}^*) - m_{xy}^* = 0. \tag{9.17}$$

The solution leads to two values for $\tilde{\beta}$, one positive and one negative. The choice between the two is determined by the value of

$$\sum (y_i^{*\prime} - \tilde{\beta}x_i^{*\prime})^2 = m_{yy}^* - 2\tilde{\beta}m_{xy}^* + \tilde{\beta}^2 m_{xx}^*,$$

that is, by the value of the sum of squared deviations from the fitted regression line. Since we want this to be small, we choose that value of $\tilde{\beta}$ which has the same sign as m_{xy}^*. The corresponding consistent estimator of α is

$$\tilde{\alpha} = \bar{Y}^* - \tilde{\beta}\bar{X}^*. \tag{9.18}$$

It can be shown that $\tilde{\alpha}$ and $\tilde{\beta}$ represent the maximum likelihood estimators of the respective parameters and, therefore, are asymptotically efficient.[5]

We can gain some insight into the principle of weighted regression estimation—and explain the basis for the name—by comparing it with the least squares estimation. Suppose the "explanatory" variable X is measured without error. Then the errors-in-variables model reduces to

$$Y_i^* = \alpha + \beta X_i + v_i,$$

and ordinary least squares estimators are consistent, besides having all other desirable properties. Note that here the least squares estimation is based on the idea of minimizing the sum of squared deviations of the observed Y^*'s from the regression line. This procedure is called "minimizing in the direction of Y"; it amounts to minimizing the sum of squares of the *vertical* distances of the observed points from the regression line. A case where X is observed without errors is one where σ_w^2 equal zero since if there are no errors of measurement, their variance is clearly zero. This implies that $\lambda = 0$. Substituting zero for λ into (9.17) leads to

$$\tilde{\beta} = \frac{m_{xy}^*}{m_{xx}^*},$$

which is the formula for the least squares estimator. At the other extreme, suppose that there are no errors in measuring Y. In this case, the errors-in-variables model reduces to

$$Y_i = \alpha + \beta(X_i^* - w_i)$$

or

$$X_i^* = -\frac{\alpha}{\beta} + \frac{1}{\beta}Y_i + w_i.$$

Here we can regard X_i^* as the "dependent" variable, and Y_i as the "explanatory" variable. The least squares estimator of $(1/\beta)$, which is consistent, is

$$\widehat{\left(\frac{1}{\beta}\right)} = \frac{m_{xy}^*}{m_{yy}^*}.$$

This leads to a consistent estimator of β, given as

$$\hat{\hat{\beta}} = \frac{m_{yy}^*}{m_{xy}^*}.$$

In obtaining this estimator we are, in fact, minimizing the sum of the squares of deviations of the observed X^*'s from the regression line, i.e., we are "minimizing in the direction of X." This amounts to minimizing the sum of squares of the *horizontal* distances of the observed points from the regression line. Note that

[5] See Johnston, *op. cit.*, pp. 152–155. A rough (and highly complicated) formula for the asymptotic variances of these estimators is presented in A. Madansky, "The Fitting of Straight Lines When Both Variables Are Subject to Error," *Journal of the American Statistical Association*, Vol. 54, March 1959, pp. 179–180.

observing Y without errors means that $\sigma_v^2 = 0$ and therefore that $\lambda \to \infty$. Dividing (9.17) by λ gives

$$\tilde{\beta}^2 m_{xy}^* + \tilde{\beta}\left(\frac{m_{xx}^*}{\lambda} - m_{yy}^*\right) - \frac{m_{xy}^*}{\lambda} = 0.$$

As $\lambda \to \infty$, this reduces to

$$\tilde{\beta}^2 m_{xy}^* - \tilde{\beta} m_{yy}^* = 0$$

or

$$\tilde{\beta} = \frac{m_{yy}^*}{m_{xy}^*},$$

which is exactly the same result as for $\hat{\hat{\beta}}$. This shows how the size of λ determines the direction of the minimization. When the value of λ lies between 0 and ∞, it serves as a "weighting" factor in placing the direction of the minimization between X and Y.

Example Continuing with the example on the relationship between log (V/PL) and log (W/P), let us calculate the weighted regression estimates of α and β on the assumption that $\lambda = 1$. The relevant calculations are

$$m_{xx}^* = 20.1834/11^2,$$

$$m_{yy}^* = 14.4456/11^2,$$

$$m_{xy}^* = 16.9577/11^2,$$

and therefore

$$m_{xx}^* - m_{yy}^* = 5.7378/11^2.$$

Substitution into (9.17) gives

$$\tilde{\beta} = \frac{-5.7378 + \sqrt{5.7378^2 + 4 \times 16.9577^2}}{2 \times 16.9577} = 0.8452.$$

Similarly, using (9.18), we obtain

$$\tilde{\alpha} = -2.3023.$$

Conclusion

This completes our discussion on errors of measurement. As pointed out at the outset, measurement errors are likely to be present in most, if not all, economic observations. We have found that it is very difficult to deal with the estimation problem where there are stochastic disturbances as well as errors of measurement—a situation described by the model with "errors in variables and errors in equation." The common practice in modern econometrics has been to neglect the errors of measurement and to concentrate on the "errors-in-equation model." The motivation has been not so much the belief that our data are perfect, but the belief that errors of measurement are unimportant compared with the role of the stochastic disturbances in economic relations. We shall carry on in the same spirit, realizing that the area of errors of measurement represents a challenge in the econometric work of the future.

9–2 Estimation from Grouped Data

Survey data are frequently presented in the form of a table summarizing the values for individual observations. Such tabular information has often been used for estimating the coefficients of a regression equation. One reason for this is the fact that tabular results are likely to be readily accessible, whereas the retrieval of the individual observations may be time-consuming and costly. Another reason for using condensed summaries of the sample observations is often the desire to avoid large-scale computations that may otherwise be necessary. In this section we shall inquire how the use of condensed sample information affects the properties of the estimators of the regression coefficients in a simple regression model. We shall consider two types of condensed tabular information, one representing the case where the observations are grouped according to the value of one variable, and the other where the observations are grouped according to the values of both variables. The respective tables are usually distinguished as *one-way* or *two-way* classification tables. Obviously, a one-way classification table represents a greater amount of condensation of the sample information than a two-way classification table. Another way of stating this is to say that a one-way classification table involves a greater loss of information than a two-way classification table.

One-Way Grouping

Consider a simple linear regression model as described by (7.1) through (7.6). As will be recalled, this means that the explanatory variable X is nonstochastic and that the regression disturbance ε has zero mean and is normal, homoskedastic, and nonautoregressive. (The conclusions of this section, however, also apply to the case where X is stochastic but independent of ε.) Suppose the n sample observations are divided into G groups. Let n_1 be the number of observations in the first group, n_2 the number of observations in the second group, and so on. Since there are altogether n observations, we must have

$$\sum_{g=1}^{G} n_g = n.$$

Let us denote the ith observation in the gth group by the double subscript ig, so that the regression equation can be written as

$$(9.19) \qquad Y_{ig} = \alpha + \beta X_{ig} + \varepsilon_{ig} \qquad (i = 1, 2, \ldots, n_g;\ g = 1, 2, \ldots, G).$$

Suppose now that instead of being given a complete enumeration of all observations in each group, we are only given their number and the mean values (or totals) of X and Y, presented as follows:

Group	Number of Observations	Mean of X	Mean of Y
1	n_1	$\bar{X}_1$	$\bar{Y}_1$
2	n_2	$\bar{X}_2$	$\bar{Y}_2$
⋮	⋮	⋮	⋮
G	n_g	$\bar{X}_G$	$\bar{Y}_G$

where

$$\bar{X}_g = \frac{1}{n_g}\sum_{i=1}^{n_g} X_{ig} \quad \text{and} \quad \bar{Y}_g = \frac{1}{n_g}\sum_{i=1}^{n_g} Y_{ig} \quad (g = 1, 2, \ldots, G).$$

The problem now is to derive estimation formulas for the regression coefficients using the group means, and to determine how the properties of the resulting estimators compare with the properties of the ordinary least squares estimators based on individual observations. Let us take the regression equation (9.19) and "condense" it by averaging over all observations within each group. In this way we obtain

$$\bar{Y}_g = \alpha + \beta\bar{X}_g + \bar{\varepsilon}_g \qquad (g = 1, 2, \ldots, G). \tag{9.20}$$

That is, we are replacing the original n observations with a smaller number of G groups means. Now, if X_{ig} is nonstochastic, $\bar{X}_g$ will also be nonstochastic so that we have to worry only about $\bar{\varepsilon}_g$. First, we note that

$$E(\bar{\varepsilon}_g) = E\frac{1}{n_g}(\varepsilon_{1g} + \varepsilon_{2g} + \cdots + \varepsilon_{n_g g}) = 0,$$

which means that ordinary least squares estimators of α and β based on group means are unbiased. Next, for $g \neq h$,

$$E(\bar{\varepsilon}_g\bar{\varepsilon}_h) = E\left[\frac{1}{n_g}(\varepsilon_{1g} + \varepsilon_{2g} + \cdots + \varepsilon_{n_g g})\right]\left[\frac{1}{n_h}(\varepsilon_{1h} + \varepsilon_{2h} + \cdots + \varepsilon_{n_h h})\right] = 0,$$

which means that $\bar{\varepsilon}_g$ is nonautoregressive. Finally,

$$\text{Var}(\bar{\varepsilon}_g) = \frac{1}{n_g^2}(\sigma^2 + \sigma^2 + \cdots + \sigma^2) = \frac{n_g\sigma^2}{n_g^2} = \frac{\sigma^2}{n_g},$$

which means that, unless the number of observations is the same in every group, the disturbance in (9.20) is *heteroskedastic*.

The heteroskedastic nature of $\bar{\varepsilon}_g$ implies that ordinary least squares estimators of α and β using group means as "observations" are not efficient. To make efficient use of the group means, we have to use the estimation formulas designed for heteroskedastic regressions. These formulas were developed earlier and are given by (8.1) through (8.4). With respect to $\bar{\varepsilon}_g$, we are in a fortunate position of knowing exactly how its variance changes from "observation" to "observation," i.e., from group to group, because n_g is known. To adapt formulas (8.1) through (8.4) to the use of group means, we replace the subscript i by g, put "bars" over the X's and the Y's, and replace w by (n_g/σ^2). The resulting estimators of α and β, say, $\tilde{\alpha}$ and $\tilde{\beta}$, are

$$(9.21)\quad \tilde{\beta} = \frac{[(\sum n_g)(\sum n_g\bar{X}_g\bar{Y}_g) - (\sum n_g\bar{X}_g)(\sum n_g\bar{Y}_g)]/\sigma^4}{[(\sum n_g)(\sum n_g\bar{X}_g^2) - (\sum n_g\bar{X}_g)^2]/\sigma^4} = \frac{\sum n_g\bar{X}_g\bar{Y}_g - n\bar{X}\bar{Y}}{\sum n_g\bar{X}_g^2 - n\bar{X}^2}$$

$$= \frac{\sum n_g(\bar{X}_g - \bar{X})(\bar{Y}_g - \bar{Y})}{\sum n_g(\bar{X}_g - \bar{X})^2}$$

and

$$(9.22)\quad \tilde{\alpha} = \frac{(\sum n_g\bar{Y}_g)/\sigma^2}{(\sum n_g)/\sigma^2} - \tilde{\beta}\frac{(\sum n_g\bar{X}_g)/\sigma^2}{(\sum n_g)/\sigma^2} = \bar{Y} - \tilde{\beta}\bar{X},$$

where $\bar{X}$ is the overall sample mean of X and $\bar{Y}$ the overall sample mean of Y. In simplifying the expressions for $\tilde{\alpha}$ and $\tilde{\beta}$ we have made use of the following equalities:

$$\sum_g n_g = n_1 + n_2 + \cdots + n_G = n,$$

$$\sum_g n_g\bar{X}_g = n_1\bar{X}_1 + n_2\bar{X}_2 + \cdots + n_G\bar{X}_G = \sum_i X_{i1} + \sum_i X_{i2} + \cdots + \sum_i X_{iG}$$

$$= \sum_i\sum_g X_{ig} = n\bar{X},$$

$$\sum_g n_g\bar{Y}_g = n_1\bar{Y}_1 + n_2\bar{Y}_2 + \cdots + n_G\bar{Y}_G = n\bar{Y}.$$

The variances of $\tilde{\alpha}$ and $\tilde{\beta}$ are

$$(9.23)\quad \mathrm{Var}(\tilde{\beta}) = \frac{(\sum n_g)/\sigma^2}{[(\sum n_g)(\sum n_g\bar{X}_g^2) - (\sum n_g\bar{X}_g)^2]/\sigma^4}$$

$$= \frac{\sigma^2}{\sum n_g(\bar{X}_g - \bar{X})^2}$$

and

$$(9.24)\quad \mathrm{Var}(\tilde{\alpha}) = \frac{(\sum n_g\bar{X}_g^2)/\sigma^2}{[(\sum n_g)(\sum n_g\bar{X}_g^2) - (\sum n_g\bar{X}_g)^2]/\sigma^4}$$

$$= \sigma^2\left[\frac{1}{n} + \frac{\bar{X}^2}{\sum n_g(\bar{X}_g - \bar{X})^2}\right].$$

A question of particular interest to us is how the variances of $\tilde{\alpha}$ and $\tilde{\beta}$ compare with the variances of the ordinary least squares estimators based on ungrouped observations. We know that by grouping the observations and estimating the regression coefficients from group means rather than from the individual observations, we are losing some information contained in the sample, namely, the information about the variation of the observations *within* each group. Therefore, we would expect that we would lose some efficiency in going from estimation based on all individual observations to estimation based on group means. We shall see whether, and to what extent, this is true by evaluating the ratio of $\mathrm{Var}(\tilde{\beta})$ to $\mathrm{Var}(\hat{\beta})$, where $\hat{\beta}$ denotes the least squares estimator of β based on individual observations. Now, from (7.23) the variance of $\hat{\beta}$ is

$$\mathrm{Var}(\hat{\beta}) = \frac{\sigma^2}{\sum_i \sum_g (X_{ig} - \bar{X})^2}.$$

Note that the denominator on the right-hand side of this expression can be written as

$$\begin{aligned}\sum_i \sum_g (X_{ig} - \bar{X})^2 &= \sum_i \sum_g [(X_{ig} - \bar{X}_g) + (\bar{X}_g - \bar{X})]^2 \\ &= \sum_i \sum_g (X_{ig} - \bar{X}_g)^2 + \sum_i \sum_g (\bar{X}_g - \bar{X})^2 \\ &\quad + 2 \sum_i \sum_g (X_{ig} - \bar{X}_g)(\bar{X}_g - \bar{X}) \\ &= \sum_i \sum_g (X_{ig} - \bar{X}_g)^2 + \sum_g n_g(\bar{X}_g - \bar{X})^2.\end{aligned}$$

The ratio of the two variances then is

$$(9.25) \qquad \frac{\mathrm{Var}(\tilde{\beta})}{\mathrm{Var}(\hat{\beta})} = \frac{\sigma^2 / \sum_g n_g(\bar{X}_g - \bar{X})^2}{\sigma^2 / [\sum_i \sum_g (X_{ig} - \bar{X}_g)^2 + \sum_g n_g(\bar{X}_g - \bar{X})^2]} = 1 + \frac{\sum_i \sum_g (X_{ig} - \bar{X}_g)^2}{\sum_g n_g(\bar{X}_g - \bar{X})^2}.$$

This ratio is always greater than, or at best equal to, unity. The last term on the right-hand side measures the loss of efficiency resulting from the use of grouped data instead of individual observations. Note that the size of the numerator reflects the variation of the values of X *within* each group around the group mean, while the size of the denominator reflects the variation of the group means of X around the overall sample mean. Thus we will lose no efficiency by grouping if there is no variation of the values of X within each group, and the loss of efficiency will be small if this variation is small compared with the variation of the group means of X around the overall mean. In other words, there will always be some loss of efficiency by going from individual observations to groups unless the X's within each group are all equal. *This conclusion holds whether the groups contain the same number of observations or not.* Having groups of equal size would make $\bar{\varepsilon}_g$ homoskedastic but would not prevent a loss of efficiency as a result of grouping.

When estimating the regression coefficients from grouped data, we can use formulas (9.21) and (9.22) since they can be readily evaluated, but the expressions for the variances of these estimators involve an unknown parameter σ^2. To find an unbiased estimator of σ^2, we first determine the mathematical expectation of the weighted sum of squared residuals, using as weights the number of observations in each group. That is,

$$E\sum_{g=1}^{G} n_g(\bar{Y}_g - \tilde{\alpha} - \tilde{\beta}\bar{X}_g)^2 = E\sum_g n_g[(\bar{Y}_g - \bar{Y}) - \tilde{\beta}(\bar{X}_g - \bar{X})]^2$$

$$= E\sum_g n_g[-(\tilde{\beta} - \beta)(\bar{X}_g - \bar{X}) + (\bar{\varepsilon}_g - \bar{\varepsilon})]^2$$

$$= E(\tilde{\beta} - \beta)^2\sum_g n_g(\bar{X}_g - \bar{X})^2 + E\sum_g n_g(\bar{\varepsilon}_g - \bar{\varepsilon})^2$$

$$- 2E(\tilde{\beta} - \beta)\sum_g n_g(\bar{X}_g - \bar{X})(\bar{\varepsilon}_g - \bar{\varepsilon}).$$

Now,

$$E(\tilde{\beta} - \beta)^2\sum_g n_g(\bar{X}_g - \bar{X})^2 = \left[\frac{\sigma^2}{\sum_g n_g(\bar{X}_g - \bar{X})^2}\right]\sum_g n_g(\bar{X}_g - \bar{X})^2 = \sigma^2,$$

$$E\sum_g n_g(\bar{\varepsilon}_g - \bar{\varepsilon})^2 = E\sum_g n_g\bar{\varepsilon}_g^2 + E\bar{\varepsilon}^2\sum_g n_g - 2E\bar{\varepsilon}\sum_g n_g\bar{\varepsilon}_g$$

$$= \sum_g n_g\left(\frac{\sigma^2}{n_g}\right) + \left(\frac{\sigma^2}{n}\right)\sum_g n_g - 2\left(\frac{\sigma^2}{n}\right)\sum_g n_g$$

$$= G\sigma^2 + \sigma^2 - 2\sigma^2 = (G - 1)\sigma^2,$$

and

$$-2E(\tilde{\beta} - \beta)\sum_g n_g(\bar{X}_g - \bar{X})(\bar{\varepsilon}_g - \bar{\varepsilon}) = -2E(\tilde{\beta} - \beta)^2\sum_g n_g(\bar{X}_g - \bar{X})^2 = -2\sigma^2.$$

Therefore,

$$E\sum_g n_g(\bar{Y}_g - \tilde{\alpha} - \tilde{\beta}\bar{X}_g)^2 = \sigma^2 + (G - 1)\sigma^2 - 2\sigma^2 = (G - 2)\sigma^2.$$

Thus an unbiased estimator of σ^2, say, $\tilde{s}^2$, is

(9.26) $$\tilde{s}^2 = \frac{1}{G - 2}\sum_g n_g(\bar{Y}_g - \tilde{\alpha} - \tilde{\beta}\bar{X}_g)^2.$$

For the purpose of calculation, this expression may be simplified as follows:

(9.26a) $$\tilde{s}^2 = \frac{1}{G - 2}\sum_g n_g[\bar{Y}_g - (\bar{Y} - \tilde{\beta}\bar{X}) - \tilde{\beta}\bar{X}_g]^2$$

$$= \frac{1}{G - 2}\left[\sum_g n_g(\bar{Y}_g - \bar{Y})^2 - \tilde{\beta}^2\sum_g n_g(\bar{X}_g - \bar{X})^2\right].$$

By using $\tilde{s}^2$ as the estimator of σ^2 in (9.23) and (9.24), we obtain estimators of the variances of $\tilde{\alpha}$ and $\tilde{\beta}$. These are

$$\text{(9.27)} \qquad s_{\tilde{\beta}}^2 = \frac{\tilde{s}^2}{\sum n_g(\bar{X}_g - \bar{X})^2},$$

$$\text{(9.28)} \qquad s_{\tilde{\alpha}}^2 = \tilde{s}^2\left[\frac{1}{n} + \frac{\bar{X}^2}{\sum n_g(\bar{X}_g - \bar{X})^2}\right].$$

These estimators are unbiased, consistent, and asymptotically efficient among the class of all estimators that are based on the same information.

A final point of interest in connection with sample data grouped in the form of a one-way classification table concerns the behavior of the coefficient of determination (R^2) as we go from individual observations to group means. When the estimation is done on the basis of individual observations, the value of R^2 is calculated as

$$\text{(9.29)} \qquad R^2 = \frac{\hat{\beta}^2 \sum_i \sum_g (X_{ig} - \bar{X})^2}{\sum_i \sum_g (Y_{ig} - \bar{Y})^2},$$

where $\hat{\beta}$ is an ordinary least squares estimator of β based on individual observations. On the other hand, when we estimate the regression coefficients by using group means, the value of R^2 is calculated as

$$\text{(9.30)} \qquad R^2 = 1 - \frac{\sum_g (\bar{Y}_g - \tilde{\alpha} - \tilde{\beta}\bar{X}_g)^2}{\sum_g (\bar{Y}_g - \bar{\bar{Y}})^2},$$

where

$$\begin{aligned}\sum_g (\bar{Y}_g - \tilde{\alpha} - \tilde{\beta}\bar{X}_g)^2 &= \sum_g [\bar{Y}_g - (\bar{Y} - \tilde{\beta}\bar{X}) - \tilde{\beta}\bar{X}_g]^2 \\ &= \sum_g (\bar{Y}_g - \bar{Y})^2 - 2\tilde{\beta}\sum_g (\bar{Y}_g - \bar{Y})(\bar{X}_g - \bar{X}) \\ &\quad + \tilde{\beta}^2 \sum_g (\bar{X}_g - \bar{X})^2\end{aligned}$$

and

$$\sum_g (\bar{Y}_g - \bar{\bar{Y}})^2 = \sum_g \bar{Y}_g^2 - \frac{1}{G}\left(\sum_g \bar{Y}_g\right)^2.$$

It has been shown that the value of R^2 calculated by (9.30) tends to be higher than that calculated by (9.29).[6] That is, as we go from individual observations to group means, the value of R^2 tends to increase. Since the underlying sample is the same whether we use individual observations or group means, the increase in

[6] See J. S. Cramer, "Efficient Grouping, Regression and Correlation in Engel Curve Analysis," *Journal of the American Statistical Association*, Vol. 59, March 1964, pp. 233–250.

the value of R^2 is entirely due to grouping and should be interpreted as such. It simply reflects the fact that the group means tend to be less dispersed around the fitted regression line than the individual observations.

EXAMPLE A sample survey of immigrants in Australia conducted in 1959 by the Department of Demography of the Australian National University contained information on weekly income and consumption expenditure of immigrant families. The results for the 181 British immigrants included in the sample survey are given in Table 9–2.

Table 9–2

Income Class	Number of Observations (n_g)	Mean Income* ($\bar{X}_g$)	Mean Consumption Expenditure* ($\bar{Y}_g$)
Under 18	51	15.5	13.900
18 and under 20	22	19.0	15.291
20 and under 22	22	21.0	18.195
22 and under 24	23	23.0	20.104
24 and under 26	13	25.0	20.985
26 and under 28	12	27.0	22.742
28 and under 30	14	29.0	24.414
30 and under 32	9	31.0	24.089
32 and under 34	7	33.0	29.286
34 and under 36	4	35.0	27.000
36 and over	4	37.0	29.500

Data made available by Dr. J. Zubrzycki of the Australian National University.
* In Australian pounds per week.

Suppose we wish to estimate the coefficients of a linear consumption function,

$$Y = \alpha + \beta X + \varepsilon,$$

from this information. The results of the basic calculations are

$$\bar{X} = \frac{1}{181} \sum_g n_g \bar{X}_g = 22.390,$$

$$\bar{Y} = \frac{1}{181} \sum_g n_g \bar{Y}_g = 19.024,$$

$$\bar{\bar{Y}} = \frac{1}{11} \sum_g \bar{Y}_g = 22.319,$$

$$\sum_g n_g(\bar{X}_g - \bar{X})(\bar{Y}_g - \bar{Y}) = \sum_g n_g \bar{X}_g \bar{Y}_g - 181(\bar{X}\bar{Y}) = 82{,}153.2 - 77{,}096.5$$

$$= 5056.7,$$

$$\sum_g n_g(\bar{X}_g - \bar{X})^2 = \sum_g n_g \bar{X}_g^2 - 181(\bar{X}^2) = 97{,}358.8 - 90{,}735.5$$

$$= 6623.3,$$

$$\sum_g n_g(\bar{Y}_g - \bar{Y})^2 = \sum_g n_g \bar{Y}_g^2 - 181(\bar{Y}^2) = 69{,}475.8 - 65{,}506.2$$

$$= 3969.6,$$

$$\sum_g (\bar{Y}_g - \bar{\bar{Y}})^2 = 273.7,$$

$$\sum_g (\bar{Y}_g - \tilde{\alpha} - \tilde{\beta}\bar{X}_g)^2 = 12.069.$$

Therefore,

$$\tilde{\beta} = \frac{5056.7}{6623.3} = 0.763,$$

$$\tilde{\alpha} = 19.024 - 0.763 \times 22.390 = 1.940,$$

$$\tilde{s}^2 = \frac{113.7201}{9} = 12.6356,$$

$$\tilde{s}^2_{\tilde{\alpha}} = 12.6356\left[\frac{1}{181} + \frac{22.390^2}{6623.3}\right] = 1.026188,$$

$$\tilde{s}^2_{\tilde{\beta}} = \frac{12.6356}{6623.3} = 0.001908,$$

$$R^2 = 1 - \frac{12.069}{273.7} = 0.956.$$

The estimated regression equation then is

$$\bar{Y}_g = \underset{(1.012)}{1.940} + \underset{(0.044)}{0.763}\bar{X}_g + e_g, \qquad R^2 = 0.956.$$

Two-Way Grouping

Let us now consider the case where the sample information is condensed in the form of a "two-way" classification table. In this case, the observations are grouped according to the values of the explanatory and the dependent variable. Suppose the values of X are divided into G groups, and those of Y into H groups. Each of the G groups is represented by the respective group mean of X and corresponds to one row, and each of the H groups is represented by the respective group mean of Y and corresponds to one column. The body of the table consists of $G \times H$ cells, each cell showing the appropriate number of observations. A cell with no observations is called "empty." There is at least one nonempty cell in each row and in each column. The following notation will be adopted:

$\bar{X}_{g\cdot}$	group mean of X in the gth row (same for each column)
$\bar{Y}_{gh}$	group mean of Y in the gth row and hth column
J	total number of nonempty cells ($J \leq G \times H$)
n_{gh}	number of observations in the cell corresponding to gth row and hth column
$n_{g\cdot}$	number of observations in gth row
$n_{\cdot h}$	number of observations in hth column
n	total number of all observations in the sample

This implies that

$$\sum_{g=1}^{G} \sum_{h=1}^{H} n_{gh} = n,$$

$$\sum_{g=1}^{G} n_{g\cdot} = n,$$

and

$$\sum_{h=1}^{H} n_{\cdot h} = n.$$

The tabular information is presented in the following form:

	$\bar{Y}_{\cdot 1}$	$\bar{Y}_{\cdot 2}$	$\ldots$	$\bar{Y}_{\cdot H}$	
$\bar{X}_{1\cdot}$	n_{11}	n_{12}	$\ldots$	n_{1H}	$n_{1\cdot}$
$\bar{X}_{2\cdot}$	n_{21}	n_{22}	$\ldots$	n_{2H}	$n_{2\cdot}$
$\vdots$	$\vdots$	$\vdots$		$\vdots$	$\vdots$
$\bar{X}_{G\cdot}$	n_{G1}	n_{G2}	$\ldots$	n_{GH}	$n_{G\cdot}$
	$n_{\cdot 1}$	$n_{\cdot 2}$	$\ldots$	$n_{\cdot H}$	n

If we use a triple subscript igh to designate the ith observation in the gth row and hth column, the regression equation describing the relationship between X and Y can be written as

$$Y_{igh} = \alpha + \beta X_{igh} + \varepsilon_{igh} \qquad (i = 1, 2, \ldots, n_{gh}; \; g = 1, 2, \ldots, G; \; h = 1, 2, \ldots, H). \tag{9.31}$$

Since we are not given the individual observations, we have to estimate the regression coefficients α and β from the row and column averages. Let us consider this in detail. For any row (i.e., for any group mean of X), say, the gth, we can have H different values of the dependent variable, namely,

$$\begin{aligned}
\bar{Y}_{g1} &= \alpha + \beta \bar{X}_{g\cdot} + \bar{\varepsilon}_{g1} \\
\bar{Y}_{g2} &= \alpha + \beta \bar{X}_{g\cdot} + \bar{\varepsilon}_{g2} \\
&\vdots \\
\bar{Y}_{gH} &= \alpha + \beta \bar{X}_{g\cdot} + \bar{\varepsilon}_{gH} ,
\end{aligned}$$

or, in a summary form,

$$(9.32)\qquad \bar{Y}_{gh} = \alpha + \beta \bar{X}_{g\cdot} + \bar{\varepsilon}_{gh} \qquad (g = 1, 2, \ldots, G;\ h = 1, 2, \ldots, H),$$

where

$$\bar{\varepsilon}_{gh} = \frac{1}{n_{gh}} \sum_{i=1}^{n_{gh}} \varepsilon_{igh}.$$

It is easy to see that $\bar{\varepsilon}_{gh}$ satisfies all the basic assumptions *except* homoskedasticity. In fact, we have

$$\text{Var}(\bar{\varepsilon}_{gh}) = \frac{\sigma^2}{n_{gh}},$$

which means that the variance of $\bar{\varepsilon}_{gh}$ does, in general, change from cell to cell.

Because of the heteroskedasticity of $\bar{\varepsilon}_{gh}$, the appropriate estimation formulas for the regression coefficients and their variances are (8.1) through (8.4). To adapt these formulas to the problem at hand, we replace the subscript i by $g\cdot$ in the case of X and by $\cdot h$ in the case of Y, put "bars" over the X's and the Y's, carry out all the summations over both g *and* h, and replace the term w by (n_{gh}/σ^2). The resulting estimators of α and β, say, $\tilde{\tilde{\alpha}}$ and $\tilde{\tilde{\beta}}$, are

$$(9.33)\qquad \tilde{\tilde{\beta}} = \frac{[(\sum_g \sum_h n_{gh})(\sum_g \sum_h n_{gh}\bar{X}_{g\cdot}\bar{Y}_{gh}) - (\sum_g \sum_h n_{gh}\bar{X}_{g\cdot})(\sum_g \sum_h n_{gh}\bar{Y}_{gh})]/\sigma^4}{[(\sum_g \sum_h n_{gh})(\sum_g \sum_h n_{gh}\bar{X}_{g\cdot}^2) - (\sum_g \sum_h n_{gh}\bar{X}_{g\cdot})^2]/\sigma^4}$$

and

$$(9.34)\qquad \tilde{\tilde{\alpha}} = \frac{(\sum_g \sum_h n_{gh}\bar{Y}_{gh})/\sigma^2}{(\sum_g \sum_h n_{gh})/\sigma^2} - \tilde{\tilde{\beta}}\,\frac{(\sum_g \sum_h n_{gh}\bar{X}_{g\cdot})/\sigma^2}{(\sum_g \sum_h n_{gh})/\sigma^2}.$$

Now,

$$\begin{aligned}\sum_g \sum_h n_{gh}\bar{X}_{g\cdot}\bar{Y}_{gh} &= \sum_g (n_{g1}\bar{X}_{g\cdot}\bar{Y}_{g1} + n_{g2}\bar{X}_{g\cdot}\bar{Y}_{g2} + \cdots + n_{gH}\bar{X}_{g\cdot}\bar{Y}_{gH})\\ &= \sum_g n_{g\cdot}\bar{X}_{g\cdot}\left[\frac{n_{g1}\bar{Y}_{g1} + n_{g2}\bar{Y}_{g2} + \cdots + n_{gH}\bar{Y}_{gH}}{n_{g\cdot}}\right]\\ &= \sum_g n_{g\cdot}\bar{X}_{g\cdot}\bar{Y}_{g\cdot},\end{aligned}$$

where $\bar{Y}_{g\cdot}$ is the mean of Y over the gth row, i.e., the mean of the values of Y belonging to the gth group of values of X. Similarly,

$$\sum_g \sum_h n_{gh}\bar{X}_{g\cdot} = \sum_g (n_{g1}\bar{X}_{g\cdot} + n_{g2}\bar{X}_{g\cdot} + \cdots + n_{gH}\bar{X}_{g\cdot}) = \sum_g n_{g\cdot}\bar{X}_{g\cdot},$$

$$\sum_g \sum_h n_{gh}\bar{Y}_{gh} = \sum_g (n_{g1}\bar{Y}_{g1} + n_{g2}\bar{Y}_{g2} + \cdots + n_{gH}\bar{Y}_{gH}) = \sum_g n_{g\cdot}\bar{Y}_{g\cdot},$$

$$\sum_g \sum_h n_{gh}\bar{X}_{g\cdot}^2 = \sum_g (n_{g1}\bar{X}_{g\cdot}^2 + n_{g2}\bar{X}_{g\cdot}^2 + \cdots + n_{gH}\bar{X}_{g\cdot}^2) = \sum_g n_{g\cdot}\bar{X}_{g\cdot}^2,$$

and, of course,

$$\sum_g \sum_h n_{gh} = \sum_g n_{g\cdot\cdot}$$

Substituting these results into (9.33) and (9.34), we obtain

$$(9.35) \qquad \tilde{\tilde{\beta}} = \frac{(\sum n_{g\cdot})(\sum n_{g\cdot}\bar{X}_{g\cdot}\bar{Y}_{g\cdot}) - (\sum n_{g\cdot}\bar{X}_{g\cdot})(\sum n_{g\cdot}\bar{Y}_{g\cdot})}{(\sum n_{g\cdot})(\sum n_{g\cdot}\bar{X}_{g\cdot}^2) - (\sum n_{g\cdot}\bar{X}_{g\cdot})^2}$$

and

$$(9.36) \qquad \tilde{\tilde{\alpha}} = \left[\frac{\sum n_{g\cdot}\bar{Y}_{g\cdot}}{\sum n_{g\cdot}}\right] - \tilde{\tilde{\beta}}\left[\frac{\sum n_{g\cdot}\bar{X}_{g\cdot}}{\sum n_{g\cdot}}\right] = \bar{Y} - \tilde{\tilde{\beta}}\bar{X}.$$

These results are precisely the same as those given by (9.21) and (9.22). *This means that the regression coefficients estimated from a two-way classification table are exactly the same as those estimated from a one-way classification table.* In other words, the information contained in the two-way classification table that is in addition to the information provided by the one-way classification table is irrelevant to the construction of efficient estimators of the regression coefficients.

Since the formulas for $\tilde{\tilde{\alpha}}$ and $\tilde{\tilde{\beta}}$ are the same as those for $\tilde{\alpha}$ and $\tilde{\beta}$, the formulas for their variances will also be the same. These are given by (9.23) and (9.24). As pointed out earlier, these formulas contain an unknown parameter σ^2 that has to be estimated. What we have to do, then, is to check whether the *estimator* of σ^2 obtained from a one-way classification table, i.e., $\tilde{s}^2$ defined by (9.26), will also remain the same when a two-way classification table is used. First, we determine the mathematical expectation of the weighted sum of squared residuals, using as weights the number of observations in each cell. That is,

$$\begin{aligned}
E\sum_g \sum_h n_{gh}(\bar{Y}_{gh} - \tilde{\alpha} - \tilde{\beta}\bar{X}_{g\cdot})^2 &= E\sum_g \sum_h n_{gh}[(\bar{Y}_{gh} - \bar{Y}) - \tilde{\beta}(\bar{X}_{g\cdot} - \bar{X})]^2 \\
&= E\sum_g \sum_h n_{gh}[-(\tilde{\beta} - \beta)(\bar{X}_{g\cdot} - \bar{X}) \\
&\qquad + (\bar{\varepsilon}_{gh} - \bar{\varepsilon})]^2 \\
&= E(\tilde{\beta} - \beta)^2 \sum_g \sum_h n_{gh}(\bar{X}_{g\cdot} - \bar{X})^2 \\
&\qquad + E\sum_g \sum_h n_{gh}(\bar{\varepsilon}_{gh} - \bar{\varepsilon})^2 \\
&\qquad - 2E(\tilde{\beta} - \beta)\sum_g \sum_h n_{gh}(\bar{X}_{g\cdot} - \bar{X})(\bar{\varepsilon}_{gh} - \bar{\varepsilon}).
\end{aligned}$$

Now,

$$E(\tilde{\beta} - \beta)^2 \sum_g \sum_h n_{gh}(\bar{X}_{g\cdot} - \bar{X})^2 = \sigma^2,$$

$$E \sum_g \sum_h n_{gh}(\bar{\varepsilon}_{gh} - \bar{\varepsilon})^2 = E \sum_g \sum_h n_{gh}\bar{\varepsilon}_{gh}^2 + E\bar{\varepsilon}^2 \sum_g \sum_h n_{gh} - 2E\bar{\varepsilon} \sum_g \sum_h n_{gh}\bar{\varepsilon}_{gh}$$

$$= J\sigma^2 + \sigma^2 - 2\sigma^2 = (J - 1)\sigma^2,$$

and

$$-2E(\tilde{\beta} - \beta) \sum_g \sum_h n_{gh}(\bar{X}_{g\cdot} - \bar{X})(\bar{\varepsilon}_{gh} - \bar{\varepsilon}) = -2E(\tilde{\beta} - \beta)^2 \sum_g \sum_h n_{gh}(\bar{X}_{g\cdot} - \bar{X})^2 = -2\sigma^2.$$

Therefore,

$$E \sum_g \sum_h n_{gh}(\bar{Y}_{gh} - \alpha - \beta \bar{X}_{g\cdot})^2 = \sigma^2 + (J - 1)\sigma^2 - 2\sigma^2 = (J - 2)\sigma^2.$$

Thus, an unbiased estimator of σ^2, say, $\tilde{\tilde{s}}^2$, is

$$\tilde{\tilde{s}}^2 = \frac{1}{J - 2} \sum_g \sum_h n_{gh}(\bar{Y}_{gh} - \tilde{\alpha} - \tilde{\beta}\bar{X}_{g\cdot})^2, \tag{9.37}$$

which is different from $\tilde{s}^2$, the estimator of σ^2 from a one-way classification table. For the purpose of calculation, we note that

$$\sum_g \sum_h n_{gh}(\bar{Y}_{gh} - \tilde{\alpha} - \tilde{\beta}\bar{X}_{g\cdot})^2 = \sum_g \sum_h n_{gh}(\bar{Y}_{gh} - \bar{Y})^2 - \tilde{\beta}^2 \sum_g \sum_h n_{gh}(\bar{X}_{g\cdot} - \bar{X})^2$$

$$= \sum_h n_{\cdot h}(\bar{Y}_{\cdot h} - \bar{Y})^2 - \tilde{\beta}^2 \sum_g n_{g\cdot}(\bar{X}_{g\cdot} - \bar{X})^2.$$

Although we shall not give a formal proof, it is obvious that $\tilde{\tilde{s}}^2$ is a more efficient estimator of σ^2 than $\tilde{s}^2$. This is because $\tilde{\tilde{s}}^2$ uses more information about the *variation* of the dependent variable than $\tilde{s}^2$. The use of $\tilde{\tilde{s}}^2$ as an estimator of σ^2 in (9.23) and (9.24) leads to new estimators of $\text{Var}(\tilde{\alpha})$ and $\text{Var}(\tilde{\beta})$, namely,

$$\tilde{\tilde{s}}_{\tilde{\beta}}^2 = \frac{\tilde{\tilde{s}}^2}{\sum_g n_{g\cdot}(\bar{X}_{g\cdot} - \bar{X})^2} \tag{9.38}$$

and

$$\tilde{\tilde{s}}_{\tilde{\alpha}} = \tilde{\tilde{s}}^2\left[\frac{1}{n} + \frac{\bar{X}^2}{\sum_g n_{g\cdot}(\bar{X}_{g\cdot} - \bar{X})^2}\right]. \tag{9.39}$$

Again, these estimators are unbiased, consistent, and asymptotically efficient among all estimators that use the same information.

Finally, we may want to determine the value of the coefficient of determination. By analogy with (9.30), the formula for R^2 calculated from a two-way classification table is

$$R^2 = 1 - \frac{\sum_g \sum_h (\bar{Y}_{gh} - \tilde{\alpha} - \tilde{\beta}\bar{X}_{g\cdot})^2}{\sum_g \sum_h (\bar{Y}_{gh} - \bar{\bar{Y}})^2}, \tag{9.40}$$

where

$$\sum_g \sum_h (\bar{Y}_{gh} - \tilde{\alpha} - \tilde{\beta}\bar{X}_{g\cdot})^2 = \sum_g \sum_h (\bar{Y}_{gh} - \bar{Y})^2 + \tilde{\beta}^2 \sum_g \sum_h (\bar{X}_{g\cdot} - \bar{X})^2$$
$$- 2\tilde{\beta} \sum_g \sum_h (\bar{Y}_{gh} - \bar{Y})(\bar{X}_{g\cdot} - \bar{X})$$

and

$$\sum_g \sum_h (\bar{Y}_{gh} - \bar{\bar{Y}})^2 = \sum_g \sum_h \bar{Y}_{gh}^2 - \frac{1}{J} \sum_g \sum_h \bar{Y}_{gh}.$$

All these summations are carried out over the nonempty cells only. Since the two-way classification table allows for greater dispersion of the observations than the one-way classification table, we would expect the value of R^2 calculated by (9.40) to be smaller than that calculated by (9.30).

If X is a stochastic variable (independent of the regression disturbance), we may be interested in calculating the value of the coefficient of correlation between X and Y. For a two-way classification table this value, unlike that of R^2 in (9.40), is usually calculated by taking into account the frequencies in individual cells. If the coefficient of correlation between X and Y is denoted by r_{XY}, then its value can be obtained from

$$r_{XY}^2 = \frac{[\sum\sum n_{gh}(\bar{X}_{gh} - \bar{X})(\bar{Y}_{gh} - \bar{Y})]^2}{[\sum\sum n_{gh}(\bar{X}_{gh} - \bar{X})^2][\sum\sum n_{gh}(\bar{Y}_{gh} - \bar{Y})^2]}. \tag{9.41}$$

The formulas for the estimated regression coefficients and their standard errors, of course, remain unchanged.

Example The sample survey results on income and expenditure of 181 British migrants in Australia used in the previous example are also available in the form of a two-way classification table, as given in Table 9–3. Here X = income and Y = consumption expenditure. The estimates of the coefficients of a linear consumption function will be the same as those calculated from Table 9–2. However, we have to calculate new estimates of the standard errors and a new value of R^2. The basic results are (assuming that all cell means are correctly centered)

$$J = 45,$$

$$\sum_g \sum_h n_{gh}(\bar{Y}_{gh} - \bar{Y})^2 = 6150.8,$$

$$\sum_g \sum_h n_{gh}(\bar{Y}_{gh} - \tilde{\alpha} - \tilde{\beta}\bar{X}_{g\cdot})^2 = 2292.5,$$

$$\sum_g \sum_h (\bar{Y}_{gh} - \bar{\bar{Y}})^2 = 1538.0,$$

$$\sum_g \sum_h (\bar{Y}_{gh} - \tilde{\alpha} - \tilde{\beta}\bar{X}_{g\cdot})^2 = 983.0.$$

Then,
$$\tilde{\tilde{s}}^2 = \frac{1}{45-2} \times 2292.5 = 53.31,$$
$$\tilde{\tilde{s}}^2_{\tilde{\alpha}} = 4.3298,$$
$$\tilde{\tilde{s}}^2_{\tilde{\beta}} = 0.008050,$$
and
$$R^2 = 1 - \frac{983.0}{1538.0} = 0.361.$$

Table 9-3

X	Y										$n_{g\cdot}$
	13.9	19.0	21.0	23.0	25.0	27.0	29.0	31.0	33.0	35.0	
15.5	51										51
19.0	16	6									22
21.0	7	7	7	1							22
23.0	6	4	2	7	4						23
25.0	2	3	2	2	4						13
27.0	1	1	2	3	3	2					12
29.0	2		1	3	2		6				14
31.0	2		2	1			1	2	1		9
33.0				2			1	1	3		7
35.0		1		1					2		4
37.0					1	1		1		1	4
$n_{\cdot h}$	87	22	16	20	14	3	8	4	6	1	181

The estimated consumption function then is

$$\bar{Y}_{gh} = \underset{(2.079)}{1.940} + \underset{(0.090)}{0.763}\bar{X}_{g\cdot} + e_{gh}, \qquad R^2 = 0.361, \quad r^2_{XY} = 0.628.$$

Concluding Remarks

The preceding analysis provided us with an interesting result, namely, that regression coefficients may be estimated just as efficiently from a two-way classification table as from a one-way classification table. However, the variances of these estimators can be estimated more efficiently from a two-way table than from a one-way table. Note that the results of the tests of significance of the estimated regression coefficients based on a two-way table may be different from the results based on the corresponding one-way table, since congesting the data amounts to throwing away sample information. In this way the researcher may (consciously or not) falsify the picture. Another point to be noted is that in our discussion we have taken for granted that the group means are the actual sample means for the respective groups. However, if instead of the group means, the table shows only the *limits* of the corresponding intervals, the group means are not known. The usual practice in this case is to use the midpoint of each interval as representing the respective group mean. But if this is not true, then the midpoint is an incorrect measure of the group mean, and we have the problem of errors of measurement on our hands. As pointed out in Section 9.1, this may not be harmful if the errors occur only in measuring the values of the dependent variable, but if the explanatory variable is measured with error, then we have a real problem. This ought to be kept in mind when dealing with tabular information.

9–3 Estimation When Some Observations Are Missing

We shall consider now the question of estimating the parameters of the regression equation

$$Y_i = \alpha + \beta X_i + \varepsilon_i$$

when some of the sample values are missing. That is, we shall be concerned with the situation where some of the pairs of observations $(X_1, Y_1), (X_2, Y_2), \ldots, (X_n, Y_n)$ are incomplete in the sense that *one* of the values is missing. Missing observations are sometimes encountered in the case of cross-section or time-series data. For instance, when estimating a family consumption function from survey data, one finds that some families may have failed to report their income, while others may have omitted to state their consumption expenditure. Or, in the case of time series, the values of either variable may not be given for certain periods of time because of a change in the recording procedure, or for a number of other reasons. The question then is whether, when estimating the regression coefficients, we should discard the incomplete pairs of observations or whether the partial information contained in them could be put to some use.

In discussing the problem of using the information contained in the incomplete pairs of observations, we shall confine ourselves to situations where all the basic assumptions about the disturbance term—that is, assumptions (7.2) through (7.5)—are valid. However, we shall distinguish between the case where X is nonstochastic and the case where X is stochastic but independent of the disturbance. If we use only the complete pairs of observations, then the least squares estimators of α and β are

$$\hat{\beta}_c = \frac{\sum_c (X_i - \bar{X}_c)(Y_i - \bar{Y}_c)}{\sum_c (X_i - \bar{X}_c)^2}, \tag{9.42}$$

and

$$\hat{\alpha}_c = \bar{Y}_c - \hat{\beta}_c \bar{X}_c, \tag{9.43}$$

where $\bar{X}_c$ and $\bar{Y}_c$ are the sample means of X and of Y calculated from the complete pairs, and $\sum_c$ denotes the summation over all such pairs. The estimators $\hat{\alpha}_c$ and $\hat{\beta}_c$ are unbiased and efficient in the class of all estimators of α and β that use the same information.

Nonstochastic Explanatory Variable

In the case where X is nonstochastic, the values of X are under the control either of the investigator or of the original "experimenter." Of course, this is to be interpreted in a broad sense—for instance, viewing the government as conducting an "experiment" whenever it incurs some expenditure. The implication of this is that those pairs of observations for which the values of Y are not shown give no information about the outcome of the "experiment" and should not be counted as a part of the sample at all. Thus the only interesting case in this context is that where some of the X's are missing while all the values of Y are available. The incomplete pairs give us information about Y, i.e., about the outcome of the "experiment," but not about the conditioning variable X. We will first determine the loss of efficiency that results from using only the complete pairs instead of all of the pairs *if* they were all complete. Then we will try to use the incomplete pairs in an effort to make the loss of efficiency smaller. In the process, and throughout this section, we will use the following notation, in addition to the symbols already used in (9.42) and (9.43):

$\sum_x$ the summation over all pairs for which X is observed

$\sum_y$ the summation over all pairs for which Y is observed

$\sum_{0x}$ the summation over all pairs for which X is not observed

$\sum_{0y}$ the summation over all pairs for which Y is not observed

n_c number of complete pairs

n_x number of pairs for which X is observed

n_y number of pairs for which Y is observed

m_x number of pairs for which X is not observed

m_y number of pairs for which Y is not observed

$\bar{X}_x = \frac{1}{n_x}\sum_x X_i$, etc.

Note that

$$n_c + m_x + m_y = n,$$

$$n_c + m_y = n_x,$$

$$n_c + m_x = n_y.$$

In the present context, where all of the values of Y are available, we have

$$n_x = n_c,$$
$$n_y = n,$$
$$m_y = 0,$$
$$\bar{X}_x = \bar{X}_c.$$

If we use only the complete pairs of observations, the variance of the least squares estimator of β is

$$\text{Var}(\hat{\beta}_c) = \frac{\sigma^2}{\sum_x (X_i - \bar{X}_x)^2}, \tag{9.44}$$

If *all* pairs were complete, the variance of the least squares estimator of β, say, $\hat{\beta}_y$, would be

$$\text{Var}(\hat{\beta}_y) = \frac{\sigma^2}{\sum_y (X_i - \bar{X}_y)^2}. \tag{9.45}$$

The loss of efficiency due to the fact that some pairs of observations do not show a value for X (and we use only the complete pairs) can be measured by the ratio $\text{Var}(\hat{\beta}_c)$ to $\text{Var}(\hat{\beta}_y)$, i.e., by

$$\frac{\text{Var}(\hat{\beta}_c)}{\text{Var}(\hat{\beta}_y)} = \frac{\sum_y (X_i - \bar{X}_y)^2}{\sum_x (X_i - \bar{X}_x)^2}. \tag{9.46}$$

Now,

$$\begin{aligned}\sum_y (X_i - \bar{X}_y)^2 &= \sum_x (X_i - \bar{X}_y)^2 + \sum_{0x} (X_i - \bar{X}_y)^2 \\ &= \sum_x [(X_i - \bar{X}_x) + (\bar{X}_x - \bar{X}_y)]^2 \\ &\quad + \sum_{0x} [(X_i - \bar{X}_{0x}) + (\bar{X}_{0x} - \bar{X}_y)]^2 \\ &= \sum_x (X_i - \bar{X}_x)^2 + n_x(\bar{X}_x - \bar{X}_y)^2 + \sum_{0x} (X_i - \bar{X}_{0x})^2 \\ &\quad + m_x(\bar{X}_{0x} - \bar{X}_y)^2.\end{aligned}$$

By using the fact that

$$\bar{X}_y = \frac{1}{n}(n_x\bar{X}_x + m_x\bar{X}_{0x}),$$

we can write

$$n_x(\bar{X}_x - \bar{X}_y)^2 = n_x\left[\bar{X}_x - \frac{1}{n}(n_x\bar{X}_x + m_x\bar{X}_{0x})\right]^2 = \frac{n_x m_x^2}{n^2}(\bar{X}_x - \bar{X}_{0x})^2,$$

and

$$m_x(\bar{X}_{0x} - \bar{X}_y)^2 = m_x\left[\bar{X}_{0x} - \frac{1}{n}(n_x\bar{X}_x + m_x\bar{X}_{0x})\right]^2 = \frac{n_x^2 m_x}{n^2}(\bar{X}_x - \bar{X}_{0x})^2.$$

Therefore,

$$\text{(9.46a)} \qquad \frac{\text{Var}(\hat{\beta}_c)}{\text{Var}(\hat{\beta}_y)} = 1 + \frac{\sum_{0x}(X_i - \bar{X}_{0x})^2 + (n_x m_x/n)(\bar{X}_x - \bar{X}_{0x})^2}{\sum_x (X_i - \bar{X}_x)^2}.$$

This result shows that the loss of efficiency will be small if the missing values of X have a small dispersion and, at the same time, the mean of the missing values of X is close to the mean of the available values of X. There will be no loss of efficiency involved (in finite samples) if and only if each one of the missing values of X is equal to the mean of the available values of X. Of course, since the missing values of X are not known, the ratio (9.46a) cannot be evaluated, but it can be estimated from the available sample information as shown below.

Let us try now to utilize the information contained in the pairs of observations for which the values of X are missing. These missing values can be viewed as unknown parameters that can be estimated alongwith the regression coefficients and σ^2. We will denote the missing values of X by ξ_i; according to our notation, their number will be m_x. The likelihood function for $(Y_1, Y_2, \ldots, Y_n)$ then is

$$L = -\frac{n}{2}\log 2\pi - \frac{n}{2}\log\sigma^2 - \frac{1}{2\sigma^2}\sum_x (Y_i - \alpha - \beta X_i)^2 - \frac{1}{2\sigma^2}\sum_{0x}(Y_i - \alpha - \beta\xi_i)^2.$$

By differentiating L with respect to α, β, σ^2, and each of the ξ_i's, putting each of the derivatives equal to zero, and solving for the values of the unknown parameters, we obtain the respective maximum likelihood estimators. It is a matter of simple algebra to show that the maximum likelihood estimators of α and β are exactly the same as the least squares estimators (9.42) and (9.43), that the estimator of σ^2 is the same as that based on complete pairs only, and that the estimators of ξ_i are

$$\text{(9.47)} \qquad \hat{\xi}_i = \frac{Y_i - \hat{\alpha}_c}{\hat{\beta}_c}.$$

This means that the maximum likelihood estimation method applied to all observations for which Y is observed provides estimates of the missing values of X but leaves the estimates of α, β, and σ^2 as they are when estimated only from the complete pairs. This is somewhat disappointing. Nevertheless, we are a little ahead because we can at least use the estimates of the missing values of X to get some idea about the loss of efficiency resulting from the presence of incomplete pairs of observations. This can be done by substituting $\hat{\xi}_i$ for the missing values of X in (9.46a). The result is

$$\text{(9.48)} \qquad \text{Est.}\left[\frac{\text{Var}(\hat{\beta}_c)}{\text{Var}(\hat{\beta}_y)}\right] = 1 + \frac{\sum_{0x} (\hat{\xi}_i - \bar{\hat{\xi}})^2 + (n_x m_x/n)(\bar{X}_x - \bar{\hat{\xi}})^2}{\sum_x (X_i - \bar{X}_x)^2}.$$

The estimator $\hat{\xi}_i$ has the desirable asymptotic properties possessed by other maximum likelihood estimators, provided the number of missing values of X does not grow with sample size.

Example In the example in Section 7–3, we were concerned with estimating the coefficients of a linear relation between price (X) and quantity or oranges sold (Y) in a given supermarket over twelve consecutive days. The observations were:

X:	100	90	80	70	70	70	70	65	60	60	55	50
Y:	55	70	90	100	90	105	80	110	125	115	130	130

The results of the relevant calculations were as follows:

$$\bar{X} = 70,$$
$$\sum (X_i - \bar{X})^2 = 2250,$$
$$\hat{\alpha} = 210.460,$$
$$\hat{\beta} = -1.578.$$

Suppose now that, in addition to the 12 pairs of observations, we also had the information that the quantity sold on the thirteenth day was 37 pounds but that no price has been reported. That is, $Y_{13} = 37$. This observation has been discarded. We wish to know how much efficiency we would have gained in estimating β if X_{13} had been known. First, we use (9.47) to estimate X_{13} as

$$\hat{\xi}_{13} = \frac{Y_{13} - \hat{\alpha}}{\hat{\beta}} = \frac{37 - 210.460}{-1.578} = 110.$$

Then, the estimated ratio of $\text{Var}(\hat{\beta}_c)$ to $\text{Var}(\hat{\beta}_y)$ is

$$1 + \frac{0 + [(12 \times 1)/13](70 - 110)^2}{2250} = 1.6564,$$

which means that the loss of efficiency is estimated to be 65.64%.

An alternative way of using the information contained in the incomplete pairs of observations is to fill in the gaps by using some approximations of the missing values of X. This approach is probably fairly common in practice. The approximations are obtained by, e.g., interpolation from the observed values of X, or by reference to some other variable Z that is correlated with X. However, if we replace the missing values of X with some approximations, we introduce errors of measurement into the values of the explanatory variable and, as a consequence, obtain inconsistent estimates of the regression coefficients. This was explained in detail in Section 9-1. How serious this inconsistency will be depends, of course, on the extent of the errors of approximation. In fact, what is being done in this case is giving up consistency in the hope of reducing the variance of the estimator. If we are reasonably certain that the errors of approximation are small while the gain in efficiency is potentially large, this may be a rational procedure. Otherwise, the trade may result in a loss.

Stochastic Explanatory Variable

Let us now turn to the case where X is a stochastic variable that is distributed independently of the disturbance. The formulas for the least squares estimators of the regression coefficients based on complete pairs of observations remain unchanged, and so do the formulas for their variances—except that the latter have to be interpreted as conditional upon the given set of available values of X. Each pair of the observed values of X and Y now comes from a bivariate probability distribution. Our problem is to estimate the regression coefficients when some of the pairs of observations are incomplete. Other than disregarding the incomplete pairs, we may try to fill in the gaps and *then* apply the least squares estimation. One way of filling the gaps is to ask which value of X, or of Y, would one expect to observe *before* making the observation. Commonly, this would be the mathematical expectation of X or of Y, i.e., their means. Since the means are unknown, we can use the available sample means as estimators. That is, we may complete the missing observations in the incomplete pairs by using the available sample means of the respective variables. The least squares estimators of α and β obtained from the sample completed in this way are called *zero order regression estimators.*[7] They are defined as follows:

$$(9.49) \qquad \hat{\beta}_0 = \frac{\sum_c (X_i - \bar{X}_x)(Y_i - \bar{Y}_y) + \sum_{0x} (\bar{X}_x - \bar{X}_x)(Y_i - \bar{Y}_y)}{\sum_c (X_i - \bar{X}_x)^2 + \sum_{0x} (\bar{X}_x - \bar{X}_x)^2 + \sum_{0y} (X_i - \bar{X}_x)^2}$$

$$+ \frac{\sum_{0y} (X_i - \bar{X}_x)(\bar{Y}_y - \bar{Y}_y)}{\sum_c (X_i - \bar{X}_x)^2 + \sum_{0x} (\bar{X}_x - \bar{X}_x)^2 + \sum_{0y} (X_i - \bar{X}_x)^2}$$

$$= \frac{\sum_c (X_i - \bar{X}_x)(Y_i - \bar{Y}_y)}{\sum_x (X_i - \bar{X}_x)^2}$$

and

$$(9.50) \qquad \hat{\alpha}_0 = \bar{Y}_y - \hat{\beta}_0 \bar{X}_x.$$

[7] See A. A. Afifi and R. M. Elashoff, "Missing Observations in Multivariate Statistics II. Point Estimation in Simple Linear Regression," *Journal of the American Statistical Association*, Vol. 62, March 1967, pp. 10–29.

In order to see whether these estimators are unbiased, we substitute

$$Y_i - \bar{Y}_y = \beta(X_i - \bar{X}_y) + (\varepsilon_i - \bar{\varepsilon}_y)$$

into (9.49) to get

$$\hat{\beta}_0 = \frac{\sum_c (X_i - \bar{X}_x)[\beta(X_i - \bar{X}_y) + (\varepsilon_i - \bar{\varepsilon}_y)]}{\sum_x (X_i - \bar{X}_x)^2}.$$

The mathematical expectation of $\hat{\beta}_0$, conditional upon the observed values of X, is

$$E(\hat{\beta}_0) = \frac{\beta \sum_c (X_i - \bar{X}_c + \bar{X}_c - \bar{X}_x)[X_i - \bar{X}_c + \bar{X}_c - E(\bar{X}_y)]}{\sum_x (X_i - \bar{X}_x)^2}$$

$$= \frac{\beta \sum_c (X_i - \bar{X}_c)^2 + n_c(\bar{X}_c - \bar{X}_x)[\bar{X}_x - E(\bar{X}_y)]}{\sum_x (X_i - \bar{X}_x)^2}.$$

But $$E(\bar{X}_y) = E\left[\frac{1}{n_y}\left(\sum_c X_i + \sum_{0x} X_i\right)\right] = \frac{1}{n_y}(n_c \bar{X}_c + m_x \mu_x),$$

where μ_x, which is the population mean of X, is used to replace $E(\bar{X}_{0x})$, since $\bar{X}_{0x}$ is not observed. Therefore,

$$E(\hat{\beta}_0) = \frac{\beta\left[\sum_c (X_i - X_c)^2 + (n_c m_x/n_y)(\bar{X}_c - \bar{X}_x)(\bar{X}_c - \mu_x)\right]}{\sum_x (X_i - \bar{X}_x)^2} \neq \beta.$$

The conclusion, then, is that the zero order regression estimator of β is, in general, *biased*. The same is true of the zero order regression estimator of α.

Before we leave the zero order regression method, let us consider some special cases. First, suppose that the values of X are all available and only some of the Y's are missing. In this case,

$$n_x = n,$$

$$n_y = n_c,$$

$$m_x = 0,$$

$$\bar{X}_{0x} = 0.$$

Then,

$$E(\hat{\beta}_0) = \beta \frac{\sum_c (X_i - \bar{X}_c)^2}{\sum_x (X_i - \bar{X}_x)^2},$$

so that, unless $\bar{X}_c = \bar{X}_x$, $\hat{\beta}_0$ is still biased. Alternatively, suppose that the values of Y are all available but some of the X's are missing. Then,

$$n_x = n_c,$$

$$n_y = n,$$

$$m_y = 0,$$

$$\bar{X}_x = \bar{X}_c,$$

and

$$E(\hat{\beta}_0) = \frac{\beta \sum_c (X_i - \bar{X}_c)^2}{\sum_c (X_i - \bar{X}_c)^2} = \beta,$$

so that in this case the zero order regression estimator of β is unbiased. However, the variance of $\hat{\beta}_0$, conditional upon the observed X's, in this case is

$$\mathrm{Var}(\hat{\beta}_0) = E(\hat{\beta}_0 - \beta)^2 = E\left[\frac{\sum_x (X_i - \bar{X}_x)(\varepsilon_i - \bar{\varepsilon}_y)}{\sum_x (X_i - \bar{X}_x)^2}\right]^2 = \frac{\sigma^2}{\sum_x (X_i - \bar{X}_x)^2},$$

which is the same as the expression for $\mathrm{Var}(\hat{\beta}_c)$ given by (9.44). This means that we have nothing to gain in the way of efficiency by using $\hat{\beta}_0$ instead of $\hat{\beta}_c$.

The zero order regression method of estimation is based on the idea of replacing each of the missing values of X by $\bar{X}_x$, and each of the missing values of Y by $\bar{Y}_y$. An alternative idea is to replace the missing values of X by a parameter ξ, and the missing values of Y by a parameter η. Since each of the missing values of X is replaced by the same parameter ξ and each of the missing values of Y is replaced by the same parameter η, this procedure brings in only two additional unknown parameters, regardless of sample size and the number of missing values. The regression coefficients α and β can then be estimated simultaneously with ξ and η. This can be done by minimizing

$$\sum_c (Y_i - \alpha - \beta X_i)^2 + \sum_{0x} (Y_i - \alpha - \beta\xi)^2 + \sum_{0y} (\eta - \alpha - \beta X_i)^2$$

with respect to α, β, ξ, and η. The resulting estimators, known as *modified zero order regression estimators*,[8] are

(9.51) $$\hat{\beta}_m = \frac{\sum_c (X_i - \bar{X}_c)(Y_i - \bar{Y}_c)}{\sum_c (X_i - \bar{X}_c)^2 + \sum_{0y} (X_i - \bar{X}_{0y})^2}$$

and

(9.52) $$\hat{\alpha}_m = \bar{Y}_c - \hat{\beta}_m \bar{X}_c.$$

[8] *Ibid.*

The estimators of ξ and η, which are of only incidental interest, are

$$\hat{\xi} = \frac{\bar{Y}_{0x} - \hat{\alpha}_m}{\hat{\beta}_m}$$

and

$$\hat{\eta} = \hat{\alpha}_m + \hat{\beta}_m \bar{X}_{0y}.$$

Let us examine $\hat{\alpha}_m$ and $\hat{\beta}_m$ for unbiasedness. For $\hat{\beta}_m$ we have

$$\hat{\beta}_m = \frac{\beta \sum_c (X_i - \bar{X}_c)^2 + \sum_c (X_i - \bar{X}_c)(\varepsilon_i - \bar{\varepsilon}_c)}{\sum_c (X_i - \bar{X}_c)^2 + \sum_{0y} (X_i - \bar{X}_{0y})^2} \tag{9.51a}$$

and the mathematical expectation of $\hat{\beta}_m$, conditional upon the observed X's, is

$$E(\hat{\beta}_m) = \frac{\beta \sum_c (X_i - \bar{X}_c)^2}{\sum_c (X_i - \bar{X}_c)^2 + \sum_{0y} (X_i - \bar{X}_y)^2} \neq \beta.$$

This means that the modified zero order regression estimator of β is, in general, *biased.* The same is true of the modified zero order regression estimator of α.

Again, let us examine some special cases. First, suppose that all of the values of X are available and only some of the Y's are missing. In this case it is easy to show that formulas (9.51) and (9.52) remain the same, which means that we do not get any further ahead. Suppose, on the other hand, that all of the values of Y are available and only some of the X's are missing. In this case formulas (9.51) and (9.52) become the same as (9.42) and (9.43). This means that the estimators $\hat{\alpha}_m$ and $\hat{\beta}_m$ are exactly equal to the ordinary least squares estimators based on complete pairs of observations only.

Summary

To sum up, when we deal with samples in which some pairs of observations are incomplete, the information contained in the incomplete pairs is of relatively little use when estimating the regression coefficients. When X is nonstochastic, the information contained in the pairs for which only the Y's are given enables us to get an estimate of the loss of efficiency due to the fact that some of the X's are missing. If this loss is substantial, it may be worthwhile to go to the trouble of attempting to recover the missing values of X, or to find some good approximations for them. When X is stochastic and we use either the zero order regression method or its modified version, we get estimators that are generally biased. If only values of X are missing, both methods will lead to unbiased estimates of β, but these will be no more efficient than the ordinary least squares estimates based on complete pairs only. One redeeming feature of the estimators of the regression coefficients obtained by the zero order regression method or its modified version is the fact that when the correlation between X and Y is low, the mean square error of these estimators is less than that of the ordinary least squares estimators based on complete pairs.[9] Thus, under certain circumstances,

[9] For a proof and an elaboration of this statement, see *ibid.*

either one of the former methods may be preferable to estimation from complete pairs only.

EXERCISES

9–1. Assuming the "errors-in-variables" model, estimate the relationship between $\log(V/PL)$ and $\log(W/P)$ from the data for the furniture industry given in Table 9–1. Use the weighted regression method with $\lambda = 2$.

9–2. Suppose the income classes given in Table 9–2 in the text are combined as follows:

Income Class	Number of Observations (n_g)
Under 18	51
18 and under 22	44
22 and under 26	36
26 and under 30	26
30 and under 34	16
34 and over	8

Calculate the appropriate values of $\bar{X}_g$ and $\bar{Y}_g$ and use these to estimate the coefficients of

$$Y = \alpha + \beta X + \varepsilon$$

and their standard errors. Compare your results with those based on the information as originally given in Table 9–2.

9–3. Provide a derivation of formula (9–47).

9–4. Consider the following observations on X (price of oranges) and Y (quantity of oranges sold):

X	Y
100	55
90	70
80	90
70	100
70	90
70	105
70	80
65	110
60	125
60	115
55	130
50	130
—	130
—	140

Estimate the loss of efficiency in estimating β as a result of disregarding the last two incomplete observations.

9–5. Given the sample moments of the observed values of X and Y, the weighted regression estimator of β—as defined by (9–7)—becomes a function of λ. For the example presented in the text we found

$$m_{xx} = 20.1834/121,$$

$$m_{yy} = 14.4456/121,$$

$$m_{xy} = 16.9577/121.$$

Calculate the values of $\hat{\beta}$ for different values of λ and plot the results in a diagram.

10 Multiple Regression

The regression model introduced in Chapter 7 is applicable to relationships that include only one explanatory variable. When the model is extended to include more than one explanatory variable, we speak of a *multiple regression* model. Relationships that can be described by a multiple regression model are very common in economics. For example, in production functions, output is typically a function of several inputs; in consumption functions, the dependent variable may be influenced by income as well as other factors; and in demand functions, the traditional explanatory variables are the price of the product, the prices of substitutes, and income.

The multiple regression model designed to describe these relationships is a natural extension of the simple regression model. In fact, most of the results derived for the simple regression model can easily be generalized so that they apply to the multiple regression case. The basic results concerning estimation are presented in Section 10–1; hypothesis testing and prediction are discussed in Section 10–2. The subject of Section 10–3 is multicollinearity—a feature that characterizes regression models with two or more explanatory variables. Finally, in Section 10–4 we examine the validity of the results of the preceding sections when the regression equation is not correctly specified.

10–1 Estimation of Regression Parameters

A common type of theoretical proposition in economics states that changes in one variable can be explained by reference to changes in *several* other variables. Such a relationship is described in a simple way by a multiple linear regression equation of the form

$$Y_i = \beta_1 + \beta_2 X_{i2} + \beta_3 X_{i3} + \cdots + \beta_K X_{iK} + \varepsilon_i, \tag{10.1}$$

where Y denotes the dependent variable, the X's denote the explanatory variables, and ε is a stochastic disturbance. The subscript i refers to the ith observation; the second subscript used in describing the explanatory variables identifies the variable in question. The number of the explanatory variables is $K - 1$, so that for $K = 2$ equation (10.1) reduces to a simple regression equation. An alternative way of writing (10.1) is

$$(10.1a) \qquad Y_i = \beta_1 X_{i1} + \beta_2 X_{i2} + \cdots + \beta_K X_{iK} + \varepsilon_i,$$

where $X_{i1} = 1$ for all $i = 1, 2, \ldots, n$. Writing X_{i1} for 1 as the multiplication factor of β_1 makes the regression equation look symmetric without bringing about any real change. To complete the specification of the regression model, we add the following *basic assumptions*:

(10.2) ε_i is normally distributed,

(10.3) $E(\varepsilon_i) = 0,$

(10.4) $E(\varepsilon_i^2) = \sigma^2,$

(10.5) $E(\varepsilon_i \varepsilon_j) = 0 \quad (i \neq j),$

(10.6) Each of the explanatory variables is nonstochastic with values fixed in repeated samples and such that, for any sample size, $\sum_{i=1}^{n} (X_{ik} - \bar{X}_k)^2/n$ is a finite number different from zero for every $k = 2, 3, \ldots, K$.

(10.7) The number of observations exceeds the number of coefficients to be estimated.

(10.8) No exact linear relation exists between any of the explanatory variables.

These assumptions are taken to apply to all observations. The full specification of the model given by (10.1) through (10.8) describes the so-called "classical normal linear regression model" in the context of multiple regression. Assumptions (10.2) through (10.5) involve the disturbance term and are exactly the same as assumptions (7.2) through (7.5) of the simple regression model. The last three assumptions refer to the explanatory variables. Assumption (10.6) is the same as assumption (7.6) except that it is extended to a larger number of explanatory variables. Assumptions (10.7) and (10.8) are new. Assumption (10.7) makes a provision for a sufficient number of "degrees of freedom" in estimation. Assumption (10.8) states that none of the explanatory variables is to be perfectly correlated with any other explanatory variable or with any linear combination of other explanatory variables. This assumption is also necessary for estimation, as will soon become clear.

Given the above specification of the multiple regression model, the distribution of Y_i is normal, as in the case of the simple regression model.

The mean of Y_i is

$$(10.9) \qquad E(Y_i) = \beta_1 + \beta_2 X_{i2} + \beta_3 X_{i3} + \cdots + \beta_K X_{iK},$$

and its variance is

$$(10.10) \qquad \operatorname{Var}(Y_i) = E[Y_i - E(Y_i)]^2 = \sigma^2.$$

Note that by using (10.9) we can interpret the regression coefficients as follows:

β_1 = the mean of Y_i when each of the explanatory variables is equal to zero;

β_k = the change in $E(Y_i)$ corresponding to a unit change in the kth explanatory variable, holding the remaining explanatory variables constant

$$= \frac{\partial E(Y_i)}{\partial X_{ik}} \quad (k = 2, 3, \ldots, K).$$

β_1 is sometimes called the *intercept* (or the *regression constant*), and $\beta_2, \beta_3, \ldots, \beta_K$ are referred to as the *regression slopes* (or the *partial regression coefficients*).

This interpretation of the regression coefficients has an important implication for their estimation. Consider, for instance, the problem of estimating β_K. Given that β_K measures the effect of X_{iK} on $E(Y_i)$ while $X_{i2}, X_{i3}, \ldots, X_{i,K-1}$ are being held constant, an obvious way of estimating β_K would be by using observations made when all the explanatory variables other than X_{iK} are, in fact, constant. That is, the observations would be obtained from a controlled experiment in which all explanatory variables other than X_{iK} were keptat fixed and unchanged levels. Let us see what would happen to the estimation problem in such a case. In particular, let the level of X_{i2} be kept at ξ_2, that of X_{i3} at ξ_3, and so on, and let X_{iK} vary. Then the regression equation (10.1) can be written as

$$Y_i = \beta_1 + \beta_2\xi_2 + \beta_3\xi_3 + \cdots + \beta_{K-1}\xi_{K-1} + \beta_K X_{iK} + \varepsilon_i$$

or

$$Y_i = \alpha + \beta_K X_{iK} + \varepsilon_i,$$

which clearly shows that in this case we are back in the realm of simple regression. This is precisely what the laboratories conducting experiments in natural sciences are frequently trying to do. It follows then that if we want to keep the assumption of nonstochastic explanatory variables and at the same time have a justification for the existence of a multiple regression model, we have to exclude the possibility that the values of the explanatory variables are controllable by the investigator. Thus we consider only those situations in which the "experiment" has been conducted by somebody other than the econometrician, and for a purpose other than estimating the regression coefficients or testing hypotheses about them. Of course, this is a common way in which economic data are acquired. The "laboratory" is the society and the econometrican is, by and large, a mere onlooker.

The description of the classical normal linear regression model is commonly presented in *matrix notation*. First, equation (10.1a) can be written as

$$\mathbf{Y} = \mathbf{X}\boldsymbol{\beta} + \boldsymbol{\epsilon}, \tag{10.1b}$$

where

$$\mathbf{Y} = \begin{bmatrix} Y_1 \\ Y_2 \\ \vdots \\ Y_n \end{bmatrix}, \quad \mathbf{X} = \begin{bmatrix} X_{11} & X_{12} & \cdots & X_{1K} \\ X_{21} & X_{22} & \cdots & X_{2K} \\ \vdots & \vdots & & \vdots \\ X_{n1} & X_{n2} & \cdots & X_{nK} \end{bmatrix}, \quad \boldsymbol{\beta} = \begin{bmatrix} \beta_1 \\ \beta_2 \\ \vdots \\ \beta_K \end{bmatrix}, \quad \boldsymbol{\epsilon} = \begin{bmatrix} \varepsilon_1 \\ \varepsilon_2 \\ \vdots \\ \varepsilon_n \end{bmatrix}.$$

This means that the dimensions of the matrices and vectors involved are as follows:

$$\mathbf{Y} \rightarrow (n \times 1),$$

$$\mathbf{X} \rightarrow (n \times K),$$

$$\boldsymbol{\beta} \rightarrow (K \times 1),$$

$$\boldsymbol{\epsilon} \rightarrow (n \times 1).$$

Note in particular that each row in the **X** matrix represents a set of values of the explanatory variables pertaining to one observation, while each column represents a set of values for one explanatory variable over the n sample observations. The first column of **X** consists entirely of 1's. The assumptions (10.2) through (10.5) can be stated in matrix notation as

(10.2a–3a) $\boldsymbol{\epsilon} \sim N(\mathbf{0}, \boldsymbol{\Sigma})$, where $\mathbf{0}$ is a column vector of zeros and $\boldsymbol{\Sigma} \rightarrow (n \times n)$,

(10.4a–5a) $\boldsymbol{\Sigma} = \sigma^2 \mathbf{I_n}$, where $\mathbf{I_n}$ is an identity matrix of order $(n \times n)$, with units in the principal diagonal and zeros everywhere else.

The statement in (10.4a–5a) combines the assumptions of homoskedasticity and nonautoregression; the disturbances that satisfy both of these assumptions are called "spherical." Finally, assumptions (10.6) through (10.8) concerning the explanatory variables can be transcribed as

(10.6a–8a) The elements of the matrix **X** are nonstochastic with values fixed in repeated samples, and the matrix $(1/n)(\mathbf{X'X})$ is nonsingular and such that, for any sample size, its elements are finite.

Least Squares Estimation

Consider now the derivation of the *least squares estimators* of the regression coefficients. The sum of squares to be minimized is

$$S = \sum_{i=1}^{n} (Y_i - \beta_1 - \beta_2 X_{i2} - \beta_3 X_{i3} - \cdots - \beta_K X_{iK})^2.$$

Differentiating S with respect to $\beta_1, \beta_2, \ldots, \beta_K$, we get

$$\frac{\partial S}{\partial \beta_1} = -2 \sum_i (Y_i - \beta_1 - \beta_2 X_{i2} - \beta_3 X_{i3} - \cdots - \beta_K X_{iK}),$$

$$\frac{\partial S}{\partial \beta_2} = -2 \sum_i X_{i2}(Y_i - \beta_1 - \beta_2 X_{i2} - \beta_3 X_{i3} - \cdots - \beta_K X_{iK}),$$

$$\vdots$$

$$\frac{\partial S}{\partial \beta_K} = -2 \sum_i X_{iK}(Y_i - \beta_1 - \beta_2 X_{i2} - \beta_3 X_{i3} - \cdots - \beta_K X_{iK}).$$

Equating each derivative to zero and rearranging terms gives us the following least squares normal equations:

$$\sum_i Y_i = \hat{\beta}_1 n + \hat{\beta}_2 \sum_i X_{i2} + \hat{\beta}_3 \sum_i X_{i3} + \cdots + \hat{\beta}_K \sum_i X_{iK},$$

$$\sum_i X_{i2} Y_i = \hat{\beta}_1 \sum_i X_{i2} + \hat{\beta}_2 \sum_i X_{i2}^2 + \hat{\beta}_3 \sum_i X_{i2} X_{i3} + \cdots + \hat{\beta}_K \sum_i X_{i2} X_{iK},$$

$$\vdots$$

$$\sum_i X_{iK} Y_i = \hat{\beta}_1 \sum_i X_{iK} + \hat{\beta}_2 \sum_i X_{i2} X_{iK} + \hat{\beta}_3 \sum_i X_{i3} X_{iK} + \cdots + \hat{\beta}_K \sum_i X_{iK}^2.$$

These equations represent a simple generalization of (7.10) and (7.11). (A simple rule for memorizing the formation of the least squares normal equations is given in footnote 4 on page 207.) Note that this system of normal equations could not be solved for the unknown $\hat{\beta}$'s if either (1) the number of explanatory variables *plus* one exceeded the number of observations or (2) any one of the explanatory variables represented an exact linear combination of other explanatory variables. In the former case, the number of equations would be less than the number of unknowns; in the latter case, the equations would not be independent.

To solve the least squares normal equations, we note that the first equation can be written as

$$\hat{\beta}_1 = \bar{Y} - \hat{\beta}_2 \bar{X}_2 - \hat{\beta}_3 \bar{X}_3 - \cdots - \hat{\beta}_K \bar{X}_K, \tag{10.11}$$

where $\bar{Y} = \frac{1}{n} \sum_i Y_i$ and $\bar{X}_k = \frac{1}{n} \sum_i X_{ik}$ $\quad (k = 2, 3, \ldots, K)$.

Substitution of (10.11) into the remaining normal equations gives, after some simplifications,

$$m_{Y2} = m_{22}\hat{\beta}_2 + m_{23}\hat{\beta}_3 + \cdots + m_{2K}\hat{\beta}_K,$$

$$m_{Y3} = m_{23}\hat{\beta}_2 + m_{33}\hat{\beta}_3 + \cdots + m_{3K}\hat{\beta}_K,$$

$$\vdots$$

$$m_{YK} = m_{2K}\hat{\beta}_2 + m_{3K}\hat{\beta}_3 + \cdots + m_{KK}\hat{\beta}_K,$$

where $m_{Yk} = \sum_i (Y_i - \bar{Y})(X_{ik} - \bar{X}_k)$

and $m_{jk} = \sum_i (X_{ij} - \bar{X}_j)(X_{ik} - \bar{X}_k) \quad (j, k = 2, 3, \ldots, K)$.

These equations can be solved for $\hat{\beta}_2, \hat{\beta}_3, \ldots, \hat{\beta}_K$. The solution is quite straightforward but somewhat laborious. For the case of two explanatory variables (i.e., $K = 3$), we have

$$\hat{\beta}_2 = \frac{\begin{vmatrix} m_{Y2} & m_{23} \\ m_{Y3} & m_{33} \end{vmatrix}}{\begin{vmatrix} m_{22} & m_{23} \\ m_{23} & m_{33} \end{vmatrix}} = \frac{m_{Y2}m_{33} - m_{Y3}m_{23}}{m_{22}m_{33} - m_{23}^2}, \tag{10.12}$$

(10.13)
$$\hat{\beta}_3 = \frac{\begin{vmatrix} m_{22} & m_{Y2} \\ m_{23} & m_{Y3} \end{vmatrix}}{\begin{vmatrix} m_{22} & m_{23} \\ m_{23} & m_{33} \end{vmatrix}} = \frac{m_{Y3}m_{22} - m_{Y2}m_{23}}{m_{22}m_{33} - m_{23}^2}.$$

The least squares normal equations can be presented in matrix notation as

$$(\mathbf{X'Y}) = (\mathbf{X'X})\hat{\boldsymbol{\beta}},$$

where

$$(\mathbf{X'Y}) = \begin{bmatrix} \sum Y_i \\ \sum X_{i2}Y_i \\ \vdots \\ \sum X_{iK}Y_i \end{bmatrix}, \qquad (\mathbf{X'X}) = \begin{bmatrix} n & \sum X_{i2} & \dots & \sum X_{iK} \\ \sum X_{i2} & \sum X_{i2}^2 & \dots & \sum X_{i2}X_{iK} \\ \vdots & \vdots & & \vdots \\ \sum X_{iK} & \sum X_{i2}X_{iK} & \dots & \sum X_{iK}^2 \end{bmatrix},$$

$$\hat{\boldsymbol{\beta}} = \begin{bmatrix} \hat{\beta}_1 \\ \hat{\beta}_2 \\ \vdots \\ \hat{\beta}_K \end{bmatrix}.$$

The solution for $\hat{\boldsymbol{\beta}}$ then simply becomes

(10.14)
$$\hat{\boldsymbol{\beta}} = (\mathbf{X'X})^{-1}(\mathbf{X'Y}).$$

Alternatively, we can eliminate $\hat{\beta}_1$ by substitution from (10.11), and then solve the reduced system of equations to get

(10.15)
$$\underline{\hat{\boldsymbol{\beta}}} = (\underline{\mathbf{X}}'\underline{\mathbf{X}})^{-1}(\underline{\mathbf{X}}'\underline{\mathbf{Y}}),$$

where

$$\underline{\hat{\boldsymbol{\beta}}} = \begin{bmatrix} \hat{\beta}_2 \\ \hat{\beta}_3 \\ \vdots \\ \hat{\beta}_K \end{bmatrix}, \qquad (\underline{\mathbf{X}}'\underline{\mathbf{X}}) = \begin{bmatrix} m_{22} & m_{23} & \dots & m_{2K} \\ m_{23} & m_{33} & \dots & m_{3K} \\ \vdots & \vdots & & \vdots \\ m_{2K} & m_{3K} & \dots & m_{KK} \end{bmatrix}, \qquad (\underline{\mathbf{X}}'\underline{\mathbf{Y}}) = \begin{bmatrix} m_{Y2} \\ m_{Y3} \\ \vdots \\ m_{YK} \end{bmatrix}.$$

EXAMPLE In Section 7–3, we illustrated the method of least squares in the simple regression context by estimating the relationship between price and quantity of oranges sold in a supermarket on twelve consecutive days. Let us modify this example by postulating that the quantity sold depends not only on price but also on the amount spent on advertising the product. That is, let

$$Y_i = \beta_1 + \beta_2 X_{i2} + \beta_3 X_{i3} + \varepsilon_i,$$

where Y_i = quantity (pounds) of oranges sold, X_{i2} = price in cents per pound, and X_{i3} = advertising expenditure in dollars. The data are given in Table 10-1. The

Table 10-1

Quantity, lb	Price, ¢/lb	Advertising Expenditure, $
55	100	5.50
70	90	6.30
90	80	7.20
100	70	7.00
90	70	6.30
105	70	7.35
80	70	5.60
110	65	7.15
125	60	7.50
115	60	6.90
130	55	7.15
130	50	6.50

results of the basic calculations are

$$\bar{Y} = 100, \qquad m_{22} = 2250, \qquad m_{Y2} = -3550,$$

$$\bar{X}_2 = 70, \qquad m_{33} = 4.86, \qquad m_{Y3} = 125.25,$$

$$\bar{X}_3 = 6.7, \qquad m_{23} = -54, \qquad m_{YY} = 6300.$$

(The quantity $m_{YY} = \sum_i (Y_i - \bar{Y})^2$ will be used in later examples.) The estimates of the regression coefficients are

$$\hat{\beta}_2 = \frac{-3550 \times 4.86 - (-54) \times 125.25}{2250 \times 4.86 - (-54)^2} = \frac{-10{,}631.5}{8019} = -1.326,$$

$$\hat{\beta}_3 = \frac{2250 \times 125.25 - (-54) \times (-3550)}{8019} = \frac{90{,}112.5}{8019} = 11.237,$$

and $\qquad \hat{\beta}_1 = 100 - (-1.326) \times 70 - 11.237 \times 6.7 = 117.532.$

Therefore, the estimated regression equation is

$$Y_i = 117.532 - 1.326\, X_{i2} + 11.237\, X_{i3} + e_i.$$

This implies that we estimate that a 10¢ reduction in the price of oranges, with advertising expenditure unchanged, would increase sales by about 13 pounds, while a $1 increase in advertising expenditure, with price unchanged, would increase sales by about 11 pounds.

Best Linear Unbiased Estimation

Let us now derive the *best linear unbiased estimators* (BLUE) for the multiple regression model. For simplicity, we shall use a model with two explanatory variables; an extension to the general case only requires more involved algebraic expressions. Suppose, then, that we wish to derive the BLUE of, say, β_2, of the model

$$Y_i = \beta_1 + \beta_2 X_{i2} + \beta_3 X_{i3} + \varepsilon_i .$$

By the condition of linearity, we have

$$\tilde{\beta}_2 = \sum_i a_i Y_i ,$$

where a_i ($i = 1, 2, \ldots, n$) are some constants to be determined. The mathematical expectation of $\tilde{\beta}_2$ is

$$\begin{aligned} E(\tilde{\beta}_2) &= E \sum_i a_i Y_i = E \sum_i a_i(\beta_1 + \beta_2 X_{i2} + \beta_3 X_{i3} + \varepsilon_i) \\ &= \beta_1 \sum_i a_i + \beta_2 \sum_i a_i X_{i2} + \beta_3 \sum_i a_i X_{i3} , \end{aligned}$$

so that, for $\tilde{\beta}_2$ to be unbiased, we require

$$\sum_i a_i = 0,$$

$$\sum_i a_i X_{i2} = 1,$$

$$\sum_i a_i X_{i3} = 0.$$

The variance of $\tilde{\beta}_2$ is

$$\mathrm{Var}(\tilde{\beta}_2) = E\Big[\sum_i a_i Y_i - E\Big(\sum_i a_i Y_i\Big)\Big]^2 = E\Big(\sum_i a_i \varepsilon_i\Big)^2 = \sigma^2 \sum_i a_i^2 .$$

That is, we have to find those values of a_i that would minimize

$$\sigma^2 \sum_i a_i^2 ,$$

subject to the conditions that

$$\sum_i a_i = 0,$$

$$\sum_i a_i X_{i2} = 1,$$

$$\sum_i a_i X_{i3} = 0.$$

Using the Lagrange multiplier method, we form

$$H = \sigma^2 \sum_i a_i^2 - \lambda_1\Big(\sum_i a_i\Big) - \lambda_2\Big(\sum_i a_i X_{i2} - 1\Big) - \lambda_3\Big(\sum_i a_i X_{i3}\Big).$$

Differentiating H with respect to $a_1, a_2, \ldots, a_n, \lambda_1, \lambda_2$, and λ_3 and putting each derivative equal to zero, we obtain

$$2a_i\sigma^2 - \lambda_1 - \lambda_2 X_{i2} - \lambda_3 X_{i3} = 0 \qquad (i = 1, 2, \ldots, n), \tag{10.16}$$

$$-\Big(\sum_i a_i\Big) = 0, \tag{10.17}$$

$$-\Big(\sum_i a_i X_{i2}\Big) + 1 = 0, \tag{10.18}$$

$$-\Big(\sum_i a_i X_{i3}\Big) = 0. \tag{10.19}$$

This gives us $(n + 3)$ equations to be solved for the unknown $a_1, a_2, \ldots, a_n, \lambda_1, \lambda_2$, and λ_3. We start by adding the n equations of (10.16). This leads to

$$2\sigma^2 \sum_i a_i - n\lambda_1 - \lambda_2 \sum_i X_{i2} - \lambda_3 \sum_i X_{i3} = 0. \tag{10.20}$$

Next, we multiply both sides of (10.16) by X_{i2} and add the resulting equations to get

$$2\sigma^2 \sum_i a_i X_{i2} - \lambda_1 \sum_i X_{i2} - \lambda_2 \sum_i X_{i2}^2 - \lambda_3 \sum_i X_{i2}X_{i3} = 0. \tag{10.21}$$

Finally, we multiply both sides of (10.16) by X_{i3} and add again:

$$2\sigma^2 \sum_i a_i X_{i3} - \lambda_1 \sum_i X_{i3} - \lambda_2 \sum_i X_{i2}X_{i3} - \lambda_3 \sum_i X_{i3}^2 = 0, \tag{10.22}$$

Substitution for $\sum_i a_i$, $\sum_i a_i X_{i2}$, and $\sum_i a_i X_{i3}$ from (10.17), (10.18), and (10.19) into (10.20), (10.21), and (10.22) then leads to

$$-n\lambda_1 - \lambda_2 \sum_i X_{i2} - \lambda_3 \sum_i X_{i3} = 0, \tag{10.20a}$$

$$-\lambda_1 \sum_i X_{i2} - \lambda_2 \sum_i X_{i2}^2 - \lambda_3 \sum_i X_{i2}X_{i3} = -2\sigma^2, \tag{10.21a}$$

$$-\lambda_1 \sum_i X_{i3} - \lambda_2 \sum_i X_{i2}X_{i3} - \lambda_3 \sum_i X_{i3} = 0. \tag{10.22a}$$

Now from (10.20a) we get

$$\lambda_1 = -\lambda_2 \bar{X}_2 - \lambda_3 \bar{X}_3.$$

We can then substitute this expression for λ_1 into (10.21a) and (10.22a), which yields

$$\lambda_2 m_{22} + \lambda_3 m_{23} = 2\sigma^2,$$
$$\lambda_2 m_{23} + \lambda_3 m_{33} = 0.$$

Therefore,

$$\lambda_2 = \frac{2\sigma^2 m_{33}}{m_{22}m_{33} - m_{23}^2}$$

and

$$\lambda_3 = \frac{-2\sigma^2 m_{23}}{m_{22}m_{33} - m_{23}^2},$$

which implies that

$$\lambda_1 = \frac{2\sigma^2(-\bar{X}_2 m_{33} + \bar{X}_3 m_{23})}{m_{22}m_{33} - m_{23}^2}.$$

In this way, we have obtained the solution for λ_1, λ_2, and λ_3. Now from (10.16), we have

$$a_i = \frac{1}{2\sigma^2}(\lambda_1 + \lambda_2 X_{i2} + \lambda_3 X_{i3}),$$

which, after substituting for the λ's, becomes

$$a_i = \frac{-\bar{X}_2 m_{33} + \bar{X}_3 m_{23} + m_{33}X_{i2} - m_{23}X_{i3}}{m_{22}m_{33} - m_{23}^2}. \tag{10.23}$$

Therefore

$$\tilde{\beta}_2 = \sum_i a_i Y_i = \frac{-n\bar{Y}\bar{X}_2 m_{33} + n\bar{Y}\bar{X}_3 m_{23} + m_{33}\sum X_{i2}Y_i - m_{23}\sum X_{i3}Y_i}{m_{22}m_{33} - m_{23}^2}$$

$$= \frac{m_{33}m_{Y2} - m_{23}m_{Y3}}{m_{22}m_{33} - m_{23}^2},$$

which is precisely the same formula as that for the least squares estimator of β_2 given by (10.12). Similarly, we could show that $\tilde{\beta}_3 = \hat{\beta}_3$ and $\tilde{\beta}_1 = \hat{\beta}_1$. Therefore, *least squares estimators of the regression coefficients are* BLUE. This conclusion applies to regression models with any number of explanatory variables.

The BLUE method provides us not only with a formula for $\tilde{\beta}_2$ but also one for the variance of $\tilde{\beta}_2$. In particular,

$$\text{Var}(\tilde{\beta}_2) = \sigma^2 \sum_i a_i^2.$$

Now, by multiplying both sides of (10.23) by a_i, adding over all observations, and substituting for $\sum a_i$, $\sum a_i X_{i2}$, and $\sum a_i X_{i3}$, we obtain

$$\sum_i a_i^2 = \frac{m_{33}}{m_{22}m_{33} - m_{23}^2}.$$

This means that

$$\text{Var}(\tilde{\beta}_2) = \frac{\sigma^2 m_{33}}{m_{22}m_{33} - m_{23}^2}. \tag{10.24}$$

The result for the variance of $\tilde{\beta}_3$, which will not be derived here, is

$$\text{Var}(\tilde{\beta}_3) = \frac{\sigma^2 m_{22}}{m_{22}m_{33} - m_{23}^2}. \tag{10.25}$$

Maximum Likelihood Estimation

Next we come to the derivation of the *maximum likelihood estimators* of the parameters of a multiple normal linear regression model. This represents a direct extension of the procedure developed in connection with the simple regression model. When we set up the likelihood function as in (7.26) but allow for more than one explanatory variable, we get

$$L = -\frac{n}{2}\log(2\pi) - \frac{n}{2}\log\sigma^2 - \frac{1}{2\sigma^2}\sum_i (Y_i - \beta_1 - \beta_2 X_{i2} - \beta_3 X_{i3} - \cdots - \beta_K X_{iK})^2.$$

The maximum likelihood estimators are obtain by differentiating L with respect to $\beta_1, \beta_2, \ldots, \beta_K$, and σ^2, and by putting each of these derivatives equal to zero. It is easy to see that the first K of these equations, which can be solved for the values of the β's, are exactly the same as the least squares normal equations. This means that the *maximum likelihood estimators of the regression coefficients are equivalent to the least squares estimators.* The maximum likelihood estimator of σ^2 is

(10.26) $$\hat{\hat{\sigma}}^2 = \frac{1}{n}\sum_i (Y_i - \hat{\beta}_1 - \hat{\beta}_2 X_{i2} - \hat{\beta}_3 X_{i3} - \cdots - \hat{\beta}_K X_{iK})^2$$

or

(10.26a) $$\hat{\hat{\sigma}}^2 = \frac{1}{n}\sum_i e_i^2,$$

where the terms e_i represent the least squares residuals.

10-2 Further Results of Statistical Inference

From the preceding discussion on estimation of the coefficients of a multiple regression model, we conclude that, as in the case of the simple regression model, each of the three estimation methods considered leads to exactly the same formulas. The implication is that the least squares estimators of the regression coefficients have all the desirable properties. We shall now describe some other features of these estimators and discuss their use for testing hypotheses and for prediction.

Variances and Covariances of the Least Squares Estimators

The formulas for the variances of the estimated regression coefficients of a model with two explanatory variables are presented in (10.24) and (10.25). Generalization of these formulas to models with a larger number of explanatory variables is quite straightforward. For the case of $(K - 1)$ variables, the result is

(10.27) $$E(\underline{\hat{\beta}} - \underline{\beta})(\underline{\hat{\beta}} - \underline{\beta})' = \sigma^2(\underline{X}'\underline{X})^{-1},$$

or, explicitly,

(10.27a)
$$\begin{bmatrix} \mathrm{Var}(\hat{\beta}_2) & \mathrm{Cov}(\hat{\beta}_2,\hat{\beta}_3) & \cdots & \mathrm{Cov}(\hat{\beta}_2,\hat{\beta}_K) \\ \mathrm{Cov}(\hat{\beta}_2,\hat{\beta}_3) & \mathrm{Var}(\hat{\beta}_3) & \cdots & \mathrm{Cov}(\hat{\beta}_3,\hat{\beta}_K) \\ \vdots & \vdots & & \vdots \\ \mathrm{Cov}(\hat{\beta}_2,\hat{\beta}_K) & \mathrm{Cov}(\hat{\beta}_3,\hat{\beta}_K) & \cdots & \mathrm{Var}(\hat{\beta}_K) \end{bmatrix} = \sigma^2 \begin{bmatrix} m_{22} & m_{23} & \cdots & m_{2K} \\ m_{23} & m_{33} & \cdots & m_{3K} \\ \vdots & \vdots & & \vdots \\ m_{2K} & m_{3K} & \cdots & m_{KK} \end{bmatrix}^{-1}.$$

The matrix $[\sigma^2(\underline{X}'\underline{X})^{-1}]$, whose dimension is $(K-1)\times(K-1)$, represents the *variance-covariance matrix* of the least squares estimators of the regression slopes. In this matrix the variances of the estimators are displayed along the main diagonal, while the covariances of the estimators are given by the off-diagonal terms.

So far we have not derived the formula for the variance of the regression intercept. We shall do this now, first for the model with two explanatory variables and then for the general case. In the case of two explanatory variables, we have

$$\hat{\beta}_1 = \bar{Y} - \hat{\beta}_2\bar{X}_2 - \hat{\beta}_3\bar{X}_3 = \beta_1 + \beta_2\bar{X}_2 + \beta_3\bar{X}_3 + \bar{\varepsilon} - \hat{\beta}_2\bar{X}_2 - \hat{\beta}_3\bar{X}_3,$$

so that

$$\hat{\beta}_1 - \beta_1 = -(\hat{\beta}_2 - \beta_2)\bar{X}_2 - (\hat{\beta}_3 - \beta_3)\bar{X}_3 + \bar{\varepsilon}.$$

This means that

$$(10.28)\qquad \mathrm{Var}(\hat{\beta}_1) = \bar{X}_2^2\mathrm{Var}(\hat{\beta}_2) + \bar{X}_3^2\mathrm{Var}(\hat{\beta}_3) + 2\bar{X}_2\bar{X}_3\mathrm{Cov}(\hat{\beta}_2,\hat{\beta}_3) - 2\bar{X}_2E\bar{\varepsilon}(\hat{\beta}_2 - \beta_2) - 2\bar{X}_3E\bar{\varepsilon}(\hat{\beta}_3 - \beta_3) + \mathrm{Var}(\bar{\varepsilon}).$$

The first three terms on the right-hand side of (10.28) can be determined from (10.27). To determine the next two terms, we note first that

$$\begin{aligned} m_{Y2} &= \sum_i (Y_i - \bar{Y})(X_{i2} - \bar{X}_2) \\ &= \sum_i [\beta_2(X_{i2} - \bar{X}_2) + \beta_3(X_{i3} - \bar{X}_3) + (\varepsilon_i - \bar{\varepsilon})](X_{i2} - \bar{X}_2) \\ &= \beta_2 m_{22} + \beta_3 m_{23} + \sum_i (X_{i2} - \bar{X}_2)\varepsilon_i \end{aligned}$$

and $$m_{Y3} = \beta_2 m_{23} + \beta_3 m_{33} + \sum_i (X_{i3} - \bar{X}_3)\varepsilon_i.$$

These expressions can be substituted into (10.12) to get

$$\hat{\beta}_2 = \frac{m_{33}[\beta_2 m_{22} + \beta_3 m_{23} + \sum (X_{i2} - \bar{X}_2)\varepsilon_i]}{m_{22}m_{33} - m_{23}^2} - \frac{m_{23}[\beta_2 m_{23} + \beta_3 m_{33} + \sum (X_{i3} - \bar{X}_3)\varepsilon_i]}{m_{22}m_{33} - m_{23}^2}$$

or

$$(10.29)\qquad \hat{\beta}_2 - \beta_2 = \frac{m_{33}\sum (X_{i2} - \bar{X}_2)\varepsilon_i - m_{23}\sum (X_{i3} - \bar{X}_3)\varepsilon_i}{m_{22}m_{33} - m_{23}^2}.$$

Similarly, by substituting for m_{Y2} and m_{Y3} into (10.13), we obtain

$$(10.30)\qquad \hat{\beta}_3 - \beta_3 = \frac{m_{22}\sum (X_{i3} - \bar{X}_3)\varepsilon_i - m_{23}\sum (X_{i2} - \bar{X}_2)\varepsilon_i}{m_{22}m_{33} - m_{23}^2}.$$

Therefore,

$$E(\hat{\beta}_2 - \beta_2)\bar{\varepsilon} = \frac{m_{33} \sum (X_{i2} - \bar{X}_2)E(\varepsilon_i\bar{\varepsilon}) - m_{23} \sum (X_{i3} - \bar{X}_3)E(\varepsilon_i\bar{\varepsilon})}{m_{22}m_{33} - m_{23}^2} = 0,$$

and also

$$E(\hat{\beta}_3 - \beta_3)\bar{\varepsilon} = 0.$$

Finally, we know that

$$\mathrm{Var}(\bar{\varepsilon}) = \frac{\sigma^2}{n}.$$

Collecting all these results and substituting into (10.28) gives

$$\text{(10.31)} \qquad \mathrm{Var}(\hat{\beta}_1) = \bar{X}_2^2\mathrm{Var}(\hat{\beta}_2) + \bar{X}_3^2\mathrm{Var}(\hat{\beta}_3) + 2\bar{X}_2\bar{X}_3\mathrm{Cov}(\hat{\beta}_2,\hat{\beta}_3) + \frac{\sigma^2}{n}$$

$$= \sigma^2\left[\frac{1}{n} + \frac{\bar{X}_2^2 m_{33} + \bar{X}_3^2 m_{22} - 2\bar{X}_2\bar{X}_3 m_{23}}{m_{22}m_{33} - m_{23}^2}\right].$$

By analogy, the variance of $\hat{\beta}_1$ in a model with $(K - 1)$ explanatory variables is

$$\text{(10.32)} \qquad \mathrm{Var}(\hat{\beta}_1) = \sum_k \bar{X}_k^2\mathrm{Var}(\hat{\beta}_k) + 2 \sum_{j<k} \bar{X}_j\bar{X}_k\mathrm{Cov}(\hat{\beta}_j,\hat{\beta}_k) + \frac{\sigma^2}{n}$$

$$(j, k = 2, 3, \ldots, K; \quad j < k).$$

This expression can be rewritten in matrix notation as

$$\text{(10.32a)} \qquad \mathrm{Var}(\hat{\beta}_1) = \underline{\bar{\mathbf{X}}}'E(\underline{\hat{\boldsymbol{\beta}}} - \underline{\boldsymbol{\beta}})(\underline{\hat{\boldsymbol{\beta}}} - \underline{\boldsymbol{\beta}})'\underline{\bar{\mathbf{X}}} = \sigma^2\underline{\bar{\mathbf{X}}}'(\underline{\mathbf{X}}'\underline{\mathbf{X}})^{-1}\underline{\bar{\mathbf{X}}},$$

where

$$\underline{\bar{\mathbf{X}}} = \begin{bmatrix} \bar{X}_2 \\ \bar{X}_3 \\ \vdots \\ \bar{X}_K \end{bmatrix}.$$

An alternative way of writing the formulas for the variances and covariances of the least squares estimators of the regression coefficients is

$$\text{(10.33)} \qquad E(\hat{\boldsymbol{\beta}} - \boldsymbol{\beta})(\hat{\boldsymbol{\beta}} - \boldsymbol{\beta})' = \sigma^2(\mathbf{X}'\mathbf{X})^{-1}$$

or, explicitly,

$$\text{(10.33a)} \qquad \begin{bmatrix} \mathrm{Var}(\hat{\beta}_1) & \mathrm{Cov}(\hat{\beta}_1,\hat{\beta}_2) & \ldots & \mathrm{Cov}(\hat{\beta}_1,\hat{\beta}_K) \\ \mathrm{Cov}(\hat{\beta}_1,\hat{\beta}_2) & \mathrm{Var}(\hat{\beta}_2) & \ldots & \mathrm{Cov}(\hat{\beta}_2,\hat{\beta}_K) \\ \vdots & \vdots & & \vdots \\ \mathrm{Cov}(\hat{\beta}_1,\hat{\beta}_K) & \mathrm{Cov}(\hat{\beta}_2,\hat{\beta}_K) & \ldots & \mathrm{Var}(\hat{\beta}_K) \end{bmatrix}$$

$$= \sigma^2 \begin{bmatrix} n & \sum X_{i2} & \ldots & \sum X_{iK} \\ \sum X_{i2} & \sum X_{i2}^2 & \ldots & \sum X_{i2}X_{iK} \\ \vdots & \vdots & & \vdots \\ \sum X_{iK} & \sum X_{i2}X_{iK} & \ldots & \sum X_{iK}^2 \end{bmatrix}^{-1}.$$

Formula (10.33), which represents the variance-covariance matrix of the estimated regression coefficients, contains the variances and covariances of *all* estimated coefficients, including the regression constant. Of course, this formula gives the same values for the variance of $\hat{\beta}_1$ and for the variances and covariances of $\hat{\beta}_2, \hat{\beta}_3, \ldots, \hat{\beta}_K$ as formulas (10.27) and (10.32). In addition, (10.33) gives the covariances of $\hat{\beta}_1$ with $\hat{\beta}_2, \hat{\beta}_3, \ldots, \hat{\beta}_K$. If the latter is not needed and we wish to minimize the calculation required, then formulas (10.27) and (10.32) are preferable to (10.33).

Estimation of σ^2

The variances and covariances of the least squares estimators of the regression coefficients all involve the parameter σ^2, the value of which has to be estimated. To find an unbiased estimator of σ^2, we first determine the mathematical expectation of the sum of squares of the least squares residuals. For the case of two explanatory variables, this is

$$\begin{aligned} E\sum_i (Y_i - \hat{\beta}_1 - \hat{\beta}_2 X_{i2} - \hat{\beta}_3 X_{i3})^2 &= E\sum_i [(Y_i - \bar{Y}) - \hat{\beta}_2(X_{i2} - \bar{X}_2) \\ &\quad - \hat{\beta}_3(X_{i3} - \bar{X}_3)]^2 \\ &= E\sum_i [\beta_2(X_{i2} - \bar{X}_2) + \beta_3(X_{i3} - \bar{X}_3) \\ &\quad + (\varepsilon_i - \bar{\varepsilon}) - \hat{\beta}_2(X_{i2} - \bar{X}_2) \\ &\quad - \hat{\beta}_3(X_{i3} - \bar{X}_3)]^2 \\ &= m_{22}\mathrm{Var}(\hat{\beta}_2) + m_{33}\mathrm{Var}(\hat{\beta}_3) \\ &\quad + 2m_{23}\mathrm{Cov}(\hat{\beta}_2, \hat{\beta}_3) \\ &\quad - 2E(\hat{\beta}_2 - \beta_2)\sum_i (X_{i2} - \bar{X}_2)\varepsilon_i \\ &\quad - 2E(\hat{\beta}_3 - \beta_3)\sum_i (X_{i3} - \bar{X}_3)\varepsilon_i \\ &\quad + E\sum_i (\varepsilon_i - \bar{\varepsilon})^2. \end{aligned}$$

Now by (10.29) we have

$$-2E(\hat{\beta}_2 - \beta_2)\sum_i (X_{i2} - \bar{X}_2)\varepsilon_i = \frac{-2\sigma^2(m_{22}m_{33} - m_{23}^2)}{m_{22}m_{33} - m_{23}^2} = -2\sigma^2,$$

and by (10.30) we have

$$-2E(\hat{\beta}_3 - \beta_3)\sum_i (X_{i3} - \bar{X}_3)\varepsilon_i = -2\sigma^2.$$

Also,

$$\begin{aligned} E\sum_i (\varepsilon_i - \bar{\varepsilon})^2 &= E\left(\sum \varepsilon_i^2\right) - 2E\left(\sum \varepsilon_i\bar{\varepsilon}\right) + nE(\bar{\varepsilon}^2) = n\sigma^2 - 2\sigma^2 + \sigma^2 \\ &= (n-1)\sigma^2. \end{aligned}$$

Therefore,

$$E \sum_i (Y_i - \hat{\beta}_1 - \hat{\beta}_2 X_{i2} - \hat{\beta}_3 X_{i3})^2 = \frac{\sigma^2(m_{22}m_{33} + m_{22}m_{33} - 2m_{23}^2)}{m_{22}m_{33} - m_{23}^2}$$

$$- 2\sigma^2 - 2\sigma^2 + (n - 1)\sigma^2$$

$$= (n - 3)\sigma^2.$$

An unbiased estimator of σ^2, say, s^2, for a regression model with two explanatory variables then is

$$s^2 = \frac{1}{n - 3} \sum_i (Y_i - \hat{\beta}_1 - \hat{\beta}_2 X_{i2} - \hat{\beta}_3 X_{i3})^2. \tag{10.34}$$

This formula can be generalized to apply to the case of $(K - 1)$ explanatory variables as follows:

$$s^2 = \frac{1}{n - K} \sum_i (Y_i - \hat{\beta}_1 - \hat{\beta}_2 X_{i2} - \hat{\beta}_3 X_{i3} - \cdots - \hat{\beta}_K X_{iK})^2. \tag{10.35}$$

Since asymptotically s^2 is equivalent to $\hat{\hat{\sigma}}^2$, the maximum likelihood estimator of σ^2, it follows that s^2 has the same optimal asymptotic properties as $\hat{\hat{\sigma}}^2$.

For computing the value of s^2, formulas (10.34) and (10.35) can be simplified to avoid the calculation of individual residuals. Let us begin with the case of two explanatory variables,

$$s^2 = \frac{1}{n - 3} \sum_i [(Y_i - \bar{Y}) - \hat{\beta}_2(X_{i2} - \bar{X}_2) - \hat{\beta}_3(X_{i3} - \bar{X}_3)]^2$$

$$= \frac{1}{n - 3}(m_{YY} + \hat{\beta}_2^2 m_{22} + \hat{\beta}_3^3 m_{33} - 2\hat{\beta}_2 m_{Y2} - 2\hat{\beta}_3 m_{Y3} + 2\hat{\beta}_2\hat{\beta}_3 m_{23}).$$

But from the least squares normal equations, we have

$$m_{Y2} = \hat{\beta}_2 m_{22} + \hat{\beta}_3 m_{23},$$

$$m_{Y3} = \hat{\beta}_2 m_{23} + \hat{\beta}_3 m_{33}.$$

Therefore,

$$\hat{\beta}_2^2 m_{22} + \hat{\beta}_2\hat{\beta}_3 m_{23} - \hat{\beta}_2 m_{Y2} = 0,$$

$$\hat{\beta}_2\hat{\beta}_3 m_{23} + \hat{\beta}_3^2 m_{33} - \hat{\beta}_3 m_{Y3} = 0.$$

Thus s^2 becomes

$$s^2 = \frac{1}{n - 3}(m_{YY} - \hat{\beta}_2 m_{Y2} - \hat{\beta}_3 m_{Y3}). \tag{10.34a}$$

This can be generalized to the case of $(K - 1)$ explanatory variables so that (10.35) becomes

$$s^2 = \frac{1}{n - K}(m_{YY} - \hat{\beta}_2 m_{Y2} - \hat{\beta}_3 m_{Y3} - \cdots - \hat{\beta}_K m_{YK}). \tag{10.35a}$$

These formulas are computationally more convenient than (10.34) and (10.35). By using s^2 in place of σ^2 in (10.27) and (10.32)—or in (10.33)—we obtain unbiased estimators of the variances and covariances of the least squares estimators of the regression coefficients. The *confidence intervals* for the regression coefficients can be constructed by noting that

$$\frac{\hat{\beta}_k - \beta_k}{s_{\hat{\beta}_k}} \sim t_{n-K} \qquad (k = 1, 2, \ldots, K),$$

where $s_{\hat{\beta}_k}$ represents the estimated standard error of $\hat{\beta}_k$.

EXAMPLE To illustrate the use of the preceding formulas, let us construct the 95% confidence intervals for the coefficients of the regression model described in the previous example. Substituting the numerical results into (10.34a), we get

$$\begin{aligned} s^2 &= \frac{1}{12-3}[6300 - (-1.326)\times(-3550) - 11.237\times 125.25] \\ &= \frac{185.27}{9} = 20.586. \end{aligned}$$

This result, combined with formulas (10.24), (10.25), and (10.31), gives

$$s^2_{\hat{\beta}_2} = \frac{20.586\times 4.86}{2250\times 4.86 - (-54)^2} = 0.012476,$$

$$s^2_{\hat{\beta}_3} = \frac{20.586\times 2250}{2250\times 4.86 - (-54)^2} = 5.7761,$$

and

$$\begin{aligned} s^2_{\hat{\beta}_1} &= 20.586\left[\frac{1}{12} + \frac{70^2\times 4.86 + 6.7^2\times 2250 - 2\times 70\times 6.7\times(-54)}{2250\times 4.86 - (-54)^2}\right] \\ &= 452.1700. \end{aligned}$$

Therefore, the estimated standard errors of $\hat{\beta}_1$, $\hat{\beta}_2$, and $\hat{\beta}_3$ are

$$\begin{aligned} s_{\hat{\beta}_1} &= 21.264, \\ s_{\hat{\beta}_2} &= 0.112, \\ s_{\hat{\beta}_3} &= 2.403. \end{aligned}$$

The tabulated t value for $12 - 3 = 9$ degrees of freedom and 0.025 two-tail probability is 2.262. Therefore, the 95% confidence intervals for the regression coefficient are

$$117.532 - 2.262\times 21.264 \leq \beta_1 \leq 117.532 + 2.262\times 21.264$$

or

$$69.43 \leq \beta_1 \leq 165.63,$$

$$-1.326 - 2.262\times 0.112 \leq \beta_2 \leq -1.326 + 2.262\times 0.112$$

or

$$-1.58 \leq \beta_2 \leq -1.07,$$

$$11.237 - 2.262\times 2.403 \leq \beta_3 \leq 11.237 + 2.262\times 2.403$$

or

$$5.80 \leq \beta_3 \leq 16.67.$$

Confidence Interval for $E(Y_i)$

The confidence intervals that we have described indicate the precision of the estimators of each of the regression coefficients considered separately. The precision of the estimated regression equation as a whole is indicated by a *confidence band.* This can be derived as a confidence interval for $E(Y_i)$, using the fitted value $\hat{Y}_i$ as its estimator. We note that $\hat{Y}_i$ is normally distributed with mean equal to $E(Y_i)$. Its variance, in the case of two explanatory variables, is

$$\sigma^2_{\hat{Y}_i} = E[\hat{Y}_i - E(\hat{Y}_i)]^2 = E[\hat{Y}_i - E(Y_i)]^2$$
$$= E[(\hat{\beta}_1 - \beta_1) + (\hat{\beta}_2 - \beta_2)X_{i2} + (\hat{\beta}_3 - \beta_3)X_{i3}]^2.$$

But $\hat{\beta}_1 - \beta_1 = -(\hat{\beta}_2 - \beta_2)\bar{X}_2 - (\hat{\beta}_3 - \beta_3)\bar{X}_3 + \bar{\varepsilon}$,

which gives

$$\text{(10.36)} \quad \sigma^2_{\hat{Y}_i} = E[(\hat{\beta}_2 - \beta_2)(X_{i2} - \bar{X}_2) + (\hat{\beta}_3 - \beta_3)(X_{i3} - \bar{X}_3) + \bar{\varepsilon}]^2$$
$$= (X_{i2} - \bar{X}_2)^2\text{Var}(\hat{\beta}_2) + (X_{i3} - \bar{X}_3)^2\text{Var}(\hat{\beta}_3)$$
$$+ 2(X_{i2} - \bar{X}_2)(X_{i3} - \bar{X}_3)\text{Cov}(\hat{\beta}_2,\hat{\beta}_3) + \frac{\sigma^2}{n}.$$

For a model with $(K - 1)$ explanatory variables, we have

$$\text{(10.37)} \quad \sigma^2_{\hat{Y}_i} = \sum_k (X_{ik} - \bar{X}_k)^2\text{Var}(\hat{\beta}_k)$$
$$+ 2\sum_{j<k} (X_{ij} - \bar{X}_j)(X_{ik} - \bar{X}_k)\text{Cov}(\hat{\beta}_j,\hat{\beta}_k) + \frac{\sigma^2}{n}$$
$$(j, k = 2, 3, \ldots, K; \;\; j < k),$$

or, in matrix notation,

$$\text{(10.37a)} \quad \sigma^2_{\hat{Y}_i} = (\underline{\mathbf{X}}_i - \underline{\bar{\mathbf{X}}})'E(\underline{\hat{\boldsymbol{\beta}}} - \underline{\boldsymbol{\beta}})(\underline{\hat{\boldsymbol{\beta}}} - \underline{\boldsymbol{\beta}})'(\underline{\mathbf{X}}_i - \underline{\bar{\mathbf{X}}}) + \frac{\sigma^2}{n}$$
$$= \sigma^2\left[(\underline{\mathbf{X}}_i - \underline{\bar{\mathbf{X}}})'(\underline{\mathbf{X}}'\underline{\mathbf{X}})^{-1}(\underline{\mathbf{X}}_i - \underline{\bar{\mathbf{X}}}) + \frac{1}{n}\right],$$

where

$$(\underline{\mathbf{X}}_i - \underline{\bar{\mathbf{X}}}) = \begin{bmatrix} X_{i2} - \bar{X}_2 \\ X_{i3} - \bar{X}_3 \\ \vdots \\ X_{iK} - \bar{X}_K \end{bmatrix}.$$

The expression for $\sigma^2_{\hat{Y}_i}$ involves the parameter σ^2 whose value is not known. If we replace σ^2 by its unbiased estimator s^2, we obtain an unbiased estimator of $\sigma^2_{\hat{Y}_i}$, say $s^2_{\hat{Y}_i}$. The confidence band for $E(Y_i)$ can then be constructed by noting that

$$\frac{\hat{Y}_i - E(Y_i)}{s_{\hat{Y}_i}} \sim t_{n-K}.$$

From this, we can determine the confidence interval for $E(Y_i)$ for *any* set of values of the explanatory variables. Note that this interval will be narrowest when the value of each explanatory variable is equal to its sample mean (in which case $s_{\hat{Y}_i}$ will be equal to $s/\sqrt{n}$) and that the interval will get wider and wider as we move away from the sample means of the X's in either direction.

Decomposition of the Sample Variation of Y

Defining, as in the case of simple regression, the sample variation of Y by $\sum(Y_i - \bar{Y})^2$, we have

$$\sum_i (Y_i - \bar{Y})^2 = \sum_i [(\hat{Y}_i + e_i) - \bar{Y}]^2$$

$$= \sum_i (\hat{Y}_i - \bar{Y})^2 + \sum_i e_i^2 + 2\sum_i (\hat{Y}_i - \bar{Y})e_i,$$

where, as before, the terms e_i represent the least squares residuals. Now, from the least squares normal equations we find that

$$\sum_i (\hat{Y}_i - \bar{Y})e_i = \sum_i (\hat{\beta}_1 + \hat{\beta}_2 X_{i2} + \hat{\beta}_i X_{i3} + \cdots + \hat{\beta}_K X_{iK})e_i - \bar{Y}\sum_i e_i = 0.$$

Thus

$$\underbrace{\sum_i (Y_i - \bar{Y})^2}_{\text{SST}} = \underbrace{\sum_i (\hat{Y}_i - \bar{Y})^2}_{\text{SSR}} + \underbrace{\sum_i e_i^2}_{\text{SSE}}.$$

Now, for the case of two explanatory variables we decompose SSR as follows:

$$\text{(10.38)} \qquad \text{SSR} = \sum_i (\hat{\beta}_1 + \hat{\beta}_2 X_{i2} + \hat{\beta}_3 X_{i3} - \bar{Y})^2$$

$$= \sum_i [(\bar{Y} - \hat{\beta}_2 \bar{X}_2 - \hat{\beta}_3 \bar{X}_3) + \hat{\beta}_2 X_{i2} + \hat{\beta}_3 X_{i3} - \bar{Y}]^2$$

$$= \hat{\beta}_2^2 m_{22} + \hat{\beta}_3^2 m_{33} + 2\hat{\beta}_2 \hat{\beta}_3 m_{23}.$$

In this case SSR, which represents the estimated regression effect on Y, consists of three terms. The first term corresponds to the effect of X_{i2}, the second to the effect of X_{i3}, and the third to the combined effect of both variables. The combined effect of X_{i2} and X_{i3} reflects the fact that X_{i2} and X_{i3} may vary together to some extent. This joint variation of X_{i2} and X_{i3} accounts for a part of the variation of Y_i. The individual contributions of X_{i2} and X_{i3} to the variation of Y_i cannot be separated completely unless X_{i2} and X_{i3} are uncorrelated, that is, unless m_{23} is equal to zero. The decomposition of SSR given in (10.38) can be generalized to the case of $(K - 1)$ explanatory variables:

$$\text{(10.39)} \quad \text{SSR} = \sum_k \hat{\beta}_k^2 m_{kk} + 2\sum_{j<k} \hat{\beta}_j \hat{\beta}_k m_{jk} \qquad (j, k = 2, 3, \ldots, K;\ j < k),$$

or, in matrix notation,

$$\text{(10.39a)} \qquad \text{SSR} = \hat{\boldsymbol{\beta}}'(\mathbf{X}'\mathbf{X})\hat{\boldsymbol{\beta}}.$$

If we are interested only in the total value of SSR and not in its components then we can obtain a computationally more convenient formula from (10.39) by a substitution from the least squares normal equation:

$$\text{SSR} = \sum_{k=2}^{K} \hat{\beta}_k m_{Yk}, \tag{10.40}$$

or, in matrix notation,

$$\text{SSR} = \hat{\underline{\beta}}'(\underline{X}'\underline{Y}). \tag{10.40a}$$

The previous results are also utilized in calculating the value of the *coefficient of determination.* This is defined, as in (7.45), by

$$R^2 = \frac{\text{SSR}}{\text{SST}} = 1 - \frac{\text{SSE}}{\text{SST}}.$$

Some research workers prefer to measure the "goodness of fit" in the case of multiple regression by a somewhat different formula known as the "*corrected coefficient of determination.*" This is usually denoted by $\bar{R}^2$ and defined by

$$\bar{R}^2 = R^2 - \frac{K-1}{n-K}(1 - R^2). \tag{10.41}$$

This measure takes into account the number of explanatory variables in relation to the number of observations. The purpose of $\bar{R}^2$ is to facilitate comparisons of the "goodness of fit" of several regression equations that may vary with respect to the number of explanatory variables and the number of observations. Note that

$$\bar{R}^2 \leq R^2,$$

with $\bar{R}^2$ being equal to R^2 in finite samples only if R^2 is equal to unity. Asymptotically the two measures are, of course, equal. Also note that, unlike R^2, $\bar{R}^2$ may have negative values. For instance, if $n = 10$, $K = 2$, and $R^2 = 0.1$, then $\bar{R}^2 = -0.0125$.

EXAMPLE From the data of the previous example, we can decompose the sample variation of Y as follows.

Source	Formula	Value	
X_{i2}	$\hat{\beta}_2^2 m_{22}$	$(-1.326)^2 \times 2250$	$= 3956$
X_{i3}	$\hat{\beta}_3^2 m_{33}$	$(11.237)^2 \times 4.86$	$= 614$
X_{i2} and X_{i3}	$2\hat{\beta}_2\hat{\beta}_3 m_{23}$	$2 \times (-1.326) \times 11.237 \times (-54)$	$= 1609$
SSR		$3956 + 614 + 1609$	$= 6179$
SSE	$m_{YY} - \text{SSR}$	$6300 - 6179$	$= 121$
SST	m_{YY}		6300

The value of the coefficient of determination is

$$R^2 = \frac{6179}{6300} = 0.981,$$

which indicates that 98% of the sample variation of the quantity of oranges sold can be attributed to the estimated effect of price variation and of variation in advertising expenditure.

Testing Hypotheses

With respect to *testing hypotheses*, the multiple regression model offers more opportunities than the simple regression model. First of all, there is the test of the hypothesis that the value of, say, β_k, is equal to some specific number. That is,

$$H_0: \quad \beta_k = \gamma_k,$$

which is to be tested against a two-sided or a one-sided alternative. The statistic that we can use to test H_0 is

$$\text{(10.42)} \qquad \frac{\hat{\beta}_k - \gamma_k}{s_{\hat{\beta}_k}} \sim t_{n-K} \quad (k = 2, 3, \ldots, K).$$

Most frequently we are interested in testing the hypothesis that β_k is equal to zero. When $k = 1$, such a hypothesis implies that the intercept is equal to zero, namely, that the regression plane passes through the origin. When $k = 2, 3, \ldots,$ K, the hypothesis that $\beta_k = 0$ means that the variable X_{ik} has no influence on the mean of Y_i; if the hypothesis is not rejected, we conclude that X_{ik} is not a relevant variable in the regression equation.

A more extensive hypothesis is that *none* of the explanatory variables has an influence on the mean of Y_i. In this case we test

$$H_0: \quad \beta_2 = \beta_3 = \cdots = \beta_K = 0$$

against the alternative that H_0 is not true; i.e., that at least one of the regression slopes is different from zero. If H_0 is true, then the variation of Y from observation to observation is not affected by changes in any one of the explanatory variables, but is purely random. However, if that is true, then the observed value of SSR ("sum of squares due to regression") differs from zero only because of sampling. Since by (10.39)

$$\text{SSR} = \sum_k \hat{\beta}_k^2 m_{kk} + 2 \sum_{j<k} \hat{\beta}_j \hat{\beta}_k m_{jk} \qquad (j, k = 2, 3, \ldots, K; \;\; j < k),$$

it is obvious that if the $\hat{\beta}$'s were replaced by the β's and the null hypothesis were correct, SSR would be equal to zero and, therefore, SSE would be equal to SST. Now, it can be shown[1] that if the null hypothesis is true, then

$$\text{(10.43)} \qquad \frac{\text{SSR}/(K-1)}{\text{SSE}/(n-K)} \sim F_{K-1,\, n-K}$$

[1] See, e.g., J. Johnston, *Econometric Methods* (New York: McGraw-Hill, 1963), pp. 119–122.

where $F_{K-1,n-K}$ represents the F distribution with $(K - 1)$ and $(n - K)$ degrees of freedom. If the value of the expression in (10.43) is not significantly different from zero, the sample offers no evidence that the explanatory variables have any effect on the mean of Y_i. Incidentally, the value of the F statistic in (10.43) can be calculated by using R^2 since

$$\frac{\text{SSR}/(K-1)}{\text{SSE}/(n-K)} = \left[\frac{n-K}{K-1}\right]\left[\frac{\text{SSR/SST}}{1-(\text{SSR/SST})}\right] = \left[\frac{n-K}{K-1}\right]\left[\frac{R^2}{1-R^2}\right].$$

Note that if any one of the estimated regression coefficients $\hat{\beta}_2, \hat{\beta}_3, \ldots, \hat{\beta}_K$ is significantly different from zero according to the t test of (10.42), then the value of the F statistic in (10.43) will also be significantly different from zero, providing the tests are carried out at the same level of significance and against the same alternative.[2] However, it is quite possible to find that *none* of $\hat{\beta}_2, \hat{\beta}_3, \ldots, \hat{\beta}_K$ is significantly different from zero according to the t test and, at the same time, to reject the hypothesis that $\beta_2 = \beta_3 = \cdots = \beta_K = 0$ by the F test. This could arise in the case where the explanatory variables are highly correlated with each other. In such a situation the separate influences of each of the explanatory variables on the dependent variable may be weak while their joint influence may be quite strong.

The relationship between the values of the individual t statistics in the test of

$$H_0\colon \quad \beta_k = 0 \qquad (k = 2, 3, \ldots, K)$$

and the value of the F statistic in the test of

$$H_0\colon \quad \beta_2 = \beta_3 = \cdots = \beta_K$$

can be made explicit by expressing the F statistic in terms of the t statistics. We shall do this for the case of two explanatory variables. From (10.38) we have

$$\text{SSR} = \hat{\beta}_2^2 m_{22} + \hat{\beta}_3^2 m_{33} + 2\hat{\beta}_2\hat{\beta}_3 m_{23},$$

and from (10.34) we know that

$$\frac{\text{SSE}}{(n-3)} = s^2.$$

Therefore,

$$F_{2,n-3} = \frac{\text{SSR}/2}{\text{SSE}/(n-3)} = \frac{\hat{\beta}_2^2 m_{22} + \hat{\beta}_3^2 m_{33} + 2\hat{\beta}_2\hat{\beta}_3 m_{23}}{2s^2}. \tag{10.44}$$

[2] Strictly speaking, this is not absolutely true. R. C. Geary and C. E. V. Leser in "Significance Tests in Multiple Regression," *The American Statistician*, Vol. 22, February 1968, pp. 20–21, give an example where all t values are significant but the F value is not. They note, however, that this situation is rare and "the possibility of its existence represents little more than a curiosity."

Now let us denote the values of the t statistics for β_2 and β_3 by t_2 and t_3 respectively. Then

$$t_2 = \frac{\hat{\beta}_2}{s_{\hat{\beta}_2}} \quad \text{and} \quad t_3 = \frac{\hat{\beta}_3}{s_{\hat{\beta}_3}}.$$

By reference to (10.24) and (10.25) we can write

$$t_2^2 = \frac{\hat{\beta}_2^2(m_{22}m_{33} - m_{23}^2)}{s^2 m_{33}},$$

$$t_3^2 = \frac{\hat{\beta}_3^2(m_{22}m_{33} - m_{23}^2)}{s^2 m_{22}},$$

or

$$\hat{\beta}_2^2 = \frac{t_2^2 s^2 m_{33}}{m_{22}m_{33} - m_{23}^2},$$

$$\hat{\beta}_3^2 = \frac{t_3^2 s^2 m_{22}}{m_{22}m_{33} - m_{23}^2},$$

and also

$$\hat{\beta}_2\hat{\beta}_3 = \frac{t_2 t_3 s^2 \sqrt{m_{22}}\sqrt{m_{33}}}{m_{22}m_{33} - m_{23}^2}.$$

Substitution into (10.44) then gives

$$\text{(10.44a)} \qquad F_{2,n-3} = \frac{t_2^2 s^2 m_{22} m_{33} + t_3^2 s^2 m_{22} m_{33} + 2t_2 t_3 s^2(\sqrt{m_{22}}\sqrt{m_{33}})m_{23}}{2s^2(m_{22}m_{33} - m_{23}^2)}.$$

If we use the symbol r_{23} to represent the sample coefficient of correlation between X_{i2} and X_{i3}, that is, if we define

$$r_{23} = \frac{m_{23}}{\sqrt{m_{22}}\sqrt{m_{33}}},$$

then (10.44a) simplifies to

$$\text{(10.44b)} \qquad F_{2,n-3} = \frac{t_2^2 + t_3^2 + 2t_2 t_3 r_{23}}{2(1 - r_{23}^2)}.$$

This shows quite clearly that if r_{23}^2 is not far from unity, the value of $F_{2,n-3}$ will be quite large even if both t_2 and t_3 are small. Thus neither $\hat{\beta}_2$ nor $\hat{\beta}_3$ may be significantly different from zero and yet the value of $F_{2,n-3}$ may be highly significant.[3]

Example Consider a regression model

$$Y_i = \beta_1 + \beta_2 X_{i2} + \beta_3 X_{i3} + \varepsilon_i.$$

[3] For a systematic exploration of this point, see K. Fox, *Intermediate Economic Statistics* (New York: Wiley, 1968), pp. 259–265. Our example given in the text represents a slight modification of one of the many illustrations given by Fox.

Suppose $n = 20$, and the calculated sample moments are

$$m_{YY} = 100, \qquad m_{22} = 100,$$
$$m_{Y2} = 90, \qquad m_{33} = 100,$$
$$m_{Y3} = 90, \qquad m_{23} = 95.$$

Then
$$\hat{\beta}_2 = \frac{90\times 100 - 90\times 95}{100\times 100 - 95^2} = 0.461,$$

and
$$\hat{\beta}_3 = \frac{90\times 100 - 90\times 95}{100\times 100 - 95^2} = 0.461.$$

Further,

$$\text{SSR} = 0.461^2\times 100 + 0.461^2\times 100 + 2\times 0.461\times 0.461\times 95 = 83,$$
$$\text{SST} = 100,$$
$$\text{SSE} = 17.$$

Therefore,
$$s^2 = \frac{17}{17} = 1,$$

and
$$s^2_{\hat{\beta}_2} = \frac{1\times 100}{100\times 100 - 95^2} = 0.102564,$$
$$s^2_{\hat{\beta}_3} = \frac{1\times 100}{100\times 100 - 95^2} = 0.102564.$$

Consequently,
$$t_2 = \frac{0.461}{\sqrt{0.102564}} = 1.444,$$
$$t_3 = \frac{0.461}{\sqrt{0.102564}} = 1.444.$$

Since the tabulated t value for 17 degrees of freedom at the 5% level of significance (i.e., $t_{17,\,0.025}$) is 2.110, which exceeds 1.444, neither $\hat{\beta}_2$ nor $\hat{\beta}_3$ is significantly different from zero at the 5% level of significance. On the other hand, the value

$$F = \frac{83/2}{1} = 41.5$$

is very much higher than the tabulated value of $F_{2,\,17}$ at the 5% level of significance, which is 3.59. Thus, by the t test we cannot reject the hypothesis that $\beta_2 = 0$ or the hypothesis that $\beta_3 = 0$, and yet by the F test we reject the hypothesis that $\beta_2 = \beta_3 = 0$. The reason is the fact that the separate contributions of X_{i2} and X_{i3} to the explanation of the variation of Y_i are weak, whereas their joint contribution, which cannot be decomposed, is quite strong. In fact,

$$\hat{\beta}_2^2 m_{22} = 21.3$$
$$\hat{\beta}_3^2 m_{33} = 21.3$$
$$2\hat{\beta}_2\hat{\beta}_3 m_{23} = 40.4$$
$$\overline{\qquad\text{SSR} = 83.0,\qquad}$$

which shows that the joint contribution of X_{i2} and X_{i3} to SSR is almost twice as large as the separate contribution of either X_{i2} or X_{i3}. Note that in this example $r_{23} = 0.95$, indicating a high degree of sample correlation between X_{i2} and X_{i3}.

A somewhat different test concerns the influence of additional explanatory variables on the mean of Y_i. In particular, consider two theories, one stating that the regression equation is

$$Y_i = \beta_1 + \beta_2 X_{i2} + \beta_3 X_{i3} + \cdots + \beta_K X_{iK} + \varepsilon_i,$$

while the competing theory states that Y_i depends not only on $X_{i2}, X_{i3}, \ldots, X_{iK}$ but also on additional explanatory variables $X_{i,K+1}, X_{i,K+2}, \ldots, X_{iQ}$ $(Q > K)$, that is,

$$Y_i = \beta_1 + \beta_2 X_{i2} + \beta_3 X_{i3} + \cdots + \beta_K X_{iK} + \beta_{K+1} X_{i,K+1} + \cdots + \beta_Q X_{iQ} + \varepsilon_i.$$

In this case, the second theory can be tested by testing the hypothesis

$$H_0\colon \quad \beta_{K+1} = \beta_{K+2} = \cdots = \beta_Q = 0$$

against the alternative that H_0 is not true. To formulate the appropriate test, we introduce a new notation, using the subscript K to denote the values pertaining to the original set of explanatory variables, and the subscript Q to denote the values to the extended set of explanatory variables. Values with no subscript apply to either set. We can write

$$\text{SST} = \text{SSR}_K + \text{SSE}_K$$

and also

$$\text{SST} = \text{SSR}_Q + \text{SSE}_Q.$$

If the additional explanatory variables are not relevant in explaining the variation of Y_i, then, in the population, SSR_K and SSR_Q would be the same and the observed difference between them would be entirely due to sampling error. If the null hypothesis is true, then it can be shown[4] that

$$\frac{(\text{SSR}_Q - \text{SSR}_K)/(Q - K)}{\text{SSE}_Q/(n - Q)} \sim F_{Q-K,\,n-Q}. \tag{10.45}$$

This can be used to test H_0 at a specified level of significance. It is not difficult to show that

$$\text{SSR}_Q \geq \text{SSR}_K$$

so that the expression in (10.45) can never be negative. An implication of this is that

$$\frac{\text{SSR}_Q}{\text{SST}} \geq \frac{\text{SSR}_K}{\text{SST}};$$

that is,

$$R_Q^2 \geq R_K^2.$$

[4] See, e.g., A. S. Goldberger, *Econometric Theory* (New York: Wiley, 1964), pp. 174–175.

This means that adding new explanatory variables into a regression equation can never result in a reduction in the value of the coefficient of determination. However, this is not necessarily true of $\bar{R}^2$.

EXAMPLE In a paper on the short-run consumption function for the United States,[5] two of the proposed functions were

$$C_t = \beta_1 + \beta_2 Y_t + \varepsilon_t$$

and

$$C_t = \beta_1 + \beta_2 Y_t + \beta_3 C_{t-1} + \beta_4 L_{t-1} + \varepsilon_t,$$

where C = consumption, Y = income, and L = liquid assets. Let us test the hypothesis

$$H_0\colon \quad \beta_3 = \beta_4 = 0$$

against the alternative that H_0 is not true at, say, the 1% level of significance. To use the F test of (10.45), we have to calculate

$$F = \left[\frac{\text{SSR}_Q - \text{SSR}_K}{\text{SSE}_Q}\right]\left[\frac{n-Q}{Q-K}\right].$$

We have $n = 31$, $Q = 4$, $K = 2$. The values of SSR and SSE are not given in the paper but can be determined from the values of $\bar{R}^2$'s, which are

$$\bar{R}^2_Q = 0.984 \qquad \text{and} \qquad \bar{R}^2_K = 0.944.$$

First, we find the values of "uncorrected" R^2's. Since

$$\bar{R}^2_K = R^2_K - \frac{K-1}{n-K}(1 - R^2_K),$$

we can solve for R^2_K to get

$$R^2_K = \frac{(n-K)\bar{R}^2_K + (K-1)}{n-1} = 0.946$$

and, similarly,

$$R^2_Q = 0.986.$$

The value of the appropriate F statistic then is

$$F = \frac{(\text{SSR}_Q/\text{SST}) - (\text{SSR}_K/\text{SST})}{1 - (\text{SSR}_Q/\text{SST})}\left[\frac{n-Q}{Q-K}\right] = \left[\frac{R^2_Q - R^2_K}{1 - R^2_Q}\right]\left[\frac{n-Q}{Q-K}\right] = 38.57.$$

Since the tabulated value of $F_{2,27}$ at the 1% level of significance is 5.49, the null hypothesis has to be rejected. That is, the evidence strongly suggests that the addition of lagged consumption and lagged liquid assets contributes to the explanation of variations in current consumption.

Another hypothesis that is sometimes of interest is

$$H_0\colon \quad \beta_j = \beta_k \qquad (j \neq k),$$

[5] Arnold Zellner, "The Short-Run Consumption Function," *Econometrica*, Vol. 25, October 1957, pp. 552–567.

which can be tested against a one-sided or a two-sided alternative. For instance, one form of the aggregate consumption function proposed in the literature is

$$C_t = \beta_1 + \beta_2 W_t + \beta_3 P_t + \beta_4 C_{t-1} + \varepsilon_t,$$

where C = consumption, W = wage income, and P = nonwage income. An interesting hypothesis is that the marginal propensity to consume of the wage earners is equal to that of the nonwage earners, i.e., that $\beta_2 = \beta_3$. To test the hypothesis that two regression coefficients are equal, we consider the distribution of the difference of the corresponding least squares estimators. In general we have

$$E(\hat{\beta}_j - \hat{\beta}_k) = \beta_j - \beta_k$$

and $$\text{Var}(\hat{\beta}_j - \hat{\beta}_k) = \text{Var}(\hat{\beta}_j) + \text{Var}(\hat{\beta}_k) - 2\,\text{Cov}(\hat{\beta}_j, \hat{\beta}_k).$$

Thus, if the null hypthesis is true,

$$(\hat{\beta}_j - \hat{\beta}_k) \sim N(0, \sigma^2_{\hat{\beta}_j - \hat{\beta}_k}).$$

An unbiased estimator of $\sigma^2_{\hat{\beta}_j - \hat{\beta}_k}$, say, $s^2_{\hat{\beta}_j - \hat{\beta}_k}$, can be obtained by using s^2 as an estimator of σ^2. It then follows that

$$\frac{\hat{\beta}_j - \hat{\beta}_k}{s_{\hat{\beta}_j - \hat{\beta}_k}} \sim t_{n-K}. \tag{10.46}$$

If the value of this statistic is significantly different from zero, the hypothesis that the two regression coefficients are equal is to be rejected. A test of the hypothesis that more than two regression coefficients are equal is described by Goldberger.[6]

A hypothesis which is similar to the preceding one is the proposition that the sum of two regression coefficients is equal to a given number. For instance, in the Cobb-Douglas production function

$$Y_i = \beta_1 + \beta_2 X_{i2} + \beta_3 X_{i3} + \varepsilon_i,$$

where Y_i = log output, X_{i2} = log labor input, and X_{i3} = log capital input, the hypothesis of constant returns to scale is equivalent to the hypothesis

$$H_0\colon\quad \beta_2 + \beta_3 = 1.$$

In general, the hypothesis

$$H_0\colon\quad \beta_j + \beta_k = a$$

can be tested by noting that

$$\left[\frac{\hat{\beta}_j + \hat{\beta}_k - a}{s_{\hat{\beta}_j + \hat{\beta}_k}}\right] \sim t_{n-k}, \tag{10.47}$$

where $$s_{\hat{\beta}_j + \hat{\beta}_k} = \sqrt{s^2_{\hat{\beta}_j} + s^2_{\hat{\beta}} + 2\,\text{Est. Cov}(\hat{\beta}_j, \hat{\beta}_k)}.$$

This test can easily be extended to a sum of more than two regression coefficients.

[6] Goldberger, *op. cit.*, p. 175, theorem (7.19).

The final test concerns the equality of two regression equations. In particular, consider a regression equation

$$Y_i = \beta_1 + \beta_2 X_{i2} + \beta_3 X_{i3} + \cdots + \beta_K X_{iK} + \varepsilon_i,$$

which has been estimated from a sample of n observations. Suppose now that we obtain m $(> K)$ additional observations and wish to test the hypothesis that the additional observations come from the same population as the first n observations. For example, data on the aggregate consumption function frequently cover the prewar as well as the postwar period. If we concede the possibility that the parameters of the postwar consumption function may be different from those of the prewar consumption function, we would test the null hypothesis that the parameters of the consumption function have *not* changed. In particular, we may write

$$Y_i = \beta_1 + \beta_2 X_{i2} + \beta_3 X_{i3} + \cdots + \beta_K X_{iK} + \varepsilon_i \quad (i = 1, 2, \ldots, n)$$

and

$$Y_i = \gamma_1 + \gamma_2 X_{i2} + \gamma_3 X_{i3} + \cdots + \gamma_K X_{iK} + \varepsilon_i \quad (i = n + 1, n + 2, \ldots, n + m).$$

The null hypothesis then would be

$$H_0: \quad \beta_1 = \gamma_1, \quad \beta_2 = \gamma_2, \quad \ldots, \quad \beta_K = \gamma_K.$$

This is to be tested against the hypothesis that H_0 is not true. The derivation of the appropriate test is described in the literature.[7] The relevant test statistic is obtained by applying the least squares estimation method to the first set of data $(i = 1, 2, \ldots, n)$, to the second set of data $(i = n + 1, n + 2, \ldots, n + m)$, and to the two sets of data combined $(i = 1, 2, \ldots, n + m)$. To estimate the regression coefficients from the combined set of data, let us write the regression equation as

$$Y_i = \delta_1 + \delta_2 X_{i2} + \delta_3 X_{i3} + \cdots + \delta_K X_{iK} + \varepsilon_i \qquad (i = 1, 2, \ldots, n + m).$$

Further, let us denote the sum of squares of the least squares residuals as follows:

$$\text{SSE}_1 = \sum_{i=1}^{n} (Y_i - \hat{\beta}_1 - \hat{\beta}_2 X_{i2} - \hat{\beta}_3 X_{i3} - \cdots - \hat{\beta}_K X_{iK})^2,$$

$$\text{SSE}_2 = \sum_{i=n+1}^{n+m} (Y_i - \hat{\gamma}_1 - \hat{\gamma}_2 X_{i2} - \hat{\gamma}_3 X_{i3} - \cdots - \hat{\gamma}_K X_{iK})^2,$$

and

$$\text{SSE}_C = \sum_{i=1}^{n+m} (Y_i - \hat{\delta}_1 - \hat{\delta}_2 X_{i2} - \hat{\delta}_3 X_{i3} - \cdots - \hat{\delta}_K X_{iK})^2.$$

It has been shown, then, that

$$\frac{(\text{SSE}_C - \text{SSE}_1 - \text{SSE}_2)/K}{(\text{SSE}_1 + \text{SSE}_2)/(n + m - 2K)} \sim F_{K,\, n+m-2K}. \tag{10.48}$$

[7] See, e.g., Johnston, *op. cit.*, pp. 136–138.

This can be used in testing H_0, but there are two points to be noted:

1. The test statistic in (10.48) is applicable only if the number of additional observations exceeds the number of explanatory variables *plus* one; i.e., if $m > K$. If $m < K$, a somewhat different test must be used.[8]
2. The formulation of the hypothesis leading to (10.48) is such that it allows for *all* of the regression parameters to change as we go from one set of data to another. Tests of the hypothesis involving only *some* of the regression coefficients will be described in Section 11–1 dealing with binary variables.

Prediction

Having discussed some of the most useful tests that can be carried out with the help of a multiple regression model, we turn our attention to the problem of *forecasting* the value of the dependent variable for a given set of values of the explanatory variables. More formally, let the given values of the explanatory variables be $X_{02}, X_{03}, \ldots, X_{0K}$, and let the corresponding value of the dependent variable be Y_0. We are interested in forecasting Y_0. As pointed out in connection with the simple regression model, the best predictor of Y_0 is $E(Y_0)$ because the variance of Y_0 around $E(Y_0)$ is smaller than around any other point. Since $E(Y_0)$ is not known, we use $\hat{Y}_0$, the least squares fitted value of Y_0, in its place. Since

$$\hat{Y}_0 = \hat{\beta}_1 + \hat{\beta}_2 X_{02} + \hat{\beta}_3 X_{03} + \cdots + \hat{\beta}_K X_{0K},$$

it follows that $\hat{Y}_0$ is normally distributed with mean

$$E(\hat{Y}_0) = \beta_1 + \beta_2 X_{02} + \beta_3 X_{03} + \cdots + \beta_K X_{0K}.$$

The variance of $\hat{Y}_0$ is, according to (10.37),

$$\begin{aligned}\mathrm{Var}(\hat{Y}_0) &= \sigma^2_{\hat{Y}_0}\\ &= \sum_k (X_{0k} - \bar{X}_k)^2 \,\mathrm{Var}(\hat{\beta}_k) + 2\sum_{j<k} (X_{0j} - \bar{X}_j)(X_{0k} - \bar{X}_k)\,\mathrm{Cov}(\hat{\beta}_j, \hat{\beta}_k)\\ &\quad + \frac{\sigma^2}{n} \qquad (j, k = 2, 3, \ldots, K;\quad j < k),\end{aligned}$$

or, in matrix notation,

$$\mathrm{Var}(\hat{Y}_0) = \sigma^2\left[(\underline{\mathbf{X}}_0 - \underline{\bar{\mathbf{X}}})'(\underline{\mathbf{X}}'\underline{\mathbf{X}})^{-1}(\underline{\mathbf{X}}_0 - \underline{\bar{\mathbf{X}}}) + \frac{1}{n}\right],$$

where

$$(\underline{\mathbf{X}}_0 - \underline{\bar{\mathbf{X}}}) = \begin{bmatrix} X_{02} - \bar{X}_2 \\ X_{03} - \bar{X}_3 \\ \vdots \\ X_{0K} - \bar{X}_K \end{bmatrix}.$$

[8] *Ibid.*, p. 138, eq. (4–65).

We are, of course, primarily interested in the *forecast error*, that is, in $(Y_0 - \hat{Y}_0)$. This random variable is normally distributed with mean

$$E(Y_0 - \hat{Y}_0) = 0$$

and variance

$$\sigma_F^2 = \text{Var}(Y_0 - \hat{Y}_0) = \text{Var}(Y_0) + \text{Var}(\hat{Y}_0) - 2\,\text{Cov}(Y_0, \hat{Y}_0).$$

Now

$$\text{Var}(Y_0) = \sigma^2,$$

$$\text{Var}(\hat{Y}_0) = \sigma^2_{\hat{Y}_0},$$

and

$$-2\,\text{Cov}(Y_0, \hat{Y}_0) = -2E[Y_0 - E(Y_0)][\hat{Y}_0 - E(\hat{Y}_0)]$$
$$= -2E\varepsilon_0[\hat{Y}_0 - E(Y_0)] = 0.$$

Therefore,

$$\sigma_F^2 = \sigma^2 + \frac{\sigma^2}{n} + \sum_k (X_{0k} - \bar{X}_k)^2\,\text{Var}(\hat{\beta}_k) + 2\sum_{j<k}(X_{0j} - \bar{X}_j)(X_{0k} - \bar{X}_k)\,\text{Cov}(\hat{\beta}_j, \hat{\beta}_k), \tag{10.49}$$

or, in matrix notation,

$$\sigma_F^2 = \sigma^2\left[1 + \frac{1}{n} + (\underline{\mathbf{X}}_0 - \underline{\bar{\mathbf{X}}})'(\underline{\mathbf{X}}'\underline{\mathbf{X}})^{-1}(\underline{\mathbf{X}}_0 - \underline{\bar{\mathbf{X}}})\right]. \tag{10.49a}$$

As with the simple regression model, the shorter the distance between the given values of the explanatory variables and their respective sample means, the smaller the variance of the forecast error. An unbiased estimator of σ_F^2 can be obtained by replacing σ^2 by s^2. If we denote the resulting estimator by s_F^2, then

$$\frac{Y_0 - \hat{Y}_0}{s_F} \sim t_{n-K}. \tag{10.50}$$

From this result, we can construct a forecast interval that will contain the actual value of Y_0 with whatever probability we choose. Designating one *minus* the chosen probability level by λ $(0 < \lambda < 1)$, we have

$$\hat{Y}_0 - t_{n-K,\lambda/2}s_F \leq Y_0 \leq \hat{Y}_0 + t_{n-K,\lambda/2}s_F.$$

The expression in (10.50) can also be used to test the hypothesis that a new observation, say, $(n + 1)$th, comes from the same population as the n observations that were used for estimating the regression parameters.

EXAMPLE In the first example of this section, we estimated a regression equation describing the demand for oranges. The sample consisted of twelve observations on the quantity of oranges sold, their price, and the amount spent on advertising (see Table 10-1). The estimated regression equation is

$$\hat{Y}_i = 117.532 - 1.326X_{i2} + 11.237X_{i2},$$

where Y_i = quantity of oranges sold, X_{i2} = price, and X_{i3} = advertising expenditure. Now suppose that no oranges are sold until a new shipment arrives, which is several weeks later. Then, the record for the first day of trading shows

$$Y_0 = 100, \qquad X_{02} = 80, \qquad \text{and} \qquad X_{03} = 7.$$

The problem is to decide whether the demand function has changed since the time of the previous shipment of oranges. Here, we have

$$\hat{Y}_0 = 117.532 - 1.326 \times 80 + 11.237 \times 7 = 90.111.$$

This is the "forecast" value of Y. The estimated variance of the forecast error is

$$s_F^2 = \left[s^2 + \frac{s^2}{n} + (X_{02} - \bar{X}_2)^2 s_{\hat{\beta}_2}^2 + (X_{03} - \bar{X}_3)^2 s_{\hat{\beta}_3}^2 \right.$$
$$\left. + 2(X_{02} - \bar{X}_2)(X_{03} - \bar{X}_3)\text{Est. Cov}(\hat{\beta}_2, \hat{\beta}_3)\right].$$

Now, from the previous calculations, we have

$$s^2 = 20.586, \qquad s_{\hat{\beta}_2}^2 = 0.012476,$$
$$\bar{X}_2 = 70, \qquad s_{\hat{\beta}_3}^2 = 5.7761,$$
$$\bar{X}_3 = 6.7, \qquad \text{Est. Cov}(\hat{\beta}_2, \hat{\beta}_3) = 0.138628.$$

Therefore,

$$s_F^2 = 20.586\left[1 + \frac{1}{12} + (80 - 70)^2 \times 0.012476 + (7 - 6.7)^2 \times 5.7761\right.$$
$$\left. + 2 \times (80 - 70) \times (7 - 6.7) \times 0.138628\right]$$
$$= 75.808974,$$
$$s_F = 8.706.$$

The 95% confidence interval for Y_0 can be constructed by noting that the tabulated value of $t_{9,0.025}$ is 2.262. Therefore we have

$$90.111 - 2.262 \times 8.706 \leq Y_0 \leq 90.111 + 2.262 \times 8.706$$

or

$$70.418 \leq Y_0 \leq 109.804.$$

The observed value of Y_0 is 100, which falls well within the 95% interval.

Change in the Units of Measurement

Let us now consider the effect of *changing the units of measurement* on the previously derived results. Let

$$Y_i, X_{i2}, X_{i3}, \ldots, X_{iK}$$

denote the values of the respective variables measured in terms of some "original" units, and let

$$Y_i^*, X_{i2}^*, X_{i3}^*, \ldots, X_{iK}^*$$

denote the values of these variables in terms of some "new" units. First, we shall discuss the case

$$Y_i^* = d_Y Y_i,$$

$$X_{i2}^* = d_2 X_{i2}$$

$$X_{i3}^* = d_3 X_{i3},$$

$$\vdots$$

$$X_{iK}^* = d_K X_{iK},$$

where the d's are some known positive numbers. (Note that when for any particular variable $d = 1$, no change in the units of measurement has occurred.) This case of multiplicative changes in the units of measurement covers changes such as switching from cents to dollars ($d = 0.01$), or expressing a variable in terms of a simple index (for example, $d_k = 1/X_{1k}$). The sample means and second moments for the "starred" variables are

$$\bar{Y}^* = d_Y \bar{Y},$$

$$\bar{X}_k^* = d_k \bar{X}_k,$$

$$m_{jk}^* = \sum_i (d_j X_{ij} - d_j \bar{X}_j)(d_k X_{ik} - d_k \bar{X}_k) = d_j d_k m_{jk},$$

$$m_{Yk}^* = d_Y d_k m_{Yk},$$

$$m_{YY}^* = d_Y^2 m_{YY} \qquad (j, k = 2, 3, \ldots, K).$$

Let us see how these changes affect the values of the estimated coefficients and their standard errors. For the regression model with two explanatory variables we have, from (10.11), (10.12), and (10.13),

$$\hat{\beta}_2^* = \frac{(d_Y d_2 m_{Y2})(d_3^2 m_{33}) - (d_Y d_3 m_{Y3})(d_2 d_3 m_{23})}{(d_2^2 m_{22})(d_3^2 m_{33}) - (d_2 d_3 m_{23})^2} = \left(\frac{d_Y}{d_2}\right)\hat{\beta}_2,$$

$$\hat{\beta}_3^* = \frac{(d_Y d_3 m_{Y3})(d_2^2 m_{22}) - (d_Y d_2 m_{Y2})(d_2 d_3 m_{23})}{(d_2^2 m_{22})(d_3^2 m_{33}) - (d_2 d_3 m_{23})^2} = \left(\frac{d_Y}{d_3}\right)\hat{\beta}_3,$$

and $\qquad \hat{\beta}_1^* = d_Y \bar{Y} - \hat{\beta}_2^*(d_2 \bar{X}_2) - \hat{\beta}_3^*(d_3 \bar{X}_3) = d_Y \hat{\beta}_1.$

For the estimator of σ^2 we have, from (10.34a),

$$s^{*2} = \frac{1}{n-K}(m_{YY}^* - \hat{\beta}_2^* m_{Y2}^* - \hat{\beta}_3^* m_{Y3}^*) = d_Y^2 s^2.$$

Therefore, by reference to (10.24) and (10.25),

$$s_{\hat{\beta}_2}^{*2} = \frac{(d_Y^2 s^2)(d_3^2 m_{33})}{(d_2^2 m_{22})(d_3^2 m_{33}) - (d_2 d_3 m_{23})^2} = \left(\frac{d_Y}{d_2}\right)^2 s_{\hat{\beta}_2}^2,$$

$$s_{\hat{\beta}_3}^{*2} = \frac{(d_Y^2 s^2)(d_2^2 m_{22})}{(d_2^2 m_{22})(d_3^2 m_{33}) - (d_2 d_3 m_{23})^2} = \left(\frac{d_Y}{d_3}\right)^2 s_{\hat{\beta}_3}^2,$$

and, by reference to (10.31),

$$s_{\hat{\beta}_1}^{*2} = (d_2 \bar{X}_2)^2 \left(\frac{d_Y}{d_2}\right)^2 s_{\hat{\beta}_2}^2 + (d_3 \bar{X}_3)^2 \left(\frac{d_Y}{d_3}\right)^2 s_{\hat{\beta}_3}^2$$

$$+ 2(d_2 \bar{X}_2)(d_3 \bar{X}_3)\left[\frac{(d_Y^2 s^2)(d_2 d_3 m_{23})}{(d_2^2 m_{22})(d_3^2 m_{33}) - (d_2 d_3 m_{23})^2}\right] + \frac{d_Y^2 s^2}{n} = d_Y^2 s_{\hat{\beta}_1}^2.$$

This means that the values of the estimated regression coefficients and of their standard errors are affected by changes in the units of measurement. However, these changes do not affect the value of the t statistic, which is used for testing the hypothesis that $\beta_k = 0$ $(k = 1, 2, \ldots, K)$:

$$\frac{\hat{\beta}_k^*}{s_{\hat{\beta}_k}^*} = \frac{(d_Y/d_k)\hat{\beta}_k}{(d_Y/d_k)s_{\hat{\beta}_k}} = \frac{\hat{\beta}_k}{s_{\hat{\beta}_k}}.$$

The same is also true of the F statistic:

$$\frac{\text{SSR}^*/(K-1)}{\text{SSE}^*/(n-K)} = \left[\frac{n-K}{K-1}\right]\left[\frac{\text{SST}^* - \text{SSE}^*}{\text{SSE}^*}\right] = \left[\frac{n-K}{K-1}\right]\left[\frac{m_{YY}^* - (n-K)s^*}{(n-K)s^*}\right]$$

$$= \left[\frac{n-K}{K-1}\right]\left[\frac{(d_Y^2 m_{YY}) - (n-K)(d_Y^2 s^2)}{(n-K)(d_Y^2 s^2)}\right] = \frac{\text{SSR}/(K-1)}{\text{SSE}/(n-K)}.$$

Finally, the value of R^2 is also unchanged:

$$R^{*2} = 1 - \frac{\text{SSE}^*}{\text{SST}^*} = 1 - \frac{(n-K)d_Y^2 s^2}{d_Y^2 m_{YY}} = R^2.$$

It can be demonstrated that these results apply to regression equations with *any* number of explanatory variables as well.

EXAMPLE In an earlier example we estimated the demand equation for oranges as

$$\underset{(21.264)}{Y_i = 117.532} - \underset{(0.112)}{1.326 X_{i2}} + \underset{(2.403)}{11.237 X_{i3}} + e_i, \qquad R^2 = 0.981,$$

where Y_i = quantity in pounds, X_{i2} = price in cents, and X_{i3} = advertising expenditure in dollars. Suppose we wish to measure the price (X_{i2}) in dollars instead of cents. Then, we have

$$d_Y = 1, \qquad d_2 = 0.01, \qquad \text{and} \qquad d_3 = 1.$$

The estimated regression equation becomes

$$\underset{(21.264)}{Y_i = 117.532} - \underset{(11.2)}{132.6 X_{i2}^*} + \underset{(2.403)}{11.237 X_{i3}} + e_i, \qquad R^2 = 0.981.$$

Sometimes the change in the units of measurement is additive rather than multiplicative. This happens frequently when the variables enter into the regression equation in a logarithmic form. For instance, in the case of the Cobb-Douglas production function, the traditional model is

$$Y_i = \beta_1 + \beta_2 X_{i2} + \beta_3 X_{i3} + \varepsilon_i,$$

where Y_i = log output, X_{i2} = log labor input, and X_{i3} = log capital input. Then, if the units of measuring the labor input are changed, say, from thousands of workers to millions of workers, we have

$$X_{i2}^* = \log L_i^* = \log d_L L_i = \log d_L + \log L_i = (\log d_L) + X_{i2}.$$

In general, let

$$\begin{aligned} Y_i^* &= g_Y + Y_i, \\ X_{i2}^* &= g_2 + X_{i2}, \\ X_{i3}^* &= g_3 + X_{i3}. \\ &\vdots \\ X_{iK}^* &= g_K + X_{iK}. \end{aligned}$$

In this case,

$$\begin{aligned} \bar{Y}^* &= g_Y + \bar{Y}, \\ \bar{X}_k^* &= g_k + \bar{X}_k, \\ m_{jk}^* &= m_{jk}, \\ m_{Yk}^* &= m_{Yk}, \\ m_{YY}^* &= m_{YY} \qquad (j, k = 2, 3, \ldots, K). \end{aligned}$$

Therefore,

$$\hat{\beta}_k^* = \hat{\beta}_k \qquad \text{for } k = 2, 3, \ldots, K;$$

but

$$\begin{aligned} \hat{\beta}_1^* &= \bar{Y}^* - \hat{\beta}_2^* \bar{X}_2^* - \hat{\beta}_3^* \bar{X}_3^* - \cdots - \hat{\beta}_K^* \bar{X}_K^* \\ &= \hat{\beta}_1 + (g_Y - \hat{\beta}_2 g_2 - \hat{\beta}_3 g_3 - \cdots - \hat{\beta}_K g_K). \end{aligned}$$

That is, the estimates of the regression slopes remain unaffected but the estimate of the intercept is changed. Similarly, the estimates of the variances of $\hat{\beta}_2^*$, $\hat{\beta}_3^*, \ldots, \hat{\beta}_K^*$ remain unchanged but the estimated variance of $\hat{\beta}_1^*$ will change. The values of t statistics, of the F statistic, and of R^2 stay the same.

To sum up, the general principle concerning units of measurement is that a linear transformation of the variables in a linear regression equation does not affect the values of the essential test statistics and of R^2. The values of the estimated regression coefficients might change, but the change can easily be determined by reference to the parameters of the linear transformation.

A Note on Basic Assumptions and Data

In Chapter 8 we discussed the consequences of violating the basic assumptions of the classical normal linear regression model in the context of simple regression. The conclusions reached there hold either completely or only with simple and obvious modifications in the context of multiple regression. In particular, the remarks concerning the assumption of normal distribution and of zero mean of ε_i apply equally to the multiple regression model. With respect to heteroskedasticity, the discussion and the findings of Section 8–1 can be extended to the multiple regression case simply by allowing for more than one explanatory variable. The same is true of the results for models with autoregressive disturbances (Section 8–2) and for models with stochastic regressors (Section 8–3).

The problems of data deficiency studied in Chapter 9 also arise in multiple regression models. The derivations and the statements made in the context of simple regression models can, for the most part, be extended to multiple regression without much difficulty.

10–3 Multicollinearity

By assumption (10.8) of the classical normal linear regression model we require that none of the explanatory variables be perfectly correlated with any other explanatory variable *or* with any linear combination of other explanatory variables. When this assumption is violated, we speak of *perfect multicollinearity*. On the other hand, whenever all explanatory variables are uncorrelated with each other, we speak of *absence of multicollinearity*. The cases in between are then described by various degrees of multicollinearity. Of particular interest are cases of a *high degree of multicollinearity*, which arise whenever one explanatory variable is highly correlated with another explanatory variable *or* with a linear combination of other explanatory variables.

Before discussing multicollinearity in detail, two points should be made clear.

1. Multicollinearity is a question of degree and not of kind. The meaningful distinction is not between the presence and the absence of multicollinearity, but between its various degrees.
2. Since multicollinearity refers to the condition of the explanatory variables that are assumed to be nonstochastic, it is a feature of the sample and not of the population.[9]

Therefore, we do not "test for multicollinearity" but can, if we wish, measure its degree in any particular sample. In the discussion that follows, we will be concerned with the implication of various degrees of multicollinearity for estimation of the regression coefficients.

[9] If the explanatory variables are stochastic and there is an underlying relation among them in the population, such a relation should be specified as a part of the model. If such a relation does not exist in the population, we still may (and generally will) find *some* relation between the explanatory variables in the sample. Then again, multicollinearity is a feature of the sample, not of the population.

Absence of Multicollinearity

Let us start with the case of *no multicollinearity*, when the explanatory variables are uncorrelated with each other. In this case the matrix $(\underline{\mathbf{X}}'\underline{\mathbf{X}})$ is diagonal. In a regression model with two explanatory variables

$$Y_i = \beta_1 + \beta_2 X_{i2} + \beta_3 X_{i3} + \varepsilon_i,$$

where $m_{23} = 0$, the least squares normal equations for $\hat{\beta}_2$ and $\hat{\beta}_3$ become

$$m_{Y2} = \hat{\beta}_2 m_{22}, \qquad m_{Y3} = \hat{\beta}_3 m_{33}.$$

Therefore,

$$\hat{\beta}_2 = \frac{m_{Y2}}{m_{22}}, \qquad \hat{\beta}_3 = \frac{m_{Y3}}{m_{33}}.$$

These formulas are exactly the same as those for the *simple* regression of Y_i on X_{i2}, and of Y_i on X_{i3}.

The preceding result seems to suggest that, when X_{i2} and X_{i3} are uncorrelated, we might abandon the multiple regression model with two explanatory variables and replace it by two simple regression models

$$Y_i = \alpha_2 + \beta_2 X_{i2} + \varepsilon_i.$$

and

$$Y_i = \alpha_3 + \beta_3 X_{i3} + \varepsilon_i.$$

However, this would create difficulties. In the first place, neither one of the simple regressions will enable us to get an estimator of the regression constant β_1, although this is not so important since the least squares estimator of β_1 is simply

$$\hat{\beta}_1 = \bar{Y} - \hat{\beta}_2 \bar{X}_2 - \hat{\beta}_3 \bar{X}_3.$$

More important is that using the simple regressions for estimating the variances of $\hat{\beta}_2$ and $\hat{\beta}_3$ results in *biased* estimates. This can be seen as follows. From (10.24) we know that the variance of $\hat{\beta}_2$ is

$$\text{Var}(\hat{\beta}_2) = \frac{\sigma^2 m_{33}}{m_{22}m_{33} - m_{23}^2},$$

which for $m_{23} = 0$ becomes

$$\text{Var}(\hat{\beta}_2) = \frac{\sigma^2}{m_{22}}.$$

Now the estimator of $\text{Var}(\hat{\beta}_2)$ based on the simple regression is

$$s_{\hat{\beta}_2}^2 = \frac{s_2^2}{m_{22}},$$

where

$$s_2^2 = \frac{1}{n-2}\sum_i [(Y_i - \bar{Y}) - \hat{\beta}_2(X_{i2} - \bar{X}_2)]^2.$$

Taking the mathematical expectation of s_2^2, we get

$$E(s_2^2) = \frac{1}{n-2} E \sum_i [\beta_2(X_{i2} - \bar{X}_2) + \beta_3(X_{i3} - \bar{X}_3) + (\varepsilon_i - \bar{\varepsilon}) - \hat{\beta}_2(X_{i2} - \bar{X}_2)]^2$$

$$= \frac{1}{n-2} [m_{22}\text{Var}(\hat{\beta}_2) + \beta_3^2 m_{33} - 2m_{22}\text{Var}(\hat{\beta}_2) + (n-1)\sigma^2]$$

$$= \frac{1}{n-2} [(n-2)\sigma^2 + \beta_3^2 m_{33}],$$

so that

$$E(s_{\hat{\beta}_2}^2) = \text{Var}(\hat{\beta}_2) + \frac{\beta_3^2 m_{33}}{m_{22}(n-2)}.$$

Similarly,

$$E(s_{\hat{\beta}_3}^2) = \text{Var}(\hat{\beta}_3) + \frac{\beta_2^2 m_{22}}{m_{33}(n-2)}.$$

This means that the simple regression estimators of the variances of $\hat{\beta}_2$ and $\hat{\beta}_3$ have an upward bias. This result can be generalized to regression models with any number of mutually uncorrelated explanatory variables.

Perfect Multicollinearity

Next we turn our attention to the case of *perfect multicollinearity*. For the multiple regression model with two explanatory variables, perfect multicollinearity means that we can write

$$X_{i2} = a + bX_{i3}, \tag{10.51}$$

where a and b are some fixed numbers and $b \neq 0$. In this case, the sample coefficient of correlation between X_{i2} and X_{i3} is

$$r_{23} = \frac{\sum (a + bX_{i3} - a - b\bar{X}_3)(X_{i3} - \bar{X}_3)}{\sqrt{\sum (a + bX_{i3} - a - b\bar{X}_3)^2}\sqrt{\sum (X_{i3} - \bar{X}_3)^2}} = \frac{bm_{33}}{\sqrt{b^2 m_{33}}\sqrt{m_{33}}},$$

so that

$$r_{23}^2 = 1.$$

Consider now the least squares estimators of the regression coefficients. The least squares normal equations for the model with two explanatory variables are

$$m_{Y2} = \hat{\beta}_2 m_{22} + \hat{\beta}_3 m_{23},$$

$$m_{Y3} = \hat{\beta}_2 m_{23} + \hat{\beta}_3 m_{33}.$$

But by (10.51) we have

$$m_{Y2} = bm_{Y3},$$

$$m_{22} = b^2 m_{33},$$

$$m_{23} = bm_{33}.$$

Therefore, the least squares normal equations become

$$bm_{Y3} = b(\hat{\beta}_2 bm_{33} + \hat{\beta}_3 m_{33}),$$

$$m_{Y3} = \hat{\beta}_2 bm_{33} + \hat{\beta}_3 m_{33}.$$

This shows that the first normal equation is exactly equal to the second normal equation multiplied by b. Therefore, the two equations are not independent, and the solution for $\hat{\beta}_2$ and $\hat{\beta}_3$ is indeterminate.

Let us now consider the case of three explanatory variables to illustrate a special feature of multicollinearity that does not show up in the two-variable case. In this case the presence of perfect multicollinearity means that we can write

$$X_{i2} = a + b_3 X_{i3} + b_4 X_{i4}, \tag{10.52}$$

where a, b_3, and b_4 are some fixed numbers. Suppose both b_3 and b_4 are different from zero. The sample coefficient of correlation between X_{i2} and X_{i3} is

$$\begin{aligned} r_{23} &= \frac{m_{23}}{\sqrt{m_{22}}\sqrt{m_{33}}}, \\ &= \frac{b_3 m_{33} + b_4 m_{34}}{\sqrt{b_3^2 m_{33} + b_4^2 m_{44} + 2b_3 b_4 m_{34}}\sqrt{m_{33}}}, \\ &= \frac{b_3\sqrt{m_{33}} + b_4 r_{34}\sqrt{m_{44}}}{\sqrt{(b_3\sqrt{m_{33}} + b_4 r_{34}\sqrt{m_{44}})^2 + b_4^2 m_{44}(1 - r_{34}^2)}}, \end{aligned}$$

where r_{34} is the sample coefficient of correlation between X_{i3} and X_{i4}. Similarly, the sample coefficient of correlation between X_{i2} and X_{i4} is

$$r_{24} = \frac{b_3 r_{34}\sqrt{m_{33}} + b_4\sqrt{m_{44}}}{\sqrt{(b_3 r_{34}\sqrt{m_{33}} + b_4\sqrt{m_{44}})^2 + b_3^2 m_{33}(1 - r_{34}^2)}}.$$

These results clearly show that the presence of perfect multicollinearity does *not* necessarily mean that the correlation between any two explanatory variables must be perfect, or even particularly high, when the total number of explanatory variables is greater than two. For example, when

$$X_{i2} = X_{i3} + X_{i4},$$

$$m_{33} = m_{44},$$

and

$$r_{34} = -0.5,$$

then

$$r_{23} = \frac{1 - 0.5}{\sqrt{(1 - 0.5)^2 + (1 - 0.5^2)}} = 0.5$$

and

$$r_{24} = \frac{-0.5 + 1}{\sqrt{(-0.5 + 1)^2 + (1 - 0.5^2)}} = 0.5.$$

In this case we have perfect multicollinearity, and yet none of the correlation coefficients is greater than one half in absolute value. This is important because it means that when there are more than two explanatory variables, we cannot simply look at the coefficients of correlation and conclude that the sample is *not* perfectly (or highly) multicollinear. On the other hand, if the correlation between any one pair of explanatory variables is perfect, then there *is* perfect multicollinearity present in the sample. For perfect correlation between, say, X_{i2} and X_{i3}, implies that X_{i2} is an exact linear function of X_{i3} so that we can write

$$X_{i2} = a + b_3 X_{i3} \quad (b_3 \neq 0),$$

which is equivalent to (10.52) with $b_4 = 0$. Thus, *perfect correlation between two explanatory variables is a sufficient but not necessary condition for the presence of perfect multicollinearity* in the sample when the number of explanatory variables exceeds two.

Now let us see what happens to the least squares estimators of the regression coefficients under conditions of perfect multicollinearity when the regression model contains three explanatory variables. The least squares normal equations are

$$m_{Y2} = \hat{\beta}_2 m_{22} + \hat{\beta}_3 m_{23} + \hat{\beta}_4 m_{24},$$
$$m_{Y3} = \hat{\beta}_2 m_{23} + \hat{\beta}_3 m_{33} + \hat{\beta}_4 m_{34},$$
$$m_{Y4} = \hat{\beta}_2 m_{24} + \hat{\beta}_3 m_{34} + \hat{\beta}_4 m_{44}.$$

But from (10.52) we have

$$m_{Y2} = b_3 m_{Y3} + b_4 m_{Y4},$$
$$m_{22} = b_3^2 m_{33} + b_4^2 m_{44} + 2b_3 b_4 m_{34},$$
$$m_{23} = b_3 m_{33} + b_4 m_{34},$$
$$m_{24} = b_3 m_{34} + b_4 m_{44}.$$

Substitution of these expressions into the least squares normal equations leads to

$$b_3 m_{Y3} + b_4 m_{Y4} = \hat{\beta}_2(b_3^2 m_{33} + b_4^2 m_{44} + 2b_3 b_4 m_{34}) + \hat{\beta}_3(b_3 m_{33} + b_4 m_{34}) + \hat{\beta}_4(b_3 m_{34} + b_4 m_{44}),$$
$$m_{Y3} = \hat{\beta}_2(b_3 m_{33} + b_4 m_{34}) + \hat{\beta}_3 m_{33} + \hat{\beta}_4 m_{34},$$
$$m_{Y4} = \hat{\beta}_2(b_3 m_{34} + b_4 m_{44}) + \hat{\beta}_3 m_{34} + \hat{\beta}_4 m_{44}.$$

Thus the first normal equation is simply equal to the second normal equation multiplied by b_3 *plus* the third normal equation multiplied by b_4. Therefore, under perfect multicollinearity, the three normal equations are not independent and cannot be solved by $\hat{\beta}_2$, $\hat{\beta}_3$, and $\hat{\beta}_4$. This result can be extended to regression models with any number of explanatory variables. Since by (10.14) the vector of the least squares estimators of the regression coefficients is

$$\hat{\beta} = (\mathbf{X}'\mathbf{X})^{-1}(\mathbf{X}'\mathbf{Y}),$$

the existence of an exact linear relation between the explanatory variables means that one of the columns of $(\mathbf{X}'\mathbf{X})$ is an exact linear function of another one or more columns. Thus $(\mathbf{X}'\mathbf{X})$ is a singular matrix and its inverse does not exist.

Given that the least squares estimators of the regression coefficients are indeterminate when there is perfect multicollinearity in the sample, what else can be done? Unfortunately, not very much. When there is perfect multicollinearity, the sample simply does not give us any information about the response of the dependent variable to changes in one of the explanatory variables while "holding the remaining explanatory variables constant." The traditional suggestion has been to use information about the regression coefficients from sources other than the sample on hand. For instance, if in the model

$$Y_i = \beta_1 + \beta_2 X_{i2} + \beta_3 X_{i3} + \varepsilon_i,$$

the two explanatory variables are perfectly correlated but we know—or are willing to assume—that

$$\frac{\beta_3}{\beta_2} = k,$$

where k is a known fixed number, then estimation of the regression coefficients becomes possible. By substituting

$$\beta_3 = k\beta_2$$

into the regression model, we obtain

$$Y_i = \beta_1 + \beta_2 X_{i2} + k\beta_2 X_{i3} + \varepsilon_i$$

or

$$Y_i = \beta_1 + \beta_2 Z_i + \varepsilon_i,$$

where Z_i is measured by $(X_{i2} + kX_{i3})$. In this case, we can obtain a least squares estimator of β_1 and β_2, and infer an estimator of β_3. These estimators can be viewed as conditional upon the given value of k. If there are several values of k that appear as likely candidates, we may obtain a set of different estimators, each conditional upon a different value of k.[10]

Cases in which we know the ratio of, or have some other exact information about, two regression coefficients are relatively rare. More frequently, we may have an estimate of one or more of the regression coefficients from a different sample. For instance, we may have a sample of time-series observations to estimate a regression model, together with an unbiased estimate of one of the regression coefficients from cross-section survey data. This might be the case in the estimation of a demand function for a particular commodity as a function of price and income. If the observations are made over time, an estimate of the income

[10] In a case like this the Bayesian approach to estimation may appear particularly attractive. See, e.g., D. V. Lindley, *Introduction to Probability and Statistics from a Bayesian Viewpoint, Part 2—Inference* (Cambridge, England: The University Press, 1964), Chapter 8.

coefficient is frequently available from a cross-section sample. Suppose the regression model to be estimated is

$$Y_t = \beta_1 + \beta_2 X_{t2} + \beta_3 X_{t3} + \varepsilon_t,$$

and we have an unbiased estimator of β_3, say $\hat{\hat{\beta}}_3$, from an independent cross-section sample. Then, the regression model can be rewritten as

$$(Y_t - \hat{\hat{\beta}}_3 X_{t3}) = \beta_1 + \beta_2 X_{t2} - (\hat{\hat{\beta}}_3 - \beta_3) X_{t3} + \varepsilon_t$$

or

$$Y_t^* = \beta_1 + \beta_2 X_{t2} + u_t.$$

The least squares estimator of $\hat{\beta}_2$ becomes

$$\text{(10.53)} \qquad \hat{\beta}_2 = \frac{\sum (Y_t^* - \bar{Y}^*)(X_{t2} - \bar{X}_2)}{\sum (X_{t2} - \bar{X}_2)^2}$$

$$= \frac{\sum (Y_t - \hat{\hat{\beta}}_3 X_{t3} - \bar{Y} + \hat{\hat{\beta}}_3 \bar{X}_3)(X_{t2} - \bar{X}_2)}{\sum (X_{t2} - X_2)^2}$$

$$= \frac{m_{Y2} - \hat{\hat{\beta}}_3 m_{23}}{m_{22}}.$$

The mean and the variance of $\hat{\beta}_2$ are

$$\text{(10.54)} \qquad E(\hat{\beta}_2) = \frac{1}{m_{22}} E\Big[\beta_2 m_{22} + \beta_3 m_{23} + \sum_t (X_{t2} - \bar{X}_2)\varepsilon_t - \hat{\hat{\beta}}_3 m_{23}\Big] = \beta_2,$$

$$\text{(10.55)} \qquad \mathrm{Var}(\hat{\beta}_2) = E(\hat{\beta}_2 - \beta_2)^2$$

$$= \frac{1}{m_{22}^2} E\Big[-(\hat{\hat{\beta}}_3 - \beta_3) m_{23} + \sum_t (X_{t2} - \bar{X}_2)\varepsilon_t\Big]^2$$

$$= \frac{1}{m_{22}^2} [m_{23}^2 \mathrm{Var}(\hat{\hat{\beta}}_3) + \sigma^2 m_{22}]$$

$$= \frac{\sigma^2}{m_{22}} + \frac{m_{23}^2 \mathrm{Var}(\hat{\hat{\beta}}_3)}{m_{22}^2}.$$

Since, under perfect multicollinearity,

$$m_{23}^2 = m_{22} m_{33},$$

the variance of $\hat{\beta}_2$ becomes

$$\text{(10.56)} \qquad \mathrm{Var}(\hat{\beta}_2) = \frac{\sigma^2}{m_{22}} + \frac{m_{33} \mathrm{Var}(\hat{\hat{\beta}}_3)}{m_{22}}.$$

In empirical applications the formula for the variance of $\hat{\beta}_2$ has often been simplified by being viewed as conditional upon the given value of $\hat{\hat{\beta}}_3$, which amounts to treating $\hat{\hat{\beta}}_3$ as a fixed number.

An objection to dealing with the multicollinearity problem by obtaining information from sources other than the sample on hand is that it calls for something that should be done in any case. Normally, we suppose that in specifying the regression model and the estimation procedure we use *all* of the available information about the population. There is no reason for us to wait for the presence of perfect multicollinearity before we search for all the relevant information, except when the search is very costly. Had we exhausted all sources of information by the time we came to estimation, the proposed remedy for the multicollinearity problem would not apply. Furthermore, with respect to the use of an estimate from another sample, we might also question the wisdom of using only this information from such a sample and disregarding the rest.

High Degree of Multicollinearity

So far we have considered the two extreme cases of multicollinearity, the case of no multicollinearity and the case of perfect multicollinearity. Neither extreme is very frequent in practical applications, but most data exhibit some—though not perfect—multicollinearity. In a regression model with two explanatory variables, the relation between the explanatory variables in the sample can be described in a general way as

$$X_{i2} = a + bX_{i3} + v_i, \tag{10.57}$$

where a and b are some fixed numbers and v_i is a "residual" such that $\sum v_i = \sum v_i X_{i3} = 0$. If we define m_{vv} as

$$m_{vv} = \sum_i v_i^2,$$

then the case of $m_{vv} = 0$ represents perfect multicollinearity, and the case of $m_{vv} = m_{22}$ signifies the absence of multicollinearity. (Note that m_{22} is equal to the maximum attainable value of m_{vv}.) Both of these are special cases of (10.57). The sample coefficient of correlation between X_{i2} and X_{i3} is

$$r_{23} = \frac{\sum (a + bX_{i3} + v_i - a - b\bar{X}_3)(X_{i3} - \bar{X}_3)}{\sqrt{\sum (a + bX_{i3} + v_i - a - b\bar{X}_3)^2}\sqrt{\sum (X_{i3} - \bar{X}_3)^2}}$$

$$= \frac{bm_{33}}{\sqrt{b^2 m_{33} + m_{vv}}\sqrt{m_{33}}}$$

or

$$r_{23}^2 = \frac{b^2 m_{33}}{b^2 m_{33} + m_{vv}}.$$

When $m_{vv} = 0$, then $r_{23}^2 = 1$; and when $m_{vv} = m_{22}$ (which implies that $b = 0$), then $r_{23}^2 = 0$. Most frequently, m_{vv} will lie between these two extremes, with r_{23}^2 lying between 0 and 1. Consider now the least squares normal equations for the model with two explanatory variables. First, from (10.57) we have

$$m_{Y2} = bm_{Y3} + m_{Yv} \quad \left(\text{where } m_{Yv} = \sum_i (Y_i - \bar{Y})v_i\right),$$

$$m_{22} = b^2 m_{33} + m_{vv},$$

$$m_{23} = bm_{33}.$$

Therefore, the least squares normal equations can be written as

$$bm_{Y3} + m_{Yv} = \hat{\beta}_2(b^2m_{33} + m_{vv}) + \hat{\beta}_3 bm_{33},$$

$$m_{Y3} = \hat{\beta}_2 bm_{33} + \hat{\beta}_3 m_{33}.$$

When $m_{vv} = 0$ (and therefore $m_{Yv} = 0$), the solution for $\hat{\beta}_2$ and $\hat{\beta}_3$ becomes indeterminate; for all other values of m_{vv} a solution exists. It is easy to see that this is also true for models with more than two explanatory variables. This means that as long as there is no *perfect* multicollinearity (and $n \geq K$), we can always obtain a determinate solution for the least squares estimators of the regression coefficients, unless we run into the problem of rounding errors.

Let us now examine the connection between the degree of multicollinearity and the properties of the least squares estimators of the regression coefficients. Under the basic assumptions of the classical normal linear regression model, the least squares estimators of the regression coefficients have all the desirable properties. But, as pointed out in Section 7–4, knowing that the least squares estimators have these properties is only cold comfort to us if their variances are such that the resulting estimates are highly unreliable. That is, knowing that our estimators have the smallest possible variance (among all unbiased estimators) is not very helpful if, at the same time, this variance happens to be very large. And this is how multicollinearity comes in. Consider a regression model with two explanatory variables. According to (10.24) and (10.25) the variances of $\hat{\beta}_2$ and $\hat{\beta}_3$ are

$$\operatorname{Var}(\hat{\beta}_2) = \frac{\sigma^2 m_{33}}{m_{22}m_{33} - m_{23}^2} = \frac{\sigma^2}{m_{22}(1 - r_{23}^2)},$$

$$\operatorname{Var}(\hat{\beta}_3) = \frac{\sigma^2 m_{22}}{m_{22}m_{33} - m_{23}^2} = \frac{\sigma^2}{m_{33}(1 - r_{23}^2)},$$

and by (10.27) their covariance is

$$\operatorname{Cov}(\hat{\beta}_2, \hat{\beta}_3) = \frac{-\sigma^2 m_{23}}{m_{22}m_{33} - m_{23}^2} = \frac{-\sigma^2 r_{23}}{\sqrt{m_{22}}\sqrt{m_{33}}(1 - r_{23}^2)},$$

This shows clearly that when r_{23}^2 is close to unity, the variances and the covariance of $\hat{\beta}_2$ and $\hat{\beta}_3$ are very large. (In the case when $r_{23}^2 = 1$, they would be infinite.) Since in the case of two explanatory variables the value of r_{23}^2 indicates the degree of multicollinearity, the preceding result implies that the higher the degree of multicollinearity, the larger the variances and the covariance of $\hat{\beta}_2$ and $\hat{\beta}_3$. When there are more than two explanatory variables, the variance-covariance matrix of the least squares estimators of the regression coefficients is

$$E(\hat{\boldsymbol{\beta}} - \boldsymbol{\beta})(\hat{\boldsymbol{\beta}} - \boldsymbol{\beta})' = \sigma^2(\mathbf{X}'\mathbf{X})^{-1},$$

as given by (10.33). A high degree of multicollinearity means that in the matrix $(\mathbf{X}'\mathbf{X})$ one column is close to being a linear combination of one or more of the remaining columns. This implies that the determinant of $(\mathbf{X}'\mathbf{X})$ is numerically small so that the elements of $(\mathbf{X}'\mathbf{X})^{-1}$—and, therefore, the variances and covariances of the estimated regression coefficients—are large.

We thus conclude that a high degree of multicollinearity is harmful in the sense that the estimates of the regression coefficients are highly imprecise. The imprecision arises because of the large variances of the least squares estimators. Although these variances are not known, their estimates can be obtained by using formula (10.35a) for estimating σ^2. However, it should be noted that large variances of the estimated regression coefficients may exist even if there is no multicollinearity at all, either because the explanatory variables have a small dispersion or because σ^2 itself is large. If we want to put the blame on multicollinearity, we ought to be able to measure its degree. In the case of models with two explanatory variables, we can use the value of r_{23}^2 for this purpose, but when there are more than two explanatory variables, measurement of the degree of multicollinearity becomes more complicated. This is because, as we demonstrated earlier, the presence of a high degree of multicollinearity, or even of perfect multicollinearity, does not generally imply that the correlation between any two explanatory variables must be particularly high.

Measures of Multicollinearity

The problem of measuring multicollinearity in models with more than two explanatory variables has been attacked in a number of ways. Some research workers have used the value of the determinant of $(\mathbf{X}'\mathbf{X})$ since this is low when the degree of multicollinearity is high, and it is zero when multicollinearity is perfect. This measure has the disadvantage of not being bounded and of being affected by the dispersion of the explanatory variables in addition to their interrelation. For instance, if we used this measure for the model with two explanatory variables, we would get

$$\text{Det}\begin{bmatrix} n & \sum X_{i2} & \sum X_{i3} \\ \sum X_{i2} & \sum X_{i2}^2 & \sum X_{i2}X_{i3} \\ \sum X_{i3} & \sum X_{i2}X_{i3} & \sum X_{i3}^2 \end{bmatrix} = n(m_{22}m_{33} - m_{23}^2) = nm_{22}m_{33}(1 - r_{23}^2).$$

Thus two sets of sample data with the same number of observations and the *same value of* r_{23}^2 would give different values of the determinant if the product of m_{22} and m_{33} were not the same in the two samples.

Another measure of multicollinearity, which is built into some of the least squares regression programs for electronic computers, is defined in terms of what is called "R^2 delete." In these programs the computer calculates not only the usual R^2 for the regression equation in question, but also those R^2's that are obtained by omitting each of the explanatory variables in turn. The R^2's obtained in this way are called the "R^2 deletes." Thus, for example, for a regression equation with three explanatory variables, X_{2i}, X_{3i}, and X_{4i}, we would have three "R^2 deletes," one from regressing Y_i on X_{2i} and X_{3i}, one from regressing Y_i on X_{2i} and X_{4i}, and one from regressing Y_i on X_{3i} and X_{4i}. If there is a high degree of multicollinearity in the sample, then at least one of the explanatory variables will vary largely in accordance with the variation of some other one or more explanatory variables. The introduction of this variable into the regression equation will therefore lead to only a small increase in the value of R^2. Thus a high degree of multicollinearity will be reflected by the fact that the difference between R^2 and the highest of the "R^2 deletes" will be small.

A relatively simple measure of the degree of multicollinearity is suggested by the fact that a high degree of multicollinearity simply means that at least one of the explanatory variables can be represented as a linear function of one or more of the remaining explanatory variables *plus* a small residual. If we "regress" each of the explanatory variables on all the remaining explanatory variables, we can obtain a measure of the "goodness of fit" by calculating the value of R^2 in each case. If any one of these R^2's is close to unity, the degree of multicollinearity is high. Or, in general, the highest of these R^2's can be taken as a measure of the degree of multicollinearity present in the sample. However, this measure, as well as all the other measures we have described, suffers from the lack of a clear definition of what constitutes a "high" degree of multicollinearity. Given that *some* multicollinearity almost always exists, the question is, At what point does the degree of multicollinearity cease to be "normal" and become "harmful"? This question has not been satisfactorily resolved. According to one criterion sometimes used in practice, multicollinearity is regarded as harmful if at, say, the 5% level of significance, the value of the F statistic is significantly different from zero but none of the t statistics for the regression coefficients (other than the regression constant) is. In this case we would *reject* the hypothesis that there is no relationship between Y_i on one side and $X_{i2}, X_{i3}, \ldots, X_{iK}$ on the other side, but we would *not reject* the hypothesis that any one of the explanatory variables is irrelevant in influencing Y_i. Such a situation indicates that the separate influence of each of the explanatory variables is weak relative to their joint influence on Y_i. This is symptomatic of a high degree of multicollinearity, which prevents us from disentangling the separate influences of the explanatory variables. The disadvantage of this criterion is that it is too strong in the sense that multicollinearity is considered as harmful only when all of the influences of the explanatory variables on Y cannot be disentangled.

Let us now assume that we have a sample with a degree of multicollinearity that is definitely considered as harmful. What can be done about it? If we have used up all the prior information in specifying the model and have no information from other samples, there is not very much that we can do. Some applied research workers, faced with this problem in time-series observations, have transformed the data to first differences. That is, instead of estimating

$$Y_t = \beta_1 + \beta_2 X_{t2} + \beta_3 X_{t3} + \cdots + \beta_K X_{tK} + \varepsilon_t,$$

the least squares estimation method is applied to

$$Y_t - Y_{t-1} = \alpha + \beta_2(X_{t2} - X_{t-1,2}) + \beta_3(X_{t3} - X_{t-1,3}) + \cdots + \beta_K(X_{tK} - X_{t-1,K}) + (\varepsilon_t - \varepsilon_{t-1}).$$

Under some circumstances, this transformation may reduce the degree of multicollinearity. However, it introduces autoregression in the disturbances that are otherwise independent. As noted, autoregression has undesirable consequences for the properties of the least squares estimators. This makes working with first differences instead of the original data a dubious practice.

Since very little can be done about multicollinearity after all of the information on hand has been used, the only thing left is to increase the stock of information. One possible way of doing this is to increase the sample size. For instance, consider the variances of $\hat{\beta}_2$ and $\hat{\beta}_3$ in a model with two explanatory variables. These are

$$\text{Var}(\hat{\beta}_2) = \frac{\sigma^2}{m_{22}(1 - r_{23}^2)},$$

$$\text{Var}(\hat{\beta}_3) = \frac{\sigma^2}{m_{33}(1 - r_{23}^2)}.$$

An increase in sample size may increase m_{22} and m_{33}, or reduce r_{23}^2, or do both at the same time. The increase in m_{22} and m_{33} will occur in all cases in which the additional values of X_{i2} and X_{i3} are different from $\bar{X}_2$ and $\bar{X}_3$, as they are quite likely to be. On the other hand, it is difficult to foresee what will happen to r_{23}^2 as n increases, given that the X's are nonstochastic and not under our control. In fact, r_{23}^2 might increase to the extent that the variances of $\hat{\beta}_2$ and $\hat{\beta}_3$ actually *increase*. One way of avoiding this is to enlarge the size of the sample in such a way that m_{22} and m_{33} are *substantially* increased, for example, by combining time-series and cross-section data.

The problem of encountering a high degree of multicollinearity in the sample is frequently surrounded by a confusion in the applied literature. There is a tendency on the part of some applied research workers to point to the high degree of multicollinearity in the sample as the reason why the estimated regression coefficients are not significantly different from zero. The reader is led to believe that if the degree of multicollinearity were lower, the estimated regression coefficients would turn out to be significant. This may be so, but it certainly does not follow from the presented results. For this reason it is important to realize that a high degree of multicollinearity is simply a feature of the sample that contributes to the unreliability of the estimated coefficients, but has no relevance for the conclusions drawn as a *result* of this unreliability. If the estimated regression coefficients are highly unreliable—that is, if they have large variances—the acceptance region for the hypothesis that a given regression coefficient is zero will be wide. In turn, this means that the power of the test is weak. Thus the test is not very helpful in discriminating between true and false hypotheses. This is all that can be said regardless of the reason for the large variances in the first place.

10-4 Specification Errors

The specification of a regression model consists of a formulation of the regression equation and of statements or assumptions concerning the regressors and the disturbance term. A "specification error," in the broad sense of the term, occurs whenever the formulation of the regression equation or one of the underlying assumptions is incorrect. In a narrower sense of the term, *specification error* refers only to the errors in formulating the appropriate regression equation, and this is the interpretation adopted here. Several kinds of such errors will be considered, in particular those resulting from:

1. Omission of a relevant explanatory variable.
2. Disregard of a qualitative change in one of the explanatory variables.
3. Inclusion of an irrelevant explanatory variable.
4. Incorrect mathematical form of the regression equation.
5. Incorrect specification of the way in which the disturbance enters the regression equation.

Although we shall consider only the cases in which the explanatory variables are nonstochastic, the conclusions would remain essentially unchanged even if the explanatory variables were stochastic, providing they were independent of the regression disturbance. Our main concern will be with determining the consequences of each type of specification error for the least squares estimators of the regression coefficients and their standard errors.

Omission of a Relevant Explanatory Variable

Let us consider a specification error due to *omitting a relevant explanatory variable* from the regression equation. In particular, suppose the correct specification of the regression equation is

$$Y_i = \beta_1 + \beta_2 X_{i2} + \beta_3 X_{i3} + \varepsilon_i, \tag{10.58}$$

but we estimate

$$Y_i = \beta_1 + \beta_2 X_{i2} + \varepsilon_i^*. \tag{10.59}$$

Such an error may be committed when no observations on X_{i3} are available, or when the researcher is not aware of the fact that X_{i3} should be included in the regression equation if the maintained hypothesis is to be correctly specified. Now if (10.59) were correct, the least squares estimators of β_1 and β_2 would be unbiased and efficient for all sample sizes. Let us see what happens to these estimators given that (10.58) rather than (10.59) is the correct formulation. For $\hat{\beta}_2$ we have

$$E(\hat{\beta}_2) = E\left[\frac{\sum (X_{i2} - \bar{X}_2)(Y_i - \bar{Y})}{\sum (X_{i2} - \bar{X}_2)^2}\right].$$

But from (10.58) we know that

$$(Y_i - \bar{Y}) = \beta_2(X_{i2} - \bar{X}_2) + \beta_3(X_{i3} - \bar{X}_3) + (\varepsilon_i - \bar{\varepsilon})$$

so that

$$E(\hat{\beta}_2) = \beta_2 + \beta_3 d_{32},$$

where

$$d_{32} = \frac{\sum (X_{i2} - \bar{X}_2)(X_{i3} - \bar{X}_3)}{\sum (X_{i2} - \bar{X}_2)^2}.$$

Similarly, for $\hat{\beta}_1$ we have

$$E(\hat{\beta}_1) = E(\bar{Y} - \hat{\beta}_2\bar{X}_2) = \beta_1 + \beta_2\bar{X}_2 + \beta_3\bar{X}_3 - (\beta_2 + \beta_3 d_{32})\bar{X}_2$$
$$= \beta_1 + \beta_3 d_{31},$$

where
$$d_{31} = \bar{X}_3 - d_{32}\bar{X}_2.$$

Note that the expressions for d_{31} and d_{32} are, in fact, the formulas for the least squares coefficients of the equation

(10.60) $$X_{i3} = d_{31} + d_{32}X_{i2} + \text{residual}.$$

Since X_{i2} and X_{i3} are nonstochastic, equation (10.60) can be viewed only as a purely descriptive regression equation. In this equation the "dependent' variable is represented by the omitted variable X_{i3}, and the "explanatory" variable by the included variable X_{i2}. Given that β_3 is different from zero, the least squares estimator of β_2 based on (10.59) will be *biased* unless d_{32} equals zero, i.e., unless X_{i2} and X_{i3} are uncorrelated. If β_3 and d_{32} are both of the same sign, the bias of $\hat{\beta}_2$ will be positive; otherwise it will be negative. This means that the direction of the bias of $\hat{\beta}_2$ depends on

1. The sign of β_3.
2. The direction of the correlation between the omitted and the included explanatory variable.

If the correlation between X_{i2} and X_{i3} does not disappear as the sample size increases, i.e., if

$$\lim_{n\to\infty} d_{32} \neq 0,$$

$\hat{\beta}_2$ will also be inconsistent. Furthermore, the least squares estimator of β_1 based on (10.59) will be biased as long as

$$\bar{X}_3 - d_{32}\bar{X}_2 \neq 0,$$

and it will be inconsistent as long as

$$\lim_{n\to\infty} (\bar{X}_3 - d_{32}\bar{X}_2) \neq 0.$$

The foregoing seems to suggest that if the omitted explanatory variable is *uncorrelated* with the included explanatory variable, its omission may not lead to serious consequences for least squares estimation. Let us examine this point in detail. Suppose that X_{i2} and X_{i3} are uncorrelated; that is, suppose $d_{32} = 0$. Then $\hat{\beta}_2$ based on (10.59) is unbiased, and its variance is

$$\text{Var}(\hat{\beta}_2) = E(\hat{\beta}_2 - \beta_2)^2 = \frac{\sigma^2}{\sum (X_{i2} - \bar{X}_2)^2}.$$

The estimator of $\text{Var}(\hat{\beta}_2)$ based on (10.59) is

$$s^2_{\hat{\beta}_2} = \frac{s^2}{\sum (X_{i2} - \bar{X}_2)^2} = \frac{\sum [(Y_i - \bar{Y}) - \hat{\beta}_2(X_{i2} - \bar{X}_2)]^2/(n-2)}{\sum (X_{i2} - \bar{X}_2)^2}$$

$$= \frac{\sum [-(\hat{\beta}_2 - \beta_2)(X_{i2} - \bar{X}_2) + \beta_3(X_{i3} - \bar{X}_3) + (\varepsilon_i - \bar{\varepsilon})]^2}{(n-2)\sum (X_{i2} - \bar{X}_2)^2}.$$

The mathematical expectation of $s^2_{\hat{\beta}_2}$ is then given by

$$E(s^2_{\hat{\beta}_2}) = \frac{m_{22}\text{Var}(\hat{\beta}_2) + \beta_3^2 m_{33} - 2m_{22}\text{Var}(\hat{\beta}_2) + (n-1)\sigma^2}{(n-2)m_{22}}$$

$$= \text{Var}(\hat{\beta}_2) + \frac{\beta_3^2 m_{33}}{(n-2)m_{22}}.$$

This implies that in this case the estimator of $\text{Var}(\hat{\beta}_2)$ is positively biased. Therefore, the usual tests of significance concerning β_2 are not valid, since they will tend to accept the null hypothesis more frequently than is justified by the given level of significance. Further, the mathematical expectation of the least squares estimator of β_1 based on (10.59) is

$$E(\hat{\beta}_1) = E(\bar{Y} - \hat{\beta}_2\bar{X}_2) = \beta_1 + \beta_2\bar{X}_2 + \beta_3\bar{X}_3 - \beta_2\bar{X}_2 = \beta_1 + \beta_3\bar{X}_3,$$

which means that $\hat{\beta}_1$ is biased unless $\bar{X}_3 = 0$.

Our results concerning the least squares estimation of β_1 and β_2 on the basis of (10.59), given that (10.58) is the correct specification, can be summarized as follows: if the omitted explanatory variable is correlated with the included explanatory variable, the estimators of β_1 and β_2 will be biased and inconsistent. If the omitted explanatory variable is *not* correlated with the included variable, the estimator of β_1 will still be biased and inconsistent, at least in general, but the estimator of β_2 will be unbiased. However, the estimator of the *variance* of $\hat{\beta}_2$ will contain an upward bias, so that the usual tests of significance and confidence intervals for β_2 will tend to lead to unduly conservative conclusions.

The preceding analysis can easily be extended to the case involving a larger number of explanatory variables. Suppose the correct specification of the regression equation is

(10.61) $$Y_i = \beta_1 + \beta_2 X_{i2} + \beta_3 X_{i3} + \beta_4 X_{i4} + \varepsilon_i,$$

but we estimate

(10.62) $$Y_i = \beta_1 + \beta_2 X_{i2} + \beta_3 X_{i3} + \varepsilon_i^*.$$

The least squares estimator of β_2 based on (10.62) is

$$\hat{\beta}_2 = \frac{m_{Y2}m_{33} - m_{Y3}m_{23}}{m_{22}m_{33} - m_{23}^2}.$$

Now,

$$E(m_{Y2}) = \beta_2 m_{22} + \beta_3 m_{23} + \beta_4 m_{24},$$

$$E(m_{Y3}) = \beta_2 m_{23} + \beta_3 m_{33} + \beta_4 m_{34},$$

so that

$$E(m_{Y2}m_{33} - m_{Y3}m_{23}) = \beta_2(m_{22}m_{33} - m_{23}^2) + \beta_4(m_{24}m_{33} - m_{34}m_{23}).$$

Therefore,

$$E(\hat{\beta}_2) = \beta_2 + \beta_4 d_{42},$$

where

$$d_{42} = \frac{m_{42}m_{33} - m_{43}m_{23}}{m_{22}m_{33} - m_{23}^2}.$$

Note that the expression for d_{42} is exactly the same as the formula of the least squares coefficient of X_{i2} in the equation

$$(10.63) \qquad X_{i4} = d_{41} + d_{42}X_{i2} + d_{43}X_{i3} + \text{residual}.$$

In (10.63) the omitted explanatory variable X_{i4} is "regressed" on the two included explanatory variables X_{i2} and X_{i3}. Similarly,

$$E(\hat{\beta}_3) = \beta_3 + \beta_4 d_{43} \qquad \text{and} \qquad E(\hat{\beta}_1) = \beta_1 + \beta_4 d_{41}.$$

Thus the conclusion in this case is the same as when a smaller number of explanatory variables is involved.

EXAMPLE In a study of production functions for Indian industry, Murti and Sastry[11] use data on outputs and inputs for a sample of 320 firms, and obtain the following estimates of the Cobb-Douglas production function:

$$\log x_i = \log 0.68 + 0.53 \log n_i + 0.50 \log k_i + e_i,$$

where x = net value of output, n = wages and salaries, k = value of net assets, and the subscript i refers to the ith firm. If the "management" input varies systematically from firm to firm so that it cannot be regarded as a part of the random disturbance, the above equation is misspecified. If the management input—which, of course, is very difficult to measure—were brought into the production function in the same way as n_i and k_i, the sign of its coefficient clearly would be positive. The descriptive least squares regression linking the "management" input m_i with the two included explanatory variables n_i and k_i is

$$\log m_i = d_{41} + d_{42} \log n_i + d_{43} \log k_i + \text{residual}.$$

We can then speculate about the signs of d_{42} and d_{43}. If the firms with a high level of capital input possess a superior management input compared to the firms that are more labor-intensive, d_{42} would be negative and d_{43} positive. Under those circumstances—and in the absence of other violations of the assumptions of the classical normal linear regression model—the estimate of the coefficient of $\log n_i$ would be biased downward and that of the coefficient of $\log k_i$ would be biased upward.

Qualitative Change in Explanatory Variables

Consider now the specification error that arises as a result of a *qualitative*

[11] V. N. Murti and V. K. Sastry, "Production Functions for Indian Industry," *Econometrica*, Vol. 25, April 1957, pp. 205–221.

change in one or more of the explanatory variables as we go from one observation to another. In particular, suppose the correctly specified regression equation is

$$Y_i = \beta_1 + \beta_2 X_{i2} + \beta_3 X_{i3} + \varepsilon_i, \tag{10.64}$$

but we do not observe X_{i2} and use X_{i2}^*, which is defined as

$$X_{i2}^* = X_{i2} + Q_{i2}, \tag{10.65}$$

where Q_{i2} is a factor representing the quality change in X_{i2}^*. Suppose also that Q_{i2} is nonstochastic and that it cannot be measured. Such a situation may arise in the case of a production function where the quality of the labor input has been improving over time. Yet the theoretical concept of a production function refers to a relationship between homogeneous output and homogeneous inputs. The effect of such a change on least squares estimation can be determined as follows. Substituting for X_{i2} from (10.65) into (10.64), we obtain

$$\begin{aligned} Y_i &= \beta_1 + \beta_2(X_{i2}^* - Q_{i2}) + \beta_3 X_{i3} + \varepsilon_i \\ &= \beta_1 + \beta_2 X_{i2}^* + \beta_3 X_{i3} - \beta_2 Q_{i2} + \varepsilon_i. \end{aligned} \tag{10.66}$$

If we then estimate

$$Y_i = \beta_1 + \beta_2 X_{i2}^* + \beta_3 X_{i3} + \varepsilon_i^*, \tag{10.67}$$

instead of (10.66), we encounter the same specification error as if we left out a relevant explanatory variable. The mathematical expectations of the least squares estimators of β_1, β_2, and β_3 based on (10.67) then are

$$E(\hat{\beta}_1) = \beta_1 - \beta_2 d_{41},$$

$$E(\hat{\beta}_2) = \beta_2 - \beta_2 d_{42},$$

$$E(\hat{\beta}_3) = \beta_3 - \beta_2 d_{43},$$

where the d's are the least squares coefficients of

$$Q_{i2} = d_{41} + d_{42} X_{i2}^* + d_{43} X_{i3} + \text{residual}. \tag{10.68}$$

In the case of a production function all the β's would be positive. Furthermore, for observations in the form of a time series, d_{42} and d_{43} may be expected to be positive since all three variables in (10.68) have been growing over time, at least since the Second World War. This would imply that both $\hat{\beta}_2$ and $\hat{\beta}_3$ are biased downward. This analysis can be extended easily to the case where the number of explanatory variables is larger than two, or to the case involving a qualitative change in more than one explanatory variable.

Inclusion of an Irrelevant Explanatory Variable

Another type of specification error occurs when the set of relevant explanatory variables is enlarged by the inclusion of one or more *irrelevant variables.* (Regression equations that are formulated by including all conceivable candidates in the set of explanatory variables without much attention to the underlying theory are, for obvious reasons, sometimes called "kitchen sink models.") For instance, suppose the correctly specified regression equation is

$$Y_i = \beta_1 + \beta_2 X_{i2} + \varepsilon_i, \tag{10.69}$$

but we estimate

$$Y_i = \beta_1 + \beta_2 X_{i2} + \beta_3 X_{i3} + \varepsilon_i^*. \tag{10.70}$$

The specification error involved in using (10.70) rather than (10.69) occurs because we ignore the restriction that $\beta_3 = 0$ in formulating our maintained hypothesis. Let us see what happens to the least squares estimators of the regression coefficients if we base our estimation on (10.70). First the mathematical expectation of $\hat{\beta}_3$ is

$$E(\hat{\beta}_3) = E\left[\frac{m_{Y3}m_{22} - m_{Y2}m_{23}}{m_{22}m_{33} - m_{23}^2}\right].$$

But from (10.69) we know that

$$E(m_{Y2}) = \beta_2 m_{22} \qquad \text{and} \qquad E(m_{Y3}) = \beta_2 m_{23}$$

so that

$$E(\hat{\beta}_3) = \frac{\beta_2 m_{22} m_{23} - \beta_2 m_{22} m_{23}}{m_{22}m_{33} - m_{23}^2} = 0.$$

That is, the mean of $\hat{\beta}_3$ is equal to the true value of β_3, which is zero. The probability that in any given sample we observe a value of $\hat{\beta}_3$ that is significantly different from zero is then equal to the chosen level of significance. Next, the mathematical expectation of $\hat{\beta}_2$ is

$$E(\hat{\beta}_2) = E\left[\frac{m_{Y2}m_{33} - m_{Y3}m_{23}}{m_{22}m_{33} - m_{23}^2}\right] = \beta_2.$$

Also, $\quad E(\hat{\beta}_1) = E(\bar{Y} - \hat{\beta}_2\bar{X}_2 - \hat{\beta}_3\bar{X}_3) = (\beta_1 + \beta_2\bar{X}_2) - \beta_2\bar{X}_2 = \beta_1.$

These results show that the estimators of the coefficients of (10.70) are all unbiased. As for their variances, we have

$$\text{Var}(\hat{\beta}_2) = \frac{\sigma^2 m_{33}}{m_{22}m_{33} - m_{23}^2} = \frac{\sigma^2}{m_{22}(1 - r_{23}^2)},$$

where r_{23} is the coefficient of correlation between X_{i2} and X_{i3}. Now, if β_2 were estimated on the basis of the correctly specified regression equation (10.69), its variance, say, $\text{Var}(\hat{\beta}_2^*)$, would be equal to

$$\text{Var}(\hat{\beta}_2^*) = \frac{\sigma^2}{m_{22}}.$$

The ratio of the two variances is

$$\frac{\text{Var}(\hat{\beta}_2)}{\text{Var}(\hat{\beta}_2^*)} = \frac{1}{1 - r_{23}^2}.$$

Since $0 \leq r_{23}^2 \leq 1$, it follows that

$$\frac{\mathrm{Var}(\hat{\beta}_2)}{\mathrm{Var}(\hat{\beta}_2^*)} \geq 1,$$

where the equality holds only for $r_{23} = 0$, i.e., only if X_{i2} and X_{i3} are uncorrelated. The implication of this result is that $\hat{\beta}_2$ is generally *not efficient*. Similarly, by working through the formulas for $\mathrm{Var}(\hat{\beta}_1)$ and $\mathrm{Var}(\hat{\beta}_1^*)$—where $\hat{\beta}_1$ and $\hat{\beta}_1^*$ refer to the least squares estimators of β_1 from (10.70) and (10.69) respectively—we could show that $\hat{\beta}_1$ is also not efficient unless

$$(\bar{X}_3\sqrt{m_{22}} - \bar{X}_2 r_{23}\sqrt{m_{33}}) = 0.$$

Consider now the estimated variances of the least squares coefficients of (10.70). The formulas for $\mathrm{Var}(\hat{\beta}_1)$, $\mathrm{Var}(\hat{\beta}_2)$, and $\mathrm{Var}(\hat{\beta}_3)$ involve only one unknown parameter, σ^2, which is estimated by

$$\begin{aligned} s^2 &= \frac{1}{n-3}\sum_i [(Y_i - \bar{Y}) - \hat{\beta}_2(X_{i2} - \bar{X}_2) - \hat{\beta}_3(X_{i3} - \bar{X}_3)]^2 \\ &= \frac{1}{n-3}\sum_i [\beta_2(X_{i2} - \bar{X}_2) + (\varepsilon_i - \bar{\varepsilon}) - \hat{\beta}_2(X_{i2} - \bar{X}_2) - \hat{\beta}_3(X_{i3} - \bar{X}_3)]^2 \\ &= \frac{1}{n-3}\sum_i [-(\hat{\beta}_2 - \beta_2)(X_{i2} - \bar{X}_2) - \hat{\beta}_3(X_{i3} - \bar{X}_3) + (\varepsilon_i - \bar{\varepsilon})]^2. \end{aligned}$$

The mathematical expectation of s^2 is

$$\begin{aligned} E(s^2) = \frac{1}{n-3}\Big[&m_{22}\mathrm{Var}(\hat{\beta}_2) + m_{33}\mathrm{Var}(\hat{\beta}_3) + (n-1)\sigma^2 + 2m_{23}\mathrm{Cov}(\hat{\beta}_2, \hat{\beta}_3) \\ &- 2E(\hat{\beta}_2 - \beta_2)\sum_i (X_{i2} - \bar{X}_2)\varepsilon_i - 2E\hat{\beta}_3\sum_i (X_{i3} - \bar{X}_3)\varepsilon_i\Big]. \end{aligned}$$

But

$$\begin{aligned} &-2E(\hat{\beta}_2 - \beta_2)\sum_i (X_{i2} - \bar{X}_2)\varepsilon_i \\ &= -2E\left[\frac{m_{33}\sum(X_{i2} - \bar{X}_2)\varepsilon_i - m_{23}\sum(X_{i3} - \bar{X}_3)\varepsilon_i}{m_{22}m_{33} - m_{23}^2}\right]\sum(X_{i2} - \bar{X}_2)\varepsilon_i = -2\sigma^2, \\ &-2E\hat{\beta}_3\sum_i (X_{i3} - \bar{X}_3)\varepsilon_i \\ &= -2E\left[\frac{m_{22}\sum(X_{i3} - \bar{X}_3)\varepsilon_i - m_{23}\sum(X_{i2} - \bar{X}_2)\varepsilon_i}{m_{22}m_{33} - m_{23}^2}\right]\sum(X_{i3} - \bar{X}_3)\varepsilon_i = -2\sigma^2, \end{aligned}$$

so that

$$E(s^2) = \frac{1}{n-3}\left[\frac{\sigma^2(m_{22}m_{33} + m_{33}m_{22} - 2m_{23}^2)}{m_{22}m_{33} - m_{23}^2} + (n-1)\sigma^2 - 4\sigma^2\right] = \sigma^2.$$

This means that the estimator of σ^2 based on (10.70) is unbiased. Therefore, the estimators of $\mathrm{Var}(\hat{\beta}_1)$, $\mathrm{Var}(\hat{\beta}_2)$, and $\mathrm{Var}(\hat{\beta}_3)$ are also unbiased. This result holds whether X_{i2} and X_{i3} are correlated or not. The conclusion, then, is that if the specification error consists of including some irrelevant explanatory variables in the regression equation, the least squares estimators of the regression coefficients are unbiased but not efficient. The estimators of their variances are also unbiased, so that, in the absence of other complications, the usual tests of significance and confidence intervals for the regression parameters are valid. These results have been derived for a simple regression model, but it is not difficult to show that they apply to models with a larger number of explanatory variables as well.

Nonlinearity

Another specification error arises in the case where the correctly specified regression equation is *nonlinear* but we estimate what may be viewed as its linear approximation. Since linear relations are widely used in applied econometric research, this kind of error is likely to be committed quite often. Suppose that the correctly specified regression equation is given by

$$Y_i = f(X_i) + \varepsilon_i, \tag{10.71}$$

where $f(X_i)$ is some function of X_i. We assume that this function is continuous and possesses a continuous pth derivative, p being some positive integer. Then, with the use of Taylor's theorem[12] we can expand $f(X_i)$ around, say $\bar{X}$, and write (10.71) as

$$\begin{aligned} Y_i = f(\bar{X}) + (X_i - \bar{X})f'(\bar{X}) + \frac{(X_i - \bar{X})^2}{2!} f''(\bar{X}) \\ + \cdots + \frac{(X_i - \bar{X})^p}{p!} f^{(p)}(\bar{X}) + R_{p+1} + \varepsilon_i, \end{aligned} \tag{10.71a}$$

where

$$f(\bar{X}) = f(X_i)\Big|_{X_i = \bar{X}},$$

$$f'(\bar{X}) = \frac{df(X_i)}{dX_i}\Big|_{X_i = \bar{X}},$$

$$f''(\bar{X}) = \frac{d^2f(X_i)}{dX_i^2}\Big|_{X_i = \bar{X}},$$

$$\vdots$$

$$R_{p+1} = \text{remainder}.$$

By rearranging the terms on the right-hand side of (10.71a), we end up with

$$Y_i = \beta_1 + \beta_2 X_i + \beta_3 X_i^2 + \cdots + \varepsilon_i, \tag{10.71b}$$

where

$$\beta_1 = f(\bar{X}) - \bar{X}f'(\bar{X}) + \frac{\bar{X}^2}{2!} f''(\bar{X}) - \cdots,$$

[12] See, e.g., A. C. Chiang, *Fundamental Methods of Mathematical Economics* (New York: McGraw-Hill, 1967), pp. 256–260.

$$\beta_2 = f'(\bar{X}) - \bar{X}f''(\bar{X}) + \frac{\bar{X}^2}{2!}f'''(\bar{X}) - \cdots,$$

and so on. That is, the β's are expressions in terms of $\bar{X}$ and the parameters of $f(X_i)$ and can be regarded as parametric regression coefficients. If we then estimate a linear approximation of (10.71), i.e.,

$$(10.72) \qquad Y_i = \beta_1 + \beta_2 X_i + \varepsilon_i^*,$$

we are, in fact, omitting the relevant "explanatory variables" from the regression equation. The consequences of such an error were discussed in the early part of this section.

The preceding finding can be illustrated as follows. Suppose the correctly specified regression equation is represented by a parabolic function,

$$(10.73) \qquad Y_i = \beta_1 + \beta_2 X_i + \beta_3 X_i^2 + \varepsilon_i.$$

If we then approximate (10.73) by (10.72) and use the least squares estimation method, we can determine the properties of the resulting estimators in the same way as with (10.58) and (10.59). The specification error involved in estimating (10.72) in place of (10.73) is simply the omission of X_i^2 from the regression equation. Therefore, we have

$$E(\hat{\beta}_2) = \beta_2 + \beta_3 d_{32} \qquad \text{and} \qquad E(\hat{\beta}_1) = \beta_1 + \beta_3 d_{31},$$

where d_{31} and d_{32} represent the least squares coefficients of

$$(10.74) \qquad X_i^2 = d_{31} + d_{32} X_i + \text{residual}.$$

In general, d_{32} will be different from zero, so that the estimator of β_2 (and of β_1) will be biased and inconsistent. The magnitude of the bias will depend on the size of β_3, which determines the curvature of the correctly specified regression equation, and on the values of X in the sample.

Incorrect Specification of the Disturbance Term

For another type of misspecification, consider the situation in which the *stochastic disturbance is brought into the regression equation in an incorrect way.* In particular, let the correctly specified regression equation be

$$(10.75) \qquad Y_i = f(X_i)\varepsilon_i,$$

where ε_i follows a log-normal distribution with mean zero and variance σ^2, i.e.,

$$\log_e \varepsilon_i \sim N(0, \sigma^2).$$

Note that here we have[13]

$$E(\varepsilon_i) = e^{\sigma^2/2},$$

$$\text{Var}(\varepsilon_i) = e^{\sigma^2}(e^{\sigma^2} - 1).$$

[13] See Goldberger, *op. cit.*, p. 215.

Suppose now that instead of (10.75) we assume

$$Y_i = f(X_i) + \varepsilon_i^*. \tag{10.76}$$

Then we have

$$\varepsilon_i^* = Y_i - f(X_i) = f(X_i)\varepsilon_i - f(X_i) = f(X_i)(\varepsilon_i - 1).$$

Consequently,
$$E(\varepsilon_i^*) = f(X_i)(e^{\sigma^2/2} - 1)$$
and
$$\mathrm{Var}(\varepsilon_i^*) = [f(X_i)]^2[e^{\sigma^2}(e^{\sigma^2} - 1)].$$

This means that ε_i^* does not satisfy the assumptions of zero mean and of homoskedasticity. Also, if ε_i is log-normal, ε_i^* cannot be normally distributed. The implications for the properties of the estimators of the parameters of (10.75) can be determined in detail when the mathematical form of $f(X_i)$ is spelled out. For example, let the correctly specified regression equation be

$$Y_i = \gamma X_i \varepsilon_i, \tag{10.77}$$

with $\log_e \varepsilon_i$ satisfying all the assumptions of the classical normal regression model. Suppose that instead of (10.77), we postulate

$$Y_i = \gamma X_i + \varepsilon_i^*. \tag{10.78}$$

Then the least squares estimator of γ based on (10.78) is

$$\hat{\gamma} = \frac{\sum Y_i X_i}{\sum X_i^2} = \frac{\gamma \sum X_i^2 \varepsilon_i}{\sum X_i^2}.$$

The mathematical expectation of $\hat{\gamma}$ is

$$E(\hat{\gamma}) = \gamma e^{\sigma^2/2},$$

which means that $\hat{\gamma}$ is *biased*. Also,

$$\operatorname{plim} \hat{\gamma} = \frac{\gamma \operatorname{plim}(\sum X_i^2 \varepsilon_i)/n}{\operatorname{plim}(\sum X_i^2)/n} = \gamma e^{\sigma^2/2},$$

which means that $\hat{\gamma}$ is inconsistent.

In the preceding case we assumed that the disturbance term in the correctly specified regression equation entered in a multiplicative way, while in the misspecified regression equation the disturbance was additive. Let us now examine the reverse situation. Suppose that the correctly specified regression equation is

$$Y_i = f(X_i) + \varepsilon_i, \tag{10.79}$$

where ε_i satisfies all the assumptions of the classical normal regression model, and suppose that we incorrectly assume

$$Y_i = f(X_i)\varepsilon_i^*. \tag{10.80}$$

Then, we have

$$\varepsilon_i^* = \frac{Y_i}{f(X_i)} = 1 + \frac{\varepsilon_i}{f(X_i)}.$$

Consequently,
$$E(\varepsilon_i^*) = 1$$
and
$$\text{Var}(\varepsilon_i^*) = \frac{\sigma^2}{[f(X_i)]^2}.$$

To illustrate this case, consider that the correctly specified regression equation is of the form

$$(10.81) \qquad Y_i = \alpha X_i^\beta + \varepsilon_i,$$

but we estimate

$$(10.82) \qquad \log Y_i = \log \alpha + \beta \log X_i + \varepsilon_i^*.$$

The least squares estimator of β based on (10.82) is

$$\hat{\beta} = \frac{\sum [\log Y_i - (\sum \log Y_i)/n][\log X_i - (\sum \log X_i)/n]}{\sum [\log X_i - (\sum \log X_i)/n]^2}.$$

But from (10.81) we have

$$\log Y_i = \log (\alpha X_i^\beta + \varepsilon_i) = \log \alpha + \beta \log X_i + \log [1 + (\varepsilon_i/\alpha X_i^\beta)].$$

Therefore,

$$\hat{\beta} = \beta + \frac{\{\sum [\log X_i - (\sum \log X_i)/n] \log [1 + (\varepsilon_i/\alpha X_i^\beta)]\}/n}{\{\sum [\log X_i - (\sum \log X_i)/n]^2\}/n}.$$

With the help of Taylor's expansion, we can write[14]

$$E \log [1 + (\varepsilon_i/\alpha X_i^\beta)] = E[(\varepsilon_i/\alpha X_i^\beta) - \tfrac{1}{2}(\varepsilon_i/\alpha X_i^\beta)^2 + \tfrac{1}{3}(\varepsilon_i/\alpha X_i^\beta)^3 - \cdots]$$
$$= -[\tfrac{1}{2}E(\varepsilon_i^2)/(\alpha X_i^\beta)^2 + \tfrac{1}{4}E(\varepsilon_i^4)/(\alpha X_i^\beta)^4 + \cdots].$$

Then it follows that

$$E(\hat{\beta}) \neq \beta$$

and also

$$\text{plim } \hat{\beta} \neq \beta.$$

Thus we reach the conclusion that $\hat{\beta}$ is biased and inconsistent.

Specification Error Tests

The above examination of the consequences of committing different types of specification errors has shown that, with the exception of the case of including irrelevant explanatory variables in the regression equation, all the specification errors that we have considered lead to biasedness and inconsistency of the least squares estimators. In the case of including irrelevant explanatory variables, the least squares estimators are unbiased and consistent but not efficient. Thus it is important that we try to avoid specification errors as much as possible or, if they are unavoidable, that we at least become aware of their presence. We have mentioned two possible reasons for committing a specification error. One is that the

[14] See, e.g., T. Yamane, *Mathematics for Economists* (Englewood Cliffs, N.J.: Prentice-Hall, 1962), p. 170.

regression equation cannot be estimated in its correctly specified form because of data limitations. In such a case the preceding analysis, adapted to the problem at hand, may enable us to get at least some idea about the seriousness of the bias and its direction. The second reason for committing a specification error is our lack of knowledge as to the correct specification of the regression equation. In this case we would like to be able to *test* whether or not we have misspecified the regression equation. This is precisely how we approached the problem in connection with the assumptions about the regression disturbance in Chapter 8, where we described some of the tests for homoskedasticity and for nonautoregression. Here we consider some tests for specification errors involving inclusion of irrelevant and omission of relevant explanatory variables; tests for linearity of the regression equation will be discussed in Section 11–3.

Let us start with the problem of *testing the hypothesis that the regression equation as specified includes some irrelevant explanatory variables.* Suppose the regression equation is specified as

$$Y_i = \beta_1 + \beta_2 X_{i2} + \cdots + \beta_K X_{iK} + \beta_{K+1} X_{i,K+1} + \cdots + \beta_Q X_{iQ} + \varepsilon_i .$$

Suppose further that there exists a competing theory according to which the variables $X_{i,K+1}, X_{i,K+2}, \ldots, X_{iQ}$ are irrelevant. Then, the null hypothesis can be stated as

$$H_0\colon \quad \beta_{K+1} = \beta_{K+2} = \cdots = \beta_Q = 0,$$

and the alternative hypothesis as

$$H_A\colon \quad H_0 \text{ is not true.}$$

The appropriate test is the F test described by (10.45). This test will enable us to discriminate between the two theories. The difficulty about applying this test in practice is that our theories are often not as sharply formulated as presupposed by the test. Quite frequently we know of no unique way of classifying the explanatory variables into two groups, one containing the variables that should be included and the other the variables that are candidates for exclusion. For instance, if our regression equation is specified as

$$Y_i = \beta_1 + \beta_2 X_{i2} + \beta_3 X_{i3} + \beta_4 X_{i4} + \varepsilon_i ,$$

we may concede, as possible alternatives, regression equations that contain any one or any two of X_{i2}, X_{i3}, and X_{i4} as the explanatory variables. If all three variables are highly intercorrelated, trying out all possible regressions will not help either. What may happen is that, in regressions with more than one explanatory variable, we do *not reject* the hypotheses

$$\beta_2 = 0,$$

$$\beta_3 = 0,$$

$$\beta_4 = 0,$$

but we *do reject* the hypotheses

$$\beta_2 = \beta_3 = \beta_4 = 0,$$
$$\beta_2 = \beta_3 = 0,$$
$$\beta_2 = \beta_4 = 0,$$
$$\beta_3 = \beta_4 = 0.$$

That is, we may find that the joint variation of the X's explains a high proportion of the variation of Y, but that this joint variation cannot be disentangled to allocate credits to individual variables.

The preceding problem is difficult to resolve by the existing sample data alone. However, it may be possible to distinguish between alternative regression models by reference to their respective forecasting performances. To illustrate this, consider the following set of alternative models:

$$\text{Model 1:} \quad Y_i = \beta_1 + \beta_2 X_{i2} + \beta_3 X_{i3} + \beta_4 X_{i4} + \varepsilon_i;$$
$$\text{Model 2:} \quad Y_i = \beta_1 + \beta_2 X_{i2} + \beta_3 X_{i3} + \varepsilon_i;$$
$$\text{Model 3:} \quad Y_i = \beta_1 + \beta_2 X_{i2} + \beta_4 X_{i4} + \varepsilon_i;$$
$$\text{Model 4:} \quad Y_i = \beta_1 + \beta_3 X_{i3} + \beta_4 X_{i4} + \varepsilon_i.$$

Suppose now that we expect to observe an additional value of Y, say, Y_{n+1}, for which the appropriate values of the X's are known. Then, for each of the models we can construct the forecast interval

$$\hat{Y}_{n+1} \pm t s_F,$$

as given by (10.50). The value of Y_{n+1} will fall within the forecast interval corresponding to the correct model with a given level of probability, say, 95%. After observing Y_{n+1}, we shall find one of the following:

(1) None of the intervals contains Y_{n+1}.
(2) Y_{n+1} lies within the interval corresponding to Model 1 but not within any other interval.
(3) The outcome is different from (1) and (2).

If the outcome is that described by (1), we have to reject all the models and look for another theory. If (2) occurs, we reject Models 2, 3, and 4, and our test is completed. In case of (3), the result of the test is inconclusive. Then, we have to wait for further observations and continue testing. If the correct model is 1, the other models will be eventually eliminated. If the correct model is, say, Model 2, then Models 3 and 4 will be eventually eliminated, and the contest will be confined to Models 1 and 2. Given that Model 2 is correct, both 1 and 2 will give unbiased forecasts, but the variance of the forecast error will be greater for 1 than for 2. It should be noted, though, that if forecasts are made more than once, the appropriate test is an F test, which is described elsewhere.[15]

[15] See Johnston, *op. cit.*, pp. 137–138.

Let us now consider *testing for the specification error that involves omitting a relevant explanatory variable from the regression equation.* For instance, suppose that we have two competing models,

$$\text{Model A:} \quad Y_i = \beta_1 + \beta_2 X_{i2} + \varepsilon_i,$$

$$\text{Model B:} \quad Y_i = \beta_1 + \beta_3 X_{i3} + \varepsilon_i.$$

If Model A is correct, β_3 must be equal to zero. To carry out a test that would discriminate between these models, we can form a "general" model,

$$Y_i = \beta_1 + \beta_2 X_{i2} + \beta_3 X_{i3} + \varepsilon_i,$$

and test the hypothesis that $\beta_3 = 0$. However, if X_{i2} and X_{i3} are highly correlated, we may well find that neither $\hat{\beta}_2$ nor $\hat{\beta}_3$ is significantly different from zero, but that the joint effect of X_{i2} and X_{i3} is definitely significant. If that is the case, we may have to wait for additional observations. If there is only *one* model, the problem of testing for a specification error involving the omission of a relevant explanatory variable becomes more difficult. We can wait for additional observations and consider each one of them as potential evidence against the model. If the model is correct, the probability that a future value of Y will fall outside the forecast interval is small. The difficulty is that there may be other models—about which we do not know—whose forecast intervals may largely overlap the forecast interval of the model that we are testing. In this case it may take many additional observations before our model is rejected even if it is incorrect.

There is an obvious disadvantage to waiting for additional observations before making a pronouncement concerning the presence of specification errors. An alternative approach involves reliance on the fact that, if the model is correctly specified, the regression disturbances (and, therefore, the residuals that represent their sample counterparts) have to exhibit certain properties. In particular, if we omit some relevant explanatory variables from the regression equation, the mean of the disturbance will no longer be equal to zero and its variance will no longer be constant. We can test for this kind of specification error by examining the behavior of the regression residuals. Several such tests have been developed recently by J. B. Ramsey and can be used in this context.[16] These tests require a somewhat involved description, which will not be presented here, but they are very useful and represent an important advance in dealing with the problem of specification errors.

EXERCISES

10–1. Consider the following multiple regression equation:

$$Y_i = \beta_1 + \beta_2 X_{i2} + \beta_3 X_{i3} + \cdots + \beta_K X_{iK} + \beta_{K+1} X_{i,K+1} + \cdots + \beta_Q X_{iQ} + \varepsilon_i.$$

[16] See James B. Ramsey, "Tests for Specification Errors, in Classical Linear Least Squares Regression Analysis," *Journal of the Royal Statistical Society*, Series B, Vol. 31, 1969, pp. 350–371.

Prove that

a. $\text{SSR}_Q \geq \text{SSR}_K$.

b. $R_Q^2 \geq R_K^2$.

10–2. Given the definitions of $\underline{\hat{\boldsymbol{\beta}}}$, $\underline{\mathbf{X}}$, and $\underline{\mathbf{Y}}$ as stated in connection with (10.15), prove that

a. $\underline{\hat{\boldsymbol{\beta}}} = (\underline{\mathbf{X}}'\underline{\mathbf{X}})^{-1}(\underline{\mathbf{X}}'\underline{\mathbf{Y}})$.

b. $\text{Var}(\underline{\hat{\boldsymbol{\beta}}}) = \sigma^2(\underline{\mathbf{X}}'\underline{\mathbf{X}})^{-1}$.

c. $\underline{\mathbf{Y}}'\underline{\mathbf{Y}} = \mathbf{Y}'\mathbf{Y} - \left(\sum_t Y_t\right)^2 / n$.

10–3. Given the least squares estimates

$$Y_t = 5 + \underset{(1)}{3X_{t1}} + \underset{(2)}{10X_{t2}} + e_t \qquad (n = 100),$$

and given that the sample coefficient of correlation between the two explanatory variables is 0.5, find the value of R^2.

10–4. Consider $\mathbf{Y} = \mathbf{X}\boldsymbol{\beta} + \boldsymbol{\epsilon}$ with K (the number of explanatory variables including the constant) equal to two. Show, by writing out all matrices in full, that the least squares formulas for the multiple regression model give the same answer as the formulas for the simple regression model developed in Section 7–3 without the use of matrix algebra.

10–5. It has been suggested that corporate investment behavior can be described by the relationship

$$I_t = \beta_1 + \beta_2 F_{t-1} + \beta_3 K_{t-1} + \varepsilon_t,$$

where I_t = current gross investment, F_{t-1} = end-of-period value of outstanding shares, and K_{t-1} = end-of-period capital stock. From the data for General Motors Corporation given in Table 10–2:

a. Obtain least squares estimates of the regression coefficients and their estimated standard errors.

b. Calculate the value of R^2 and test for the existence of a relationship.

c. The values of F_{t-1} and K_{t-1} for the year 1954 are 5593.6 and 2226.3, respectively. What is the forecast value of I_{1954} and its 95% forecast interval? (The actual value of I_{1954} was 1486.7.)

10–6. For the regression model

$$Y_i = \beta_1 + \beta_2 X_{i2} + \beta_3 X_{i3} + \varepsilon_i,$$

derive the formula for the best-linear-unbiased estimator of β_1 and its variance.

10–7. Consider a regression model with three explanatory variables, i.e., with $K = 4$. Derive the expression for the F statistic,

$$F_{3,\,n-4} = \frac{\text{SSR}/3}{\text{SSE}/(n-4)}$$

in terms of the t statistics.

Table 10–2*

Year	I_t	F_{t-1}	K_{t-1}
1935	317.6	3078.5	2.8
1936	391.8	4661.7	52.6
1937	410.6	5387.1	156.9
1938	257.7	2792.2	209.2
1939	330.8	4313.2	203.4
1940	461.2	4643.9	207.2
1941	512.0	4551.2	255.2
1942	448.0	3244.1	303.7
1943	499.6	4053.7	264.1
1944	547.5	4379.3	201.6
1945	561.2	4840.9	265.0
1946	688.1	4900.9	402.2
1947	568.9	3526.5	761.5
1948	529.2	3254.7	922.4
1949	555.1	3700.2	1020.1
1950	642.9	3755.6	1099.0
1951	755.9	4833.0	1207.7
1952	891.2	4924.9	1430.5
1953	1304.4	6241.7	1777.3

Source: J. C. G. Boot and G. M. deWitt, "Investment Demand: An Empirical Contribution to the Aggregation Problem," *International Economic Review*, Vol. 1, January 1960, pp. 3–30.

* All values (in millions of dollars) are deflated by appropriate price indexes.

10–8. Suppose a correctly specified regression model is given as

$$Y_t = \alpha + \beta X_t + \varepsilon_t.$$

All assumptions of the classical normal linear regression model are satisfied. Now suppose that we do not have observations on X, and that in its place we use as a "proxy" some other nonstochastic variable Z; i.e., we estimate

$$Y_t = \alpha + \beta Z_t + \varepsilon_t^*.$$

a. What are the properties of the resulting least squares estimates of α and β, and of their estimated variances?

b. Does the replacement of X_t by Z_t affect the validity of the standard test of the hypothesis that $\beta = 0$? Would it make any difference if Z_t were not a "good proxy" for X_t, that is, if X_t and Z_t were not highly correlated?

10–9. Let E_i = total weekly planned expenditure of the ith household, X_{ig} = expenditure of the ith household on the gth commodity, and N_i = number of persons in the ith household. The variable N_i is nonstochastic. Consider the following model:

$$X_{ig} = \alpha_g + \beta_g E_i + \gamma_g N_i + u_{ig} \quad (i = 1, 2, \ldots, n;\ g = 1, 2, \ldots, G;\ n > G).$$

Further,

$$E_i = \sum_{g=1}^{G} X_{ig} + v_i,$$

$$v_i = -\sum_{g=1}^{G} u_{ig}.$$

We assume that

$$E(u_{ig}) = 0,$$

$$E(\mathbf{u_g u_g'}) = \sigma_{gg}\mathbf{I_n},$$

$$E(\mathbf{u_g u_h'}) = \mathbf{0} \quad (g \neq h),$$

where

$$\mathbf{u_g'} = [u_{1g} \quad u_{2g} \quad \dots \quad u_{ng}].$$

Suppose we have obtained observations on E_i and X_{ig} and have fitted the following equation by the ordinary least squares method:

$$X_{ig} = a_g + b_g E_i + e_{ig}, \quad g = 1, 2, \dots, G.$$

a. Under what conditions, if any, will b_g be an unbiased estimate of β_g?

b. Under what conditions, if any, will α_g be an unbiased estimate of α_g?

11 Formulation and Estimation of Special Models

Multiple regression, because of its flexibility, is a suitable analytical tool for problems of statistical inference under conditions in which the imposition of prior knowledge about the regression equation leads to a departure from the standard linear regression model. In this chapter we consider four types of departures. Section 11–1 deals with the formulation and estimation of relationships that involve qualitative or binary variables. Included here are the well-known statistical techniques of "analysis of variance" and "analysis of covariance," both of which can be regarded as regression models with qualitative explanatory variables. In Section 11–2 we take up the problem of incorporating various prior restrictions on the coefficients of a linear relationship when carrying out the estimation. Section 11–3 contains description of some nonlinear models and deals with the problems of estimation and of testing for linearity. Finally, in Section 11–4 we examine models in which the response of the dependent variable to changes in the explanatory variables may be delayed. These models, which are known as "distributed lag models," have recently assumed an important place in many areas of applied economic research.

11–1 Models with Binary Variables

Some phenomena that we observe cannot be measured but only counted. This is true of all qualitative characteristics of objects, people, time periods, etc. Our observation then consists of noting whether the given characteristic is or is not present. For instance, when the unit of observation is an adult man, we may note whether he is or is not a house owner, whether he has or has not a college degree, whether he does or does not smoke, or anything else that is relevant to the problem at hand. Since we can assign a value of 1 to the presence, and 0 to the absence of the attribute in question, we may view it as a variable that is restricted to two values. (Of course, it is not necessary that the two values be 0 and 1. We may, if we wish, choose any other two values to represent the presence and the absence of the given attribute. For obvious reasons, 0 and 1 are chosen most commonly.) Such a variable is then called a "binary" or a "dummy" variable. We will discuss the problem of formulating and estimating models in which qualitative variables appear on either side of the regression equation, starting with simple models and progressing to more complex ones.

Single Qualitative Explanatory Variable

A simple regression model in which the explanatory variable is represented by a binary variable can be illustrated by the salaries offered to economics graduate students entering the academic labor market. Assume that these salaries are normally distributed with variance σ^2 and mean equal to μ_1 for candidates who have already received their Ph.D., and μ_0 for those who have not. This situation can be described by a regression model, with salary as the dependent variable and degree qualification as the explanatory variable. Formally,

$$Y_i = \alpha + \beta X_i + \varepsilon_i, \tag{11.1}$$

where Y_i is the salary of the ith candidate, and X_i is a binary variable such that

$$\begin{aligned} X_i &= 1 \quad \text{if the candidate has a Ph.D.,} \\ &= 0 \quad \text{otherwise.} \end{aligned}$$

The disturbance ε_i is a random variable that satisfies all the basic assumptions of the classical normal linear regression model. The mean values of Y_i corresponding to the two values of X_i are

$$E(Y_i \mid X_i = 0) = \alpha,$$

$$E(Y_i \mid X_i = 1) = \alpha + \beta.$$

Therefore,

$$\alpha = \mu_0,$$

and

$$\alpha + \beta = \mu_1,$$

or

$$\beta = \mu_1 - \mu_0.$$

This means that the intercept of the population regression line (11.1) measures the mean salary of a non-Ph.D., and the slope measures the difference between the mean salary of a Ph.D. and that of a non-Ph.D. A test of the hypothesis that β is zero is then equivalent to the test that there is no difference between the mean salary of a Ph.D. and that of a non-Ph.D.

The coefficients of the regression equation (11.1) can be estimated by the method of the least squares. Under the assumptions of the classical normal linear regression model, the resulting estimates will have all the desirable properties. Recall that the formulas for the least squares estimators are

$$\hat{\beta} = \frac{\sum (X_i - \bar{X})(Y_i - \bar{Y})}{\sum (X_i - \bar{X})^2},$$

$$\hat{\alpha} = \bar{Y} - \hat{\beta}\bar{X}.$$

Let n_1 = number of candidates with a Ph.D. in the sample,

n_0 = number of candidates without a Ph.D. in the sample,

$\bar{Y}_1$ = sample mean salary of a candidate with a Ph.D.,

$\bar{Y}_0$ = sample mean salary of a candidate without a Ph.D.

Then

$$\sum_{i=1}^{n} X_i = n_1,$$

$$\sum_{i=1}^{n} X_i^2 = n_1,$$

$$\sum_{i=1}^{n} Y_i = n_1 \bar{Y}_1 + n_0 \bar{Y}_0,$$

$$\sum_{i=1}^{n} X_i Y_i = n_1 \bar{Y}_1.$$

Therefore,

$$\sum_i (X_i - \bar{X})(Y_i - \bar{Y}) = \sum_i X_i Y_i - \frac{1}{n}\Big(\sum_i X_i\Big)\Big(\sum_i Y_i\Big)$$

$$= n_1 \bar{Y}_1 - \frac{n_1}{n}(n_1 \bar{Y}_1 + n_0 \bar{Y}_0) = \frac{n_0 n_1}{n}(\bar{Y}_1 - \bar{Y}_0)$$

and

$$\sum_i (X_i - \bar{X})^2 = \sum_i X_i^2 - \frac{1}{n}\Big(\sum_i X_i\Big)^2 = n_1 - \frac{n_1^2}{n} = \frac{n_0 n_1}{n}.$$

This gives

$$\hat{\beta} = \frac{(n_0 n_1/n)(\bar{Y}_1 - \bar{Y}_0)}{n_0 n_1/n} = \bar{Y}_1 - \bar{Y}_0$$

and

$$\hat{\alpha} = \frac{1}{n}(n_1 \bar{Y}_1 + n_0 \bar{Y}_0) - (\bar{Y}_1 - \bar{Y}_0)\frac{n_1}{n} = \bar{Y}_0.$$

Thus the least squares estimator of the regression slope is equal to the difference between the sample mean salary of a Ph.D. and that of a non-Ph.D., and the least squares estimator of the regression intercept is equal to the sample mean salary of a non-Ph.D. The t test of the hypothesis that β is equal to zero described in (7.46) is in this case exactly the same as the t test of the hypothesis that two population means are equal. The latter is derived from (5.2). (The test statistic $\hat{\beta}/s_{\hat{\beta}}$ is the same as the test statistic in (5.2), after replacing σ_1^2 and σ_2^2 by s^2.)

In the preceding illustration the characteristic represented by the explanatory variable was dichotomous; i.e., only two possibilities were considered as relevant. But we can handle equally well models in which the explanatory characteristic is polychotomous. The only consequence of this complication is that we need more than one binary variable to describe such a characteristic. For instance, suppose the starting salaries of the high school teachers of English are normally distributed with variance σ^2, the mean depending on whether the highest degree attained by the candidate is a B.A., an M.A., or a Ph.D. Let the mean starting salary for a B.A. be equal to μ_A; that for an M.A., μ_B; and that for a Ph.D., μ_C. The appropriate regression equation can be represented by

$$Y_i = \beta_1 + \beta_2 X_{i2} + \beta_3 X_{i3} + \varepsilon_i, \tag{11.2}$$

where Y_i is the salary of the ith candidate, and

$$\begin{aligned} X_{i2} &= 1 \quad \text{if the highest degree of the candidate is a Ph.D.,} \\ &= 0 \quad \text{otherwise;} \\ X_{i3} &= 1 \quad \text{if the highest degree of the candidate is an M.A.,} \\ &= 0 \quad \text{otherwise.} \end{aligned}$$

Note that when $X_{i2} = 1$, X_{i3} must be equal to zero, and vice versa. The mean values of Y_i corresponding to different values of the regressors are

$$\begin{aligned} E(Y_i \mid X_{i2} = 1, X_{i3} = 0) &= \beta_1 + \beta_2, \\ E(Y_i \mid X_{i2} = 0, X_{i3} = 1) &= \beta_1 + \beta_3, \\ E(Y_i \mid X_{i2} = 0, X_{i3} = 0) &= \beta_1. \end{aligned}$$

It follows then that

$$\begin{aligned} \beta_1 &= \mu_A, \\ \beta_2 &= \mu_C - \mu_A, \\ \beta_3 &= \mu_B - \mu_A. \end{aligned}$$

This result is analogous to that obtained for the dichotomous classification of (11.1).

Note that the trichotomy in the preceding model is represented by *two* binary variables, each assuming a value of 0 or 1. It would be incorrect to use *one* variable with three values, say, 0 for a B.A., 1 for an M.A., and 2 for a Ph.D. If we did that and formed the regression model as

$$Y_i = \alpha + \beta W_i + \varepsilon_i,$$

where W_i is the explanatory variable with values 0, 1, and 2, we would have

$$\begin{aligned} E(Y_i \mid W_i = 0) &= \alpha, \\ E(Y_i \mid W_i = 1) &= \alpha + \beta, \\ E(Y_i \mid W_i = 2) &= \alpha + 2\beta. \end{aligned}$$

However, this implies that the difference between the mean salary of an M.A. and a B.A. is

$$(\alpha + \beta) - \alpha = \beta,$$

and the difference between the mean salary of a Ph.D. and an M.A. is

$$(\alpha + 2\beta) - (\alpha + \beta) = \beta.$$

That is, by using one variable with values 0, 1, and 2 (or any three equidistant values) we are, in fact, assuming that the difference between the salary of a Ph.D. and an M.A. is the same as that between the salary of an M.A. and a B.A. Unless we know a priori that this is the case, we are not justified in making such an assumption.

Note also that we cannot represent the trichotomy by three rather than by two binary variables (unless we drop the constant term in the regression equation). For if we did and formed the regression model as

$$Y_i = \beta_1 + \beta_2 X_{i2} + \beta_3 X_{i3} + \beta_4 X_{i4} + \varepsilon_i,$$

where X_{i2} and X_{i3} are defined as before and

$$X_{i4} = 1 \quad \text{if the highest degree of the candidate is a B.A.,}$$
$$= 0 \quad \text{otherwise,}$$

the solution for $\hat{\beta}_1$, $\hat{\beta}_2$, $\hat{\beta}_3$, and $\hat{\beta}_4$ would be indeterminate. The reason is that

$$X_{i4} = 1 - X_{i2} - X_{i3}$$

and the least squares normal equations are not independent, or (what amounts to the same thing) $\mathbf{X'X}$ is a singular matrix. This holds quite generally: when the explanatory characteristic leads to a classification into G types, we use $(G - 1)$ binary variables for its representation.

Models with a single qualitative variable have been traditionally formulated in statistical texts as "one-way analysis of variance" models rather than as regression models with binary regressors. The two approaches are equivalent in the sense that they describe the same phenomenon and lead to the same test results about it. Consider a normally distributed random variable Y whose mean depends on a given polychotomous characteristic that leads to a classification into G types. The variance of Y is constant, and the observations are assumed to be independent. By the "analysis of variance" approach we divide all of the observed values of Y into G groups according to the given characteristic, and formulate the model as

$$(11.3) \qquad Y_{tg} = \mu + \alpha_g + \varepsilon_{tg} \qquad (t = 1, 2, \ldots, n_g;\ g = 1, 2, \ldots, G).$$

Here Y_{tg} is the tth observation on Y in the gth group, μ is the "grand mean," α_g is the deviation of the mean of the gth group from μ, and ε_{tg} is a stochastic disturbance. Note that

$$\sum_{g=1}^{G} \alpha_g = 0.$$

Let us now compare the "analysis of variance" model with the corresponding regression model. The latter is given by

(11.4) $$Y_{tg} = \beta_1 + \beta_2 X_{t2} + \beta_3 X_{t3} + \cdots + \beta_G X_{tG} + \varepsilon_{tg},$$

where $X_{tg} = 1$ if the observation belongs to the gth group,

$= 0$ otherwise $\quad (g = 2, 3, \ldots, G)$.

To specify the coefficients of (11.4) in terms of the parameters of (11.3) and vice versa, we compare the two formulations for each group separately (Table 11–1).

Table 11–1

Group	Analysis of Variance Model	Regression Model
1	$E(Y_{t1}) = \mu + \alpha_1$	$E(Y_{t1}) = \beta_1$
2	$E(Y_{t2}) = \mu + \alpha_2$	$E(Y_{t2}) = \beta_1 + \beta_2$
$\vdots$	$\vdots$	$\vdots$
G	$E(Y_{tG}) = \mu + \alpha_G$	$E(Y_{tG}) = \beta_1 + \beta_G$

That is,

$$\mu + \alpha_1 = \beta_1,$$
$$\mu + \alpha_2 = \beta_1 + \beta_2,$$
$$\vdots$$
$$\mu + \alpha_G = \beta_1 + \beta_G,$$

or

$$\mu = \beta_1 + \frac{1}{G}(\beta_2 + \beta_3 + \cdots + \beta_G),$$
$$\alpha_1 = -\frac{1}{G}(\beta_2 + \beta_3 + \cdots + \beta_G),$$
$$\alpha_2 = \beta_2 - \frac{1}{G}(\beta_2 + \beta_3 + \cdots + \beta_G),$$
$$\vdots$$
$$\alpha_G = \beta_G - \frac{1}{G}(\beta_2 + \beta_3 + \cdots + \beta_G).$$

The hypothesis, tested with the help of the analysis of variance model, is that there is no difference between the group means; i.e.,

$$H_0: \quad \alpha_1 = \alpha_2 = \cdots = \alpha_G = 0,$$
$$H_A: \quad H_0 \text{ is not true.}$$

It is easy to see that this null hypothesis is exactly equivalent to the hypothesis that the slopes of the regression equation (11.4) are jointly equal to zero; that is,

$$H_0: \quad \beta_2 = \beta_3 = \cdots = \beta_G = 0,$$

$$H_A: \quad H_0 \text{ is not true.}$$

As we have shown earlier, to carry out a test of H_0 within the framework of the regression model, we use the F test described by (10.43). This is equivalent to the F test for the analysis of variance models that is traditionally given in the textbooks on statistics.[1] The regression model can also be used for testing the hypothesis that any one of the β coefficients is singly equal to zero, but the analysis of variance model is not readily suited for such a test.

Several Qualitative Explanatory Variables

Let us now extend the formulation of the regression models with qualitative explanatory variables to take into account more than one characteristic. Consider the following modification of the earlier example on the salaries of high school English teachers. Suppose the mean salary depends not only on the highest degree attained by the candidate, but also on whether the high school making the offer is public or private. The difference between the mean salaries in the public and the private school systems is presumed to be the same whatever the degree qualification. Again, we assume that salaries are normally distributed with variance σ^2 and that the observations are independent. Let

μ_{A0} = mean salary for a B.A. in a private school;

μ_{A1} = mean salary for a B.A. in a public school;

μ_{B0} = mean salary for an M.A. in a private school;

μ_{B1} = mean salary for an M.A. in a public school;

μ_{C0} = mean salary for a Ph.D. in a private school;

μ_{C1} = mean salary for a Ph.D. in a public school.

Then a regression model can be formulated as

$$Y_i = \beta_1 + \beta_2 X_{i2} + \beta_3 X_{i3} + \gamma Z_i + \varepsilon_i, \tag{11.5}$$

where Y_i, X_{i2} and X_{i3} are defined as in (11.2), and

$Z_i = 1$ if the school to which the ith candidate is applying is a public school,

$= 0$ otherwise.

[1] See, e.g., J. E. Freund, *Mathematical Statistics* (Englewood Cliffs, N.J.: Prentice-Hall, 1962), p. 335, formula (14.2.5).

Note again that when $X_{i2} = 1$, X_{i3} must be equal to zero. The mean values of Y_i corresponding to different values of the regressors are

$$E(Y_i \mid X_{i2} = 1, X_{i3} = 0, Z_i = 1) = \beta_1 + \beta_2 + \gamma,$$

$$E(Y_i \mid X_{i2} = 0, X_{i3} = 1, Z_i = 1) = \beta_1 + \beta_3 + \gamma,$$

$$E(Y_i \mid X_{i2} = 0, X_{i3} = 0, Z_i = 1) = \beta_1 + \gamma,$$

$$E(Y_i \mid X_{i2} = 1, X_{i3} = 0, Z_i = 0) = \beta_1 + \beta_2,$$

$$E(Y_i \mid X_{i2} = 0, X_{i3} = 1, Z_i = 0) = \beta_1 + \beta_3,$$

$$E(Y_i \mid X_{i2} = 0, X_{i3} = 0, Z_i = 0) = \beta_1.$$

From this it follows that

$$\beta_1 = \mu_{A0},$$

$$\beta_2 = \mu_{C0} - \mu_{A0} = \mu_{C1} - \mu_{A1},$$

$$\beta_3 = \mu_{B0} - \mu_{A0} = \mu_{B1} - \mu_{A1},$$

$$\gamma = \mu_{A1} - \mu_{A0} = \mu_{B1} - \mu_{B0} = \mu_{C1} - \mu_{C0}.$$

That is, β_1 measures the mean salary of a B.A. in a private high school, β_2 measures the difference between the mean salary of a Ph.D. and a B.A. (which is presumed to be the same in both school systems), β_3 measures the difference between the mean salary of an M.A. and a B.A. (also the same in both school systems), and γ represents the difference between the mean salaries in the public and the private schools.

The preceding regression model is represented in statistical texts as a "two-way analysis of variance" model. The two approaches are again equivalent. Consider a random variable Y with values that can be classified according to two criteria, one criterion leading to a classification into G groups and the other to a classification into H groups. The observations on Y can then be arranged in the form of a two-way classification table with G columns and H rows. In this table each cell contains all observations belonging to the appropriate row and column. (The "analysis of variance" model usually assumes an equal number of observations per cell. This assumption is not needed for the regression formulation.) The two-way analysis of variance model is formulated as

$$(11.6) \qquad Y_{tgh} = \mu + \alpha_g + \lambda_h + \varepsilon_{tgh}$$

$$(t = 1, 2, \ldots, n_{gh};\ g = 1, 2, \ldots, G;\ h = 1, 2, \ldots, H).$$

Here Y_{tgh} is the tth observation on Y in the gth column and hth row, μ is the "grand mean," α_g is the deviation of the mean of the gth column from μ, λ_h is the deviation of the mean of the hth row from μ, and ε_{tgh} is a stochastic disturbance. Note that

$$\sum_{g=1}^{G} \alpha_g = 0, \qquad \sum_{h=1}^{H} \lambda_h = 0.$$

We may compare this formulation with the corresponding regression model:

$$(11.7)\qquad Y_{tgh} = \beta_1 + \beta_2 X_{t2} + \beta_3 X_{t3} + \cdots + \beta_G X_{tG} + \gamma_2 Z_{t2} + \gamma_3 Z_{t3} + \cdots + \gamma_H Z_{tH} + \varepsilon_{tgh},$$

where

$$X_{tg} = 1 \quad \text{if the observation belongs to the } g\text{th column,}$$
$$= 0 \quad \text{otherwise} \quad (g = 2, 3, \ldots, G);$$
$$Z_{th} = 1 \quad \text{if the observation belongs to the } h\text{th row,}$$
$$= 0 \quad \text{otherwise} \quad (h = 2, 3, \ldots, H).$$

To determine the relationship between the coefficients of (11.6) and the parameters of (11.7), we compare the means of Y for each cell, as shown in Table 11-2.

Table 11-2

Column	Row	Analysis of Variance Model	Regression Model
1	1	$E(Y_{t11}) = \mu + \alpha_1 + \lambda_1$	$E(Y_{t11}) = \beta_1$
1	2	$E(Y_{t12}) = \mu + \alpha_1 + \lambda_2$	$E(Y_{t12}) = \beta_1 + \gamma_2$
$\vdots$	$\vdots$	$\vdots$	$\vdots$
1	H	$E(Y_{t1H}) = \mu + \alpha_1 + \lambda_H$	$E(Y_{t1H}) = \beta_1 + \gamma_H$
2	1	$E(Y_{t21}) = \mu + \alpha_2 + \lambda_1$	$E(Y_{t21}) = \beta_1 + \beta_2$
2	2	$E(Y_{t22}) = \mu + \alpha_2 + \lambda_2$	$E(Y_{t22}) = \beta_1 + \beta_2 + \gamma_2$
$\vdots$	$\vdots$	$\vdots$	$\vdots$
G	H	$E(Y_{tGH}) = \mu + \alpha_G + \lambda_H$	$E(Y_{tGH}) = \beta_1 + \beta_G + \gamma_H$

From this, we find that

$$\mu = \beta_1 + \frac{1}{G}(\beta_2 + \beta_3 + \cdots + \beta_G) + \frac{1}{H}(\gamma_2 + \gamma_3 + \cdots + \gamma_H),$$

$$\alpha_1 = -\frac{1}{G}(\beta_2 + \beta_3 + \cdots + \beta_G),$$

$$\alpha_2 = \beta_2 - \frac{1}{G}(\beta_2 + \beta_3 + \cdots + \beta_G),$$

$$\vdots$$

$$\alpha_G = \beta_G - \frac{1}{G}(\beta_2 + \beta_3 + \cdots + \beta_G),$$

$$\lambda_1 = -\frac{1}{H}(\gamma_2 + \gamma_3 + \cdots + \gamma_H),$$

$$\lambda_2 = \gamma_2 - \frac{1}{H}(\gamma_2 + \gamma_3 + \cdots + \gamma_H),$$

$$\vdots$$

$$\lambda_H = \gamma_H - \frac{1}{H}(\gamma_2 + \gamma_3 + \cdots + \gamma_H).$$

The two-way analysis of variance model is used for testing the hypotheses

$$H_0: \quad \alpha_1 = \alpha_2 = \cdots = \alpha_G = 0$$

and

$$H_0: \quad \lambda_1 = \lambda_2 = \cdots = \lambda_H = 0.$$

These hypotheses have their exact counterparts in terms of the coefficients of the regression model (11.7). The first hypothesis is equivalent to the hypothesis that $\beta_2, \beta_3, \ldots, \beta_G$ are jointly equal to zero; i.e.,

$$H_0: \quad \beta_2 = \beta_3 = \cdots = \beta_G = 0.$$

The second hypothesis is equivalent to the hypothesis that $\gamma_2, \gamma_3, \ldots, \gamma_H$ are jointly equal to zero; i.e.,

$$H_0: \quad \gamma_2 = \gamma_3 = \cdots = \gamma_H = 0.$$

The appropriate test for these hypotheses is the F test described by (10.45). This test is equivalent to the F test for the analysis of variance models given in the statistical texts. The models (11.6) and (11.7), and the comparison, can be generalized to a larger number of explanatory characteristics by simple analogy.

Interaction Terms

The regression model with two, or more, explanatory characteristics can be generalized further by introducing "interaction terms." Consider the preceding example on the starting salaries of the high school English teachers. In this example we presume that the mean salary depends on the degree qualification of the candidate and on the type of high school, and that the difference between the mean salaries in the public and in the private school systems is the same for all degree qualifications. Suppose now that we do not wish to make the latter presumption. Then the regression model (11.5) can be modified as follows:

$$(11.8) \qquad Y_i = \beta_1 + \beta_2 X_{i2} + \beta_3 X_{i3} + \gamma Z_i + \delta_2 X_{i2} Z_i + \delta_3 X_{i3} Z_i + \varepsilon_i,$$

where all the variables are defined as in (11.5). The mean values of Y_i corresponding to different values of the regressors are

$$E(Y_i \mid X_{i2} = 1, X_{i3} = 0, Z_i = 1) = \beta_1 + \beta_2 + \gamma + \delta_2,$$

$$E(Y_i \mid X_{i2} = 0, X_{i3} = 1, Z_i = 1) = \beta_1 + \beta_3 + \gamma + \delta_3,$$

$$E(Y_i \mid X_{i2} = 0, X_{i3} = 0, Z_i = 1) = \beta_1 + \gamma,$$

$$E(Y_i \mid X_{i2} = 1, X_{i3} = 0, Z_i = 0) = \beta_1 + \beta_2,$$

$$E(Y_i \mid X_{i2} = 0, X_{i3} = 1, Z_i = 0) = \beta_1 + \beta_3,$$

$$E(Y_i \mid X_{i2} = 0, X_{i3} = 0, Z_i = 0) = \beta_1.$$

This means that we can define the regression coefficients in terms of the mean salaries as follows:

$$\beta_1 = \mu_{A0},$$

$$\beta_2 = \mu_{C0} - \mu_{A0},$$

$$\beta_3 = \mu_{B0} - \mu_{A0},$$

$$\gamma = \mu_{A1} - \mu_{A0},$$

$$\delta_2 = (\mu_{C1} - \mu_{C0}) - (\mu_{A1} - \mu_{A0}),$$

$$\delta_3 = (\mu_{B1} - \mu_{B0}) - (\mu_{A1} - \mu_{A0}).$$

The differences in the mean salary in the public and the private systems are

$$\text{B.A.:} \quad \mu_{A1} - \mu_{A0} = \gamma,$$

$$\text{M.A.:} \quad \mu_{B1} - \mu_{B0} = \gamma + \delta_3,$$

$$\text{Ph.D.:} \quad \mu_{C1} - \mu_{C0} = \gamma + \delta_2.$$

The regression model (11.8) is equivalent to a model presented as a "two-way analysis of variance with interactions" in statistical literature. A demonstration of the equivalence of the two models would follow the same lines as in the previously discussed cases, and will not be presented here.

Qualitative and Quantitative Explanatory Variables

In the preceding models all of the included regressors were represented by binary variables. Such models are really not very frequent in economics. More frequently, we encounter models in which *some* regressors are binary and others are not. A traditional example is a consumption function estimated from time-series data that include a major war period. In this model the mean consumption is presumed to depend on income and on whether the period is one of peace or one of war. A simple way of representing this model is

$$C_t = \beta_1 + \beta_2 Y_t + \gamma Z_t + \varepsilon_t, \tag{11.9}$$

where C represents consumption, Y represents income, and Z is a binary variable such that

$$Z_t = 1 \quad \text{if } t \text{ is a wartime period,}$$

$$= 0 \quad \text{otherwise.}$$

Then, we have

$$C_t = (\beta_1 + \gamma) + \beta_2 Y_t + \varepsilon_t \quad \text{(wartime)},$$

$$C_t = \beta_1 + \beta_2 Y_t + \varepsilon_t \quad \text{(peacetime)}.$$

Thus we are, in fact, postulating that in wartime the intercept of the consumption function changes from β_1 to $\beta_1 + \gamma$. A graphic illustration is given in Figure 11–1.

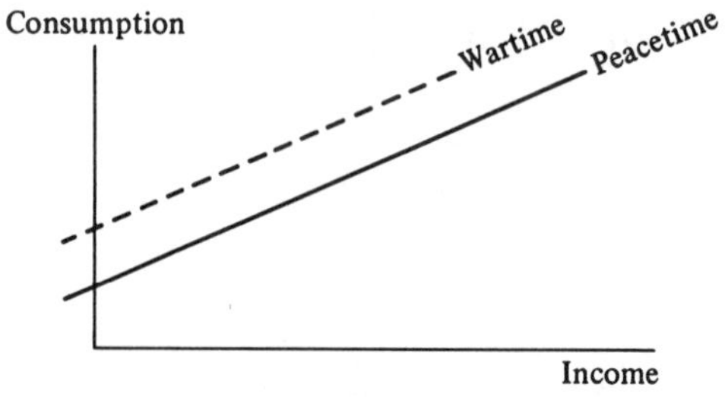

Figure 11–1

If the intercept is viewed as representing the "subsistence level" of consumption, this model implies that the subsistence level changes during the war. Such a change is put forward as a hypothesis to be tested, i.e.,

$$H_0: \quad \gamma = 0,$$

$$H_A: \quad \gamma \neq 0.$$

Statistical texts show an equivalent formulation of models such as (11.9) under the name of "analysis of covariance."

The effect of war can be brought into the consumption function differently if we postulate that the war conditions affect the slope and not the intercept of the consumption function. According to this theoretical formulation, the regression model is

$$C_t = \beta_1 + \beta_2 Y_t + \delta Y_t Z_t + \varepsilon_t, \tag{11.10}$$

where the variables are defined as before. In this case we have

$$C_t = \beta_1 + (\beta_2 + \delta) Y_t + \varepsilon_t \quad \text{(wartime)},$$

$$C_t = \beta_1 + \beta_2 Y_t + \varepsilon_t \quad \text{(peacetime)}.$$

Equation (11.10) implies that the effect of the war is to change the marginal propensity to consume as shown in Figure 11–2. This implication can be checked by testing the hypothesis that δ is zero.

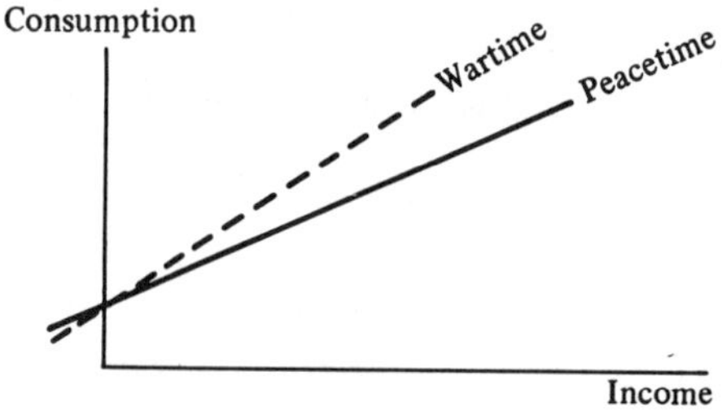

Figure 11–2

The third and final possibility of distinguishing between wartime and peacetime observations is to let *both* the intercept and the slope of the consumption function change in wartime. The regression equation would become

$$C_t = \beta_1 + \beta_2 Y_t + \gamma Z_t + \delta Y_t Z_t + \varepsilon_t. \tag{11.11}$$

Then, we would have

$$C_t = (\beta_1 + \gamma) + (\beta_2 + \delta) Y_t + \varepsilon_t \quad \text{(wartime)},$$

$$C_t = \beta_1 + \beta_2 Y_t + \varepsilon_t \quad \text{(peacetime)}.$$

These relations are illustrated in Figure 11-3. The interesting point about (11.11) is that the least squares estimators of the regression coefficients are exactly the same as those that would be obtained from two separate regressions of C_t on Y_t, one estimated from the peacetime observations and the other from the wartime observations. The proof is obtained by a straightforward application of the least squares formulas and will not be presented here. The only difference between the two approaches to estimation concerns σ^2. If, as we normally assume, the variance of ε_t is unchanged throughout the entire period, then its estimate from (11.11) based on *all* observations will be efficient, whereas the two estimates obtained from the two separate subsamples will not be. This is because the estimate of σ^2 based on either subsample does not utilize the information about σ^2 contained in the other subsample.

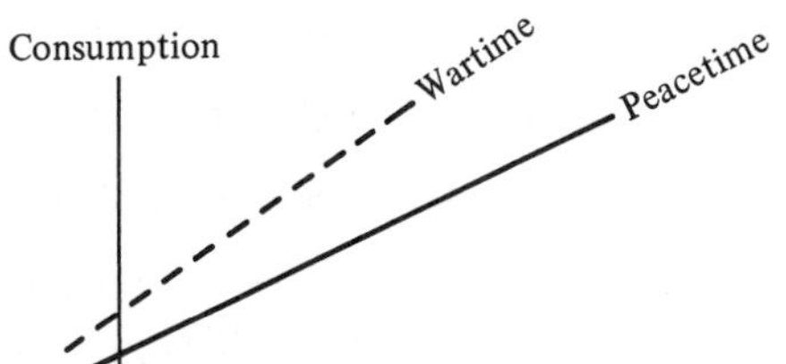

Figure 11-3

Another use of models with quantitative and qualitative explanatory variables occurs when testing the hypothesis of *asymmetric response*. According to this hypothesis the change in $E(Y_i)$ in response to a unit *increase* of a given explanatory variable is different in absolute magnitude from the change in response to a unit *decrease* of the same explanatory variable. Behavior of this sort is implied in statements such as "wages are sticky downwards," and in the claim that consumers respond more readily to an increase in income than to a decrease. For such behavior the standard formulation of the linear regression equation would be inappropriate. However, asymmetric response of $E(Y_i)$ to changes in an explanatory variable can be incorporated into the regression equation by introducing a binary variable. Consider a simple regression model,

$$Y_t = \alpha + \beta X_t + \varepsilon_t,$$

for which all of the basic assumptions are satisfied. In this model a unit increase in X_t leads to a change in $E(Y_t)$ equal to β, and a unit decrease in X_t leads to a change in $E(Y_t)$ equal to $-\beta$. If we want to make the response of $E(Y_t)$ assymmetric, we can write

$$(11.12) \qquad Y_t = \alpha + \beta X_t + \gamma X_t Z_t + \varepsilon_t$$

where

$$Z_t = 1 \quad \text{when } X_t \leq X_{t-1},$$
$$= 0 \quad \text{otherwise.}$$

The test of the asymmetric response hypothesis is equivalent to testing that $\gamma = 0$. Note that the asymmetric response model can be used not only with time series but also with cross-section data, providing we have some information about the value of the relevant explanatory variable in the period preceding the time of the survey.

Models with quantitative *and* qualitative explanatory variables are used most frequently in connection with regression models that include seasonal effects. These models are usually estimated from quarterly or monthly observations. For instance, consider the following simple regressions:

$$(11.13) \qquad \begin{aligned} Y_t &= \alpha_1 + \beta X_t + \varepsilon_t \quad \text{(spring quarter)},\\ Y_t &= \alpha_2 + \beta X_t + \varepsilon_t \quad \text{(summer quarter)},\\ Y_t &= \alpha_3 + \beta X_t + \varepsilon_t \quad \text{(fall quarter)},\\ Y_t &= \alpha_4 + \beta X_t + \varepsilon_t \quad \text{(winter quarter)}. \end{aligned}$$

Here the seasonal effects are presumed to shift the intercept of the regression function. The model can be described by a single regression equation extended by the introduction of binary regressors representing the seasonal factors:

$$(11.14) \qquad Y_t = \alpha + \beta X_t + \gamma_2 Q_{t2} + \gamma_3 Q_{t3} + \gamma_4 Q_{t4} + \varepsilon_t,$$

where

$$\begin{aligned} Q_{t2} &= 1 \quad \text{if } t \text{ is a summer quarter},\\ &= 0 \quad \text{otherwise};\\ Q_{t3} &= 1 \quad \text{if } t \text{ is a fall quarter},\\ &= 0 \quad \text{otherwise};\\ Q_{t4} &= 1 \quad \text{if } t \text{ is a winter quarter},\\ &= 0 \quad \text{otherwise}. \end{aligned}$$

Note that the quarterly seasonal effects are represented by three, not four, binary regressors; otherwise, the least squares estimators of the regression coefficients would be indeterminate. A comparison of (11.14) and (11.13) reveals that

$$\alpha = \alpha_1,$$

$$\alpha + \gamma_2 = \alpha_2,$$

$$\alpha + \gamma_3 = \alpha_3,$$

$$\alpha + \gamma_4 = \alpha_4.$$

To examine the relevance of the seasonal effects in a regression model such as (11.14), we test the hypothesis that γ_2, γ_3, and γ_4 are jointly zero; that is,

$$H_0: \quad \gamma_2 = \gamma_3 = \gamma_4 = 0,$$

$$H_A: \quad H_0 \text{ is not true.}$$

The appropriate test then is the F test of (10.45).

An alternative way of introducing the seasonal factors into a regression model is

(11.15)
$$Y_t = \alpha + \beta_1 X_t + \varepsilon_t \quad \text{(spring quarter)},$$
$$Y_t = \alpha + \beta_2 X_t + \varepsilon_t \quad \text{(summer quarter)},$$
$$Y_t = \alpha + \beta_3 X_t + \varepsilon_t \quad \text{(fall quarter)},$$
$$Y_t = \alpha + \beta_4 X_t + \varepsilon_t \quad \text{(winter quarter)}.$$

In this case, the seasonal factors are supposed to affect the slope of the regression equation but not its intercept. A compact representation of (11.15) is

(11.16)
$$Y_t = \alpha + \beta X_t + \delta_2 Q_{t2} X_t + \delta_3 Q_{t3} X_t + \delta_4 Q_{t4} X_t + \varepsilon_t,$$

where the Q's are defined as in (11.14). By comparing (11.16) with (11.15), we can see that

$$\beta = \beta_1,$$

$$\beta + \delta_2 = \beta_2,$$

$$\beta + \delta_3 = \beta_3,$$

$$\beta + \delta_4 = \beta_4.$$

The relevance of the seasonal effects can be examined by testing the hypothesis that δ_2, δ_3, and δ_4 are jointly zero; i.e.,

$$H_0: \quad \delta_2 = \delta_3 = \delta_4 = 0,$$

$$H_A: \quad H_0 \text{ is not true.}$$

As a final possibility, we could let both the intercept and the slope be affected by the seasonal factors. From the point of view of estimating the regression coefficients, such a formulation is equivalent to splitting the sample into four subsamples, as discussed earlier in connection with Equation (11.11).

A Note on the Use of Deseasonalized Data

While we are on the subject of seasonal factors in regression equations, we may consider the implications of using "deseasonalized" time-series data in regression analysis. A common practice is to form the regression equation as

$$\tilde{Y}_t = \alpha + \beta\tilde{X}_t + \varepsilon_t,$$

where $\tilde{Y}$ and $\tilde{X}$ are the "deseasonalized" values of X and Y. "Deseasonalizing" means removing regular oscillatory movement of a one-year period from the original time series. This is done either by the statistical agency that makes the data available, or by the econometrician himself. In our discussion we assume that the deseasonalizing has been successful in the sense that the seasonal elements have been completely removed from the series. These elements are usually considered to be additive or multiplicative. In the additive case, we can write

$$Y_t = \tilde{Y}_t + D_{tY},$$

$$X_t = \tilde{X}_t + D_{tX},$$

where D_{tY} and D_{tX} represent seasonal deviations contained in the respective series. Note that for, say, quarterly data,

$$D_{tY} = D_{t+4,\,Y},$$

$$D_{tX} = D_{t+4,\,X},$$

and

$$D_{tY} + D_{t+1,\,Y} + D_{t+2,\,Y} + D_{t+3,\,Y} = 0,$$

$$D_{tX} + D_{t+1,\,X} + D_{t+2,\,X} + D_{t+3,\,X} = 0,$$

for all t. If any series contains no seasonal elements, the corresponding D's would all be zero. The regression equation

$$\tilde{Y}_t = \alpha + \beta\tilde{X}_t + \varepsilon_t$$

then implies that

$$(Y_t - D_{tY}) = \alpha + \beta(X_t - D_{tX}) + \varepsilon_t \tag{11.17}$$

or

$$Y_t = (\alpha + D_{tY} - \beta D_{tX}) + \beta X_t + \varepsilon_t. \tag{11.17a}$$

That is, in this case the seasonal factors are assumed to operate by shifting the intercept of the regression function. This is equivalent to the formulation given by (11.13) or (11.14).

In the case of multiplicative seasonal elements, we can write

$$Y_t = \tilde{Y}_t S_{tY} \quad \text{and} \quad X_t = \tilde{X}_t S_{tX},$$

where S_{tY} and S_{tX} represent seasonal indexes pertaining to the respective series. Note that for, say, quarterly data,

$$S_{tY} = S_{t+4,\,Y} \qquad \text{and} \qquad S_{tX} = S_{t+4,\,X},$$

and

$$S_{tY} \times S_{t+1,\,Y} \times S_{t+2,\,Y} \times S_{t+3,\,Y} = 1,$$

$$S_{tX} \times S_{t+1,\,X} \times S_{t+2,\,X} \times S_{t+3,\,X} = 1$$

for all t. If any series contains no seasonal elements, the corresponding S's would all be equal to unity. The regression equation

$$\tilde{Y}_t = \alpha + \beta \tilde{X}_t + \varepsilon_t$$

in this case implies

(11.18) $$\frac{Y_t}{S_{tY}} = \alpha + \beta \frac{X_t}{S_{tX}} + \varepsilon_t$$

or

(11.18a) $$Y_t = \alpha S_{tY} + \beta \frac{S_{tY}}{S_{tX}} X_t + \varepsilon_t^*,$$

where $$\varepsilon_t^* = S_{tY}\varepsilon_t.$$

Here it is assumed that the seasonal elements affect both the intercept and the slope of the regression equation and that the disturbance is heteroskedastic with variance equal to $\sigma^2 S_{tY}^2$. When a research worker is applying the least squares method to the deseasonalized data while making the usual basic assumptions about the disturbance as in (11.18), then he is implying *something* about the relationship between X and Y in the real, "nondeseasonalized" world. These implications are spelled out by (11.18a). If (11.18a) does not provide a true description of the relationship between X and Y, then the least squares estimators of α and β (based on deseasonalized data) do not, in general, possess the desirable properties that they would otherwise have.

Binary Dependent Variable

At this point we turn our attention to regression models in which the *dependent* variable is binary while the explanatory variables are quantitative. As an example, consider a regression model designed to explain the ownership of a certain appliance—for instance, a dishwasher. Suppose the postulated regression equation is

(11.19) $$Y_i = \alpha + \beta X_i + \varepsilon_i,$$

where X_i represents the income of the ith family, and Y_i is a binary variable such that

$$\begin{aligned} Y_i &= 1 \quad \text{if the } i\text{th family owns a dishwasher,} \\ &= 0 \quad \text{otherwise.} \end{aligned}$$

The explanatory variable X_i is assumed to be nonstochastic or, if stochastic, independent of ε_i. The disturbance ε_i is a random variable that has a zero mean and is independent of ε_j $(i \neq j)$. Since Y_i can only assume two different values, 0 and 1, we have, by the definition of mathematical expectation given by (3.23),

$$E(Y_i) = 1 \times f_i(1) + 0 \times f_i(0) = f_i(1),$$

where $f_i(1)$ is the probability that a family with income X_i has a dishwasher. Note that since from (11.19)

$$E(Y_i) = \alpha + \beta X_i,$$

the probability $f_i(1)$ is supposed to be different for different income levels. Thus $E(Y_i)$ can be interpreted as measuring the proportion of all families with income X_i who have a dishwasher. This implies that

$$0 \leq \alpha + \beta X_i \leq 1.$$

Let us now consider the disturbance ε_i. Since from (11.19)

$$\varepsilon_i = Y_i - \alpha - \beta X_i,$$

and since Y_i can only be equal to 0 or 1, it follows that for any given income X_i the disturbance can assume only two different values, $(-\alpha - \beta X_i)$ and $(1 - \alpha - \beta X_i)$. This means that ε_i is *not* normally distributed but has a discrete distribution defined as

ε_i	$f(\varepsilon_i)$
$-\alpha - \beta X_i$	f
$1 - \alpha - \beta X_i$	$1 - f$
	1

The probabilities f and $(1 - f)$ can be determined by utilizing the assumption that $E(\varepsilon_i) = 0$. This means that

$$(-\alpha - \beta X_i)f + (1 - \alpha - \beta X_i)(1 - f) = 0,$$

which gives

$$f = 1 - \alpha - \beta X_i.$$

Therefore the variance of ε_i is

(11.20)
$$E(\varepsilon_i^2) = (-\alpha - \beta X_i)^2(1 - \alpha - \beta X_i) + (1 - \alpha - \beta X_i)^2(\alpha + \beta X_i)$$
$$= (\alpha + \beta X_i)(1 - \alpha - \beta X_i) = E(Y_i)[1 - E(Y_i)].$$

This means that ε_i is heteroskedastic, since its variance depends on $E(Y_i)$.

Because of the special nature of the dependent variable in (11.19), there are some problems of estimation and prediction. The first problem is that, because of the heteroskedastic nature of the disturbance, the least squares estimators of α and β, although unbiased, are not efficient. This problem may be overcome, at least for large samples, by using the estimation formulas (8.1) and (8.3), which are designed for heteroskedastic models and involve the variances of ε_i that are unknown. In our case we obtain consistent estimates of the variances by

$$\hat{\sigma}_i^2 = \hat{Y}_i(1 - \hat{Y}_i), \tag{11.21}$$

where $\hat{Y}_i$ is the least squares fitted value of Y_i. The second problem concerns the distribution of the estimators of α and β. Because ε_i is not normally distributed, the estimators of α and β also are not normally distributed, and thus the classical tests of significance do not apply. Should we want to test a hypothesis about α or β, we would have to derive the acceptance region from the known distribution of ε_i. However, there is no difficulty about determining the asymptotic means and variances of the estimators of α and β: the asymptotic means are equal to the true values and the asymptotic variances can be derived from formulas (8.2) and (8.4). The third and final problem concerns prediction. Since $E(Y_i)$ is interpreted as a probability, its range is confined to the interval from 0 to 1. However, the predicted value of Y is a point on a straight line and, therefore, its range is from $-\infty$ to $+\infty$ (unless the sample regression line is perfectly horizontal, of course). There are several ways of overcoming this difficulty. Perhaps the simplest is to let the estimates of α and β be $\overset{\triangle}{\alpha}$ and $\overset{\triangle}{\beta}$, and let

$$\overset{\triangle}{Y}_i = \overset{\triangle}{\alpha} + \overset{\triangle}{\beta} X_i .$$

Then we can use as a predictor of the value of Y for a given value of X, say X_0, the value $\overset{\square}{Y}_0$ defined as follows:

$$\begin{aligned} \overset{\square}{Y}_0 &= \overset{\triangle}{Y}_0 \quad \text{if} \quad 0 < \overset{\triangle}{Y}_0 < 1, \\ &= 1 \quad \text{if} \quad \overset{\triangle}{Y}_0 \geq 1, \\ &= 0 \quad \text{if} \quad \overset{\triangle}{Y}_0 \leq 0, \end{aligned}$$

An illustration of this method of prediction is given in Figure 11–4. There are,

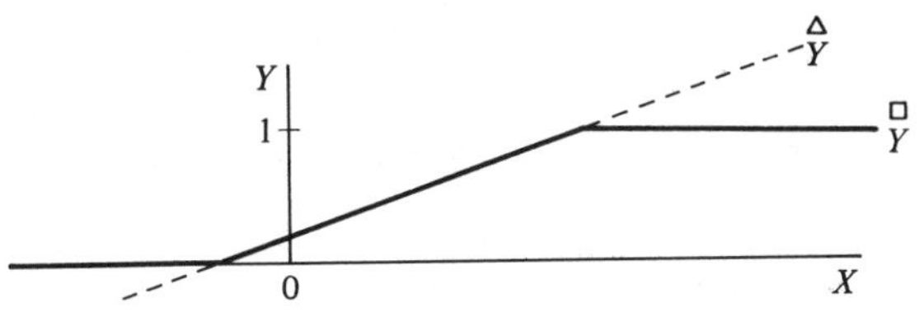

Figure 11–4

of course, difficulties about making exact probability statements concerning Y_0 since the distribution of $\overset{\square}{Y}_0$ is not determined.[2]

Qualitative Dependent and Explanatory Variables

We consider now a model in which both the dependent and the explanatory variables are qualitative. The preceding case of a qualitative dependent variable was discussed with the understanding that the characteristic in question was dichotomous. Here we no longer make such a restriction and allow the dependent characteristic to be polychotomous. However, we confine the analysis to the case in which there is only *one* explanatory characteristic. An example would be a model in which income—classified into some broad groups such as low, medium, and high—is considered to be dependent on the level of education. The sample results for such a model are usually presented in the form of the so-called *contingency table* (see Table 11–3). This is a two-way classification table with the

Table 11–3

		Explanatory Characteristic (X)						
		1	2	...	h	...	H	
	1	n_{11}	n_{12}	...	n_{1h}	...	n_{1H}	$n_{1\cdot}$
Dependent Characteristic (Y)	2	n_{21}	n_{22}	...	n_{2h}	...	n_{2H}	$n_{2\cdot}$
	$\vdots$	$\vdots$	$\vdots$		$\vdots$		$\vdots$	$\vdots$
	g	n_{g1}	n_{g2}	...	n_{gh}	...	n_{gH}	$n_{g\cdot}$
	$\vdots$	$\vdots$	$\vdots$	...	$\vdots$	...	$\vdots$	$\vdots$
	G	n_{G1}	n_{G2}	...	n_{Gh}	...	n_{GH}	$n_{G\cdot}$
		$n_{\cdot 1}$	$n_{\cdot 2}$	...	$n_{\cdot h}$	...	$n_{\cdot H}$	n

rows representing classifications according to, say, the dependent characteristic, and the columns representing classifications according to the explanatory characteristic. The number shown in each cell is the number of observations corresponding to the particular row and column. The entries in the body of the table represent the number of observations in the cell, and the entries on the margin are the row or column totals.

The motivation behind constructing the contingency table is the belief that there is a relation between the two characteristics. A test of this proposition would involve examining the sample data to see whether they do or do not refute such a proposition. The regression model is not well suited for such a test, but there is a *chi-square contingency table test* which has been designed for this purpose. In this test we use a test statistic that is constructed by comparing the

[2] An alternative approach to the problem of having a binary dependent variable is provided by the *probit analysis model*. See, e.g., J. Tobin, "Estimation of relationships for limited dependent variables," *Econometrica*, Vol. 26, January 1958, pp. 24–36.

actual number of observations, or frequencies, in each cell with the number that would occur if there were no relation between X and Y, which is usually called the "theoretical" frequency. The "theoretical" frequencies are determined by reference to "independence in probability," as defined by Theorem 5 of Section 3–3. According to this theorem, if two events are independent, then their joint probability is equal to the product of their respective marginal probabilities. This means that if X and Y are independent, then the probability that an observation drawn at random belongs to the gth row and hth column is

$$P(g \cap h) = P(g)P(h).$$

Here $P(g)$ is the probability that a random observation belongs to the gth row, and $P(h)$ is the probability that a random observation belongs to the hth column. Thus, if we knew $P(g)$ and $P(h)$, we could determine what $P(g \cap h)$ would be under independence between X and Y. Since we do *not* know $P(g)$ and $P(h)$, we estimate them by the respective sample proportions, i.e.,

$$\text{Est. } P(g) = \frac{n_{g\cdot}}{n},$$

$$\text{Est. } P(h) = \frac{n_{\cdot h}}{n}.$$

Now let e_{gh} designate the desired "theoretical" frequency for the cell in the gth row and hth column. Then we can write

$$\text{(11.22)} \qquad \frac{e_{gh}}{n} = \text{Est. } P(g \cap h) = \text{Est. } P(g) \times \text{Est. } P(h) = \frac{n_{g\cdot}}{n} \times \frac{n_{\cdot h}}{n},$$

or

$$\text{(11.22a)} \qquad e_{gh} = \frac{n_{g\cdot} \times n_{\cdot h}}{n}.$$

An intuitive justification for (11.22) can be made as follows. Suppose Y is income and X is education, and suppose the gth row represents a "medium income" group and the hth column a "high school diploma" group. Then if there were no relation between income and education, we would expect the proportion of medium income earners among the high school graduates to be the same as the proportion of medium income earners in the population as a whole. By using sample proportions instead of the population proportions, we have

$$\frac{e_{gh}}{n_{\cdot h}} = \frac{n_{g\cdot}}{n},$$

where $n_{\cdot h}$ in this case stands for the total number of high school graduates and $n_{g\cdot}$ for the total number of medium income earners. This equation is equivalent to (11.22) or (11.22a).

The chi-square contingency table test is a test of the hypothesis that there is *no* relation between X and Y. If this hypothesis is true, then the main reason for the difference between the actual and the "theoretical" frequencies would be the sampling errors. The statistic to be used for testing is

$$\sum_{g=1}^{G} \sum_{h=1}^{H} \frac{(n_{gh} - e_{gh})^2}{e_{gh}}.$$

It can be shown that this statistic has a distribution that, for large samples, can be approximated by the chi-square distribution.[3] In particular, if the sample is large, then

$$\sum_{g=1}^{G} \sum_{h=1}^{H} \frac{(n_{gh} - e_{gh})^2}{e_{gh}} \sim \chi^2_{(G-1)\times(H-1)}, \tag{11.23}$$

where the subscript $(G - 1)\times(H - 1)$ refers to the number of the appropriate degrees of freedom. This number is determined by the fact that with the given row and column totals, only $(G - 1)\times(H - 1)$ cells can be filled at will; once this is done, the numbers in the remaining cells are automatically determined. With respect to the requirement of a "large" sample size, the criterion used in practice is that none of the "theoretical" frequencies is less than 5. Consequently, it is sometimes necessary to combine cells to bring the number of frequencies up to the required minimum. When the value of the test statistic calculated on the basis of the sample observations exceeds the tabulated value of chi-square for the chosen level of significance, the null hypothesis will be rejected. Note that since the evidence against the null hypothesis can only take the form of a large value of the calculated test statistic, the appropriate test is a *one-tail* test. The chi-square contingency table test is very similar to the chi-square "goodness of fit" test discussed at the end of Section 5–2.

11–2 Models with Restricted Coefficients

Here our problem is how to incorporate into our estimation procedure some prior information about the regression coefficient (or coefficients). Such information can be viewed as providing certain restrictions on one or more given regression coefficients. For instance, if we know a priori that the population regression line passes through the origin, then, if we use this prior knowledge, we are required to restrict the value of the intercept of the sample regression line to zero. The incorporation of this prior knowledge into the estimation procedure has two distinct aspects. First, we do not estimate the intercept, since its value is known; second, we estimate the slope of the regression line in such a way that the estimator has the usual desirable properties *under the condition* that the intercept is zero. The second aspect is quite important because an estimator that has all the desirable properties under general conditions does not necessarily retain these properties when the conditions become special in some way. In our example, "general conditions" mean that the regression line can be anywhere in

[3] See, e.g., A. M. Mood and F. A. Graybill, *Introduction to the Theory of Statistics* (New York: McGraw-Hill, 1963), p. 318.

the plane. Once we specify that the regression line *must* pass through the origin, we impose a restriction that reduces the degree of generality.

In this section we consider several types of restrictions, some imposed by prior information about the *value* of the individual regression coefficients and others imposed by the *relations* among the individual regression coefficients.

Fixed-Value Restrictions

To illustrate the case where we have exact information about the value of one of the regression coefficients, we use a regression equation with two explanatory variables,

$$Y_i = \beta_1 + \beta_2 X_{i2} + \beta_3 X_{i3} + \varepsilon_i,$$

but the analysis applies, and can be easily extended, to equations with a larger number of explanatory variables. Suppose now that we know the value of the intercept a priori; in particular, suppose

$$\beta_1 = 0,$$

as is most commonly the case. Then, the regression equation becomes

$$Y_i = \beta_2 X_{i2} + \beta_3 X_{i3} + \varepsilon_i. \tag{11.24}$$

This specification of the regression equation now incorporates our prior knowledge about the value of the intercept as required. The least squares estimators of β_2 and β_3 can be obtained by minimizing the sum of squares S given by

$$S = \sum_i (Y_i - \beta_2 X_{i2} - \beta_3 X_{i3})^2.$$

Differentiating S with respect to β_2 and β_3, we obtain

$$\frac{\partial S}{\partial \beta_2} = -2 \sum_i X_{i2}(Y_i - \beta_2 X_{i2} - \beta_3 X_{i3}),$$

$$\frac{\partial S}{\partial \beta_3} = -2 \sum_i X_{i3}(Y_i - \beta_2 X_{i2} - \beta_3 X_{i3}).$$

Equating each derivative to zero and rearranging terms, we obtain the following least squares normal equations:

$$\sum_i Y_i X_{i2} = \hat{\beta}_2 \sum_i X_{i2}^2 + \hat{\beta}_3 \sum_i X_{i2} X_{i3},$$

$$\sum_i Y_i X_{i3} = \hat{\beta}_2 \sum_i X_{i2} X_{i3} + \hat{\beta}_3 \sum_i X_{i3}^2.$$

(By comparison with (10.12) and (10.13), these equations are the same as those that would be obtained for the unrestricted least squares estimators if $\bar{Y}$, $\bar{X}_2$, and $\bar{X}_3$ were all zero.) The resulting estimators of β_2 and β_3 are

$$\hat{\beta}_2 = \frac{(\sum Y_i X_{i2})(\sum X_{i3}^2) - (\sum Y_i X_{i3})(\sum X_{i2} X_{i3})}{(\sum X_{i2}^2)(\sum X_{i3}^2) - (\sum X_{i2} X_{i3})^2}, \tag{11.25}$$

$$\hat{\beta}_3 = \frac{(\sum Y_i X_{i3})(\sum X_{i2}^2) - (\sum Y_i X_{i2})(\sum X_{i2} X_{i3})}{(\sum X_{i2}^2)(X_{i3}^2) - (\sum X_{i2} X_{i3})^2}.$$

To derive the formulas for the variances of $\hat{\beta}_2$ and $\hat{\beta}_3$, we note that

$$\hat{\beta}_2 = \beta_2 + \frac{(\sum X_{i3}^2)(\sum X_{i2}\varepsilon_i) - (\sum X_{i2}X_{i3})(\sum X_{i3}\varepsilon_i)}{(\sum X_{i2}^2)(\sum X_{i3}^2) - (\sum X_{i2}X_{i3})^2},$$

$$\hat{\beta}_3 = \beta_3 + \frac{(\sum X_{i2}^2)(\sum X_{i3}\varepsilon_i) - (\sum X_{i2}X_{i3})(\sum X_{i2}\varepsilon_i)}{(\sum X_{i2}^2)(\sum X_{i3}^2) - (\sum X_{i2}X_{i3})^2}.$$

Therefore,

$$(11.26)\quad \mathrm{Var}(\hat{\beta}_2) = E(\hat{\beta}_2 - \beta_2)^2 = \frac{\sigma^2 \sum X_{i3}^2}{(\sum X_{i2}^2)(\sum X_{i3}^2) - (\sum X_{i2}X_{i3})^2},$$

$$\mathrm{Var}(\hat{\beta}_3) = E(\hat{\beta}_3 - \beta_3)^2 = \frac{\sigma^2 \sum X_{i2}^2}{(\sum X_{i2}^2)(\sum X_{i3}^2) - (\sum X_{i2}X_{i3})^2},$$

$$\mathrm{Cov}(\hat{\beta}_2,\hat{\beta}_3) = E(\hat{\beta}_2 - \beta_2)(\hat{\beta}_3 - \beta_3) = \frac{-\sigma^2 \sum X_{i2}X_{i3}}{(\sum X_{i2}^2)(\sum X_{i3}^2) - (\sum X_{i2}X_{i3})^2}.$$

It can be shown, by following the steps outlined in the first part of Section 10–1, that $\hat{\beta}_2$ and $\hat{\beta}_3$ have all the desirable properties. The variances of $\hat{\beta}_2$ and $\hat{\beta}_3$ can be estimated by references to (11.26), after we replace σ^2 by its unbiased estimator s^2 defined as

$$(11.27)\qquad s^2 = \frac{1}{n-2}\sum_i (Y_i - \hat{\beta}_2 X_{i2} - \hat{\beta}_3 X_{i3})^2.$$

Note that in (11.27) we divide the sum of the squares of residuals by $(n - 2)$—rather than by $(n - 3)$, as in (10.34)—since only two regression coefficients are unknown. All of these results can be easily generalized to apply to regression models with more than two explanatory variables.

The preceding case demonstrates the gain achieved by incorporating the prior knowledge about a regression coefficient in the estimation procedure. The gain is essentially twofold. First, we do not have to estimate β_1 since its value is known. Second, the restricted least squares estimators of β_2 and β_3, i.e., those estimators which incorporate the information that $\beta_1 = 0$, have a smaller variance than the ordinary unrestricted least squares estimators. The second type of gain represents a less obvious but very important feature of estimation with restrictions. For example, let $\hat{\beta}_2$ stand for the restricted estimator of β_2 as defined by (11.25), and let $\hat{\beta}_2^{ORD}$ represent the ordinary unrestricted least squares estimator of β_2 as defined by (10.12). The ratio of the variances of the two estimators is

$$(11.28)\quad \frac{\mathrm{Var}(\hat{\beta}_2^{ORD})}{\mathrm{Var}(\hat{\beta}_2)} = \frac{\sigma^2 m_{33}/(m_{22}m_{33} - m_{23}^2)}{\sigma^2 \sum X_{i3}^2/[(\sum X_{i2}^2)(\sum X_{i3}^2) - (\sum X_{i2}X_{i3})^2]}$$

$$= \frac{m_{33}[(m_{22} + n\bar{X}_2^2)(m_{33} + n\bar{X}_3^2) - (m_{23} + n\bar{X}_2\bar{X}_3)^2]}{(m_{33} + n\bar{X}_3^2)(m_{22}m_{33} - m_{23}^2)}$$

$$= 1 + \frac{n(\bar{X}_2 m_{33} - \bar{X}_3 m_{23})^2}{(m_{33} + n\bar{X}_3^2)(m_{22}m_{33} - m_{23}^2)},$$

which is clearly greater than, or at best equal to, one. Thus

$$\mathrm{Var}(\hat{\beta}_2^{ORD}) \geq \mathrm{Var}(\hat{\beta}_2).$$

A similar proof could be presented with respect to β_3. Note, however, that while the restricted estimators of β_2 and β_3 have smaller variances than their unrestricted counterparts, the value of R^2 is higher for the unrestricted sample regression line than for the restricted one. This is because the unrestricted least squares estimation leads to the maximum value of R^2 so that *any* departure from it must result in a decrease.

Suppose now that the prior information about the value of a regression coefficient concerns not the intercept but, say, β_3. Then the regression equation

$$Y_i = \beta_1 + \beta_2 X_{i2} + \beta_3 X_{i3} + \varepsilon_i$$

can be written as

$$Y_i^* = \beta_1 + \beta_2 X_{i2} + \varepsilon_i, \tag{11.29}$$

where Y_i^* is measured by $(Y_i - \beta_3 X_{i3})$. The least squares estimators of β_1 and β_2 of (11.29), to be called $\hat{\beta}_1$ and $\hat{\beta}_2$, have all the desirable properties. Note that in this case the variance of $\hat{\beta}_2$ is

$$\mathrm{Var}(\hat{\beta}_2) = \frac{\sigma^2}{m_{22}},$$

whereas the variance of the unrestricted least squares estimator of β_2 is

$$\mathrm{Var}(\hat{\beta}_2^{ORD}) = \frac{\sigma^2 m_{33}}{m_{22}m_{33} - m_{23}^2}.$$

The ratio of these variances then is

$$\frac{\mathrm{Var}(\hat{\beta}_2^{ORD})}{\mathrm{Var}(\hat{\beta}_2)} = \frac{\sigma^2 m_{33}/(m_{22}m_{33} - m_{23}^2)}{\sigma^2/m_{22}} = \frac{m_{22}m_{33}}{m_{22}m_{33} - m_{23}^2} = \frac{1}{1 - r_{23}^2}, \tag{11.30}$$

where r_{23}^2 is the sample coefficient of correlation between X_{i2} and X_{i3}. Therefore, unless r_{23}^2 is zero, there is always a gain in efficiency if we use the information about β_3 when estimating β_2. This gain is particularly great if r_{23}^2 is close to unity, i.e., if the two explanatory variables are highly correlated in the sample.

Inequality Constraints

In many cases prior information about a regression coefficient is not given as a definite equality, but instead takes the form of an inequality. For instance, in the case of a linear consumption function, we know a priori that the coefficient attached to income (i.e., the marginal propensity to consume) lies between 0 and 1. In general, suppose the prior information about the regression coefficient β_k is

$$a \leq \beta_k \leq b,$$

where a and b are some known numbers, and $b > a$. Here we have the problem of estimating the coefficients of a regression equation subject to an inequality constraint on one or more of the regression coefficients. This kind of constraint is considerably more awkward to incorporate into our estimation procedure than a definite equality. The simplest way is to obtain a least squares estimator of β_k by ignoring the inequality constraint altogether, and to define the constrained estimator of β_k, say, $\hat{\beta}_k$, as follows:

$$\begin{aligned} \hat{\beta}_k &= \hat{\beta}_k^{ORD} && \text{if } a \leq \hat{\beta}_k^{ORD} \leq b, \\ &= a && \text{if } \quad \hat{\beta}^{ORD} < a, \\ &= b && \text{if } \quad \hat{\beta}^{ORD} > b, \end{aligned} \tag{11.31}$$

where $\hat{\beta}_k^{ORD}$ is the ordinary, unrestricted estimator of β_k. Of course, since $\hat{\beta}_k$ is confined to a limited range, its distribution is no longer normal. However, as the sample size increases, the probability of getting the ordinary, unrestricted estimates outside the interval specified by the inequality becomes small, unless β_k is equal to either a or b. Thus, for large samples, we may regard the normal distribution as a reasonable approximation of the distribution of $\hat{\beta}_k$ of (11.31). Obviously, the closer the true value of β_k is to the center of the interval, the better the approximation will be. This approach to estimating the regression coefficients that are subject to inequality constraints has the disadvantage that the information about β_k is ignored in estimating the remaining regression coefficients. An alternative approach, which is free of this disadvantage, is to obtain estimators of the regression coefficient by maximizing the appropriate likelihood function subject to the inequality constraint (or constraints). This is a problem in quadratic programming, and its solution is complicated.[4]

A still different approach to estimation of the regression coefficients subject to inequality constraints has been suggested by Theil and Goldberger and is known as "mixed estimation."[5] The authors point out that the inequality constraint

$$a \leq \beta_k \leq b$$

is really a statement by which we assert that we consider it certain that β_k lies between a and b. This can be viewed as if we were making probability statements about β_k, i.e., as if we were saying that the probability of β_k lying outside the interval $a \leq \beta_k \leq b$ is zero and the probability of β_k lying inside that interval is one. However, if we make such statements when distinguishing between the values of β_k outside and inside the interval $a \leq \beta_k \leq b$, we may also be willing to make a further probability statement about β_k *within* the interval $a \leq \beta_k \leq b$. One such statement (which is presumably fairly common) is that we have no idea at all

[4] This approach is developed in G. C. Judge and T. Takayama, "Inequality Restrictions in Regression Analysis," *Journal of the American Statistical Association*, Vol. 61, March 1966, pp. 166–181.

[5] H. Theil and A. S. Goldberger, "On Pure and Mixed Statistical Estimation in Economics," *International Economic Review*, Vol. 2, January 1961, pp. 65–78. The method is called "mixed" because it includes elements of the classical as well as the Bayesian approaches to estimation.

about the location of β_k within the interval. This can be interpreted as meaning that, as far as we know, all values of β_k within the interval are *equally likely*, i.e., that the distribution of β_k within the interval is uniform. In this case, we can write

$$\beta_k = \frac{a+b}{2} + u, \tag{11.32}$$

where u has a continuous uniform distribution with mean

$$E(u) = 0$$

and variance[6]

$$\mathrm{Var}(u) = \frac{(b-a)^2}{12}.$$

This specification can be incorporated into our estimation procedure by using the "mixed" method of Theil and Goldberger.[7]

The main idea behind the "mixed" estimation method is to combine the prior information about one or more of the regression coefficients with the information provided by the sample. This can be achieved by using the inequality restriction as if it were an additional observation, and then applying the least squares method to the "extended" sample. First, we can rewrite (11.32) as

$$\frac{a+b}{2} = \beta_1 \times 0 + \beta_2 \times 0 + \cdots + \beta_k \times 1 + \cdots + \beta_K \times 0 + (-u), \tag{11.32a}$$

which can be viewed as the $(n+1)$th observation on

$$Y_i = \beta_1 X_{i1} + \beta_2 X_{i2} + \cdots + \beta_k X_{ik} + \cdots + \beta_K X_{iK} + \varepsilon_i,$$

with $(-u)$ serving as the disturbance. However, since each of the ε's has a variance equal to σ^2, while the variance of $(-u)$ is $(b-a)^2/12$, the $(n+1)$th observation as stated in (11.32a) would bring in heteroskedasticity. This can be easily remedied by multiplying both sides of (11.32a) by $\sigma\sqrt{12}/(b-a)$ to get

(11.32b)

$$\frac{(b+a)\sigma\sqrt{3}}{b-a} = \beta_1 \times 0 + \beta_2 \times 0 + \cdots + \beta_k \times \left[\frac{\sigma\sqrt{12}}{b-a}\right] + \cdots + \beta_K \times 0 + u^*$$

[6] See, e.g., Freund, *op. cit.*, p. 146.

[7] Another specification would be obtained if we believed that the values of β_k in the middle of the interval $a \leq \beta_k \leq b$ were more likely than the values near the boundaries. Then we might specify the variance of u to be such that

$$\frac{a+b}{2} + 2\sqrt{\mathrm{Var}(u)} = b \quad \text{and} \quad \frac{a+b}{2} - 2\sqrt{\mathrm{Var}(u)} = a,$$

relying on the fact that, for many distributions, the values of the variable outside the range of two standard deviations on either side of the mean occur very rarely. This would give

$$\mathrm{Var}(u) = \frac{(b-a)^2}{16}.$$

This specification is the one used by Theil and Goldberger, *op. cit.*

where
$$u^* = \frac{-u\sigma\sqrt{12}}{b-a},$$

so that

$$\text{Var}(u^*) = \left[\frac{12\sigma^2}{(b-a)^2}\right]\text{Var}(u) = \sigma^2,$$

as desired. Then, the observations in the "extended" sample are:

i	Y_i	X_{i1}	X_{i2}	$\ldots$	X_{ik}	$\ldots$	X_{iK}
1	Y_1	1	X_{12}	$\ldots$	X_{1k}	$\ldots$	X_{1K}
2	Y_2	1	X_{22}	$\ldots$	X_{2k}	$\ldots$	X_{2K}
$\vdots$	$\vdots$	$\vdots$	$\vdots$		$\vdots$		$\vdots$
n	Y_n	1	X_{n2}	$\ldots$	X_{nk}	$\ldots$	X_{nK}
$n+1$	$\frac{(b+a)\sigma\sqrt{3}}{b-a}$	0	0	$\ldots$	$\frac{\sigma\sqrt{12}}{b-a}$	$\ldots$	0

The value of the $(n+1)$th observation on Y is not known because σ is not known. However, σ can be estimated by s [as defined by (10.34)] from the first n observations. As we have shown, s^2 is an unbiased, consistent, and asymptotically efficient estimator of σ^2. The least squares normal equations for the "mixed" estimators of the regression coefficients then are

(11.33)
$$\begin{aligned}
\sum_i Y_i &= \hat{\beta}_1 n + \hat{\beta}_2 \sum_i X_{i2} + \cdots + \hat{\beta}_k \sum_i X_{ik} \\
&\quad + \cdots + \hat{\beta}_K \sum_i X_{iK}, \\
\sum_i Y_i X_{i2} &= \hat{\beta}_1 \sum_i X_{i2} + \hat{\beta}_2 \sum_i X_{i2}^2 + \cdots + \hat{\beta}_k \sum_i X_{i2} X_{ik} \\
&\quad + \cdots + \hat{\beta}_K \sum_i X_{i2} X_{iK}, \\
&\vdots \\
\sum_i Y_i X_{ik} + \frac{6s^2(b+a)}{(b-a)^2} &= \hat{\beta}_1 \sum_i X_{ik} + \hat{\beta}_2 \sum_i X_{i2} X_{ik} \\
&\quad + \cdots + \hat{\beta}_k \left[\sum_i X_{ik}^2 + \frac{12s^2}{(b-a)^2}\right] \\
&\quad + \cdots + \hat{\beta}_K \sum_i X_{ik} X_{iK}, \\
&\vdots \\
\sum_i Y_i X_{iK} &= \hat{\beta}_1 \sum_i X_{iK} + \hat{\beta}_2 \sum_i X_{i2} X_{iK} + \cdots + \hat{\beta}_k \sum_i X_{ik} X_{iK} \\
&\quad + \cdots + \hat{\beta}_K \sum_i X_{iK}^2,
\end{aligned}$$

where all summations run from $i = 1$ to $i = n$. In the case of two explanatory variables with the constraint

$$a \leq \beta_2 \leq b,$$

the "mixed" estimators are

$$\hat{\beta}_1 = \bar{Y} - \hat{\beta}_2\bar{X}_2 - \hat{\beta}_3\bar{X}_3, \tag{11.34}$$

$$\hat{\beta}_2 = \frac{m^*_{Y2}m_{33} - m_{Y3}m_{23}}{m^*_{22}m_{33} - m^2_{23}},$$

$$\hat{\beta}_3 = \frac{m_{Y3}m^*_{22} - m^*_{Y2}m_{23}}{m^*_{22}m_{33} - m^2_{23}},$$

where

$$m^*_{Y2} = m_{Y2} + \frac{6s^2(b + a)}{(b - a)^2},$$

$$m^*_{22} = m_{22} + \frac{12s^2}{(b - a)^2}.$$

Except for the obvious modifications, these formulas are the same as those for the ordinary, unrestricted least squares estimators given by (10.11) through (10.13). The variances of the "mixed" estimators can be estimated as follows:

$$\text{Est. Var}(\hat{\beta}_2) = \frac{s^2m_{33}}{m^*_{22}m_{33} - m^2_{23}}. \tag{11.35}$$

$$\text{Est. Var}(\hat{\beta}_3) = \frac{s^2m^*_{22}}{m^*_{22}m_{33} - m^2_{23}}.$$

These results have been obtained by analogy with (10.24) and (10.25). The "mixed" estimators as defined by (11.34) are consistent and asymptotically efficient under the given specification, but unbiasedness is difficult to prove because the formulas involve s^2 in a nonlinear way. Note, though, that we cannot rule out the possibility that the "mixed" estimator of β_2 falls outside the specified interval. If this should happen, it would reflect the fact that, given the maintained hypothesis of the model, the sample is in disagreement with our prior information about β_2.

Example We may illustrate the method of "mixed" estimation by estimating the coefficients of the quarterly consumption function for the United States,

$$C_t = \alpha + \beta Y_t + \varepsilon_t,$$

where C = consumption and Y = income. The prior information concerning β is

$$0 \leq \beta \leq 1.$$

This function has been estimated by Zellner[8] without the inequality constraint with

[8] A. Zellner, "The Short Run Consumption Function," *Econometrica*, Vol. 25, October 1957, pp. 552–567.

the following result:

$$C_t = 38.09 + \underset{(0.033)}{0.747}\,Y_t + e_t, \qquad \bar{R}^2 = 0.944.$$

If we wish to impose the inequality restriction on β and use the "mixed" estimation method, we put

$$\beta = \tfrac{1}{2} + u,$$

where $$E(u) = 0 \quad \text{and} \quad \text{Var}(u) = \frac{1}{12}.$$

The least squares normal equations then become

$$\sum_t C_t = \hat{\alpha}n + \hat{\beta}\sum_t Y_t,$$

$$\sum_t C_t Y_t + 6s^2 = \hat{\alpha}\sum_t Y_t + \hat{\beta}\Big(\sum_t Y_t^2 + 12s^2\Big).$$

By eliminating $\hat{\alpha}$ we obtain

$$\sum (C_t - \bar{C})(Y_t - \bar{Y}) + 6s^2 = \hat{\beta}\Big[\sum (Y_t - \bar{Y})^2 + 12s^2\Big].$$

Now, from Zellner's results, we find that

$$\sum (C_t - \bar{C})(Y_t - \bar{Y}) = 0.747 \times \sum (Y_t - \bar{Y})^2$$

and $$\frac{s^2}{\sum (Y_t - \bar{Y})^2} = 0.033^2,$$

or $$s^2 = 0.033^2 \times \sum (Y_t - \bar{Y})^2.$$

Therefore,

$$0.747 \times \sum (Y_t - \bar{Y})^2 + 6 \times 0.033^2 \times \sum (Y_t - \bar{Y})^2$$
$$= \hat{\beta}\Big[\sum (Y_t - \bar{Y})^2 + 12 \times 0.033^2 \times \sum (Y_t - \bar{Y})^2\Big].$$

This can be solved for $\hat{\beta}$ because the term $\sum (Y_t - \bar{Y})^2$ cancels out. The result is

$$\hat{\beta} = 0.744$$

and $$\hat{\alpha} = \bar{C} - 0.744\,\bar{Y} = (38.09 + 0.747\,\bar{Y}) - 0.744\,\bar{Y}$$
$$= 38.09 + 0.003 \times 200.55 = 38.69.$$

Finally,

$$\text{Est. Var}(\hat{\beta}) = \frac{s^2}{\sum (Y_t - \bar{Y})^2 + 12s^2} = \frac{0.033^2 \times \sum (Y_t - \bar{Y})^2}{\sum (Y_t - \bar{Y})^2 + 12 \times 0.033^2 \times \sum (Y_t - \bar{Y})^2}$$
$$= 0.001075.$$

The result of the "mixed" estimation of the consumption function therefore is

$$C_t = 38.69 + \underset{(0.033)}{0.744}\,Y_t + e_t.$$

As can be seen, the incorporation of the inequality restriction into the estimation procedure has resulted in only a very slight change in the estimated regression equation in this case.

Linear Restrictions

Frequently, the prior information available is not about the values of the individual regression coefficients, but about the relations among them. For instance, we may know a priori that one coefficient is equal to the sum of two other coefficients, or that certain coefficients form a geometric progression. These restrictions can be divided into two types, depending upon whether the relation between the coefficients is linear or nonlinear. We will discuss the *linear restrictions* first because they are simpler. In either case, we find it convenient to compare the regression equation in which the restrictions are explicitly taken into account with the regression equation in which the restrictions are ignored. The parameters of the former will be called "restricted," and those of the latter "unrestricted." Such a juxtaposition will enable us to introduce the concept of "identification," which plays an important role in many econometric problems. Our discussion will be carried out in terms of examples that illustrate the type of problem and its solution and that can be easily modified to fit other cases.

Consider the problem of estimating a regression model with one explanatory variable and with additive seasonal effects. That is,

$$\begin{aligned}
Y_t &= \alpha_1 + \beta X_t + \varepsilon_t \quad \text{(spring quarter)},\\
Y_t &= \alpha_2 + \beta X_t + \varepsilon_t \quad \text{(summer quarter)},\\
Y_t &= \alpha_3 + \beta X_t + \varepsilon_t \quad \text{(fall quarter)},\\
Y_t &= \alpha_4 + \beta X_t + \varepsilon_t \quad \text{(winter quarter)}.
\end{aligned}$$

By introducing binary variables for the last three quarters, we can rewrite the above compactly:

$$(11.36)\qquad Y_t = \alpha_1 + \beta X_t + (\alpha_2 - \alpha_1)Q_{t2} + (\alpha_3 - \alpha_1)Q_{t3} + (\alpha_4 - \alpha_1)Q_{t4} + \varepsilon_t,$$

where

$$\begin{aligned}
Q_{t2} &= 1 \quad \text{if } t \text{ is a summer quarter},\\
&= 0 \quad \text{otherwise};\\
Q_{t3} &= 1 \quad \text{if } t \text{ is a fall quarter},\\
&= 0 \quad \text{otherwise};\\
Q_{t4} &= 1 \quad \text{if } t \text{ is a winter quarter},\\
&= 0 \quad \text{otherwise}.
\end{aligned}$$

Here we have five restricted parameters: α_1, α_2, α_3, α_4, and β. The restrictions in this case are that α_2 must be equal to the coefficient of Q_{t2} *plus* the intercept, α_3 to the coefficient of Q_{t3} *plus* the intercept, and α_4 to the coefficient of Q_{t4} *plus* the intercept. The unrestricted form of (11.36) is

$$(11.36a)\qquad Y_t = \beta_1 + \beta_2 Q_{t2} + \beta_3 Q_{t3} + \beta_4 Q_{t4} + \beta_5 X_t + \varepsilon_t.$$

When we compare the unrestricted coefficients of (11.36a) with the restricted parameters of (11.36), we can see that

$$\begin{aligned}\beta_1 &= \alpha_1,\\ \beta_2 &= \alpha_2 - \alpha_1,\\ \beta_3 &= \alpha_3 - \alpha_1,\\ \beta_4 &= \alpha_4 - \alpha_1,\\ \beta_5 &= \beta.\end{aligned}$$

In this case there is a one-to-one correspondence between the unrestricted and the restricted parameters and a unique solution for the restricted parameters in terms of the unrestricted parameters. In particular,

$$\begin{aligned}\alpha_1 &= \beta_1,\\ \alpha_2 &= \beta_2 + \beta_1,\\ \alpha_3 &= \beta_3 + \beta_1,\\ \alpha_4 &= \beta_4 + \beta_1,\\ \beta &= \beta_5.\end{aligned}$$

A case like this is called *exact identification* to indicate the fact that the restricted parameters can be uniquely "identified" by reference to the unrestricted coefficients.

The practical importance of exact identification is that we can obtain least squares of estimates of the unrestricted coefficients and use them to obtain estimates of the restricted parameters. Since the estimates of the restricted parameters are all linear functions of the estimates of the unrestricted coefficients, all of the desirable properties of the latter will be carried over to the former. The variances of the estimated restricted parameters can be determined from the variances and covariances of the estimated unrestricted coefficients. In particular,

$$\begin{aligned}\text{Var}(\hat{\alpha}_1) &= \text{Var}(\hat{\beta}_1),\\ \text{Var}(\hat{\alpha}_2) &= \text{Var}(\hat{\beta}_1) + \text{Var}(\hat{\beta}_2) + 2\,\text{Cov}(\hat{\beta}_1,\hat{\beta}_2),\\ \text{Var}(\hat{\alpha}_3) &= \text{Var}(\hat{\beta}_1) + \text{Var}(\hat{\beta}_3) + 2\,\text{Cov}(\hat{\beta}_1,\hat{\beta}_3),\\ \text{Var}(\hat{\alpha}_4) &= \text{Var}(\hat{\beta}_1) + \text{Var}(\hat{\beta}_4) + 2\,\text{Cov}(\hat{\beta}_1,\hat{\beta}_4),\\ \text{Var}(\hat{\beta}) &= \text{Var}(\hat{\beta}_5).\end{aligned}$$

The same relations hold between the respective estimates of the variances. Note that the same results for the estimates of the restricted parameters would be obtained by rewriting (11.36) as

$$Y_t = \alpha_1 Q_{t1} + \alpha_2 Q_{t2} + \alpha_3 Q_{t3} + \alpha_4 Q_{t4} + \beta X_t + \varepsilon_t. \tag{11.36b}$$

where

$$\begin{aligned} Q_{t1} &= 1 \quad \text{if } t \text{ is a spring quarter},\\ &= 0 \quad \text{otherwise}.\end{aligned}$$

Equation (11.36b) is restricted to pass through the origin, and can be estimated by the method of least squares, as described at the outset of this section. The resulting estimates and their variances are precisely the same as those obtained from the unrestricted estimates of (11.36a).

Consider now a different case of linear restrictions, namely, one in which the sum of two or more of the regression coefficients is equal to a given number. A well-known example of such a restriction is the Cobb-Douglas production function characterized by constant returns to scale. Here we require that the sum of the regression slopes be equal to unity. Specifically,

$$Y_i = \alpha_1 + \alpha_2 X_{i2} + (1 - \alpha_2)X_{i3} + \varepsilon_i, \tag{11.37}$$

where Y_i = log output, X_{i2} = log labor input, and X_{i3} = log capital input. We have two restricted parameters: α_1 and α_2. The unrestricted form of (11.37) is

$$Y_i = \beta_1 + \beta_2 X_{i2} + \beta_3 X_{i3} + \varepsilon_i. \tag{11.37a}$$

The relationship between the unrestricted and the restricted parameters is

$$\beta_1 = \alpha_1,$$
$$\beta_2 = \alpha_2,$$
$$\beta_3 = 1 - \alpha_2.$$

In this case, the number of unrestricted coefficients exceeds the number of the restricted parameters, and there is no unique solution for α_2. In fact,

$$\alpha_1 = \beta_1,$$
$$\alpha_2 = \beta_2,$$

and

$$\alpha_2 = 1 - \beta_3.$$

This case is called *overidentification*, alluding to the fact that there is more than one solution to "identify" the restricted parameter α_2.

Under the conditions of overidentification, we cannot proceed with estimation (as we can with exact identification) by estimating the unrestricted equation and then translating the results to obtain estimates of the restricted parameters. Rather, we must turn directly to the restricted equation (11.37). The least squares estimators of the restricted parameters can be obtained by minimizing

$$\sum_i [Y_i - \alpha_1 - \alpha_2 X_{i2} - (1 - \alpha_2)X_{i3}]^2$$

with respect to α_1 and α_2. It can be easily shown that the resulting estimates are exactly the same as those obtained by applying the least squares method to

$$Y_i^* = \alpha_1 + \alpha_2 X_{i2}^* + \varepsilon_i, \tag{11.37b}$$

where Y_i^* is measured by $(Y_i - X_{i3})$ and X_{i2}^* by $(X_{i2} - X_{i3})$. Equation (11.37b) represents just another way of writing (11.37) by rearranging its terms. This possibility is always open whenever we have overidentification and whenever the restrictions are linear.

As a third and final case of linear restrictions, we consider the case where the number of the restricted parameters is larger than the number of unrestricted coefficients. For example, suppose that family expenditure on fruit can be described by the following regression equation:

$$F_i = \alpha_F + \beta_F Y_i + \varepsilon_{iF},$$

where F_i = family expenditure on fruit, and Y_i = family income. Suppose further that family expenditure on vegetables can be described by

$$V_i = \alpha_V + \beta_V Y_i + \varepsilon_{iV},$$

where V_i = family expenditure on vegetables. Now if, as is commonly the case, the sample does not provide separate information on expenditure on fruit and on vegetables but only their total, we have to combine the foregoing regressions to get

$$G_i = (\alpha_F + \alpha_V) + (\beta_F + \beta_V)Y_i + \varepsilon_i, \tag{11.38}$$

where $G_i = F_i + V_i$, and $\varepsilon_i = \varepsilon_{iF} + \varepsilon_{iV}$. The unrestricted version of (11.38) is

$$G_i = \alpha + \beta Y_i + \varepsilon_i. \tag{11.38a}$$

when we compare the coefficients of the two equations, we get

$$\alpha = \alpha_F + \alpha_V \quad \text{and} \quad \beta = \beta_F + \beta_V.$$

Here we have four restricted parameters and only two unrestricted coefficients. Clearly, we cannot express the restricted parameters in terms of the unrestricted coefficients. This is known as the case of *underidentification*, in which the restricted parameters cannot be estimated on the basis of the available sample information.

Nonlinear Restrictions

As our first case of nonlinear restrictions we consider *exact identification*. This can be illustrated by a simple version of the so-called "stock adjustment model." Suppose the volume of stock of a commodity that a firm "desires" to hold is equal to a given linear function of sales, i.e.,

$$Y_t^* = \alpha + \beta X_t,$$

where Y_t^* = desired level of stock at the end of period t, and X_t = sales during the period t. Y^* is, in general, not observable. Now suppose further that the adjustment on the part of each firm to the desired level in any one period is not complete, so that

$$Y_t - Y_{t-1} = \gamma(Y_t^* - Y_{t-1}) + \varepsilon_t,$$

where Y_t = actual level of stock at the end of period t. The parameter γ is called the "adjustment coefficient," and its value lies between 0 and 1. A value of γ close to zero indicates that only a small part of the gap between the desired and the actual level of stock is closed during any one period, while a value of γ close to unity indicates that a large part of the gap is closed. The disturbance ε_t is brought in to allow for random influences in carrying out the adjustment. Substituting for Y_t^* and rearranging terms, we obtain

$$Y_t = \alpha\gamma + \beta\gamma X_t + (1 - \gamma)Y_{t-1} + \varepsilon_t. \tag{11.39}$$

This is an equation that explains investment in stock. All variables in this equation except ε_t are observable. In (11.39) we have three "restricted" parameters: α, β, and γ. The unrestricted counterpart of (11.39) is

$$Y_t = \beta_1 + \beta_2 X_t + \beta_3 Y_{t-1} + \varepsilon_t. \tag{11.39a}$$

The coefficients of (11.39a) are related to the parameters of (11.39) as follows:

$$\beta_1 = \alpha\gamma,$$

$$\beta_2 = \beta\gamma,$$

$$\beta_3 = 1 - \gamma.$$

In this case, we can obtain a unique solution for the restricted parameters in terms of the unrestricted coefficients; that is, we have *exact identification.* The solution is

$$\alpha = \frac{\beta_1}{1 - \beta_3},$$

$$\beta = \frac{\beta_2}{1 - \beta_3},$$

$$\gamma = 1 - \beta_3.$$

Note that α and β are *nonlinear* functions of the unrestricted β's.

To estimate the parameters of (11.39), we obtain least squares estimates of the unrestricted coefficients of (11.39a), and use the solution for α, β, and γ to obtain the corresponding estimates of these parameters. [The inequality restrictions on γ, and consequently on β_3, can be taken care of by following the rule specified in (11.31).] As for the desirable properties of the resulting estimators, we note that those estimators which are nonlinear functions of the unconstrained coefficients inherit the desirable asymptotic, but *not* small-sample, properties from the unconstrained estimators. The reason is that unbiasedness does not "carry over" *via* nonlinear functions (see Theorem 17 and the subsequent remarks in Section 6–1). In the present case, the unconstrained estimators themselves are not unbiased because of the presence of Y_{t-1} among the explanatory variables, so that *none* of the constrained estimators can be claimed to be unbiased. The variance of the restricted estimator of γ can be determined by reference to the variance of the unrestricted $\hat{\beta}_3$ if we note that

$$\text{Var}(\hat{\gamma}) = \text{Var}(\hat{\beta}_3).$$

The determination of the variances of $\hat{\alpha}$ and $\hat{\beta}$ is somewhat more troublesome because $\hat{\alpha}$ and $\hat{\beta}$ are not linear functions of the unrestricted estimators. However, there is an approximate formula that can be used in this case. The formula refers to the general case where an estimator, say $\hat{\alpha}$, is a function of k other estimators such as, $\hat{\beta}_1, \hat{\beta}_2, \ldots, \hat{\beta}_k$; i.e.,

$$\hat{\alpha} = f(\hat{\beta}_1, \hat{\beta}_2, \ldots, \hat{\beta}_k).$$

Then the large-sample variance of $\hat{\alpha}$ can be approximated[9] as

$$\text{(11.40)} \qquad \text{Var}(\hat{\alpha}) \approx \sum_k \left[\frac{\partial f}{\partial \hat{\beta}_k}\right]^2 \text{Var}(\hat{\beta}_k) + 2 \sum_{j<k} \left[\frac{\partial f}{\partial \hat{\beta}_j}\right]\left[\frac{\partial f}{\partial \hat{\beta}_k}\right] \text{Cov}(\hat{\beta}_j, \hat{\beta}_k)$$

$$(j, k = 1, 2, \ldots, K; j < k).$$

(The approximation is obtained by using Taylor expansion for $f(\hat{\beta}_1, \hat{\beta}_2, \ldots, \hat{\beta}_k)$ around $\hat{\beta}_1, \hat{\beta}_2, \ldots, \hat{\beta}_k$, dropping terms of the order of two or higher, and then obtaining the variance by the usual formula.) For example, for

$$\hat{\alpha} = \frac{\hat{\beta}_1}{1 - \hat{\beta}_3},$$

we have

$$\text{Var}(\hat{\alpha}) \approx \left[\frac{1}{1 - \hat{\beta}_3}\right]^2 \text{Var}(\hat{\beta}_1) + \left[\frac{\hat{\beta}_1}{(1 - \hat{\beta}_3)^2}\right]^2 \text{Var}(\hat{\beta}_3)$$

$$+ 2\left[\frac{1}{1 - \hat{\beta}_3}\right]\left[\frac{\hat{\beta}_1}{(1 - \hat{\beta}_3)^2}\right] \text{Cov}(\hat{\beta}_1, \hat{\beta}_3).$$

This formula can be used to approximate the large-sample variance of $\hat{\alpha}$. Since the large-sample variances and covariances of the unrestricted estimators can be readily estimated by the application of the standard formulas, there is no problem in estimating the large-sample variances of the restricted estimators.

An alternative approach to estimating the parameters of (11.39) is to minimize the sum of squares S given by

$$S = \sum_{t=2}^{n} [Y_t - \alpha\gamma - \beta\gamma X_t - (1 - \gamma) Y_{t-1}]^2$$

with respect to α, β, and γ. The resulting estimators of these parameters are called *nonlinear least squares estimators*. It can easily be shown that these estimators are exactly the same as those obtained from the estimated unconstrained coefficients of (11.39a). Further, since the logarithmic likelihood function for $Y_2, Y_3, \ldots, Y_n$ (conditional on Y_1) is

$$L = -\frac{n}{2} \log 2\pi\sigma^2 - \frac{1}{2\sigma^2} \sum_{t=2}^{n} [Y_t - \alpha\gamma - \beta\gamma X_t - (1 - \gamma) Y_{t-1}]^2,$$

minimizing S with respect to α, β, and γ is equivalent to maximizing L with respect to the same parameters. Thus, if the regression disturbance is normally

[9] See L. R. Klein, *A Textbook of Econometrics* (Evanston, Illinois: Row, Peterson, 1953), p. 258.

distributed, nonlinear least squares estimators are the same as maximum likelihood estimators. Therefore, we can estimate their asymptotic variances by using the appropriate information matrix.

EXAMPLE The case of nonlinear restrictions under conditions of exact identification is encountered in connection with one of the consumption function models considered by Zellner.[10] This model is not a "stock adjustment model" in the strict sense, but it has the same basic features. If we use a simple variant of the "permanent income hypothesis," we can postulate the consumption function as

$$C_t = \alpha + k(1 - \lambda)Y_t + \lambda C_{t-1} + u_t$$

where C = real consumption, and Y = real income. The unrestricted counterpart of this equation is

$$C_t = \beta_1 + \beta_2 Y_t + \beta_3 C_{t-1} + u_t.$$

The disturbance term u_t was assumed to be nonautoregressive. Zellner estimated the unrestricted function from 31 quarterly observations for the United States with the following result:

$$C_t = \underset{}{0.10} + \underset{(0.093)}{0.128 Y_t} + \underset{(0.127)}{0.870 C_{t-1}} + e_t, \qquad \bar{R}^2 = 0.978.$$

Therefore, the estimates of the restricted parameters are

$$\hat{\alpha} = \hat{\beta}_1 = 0.10,$$

$$\hat{k} = \frac{\hat{\beta}_2}{1 - \hat{\beta}_3} = 0.985,$$

$$\hat{\lambda} = \hat{\beta}_3 = 0.870.$$

The estimate of the large-sample standard error of $\hat{\lambda}$ can be obtained directly from the unrestricted result. The estimated large-sample standard error of $\hat{k}$ can be found by using the approximation formula (11.40), i.e., by noting that

$$\operatorname{Var}(\hat{k}) = \left[\frac{1}{1 - \hat{\beta}_3}\right]^2 \operatorname{Var}(\hat{\beta}_2) + \left[\frac{\hat{\beta}_2}{(1 - \hat{\beta}_3)^2}\right]^2 \operatorname{Var}(\hat{\beta}_3)$$

$$+ 2\left[\frac{1}{1 - \hat{\beta}_3}\right]\left[\frac{\hat{\beta}_2}{(1 - \hat{\beta}_3)^2}\right] \operatorname{Cov}(\hat{\beta}_2, \hat{\beta}_3).$$

Estimates of $\operatorname{Var}(\hat{\beta}_2)$ and $\operatorname{Var}(\hat{\beta}_3)$ are directly available from Zellner's results. The estimate of $\operatorname{Cov}(\hat{\beta}_2, \hat{\beta}_3)$ can be obtained by noting that

$$\operatorname{Cov}(\hat{\beta}_2, \hat{\beta}_3) = \frac{-\sigma^2 m_{23}}{m_{22}m_{33} - m_{23}^2} = \frac{-\sigma^2 r_{23}\sqrt{m_{22}}\sqrt{m_{33}}}{m_{22}m_{33} - m_{23}^2} = -r_{23}\sqrt{\operatorname{Var}(\hat{\beta}_2)}\sqrt{\operatorname{Var}(\hat{\beta}_3)},$$

so that the only additional information needed is the value of r_{23}, the sample coefficient of correlation between Y_t and C_{t-1}. This value can be found from the relation

[10] *Op. cit.* The theoretical development is not given in Zellner's paper but can be found in A. Zellner, D. S. Huang, and L. C. Chau, "Further Analysis of the Short-Run Consumption Function with Emphasis on the Role of Liquid Assets," *Econometrica*, Vol. 33, July 1965, pp. 571–581.

between the F statistic and the two t statistics. First, since $\bar{R}^2 = 0.978$, it follows from (10.41) that

$$R^2 = 0.9795.$$

Therefore, by reference to (10.43),

$$F = \frac{R^2/(3-1)}{(1-R^2)/(31-3)} = 669.$$

This enables us to utilize (10.44b):

$$669 = \frac{(0.128/0.093)^2 + (0.870/0.127)^2 + 2(0.128/0.093)(0.870/0.127)r_{23}}{2(1-r_{23}^2)}.$$

This is a quadratic equation in r_{23} which has one positive and one negative root. We choose the positive root since the sample correlation between Y_t and C_{t-1} is clearly positive. This gives

$$r_{23} = 0.975,$$

and

$$\text{Est. Cov}(\hat{\beta}_2, \hat{\beta}_3) = -0.975 \times 0.093 \times 0.127 = -0.011515.$$

Therefore,

$$\text{Est. Var}(\hat{k}) = \left[\frac{1}{1-0.870}\right]^2 0.093^2 + \left[\frac{0.128}{(1-0.870)^2}\right]^2 0.127^2$$

$$+ \left[\frac{1}{1-0.870}\right]\left[\frac{0.128}{(1-0.870)^2}\right](-0.011515) = 0.095175.$$

Thus, the estimated large-sample standard errors of the restricted estimators are

$$s_{\hat{\lambda}} = 0.127 \quad \text{and} \quad s_{\hat{k}} = 0.308.$$

This means that both $\hat{\lambda}$ and $\hat{k}$ are highly significant.

To illustrate *overidentifying nonlinear restrictions*, we use a simple regression model in which the disturbance follows a first-order autoregressive scheme. In particular, suppose we have

$$Y_t = \alpha + \beta X_t + \varepsilon_t,$$

$$\varepsilon_t = \rho\varepsilon_{t-1} + u_t,$$

where $u_t \sim N(0, \sigma_u^2)$, and $E(u_t\varepsilon_{t-1}) = 0$. As mentioned in Section 8–2, the regression equation can be transformed in such a way that the autoregressive disturbance ε_t is eliminated. By lagging the regression equation by one period, multiplying it by ρ, and deducting the result from the original form of the regression equation, we obtain

$$Y_t - \rho Y_{t-1} = \alpha(1-\rho) + \beta(X_t - \rho X_{t-1}) + u_t.$$

This equation appears as (8.52) in Section 8–2. Alternatively,

(11.41) $$Y_t = \alpha(1-\rho) + \beta X_t - \beta\rho X_{t-1} + \rho Y_{t-1} + u_t,$$

which is a multiple regression equation with parameters α, β, and ρ. The unrestricted counterpart of (11.41) is

$$(11.41a) \qquad Y_t = \beta_1 + \beta_2 X_t + \beta_3 X_{t-1} + \beta_4 Y_{t-1} + u_t.$$

By comparing the two versions, we see that

$$\beta_1 = \alpha(1 - \rho),$$

$$\beta_2 = \beta,$$

$$\beta_3 = -\beta\rho,$$

$$\beta_4 = \rho.$$

That is, we have four unrestricted coefficients and only three restricted parameters. Since there is no unique solution for any of the restricted parameters in terms of the unrestricted coefficients, we clearly have a case of *overidentification.* However, there is no great difficulty about estimating the restricted parameters by the nonlinear least squares method; i.e., we can minimize

$$S = \sum_{t=2}^{n} [Y_t - \alpha(1 - \rho) - \beta X_t + \beta\rho X_{t-1} - \rho Y_{t-1}]^2$$

with respect to α, β, and ρ. The resulting estimates are equivalent to the maximum likelihood estimates (conditional on Y_1), and their asymptotic variances can be estimated by reference to the information matrix. A convenient way of carrying out the calculations on a digital computer is described in Section 8–2, where we also discuss several alternative estimation methods designed for this model. The maximum likelihood estimation method is available for any kind of overidentification; but in some cases the computations are highly complicated, and it is not always guaranteed that the maximum of the likelihood function is not a local one rather than a global one.

Finally, we consider *underidentification.* We shall illustrate this in the context of a model in which some parameters are overidentified and some are underidentified. Consider another consumption function model developed and estimated by Zellner, Huang, and Chau:[11]

$$(11.42) \qquad C_t = (k - \alpha\eta)(1 - \lambda)Y_t + \alpha L_{t-1} - \alpha\lambda L_{t-2} + \lambda C_{t-1} + u_t,$$

where

$$u_t = \varepsilon_t - \lambda\varepsilon_{t-1},$$

and L = actual holdings of liquid assets at the end of the period. Thus we have four parameters—α, λ, k, and η—to estimate. The unrestricted version of (11.42) is

$$(11.42a) \qquad C_t = \beta_1 Y_t + \beta_2 L_{t-1} + \beta_3 L_{t-2} + \beta_4 C_{t-1} + u_t.$$

[11] *Ibid.*

There are then four unrestricted coefficients in (11.42a). The relation between the parameters of (11.42) and the coefficients of (11.42a) is

$$\beta_1 = (k - \alpha\eta)(1 - \lambda),$$

$$\beta_2 = \alpha,$$

$$\beta_3 = -\alpha\lambda,$$

$$\beta_4 = \lambda.$$

From this, we can see that

$$\alpha = \beta_2 \quad \text{or} \quad \alpha = -\frac{\beta_3}{\beta_4},$$

and

$$\lambda = \beta_4 \quad \text{or} \quad \lambda = -\frac{\beta_3}{\beta_2}.$$

Thus, α and λ are overidentified, but no solution exists for k and η. This means that k and η are underidentified. The implication of this is that α and λ can be estimated by the nonlinear least squares method, but no estimates of k and η are obtainable from the sample. All that can be done is to get an estimate of $(k - \alpha\eta)$.

EXAMPLE The estimates of the parameters of (11.42) have been obtained by Zellner, Huang, and Chau from quarterly data for the United States on the assumption that u_t is nonautoregressive. The result of the nonlinear least squares estimation is

$$C_t = \underset{(0.085)}{0.475\,Y_t} + \underset{(0.045)}{0.226L_{t-1}} - 0.085L_{t-2} + \underset{(0.106)}{0.378C_{t-1}} + e_t.$$

Thus,

$$\hat{\alpha} = 0.226,$$

$$\hat{\lambda} = 0.378,$$

$$\hat{k} - 0.226\hat{\eta} = 0.763.$$

This equation was also estimated by the nonlinear least squares method with the addition of a constant term:

$$C_t = -12.470 + \underset{(0.080)}{0.538\,Y_t} + \underset{(0.050)}{0.376L_{t-1}} - 0.091L_{t-2} + \underset{(0.105)}{0.242C_{t-1}} + e_t.$$

The result of the unrestricted least squares estimation of the previous equation is

$$C_t = \underset{(3.606)}{-1.082} + \underset{(0.085)}{0.517\,Y_t} + \underset{(0.172)}{0.560L_{t-1}} - \underset{(0.181)}{0.296L_{t-2}} + \underset{(0.110)}{0.273C_{t-1}} + e_t.$$

Note that the unrestricted estimates are numerically different from the restricted estimates, but for some coefficients the differences are not overwhelming.

The Effect of Restrictions on R^2 and the Variance of the Forecast Error

In the case where the restricted parameters are exactly identified in terms of the unrestricted coefficients, the restricted estimates lead to the same sample regression equation as the unrestricted estimates. This means that the value of

R^2 and the forecast of the value of the dependent variable are the same for both sets of estimates. However, if the restricted estimation is carried out under conditions of overidentification, then the sample regression line based on the restricted estimates will be different from the sample regression line based on the unrestricted estimates. Since the unrestricted least squares estimates minimize the sum of squares of the residuals, they lead to the maximum attainable value of R^2. This necessarily implies that the value of R^2 for the restricted sample regression equation will be lower than, or equal to, the value of R^2 for the unrestricted sample regression equation. This fact has been used sometimes as an argument for supposing that a forecast of the value of the dependent variable based on the unrestricted estimates is better than one based on the restricted estimates. If we interpret the word "better" as meaning "having a smaller (or equal) variance of the forecast error," then the argument is fallacious. We shall prove this for the case of overidentification under linear restrictions, but the proof could be extended to apply to nonlinear restrictions as well. (In the case of nonlinear restrictions, the proof is complicated by the fact that the restricted estimators are nonlinear functions of the disturbances. However, a proof in terms of asymptotic variances and covariances is quite feasible.)

Consider, for instance, the regression equation (11.37), which we have used to illustrate overidentification with linear restrictions. The equation was presented as

$$Y_i = \alpha_1 + \alpha_2 X_{i2} + (1 - \alpha_2)X_{i3} + \varepsilon_i,$$

with the unrestricted version given by (11.37a) as

$$Y_i = \beta_1 + \beta_2 X_{i2} + \beta_3 X_{i3} + \varepsilon_i.$$

Suppose now that we wish to forecast the value of Y for some given values of the two explanatory variables, say X_{02} and X_{03}. Using the unrestricted regression equation, we would forecast the value of Y by, say, $\hat{Y}_0$, defined as

$$\hat{Y}_0 = \hat{\beta}_1 + \hat{\beta}_2 X_{02} + \hat{\beta}_3 X_{03},$$

where the $\hat{\beta}$'s represent the unrestricted least squares estimates of the β's. Using the formula (10.49), we can determine the variance of the forecast error of $\hat{Y}_0$ as

$$(11.43)\quad E(\hat{Y}_0 - Y_0)^2 = \sigma^2 + \frac{\sigma^2}{u} + (X_{02} - \bar{X}_2)^2\mathrm{Var}(\hat{\beta}_2) + (X_{03} - \bar{X}_3)^2\mathrm{Var}(\hat{\beta}_3)$$
$$+ 2(X_{02} - \bar{X}_2)(X_{03} - \bar{X}_3)\mathrm{Cov}(\hat{\beta}_2, \hat{\beta}_3)$$
$$= \sigma^2\left[1 + \frac{1}{n} + \frac{(X_{02} - \bar{X}_2)^2 m_{33} + (X_{03} - \bar{X}_3)^2 m_{22}}{m_{22}m_{33} - m_{23}^2} - \frac{2(X_{02} - \bar{X}_2)(X_{03} - \bar{X}_3)m_{23}}{m_{22}m_{33} - m_{23}^2}\right].$$

On the other hand, if we use the restricted regression equation for forecasting the value of Y, we use $\tilde{Y}_0$ defined as

$$\tilde{Y}_0 = \hat{\alpha}_1 + \hat{\alpha}_2 X_{02} + (1 - \hat{\alpha}_2)X_{03},$$

where the $\hat{\alpha}$'s represent the restricted least squares estimates of the α's. The variance of the forecast error in this case is

$$(11.44)\quad E(\tilde{Y}_0 - Y_0)^2 = E[(\tilde{Y}_0 - X_{03}) - (Y_0 - X_{03})]^2$$

$$= \sigma^2 + \frac{\sigma^2}{n} + [(X_{02} - X_{03}) - (\bar{X}_2 - \bar{X}_3)]^2 \text{Var}(\hat{\alpha}_2)$$

$$= \sigma^2\left[1 + \frac{1}{n} + \frac{(X_{02} - \bar{X}_2)^2 + (X_{03} - \bar{X}_3)^2}{m_{22} + m_{33} - 2m_{23}} - \frac{2(X_{02} - \bar{X}_2)(X_{03} - \bar{X}_3)}{m_{22} + m_{33} - 2m_{23}}\right].$$

Let us now compare (11.43) with (11.44). The difference between the two is

(11.45)

$$E(\hat{Y}_0 - Y_0)^2 - E(\tilde{Y}_0 - Y_0)^2$$

$$= \sigma^2\left[\frac{(X_{02} - \bar{X}_2)^2 m_{33} + (X_{03} - \bar{X}_3)^2 m_{22} - 2(X_{02} - \bar{X}_2)(X_{03} - \bar{X}_3) m_{23}}{m_{22}m_{33} - m_{23}^2} - \frac{(X_{02} - \bar{X}_2)^2 + (X_{03} - \bar{X}_3)^2 - 2(X_{02} - \bar{X}_2)(X_{03} - \bar{X}_3)}{m_{22} + m_{33} - 2m_{23}}\right]$$

$$= \sigma^2\left\{\frac{[(X_{02} - \bar{X}_2)(m_{33} - m_{23}) + (X_{03} - \bar{X}_3)(m_{22} - m_{23})]^2}{(m_{22}m_{33} - m_{23}^2)(m_{22} + m_{33} - 2m_{23})}\right\}.$$

This expression is clearly positive (or zero), which indicates that the variance of the forecast error for the unrestricted predictor $\hat{Y}_0$ is larger than, or at best equal to, the variance of the forecast error for the restricted predictor $\tilde{Y}_0$. This means that the restricted regression equation leads to a better forecasting procedure than the unrestricted regression equation.

The Role of Prior Restrictions in Estimation

A useful way of ending this section may be by making a few remarks on the relevance of prior restrictions in estimation. Prior restrictions on the regression coefficients represent information about the population regression equation. If this information is correct, then we may increase the efficiency of our estimators by incorporating this information into our estimation procedure. The extent of this increase in efficiency depends on the type of information (i.e., how *specific* it is) and on the variances of the unconstrained estimators, assuming that these variances exist and that the unconstrained estimators are squared-error consistent. For instance, suppose the prior restriction is in the form of a statement that a given regression coefficient, say, β, is positive. Then, if the variance of the unconstrained estimator of β is small, we may get samples with a negative estimate of β only very rarely. Therefore, the restriction may not, for all practical purposes, be "restrictive" at all. In this case, the value of the prior information may be negligible. This brings up another aspect of prior information—namely, that its value diminishes with the size of the sample. This is because the variances of the unconstrained estimators will, in general, decrease as the sample size increases. This is true regardless of how specific the restrictions are. For example, even such a specific restriction as one that confines β to a given number is not of much value to us if, in fact, the estimates of β are highly concentrated in the near vicinity of the true value of the parameter. In the limit (i.e., when $n \rightarrow \infty$), prior information is of no more use. However, if the estimates tend to be highly concentrated around a value different from that specified by the restriction, then either our prior information is false, or the model is misspecified and the claim that the unconstrained estimator is consistent is not justified. Unfortunately, in economics our samples are typically small and generation of additional observations is severely limited, so that prior information is highly valuable. For this reason its use—frequently neglected in applied econometric work—ought to be strongly encouraged.

11-3 Nonlinear Models

The models that we have considered so far have, with a few minor exceptions, all been characterized by linear regression equations. However, this is not as restrictive as it might at first appear for the following reasons. First, all the results for the linear regression models derived in the preceding chapters may apply without any modification to regression models that are nonlinear with respect to the variables but linear with respect to the parameters to be estimated. Second, regression models that are nonlinear with respect to the variables *as well as* with respect to the parameters to be estimated can be analyzed by using many of the basic principles and results derived in connection with purely linear models. Nonlinear regression models can thus be classified into two groups according to whether they are or are not linear with respect to the parameters to be estimated. We may call the first type "models that are intrinsically linear," and the second type "models that are intrinsically nonlinear." We shall discuss each type separately. In addition, we shall also consider the problem of how to test for linearity in the case where the functional form of the regression equation is in doubt.

Intrinsically Linear Models

A nonlinear model that is intrinsically linear is, as indicated, *nonlinear* with respect to the variables but *linear* with respect to the parameters to be estimated. The basic common characteristic of such models is that they can be converted into ordinary linear models by a suitable transformation of the variables. Frequently, such a transformation amounts to nothing more than relabeling one or more of the variables. We have already used some of these models without even having to pause over the fact that some of the variables entered the regression equation in a nonlinear way. Our present intention is to consider intrinsically linear models in a systematic way and with some attention to detail. As the first case, we take a model in which the regressors are represented by a *power series* in X_i:

$$Y_i = \beta_1 + \beta_2 X_i + \beta_3 X_i^2 + \cdots + \beta_K X_i^{K-1} + \varepsilon_i, \tag{11.46}$$

where X_i is nonstochastic and bounded, and ε_i satisfies all the assumptions of the classical normal linear regression model. For instance, the specification may call first for an increase and then for a decrease in $E(Y_i)$ in response to increases in X_i, as in the relationship between income and age of an individual. In this case, the power series would be given by a parabola

$$Y_i = \beta_1 + \beta_2 X_i + \beta_2 X_i^2 + \varepsilon_i,$$

as illustrated in Figure 11–5. But whatever the degree of the polynomial in (11.46), the equation can be rewritten as

$$Y_i = \beta_1 + \beta_2 Z_{i2} + \beta_3 Z_{i3} + \cdots + \beta_K Z_{iK} + \varepsilon_i, \tag{11.46a}$$

where $Z_{i2} = X_i, Z_{i3} = X_i^2, \ldots, Z_{iK} = X_i^{K-1}$. Then, if the number of observations exceeds K, the ordinary least squares estimators of the regression coefficients of (11.46a) will have the desirable properties. However, the Z's will often

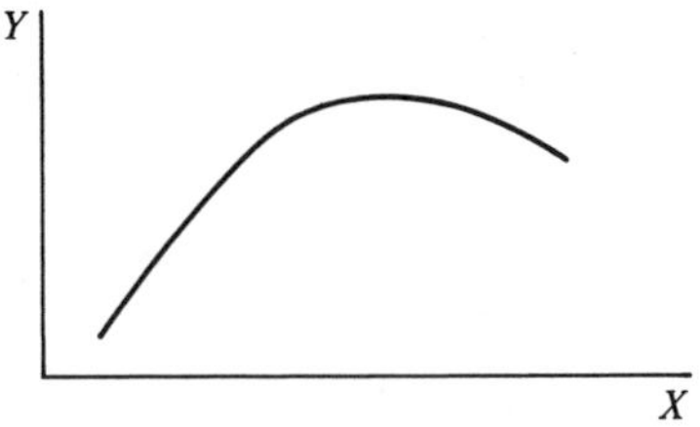

Figure 11–5

be highly correlated, so that the variances of the estimated regression coefficients may be quite large.[12] One nice feature of the power function (11.46) or its equivalent (11.46a) is that we can easily test the hypothesis that the degree of the polynomial is less than $(K - 1)$. For example, we may wish to test the hypothesis that the regression equation is linear against the alternative hypothesis that the regression equation is represented by a polynomial of degree $(K - 1)$. The formulation would be

$$H_0: \quad \beta_3 = \beta_4 = \cdots = \beta_K = 0,$$

$$H_A: \quad H_0 \text{ is not true}.$$

[12] If the sample values of X_i are equally spaced, the computations of the least squares estimates can be simplified by the use of the so-called "orthogonal polynomial transformation"; see, e.g., R. L. Anderson and T. A. Bancroft, *Stastitical Theory in Research* (New York: McGraw-Hill, 1952), pp. 207–214. Of course, this does not affect the variances of the least squares estimates of the β's.

The relevant test procedure is described in Section 10-2, with the test statistic given by the formula (10.45).

The preceding discussion is of some relevance not only for the regression models in which the explanatory variable (or variables) enters in the form of a power function, but also for any nonlinear regression model in general. The reason is that any function $f(x)$ that is continuous and has a continuous pth derivative can be written as

$$(11.47)\quad f(x) = f(a) + (x-a)f'(a) + \frac{(x-a)^2}{2!}f''(a) + \frac{(x-a)^3}{3!}f'''(a) + \cdots + \frac{(x-a)^p}{p!}f^{(p)}(a) + R_{p+1},$$

where a is any fixed number in the domain of X and

$$f(a) = f(x)\Big|_{x=a},$$

$$f'(a) = \frac{df(x)}{dx}\Big|_{x=a},$$

$$f''(a) = \frac{d^2f(x)}{dx}\Big|_{x=a}$$

$$\vdots$$

$$R_{p+1} = \text{remainder}.$$

The series given in (11.47) is called the *Taylor's series expansion* of $f(x)$ about the point $x = a$. If p is sufficiently large, the remainder R_{p+1} will be small. Therefore, by disregarding R_{p+1} we obtain an approximation of $f(x)$, which we can make as close as we like by a suitable choice of p.

Example 1 Let $f(x) = b_0 + b_1x + b_2x^2 + b_3x^3$, and let $p = 3$. Suppose we expand $f(x)$ around $x = 0$. Then we have

$$f(0) = b_0,$$

$$f'(0) = (b_1 + 2b_2x + 3b_3x^2)_{x=0} = b_1,$$

$$f''(0) = (2b_2 + 6b_3x)_{x=0} = 2b_2,$$

$$f'''(0) = 6b_3,$$

so that

$$f(x) = b_0 + (x-0)b_1 + \frac{(x-0)^2}{2}2b_2 + \frac{(x-0)^3}{6}6b_3$$

$$= b_0 + b_1x + b_2x^2 + b_3x^3,$$

which is exactly correct.

EXAMPLE 2 Let $f(x) = e^{bx}$, $p = 3$, and $a = 0$. Then we have

$$f(0) = 1,$$
$$f'(0) = (be^{bx})_{x=0} = b,$$
$$f''(0) = (b^2e^{bx})_{x=0} = b^2,$$
$$f'''(0) = (b^3e^{bx})_{x=0} = b^3,$$

so that
$$f(x) \approx 1 + bx + \left[\frac{b^2}{2}\right]x^2 + \left[\frac{b^3}{6}\right]x^3.$$

If, for instance, $b = 1$, then the approximate values of $f(x)$ for various values of x are

x	Exact $f(x)$	Approximate $f(x)$
0	1.0000	1.0000
0.5	1.6487	1.6458
1	2.7183	2.6667
2	7.3891	6.3333
3	20.0860	13.0000

As shown, the approximation becomes poorer as we move away from the value around which the series is being expanded.

The Taylor's series expansion can be extended to apply to a function of more than one variable. In particular, the expansion for *two* variables is given by

$$(11.48)\qquad f(x,z) = f(a,b) + f_x(a,b)(x - a) + f_z(a,b)(z - b) + \frac{1}{2!}[f_{xx}(a,b)(x - a)^2 + 2f_{xz}(a,b)(x - a)(z - b) + f_{zz}(a,b)(z - b)^2] + \cdots,$$

where
$$f_x(a,b) = \left.\frac{\partial f(x,z)}{\partial x}\right|_{\substack{x=a\\z=b}},$$

$$f_z(a,b) = \left.\frac{\partial f(x,z)}{\partial z}\right|_{\substack{x=a\\z=b}},$$

$$f_{xx}(a,b) = \left.\frac{\partial^2 f(x,z)}{\partial x^2}\right|_{\substack{x=a\\z=b}},$$

$$f_{xz}(a,b) = \left.\frac{\partial^2 f(x,z)}{\partial x \partial z}\right|_{\substack{x=a\\z=b}},$$

$$f_{zz}(a,b) = \left. \frac{\partial^2 f(x,z)}{\partial z^2} \right|_{\substack{x=a \\ z=b}},$$

etc. Formula (11.48) has been used to obtain linear approximations of products and ratios of two variables by expanding the series about the sample means of the two variables and retaining only the first three terms of the expansion.[13] Specifically,

$$\text{(11.49)} \quad X_i Z_i \approx \bar{X}\bar{Z} + \bar{Z}(X_i - \bar{X}) + \bar{X}(Z_i - \bar{Z}) \approx \bar{Z}X_i + \bar{X}Z_i - \bar{X}\bar{Z},$$

$$\text{(11.50)} \quad \frac{X_i}{Z_i} \approx \frac{\bar{X}}{\bar{Z}} + \frac{1}{\bar{Z}}(X_i - \bar{X}) + \left[-\frac{\bar{X}}{\bar{Z}^2}\right](Z_i - \bar{Z})$$

$$\approx \frac{\bar{X}}{\bar{Z}} + \left[\frac{1}{\bar{Z}}\right]X_i - \left[\frac{\bar{X}}{\bar{Z}^2}\right]Z_i.$$

Consider now a regression equation in which the change in $E(Y_i)$ corresponding to a unit change in X_{ij} depends on the level of X_{ik}. Formally, suppose the mean value of the dependent variable is some function of two nonstochastic explanatory variables X_{i2} and X_{i3}

$$E(Y_i) = f(X_{i2}, X_{i3})$$

such that

$$\frac{\partial E(Y_i)}{\partial X_{i2}} = g(X_{i3})$$

and

$$\frac{\partial E(Y_i)}{\partial X_{i3}} = h(X_{i2}),$$

where $g(X_{i3})$ and $h(X_{i2})$ are some functions whose mathematical form is specified a priori. There are many situations in which such a model is appropriate. For example, in estimations of Engel curves from cross-section data, family expenditure on a given commodity is frequently considered to be dependent on family income and family size. It may be reasonable to expect that families of different sizes respond to a given change in income in a different way, and that families in different income brackets respond differently to a change in family size. The simplest formulation of such a model is obtained by introducing a so-called *interaction term*, defined as a multiple of the product of the two explanatory variables, into the linear regression equation:

$$\text{(11.51)} \quad Y_i = \beta_1 + \beta_2 X_{i2} + \beta_3 X_{i3} + \beta_4 X_{i2} X_{i3} + \varepsilon_i.$$

In this model

$$\frac{\partial E(Y_i)}{\partial X_{i2}} = \beta_2 + \beta_4 X_{i3}$$

and

$$\frac{\partial E(Y_i)}{\partial X_{i3}} = \beta_3 + \beta_4 X_{i2}.$$

[13] See Klein, *op. cit.*, pp. 120–121.

The functions $g(X_{i3})$ and $h(X_{i2})$ are both linear functions of the respective variables and have a common slope equal to β_4. Equation (11.51) is intrinsically linear because we can write $X_{i2}X_{i3} = X_{i4}$.

The presence of the interaction terms in a regression equation has an important implication for the test of the hypothesis that a given explanatory variable is not relevant in the regression model in question, i.e., that it does not influence $E(Y_i)$. When there are interaction terms in the equation, then any given explanatory variable may be represented by not one but several regressors. The hypothesis that this variable does not influence $E(Y_i)$ means that the coefficients of *all* regressors involving this variable are jointly zero. Therefore, the appropriate test of such a hypothesis is the F test described by (10.45). Usually we are also interested in testing the hypothesis that the change in $E(Y_i)$ corresponding to a unit increase in X_{ik} is constant. This is equivalent to testing the hypothesis that the coefficients of the interaction "variables" are equal to zero.

EXAMPLE The use of the multiple regression model of Section 10–1 was illustrated by estimating the demand for oranges as a linear function of price and the amount spent on advertising. Let us now modify this example by specifying that the regression equation should also include the interaction term. That is, let

$$Y_i = \beta_1 + \beta_2 X_{i2} + \beta_3 X_{i3} + \beta_4 X_{i2} X_{i3} + \varepsilon_i,$$

where Y_i = quantity of oranges sold, X_{i2} = price, and X_{i3} = advertising expenditure. The details for the twelve available sample observations are given in Table 10–1. The results of the basic calculations are

$$\begin{aligned}
&m_{22} = 2250,\\
&m_{23} = -54, \qquad m_{33} = 4.8573,\\
&m_{24} = 10{,}237.5, \qquad m_{34} = 15.6854, \qquad m_{44} = 66{,}503.85,\\
&m_{Y2} = -3550, \qquad m_{Y3} = 125.2500, \qquad m_{Y4} = -13{,}542.50,\\
&m_{YY} = 6300.
\end{aligned}$$

(The subscript "4" denotes the interaction "variable" $X_{i2}X_{i3}$.) The estimated regression equation then is

$$\underset{}{Y_i} = -93.100 + \underset{(0.832)}{1.508 X_{i2}} + \underset{(9.803)}{43.990 X_{i3}} - \underset{(0.119)}{0.446 X_{i2} X_{i3}} + e_i, \qquad R^2 = 0.984.$$

These results can be used for testing several interesting hypotheses. First, we shall test the hypothesis that X_{i2} does not influence $E(Y_i)$. Formally,

$$H_0: \quad \beta_2 = \beta_4 = 0,$$

$$H_A: \quad H_0 \text{ is not true.}$$

According to the test described in (10.45), the acceptance region for, say, the 5% level of significance, is

$$\frac{(\text{SSR}_Q - \text{SSR}_K)/(Q - K)}{\text{SSE}_Q/(n - Q)} \leq F_{Q-K,\, n-Q,\, 0.05}.$$

In this problem, we have $n = 12$, $Q = 4$, and $K = 2$, so that $F_{2,8,0.05} = 4.46$, as shown in the table of the F distribution. Now, from our sample we have

$$\text{SSR}_Q = 1.508 \times (-3550) + 43.990 \times 125.25 + (-0.446) \times (-13{,}542.5) = 6198,$$

$$\text{SSE}_Q = 6300 - 6198 = 102.$$

The value of SSR_K is to be obtained by regressing Y_i on X_{i3} alone, i.e., by applying the least squares estimation method to

$$Y_i = \beta_1^* + \beta_3^* X_{i3} + \varepsilon_i^*.$$

Then,

$$\text{SSR}_K = \hat{\beta}_3^* m_{Y3} = \left[\frac{m_{Y3}}{m_{33}}\right] m_{Y3} = \frac{125.25^2}{4.86} = 3228.$$

Therefore,

$$\frac{(\text{SSR}_Q - \text{SSR}_K)/(Q - K)}{\text{SSE}_Q/(n - Q)} = \frac{(6198 - 3228)/(4 - 2)}{102/(12 - 4)} = 116.5,$$

which is considerably greater than the critical value 4.46. Therefore we reject the hypothesis that X_{i2} has no influence on $E(Y_i)$, and we do so even though the t ratio for the coefficient of X_{i2} is less than 2.0. Next, we shall test the same hypothesis with respect to X_{i3}. The acceptance region is exactly the same as for the first test, and so are all the other calculations except for SSR_K. The value of SSR_K will be obtained by regressing Y_i on X_{i2}, that is, by estimating the coefficients of

$$Y_i = \beta_1^{**} + \beta_2^{**} X_{i2} + \varepsilon_i^{**}.$$

Then, we have

$$\text{SSR}_K = \hat{\beta}_2^{**} m_{Y2} = \left[\frac{m_{Y2}}{m_{22}}\right] m_{Y2} = \frac{(-3550)^2}{2250} = 5602.$$

The value of the appropriate test statistic then becomes

$$\frac{(\text{SSR}_Q - \text{SSR}_K)/(Q - K)}{\text{SSE}_Q/(n - Q)} = \frac{(6198 - 5602)/(4 - 2)}{102/(12 - 4)} = 23.4,$$

which again is larger than the critical value, 4.46. Finally, we shall test the hypothesis that the coefficient attached to the interaction "variable" $X_{i2}X_{i3}$ is zero; i.e.,

$$H_0\colon \quad \beta_4 = 0,$$

$$H_A\colon \quad \beta_4 \neq 0.$$

The tabulated t value for a two-sided test at the 5% level of significance and with eight degrees of freedom is 2.306. Therefore, the 5% acceptance region is

$$-2.306 \le \frac{\hat{\beta}_4}{s_{\hat{\beta}_4}} \le 2.306.$$

Since in our case

$$\frac{\hat{\beta}_4}{s_{\hat{\beta}_4}} = \frac{-0.446}{0.119} = -3.748,$$

the null hypothesis has to be rejected.

Another intrinsically linear model involves a regression equation that is linear in terms of the logarithms of the variables. This is known as the *multiplicative model* and can be described as

$$(11.52) \qquad Y_i = \alpha X_{i2}^{\beta_2} X_{i3}^{\beta_3} \cdots X_{iK}^{\beta_K} 10^{\varepsilon_i}.$$

A notable feature of this model is the fact that the elasticity of $E(Y_i)$ with respect to any of the explanatory variables is constant, i.e., that

$$\frac{\partial E(Y_i)}{\partial X_{ik}} \frac{X_{ik}}{E(Y_i)} = \beta_k \qquad (k = 2, 3, \ldots, K).$$

An example of such a model is the Cobb-Douglas production function. By taking logarithms (to base 10) of both sides of (11.52), we obtain

$$(11.52a) \quad \log Y_i = \log a + \beta_2 \log X_{i2} + \beta_3 \log X_{i3} + \cdots + \beta_K \log X_{iK} + \varepsilon_i,$$

which can be written as

$$(11.52b) \qquad Y_i^* = \alpha^* + \beta_2 X_{i2}^* + \beta_3 X_{i3}^* + \cdots + \beta_K X_{iK}^* + \varepsilon_i,$$

where the starred symbols represent the logarithms of the unstarred counterparts. Equation (11.52b) is clearly an ordinary linear multiple regression equation, and its estimation can proceed along the usual lines. Two points are worth mentioning, though. First, equation (11.52b) is linear with respect to α^* and the β's, but not with respect to α. Thus, if the assumptions of the classical normal linear regression model are satisfied, the ordinary least squares estimators of $\alpha^*, \beta_2, \beta_3, \ldots, \beta_K$ will have the desirable properties. Since

$$\alpha^* = \log \alpha,$$

the estimator of α will be given by

$$\hat{\alpha} = \text{antilog } \hat{\alpha}^*.$$

While $\hat{\alpha}$ inherits all the desirable asymptotic properties from $\hat{\alpha}^*$, the small-sample properties of $\hat{\alpha}^*$, and in particular its unbiasedness, do not carry over to $\hat{\alpha}$. Second, if we assume that ε_i is normally distributed with zero mean and variance σ^2, then we can write

$$(11.52c) \qquad Y_i = \alpha X_{i2}^{\beta_2} X_{i3}^{\beta_3} \cdots X_{iK}^{\beta_K} \eta_i$$

and assume that the *logarithm* (to base 10) of η_i is normally distributed with mean zero and variance σ^2. The distribution of η_i itself would be called *log-normal.* However, if the regression equation were specified as

$$Y_i = \alpha X_{i2}^{\beta_2} X_{i3}^{\beta_3} \cdots X_{iK}^{\beta_K} + \varepsilon_i,$$

no transformation of the variables could lead to a regression equation that would be linear in the β's, so the equation would have to be classified as intrinsically nonlinear.

There exist many other nonlinear models that can be converted to linear models by a suitable transformation. The following cases have been selected to illustrate the general approach. One frequently applicable nonlinear relation is a *hyperbola*,

(11.53) $$Y_i = \alpha + \beta\frac{1}{X_i} + \varepsilon_i \qquad (\beta < 0),$$

which describes a situation where the mean value of Y_i approaches an upper limit as X_i tends to increase, as illustrated in Figure 11-6. This model might be

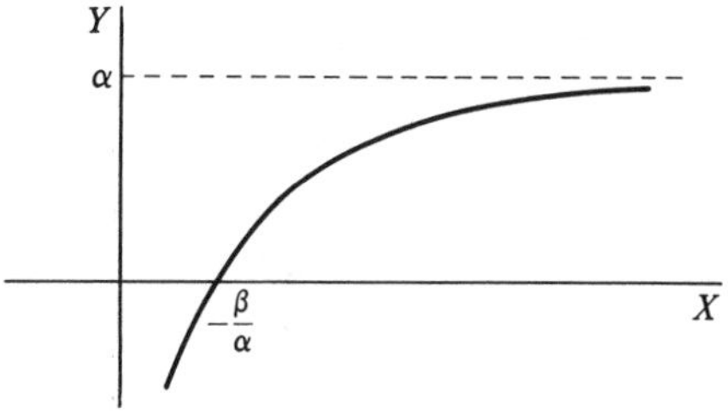

Figure 11-6

applicable, for instance, when one considers the consumption of food as dependent on income. Note that

$$\frac{dE(Y_i)}{dX_i} = -\frac{\beta}{X_i^2},$$

which shows that the change in $E(Y_i)$ corresponding to a change in X_i is inversely related to the square of X_i. Equation (11.53) can be converted into a linear function by simply putting

$$\frac{1}{X_i} = Z_i.$$

In this way, we obtain

(11.53a) $$Y_i = \alpha + \beta Z_i + \varepsilon_i.$$

A relationship similar to (11.53) is represented by a *semilog function*,

(11.54) $$Y_i = \alpha + \beta \log X_i + \varepsilon_i \qquad (\beta > 0).$$

If the base of log X_i is $e = 2.71828\ldots$, then[14]

$$\frac{dE(Y_i)}{dX_i} = \frac{\beta}{X_i},$$

[14] Note that logarithms to base 10 (i.e., common logarithms) can be converted to logarithms to base *e* (i.e., natural logarithms) by multiplying the common logarithms by 2.3025850930. Multiplication by 0.4342944819 converts natural logarithms to common logarithms.

which shows that the change in $E(Y_i)$ corresponding to a change in X_i is inversely related to the value of X_i. The main difference between (11.53) and (11.54) is that in (11.54), unlike in (11.53), the value of $E(Y_i)$ can grow without limit. Equation (11.54) can be changed into a linear relationship by putting

$$\log X_i = Z_i .$$

A variation of (11.54) is represented by a function in which the logarithmic operator is attached to the dependent rather than to the explanatory variable, i.e.,

$$\log Y_i = \alpha + \beta X_i + \varepsilon_i . \tag{11.55}$$

If the base of $\log Y_i$ is e, this relationship can be rewritten as

$$Y_i = e^{\alpha + \beta X_i + \varepsilon_i}, \tag{11.55a}$$

which is called an *exponential function.* A notable feature of (11.55a) is that, for equally spaced values of X_i, the ratio of each two consecutive values of $E(Y_i)$ is equal to the same constant. For instance, if

$$X_{i+1} - X_i = 1,$$

then
$$\frac{E(Y_{i+1})}{E(Y_i)} = \frac{e^{\alpha + \beta X_{i+1}} E(e^{\varepsilon_{i+1}})}{e^{\alpha + \beta X_i} E(e^{\varepsilon_i})} = e^{\beta} .$$

A simple transformation

$$\log Y_i = Y_i^*$$

allows us to express (11.55) as a linear function

$$Y_i^* = \alpha + \beta X_i + \varepsilon_i . \tag{11.55b}$$

In all of the preceding regression models, and in many others, the problem of estimating the regression parameters is simplified by our ability to reduce the models to linearity. The only aspect of the transformation that deserves careful attention concerns the stochastic disturbance. In the cases presented, the stochastic disturbance was always introduced into the relationship in such a way that we could proceed with the linear transformation without any difficulty. However, the specification of the model—including the manner in which the disturbance is introduced—should not be dictated by mathematical or computational convenience. It is important to keep in mind that such a specification represents a commitment on our part concerning our prior knowledge and beliefs about the relationship that is being modeled. Since the stochastic disturbance determines the distribution of the dependent variable for any set of fixed values of the explanatory variables, its role in the regression model is quite crucial. Clearly, we need to be aware of the implications of the particular specification put forward. For instance, in the case of the Cobb-Douglas production function described by (11.52), the particular way in which the disturbance is introduced into the equation implies that the distribution of outputs for any given set of inputs is log-normal, i.e., skewed. This, then, must be our view of the world if we wish to insist on that given specification.

Intrinsically Nonlinear Models

Let us now turn to the *intrinsically nonlinear models*, i.e., models that are nonlinear with respect to the variables as well as with respect to the parameters. There is, of course, a great variety of these models; our discussion will be confined to a few interesting cases. Consider the relationship

$$Y_i = \alpha X_{i2}^{\beta_2} X_{i3}^{\beta_3} + \varepsilon_i \tag{11.56}$$

which is essentially the same as the multiplicative model (11.52) *except* that the disturbance enters as an additive rather than a multiplicative term. A relationship of this sort could, for instance, describe a demand function for some commodity, with Y_i standing for quantity demanded, X_{i2} for price, and X_{i3} for income. Since

$$\frac{\partial E(Y_i)}{\partial X_{i2}} \frac{X_{i2}}{E(Y_i)} = \beta_2$$

and

$$\frac{\partial E(Y_i)}{\partial X_{i3}} \frac{X_{i3}}{E(Y_i)} = \beta_3,$$

β_2 and β_3 would represent the price and the income elasticity, respectively. Now, as we pointed out earlier, there exists no transformation that would convert (11.56) into a linear relationship with respect to the parameters. However, if X_{i2} and X_{i3} are nonstochastic—or, if stochastic, independent of ε_i—and if ε_i satisfies all the assumptions of the classical normal regression model, we can use the maximum likelihood method of estimation. The likelihood function for a sample of size n is

$$L = -\frac{n}{2}\log 2\pi - \frac{n}{2}\log \sigma^2 - \frac{1}{2\sigma^2}\sum_{i=1}^{n} (Y_i - \alpha X_{i2}^{\beta_2} X_{i3}^{\beta_3})^2. \tag{11.57}$$

The next step is to differentiate L with respect to α, β_2, β_3, and σ^2 and put the respective derivatives equal to zero. This leads to a system of four equations, which are nonlinear with respect to the four unknowns. An algebraic solution of this system is difficult, but there may be no difficulty about getting a solution with an electronic computer, since programs for nonlinear estimation are now available. These programs are essentially based on a systematic "trial-and-error" approach; i.e., the computer is asked to calculate the value of L for a number of different combinations of the parameter values until the maximum value of L is found. The values of the parameters corresponding to this maximum value of L are the desired maximum likelihood estimates and have the desirable asymptotic properties.

Another interesting intrinsically nonlinear model is the *logistic model*, represented as

$$Y_i = \frac{\gamma}{1 + e^{\alpha + \beta X_i}} + \varepsilon_i \qquad (\gamma > 0,\ \beta < 0), \tag{11.58}$$

where $e = 2.71828\ldots$. In this case, the population regression line is given by a logistic "growth curve" as shown in Figure 11–7. Note that $E(Y_i)$ is confined to the values between 0 and γ. The values of Y_i are, of course, not restricted. Again, we can obtain the maximum likelihood estimates of the parameters of (11.58) with a computer. The estimation problem becomes seemingly simplified if the specification of the logistic curve is

$$Y_i = \frac{\gamma}{1 + e^{\alpha + \beta X_i + \varepsilon_i}} \tag{11.59}$$

since in this case we can write

$$\log\left(\frac{\gamma}{Y_i} - 1\right) = \alpha + \beta X_i + \varepsilon_i. \tag{11.59a}$$

The apparent simplification is because now only one parameter, γ, enters the regression equation in a nonlinear way. However, it should be noted that the

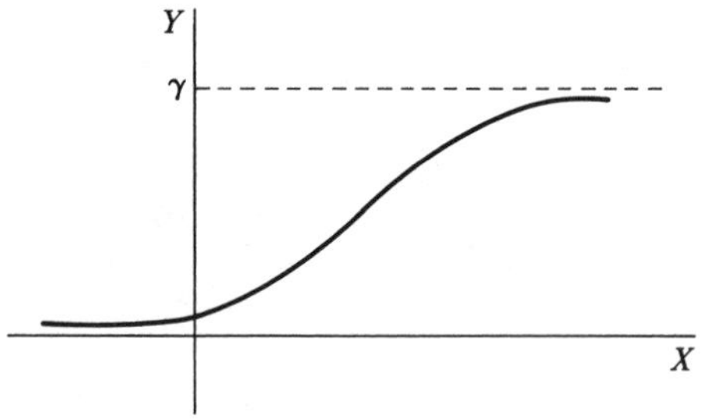

Figure 11–7

model (11.59) is markedly different from that given by (11.58). In particular, in (11.58) the values of Y_i for any given value of X_i can extend from $-\infty$ to $+\infty$, whereas in (11.59) the values of Y_i are confined to the interval from 0 to γ. This implies that, in (11.59), the dependent variable Y_i cannot have a normal distribution. The same complication was encountered in Section 11–1 in the case of a qualitative dependent variable.

As a final illustration of an intrinsically nonlinear model, we consider the so-called CES (constant elasticity of substitution) production function represented as

$$Q_i = \gamma[\delta K_i^{-\rho} + (1 - \delta)L_i^{-\rho}]^{-\nu/\rho} e^{\varepsilon_i} \tag{11.60}$$

$$(\gamma > 0;\ 1 > \delta > 0;\ \nu > 0;\ \rho \geq -1),$$

where Q_i = output, K_i = capital input, L_i = labor input, and $e = 2.71828\ldots$. The parameter γ is known as the "efficiency parameter," the parameter δ as the "distribution parameter," the parameter ν as the "returns-to-scale parameter," and the parameter ρ as the "substitution parameter," This type of production function has gained a great degree of popularity because it subsumes a number of other more specialized production functions. This degree of generality is achieved through the "substitution parameter" ρ, since the CES production function reduces to the Cobb–Douglas production function for $\rho = 0$, and to the "fixed-proportions" production function for $\rho \to \infty$. By taking logarithms (to base e) of both sides of (11.60), we obtain

$$\text{(11.60a)} \qquad \log Q_i = \log \gamma - \frac{\nu}{\rho} \log [\delta K_i^{-\rho} + (1 - \delta) L_i^{-\rho}] + \varepsilon_i .$$

If K_i and L_i are nonstochastic—or, if stochastic, independent of ε_i—we can set up the likelihood function in the usual way and obtain the maximum likelihood estimates of γ, δ, ν, and ρ with a computer.

An alternative and a considerably more simple estimation of the parameters of the CES production function is possible if we replace (11.60a) by its approximation that is linear with respect to ρ. By using Taylor's series formula (11.47), expanding $\log Q_i$ around $\rho = 0$, and dropping the terms involving powers of ρ higher than one, we obtain[15]

$$\text{(11.60b)} \qquad \begin{aligned} \log Q_i = {} & \log \gamma + \nu\delta \log K_i + \nu(1 - \delta) \log L_i \\ & - \tfrac{1}{2}\rho\nu\delta(1 - \delta)[\log K_i - \log L_i]^2 + \varepsilon_i . \end{aligned}$$

Note that the right-hand side of (11.60b) can be conveniently separated into two parts, one corresponding to the Cobb–Douglas production function and one representing a "correction" due to the departure of ρ from zero. The latter part, given by the term $-[\rho\nu\delta(1 - \delta)/2][\log K_i - \log L_i]^2$, will disappear if $\rho = 0$. The estimation of the parameters of (11.60b) is the same as in the case of estimation with nonlinear restrictions under exact identification. The "unrestricted" version of (11.60b) is

$$\text{(11.60c)} \quad \log Q_i = \beta_1 + \beta_2 \log K_i + \beta_3 \log L_i + \beta_4[\log K_i - \log L_i]^2 + \varepsilon_i ,$$

which represents an intrinsically linear regression model. If the estimate of β_4 is not significantly different from zero, we would reject the CES model in favor of the Cobb–Douglas model. The parameters of (11.60b) are related to the coefficients of (11.60c) as follows:

$$\gamma = \text{antilog } \beta_1 ,$$

$$\delta = \frac{\beta_2}{\beta_2 + \beta_3} ,$$

$$\nu = \beta_2 + \beta_3 ,$$

$$\rho = \frac{-2\beta_4(\beta_2 + \beta_3)}{\beta_2\beta_3} .$$

[15] All logarithms are natural logarithms. If common logarithms were to be used, the term involving $[\log K_i - \log L_i]^2$ would have to be multiplied by 2.302585.

Thus we can use ordinary least squares estimates of the β's to obtain estimates of the parameters of (11.60b). The estimated standard errors can be calculated by using the approximation formula (11.40). If (11.60b) is a reasonable approximation of (11.60a), and if the appropriate assumptions about K_i, L_i, and ε_i hold, the estimates of the production function parameters obtained in this way will be very nearly asymptotically efficient.

EXAMPLE To illustrate the estimation of the CES production function we use the data on inputs and output of 25 firms given in Table 11–4. The maximum likelihood method yields the following estimates of the production function parameters:

Table 11–4

Firm No.	K_i	L_i	Q_i
1	8	23	106.00
2	9	14	81.08
3	4	38	72.80
4	2	97	57.34
5	6	11	66.79
6	6	43	98.23
7	3	93	82.68
8	6	49	99.77
9	8	36	110.00
10	8	43	118.93
11	4	61	95.05
12	8	31	112.83
13	3	57	64.54
14	6	97	137.22
15	4	93	86.17
16	2	72	56.25
17	3	61	81.10
18	3	97	65.23
19	9	89	149.56
20	3	25	65.43
21	1	81	36.06
22	4	11	56.92
23	2	64	49.59
24	3	10	43.21
25	6	71	121.24

$$\log \hat{\gamma} = 1.0564,$$

$$\hat{\delta} = 0.4064,$$

$$\hat{\nu} = 0.8222,$$

$$\hat{\rho} = 0.6042.$$

The estimates of the asymptotic standard errors of the maximum likelihood estimates were not calculated. Using the approximation of the CES production function given by (11.60b), we obtain

$$\log \tilde{\gamma} = 1.2371,$$

$$\underset{(0.0291)}{\tilde{\delta} = 0.4723},$$

$$\underset{(0.0525)}{\tilde{\nu} = 0.8245},$$

$$\underset{(0.1899)}{\tilde{\rho} = 0.4334}.$$

The figures in parentheses represent estimates of the asymptotic standard errors. The results show that the sample provides no strong evidence against the CES model.

In general, the parameters of an intrinsically nonlinear model may be estimated by setting up the likelihood function and finding the maximum likelihood estimates. Under the classical assumptions concerning the stochastic disturbance and the explanatory variables, the resulting estimates will have all the desirable asymptotic properties. Of course, the application of the maximum likelihood method is contingent on the assumption that ε_i is normally distributed. If we do not wish to make this assumption, we can obtain our estimates by minimizing the sum of squared deviations of the observed values from the fitted values of Y, i.e., by the least squares method. Since the parameters to be estimated enter in a nonlinear way, this method is usually called the *nonlinear least squares method*. The principal difference between this and the ordinary (linear) least squares method is that in the linear case the estimates can be expressed as linear functions of the disturbances. This is not generally possible in the nonlinear case. The estimates obtained by the nonlinear least squares method are exactly the same as the maximum likelihood estimates whenever the maximization of the likelihood function is achieved by the minimization of the sum of squared deviations of the observed from the fitted values of Y. It can be shown that even without the assumption of normality the *asymptotic* distribution of the nonlinear least squares estimates is then normal and has the same mean and variance as the maximum likelihood estimates for the normal disturbance case.[16] Thus the assumption of normality of the stochastic disturbance is not always crucial.

The troublesome aspect of the nonlinear estimation is the actual finding of the estimates. As we mentioned earlier, the estimates are obtained with a computer by systematic "trial and error." Essentially, the computer substitutes different values of the parameters into the likelihood function, calculates the value of the function, and repeats this until there can be no further increase in the value of the likelihood function. This works fine if the likelihood function

[16] See E. Malinvaud, *Statistical Methods of Econometrics* (Chicago: Rand McNally, 1966), pp. 290–299.

has only one well-defined peak, but there may be problems if the likelihood function either has more than one peak or is very flat at the top. These possibilities are illustrated in Figure11–8 for the case in which the search is related to a single parameter θ. In Figure 11–8(a) the likelihood function has one well-defined peak and there is no problem about finding $\hat{\theta}$. In Figure 11–8(b) the likelihood function displays two peaks, the lower peak representing a local and the higher peak a global maximum of the function. Here the difficulty arises because if the computer starts its search for the maximizing value of θ in the vicinity of $\hat{\theta}_1$, it will stop at $\hat{\theta}_1$ and present this as the maximum likelihood estimate of θ, while the correct maximum likelihood estimate of θ is really $\hat{\theta}_2$. There is not much that can be done about that, except to require the computer to scan the entire range of possible values of θ. However, if this range is infinite, the computer is faced with a task that it cannot fulfill. However, frequently the range of admissible parameter values is finite, in which case the problem of finding the global maximum may become manageable. A good example is the marginal propensity to consume, which is confined to values between 0 and 1, or the autoregression

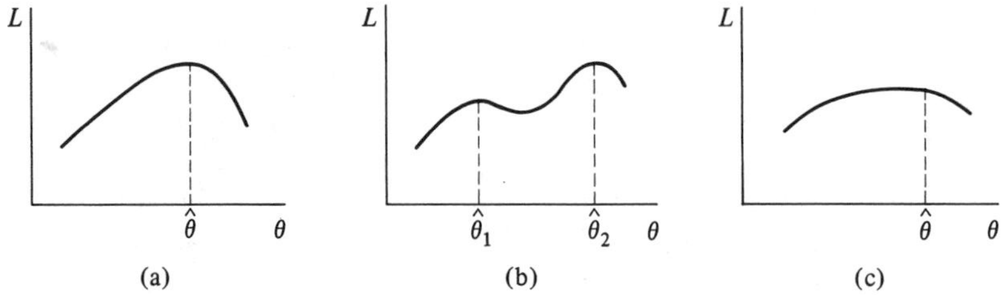

Figure 11–8

parameter ρ, which is confined to values between -1 and $+1$. The case of a relatively flat likelihood function, depicted by Figure 11–8(c), poses yet another problem. The likelihood function in this case is clearly very sensitive to changes in the sample data. This means that even a slight error of measurement or an error of rounding might shift the maximizing value of θ quite markedly, which does not inspire a high degree of confidence in the resulting estimate.

Tests for Linearity

Our discussion, thus far, of estimating the parameters of a nonlinear model has presupposed that the functional form of the population regression equation is known, or assumed, a priori. If this is not the case, we may want to consider the specification of the functional form as a testable rather than a maintained hypothesis. In this context the most interesting hypothesis is that of linearity. That is, frequently we may wish to test the hypothesis that the population regression equation is linear with respect to the variables against some alternative hypothesis. The hypothesis of linearity can be tested in a number of ways, but unfortunately none of the tests is without drawbacks.

The simplest test of linearity is in the case in which the alternative hypothesis is that the regression equation involves a power function of a given degree. This test was already described in connection with (11.46) and (11.46a). Its disadvantage is that we have to commit ourselves to a power function of a specific degree as the alternative to the linear model. Note that the basic idea of this test rests on the fact that a linear function is a special case of a power function, namely, a power function of degree one. If the coefficients attached to the higher powers of the explanatory variable are all zero, the given power function reduces to a simple linear regression. This idea can be exploited by specifying other functional forms, which include linearity as a special case. One such specification[17] is

$$\text{(11.61)} \qquad \frac{Y_i^\lambda - 1}{\lambda} = \alpha + \beta\left(\frac{X_i^\lambda - 1}{\lambda}\right) + \varepsilon_i.$$

Let us examine this function for some selected values of λ. First, for $\lambda = 0$, the expressions $(Y_i^\lambda - 1)/\lambda$ and $(X_i^\lambda - 1)/\lambda$ appear to be indeterminate. However, we note that any finite positive number, say, Z, can be written as

$$Z = e^{\log Z},$$

where the base of the logarithm is e, and that $e^{\log Z}$ can be expanded as

$$e^{\log Z} = 1 + \log Z + \frac{1}{2!}(\log Z)^2 + \frac{1}{3!}(\log Z)^3 + \cdots.$$

Therefore, it follows that

$$\begin{aligned} \frac{Y_i^\lambda - 1}{\lambda} &= \frac{1}{\lambda}\left[1 + \lambda \log Y_i + \frac{1}{2!}(\lambda \log Y_i)^2 + \cdots - 1\right] \\ &= \log Y_i + \frac{\lambda}{2!}(\log Y_i)^2 + \frac{\lambda^2}{3!}(\log Y_i)^3 + \cdots \end{aligned}$$

For $\lambda = 0$,

$$\frac{Y_i^\lambda - 1}{\lambda} = \log Y_i,$$

and, similarly,

$$\frac{X_i^\lambda - 1}{\lambda} = \log X_i.$$

This means that for $\lambda = 0$ (and for X_i and Y_i positive) the regression equation (11.61) reduces to

$$\log Y_i = \alpha + \beta \log X_i + \varepsilon_i.$$

Further, for $\lambda = 1$, we obtain

$$(Y_i - 1) = \alpha + \beta(X_i - 1) + \varepsilon_i$$

[17] This specification was proposed in G. E. P. Box and D. R. Cox, "An Analysis of Transformations," *Journal of the Royal Statistical Society, Series B*, Vol. 26, 1964, pp. 211–243.

or
$$Y_i = \alpha^* + \beta X_i + \varepsilon_i,$$
where
$$\alpha^* = \alpha - \beta + 1,$$
which is a simple linear regression model.

In general, different values of λ in (11.61) lead to different functional specifications of the regression equation.[18] This allows us to test the linear hypothesis against the alternative hypothesis that the regression equation is some nonlinear function within the family of functions defined by (11.61). Formally,

$$H_0: \quad \lambda = 1,$$
$$H_A: \quad \lambda \neq 1.$$

To carry out the test, we need an estimate of λ and its standard error. Clearly, λ can be estimated along with the other parameters of (11.61) by the maximum likelihood method. In setting up the likelihood function for $Y_1, Y_2, \ldots, Y_n$, we have to derive the distribution of the Y's from the distribution of the ε's, which is assumed to be normal. By Theorem 18 of Section 7–3 (the "change-of-variable" theorem), we have

$$f(Y_i) = \left|\frac{d\varepsilon_i}{dY_i}\right| f(\varepsilon_i).$$

But
$$\varepsilon_i = \left(\frac{Y_i^\lambda - 1}{\lambda}\right) - \alpha - \beta\left(\frac{X_i^\lambda - 1}{\lambda}\right)$$
so that
$$\frac{d\varepsilon_i}{dY_i} = Y_i^{\lambda - 1}.$$

Therefore, the likelihood function for $Y_1, Y_2, \ldots, Y_n$ is

$$(11.62) \qquad L = (\lambda - 1)\sum_i \log Y_i - \frac{n}{2}\log(2\pi) - \frac{n}{2}\log\sigma^2 - \frac{1}{2\sigma^2}\sum_i\left[\left(\frac{Y_i^\lambda - 1}{\lambda}\right) - \alpha - \beta\left(\frac{X_i^\lambda - 1}{\lambda}\right)\right]^2.$$

The maximizing values of λ, α, β, and σ^2 can be found with an electronic computer, and the respective standard errors can be estimated by reference to the appropriate information matrix. In large samples the maximum likelihood estimates will be distributed normally, or at least approximately so.

The hypothesis that the population regression equation is linear with respect to the variables can also be tested without specifying the alternative functional form or forms. This can be done by considering some of the implications of linearity in a more general way. The rather obvious implication of linearity is

[18] Some attention has to be paid to the restrictions on the values of the dependent variable. Since, under the assumption of normality, the range of ε_i extends from $-\infty$ to $+\infty$, this should also be the range of $(Y_i^\lambda - 1)/\lambda$. However, for some values of λ (e.g., $\lambda = \frac{1}{2}$) this may not be possible, in which case only *approximate* normality can be required. This point was originally raised by J. B. Ramsey.

that the slope and the intercept of the regression equation must remain constant over *all* values of the explanatory variable. What we can do, then, is to divide the sample observations into a number of subsamples, each subsample corresponding to a different and nonoverlapping interval of values of the explanatory variable. We can estimate the slope and the intercept for each subsample and test whether there are any significant differences from one subsample to another.

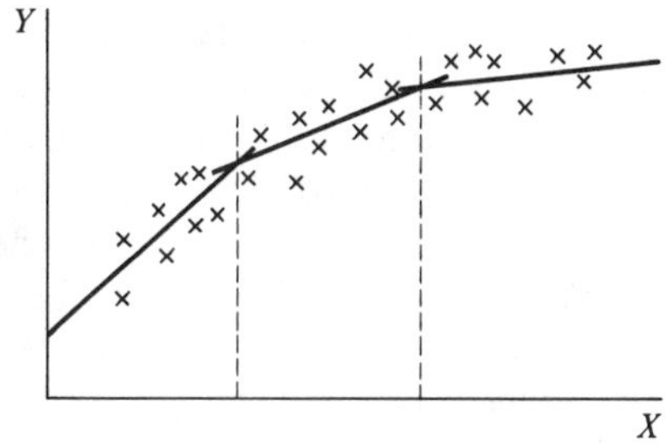

Figure 11-9

This is illustrated in Figure 11-9. To indicate how the test is carried out, we consider a sample of n observations, with the observations being arranged so that

$$X_1 \leq X_2 \leq X_3 \leq \cdots \leq X_n.$$

Suppose the sample is divided into three subsamples, with the values of the explanatory variable allocated as follows:

Subsample 1: $X_1, X_2, \ldots, X_k,$

Subsample 2: $X_{k+1}, X_{k+2}, \ldots, X_m,$

Subsample 3: $X_{m+1}, X_{m+2}, \ldots, X_n.$

The regression model can be set up as

$$Y_i = \beta_1 + \beta_2 X_i + \gamma_1 Z_{i1} + \gamma_2 X_i Z_{i1} + \gamma_3 Z_{i2} + \gamma_4 X_i Z_{i2} + \varepsilon_i, \tag{11.63}$$

where

$$Z_{i1} = 1 \quad \text{if } i \text{ belongs to Subsample 1,}$$
$$= 0 \quad \text{otherwise;}$$
$$Z_{i2} = 1 \quad \text{if } i \text{ belongs to Subsample 2,}$$
$$= 0 \quad \text{otherwise.}$$

The hypothesis of linearity can then be tested by testing

$$H_0: \quad \gamma_1 = \gamma_2 = \gamma_3 = \gamma_4 = 0$$

$$H_A: \quad H_0 \text{ is not true.}$$

The appropriate F test, described in (10.45), has a disadvantage in that its result may depend on the way in which the sample is divided up. If the number of subsamples is too small, a departure from linearity may remain concealed, and if the number of subsamples is large, we lose many degrees of freedom and thus weaken the power of the test. As a compromise, it has been suggested that in practical applications three or four samples should be sufficient.[19]

Another test of linearity which does not rely on the specification of the alternative functional form is based on the scatter of the residuals around the sample regression line. The idea is to rely on the fact that, under the assumptions of the classical normal linear regression model, the disturbances are *randomly* scattered around the population regression line. If the population regression is *not* linear, the scatter of the disturbances around a straight line will no longer be random. In Figure 11–10 we can see how, because of the nonlinearity of the relation, the deviations from the straight line tend to be at first negative, then positive, and then negative again. This suggests that we can test linearity by determining whether the sequence of the deviations from the regression line is randomly arranged.

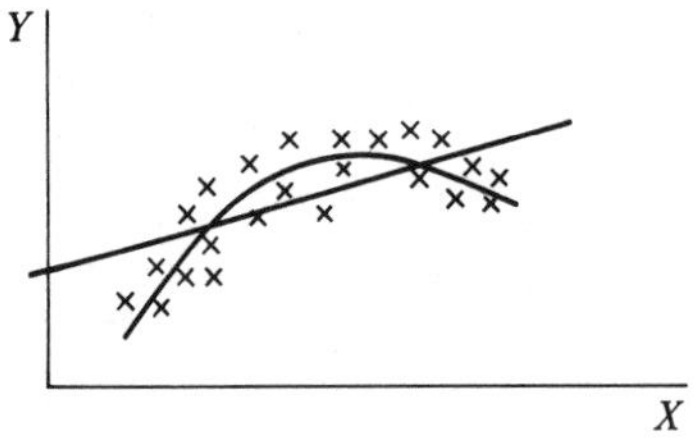

Figure 11–10

An obvious difficulty about carrying out a test of this sort arises because the deviations from the population regression line (i.e., the disturbances) are not observable. All that we have are the deviations from the sample regression line (i.e., the residuals). The trouble is that the residuals are not independent even if the disturbances themselves are. In particular, we have, for $i \neq j$,

$$(11.64)\quad \begin{aligned} \text{Cov}(e_i, e_j) &= E(y_i' - \hat{\beta}x_i')(y_j' - \hat{\beta}x_j') \\ &= E(\beta x_i' + \varepsilon_i' - \hat{\beta}x_i')(\beta x_j' + \varepsilon_j' - \hat{\beta}x_j') \\ &= x_i'x_j'E(\hat{\beta} - \beta)^2 - E(\hat{\beta} - \beta)\varepsilon_i'x_j' - E(\hat{\beta} - \beta)\varepsilon_j'x_i' + E(\varepsilon_i'\varepsilon_j') \\ &= -x_i'x_j'\left[\frac{\sigma^2}{\sum x_i'^2}\right] - \frac{\sigma^2}{n}, \end{aligned}$$

which is clearly nonzero. This difference between the e's and the ε's has been

[19] Malinvaud, *op. cit.*, p. 270.

taken into account by the Durbin–Watson test described in Section 8–2, which was originally designed for testing the hypothesis that the disturbances are uncorrelated over time against the hypothesis that they follow a first-order autoregressive scheme. If the residuals are arranged according to increasing values of the explanatory variable rather than according to time, this test can be used to check whether the deviations from the population regression line are random. However, the Durbin–Watson test is not without disadvantages. If the ordering of the residuals according to time is similar to their ordering according to increasing values of the explanatory variable, we would be using very much the same test for linearity as for nonautoregression of the disturbances over time. This difficulty is due to the fact that, when the orderings are similar, both nonlinearity and autoregression in the disturbances tend to have the same implication with respect to the residuals.

The construction of the Durbin–Watson test has been motivated by the fact that the least squares residuals are not mutually independent even if the disturbances are. This has been shown explicitly in (11.64). However, we note that the expression for the covariance of e_i and e_j $(i \neq j)$ tends to approach zero as the sample size increases to infinity, so that in large samples the residuals will be close to being independent if the disturbances are. Thus, in large samples we can use any general test for "randomness" without risking too large an error. One such test involves examining the peaks and troughs of a series to see whether they may be considered a result of pure chance. We can apply this test to the sequence of residuals arranged in accordance with increasing values of the explanatory variable. A residual e_i is defined as a "peak" if

$$e_{i-1} < e_i > e_{i+1}$$

and as a "trough" if

$$e_{i-1} > e_i < e_{i+1}.$$

If two or more successive residuals have the same value and this value exceeds the neighboring values, we regard them as determining *one* peak, and similarly for troughs. A general name for either a peak or a trough is a "turning point." It can be shown[20] that in a series of n independent values the total number of turning points, say, p, is—for a large n—approximately normally distributed with mean

$$E(p) = \frac{2(n-2)}{3} \tag{11.65}$$

and variance

$$\text{Var}(p) = \frac{16n - 29}{90}. \tag{11.66}$$

[20] G. Udny Yule and M. G. Kendall, *An Introduction to the Theory of Statistics* (London: Charles Griffin, 1950), p. 638.

The test of independence then involves counting the number of turning points in the series of the residuals (arranged according to increasing values of X) and checking whether this number is significantly different from $E(p)$. That is, the hypothesis of independence (and, therefore, presumably of linearity) is

$$H_0: \quad E(p) = \frac{2(n-2)}{3}$$

with a two-sided H_A. The appropriate test statistic for large samples would be

$$\frac{p - 2(n-2)/3}{\sqrt{(16n - 29)/90}} \sim N(0, 1). \tag{11.67}$$

This test does not require the assumption that the disturbances are normally distributed. Its disadvantage, as in the case of the Durbin–Watson test, is that if the ordering of the residuals according to increasing values of X and according to time is similar, we cannot distinguish between nonlinearity and autoregression of the disturbances over time.

In addition to the various disadvantages specific to each, all tests of linearity suffer from one particular weakness that detracts from their usefulness: the sample data do not provide any information about the shape of the regression line outside the interval covered by the observed values of the explanatory variable. If the population regression is approximately linear *within* this interval and nonlinear outside, then no test can possibly detect the nonlinearity of the population regression. This situation is illustrated in Figure 11–11. There is nothing

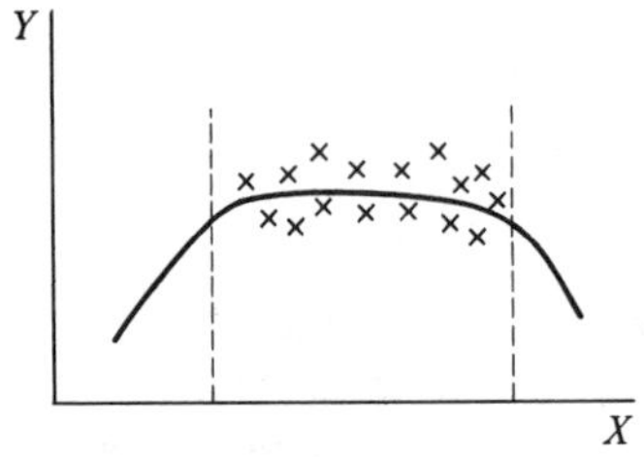

Figure 11–11

that can be done about this with the given sample data. The only possible way to avoid this difficulty is to enlarge the sample and extend the interval encompassed by the observed values of the explanatory variable. Indeed, if the linearity of the population regression is suspect a priori, this would certainly be the recommended procedure. In the past most of the applied work in econometrics has been with linear models only, largely on the grounds of computational simplicity. However, with the spread of electronic computers, this reason has lost some force. There is little excuse for not using nonlinear models when suggested by theory, or for not testing for linearity when its assumption is open to doubt.

11-4 Distributed Lag Models

A simple regression equation designed to explain variations over time in the mean value of the dependent variable is given by

$$Y_t = \alpha + \beta X_t + \varepsilon_t,$$

where ε_t is a random variable with zero mean (conforming to other assumptions as specified), and X_t is either nonstochastic or, if stochastic, independent of ε_t. In setting up the regression equation in this way we are, in fact, assuming that the current value of Y may depend on the current value of X but *not* on any of the past values of X. A more general formulation, which would allow for the current as well as the past values of X to affect Y, would be written as

$$(11.68) \qquad Y_t = \alpha + \beta_0 X_t + \beta_1 X_{t-1} + \beta_2 X_{t-2} + \cdots + \beta_m X_{t-m} + \varepsilon_t.$$

This equation is the basis for the discussion of the present section. For simplicity we shall limit ourselves to the case of a nonstochastic X; a modification to allow for the case in which X is stochastic but independent of ε is quite straightforward.

The regression equation (11.68), extended by the relevant assumptions concerning the behavior of X and ε, is called a *distributed lag model* because the influence of the explanatory variable on $E(Y_t)$ is distributed over a number of lagged values of X. This number, m, may be either finite or infinite. However, we assume that the β's have a finite sum; i.e.,

$$\sum_{i=0}^{m} \beta_i < \infty .$$

This assumption is needed to eliminate the possibility of explosive values of $E(Y_t)$. We also define the *average lag* as the weighted mean of all the lags involved, with weights given by the relative size of the respective β coefficients. Formally,

$$\text{Average lag} = \frac{\sum i\beta_i}{\sum \beta_i},$$

where the summations run from $i = 0$ to $i = m$. Equation (11.68) could (at least in principle) be estimated by the least squares method, or by some other method which leads to estimates with some desirable properties under the given specifications about ε. Of course, if m is large, we may not have enough observations to estimate all the parameters. However, even if we do have enough observations, we are likely to encounter a high degree of multicollinearity, which would have a detrimental effect on the standard errors of the estimated coefficients. As a matter of fact, a distributed lag model has rarely been posited and estimated in as general a form as that specified in (11.68). Most frequently some restrictions are placed on the regression coefficients $\beta_0, \beta_1, \ldots, \beta_m$, so that the number of the regression parameters becomes substantially reduced. In practical applications these restrictions have been of two kinds—one resulting from the requirement that the β's should be declining in a geometric progression, and the other from the requirement that the β's should first be increasing and then decreasing.

Geometric Lag

By far the most popular form of a distributed lag is that of a *geometric lag distribution* characterized as

$$(11.69) \qquad Y_t = \alpha + \beta_0(X_t + \lambda X_{t-1} + \lambda^2 X_{t-2} + \cdots) + \varepsilon_t,$$

where $\qquad 0 \leq \lambda < 1.$

Here the effect of X on $E(Y_t)$ extends indefinitely into the past (i.e., $m \to \infty$), but the coefficients decline in a fixed proportion so that the effect of the distant values of X eventually becomes negligible. This model has been rationalized in two different ways, each leading to the same description of the population regression equation, but each having a different implication for the behavior of the regression disturbance. The first rationalization is known as the *adaptive expectation model* and is based on the following reasoning. Suppose a simple regression model is modified so that $E(Y_t)$ is a linear function not of X_t but of the "expected" or "permanent" level of X at time t, say, X_t^*. One example would be a demand relationship in which the quantity demanded is a function of expected price, or a consumption function with "permanent income" as the explanatory variable. Then,

$$(11.70) \qquad Y_t = \alpha + \beta X_t^* + \varepsilon_t,$$

where, as before, ε_t is a random variable with zero mean. Since X_t^* is not directly observable, we have to state how it is determined. Here, we postulate that

$$(11.71) \qquad X_t^* - X_{t-1}^* = (1 - \lambda)(X_t - X_{t-1}^*),$$

or equivalently,

$$(11.71a) \qquad X_t^* = (1 - \lambda)X_t + \lambda X_{t-1}^*,$$

where $\qquad 0 \leq \lambda < 1.$

This presupposes that the expected or permanent value of X at time t is represented by a weighted average of the current value of X and the value of X expected in the preceding period. Such a formation of expectations is based on the idea that the current expectations are derived by modifying previous expectations in light of the current experience. Thus, for instance, in the case of a demand relationship, X_t may be the price at the beginning of the current period, and X_{t-1}^* may be the average price expected to have prevailed during the preceding period. Or, in the case of a consumption function, the current "permanent" income may be determined by revising the last period's level of the "permanent" income in light of the current income experience. Note that (11.71a) can also be written as

$$(11.71b) \qquad X_t^* = (1 - \lambda)(X_t + \lambda X_{t-1} + \lambda^2 X_{t-2} + \cdots).$$

The equivalence of (11.71a) and (11.71b) can be demonstrated by making use of the so-called "Koyck transformation."[21] By lagging (11.71b) by one period and by multiplying both sides by λ, we obtain

$$\lambda X_{t-1}^* = (1 - \lambda)(\lambda X_{t-1} + \lambda^2 X_{t-2} + \cdots).$$

Deducting this equation from (11.71b) leads to

$$X_t^* - \lambda X_{t-1}^* = (1 - \lambda)X_t,$$

which is the same as (11.71a). Therefore, (11.71a) and (11.71b) are equivalent. The substitution for X_t^* from (11.71b) into (11.70) gives

$$(11.72) \qquad Y_t = \alpha + \beta(1 - \lambda)(X_t + \lambda X_{t-1} + \lambda^2 X_{t-2} + \cdots) + \varepsilon_t,$$

which represents the geometric lag model (11.69) with $\beta_0 = \beta(1 - \lambda)$. The size of the average lag in this case is

$$\frac{\beta(1 - \lambda)(0 + \lambda + 2\lambda^2 + 3\lambda^3 + \cdots)}{\beta(1 - \lambda)(1 + \lambda + \lambda^2 + \lambda^3 + \cdots)} = \frac{\beta(1 - \lambda)[\lambda/(1 - \lambda)^2]}{\beta(1 - \lambda)[1/(1 - \lambda)]} = \frac{\lambda}{1 - \lambda}.$$

Equation (11.72) is clearly awkward from the point of view of estimation because of the infinite number of regressors. It can, however, be simplified by the application of the Koyck transformation. By lagging (11.72) by one period, multiplying through by λ, and subtracting the result from (11.72), we obtain

$$(11.73) \qquad Y_t = \alpha(1 - \lambda) + \beta(1 - \lambda)X_t + \lambda Y_{t-1} + \eta_t$$

where

$$\eta_t = \varepsilon_t - \lambda\varepsilon_{t-1}.$$

The adaptive expectation model is sometimes formulated in a slightly different way. The form of the relationship given by (11.70) is retained, but the formation of the expectations is postulated as

$$(11.74) \qquad X_t^* - X_{t-1}^* = (1 - \lambda)(X_{t-1} - X_{t-1}^*),$$

where again

$$0 \leq \lambda < 1.$$

Equation (11.74) differs from (11.71) in that X_t is replaced by X_{t-1}. Such a formulation would be appropriate where X_t is not known in advance so that expectations have to be revised by comparing X_{t-1}^* with X_{t-1}, the most recent available information on X. Equation (11.74) can be rewritten as

$$(11.74a) \qquad X_t^* = (1 - \lambda)X_{t-1} + \lambda X_{t-1}^*,$$

which, in turn, implies that

$$(11.74b) \qquad X_t^* = (1 - \lambda)(X_{t-1} + \lambda X_{t-2} + \lambda^2 X_{t-3} + \cdots).$$

[21] L. M. Koyck, *Distributed Lags and Investment Analysis* (Amsterdam: North-Holland Publishing Company, 1954).

Substitution for X_t^* from (11.74) into (11.70) and application of the Koyck transformation to the result gives

$$Y_t = \alpha(1 - \lambda) + \beta(1 - \lambda)X_{t-1} + \lambda Y_{t-1} + \eta_t, \tag{11.75}$$

where $\eta_t = \varepsilon_t - \lambda\varepsilon_{t-1}.$

The only difference between (11.73) and (11.75) is that in the latter equation X_t is replaced by X_{t-1}. This does not affect the problem of estimating the regression parameters.

An alternative rationalization of the geometric lag is provided by the so-called *partial adjustment* or *habit persistence* model. Suppose the *desired* level of Y at time t, say, Y_t^*, is given by a linear function of some explanatory variable X_t *plus* a disturbance ε_{t1}; i.e.,

$$Y_t^* = \alpha + \beta X_t + \varepsilon_{t1}. \tag{11.76}$$

For instance, the mean desired level of inventory held by a firm may be a linear function of sales (see the "stock adjustment model" in Section 11–2), or the mean desired level of consumption may be a linear function of wealth. The values of Y^* are not directly observable, but we assume that an attempt is being made to bring the actual level of Y to its desired level, and that such an attempt is only partially successful during any one period. The reasons why a complete adjustment of Y to Y^* is not achieved in a single period may be varied; they may include technological constraints, institutional rigidities, persistence of habit, etc.[22] The relationship between the actual and the desired level of Y may be specified as follows:

$$Y_t - Y_{t-1} = \gamma(Y_t^* - Y_{t-1}) + \varepsilon_{t2} \tag{11.77}$$

where $0 < \gamma \leq 1,$

and ε_{t2} is a random disturbance. The coefficient γ is called the "adjustment coefficient" since it indicates the rate of adjustment of Y to Y^*. Solving (11.77) for Y_t^*, we obtain

$$Y_t^* = \frac{1}{\gamma} Y_t + \frac{\gamma - 1}{\gamma} Y_{t-1} - \frac{1}{\gamma} \varepsilon_{t2}. \tag{11.77a}$$

Substitution for Y_t^* from (11.77a) into (11.76) gives

$$Y_t = \alpha\gamma + \beta\gamma X_t + (1 - \gamma)Y_{t-1} + \xi_t, \tag{11.78}$$

where $\xi_t = \gamma\varepsilon_{t1} + \varepsilon_{t2}.$

Equation (11.78) is formally the same as the adaptive expectation model characterized by (11.73) *except* that the disturbance in (11.73), unlike that in (11.78), is generated by events of the preceding as well as the present period.

[22] For a more precisely formulated rationale within a particular context, see Z. Griliches, "Distributed Lags: A Survey," *Econometrica*, Vol. 35, January 1967, p. 43.

Note also that (11.78) describes a geometric lag of the form

$$(11.78a) \quad Y_t = \alpha + \beta\gamma[X_t + (1-\gamma)X_{t-1} + (1-\gamma)^2 X_{t-2} + \cdots] + \zeta_t,$$

where $\zeta_t = \xi_t + (1-\gamma)\xi_{t-1} + (1-\gamma)^2\xi_{t-2} + \cdots$

As in the case of the adaptive expectation model, the partial adjustment model is also sometimes formulated so that the geometric lag starts with X_{t-1} instead of X_t. This is derived by retaining the specification of the adjustment process exactly as in (11.77), but reformulating the determination of the desired level of Y as

$$(11.79) \quad Y_t^* = \alpha + \beta X_{t-1} + \varepsilon_{t1}.$$

In this formulation, the current desired level of Y depends on the preceding rather than the current level of X. By substituting for Y_t^* from (11.77a) into (11.79) and rearranging the terms, we obtain

$$(11.80) \quad Y_t = \alpha\gamma + \beta\gamma X_{t-1} + (1-\gamma)Y_{t-1} + \xi_t$$

where

$$\xi_t = \gamma\varepsilon_{t1} + \varepsilon_{t2}.$$

Again, (11.80) is formally the same as the alternative version of the adaptive expectation model presented in (11.75), except for the specification of the disturbance. From the point of view of estimating the regression parameters, equation (11.80) involves exactly the same considerations as (11.78).

As a matter of interest, we note that the adaptive expectation and the partial adjustment model can be combined into one *compound geometric lag* model. By comparing equation (11.70) of the adaptive expectation model with equation (11.76) of the partial adjustment model, we can see that each represents a straightforward modification of the simple regression model

$$Y_t = \alpha + \beta X_t + \varepsilon_t.$$

In the adaptive expectation model, X_t is replaced by its "expected" value X_t^*; and in the partial adjustment model, Y_t is replaced by its "desired" value Y_t^*. Combining the two specifications, we have

$$(11.81) \quad Y_t^* = \alpha + \beta X_t^* + \varepsilon_{t1}.$$

This means that the mean desired value of Y is a linear function of the expected level of X. To complete the model, we have to state how the unobservable X_t^* and Y_t^* are assumed to be determined. We assume that X_t^* is determined by (11.71b) of the adaptive expectation model, and that Y_t^* is determined by (11.77a) of the partial adjustment model. By making the appropriate substitutions in (11.81), we obtain

$$(11.82) \quad Y_t = \alpha\gamma + \beta\gamma(1-\lambda)(X_t + \lambda X_{t-1} + \lambda^2 X_{t-2} + \cdots) + (1-\gamma)Y_{t-1} + \xi_t,$$

where

$$\xi_t = \gamma\varepsilon_{t1} + \varepsilon_{t2}.$$

Equation (11.82) can be simplified by applying the Koyck transformation, so that

$$(11.83)\qquad Y_t = \alpha\gamma(1-\lambda)+\beta\gamma(1-\lambda)X_t+[(1-\gamma)+\lambda]Y_{t-1}-(1-\gamma)\lambda Y_{t-2}+\omega_t,$$

where

$$\omega_t = \xi_t - \lambda\xi_{t-1}.$$

Note that, by analogy with (11.78a), equation (11.83) can be written as

$$(11.83a)\qquad Y_t = \alpha + \beta\gamma[X_t^* + (1-\gamma)X_{t-1}^* + (1-\gamma)^2 X_{t-2}^* + \cdots] + \zeta_t,$$

where

$$\zeta_t = \xi_t + (1-\gamma)\xi_{t-1} + (1-\gamma)^2\xi_{t-2} + \cdots$$

This shows why the model is called a compound geometric lag model: the regression coefficients of (11.83a) follow a geometric progression while each of X_t^*, X_{t-1}^*, $X_{t-2}^*, \ldots,$ is a weighted average of the preceding values of X with the weights also following a geometric progression. The model reduces to a pure adaptive expectation model if $\gamma = 1$, to a pure partial adjustment model if $\lambda = 0$, and to a simple regression model if $\gamma = 1$ *and* $\lambda = 0$.

Before turning our attention to the problem of estimating the regression coefficients of the geometric lag models, we should consider the formulation of models in which the distributed lag extends over more than one explanatory variable. In particular, let us take a model in which there are two explanatory variables, X and Z, each exerting its effect on $E(Y_t)$ through its own geometrically distributed lag:

$$(11.84)\qquad Y_t = \alpha + \beta_0(X_t + \lambda X_{t-1} + \lambda^2 X_{t-2} + \cdots) + \delta_0(Z_t + \mu Z_{t-1} + \mu^2 Z_{t-2} + \cdots) + \varepsilon_t,$$

where

$$0 \leq \lambda < 1 \quad \text{and} \quad 0 \leq \mu < 1.$$

For example, the demand for money may depend on "permanent" income and on an "expected" rate of interest. Equation (11.84) can be reduced to a more manageable form by applying the Koyck transformation twice in succession. First, we lag (11.84) by one period, multiply both sides by λ, and deduct the resulting equation from (11.84). This gives

$$(11.84a)\qquad Y_t = \alpha(1-\lambda) + \lambda Y_{t-1} + \delta_0[Z_t + (\mu-\lambda)Z_{t-1} + \mu(\mu-\lambda)Z_{t-2} + \mu^2(\mu-\lambda)Z_{t-3} + \cdots] + \beta_0 X_t + \varepsilon_t - \lambda\varepsilon_{t-1}.$$

Next, we lag (11.84a) by one period, multiply both sides by μ, and deduct the resulting equation from (11.84a). The result is

$$(11.84b)\qquad Y_t = \alpha(1-\lambda)(1-\mu) + (\lambda+\mu)Y_{t-1} - \lambda\mu Y_{t-2} + \beta_0 X_t - \beta_0\mu X_{t-1} + \delta_0 Z_t - \delta_0\lambda Z_{t-1} + \eta_t^*,$$

where

$$\eta_t^* = \varepsilon_t - (\lambda+\mu)\varepsilon_{t-1} + \lambda\mu\varepsilon_{t-2},$$

which is a regression equation with six regressors (in addition to the constant term). It is clear that we could handle models with any number of distributed lags in a similar manner.

Let us now consider the problem of estimating the parameters of a geometrically distributed lag model,

$$Y_t = \alpha + \beta_0(X_t + \lambda X_{t-1} + \lambda^2 X_{t-2} + \cdots) + \varepsilon_t,$$

where ε_t is a random normal variable with mean zero and variance σ^2. Suppose further that the relation is generated by an *adaptive expectation* mechanism, as described by equations (11.70) and (11.71). Estimation of the parameters of this model depends on whether we assume the ε's to be mutually independent or not. We shall start with the case where the ε's are mutually independent; i.e., we assume that the disturbances are normally distributed and

$$E(\varepsilon_t \varepsilon_s) = 0 \qquad (t \neq s). \tag{11.85}$$

The geometric lag model is clearly not suitable for estimation in its original form since it involves an infinite number of regressors. However, by applying the Koyck transformation, we can write

$$Y_t = \alpha(1 - \lambda) + \beta(1 - \lambda)X_t + \lambda Y_{t-1} + \eta_t,$$

or

$$Y_t = \alpha_0 + \beta_0 X_t + \lambda Y_{t-1} + \eta_t,$$

where

$$\alpha_0 = \alpha(1 - \lambda),$$

$$\beta_0 = \beta(1 - \lambda),$$

and

$$\eta_t = \varepsilon_t - \lambda\varepsilon_{t-1}.$$

This equation was presented earlier as (11.73). Its form is relatively simple, but this simplification has not been achieved without cost. The trouble with (11.73) is that the "new" disturbance η_t is correlated with Y_{t-1}, which is now one of the explanatory variables. In particular,

$$\begin{aligned} E(\eta_t Y_{t-1}) &= E(\varepsilon_t - \lambda\varepsilon_{t-1})[\alpha + \beta(X_{t-1} + \lambda X_{t-2} + \cdots) + \varepsilon_{t-1}] \\ &= -\lambda\sigma^2. \end{aligned}$$

This means that the ordinary least squares estimates of the coefficients of (11.73) are *inconsistent* (see Section 8–3), and we have to resort to other estimation methods.

Consistent estimates of the coefficients of (11.73) under the assumption specified in (11.85) can be obtained in several ways. Perhaps the simplest is to use the *method of instrumental variables*, which we have described in connection with the "errors-in-variables" models in Section 9–1. Since equation (11.73) involves two explanatory variables, we have to find two instrumental variables, say, Z_1 and Z_2. These variables should satisfy the following conditions:

1. $\text{plim} \sum_t (Z_{1t} - \bar{Z}_1)\eta_t/n = 0$ and $\text{plim} \sum_t (Z_{2t} - \bar{Z}_2)\eta_t/n = 0$.
2. $\text{plim} \sum_t (Z_{1t} - \bar{Z}_1)X_t/n$ and $\text{plim} \sum_t (Z_{2t} - \bar{Z}_2)Y_{t-1}/n$ are both finite numbers different from zero.

An additional condition, which is not necessary for consistency but which helps to reduce the asymptotic variance of the instrumental variables estimator, is that the instrumental variables should be highly correlated with the respective regressors. It has been suggested that the following instrumental variables be used:

$$Z_{1t} = X_t, \qquad \text{and} \qquad Z_{2t} = X_{t-1}.$$

That is, the instrumental variable for the first regressor, X_t, is to be X_t itself, and the instrumental variable for the second regressor, Y_{t-1}, is to be X_{t-1}. Clearly, since X_t is nonstochastic, it serves as an ideal instrumental variable for itself since it satisfies the necessary conditions and is "perfectly correlated" with X_t. The second instrumental variable also satisfies the necessary conditions and is likely to be correlated with Y_{t-1}. The normal equations for the instrumental variables estimates then are

$$\sum_t Y_t = \alpha_0^\dagger(n-1) + \beta_0^\dagger \sum_t X_t + \lambda^\dagger \sum Y_{t-1},$$

$$\sum_t X_t Y_t = \alpha_0^\dagger \sum_t X_t + \beta_0^\dagger \sum_t X_t^2 + \lambda^\dagger \sum X_t Y_{t-1},$$

$$\sum_t X_{t-1} Y_t = \alpha_0^\dagger \sum X_{t-1} + \beta_0^\dagger \sum_t X_t X_{t-1} + \lambda^\dagger \sum X_{t-1} Y_{t-1},$$

or, in matrix notation,

$$\mathbf{Z'Y} = (\mathbf{Z'X})\mathbf{b}^\dagger,$$

where

$$\mathbf{Y} = \begin{bmatrix} Y_2 \\ Y_3 \\ \vdots \\ Y_n \end{bmatrix}, \quad \mathbf{Z} = \begin{bmatrix} 1 & X_2 & X_1 \\ 1 & X_3 & X_2 \\ \vdots & \vdots & \vdots \\ 1 & X_n & X_{n-1} \end{bmatrix}, \quad \mathbf{X} = \begin{bmatrix} 1 & X_2 & Y_1 \\ 1 & X_3 & Y_2 \\ \vdots & \vdots & \vdots \\ 1 & X_n & Y_{n-1} \end{bmatrix}, \quad \mathbf{b}^\dagger = \begin{bmatrix} \alpha_0^\dagger \\ \beta_0^\dagger \\ \lambda^\dagger \end{bmatrix}.$$

Note that since the first available observation on Y_t is Y_1, the summation goes from $t = 2$ to $t = n$. The solution of the normal equations is

(11.86) $$\mathbf{b}^\dagger = (\mathbf{Z'X})^{-1}(\mathbf{Z'Y}).$$

The asymptotic variance-covariance matrix of $\mathbf{b}^\dagger$ can be estimated as follows:

(11.87) $$\text{Est. Asympt. Var-Cov}(\mathbf{b}^\dagger) = s^{*2}(\mathbf{Z'X})^{-1}(\mathbf{Z'AZ})(\mathbf{X'Z})^{-1},$$

where $$s^{*2} = \frac{1}{n-4} \sum_{t=2}^{n} (Y_t - \alpha_0^\dagger - \beta_0^\dagger X_t - \lambda^\dagger Y_{t-1})^2$$

and A is a n x n matrix with $a_{tt} = 1$, $a_{t-1,t} = a_{t,t+1} = \lambda^\dagger/(1 + \lambda^{\dagger 2})$, and zeros everywhere else. From the consistent estimates of α_0, β_0 and λ we can easily derive consistent estimates of α and β.

An alternative approach to estimating the coefficients of (11.73) is based on the *maximum likelihood* principle. The estimators can then be developed as follows.[23] Equation (11.73) can be rewritten as

$$(Y_t - \varepsilon_t) = \alpha(1 - \lambda) + \beta(1 - \lambda)X_t + \lambda(Y_{t-1} - \varepsilon_{t-1}),$$

or

$$E(Y_t) = \alpha_0 + \beta_0 X_t + \lambda E(Y_{t-1}).$$

However, since

$$\begin{aligned} E(Y_{t-1}) &= \alpha_0 + \beta_0 X_{t-1} + \lambda E(Y_{t-2}), \\ E(Y_{t-2}) &= \alpha_0 + \beta_0 X_{t-2} + \lambda E(Y_{t-3}), \\ &\vdots \\ E(Y_1) &= \alpha_0 + \beta_0 X_1 + \lambda E(Y_0), \end{aligned}$$

we can also write

$$(11.88)\quad E(Y_t) = \alpha_0(1 + \lambda + \lambda^2 + \cdots + \lambda^{t-1}) + \beta_0(X_t + \lambda X_{t-1} + \lambda^2 X_{t-2} + \cdots + \lambda^{t-1}X_1) + \lambda^t E(Y_0).$$

Using the formula for the sum of a geometric progression, and the fact that $\alpha_0 = \alpha(1 - \lambda)$, we can reformulate (11.88) as

$$(11.88a)\quad Y_t = \alpha + \beta_0 W_t^{(\lambda)} + (\theta_0 - \alpha)\lambda^t + \varepsilon_t,$$

where

$$W_t^{(\lambda)} = X_t + \lambda X_{t-1} + \lambda^2 X_{t-2} + \cdots + \lambda^{t-1} X_1$$

and

$$\theta_0 = E(Y_0).$$

The value of $E(Y_0)$ is the initial mean value of Y and can be regarded as a parameter. Note that if λ were known, equation (11.88a) would be a linear multiple regression equation with two explanatory variables, $W_t^{(\lambda)}$ and λ^t, and could be estimated by the ordinary least squares method. Of course, λ is generally not known and has to be estimated along with α, β_0, and θ_0. The logarithmic likelihood function for $Y_1, Y_2, \dots, Y_n$ is

$$(11.89)\quad L = -\frac{n}{2}\log(2\pi\sigma^2) - \frac{1}{2\sigma^2}\sum_{t=1}^{n}[Y_t - \alpha - \beta_0 W_t^{(\lambda)} - (\theta_0 - \alpha)\lambda^t]^2.$$

Maximizing L with respect to α, β_0, λ, and θ_0 is equivalent to minimizing

$$S^{(\lambda)} = \sum_{t=1}^{n}[Y_t - \alpha - \beta_0 W_t^{(\lambda)} - (\theta_0 - \alpha)\lambda^t]^2$$

[23] These estimators have been derived in the appendix of the paper by L. R. Klein, "The Estimation of Distributed Lags," *Econometrica*, Vol. 26, October 1958, pp. 553–565, and operationally developed in P. J. Dhrymes, "Efficient Estimation of Distributed Lags with Autocorrelated Error Terms," *International Economic Review*, Vol. 10, February 1969, pp. 47–67, and in A. Zellner and M. S. Geisel, "Analysis of Distributed Lag Models with Applications to Consumption Function Estimation," manuscript, University of Chicago (January, 1968), forthcoming in *Econometrica*. Our presentation of the method follows closely that of Zellner and Geisel.

with respect to the same parameters. Since we know that $0 \leq \lambda < 1$, we can easily calculate the minimizing values of α, β_0, and θ_0, and the corresponding value of $S^{(\lambda)}$, for different values of λ from 0 to 0.95 or 0.99. Then we select those values of α, β_0, and θ_0, and λ that lead to the smallest value of $S^{(\lambda)}$. These values will be the maximum likelihood estimates of the respective parameters. If we have no information about X other than the sample values of $X_1, X_2, \ldots, X_n$, the maximum likelihood estimates of α, β_0, and λ obtained in this way will be asymptotically efficient. Their asymptotic variances can be estimated by using the appropriate information matrix.

EXAMPLE The preceding method has been applied to estimating the parameters of a consumption function model from United States quarterly observations 1947(I) to 1960(IV).[24] The consumption function is derived from an adaptive expectation model and can be described as

$$C_t = \beta Y_t^* + \varepsilon_t,$$

$$Y_t^* - Y_{t-1}^* = (1 - \lambda)(Y_t - Y_{t-1}^*),$$

where C = measured real consumption, Y^* = "normal" or "permanent" real income, and Y = measured real income. By combining the two equations and eliminating Y^*, we obtain

$$C_t = \beta(1 - \lambda) Y_t + \lambda C_t + \varepsilon_t - \lambda \varepsilon_{t-1}.$$

The coefficients have been estimated from

$$C_t = \beta(1 - \lambda) W_t^{(\lambda)} + \theta_0 \lambda^t + \varepsilon_t,$$

where

$$W_t^{(\lambda)} = Y_t + \lambda Y_{t-1} + \cdots + \lambda^{t-1} Y_1$$

and

$$\theta_0 = E(Y_0).$$

The sum of squared residuals (divided by the number of observations) has been calculated for different values of λ between 0 and 1; the results are shown in Figure 11–12. The curve has a local minimum at $\lambda = 0.45$, and a global minimum at $\lambda = 0.963$. The latter is then the maximum likelihood estimate of λ. The corresponding estimates of β and θ_0 are

$$\hat{\beta} = 1.129, \quad \text{and} \quad \hat{\theta}_0 = 191.53.$$

Since β is supposed to measure the marginal propensity to consume out of "normal" income, a value larger than one is unreasonable a priori. Therefore, the results cannot be considered as acceptable. (Zellner and Geisel note that this result may be due to inadequacies of the particular model and/or data. If both the model and the data are thought to be adequate, then we should incorporate the restriction $0 < \beta < 1$ into our estimation procedure.)

[24] See Zellner and Geisel, *op. cit.* The data on personal consumption expenditures and personal disposable income, both series price-deflated and seasonally adjusted, are presented in Z. Griliches *et al.*, "Notes on Estimated Aggregate Quarterly Consumption Function," *Econometrica*, Vol. 30, July 1962, pp. 491–500.

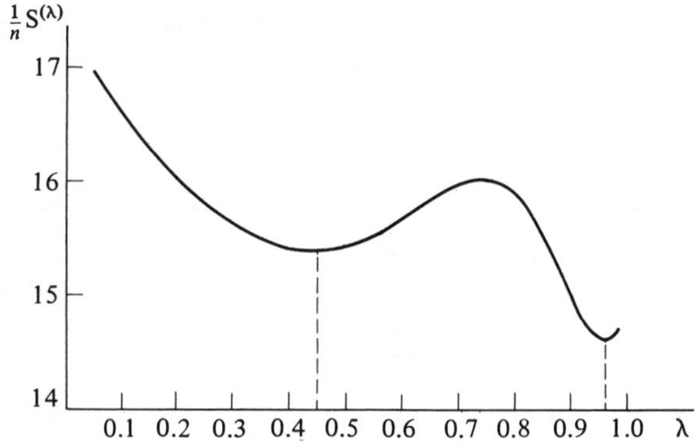

Figure 11–12

A still different approach to estimating the coefficients of (11.73) is possible if we note that

$$(Y_t - \varepsilon_t) = \alpha(1 - \lambda) + \beta(1 - \lambda)X_t + \lambda(Y_{t-1} - \varepsilon_{t-1})$$

is formally similar to an "errors-in-variables" model discussed in Section 9–1. That is, we may view ε_t as an "error" involved in measuring $E(Y_t)$, and ε_{t-1} as an "error" involved in measuring $E(Y_{t-1})$. Since, by assumption, ε is homoskedastic, the variance of ε_t is equal to that of ε_{t-1}. Therefore, we can use the *weighted regression method* by assigning equal weights to each of the errors. In particular, we can minimize

$$S = \sum_t \varepsilon_t^2 + \sum_t \varepsilon_{t-1}^2 = \sum_t [Y_t - \alpha(1 - \lambda) - \beta(1 - \lambda)X_t - \lambda\theta_{t-1}]^2 + \sum_t [Y_{t-1} - \theta_{t-1}]^2, \tag{11.90}$$

where $$\theta_{t-1} = E(Y_{t-1}),$$

with respect to α, β, λ, and each of the θ's. Since the first known value of Y is Y_1, the summation has to run from $t = 2$ to $t = n$. The first-order conditions for minimization are

$$\sum_t (Y_t - \tilde{\alpha}_0 - \tilde{\beta}_0 X_t - \tilde{\lambda}\tilde{\theta}_{t-1}) = 0,$$

$$\sum_t X_t(Y_t - \tilde{\alpha}_0 - \tilde{\beta}_0 X_t - \tilde{\lambda}\tilde{\theta}_{t-1}) = 0,$$

$$\sum_t \tilde{\theta}_{t-1}(Y_t - \tilde{\alpha}_0 - \tilde{\beta}_0 X_t - \tilde{\lambda}\tilde{\theta}_{t-1}) = 0,$$

$$\tilde{\lambda}(Y_t - \tilde{\alpha}_0 - \tilde{\beta}_0 X_t - \tilde{\lambda}\tilde{\theta}_{t-1}) + (Y_{t-1} - \tilde{\theta}_{t-1}) = 0,$$

where
$$\tilde{\alpha}_0 = \tilde{\alpha}(1 - \tilde{\lambda}),$$
$$\tilde{\beta}_0 = \tilde{\beta}(1 - \tilde{\lambda}),$$
$$t = 2, 3, \ldots, n.$$

From the first condition, we have

$$\tilde{\alpha}_0 = \bar{Y} - \tilde{\beta}_0 \bar{X} - \tilde{\lambda}\left[\frac{1}{n-1}\sum_t \tilde{\theta}_{t-1}\right].$$

Substituting this result into the remaining first-order conditions, we can eliminate $\tilde{\alpha}_0$ and then express all variables in terms of deviations from their respective sample means. Having done that, we can express the last condition as

$$\tilde{\theta}'_{t-1} = \frac{\tilde{\lambda}(y'_t - \tilde{\beta}_0 x'_t) + y'_{t-1}}{1 + \tilde{\lambda}^2},$$

where
$$\tilde{\theta}'_{t-1} = \tilde{\theta}_{t-1} - \frac{1}{n-1}\sum_t \tilde{\theta}_{t-1},$$
$$y'_t = Y_t - \bar{Y},$$
$$x'_t = X_t - \bar{X},$$
$$y'_{t-1} = Y_{t-1} - \frac{1}{n-1}\sum_t Y_{t-1}.$$

Substitution for $\tilde{\theta}'_{t-1}$ into the second and third of the first-order conditions and elimination of $\tilde{\beta}_0$ lead to

$$\tilde{\lambda}^2\left[\frac{\sum x'_t y'_t \sum x'_t y'_{t-1}}{\sum x'^2_t} - \sum y'_t y'_{t-1}\right] + \tilde{\lambda}\left[\frac{(\sum x'_t y'_{t-1})^2 - (\sum x'_t y'_t)^2}{\sum x'^2_t} + \sum y'^2_t - \sum y'^2_{t-1}\right] + \left[\sum y'_t y'_{t-1} - \frac{\sum x'_t y'_t \sum x'_t y'_{t-1}}{\sum x'^2_t}\right] = 0. \tag{11.91}$$

From the two roots of (11.91), we choose the value of $\tilde{\lambda}$ that minimizes S. Having obtained a solution for $\tilde{\lambda}$, we can easily calculate the estimated values of α, β, and the θ's. These estimates are consistent but not necessarily asymptotically efficient.[25]

Let us now change the specification of the adaptive expectation model by

[25] The weighted regression approach to estimating the parameters of a distributed lag model was suggested and developed in Klein (1958), *op. cit.* The relationship between this method and the maximum likelihood method is described in the appendix of the paper. See also T. Amemiya and W. A. Fuller, "A Comparative Study of Alternative Estimators in a Distributed Lag Model," *Econometrica*, Vol. 35, July–October 1967, pp. 509–529.

dropping the assumption of mutual independence of the ε's as implied by (11.85), and replacing it by

(11.92) $$\varepsilon_t = \rho\varepsilon_{t-1} + u_t,$$

with $$E(\varepsilon_{t-1}u_t) = 0,$$

$$u_t \sim N(0, \sigma_u^2),$$

and $$\varepsilon_0 \sim N\left(0, \frac{\sigma_u^2}{1-\rho^2}\right).$$

First, we note that in the special case in which $\rho = \lambda$, the problem of estimating the coefficients of (11.73) becomes greatly simplified. The reason is that in this case the "transformed" disturbance η_t is now equal to u_t; that is, it is nonautoregressive and uncorrelated with Y_{t-1}. Under these circumstances the ordinary least squares method applied to (11.73) leads to estimates which have all the desirable asymptotic properties. Of course, the assumption that the η's are mutually independent is quite restrictive; it is unfortunate that we cannot test it by using the Durbin–Watson test, but this test is not applicable in this case. Theoretically, the contention that $\rho = \lambda$ is difficult to justify.

The problem of estimating the coefficients of (11.73) subject to the assumption (11.92) when $\lambda \neq \rho$ is more complicated. As in the case of independent ε's, the ordinary least squares estimates are inconsistent, and we must use alternative methods of estimation. Again, the simplest way of getting consistent estimates is by the *method of instrumental variables.* Alternatively, we may rely on the maximum likelihood principle and develop *maximum likelihood estimators* of the parameters of (11.73) and (11.92), in which case we rewrite (11.73) as

$$E(Y_t) = \alpha(1-\lambda) + \beta(1-\lambda)X_t + \lambda E(Y_{t-1})$$

and $$\rho E(Y_{t-1}) = \alpha(1-\lambda)\rho + \beta(1-\lambda)\rho X_{t-1} + \lambda\rho E(Y_{t-2}).$$

Deducting the second expression from the first, we obtain

(11.93) $$\begin{aligned} E(Y_t) - \rho E(Y_{t-1}) &= \alpha(1-\lambda)(1-\rho) + \beta(1-\lambda)(X_t - \rho X_{t-1}) \\ &\quad + \lambda[E(Y_{t-1}) - \rho E(Y_{t-2})] \\ &= \alpha(1-\lambda)(1-\rho)(1 + \lambda + \lambda^2 + \cdots + \lambda^{t-1}) \\ &\quad + \beta(1-\lambda)[(X_t - \rho X_{t-1}) + \lambda(X_{t-1} - \rho X_{t-2}) \\ &\quad + \cdots + \lambda^{t-1}(X_1 - \rho X_0)] \\ &\quad + \lambda^t[E(Y_0) - \rho E(Y_{-1})]. \end{aligned}$$

If we now use (11.92) and introduce simplifying notation, we can write (11.93) as

(11.93a) $$(Y_t - \rho Y_{t-1}) = \alpha^* + \beta_0 W_t^{(\lambda,\rho)} + \delta_0\lambda^t + u_t,$$

where

$$W_t^{(\lambda,\rho)} = (X_t - \rho X_{t-1}) + \lambda(X_{t-1} - \rho X_{t-2}) + \cdots + \lambda^{t-2}(X_2 - \rho X_1) + \lambda^{t-1}X_1,$$

$$\alpha^* = \alpha(1 - \rho),$$

$$\beta_0 = \beta(1 - \lambda),$$

$$\delta_0 = E(Y_0) - \rho E(Y_{-1}) - \alpha^* - \frac{\beta_0 \rho X_0}{\lambda}.$$

If λ and ρ were known, (11.93a) would be a linear multiple regression equation with two explanatory variables, $W_t^{(\lambda,\rho)}$ and λ^t. When, as usual, this is not the case, we can set up the likelihood function for $Y_2, Y_3, \ldots, Y_n$ (conditional on Y_1) as

$$(11.94) \qquad L = -\frac{n-1}{2}\log(2\pi\sigma_u^2) - \frac{1}{2\sigma_u^2}\sum_{t=2}^{n}[Y_t - \rho Y_{t-1} - \alpha^* - \beta_0 W_t^{(\lambda,\rho)} - \delta_0\lambda^t]^2.$$

Maximizing L with respect to α^*, β_0, δ_0, λ, and ρ is equivalent to minimizing

$$S^{(\lambda,\rho)} = \sum_{t=2}^{n}[Y_t - \rho Y_{t-1} - \alpha^* - \beta_0 W_t^{(\lambda,\rho)} - \delta_0\lambda^t]^2$$

with respect to the same parameters. Since we know that $0 \leq \lambda < 1$ and $-1 < \rho < 1$, we can take different pairs of values of λ and ρ, and for each pair calculate the corresponding estimates of α^*, β_0, and δ_0. Of all the results, we choose that set of values of the parameters which corresponds to the smallest value of $S^{(\lambda,\rho)}$. The estimates of α, β, λ, and ρ will be asymptotically efficient; their asymptotic variances can be determined by reference to the appropriate information matrix.

EXAMPLE Zellner and Geisel[26] have applied the above method to the consumption model described in the preceding example, using the same set of observations. The results are

$$\hat{\beta} = \underset{(0.46)}{0.94},$$

$$\hat{\lambda} = \underset{(0.085)}{0.66},$$

$$\hat{\rho} = \underset{(0.076)}{0.69}.$$

The figures in parentheses are the estimated asymptotic standard errors. The results show that the estimate of λ is very close to that of ρ, which indicates that the assumption $\lambda = \rho$ may not have been too unreasonable in this case.

[26] *Op. cit.*

Let us now consider estimating the parameters of a geometrically distributed lag relation generated by a *partial adjustment* (or *habit persistence*) mechanism. Such a relation was represented by equation (11.78) as

$$Y_t = \alpha\gamma + \beta\gamma X_t + (1-\gamma)Y_{t-1} + \xi_t,$$

where ξ_t is a normally distributed random variable with mean zero and variance σ^2. The specification of the partial adjustment model does not lead to any further restrictions on ξ_t, which makes estimation much simpler than in the case of the adaptive expectation model. If it can be assumed that $E(\xi_t\xi_s) = 0$ for all $t \neq s$, then we can use the ordinary least squares method and obtain consistent and asymptotically efficient estimates of the parameters of (11.78). On the other hand, if ξ_t follows a first-order autoregression scheme, i.e., if

$$\xi_t = \rho\xi_{t-1} + u_t, \tag{11.95}$$

where

$$E(\xi_{t-1}u_t) = 0,$$

$$u_t \sim N(0, \sigma_u^2),$$

and

$$\xi_0 \sim N\left(0, \frac{\sigma_u^2}{1-\rho^2}\right),$$

then the ordinary least squares method applied to (11.78) would lead to inconsistent estimates. In this case, we can use a transformation of (11.78) that eliminates ξ_t and leads to

$$\begin{aligned}(Y_t - \rho Y_{t-1}) = \alpha\gamma(1-\rho) &+ \beta\gamma(X_t - \rho X_{t-1}) \\ &+ (1-\gamma)(Y_{t-1} - \rho Y_{t-2}) + u_t.\end{aligned} \tag{11.96}$$

The maximum likelihood of α, β, γ, and ρ (conditional on Y_1) can then be obtained by maximizing

$$\begin{aligned}L = -\frac{n-1}{2}\log(2\pi\sigma_u^2) - \frac{1}{2\sigma_u^2}\sum_{t=2}^{n}[(Y_t - \rho Y_{t-1}) - \alpha\gamma(1-\rho) \\ - \beta\gamma(X_t - \rho X_{t-1}) - (1-\gamma)(Y_{t-1} - \rho Y_{t-2})]^2\end{aligned} \tag{11.97}$$

with respect to the unknown parameters. The resulting estimates will have all the desirable asymptotic properties.[27]

Pascal Lag

In some instances, a distributed lag model with the weights declining geometrically from the current period into the past may not be altogether appropriate. For example, in a model relating current capital expenditures to current and past capital appropriations, it is much more reasonable to expect that the weights attached to capital appropriations at times t, $t-1$, $t-2$, . . ., would

[27] See Malinvaud, *op. cit.*, p. 469. For a test of the hypothesis that ξ_t is nonautoregressive, see J. Durbin, "Testing for Serial Correlation in Least-Squares Regression When Some of the Regressors Are Lagged Dependent Variables," *Econometrica*, Vol. 38, May 1970, pp. 410–421.

first rise and then decline instead of declining all the way. Such a distribution of weights may be called an *inverted V-lag distribution.* There are many ways in which such a lag distribution can be formulated. One possibility is to use the so-called *Pascal lag distribution.* This distribution can be described as follows. First rewrite (11.68) as

$$\text{(11.68a)} \qquad Y_t = \alpha + \beta(w_0 X_t + w_1 X_{t-1} + w_2 X_{t-2} + \cdots) + \varepsilon_t,$$

where ε_t is a normally distributed disturbance with mean zero and variance σ^2. The weights corresponding to the Pascal lag model then are given as

$$w_i = \binom{i+r-1}{i}(1-\lambda)^r\lambda^i = \frac{(i+r-1)!}{i!(r-1)!}(1-\lambda)^r\lambda^i \qquad (i = 0, 1, 2, \ldots),$$

where r is some positive integer and λ a parameter to be estimated. The regression equation then becomes

$$\text{(11.98)} \quad Y_t = \alpha + \beta(1-\lambda)^r\left[X_t + r\lambda X_{t-1} + \frac{r(r+1)}{2!}\lambda^2 X_{t-2} + \cdots\right] + \varepsilon_t.$$

Note that when $r = 1$, we get $w_i = (1-\lambda)\lambda^i$, which means that the Pascal distribution reduces to a geometric lag distribution. For values of r greater than one, we may get inverted V-lag distributions. Figure 11–13 shows the distribution of weights for $\lambda = 0.6$ and for different values of r.

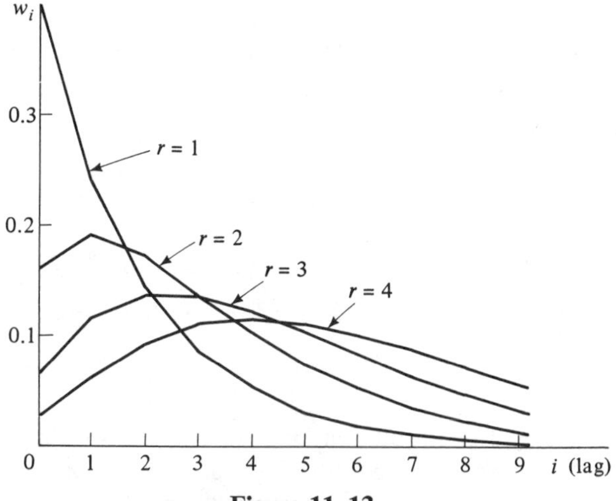

Figure 11–13

The estimation of the parameters in the case of a Pascal lag model is more complicated than with a geometric lag model. Consider, for instance, the case $r = 2$. The Pascal lag relation then is

$$\text{(11.99)} \qquad Y_t = \alpha + \beta(1-\lambda)^2(X_t + 2\lambda X_{t-1} + 3\lambda^2 X_{t-2} + \cdots) + \varepsilon_t.$$

This equation can be simplified by applying the following transformation. First, lag (11.99) by one period and multiply through by -2λ. This gives

$$(11.99a)\qquad -2\lambda Y_{t-1} = -2\alpha\lambda + \beta(1-\lambda)^2(-2\lambda X_{t-1} - 4\lambda^2 X_{t-2} - 6\lambda^3 X_{t-3} - \cdots) - 2\lambda\varepsilon_{t-1}.$$

Next, lag (11.99) by two periods and multiply through by λ^2. The result is

$$(11.99b)\qquad \lambda^2 Y_{t-2} = \alpha\lambda^2 + \beta(1-\lambda)^2(\lambda^2 X_{t-2} + 2\lambda^3 X_{t-3} + 3\lambda^4 X_{t-4} + \cdots) + \lambda^2\varepsilon_{t-2}.$$

Now add (11.99), (11.99a), and (11.99b) to obtain

$$(11.100)\qquad Y_t = \alpha(1-\lambda)^2 + \beta(1-\lambda)^2 X_t + 2\lambda Y_{t-1} - \lambda^2 Y_{t-2} + \eta_t,$$

where
$$\eta_t = \varepsilon_t - 2\lambda\varepsilon_{t-1} + \lambda^2\varepsilon_{t-2}.$$

Unless η_t is nonautoregressive, estimation of (11.100) by the ordinary least squares method leads to inconsistent estimates. To obtain consistent estimates, we can use the *method of instrumental variables.* To allow for the fact that (11.100) is overidentified, we rewrite it as

$$(11.100a)\qquad Y_t^* = \alpha_0 + \beta_0 X_t + \gamma_0 Y_{t-1}^* + \eta_t,$$

where
$$Y_t^* = Y_t - \lambda Y_{t-1},$$
$$Y_{t-1}^* = Y_{t-1} - \lambda Y_{t-2},$$
$$\alpha_0 = \alpha(1-\lambda)^2,$$
$$\beta_0 = \beta(1-\lambda)^2,$$
$$\gamma_0 = \lambda.$$

Then we use, as instrumental variables for X_t and Y_{t-1}^*,

$$Z_{1t} = X_t \qquad \text{and} \qquad Z_{2t} = X_{t-1},$$

and calculate the estimates of α_0, β_0, and γ_0 for different values of λ between 0 and 1. Of all the results, we choose that set of values of α_0, β_0, and γ_0 for which γ_0 is equal to λ, or at least approximately so.

Equation (11.100) could also be estimated by the *maximum likelihood method.* Note that it can also be written as

$$(Y_t - \varepsilon_t) = \alpha(1-\lambda)^2 + \beta(1-\lambda)^2 X_t + 2\lambda(Y_{t-1} - \varepsilon_{t-1}) - \lambda^2(Y_{t-2} - \varepsilon_{t-2}),$$

or

$$E(Y_t) = \alpha_0 + \beta_0 X_t + 2\lambda E(Y_{t-1}) - \lambda^2 E(Y_{t-2}).$$

However, since

$$E(Y_{t-1}) = \alpha_0 + \beta_0 X_{t-1} + 2\lambda E(Y_{t-2}) - \lambda^2 E(Y_{t-3}),$$
$$E(Y_{t-2}) = \alpha_0 + \beta_0 X_{t-2} + 2\lambda E(Y_{t-3}) - \lambda^2 E(Y_{t-4}),$$
$$\vdots$$
$$E(Y_1) = \alpha_0 + \beta_0 X_1 + 2\lambda E(Y_0) - \lambda^2 E(Y_{-1}),$$

we can also write

$$\text{(11.101)} \quad E(Y_t) = \alpha_0(1 + 2\lambda + 3\lambda^2 + \cdots + t\lambda^{t-1}) + \beta_0(X_t + 2\lambda X_{t-1} + 3\lambda^2 X_{t-2} + \cdots + t\lambda^{t-1}X_1) + (t+1)\lambda^t E(Y_0) - t\lambda^{t+1}E(Y_{-1}).$$

Further,

$$\alpha_0(1 + 2\lambda + 3\lambda^2 + \cdots + t\lambda^{t-1}) = \frac{\alpha_0}{1-\lambda}(1 + \lambda + \lambda^2 + \cdots + \lambda^{t-1} - t\lambda^t)$$
$$= \frac{\alpha_0(1-\lambda^t)}{(1-\lambda)^2} - \frac{\alpha_0 t\lambda^t}{(1-\lambda)}$$
$$= \alpha(1-\lambda^t) - \alpha(1-\lambda)t\lambda^t.$$

Thus, (11.101) can be written as

$$\text{(11.101a)} \quad Y_t = \alpha + \beta_0 W_{2t}^{(\lambda)} + \delta_0\lambda^t + \phi_0 t\lambda^t + \varepsilon_t$$

where
$$W_{2t}^{(\lambda)} = X_t + 2\lambda X_{t-1} + 3\lambda^2 X_{t-2} + \cdots + t\lambda^{t-1}X_1,$$
$$\beta_0 = \beta(1-\lambda)^2,$$
$$\delta_0 = E(Y_0) - \alpha,$$
$$\phi_0 = E(Y_0) - \lambda E(Y_{-1}) - \alpha(1-\lambda).$$

If λ were known, equation (11.101a) would be a linear regression equation with three regressors: $W_{2t}^{(\lambda)}$, λ^t, and $t\lambda^t$. Of course, in most cases, λ is not known. If it is assumed that the ε's are mutually independent, then we can obtain the maximum likelihood estimates of the unknown parameters by minimizing

$$S^{(\lambda)} = \sum_{t=1}^{n} (Y_t - \alpha - \beta_0 W_{2t}^{(\lambda)} - \delta_0\lambda^t - \phi_0 t\lambda^t)^2$$

with respect to α, β_0, δ_0, and ϕ_0 for different values of λ between 0 and 1. The maximum likelihood estimates of α, β, δ_0, and λ will then be those values which lead to the smallest value of $S^{(\lambda)}$. Under the stated assumptions the estimates of α, β, and λ will have all the desirable asymptotic properties. If the ε's follow a first-order autoregression scheme, we can transform (11.100) into

$$E(Y_t) - \rho E(Y_{t-1}) = \alpha_0(1-\rho) + \beta_0(X_t - \rho X_{t-1}) + 2\lambda[E(Y_{t-1}) - \rho E(Y_{t-2})] - \lambda^2[E(Y_{t-2}) - \rho E(Y_{t-3})] + u_t$$

and then proceed as with (11.93) and (11.93a).

The approach to the problem of estimating the parameters of a Pascal lag model for $r = 3$, 4, etc., could be similar to that for $r = 2$. Of course, the degree of complexity of the estimation problem increases with r. If the value of r cannot be assumed a priori, we have to calculate the value of the likelihood function for each r and then choose the value of r that leads to the maximum value of the likelihood function. While there is no difficulty about such a procedure in principle, its implementation is involved and may not be practicable.

The transformation of the Pascal lag relation presented in (11.100) for $r = 2$ can be extended to any nonnegative integer value of r as follows:

$$Y_t + \binom{r}{1}(-\lambda)^1 Y_{t-1} + \binom{r}{2}(-\lambda)^2 Y_{t-2} + \cdots + \binom{r}{r}(-\lambda)^r Y_{t-r}$$
$$= \alpha(1-\lambda)^r + \beta(1-\lambda)^r X_t + \varepsilon_t + \binom{r}{1}(-\lambda)^1 \varepsilon_{t-1} + \cdots + \binom{r}{r}(-\lambda)^r \varepsilon_{t-r}. \tag{11.102}$$

Note that in (11.102) the coefficients of the current and lagged Y's (and ε's) are all constrained to be equal to specific functions of λ. If we generalize the form of (11.102) by removing these constraints, we obtain

$$Y_t + \delta_1 Y_{t-1} + \delta_2 Y_{t-2} + \cdots + \delta_r Y_{t-r}$$
$$= \alpha_0 + \beta_0 X_t + \varepsilon_t + \delta_1 \varepsilon_{t-1} + \cdots + \delta_r \varepsilon_{t-r}. \tag{11.103}$$

Equation (11.103) describes the so-called *rational distributed lag model* introduced by Jorgenson.[28] The estimation of this model could proceed along the lines similar to those applied to the Pascal lag model.

The complexity of the estimation problem in the case of general inverted V-lag models has led to the search for simpler formulations. One such simplification is available if we are willing to assume that the weights attached to X_t, $X_{t-1}, \ldots,$ reach a peak in one of the past $(h-1)$ periods, and that they decline geometrically after that. The distributed lag relation can then be formulated as

$$Y_t = \alpha + \beta_0 X_t + \beta_1 X_{t-1} + \cdots + \beta_{h-1} X_{t-h+1}$$
$$+ \beta_h (X_{t-h} + \lambda X_{t-h-1} + \lambda^2 X_{t-h-2} + \cdots) + \varepsilon_t. \tag{11.104}$$

By the application of the Koyck transformation, this becomes

$$Y_t = \alpha_0 + \beta_0 X_t + \beta_1^* X_{t-1} + \beta_2^* X_{t-2}$$
$$+ \cdots + \beta_h^* X_{t-h} + \lambda Y_{t-1} + \eta_t, \tag{11.104a}$$

where

$$\alpha_0 = \alpha(1-\lambda),$$
$$\beta_1^* = \beta_1 - \beta_0\lambda,$$
$$\beta_2^* = \beta_2 - \beta_1\lambda,$$
$$\vdots$$
$$\beta_h^* = \beta_h - \beta_{h-1}\lambda,$$
$$\eta_t = \varepsilon_t - \lambda\varepsilon_{t-1}.$$

[28] D. W. Jorgenson, "Rational Distributed Lag Functions," *Econometrica*, Vol. 34, January 1966, pp. 135–149.

The estimation of (11.104a) can be carried out in the same way as that of the conventional geometric lag model discussed earlier.

Polynomial Lag

A different formulation of the inverted V-lag model is possible in a situation in which we can assume that the weights w in

$$Y_t = \alpha + \beta(w_0 X_t + w_1 X_{t-1} + \cdots + w_m X_{t-m}) + \varepsilon_t$$

follow a polynomial of a given degree. Such models are called *polynomial lag models*. To formulate them we have to specify the appropriate degree of the polynomial and state the number of periods before the weights can be assumed to be zero. In the example on capital expenditures and appropriations, we assume that current capital expenditures are influenced neither by capital appropriations made more than m periods ago, nor by those to be made in the future. Thus we wish to fit a polynomial of, say, pth degree to the weights w_{-1}, $w_0, w_1, \ldots, w_m, w_{m+1}$ in such a way that

$$w_{-1} = 0 \quad \text{and} \quad w_{m+1} = 0.$$

The weights $w_{-2}, w_{-3}, \ldots,$ and $w_{m+2}, w_{m+3}, \ldots,$ do not lie on the polynomial but are all assumed to be zero. The estimation problem is quite straightforward. Suppose the degree of the polynomial is chosen to be four. Then to make each of the weights $w_{-1}, w_0, w_1, \ldots, w_{m+1}$ lie along a fourth-degree polynomial curve, we specify

$$w_i = \lambda_0 + \lambda_1 i + \lambda_2 i^2 + \lambda_3 i^3 + \lambda_4 i^4, \quad (i = -1, 0, 1, 2, \ldots, m, m+1). \tag{11.105}$$

Our polynomial lag model then becomes

$$\begin{aligned} Y_t = \alpha + \beta[\lambda_0 X_t &+ (\lambda_0 + \lambda_1 + \lambda_2 + \lambda_3 + \lambda_4) X_{t-1} \\ &+ (\lambda_0 + 2\lambda_1 + 2^2\lambda_2 + 2^3\lambda_3 + 2^4\lambda_4) X_{t-2} \\ &+ \cdots + (\lambda_0 + m\lambda_1 + m^2\lambda_2 + m^3\lambda_3 + m^4\lambda_4) X_{t-m}] + \varepsilon_t, \end{aligned} \tag{11.106}$$

which can be concentrated as

$$Y_t = \alpha + \beta\lambda_0 Z_{t0} + \beta\lambda_1 Z_{t1} + \cdots + \beta\lambda_4 Z_{t4} + \varepsilon_t \tag{11.106a}$$

where

$$\begin{aligned} Z_{t0} &= X_t + X_{t-1} + \cdots + X_{t-m}, \\ Z_{t1} &= X_{t-1} + 2X_{t-2} + \cdots + mX_{t-m}, \\ &\vdots \\ Z_{t4} &= X_{t-1} + 2^4 X_{t-2} + \cdots + m^4 X_{t-m}. \end{aligned}$$

Equation (11.106a) involves altogether seven parameters. This number can be reduced by imposing the restrictions that $w_{-1} = 0$ and $w_{m+1} = 0$, i.e., that

$$\lambda_0 - \lambda_1 + \lambda_2 - \lambda_3 + \lambda_4 = 0, \tag{11.107}$$

$$\lambda_0 + (m+1)\lambda_1 + (m+1)^2\lambda_2 + (m+1)^3\lambda_3 + (m+1)^4\lambda_4 = 0. \tag{11.108}$$

These equations can be solved for, say, λ_0 and λ_1, which leads to

$$\lambda_0 = -(m+1)\lambda_2 - m(m+1)\lambda_3 - (m+1)(m^2+m+1)\lambda_4$$

and $$\lambda_1 = -m\lambda_2 - (m^2+m+1)\lambda_3 - m(m^2+2m+2)\lambda_4.$$

Substituting these results into (11.104a) yields

(11.109) $$Y_t = \alpha + \beta\lambda_2 W_{t2} + \beta\lambda_3 W_{t3} + \beta\lambda_4 W_{t4} + \varepsilon_t,$$

where
$$W_{t2} = -(m+1)Z_{t0} - mZ_{t1} + Z_{t2},$$
$$W_{t3} = -m(m+1)Z_{t0} - (m^2+m+1)Z_{t1} + Z_{t3},$$
$$W_{t4} = -(m+1)(m^2+m+1)Z_{t0} - m(m^2+2m+2)Z_{t1} + Z_{t4}.$$

For instance, if m is chosen to be 7, the W's are defined as

$$\begin{aligned} W_{t2} &= -8Z_{t0} - 7Z_{t1} + Z_{t2} \\ &= -8X_t - 14X_{t-1} - 18X_{t-2} - 20X_{t-3} - 20X_{t-4} - 18X_{t-5} \\ &\quad -14X_{t-6} - 8X_{t-7}, \\ W_{t3} &= -56Z_{t0} - 57Z_{t1} + Z_{t3} \\ &= -56X_t - 112X_{t-1} - 162X_{t-2} - 200X_{t-3} - 220X_{t-4} \\ &\quad -216X_{t-5} - 182X_{t-6} - 112X_{t-7}, \\ W_{t4} &= -456Z_{t0} - 455Z_{t1} + Z_{t4} \\ &= -456X_t - 910X_{t-1} - 1350X_{t-2} - 1740X_{t-3} - 2020X_{t-4} \\ &\quad -2106X_{t-5} - 1890X_{t-6} - 1240X_{t-7}. \end{aligned}$$

Note that the parameter β is still not identified; in practice, its value is usually taken to be unity. The parameters α, λ_2, λ_3, and λ_4 of (11.109) can be estimated by ordinary least squares. If ε_t satisfies all the assumptions of the classical normal regression model, the resulting estimates will have all the desirable properties. In case of autocorrelation, we can use one of the estimation methods described in Section 8–2. The estimated values of the λ's can be substituted into (11.105) to obtain estimates of the weights $w_0, w_1, \ldots, w_m$.[29] If we should require that the weights add up to 1, we would impose a further restriction on the λ's, namely,

$$\lambda_0(m+1) + \lambda_1 \sum_i i + \lambda_2 \sum_i i^2 + \lambda_3 \sum_i i^3 + \lambda_4 \sum_i i^4 = 1.$$

In this case equation (11.109) would be further reduced to involve only two, rather than three, regressors.

[29] In S. Almon, "The Distributed Lag Between Capital Appropriations and Expenditures," *Econometrica*, Vol. 33, January 1965, pp. 178–196, the parameters of the model are estimated with the help of the so-called "Lagrangian interpolation." However, the results should be identical to those obtained by the straightforward application of the ordinary least squares method as described by us.

EXAMPLE The polynomial lag model was used by Almon[30] to estimate the relationship between current capital expenditures and current and past capital appropriations in the United States manufacturing industries. The degree of the polynomial in each case was 4, but the length of the lag was taken to be different for different industries. The data used for estimation were given by the quarterly observations for the years 1953–1961. The model was specified as

$$Y_t = \alpha_1 S_{t1} + \alpha_2 S_{t2} + \alpha_3 S_{t3} + \alpha_4 S_{t4} + w_0 X_t + w_1 X_{t-1} + \cdots + w_m X_{t-m} + \varepsilon_t,$$

where Y represents capital expenditures, the S's represent seasonal dummy variables, and the X's represent capital appropriations. The parameter α_4 was set to be equal to $(-\alpha_1 - \alpha_2 - \alpha_3)$. The weights were restricted by the conditions that $w_{-1} = 0$ and $w_{m+1} = 0$, but they were not required to add up to unity. The result for "all manufacturing industries" was as follows:

$$\begin{aligned} Y_t = {} & -283S_{t1} + 13S_{t2} - 50S_{t3} + 320S_{t4} + \underset{(0.023)}{0.048X_t} + \underset{(0.016)}{0.099X_{t-1}} + \underset{(0.013)}{0.141X_{t-2}} \\ & + \underset{(0.023)}{0.165X_{t-3}} + \underset{(0.023)}{0.167X_{t-4}} + \underset{(0.013)}{0.146X_{t-5}} + \underset{(0.016)}{0.105X_{t-6}} + \underset{(0.024)}{0.053X_{t-7}} + e_t. \end{aligned}$$

As can be seen, the chosen length of the lag in this case was 7 periods. The weights add up to 0.922; the difference between 0.922 and 1 can be very nearly accounted for by cancellations. The estimated weights are shown graphically in Figure 11–14.

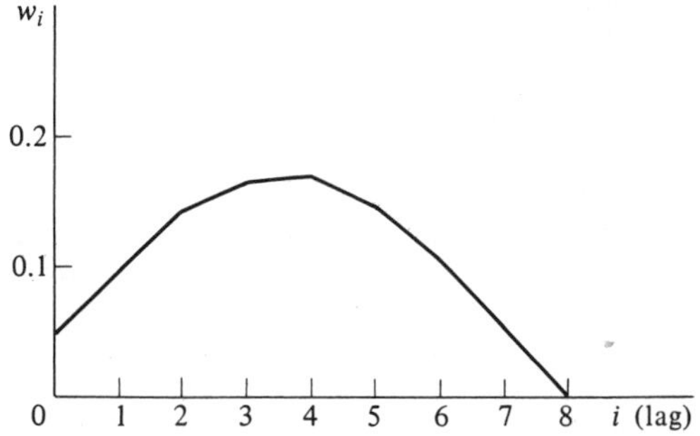

Figure 11–14

The difficulty about using the polynomial lag model is that we have to specify a priori the degree of the polynomial and the length of the lag. Concerning the latter, however, some help may be obtained from the data. One possibility is to keep on extending the length of the lag until the contribution of the additional X's to the regression sum of squares is no longer statistically significant. But if the X's are highly correlated, this criterion may not work very well. Another possibility is to choose that length of the lag which results in the highest value of $\bar{R}^2$, i.e., of the coefficient of determination corrected for the "number of degrees of freedom." However, this also may not always work well since the differences

[30] *Ibid.*

between several values of $\bar{R}^2$ may be very small. Nevertheless, one or the other of these criteria, *plus* other considerations (for example, that all weights should be positive), may help in choosing the "best" lag for the problem at hand.

EXERCISES

11–1. Three salesmen employed by a certain firm had the following weekly earnings in five consecutive days:

Salesman:	A	B	C
Weekly earnings ($):	928	924	793

An analysis-of-variance test of the null hypothesis that the mean earnings of the three salesmen are the same has been carried out, and the value of the F statistic found to be 5.00. Consider this problem as one of regression analysis, with the regression equation given by

$$Y_{ig} = \beta_1 + \beta_2 X_{i2} + \beta_3 X_{i3} + \varepsilon_i,$$

where

$$\begin{aligned} X_{i2} &= 1 \quad \text{if } i \text{ belongs to B,} \\ &= 0 \quad \text{otherwise;} \\ X_{i3} &= 1 \quad \text{if } i \text{ belongs to C,} \\ &= 0 \quad \text{otherwise;} \\ i &= 1, 2, \ldots, 5; \\ g &= 1, 2, 3. \end{aligned}$$

Find the least squares estimates of the regression coefficients and their estimated standard errors. Also, calculate the value of R^2.

11–2. Demonstrate the equivalence of the regression model (11.8) and a "two-way analysis of variance" model with interactions.

11–3. The least squares estimates of a regression model are:

$$\underset{(1)}{Y_t = 10} + \underset{(\sqrt{0.5})}{5X_t} + e_t.$$

The explanatory variable X_t is a binary variable. Suppose that in checking the results it was found that the values of X_t were punched by mistake as 0 and 2 instead of 0 and 1. Make the appropriate corrections.

11–4. The survey records for a sample of twelve families show the weekly consumption expenditures and weekly incomes given in Table 11–5. Families whose income is marked by an asterisk (*) have reported that their income is higher than in the previous year. Test the relevance of the asymmetric response model.

Table 11–5

Family No.	Income	Consumption Expenditure
1	80	70
2	95*	76
3	105	91
4	115	100
5	125*	105
6	135*	113
7	145	122
8	155	120
9	165*	146
10	175*	135
11	185*	147
12	200*	155

11–5. Consider the following consumption function model:

$$C_t = \beta_1 + \beta_2 Y_t + \beta_3 Z_t + \beta_4 Y_t Z_t + \varepsilon_t,$$

where C = consumption, Y = income, and $Z_t = 1$ in wartime and 0 otherwise. Prove that the least squares estimates of the regression coefficients could have been obtained equally well from two separate regressions of C_t on Y_t, one estimated from the peacetime observations and one estimated from the wartime observations.

11–6. A production function model is specified as

$$Y_i = \beta_1 + \beta_2 X_{i2} + \beta_3 X_{i3} + \varepsilon_i,$$

where Y_i = log output, X_{i2} = log labor input, and X_{i3} log capital input. The subscript i refers to the ith firm. There are 23 observations in the sample, and the moment matrices (in terms of deviations from sample means) are

$$(\underline{\mathbf{X}}'\underline{\mathbf{X}}) = \begin{bmatrix} 12 & 8 \\ 8 & 12 \end{bmatrix}, \qquad (\underline{\mathbf{X}}'\underline{\mathbf{Y}}) = \begin{bmatrix} 10 \\ 8 \end{bmatrix}, \qquad (\underline{\mathbf{Y}}'\underline{\mathbf{Y}}) = 10.$$

a. Find the least squares estimates of the regression coefficients β_2 and β_3, and their estimated standard errors. Calculate the value of R^2.

b. Carry out the test for constant returns to scale (i.e., test the hypothesis that $\beta_2 + \beta_3 = 1$).

c. Suppose now that you wish to impose the restriction that $\beta_2 + \beta_3 = 1$ a priori and to estimate the production function in that way. What, then are the least squares estimate of β_2 and its estimated standard error? Also, what is the value of R^2 under this specification?

11–7. Consider the "stock adjustment" model

$$Y_t = \alpha\gamma + \beta\gamma X_t + (1 - \gamma) Y_{t-1} + \varepsilon_t.$$

Give the formula for the nonlinear least squares estimator of α, say, $\hat{\alpha}$. Derive the formula for the estimated variance of $\hat{\alpha}$ by using

a. The approximation formula (11.40).

b. The maximum likelihood information matrix.

11–8. The results of simple least squares regression of Y on X_1 and X_2 are

$$Y_t = 10 + \underset{(2)}{12X_{1t}} + \underset{(1)}{4X_{2t}} + e_t.$$

Further, the sample coefficient of correlation between X_1 and X_2 is 0.5. Suppose now that it is suggested that a preferable specification of the model would have been one in which Y were regressed on a weighted average of X_1 and X_2, so that the regression equation would become

$$Y_t = \beta_1 + \beta_2(w_1X_{1t} + w_2X_{2t}) + \varepsilon_t,$$

where $w_2 = 1 - w_1$. Find the nonlinear least squares estimates of β_2 and w_1, and their estimated standard errors.

11–9. Using the data on consumption, income, and holdings of liquid assets in the United States presented in Table 11–6, estimate the aggregate consumption function

$$C_t = \beta_1 + \beta_2 Y_t + \beta_3 L_t + \varepsilon_t,$$

subject to the constraint that

$$\tfrac{1}{2} \leq \beta_2 \leq 1.$$

11–10. Suppose the aggregate consumption function is specified as

$$C_t = \beta_1 + \beta_2 Y_t + \beta_3 L_t + \beta_4 Y_t L_t + \varepsilon_t.$$

Using the data given in Table 11–6:

a. Obtain the least squares estimates of the regression coefficients and their estimated standard errors.

b. Calculate the value of R^2 and test for the existence of a relationship.

c. Test the hypothesis that $\beta_4 = 0$.

11–11. Let $Y_i = Q_i/L_i$ and $X_i = K_i/L_i$, where Q_i = output, L_i = labor input, K_i = capital input, and the subscript i refers to the ith firm. Using the data presented in Table 11–4, estimate the following relationship:

$$\frac{Y_i^\lambda - 1}{\lambda} = \alpha + \beta\left(\frac{X_i^\lambda - 1}{\lambda}\right) + \varepsilon_i.$$

Test the hypothesis that $\lambda = 0$.

11–12. Consider the following distributed lag model:

$$Y_t = \alpha + \beta(w_0X_t + w_1X_{t-1} + w_2X_{t-2} + w_3X_{t-3}) + \varepsilon_t.$$

Table 11–6*

		C_t	Y_t	L_t
1955	I	248.7	263.0	207.6
	II	253.7	271.5	209.4
	III	259.9	276.5	211.1
	IV	261.8	281.4	213.2
1956	I	263.2	282.0	214.1
	II	263.7	286.2	216.5
	III	263.4	287.7	217.3
	IV	266.9	291.0	217.3
1957	I	268.9	291.1	218.2
	II	270.4	294.6	218.5
	III	273.4	296.1	219.8
	IV	272.1	293.3	219.5
1958	I	268.9	291.3	220.5
	II	270.9	292.6	222.7
	III	274.4	299.9	225.0
	IV	278.7	302.1	229.4
1959	I	283.8	305.9	232.2
	II	289.7	312.5	235.2
	III	290.8	311.3	237.2
	IV	292.8	313.2	237.7
1960	I	295.4	315.4	238.0
	II	299.5	320.3	238.4
	III	298.6	321.0	240.1
	IV	299.6	320.1	243.3
1961	I	297.0	318.4	246.1
	II	301.6	324.8	250.0

Source: Z. Griliches *et al.* "Notes on Estimated Aggregate Quarterly Consumption Functions," *Econometrica*, Vol. 30, July 1962, p. 500.

* All values (in billions of dollars) are price deflated and seasonally adjusted.

The weights w_i ($i = 0, 1, 2, 3$) are assumed to lie along a second-degree polynomial, and they are required to satisfy the following restrictions:

$$w_0 + w_1 + w_2 + w_3 = 1,$$

$$w_{-1} = 0,$$

$$w_4 = 0.$$

Show how you can estimate the coefficients of this model by using ordinary least squares estimation.

12 Generalized Linear Regression Model and Its Applications

The classical regression model is based on rather restrictive assumptions concerning the behavior of the regression disturbance. An alternative model, known as the "generalized linear regression model," is considerably less restrictive in this respect. This model and its implications for estimating the regression coefficients are discussed in Section 12–1. An interesting application of this model to observations on a number of cross-sectional units over time is described in Section 12–2. Since such observations are now becoming more commonly available, the development of appropriate estimation procedures is very useful. Another and very ingenious application of the generalized linear regression model can be made when estimating a set of regression equations whose disturbances are correlated. The discussion of this application, which also provides a logical bridge between single-equation models and simultaneous equation models (to be discussed in Chapter 13), is presented in Section 12–3.

12–1 Generalized Linear Regression Model

The classical normal linear regression model is characterized by a number of assumptions concerning the stochastic disturbance in the regression equation, including homoskedasticity and nonautocorrelation. Specifically, the disturbance term ε_i in

$$Y_i = \beta_1 + \beta_2 X_{i2} + \beta_3 X_{i3} + \cdots + \beta_K X_{iK} + \varepsilon_i$$

is supposed to satisfy the following requirements:

$$E(\varepsilon_i^2) = \sigma^2 \quad \text{for all } i,$$

$$E(\varepsilon_i \varepsilon_j) = 0 \quad \text{for all } i \neq j.$$

These assumptions are given by (10.4) and (10.5); in the matrix notation they can be described, as in (10.4a–10.5a), by

$$E(\boldsymbol{\epsilon}\boldsymbol{\epsilon}') = \sigma^2 \mathbf{I_n},$$

where

$$\boldsymbol{\epsilon} = \begin{bmatrix} \varepsilon_1 \\ \varepsilon_2 \\ \vdots \\ \varepsilon_n \end{bmatrix}$$

and $\mathbf{I}_n$ is an identity matrix of order $(n \times n)$. If we do not make these two assumptions—but retain all the other assumptions of the classical normal linear regression model—we have the so-called *generalized linear regression model.* (Some authors also drop the assumption of normality of ε_i.) The full description of this model is

(12.1) $Y_i = \beta_1 + \beta_2 X_{i2} + \beta_3 X_{i3} + \cdots + \beta_K X_{iK} + \varepsilon_i.$

(12.2) The joint distribution of $\varepsilon_1, \varepsilon_2, \ldots, \varepsilon_n$ is multivariate normal,

(12.3) $E(\varepsilon_i) = 0, \qquad i = 1, 2, \ldots, n.$

(12.4) $E(\varepsilon_i \varepsilon_j) = \sigma_{ij}, \qquad i, j = 1, 2, \ldots, n.$

(12.5) Each of the explanatory variables is nonstochastic and such that, for any sample size,

$$\frac{1}{n} \sum_{i=1}^{n} (X_{ik} - \bar{X}_k)^2$$

is a finite number different from zero for every $k = 2, 3, \ldots, K$.

(12.6) The number of observations exceeds the number of explanatory variables *plus* one, i.e., $n > K$.

(12.7) No exact linear relation exists between any of the explanatory variables.

Note that according to (12.3) and (12.4), σ_{ii} is the variance of ε_i, and σ_{ij} $(i \neq j)$ is the covariance of ε_i and ε_j. If we use matrix notation we can restate (12.1) as

(12.1a) $$\mathbf{Y} = \mathbf{X}\boldsymbol{\beta} + \boldsymbol{\epsilon},$$

where $\mathbf{Y}$ is an $(n \times 1)$ vector of the sample values of Y, $\mathbf{X}$ is an $(n \times K)$ matrix of the sample values of $X_{i1}, X_{i2}, \ldots, X_{iK}$ (with $X_{i1} = 1$ for all i), $\boldsymbol{\beta}$ is a $(K \times 1)$ vector of the regression coefficients, and $\boldsymbol{\epsilon}$ is an $(n \times 1)$ vector of the sample values of ε. The assumption (12.4) can be written as

(12.4a) $$E(\boldsymbol{\epsilon}\boldsymbol{\epsilon}') = \boldsymbol{\Omega},$$

where $$\boldsymbol{\Omega} = \begin{bmatrix} \sigma_{11} & \sigma_{12} & \cdots & \sigma_{1n} \\ \sigma_{21} & \sigma_{22} & \cdots & \sigma_{2n} \\ \vdots & \vdots & & \vdots \\ \sigma_{n1} & \sigma_{n2} & \cdots & \sigma_{nn} \end{bmatrix}.$$

This model is called "generalized" because it includes other models as special cases. The classical normal linear regression model is one such special case, in which $\mathbf{\Omega}$ is a diagonal matrix with σ^2 in place of each of the diagonal elements. Another special case is the heteroskedastic model; here $\mathbf{\Omega}$ is again diagonal, but the diagonal elements are not necessarily all the same. For the model in which the disturbances follow a first-order autoregressive scheme, the matrix $\mathbf{\Omega}$ becomes

$$\mathbf{\Omega} = \sigma^2 \begin{bmatrix} 1 & \rho & \rho^2 & \cdots & \rho^{n-1} \\ \rho & 1 & \rho & \cdots & \rho^{n-2} \\ \vdots & \vdots & \vdots & & \vdots \\ \rho^{n-1} & \rho^{n-2} & \rho^{n-3} & \cdots & 1 \end{bmatrix}.$$

Let us now turn to the problem of estimating the parameters of the generalized linear regression model. We will assume for the present that the variances and covariances of the disturbances (i.e., the elements of the $\mathbf{\Omega}$ matrix) are known. First, we note that since the *ordinary least squares estimators* of the regression coefficients are obtained by minimizing

$$\sum_{i=1}^{n} (Y_i - \beta_1 - \beta_2 X_{i2} - \cdots - \beta_K X_{iK})^2,$$

they are exactly the same as the least squares estimators of the classical normal linear regression model; that is,

$$\hat{\boldsymbol{\beta}} = (\mathbf{X}'\mathbf{X})^{-1}(\mathbf{X}'\mathbf{Y}).$$

Note that

$$E(\hat{\boldsymbol{\beta}}) = E(\mathbf{X}'\mathbf{X})^{-1}\mathbf{X}'[\mathbf{X}\boldsymbol{\beta} + \boldsymbol{\epsilon}] = \boldsymbol{\beta} + E(\mathbf{X}'\mathbf{X})^{-1}(\mathbf{X}'\boldsymbol{\epsilon}) = \boldsymbol{\beta}$$

and
$$\operatorname{plim} \hat{\boldsymbol{\beta}} = \boldsymbol{\beta} + \operatorname{plim} \left[\frac{1}{n}\mathbf{X}'\mathbf{X}\right]^{-1}\left[\frac{1}{n}\mathbf{X}'\boldsymbol{\epsilon}\right] = \boldsymbol{\beta}.$$

This shows the ordinary least squares estimators of $\boldsymbol{\beta}$ of the generalized linear regression model are unbiased and consistent.

Next, we derive the *best linear unbiased estimators* (BLUE) of the regression coefficients. To find the BLUE of β_1, we put

$$\tilde{\beta}_1 = \sum_{i=1}^{n} a_i Y_i$$

where $a_1, a_2, \ldots, a_n$ are some constants to be determined. In matrix notation we write

$$\tilde{\beta}_1 = \mathbf{Y}'\mathbf{a},$$

where
$$\mathbf{a} = \begin{bmatrix} a_1 \\ a_2 \\ \vdots \\ a_n \end{bmatrix}.$$

The mathematical expectation of $\tilde{\beta}_1$ is

$$E(\tilde{\beta}_1) = E\Big(\sum_i a_i Y_i\Big) = \beta_1 \sum_i a_i + \beta_2 \sum_i a_i X_{i2} + \cdots + \beta_K \sum_i a_i X_{iK}.$$

By the condition of unbiasedness of $\tilde{\beta}_1$, we then require that

$$\sum_i a_i = 1,$$
$$\sum_i a_i X_{i2} = 0,$$
$$\vdots$$
$$\sum_i a_i X_{iK} = 0,$$

or, in matrix notation,

$$\mathbf{X'a} = \boldsymbol{\iota}_1,$$

where $\boldsymbol{\iota}_1$ is a $(K \times 1)$ vector defined as

$$\boldsymbol{\iota}_1 = \begin{bmatrix} 1 \\ 0 \\ \vdots \\ 0 \end{bmatrix}.$$

The variance of $\tilde{\beta}_1$ is

$$\mathrm{Var}(\tilde{\beta}_1) = E\Big[\sum_i a_i Y_i - E\Big(\sum_i a_i Y_i\Big)\Big]^2 = E\Big(\sum_i a_i \varepsilon_i\Big)^2 = \sum_{i=1}^{n} \sum_{j=1}^{n} a_i a_j \sigma_{ij},$$

or
$$\mathrm{Var}(\tilde{\beta}_1) = \mathbf{a}'\boldsymbol{\Omega}\mathbf{a}.$$

Thus we have to find those values of $a_1, a_2, \ldots, a_n$ which would minimize $\mathrm{Var}(\tilde{\beta}_1)$ subject to $\mathbf{X'a} = \boldsymbol{\iota}_1$. Using the Lagrange multiplier method, we form

$$H = \sum_{i=1}^{n} \sum_{j=1}^{n} a_i a_j \sigma_{ij} - \lambda_1 \Big(\sum_{i=1}^{n} a_i - 1\Big) - \lambda_2 \sum_{i=1}^{n} a_i X_{i2} - \cdots - \lambda_K \sum_{i=1}^{n} a_i X_{iK}.$$

Differentiating H with respect to $a_1, a_2, \ldots, a_n, \lambda_1, \lambda_2, \ldots, \lambda_K$ and putting each derivative equal to zero, we obtain

$$2(a_1\sigma_{11} + a_2\sigma_{12} + \cdots + a_n\sigma_{1n}) - \lambda_1 - \lambda_2 X_{12} - \cdots - \lambda_K X_{1K} = 0,$$

$$2(a_1\sigma_{21} + a_2\sigma_{22} + \cdots + a_n\sigma_{2n}) - \lambda_1 - \lambda_2 X_{22} - \cdots - \lambda_K X_{2K} = 0,$$

$$\vdots$$

$$2(a_1\sigma_{n1} + a_2\sigma_{n2} + \cdots + a_n\sigma_{nn}) - \lambda_1 - \lambda_2 X_{n2} - \cdots - \lambda_K X_{nK} = 0,$$

$$-\Big(\sum_i a_i - 1\Big) = 0,$$

$$-\sum_i a_i X_{i2} = 0,$$

$$\vdots$$

$$-\sum_i a_i X_{iK} = 0.$$

In matrix notation this can be written as

(12.8) $$2\mathbf{\Omega a} - \mathbf{X\lambda} = \mathbf{0}$$

(12.9) $$\mathbf{X'a} = \boldsymbol{\iota}_1,$$

where $$\boldsymbol{\lambda} = \begin{bmatrix} \lambda_1 \\ \lambda_2 \\ \vdots \\ \lambda_K \end{bmatrix}$$

and $\mathbf{0}$ is an $(n \times 1)$ vector of zeros. From (12.8) we obtain

(12.8a) $$\mathbf{a} = \tfrac{1}{2}\mathbf{\Omega}^{-1}\mathbf{X\lambda}.$$

Substitution of this expression for $\mathbf{a}$ into (12.9) gives

(12.10) $$\tfrac{1}{2}\mathbf{X'\Omega}^{-1}\mathbf{X\lambda} = \boldsymbol{\iota}_1,$$

or

(12.10a) $$\boldsymbol{\lambda} = 2(\mathbf{X'\Omega}^{-1}\mathbf{X})^{-1}\boldsymbol{\iota}_1.$$

Substituting for $\boldsymbol{\lambda}$ from (12.10a) into (12.8a), we find

(12.11) $$\mathbf{a} = \mathbf{\Omega}^{-1}\mathbf{X}(\mathbf{X'\Omega}^{-1}\mathbf{X})^{-1}\boldsymbol{\iota}_1.$$

Therefore,

(12.12) $$\tilde{\beta}_1 = \mathbf{Y'a} = (\mathbf{Y'\Omega}^{-1}\mathbf{X})(\mathbf{X'\Omega}^{-1}\mathbf{X})^{-1}\boldsymbol{\iota}_1$$
$$= \boldsymbol{\iota}_1'(\mathbf{X'\Omega}^{-1}\mathbf{X})^{-1}(\mathbf{X'\Omega}^{-1}\mathbf{Y}).$$

This then is the BLUE of β_1.[1] Further, since

$$\mathrm{Var}(\tilde{\beta}_1) = \mathbf{a'\Omega a},$$

[1] The proof that this result corresponds to a minimum and not to a maximum variance can be found in J. Johnston, *Econometric Methods* (New York: McGraw-Hill, 1963), pp. 183–184.

we can use (12.11) to determine

$$(12.13)\qquad \operatorname{Var}(\tilde{\beta}_1) = [\boldsymbol{\iota}_1'(\mathbf{X}'\boldsymbol{\Omega}^{-1}\mathbf{X})^{-1}\mathbf{X}'\boldsymbol{\Omega}^{-1}]\boldsymbol{\Omega}[\boldsymbol{\Omega}^{-1}\mathbf{X}(\mathbf{X}'\boldsymbol{\Omega}^{-1}\mathbf{X})^{-1}\boldsymbol{\iota}_1]$$
$$= \boldsymbol{\iota}_1'(\mathbf{X}'\boldsymbol{\Omega}^{-1}\mathbf{X})^{-1}\boldsymbol{\iota}_1.$$

The procedure for deriving the BLUE of β_1 and its variance can be used also with the other regression coefficients. The results are

$$\tilde{\beta}_2 = \boldsymbol{\iota}_2'(\mathbf{X}'\boldsymbol{\Omega}^{-1}\mathbf{X})^{-1}(\mathbf{X}'\boldsymbol{\Omega}^{-1}\mathbf{Y}),$$
$$\operatorname{Var}(\tilde{\beta}_2) = \boldsymbol{\iota}_2'(\mathbf{X}'\boldsymbol{\Omega}^{-1}\mathbf{X})^{-1}\boldsymbol{\iota}_2,$$
$$\vdots$$
$$\tilde{\beta}_K = \boldsymbol{\iota}_K'(\mathbf{X}'\boldsymbol{\Omega}^{-1}\mathbf{X})^{-1}(\mathbf{X}'\boldsymbol{\Omega}^{-1}\mathbf{Y}),$$
$$\operatorname{Var}(\tilde{\beta}_K) = \boldsymbol{\iota}_K'(\mathbf{X}'\boldsymbol{\Omega}^{-1}\mathbf{X})^{-1}\boldsymbol{\iota}_K.$$

In general,

$$\tilde{\beta}_k = \boldsymbol{\iota}_k'(\mathbf{X}'\boldsymbol{\Omega}^{-1}\mathbf{X})^{-1}(\mathbf{X}'\boldsymbol{\Omega}^{-1}\mathbf{Y}),$$
$$\operatorname{Var}(\tilde{\beta}_k) = \boldsymbol{\iota}_k'(\mathbf{X}'\boldsymbol{\Omega}^{-1}\mathbf{X})^{-1}\boldsymbol{\iota}_k, \qquad (k = 1, 2, \ldots, K),$$

where $\boldsymbol{\iota}_k$ is a $(K \times 1)$ vector with the kth element equal to one and each of the remaining elements equal to zero. These results can be summarized by writing

$$(12.14)\qquad \tilde{\boldsymbol{\beta}} = (\mathbf{X}'\boldsymbol{\Omega}^{-1}\mathbf{X})^{-1}(\mathbf{X}'\boldsymbol{\Omega}^{-1}\mathbf{Y}),$$

$$(12.15)\qquad E(\tilde{\boldsymbol{\beta}} - \boldsymbol{\beta})(\tilde{\boldsymbol{\beta}} - \boldsymbol{\beta})' = (\mathbf{X}'\boldsymbol{\Omega}^{-1}\mathbf{X})^{-1},$$

where

$$\tilde{\boldsymbol{\beta}} = \begin{bmatrix} \tilde{\beta}_1 \\ \tilde{\beta}_2 \\ \vdots \\ \tilde{\beta}_K \end{bmatrix}.$$

The estimator $\tilde{\boldsymbol{\beta}}$ is usually called *Aitken's generalized least squares estimator.*[2] If we denote the elements of the inverse of $\boldsymbol{\Omega}$ by appropriate superscripts, that is, if we put

$$\boldsymbol{\Omega}^{-1} = \begin{bmatrix} \sigma^{11} & \sigma^{12} & \cdots & \sigma^{1n} \\ \sigma^{21} & \sigma^{22} & \cdots & \sigma^{2n} \\ \vdots & \vdots & & \vdots \\ \sigma^{n1} & \sigma^{n2} & & \sigma^{nn} \end{bmatrix},$$

[2] A. C. Aitken, "On Least Squares and Linear Combination of Observations," *Proceedings of the Royal Society of Edinburgh*, Vol. 55, 1934–35, pp. 42–48.

then we can describe the elements of $(\mathbf{X}'\mathbf{\Omega}^{-1}\mathbf{X})$ and $(\mathbf{X}'\mathbf{\Omega}^{-1}\mathbf{Y})$ and write

$$\tilde{\boldsymbol{\beta}} = \begin{bmatrix} \sum_i\sum_j \sigma^{ij}X_{i1}^2 & \sum_i\sum_j \sigma^{ij}X_{i1}X_{j2} & \cdots & \sum_i\sum_j \sigma^{ij}X_{i1}X_{jK} \\ \sum_i\sum_j \sigma^{ij}X_{i2}X_{j1} & \sum_i\sum_j \sigma^{ij}X_{i2}^2 & \cdots & \sum_i\sum_j \sigma^{ij}X_{i2}X_{jK} \\ \vdots & \vdots & & \vdots \\ \sum_i\sum_j \sigma^{ij}X_{iK}X_{j1} & \sum_i\sum_j \sigma^{ij}X_{iK}X_{j2} & \cdots & \sum_i\sum_j \sigma^{ij}X_{iK}^2 \end{bmatrix}^{-1} \begin{bmatrix} \sum_i\sum_j \sigma^{ij}X_{i1}Y_j \\ \sum_i\sum_j \sigma^{ij}X_{i2}Y_j \\ \vdots \\ \sum_i\sum_j \sigma^{ij}X_{iK}Y_j \end{bmatrix}.$$

Further, if

$$\underline{\tilde{\boldsymbol{\beta}}} = \begin{bmatrix} \tilde{\beta}_2 \\ \tilde{\beta}_3 \\ \vdots \\ \tilde{\beta}_K \end{bmatrix}, \qquad \underline{\mathbf{X}} = \begin{bmatrix} (X_{12} - \tilde{X}_2) & (X_{13} - \tilde{X}_3) & \cdots & (X_{1K} - \tilde{X}_K) \\ (X_{22} - \tilde{X}_2) & (X_{23} - \tilde{X}_3) & \cdots & (X_{2K} - \tilde{X}_K) \\ \vdots & \vdots & & \vdots \\ (X_{n2} - \tilde{X}_2) & (X_{n3} - \tilde{X}_3) & \cdots & (X_{nK} - \tilde{X}_K) \end{bmatrix},$$

$$\underline{\mathbf{Y}} = \begin{bmatrix} Y_1 - \tilde{Y} \\ Y_2 - \tilde{Y} \\ \vdots \\ Y_n - \tilde{Y} \end{bmatrix},$$

where $\tilde{X}_2 = \sum_i \sum_j \sigma^{ij} X_{j2} \Big/ \sum_i \sum_j \sigma^{ij}$, etc., then

(12.16) $$\underline{\tilde{\boldsymbol{\beta}}} = (\underline{\mathbf{X}}'\mathbf{\Omega}^{-1}\underline{\mathbf{X}})^{-1}(\underline{\mathbf{X}}'\mathbf{\Omega}^{-1}\underline{\mathbf{Y}})$$

and

(12.17) $$E(\underline{\tilde{\boldsymbol{\beta}}} - \underline{\boldsymbol{\beta}})(\underline{\tilde{\boldsymbol{\beta}}} - \underline{\boldsymbol{\beta}})' = (\underline{\mathbf{X}}'\mathbf{\Omega}^{-1}\underline{\mathbf{X}})^{-1}.$$

The *maximum likelihood estimators* of the regression coefficients can be derived by noting that, under the assumptions of the model, the joint distribution of $\varepsilon_1, \varepsilon_2, \ldots, \varepsilon_n$ is given by[3]

$$f(\varepsilon_1, \varepsilon_2, \ldots, \varepsilon_n) = (2\pi)^{-(n/2)}|\mathbf{\Omega}|^{-(1/2)}e^{-(1/2)\boldsymbol{\varepsilon}'\mathbf{\Omega}^{-1}\boldsymbol{\varepsilon}},$$

where $|\mathbf{\Omega}|$ represents the determinant of the matrix $\mathbf{\Omega}$. The logarithmic likelihood function for $Y_1, Y_2, \ldots, Y_n$ is given by[4]

(12.18) $$\begin{aligned} L &= -\frac{n}{2}\log(2\pi) - \frac{1}{2}\log|\mathbf{\Omega}| - \frac{1}{2}(\mathbf{Y} - \mathbf{X}\boldsymbol{\beta})'\mathbf{\Omega}^{-1}(\mathbf{Y} - \mathbf{X}\boldsymbol{\beta}) \\ &= -\frac{n}{2}\log(2\pi) - \frac{1}{2}\log|\mathbf{\Omega}| \\ &\quad -\frac{1}{2}(\mathbf{Y}'\mathbf{\Omega}^{-1}\mathbf{Y} - 2\mathbf{Y}'\mathbf{\Omega}^{-1}\mathbf{X}\boldsymbol{\beta} + \boldsymbol{\beta}'\mathbf{X}'\mathbf{\Omega}^{-1}\mathbf{X}\boldsymbol{\beta}). \end{aligned}$$

[3] See A. S. Goldberger, *Econometric Theory* (New York: Wiley, 1964), p. 104. If the ε's in the sample are *not* independent of any ε outside the sample, the joint distribution is conditional on the latter.

[4] For the theorem relating to the transformation from the ε's to the Y's, see *ibid.*, p. 106.

By differentiating L with respect to $\boldsymbol{\beta}$ and putting the result equal to zero, we obtain

$$-\tfrac{1}{2}(-2\mathbf{X}'\boldsymbol{\Omega}^{-1}\mathbf{Y} + 2\mathbf{X}'\boldsymbol{\Omega}^{-1}\mathbf{X}\hat{\boldsymbol{\beta}}) = \mathbf{0},$$

where $\mathbf{0}$ is a $(K \times 1)$ vector of zeros. This gives

$$\hat{\boldsymbol{\beta}} = (\mathbf{X}'\boldsymbol{\Omega}^{-1}\mathbf{X})^{-1}(\mathbf{X}'\boldsymbol{\Omega}^{-1}\mathbf{Y}),$$

which is exactly the same expression as that for Aitken's generalized least squares estimator of β given by (12.14). It can be shown that this estimator has, under fairly general conditions, the desirable properties of consistency, asymptotic efficiency, and asymptotic normality.[5]

Let us now consider some special cases. First, if

$$\boldsymbol{\Omega} = \sigma^2\mathbf{I_n},$$

that is, if the generalized model reduces to the *classical* model, we have

$$\boldsymbol{\Omega}^{-1} = \frac{1}{\sigma^2}\mathbf{I_n},$$

and Aitken's generalized estimator is the same as the ordinary least squares estimator. Second, if

$$\boldsymbol{\Omega} = \begin{bmatrix} \sigma_{11} & 0 & \dots & 0 \\ 0 & \sigma_{22} & \dots & 0 \\ \vdots & \vdots & & \vdots \\ 0 & 0 & \dots & \sigma_{nn} \end{bmatrix},$$

that is, if the generalized model reduces to a purely *heteroskedastic* model, then

$$\boldsymbol{\Omega}^{-1} = \begin{bmatrix} \frac{1}{\sigma_{11}} & 0 & \dots & 0 \\ 0 & \frac{1}{\sigma_{22}} & \dots & 0 \\ \vdots & \vdots & & \vdots \\ 0 & 0 & \dots & \frac{1}{\sigma_{nn}} \end{bmatrix},$$

and Aitken's generalized estimator is the same as the best linear unbiased estimator developed for the heteroskedastic model (see formulas (8.1) through (8.4)

[5] See A. Zellner, "An Efficient Method of Estimating Seemingly Unrelated Regressions and Tests for Aggregation Bias," *Journal of the American Statistical Association*, Vol. 57, June 1962, pp. 348–368.

and their extension to a multiple regression model in Section 8–1). Finally, if

$$\mathbf{\Omega} = \sigma^2 \begin{bmatrix} 1 & \rho & \rho^2 & \dots & \rho^{n-1} \\ \rho & 1 & \rho & \dots & \rho^{n-2} \\ \vdots & \vdots & \vdots & & \vdots \\ \rho^{n-1} & \rho^{n-2} & \rho^{n-3} & \dots & 1 \end{bmatrix},$$

that is, if the disturbance follows a first-order autoregressive scheme, we obtain

$$\mathbf{\Omega}^{-1} = \frac{1}{\sigma^2(1-\rho^2)} \begin{bmatrix} 1 & -\rho & 0 & 0 & \dots & 0 & 0 \\ -\rho & (1+\rho^2) & -\rho & 0 & \dots & 0 & 0 \\ \vdots & \vdots & \vdots & \vdots & & \vdots & \vdots \\ 0 & 0 & 0 & 0 & \dots & -\rho & 1 \end{bmatrix}.$$

In this case Aitken's generalized estimator is the same as the best-linear-unbiased estimator derived for the regression model with autoregressive disturbances (see formulas (8.38) through (8.41) and their extension to a multiple regression model in Section 8–2).

The preceding discussion has been carried out on the presumption that $\mathbf{\Omega}$, the variance-covariance matrix of the disturbances, is known. In many cases, of course, this is not the case and, therefore, Aitken's generalized least squares estimation procedure is not operational. However, suppose that we can find a *consistent estimator* of $\mathbf{\Omega}$, say, $\hat{\mathbf{\Omega}}$, and that we substitute $\hat{\mathbf{\Omega}}$ for $\mathbf{\Omega}$ in Aitken's formula to get

$$\tilde{\tilde{\boldsymbol{\beta}}} = (\mathbf{X}'\hat{\mathbf{\Omega}}^{-1}\mathbf{X})^{-1}(\mathbf{X}'\hat{\mathbf{\Omega}}^{-1}\mathbf{Y}). \tag{12.19}$$

Under general conditions,[6] $\tilde{\tilde{\boldsymbol{\beta}}}$ has the same asymptotic properties as Aitken's estimator; i.e., it is consistent, asymptotically efficient, and asymptotically normal. The asymptotic variance-covariance matrix of $\tilde{\tilde{\boldsymbol{\beta}}}$ is given by

$$\text{Asympt. Var-Cov}(\tilde{\tilde{\boldsymbol{\beta}}}) = (\mathbf{X}'\mathbf{\Omega}^{-1}\mathbf{X})^{-1}. \tag{12.20}$$

Thus the problem is to find a consistent estimator of $\mathbf{\Omega}$. If there are no prior restrictions on any of its elements, the $\mathbf{\Omega}$ matrix involves $n(n+1)/2$ unknown parameters. It is clear that, with only n observations, estimation under these circumstances becomes impossible. Therefore, we can consider only those models for which we have at least some information—or are willing to make some assumptions—about the elements of $\mathbf{\Omega}$. One such model is the heteroskedastic model. However, even here the number of unknown elements of $\mathbf{\Omega}$ is n, which, together with the K regression coefficients, makes impossible demands on the sample data. In this case consistent estimation becomes possible only if we make

[6] For a proof see *ibid.*

some further restrictions on the parameters (see Section 8–1). Another model in which the elements of $\mathbf{\Omega}$ are restricted is the regression model with autocorrelated disturbances. If the disturbances are homoskedastic and follow a first-order autoregressive scheme, $\mathbf{\Omega}$ involves only two unknown parameters, σ^2 and ρ, which can be readily estimated. This model and its estimation was discussed in Section 8–2. We now discuss other restrictions on $\mathbf{\Omega}$ that arise in other contexts.

12–2 Pooling of Cross-section and Time-Series Data

The question of the appropriate restrictions on $\mathbf{\Omega}$ is of special interest and significance in connection with *pooling cross-section and time-series observations*, as in the case of observations for a number of households (states, countries, etc.) over several periods of time. Here the behavior of the disturbances over the cross-sectional units (households, states, countries, etc.) is likely to be different from the behavior of the disturbances of a given cross-sectional unit over time. In particular, the relationship between the disturbances of two households at some specific time may differ from the relationship between the disturbances of a specific household at two different periods of time. Clearly, various kinds of prior specifications with respect to the disturbances will lead to various kinds of restrictions on $\mathbf{\Omega}$. In general, the regression equation for this type of data can be written as

$$Y_{it} = \beta_1 X_{it,1} + \beta_2 X_{it,2} + \cdots + \beta_K X_{it,K} + \varepsilon_{it} \quad (i = 1, 2, \ldots, N;\, t = 1, 2, \ldots, T).$$

That is, the sample data are represented by observations on N cross-section units over T periods of time. There are altogether $n = N \times T$ observations. The explanatory variables and the regression disturbance are presumed to satisfy the assumptions of the generalized linear regression model. In most (although not necessarily in all) cases, we will have $X_{it,1} = 1$ for all i and t. In matrix notation the regression equation can be written as

$$\mathbf{Y} = \mathbf{X}\boldsymbol{\beta} + \boldsymbol{\epsilon},$$

where

$$\mathbf{Y} = \begin{bmatrix} Y_{11} \\ Y_{12} \\ \vdots \\ Y_{1T} \\ Y_{21} \\ Y_{22} \\ \vdots \\ Y_{NT} \end{bmatrix}, \quad \mathbf{X} = \begin{bmatrix} X_{11,1} & X_{11,2} & \cdots & X_{11,K} \\ X_{12,1} & X_{12,2} & \cdots & X_{12,K} \\ \vdots & \vdots & & \vdots \\ X_{1T,1} & X_{1T,2} & \cdots & X_{1T,K} \\ X_{21,1} & X_{21,2} & \cdots & X_{21,K} \\ X_{22,1} & X_{22,2} & \cdots & X_{22,K} \\ \vdots & \vdots & & \vdots \\ X_{NT,1} & X_{NT,2} & \cdots & X_{NT,K} \end{bmatrix}, \quad \boldsymbol{\epsilon} = \begin{bmatrix} \varepsilon_{11} \\ \varepsilon_{12} \\ \vdots \\ \varepsilon_{1T} \\ \varepsilon_{21} \\ \varepsilon_{22} \\ \vdots \\ \varepsilon_{NT} \end{bmatrix},$$

and
$$\boldsymbol{\beta} = \begin{bmatrix} \beta_1 \\ \beta_2 \\ \vdots \\ \beta_K \end{bmatrix}.$$

Therefore,

(12.21)
$$\boldsymbol{\Omega} = \begin{bmatrix} E(\varepsilon_{11}^2) & E(\varepsilon_{11}\varepsilon_{12}) & \dots & E(\varepsilon_{11}\varepsilon_{1T}) & E(\varepsilon_{11}\varepsilon_{21}) & E(\varepsilon_{11}\varepsilon_{22}) & \dots & E(\varepsilon_{11}\varepsilon_{NT}) \\ E(\varepsilon_{12}\varepsilon_{11}) & E(\varepsilon_{12}^2) & \dots & E(\varepsilon_{12}\varepsilon_{1T}) & E(\varepsilon_{12}\varepsilon_{21}) & E(\varepsilon_{12}\varepsilon_{22}) & \dots & E(\varepsilon_{12}\varepsilon_{NT}) \\ \vdots & \vdots & & \vdots & \vdots & \vdots & & \vdots \\ E(\varepsilon_{1T}\varepsilon_{11}) & E(\varepsilon_{1T}\varepsilon_{12}) & \dots & E(\varepsilon_{1T}^2) & E(\varepsilon_{1T}\varepsilon_{21}) & E(\varepsilon_{1T}\varepsilon_{22}) & \dots & E(\varepsilon_{1T}\varepsilon_{NT}) \\ E(\varepsilon_{21}\varepsilon_{11}) & E(\varepsilon_{21}\varepsilon_{12}) & \dots & E(\varepsilon_{21}\varepsilon_{1T}) & E(\varepsilon_{21}^2) & E(\varepsilon_{21}\varepsilon_{22}) & \dots & E(\varepsilon_{21}\varepsilon_{NT}) \\ E(\varepsilon_{22}\varepsilon_{11}) & E(\varepsilon_{22}\varepsilon_{12}) & \dots & E(\varepsilon_{22}\varepsilon_{1T}) & E(\varepsilon_{22}\varepsilon_{21}) & E(\varepsilon_{22}^2) & \dots & E(\varepsilon_{22}\varepsilon_{NT}) \\ \vdots & \vdots & & \vdots & \vdots & \vdots & & \vdots \\ E(\varepsilon_{NT}\varepsilon_{11}) & E(\varepsilon_{NT}\varepsilon_{12}) & \dots & E(\varepsilon_{NT}\varepsilon_{1T}) & E(\varepsilon_{NT}\varepsilon_{21}) & E(\varepsilon_{NT}\varepsilon_{22}) & \dots & E(\varepsilon_{NT}^2) \end{bmatrix}.$$

This specification provides a general framework for the discussion of different models designed to deal with pooled cross-section and time-series observations.

A Cross-sectionally Heteroskedastic and Time-wise Autoregressive Model

One approach to the specification of the behavior of the disturbances when we deal with cross-section and time-series data is to combine the assumptions that we frequently make about cross-sectional observations with those that are usually made when dealing with time series. As for the cross-sectional observations—for example, observations on individual households at a point (or period) of time—it is frequently assumed that the regression disturbances are mutually independent but heteroskedastic.[7] Concerning the time-series data, one usually suspects that the disturbances are autoregressive though not necessarily heteroskedastic. When dealing with pooled cross-section and time-series observations, we may combine these assumptions and adopt a *cross-sectionally heteroskedastic and time-wise autoregressive model.* The particular characterization of this model is as follows:

(12.22) $$E(\varepsilon_{it}^2) = \sigma_i^2 \qquad \text{(heteroskedasticity)}$$

(12.23) $$E(\varepsilon_{it}\varepsilon_{jt}) = 0 \quad (i \neq j) \qquad \text{(cross-sectional independence)}$$

(12.24) $$\varepsilon_{it} = \rho_i \varepsilon_{i,t-1} + u_{it} \qquad \text{(autoregression)}$$

[7] See, e.g., S. J. Prais and H. S. Houthakker, *The Analysis of Family Budgets* (Cambridge, England: The University Press, 1955). The assumption of mutual independence of the cross-sectional units will be relaxed later.

where
$$u_{it} \sim N(0, \sigma_{ui}^2),$$
$$\varepsilon_{i0} \sim N\left(0, \frac{\sigma_{ui}^2}{1-\rho_i^2}\right),$$
and
$$E(\varepsilon_{i,t-1}u_{jt}) = 0 \quad \text{for all } i, j.$$

Note that in this model we allow the value of the parameter ρ to vary from one cross-sectional unit to another. From these specifications we deduce:

$$E(\varepsilon_{it}\varepsilon_{is}) = \rho^{t-s}\sigma_i^2 \qquad (t \geq s),$$
$$E(\varepsilon_{it}\varepsilon_{js}) = 0 \qquad (i \neq j).$$

By making the appropriate substitution into (12.21), we find that for this model

(12.25)
$$\mathbf{\Omega} = \begin{bmatrix} \sigma_1^2\mathbf{P}_1 & \mathbf{0} & \dots & \mathbf{0} \\ \mathbf{0} & \sigma_2^2\mathbf{P}_2 & \dots & \mathbf{0} \\ \vdots & \vdots & & \vdots \\ \mathbf{0} & \mathbf{0} & \dots & \sigma_N^2\mathbf{P}_\mathbf{N} \end{bmatrix},$$

where
$$\mathbf{P_i} = \begin{bmatrix} 1 & \rho_i & \rho_i^2 & \dots & \rho_i^{T-1} \\ \rho_i & 1 & \rho_i & \dots & \rho_i^{T-2} \\ \vdots & \vdots & \vdots & & \vdots \\ \rho_i^{T-1} & \rho_i^{T-2} & \rho_i^{T-3} & \dots & 1 \end{bmatrix},$$

and each of the $\mathbf{0}$'s represents a $(T \times T)$ matrix of zeros.

To find consistent estimates of the elements of (12.25), we can proceed in the following way. First, we apply the ordinary least squares method to all $N \times T$ observations. The resulting estimates of the regression coefficients are unbiased and consistent, and can be used to calculate the regression residuals e_{it}. From these residuals, we can obtain estimates of ρ_i, say, $\hat{\rho}_i$, by

(12.26)
$$\hat{\rho}_i = \frac{\sum e_{it}e_{i,t-1}}{\sum e_{i,t-1}^2} \qquad (t = 2, 3, \dots, T).$$

As pointed out in Section 8–2, $\hat{\rho}_i$ is a consistent estimator of ρ_i. Next, we use the $\hat{\rho}_i$'s to transform the observations in accordance with (8.52); that is, we form

(12.27)
$$Y_{it}^* = \beta_1 X_{it,1}^* + \beta_2 X_{it,2}^* + \cdots + \beta_K X_{it,K}^* + u_{it}^*,$$

where
$$Y_{it}^* = Y_{it} - \hat{\rho}_i Y_{i,t-1},$$
$$X_{it,k}^* = X_{it,k} - \hat{\rho}_i X_{i,t-1,k} \qquad (k = 1, 2, \dots, K),$$
$$u_{it}^* = \varepsilon_{it} - \hat{\rho}_i \varepsilon_{i,t-1},$$
$$t = 2, 3, \dots, T,$$
$$i = 1, 2, \dots, N.$$

The purpose here is to estimate σ_i^2 from observations that are, at least asymptotically, nonautoregressive. To this end, we can apply the ordinary least squares method to (12.27) for which we have $N(T - 1)$ observations. The resulting regression residuals, say, $\hat{u}_{it}^*$, can be used to estimate the variances of u_{it} (i.e., σ_{ui}^2) by

$$s_{ui}^2 = \frac{1}{T - K - 1} \sum_{t=2}^{T} \hat{u}_{it}^{*2}. \tag{12.28}$$

Since

$$\sigma_{ui}^2 = \sigma_i^2(1 - \rho_i^2),$$

it follows that σ_i^2 can be estimated by

$$s_i^2 = \frac{s_{ui}^2}{1 - \hat{\rho}_i^2}. \tag{12.29}$$

Since $\hat{\rho}_i$ is a consistent estimator of ρ_i and s_{ui}^2 is a consistent estimator of σ_{ui}^2, s_i^2 is a consistent estimator of σ_i^2.

Having obtained consistent estimators of ρ_i and σ_i^2, we have completed the task of deriving consistent estimators of the elements of $\mathbf{\Omega}$. By substituting for $\hat{\mathbf{\Omega}}$ into (12.19) and replacing $\mathbf{\Omega}$ by $\hat{\mathbf{\Omega}}$ in (12.20), we obtain the desired estimates of the regression coefficients and their variances. Since the evaluation of (12.19) and (12.20) is quite burdensome computationally, we may choose a slightly different procedure, which leads to almost identical results and is computationally less demanding. The idea is to subject the observations to a double transformation—one transformation designed to remove autoregression and the other to remove heteroskedasticity—and then use the ordinary least squares method on the transformed data. The autoregressive transformation is described by (12.27), so that we only have to worry about the transformation to remove heteroskedasticity. This transformation can be carried out by dividing both sides of (12.27) by s_{ui} obtained from (12.28), which leads to

$$Y_i^{**} = \beta_1 X_{it,1}^{**} + \beta_2 X_{it,2}^{**} + \cdots + \beta_K X_{it,K}^{**} + u_{it}^{**}, \tag{12.30}$$

where

$$Y_{it}^{**} = \frac{Y_i^*}{s_{ui}},$$

$$X_{it,k}^{**} = \frac{X_{it,k}^*}{s_{ui}} \qquad (k = 1, 2, \ldots, K),$$

$$u_{it}^{**} = \frac{u_{it}^*}{s_{ui}},$$

$$t = 2, 3, \ldots, T,$$

$$i = 1, 2, \ldots, N.$$

The disturbance u_{it}^{**} is asymptotically nonautoregressive and homoskedastic. The equation (12.30) can then be estimated by the ordinary least squares method, utilizing all of the $N(T - 1)$ pooled observations.[8]

[8] The difference between the estimation results obtained by using the modified Aitken's formula (12.19) and those obtained by the ordinary least squares method applied to (12.30) is due to the fact that, in the latter case, we drop one observation for each cross-sectional unit. This difference is described in detail in, e.g., Johnston, *op. cit.*, pp. 185–186.

A somewhat different version of the cross-sectionally heteroskedastic and time-wise autoregressive model is obtained when we assume that the parameter ρ has the same value for all cross-sectional units; i.e., when

$$\rho_i = \rho_j = \rho \quad \text{for all } i, j = 1, 2, \ldots, N.$$

In this case, the matrix $\boldsymbol{\Omega}$ becomes

$$(12.31) \qquad \boldsymbol{\Omega} = \begin{bmatrix} \sigma_1^2\mathbf{P} & \mathbf{0} & \ldots & \mathbf{0} \\ \mathbf{0} & \sigma_2^2\mathbf{P} & \ldots & \mathbf{0} \\ \vdots & \vdots & & \vdots \\ \mathbf{0} & \mathbf{0} & \ldots & \sigma_N^2\mathbf{P} \end{bmatrix},$$

where

$$\mathbf{P} = \begin{bmatrix} 1 & \rho & \rho^2 & \ldots & \rho^{T-1} \\ \rho & 1 & \rho & \ldots & \rho^{T-2} \\ \vdots & \vdots & \vdots & & \vdots \\ \rho^{T-1} & \rho^{T-2} & \rho^{T-3} & \ldots & 1 \end{bmatrix}.$$

The estimation of the regression coefficients can proceed in exactly the same way as in the previous case, except that formula (12.26) for $\hat{\rho}_i$ is replaced by

$$(12.32) \quad \hat{\rho} = \frac{\sum_i \sum_t e_{it}e_{i,t-1}}{\sum_i \sum_t e_{i,t-1}^2} \qquad (i = 1, 2, \ldots, N;\ t = 2, 3, \ldots, T),$$

and the variables in (12.27) are transformed by using $\hat{\rho}$ instead of $\hat{\rho}_i$. The remaining steps in the estimation procedure are unchanged.

A Cross-sectionally Correlated and Time-wise Autoregressive Model

In many circumstances the most questionable assumption of the preceding model is that the cross-sectional units are mutually independent. For instance, when the cross-sectional units are geographical regions with arbitrarily drawn boundaries—such as the states of the United States—we would not expect this assumption to be well satisfied. If we then generalize the preceding model by dropping the assumption of mutual independence, we have what may be termed a *cross-sectionally correlated and time-wise autoregressive model.* The specification of the behavior of the disturbances in this model is as follows:

$$(12.33) \qquad E(\varepsilon_{it}^2) = \sigma_{ii} \qquad \text{(heteroskedasticity)},$$

$$(12.34) \qquad E(\varepsilon_{it}\varepsilon_{jt}) = \sigma_{ij} \qquad \text{(mutual correlation)},$$

$$(12.35) \qquad \varepsilon_{it} = \rho_i\varepsilon_{i,t-1} + u_{it} \qquad \text{(autoregression)},$$

where

$$u_{it} \sim N(0, \phi_{ii}),$$

$$E(\varepsilon_{i,t-1}u_{jt}) = 0,$$

$$E(u_{it}u_{jt}) = \phi_{ij},$$

$$E(u_{it}u_{js}) = 0 \qquad (t \neq s),$$

$$i, j = 1, 2, \ldots, N.$$

The initial value of ε is assumed to have the following properties:

$$\varepsilon_{i0} \sim N\left(0, \frac{\phi_{ii}}{1 - \rho_i^2}\right),$$

$$E(\varepsilon_{i0}\varepsilon_{j0}) = \frac{\phi_{ij}}{1 - \rho_i \rho_j}.$$

Note that the variances of the u's have now been denoted by the symbol ϕ rather than by σ_u^2, as in the preceding, simpler model. The matrix $\mathbf{\Omega}$ for the present model is

$$\mathbf{\Omega} = \begin{bmatrix} \sigma_{11}\mathbf{P}_{11} & \sigma_{12}\mathbf{P}_{12} & \cdots & \sigma_{1N}\mathbf{P}_{1N} \\ \sigma_{21}\mathbf{P}_{21} & \sigma_{22}\mathbf{P}_{22} & \cdots & \sigma_{2N}\mathbf{P}_{2N} \\ \vdots & \vdots & & \vdots \\ \sigma_{N1}\mathbf{P}_{N1} & \sigma_{N2}\mathbf{P}_{N2} & \cdots & \sigma_{NN}\mathbf{P}_{NN} \end{bmatrix}, \tag{12.36}$$

where

$$\mathbf{P}_{ij} = \begin{bmatrix} 1 & \rho_j & \rho_j^2 & \cdots & \rho_j^{T-1} \\ \rho_i & 1 & \rho_j & \cdots & \rho_j^{T-2} \\ \rho_i^2 & \rho_i & 1 & \cdots & \rho_j^{T-3} \\ \vdots & \vdots & \vdots & & \vdots \\ \rho_i^{T-1} & \rho_i^{T-2} & \rho_i^{T-3} & \cdots & 1 \end{bmatrix}.$$

To obtain consistent estimates of the elements of $\mathbf{\Omega}$, we first apply the ordinary least squares method to all of the pooled observations, and calculate the corresponding residuals e_{it}. These residuals are used for obtaining ρ_i by application of the formula (12.26). With the help of $\hat{\rho}_i$, we transform the variables and form (12.27). To this equation we again apply the ordinary least squares method and calculate the residuals $\hat{u}_{it}^*$. The variances and covariances of the ε's (i.e., σ_{ij}) can then be estimated by

$$s_{ij} = \frac{\hat{\phi}_{ij}}{1 - \hat{\rho}_i \hat{\rho}_j}, \tag{12.37}$$

where

$$\hat{\phi}_{ij} = \frac{1}{T - K - 1} \sum_{t=2}^{T} \hat{u}_{it}^* \hat{u}_{jt}^*.$$

In this way we obtain consistent estimates of ρ_i and σ_{ij} and, therefore, of $\mathbf{\Omega}$. This enables us to use the formulas (12.19) and (12.20), and thus to obtain asymptotically efficient estimates of the regression coefficients and of their variances.

This procedure can be simplified by applying the modified Aitken's estimation formulas (12.19) and (12.20) to the *transformed* variables, that is, by using an estimator of $\boldsymbol{\beta}$

$$\overset{\approx}{\boldsymbol{\beta}} = (\mathbf{X}^{*\prime}\hat{\mathbf{\Phi}}^{-1}\mathbf{X}^*)^{-1}(\mathbf{X}^{*\prime}\hat{\mathbf{\Phi}}^{-1}\mathbf{Y}^*) \tag{12.38}$$

with

$$\text{Asympt. Var-Cov}(\tilde{\tilde{\tilde{\boldsymbol{\beta}}}}) = (\mathbf{X}^{*\prime}\hat{\boldsymbol{\Phi}}^{-1}\mathbf{X}^*)^{-1}. \tag{12.39}$$

Here $\mathbf{Y}^*$ is an $N(T-1)\times 1$ vector of the transformed observations of $Y_{it}^* = Y_{it} - \hat{\rho}_i Y_{i,t-1}$, and $\mathbf{X}^*$ is an $N(T-1)\times K$ matrix of the transformed observations $X_{it,k}^* = X_{it,k} - \hat{\rho}_i X_{i,t-1,k}$ $(t = 2, 3, \ldots, T; i = 1, 2, \ldots, N; k = 1, 2, \ldots, K)$. The matrix $\hat{\boldsymbol{\Phi}}$ is the estimated variance-covariance matrix of the u's, and it is of the order $N(T-1)\times N(T-1)$. Its full description is

$$\hat{\boldsymbol{\Phi}} = \begin{bmatrix} \hat{\phi}_{11}\mathbf{I}_{T-1} & \hat{\phi}_{12}\mathbf{I}_{T-1} & \cdots & \hat{\phi}_{1N}\mathbf{I}_{T-1} \\ \hat{\phi}_{21}\mathbf{I}_{T-1} & \hat{\phi}_{22}\mathbf{I}_{T-1} & \cdots & \hat{\phi}_{2N}\mathbf{I}_{T-1} \\ \vdots & \vdots & & \vdots \\ \hat{\phi}_{N1}\mathbf{I}_{T-1} & \hat{\phi}_{N2}\mathbf{I}_{T-1} & \cdots & \hat{\phi}_{NN}\mathbf{I}_{T-1} \end{bmatrix}, \tag{12.40}$$

where the $\hat{\phi}_{ij}$'s are as defined in (12.37), and $\mathbf{I}_{T-1}$ is an identity matrix of order $(T-1)\times(T-1)$. In general, the value of the estimator in (12.38) will be different from that obtained by using (12.19), but the asymptotic properties of the two estimators are the same.

An Error Components Model

A different approach to the specification of the behavior of the disturbances when combining cross-section and time-series data has been adopted by the proponents of the so-called *error components model.* The basic assumption here is that the regression disturbance is composed of three independent components —one component associated with time, another associated with the cross-sectional units, and the third varying in both dimensions. Specifically,

$$\varepsilon_{it} = u_i + v_t + w_{it} \qquad (i = 1, 2, \ldots, N;\ t = 1, 2, \ldots, T), \tag{12.41}$$

where

$$u_i \sim N(0, \sigma_u^2),$$

$$v_t \sim N(0, \sigma_v^2),$$

$$w_{it} \sim N(0, \sigma_w^2),$$

and the components u_i, v_t, and w_{it} satisfy the following conditions:

$$E(u_i v_t) = E(u_i w_{it}) = E(v_t w_{it}) = 0,$$

$$E(u_i u_j) = 0 \quad (i \neq j),$$

$$E(v_t v_s) = 0 \quad (t \neq s),$$

$$E(w_{it} w_{is}) = E(w_{it} w_{jt}) = E(w_{it} w_{js}) = 0 \qquad (i \neq j;\ t \neq s).$$

Note that this implies that ε_{it} is *homoskedastic* with variance given by

$$\text{Var}(\varepsilon_{it}) = \sigma^2 = \sigma_u^2 + \sigma_v^2 + \sigma_w^2.$$

The coefficient of correlation between ε_{it} and ε_{jt} $(i \neq j)$—i.e., between the disturbances of two different cross-sectional units at a given point of time—is

$$\frac{\mathrm{Cov}(\varepsilon_{it}, \varepsilon_{jt})}{\sqrt{\mathrm{Var}(\varepsilon_{it})\mathrm{Var}(\varepsilon_{jt})}} = \frac{\sigma_v^2}{\sigma_u^2 + \sigma_v^2 + \sigma_w^2} \qquad (i \neq j).$$

The coefficient of correlation between ε_{it} and ε_{is} $(i \neq s)$—i.e., between the disturbances of a given cross-sectional unit at two different points of time—is

$$\frac{\mathrm{Cov}(\varepsilon_{it}, \varepsilon_{is})}{\sqrt{\mathrm{Var}(\varepsilon_{it})\mathrm{Var}(\varepsilon_{is})}} = \frac{\sigma_u^2}{\sigma_u^2 + \sigma_v^2 + \sigma_w^2} \qquad (t \neq s).$$

This last feature of the error components model means that, for each cross-sectional unit, the correlation of the disturbances over time remains *unchanged* no matter how far apart in time the disturbances are. This contrasts sharply with the usual assumption of first-order autoregression, which implies that the degree of correlation declines geometrically with the time distance involved. Finally, the coefficient of correlation between ε_{it} and ε_{js} is

$$\frac{\mathrm{Cov}(\varepsilon_{it}, \varepsilon_{js})}{\sqrt{\mathrm{Var}(\varepsilon_{it})\mathrm{Var}(\varepsilon_{js})}} = 0 \qquad (i \neq j;\ t \neq s).$$

By substituting these results into (12.21), we find that the matrix $\mathbf{\Omega}$ for the error components model is

$$(12.42) \qquad \mathbf{\Omega} = \begin{bmatrix} \sigma_u^2\mathbf{A_T} & \sigma_v^2\mathbf{I_T} & \cdots & \sigma_v^2\mathbf{I_T} \\ \sigma_v^2\mathbf{I_T} & \sigma_u^2\mathbf{A_T} & \cdots & \sigma_v^2\mathbf{I_T} \\ \vdots & \vdots & & \vdots \\ \sigma_v^2\mathbf{I_T} & \sigma_v^2\mathbf{I_T} & \cdots & \sigma_u^2\mathbf{A_T} \end{bmatrix},$$

where $\mathbf{A_T}$ is a $(T \times T)$ matrix defined as

$$\mathbf{A_T} = \begin{bmatrix} \frac{\sigma^2}{\sigma_u^2} & 1 & \cdots & 1 \\ 1 & \frac{\sigma^2}{\sigma_u^2} & \cdots & 1 \\ \vdots & \vdots & & \vdots \\ 1 & 1 & \cdots & \frac{\sigma^2}{\sigma_u^2} \end{bmatrix}$$

and $\mathbf{I_T}$ is an identity matrix of order $T \times T$. The elements of the $\mathbf{\Omega}$ matrix can be estimated as follows:[9]

[9] See T. D. Wallace and A. Hussain, "The Use of Error Components Models in Combining Cross-Section with Time-Series Data," *Econometrica*, Vol. 37, January 1969, pp. 55–72.

$$(12.43)\quad \hat{\sigma}_w^2 = \frac{1}{(N-1)(T-1)} \sum_{i=1}^{N} \sum_{t=1}^{T} \left[e_{it} - \frac{1}{T}\sum_{t=1}^{T} e_{it} - \frac{1}{N}\sum_{i=1}^{N} e_{it} \right]^2,$$

$$\hat{\sigma}_u^2 = \frac{1}{T}\left\{ \frac{1}{(N-1)T} \sum_{i=1}^{N} \left[\sum_{t=1}^{T} e_{it} \right]^2 - \hat{\sigma}_w^2 \right\},$$

$$\hat{\sigma}_v^2 = \frac{1}{N}\left\{ \frac{1}{N(T-1)} \sum_{t=1}^{T} \left[\sum_{i=1}^{N} e_{it} \right]^2 - \hat{\sigma}_w^2 \right\},$$

where e_{it} represents residuals obtained by applying the ordinary least squares method to the pooled data. Using these estimates and the formulas (12.19) and (12.20), we obtain estimates of the regression coefficients that have the same properties as Aitken's generalized least squares estimator.[10]

A Covariance Model

Another model that is commonly used when dealing with pooled cross-section and time-series observations is the so-called *covariance model*. We mention this as a postscript to the present section because the covariance model is generally treated within the framework of the classical regression model rather than as a generalized regression model. The idea behind the covariance model is the supposition that each cross-sectional unit and each time period are characterized by their own special intercept. This feature is incorporated into the regression equation by the introduction of binary variables. The regression equation then becomes

$$(12.44)\quad Y_{it} = \beta_1 + \beta_2 X_{it,2} + \cdots + \beta_K X_{it,K} + \gamma_2 Z_{2t} + \gamma_3 Z_{3t} + \cdots + \gamma_N Z_{Nt} + \delta_2 W_{i2} + \delta_3 W_{i3} + \cdots + \delta_T W_{iT} + \varepsilon_{it},$$

where

$$\begin{aligned} Z_{it} &= 1 \quad \text{for the } i\text{th cross-sectional unit,} \\ &= 0 \quad \text{otherwise} \qquad (i = 2, 3, \ldots, N); \\ W_{it} &= 1 \quad \text{for the } t\text{th time period,} \\ &= 0 \quad \text{otherwise} \qquad (t = 2, 3, \ldots, T). \end{aligned}$$

The disturbance ε_{it} is supposed to satisfy the assumptions of the classical normal linear regression model. (We could, of course, allow ε_{it} to be autoregressive or heteroskedastic and then choose an appropriate estimation method.) Note that with the foregoing specification of the regression equation, we have

$$\begin{aligned} Y_{11} &= \beta_1 + \beta_2 X_{11,2} + \cdots + \beta_K X_{11,K} + \varepsilon_{11}, \\ Y_{12} &= (\beta_1 + \delta_2) + \beta_2 X_{12,2} + \cdots + \beta_K X_{12,K} + \varepsilon_{12}, \\ &\vdots \\ Y_{1T} &= (\beta_1 + \delta_T) + \beta_2 X_{1T,2} + \cdots + \beta_K X_{1T,K} + \varepsilon_{1T}, \\ Y_{21} &= (\beta_1 + \gamma_2) + \beta_2 X_{21,2} + \cdots + \beta_K X_{21,K} + \varepsilon_{21}, \\ Y_{22} &= (\beta_1 + \gamma_2 + \delta_2) + \beta_2 X_{22,2} + \cdots + \beta_K X_{22,K} + \varepsilon_{22}, \\ &\vdots \\ Y_{NT} &= (\beta_1 + \gamma_N + \delta_T) + \beta_2 X_{NT,2} + \cdots + \beta_K X_{NT,K} + \varepsilon_{NT}. \end{aligned}$$

[10] For a proof, see *ibid.*

Equation (12.44) contains $K + (N - 1) + (T - 1)$ regression coefficients to be estimated from $N \times T$ observations. If the model is correctly specified and the classical assumptions are satisfied, the ordinary least squares estimates of the regression coefficients will be unbiased and efficient.

12–3 Seemingly Unrelated Regressions

Under the assumptions of the classical normal linear regression model, the least squares estimators of the regression coefficients were found to be unbiased and efficient. This result was derived on the understanding that the specification of the model represents *all* there is to know about the regression equation and the variables involved. If there exists some other piece of information that has not been taken into account, then the result concerning the properties of the least squares estimators can no longer be considered established. One such additional piece of information would be the knowledge that the disturbance in the regression equation under consideration could be correlated with the disturbance in some other regression equation (see fn. 2, page 202). In the present section we shall consider such a situation and examine the implications for estimation of the regression coefficients.

Suppose we are concerned with the problem of estimating the coefficients of any one or all of the following M regression equations:

(12.45)
$$\begin{aligned} Y_{1t} &= \beta_{11}X_{1t,1} + \beta_{12}X_{1t,2} + \cdots + \beta_{1K_1}X_{1t,K_1} + \varepsilon_{1t}, \\ Y_{2t} &= \beta_{21}X_{2t,1} + \beta_{22}X_{2t,2} + \cdots + \beta_{2K_2}X_{2t,K_2} + \varepsilon_{2t}, \\ &\vdots \\ Y_{Mt} &= \beta_{M1}X_{Mt,1} + \beta_{M2}X_{Mt,2} + \cdots + \beta_{MK_M}X_{Mt,K_M} + \varepsilon_{Mt}, \\ t &= 1, 2, \ldots, T. \end{aligned}$$

Using matrix notation, we can write

(12.45a)
$$\begin{aligned} \mathbf{Y_1} &= \mathbf{X_1}\boldsymbol{\beta}_1 + \boldsymbol{\epsilon}_1, \\ \mathbf{Y_2} &= \mathbf{X_2}\boldsymbol{\beta}_2 + \boldsymbol{\epsilon}_2, \\ &\vdots \\ \mathbf{Y_M} &= X_{\mathbf{M}}\boldsymbol{\beta}_{\mathbf{M}} + \boldsymbol{\epsilon}_{\mathbf{M}}, \end{aligned}$$

or

(12.45b)
$$\mathbf{Y_m} = \mathbf{X_m}\boldsymbol{\beta}_{\mathbf{m}} + \boldsymbol{\epsilon}_{\mathbf{m}} \qquad (m = 1, 2, \ldots, M),$$

where $\mathbf{Y_m}$ is a $(T \times 1)$ vector of the sample values of the dependent variable, $\mathbf{X_m}$ is a $(T \times K_m)$ matrix of the sample values of the explanatory variables, $\boldsymbol{\beta}_{\mathbf{m}}$ is a $(K_m \times 1)$ vector of the regression coefficients, and $\boldsymbol{\epsilon}_{\mathbf{m}}$ is a $(T \times 1)$ vector of the sample values of the disturbances. We assume that $\boldsymbol{\epsilon}_{\mathbf{m}}$ is normally distributed with mean

(12.46)
$$E(\varepsilon_{mt}) = 0 \qquad (t = 1, 2, \ldots, T)$$

and that its variance-covariance matrix is given by

(12.47) $$E(\boldsymbol{\epsilon}_m\boldsymbol{\epsilon}_m') = \sigma_{mm}\mathbf{I}_T,$$

where $\mathbf{I}_T$ is an identity matrix of order $(T \times T)$. The explanatory variables are taken to be nonstochastic and such that $(\mathbf{X}_m'\mathbf{X}_m)/T$ is nonsingular and its limit (for $T \to \infty$) exists. This means that each of the equations is expected to satisfy the assumptions of the classical normal linear regression model. Now, suppose further that we cannot rule out the possibility that the regression disturbances in different equations are *mutually correlated*. In this case we have

(12.48) $$E(\boldsymbol{\epsilon}_m\boldsymbol{\epsilon}_p') = \sigma_{mp}\mathbf{I}_T \qquad (m, p = 1, 2, \ldots, M).$$

Thus σ_{mp} is the covariance of the disturbances of the mth and the pth equation, which is assumed to be constant over all observations. This covariance represents the *only* link between the mth and the pth equation. Because this link is rather subtle, the system of M equations is called a system of *seemingly unrelated regression equations*. Examples of such regressions would be demand functions for various commodities or production functions for different industries, with observations made over time (or over some cross-sectional units). The disturbance in the demand equation for commodity A is likely to be correlated with the disturbance in the demand equations for commodities B, C, etc. Similarly, the disturbance in the production function for one industry may be correlated with the disturbances in the production functions for other industries. Note that if the regression equations (12.45) are such that the regression coefficients in each equation are the *same* as the regression coefficients in any other equation, the whole system would reduce to a single equation, and the observations would represent pooled cross-section and time-series data.

Estimation When the Variance-Covariance Matrix Is Known

Let us now turn to the problem of estimating the coefficients of the seemingly unrelated regression equations. One possible approach is to apply the ordinary least squares method to each equation separately. This would give

$$\hat{\boldsymbol{\beta}}_m = (\mathbf{X}_m'\mathbf{X}_m)^{-1}(\mathbf{X}_m'\mathbf{Y}_m)$$

and $$E(\hat{\boldsymbol{\beta}}_m - \boldsymbol{\beta}_m)(\hat{\boldsymbol{\beta}}_m - \boldsymbol{\beta}_m)' = \sigma_{mm}(\mathbf{X}_m'\mathbf{X}_m)^{-1}.$$

Note that

$$E(\hat{\boldsymbol{\beta}}_m) = \boldsymbol{\beta}_m + E(\mathbf{X}_m'\mathbf{X}_m)^{-1}(\mathbf{X}_m'\boldsymbol{\epsilon}_m) = \boldsymbol{\beta}_m$$

and $$\text{plim } \hat{\boldsymbol{\beta}}_m = \boldsymbol{\beta}_m + \text{plim}\left[\frac{1}{T}\mathbf{X}_m'\mathbf{X}_m\right]^{-1}\left[\frac{1}{T}\mathbf{X}_m'\boldsymbol{\epsilon}_m\right] = \boldsymbol{\beta}_m,$$

which means that the ordinary least squares estimators of the regression coefficients are unbiased and consistent. Thus the major question is that of efficiency. By estimating each equation separately and independently, we are disregarding the information about the mutual correlation of the disturbances, and the efficiency of the estimators becomes questionable.

To take into account the correlation of the disturbances across equations, we compress (12.45) into one big equation. This can be done by noting that each equation of the system can be written as

$$\text{(12.49)}\quad \mathbf{Y_m} = \mathbf{X_1^{(m)}}\boldsymbol{\beta}_1 + \mathbf{X_2^{(m)}}\boldsymbol{\beta}_2 + \cdots + \mathbf{X_M^{(m)}}\boldsymbol{\beta}_\mathbf{M} + \boldsymbol{\epsilon}_\mathbf{m} \qquad (m = 1, 2, \ldots, M),$$

where

$$\mathbf{X_p^{(m)}} = \mathbf{X_p} \quad \text{if } m = p,$$
$$= \mathbf{0} \quad \text{if } m \neq p,$$

with $\mathbf{0}$ representing a $(T \times K_p)$ matrix of zeros. By redefining the explanatory variables in this way, we obtain a set of regression equations in which each equation contains exactly the same regression coefficients as any other. Thus, we are formally in the same situation as when we are dealing with pooled cross-section and time-series observations on a single equation. Equations (12.49) can also be represented as

$$\text{(12.49a)}\quad \begin{bmatrix} \mathbf{Y_1} \\ \mathbf{Y_2} \\ \vdots \\ \mathbf{Y_M} \end{bmatrix} = \begin{bmatrix} \mathbf{X_1^{(1)}} & \mathbf{X_2^{(1)}} & \cdots & \mathbf{X_M^{(1)}} \\ \mathbf{X_1^{(2)}} & \mathbf{X_2^{(2)}} & \cdots & \mathbf{X_M^{(2)}} \\ \vdots & \vdots & & \vdots \\ \mathbf{X_1^{(M)}} & \mathbf{X_2^{(M)}} & \cdots & \mathbf{X_M^{(M)}} \end{bmatrix} \begin{bmatrix} \boldsymbol{\beta}_1 \\ \boldsymbol{\beta}_2 \\ \vdots \\ \boldsymbol{\beta}_\mathbf{M} \end{bmatrix} + \begin{bmatrix} \boldsymbol{\epsilon}_1 \\ \boldsymbol{\epsilon}_2 \\ \vdots \\ \boldsymbol{\epsilon}_\mathbf{M} \end{bmatrix},$$

or

$$\text{(12.49b)}\quad \begin{bmatrix} \mathbf{Y_1} \\ \mathbf{Y_2} \\ \vdots \\ \mathbf{Y_M} \end{bmatrix} = \begin{bmatrix} \mathbf{X_1} & \mathbf{0} & \cdots & \mathbf{0} \\ \mathbf{0} & \mathbf{X_2} & \cdots & \mathbf{0} \\ \vdots & \vdots & & \vdots \\ \mathbf{0} & \mathbf{0} & \cdots & \mathbf{X_M} \end{bmatrix} \begin{bmatrix} \boldsymbol{\beta}_1 \\ \boldsymbol{\beta}_2 \\ \vdots \\ \boldsymbol{\beta}_\mathbf{M} \end{bmatrix} + \begin{bmatrix} \boldsymbol{\epsilon}_1 \\ \boldsymbol{\epsilon}_2 \\ \vdots \\ \boldsymbol{\epsilon}_\mathbf{M} \end{bmatrix}.$$

This can be written more compactly as

$$\text{(12.49c)}\quad \mathbf{Y} = \mathbf{X}\boldsymbol{\beta} + \boldsymbol{\epsilon},$$

where $\mathbf{Y}$ is a $(MT \times 1)$ vector, $\mathbf{X}$ is a $(MT \times \sum_{m=1}^{M} K_m)$ matrix, $\boldsymbol{\beta}$ is a $(\sum_{m=1}^{M} K_m \times 1)$ matrix, and the dimension of $\boldsymbol{\epsilon}$ is $(MT \times 1)$. Note that, by the assumptions (12.46) through (12.48), the variance-covariance matrix of $\boldsymbol{\epsilon}$ is

$$\text{(12.50)}\quad \boldsymbol{\Omega} = E(\boldsymbol{\epsilon\epsilon}')$$

$$= \begin{bmatrix} E(\boldsymbol{\epsilon}_1\boldsymbol{\epsilon}_1') & E(\boldsymbol{\epsilon}_1\boldsymbol{\epsilon}_2') & \cdots & E(\boldsymbol{\epsilon}_1\boldsymbol{\epsilon}_\mathbf{M}') \\ E(\boldsymbol{\epsilon}_2\boldsymbol{\epsilon}_1') & E(\boldsymbol{\epsilon}_2\boldsymbol{\epsilon}_2') & \cdots & E(\boldsymbol{\epsilon}_2\boldsymbol{\epsilon}_\mathbf{M}') \\ \vdots & \vdots & & \vdots \\ E(\boldsymbol{\epsilon}_\mathbf{M}\boldsymbol{\epsilon}_1') & E(\boldsymbol{\epsilon}_\mathbf{M}\boldsymbol{\epsilon}_2') & \cdots & E(\boldsymbol{\epsilon}_\mathbf{M}\boldsymbol{\epsilon}_\mathbf{M}') \end{bmatrix} = \begin{bmatrix} \sigma_{11}\mathbf{I_T} & \sigma_{12}\mathbf{I_T} & \cdots & \sigma_{1M}\mathbf{I_T} \\ \sigma_{21}\mathbf{I_T} & \sigma_{22}\mathbf{I_T} & \cdots & \sigma_{2M}\mathbf{I_T} \\ \vdots & \vdots & & \vdots \\ \sigma_{M1}\mathbf{I_T} & \sigma_{M2}\mathbf{I_T} & \cdots & \sigma_{MM}\mathbf{I_T} \end{bmatrix},$$

where, as before, $\mathbf{I_T}$ is an identity matrix of order $(T \times T)$. The information about the correlation of the disturbances across equations is then contained in the description of the $\boldsymbol{\Omega}$ matrix, and it can be taken into account in that form.

The equation (12.49c), together with the assumptions about $\mathbf{X}$ and $\boldsymbol{\epsilon}$, can be viewed as a generalized linear regression model (discussed in Section 12–1). The best linear unbiased estimator of $\boldsymbol{\beta}$ for this model is given by Aitken's generalized least squares formula as

$$\tilde{\boldsymbol{\beta}} = (\mathbf{X}'\boldsymbol{\Omega}^{-1}\mathbf{X})^{-1}(\mathbf{X}'\boldsymbol{\Omega}^{-1}\mathbf{Y}). \tag{12.51}$$

In the context of the seemingly unrelated regressions, this becomes

$$\tilde{\boldsymbol{\beta}} = \begin{bmatrix} \sigma^{11}(\mathbf{X}_1'\mathbf{X}_1) & \sigma^{12}(\mathbf{X}_1'\mathbf{X}_2) & \dots & \sigma^{1M}(\mathbf{X}_1'\mathbf{X}_\mathbf{M}) \\ \sigma^{21}(\mathbf{X}_2'\mathbf{X}_1) & \sigma^{22}(\mathbf{X}_2'\mathbf{X}_2) & \dots & \sigma^{2M}(\mathbf{X}_2'\mathbf{X}_\mathbf{M}) \\ \vdots & \vdots & & \vdots \\ \sigma^{M1}(\mathbf{X}_\mathbf{M}'\mathbf{X}_1) & \sigma^{M2}(\mathbf{X}_\mathbf{M}'\mathbf{X}_2) & \dots & \sigma^{MM}(\mathbf{X}_\mathbf{M}'\mathbf{X}_\mathbf{M}) \end{bmatrix}^{-1} \begin{bmatrix} \sum_{m=1}^{M} \sigma^{1m}(\mathbf{X}_1'\mathbf{Y}_\mathbf{m}) \\ \sum_{m=1}^{M} \sigma^{2m}(\mathbf{X}_2'\mathbf{Y}_\mathbf{m}) \\ \vdots \\ \sum_{m=1}^{M} \sigma^{Mm}(\mathbf{X}_\mathbf{m}'\mathbf{Y}_\mathbf{m}) \end{bmatrix}, \tag{12.51a}$$

where σ^{mp} represents the element that appears in the mth row and pth column of the inverse of the matrix

$$\begin{bmatrix} \sigma_{11} & \sigma_{12} & \dots & \sigma_{1M} \\ \sigma_{21} & \sigma_{22} & \dots & \sigma_{2M} \\ \vdots & \vdots & & \vdots \\ \sigma_{M1} & \sigma_{M2} & \dots & \sigma_{MM} \end{bmatrix}.$$

Further, the variance-covariance matrix of $\tilde{\boldsymbol{\beta}}$ is given by

$$E(\tilde{\boldsymbol{\beta}} - \boldsymbol{\beta})(\tilde{\boldsymbol{\beta}} - \boldsymbol{\beta})' = (\mathbf{X}'\boldsymbol{\Omega}^{-1}\mathbf{X})^{-1}. \tag{12.52}$$

Under the assumption of normality, $\tilde{\boldsymbol{\beta}}$ also represents the maximum likelihood estimator of $\boldsymbol{\beta}$. Since the ordinary least squares estimator of $\boldsymbol{\beta}$ is

$$\hat{\boldsymbol{\beta}} = (\mathbf{X}'\mathbf{X})^{-1}(\mathbf{X}'\mathbf{Y}),$$

which is, in general, different from $\tilde{\boldsymbol{\beta}}$, ordinary least squares estimation of the seemingly unrelated regressions is *not efficient.*

An interesting question concerning the application of Aitken's generalized estimator to seemingly unrelated regressions relates to the special conditions under which this estimator is, in fact, equivalent to the ordinary least squares estimator. One such obvious case exists when the equations are not seemingly but *actually* unrelated; that is, when

$$\sigma_{mp} = 0$$

for all $m \neq p$. In this case $\tilde{\boldsymbol{\beta}}$ becomes

$$\tilde{\boldsymbol{\beta}} = \begin{bmatrix} \sigma^{11}(\mathbf{X}_1'\mathbf{X}_1) & 0 & \dots & 0 \\ 0 & \sigma^{22}(\mathbf{X}_2'\mathbf{X}_2) & \dots & 0 \\ \vdots & \vdots & & \vdots \\ 0 & 0 & \dots & \sigma^{MM}(\mathbf{X}_\mathbf{M}'\mathbf{X}_\mathbf{M}) \end{bmatrix}^{-1} \begin{bmatrix} \sigma^{11}(\mathbf{X}_1'\mathbf{Y}_1) \\ \sigma^{22}(\mathbf{X}_2'\mathbf{Y}_2) \\ \vdots \\ \sigma^{MM}(\mathbf{X}_\mathbf{M}'\mathbf{Y}_\mathbf{M}) \end{bmatrix}$$

$$= (\mathbf{X}'\mathbf{X})^{-1}(\mathbf{X}'\mathbf{Y}),$$

which is the formula for the least squares estimator. The two estimators are also equivalent when each of the seemingly unrelated regressions involves exactly the *same* explanatory variables; that is, when

$$\mathbf{X_m} = \mathbf{X_p}$$

for all m and p. We shall prove the equivalence of Aitken's and ordinary least squares formulas in this case for a set of two equations, but the proof can be extended to any number of equations. (The proof could also be extended to where $\mathbf{X_m}$ and $\mathbf{X_p}$ are not exactly the same but $\mathbf{X_m}$ is a linear combination of $\mathbf{X_p}$.) Now, for $M = 2$ and $\mathbf{X_1} = \mathbf{X_2}$, Aitken's generalized estimator is

$$\begin{bmatrix} \tilde{\boldsymbol{\beta}}_1 \\ \tilde{\boldsymbol{\beta}}_2 \end{bmatrix} = \begin{bmatrix} \sigma^{11}(\mathbf{X}_1'\mathbf{X}_1) & \sigma^{12}(\mathbf{X}_1'\mathbf{X}_1) \\ \sigma^{21}(\mathbf{X}_1'\mathbf{X}_1) & \sigma^{22}(\mathbf{X}_1'\mathbf{X}_1) \end{bmatrix}^{-1} \begin{bmatrix} \sigma^{11}(\mathbf{X}_1'\mathbf{Y}_1) + \sigma^{12}(\mathbf{X}_1'\mathbf{Y}_2) \\ \sigma^{21}(\mathbf{X}_1'\mathbf{Y}_1) + \sigma^{22}(\mathbf{X}_1'\mathbf{Y}_2) \end{bmatrix},$$

or

$$\begin{bmatrix} \sigma^{11}(\mathbf{X}_1'\mathbf{X}_1)\tilde{\boldsymbol{\beta}}_1 + \sigma^{12}(\mathbf{X}_1'\mathbf{X}_1)\tilde{\boldsymbol{\beta}}_2 \\ \sigma^{21}(\mathbf{X}_1'\mathbf{X}_1)\tilde{\boldsymbol{\beta}}_1 + \sigma^{22}(\mathbf{X}_1'\mathbf{X}_1)\tilde{\boldsymbol{\beta}}_2 \end{bmatrix} = \begin{bmatrix} \sigma^{11}(\mathbf{X}_1'\mathbf{Y}_1) + \sigma^{12}(\mathbf{X}_1'\mathbf{Y}_2) \\ \sigma^{21}(\mathbf{X}_1'\mathbf{Y}_1) + \sigma^{22}(\mathbf{X}_1'\mathbf{Y}_2) \end{bmatrix}.$$

But

$$\begin{bmatrix} \sigma^{11} & \sigma^{12} \\ \sigma^{21} & \sigma^{22} \end{bmatrix} = \begin{bmatrix} \sigma_{11} & \sigma_{12} \\ \sigma_{12} & \sigma_{22} \end{bmatrix}^{-1} = \frac{1}{\sigma_{11}\sigma_{22} - \sigma_{12}^2} \begin{bmatrix} \sigma_{22} & -\sigma_{12} \\ -\sigma_{12} & \sigma_{11} \end{bmatrix},$$

so that we have

$$\sigma_{22}(\mathbf{X}_1'\mathbf{X}_1)\tilde{\boldsymbol{\beta}}_1 - \sigma_{12}(\mathbf{X}_1'\mathbf{X}_1)\tilde{\boldsymbol{\beta}}_2 = \sigma_{22}(\mathbf{X}_1'\mathbf{Y}_1) - \sigma_{12}(\mathbf{X}_1'\mathbf{Y}_2),$$

$$-\sigma_{12}(\mathbf{X}_1'\mathbf{X}_1)\tilde{\boldsymbol{\beta}}_1 + \sigma_{11}(\mathbf{X}_1'\mathbf{X}_1)\tilde{\boldsymbol{\beta}}_2 = -\sigma_{12}(\mathbf{X}_1'\mathbf{Y}_1) + \sigma_{11}(\mathbf{X}_1'\mathbf{Y}_2).$$

The solution for $\tilde{\boldsymbol{\beta}}_1$ and $\tilde{\boldsymbol{\beta}}_2$ is then

$$\tilde{\boldsymbol{\beta}}_1 = (\mathbf{X}_1'\mathbf{X}_1)^{-1}(\mathbf{X}_1'\mathbf{Y}_1) \quad \text{and} \quad \tilde{\boldsymbol{\beta}}_2 = (\mathbf{X}_1'\mathbf{X}_1)^{-1}(\mathbf{X}_1'\mathbf{Y}_2),$$

which is the same as the ordinary least squares results.

To illustrate the difference between Aitken's and the ordinary least squares estimators of the coefficients of seemingly unrelated regressions, we consider a simple system of two equations. Suppose we have

(12.53)
$$Y_{1t} = \beta_{11} + \beta_{12}X_{1t} + \varepsilon_{1t},$$
$$Y_{2t} = \beta_{21} + \beta_{22}X_{2t} + \varepsilon_{2t},$$

or

(12.53a)
$$\mathbf{Y}_1 = \mathbf{X}_1\boldsymbol{\beta}_1 + \boldsymbol{\epsilon}_1 \quad \text{and} \quad \mathbf{Y}_2 = \mathbf{X}_2\boldsymbol{\beta}_2 + \boldsymbol{\epsilon}_2,$$

where
$$\mathbf{X}_r = \begin{bmatrix} 1 & X_{r1} \\ 1 & X_{r2} \\ \vdots & \vdots \\ 1 & X_{rT} \end{bmatrix}, \quad \boldsymbol{\beta}_r = \begin{bmatrix} \beta_{r1} \\ \beta_{r2} \end{bmatrix} \quad (r = 1, 2).$$

In this case,

$$\mathbf{\Omega}^{-1} = \frac{1}{\sigma_{11}\sigma_{22} - \sigma_{12}^2}\begin{bmatrix} \sigma_{22}\mathbf{I_T} & -\sigma_{12}\mathbf{I_T} \\ -\sigma_{12}\mathbf{I_T} & \sigma_{11}\mathbf{I_T} \end{bmatrix}.$$

Aitken's generalized estimator of the regression coefficients then is

$$\begin{bmatrix} \tilde{\boldsymbol{\beta}}_1 \\ \tilde{\boldsymbol{\beta}}_2 \end{bmatrix} = \begin{bmatrix} \sigma_{22}(\mathbf{X}_1'\mathbf{X}_1) & -\sigma_{12}(\mathbf{X}_1'\mathbf{X}_2) \\ -\sigma_{12}(\mathbf{X}_2'\mathbf{X}_1) & \sigma_{11}(\mathbf{X}_2'\mathbf{X}_2) \end{bmatrix}^{-1} \begin{bmatrix} \sigma_{22}(\mathbf{X}_1'\mathbf{Y}_1) & -\sigma_{12}(\mathbf{X}_1'\mathbf{Y}_2) \\ -\sigma_{12}(\mathbf{X}_2'\mathbf{Y}_1) & +\sigma_{11}(\mathbf{X}_2'\mathbf{Y}_2) \end{bmatrix}.$$

This leads to the following system of "Aitken's generalized least squares normal equations":

$$\sigma_{22}\sum_t (Y_{1t} - \tilde{\beta}_{11} - \tilde{\beta}_{12}X_{1t}) - \sigma_{12}\sum_t (Y_{2t} - \tilde{\beta}_{21} - \tilde{\beta}_{22}X_{2t}) = 0,$$

$$\sigma_{22}\sum_t X_{1t}(Y_{1t} - \tilde{\beta}_{11} - \tilde{\beta}_{12}X_{1t}) - \sigma_{12}\sum_t X_{1t}(Y_{2t} - \tilde{\beta}_{21} - \tilde{\beta}_{22}X_{2t}) = 0,$$

$$-\sigma_{12}\sum_t (Y_{1t} - \tilde{\beta}_{11} - \tilde{\beta}_{12}X_{1t}) + \sigma_{11}\sum_t (Y_{2t} - \tilde{\beta}_{21} - \tilde{\beta}_{22}X_{2t}) = 0,$$

$$-\sigma_{12}\sum_t X_{2t}(Y_{1t} - \tilde{\beta}_{11} - \tilde{\beta}_{12}X_{1t}) + \sigma_{11}\sum_t X_{2t}(Y_{2t} - \tilde{\beta}_{21} - \tilde{\beta}_{22}X_{2t}) = 0.$$

The first and third of these equations can be solved for $\tilde{\beta}_{11}$ and $\tilde{\beta}_{21}$ to give

(12.54)
$$\tilde{\beta}_{11} = \bar{Y}_1 - \tilde{\beta}_{12}\bar{X}_1,$$
$$\tilde{\beta}_{21} = \bar{Y}_2 - \tilde{\beta}_{22}\bar{X}_2.$$

Substituting these results into the remaining equations and solving for $\tilde{\beta}_{12}$ and $\tilde{\beta}_{22}$, we obtain

(12.55)

$$\tilde{\beta}_{12} = \frac{\sigma_{11}m_{X_2X_2}(\sigma_{22}m_{X_1Y_1} - \sigma_{12}m_{X_1Y_2}) + \sigma_{12}m_{X_1X_2}(\sigma_{11}m_{X_2Y_2} - \sigma_{12}m_{X_2Y_1})}{\sigma_{11}\sigma_{22}m_{X_1X_1}m_{X_2X_2} - \sigma_{12}^2 m_{X_1X_2}^2},$$

$$\tilde{\beta}_{22} = \frac{\sigma_{12}m_{X_1X_2}(\sigma_{22}m_{X_1Y_1} - \sigma_{12}m_{X_1Y_2}) + \sigma_{22}m_{X_1X_1}(\sigma_{11}m_{X_2Y_2} - \sigma_{12}m_{X_2Y_1})}{\sigma_{11}\sigma_{22}m_{X_1X_1}m_{X_2X_2} - \sigma_{12}^2 m_{X_1X_2}^2},$$

where
$$m_{X_rX_s} = \sum_t (X_{rt} - \bar{X}_r)(X_{st} - \bar{X}_s),$$
$$m_{X_rY_s} = \sum_t (X_{rt} - \bar{X}_r)(Y_{st} - \bar{Y}_s),$$
$$r, s = 1, 2.$$

Note that if ε_{1t} and ε_{2t} are uncorrelated (i.e., if $\sigma_{12} = 0$), the formulas for $\tilde{\beta}_{12}$ and $\tilde{\beta}_{22}$ become

$$\tilde{\beta}_{12} = \frac{\sigma_{11}\sigma_{22}m_{X_2X_2}m_{X_1Y_1}}{\sigma_{11}\sigma_{22}m_{X_1X_1}m_{X_2X_2}} = \frac{m_{X_1Y_1}}{m_{X_1X_1}},$$

$$\tilde{\beta}_{22} = \frac{\sigma_{11}\sigma_{22}m_{X_1X_1}m_{X_2Y_2}}{\sigma_{11}\sigma_{22}m_{X_1X_1}m_{X_2X_2}} = \frac{m_{X_2Y_2}}{m_{X_2Y_2}},$$

which is the same result as that for the ordinary least squares estimators. Similarly, if $X_{1t} = X_{2t}$ (i.e., if both equations involve the same explanatory variable), we obtain

$$\tilde{\beta}_{12} = \frac{\sigma_{11}m_{X_1X_1}(\sigma_{22}m_{X_1Y_1} - \sigma_{12}m_{X_1Y_2}) + \sigma_{12}m_{X_1X_1}(\sigma_{11}m_{X_1Y_2} - \sigma_{12}m_{X_1Y_1})}{\sigma_{11}\sigma_{22}m_{X_1X_1}^2 - \sigma_{12}^2 m_{X_1X_1}^2}$$

$$= \frac{(\sigma_{11}\sigma_{22} - \sigma_{12}^2)m_{X_1X_1}m_{X_1Y_1}}{(\sigma_{11}\sigma_{22} - \sigma_{12}^2)m_{X_1X_1}^2} = \frac{m_{X_1Y_1}}{m_{X_1X_1}},$$

$$\tilde{\beta}_{22} = \frac{\sigma_{12}m_{X_1X_1}(\sigma_{22}m_{X_1Y_1} - \sigma_{12}m_{X_1Y_2}) + \sigma_{22}m_{X_1X_1}(\sigma_{11}m_{X_1Y_2} - \sigma_{12}m_{X_1Y_1})}{\sigma_{11}\sigma_{22}m_{X_1X_1}^2 - \sigma_{12}^2 m_{X_1X_1}^2}$$

$$= \frac{(\sigma_{11}\sigma_{22} - \sigma_{12}^2)m_{X_1X_1}m_{X_1Y_2}}{(\sigma_{11}\sigma_{22} - \sigma_{12}^2)m_{X_1X_1}^2} = \frac{m_{X_1Y_2}}{m_{X_1X_1}},$$

which again corresponds to the ordinary least squares formulas.

Because the generalized least squares estimator is BLUE, its variance is smaller than, or at best equal to, the variance of the ordinary least squares estimator. It is appropriate then to ask what the difference between variances is and on what it depends. We shall answer by reference to the simple system of two seemingly unrelated regressions we have just described. First, we note that the variance-covariance matrix of the generalized least squares estimators of β_{12} and β_{22} is

$$E(\underline{\tilde{\beta}} - \underline{\beta})(\underline{\tilde{\beta}} - \underline{\beta}) = (\underline{\mathbf{X}}'\mathbf{\Omega}^{-1}\underline{\mathbf{X}})^{-1}.$$

In this case

$$(\underline{\tilde{\beta}} - \underline{\beta}) = \begin{bmatrix} \tilde{\beta}_{12} - \beta_{12} \\ \tilde{\beta}_{22} - \beta_{22} \end{bmatrix} \quad \text{and} \quad \underline{\mathbf{X}} = \begin{bmatrix} (X_{11} - \bar{X}_1) & 0 \\ (X_{12} - \bar{X}_1) & 0 \\ \vdots & \vdots \\ (X_{1T} - \bar{X}_1) & 0 \\ 0 & (X_{21} - \bar{X}_2) \\ 0 & (X_{22} - \bar{X}_2) \\ \vdots & \vdots \\ 0 & (X_{2T} - \bar{X}_2) \end{bmatrix}$$

This means that

$$\begin{bmatrix} \operatorname{Var}(\tilde{\beta}_{12}) & \operatorname{Cov}(\tilde{\beta}_{12}, \tilde{\beta}_{22}) \\ \operatorname{Cov}(\tilde{\beta}_{12}, \tilde{\beta}_{22}) & \operatorname{Var}(\tilde{\beta}_{22}) \end{bmatrix} = (\sigma_{11}\sigma_{22} - \sigma_{12}^2)\begin{bmatrix} \sigma_{22}m_{X_1X_1} & -\sigma_{12}m_{X_1X_2} \\ -\sigma_{12}m_{X_1X_2} & \sigma_{11}m_{X_2X_2} \end{bmatrix}^{-1}$$

In particular, the variance of the generalized least squares estimator of β_{12} is

$$\operatorname{Var}(\tilde{\beta}_{12}) = \frac{(\sigma_{11}\sigma_{22} - \sigma_{12}^2)\sigma_{11}m_{X_2X_2}}{\sigma_{11}\sigma_{22}m_{X_1X_1}m_{X_2X_2} - \sigma_{12}^2 m_{X_1X_2}^2}. \tag{12.56}$$

If we let

$$\rho_{12} = \frac{\sigma_{12}}{\sqrt{\sigma_{11}\sigma_{22}}}$$

represent the coefficient of correlation between ε_{1t} and ε_{2t}, and if we let

$$r_{12} = \frac{m_{X_1X_2}}{\sqrt{m_{X_1X_1}m_{X_2X_2}}}$$

represent the sample coefficient of correlation between X_{1t} and X_{2t}, then we can write

$$\text{Var}(\tilde{\beta}_{12}) = \frac{\sigma_{11}\sigma_{22}(1 - \rho_{12}^2)\sigma_{11}m_{X_2X_2}}{\sigma_{11}\sigma_{22}(1 - \rho_{12}^2 r_{12}^2)m_{X_1X_1}m_{X_2X_2}} = \frac{\sigma_{11}}{m_{X_1X_1}} \frac{1 - \rho_{12}^2}{1 - \rho_{12}^2 r_{12}^2}.$$

On the other hand, the variance of the ordinary least squares estimator of β_{12}, say, $\hat{\beta}_{12}$, is

$$\text{Var}(\hat{\beta}_{12}) = \frac{\sigma_{11}}{m_{X_1X_1}}.$$

Therefore, the ratio of the two variances is

$$\text{(12.57)} \qquad \frac{\text{Var}(\tilde{\beta}_{12})}{\text{Var}(\hat{\beta}_{12})} = \frac{1 - \rho_{12}^2}{1 - \rho_{12}^2 r_{12}^2} \leq 1.$$

This ratio is a decreasing function of ρ_{12}^2 and an increasing function of r_{12}^2. This means that the gain in efficiency of the generalized least squares estimator over the ordinary squares estimator is greatest when the disturbances in the two equations are highly correlated and, at the same time, the explanatory variables are uncorrelated. Table 12–1 gives the values of the ratio $\text{Var}(\tilde{\beta}_{12})/\text{Var}(\hat{\beta}_{12})$ for different values of ρ_{12}^2 and r_{12}^2. Clearly, the gain in efficiency is in many cases very substantial. These results could be extended to a more complex system of seemingly unrelated regressions as well.

Table 12–1

r_{12}^2	ρ_{12}^2					
	0	0.1	0.3	0.5	0.7	0.9
0	1.000	0.900	0.700	0.500	0.300	0.100
0.1	1.000	0.909	0.722	0.526	0.323	0.110
0.3	1.000	0.928	0.769	0.588	0.380	0.137
0.5	1.000	0.947	0.823	0.667	0.461	0.182
0.7	1.000	0.967	0.886	0.769	0.588	0.270
0.9	1.000	0.989	0.959	0.909	0.811	0.526
1.0	1.000	1.000	1.000	1.000	1.000	1.000

Estimation When the Variance-Covariance Matrix Is Unknown

In the preceding discussion we assumed that the elements of the $\mathbf{\Omega}$ matrix (i.e., the variances and covariances of the regression disturbances) are known. However, if they are not known, as is generally the case, we can replace $\mathbf{\Omega}$ by a consistent estimator of $\mathbf{\Omega}$. As pointed out in Section 12–1, the resulting estimator of

$\boldsymbol{\beta}$ has the same asymptotic properties as Aitken's generalized least squares estimator. Our problem, then, is to find consistent estimators of the variances and covariances of the regression disturbances. One possibility is to estimate these variances and covariances from ordinary least squares residuals (which we call e_{mt}) as suggested by Zellner in his path-breaking paper.[11] For this, we may use

$$(12.58) \qquad \hat{\boldsymbol{\Omega}} = \begin{bmatrix} s_{11}\mathbf{I_T} & s_{12}\mathbf{I_T} & \cdots & s_{1M}\mathbf{I_T} \\ s_{21}\mathbf{I_T} & s_{22}\mathbf{I_T} & \cdots & s_{2M}\mathbf{I_T} \\ \vdots & \vdots & & \vdots \\ s_{M1}\mathbf{I_T} & s_{M2}\mathbf{I_T} & \cdots & s_{MM}\mathbf{I_T} \end{bmatrix},$$

where

$$s_{mp} = \frac{1}{T - K_m} \sum_{t=1}^{T} e_{mt}e_{pt},$$

$$K_m \geq K_p,$$

$$m, p = 1, 2, \ldots, M.$$

It is well known that s_{mm} is an unbiased and consistent estimator of σ_{mm}, and it can be shown that s_{mp} $(m \neq p)$ is a consistent estimator of σ_{mp}. (Since we are only concerned with consistency, we could use T instead of $(T - K_m)$ in calculating the estimates of σ_{mp} without affecting the asymptotic properties of the estimator of $\boldsymbol{\beta}$.) The resulting estimator of $\boldsymbol{\beta}$

$$(12.59) \qquad \tilde{\tilde{\boldsymbol{\beta}}} = (\mathbf{X}'\hat{\boldsymbol{\Omega}}^{-1}\mathbf{X})^{-1}(\mathbf{X}'\hat{\boldsymbol{\Omega}}^{-1}\mathbf{Y})$$

with

$$(12.60) \qquad \text{Asympt. Var-Cov}(\tilde{\tilde{\boldsymbol{\beta}}}) = (\mathbf{X}'\boldsymbol{\Omega}^{-1}\mathbf{X})^{-1}$$

is called a *two-stage Aitken estimator* because its value is calculated in two stages. First, we obtain the ordinary least squares estimates for each equation and use the resulting residuals to estimate the variances and covariances of the disturbances. This enables us to construct $\hat{\boldsymbol{\Omega}}$. The second stage involves substituting $\hat{\boldsymbol{\Omega}}$ into (12.59) and calculating the values of the elements of $\tilde{\tilde{\boldsymbol{\beta}}}$. (A computer program for this estimation method is called EFFEST.) The two-stage Aitken estimator of $\boldsymbol{\beta}$ is asymptotically equivalent to Aitken's generalized least squares estimator and, therefore, to the maximum likelihood estimator of $\boldsymbol{\beta}$. Thus this estimator is asymptotically efficient and its asymptotic distribution is normal. With respect to the small sample properties of the two-stage Aitken estimator, we have some theoretical and some experimental results indicating that this estimator is unbiased and efficient relative to the ordinary least squares estimator.[12]

[11] Zellner, *op. cit.*

[12] See A. Zellner, "Estimators of Seemingly Unrelated Regressions: Some Exact Finite Sample Results," *Journal of the American Statistical Association*, Vol. 58, December 1963, pp. 977–992; N. C. Kakwani, "The Unbiasedness of Zellner's Seemingly Unrelated Regression Equations Estimators," *Journal of the American Statistical Association*, Vol. 62, March 1967, pp. 141–142; J. Kmenta and R. F. Gilbert, "Small Sample Properties of Alternative Estimators of Seemingly Unrelated Regressions," *Journal of the American Statistical Association*, Vol. 63, December 1968, pp. 1180–1200.

An alternative approach to the problem of estimating the elements of $\mathbf{\Omega}$ is to use the maximum likelihood method. In accordance with (12.18), the likelihood function for $\mathbf{Y}$ in the context of seemingly unrelated regressions is

$$(12.61)\quad L = -\frac{MT}{2}\log(2\pi) - \tfrac{1}{2}\log|\mathbf{\Omega}| - \tfrac{1}{2}(\mathbf{Y} - \mathbf{X}\boldsymbol{\beta})'\mathbf{\Omega}^{-1}(\mathbf{Y} - \mathbf{X}\boldsymbol{\beta}).$$

We can differentiate L with respect to the elements of $\boldsymbol{\beta}$ *and* $\mathbf{\Omega}$, set the resulting derivatives equal to zero, and then solve for the values of the unknown parameters. For the system of two seemingly unrelated regressions described by (12.53), we have

$$\begin{aligned} L = &-\frac{2T}{2}\log(2\pi) - \frac{T}{2}\log(\sigma_{11}\sigma_{22} - \sigma_{12}^2) \\ &- \frac{1}{2(\sigma_{11}\sigma_{22} - \sigma_{12}^2)}\Big[\sigma_{22}\sum_t (Y_{1t} - \beta_{11} - \beta_{12}X_{1t})^2 \\ &+ \sigma_{11}\sum_t (Y_{2t} - \beta_{21} - \beta_{22}X_{2t})^2 \\ &- 2\sigma_{12}\sum_t (Y_{1t} - \beta_{11} - \beta_{12}X_{1t})(Y_{2t} - \beta_{21} - \beta_{22}X_{2t})\Big]. \end{aligned}$$

The first-order conditions for maximizing L with respect to the β's and the σ's are

$$\begin{aligned} \hat{\sigma}_{22}\sum_t (Y_{1t} - \hat{\beta}_{11} - \hat{\beta}_{12}X_{1t}) - \hat{\sigma}_{12}\sum_t (Y_{2t} - \hat{\beta}_{21} - \hat{\beta}_{22}X_{2t}) &= 0, \\ \hat{\sigma}_{22}\sum_t X_{1t}(Y_{1t} - \hat{\beta}_{11} - \hat{\beta}_{12}X_{1t}) - \hat{\sigma}_{12}\sum_t X_{1t}(Y_{2t} - \hat{\beta}_{21} - \hat{\beta}_{22}X_{2t}) &= 0, \\ -\hat{\sigma}_{12}\sum_t (Y_{1t} - \hat{\beta}_{11} - \hat{\beta}_{12}X_{1t}) + \hat{\sigma}_{11}\sum_t (Y_{2t} - \hat{\beta}_{21} - \hat{\beta}_{22}X_{2t}) &= 0, \\ -\hat{\sigma}_{12}\sum_t X_{2t}(Y_{1t} - \hat{\beta}_{11} - \hat{\beta}_{12}X_{1t}) + \hat{\sigma}_{11}\sum_t X_{2t}(Y_{2t} - \hat{\beta}_{21} - \hat{\beta}_{22}X_{2t}) &= 0, \\ \hat{\sigma}_{11} = \frac{1}{T}\sum_t (Y_{1t} - \hat{\beta}_{11} - \hat{\beta}_{12}X_{1t})^2&, \\ \hat{\sigma}_{22} = \frac{1}{T}\sum_t (Y_{2t} - \hat{\beta}_{21} - \hat{\beta}_{22}X_{2t})^2&, \\ \hat{\sigma}_{12} = \frac{1}{T}\sum_t (Y_{1t} - \hat{\beta}_{11} - \hat{\beta}_{12}X_{1t})(Y_{2t} - \hat{\beta}_{21} - \hat{\beta}_{22}X_{2t})&. \end{aligned}$$

Note that the first four equations are essentially the same as "Aitken's generalized least squares normal equations" derived earlier; the only difference is that the σ's are replaced by $\hat{\sigma}$'s. In the case of the two-stage Aitken estimator, the $\hat{\sigma}$'s in the first four equations are replaced by the estimates obtained from the ordinary least squares residuals and, thus, the last three equations are not used. In the case of the maximum likelihood estimator, however, the σ's are to be estimated *jointly* with the β's, using all seven equations.

The first-order conditions for maximizing L for a more complex system of seemingly unrelated regressions can be determined by a simple generalization of the case of two equations. In the first place, we have the equations corresponding to "Aitken's generalized least squares normal equations"; in the second place, we have the expressions for the estimated variances and covariances of the disturbances. Thus the maximum likelihood estimators for the general case are given by

$$\hat{\hat{\boldsymbol{\beta}}} = (\mathbf{X}'\hat{\hat{\boldsymbol{\Omega}}}^{-1}\mathbf{X})^{-1}(\mathbf{X}'\hat{\hat{\boldsymbol{\Omega}}}^{-1}\mathbf{Y}), \tag{12.62}$$

$$\hat{\hat{\boldsymbol{\Omega}}} = \begin{bmatrix} \hat{\hat{\sigma}}_{11}\mathbf{I_T} & \hat{\hat{\sigma}}_{12}\mathbf{I_T} & \cdots & \hat{\hat{\sigma}}_{1M}\mathbf{I_T} \\ \hat{\hat{\sigma}}_{21}\mathbf{I_T} & \hat{\hat{\sigma}}_{22}\mathbf{I_T} & \cdots & \hat{\hat{\sigma}}_{2M}\mathbf{I_T} \\ \vdots & \vdots & & \vdots \\ \hat{\hat{\sigma}}_{M1}\mathbf{I_T} & \hat{\hat{\sigma}}_{M2}\mathbf{I_T} & \cdots & \hat{\hat{\sigma}}_{MM}\mathbf{I_T} \end{bmatrix},$$

where
$$\hat{\hat{\sigma}}_{mp} = \frac{1}{T}(\mathbf{Y_m} - \mathbf{X_m}\hat{\hat{\boldsymbol{\beta}}}_\mathbf{m})'(\mathbf{Y_p} - \mathbf{X_p}\hat{\hat{\boldsymbol{\beta}}}_\mathbf{p}),$$

$$m, p = 1, 2, \ldots, M.$$

The analytical solution of (12.62) is quite complicated since the equations are nonlinear in the unknowns, but it can be obtained with the help of an electronic computer. The resulting estimator $\hat{\hat{\boldsymbol{\beta}}}$ has the same asymptotic properties as the two-stage Aitken estimator. There is also some evidence that the small sample properties of these two estimators are fairly similar.[13]

Example As an example of seemingly unrelated regressions, consider the following set of investment functions for individual firms:

$$I_t = \beta_{m1} + \beta_{m2}C_{t-1} + \beta_{m3}F_{t-1} + \varepsilon_{mt}$$

where I = gross investment, C = end-of-period capital stock, and F = end-of-period value of outstanding shares. The following estimates for two firms, General Electric and Westinghouse, were based on annual data for 1935–1954:[14]

General Electric

OLS $$I_t = \underset{(31.3742)}{-9.9563} + \underset{(0.0257)}{0.1517}C_{t-1} + \underset{(0.0156)}{0.0266}F_{t-1} + e_t,$$

EFFEST $$I_t = \underset{(29.3212)}{-27.7193} + \underset{(0.0250)}{0.1390}C_{t-1} + \underset{(0.0145)}{0.0383}F_{t-1} + e_t,$$

ML $$I_t = \underset{(29.6608)}{-30.7485} + \underset{(0.0255)}{0.1359}C_{t-1} + \underset{(0.0145)}{0.0405}F_{t-1} + e_t;$$

[13] See Kmenta and Gilbert, *op. cit.*

[14] From *ibid.* The results are based on the data given in J. C. G. Boot and G. M. deWitt, "Investment Demand: An Empirical Contribution to the Aggregation Problem," *International Economic Review*, Vol. 1, January 1960, pp. 3–30.

Westinghouse

$$\text{OLS} \qquad I_t = \underset{(8.0153)}{-0.5094} + \underset{(0.0561)}{0.0924}C_{t-1} + \underset{(0.0157)}{0.0529}F_{t-1} + e_t,$$

$$\text{EFFEST} \qquad I_t = \underset{(7.5452)}{-1.2520} + \underset{(0.0530)}{0.0576}C_{t-1} + \underset{(0.0145)}{0.0640}F_{t-1} + e_t,$$

$$\text{ML} \qquad I_t = \underset{(7.5149)}{-1.7016} + \underset{(0.0529)}{0.0593}C_{t-1} + \underset{(0.0144)}{0.0557}F_{t-1} + e_t.$$

As can be seen, there appears to be some—though by no means a great—gain in efficiency by going from ordinary least squares to two-stage Aitken or maximum likelihood estimation. The reason for this relatively low gain in efficiency is, at least in part, the high degree of correlation between the explanatory variables in the two equations.

Estimation of Seemingly Unrelated Regressions with Autoregressive Disturbances

As the final point connected with the problem of estimating seemingly unrelated regressions, we consider the case where the disturbances in each equation are not independent *over time*, but follow a first-order autoregressive scheme as described in Section 8–2. In this case the assumptions (12.47) and (12.48) stated at the outset of the present section are replaced by

$$(12.63) \qquad E(\boldsymbol{\epsilon}_m\boldsymbol{\epsilon}_m') = \sigma_{mm}\begin{bmatrix} 1 & \rho_m & \cdots & \rho_m^{T-1} \\ \rho_m & 1 & \cdots & \rho_m^{T-2} \\ \vdots & \vdots & & \vdots \\ \rho_m^{T-1} & \rho_m^{T-2} & \cdots & 1 \end{bmatrix},$$

$$(12.64) \qquad E(\boldsymbol{\epsilon}_m\boldsymbol{\epsilon}_p') = \sigma_{mp}\begin{bmatrix} 1 & \rho_p & \cdots & \rho_p^{T-1} \\ \rho_m & 1 & \cdots & \rho_p^{T-2} \\ \vdots & \vdots & & \vdots \\ \rho_m^{T-1} & \rho_m^{T-2} & \cdots & 1 \end{bmatrix},$$

$$m, p = 1, 2, \ldots, M,$$

where ρ_m is the coefficient of autocorrelation in the mth equation. Here, we can estimate ρ_m separately for each equation, using one of the consistent methods described in Section 8–2. Suppose the resulting estimates are called $\hat{\rho}_m$. They can be used to transform the original observations so that the system of seemingly unrelated regressions now becomes

$$(12.65) \quad (Y_{mt} - \hat{\rho}_m Y_{m,t-1}) = \beta_{m1}(X_{it,1} - \hat{\rho}_m X_{1,t-1,1}) + \beta_{m2}(X_{1t,2} - \hat{\rho}_m X_{1,t-1,2}) + \cdots + \beta_{mK_m}(X_{mt,K_m} - \hat{\rho}_m X_{m,t-1,K_m}) + u_{mt},$$

$$m = 1, 2, \ldots, M.$$

The regressions in (12.65) can be estimated by the two-stage Aitken method in the usual way. The resulting estimates of the regression coefficients have the same asymptotic properties as Aitken's generalized least squares estimates.[15]

EXERCISES

12–1. Prove the validity of equations (12.16) and (12.17).

12–2. Consider a regression equation to be estimated from observations on N households for 2 consecutive periods of time. Assume that the regression disturbances are cross-sectionally uncorrelated but time-wise autoregressive with $\rho_i = \rho_j$ for all i, j.

a. Determine the elements of $\mathbf{\Omega}$ (the variance-covariance matrix of the regression disturbances).

b. Devise an estimation procedure that would lead to a consistent estimator of $\mathbf{\Omega}$.

c. Devise a transformation of the observations that would enable us to use the ordinary least squares method to get asymptotically efficient estimates of the regression coefficients.

12–3. A regression model to be estimated from pooled cross-section and time-series data is given by

$$Y_{it} = \beta X_{it} + \varepsilon_{it} \qquad (t = 1, 2, \ldots, 21;\ i = 1, 2).$$

Alternatively, we may write

$$\begin{bmatrix} \mathbf{Y}_1 \\ \mathbf{Y}_2 \end{bmatrix} = \begin{bmatrix} \mathbf{X}_1 \\ \mathbf{X}_2 \end{bmatrix} \beta + \begin{bmatrix} \boldsymbol{\epsilon}_1 \\ \boldsymbol{\epsilon}_2 \end{bmatrix},$$

where $\mathbf{Y}_i \to (21 \times 1)$, $\mathbf{X}_i \to (21 \times 1)$, $\boldsymbol{\epsilon}_i \to (21 \times 1)$, and β is a scalar. Assume that the X's are nonstochastic and bounded, and that

$$E(\varepsilon_{it}) = 0,$$
$$E(\varepsilon_{it}\varepsilon_{is}) = 0 \qquad (t \neq s),$$
$$E(\varepsilon_{it}\varepsilon_{jt}) = \sigma_{ij}.$$

The sample data are given as follows:

$$\mathbf{X}_1'\mathbf{X}_1 = 10, \qquad \mathbf{X}_1'\mathbf{Y}_1 = 10, \qquad \mathbf{Y}_1'\mathbf{Y}_1 = 13.90,$$
$$\mathbf{X}_1'\mathbf{X}_2 = 8, \qquad \mathbf{X}_1'\mathbf{Y}_2 = 8, \qquad \mathbf{Y}_1'\mathbf{Y}_2 = 11.92,$$
$$\mathbf{X}_2'\mathbf{X}_2 = 10, \qquad \mathbf{X}_2'\mathbf{Y}_1 = 8, \qquad \mathbf{Y}_2'\mathbf{Y}_2 = 12.30.$$
$$\mathbf{X}_2'\mathbf{Y}_2 = 8,$$

Obtain an asymptotically efficient estimate of β and its estimated standard error.

[15] See R. W. Parks, "Efficient Estimation of a System of Regression Equations when Disturbances are Both Serially and Contemporaneously Correlated," *Journal of the American Statistical Association*, Vol. 62, June 1967, pp. 500–509; J. Kmenta and R. F. Gilbert, "Estimation of Seemingly Unrelated Regressions With Autoregressive Disturbances," *Journal of the American Statistical Association*, Vol. 65, March 1970, pp. 186–197.

12–4. Consider the following two regression equations:

$$\begin{aligned} Y_{1t} &= \beta_1 X_{1t} + \varepsilon_{1t} \\ Y_{2t} &= \beta_2 X_{2t} + \varepsilon_{2t} \end{aligned} \qquad (t = 1, 2, \ldots, 21).$$

Assume that the X's are nonstochastic and bounded, and that

$$\begin{aligned} \varepsilon_{it} &\sim N(0, \sigma_{ii}) && (i = 1, 2), \\ E(\varepsilon_{it}\varepsilon_{is}) &= 0 && (t \neq s), \\ E(\varepsilon_{it}\varepsilon_{jt}) &= \sigma_{ij} && (i, j = 1, 2). \end{aligned}$$

The sample results are

$$\begin{aligned} &\sum X_{1t}^2 = 10, && \sum X_{1t}Y_{1t} = 10, && \sum Y_{1t}^2 = 12.0, \\ &\sum X_{2t}^2 = 10, && \sum X_{1t}Y_{2t} = 8, && \sum Y_{2t}^2 = 12.4, \\ &\sum X_{1t}X_{2t} = 8, && \sum X_{2t}Y_{1t} = 8, && \sum Y_{1t}Y_{2t} = 10.0. \\ & && \sum X_{2t}Y_{2t} = 8, && \end{aligned}$$

Find asymptotically efficient estimates of the regression coefficients and their estimated standard errors by using

a. Zellner's two-stage Aitken method.

b. The maximum likelihood method.

12–5. A set of three seemingly unrelated regression equations is specified as

$$\begin{aligned} Y_{t1} &= \alpha_1 + \beta_1 X_{t1} + \varepsilon_{t1}, \\ Y_{t2} &= \alpha_2 + \beta_2 X_{t2} + \varepsilon_{t2}, \\ Y_{t3} &= \alpha_3 + \beta_3 X_{t3} + \varepsilon_{t3}, \end{aligned}$$

The variance-covariance matrix of the disturbances is assumed to be known. Consider two estimators of β_1, the first obtained by applying Aitken's generalized least squares estimation to all three equations, and the second by applying this method only to the first two equations. Examine the efficiency of the first estimator relative to the second.

12–6. Consider the following set of demand equations for different commodities to be estimated from time-series data:

$$V_{it} = \alpha_i + \beta_i P_{it} + \gamma_i V_t + \varepsilon_{it}$$

where V_{it} = expenditure on the ith commodity, P_{it} = price of the ith commodity, and V_t = total expenditure on all commodities. Since

$$\sum_i V_{it} = V_t,$$

the following restrictions are in effect:

$$\sum_i \alpha_i = 0, \qquad \sum_i \beta_i = 0, \qquad \sum_i \gamma_i = 1, \qquad \sum_i \varepsilon_{it} = 0.$$

Describe an estimation procedure that would yield asymptotically efficient estimates of the regression coefficients.

13 Simultaneous Equation Systems

Economic models frequently involve a *set* of relationships designed to explain the behavior of certain variables. For instance, a simple model of the market for a given commodity may involve a supply and a demand function, and may explain the equilibrium price and quantity of the commodity exchanged in the market. Similarly, a model of aggregate income may explain the determination of various income components by means of appropriately specified relationships. In such models the problem of estimating the parameters has special features that are not present when a model involves only a single relation. In particular, when a relation is a part of a system, some regressors are typically stochastic and correlated with the regression disturbance. In this case the ordinary least squares estimators of the regression coefficients are inconsistent and other methods must be devised to provide consistent estimates.

This chapter is concerned with the problem of estimating equations that belong to a system of relations, and with the analysis and interpretation of such systems. Section 13–1 contains a general description of simultaneous equation systems and introduces some basic concepts. Section 13–2 deals with the problem of identification, which is crucially important for estimation. The discussion represents a logical extension of the identification problem from the single-equation models of Section 11–2 to the multiequation models of this chapter. In Section 13–3 we describe several methods of estimating a single equation that is embedded in a simultaneous equation system, while the methods presented in Section 13–4 are designed to provide estimates for *all* equations of the system. Section 13–5 is concerned with comparing different methods of estimation and also deals with certain special problems. Finally, Section 13–6 provides an analysis and interpretation of dynamic economic systems.

13–1 Description of Simultaneous Equation Systems

The basic requirement an economic model must satisfy is that the number of the variables whose values are to be explained must be equal to the number of independent relationships in the model—i.e., to the number of different pieces of relevant information—otherwise the values of these variables would not be determinate. In addition to the variables whose values are to be explained a model may, and usually does, contain variables whose values are not immediately affected by the mechanism described by the model. The relevance of these variables lies in their role as explanatory factors. This leads to a distinction between those variables whose values are to be explained by the model and those that contribute to providing such an explanation; the former are called *endogenous* and the latter *predetermined.* Predetermined variables can be subdivided into *exogenous* and *lagged endogenous* variables. The values of the exogenous variables are completely determined outside the system under consideration, whereas the values of the lagged endogenous variables are represented by the past values of the endogenous variables of the model. Models having no lagged endogenous variables are not uncommon, but models without any predetermined variables are rather rare. For example, a model of the market for a given commodity may involve a supply and a demand relation, with current equilibrium price and quantity exchanged as the endogenous variables, and the factors that account for systematic shifts of the supply and the demand functions as the predetermined variables. *A model is said to constitute a system of simultaneous equations if all of the relationships involved are needed for determining the value of at least one of the endogenous variables included in the model.* This implies that at least one of the relationships includes more than one endogenous variable.

The definition of a simultaneous equation system can be given a more rigorous interpretation when an economic model has been specifically formulated as a set of well-defined stochastic relationships, that is, when it has been turned into what is generally called an *econometric model.* Typically, economic theory tells us which relations make up the model, which variables are to be included in each of the relations, and what is the sign of some of the partial derivatives. As a rule, economic theory has very little to say about the functional form of the relations, the time lags involved, and the values of the parameters. Also, the relations are deterministic, so that no allowance is made for the presence of stochastic disturbances. In order to put an economic model into the form of a testable proposition, it is necessary to specify the functional form of the relations, the timing of the variables, and the stochastic characterization of the system. The end result is an econometric model that is ready for estimation or testing. This model represents a summary of the prior knowledge of the investigator concerning the phenomenon in question. Given the current state of economics, this prior knowledge is derived in part from economic theory, and in part from ad hoc reasoning or guessing. For example, consider the following simplified supply-demand model for a commodity:

$$Q = f_1(P, Y) \quad \text{(demand)},$$

$$Q = f_2(P) \quad \text{(supply)},$$

$$\frac{\partial f_1}{\partial P} \leq 0, \qquad \frac{\partial f_1}{\partial Y} \geq 0, \qquad \frac{\partial f_2}{\partial P} \geq 0,$$

where Q = equilibrium quantity exchanged on the market, P = equilibrium price, and Y = income of the consumers. The variables Q and P are endogenous, and Y is exogenous. Note that both relations are needed for determining the values of the two endogenous variables, so that the system is one of simultaneous equations. An econometric model representing these relations might look as follows:

$$Q_t = \alpha_1 + \alpha_2 P_t + \alpha_3 Y_t + \varepsilon_{1t} \quad \text{(demand)},$$
$$Q_t = \beta_1 + \beta_2 P_t + \varepsilon_{2t} \quad \text{(supply)},$$
$$\alpha_2 \leq 0, \qquad \alpha_3 \geq 0, \qquad \beta_2 \geq 0, \tag{13.1}$$

where α's and β's are parameters, ε's are random disturbances, and t represents a specific period of time. Each disturbance is characterized by the assumptions of the classical normal linear regression model. The variances and the covariance of the disturbances are

$$E(\varepsilon_{1t}^2) = \sigma_{11},$$
$$E(\varepsilon_{2t}^2) = \sigma_{22},$$
$$E(\varepsilon_{1t}\varepsilon_{2t}) = \sigma_{12}.$$

Equations (13.1) are called the *structural form* of the model under study. This form is derived from economic theory. The structural equations can be solved for the endogenous variables to give

$$Q_t = \left(\frac{\alpha_2\beta_1 - \alpha_1\beta_2}{\alpha_2 - \beta_2}\right) - \left(\frac{\alpha_3\beta_2}{\alpha_2 - \beta_2}\right)Y_t + \left(\frac{-\beta_2\varepsilon_{1t} + \alpha_2\varepsilon_{2t}}{\alpha_2 - \beta_2}\right) \tag{13.2}$$
$$P_t = \left(\frac{-\alpha_1 + \beta_1}{\alpha_2 - \beta_2}\right) - \left(\frac{\alpha_3}{\alpha_2 - \beta_2}\right)Y_t + \left(\frac{-\varepsilon_{1t} + \varepsilon_{2t}}{\alpha_2 - \beta_2}\right).$$

The solution given by (13.2) is called the *reduced form* of the model. The reduced form equations show explicitly how the endogenous variables are *jointly dependent* on the predetermined variables and the disturbances of the system. In the case of (13.2), we can see that the values of Q_t and P_t are fully determined by Y_t, ε_{1t}, and ε_{2t}. The value of Y_t, on the other hand, is believed to be determined outside of the market in question and to be in no way influenced by P_t or Q_t. If Y_t is random, it is assumed to be distributed independently of ε_{1t} and ε_{2t}.

From the point of view of statistical inference, the single relevant characteristic of the simultaneous equation systems—and one that requires special consideration—is the appearance of endogenous variables among the explanatory variables of at least some of the structural equations. This leads to problems because the endogenous variables are, in general, correlated with the disturbance of the equation in which they appear. Consider the supply-demand model of (13.1). In both equations the endogenous P_t appears as an explanatory variable. But from (13.2) we can see that

$$E(P_t\varepsilon_{1t}) = \frac{-\sigma_{11} + \sigma_{12}}{\alpha_2 - \beta_2}$$

and
$$E(P_t\varepsilon_{2t}) = \frac{-\sigma_{12} + \sigma_{22}}{\alpha_2 - \beta_2},$$

which shows that P_t is correlated with both disturbances. As pointed out in Section 8–3, the existence of correlation between an explanatory variable and the disturbance leads to inconsistency of the ordinary least squares estimator of the regression coefficients. It appears, then, that the crucial aspect of the predetermined variables in a system is that they are not contemporaneously correlated with the disturbances.

In general, the structural form of a simultaneous equation system can be described as follows:

$$(13.3)\quad \begin{aligned} \beta_{11}y_{1t} + \beta_{12}y_{2t} + \cdots + \beta_{1G}y_{Gt} + \gamma_{11}x_{1t} + \gamma_{12}x_{2t} + \cdots + \gamma_{1K}x_{Kt} &= u_{1t} \\ \beta_{21}y_{1t} + \beta_{22}y_{2t} + \cdots + \beta_{2G}y_{Gt} + \gamma_{21}x_{1t} + \gamma_{22}x_{2t} + \cdots + \gamma_{2K}x_{Kt} &= u_{2t} \\ \vdots \\ \beta_{G1}y_{1t} + \beta_{G2}y_{2t} + \cdots + \beta_{GG}y_{Gt} + \gamma_{G1}x_{1t} + \gamma_{G2}x_{2t} + \cdots + \gamma_{GK}x_{K1} &= u_{Gt}. \end{aligned}$$

where the y's are endogenous variables, the x's are predetermined variables, the u's are stochastic disturbances, and $t = 1, 2, \ldots, T$. The β's and the γ's are known as the structural coefficients. There are G endogenous and K predetermined variables in the system. Generally, of course, not all endogenous and predetermined variables will appear in every equation since some of the β's and γ's will be known to be zero. Further, in each equation one of the β's is taken to be unity, thus indicating that one of the endogenous variables serves as the "dependent" variable when the equation is written out as a standard regression equation. It should also be noted that some of the equations may actually be identities, which means that all their coefficients are known and that they contain no stochastic disturbances. The whole system of equations may be written in matrix form as

$$(13.3a)\quad \mathbf{B}\mathbf{y}_t + \mathbf{\Gamma}\mathbf{x}_t = \mathbf{u}_t,$$

where

$$\mathbf{y}_t = \underset{(G\times 1)}{\begin{bmatrix} y_{1t} \\ y_{2t} \\ \vdots \\ y_{Gt} \end{bmatrix}}, \quad \mathbf{x}_t = \underset{(K\times 1)}{\begin{bmatrix} x_{1t} \\ x_{2t} \\ \vdots \\ x_{Kt} \end{bmatrix}}, \quad \mathbf{u}_t = \underset{(G\times 1)}{\begin{bmatrix} u_{1t} \\ u_{2t} \\ \vdots \\ u_{Gt} \end{bmatrix}},$$

$$\mathbf{B} = \underset{(G\times G)}{\begin{bmatrix} \beta_{11} & \beta_{12} & \cdots & \beta_{1G} \\ \beta_{21} & \beta_{22} & \cdots & \beta_{2G} \\ \vdots & \vdots & & \vdots \\ \beta_{G1} & \beta_{G2} & \cdots & \beta_{GG} \end{bmatrix}}, \quad \mathbf{\Gamma} = \underset{(G\times K)}{\begin{bmatrix} \gamma_{11} & \gamma_{12} & \cdots & \gamma_{1K} \\ \gamma_{21} & \gamma_{22} & \cdots & \gamma_{2K} \\ \vdots & \vdots & & \vdots \\ \gamma_{G1} & \gamma_{G2} & \cdots & \gamma_{GK} \end{bmatrix}}.$$

If there are constant terms in any of the equations, one of the x's will be equal to unity for all $t = 1, 2, \ldots, T$. With respect to the stochastic disturbances, we stipulate that each disturbance satisfies the assumptions of the classical normal linear regression model, i.e., that

$$u_{gt} \sim N(0, \sigma_{gg}), \qquad g = 1, 2, \ldots, G;$$
$$E(u_{gt}u_{gs}) = 0, \qquad t, s = 1, 2, \ldots, T;$$
$$t \neq s.$$

However, we do not rule out the possibility that the disturbances are correlated across equations, i.e., that

$$E(u_{gt}u_{ht}) = \sigma_{gh} \qquad (g, h = 1, 2, \ldots, G).$$

In matrix notation these assumptions become

$$\mathbf{u_t} = N(\mathbf{0}, \mathbf{\Phi}), \tag{13.4}$$

$$E(\mathbf{u_t u_s'}) = \mathbf{0}, \tag{13.5}$$

where

$$\mathbf{\Phi} = \underset{(G \times G)}{\begin{bmatrix} \sigma_{11} & \sigma_{12} & \cdots & \sigma_{1G} \\ \sigma_{21} & \sigma_{22} & \cdots & \sigma_{2G} \\ \vdots & \vdots & & \vdots \\ \sigma_{G1} & \sigma_{G2} & \cdots & \sigma_{GG} \end{bmatrix}}.$$

The matrix $\mathbf{\Phi}$ is known as the variance-covariance matrix of the structural disturbances. If there are any identities present, $\mathbf{\Phi}$ refers only to the equations that are not identities, and its dimension is appropriately reduced.

The reduced form of the system is obtained by solving the structural form equations for the values of the endogenous variables, that is, by expressing the y's in terms of the x's and the u's. The result may be written as

$$\begin{aligned} y_{1t} &= \pi_{11}x_{1t} + \pi_{12}x_{2t} + \cdots + \pi_{1K}x_{Kt} + v_{1t}, \\ y_{2t} &= \pi_{21}x_{1t} + \pi_{22}x_{2t} + \cdots + \pi_{2K}x_{Kt} + v_{2t}, \\ &\vdots \\ y_{Gt} &= \pi_{G1}x_{1t} + \pi_{G2}x_{2t} + \cdots + \pi_{GK}x_{Kt} + v_{Gt}. \end{aligned} \tag{13.6}$$

The π's represent the reduced form coefficients and the v's the reduced form disturbances. In general, each reduced form disturbance is a linear function of *all* structural disturbances. Using matrix notation, we may write (13.6) as

$$\mathbf{y_t} = \mathbf{\Pi x_t} + \mathbf{v_t}, \tag{13.6a}$$

where

$$\mathbf{\Pi} = \underset{(G \times K)}{\begin{bmatrix} \pi_{11} & \pi_{12} & \cdots & \pi_{1K} \\ \pi_{21} & \pi_{22} & \cdots & \pi_{2K} \\ \vdots & \vdots & & \vdots \\ \pi_{G1} & \pi_{G2} & \cdots & \pi_{GK} \end{bmatrix}}, \qquad \mathbf{v_t} = \underset{(G \times 1)}{\begin{bmatrix} v_{1t} \\ v_{2t} \\ \vdots \\ v_{Gt} \end{bmatrix}}.$$

The relation between the structural form and the reduced form can be derived explicitly by solving (13.3a) for y_t. This gives

$$\mathbf{y_t} = -\mathbf{B}^{-1}\mathbf{\Gamma}\mathbf{x_t} + \mathbf{B}^{-1}\mathbf{u_t}. \tag{13.6b}$$

Comparing this result with the reduced form (13.6a), we can see that

$$\mathbf{\Pi} = -\mathbf{B}^{-1}\mathbf{\Gamma} \tag{13.7}$$

and

$$\mathbf{v_t} = \mathbf{B}^{-1}\mathbf{u_t}. \tag{13.8}$$

The variance-covariance matrix of the reduced form disturbances, $\mathbf{\Psi}$, is

$$\mathbf{\Psi} = E(\mathbf{v_t}\mathbf{v_t'}) = E[\mathbf{B}^{-1}\mathbf{u_t}\mathbf{u_t'}(\mathbf{B}^{-1})'] = \mathbf{B}^{-1}\mathbf{\Phi}(\mathbf{B}^{-1})'. \tag{13.9}$$

EXAMPLE 1 The supply-demand model described by (13.1) is

$$Q_t - \alpha_1 - \alpha_2 P_t - \alpha_3 Y_t = \varepsilon_{1t},$$

$$Q_t - \beta_1 - \beta_2 P_t = \varepsilon_{2t}.$$

This can be written in the pattern of (13.3a) as

$$\begin{bmatrix} 1 & -\alpha_2 \\ 1 & -\beta_2 \end{bmatrix}\begin{bmatrix} Q_t \\ P_t \end{bmatrix} + \begin{bmatrix} -\alpha_1 & -\alpha_3 \\ -\beta_1 & 0 \end{bmatrix}\begin{bmatrix} 1 \\ Y_t \end{bmatrix} = \begin{bmatrix} \varepsilon_{1t} \\ \varepsilon_{2t} \end{bmatrix}.$$

The reduced form of the system is

$$\begin{bmatrix} Q_t \\ P_t \end{bmatrix} = \begin{bmatrix} \pi_{11} & \pi_{12} \\ \pi_{21} & \pi_{22} \end{bmatrix}\begin{bmatrix} 1 \\ Y_t \end{bmatrix} + \begin{bmatrix} v_{1t} \\ v_{2t} \end{bmatrix},$$

where

$$\begin{bmatrix} \pi_{11} & \pi_{12} \\ \pi_{21} & \pi_{22} \end{bmatrix} = -\mathbf{B}^{-1}\mathbf{\Gamma} = \begin{bmatrix} 1 & -\alpha_2 \\ 1 & -\beta_2 \end{bmatrix}^{-1}\begin{bmatrix} -\alpha_1 & -\alpha_3 \\ -\beta_1 & 0 \end{bmatrix}$$

$$= -\left[\frac{1}{\alpha_2 - \beta_2}\right]\begin{bmatrix} -\beta_2 & \alpha_2 \\ -1 & 1 \end{bmatrix}\begin{bmatrix} -\alpha_1 & -\alpha_3 \\ -\beta_1 & 0 \end{bmatrix}$$

$$= -\left[\frac{1}{\alpha_2 - \beta_2}\right]\begin{bmatrix} (\alpha_1\beta_2 - \alpha_2\beta_1) & \alpha_3\beta_2 \\ (\alpha_1 - \beta_1) & \alpha_3 \end{bmatrix}$$

and

$$\begin{bmatrix} v_{1t} \\ v_{2t} \end{bmatrix} = \mathbf{B}^{-1}\begin{bmatrix} \varepsilon_{1t} \\ \varepsilon_{2t} \end{bmatrix} = \left[\frac{1}{\alpha_2 - \beta_2}\right]\begin{bmatrix} -\beta_2 & \alpha_2 \\ -1 & 1 \end{bmatrix}\begin{bmatrix} \varepsilon_{1t} \\ \varepsilon_{2t} \end{bmatrix} = \left[\frac{1}{\alpha_2 - \beta_2}\right]\begin{bmatrix} -\beta_2\varepsilon_{1t} + \alpha_2\varepsilon_{2t} \\ -\varepsilon_{1t} + \varepsilon_{2t} \end{bmatrix}.$$

Of course, these results are the same as those given by (13.2).

EXAMPLE 2 The following represents a highly simplified model of the economy:

$$C_t = \alpha_0 + \alpha_1 Y_t + \alpha_2 C_{t-1} + u_{1t} \quad \text{(consumption)},$$

$$I_t = \beta_0 + \beta_1 r_t + \beta_2 I_{t-1} + u_{2t} \quad \text{(investment)},$$

$$r_t = \gamma_0 + \gamma_1 Y_t + \gamma_2 M_t + u_{3t} \quad \text{(money market)},$$

$$Y_t = C_t + I_t + G_t \quad \text{(income identity)}.$$

where C = consumption, Y = income, I = investment, r = rate of interest, M = money supply, and G = government expenditure. The variables C_t, I_t, Y_t, and r_t are endogenous; the remaining variables are predetermined. We can describe the model as

$$\begin{bmatrix} 1 & 0 & -\alpha_1 & 0 \\ 0 & 1 & 0 & -\beta_1 \\ 0 & 0 & -\gamma_1 & 1 \\ -1 & -1 & 1 & 0 \end{bmatrix} \begin{bmatrix} C_t \\ I_t \\ Y_t \\ r_t \end{bmatrix} + \begin{bmatrix} -\alpha_0 & -\alpha_2 & 0 & 0 & 0 \\ -\beta_0 & 0 & -\beta_2 & 0 & 0 \\ -\gamma_0 & 0 & 0 & -\gamma_2 & 0 \\ 0 & 0 & 0 & 0 & -1 \end{bmatrix} \begin{bmatrix} 1 \\ C_{t-1} \\ I_{t-1} \\ M_t \\ G_t \end{bmatrix} = \begin{bmatrix} u_{1t} \\ u_{2t} \\ u_{3t} \\ 0 \end{bmatrix}.$$

The reduced form of this system is

$$\begin{bmatrix} C_t \\ I_t \\ Y_t \\ r_t \end{bmatrix} = \frac{1}{\Delta} \begin{bmatrix} \alpha_0(1-\beta_1\gamma_1) + \alpha_1(\beta_0+\beta_1\gamma_0) & \alpha_1\alpha_2 & \alpha_1\beta_2 & \alpha_1\beta_1\gamma_2 & \alpha_1 \\ \alpha_0\beta_1\gamma_1 + (1-\alpha_1)(\beta_0+\beta_1\gamma_0) & \alpha_2\beta_1\gamma_1 & (1-\alpha_1)\beta_2 & (1-\alpha_1)\beta_1\gamma_1 & \beta_1\gamma_1 \\ \alpha_0+\beta_0+\beta_1\gamma_0 & \alpha_2 & \beta_2 & \beta_1\gamma_2 & 1 \\ (\alpha_0+\beta_0)\gamma_1 + (1-\alpha_1)\gamma_0 & \alpha_2\gamma_1 & \beta_2\gamma_1 & (1-\alpha_1)\gamma_2 & \gamma_1 \end{bmatrix} \begin{bmatrix} 1 \\ C_{t-1} \\ I_{t-1} \\ M_t \\ G_t \end{bmatrix}$$

$$+ \frac{1}{\Delta} \begin{bmatrix} 1-\beta_1\gamma_1 & \alpha_1 & \alpha_1\beta_1 \\ \beta_1\gamma_1 & (1-\alpha_1) & (1-\alpha_1)\beta_1 \\ 1 & 1 & \beta_1 \\ \gamma_1 & \gamma_1 & (1-\alpha_1) \end{bmatrix} \begin{bmatrix} u_{1t} \\ u_{2t} \\ u_{3t} \end{bmatrix},$$

where $\Delta = 1 - \alpha_1 - \beta_1\gamma_1$.

Types of Structural Models

The position of the zero elements in the **B** matrix indicates which endogenous variables do not appear in different structural equations. This is used as a criterion for distinguishing between various types of structures.

(a) If **B** is *diagonal*, i.e., if

$$\mathbf{B} = \begin{bmatrix} \beta_{11} & 0 & \dots & 0 \\ 0 & \beta_{22} & \dots & 0 \\ \vdots & \vdots & & \\ 0 & 0 & \dots & \beta_{GG} \end{bmatrix},$$

only one endogenous variable appears in each equation. This means that the equations are not simultaneous but *seemingly unrelated*. This case has been discussed in Section 12-3.

(b) If **B** is *block-diagonal*, i.e., if

$$\mathbf{B} = \begin{bmatrix} \mathbf{B}_1 & \mathbf{0} & \dots & \mathbf{0} \\ \mathbf{0} & \mathbf{B}_2 & \dots & \mathbf{0} \\ \vdots & \vdots & & \vdots \\ \mathbf{0} & \mathbf{0} & \dots & \mathbf{B}_R \end{bmatrix},$$

where $\mathbf{B}_1, \mathbf{B}_2, \ldots, \mathbf{B}_R$ are square matrices and the $\mathbf{0}$'s represent zero-matrices of appropriate dimensions, then each block contains its own set of endogenous variables. In this case we have not one but R systems of simultaneous equations. Each block constitutes a separate system since, in the derivation of the reduced form solutions, we utilize only the structural equations of the same block. This can be clearly seen if we partition the structural equations in the following way:

$$\begin{bmatrix} \mathbf{B}_1 & \mathbf{0} & \ldots & \mathbf{0} \\ \mathbf{0} & \mathbf{B}_2 & \ldots & \mathbf{0} \\ \vdots & \vdots & & \vdots \\ \mathbf{0} & \mathbf{0} & \ldots & \mathbf{B}_R \end{bmatrix} \begin{bmatrix} \mathbf{y}_t^{(1)} \\ \mathbf{y}_t^{(2)} \\ \vdots \\ \mathbf{y}_t^{(R)} \end{bmatrix} + \begin{bmatrix} \mathbf{\Gamma}_1 \\ \mathbf{\Gamma}_2 \\ \vdots \\ \mathbf{\Gamma}_R \end{bmatrix} \mathbf{x}_t = \begin{bmatrix} \mathbf{u}_t^{(1)} \\ \mathbf{u}_t^{(2)} \\ \vdots \\ \mathbf{u}_t^{(R)} \end{bmatrix},$$

where $\mathbf{y}_t^{(r)}$ is a $(G_r \times 1)$ vector of the endogenous variables appearing in the rth block, $\mathbf{u}_t^{(r)}$ is a $(G_r \times 1)$ vector of the corresponding structural disturbances, and $\mathbf{\Gamma}_r$ is a $(G_r \times K)$ matrix of the γ coefficients in the structural equations of the rth block $(r = 1, 2, \ldots, R)$. The reduced form solution for $\mathbf{y}_t^{(r)}$ is

$$\mathbf{y}_t^{(r)} = -\mathbf{B}_r^{-1}\mathbf{\Gamma}_r\mathbf{x}_t + \mathbf{B}_r^{-1}\mathbf{u}_t^{(r)} \qquad (r = 1, 2, \ldots, R).$$

In this result there is no reference to any equation outside of the rth block. When the $\mathbf{B}$ matrix is block-diagonal, we speak of a *nonintegrated structure*. If the variance-covariance matrix of the structural disturbances is also block-diagonal in the same way as the $\mathbf{B}$ matrix, then each block can be treated as a separate system when it comes to estimation. However, if the variance-covariance matrix of the structural disturbances is not block-diagonal, then the blocks are only "seemingly" unrelated. We may add that there is also another, stricter kind of nonintegration known as *dynamic nonintegration*. This condition prevails when the structural equations in any one block do not involve current *as well as* lagged endogenous variables from any other block. This kind of nonintegration implies that not only the current value but also the path through time of an endogenous variable are determined entirely by reference to the equations of the block in which the variable in question appears. We shall comment further on this in Section 13–6.

(c) If $\mathbf{B}$ is triangular, i.e., if

$$\mathbf{B} = \begin{bmatrix} \beta_{11} & 0 & \ldots & 0 \\ \beta_{21} & \beta_{22} & \ldots & 0 \\ \vdots & & & \vdots \\ \beta_{G1} & \beta_{G2} & \ldots & \beta_{GG} \end{bmatrix},$$

the system is known as *recursive*. In this case the solution for the gth endogenous variable involves only the first g structural equations. This means that all G structural equations are needed for the solution only in the case of the last endogenous variable y_{Gt}. The first structural equation involves only one endogenous variable so that it coincides with the first reduced form equation.

(d) If **B** is *block-triangular*, i.e., if

$$\mathbf{B} = \begin{bmatrix} \mathbf{B}_{11} & \mathbf{0} & \cdots & \mathbf{0} \\ \mathbf{B}_{21} & \mathbf{B}_{22} & \cdots & \mathbf{0} \\ \vdots & & & \\ \mathbf{B}_{R1} & \mathbf{B}_{R2} & \cdots & \mathbf{B}_{RR} \end{bmatrix},$$

where the **B**'s are matrices of given dimensions, the system is called *block-recursive*. This system has the same characteristics as the recursive system just described, except that reference is made to blocks of equations rather than to individual equations themselves.

(e) If **B** is neither diagonal nor triangular (block or otherwise), we speak of an *integrated structure*. Such structures have commanded the greatest attention of econometricians and provide the main subject for our discussion of simultaneous equation systems. A system of equations characterized by an integrated structure is sometimes called a *general interdependent system*.

13–2 The Identification Problem

Because there are endogenous variables among the explanatory variables in simultaneous equations, ordinary least squares estimators of the structural coefficients are not consistent, at least in general. However, in the reduced form equations the explanatory variables are represented by the predetermined variables of the system so that ordinary least squares estimators of the reduced form coefficients are consistent. This suggests that we may try to estimate the structural coefficients via the reduced form. The question then is whether we can derive estimates of the structural coefficients from the consistent estimates of the reduced form coefficients. Obviously, we can do this providing we can express the structural coefficients—the β's and the γ's—in terms of the reduced form coefficients—the π's. Thus the problem is one of *identification*, as was discussed in the context of a single equation model in Section 11–2. At present we face the same problem with a system of equations. The reduced form equations described by (13.6a) as

$$\mathbf{y}_t = \mathbf{\Pi x}_t + \mathbf{v}_t$$

represent the unrestricted version of these equations, while the form (13.6b) given by

$$\mathbf{y}_t = -\mathbf{B}^{-1}\mathbf{\Gamma x}_t + \mathbf{B}^{-1}\mathbf{u}_t$$

represents the restricted version. As with a single equation model, when there is a one-to-one correspondence between the restricted and the unrestricted parameters (in the sense that there is a unique solution for the restricted parameters in terms of the unrestricted coefficients) we have *exact identification*. On the other hand, when the number of the unrestricted coefficients exceeds the number of the restricted parameters and there is no unique solution, we have *overidentification.* Finally, if the number of unrestricted coefficients is insufficient for the solution, we have *underidentification.* An equation is said to be identified if it is either exactly identified or overidentified.

We may illustrate the identification problem by reference to the supply-demand model (13.1):

$$Q_t = \alpha_1 + \alpha_2 P_t + \alpha_3 Y_t + \varepsilon_{1t} \quad \text{(demand)},$$

$$Q_t = \beta_1 + \beta_2 P_t + \varepsilon_{2t} \quad \text{(supply)},$$

and its reduced form (13.2):

$$Q_t = \pi_{11} + \pi_{12} Y_t + v_{1t},$$

$$P_t = \pi_{21} + \pi_{22} Y_t + v_{2t}.$$

The simplest way of finding out whether it is possible to express the α's and the β's in terms of the π's is to substitute for Q_t and P_t from the reduced form (13.2) into the structural form (13.1). This gives

$$(\pi_{11} + \pi_{12} Y_t + v_{1t}) = \alpha_1 + \alpha_2(\pi_{21} + \pi_{22} Y_t + v_{2t}) + \alpha_3 Y_t + \varepsilon_{1t} \quad \text{(demand)},$$

$$(\pi_{11} + \pi_{12} Y_t + v_{1t}) = \beta_1 + \beta_2(\pi_{21} + \pi_{22} Y_t + v_{2t}) + \varepsilon_{2t} \quad \text{(supply)}.$$

In light of the definition of v_{1t} and v_{2t} given earlier, the stochastic disturbances in each equation cancel out, and we are left with

$$\pi_{11} + \pi_{12} Y_t = (\alpha_1 + \alpha_2 \pi_{21}) + (\alpha_2 \pi_{22} + \alpha_3) Y_t \quad \text{(demand)},$$

$$\pi_{11} + \pi_{12} Y_t = (\beta_1 + \beta_2 \pi_{21}) + \beta_2 \pi_{22} Y_t \quad \text{(supply)}.$$

The equalities implied by the demand equation are

$$\pi_{11} = \alpha_1 + \alpha_2 \pi_{21} \quad \text{and} \quad \pi_{12} = \alpha_2 \pi_{22} + \alpha_3.$$

Since there are only two equalities, we cannot solve for the three unknowns represented by α_1, α_2, and α_3. The equalities for the supply equation are

$$\pi_{11} = \beta_1 + \beta_2 \pi_{21} \quad \text{and} \quad \pi_{12} = \beta_2 \pi_{22}.$$

This leads to

$$\beta_1 = \pi_{11} - \frac{\pi_{12}\pi_{21}}{\pi_{22}},$$

$$\beta_2 = \frac{\pi_{12}}{\pi_{22}}.$$

Thus the demand equation is underidentified, and the supply equation is exactly identified.

Clearly, it would be desirable to have some general rule for determining the identification status of any given structural equation. Such a rule can be derived in the following way. The structural equations are

$$\mathbf{B}\mathbf{y}_t + \mathbf{\Gamma}\mathbf{x}_t = \mathbf{u}_t,$$

while the reduced form equations are

$$\mathbf{y}_t = \mathbf{\Pi}\mathbf{x}_t + \mathbf{v}_t.$$

By substituting for $\mathbf{y}_t$ from the reduced form expression into the structural form, we obtain

$$\mathbf{B}\mathbf{\Pi}\mathbf{x}_t + \mathbf{B}\mathbf{v}_t + \mathbf{\Gamma}\mathbf{x}_t = \mathbf{u}_t.$$

But since

$$\mathbf{v}_t = \mathbf{B}^{-1}\mathbf{u}_t,$$

we can write

$$\mathbf{B}\mathbf{\Pi}\mathbf{x}_t = -\mathbf{\Gamma}\mathbf{x}_t$$

or

$$\mathbf{B}\mathbf{\Pi} = -\mathbf{\Gamma}.$$

This is the relation used in determining the identification status of the demand and the supply equations. We shall now try to use this relation for deriving a general identification criterion for each structural equation. Writing out the matrices in full, we have

$$\begin{bmatrix} \beta_{11} & \beta_{12} & \cdots & \beta_{1G} \\ \beta_{21} & \beta_{22} & \cdots & \beta_{2G} \\ \vdots & \vdots & & \vdots \\ \beta_{G1} & \beta_{G2} & \cdots & \beta_{GG} \end{bmatrix} \begin{bmatrix} \pi_{11} & \pi_{12} & \cdots & \pi_{1K} \\ \pi_{21} & \pi_{22} & \cdots & \pi_{2K} \\ \vdots & \vdots & & \vdots \\ \pi_{G1} & \pi_{G2} & \cdots & \pi_{GK} \end{bmatrix} = - \begin{bmatrix} \gamma_{11} & \gamma_{12} & \cdots & \gamma_{1K} \\ \gamma_{21} & \gamma_{22} & \cdots & \gamma_{2K} \\ \vdots & \vdots & & \vdots \\ \gamma_{G1} & \gamma_{G2} & \cdots & \gamma_{GK} \end{bmatrix}.$$

For a single equation of the system, say, the gth, this becomes

$$(13.10) \quad [\beta_{g1} \quad \beta_{g2} \quad \cdots \quad \beta_{gG}] \begin{bmatrix} \pi_{11} & \pi_{12} & \cdots & \pi_{1K} \\ \pi_{21} & \pi_{22} & \cdots & \pi_{2K} \\ \vdots & \vdots & & \vdots \\ \pi_{G1} & \pi_{G2} & \cdots & \pi_{GK} \end{bmatrix} = -[\gamma_{g1} \quad \gamma_{g2} \quad \cdots \quad \gamma_{gK}]$$

or

$$(13.10a) \quad \boldsymbol{\beta}_g\mathbf{\Pi} = -\boldsymbol{\gamma}_g,$$

where

$$\boldsymbol{\beta}_g = [\beta_{g1} \quad \beta_{g2} \quad \cdots \quad \beta_{gG}],$$

$$\boldsymbol{\gamma}_g = [\gamma_{g1} \quad \gamma_{g2} \quad \cdots \quad \gamma_{gK}].$$

If all of the endogenous and the predetermined variables of the system do not appear in the gth equation, some of the β's and some of the γ's will be equal to zero.

Let G^{Δ} = number of endogenous variables which appear in the gth equation (i.e., number of the nonzero elements in $\boldsymbol{\beta}_g$);

$G^{\Delta\Delta} = G - G^{\Delta}$;

K^* = number of predetermined variables which appear in the gth equation (i.e., number of the nonzero elements in $\boldsymbol{\gamma}_g$);

$K^{**} = K - K^*$.

Without a loss of generality, we assume that the elements of $\boldsymbol{\beta}_g$ and $\boldsymbol{\gamma}_g$ are arranged in such a way that the nonzero elements appear first, being followed by the zero elements. Then we can partition $\boldsymbol{\beta}_g$ and $\boldsymbol{\gamma}_g$ as

(13.11)
$$\boldsymbol{\beta}_g = [\boldsymbol{\beta}_{\Delta} \quad \mathbf{0}_{\Delta\Delta}],$$
$$\boldsymbol{\gamma}_g = [\boldsymbol{\gamma}_* \quad \mathbf{0}_{**}],$$

where
$$\boldsymbol{\beta}_{\Delta} = [\beta_{g1} \quad \beta_{g2} \quad \ldots \quad \beta_{gG^{\Delta}}] \rightarrow 1 \times G^{\Delta},$$
$$\mathbf{0}_{\Delta\Delta} = [0 \quad 0 \quad \ldots \quad 0] \rightarrow 1 \times G^{\Delta\Delta},$$
$$\boldsymbol{\gamma}_* = [\gamma_{g1} \quad \gamma_{g2} \quad \ldots \quad \gamma_{gK^*}] \rightarrow 1 \times K^*,$$
$$\mathbf{0}_{**} = [0 \quad 0 \quad \ldots \quad 0] \rightarrow 1 \times K^{**}.$$

The matrix $\boldsymbol{\Pi}$ can be partitioned in a corresponding way:

(13.12)
$$\boldsymbol{\Pi} = \begin{bmatrix} \boldsymbol{\Pi}_{\Delta *} & \boldsymbol{\Pi}_{\Delta **} \\ \boldsymbol{\Pi}_{\Delta\Delta *} & \boldsymbol{\Pi}_{\Delta\Delta **} \end{bmatrix},$$

where
$$\boldsymbol{\Pi}_{\Delta *} \rightarrow (G^{\Delta} \times K^*),$$
$$\boldsymbol{\Pi}_{\Delta **} \rightarrow (G^{\Delta} \times K^{**}),$$
$$\boldsymbol{\Pi}_{\Delta\Delta *} \rightarrow (G^{\Delta\Delta} \times K^*),$$
$$\boldsymbol{\Pi}_{\Delta\Delta **} \rightarrow (G^{\Delta\Delta} \times K^{**}).$$

By using (13.11) and (13.12), we can rewrite (13.10a) as

(13.13)
$$[\boldsymbol{\beta}_{\Delta} \quad \mathbf{0}_{\Delta\Delta}] \begin{bmatrix} \boldsymbol{\Pi}_{\Delta *} & \boldsymbol{\Pi}_{\Delta **} \\ \boldsymbol{\Pi}_{\Delta\Delta *} & \boldsymbol{\Pi}_{\Delta\Delta **} \end{bmatrix} = -[\boldsymbol{\gamma}_* \quad \mathbf{0}_{**}].$$

This leads to the following equalities:

(13.14)
$$\underset{(1 \times G^{\Delta})(G^{\Delta} \times K^*)}{\boldsymbol{\beta}_{\Delta} \boldsymbol{\Pi}_{\Delta *}} = \underset{(1 \times K^*)}{-\boldsymbol{\gamma}_*},$$

(13.15)
$$\underset{(1 \times G^{\Delta})(G^{\Delta} \times K^{**})}{\boldsymbol{\beta}_{\Delta} \boldsymbol{\Pi}_{\Delta **}} = \underset{(1 \times K^{**})}{\mathbf{0}_{**}}.$$

Since one of the β's in each structural equation equals unity, the equalities (13.14) and (13.15) involve $(G^{\Delta} - 1)$ unknown β's and K^* unknown γ's. The equality (13.15) is particularly important since it does not involve any γ's. If we can solve (13.15) for $\boldsymbol{\beta}_\Delta$, we can solve for $\boldsymbol{\gamma}_*$ easily from (13.14). Now, equality (13.15) contains altogether K^{**} equations, one for each element of the $(1 \times K^{**})$ vector. Clearly, if we want to obtain a solution for the $(G^\Delta - 1)$ unknown elements of $\boldsymbol{\beta}_\Delta$, we need at least $(G^\Delta - 1)$ equations. That means that we require that

(13.16) $$K^{**} \geq G^\Delta - 1.$$

This is known as the *order condition* for identifiability. This condition, in fact, states that a necessary condition for identification of a given structural equation is that the number of predetermined variables excluded from the given equation is at least as large as the number of endogenous variables included in the equation less one. Note that this is only a *necessary* and not a sufficient condition for identification since the K^{**} equations in (13.15) may not be independent. That is, it may happen that the equations in (13.15) contain fewer than $G^\Delta - 1$ different pieces of information about the relation between the β's and the π's. Thus a necessary *and* sufficient condition for identification is that the number of independent equations in (13.15) is $G^\Delta - 1$. This will be the case if and only if the order of the largest non-zero determinant that can be formed from all square submatrices of $\boldsymbol{\Pi}_{\Delta**}$ is $G^\Delta - 1$, i.e., if and only if

(13.17) $$\text{rank}\,(\boldsymbol{\Pi}_{\Delta**}) = G^\Delta - 1.$$

This is known as the *rank condition* for identifiability.

A convenient way of determining the rank of $\boldsymbol{\Pi}_{\Delta**}$ involves partitioning the matrices of the structural coefficients as follows:

$$\mathbf{B} = \begin{bmatrix} \boldsymbol{\beta}_\Delta & \mathbf{0}_{\Delta\Delta} \\ \mathbf{B}_\Delta & \mathbf{B}_{\Delta\Delta} \end{bmatrix}, \qquad \boldsymbol{\Gamma} = \begin{bmatrix} \boldsymbol{\gamma}_* & \mathbf{0}_{**} \\ \boldsymbol{\Gamma}_* & \boldsymbol{\Gamma}_{**} \end{bmatrix},$$

where $\boldsymbol{\beta}_\Delta$, $\boldsymbol{\gamma}_*$, $\mathbf{0}_{\Delta\Delta}$, and $\mathbf{0}_{**}$ are row vectors defined as in (13.11), and

$$\mathbf{B}_\Delta \to (G - 1) \times G^\Delta,$$

$$\mathbf{B}_{\Delta\Delta} \to (G - 1) \times G^{\Delta\Delta},$$

$$\boldsymbol{\Gamma}_* \to (G - 1) \times K^*,$$

$$\boldsymbol{\Gamma}_{**} \to (G - 1) \times K^{**}.$$

Note that $\mathbf{B}_{\Delta\Delta}$ and $\boldsymbol{\Gamma}_{**}$ are matrices of the structural coefficients for the variables omitted from the gth equation but included in other structural equations. If we now form a new matrix $\boldsymbol{\Delta}$ defined as

$$\boldsymbol{\Delta} = [\mathbf{B}_{\Delta\Delta} \quad \boldsymbol{\Gamma}_{**}],$$

then

(13.17a) $$\text{rank}\,(\boldsymbol{\Pi}_{\Delta**}) = \text{rank}\,(\boldsymbol{\Delta}) - G^{\Delta\Delta}.$$

This can be proved as follows. Let $\boldsymbol{\Delta}_*$ be defined as

$$\boldsymbol{\Delta}_* = \begin{bmatrix} \mathbf{0}_{**} & \mathbf{0}_{\Delta\Delta} \\ \boldsymbol{\Gamma}_{**} & \mathbf{B}_{\Delta\Delta} \end{bmatrix}.$$

Clearly, the rank of $\boldsymbol{\Delta}_*$ is the same as that of $\boldsymbol{\Delta}$ since the rank of a matrix is not affected by enlarging the matrix by a row of zeros, or by switching any columns. Now, $\boldsymbol{\Delta}_*$ can be written as

$$\boldsymbol{\Delta}_* = \begin{bmatrix} \boldsymbol{\beta}_\Delta & \mathbf{0}_{\Delta\Delta} \\ \mathbf{B}_\Delta & \mathbf{B}_{\Delta\Delta} \end{bmatrix} \begin{bmatrix} -\boldsymbol{\Pi}_{\Delta**} & \mathbf{0}_{\Delta,\Delta\Delta} \\ -\boldsymbol{\Pi}_{\Delta\Delta**} & \mathbf{I}_{\Delta\Delta} \end{bmatrix},$$

where $\mathbf{0}_{\Delta,\Delta\Delta}$ is $G^\Delta \times G^{\Delta\Delta}$ matrix of zeros, and $\mathbf{I}_{\Delta\Delta}$ is an identity matrix of order $G^{\Delta\Delta} \times G^{\Delta\Delta}$. To see that, we carry out the multiplication indicated in the above equality to obtain

$$\boldsymbol{\Delta}_* = \begin{bmatrix} -\boldsymbol{\beta}_\Delta \boldsymbol{\Pi}_{\Delta**} & \mathbf{0}_{\Delta\Delta} \\ (-\mathbf{B}_\Delta \boldsymbol{\Pi}_{\Delta**} - \mathbf{B}_{\Delta\Delta}\boldsymbol{\Pi}_{\Delta\Delta**}) & \mathbf{B}_{\Delta\Delta} \end{bmatrix}.$$

But by (13.15)

$$-\boldsymbol{\beta}_\Delta \boldsymbol{\Pi}_{\Delta**} = \mathbf{0}_{**},$$

and from the equality $\mathbf{B}\boldsymbol{\Pi} = -\boldsymbol{\Gamma}$ it follows that

$$-\mathbf{B}_\Delta \boldsymbol{\Pi}_{\Delta**} - \mathbf{B}_{\Delta\Delta}\boldsymbol{\Pi}_{\Delta\Delta**} = \boldsymbol{\Gamma}_{**}.$$

Utilizing the theorem[1] that if a matrix $\mathbf{A}$ is multiplied by a nonsingular matrix, the product has the same rank as $\mathbf{A}$, we can write

$$\begin{aligned}
\text{rank}(\boldsymbol{\Delta}_*) &= \text{rank}(\mathbf{B}^{-1}\boldsymbol{\Delta}_*) \\
&= \text{rank}\begin{bmatrix} -\boldsymbol{\Pi}_{\Delta**} & \mathbf{0}_{\Delta,\Delta\Delta} \\ -\boldsymbol{\Pi}_{\Delta\Delta**} & \mathbf{I}_{\Delta\Delta} \end{bmatrix} \\
&= \text{rank}\begin{bmatrix} -\boldsymbol{\Pi}_{\Delta**} & \mathbf{0}_{\Delta,\Delta\Delta} \\ -\boldsymbol{\Pi}_{\Delta\Delta**} & \mathbf{I}_{\Delta\Delta} \end{bmatrix} \begin{bmatrix} \mathbf{I}_{**} & \mathbf{0}_{**,\Delta\Delta} \\ \boldsymbol{\Pi}_{\Delta\Delta**} & \mathbf{I}_{\Delta\Delta} \end{bmatrix} \\
&= \text{rank}\begin{bmatrix} -\boldsymbol{\Pi}_{\Delta**} & \mathbf{0}_{\Delta,\Delta\Delta} \\ \mathbf{0}_{\Delta\Delta,**} & \mathbf{I}_{\Delta\Delta} \end{bmatrix} \\
&= \text{rank}(\boldsymbol{\Pi}_{\Delta**}) + G^{\Delta\Delta},
\end{aligned}$$

where $\mathbf{0}_{**,\Delta\Delta}$ and $\mathbf{0}_{\Delta\Delta,**}$ are zero matrices of order $K^{**} \times G^{\Delta\Delta}$ and $G^{\Delta\Delta} \times K^{**}$, respectively, and $\mathbf{I}_{**}$ is an identity matrix of order $K^{**} \times K^{**}$. This completes the proof of (13.17a). It is clearly much easier to determine the rank of $\boldsymbol{\Pi}_{\Delta**}$ from (13.17a) than from the direct solution for $\boldsymbol{\Pi}_{\Delta**}$ in terms of the structural coefficients.

The order and rank conditions enable us to set up the following general rule for determining the identification status of a structural equation.

1. If $K^{**} > G^\Delta - 1$ and $\text{rank}(\boldsymbol{\Pi}_{\Delta**}) = G^\Delta - 1$, we have overidentification.

[1] See, e.g., J. Johnston, *Econometric Methods* (New York: McGraw-Hill, 1963), p. 92.

2. If $K^{**} = G^{\Delta} - 1$ and $\text{rank}(\mathbf{\Pi}_{\Delta**}) = G^{\Delta} - 1$, we have exact identification.
3. If $K^{**} \geq G^{\Delta} - 1$ and $\text{rank}(\mathbf{\Pi}_{\Delta**}) < G^{\Delta} - 1$, the structural equation is underidentified.
4. If $K^{**} < G^{\Delta} - 1$, the structural equation is underidentified.

EXAMPLE 1 The supply-demand model described by (13.1) is

$$Q_t = \alpha_1 + \alpha_2 P_t + \alpha_3 Y_t + \varepsilon_{1t} \quad \text{(demand)},$$

$$Q_t = \beta_1 + \beta_2 P_t + \varepsilon_{2t} \quad \text{(supply)},$$

Consider the identification status of the demand equation first. There are two included endogenous variables, Q_t and P_t, so that

$$G^{\Delta} - 1 = 1.$$

Since no predetermined variables of the system are excluded from the demand equation, we have

$$K^{**} = 0.$$

Therefore,

$$K^{**} < G^{\Delta} - 1,$$

which means that the order condition is not satisfied, and, therefore, the demand equation is *underidentified.*

Turning now to the supply equation, we note that there are again two included endogenous variables, Q_t and P_t, i.e., that

$$G^{\Delta} - 1 = 1,$$

but there is now one predetermined variable, Y_t, which appears in the system but not in the supply equation. Thus, in this case we have

$$K^{**} = 1,$$

so that the order condition is satisfied. With respect to the rank condition, we have

$$\text{rank}(\mathbf{\Delta}) = \text{rank}[-\alpha_3] = 1.$$

Then, by (13.17a),

$$\text{rank}(\mathbf{\Pi}_{\Delta**}) = 1 - 0 = 1,$$

and the rank condition is also satisfied. Note that equality (13.15) for the supply equation of our model is

$$[1 \quad -\beta_2]\begin{bmatrix}\pi_{QY} \\ \pi_{PY}\end{bmatrix} = 0,$$

which involves one equation and one unknown; i.e., the supply function is *exactly* identified.

EXAMPLE 2 An aggregate model of the economy has been given as follows:

$$C_t = \alpha_0 + \alpha_1 Y_t + \alpha_2 C_{t-1} + u_t \quad \text{(consumption)},$$
$$I_t = \beta_0 + \beta_1 r_t + \beta_2 I_{t-1} + u_{2t} \quad \text{(investment)},$$
$$r_t = \gamma_0 + \gamma_1 Y_t + \gamma_2 M_t + u_{3t} \quad \text{(money market)},$$
$$Y_t = C_t + I_t + G_t \quad \text{(income identity)}.$$

For each of the first three structural equations, we have

$$G^{\Delta} - 1 = 1,$$
$$K^{**} = 3,$$

so that the order condition is satisfied in every case. As for the rank condition, the rank of $\boldsymbol{\Delta}$ for the *consumption function* is

$$\text{rank}(\boldsymbol{\Delta}) = \text{rank}\begin{bmatrix} 1 & -\beta_1 & -\beta_2 & 0 & 0 \\ 0 & 1 & 0 & -\gamma_2 & 0 \\ -1 & 0 & 0 & 0 & 1 \end{bmatrix} = 3.$$

Therefore, $$\text{rank}(\boldsymbol{\Pi}_{\Delta**}) = 3 - 2 = 1,$$

so that the rank condition is satisfied. This means that the consumption function is *identified.* Note that the equality (13.15) in the case of our consumption function becomes

$$[1 \quad -\alpha_1]\begin{bmatrix} \pi_{CI_{-1}} & \pi_{CM} & \pi_{CG} \\ \pi_{YI_{-1}} & \pi_{YM} & \pi_{YG} \end{bmatrix} = [0 \quad 0 \quad 0].$$

That is, there are three equations to determine one unknown; i.e., the consumption function is *overidentified.* The derivation of the rank condition for the remaining two structural equations would follow along the same lines.

The above order and rank conditions for identifiability have been stated in terms of population parameters on the assumption that none of the structural parameters is equal to zero. However, we do not know what the values of these parameters really are and, in fact, may want to test the hypothesis that they *are* equal to zero. If this hypothesis were not rejected in every case, some variables would be considered irrelevant and, therefore, should not be counted. For instance, to determine whether a given structural equation satisfies the order condition for identifiability, we count the number of predetermined variables excluded from the equation. But if some of these variables are irrelevant, they should not be counted. This means that a structural equation that appears to satisfy the order condition a priori may not, in fact, satisfy this condition when the irrelevant variables have been discarded. Therefore, we may want to consider the identifiability of an equation as a hypothesis to be tested instead of relying on prior specification. A description of a suggested test procedure can be found in the literature.[2]

[2] R. L. Basmann, "On Finite Sample Distributions of Generalized Classical Linear Identifiability Test Statistics," *Journal of the American Statistical Association*, Vol. 55, December 1960, pp. 650–659.

Identification Through Restrictions on the Disturbance Variance-Covariance Matrix

The preceding examination of the identifiability conditions has been confined to the specification of the structural equation and no reference has been made to the variance-covariance matrix of the disturbances. We have shown that a structural equation can be identified by specifying that some of the variables appearing in the system are omitted from the equation in question. Since omitting a variable from a linear equation is equivalent to specifying that the corresponding β or γ coefficient is equal to zero, it can be said that identification of an equation is achieved by *zero restrictions* on some of the coefficients. (Of course, identification could also be achieved by *nonzero* restrictions on the structural coefficients, e.g., by specifying that some coefficients are equal to given numbers that are not necessarily zero, or by specifying the ratio or ratios between coefficients in a linear equation.) But if this is the case, it should also be possible to achieve identification by prior restrictions on some of the elements of the variance-covariance matrix of the regression disturbances. We shall illustrate this by reference to the supply-demand model (13.1). In examining the identification status of the structural equations we concluded that, given the zero restrictions on the structural coefficients, the demand equation is underidentified while the supply equation is exactly identified. Let us now add a further restriction by specifying that the disturbances in the two equations are mutually independent, i.e., that

$$E(\varepsilon_{1t}\varepsilon_{2t}) = 0$$

for all t. Our previous results, obtained by utilizing the zero restrictions on the structural coefficients, have led to the following relations between the structural and the reduced form coefficients:

$$\pi_{11} = \alpha_1 + \alpha_2\pi_{21}, \qquad \pi_{11} = \beta_1 + \beta_2\pi_{21},$$

$$\pi_{12} = \alpha_2\pi_{22} + \alpha_3, \qquad \pi_{12} = \beta_2\pi_{22}.$$

As noted earlier, we can solve these equations for the β's but not for the α's. However, now we may add another relation that follows from the zero restriction on the covariance of the two disturbances. First, we note that the reduced form disturbances are given by

$$v_{1t} = \frac{-\beta_2\varepsilon_{1t} + \alpha_2\varepsilon_{2t}}{\alpha_2 - \beta_2},$$

$$v_{2t} = \frac{-\varepsilon_{1t} + \varepsilon_{2t}}{\alpha_2 - \beta_2}.$$

Therefore we can write

$$\varepsilon_{1t} = v_{1t} - \alpha_2 v_{2t},$$

$$\varepsilon_{2t} = v_{1t} - \beta_2 v_{2t}.$$

Thus the restriction

$$E(\varepsilon_{1t}\varepsilon_{2t}) = 0$$

implies that

$$E(v_{1t} - \alpha_2 v_{2t})(v_{1t} - \beta_2 v_{2t}) = 0$$

or

$$\psi_{11} - \alpha_2\psi_{12} - \beta_2\psi_{12} + \alpha_2\beta_2\psi_{22} = 0, \tag{13.18}$$

where the ψ's represent the elements of the variance-covariance matrix of the reduced form disturbances. Since we know that

$$\beta_2 = \frac{\pi_{12}}{\pi_{22}},$$

we can solve (13.18) for α_2 to obtain

$$\alpha_2 = \frac{\pi_{12}\psi_{12} - \pi_{22}\psi_{11}}{\pi_{12}\psi_{22} - \pi_{22}\psi_{12}}.$$

Also, since

$$\alpha_1 = \pi_{11} - \alpha_2\pi_{21}$$

and

$$\alpha_3 = \pi_{12} - \alpha_2\pi_{22},$$

we can solve for α_1 and α_3. Thus, with the added restriction on the covariance of the structural disturbances, the previously underidentified demand equation becomes identified.

Underidentification

The question of identification is important because of its implications for estimation and hypothesis testing. If a structural equation is identified, we can obtain consistent estimators of its coefficients. In the case of underidentification, however, it is not possible to derive consistent estimators of the structural coefficients. Of course, we can estimate the coefficients of an underidentified structural equation by the method of ordinary least squares, but the resulting estimates are inconsistent. The fact that consistent estimation of the coefficients of an underidentified structural equation breaks down can be illustrated by reference to the supply-demand model (13.1). We found that—in the absence of any prior information about the variance-covariance matrix of the disturbances—the demand equation of the system is underidentified. This equation was given as

$$Q_t = \alpha_1 + \alpha_2 P_t + \alpha_3 Y_t + \varepsilon_{1t}.$$

Suppose we try to estimate the coefficients of this equation by the method of instrumental variables, which leads to consistent estimates. This method was described in connection with estimating regression models with errors in variables in Section 9–1, and in connection with distributed lag models in Section

11-4. It involves pairing each explanatory variable of the equation to be estimated with an instrumental variable. The latter is supposed to be uncorrelated with the regression disturbance, but correlated with the explanatory variable with which it is paired. In the case of our demand equation, the explanatory variables are Q_t and P_t. Since Y_t is uncorrelated with ε_{1t} by assumption, it can serve as its own instrumental variable, so that we need only to find an instrumental variable for P_t. Let this variable be called Z_t. Then the "instrumental variables normal equations" are

$$\sum_t Q_t = \alpha_1^\dagger T + \alpha_2^\dagger \sum_t P_t + \alpha_3^\dagger \sum_t Y_t,$$

$$\sum_t Q_t Z_t = \alpha_1^\dagger \sum_t Z_t + \alpha_2^\dagger \sum_t P_t Z_t + \alpha_3^\dagger \sum_t Y_t Z_t,$$

$$\sum_t Q_t Y_t = \alpha_1^\dagger \sum_t Y_t + \alpha_2^\dagger \sum_t P_t Y_t + \alpha_3^\dagger \sum_t Y_t^2,$$

where $\alpha_1^\dagger$, $\alpha_2^\dagger$, and $\alpha_3^\dagger$ are the instrumental variables estimators of the respective coefficients. The solution for, say, $\alpha_2^\dagger$, is

$$\alpha_2^\dagger = \frac{m_{QZ}m_{YY} - m_{QY}m_{YZ}}{m_{PZ}m_{YY} - m_{PY}m_{YZ}},$$

where $$m_{QZ} = \sum_t (Q_t - \bar{Q})(Z_t - \bar{Z}),$$

$$m_{YY} = \sum_t (Y_t - \bar{Y})^2,$$

etc. Since from the reduced form solution we have

$$(Q_t - \bar{Q}) = \left(\frac{-\alpha_3\beta_2}{\alpha_2 - \beta_2}\right)(Y_t - \bar{Y}) + (v_{1t} - \bar{v}_1),$$

$$(P_t - \bar{P}) = \left(\frac{-\alpha_3}{\alpha_2 - \beta_2}\right)(Y_t - \bar{Y}) + (v_{2t} - \bar{v}_2),$$

it follows that

$$\operatorname{plim} \frac{1}{T} m_{QZ} = \left(\frac{-\alpha_3\beta_2}{\alpha_2 - \beta_2}\right) \operatorname{plim} \frac{1}{T} m_{YZ},$$

$$\operatorname{plim} \frac{1}{T} m_{QY} = \left(\frac{-\alpha_3\beta_2}{\alpha_2 - \beta_2}\right) \operatorname{plim} \frac{1}{T} m_{YY},$$

$$\operatorname{plim} \frac{1}{T} m_{PZ} = \left(\frac{-\alpha_3}{\alpha_2 - \beta_2}\right) \operatorname{plim} \frac{1}{T} m_{YZ},$$

$$\operatorname{plim} \frac{1}{T} m_{PY} = \left(\frac{-\alpha_3}{\alpha_2 - \beta_2}\right) \operatorname{plim} \frac{1}{T} m_{YY}.$$

Therefore,

$$\text{plim}\ \alpha_2^\dagger = \frac{\left(\frac{-\alpha_3\beta_2}{\alpha_2-\beta_2}\right)\text{plim}\ \frac{m_{YZ}}{T}\cdot\text{plim}\ \frac{m_{YY}}{T} - \left(\frac{-\alpha_3\beta_2}{\alpha_2-\beta_2}\right)\text{plim}\ \frac{m_{YY}}{T}\cdot\text{plim}\ \frac{m_{YZ}}{T}}{\left(\frac{-\alpha_3}{\alpha_2-\beta_2}\right)\text{plim}\ \frac{m_{YZ}}{T}\cdot\text{plim}\ \frac{m_{YY}}{T} - \left(\frac{-\alpha_3}{\alpha_2-\beta_2}\right)\text{plim}\ \frac{m_{YY}}{T}\cdot\text{plim}\ \frac{m_{YZ}}{T}} = \frac{0}{0},$$

i.e., plim $\alpha_2^\dagger$ is indeterminate. Similar results can be obtained for $\alpha_1^\dagger$ and $\alpha_3^\dagger$. Thus the instrumental variables method breaks down as claimed.

Our inability to obtain consistent estimates of the structural coefficients of an underidentified equation can also be explained in a more intuitive way. In the supply-demand model (13.1), we note that the identification of the supply equation is due to the presence of the exogenous income variable in the demand function. If this variable did not appear in the demand function, both equations of the model would be underidentified. In that case all observations on price and quantity would be scattered around the single point of intersection of the mean price and the mean quantity. An increase in the number of observations in the sample would only increase the denseness of the points without providing any more information about the two lines to be estimated. With the income variable present, however, the demand function shifts with changes in income; and in this way, we observe points that are scattered around the supply function. The more points we observe, the more accurate are the estimates of the coefficients of the supply function. Since there is no exogenous variable in the supply equation, we cannot trace out the demand function in a similar way. However, if the disturbances of the two functions are mutually independent, their covariance is zero, and this additional information enables us to identify the parameters of the demand function as well. Note that since the parameters of underidentified equations cannot be consistently estimated, the hypotheses about their values cannot be refuted by sample observations. This means that the underlying theory is, from scientific viewpoint, incomplete.

13–3 Single-Equation Methods of Estimation

In Section 13–1 we emphasized that the ordinary least squares method of estimation applied to the structural equations of a simultaneous equation system in general leads to inconsistent estimates. Therefore we have to develop other methods to obtain consistent estimates of the structural coefficients. As stated, this is not possible when a structural equation is underidentified.

Our concern here is with structural equations that are identified and for which consistent methods of estimation are available. We have two categories of methods of estimating structural equations: (1) methods designed to estimate a single structural equation with only a limited reference to the rest of the system and (2) methods by which all equations of the system are estimated simultaneously. This section deals with methods belonging to the first category.

Estimation of an Exactly Identified Equation

Consider the problem of estimating an *exactly identified* structural equation belonging to a general interdependent system of simultaneous equations with no restrictions on the variance-covariance matrix of the disturbances. In this case there exists a unique solution for the structural coefficients in terms of the reduced form coefficients. The reduced form equations are given by (13.6a) as

$$\mathbf{y_t} = \mathbf{\Pi x_t} + \mathbf{v_t},$$

where $\mathbf{y_t}$ is a $(G \times 1)$ vector of the endogenous variables, $\mathbf{\Pi}$ is a $(G \times K)$ matrix of the reduced form coefficients, $\mathbf{x_t}$ is a $(K \times 1)$ vector of the predetermined variables, and $\mathbf{v_t}$ is a $(G \times 1)$ vector of the reduced form disturbances. Since the reduced form disturbances are represented by linear combinations of the structural disturbances, they satisfy all the assumptions of the classical normal linear regression model. The predetermined variables, which serve as explanatory variables in the reduced form equations, are either nonstochastic or, if stochastic, independent of the current disturbances. We shall also assume that they have finite variances and covariances as $T \to \infty$, and that there exists no exact linear relation between them. If the predetermined variables include lagged endogenous variables, we assume that the initial values of these variables are fixed. Under these assumptions, the application of the ordinary (unrestricted) least squares method to each reduced form equation leads to consistent estimates of the π's. If *all* structural equations are exactly identified, these estimates will be equivalent to the maximum likelihood estimates and will, in addition to consistency, also possess the properties of asymptotic efficiency and asymptotic normality. The ordinary least squares estimates of the reduced form coefficients can be used to determine the corresponding estimates of the structural coefficients as specified by (13.14) and (13.15). The latter are called *indirect least squares estimates.* They are, in general, given as nonlinear functions of the reduced form estimates and inherit all their asymptotic properties.

EXAMPLE To illustrate the use of the indirect least squares method, we use the supply-demand model described by (13.1):

$$Q_t = \alpha_1 + \alpha_2 P_t + \alpha_3 Y_t + \varepsilon_{1t} \quad \text{(demand)},$$

$$Q_t = \beta_1 + \beta_2 P_t + \varepsilon_{2t} \quad \text{(supply)},$$

where Q_t and P_t are endogenous and Y_t is exogenous. Without any restrictions on the variance-covariance matrix of the disturbances, the demand equation is underidentified, but the supply equation is exactly identified. The reduced form equations are

$$Q_t = \pi_{11} + \pi_{12} Y_t + v_{1t},$$

$$P_t = \pi_{21} + \pi_{22} Y_t + v_{2t}.$$

Substituting the reduced form expression for Q_t and P_t into the supply equation, we obtain

$$\pi_{11} + \pi_{12}Y_t + v_{1t} = \beta_1 + \beta_2(\pi_{21} + \pi_{22}Y_t + v_{2t}) + \varepsilon_{2t}.$$

Therefore,

$$\pi_{11} = \beta_1 + \beta_2\pi_{21},$$

$$\pi_{12} = \beta_2\pi_{22},$$

or

$$\beta_2 = \frac{\pi_{12}}{\pi_{22}},$$

$$\beta_1 = \pi_{11} - \frac{\pi_{12}\pi_{21}}{\pi_{22}}.$$

Now the ordinary least squares estimators of the reduced form coefficients are

$$\hat{\pi}_{12} = \frac{m_{QY}}{m_{YY}},$$

$$\hat{\pi}_{11} = \bar{Q} - \left(\frac{m_{QY}}{m_{YY}}\right)\bar{Y},$$

$$\hat{\pi}_{22} = \frac{m_{PY}}{m_{YY}},$$

$$\hat{\pi}_{21} = \bar{P} - \left(\frac{m_{PY}}{m_{YY}}\right)\bar{Y},$$

where

$$m_{QY} = \sum_t (Q_t - \bar{Q})(Y_t - \bar{Y}),$$

$$m_{PY} = \sum_t (P_t - \bar{P})(Y_t - \bar{Y}),$$

$$m_{YY} = \sum_t (Y_t - \bar{Y})^2.$$

Hence the indirect least squares estimators of β_1 and β_2 are

$$\tilde{\beta}_2 = \frac{m_{QY}}{m_{PY}},$$

$$\tilde{\beta}_1 = \bar{Q} - \left(\frac{m_{QY}}{m_{PY}}\right)\bar{P}.$$

The problem of estimating the coefficients of a structural equation can also be approached by resorting to the *instrumental variables method.* Suppose the structural equation that we wish to estimate is the first equation of the system, i.e.,

$$(13.19)\quad \beta_{11}y_{1t} + \beta_{12}y_{2t} + \cdots + \beta_{1G}y_{Gt} + \gamma_{11}x_{1t} + \gamma_{12}x_{2t} + \cdots + \gamma_{1K}x_{Kt} = u_{1t}.$$

This involves no loss of generality since the structural equations can be written in any order we like. Let us suppose further that β_{11} is equal to unity, and that the included endogenous and predetermined variables are $y_{1t}, y_{2t}, \ldots, y_{G^\Delta t}, x_{1t}, x_{2t}, \ldots, x_{K^*t}$. Then (13.19) can be written as

$$(13.19a)\quad y_{1t} = -\beta_{12}y_{2t} - \beta_{13}y_{3t} - \cdots - \beta_{1G^\Delta}y_{G^\Delta t} - \gamma_{11}x_{1t} - \gamma_{12}x_{2t} - \cdots - \gamma_{1K^*}x_{K^*t} + u_{1t}.$$

In matrix notation, equation (13.19a) can be expressed as

$$(13.20)\quad \mathbf{y}_1 = \mathbf{Y}_1\boldsymbol{\beta}_1 + \mathbf{X}_1\boldsymbol{\gamma}_1 + \mathbf{u}_1,$$

where

$$\underset{(T\times 1)}{\mathbf{y}_1 = \begin{bmatrix} y_{11} \\ y_{12} \\ \vdots \\ y_{1T} \end{bmatrix}}, \quad \underset{(T\times \overline{G^\Delta - 1})}{\mathbf{Y}_1 = \begin{bmatrix} y_{21} & y_{31} & \cdots & y_{G^\Delta 1} \\ y_{22} & y_{32} & \cdots & y_{G^\Delta 2} \\ \vdots & \vdots & & \vdots \\ y_{2T} & y_{3T} & \cdots & y_{G^\Delta T} \end{bmatrix}}, \quad \underset{(T\times K^*)}{\mathbf{X}_1 = \begin{bmatrix} x_{11} & x_{21} & \cdots & x_{K^*1} \\ x_{12} & x_{22} & \cdots & x_{K^*2} \\ \vdots & \vdots & & \vdots \\ x_{1T} & x_{2T} & \cdots & x_{K^*T} \end{bmatrix}},$$

$$\underset{(\overline{G^\Delta - 1}\times 1)}{\boldsymbol{\beta}_1 = \begin{bmatrix} -\beta_{12} \\ -\beta_{13} \\ \vdots \\ -\beta_{1G^\Delta} \end{bmatrix}}, \quad \underset{(K^*\times 1)}{\boldsymbol{\gamma}_1 = \begin{bmatrix} -\gamma_{11} \\ -\gamma_{12} \\ \vdots \\ -\gamma_{1K^*} \end{bmatrix}}.$$

An alternative way of writing (13.20) is

$$(13.20a)\quad \mathbf{y}_1 = \mathbf{Z}_1\boldsymbol{\alpha}_1 + \mathbf{u}_1,$$

where $\mathbf{Z}_1 = [\mathbf{Y}_1 \quad \mathbf{X}_1]$ and $\boldsymbol{\alpha}_1 = \begin{bmatrix} \boldsymbol{\beta}_1 \\ \boldsymbol{\gamma}_1 \end{bmatrix}$.

An instrumental variables estimator of the structural coefficients is

$$(13.21)\quad \boldsymbol{\alpha}^\dagger = (\mathbf{W}_1'\mathbf{Z}_1)^{-1}(\mathbf{W}_1'\mathbf{y}_1),$$

and its estimated variance-covariance matrix is

$$(13.22)\quad \text{Est. Var-Cov}(\boldsymbol{\alpha}^\dagger) = s_{11}(\mathbf{W}_1'\mathbf{Z}_1)^{-1}(\mathbf{W}_1'\mathbf{W}_1)(\mathbf{Z}_1'\mathbf{W}_1)^{-1}, \text{ estimated}$$

where $\mathbf{W}_1$ is a $T\times(G^\Delta - 1 + K^*)$ matrix of the observed values of the chosen instrumental variables. (The formulas for the instrumental variables estimator and its variance are given by (11.86) and (11.87) of Section 11-4.) The estimator s_{11} can be obtained by the formula

$$(13.23)\quad s_{11} = \frac{(\mathbf{y}_1 - \mathbf{Z}_1\boldsymbol{\alpha}_1^\dagger)'(\mathbf{y}_1 - \mathbf{Z}_1\boldsymbol{\alpha}_1^\dagger)}{(T - G^\Delta + 1 - K^*)}$$

(The consistency of the estimator will not be changed if we use any denominator D in place of $(T - G^{\Delta} + 1 - K^*)$ *providing* plim $(D/T) = 1$.) As for the choice of appropriate instrumental variables, the problem is confined to the $(G^{\Delta} - 1)$ included endogenous variables, since the predetermined variables included in the equation can serve as their own instrumental variables. Natural candidates for the "outside" instrumental variables would be the predetermined variables that appear in the system but not in the equation to be estimated. The number of these is K^{**}, which, in the case of an *exactly identified* structural equation, is just equal to $(G^{\Delta} - 1)$. Let $\underline{\mathbf{X}}_1$ be the matrix of the observed values of the excluded predetermined variables, i.e., let

$$\underline{\mathbf{X}}_1 = \begin{bmatrix} x_{K^*+1,1} & x_{K^*+2,1} & \cdots & x_{K1} \\ x_{K^*+1,2} & x_{K^*+2,2} & \cdots & x_{K2} \\ \vdots & \vdots & & \vdots \\ x_{K^*+1,T} & x_{K^*+2,T} & \cdots & x_{KT} \end{bmatrix}. \tag{13.24}$$

The order in which these variables are arranged is immaterial. Then the instrumental variables for our structural equation can be taken as

$$\mathbf{W}_1 = [\underline{\mathbf{X}}_1 \quad \mathbf{X}_1]. \tag{13.25}$$

Therefore,

$$\mathbf{W}_1'\mathbf{Z}_1 = \begin{bmatrix} \underline{\mathbf{X}}_1' \\ \mathbf{X}_1' \end{bmatrix} [\mathbf{Y}_1 \quad \mathbf{X}_1] = \begin{bmatrix} \underline{\mathbf{X}}_1'\mathbf{Y}_1 & \underline{\mathbf{X}}_1'\mathbf{X}_1 \\ \mathbf{X}_1'\mathbf{Y}_1 & \mathbf{X}_1'\mathbf{X}_1 \end{bmatrix},$$

and

$$\mathbf{W}_1'\mathbf{y}_1 = \begin{bmatrix} \underline{\mathbf{X}}_1'\mathbf{y}_1 \\ \mathbf{X}_1'\mathbf{y}_1 \end{bmatrix}.$$

Hence the instrumental variables estimator of the structural coefficients in the exactly identified case is

$$\boldsymbol{\alpha}_1^\dagger = \begin{bmatrix} \boldsymbol{\beta}_1^\dagger \\ \boldsymbol{\gamma}_1^\dagger \end{bmatrix} = \begin{bmatrix} \underline{\mathbf{X}}_1'\mathbf{Y}_1 & \underline{\mathbf{X}}_1'\mathbf{X}_1 \\ \mathbf{X}_1'\mathbf{Y}_1 & \mathbf{X}_1'\mathbf{X}_1 \end{bmatrix}^{-1} \begin{bmatrix} \underline{\mathbf{X}}_1'\mathbf{y}_1 \\ \mathbf{X}_1'\mathbf{y}_1 \end{bmatrix}. \tag{13.26}$$

Further, following (13.22) and (13.23) we define a consistent estimator of the variance-covariance matrix of $\boldsymbol{\alpha}^\dagger$ as

$$\text{Est. Var-Cov}(\boldsymbol{\alpha}^\dagger) = s_{11} \begin{bmatrix} \underline{\mathbf{X}}_1'\mathbf{Y}_1 & \underline{\mathbf{X}}_1'\mathbf{X}_1 \\ \mathbf{X}_1\mathbf{Y}_1 & \mathbf{X}_1'\mathbf{X}_1 \end{bmatrix}^{-1} \begin{bmatrix} \underline{\mathbf{X}}_1'\underline{\mathbf{X}}_1 & \underline{\mathbf{X}}_1'\mathbf{X}_1 \\ \mathbf{X}_1'\underline{\mathbf{X}}_1 & \mathbf{X}_1'\mathbf{X}_1 \end{bmatrix} \begin{bmatrix} \mathbf{Y}_1'\underline{\mathbf{X}}_1 & \mathbf{Y}_1'\mathbf{X}_1 \\ \mathbf{X}_1'\underline{\mathbf{X}}_1 & \mathbf{X}_1'\mathbf{X}_1 \end{bmatrix}^{-1}, \tag{13.27}$$

where s_{11} is determined as in (13.23).

The instrumental variables estimator (13.26) is, in fact, *exactly the same* as the indirect least squares estimator described earlier. We shall not give a general proof of this proposition, but we will demonstrate its validity with reference to the supply equation of the supply-demand model (13.1). This equation,

$$Q_t = \beta_1 + \beta_2 P_t + \varepsilon_{2t},$$

is exactly identified, with Y_t being the excluded predetermined variable. In terms of the notation used for instrumental variables estimation, we have

$$\mathbf{Z}_1 = [\mathbf{P} \quad \boldsymbol{\iota}],$$

$$\mathbf{W}_1 = [\mathbf{Y} \quad \boldsymbol{\iota}],$$

$$\mathbf{y}_1 = [\mathbf{Q}],$$

where

$$\underset{(T\times 1)}{\mathbf{Q} = \begin{bmatrix} Q_1 \\ Q_2 \\ \vdots \\ Q_T \end{bmatrix}}, \quad \underset{(T\times 1)}{\mathbf{P} = \begin{bmatrix} P_1 \\ P_2 \\ \vdots \\ P_T \end{bmatrix}}, \quad \underset{(T\times 1)}{\mathbf{Y} = \begin{bmatrix} Y_1 \\ Y_2 \\ \vdots \\ Y_T \end{bmatrix}}, \quad \underset{(T\times 1)}{\boldsymbol{\iota} = \begin{bmatrix} 1 \\ 1 \\ \vdots \\ 1 \end{bmatrix}}.$$

Then

$$\mathbf{W}_1'\mathbf{Z}_1 = \begin{bmatrix} \mathbf{Y}' \\ \boldsymbol{\iota}' \end{bmatrix} [\mathbf{P} \quad \boldsymbol{\iota}] = \begin{bmatrix} \sum_t P_t Y_t & \sum_t Y_t \\ \sum_t P_t & T \end{bmatrix},$$

and

$$\mathbf{W}_1'\mathbf{y}_1 = \begin{bmatrix} \mathbf{Y}' \\ \boldsymbol{\iota}' \end{bmatrix} [\mathbf{Q}] = \begin{bmatrix} \sum_t Q_t Y_t \\ \sum_t Q_t \end{bmatrix}.$$

Therefore, by (13.21) we have

$$(13.28) \quad \begin{bmatrix} \beta_2^\dagger \\ \beta_1^\dagger \end{bmatrix} = \frac{1}{T \sum P_t Y_t - (\sum P_t)(\sum Y_t)} \begin{bmatrix} T & -\sum_t Y_t \\ -\sum_t P_t & \sum_t P_t Y_t \end{bmatrix} \begin{bmatrix} \sum_t Q_t Y_t \\ \sum_t Q_t \end{bmatrix}$$

$$= \begin{bmatrix} \dfrac{m_{QY}}{m_{PY}} \\ \bar{Q} - \left(\dfrac{m_{QY}}{m_{PY}}\right) \bar{P} \end{bmatrix}.$$

Clearly, these formulas are exactly the same as the indirect least squares formulas.

The equivalence of the indirect least squares and the instrumental variables estimator enables us to use the instrumental variables formula for the asymptotic variance-covariance matrix of the estimated coefficients. This is very useful since the derivation of the asymptotic variance-covariance matrix of the indirect least squares estimator is otherwise awkward. For example, consider estimating the variance-covariance matrix of the estimated coefficients of the supply equation discussed in (13.1). By appropriate substitution into (13.27) we obtain

(13.29) $$\text{Est. Var-Cov}\begin{bmatrix}\beta_2^\dagger\\ \beta_1^\dagger\end{bmatrix}$$

$$= s_{22}\begin{bmatrix}\sum_t P_tY_t & \sum_t Y_t\\ \sum_t P_t & T\end{bmatrix}^{-1}\begin{bmatrix}\sum_t Y_t^2 & \sum_t Y_t\\ \sum_t Y_t & T\end{bmatrix}\begin{bmatrix}\sum_t P_tY_t & \sum_t P_t\\ \sum_t Y_t & T\end{bmatrix}^{-1}$$

$$= \frac{s_{22}}{(Tm_{PY})^2}\begin{bmatrix}T^2m_{YY} & -T(\sum P_t)m_{YY}\\ -T(\sum P_t)m_{YY} & (\sum P_t)^2m_{YY} + Tm_{PY}^2\end{bmatrix}$$

$$= s_{22}\begin{bmatrix}\left(\dfrac{m_{YY}}{m_{PY}^2}\right) & \left(\dfrac{-\bar{P}m_{YY}}{m_{PY}^2}\right)\\ \left(\dfrac{-\bar{P}m_{YY}}{m_{PY}^2}\right) & \left(\dfrac{\bar{P}^2m_{YY}}{m_{PY}^2} + \dfrac{1}{T}\right)\end{bmatrix},$$

where

(13.30) $$s_{22} = \frac{1}{T-2}\sum_t (Q_t - \beta_1^\dagger - \beta_2^\dagger P_t)^2$$

$$= \frac{1}{T-2}\left(\frac{m_{QQ}m_{PY}^2 - 2m_{QY}m_{QP}m_{PY} + m_{PP}m_{QY}^2}{m_{PY}^2}\right).$$

EXAMPLE The supply equation in (13.1) can be estimated from the annual data on the American meat market for the period 1919–1941.[3]

Q_t = per capita consumption of meat (pounds);

P_t = retail prices of meat (index, 1935–39 = 100);

Y_t = per capita disposable real income (dollars).

The sample means of these variables are

$$\bar{Q} = 166.1913,$$

$$\bar{P} = 92.3391,$$

$$\bar{Y} = 495.5652;$$

the sums of squares and cross-products of the deviations from sample means are

$$m_{QQ} = 1{,}369.53826, \qquad m_{PP} = 1{,}581.49478,$$

$$m_{QP} = -352.55217, \qquad m_{PY} = 8{,}354.59130,$$

$$m_{QY} = 3{,}671.91304, \qquad m_{YY} = 83{,}433.65217.$$

[3] From G. Tintner, *Econometrics* (New York: Wiley, 1965), p. 169.

The indirect least squares estimates of the structural coefficients of the supply equation are as follows:

$$\tilde{\beta}_2 = \frac{3{,}671.91304}{8{,}354.59130} = 0.43951,$$

$$\tilde{\beta}_1 = 166.1913 - 0.43951 \times 92.3391 = 125.60749.$$

The estimate of the variance of the structural disturbance, calculated according to (13.30), is

$$s_{22} = \frac{1{,}984.9311}{21} = 94.5205.$$

The estimated variances of the indirect least squares estimates are then obtained from (13.29) as follows:

$$\text{Est. Var}(\tilde{\beta}_2) = 94.5205\left(\frac{83{,}433.65217}{8{,}354.59130^2}\right) = 0.11298318,$$

$$\text{Est. Var}(\tilde{\beta}_1) = 94.5205\left(\frac{92.3391^2 \times 83{,}433.65217}{8{,}354.59130^2} + \frac{1}{23}\right) = 10.23547072.$$

Thus the final result of indirect least squares estimation is

$$\underset{}{Q_t} = \underset{(3.19929)}{125.60749} + \underset{(0.33613)}{0.43951}P_t + \hat{\varepsilon}_{2t}.$$

For comparison we also present the (inconsistent) ordinary least squares estimates of the supply equation:

$$Q_t = 145.60676 - 0.22292P_t + e_{2t}.$$

The estimation of an *exactly identified* structural equation when identification is achieved by *restrictions on the variance-covariance matrix* of the structural disturbances, can also be examined in the context of the supply-demand model (13.1). The demand equation

$$Q_t = \alpha_1 + \alpha_2 P_t + \alpha_3 Y_t + \varepsilon_{1t}$$

—which, in the case of no restrictions on the variance-covariance matrix of the disturbances, is underidentified—becomes exactly identified if we assume that ε_{1t} and ε_{2t} are uncorrelated, as discussed in Section 13–2. The identifying relations between the structural coefficients and the reduced form parameters are as follows. First, by substituting the reduced form expressions for Q_t and P_t into the demand equation, we obtain

(13.31) $$\pi_{11} = \alpha_1 + \alpha_2\pi_{21},$$

(13.32) $$\pi_{12} = \alpha_2\pi_{22} + \alpha_3.$$

Next, from (13.18) we know that

$$\psi_{11} - \alpha_2\psi_{12} - \beta_2\psi_{12} + \alpha_2\beta_2\psi_{22} = 0,$$

where the ψ's are the elements of the variance-covariance matrix of the reduced form disturbances and β_2 is a structural coefficient of the supply equation. Since from the results for the supply equation we get

$$\beta_2 = \frac{\pi_{12}}{\pi_{22}},$$

we can write

$$\alpha_2 = \frac{\pi_{12}\psi_{12} - \pi_{21}\psi_{11}}{\pi_{12}\psi_{22} - \pi_{22}\psi_{12}}. \tag{13.33}$$

Equations (13.31), (13.32), and (13.33) enable us to express the structural coefficients α_1, α_2, and α_3 in terms of the π's and ψ's of the reduced form equations. The reduced form parameters can be estimated by application of the ordinary least squares formulas. From the estimates of the reduced form parameters we can determine the corresponding estimates of the α's. Since both equations are now exactly identified, these estimates are maximum likelihood estimates, and their asymptotic variance-covariance matrix can be determined by reference to the information matrix for the appropriate likelihood function. Note that the likelihood function for the sample observations on Q_t and P_t of our supply-demand model is

$$L = -T\log(2\pi) - \frac{T}{2}\log(\sigma_{11}\sigma_{22}) + T\log|\alpha_2 - \beta_2|$$
$$- \frac{\sum_t (Q_t - \alpha_1 - \alpha_2 P_t - \alpha_3 Y_t)^2}{2\sigma_{11}} - \frac{\sum_t (Q_t - \beta_1 - \beta_2 P_t)^2}{2\sigma_{22}}.$$

Example We will estimate the demand equation of (13.1) on the assumption of zero covariance between ε_{1t} and ε_{2t} from the data on the American meat market given in the preceding example. First, note that the ordinary least squares estimators of the reduced form coefficients are

$$\hat{\pi}_{12} = \frac{m_{QY}}{m_{YY}},$$
$$\hat{\pi}_{11} = \bar{Q} - \hat{\pi}_{12}\bar{Y},$$
$$\hat{\pi}_{22} = \frac{m_{PY}}{m_{YY}},$$
$$\hat{\pi}_{21} = \bar{P} - \hat{\pi}_{22}\bar{Y}.$$

The variances and the covariance of the reduced form disturbances are estimated as follows:

$$\hat{\psi}_{11} = \frac{m_{QQ} - \hat{\pi}_{12}m_{QY}}{T} = \frac{m_{QQ}m_{YY} - m_{QY}^2}{Tm_{YY}},$$
$$\hat{\psi}_{22} = \frac{m_{PP} - \hat{\pi}_{22}m_{PY}}{T} = \frac{m_{PP}m_{YY} - m_{PY}^2}{Tm_{YY}},$$
$$\hat{\psi}_{12} = \frac{m_{QP} - \hat{\pi}_{12}m_{PY} - \hat{\pi}_{22}m_{QY} + \hat{\pi}_{12}\hat{\pi}_{22}m_{YY}}{T} = \frac{m_{QP}m_{YY} - m_{QY}m_{PY}}{Tm_{YY}}.$$

By substituting these results into (13.33) we find, after some simplifications,

$$\tilde{\alpha}_2 = \frac{m_{QY}m_{QP} - m_{QQ}m_{PY}}{m_{QY}m_{PP} - m_{QP}m_{PY}}$$

$$= \frac{3{,}671.91304 \times (-352.55217) - 1{,}369.53826 \times 8{,}354.59130}{3{,}671.91304 \times 1{,}581.49478 - (-352.55217) \times 8{,}354.59130} = -1.4551.$$

Further, from (13.31), we have

$$\tilde{\alpha}_1 = \hat{\pi}_{11} - \tilde{\alpha}_2\hat{\pi}_{21} = 206.5374,$$

and from (13.32),

$$\tilde{\alpha}_3 = \hat{\pi}_{12} - \tilde{\alpha}_2\hat{\pi}_{22} = 0.1897.$$

Therefore, the estimated demand equation is

$$Q_t = 206.5374 - 1.4551P_t + 0.1897Y_t + \hat{\varepsilon}_{1t}.$$

Under the assumptions of the model, these estimates are consistent and asymptotically efficient. For comparison we also present the ordinary least squares estimates, which are not consistent:

$$Q_t = 185.8452 - 0.9739P_t + 0.1418Y_t + e_{1t}.$$

Two-Stage Least Squares Estimation

In estimating an *overidentified* structural equation belonging to a general interdependent system of equations, there are several methods leading to consistent estimation that can be used. Probably the best-known single equation method is that of *two-stage least squares*. Suppose the overidentified structural equation is the first equation of the system:

$$\text{(13.34)} \qquad \mathbf{y}_1 = \mathbf{Y}_1\boldsymbol{\beta}_1 + \mathbf{X}_1\boldsymbol{\gamma}_1 + \mathbf{u}_1,$$

where $\mathbf{y}_1$ is a $(T \times 1)$ vector of the endogenous variable whose coefficient in the first equation is one, $\mathbf{Y}_1$ is a $T \times (G^\Delta - 1)$ matrix of the remaining endogenous variables in the first equation, $\mathbf{X}_1$ is a $(T \times K^*)$ matrix of the predetermined variables in the first equation, and $\mathbf{u}_1$ is a $(T \times 1)$ vector of the disturbances in this equation. An alternative way of writing (13.34) is

$$\text{(13.34a)} \qquad \mathbf{y}_1 = \mathbf{Z}_1\boldsymbol{\alpha}_1 + \mathbf{u}_1,$$

where

$$\mathbf{Z}_1 = [\mathbf{Y}_1 \quad \mathbf{X}_1] \quad \text{and} \quad \boldsymbol{\alpha}_1 = \begin{bmatrix} \boldsymbol{\beta}_1 \\ \boldsymbol{\gamma}_1 \end{bmatrix}.$$

The matrix $\mathbf{Y}_1$ can be partitioned to give

$$\mathbf{Y}_1 = [\mathbf{y}_2 \quad \mathbf{y}_3 \quad \cdots \quad \mathbf{y}_{G^\Delta}],$$

where each of the y's is a vector of order $T\times 1$. The reduced form equations for these variables are

$$\mathbf{y}_2 = \mathbf{X}\boldsymbol{\pi}_2 + \mathbf{v}_2,$$
$$\mathbf{y}_3 = \mathbf{X}\boldsymbol{\pi}_3 + \mathbf{v}_3,$$
$$\vdots$$
$$\mathbf{y}_{G^\Delta} = \mathbf{X}\boldsymbol{\pi}_{G^\Delta} + \mathbf{v}_{G^\Delta},$$

where **X** is a $(T\times K)$ matrix of *all* predetermined variables in the system, each of the $\boldsymbol{\pi}$'s represents a $(K\times 1)$ vector of the corresponding reduced form coefficients, and each of the **v**'s is a $(T\times 1)$ vector of the corresponding reduced form disturbances. Let

$$\mathbf{V}_1 = [\mathbf{v}_2 \quad \mathbf{v}_3 \quad \ldots \quad \mathbf{v}_{G^\Delta}]$$

and
$$\mathbf{Y}_1 - \mathbf{V}_1 = [\mathbf{X}\boldsymbol{\pi}_2 \quad \mathbf{X}\boldsymbol{\pi}_3 \quad \ldots \quad \mathbf{X}\boldsymbol{\pi}_{G^\Delta}].$$

Therefore (13.34) can be written as

(13.35) $$\mathbf{y}_1 = (\mathbf{Y}_1 - \mathbf{V}_1)\boldsymbol{\beta}_1 + \mathbf{X}_1\boldsymbol{\gamma}_1 + (\mathbf{u}_1 + \mathbf{V}_1\boldsymbol{\beta}_1).$$

Since $(\mathbf{Y}_1 - \mathbf{V}_1)$ depends only on **X** and does not involve any disturbance, it is uncorrelated with $(\mathbf{u}_1 + \mathbf{V}_1\boldsymbol{\beta}_1)$. Thus applying the ordinary least squares method to (13.35) would lead to consistent estimates of $\boldsymbol{\beta}_1$ and $\boldsymbol{\gamma}_1$. The difficulty is that $\mathbf{V}_1$—and therefore $(\mathbf{Y}_1 - \mathbf{V}_1)$—is not observable. However, we can replace $\mathbf{V}_1$ by the corresponding reduced form least squares residuals and use

$$\mathbf{Y}_1 - \hat{\mathbf{V}}_1 = \hat{\mathbf{Y}}_1 = [\mathbf{X}\hat{\boldsymbol{\pi}}_2 \quad \mathbf{X}\hat{\boldsymbol{\pi}}_3 \quad \ldots \quad \mathbf{X}\hat{\boldsymbol{\pi}}_{G^\Delta}].$$

Clearly,

$$\text{plim}\,(\mathbf{Y}_1 - \hat{\mathbf{V}}_1) = [\mathbf{X}\boldsymbol{\pi}_2 \quad \mathbf{X}\boldsymbol{\pi}_3 \quad \ldots \quad \mathbf{X}\boldsymbol{\pi}_{G^\Delta}] = \mathbf{Y}_1 - \mathbf{V}_1,$$

so that $(\mathbf{Y}_1 - \hat{\mathbf{V}}_1)$ and $(\mathbf{u}_1 + \hat{\mathbf{V}}_1\boldsymbol{\beta}_1)$ are *asymptotically uncorrelated.* Therefore, if we apply the ordinary least squares method to

(13.36) $$\mathbf{y}_1 = \hat{\mathbf{Y}}_1\boldsymbol{\beta}_1 + \mathbf{X}_1\boldsymbol{\gamma}_1 + \mathbf{u}_1^*,$$

where $$\mathbf{u}_1^* = \mathbf{u}_1 + \hat{\mathbf{V}}_1\boldsymbol{\beta}_1,$$

we obtain consistent estimates of $\boldsymbol{\beta}_1$ and $\boldsymbol{\gamma}_1$. These estimates are called "two-stage least squares" because the estimation process may be viewed as consisting of two successive applications of the ordinary least squares method. In the first stage we estimate the reduced form equations for $\mathbf{y}_2, \mathbf{y}_3, \ldots, \mathbf{y}_{G^\Delta}$ and calculate the fitted values of these variables. In the second stage we apply the least squares method to (13.36) where the fitted values of $\mathbf{y}_2, \mathbf{y}_3, \ldots, \mathbf{y}_{G^\Delta}$ are used as explanatory variables.

By analogy with (13.34a), equation (13.36) could also be written as

(13.36a) $$\mathbf{y}_1 = \hat{\mathbf{Z}}_1\boldsymbol{\alpha}_1 + \mathbf{u}_1^*,$$

where $$\hat{\mathbf{Z}}_1 = [\hat{\mathbf{Y}}_1 \quad \mathbf{X}_1].$$

The application of the least squares method to (13.36a) leads to

$$\text{(13.37)} \qquad \tilde{\boldsymbol{\alpha}}_1 = \begin{bmatrix} \tilde{\boldsymbol{\beta}}_1 \\ \tilde{\boldsymbol{\gamma}}_1 \end{bmatrix} = (\hat{\mathbf{Z}}'\hat{\mathbf{Z}})^{-1}(\hat{\mathbf{Z}}\mathbf{y}_1) = \begin{bmatrix} \hat{\mathbf{Y}}_1'\hat{\mathbf{Y}}_1 & \hat{\mathbf{Y}}_1'\mathbf{X}_1 \\ \mathbf{X}_1'\hat{\mathbf{Y}}_1 & \mathbf{X}_1'\mathbf{X}_1 \end{bmatrix}^{-1} \begin{bmatrix} \hat{\mathbf{Y}}_1'\mathbf{y}_1 \\ \mathbf{X}_1'\mathbf{y}_1 \end{bmatrix}.$$

(In what follows we make use of the fact that ordinary least squares residuals are orthogonal to the fitted value of the dependent variable and to each explanatory variable. This implies that $\hat{\mathbf{V}}_1'\hat{\mathbf{Y}}_1 = \mathbf{0}$ and $\hat{\mathbf{V}}_1'\mathbf{X}_1 = \mathbf{0}$.) Since

$$\begin{aligned} \hat{\mathbf{Y}}_1'\hat{\mathbf{Y}}_1 &= (\mathbf{Y}_1 - \hat{\mathbf{V}}_1)'(\mathbf{Y}_1 - \hat{\mathbf{V}}_1) = \mathbf{Y}_1'\mathbf{Y}_1 - \hat{\mathbf{V}}_1'\mathbf{Y}_1 - \mathbf{Y}_1'\hat{\mathbf{V}}_1 + \hat{\mathbf{V}}_1'\hat{\mathbf{V}}_1 \\ &= \mathbf{Y}_1'\mathbf{Y}_1 + \hat{\mathbf{V}}_1'(\hat{\mathbf{Y}}_1 + \hat{\mathbf{V}}_1) - (\hat{\mathbf{Y}}_1 + \hat{\mathbf{V}}_1)'\hat{\mathbf{V}}_1 + \hat{\mathbf{V}}_1'\hat{\mathbf{V}}_1 \\ &= \mathbf{Y}_1'\mathbf{Y}_1 - \hat{\mathbf{V}}_1'\hat{\mathbf{V}}_1 - \hat{\mathbf{V}}_1'\hat{\mathbf{V}}_1 + \hat{\mathbf{V}}_1'\hat{\mathbf{V}}_1 = \mathbf{Y}_1'\mathbf{Y}_1 - \hat{\mathbf{V}}_1'\hat{\mathbf{V}}_1, \\ \hat{\mathbf{Y}}_1'\mathbf{X}_1 &= (\mathbf{Y}_1 - \hat{\mathbf{V}}_1)'\mathbf{X}_1 = \mathbf{Y}_1'\mathbf{X}_1, \\ \mathbf{X}_1'\hat{\mathbf{Y}}_1 &= \mathbf{X}_1'(\mathbf{Y}_1 - \hat{\mathbf{V}}_1) = \mathbf{X}_1'\mathbf{Y}_1, \end{aligned}$$

and $\quad \hat{\mathbf{Y}}_1'\mathbf{y}_1 = (\mathbf{Y}_1 - \hat{\mathbf{V}}_1)'\mathbf{y}_1 = \mathbf{Y}_1'\mathbf{y}_1 - \hat{\mathbf{V}}'\mathbf{y}_1,$

equation (13.37) can be written as

$$\text{(13.38)} \qquad \tilde{\boldsymbol{\alpha}}_1 = \begin{bmatrix} \tilde{\boldsymbol{\beta}}_1 \\ \tilde{\boldsymbol{\gamma}}_1 \end{bmatrix} = \begin{bmatrix} \mathbf{Y}_1'\mathbf{Y}_1 - \hat{\mathbf{V}}_1'\hat{\mathbf{V}}_1 & \mathbf{Y}_1'\mathbf{X}_1 \\ \mathbf{X}_1'\mathbf{Y}_1 & \mathbf{X}_1'\mathbf{X}_1 \end{bmatrix}^{-1} \begin{bmatrix} \mathbf{Y}_1'\mathbf{y}_1 - \hat{\mathbf{V}}_1'\mathbf{y}_1 \\ \mathbf{X}_1'\mathbf{y}_1 \end{bmatrix}.$$

This is the form in which the formula for the two-stage least squares estimator is usually presented because it shows clearly how this estimator differs from the (inconsistent) ordinary least squares estimator, which is given as

$$\text{(13.39)} \qquad \hat{\boldsymbol{\alpha}}_1 = \begin{bmatrix} \hat{\boldsymbol{\beta}}_1 \\ \tilde{\boldsymbol{\gamma}}_1 \end{bmatrix} = \begin{bmatrix} \mathbf{Y}_1'\mathbf{Y}_1 & \mathbf{Y}_1'\mathbf{X}_1 \\ \mathbf{X}_1'\mathbf{Y}_1 & \mathbf{X}_1'\mathbf{X}_1 \end{bmatrix}^{-1} \begin{bmatrix} \mathbf{Y}_1'\mathbf{y}_1 \\ \mathbf{X}_1'\mathbf{y}_1 \end{bmatrix}.$$

The two-stage least squares estimator can also be presented as an *instrumental variables estimator*, with $\hat{\mathbf{Y}}_1$ serving as an instrument for $\mathbf{Y}_1$, and $\mathbf{X}_1$ serving as its own instrument. This can be shown as follows. According to (13.21), an instrumental variables estimator of the coefficients of the first structural equation is

$$\boldsymbol{\alpha}_1^\dagger = (\mathbf{W}_1'\mathbf{Z}_1)^{-1}(\mathbf{W}_1'\mathbf{y}_1),$$

where $\mathbf{W}_1$ is a matrix of the instrumental variables. By putting

$$\mathbf{W}_1 = [\hat{\mathbf{Y}}_1 \quad \mathbf{X}_1]$$

we obtain

$$\mathbf{W}_1'\mathbf{Z}_1 = \begin{bmatrix} \hat{\mathbf{Y}}_1' \\ \mathbf{X}_1' \end{bmatrix} [\mathbf{Y}_1 \quad \mathbf{X}_1] = \begin{bmatrix} \hat{\mathbf{Y}}_1'\mathbf{Y}_1 & \hat{\mathbf{Y}}_1'\mathbf{X}_1 \\ \mathbf{X}_1'\mathbf{Y}_1 & \mathbf{X}_1'\mathbf{X}_1 \end{bmatrix},$$

and $\quad \mathbf{W}_1'\mathbf{y}_1 = \begin{bmatrix} \hat{\mathbf{Y}}_1'\mathbf{y}_1 \\ \mathbf{X}_1'\mathbf{y}_1 \end{bmatrix}.$

But

$$\hat{\mathbf{Y}}'\mathbf{Y}_1 = (\mathbf{Y}_1 - \hat{\mathbf{V}}_1)'\mathbf{Y}_1 = \mathbf{Y}_1'\mathbf{Y}_1 - \hat{\mathbf{V}}_1'(\hat{\mathbf{Y}}_1 + \hat{\mathbf{V}}_1) = \mathbf{Y}_1'\mathbf{Y}_1 - \hat{\mathbf{V}}_1'\hat{\mathbf{V}}_1,$$

and, from previous results,

$$\hat{\mathbf{Y}}_1'\mathbf{X}_1 = \mathbf{Y}_1'\mathbf{X}_1,$$

$$\hat{\mathbf{Y}}_1'\mathbf{y}_1 = \mathbf{Y}_1'\mathbf{y}_1 - \hat{\mathbf{V}}_1'\mathbf{y}_1.$$

Therefore,

$$\boldsymbol{\alpha}_1^\dagger = \begin{bmatrix} \mathbf{Y}_1'\mathbf{Y}_1 - \hat{\mathbf{V}}_1'\hat{\mathbf{V}}_1 & \mathbf{Y}_1'\mathbf{X}_1 \\ \mathbf{X}_1'\mathbf{Y}_1 & \mathbf{X}_1'\mathbf{X}_1 \end{bmatrix}^{-1} \begin{bmatrix} \mathbf{Y}_1'\mathbf{y}_1 - \hat{\mathbf{V}}_1'\mathbf{y}_1 \\ \mathbf{X}_1'\mathbf{y}_1 \end{bmatrix}, \tag{13.40}$$

which is precisely the same formula as that for $\tilde{\boldsymbol{\alpha}}_1$ given by (13.38). Because of the equivalence of $\boldsymbol{\alpha}_1^\dagger$ and $\tilde{\boldsymbol{\alpha}}_1$, we can use formula (13.22) to estimate the asymptotic variance-covariance matrix of the two-stage least squares estimator. This gives

$$\text{Est. Var-Cov}(\tilde{\boldsymbol{\alpha}}_1) = s_{11}(\mathbf{W}_1'\mathbf{Z}_1)^{-1}(\mathbf{W}_1'\mathbf{W}_1)(\mathbf{Z}_1'\mathbf{W}_1)^{-1} = s_{11}(\mathbf{W}_1'\mathbf{Z}_1)^{-1} \tag{13.41}$$

$$= s_{11}\begin{bmatrix} \mathbf{Y}_1'\mathbf{Y}_1 - \hat{\mathbf{V}}_1'\hat{\mathbf{V}}_1 & \mathbf{Y}_1'\mathbf{X}_1 \\ \mathbf{X}_1'\mathbf{Y}_1 & \mathbf{X}_1'\mathbf{X}_1 \end{bmatrix}^{-1}.$$

Since $\sigma_{11} = \text{Var}(u_{1t})$, a consistent estimator of σ_{11} is, according to (13.23),

$$s_{11} = \frac{(\mathbf{y}_1 - \mathbf{Y}_1\tilde{\boldsymbol{\beta}}_1 - \mathbf{X}_1\tilde{\boldsymbol{\gamma}}_1)'(\mathbf{Y}_1 - \mathbf{Y}_1\tilde{\boldsymbol{\beta}}_1 - \mathbf{X}_1\tilde{\boldsymbol{\gamma}}_1)}{T - G^\Delta + 1 - K^*}. \tag{13.42}$$

The two-stage least squares estimator, although consistent, is in general not asymptotically efficient because it does not take into account the correlation of the structural disturbances across equations. However, its construction does not require a complete knowledge of the whole system; all that is needed is a listing of all predetermined variables and their sample values.

When the two-stage least squares method is applied to an exactly identified equation, the resulting estimates are the same as those obtained by the indirect least squares method. This can be proved as follows. The two-stage least squares estimator can be presented as

$$\tilde{\boldsymbol{\alpha}}_1 = (\mathbf{W}_1'\mathbf{Z}_1)^{-1}(\mathbf{W}_1'\mathbf{y}_1),$$

where $\mathbf{W}_1 = [\hat{\mathbf{Y}}_1 \quad \mathbf{X}_1]$ and $\mathbf{Z}_1 = [\mathbf{Y}_1 \quad \mathbf{X}_1]$.

Now, we can write

$$\hat{\mathbf{Y}}_1 = \underline{\mathbf{X}}_1\mathbf{A}, \tag{13.43}$$

where $\underline{\mathbf{X}}_1$ is a $(T \times K^{**})$ matrix of the excluded predetermined variables as defined by (13.24), and $\mathbf{A}$ is a $(K^{**} \times K^{**})$ matrix defined as

$$\mathbf{A} = (\underline{\mathbf{X}}_1'\underline{\mathbf{X}}_1)^{-1}(\underline{\mathbf{X}}_1'\mathbf{Y}_1).$$

Of course, the equation to be estimated has to be exactly identified; i.e., it is required that $K^{**} = G^{\Delta} - 1$, otherwise the dimension of $(\underline{\mathbf{X}}_1\mathbf{A})$ would not be the same as that of $\hat{\mathbf{Y}}_1$. The legitimacy of (13.43) can be established by substituting for $\mathbf{A}$ and premultiplying both sides by $\underline{\mathbf{X}}_1'$:

$$\underline{\mathbf{X}}_1'\hat{\mathbf{Y}}_1 = \underline{\mathbf{X}}_1'\underline{\mathbf{X}}_1(\underline{\mathbf{X}}_1'\underline{\mathbf{X}}_1)^{-1}(\underline{\mathbf{X}}_1'\mathbf{Y}) = \underline{\mathbf{X}}_1'\mathbf{Y}_1 = \underline{\mathbf{X}}_1'(\hat{\mathbf{Y}}_1 + \hat{\mathbf{V}}_1) = \underline{\mathbf{X}}_1'\hat{\mathbf{Y}}_1.$$

By substituting for $\hat{\mathbf{Y}}_1$ from (13.43) into the formula for $\tilde{\boldsymbol{\alpha}}_1$, we obtain

$$(13.44)\qquad \tilde{\boldsymbol{\alpha}}_1 = (\mathbf{W}_1'\mathbf{Z}_1)^{-1}(\mathbf{W}_1'\mathbf{y}_1) = \begin{bmatrix} \mathbf{A}'\underline{\mathbf{X}}_1'\mathbf{Y}_1 & \mathbf{A}'\underline{\mathbf{X}}_1'\mathbf{X}_1 \\ \mathbf{X}_1'\mathbf{Y}_1 & \mathbf{X}_1'\mathbf{X}_1 \end{bmatrix}^{-1} \begin{bmatrix} \mathbf{A}'\underline{\mathbf{X}}_1'\mathbf{y}_1 \\ \mathbf{X}_1'\mathbf{y}_1 \end{bmatrix}$$

$$= \left\{ \begin{bmatrix} \mathbf{A}' & \mathbf{0} \\ \mathbf{0} & \mathbf{I}_{K^*} \end{bmatrix} \begin{bmatrix} \underline{\mathbf{X}}_1'\mathbf{Y}_1 & \underline{\mathbf{X}}_1'\mathbf{X}_1 \\ \mathbf{X}_1'\mathbf{Y}_1 & \mathbf{X}_1'\mathbf{X}_1 \end{bmatrix} \right\}^{-1} \begin{bmatrix} \mathbf{A}' & \mathbf{0} \\ \mathbf{0} & \mathbf{I}_{K^*} \end{bmatrix} \begin{bmatrix} \underline{\mathbf{X}}_1'\mathbf{y}_1 \\ \mathbf{X}_1'\mathbf{y}_1 \end{bmatrix}$$

$$= \begin{bmatrix} \underline{\mathbf{X}}_1'\mathbf{Y}_1 & \underline{\mathbf{X}}_1'\mathbf{X}_1 \\ \mathbf{X}_1'\mathbf{Y}_1 & \mathbf{X}_1'\mathbf{X}_1 \end{bmatrix}^{-1} \begin{bmatrix} \underline{\mathbf{X}}_1'\mathbf{y}_1 \\ \mathbf{X}_1'\mathbf{y}_1 \end{bmatrix}.$$

This expression for $\tilde{\boldsymbol{\alpha}}_1$ is precisely the same as that for the indirect least squares estimator given by (13.26).

EXAMPLE Following is a simplified model designed to explain variations in the consumption and prices of food:

$$(13.45)\qquad Q_t = \alpha_1 + \alpha_2 P_t + \alpha_3 D_t + u_{1t} \qquad \text{(demand)},$$

$$Q_t = \beta_1 + \beta_2 P_t + \beta_3 F_t + \beta_4 A_t + u_{2t} \quad \text{(supply)}.$$

Here Q_t = food consumption per head, P_t = ratio of food prices to general consumer prices, D_t = disposable income in constant prices, F_t = ratio of preceding year's prices received by farmers for products to general consumer prices, and A_t = time in years. The variables Q_t and P_t are endogenous, while D_t, F_t, and A_t are predetermined. The demand equation is overidentified; the supply equation is exactly identified. Instead of estimating this model from actual data, we will *simulate* the sample observations on prices and quantities by presetting the values of the parameters, specifying the sample values of the predetermined variables, and drawing the values of the disturbances at random from a normal population. Using such an artificial sample, we may try various methods to compare the estimates of the parameters with their true values. Specifically, let the true model be

$$(13.45a)\qquad Q_t = 96.5 - 0.25P_t + 0.30D_t + u_{1t} \qquad \text{(demand)},$$

$$Q_t = 62.5 + 0.15P_t + 0.20F_t + 0.36A_t + u_{2t} \quad \text{(supply)}.$$

The true reduced form for this model is

$$(13.46)\qquad Q_t = 75.25 + 0.1125D_t + 0.125F_t + 0.225A_t + v_{1t},$$

$$P_t = 85.00 + 0.75D_t - 0.50F_t - 0.90A_t + v_{2t}.$$

Suppose now that we draw two sets of 20 values of random $N(0, 1)$ deviates from the table in Appendix D. Let us call the values belonging to the first set ε_{1t} and those belonging to the second set ε_{2t} ($t = 1, 2, \ldots, 20$). The values of the reduced form disturbances are then constructed as

$$v_{1t} = 2\varepsilon_{1t},$$

$$v_{2t} = -0.5\, v_{1t} + \varepsilon_{2t}.$$

This implies the following variance-covariance matrix of the reduced form disturbances:

$$\mathbf{\Psi} = \begin{bmatrix} 4 & -2 \\ -2 & 2 \end{bmatrix}.$$

Since for our model

$$u_{1t} = v_{1t} + 0.25 v_{2t},$$

$$u_{2t} = v_{1t} - 0.15 v_{2t},$$

the variance-covariance matrix of the structural disturbances is

$$\mathbf{\Phi} = \begin{bmatrix} 3.125 & 3.725 \\ 3.725 & 4.645 \end{bmatrix}.$$

The choice of the values of the elements of $\mathbf{\Psi}$ is, of course, arbitrary. The sample values of D_t and F_t are taken from a paper by Girschick and Haavelmo.[4] They represent actual values for the United States economy for the years 1922–1941, expressed in terms of index numbers with the average for 1935–39 = 100. The values of Q_t and P_t are calculated according to (13.46). The resulting sample data are given in Table 13–1. The ordinary least squares estimates of the reduced form equations are

$$Q_t = 72.2778 + 0.1126 D_t + 0.1646 F_t + 0.1648 A_t + \hat{v}_{1t}, \qquad R^2 = 0.7076,$$

$$P_t = 87.3149 + 0.7020 D_t - 0.5206 F_t - 0.5209 A_t + \hat{v}_{2t}, \qquad R^2 = 0.8719.$$

These may be compared with the true reduced form equations given by (13.46). Applying the two-stage least squares method to the structural equations in (13.45), we obtain

$$\underset{}{Q_t} = \underset{(7.9208)}{94.6333} - \underset{(0.0965)}{0.2436 P_t} + \underset{(0.0469)}{0.3140 D_t} + \tilde{u}_{1t} \qquad \text{(demand)},$$

$$Q_t = \underset{(12.0105)}{49.5324} + \underset{(0.0999)}{0.2401 P_t} + \underset{(0.0472)}{0.2556 F_t} + \underset{(0.0996)}{0.2529 A_t} + \tilde{u}_{2t} \qquad \text{(supply)}.$$

The figures in parentheses are the estimated standard errors. These results may be compared with the true structural equations (13.45a). It is also interesting to show the (inconsistent) ordinary least squares estimates of the two structural equations:

$$Q_t = 99.8954 - 0.3163 P_t + 0.3346 D_t + \hat{u}_{1t} \qquad \text{(demand)},$$
$$R^2 = 0.7638,$$

$$Q_t = 58.2754 + 0.1604 P_t + 0.2481 F_t + 0.2483 A_t + \hat{u}_{2t} \qquad \text{(supply)},$$
$$R^2 = 0.6548.$$

[4] M. A. Girschick and T. Haavelmo, "Statistical Analysis of the Demand for Food: Examples of Simultaneous Estimation of Structural Equations," *Econometrica*, Vol. 15, April 1947, pp. 79–110; reprinted in W. C. Hood and T. C. Koopmans (eds.), *Studies in Econometric Method* (New York: Wiley, 1953).

Table 13-1

Q_t	P_t	D_t	F_t	A_t
98.485	100.323	87.4	98.0	1
99.187	104.264	97.6	99.1	2
102.163	103.435	96.7	99.1	3
101.504	104.506	98.2	98.1	4
104.240	98.001	99.8	110.8	5
103.243	99.456	100.5	108.2	6
103.993	101.066	103.2	105.6	7
99.900	104.763	107.8	109.8	8
100.350	96.446	96.6	108.7	9
102.820	91.228	88.9	100.6	10
95.435	93.085	75.1	81.0	11
92.424	98.801	76.9	68.6	12
94.535	102.908	84.6	70.9	13
98.757	98.756	90.6	81.4	14
105.797	95.119	103.1	102.3	15
100.225	98.451	105.1	105.0	16
103.522	86.498	96.4	110.5	17
99.929	104.016	104.4	92.5	18
105.223	105.769	110.7	89.3	19
106.232	113.490	127.1	93.0	20

k-Class Estimators

The formula for the two-stage least squares estimator as given by (13.38) can be generalized to cover a whole class of different estimators. These estimators, known as *k-class estimators*, are defined as

$$(13.47)\quad \tilde{\boldsymbol{\alpha}}_1^{(k)} = \begin{bmatrix} \tilde{\boldsymbol{\beta}}_1^{(k)} \\ \boldsymbol{\gamma}_1^{(k)} \end{bmatrix} = \begin{bmatrix} \mathbf{Y}_1'\mathbf{Y}_1 - k\hat{\mathbf{V}}_1'\hat{\mathbf{V}}_1 & \mathbf{Y}_1'\mathbf{X}_1 \\ \mathbf{X}'\mathbf{Y}_1 & \mathbf{X}_1'\mathbf{X}_1 \end{bmatrix}^{-1} \begin{bmatrix} \mathbf{Y}_1'\mathbf{y}_1 - k\hat{\mathbf{V}}_1'\mathbf{y}_1 \\ \mathbf{X}_1'\mathbf{y}_1 \end{bmatrix}.$$

This formula differs from (13.38) only because $\hat{\mathbf{V}}_1'\hat{\mathbf{V}}_1$ and $\hat{\mathbf{V}}_1'\mathbf{y}_1$ are multiplied by a scalar k. This scalar can be set a priori to be equal to some number, or its value can be determined from the sample observations according to some rule. We have already encountered two k-class estimators; namely the two-stage least squares estimator for which $k = 1$, and the ordinary least squares estimator [given by (13.39)] for which $k = 0$. The fact that the ordinary least squares estimator belongs to the k-class indicates that not all k-class estimators are consistent. To find which values of k lead to consistent estimates, we first note that (13.47) can be formally expressed as a formula for an *instrumental variables estimator*. This can be shown as follows. An instrumental variables estimator of the first structural equation is, according to (13.21), defined as

$$\boldsymbol{\alpha}_1^{\dagger} = (\mathbf{W}_1'\mathbf{Z}_1)^{-1}(\mathbf{W}_1'\mathbf{y}_1),$$

where
$$\mathbf{Z}_1 = [\mathbf{Y}_1 \quad \mathbf{X}_1],$$

as before. By choosing the instrumental variables as

$$\mathbf{W}_1 = [(\mathbf{Y}_1 - k\hat{\mathbf{V}}_1) \quad \mathbf{X}_1],$$

we have

$$\boldsymbol{\alpha}_1^{\dagger} = \begin{bmatrix} (\mathbf{Y}_1 - k\hat{\mathbf{V}}_1)'\mathbf{Y}_1 & (\mathbf{Y}_1 - k\hat{\mathbf{V}}_1)'\mathbf{X}_1 \\ \mathbf{X}_1'\mathbf{Y}_1 & \mathbf{X}_1'\mathbf{X}_1 \end{bmatrix}^{-1} \begin{bmatrix} (\mathbf{Y}_1 - k\hat{\mathbf{V}}_1)'\mathbf{y}_1 \\ \mathbf{X}_1'\mathbf{y}_1 \end{bmatrix}.$$

However,

$$(\mathbf{Y}_1 - k\hat{\mathbf{V}}_1)'\mathbf{Y}_1 = \mathbf{Y}_1'\mathbf{Y}_1 - k\hat{\mathbf{V}}_1'(\hat{\mathbf{Y}}_1 + \hat{\mathbf{V}}_1) = \mathbf{Y}_1'\mathbf{Y}_1 - k\hat{\mathbf{V}}_1'\hat{\mathbf{V}}_1$$

$$(\mathbf{Y}_1 - k\hat{\mathbf{V}}_1)'\mathbf{X}_1 = \mathbf{Y}_1'\mathbf{X}_1 - k\hat{\mathbf{V}}_1'\mathbf{X}_1 = \mathbf{Y}_1'\mathbf{X}_1,$$

$$(\mathbf{Y}_1 - k\hat{\mathbf{V}}_1)'\mathbf{y}_1 = \mathbf{Y}_1'\mathbf{y}_1 - k\hat{\mathbf{V}}_1'\mathbf{y}_1;$$

therefore,

$$\text{(13.48)} \qquad \boldsymbol{\alpha}_1^{\dagger} = \begin{bmatrix} \mathbf{Y}_1'\mathbf{Y}_1 - k\hat{\mathbf{V}}_1'\hat{\mathbf{V}}_1 & \mathbf{Y}_1'\mathbf{X}_1 \\ \mathbf{X}_1'\mathbf{Y}_1 & \mathbf{X}_1'\mathbf{X}_1 \end{bmatrix}^{-1} \begin{bmatrix} \mathbf{Y}_1'\mathbf{y}_1 - k\hat{\mathbf{V}}_1'\mathbf{y}_1 \\ \mathbf{X}_1'\mathbf{y}_1 \end{bmatrix},$$

which is precisely the same as $\tilde{\boldsymbol{\alpha}}^{(k)}$ in (13.47). However, $\mathbf{W}_1$ does not qualify as a set of instrumental variables *unless* these variables are asymptotically uncorrelated with the structural disturbance $\mathbf{u}_1$, i.e., unless

$$\text{plim} \frac{1}{T} \mathbf{W}_1'\mathbf{u}_1 = \mathbf{0}.$$

That is, we require

$$\text{(13.49)} \qquad \text{plim} \frac{1}{T} (\mathbf{Y}_1 - k\hat{\mathbf{V}}_1)'\mathbf{u}_1 = \mathbf{0},$$

$$\text{(13.50)} \qquad \text{plim} \frac{1}{T} \mathbf{X}_1'\mathbf{u}_1 = \mathbf{0}.$$

Now (13.50) is always satisfied, since all predetermined variables are uncorrelated with the structural disturbances by definition. As for (13.49), we have

$$\text{(13.49a)} \quad \text{plim} \frac{1}{T} (\mathbf{Y}_1 - k\hat{\mathbf{V}}_1)'\mathbf{u}_1 = \text{plim} \frac{1}{T} \mathbf{Y}_1'\mathbf{u}_1 - \text{plim}\, k \cdot \text{plim}\, \hat{\mathbf{V}}_1'\mathbf{u}_1$$

$$= \text{plim} \frac{1}{T} (\hat{\mathbf{Y}}_1 + \hat{\mathbf{V}}_1)'\mathbf{u}_1 - \text{plim}\, k \cdot \text{plim}\, \hat{\mathbf{V}}_1'\mathbf{u}_1$$

$$= \text{plim} \frac{1}{T} \hat{\mathbf{V}}_1'\mathbf{u}_1 - \text{plim}\, k \cdot \text{plim}\, \hat{\mathbf{V}}_1'\mathbf{u}_1.$$

Since plim $(\hat{\mathbf{V}}_1'\mathbf{u}_1)/T$ is a finite number different from zero, it follows that

$$\text{plim} \frac{1}{T} (\mathbf{Y}_1 - k\hat{\mathbf{V}}_1)'\mathbf{u}_1 = 0$$

if and only if

$$\text{(13.51)} \qquad \text{plim}\, k = 1.$$

This condition is automatically fulfilled in the case of two-stage least squares estimation in which k is *always* equal to one. Further, it can be shown that the asymptotic variance-covariance matrix of all k-class estimators for which

$$\text{plim}\ \sqrt{T}(k - 1) = 0 \tag{13.52}$$

reduces to (13.41).[5] This means that all of these estimators must have the same asymptotic variance-covariance matrix as the two-stage least squares estimator. This matrix is usually estimated as follows:

$$\text{Est. Var-Cov}(\tilde{\boldsymbol{\alpha}}^{(k)}) = s_{11}\begin{bmatrix} \mathbf{Y}_1'\mathbf{Y}_1 - k\hat{\mathbf{V}}_1'\hat{\mathbf{V}}_1 & \mathbf{Y}_1'\mathbf{X}_1 \\ \mathbf{X}_1'\mathbf{Y}_1 & \mathbf{X}_1'\mathbf{X}_1 \end{bmatrix}^{-1} \tag{13.53}$$

where

$$s_{11} = \frac{(\mathbf{y}_1 - \mathbf{Z}_1\tilde{\boldsymbol{\alpha}}_1^{(k)})'(\mathbf{y}_1 - \mathbf{Z}_1\tilde{\boldsymbol{\alpha}}_1^{(k)})}{T - G^{\Delta} + 1 - K^*}. \tag{13.54}$$

This, of course, is asymptotically equivalent to (13.41).

Limited Information Maximum Likelihood Estimation

Another single equation estimator, which is known as the *limited information maximum likelihood estimator*, also belongs to the k-class family and is consistent. It is derived by maximizing the likelihood function for the observations on the endogenous variables included in the equation to be estimated. The phrase "limited information" means that, in setting up the likelihood function, we limit ourselves to those endogenous variables that appear in the equation under investigation and disregard the overidentifying restrictions on the other structural equations. Suppose this equation is again the first one of the system as described by (13.34):

$$\mathbf{y}_1 = \mathbf{Y}_1\boldsymbol{\beta}_1 + \mathbf{X}_1\boldsymbol{\gamma}_1 + \mathbf{u}_1,$$

where

$$\mathbf{Y}_1 = [\mathbf{y}_2 \quad \mathbf{y}_3 \quad \cdots \quad \mathbf{y}_{G^{\Delta}}].$$

Thus the included endogenous variables are $\mathbf{y}_{1t}, \mathbf{y}_{2t}, \ldots, \mathbf{y}_{G^{\Delta}t}$. The reduced form equations for these variables are

$$y_{1t} = \pi_{11}x_{1t} + \pi_{12}x_{2t} + \cdots + \pi_{1K}x_{Kt} + v_{1t},$$
$$y_{2t} = \pi_{21}x_{1t} + \pi_{22}x_{2t} + \cdots + \pi_{2K}x_{Kt} + v_{2t},$$
$$\vdots$$
$$y_{G^{\Delta}t} = \pi_{G^{\Delta}1}x_{1t} + \pi_{G^{\Delta}2}x_{2t} + \cdots + \pi_{G^{\Delta}K}x_{Kt} + v_{G^{\Delta}t}.$$

[5] See H. Theil, *Economic Forecasts and Policy*, 2nd ed. (Amsterdam: North-Holland Publishing Company, 1961), p. 232.

Since $v_{1t}, v_{2t}, \ldots, v_{G^{\Delta}t}$ are normally distributed stochastic disturbances, their joint distribution is[6]

$$f(v_{1t}, v_{2t}, \ldots, v_{G^{\Delta}t}) = (2\pi)^{-(G^{\Delta}/2)}|\mathbf{\Psi}_{\Delta}|^{-(1/2)}e^{-(1/2)\mathbf{v}'_{\Delta t}\mathbf{\Psi}_{\Delta}^{-1}\mathbf{v}_{\Delta t}}$$

where

$$\mathbf{v}_{\Delta t} = \begin{bmatrix} v_{1t} \\ v_{2t} \\ \vdots \\ v_{G^{\Delta}t} \end{bmatrix} \quad \text{and} \quad \mathbf{\Psi}_{\Delta} = E(\mathbf{v}_{\Delta}\mathbf{v}'_{\Delta}) = \begin{bmatrix} \psi_{11} & \psi_{12} & \cdots & \psi_{1G^{\Delta}} \\ \psi_{21} & \psi_{22} & \cdots & \psi_{2G^{\Delta}} \\ \vdots & \vdots & & \\ \psi_{G^{\Delta}1} & \psi_{G^{\Delta}2} & \cdots & \psi_{G^{\Delta}G^{\Delta}} \end{bmatrix}.$$

Under the classical assumptions concerning disturbances, the joint distribution of $v_{1t}, v_{2t}, \ldots, v_{G^{\Delta}t}$ for all sample observations is

$$(13.55)\quad f(v_{11}, v_{12}, \ldots, v_{1T}, v_{21}, v_{22}, \ldots, v_{G^{\Delta}T}) = (2\pi)^{-(TG^{\Delta}/2)}|\mathbf{\Psi}_{\Delta}|^{-(T/2)}e^{-\sum_t \mathbf{v}'_{\Delta t}\mathbf{\Psi}_{\Delta}^{-1}\mathbf{v}_{\Delta t}}.$$

We are interested in the likelihood function for the sample observations on the G^{Δ} endogenous variables included in the first structural equation. This so-called *limited information likelihood function* is obtained from (13.55) by expressing the elements of $\mathbf{v}_{\Delta t}$ in terms of the y's. Furthermore, we know that the y's are linearly connected by the structural equation that is being estimated. This fact is taken into account by maximizing the limited information likelihood function *subject* to the identifying restrictions for this equation. These restrictions, which are derived from (13.10), are

$$(13.56)\quad \begin{aligned} \pi_{11} &= -\beta_{12}\pi_{21} - \beta_{13}\pi_{31} - \cdots - \beta_{1G^{\Delta}}\pi_{G^{\Delta}1} - \gamma_{11}, \\ \pi_{12} &= -\beta_{12}\pi_{22} - \beta_{13}\pi_{32} - \cdots - \beta_{1G^{\Delta}}\pi_{G^{\Delta}2} - \gamma_{12}, \\ &\vdots \\ \pi_{1K^*} &= -\beta_{12}\pi_{2K^*} - \beta_{13}\pi_{3K^*} - \cdots - \beta_{1G^{\Delta}}\pi_{G^{\Delta}K^*} - \gamma_{1K^*}, \\ \pi_{1,K^*+1} &= -\beta_{12}\pi_{2,K^*+1} - \beta_{13}\pi_{3,K^*+1} - \cdots - \beta_{1G^{\Delta}}\pi_{G^{\Delta},K^*+1}, \\ &\vdots \\ \pi_{1K} &= -\beta_{12}\pi_{2K} - \beta_{13}\pi_{3K} - \cdots - \beta_{1G^{\Delta}}\pi_{G^{\Delta}K}. \end{aligned}$$

These restrictions can be introduced into the limited information likelihood function by putting

$$\begin{aligned} v_{1t} &= y_{1t} - \pi_{11}x_{1t} - \ldots - \pi_{1K}x_{Kt}, \\ v_{2t} &= y_{2t} - \pi_{21}x_{1t} - \cdots - \pi_{2K}x_{Kt}, \\ &\vdots \\ v_{G^{\Delta}T} &= y_{G^{\Delta}t} - \pi_{G^{\Delta}1}x_{1t} - \cdots - \pi_{G^{\Delta}K}x_{Kt}, \end{aligned}$$

and then replacing $\pi_{11}, \pi_{12}, \ldots, \pi_{1K}$ with the expressions on the right-hand side of (13.56). The resulting function then can be maximized with respect to the unknown parameters that include the structural coefficients.

[6] A. S. Goldberger, *Econometric Theory* (New York: Wiley, 1964), p. 104. If the x's are stochastic, the joint distribution of the v's should be viewed as being conditional on the sample values of the x's.

To derive the limited information maximum likelihood estimator by maximizing the restricted likelihood function is quite complicated. However, the same results can also be obtained by utilizing the so-called *least variance ratio principle.* The equivalence of the two approaches is well known and will not be proved here.[7] The least variance ratio estimates are derived as follows. The first structural equation,

$$\mathbf{y}_1 = \mathbf{Y}_1\boldsymbol{\beta}_1 + \mathbf{X}_1\boldsymbol{\gamma}_1 + \mathbf{u}_1$$

can be written as

$$\tilde{\mathbf{y}}_1 = \mathbf{X}_1\boldsymbol{\gamma}_1 + \mathbf{u}_1, \tag{13.57}$$

where

$$\tilde{\mathbf{y}}_1 = \mathbf{y}_1 - \mathbf{Y}_1\boldsymbol{\beta}_1.$$

The "composite" variable $\tilde{\mathbf{y}}_1$ represents a linear combination of the endogenous variables included in the first structural equation. If its values could be observed, we could estimate $\boldsymbol{\gamma}_1$ by the ordinary least squares method. This would lead to

$$\hat{\boldsymbol{\gamma}}_1 = (\mathbf{X}_1'\mathbf{X}_1)^{-1}\mathbf{X}_1'\tilde{\mathbf{y}}_1,$$

and the sum of the squared residuals would be

$$\text{SSE}_1 = (\tilde{\mathbf{y}}_1 - \mathbf{X}_1\hat{\boldsymbol{\gamma}}_1)'(\tilde{\mathbf{y}}_1 - \mathbf{X}_1\boldsymbol{\gamma}_1) = \tilde{\mathbf{y}}_1'\tilde{\mathbf{y}}_1 - \tilde{\mathbf{y}}_1'\mathbf{X}_1(\mathbf{X}_1'\mathbf{X}_1)^{-1}\mathbf{X}_1'\tilde{\mathbf{y}}_1.$$

Note that in (13.57) the explanatory variables consist of the predetermined variables included in the first structural equation. If this set were extended to include *all* the predetermined variables of the system, we would have

$$\tilde{\mathbf{y}}_1 = \mathbf{X}\boldsymbol{\gamma} + \mathbf{u}_1, \tag{13.58}$$

where $\mathbf{X}$ is a $(T \times K)$ matrix of all predetermined variables and

$$\underset{(K\times 1)}{\boldsymbol{\gamma}} = \begin{bmatrix} \boldsymbol{\gamma}_1 \\ \mathbf{0}_{**} \end{bmatrix}.$$

If we applied the ordinary least squares method to (13.58)—ignoring the fact that the true value of some of the γ coefficients is zero—we would get

$$\hat{\boldsymbol{\gamma}} = (\mathbf{X}'\mathbf{X})^{-1}(\mathbf{X}'\tilde{\mathbf{y}}_1),$$

and the sum of the squared residuals would be

$$\text{SSE} = (\tilde{\mathbf{y}}_1 - \mathbf{X}\boldsymbol{\gamma})'(\tilde{\mathbf{y}}_1 - \mathbf{X}\boldsymbol{\gamma}) = \tilde{\mathbf{y}}_1'\tilde{\mathbf{y}}_1 - \tilde{\mathbf{y}}_1'\mathbf{X}(\mathbf{X}'\mathbf{X})^{-1}\mathbf{X}'\tilde{\mathbf{y}}_1.$$

Since the addition of further explanatory variables can never increase the residual sum of squares, the ratio

$$\ell = \frac{\text{SSE}_1}{\text{SSE}} = \frac{\tilde{\mathbf{y}}_1'\tilde{\mathbf{y}}_1 - \tilde{\mathbf{y}}_1'\mathbf{X}_1(\mathbf{X}_1'\mathbf{X}_1)^{-1}\mathbf{X}_1'\tilde{\mathbf{y}}_1}{\tilde{\mathbf{y}}_1'\tilde{\mathbf{y}}_1 - \tilde{\mathbf{y}}_1'\mathbf{X}(\mathbf{X}'\mathbf{X})^{-1}\mathbf{X}'\tilde{\mathbf{y}}_1} \tag{13.59}$$

can never be smaller than unity.

[7] See T. C. Koopmans and W. C. Hood, "The Estimation of Simultaneous Linear Economic Relationships," in Hood and Koopmans, *op. cit.*, pp. 166–177.

The problem now is to estimate the elements of $\boldsymbol{\beta}_1$. Let us write

(13.60) $$\tilde{\mathbf{y}}_1 = \mathbf{Y}_{1\Delta}\boldsymbol{\beta}_{1\Delta},$$

where $$\mathbf{Y}_{1\Delta} = [\mathbf{y}_1 \quad \mathbf{y}_2 \quad \dots \quad \mathbf{y}_{G^\Delta}] \quad \text{and} \quad \boldsymbol{\beta}_{1\Delta} = \begin{bmatrix} 1 \\ \beta_{12} \\ \vdots \\ \beta_{1G^\Delta} \end{bmatrix}.$$

Therefore, (13.59) can be written as

(13.59a) $$\ell = \frac{\boldsymbol{\beta}'_{1\Delta}\mathbf{W}_{1*}\boldsymbol{\beta}_{1\Delta}}{\boldsymbol{\beta}'_{1\Delta}\mathbf{W}_1\boldsymbol{\beta}_{1\Delta}}$$

where $$\mathbf{W}_{1*} = \mathbf{Y}'_{1\Delta}\mathbf{Y}_{1\Delta} - (\mathbf{Y}'_{1\Delta}\mathbf{X}_1)(\mathbf{X}'_1\mathbf{X}_1)^{-1}\mathbf{X}'_1\mathbf{Y}_{1\Delta},$$
$$\mathbf{W}_1 = \mathbf{Y}'_{1\Delta}\mathbf{Y}_{1\Delta} - (\mathbf{Y}'_{1\Delta}\mathbf{X})(\mathbf{X}'\mathbf{X})^{-1}\mathbf{X}'\mathbf{Y}_{1\Delta}.$$

The least variance ratio estimator of $\boldsymbol{\beta}_{1\Delta}$ is given by those values of the β coefficients that lead to the smallest value of ℓ. Thus we have to minimize ℓ with respect to $\boldsymbol{\beta}_{1\Delta}$. Taking the first derivative of ℓ, we get

(13.61) $$\frac{\partial \ell}{\partial \boldsymbol{\beta}_{1\Delta}} = \frac{2(\mathbf{W}_{1*}\boldsymbol{\beta}_{1\Delta})(\boldsymbol{\beta}'_{1\Delta}\mathbf{W}_1\boldsymbol{\beta}_{1\Delta}) - 2(\boldsymbol{\beta}'_{1\Delta}\mathbf{W}_{1*}\boldsymbol{\beta}_{1\Delta})(\mathbf{W}_1\boldsymbol{\beta}_{1\Delta})}{(\boldsymbol{\beta}'_{1\Delta}\mathbf{W}_1\boldsymbol{\beta}_{1\Delta})^2}.$$

By setting this equal to zero, we obtain

(13.62) $$\mathbf{W}_{1*}\tilde{\tilde{\boldsymbol{\beta}}}_{1\Delta} - \left[\frac{\boldsymbol{\beta}'_{1\Delta}\mathbf{W}_{1*}\boldsymbol{\beta}_{1\Delta}}{\boldsymbol{\beta}_{1\Delta}\mathbf{W}_1\boldsymbol{\beta}_{1\Delta}}\right]\mathbf{W}_1\tilde{\tilde{\boldsymbol{\beta}}}_{1\Delta} = \mathbf{0}$$

or

(13.62a) $$(\mathbf{W}_{1*} - \ell\mathbf{W}_1)\tilde{\tilde{\boldsymbol{\beta}}}_{1\Delta} = \mathbf{0}.$$

Now, for $\tilde{\tilde{\boldsymbol{\beta}}}_{1\Delta} \neq \mathbf{0}$ we must have

(13.63) $$\text{Det}\,(\mathbf{W}_{1*} - \ell\mathbf{W}_1) = 0;$$

that is, the determinant of the matrix $(\mathbf{W}_{1*} - \ell\mathbf{W}_1)$—whose dimension is $(G^\Delta \times G^\Delta)$—must equal zero. Since all elements of $\mathbf{W}_{1*}$ and $\mathbf{W}_1$ can be determined from the sample observations, equation (13.63) becomes a polynomial of G^Δ degree in ℓ. As noted, we want ℓ to be as close to unity as possible, and thus the appropriate root of (13.63) is the smallest one, say, ℓ_1. By using ℓ_1 in place of ℓ in (13.62a), we can obtain a solution for the $(G^\Delta - 1)$ unknown elements of $\tilde{\tilde{\boldsymbol{\beta}}}_{1\Delta}$. The elements of $\boldsymbol{\gamma}_1$ are then estimated by

(13.64) $$\tilde{\tilde{\boldsymbol{\gamma}}}_1 = (\mathbf{X}'_1\mathbf{X}_1)^{-1}(\mathbf{X}'_1\tilde{\mathbf{y}}_1) = (\mathbf{X}'_1\mathbf{X}_1)^{-1}(\mathbf{X}'_1\mathbf{Y}_{1\Delta})\tilde{\tilde{\boldsymbol{\beta}}}_1.$$

These are the limited information maximum likelihood estimates.

When the limited information maximum likelihood estimator was introduced, we mentioned that it belongs to the k-class family. We can now elaborate by stating that, for this estimator,

$$k = \ell_1$$

and that

$$\operatorname{plim} \ell_1 = 1,$$

$$\operatorname{plim} \sqrt{T}(\ell_1 - 1) = 0.$$

The proof of these propositions can be found elsewhere.[8] Their implications are that the limited information maximum likelihood estimator is consistent and that it has the same asymptotic variance-covariance matrix as the two-stage least squares estimator. One difference between these two estimators is that the limited information maximum likelihood estimator is *invariant* with respect to the choice of the endogenous variable whose structural coefficient is to be equal to one, whereas the two-stage least squares estimator is not invariant in this respect. Consider the first structural equation written as

$$\beta_{11}y_{1t} + \beta_{12}y_{2t} + \cdots + \beta_{1G^\Delta}y_{G^\Delta t} + \gamma_{11}x_{1t} + \cdots + \gamma_{1K^*}x_{K^*t} = u_{1t}.$$

In deriving the two-stage least squares estimator and the limited information maximum likelihood estimator, we have taken the value of β_{11} to be equal to one. This means that the structural equation may be written as

$$y_{1t} = -\beta_{12}y_{2t} - \cdots - \beta_{1G^\Delta}y_{G^\Delta t} - \gamma_{11}x_{1t} - \cdots - \gamma_{1K^*}x_{K^*t} + u_{1t}.$$

In our notation the two-stage least squares estimate of β_{12} is $\tilde{\beta}_{12}$ and the limited information maximum likelihood estimate is $\tilde{\tilde{\beta}}_{12}$. Now suppose we change our specification and take β_{12}, rather than β_{11}, to be equal to one. Then the structural equation would be written as

$$y_{2t} = -\beta_{11}y_{1t} - \cdots - \beta_{1G^\Delta}y_{G^\Delta t} - \gamma_{11}x_{1t} - \cdots - \gamma_{1K^*}x_{K^*t} + u_{1t}.$$

The two-stage least squares estimate of β_{11} is $\tilde{\beta}_{11}$, and the limited information maximum likelihood estimate is $\tilde{\tilde{\beta}}_{11}$. Then

$$\tilde{\beta}_{11} \neq \frac{1}{\tilde{\beta}_{12}},$$

but

$$\tilde{\tilde{\beta}}_{11} = \frac{1}{\tilde{\tilde{\beta}}_{12}}.$$

This is what is meant by "invariance" of the limited information maximum likelihood estimator. In this respect it is unique among all members of the k-class family.[9] Invariance may be useful whenever economic theory offers no guidance concerning the choice of endogenous variable for which the structural coefficient is to be unity. Finally, it may be noted that when the structural equation is exactly identified, the limited information maximum likelihood method leads to the same result as the indirect least squares method.

[8] See Goldberger, *op. cit.*, pp. 341–344.

[9] See A. S. Goldberger, "An Instrumental Variable Interpretation of k-Class Estimation," *Indian Economic Journal*, Vol. 13, No. 3, 1965, pp. 424–431.

EXAMPLE We can illustrate the construction of the limited information maximum likelihood estimates by reference to the food market model (13.45). The two-equation model given by (13.45) is

$$Q_t = \alpha_1 + \alpha_2 P_t + \alpha_3 D_t + u_{1t} \qquad \text{(demand)},$$

$$Q_t = \beta_1 + \beta_2 P_t + \beta_3 F_t + \beta_4 A_t + u_{2t} \quad \text{(supply)}.$$

The sample observations ($T = 20$) are given in Table 13–1. For the demand equation, which is overidentified, we have

$$\mathbf{Y}_{1\Delta} = \begin{bmatrix} Q_1 & P_1 \\ Q_2 & P_2 \\ \vdots & \vdots \\ Q_{20} & P_{20} \end{bmatrix}, \quad \mathbf{X}_1 = \begin{bmatrix} 1 & D_1 \\ 1 & D_2 \\ \vdots & \vdots \\ 1 & D_{20} \end{bmatrix}, \quad \mathbf{X} = \begin{bmatrix} 1 & D_1 & F_1 & A_1 \\ 1 & D_2 & F_2 & A_2 \\ \vdots & \vdots & \vdots & \vdots \\ 1 & D_{20} & F_{20} & A_{20} \end{bmatrix},$$

$$\boldsymbol{\beta}_{1\Delta} = \begin{bmatrix} 1 \\ -\alpha_2 \end{bmatrix}, \quad \boldsymbol{\gamma}_1 = \begin{bmatrix} \alpha_1 \\ \alpha_3 \end{bmatrix}.$$

Then,

$$\mathbf{W}_{1*} = \begin{bmatrix} \sum Q_t^2 & \sum Q_t P_t \\ \sum Q_t P_t & \sum P_t^2 \end{bmatrix} - \begin{bmatrix} \sum Q_t & \sum Q_t D_t \\ \sum P_t & \sum P_t D_t \end{bmatrix} \begin{bmatrix} T & \sum D_t \\ \sum D_t & \sum D_t^2 \end{bmatrix}^{-1} \begin{bmatrix} \sum Q_t & \sum P_t \\ \sum Q_t D_t & \sum P_t D_t \end{bmatrix}$$

and

$$\mathbf{W}_1 = \begin{bmatrix} \sum Q_t^2 & \sum Q_t P_t \\ \sum Q_t P_t & \sum P_t^2 \end{bmatrix} - \begin{bmatrix} \sum Q_t & \sum Q_t D_t & \sum Q_t F_t & \sum Q_t A_t \\ \sum P_t & \sum P_t D_t & \sum P_t F_t & \sum P_t A_t \end{bmatrix}$$

$$\times \begin{bmatrix} T & \sum D_t & \sum F_t & \sum A_t \\ \sum D_t & \sum D_t^2 & \sum D_t F_t & \sum D_t A_t \\ \sum F_t & \sum F_t D_t & \sum F_t^2 & \sum F_t A_t \\ \sum A_t & \sum A_t D_t & \sum A_t F_t & \sum A_t^2 \end{bmatrix}^{-1} \begin{bmatrix} \sum Q_t & \sum P_t \\ \sum Q_t D_t & \sum P_t D_t \\ \sum Q_t F_t & \sum P_t F_t \\ \sum Q_t A_t & \sum P_t A_t \end{bmatrix}.$$

Thus the determinant of $(\mathbf{W}_{1*} - \ell \mathbf{W}_1)$ is a second-degree polynomial in ℓ. Its two roots are

$$\ell_1 = 1.1739 \quad \text{and} \quad \ell_2 = 12.0031.$$

Therefore, (13.62a) becomes

$$[\mathbf{W}_{1*} - 1.1739\ \mathbf{W}_1] \begin{bmatrix} 1 \\ -\tilde{\tilde{\alpha}}_2 \end{bmatrix} = \begin{bmatrix} 0 \\ 0 \end{bmatrix}. \tag{13.65}$$

The two equations in (13.65) lead to the same value of $\tilde{\tilde{\alpha}}_2$:

$$\tilde{\tilde{\alpha}}_2 = -0.2295.$$

The solution for $\tilde{\tilde{\boldsymbol{\gamma}}}_1$ is obtained from (13.64) as

$$\tilde{\tilde{\boldsymbol{\gamma}}}_1 = \begin{bmatrix} \tilde{\tilde{\alpha}}_1 \\ \tilde{\tilde{\alpha}}_3 \end{bmatrix} = \begin{bmatrix} T & \sum D_t \\ \sum D_t & \sum D_t^2 \end{bmatrix}^{-1} \begin{bmatrix} \sum Q_t & \sum P_t \\ \sum Q_t D_t & \sum P_t D_t \end{bmatrix} \begin{bmatrix} 1 \\ 0.2295 \end{bmatrix} = \begin{bmatrix} 93.6192 \\ 0.3100 \end{bmatrix}.$$

The estimated standard errors of these estimates are calculated in accordance with (13.53) and (13.54). The results for both equations of the model are

$$\underset{}{Q_t} = \underset{(8.0312)}{93.6192} - \underset{(0.0980)}{0.2295P_t} + \underset{(0.0474)}{0.3100D_t} + \tilde{\tilde{u}}_{1t} \qquad \text{(demand)},$$

$$Q_t = \underset{(12.0105)}{49.5324} + \underset{(0.0999)}{0.2401P_t} + \underset{(0.0472)}{0.2556F_t} + \underset{(0.0996)}{0.2529A_t} + \tilde{\tilde{u}}_{2t} \qquad \text{(supply)}.$$

The estimated demand equation may be compared with the true demand equation in (13.45a) as well as with the result obtained for the two-stage least squares method in the preceding example. The results for the supply equation—which is exactly identified—are precisely the same as those obtained by the two-stage least squares method.

13-4 System Methods of Estimation

The single equation estimation methods lead to estimates that are consistent but, in general, not asymptotically efficient. The reason for the lack of asymptotic efficiency is the disregard of the correlation of the disturbances across equations. (An alternative explanation for the lack of asymptotic efficiency is that single equation estimators do not take into account prior restrictions on other equations in the model.) This parallels the situation in which a regression equation belonging to a set of seemingly unrelated regressions is estimated by the ordinary least squares method (see Section 12-3). If we do not take into account the correlation between the disturbances of different structural equations, we are not using all the available information about each equation and, therefore, do not attain asymptotic efficiency. This deficiency can be overcome—as in the case of seemingly unrelated regressions—by estimating all equations of the system simultaneously. For this purpose we can use one of the so-called *system methods* described in this section.

Three-Stage Least Squares Estimation

The simplest system method is that of *three-stage least squares*, which involves a straightforward application of Aitken's generalized estimation to the system of structural equations written, in accordance with (13.36), as

$$\begin{aligned} \mathbf{y}_1 &= \hat{\mathbf{Y}}_1\boldsymbol{\beta}_1 + \mathbf{X}_1\boldsymbol{\gamma}_1 + \mathbf{u}_1^*, \\ \mathbf{y}_2 &= \hat{\mathbf{Y}}_2\boldsymbol{\beta}_2 + \mathbf{X}_2\boldsymbol{\gamma}_2 + \mathbf{u}_2^*, \\ &\vdots \\ \mathbf{y}_G &= \hat{\mathbf{Y}}_G\boldsymbol{\beta}_G + \mathbf{X}_G\boldsymbol{\gamma}_G + \mathbf{u}_G^*. \end{aligned} \tag{13.66}$$

where

$$\begin{aligned} &\mathbf{y}_g \to T\times 1, \\ &\hat{\mathbf{Y}}_g \to T\times(G_g - 1), \\ &\mathbf{X}_g \to T\times K_g, \\ &\boldsymbol{\beta}_g \to (G_g - 1)\times 1, \\ &\boldsymbol{\gamma}_g \to K_g\times 1, \\ &\mathbf{u}_g^* \to T\times 1. \end{aligned}$$

Note that G_g = number of endogenous variables included in the gth equation;

K_g = number of predetermined variables included in the gth equation;

$g = 1, 2, \ldots, G.$

If there are any identities in the system, they are simply omitted from (13.66). Alternatively, we may describe the system as

$$\text{(13.66a)} \qquad \begin{aligned} \mathbf{y}_1 &= \hat{\mathbf{Z}}_1\boldsymbol{\alpha}_1 + \mathbf{u}_1^*, \\ \mathbf{y}_2 &= \hat{\mathbf{Z}}_2\boldsymbol{\alpha}_2 + \mathbf{u}_2^*, \\ &\vdots \\ \mathbf{y}_G &= \hat{\mathbf{Z}}_G\boldsymbol{\alpha}_G + \mathbf{u}_G^*, \end{aligned}$$

where

$$\hat{\mathbf{Z}}_g = [\hat{\mathbf{Y}}_g \quad \mathbf{X}_g],$$

$$\boldsymbol{\alpha}_g = \begin{bmatrix} \boldsymbol{\beta}_g \\ \boldsymbol{\gamma}_g \end{bmatrix}.$$

A compact way of writing (13.66a) is

$$\text{(13.66b)} \qquad \begin{bmatrix} \mathbf{y}_1 \\ \mathbf{y}_2 \\ \vdots \\ \mathbf{y}_G \end{bmatrix} = \begin{bmatrix} \hat{\mathbf{Z}}_1 & \mathbf{0} & \ldots & \mathbf{0} \\ \mathbf{0} & \hat{\mathbf{Z}}_2 & \ldots & \mathbf{0} \\ \vdots & \vdots & & \vdots \\ \mathbf{0} & \mathbf{0} & \ldots & \hat{\mathbf{Z}}_G \end{bmatrix} \begin{bmatrix} \boldsymbol{\alpha}_1 \\ \boldsymbol{\alpha}_2 \\ \vdots \\ \boldsymbol{\alpha}_G \end{bmatrix} + \begin{bmatrix} \mathbf{u}_1^* \\ \mathbf{u}_2^* \\ \vdots \\ \mathbf{u}_G^* \end{bmatrix},$$

or

$$\text{(13.66c)} \qquad \mathbf{y} = \hat{\mathbf{Z}}\boldsymbol{\alpha} + \mathbf{u}^*$$

where

$$\mathbf{y} \to GT \times 1,$$

$$\hat{\mathbf{Z}} \to GT \times \sum_{g=1}^{G} (G_g - 1 + K_g),$$

$$\boldsymbol{\alpha} \to \sum_{g=1}^{G} (G_g - 1 + K_g) \times 1,$$

$$\mathbf{u}^* \to GT \times 1.$$

Describing the system of equations in the form (13.66c) enables us to apply Aitken's generalized least squares formula as given by (12.51). This leads to

$$\text{(13.67)} \qquad \bar{\bar{\boldsymbol{\alpha}}} = (\hat{\mathbf{Z}}'\boldsymbol{\Omega}^{-1}\hat{\mathbf{Z}})^{-1}(\hat{\mathbf{Z}}'\boldsymbol{\Omega}^{-1}\mathbf{y})$$

where

$$\boldsymbol{\Omega} = E(\mathbf{u}^*\mathbf{u}^{*\prime}).$$

The three-stage least squares estimator of $\boldsymbol{\alpha}$ is obtained by replacing $\boldsymbol{\Omega}$, whose elements are unknown, by $\hat{\boldsymbol{\Omega}}$, which is defined as

$$\hat{\boldsymbol{\Omega}} = \begin{bmatrix} \tilde{\psi}_{11}\mathbf{I_T} & \tilde{\psi}_{12}\mathbf{I_T} & \cdots & \tilde{\psi}_{1G}\mathbf{I_T} \\ \tilde{\psi}_{21}\mathbf{I_T} & \tilde{\psi}_{22}\mathbf{I_T} & \cdots & \tilde{\psi}_{2G}\mathbf{I_T} \\ \vdots & \vdots & & \vdots \\ \tilde{\psi}_{G1}\mathbf{I_T} & \tilde{\psi}_{G2}\mathbf{I_T} & \cdots & \tilde{\psi}_{GG}\mathbf{I_T} \end{bmatrix}, \tag{13.68}$$

where

$$\tilde{\psi}_{gh} = \frac{(\mathbf{y_g} - \mathbf{Y_g}\tilde{\boldsymbol{\beta}}_\mathbf{g} - \mathbf{X_g}\tilde{\boldsymbol{\gamma}}_\mathbf{g})'(\mathbf{y_h} - \mathbf{Y_h}\tilde{\boldsymbol{\beta}}_\mathbf{h} - \mathbf{X_h}\tilde{\boldsymbol{\gamma}}_\mathbf{h})}{(T - G_g + 1 - K_g)}, \tag{13.69}$$

$$G_g + K_g \geq G_h + K_h,$$

$$g, h = 1, 2, \ldots, G,$$

and $\tilde{\boldsymbol{\beta}}$ and $\tilde{\boldsymbol{\gamma}}$ represent the two-stage least squares estimates of the respective coefficients. (Some authors prefer using T instead of $(T - G_g + 1 - K_g)$ in the denominator of $\tilde{\psi}_{gh}$; this makes no difference to the asymptotic properties of the three-stage least squares estimator. Note, however, that $\hat{\boldsymbol{\Omega}}$ will be singular if the number of equations exceeds the number of observations.) The three-stage least squares estimator of the structural coefficients then is

$$\begin{aligned} \tilde{\tilde{\tilde{\boldsymbol{\alpha}}}} &= (\hat{\mathbf{Z}}'\hat{\boldsymbol{\Omega}}^{-1}\hat{\mathbf{Z}})^{-1}(\hat{\mathbf{Z}}'\hat{\boldsymbol{\Omega}}^{-1}\mathbf{y}) \\ &= \begin{bmatrix} \tilde{\psi}^{11}(\hat{\mathbf{Z}}_1'\hat{\mathbf{Z}}_1) & \tilde{\psi}^{12}(\hat{\mathbf{Z}}_1'\hat{\mathbf{Z}}_2) & \cdots & \tilde{\psi}^{1G}(\hat{\mathbf{Z}}_1'\hat{\mathbf{Z}}_\mathbf{G}) \\ \tilde{\psi}^{21}(\hat{\mathbf{Z}}_2'\hat{\mathbf{Z}}_1) & \tilde{\psi}^{22}(\hat{\mathbf{Z}}_2'\hat{\mathbf{Z}}_2) & \cdots & \tilde{\psi}^{2G}(\hat{\mathbf{Z}}_2'\hat{\mathbf{Z}}_\mathbf{G}) \\ \vdots & \vdots & & \vdots \\ \tilde{\psi}^{G1}(\hat{\mathbf{Z}}_\mathbf{G}'\hat{\mathbf{Z}}_1) & \tilde{\psi}^{G2}(\hat{\mathbf{Z}}_\mathbf{G}'\hat{\mathbf{Z}}_2) & \cdots & \tilde{\psi}^{GG}(\hat{\mathbf{Z}}_\mathbf{G}'\hat{\mathbf{Z}}_\mathbf{G}) \end{bmatrix}^{-1} \begin{bmatrix} \sum_g \tilde{\psi}^{1g}(\hat{\mathbf{Z}}_1'\mathbf{y_g}) \\ \sum_g \tilde{\psi}^{2g}(\hat{\mathbf{Z}}_2'\mathbf{y_g}) \\ \vdots \\ \sum_g \tilde{\psi}^{Gg}(\hat{\mathbf{Z}}_\mathbf{G}'\mathbf{y_g}) \end{bmatrix}, \end{aligned} \tag{13.70}$$

where $\tilde{\psi}^{gh}$ represents the corresponding element of the *inverse* of $\hat{\boldsymbol{\Omega}}$. As in the two-stage Aitken estimator of Section 12–3, the variance-covariance matrix of the three-stage least squares estimator can be estimated by

$$\text{Est. Var-Cov}(\tilde{\tilde{\tilde{\boldsymbol{\alpha}}}}) = (\hat{\mathbf{Z}}'\hat{\boldsymbol{\Omega}}^{-1}\hat{\mathbf{Z}})^{-1}. \tag{13.71}$$

An alternative way of deriving the three-stage least squares estimation formula can also be presented. The structural equations of the system can be written as

$$\begin{aligned} \mathbf{y}_1 &= \mathbf{Z}_1\boldsymbol{\alpha}_1 + \mathbf{u}_1, \\ \mathbf{y}_2 &= \mathbf{Z}_2\boldsymbol{\alpha}_2 + \mathbf{u}_2, \\ &\vdots \\ \mathbf{y_G} &= \mathbf{Z_G}\boldsymbol{\alpha}_\mathbf{G} + \mathbf{u_G}, \end{aligned} \tag{13.72}$$

where

$$\mathbf{Z_g} = [\mathbf{Y_g} \quad \mathbf{X_g}],$$

$$\boldsymbol{\alpha}_\mathbf{g} = \begin{bmatrix} \boldsymbol{\beta}_\mathbf{g} \\ \boldsymbol{\gamma}_\mathbf{g} \end{bmatrix}.$$

Premultiplying each equation of (13.72) by $\mathbf{X}'$ gives

$$\text{(13.73)} \qquad \begin{aligned} \mathbf{X}'\mathbf{y}_1 &= \mathbf{X}'\mathbf{Z}_1\boldsymbol{\alpha}_1 + \mathbf{X}'\mathbf{u}_1, \\ \mathbf{X}'\mathbf{y}_2 &= \mathbf{X}'\mathbf{Z}_2\boldsymbol{\alpha}_2 + \mathbf{X}'\mathbf{u}_2, \\ &\vdots \\ \mathbf{X}'\mathbf{y}_G &= \mathbf{X}'\mathbf{Z}_G\boldsymbol{\alpha}_G + \mathbf{X}'\mathbf{u}_G. \end{aligned}$$

This can be written as

$$\text{(13.73a)} \qquad \begin{bmatrix} \mathbf{X}'\mathbf{y}_1 \\ \mathbf{X}'\mathbf{y}_2 \\ \vdots \\ \mathbf{X}'\mathbf{y}_G \end{bmatrix} = \begin{bmatrix} \mathbf{X}'\mathbf{Z}_1 & \mathbf{0} & \dots & \mathbf{0} \\ \mathbf{0} & \mathbf{X}'\mathbf{Z}_2 & \dots & \mathbf{0} \\ \vdots & \vdots & & \vdots \\ \mathbf{0} & \mathbf{0} & \dots & \mathbf{X}'\mathbf{Z}_G \end{bmatrix} \begin{bmatrix} \boldsymbol{\alpha}_1 \\ \boldsymbol{\alpha}_2 \\ \vdots \\ \boldsymbol{\alpha}_G \end{bmatrix} + \begin{bmatrix} \mathbf{X}'\mathbf{u}_1 \\ \mathbf{X}'\mathbf{u}_2 \\ \vdots \\ \mathbf{X}'\mathbf{u}_G \end{bmatrix},$$

or

$$\text{(13.73b)} \qquad \bar{\bar{\mathbf{y}}} = \bar{\bar{\mathbf{Z}}}\boldsymbol{\alpha} + \bar{\bar{\mathbf{u}}},$$

where

$$\begin{aligned} &\bar{\bar{\mathbf{y}}} \to KG \times 1, \\ &\bar{\bar{\mathbf{Z}}} \to KG \times \sum_{g=1}^{G} (G_g - 1 + K_g), \\ &\boldsymbol{\alpha} \to \sum_{g=1}^{G} (G_g - 1 + K_g) \times 1, \\ &\bar{\bar{\mathbf{u}}} \to KG \times 1. \end{aligned}$$

We note that

$$E(\bar{\bar{\mathbf{u}}}\bar{\bar{\mathbf{u}}}') = \begin{bmatrix} \sigma_{11}(\mathbf{X}'\mathbf{X}) & \sigma_{12}(\mathbf{X}'\mathbf{X}) & \dots & \sigma_{1G}(\mathbf{X}'\mathbf{X}) \\ \sigma_{21}(\mathbf{X}'\mathbf{X}) & \sigma_{22}(\mathbf{X}'\mathbf{X}) & \dots & \sigma_{2G}(\mathbf{X}'\mathbf{X}) \\ \vdots & \vdots & & \vdots \\ \sigma_{G1}(\mathbf{X}'\mathbf{X}) & \sigma_{G2}(\mathbf{X}'\mathbf{X}) & \dots & \sigma_{GG}(\mathbf{X}'\mathbf{X}) \end{bmatrix},$$

where the σ's represent variances and covariances of the structural disturbances. The application of Aitken's generalized least squares formula to (13.73b) leads to

$$\text{(13.74)} \qquad \bar{\bar{\boldsymbol{\alpha}}} = (\bar{\bar{\mathbf{Z}}}'\boldsymbol{\Theta}^{-1}\bar{\bar{\mathbf{Z}}})^{-1}(\bar{\bar{\mathbf{Z}}}'\boldsymbol{\Theta}^{-1}\bar{\bar{\mathbf{y}}}),$$

where

$$\boldsymbol{\Theta} = E(\bar{\bar{\mathbf{u}}}\bar{\bar{\mathbf{u}}}').$$

Consistent estimates of the variances and covariances of the structural disturbances can be obtained by using the two-stage least squares residuals. That is, we can obtain consistent estimates of σ_{gh} by utilizing

$$\text{(13.75)} \qquad s_{gh} = \frac{(\mathbf{y}_g - \mathbf{Y}_g\tilde{\boldsymbol{\beta}}_g - \mathbf{X}_g\tilde{\boldsymbol{\gamma}}_g)'(\mathbf{y}_h - \mathbf{Y}_h\tilde{\boldsymbol{\beta}}_h - \mathbf{X}_h\tilde{\boldsymbol{\gamma}}_h)}{(T - G_g + 1 - K_g)},$$

$$G_g + K_g \geq G_h + K_h,$$

$$g, h = 1, 2, \dots, G.$$

Then $\boldsymbol{\alpha}$ can be estimated by

(13.76)

$$\hat{\hat{\boldsymbol{\alpha}}} = (\overline{\overline{\mathbf{Z}}}'\hat{\boldsymbol{\Theta}}^{-1}\overline{\overline{\mathbf{Z}}})^{-1}(\overline{\overline{\mathbf{Z}}}'\hat{\boldsymbol{\Theta}}^{-1}\overline{\overline{\mathbf{y}}})$$

$$= \begin{bmatrix} s^{11}\mathbf{Z}_1'\mathbf{X}(\mathbf{X}'\mathbf{X})^{-1}\mathbf{X}'\mathbf{Z}_1 & s^{12}\mathbf{Z}_1'\mathbf{X}(\mathbf{X}'\mathbf{X})^{-1}\mathbf{X}'\mathbf{Z}_2 & \dots & s^{1G}\mathbf{Z}_1'\mathbf{X}(\mathbf{X}'\mathbf{X})^{-1}\mathbf{X}'\mathbf{Z}_G \\ s^{21}\mathbf{Z}_2'\mathbf{X}(\mathbf{X}'\mathbf{X})^{-1}\mathbf{X}'\mathbf{Z}_1 & s^{22}\mathbf{Z}_2'\mathbf{X}(\mathbf{X}'\mathbf{X})^{-1}\mathbf{X}'\mathbf{Z}_2 & \dots & s^{2G}\mathbf{Z}_2'\mathbf{X}(\mathbf{X}'\mathbf{X})^{-1}\mathbf{X}'\mathbf{Z}_G \\ \vdots & \vdots & & \vdots \\ s^{G1}\mathbf{Z}_G'\mathbf{X}(\mathbf{X}'\mathbf{X})^{-1}\mathbf{X}'\mathbf{Z}_1 & s^{G2}\mathbf{Z}_G'\mathbf{X}(\mathbf{X}'\mathbf{X})^{-1}\mathbf{X}'\mathbf{Z}_2 & \dots & s^{GG}\mathbf{Z}_G'\mathbf{X}(\mathbf{X}'\mathbf{X})^{-1}\mathbf{X}'\mathbf{Z}_G \end{bmatrix}^{-1}$$

$$\times \begin{bmatrix} \sum_g s^{1g}\mathbf{Z}_1'\mathbf{X}(\mathbf{X}'\mathbf{X})^{-1}\mathbf{X}'\mathbf{y}_g \\ \sum_g s^{2g}\mathbf{Z}_2'\mathbf{X}(\mathbf{X}'\mathbf{X})^{-1}\mathbf{X}'\mathbf{y}_g \\ \vdots \\ \sum_g s^{Gg}\mathbf{Z}_G'\mathbf{X}(\mathbf{X}'\mathbf{X})^{-1}\mathbf{X}'\mathbf{y}_g \end{bmatrix},$$

where s^{gh} represents the corresponding element of the *inverse* of $\hat{\boldsymbol{\Theta}}$. The expression (13.76) is equivalent to (13.70). Further,

(13.77) $$\text{Est. Var-Cov}(\hat{\hat{\boldsymbol{\alpha}}}) = (\overline{\overline{\mathbf{Z}}}'\hat{\boldsymbol{\Theta}}^{-1}\overline{\overline{\mathbf{Z}}})^{-1},$$

which is equivalent to (13.71). Under the assumptions stated at the outset of this chapter, the three-stage least squares estimates of the structural coefficients are consistent and asymptotically efficient. (If the predetermined variables in the system include lagged endogenous variables, their initial values are assumed to be fixed.) In models in which it can be assumed that the structural disturbances are uncorrelated across equations, $\boldsymbol{\Theta}$ will be diagonal, and the three-stage least squares estimates will be the same as the two-stage least squares estimates. We also note that the three-stage least squares estimator, like the two-stage estimator, is *not invariant* with respect to the choice of the endogenous variable whose structural coefficient is to be unity. A final point worth mentioning is that in applying the three-stage least squares method, the omission of exactly identified equations will not affect the three-stage least squares estimates of the coefficients of the remaining equations.[10] This means that exactly identified equations add no information that is relevant for estimation of the overidentified equations of the system. The reverse, however, is not true.

EXAMPLE Continuing with the food market example, we use the results from the application of the two-stage least squares method to estimate the variance-covariance matrix of the structural disturbances. By (13.75) this is

$$\tilde{\boldsymbol{\Phi}} = \begin{bmatrix} s_{11} & s_{12} \\ s_{21} & s_{22} \end{bmatrix} = \begin{bmatrix} 3.8664 & 4.3574 \\ 4.3574 & 6.0396 \end{bmatrix}.$$

[10] See A. Zellner and H. Theil, "Three-Stage Least Squares: Simultaneous Estimation of Simultaneous Equations," *Econometrica*, Vol. 30, January, 1962, pp. 63–68.

The three-stage least squares estimates of the structural coefficients then are

$$Q_t = \underset{(7.9208)}{94.6333} - \underset{(0.0965)}{0.2436}P_t + \underset{(0.0469)}{0.3140}D_t + \tilde{\tilde{u}}_{1t} \qquad \text{(demand)},$$

$$Q_t = \underset{(11.8934)}{52.1176} + \underset{(0.0997)}{0.2289}P_t + \underset{(0.0440)}{0.2290}F_t + \underset{(0.0729)}{0.3579}A_t + \tilde{\tilde{u}}_{2t} \quad \text{(supply)}.$$

The supply equation is exactly identified and, therefore, adds no information for estimating the overidentified demand equation. Thus the three-stage least squares estimates of the demand equation are the same as those obtained by the two-stage least squares method. However, the three-stage least squares results for the supply equation are different from those obtained by the two-stage least squares method.

It may be noted that the residuals from the estimated three-stage least squares equations can be used to obtain new estimates of the variances and covariances of the structural disturbances. These can then replace the previous estimates in the three-stage least squares formula, thus leading to new estimates of the structural coefficients. The process could be repeated until there is no change in the estimated structural coefficients. The resulting estimates, known as *iterative three-stage least squares estimates*, have the same asymptotic properties as the ordinary three-stage least squares estimates.[11] For our food market example, the estimated coefficients converged at the tenth decimal place after nine iterations. The final estimates of the variance-covariance matrix of the structural disturbances are

$$\overset{\approx}{\mathbf{\Phi}} = \begin{bmatrix} 3.8664 & 5.0907 \\ 5.0907 & 6.9564 \end{bmatrix}.$$

As a result, the converged iterative three-stage least squares are

$$Q_t = \underset{(7.9208)}{94.6333} - \underset{(0.0965)}{0.2436}P_t + \underset{(0.0469)}{0.3140}D_t + \bar{\bar{u}}_{1t} \qquad \text{(demand)},$$

$$Q_t = \underset{(12.7408)}{52.5527} + \underset{(0.1069)}{0.2271}P_t + \underset{(0.0465)}{0.2245}F_t + \underset{(0.0717)}{0.3756}A_t + \bar{\bar{u}}_{2t} \quad \text{(supply)}.$$

Full Information Maximum Likelihood Estimation

Another system method designed for estimating the structural coefficients of a simultaneous equation system is the *full information maximum likelihood method*. It involves the usual application of the maximum likelihood principle to all stochastic equations of the system simultaneously. Consider the complete system

$$\mathbf{B}\mathbf{y}_t + \mathbf{\Gamma}\mathbf{x}_t = \mathbf{u}_t$$

specified in (13.3a), and the corresponding variance-covariance matrix of the disturbances

$$\mathbf{\Phi} = E(\mathbf{u}_t\mathbf{u}_t').$$

[11] See A. Madansky, "On the Efficiency of Three-Stage Least Squares Estimation," *Econometrica*, Vol. 32, January–April 1964, p. 55.

On the assumptions previously specified, the joint distribution of the elements of u_t is

$$f(\mathbf{u}_t) = (2\pi)^{-(G/2)}|\mathbf{\Phi}|^{-(1/2)}e^{-(\mathbf{u}_t'\mathbf{\Phi}^{-1}\mathbf{u}_t)/2}.$$

The probability transformation from the unobservable $\mathbf{u}_t$ to the observable $\mathbf{y}_t$ is

$$f(\mathbf{y}_t \mid \mathbf{x}_t) = f(\mathbf{u}_t)\left|\frac{\partial \mathbf{u}_t}{\partial \mathbf{y}_t}\right| = f(\mathbf{u}_t)\left|\frac{\partial(\mathbf{B}\mathbf{y}_t + \mathbf{\Gamma}\mathbf{x}_t)}{\partial \mathbf{y}_t}\right| = f(\mathbf{u}_t)|\mathbf{B}|,$$

where $|\mathbf{B}|$ is the Jacobian, given by the absolute value of the determinant of the matrix $\mathbf{B}$. Then the logarithmic likelihood function for the T observations on $\mathbf{y}_t$ conditional on the values of $\mathbf{x}_t$ is

(13.78)
$$L = -\frac{GT}{2}\log(2\pi) - \frac{T}{2}\log|\mathbf{\Phi}| + T\log|\mathbf{B}| - \frac{1}{2}\sum_{t=1}^{T}(\mathbf{B}\mathbf{y}_t + \mathbf{\Gamma}\mathbf{x}_t)'\mathbf{\Phi}^{-1}(\mathbf{B}\mathbf{y}_t + \mathbf{\Gamma}\mathbf{x}_t).$$

The maximum likelihood estimators of $\mathbf{B}$, $\mathbf{\Gamma}$, and $\mathbf{\Phi}$ are then obtained by maximizing (13.78) with respect to these parameters. These estimators are consistent, asymptotically efficient, and their asymptotic distribution is normal. This means that they have the same asymptotic properties—and the same asymptotic variance-covariance matrix—as the three-stage least squares estimators. The asymptotic variance-covariance matrix of the full information maximum likelihood estimators can be estimated in the usual way by reference to the appropriate information matrix. The full information maximum likelihood estimators are equivalent to the so-called *least generalized residual variance estimators,* which are obtained by minimizing the determinant of the variance-covariance matrix of the reduced form residuals.[12]

EXAMPLE To illustrate the construction of the logarithmic likelihood function (13.78), we use the food market model (13.45):

$$Q_t = \alpha_1 + \alpha_2 P_t + \alpha_3 D_t + u_{1t} \quad \text{(demand)},$$

$$Q_t = \beta_1 + \beta_2 P_t + \beta_3 F_t + \beta_4 A_t + u_{2t} \quad \text{(supply)}.$$

Here,

$$\mathbf{y}_t' = [Q_t \quad P_t], \qquad \mathbf{x}_t' = [1 \quad D_t \quad F_t \quad A_t]$$

and

$$\mathbf{B} = \begin{bmatrix} 1 & -\alpha_2 \\ 1 & -\beta_2 \end{bmatrix}, \quad \mathbf{\Gamma} = \begin{bmatrix} -\alpha_1 & -\alpha_3 & 0 & 0 \\ -\beta_1 & 0 & -\beta_3 & -\beta_4 \end{bmatrix}, \quad \mathbf{\Phi} = \begin{bmatrix} \sigma_{11} & \sigma_{12} \\ \sigma_{12} & \sigma_{22} \end{bmatrix}.$$

[12] See Goldberger (1964), *op. cit.*, pp. 352–356. A somewhat different interpretation of interdependent systems and an iterative method of estimation known as "fix-point" are described in E. J. Mosback and H. Wold, *Interdependent Systems, Structure and Estimation* (Amsterdam: North-Holland Publishing Company, 1970).

Then

$$|\mathbf{\Phi}| = \sigma_{11}\sigma_{22} - \sigma_{12}^2,$$
$$|\mathbf{B}| = -\beta_2 + \alpha_2,$$

and

$$(\mathbf{B}\mathbf{y}_t + \mathbf{\Gamma}\mathbf{x}_t)'\mathbf{\Phi}^{-1}(\mathbf{B}\mathbf{y}_t + \mathbf{\Gamma}\mathbf{x}_t)$$
$$= [u_{1t} \quad u_{2t}]\frac{1}{|\mathbf{\Phi}|}\begin{bmatrix} \sigma_{22} & -\sigma_{12} \\ -\sigma_{12} & \sigma_{11}\end{bmatrix}\begin{bmatrix} u_{1t} \\ u_{2t}\end{bmatrix} = \frac{1}{|\mathbf{\Phi}|}(\sigma_{22}u_{1t}^2 + \sigma_{11}u_{2t}^2 - 2\sigma_{12}u_{1t}u_{2t}),$$

where

$$u_{1t} = Q_t - \alpha_1 - \alpha_2 P_t - \alpha_3 D_t,$$
$$u_{2t} = Q_t - \beta_1 - \beta_2 P_t - \beta_3 F_t - \beta_4 A_t.$$

Therefore, the logarithmic likelihood function (13.78) becomes

$$(13.79) \quad L = -\frac{GT}{2}\log(2\pi) - \frac{T}{2}\log(\sigma_{11}\sigma_{22} - \sigma_{12}^2) + T\log|\alpha_2 - \beta_2|$$
$$- \frac{1}{2(\sigma_{11}\sigma_{22} - \sigma_{12}^2)}\Big\{\sigma_{22}\sum_{t=1}^{T}(Q_t - \alpha_1 - \alpha_2 P_t - \alpha_3 D_t)^2$$
$$+ \sigma_{11}\sum_{t=1}^{T}(Q_t - \beta_1 - \beta_2 P_t - \beta_3 F_t - \beta_4 A_t)^2$$
$$- 2\sigma_{12}\sum_{t=1}^{T}(Q_t - \alpha_1 - \alpha_2 P_t - \alpha_3 D_t)(Q_t - \beta_1 - \beta_2 P_t - \beta_3 F_t - \beta_4 A_t)\Big\}$$

where $|\alpha_2 - \beta_2|$ stands for the absolute value of $(\alpha_2 - \beta_2)$.

In the preceding exposition we did not consider the possibility that the system might include identities as well as stochastic equations. If that is the case, the variance-covariance matrix of the structural disturbances will be singular so that its inverse will not exist. One way of dealing with this problem is to eliminate all identities (and the corresponding endogenous variables) by substitution before setting up the likelihood function. For instance, consider the following model:

$$C_t = \alpha_0 + \alpha_1 Y_t + \alpha_2 C_{t-1} + u_{1t} \quad \text{(consumption)},$$
$$I_t = \beta_0 + \beta_1 r_t + \beta_2 I_{t-1} + u_{2t} \quad \text{(investment)},$$
$$r_t = \gamma_0 + \gamma_1 Y_t + \gamma_2 M_t + u_{3t} \quad \text{(money market)},$$
$$Y_t = C_t + I_t + G_t \quad \text{(income identity)},$$

where C = consumption, Y = income, I = investment, r = rate of interest, M = money supply, and G = government expenditure. The variables C_t, Y_t, I_t, and r_t are endogenous; the remaining variables are predetermined. The income identity can be eliminated by substituting for Y_t into the rest of the system. The system then becomes

$$C_t = \left(\frac{\alpha_0}{1-\alpha_1}\right) + \left(\frac{\alpha_1}{1-\alpha_1}\right)I_t + \left(\frac{\alpha_1}{1-\alpha_1}\right)G_t + \left(\frac{\alpha_2}{1-\alpha_1}\right)C_{t-1} + \left(\frac{1}{1-\alpha_1}\right)u_{1t},$$
$$I_t = \beta_0 + \beta_1 r_t + \beta_2 I_{t-1} + u_{2t},$$
$$r_t = \gamma_0 + \gamma_1 C_t + \gamma_1 I_t + \gamma_1 G_t + \gamma_2 M_t + u_{3t},$$

which involves only stochastic equations. Of course, the variance-covariance matrix $\boldsymbol{\Phi}$ of the structural disturbances must now be changed to $\boldsymbol{\Phi}^*$, which is defined as

$$\boldsymbol{\Phi}^* = \begin{bmatrix} \dfrac{\sigma_{11}}{(1-\alpha_1)^2} & \dfrac{\sigma_{12}}{(1-\alpha_1)} & \dfrac{\sigma_{13}}{(1-\alpha_1)} \\ \dfrac{\sigma_{12}}{(1-\alpha_1)} & \sigma_{22} & \sigma_{23} \\ \dfrac{\sigma_{13}}{(1-\alpha_1)} & \sigma_{23} & \sigma_{33} \end{bmatrix}.$$

The disadvantage of this approach is that it introduces nonzero restrictions into the structural equations and thus makes the derivation of the maximum likelihood estimates more complicated. An alternative way of dealing with identities without making a direct substitution is also available.[13]

EXAMPLE The full information maximum likelihood estimates of the structural equations of the food market model are:

$$\underset{}{Q_t} = \underset{(8.0312)}{93.6192} - \underset{(0.0980)}{0.2295P_t} + \underset{(0.0474)}{0.3100D_t} + \overset{\Delta}{u}_{1t} \qquad \text{(demand)},$$

$$Q_t = \underset{(12.7460)}{51.9445} + \underset{(0.1078)}{0.2373P_t} + \underset{(0.0457)}{0.2208F_t} + \underset{(0.0765)}{0.3697A_t} + \overset{\Delta}{u}_{2t} \quad \text{(supply)}.$$

We note that the estimates of the coefficients of the demand equation are identical with the limited information maximum likelihood estimates given earlier. Again, this is the result of the fact that the supply equation is exactly identified and, therefore, provides no information about the demand equation.

13-5 Comparison of Alternative Methods of Estimation and Special Problems

In discussing the methods of estimating structural equations of a general interdependent system, we have been using the food market model for which the true values of the parameters are known. Therefore, it might be interesting to compare the results obtained for this model by the different estimation methods. In making the comparison, however, we should keep in mind that we have only one sample on which to base the comparisons. In this case comparing various estimators is like comparing different guns on the basis of one shot from each. The summary of the results is shown in Table 13-2, which also includes the OLS estimates. The latter are inconsistent, but they are nevertheless sometimes used in applied work, mainly because they are simple to compute. In our particular

[13] A detailed description can be found in W. L. Ruble, "Improving the Computation of Simultaneous Stochastic Linear Equations Estimates," *Agricultural Economics Report No. 116*, Department of Agricultural Economics, Michigan State University, East Lansing, 1968, pp. 163-171.

Table 13–2

Method*	Demand			Supply			
	Constant	P_t	D_t	Constant	P_t	F_t	A_t
True values of coefficients	96.5	−0.25	0.30	62.5	0.15	0.20	0.36
			ESTIMATES				
OLS	99.8954	−0.3163	0.3346	58.2754	0.1604	0.2481	0.2483
	(7.5194)	(0.0907)	(0.0454)	(11.4629)	(0.0949)	(0.0462)	(0.0975)
2SLS	94.6333	−0.2436	0.3140	49.5324	0.2401	0.2556	0.2529
	(7.9208)	(0.0965)	(0.0469)	(12.0105)	(0.0999)	(0.0472)	(0.0996)
LIML	93.6192	−0.2295	0.3100	49.5324	0.2401	0.2556	0.2529
	(8.0312)	(0.0980)	(0.0474)	(12.0105)	(0.0999)	(0.0472)	(0.0996)
3SLS	94.6333	−0.2436	0.3140	52.1176	0.2289	0.2290	0.3579
	(7.9208)	(0.0965)	(0.0469)	(11.8934)	(0.0997)	(0.0440)	(0.0729)
I3SLS	94.6333	−0.2436	0.3140	55.5527	0.2271	0.2245	0.3756
	(7.9208)	(0.0965)	(0.0469)	(12.7408)	(0.1069)	(0.0465)	(0.0717)
FIML	93.6192	−0.2295	0.3100	51.9445	0.2373	0.2208	0.3697
	(8.0312)	(0.0980)	(0.0474)	(12.7460)	(0.1078)	(0.0457)	(0.0765)
			SAMPLING ERRORS				
OLS	3.3954	−0.0663	0.0346	−4.2246	0.0104	0.0481	−0.1117
2SLS	−1.8667	0.0064	0.0140	−12.9676	0.0901	0.0556	−0.1071
LIML	−2.8808	0.0205	0.0100	−12.9676	0.0901	0.0556	−0.1071
3SLS	−1.8667	0.0064	0.0140	−10.3824	0.0789	0.0290	−0.0021
I3SLS	−1.8667	0.0064	0.0140	−6.9473	0.0771	0.0245	0.0156
FIML	−2.8808	0.0205	0.0100	−10.5555	0.0873	0.0208	0.0097

* Notation:
OLS ordinary least squares
2SLS two-stage least squares
LIML limited information maximum likelihood
3SLS three-stage least squares
I3SLS iterative three-stage least squares
FIML full information maximum likelihood

example, their performance in estimating the supply equation compares quite well with that of the 2SLS and LIML estimators. With respect to the consistent methods, we can distinguish between the results for the overidentified demand equation and those for the exactly identified supply equation. In the case of the *demand equation*, we obtain identical results for 2SLS, 3SLS, and I3SLS, on one hand, and for LIML and FIML on the other. The reasons for this were given in the text. (However, note that, if the model contained—in addition to the exactly identified equation—*more than one* overidentified equation, the results for the system methods would differ from those for the single equation methods.) In the present case there is therefore no gain in going from the single equation methods (2SLS or LIML) to the system methods (3SLS, I3SLS, or FIML). Furthermore, the results for 2SLS and LIML do not appear to be markedly different. As for the *supply equation*, we obtain identical results for the 2SLS and LIML methods. Comparing the system methods with the single equation methods, we see that the former clearly performed better than the latter. There is, however, no clear-cut answer to the question as to *which* of the system methods performed best. On the grounds of computational effort the 3SLS is, of course, the one to be preferred. In assessing the general performance of the consistent methods, we note that *in each case* the true values of the coefficients are covered by the conventionally calculated 95% confidence intervals. This result would be expected for a large sample since the estimated standard errors are justified on asymptotic grounds, but it is gratifying to see it happen also in a sample of only 20 observations.

All simultaneous equation estimation methods discussed in this section have some desirable asymptotic properties. These properties become effective in large samples, but since our samples are mostly small, we would be more interested in knowing the *small sample properties* of these estimators. Unfortunately, our knowledge in this respect is far from complete. The results from the food market example presented in Table 13–2 relate to a single set of values of the various estimators, but they give no information about the characteristics of their sampling distributions. Ideally, we would like to know the mathematical description of the distributions of each of the estimators. Such knowledge is available only for a small number of special cases.[14] From this we can conclude that the small sample distribution of the 2SLS estimator has a finite mean, but that its variance is, at least in some cases, infinite. The shape of the distribution appears to be similar to that of the normal distribution, but its peak is taller and its tails thicker than in the case of the normal distribution. Most of the evidence on the small sample properties of the simultaneous equation estimators comes from sampling (or Monte Carlo) experiments similar to those described in Chapter 2 and in the concluding part of Section 8–2 (our food example, for instance, could serve as the first sample of a Monte Carlo experiment). Since a survey of these experiments can be found elsewhere,[15] only the main results will be reported here. For the most part, the experimenters have presented some of the basic characteristics of the sampling distributions rather than their full description. Typically, these characteristics were the mean, the variance, and the mean square error. Of course, when an estimator has no finite variance, the value of the variance or of the mean square error of an experimental sampling distribution has no meaning,

[14] See especially R. L. Basmann, "A Note on the Exact Finite Sample Frequency Functions of Generalized Classical Linear Estimators in Two Leading Over-Identified Cases," *Journal of the American Statistical Association*, Vol. 56, September 1961, pp. 619–636, and "A Note on the Exact Finite Sample Frequency Functions of Generalized Classical Linear Estimators in a Leading Three-Equation Case," *Journal of the American Statistical Association*, Vol. 58, March 1963, pp. 161–171.

[15] See Johnston, *op. cit.*, Chapter 10, and C. F. Christ, *Econometric Models and Methods* (New York: Wiley, 1966), pp. 474–481.

since it tends to increase without limit as the number of samples increases. Nevertheless, these values may serve as a basis for comparison of alternative estimators in relation to the same samples whose number is fixed. In all of the experiments the predetermined variables included only exogenous variables, but it can be conjectured that the presence of lagged endogenous variables would not alter the essence of the results obtained. While the results of different experiments do not appear to be in complete agreement in all respects, some common features have been confirmed repeatedly. In particular, the OLS estimator tends to have a larger bias but a smaller variance than 2SLS or LIML. If the mean square error is used as a criterion in comparing the single equation estimators, the results are somewhat mixed. In some cases the OLS estimator performs better than 2SLS or LIML, in others worse, and sometimes about the same. When 2SLS is compared with LIML, it appears that the former usually leads to smaller mean square errors than the latter, particularly when the exogenous variables are highly intercorrelated. As for the system estimators, the experimental results are much less numerous than those for the single equation estimators. From the available evidence it appears that the asymptotic advantage of the system methods over the single equation methods persists also in small samples, although not in an equally pronounced way. However, the FIML method appears to be more sensitive to errors of specification (such as omitting a relevant explanatory variable) than 2SLS.

In assessing various estimation methods, we are frequently concerned not only with the properties of the estimators, but also with the performance of the methods when it comes to *hypothesis testing*. In this context the most important quantity is the ratio of the estimated coefficient to its estimated standard error. This test statistic is frequently referred to as the "t ratio" in spite of the fact that the t distribution is not necessarily appropriate. When consistent simultaneous equation estimation methods are used, the asymptotic distribution of this statistic is normal. In small samples the desired acceptance regions or confidence intervals are usually determined by reference to the tabulated t distribution. This procedure is clearly not exactly valid, since the test statistic does *not* have a t distribution. The question, then, is whether the t distribution can serve as a tolerable approximation of the true distribution so that the results of the tests and of interval estimation are not seriously distorted. The available Monte Carlo evidence suggests that the distortion is usually (although not always) reasonably small. For instance, Cragg, who has conducted a large number of experiments, concludes on this point as follows:

> Usually use of the standard errors of the consistent methods would lead to reliable inferences, but this was not always the case. The standard errors of DLS were not useful for making inference about the true values of the coefficients.[16]

[16] J. G. Cragg, "On the Relative Small-Sample Properties of Several Structural-Equation Estimators," *Econometrica*, Vol. 35, January 1967, p. 109. The term "DLS" refers to the OLS estimator.

A very similar conclusion was reached by Summers.[17] This suggests that, at least from the point of view of hypothesis testing or interval estimation, the OLS method is inferior to the consistent methods of estimation.

Another relevant criterion for judging various estimators is their ability to *forecast*. In simultaneous equations the values of the endogenous variables can be predicted by reference to the reduced form equations. Suppose the $(K \times 1)$ vector of the values of the predetermined variables for the period of the forecast is $\mathbf{x}_0$. Then the forecast values of the G endogenous variables are

$$\hat{\mathbf{y}}_0 = \hat{\mathbf{\Pi}}\mathbf{x}_0,$$

where $\hat{\mathbf{\Pi}}$ is a $(G \times K)$ matrix of the reduced form coefficients estimated from the sample observations. Now, consistent estimates of $\mathbf{\Pi}$ can be obtained either by a direct application of the OLS method to the reduced form equations, or by using consistent estimates of the structural coefficients, say, $\tilde{\mathbf{B}}$ and $\tilde{\mathbf{\Gamma}}$, and setting

$$\tilde{\mathbf{\Pi}} = -\tilde{\mathbf{B}}\tilde{\mathbf{\Gamma}} \tag{13.80}$$

in accordance with (13.7). If the estimated reduced form coefficients are obtained by a direct application of OLS, they are called "unrestricted"; otherwise, they are called "derived." Unless all structural equations are exactly identified, the unrestricted and the derived reduced form coefficients will not coincide. Since the unrestricted least squares estimator of $\mathbf{\Pi}$ does not, in general, incorporate the prior restrictions imposed by the relation

$$\mathbf{\Pi} = -\mathbf{B}^{-1}\mathbf{\Gamma},$$

it will be asymptotically less efficient than the derived estimator $\tilde{\mathbf{\Pi}}$. Furthermore, since the FIML and 3SLS methods lead to asymptotically efficient estimates of $\mathbf{B}$ and $\mathbf{\Gamma}$, and since this property carries over to any single-valued functions of $\mathbf{B}$ and $\mathbf{\Gamma}$, it follows that the derived estimator of $\mathbf{\Pi}$ based on FIML or 3SLS estimates of the structural coefficients is itself asymptotically efficient. This implies that an estimator of $\mathbf{\Pi}$ derived from FIML or 3SLS leads to a smaller asymptotic variance of the forecast error than an estimator derived from 2SLS or LIML. On the basis of Monte Carlo experiments there is some evidence that these results tend to hold in small samples as well, although such ranking is to be regarded as very tentative.[18]

Recursive Systems

We have dealt so far with the estimation problem for a general interdependent system of equations. We shall now briefly consider the estimation problem in the case where the system is *recursive*. As stated in Section 13–1, a system

$$\mathbf{B}\mathbf{y}_t + \mathbf{\Gamma}\mathbf{x}_t = \mathbf{u}_t$$

[17] R. M. Summers, "A Capital Intensive Approach to the Small Sample Properties of Various Simultaneous Equation Estimators," *Econometrica*, Vol. 33, January 1965, pp. 1–41.

[18] *Ibid.*, pp. 31–22

is called recursive if the matrix **B** is triangular. A well-known example of a recursive system is the so-called "cobweb model," which may be exemplified as follows:

$$(13.81) \qquad \begin{aligned} Q_t &= \alpha_1 + \alpha_2 P_{t-1} + u_{1t} && \text{(supply)},\\ P_t &= \beta_1 + \beta_2 Q_t + \beta_3 Y_t + u_{2t} && \text{(demand)}, \end{aligned}$$

where Q = equilibrium quantity, P = equilibrium price, and Y = income (exogenous). Here

$$\mathbf{B} = \begin{bmatrix} 1 & 0 \\ -\beta_2 & 1 \end{bmatrix} \quad \text{and} \quad \mathbf{\Gamma} = \begin{bmatrix} -\alpha_1 & -\alpha_2 & 0 \\ -\beta_1 & 0 & -\beta_3 \end{bmatrix}.$$

Note that the supply equation involves only one endogenous variable and, therefore, using ordinary least squares would lead to consistent estimates. These estimates would not be asymptotically efficient, though, because they disregard the implied correlation between the disturbances of the two equations. The demand equation could be consistently estimated by ILS. Alternatively, both equations could be estimated by one of the system methods, in which case the estimates would be not only consistent but also asymptotically efficient. The notable feature of the recursive models such as (13.81) is that the calculation of the FIML estimates is greatly simplified by the fact that the Jacobian (i.e., the determinant of **B**) is equal to unity. (The foregoing presupposes that each diagonal element of **B** is unity; if this is not so, we can divide each structural equation by the appropriate coefficient β_{gg}.)

If the system

$$\mathbf{B}\mathbf{y}_t + \mathbf{\Gamma}\mathbf{x}_t = \mathbf{u}_t$$

is *diagonally recursive*—that is, if **B** is triangular and the variance-covariance matrix of the structural disturbances, **Φ**, is diagonal—the estimation problem becomes really simple. The reason is that the endogenous variables, which serve as explanatory factors in the structural equations, are *not* correlated with the disturbance of the equation in which they appear. For instance, in the demand equation of (13.81) the explanatory variables include the endogenous variable Q_t. However, if u_{1t} and u_{2t} are independent and nonautoregressive, then

$$E(Q_t u_{2t}) = E[(\alpha_1 + \alpha_2 P_{t-1} + u_{1t})u_{2t}] = 0.$$

This means that *the application of the OLS method to each of the structural equations leads to consistent and asymptotically efficient estimates.* (In the absence of lagged endogenous variables, the OLS estimates are also *unbiased.*) It should be emphasized that this is true only if the system is *diagonally* recursive, not otherwise. Finally, we note that if **B** is block-triangular and the **Φ** matrix is correspondingly block-diagonal, then the equations corresponding to each diagonal block of **Φ** can be treated as belonging to separate systems. Of course, this also simplifies estimation considerably.

Autoregressive Disturbances

As the final point connected with the problem of estimating the coefficients of structural equations in a simultaneous equation system, we consider the case in which the structural disturbances are not independent over time. In particular, suppose the structural disturbances follow a first-order *autoregressive* scheme of the type described in Section 8–2. In this case we have

$$\begin{aligned} u_{1t} &= \rho_1 u_{1,t-1} + \varepsilon_{1t}, \\ u_{2t} &= \rho_2 u_{2,t-1} + \varepsilon_{2t}, \\ &\vdots \\ u_{Gt} &= \rho_G u_{G,t-1} + \varepsilon_{Gt}. \end{aligned}$$

The ε's are *not* assumed to be independent across equations. Consider the problem of estimating the first structural equation of the system as described by (13.34):

$$\mathbf{y}_1 = \mathbf{Y}_1\boldsymbol{\beta}_1 + \mathbf{X}_1\boldsymbol{\gamma}_1 + \mathbf{u}_1.$$

The tth observation is then represented as

$$(13.82)\qquad y_{1t} = -\beta_{12}y_{2t} - \cdots - \beta_{1G^\Delta}y_{G^\Delta t} - \gamma_{11}x_{1t} - \cdots - \gamma_{1K^*}x_{K^*t} + u_{1t}.$$

For the time being we shall confine ourselves to the case in which *the predetermined variables of the system do not include any lagged endogenous variables.* In this case the OLS estimates of the reduced form coefficients are consistent. Therefore, the straightforward application of the 2SLS method leads to consistent estimates of the structural coefficients, but the estimates of the variance-covariance matrix are inconsistent. However, we can easily modify the 2SLS method to account for the autoregressive nature of u_{1t}. First, we apply the transformation described in (8.52) to (13.82) to obtain

$$\begin{aligned} (13.83)\qquad y_{1t} - \rho_1 y_{1,t-1} = {} & -\beta_{12}(y_{2t} - \rho_1 y_{2,t-1}) - \beta_{13}(y_{3t} - \rho_1 y_{3,t-1}) \\ & - \cdots - \beta_{1G^\Delta}(y_{G^\Delta t} - \rho_1 y_{G^\Delta,t-1}) \\ & -\gamma_{11}(x_{1t} - \rho_1 x_{1,t-1}) - \gamma_{12}(x_{2t} - \rho_1 x_{2,t-1}) \\ & - \cdots - \gamma_{1K^*}(x_{K^*t} - \rho_1 x_{K^*,t-1}) + \varepsilon_{1t}. \end{aligned}$$

Now, a similar transformation can be applied to each structural equation. This leads to the replacement of the autoregressive u's by the nonautoregressive ε's. The resulting system can then be solved for the current values of the endogenous variables in terms of the lagged values of the endogenous variables and current and lagged values of the exogenous variables. The equations thus obtained may be called "augmented reduced form equations" because they contain an augmented set of explanatory variables as compared to the ordinary reduced form equations. With respect to (13.83) the relevant augmented reduced form equations are those for $y_{2t}, y_{3t}, \ldots, y_{G^\Delta t}$. The coefficients of these equations can be estimated by application of the ordinary (unrestricted) least squares method.

Let us denote the resulting fitted values of the y's by $\hat{y}_{2t}, \hat{y}_{3t}, \ldots, \hat{y}_{G^{\Delta}t}$. Then we form

$$(13.84)\quad y_{1t} - \rho_1 y_{1,t-1} = -\beta_{12}(\hat{y}_{2t} - \rho_1\hat{y}_{2,t-1}) - \beta_{13}(\hat{y}_{3t} - \rho_1\hat{y}_{3,t-1}) - \cdots - \beta_{1G^{\Delta}}(\hat{y}_{G^{\Delta}t} - \rho_1\hat{y}_{G^{\Delta},t-1}) - \gamma_{11}(x_{1t} - \rho_1 x_{1,t-1}) - \gamma_{12}(x_{2t} - \rho_1 x_{2,t-1}) - \cdots - \gamma_{1K^*}(x_{K^*t} - \rho_1 x_{K^*,t-1}) + \varepsilon_{1t}^*$$

or

$$(13.84a)\quad \mathbf{y}_1^* = \hat{\mathbf{Y}}_1^*\boldsymbol{\beta}_1 + \mathbf{X}_1^*\boldsymbol{\gamma}_1 + \boldsymbol{\epsilon}_1^*,$$

where

$$\mathbf{y}_1^* = \begin{bmatrix} y_{12} - \rho_1 y_{11} \\ y_{13} - \rho_1 y_{12} \\ \vdots \\ y_{1T} - \rho_1 y_{1,T-1} \end{bmatrix},$$

$$\hat{\mathbf{Y}}_1^* = \begin{bmatrix} (\hat{y}_{22} - \rho_1\hat{y}_{21}) & (\hat{y}_{32} - \rho_1\hat{y}_{31}) & \cdots & (\hat{y}_{G^{\Delta}2} - \rho_1\hat{y}_{G^{\Delta}1}) \\ (\hat{y}_{23} - \rho_1\hat{y}_{22}) & (\hat{y}_{33} - \rho_1\hat{y}_{32}) & \cdots & (\hat{y}_{G^{\Delta}3} - \rho_1\hat{y}_{G^{\Delta}2}) \\ \vdots & \vdots & & \vdots \\ (\hat{y}_{2T} - \rho_1\hat{y}_{2,T-1}) & (\hat{y}_{3T} - \rho_1\hat{y}_{3,T-1}) & \cdots & (\hat{y}_{G^{\Delta}T} - \rho_1\hat{y}_{G^{\Delta},T-1}) \end{bmatrix},$$

and

$$\mathbf{X}_1^* = \begin{bmatrix} (x_{12} - \rho_1 x_{11}) & (x_{22} - \rho_1 x_{21}) & \cdots & (x_{K^*2} - \rho_1 x_{K^*1}) \\ (x_{13} - \rho_1 x_{12}) & (x_{23} - \rho_1 x_{22}) & \cdots & (x_{K^*3} - \rho_1 x_{K^*2}) \\ \vdots & \vdots & & \vdots \\ (x_{1T} - \rho_1 x_{1,T-1}) & (x_{2T} - \rho_1 x_{2,T-1}) & \cdots & (x_{K^*T} - \rho_1 x_{K^*,T-1}) \end{bmatrix},$$

The coefficients ρ_1, $\boldsymbol{\beta}_1$, and $\boldsymbol{\gamma}_1$ can then be estimated by applying the restricted least squares method to (13.84) as described in Section 8–2.

The 3SLS method can also be easily modified to take into account the autoregressive character of the structural disturbances. By applying the modified 2SLS method to each structural equation, we obtain consistent estimates of $\rho_1, \rho_2, \ldots, \rho_G$. These can be used to transform the variables so that the system can be written as

$$(13.85)\quad \begin{aligned} \mathbf{y}_1^{**} &= \hat{\mathbf{Y}}_1^{**}\boldsymbol{\beta}_1 + \mathbf{X}_1^{**}\boldsymbol{\gamma}_1 + \boldsymbol{\epsilon}_1^{**}, \\ \mathbf{y}_2^{**} &= \hat{\mathbf{Y}}_2^{**}\boldsymbol{\beta}_2 + \mathbf{X}_2^{**}\boldsymbol{\gamma}_2 + \boldsymbol{\epsilon}_2^{**}, \\ &\vdots \\ \mathbf{y}_G^{**} &= \hat{\mathbf{Y}}_G^{**}\boldsymbol{\beta}_G + \mathbf{X}_G^{**}\boldsymbol{\gamma}_G + \boldsymbol{\epsilon}_G^{**}, \end{aligned}$$

where the double asterisk indicates that the ρ's have been replaced by their consistent estimates; otherwise the notation in (13.85) conforms to that in (13.84a). The coefficients of (13.85) can then be estimated by two-stage Aitken's estimation method as in the case of the ordinary 3SLS method. It would also be possible to set up a joint distribution function for the ε's and use it to derive the FIML estimates for the autoregressive case, but this would be quite complicated.

The preceding discussion has been restricted to simultaneous equation systems in which the predetermined variables do not include any lagged endogenous variables. If this is not the case, the estimation problem under autoregressive disturbances becomes rather difficult. The source of this difficulty is the fact that, under these circumstances, the predetermined variables are no longer uncorrelated with the structural disturbances. One consequence is that the OLS estimates of the reduced form coefficients are inconsistent, which creates serious complications. A way out of this difficulty would be to use the method of instrumental variables. Another approach, similar to that adopted in the context of distributed lag models, has been proposed by Fisher.[19]

13–6 Analysis of Dynamic Econometric Models[20]

A simultaneous equation model represents a set of relations between the endogenous and the predetermined variables of a system. If the predetermined variables are all purely exogenous, then the model specifies how the exogenous variables, together with the stochastic disturbances, generate the values of the endogenous variables at a given point (or period) of time. This was illustrated in detail in the food market example of Section 13–2. However, if the predetermined variables also include lagged endogenous variables, then the model specifies not only how the predetermined variables (together with the disturbances) generate the current values of the endogenous variables, but also how the time paths of the exogenous variables and the disturbances determine the time paths of the endogenous variables. This is implicit in the structure of the model, but it is of some interest to have such a dynamic dependence formulated explicitly. Further questions of interest concern the stability of the system, and the influence of the past values of the exogenous variables on the current values

[19] See F. M. Fisher, *The Identification Problem in Econometrics* (New York: McGraw-Hill, 1966), pp. 168–175. The instrumental variables approach is described in R. C. Fair, "The Estimation of Simultaneous Equation Models with Lagged Endogenous Variables and First Order Serially Correlated Errors," *Econometrica*, Vol. 38, May 1970, pp. 507–516.

[20] In our exposition we present only the very basic elements of dynamic analysis applicable to simple linear systems. Considerably more sophisticated methods involving simulation, policy analysis, and nonlinear dynamic multipliers are now becoming known and may be studied. See, e.g., L. R. Klein, M. K. Evans, and M. Hartley, *Econometric Gaming* (New York: Macmillan, 1969); Gary Fromm and Paul Taubman, *Policy Simulations with an Econometric Model* (Washington: Brookings Institution, 1968); or M. K. Evans and L. R. Klein, *The Wharton Econometric Forecasting Model* (Philadelphia: University of Pennsylvania Press, 1967).

of the endogenous variables. The purpose of this section is to examine these questions, since providing the answers represents a natural and important part of the work of an econometrician. Our approach will be to illustrate the problems and their solution by reference to a specific model; in this way the special concepts of dynamic analysis will acquire a concrete meaning. However, the basic procedures can easily be adapted to other models as well.

Consider the following simple model of the economy:

$$C_t = \alpha_0 + \alpha_1 Y_t + \alpha_2 C_{t-1} + u_{1t} \quad \text{(consumption)},$$

$$I_t = \beta_0 + \beta_1 r_t + \beta_2 I_{t-1} + u_{2t} \quad \text{(investment)},$$

$$r_t = \gamma_0 + \gamma_1 Y_t + \gamma_2 M_t + u_{3t} \quad \text{(money market)},$$

$$Y_t = C_t + I_t + G_t \quad \text{(income identity)},$$

where C = consumption, Y = income, I = investment, r = rate of interest, M = money supply, and G = government expenditure. C, Y, I, and r are endogenous; M and G are exogenous. The latter may be viewed as policy variables that can be, and have been, manipulated at will by the policymakers. The reduced form of this system is

$$(13.86) \qquad C_t = \pi_{11} + \pi_{12} C_{t-1} + \pi_{13} I_{t-1} + \pi_{14} M_t + \pi_{15} G_t + v_{1t},$$

$$(13.87) \qquad I_t = \pi_{21} + \pi_{22} C_{t-1} + \pi_{23} I_{t-1} + \pi_{24} M_t + \pi_{25} G_t + v_{2t},$$

$$(13.88) \qquad Y_t = \pi_{31} + \pi_{32} C_{t-1} + \pi_{33} I_{t-1} + \pi_{34} M_t + \pi_{35} G_t + v_{3t},$$

$$(13.89) \qquad r_t = \pi_{41} + \pi_{42} C_{t-1} + \pi_{43} I_{t-1} + \pi_{44} M_t + \pi_{45} G_t + v_{4t}.$$

The reduced form coefficients can, of course, be expressed in terms of the structural coefficients. In the language of dynamic analysis, the reduced form coefficients are called *impact multipliers*, since they measure the immediate response of the endogenous variables to changes in the predetermined variables. For instance, π_{15} measures the change in the mean value of current consumption due to a unit change in current government expenditure, given the current value of the money supply and given the level of consumption and investment in the preceding period.

The reduced form equations are useful mainly for short-term forecasting. We can forecast the next period's values of the endogenous variables on the basis of our knowledge of the current values of I and C and of the forthcoming values of the policy variables. However, we cannot use the reduced form equations to determine how the system operates under continuous impact of the exogenous variables. For instance, the reduced form equation for consumption shows that the current value of consumption depends not only on the current values of G and M but also on the previous values of consumption and investment. This is not greatly illuminating because it pushes part of the responsibility for explaining the current level of consumption onto its own immediate history. To understand the mechanism of the determination of consumption and of other endogenous variables, we need a solution that would determine the level of these variables *without* reference to their immediate past. Such a solution can be obtained by manipulating the reduced form equations so that all lagged endogenous variables are eliminated. This elimination can proceed in two steps. First we reformulate the reduced form equations so that each equation contains only one endogenous variable, whether current or lagged. Then we remove the lagged endogenous variables as intended.

Let us take the reduced form equation for consumption. Here the only "foreign" lagged endogenous variable is I_{t-1}. Now, from (13.87) we have

$$(13.90) \qquad I_t - \pi_{23}I_{t-1} = \pi_{21} + \pi_{22}C_{t-1} + \pi_{24}M_t + \pi_{25}G_t + v_{2t}$$

or

$$(13.90a) \quad I_{t-1} - \pi_{23}I_{t-2} = \pi_{21} + \pi_{22}C_{t-2} + \pi_{24}M_{t-1} + \pi_{25}G_{t-1} + v_{2,t-1}.$$

Further, lagging (13.86) by one period and multiplying by $-\pi_{23}$ gives

$$(13.91) \quad -\pi_{23}C_{t-1} = -\pi_{11}\pi_{23} - \pi_{12}\pi_{23}C_{t-2} - \pi_{13}\pi_{23}I_{t-2} - \pi_{14}\pi_{23}M_{t-1} - \pi_{15}\pi_{23}G_{t-1} - \pi_{23}v_{1,t-1}.$$

By adding (13.86) and (13.91), we obtain

$$(13.92) \qquad C_t = \pi_{11}(1 - \pi_{23}) + (\pi_{12} + \pi_{23})C_{t-1} - \pi_{12}\pi_{23}C_{t-2} + \pi_{13}(I_{t-1} - \pi_{23}I_{t-2}) + \pi_{14}M_t - \pi_{14}\pi_{23}M_{t-1} + \pi_{15}G_t - \pi_{15}\pi_{23}G_{t-1} + v_{1t} - \pi_{23}v_{1,t-1}.$$

Substitution for $(I_{t-1} - \pi_{23}I_{t-2})$ from (13.90a) into (13.92) then leads to

$$(13.93) \quad C_t = [\pi_{11}(1 - \pi_{23}) + \pi_{13}\pi_{21}] + (\pi_{12} + \pi_{23})C_{t-1} + (\pi_{13}\pi_{22} - \pi_{12}\pi_{23})C_{t-2} + \pi_{14}M_t + (\pi_{13}\pi_{24} - \pi_{14}\pi_{23})M_{t-1} + \pi_{15}G_t + (\pi_{13}\pi_{25} - \pi_{15}\pi_{23})G_{t-1} + v_{1t} - \pi_{23}v_{1,t-1} + \pi_{13}v_{2,t-1},$$

or, in obvious notation,

$$(13.93a) \quad C_t = \delta + \mu_1C_{t-1} + \mu_2C_{t-2} + \kappa_0M_t + \kappa_1M_{t-1} + \nu_0G_t + \nu_1G_{t-1} + \varepsilon_t.$$

Equation (13.93), or its equivalent (13.93a), is called the *fundamental dynamic equation* for the consumption variable. Similar equations could be derived for the remaining endogenous variables of the system. Since it can be shown that in a general interdependent linear system each variable satisfies the same final autoregressive equation,[21] we will refer to consumption alone. The fundamental dynamic equation has special importance in determining the stability of the system, and we shall return to it. Our present aim is to express current consumption in terms of current and past values of the exogenous variables and

[21] See A. S. Goldberger, *Impact Multipliers and Dynamic Properties of the Klein-Goldberger Model* (Amsterdam: North-Holland Publishing Company, 1959), pp. 106–108.

disturbances, which can be done by a series of successive substitutions. First, note that by (13.93a) the expression for C_t at $t = 1$ is

$$C_1 = \delta + \mu_1 C_0 + \mu_2 C_{-1} + \kappa_0 M_1 + \kappa_1 M_0 + \nu_0 G_1 + \nu_1 G_0 + \varepsilon_1. \tag{13.94}$$

The values of C_0 and C_{-1} have been determined prior to the beginning of the series, and are called the *initial conditions*. For the purpose of dynamic analysis we shall assume them to be given. The values of M_0 and G_0 are of no special interest to us and can be merged with the constant term, so that (13.94) can be written as

$$C_1 = \eta + \mu_1 C_0 + \mu_2 C_{-1} + \kappa_0 M_1 + \nu_0 G_1 + \varepsilon_1. \tag{13.94a}$$

Next, the expression for C_t at $t = 2$ is

$$C_2 = \delta + \mu_1 C_1 + \mu_2 C_0 + \kappa_0 M_2 + \kappa_1 M_1 + \nu_0 G_2 + \nu_1 G_1 + \varepsilon_2. \tag{13.95}$$

Since C_0 is taken as given, we have only to eliminate C_1 from (13.95), by substituting from (13.94a), which gives

$$\begin{aligned} C_2 = {} & (\delta + \mu_1 \eta) + (\mu_1^2 + \mu_2) C_0 + \mu_1 \mu_2 C_{-1} \\ & + \kappa_0 M_2 + (\kappa_1 + \kappa_0 \mu_1) M_1 + \nu_0 G_2 + (\nu_1 + \nu_0 \mu_1) G_1 + \varepsilon_2 + \mu_1 \varepsilon_1. \end{aligned} \tag{13.96}$$

In a similar way we can obtain a solution for C_3, C_4, etc. The outcome is a general expression for C_t, which is

$$\begin{aligned} C_t = {} & \eta_t + \eta_1 C_0 + \eta_2 C_{-1} + \zeta_0 M_t + \zeta_1 M_{t-1} + \cdots + \zeta_{t-1} M_1 \\ & + \xi_0 G_t + \xi_1 G_{t-1} + \cdots + \xi_{t-1} G_1 + \varepsilon_t + \theta_1 \varepsilon_{t-1} + \cdots + \theta_{t-1} \varepsilon_1. \end{aligned} \tag{13.97}$$

Thus C_t is—for a set of given initial conditions—expressed purely in terms of current and lagged exogenous variables and disturbances. (If the system is stable, η_t becomes a constant for large t.) Similar expressions could be derived for the other endogenous variables. These equations are called the *final form* of the equation system. They show how the time paths of the exogenous variables determine the time path of each endogenous variable. The coefficients attached to the exogenous variables are here called the *dynamic multipliers*. Note that equations such as (13.97) can also be used to answer questions concerning the influence of some past policy action on the current level of the endogenous variables, or the extent of corrective measures necessary to bring about some desired changes in the endogenous variables over any number of future periods.

Stability Conditions and Dynamic Analysis

Let us now turn to the question of the stability of a system. In general, we say that a system is stable if, in a situation where the values of the exogenous variables are held constant through time, the mean values of the endogenous variable settle down to some constant levels. (The actual values of the endogenous variables will, of course, fluctuate because of the effect of the stochastic disturbances. We will consider only cases where the probability is very small that an otherwise stable system could turn unstable because of random disturbances.)

This means that a system is considered unstable if, for constant values of the exogenous variables, the mean values of the endogenous variables either explode or display a regular oscillatory movement. One way of determining whether a system is stable or not is to refer to the final form equations. Clearly, if the system is to settle down when the levels of the exogenous variables are unchanged, the sums of each set of dynamic multipliers must be finite. That is, the requirement for stability is that the sums

$$\sum_{i=0}^{\infty} \zeta_i \quad \text{and} \quad \sum_{i=0}^{\infty} \xi_i$$

are finite. These sums represent the *long-run* or *equilibrium multipliers* for consumption with respect to money supply and to government expenditure. Another way of finding out whether a system is stable or not is to examine the fundamental dynamic equation. If the exogenous variables are held constant (and the disturbances are disregarded), this equation becomes an ordinary linear nonhomogeneous difference equation and can be solved as such.[22] In our case we have from (13.93a)

$$C_t - \mu_1 C_{t-1} - \mu_2 C_{t-2} = \text{constant}. \tag{13.98}$$

The characteristic equation for (13.98) is

$$\lambda^2 - \mu_1 \lambda - \mu_2 = 0 \tag{13.99}$$

with roots

$$\lambda_{1,2} = \frac{\mu_1 \pm \sqrt{\mu_1^2 + 4\mu_2}}{2}.$$

The system is stable if and only if the absolute value of the largest root (or modulus) of (13.99) is smaller than one. If this is the case, we can determine the equilibrium mean value of consumption from (13.93a) as

$$C_E = \frac{\delta + \kappa_0 M_t + \kappa_1 M_{t-1} + \nu_0 G_t + \nu_1 G_{t-1}}{1 - \mu_1 - \mu_2}. \tag{13.100}$$

The stability condition is clearly important from the economic point of view. It should also be realized that the existence of stability (or, at worst, of a regular oscillatory pattern) is, in fact, assumed in the process of estimation. The assumption that the predetermined variables of the system have finite variances as $t \to \infty$ applies also to the lagged endogenous variables, and this assumption would be violated if the endogenous variables were to grow or decline without limit. If this assumption were not made, there would be difficulties in proving the asymptotic properties of estimators.

The dynamic solution given by the final form equations answers questions concerning the influence of hypothetical changes in the exogenous variables of

[22] See, e.g., R. G. D. Allen, *Mathematical Economics* (London: Macmillan, 1956), pp. 176–195.

the system. If we are interested in the effect of changes in the values of exogenous variables that actually did take place during the period under observation, we may trace these more conveniently by using first differences. In our model we have, by reference to (13.97),

$$(13.101)\quad C_t - C_{t-1} = (\eta_t - \eta_{t-1}) + \zeta_0(M_t - M_{t-1}) + \zeta_1(M_{t-1} - M_{t-2}) + \cdots + \zeta_{t-2}(M_2 - M_1) + \zeta_{t-1}M_1 + \xi_0(G_t - G_{t-1}) + \xi_1(G_{t-1} - G_{t-2}) + \cdots + \xi_{t-2}(G_2 - G_1) + \xi_{t-1}G_1 + \omega_t.$$

The first term on the right-hand side indicates the influence of the initial conditions and of the dynamics of the system operating in absence of any changes in the exogenous variables. For systems that are stable the value of this term will diminish as the system moves from the initial position, and will eventually approach zero. The terms $\zeta_{t-1}M_1$ and $\xi_{t-1}G_1$ measure the influence of the starting levels of the exogenous variables. The term ω_t summarizes the influence of the random disturbances. By substituting the actual values of the exogenous variables for the period under investigation into (13.101), we can determine the part that any policy measure played in affecting the observed change in the level of consumption.

The preceding discussion has been carried out in terms of the population parameters which are, of course, not known and must be replaced by sample estimates. Therefore, it would be desirable to accompany each estimate with its standard error. Formulas for estimating the standard errors are available for the impact multipliers of the reduced form equations, and also for the dynamic multipliers of the final form equations. As for the characteristic roots that are crucial for the determination of the stability condition of a system, a formula for the asymptotic variance of the largest root has been derived by Theil and Boot.[23] In general, however, dynamic analysis in econometrics has not yet been well developed from the viewpoint of statistical inference.

EXAMPLE A model of the United States economy for the period 1921–1941, known as Klein's Model I, has been estimated as follows:[24]

Consumption: $C_t = 16.555 + 0.017P_t + 0.216P_{t-1} + 0.810W_t + \tilde{u}_{1t};$

Investment: $I_t = 20.278 + 0.150P_t + 0.616P_{t-1} - 0.158K_{t-1} + \tilde{u}_{2t};$

Private wages: $W_t^* = 1.500 + 0.439E_t + 0.147E_{t-1} + 0.130A_t + \tilde{u}_{3t};$

Product: $Y_t + T_t = C_t + I_t + G_t;$

Income: $Y_t = P_t + W_t;$

[23] H. Theil and J. C. G. Boot, "The Final Form of Econometric Equation Systems," *Review of the International Statistical Institute*, Vol. 30, 1962, pp. 136–152.

[24] The model is presented in L. R. Klein, *Economic Fluctuations in the United States 1921–1941* (New York: Wiley, 1950), pp. 65–68. The estimates of the coefficients are two-stage least squares estimates given in A. S. Goldberger, *op. cit.* (1964), p. 365.

Capital: $K_t = K_{t-1} + I_t;$

Wages: $W_t = W_t^* + W_t^{**};$

Private product: $E_t = Y_t + T_t - W_t^{**}.$

Endogenous variables:

C	consumption	Y	national income
I	investment	K	end-of-year capital stock
W^*	private wage bill	W	total wage bill
P	profits	E	private product.

Exogenous variables:

W^{**} government wage bill

T indirect taxes

A time in years (1931 = 1)

All variables except time are measured in billions of constant (1934) dollars. We are especially interested in the income variable. The estimated fundamental dynamic equation for this variable is

$$\begin{aligned}Y_t - 1.726\,Y_{t-1} + 1.029\,Y_{t-2} - 0.183\,Y_{t-3} \\ = 4.880 + 1.773G_t - 1.493G_{t-1} + 0.154A_t - 0.294A_{t-1} + 0.162A_{t-2} \\ - 1.254T_t + 0.673T_{t-1} + 0.213T_{t-2} + 0.183T_{t-3} + 0.663\,W_t^{**} \\ - 1.443\,W_{t-1}^{**} + 1.029\,W_{t-2}^{**} - 0.183\,W_{t-3}^{**} + \tilde{\omega}_t.\end{aligned}$$

The characteristic equation

$$\lambda^3 - 1.726\,\lambda^2 + 1.029\,\lambda - 0.183 = 0$$

has as its roots

$$\lambda_1 = 0.310 \qquad \text{and} \qquad \lambda_{2,3} = 0.708 \pm 0.298i.$$

The modulus of the complex roots is $\sqrt{0.708^2 + 0.298^2} = 0.768$, which is smaller than unity. Thus, according to our estimates, the system appears stable. Table 13-3 shows the dynamic multipliers of government expenditure on income (Y) or net national product ($Y + T$). Finally, we are interested in how government expenditure affected the changes in the net national product during the period 1921–1941. Table 13-4 shows the actual changes in ($Y + T$) as well as those estimated to be due to current and past changes in government expenditure. The latter were calculated in accordance with (13.101) as

$$\xi_0(G_t - G_{t-1}) + \xi_1(G_{t-1} - G_{t-2}) + \cdots + \xi_{t-2}(G_2 - G_1).$$

Table 13-4 may be used to examine the extent of anticyclical fiscal policy effects during the period.

Table 13–3 Dynamic Multipliers of G on $(Y + T)$

Lag	Multiplier
0	1.773
1	1.567
2	0.881
3	0.232
4	−0.219
5	−0.456
6	−0.519
7	−0.466
8	−0.355
9	−0.227
10	−0.112
11	−0.025
12	0.031
13	0.058
14	0.064
15	0.057
16	0.042
17	0.027
18	0.013
19	0.002
20	−0.004
Total	2.071

Table 13–4 Changes in $(Y + T)$ Accounted by Past and Current Changes in G

Year	$\Delta(Y + T)$	Due to changes in G
1922	4.7	−0.9
1923	7.1	−1.4
1924	0.1	0.5
1925	4.0	0.8
1926	3.1	0.8
1927	0.7	2.4
1928	0.2	2.4
1929	2.8	1.8
1930	−5.6	3.0
1931	−7.2	4.2
1932	−8.6	1.6
1933	1.1	−1.8
1934	5.0	−1.4
1935	4.8	−0.5
1936	9.6	−0.8
1937	1.6	0.4
1938	−3.1	3.9
1939	8.7	5.7
1940	6.4	5.6
1941	13.2	15.2

Concluding Remarks

In conclusion, we may draw the attention of the reader to some of the main gaps that have yet to be filled. Most of the work on estimation of simultaneous equation models has relied upon the basic assumptions of the classical linear regression model. Clearly, there is a need to consider the estimation problem under circumstances in which these assumptions do not hold. Other than the problem of autoregression in the disturbances, which we noted at the end of Section 13–5, we have to develop estimators for simultaneous equation models with nonlinear equations, and with equations containing distributed lags. But perhaps the most important problems relate to errors of measurement and specification. Unfortunately, these problems have not yet been entirely satisfactorily resolved even in the simpler context of single-equation models, much less in the relatively complex framework of simultaneous equations.

EXERCISES

13–1. A highly simplified Keynesian model of the economy is

$$C_t = \alpha + \beta Y_t + \varepsilon_t,$$

$$Y_t = C_t + I_t,$$

where Y = income, C = consumption, and I = exogenous investment. Show that the ILS, 2SLS, LIML, and FIML methods of estimation lead to identical results.

13–2. Consider the following simultaneous equation model:

$$Y_{1t} = \beta_{12} Y_{2t} + \gamma_{11} + u_{1t},$$

$$Y_{2t} = \gamma_{21} + \gamma_{22} X_t + u_{2t},$$

where X is a nonstochastic exogenous variable. The disturbances are assumed to have zero means and constant variances, and to be nonautoregressive over time. Further, u_{1t} and u_{2t} are mutually independent. Compare the variances of the ordinary least squares and the indirect least squares estimator of β_{12}.

13–3. Tintner's model of the American meat market is

$$Y_{1t} = a_0 + a_1 Y_{2t} + a_2 X_{1t} + u_{1t} \qquad \text{(demand)},$$

$$Y_{1t} = b_0 + b_1 Y_{2t} + b_2 X_{2t} + b_3 X_{3t} + u_{2t} \quad \text{(supply)},$$

where u_{1t} and u_{2t} are disturbance terms, Y_{1t} and Y_{2t} are endogenous variables, and X_{1t}, X_{2t}, and X_{3t} are predetermined variables. These variables are defined as follows:

Y_1 per capita meat consumption;
Y_2 index of meat prices;
X_1 per capita disposable income;
X_2 index of meat processing costs;
X_3 index of agricultural production costs.

The $T \times 1$ disturbance vectors, $\mathbf{u}_1$ and $\mathbf{u}_2$, are assumed to have the following covariance matrix:

$$E\begin{bmatrix}\mathbf{u}_1\\ \mathbf{u}_2\end{bmatrix}[\mathbf{u}_1' \quad \mathbf{u}_2'] = \begin{bmatrix}\sigma_{11}\mathbf{I}_\mathbf{T} & \sigma_{12}\mathbf{I}_\mathbf{T}\\ \sigma_{11}\mathbf{I}_\mathbf{T} & \sigma_{22}\mathbf{I}_\mathbf{T}\end{bmatrix}.$$

a. Discuss the identification of the two equations.

b. Suppose that it is known a priori that $b_2/b_3 = K$, where K is a known number. Discuss the identification properties of the model after adding this specification.

c. Suppose instead that the term $a_3 X_{4t}$ is added to the demand equation, where X_4 is an index of prices of nonanimal proteins and fats. How does this alter the identification of the model?

13–4. Assume the following aggregate model for the economy:

$$C_t = \alpha_1 + \alpha_2 D_t + u_{1t},$$

$$I_t = \beta_1 + \beta_2 Y_t + \beta_3 Y_{t-1} + u_{2t},$$

$$Y_t = D_t + T_t,$$

$$Y_t = C_t + I_t + G_t,$$

where C = consumption, D = net national income, I = investment, Y = net national product, T = indirect taxes, and G = autonomous expenditures. The variables C, D, I, and Y are endogenous; T and G are exogenous.

a. Examine the conditions of identification of the first two equations of the model.

b. Obtain consistent estimates of the consumption and investment equations using data in Table 13–5 for the United States economy, 1921–1941.

Table 13–5*

1920	C	D	Y	I
1920	—	—	47.1	—
1921	41.9	40.6	48.3	−0.2
1922	45.0	49.1	53.0	1.9
1923	49.2	55.4	60.1	5.2
1924	50.6	56.4	60.2	3.0
1925	52.6	58.7	64.2	5.1
1926	55.1	60.3	67.3	5.6
1927	56.2	61.3	68.0	4.2
1928	57.3	64.0	68.2	3.0
1929	57.8	67.0	71.0	5.1
1930	55.0	57.7	65.4	1.0
1931	50.9	50.7	58.2	−3.4
1932	45.6	41.3	49.6	−6.2
1933	46.5	45.3	50.7	−5.1
1934	48.7	48.9	55.7	−3.0
1935	51.3	53.3	60.5	−1.3
1936	57.7	61.8	70.1	2.1
1937	58.7	65.0	71.7	2.0
1938	57.5	61.2	68.6	−1.9
1939	61.6	68.4	77.3	1.3
1940	65.0	74.1	83.7	3.3
1941	69.7	85.3	96.9	4.9

Source: L. R. Klein, *Economic Fluctuations in the United States 1921–1941* (New York: Wiley, 1950), p. 135.

* All variables measured in billions of 1934 dollars.

13–5. Using the results from Exercise 13–4:

a. Derive the fundamental dynamic equation and use it to determine whether the system is stable or not.

b. Calculate the dynamic multipliers of Y with respect to G.

c. Find the value of the long-run (equilibrium) multiplier of Y with respect to G.

13–6. Consider the following dynamic model of the market for a certain commodity:

$$
\begin{aligned}
S_t &= \alpha_0 + \alpha_1 P_t + u_{1t}, \\
D_t &= \beta_0 + \beta_1 P_t + u_{2t}, \\
P_t - P_{t-1} &= m(Q_{t-1} - Q_{t-2}) + u_{3t}, \\
S_t - D_t &= Q_t - Q_{t-1},
\end{aligned}
$$

where S_t = production, D_t = sales, P_t = price, and Q_t = end-of-period level of stock. Note that

$$\alpha_1 > 0,$$
$$\beta_1 < 0,$$
$$\alpha_0 < \beta_0,$$
$$m < 0.$$

a. Determine the identification status of the first three equations.

b. Show that the time path of Q_t is determined by a second-order homogeneous difference equation, and that the time path of P_t is determined by a first-order nonhomogeneous difference equation.

c. Derive the conditions for the existence of stability in this market.

d. Disregarding the stochastic disturbances, find the value of m for which the time path of P_t is one of regular oscillations.

Appendix

A. Algebra of Summations

Expressions involving sums are widely used in statistics. They are usually abbreviated with the help of the so-called "$\sum$ notation." The basic definition relating to this notation states that if m and n are integers and $m \leq n$, then

$$\sum_{i=m}^{n} x_i = x_m + x_{m+1} + x_{m+2} + \cdots + x_n .$$

This notation is used most frequently with sums of observations on a given variable or variables, with the subscript designating the numbering of the observations. When this notation is used, the following rules are useful:

(A.1)
$$\sum_{i=1}^{n} kx_i = k \sum_{i=1}^{n} x_i .$$

Proof:

$$\sum_{i=1}^{n} kx_i = kx_1 + kx_2 + \cdots + kx_n = k(x_1 + x_2 + \cdots + x_n) = k \sum_{i=1}^{n} x_i .$$

(A.2)
$$\sum_{i=1}^{n} k = nk .$$

Proof:

$$\sum_{i=1}^{n} k = k + k + \cdots + k = nk .$$

(A.3)
$$\sum_{i=1}^{n} (x_i + y_i) = \sum_{i=1}^{n} x_i + \sum_{i=1}^{n} y_i .$$

Proof:

$$\sum_{i=1}^{n} (x_i + y_i) = (x_i + y_1) + (x_2 + y_2) + \cdots + (x_n + y_n)$$

$$= (x_1 + x_2 + \cdots + x_n) + (y_1 + y_2 + \cdots + y_n) = \sum_{i=1}^{n} x_i + \sum_{i=1}^{n} y_i .$$

Useful formulas are established by considering the sum of the first n positive integers and the sums of their powers. The results, given without proof, are

(A.4) $$\sum_{i=1}^{n} i = 1 + 2 + \cdots + n = \tfrac{1}{2}[n(n+1)] = \tfrac{1}{2}[(n+1)^2 - (n+1)],$$

(A.5) $$\sum_{i=1}^{n} i^2 = 1^2 + 2^2 + \cdots + n^2 = \tfrac{1}{6}[n(n+1)(2n+1)]$$
$$= \tfrac{1}{3}[(n+1)^3 - \tfrac{3}{2}(n+1)^2 + \tfrac{1}{2}(n+1)],$$

(A.6) $$\sum_{i=1}^{n} i^3 = 1^3 + 2^3 + \cdots + n^3 = \tfrac{1}{4}[n^2(n+1)^2]$$
$$= \tfrac{1}{4}[(n+1)^4 - 2(n+1)^3 + (n+1)^2],$$

(A.7) $$\sum_{i=1}^{n} i^4 = 1^4 + 2^4 + \cdots + n^4 = \tfrac{1}{30}[n(n+1)(2n+1)(3n^2 + 3n - 1)]$$
$$= \tfrac{1}{5}[(n+1)^5 - \tfrac{5}{2}(n+1)^4 + \tfrac{5}{3}(n+1)^3 - \tfrac{1}{6}(n+1)].$$

The $\sum$ notation can also be extended to multiple sums. For instance, a double summation is defined as

$$\sum_{i=1}^{n}\sum_{j=1}^{m} x_{ij} = \sum_{i=1}^{n} (x_{i1} + x_{i2} + \cdots + x_{im})$$
$$= (x_{11} + x_{21} + \cdots + x_{n1}) + (x_{12} + x_{22} + \cdots + x_{n2})$$
$$+ \cdots + (x_{1m} + x_{2m} + \cdots + x_{nm}).$$

The following double-summation rules are of special interest:

(A.8) $$\sum_{i=1}^{n}\sum_{j=1}^{m} (x_{ij} + y_{ij}) = \sum_{i=1}^{n}\sum_{j=1}^{m} x_{ij} + \sum_{i=1}^{n}\sum_{j=1}^{m} y_{ij}.$$

Proof:

$$\sum_{i=1}^{n}\sum_{j=1}^{m} (x_{ij} + y_{ij}) = \sum_{j=1}^{m} (x_{1j} + y_{1j}) + \sum_{j=1}^{m} (x_{2j} + y_{2j}) + \cdots + \sum_{j=1}^{m} (x_{nj} + y_{nj})$$
$$= \sum_{j=1}^{m} (x_{1j} + x_{2j} + \cdots + x_{nj}) + \sum_{j=1}^{m} (y_{1j} + y_{2j} + \cdots + y_{nj})$$
$$= \sum_{i=1}^{n}\sum_{j=1}^{m} x_{ij} + \sum_{i=1}^{n}\sum_{j=1}^{m} y_{ij}.$$

(A.9) $$\sum_{i=1}^{n}\sum_{j=1}^{m} x_i = m \sum_{i=1}^{n} x_i.$$

Proof:

$$\sum_{i=1}^{n}\sum_{j=1}^{m} x_i = \sum_{j=1}^{m}\left[\sum_{i=1}^{n} x_i\right] = m \sum_{i=1}^{n} x_i.$$

(A.10) $$\sum_{i=1}^{n}\sum_{j=1}^{m} x_i y_j = \left[\sum_{i=1}^{n} x_i\right]\left[\sum_{j=1}^{m} y_j\right].$$

Proof:

$$\sum_{i=1}^{n}\sum_{j=1}^{m} x_i y_j = \sum_{i=1}^{n} (x_i y_1 + x_i y_2 + \cdots + x_i y_m)$$

$$= y_1 \sum_{i=1}^{n} x_i + y_2 \sum_{i=1}^{n} x_i + \cdots + y_m \sum_{i=1}^{n} x_i = \left[\sum_{i=1}^{n} x_i\right]\left[\sum_{j=1}^{m} y_j\right].$$

(A.11)
$$\sum_{i=1}^{n}\sum_{j=1}^{m} x_i y_{ij} = \sum_{i=1}^{n} x_i \sum_{j=1}^{m} y_{ij}.$$

Proof:

$$\sum_{i=1}^{n}\sum_{j=1}^{m} x_i y_{ij} = \sum_{i=1}^{n} (x_i y_{i1} + x_i y_{i2} + \cdots + x_i y_{im}) = \sum_{i=1}^{n} x_i (y_{i1} + y_{i2} + \cdots + y_{im})$$

$$= \sum_{i=1}^{n} x_i \sum_{j=1}^{m} y_{ij}.$$

(A.12)
$$\left[\sum_{i=1}^{n} x_i\right]^2 = \sum_{i=1}^{n} x_i^2 + 2\sum_{i=1}^{n-1}\sum_{j=i+1}^{n} x_i x_j = \sum_{i=1}^{n} x_i^2 + 2\sum_{i<j} x_i x_j.$$

Proof:

$$\left[\sum_{i=1}^{n} x_i\right]^2 = (x_1 + x_2 + \cdots + x_n)^2$$

$$= x_1^2 + x_2^2 + \cdots + x_n^2 + 2(x_1x_2 + x_1x_3 + \cdots + x_1x_n$$

$$+ x_2x_3 + x_2x_4 + \cdots + x_{n-1}x_n) = \sum_{i=1}^{n} x_i^2 + 2\sum_{i<j} x_i x_j.$$

A special case of (A.12) is

(A.13)
$$\sum_{i=1}^{n} (x_i - \bar{x})^2 = -2\sum_{i<j} (x_i - \bar{x})(x_j - \bar{x}).$$

Proof: Since

$$\sum_{i=1}^{n} (x_i - \bar{x}) = 0,$$

we have

$$\left[\sum_{i=1}^{n} (x_i - \bar{x})\right]^2 = \sum_{i=1}^{n} (x_i - \bar{x})^2 + 2\sum_{i<j} (x_i - \bar{x})(x_j - \bar{x}) = 0,$$

or
$$\sum_{i=1}^{n} (x_i - \bar{x})^2 = -2\sum_{i<j} (x_i - \bar{x})(x_j - \bar{x}).$$

B. Elements of Matrix Algebra

Definitions

An $(M \times N)$ matrix is defined as a rectangular array of real numbers arranged in M rows and N columns as in

(B.1)
$$\mathbf{A} = \begin{bmatrix} a_{11} & a_{12} & \dots & a_{1N} \\ a_{21} & a_{22} & \dots & a_{2N} \\ \vdots & \vdots & & \vdots \\ a_{M1} & a_{M2} & \dots & a_{MN} \end{bmatrix}.$$

The numbers a_{ij} $(i = 1, 2, \dots, M; j = 1, 2, \dots, N)$ are the *elements* of $\mathbf{A}$; the term a_{ij} itself is frequently used to designate a typical element of $\mathbf{A}$. The number of rows and columns—in the case of (B.1) given as $M \times N$—is referred to as the *order* or the *dimension* of the matrix. A matrix of order 1×1 is a *scalar*, a matrix of order $M \times 1$ is called a *column vector*, and a matrix of order $1 \times N$ is called a *row vector*. A matrix with an equal number of rows and columns is a *square matrix*. The sum of the diagonal elements of a square matrix is called the *trace* of the matrix. A *diagonal matrix* is a square matrix such that each element that does not lie along the principal diagonal is equal to zero; i.e.,

$$\mathbf{A} = \begin{bmatrix} a_{11} & 0 & \dots & 0 \\ 0 & a_{22} & \dots & 0 \\ \vdots & \vdots & & \vdots \\ 0 & 0 & \dots & a_{MM} \end{bmatrix}.$$

An *identity* or a *unit matrix* is a diagonal matrix whose diagonal elements are all equal to one; i.e.,

$$\mathbf{I} = \begin{bmatrix} 1 & 0 & \dots & 0 \\ 0 & 1 & \dots & 0 \\ \vdots & \vdots & & \vdots \\ 0 & 0 & \dots & 1 \end{bmatrix}.$$

Sometimes we use a subscript to indicate the order of the identity matrix in question, e.g., $\mathbf{I}_M$. Finally, a *zero matrix* is any matrix whose elements are all zero.

Basic Operations with Matrices

(B.2) **Equality of matrices** $\mathbf{A} = \mathbf{B}$ *if and only if* $\mathbf{A}$ *and* $\mathbf{B}$ *are of the same order and* $a_{ij} = b_{ij}$ *for all* i, j.

(B.3) **Addition of matrices** $\mathbf{A} + \mathbf{B} = \mathbf{C}$ *if and only if* $\mathbf{A}$, $\mathbf{B}$, *and* $\mathbf{C}$ *are of the same order and* $a_{ij} + b_{ij} = c_{ij}$ *for all* i, j.

EXAMPLE

$$\begin{bmatrix} 5 & 0 \\ 2 & -4 \end{bmatrix} + \begin{bmatrix} -1 & 3 \\ 3 & 5 \end{bmatrix} = \begin{bmatrix} 4 & 3 \\ 5 & 1 \end{bmatrix}.$$

(B.4) **Scalar multiplication** If k *is a scalar, then* $k\mathbf{A} = [ka_{ij}]$.

This means that if we want to multiply a matrix **A** by a scalar, we have to multiply each element of **A**.

(B.5) **Matrix multiplication** *If* **A** *is of order* $M \times N$ and **B** *is of order* $N \times P$, *then the product of the two matrices is given as*

$$\mathbf{AB} = \mathbf{C},$$

where **C** *is a matrix of order* $M \times P$ *whose element in the ith row and the jth column is given by*

$$c_{ij} = \sum_{k=1}^{N} a_{ik}b_{kj}.$$

That is, the element c_{11} is obtained by multiplying the elements of the first row of **A** by the elements of the first column of **B** and then summing over all terms; the element c_{12} is obtained by performing the same operation with the elements of the first row of **A** and the second column of **B**, and so on.

EXAMPLE 1

$$\begin{bmatrix} a_{11} & a_{12} \\ a_{21} & a_{22} \\ a_{31} & a_{32} \end{bmatrix} \begin{bmatrix} b_{11} & b_{12} \\ b_{21} & b_{22} \end{bmatrix} = \begin{bmatrix} (a_{11}b_{11} + a_{12}b_{21}) & (a_{11}b_{12} + a_{12}b_{22}) \\ (a_{21}b_{11} + a_{22}b_{21}) & (a_{21}b_{12} + a_{22}b_{22}) \\ (a_{31}b_{11} + a_{32}b_{21}) & (a_{31}b_{12} + a_{32}b_{22}) \end{bmatrix}$$

EXAMPLE 2

$$\begin{bmatrix} 1 & 2 & 3 \\ 4 & 5 & 6 \end{bmatrix} \begin{bmatrix} 7 & 10 \\ 8 & 11 \\ 9 & 12 \end{bmatrix} = \begin{bmatrix} (1\times 7 + 2\times 8 + 3\times 9) & (1\times 10 + 2\times 11 + 3\times 12) \\ (4\times 7 + 5\times 8 + 6\times 9) & (4\times 10 + 5\times 11 + 6\times 12) \end{bmatrix}$$

$$= \begin{bmatrix} 50 & 68 \\ 122 & 167 \end{bmatrix}.$$

Note that, in general,

$$\mathbf{AB} \neq \mathbf{BA}.$$

This inequality implies that we must distinguish between pre- and postmultiplication by a matrix.

Transposition

(B.6) *If* **A** *is an* $(M \times N)$ *matrix, then the* transpose *of* **A**, *denoted by* $\mathbf{A}'$, *is an* $(N \times M)$ *matrix obtained by interchanging the rows with the columns in* **A**; *i.e.*,

$$\mathbf{A}' = \begin{bmatrix} a_{11} & a_{21} & \cdots & a_{M1} \\ a_{12} & a_{22} & \cdots & a_{M2} \\ \vdots & \vdots & & \vdots \\ a_{1N} & a_{2N} & \cdots & a_{MN} \end{bmatrix}.$$

EXAMPLE

$$A = \begin{bmatrix} 2 & 5 \\ 3 & 6 \\ 4 & 7 \end{bmatrix}, \qquad A' = \begin{bmatrix} 2 & 3 & 4 \\ 5 & 6 & 7 \end{bmatrix}.$$

The following theorems apply to transposed matrices:

(B.7) $$(\mathbf{A}')' = \mathbf{A},$$

(B.8) $$(\mathbf{A} + \mathbf{B})' = \mathbf{A}' + \mathbf{B}',$$

(B.9) $$(\mathbf{AB})' = \mathbf{B}'\mathbf{A}'.$$

The proofs follow directly from the definition of matrix operations.

(B.10) *If* **A** *is a square matrix and* **A** = **A**′, *then* **A** *is symmetric.*

A well-known expression involving a transpose of a vector is known as *quadratic form.* Suppose **x** is an $(M \times 1)$ nonzero vector and **A** is a square and symmetric matrix of order $M \times M$. Then the quadratic form of **x** is a scalar defined as

(B.11) $$\mathbf{x}'\mathbf{A}\mathbf{x} = \sum_{i=1}^{M} \sum_{j=1}^{M} a_{ij} x_i x_j.$$

EXAMPLE If

$$\mathbf{x} = \begin{bmatrix} x_1 \\ x_2 \end{bmatrix} \quad \text{and} \quad \mathbf{A} = \begin{bmatrix} a_{11} & a_{12} \\ a_{21} & a_{22} \end{bmatrix},$$

then

$$\mathbf{x}'\mathbf{A}\mathbf{x} = [x_1 \quad x_2] \begin{bmatrix} a_{11} & a_{12} \\ a_{21} & a_{22} \end{bmatrix} \begin{bmatrix} x_1 \\ x_2 \end{bmatrix} = [x_1 \quad x_2] \begin{bmatrix} a_{11}x_1 + a_{12}x_2 \\ a_{21}x_1 + a_{22}x_2 \end{bmatrix}$$

$$= a_{11}x_1^2 + a_{12}x_1x_2 + a_{21}x_1x_2 + a_{22}x_2^2 = a_{11}x_1^2 + 2a_{12}x_1x_2 + a_{22}x_2^2.$$

A symmetric matrix **A** is called *positive definite* if $\mathbf{x}'\mathbf{A}\mathbf{x} > 0$, and *positive semidefinite* if $\mathbf{x}'\mathbf{A}\mathbf{x} \geq 0$. Similarly, **A** is *negative definite* if $\mathbf{x}'\mathbf{A}\mathbf{x} < 0$, and *negative semidefinite* if $\mathbf{x}'\mathbf{A}\mathbf{x} \leq 0$. Note that all variance-covariance matrices are positive definite.

Partitioned Matrices

Frequently it is convenient to *partition* a matrix into submatrices. In this case the submatrices are treated as scalar elements except that care has to be taken to insure that the rules of matrix multiplication are preserved. In particular, if

$$\mathbf{A} = \begin{bmatrix} \mathbf{P}_{11} & \mathbf{P}_{12} \\ \mathbf{P}_{21} & \mathbf{P}_{22} \end{bmatrix} \quad \text{and} \quad \mathbf{B} = \begin{bmatrix} \mathbf{Q}_{11} & \mathbf{Q}_{12} \\ \mathbf{Q}_{21} & \mathbf{Q}_{22} \end{bmatrix},$$

where the dimensions of the submatrices are

$$\mathbf{P}_{11} \to (M_1 \times N_1), \qquad \mathbf{Q}_{11} \to (N_1 \times R_1),$$

$$\mathbf{P}_{12} \to (M_1 \times N_2), \qquad \mathbf{Q}_{12} \to (N_1 \times R_2),$$

$$\mathbf{P}_{21} \to (M_2 \times N_1), \qquad \mathbf{Q}_{21} \to (N_2 \times R_1),$$

$$\mathbf{P}_{22} \to (M_2 \times N_2), \qquad \mathbf{Q}_{22} \to (N_2 \times R_2),$$

then

$$\mathbf{A}' = \begin{bmatrix} \mathbf{P}'_{11} & \mathbf{P}'_{21} \\ \mathbf{P}'_{12} & \mathbf{P}'_{22} \end{bmatrix} \tag{B.12}$$

and

$$\mathbf{AB} = \begin{bmatrix} \mathbf{P}_{11}\mathbf{Q}_{11} + \mathbf{P}_{12}\mathbf{Q}_{21} & \mathbf{P}_{11}\mathbf{Q}_{12} + \mathbf{P}_{12}\mathbf{Q}_{22} \\ \mathbf{P}_{21}\mathbf{Q}_{11} + \mathbf{P}_{22}\mathbf{Q}_{21} & \mathbf{P}_{21}\mathbf{Q}_{12} + \mathbf{P}_{22}\mathbf{Q}_{22} \end{bmatrix}. \tag{B.13}$$

Determinants

A determinant is a scalar whose value is calculated by a certain rule from a square matrix. The determinant of matrix **A** is denoted by det **A** or $|\mathbf{A}|$. The rules for calculating determinants are as follows. For a (2×2) matrix

$$\mathbf{A} = \begin{bmatrix} a_{11} & a_{12} \\ a_{21} & a_{22} \end{bmatrix},$$

the determinant is given by

$$\det \mathbf{A} = a_{11}a_{22} - a_{12}a_{21}. \tag{B.14}$$

Note that the value of det **A** has been obtained by multiplying certain elements of **A** by certain other elements, and then by assigning a positive or a negative sign to the resulting product. If we use solid lines to designate products with a positive sign, and dashed lines to designate products with a negative sign, then the rule for calculating the determinant of a (2×2) matrix can be represented schematically as in Figure B–1(a).

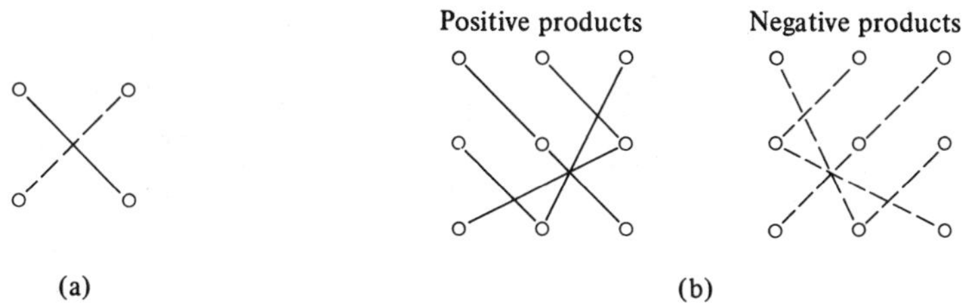

Figure B–1

For a (3×3) matrix

$$\mathbf{A} = \begin{bmatrix} a_{11} & a_{12} & a_{13} \\ a_{21} & a_{22} & a_{23} \\ a_{31} & a_{32} & a_{33} \end{bmatrix}$$

the determinant is

$$\det \mathbf{A} = a_{11}a_{22}a_{33} + a_{12}a_{23}a_{31} + a_{13}a_{32}a_{21} - a_{13}a_{22}a_{31} - a_{23}a_{32}a_{11} - a_{33}a_{21}a_{12}, \tag{B.15}$$

and the schematic representation is shown in Figure B–1(b).

For square matrices of higher order, the schematic rules for calculating determinants become messy and are rarely used. Instead we use a general rule for calculating determinants of matrices of *any* order. This rule involves the use of *minors* and *cofactors*. Suppose we take a matrix **A** of order $M \times M$ and eliminate the ith row and the jth column, i.e., eliminate the row and the column corresponding to the element a_{ij}. Then the determinant of the resulting $(M - 1) \times (M - 1)$ matrix is called a *minor* of a_{ij}. A *cofactor* of a_{ij} is simply the minor of a_{ij} multiplied by $(-1)^{i+j}$. A common term to designate a cofactor of a_{ij} is $\mathbf{A_{ij}}$. The general rule for evaluating the determinant of **A** is to take *any* row or *any* column of **A**, multiply each element by the corresponding cofactor, and then add the results. Thus the determinant of an $(M \times M)$ matrix **A** can be calculated as

$$\text{(B.16)} \qquad \det \mathbf{A} = a_{11}\mathbf{A_{11}} + a_{12}\mathbf{A_{12}} + \cdots + a_{1M}\mathbf{A_{1M}}.$$

In formula (B.16) we use the first row as the basis for calculations, but any other row, or any column, would do equally well. The importance of the "cofactor formula" (B.16) is that it enables us to reduce a determinant of any order to a linear combination of determinants of lower order. Of course, this formula also applies to the cases of $M = 2$ and $M = 3$, for which we gave special formulas in (B.14) and (B.15). For $M = 2$ we have

$$\mathbf{A} = \begin{bmatrix} a_{11} & a_{12} \\ a_{21} & a_{22} \end{bmatrix},$$

$$\mathbf{A_{11}} = a_{22},$$

$$\mathbf{A_{12}} = -a_{21},$$

so that, by (B.16),

$$\det \mathbf{A} = a_{11}(a_{22}) + a_{12}(-a_{21}) = a_{11}a_{22} - a_{12}a_{21},$$

which is the same answer as that in (B.14). Further, for $M = 3$ we have

$$\mathbf{A} = \begin{bmatrix} a_{11} & a_{12} & a_{13} \\ a_{21} & a_{22} & a_{23} \\ a_{31} & a_{32} & a_{33} \end{bmatrix},$$

$$\mathbf{A_{11}} = \det \begin{bmatrix} a_{22} & a_{23} \\ a_{32} & a_{33} \end{bmatrix} = a_{22}a_{33} - a_{23}a_{32},$$

$$\mathbf{A_{12}} = -\det \begin{bmatrix} a_{21} & a_{23} \\ a_{31} & a_{33} \end{bmatrix} = -a_{21}a_{33} + a_{23}a_{31},$$

$$\mathbf{A_{13}} = \det \begin{bmatrix} a_{21} & a_{22} \\ a_{31} & a_{32} \end{bmatrix} = a_{21}a_{32} - a_{22}a_{31},$$

so that, by (B.16),

$$\begin{aligned} \det \mathbf{A} &= a_{11}(a_{22}a_{33} - a_{23}a_{32}) + a_{12}(-a_{21}a_{33} + a_{23}a_{31}) + a_{13}(a_{21}a_{32} - a_{22}a_{31}) \\ &= a_{11}a_{22}a_{33} - a_{11}a_{23}a_{32} - a_{12}a_{21}a_{33} + a_{12}a_{23}a_{31} + a_{13}a_{21}a_{32} - a_{13}a_{22}a_{31}, \end{aligned}$$

which is the same expression as that in (B.15).

Some interesting and useful properties of determinants are

(B.17) Interchanging any two rows or any two columns of **A** changes the sign of det **A**.

(B.18) If every element of a row, or of a column, of **A** is multiplied by a scalar, then det **A** is multiplied by the same scalar.

(B.19) If any row (column) of **A** is extended by the addition of a multiple of any other row (column), the value of det **A** is unaltered.

(B.20) The value of the determinant of a matrix in which two rows (or two columns) are identical is zero.

(B.21) $\det \mathbf{A} = \det \mathbf{A}'$.

(B.22) $\det \mathbf{AB} = (\det \mathbf{A})(\det \mathbf{B})$.

Determinants are also used to describe certain properties of matrices. In particular, if $\det \mathbf{A} = 0$, then **A** is called *singular*, and if $\det \mathbf{A} \neq 0$, then **A** is called *nonsingular*. Further, the order of the largest determinant contained in an $(M \times N)$ matrix is called the *rank* of the matrix.

EXAMPLE 1 If

$$\mathbf{A} = \begin{bmatrix} 1 & 2 & 3 \\ 4 & 5 & 6 \\ 7 & 8 & 9 \end{bmatrix},$$

then

$$\det \mathbf{A} = 1 \times 5 \times 10 + 2 \times 6 \times 7 + 3 \times 8 \times 4 - 3 \times 5 \times 7 - 6 \times 8 \times 1 - 10 \times 4 \times 2 = -3.$$

The same result could have been obtained by the "cofactor formula" (B.16):

$$\det \mathbf{A} = 1 \times \det \begin{bmatrix} 5 & 6 \\ 8 & 10 \end{bmatrix} + 2 \times (-1) \det \begin{bmatrix} 4 & 6 \\ 7 & 10 \end{bmatrix} + 3 \times \det \begin{bmatrix} 4 & 5 \\ 7 & 8 \end{bmatrix}$$
$$= 1 \times 2 + 2 \times 2 + 3 \times (-3) = -3.$$

Note also that

$$\mathbf{A}' = \begin{bmatrix} 1 & 4 & 7 \\ 2 & 5 & 8 \\ 3 & 6 & 10 \end{bmatrix} \quad \text{and} \quad \det A' = -3.$$

Suppose we change **A** by (a) multiplying the first row by 4 and deducting the result from the second row, and (b) multiplying the first row by 7 and deducting the result from the third row. The resulting matrix, say, $\mathbf{A}^*$, is

$$\mathbf{A}^* = \begin{bmatrix} 1 & 2 & 3 \\ (4-4) & (5-8) & (6-12) \\ (7-7) & (8-14) & (10-21) \end{bmatrix} = \begin{bmatrix} 1 & 2 & 3 \\ 0 & -3 & -6 \\ 0 & -6 & -11 \end{bmatrix}$$

and

$$\det \mathbf{A}^* = 1 \det \begin{bmatrix} -3 & -6 \\ -6 & -11 \end{bmatrix} = -3 = \det \mathbf{A}.$$

EXAMPLE 2 Let

$$\mathbf{A} = \begin{bmatrix} 1 & 2 \\ 3 & 4 \end{bmatrix} \quad \text{and} \quad \mathbf{B} = \begin{bmatrix} 5 & 6 \\ 7 & 8 \end{bmatrix}.$$

Then

$$\det \mathbf{A} = 1 \times 4 - 2 \times 3 = -2,$$

$$\det \mathbf{B} = 5 \times 8 - 6 \times 7 = -2.$$

Now, define

$$\mathbf{C} = \mathbf{AB} = \begin{bmatrix} 1 & 2 \\ 3 & 4 \end{bmatrix} \begin{bmatrix} 5 & 6 \\ 7 & 8 \end{bmatrix} = \begin{bmatrix} 19 & 22 \\ 43 & 50 \end{bmatrix}$$

and note that

$$\det \mathbf{C} = 950 - 946 = 4 = (\det \mathbf{A})(\det \mathbf{B})$$

Matrix Inversion

The *inverse* of a square matrix **A** is a matrix that, when premultiplied or postmultiplied by **A**, yields the identity matrix. The inverse of **A** is denoted by $\mathbf{A}^{-1}$. Thus we define

(B.23) $\mathbf{B} = \mathbf{A}^{-1}$ *if and only if* $\mathbf{BA} = \mathbf{AB} = \mathbf{I}$.

Not all matrices have an inverse. The following theorem establishes the conditions under which an inverse exists:

(B.24) *The matrix* **A** *has an inverse if and only if det* $\mathbf{A} \neq 0$, *that is, if and only if* **A** *is a nonsingular matrix.*

The calculation of an inverse involves the formation of the so-called *adjoint*. The adjoint of a square matrix **A** is defined as a matrix that is formed from **A** by replacing each element of **A** by the corresponding cofactor, and by transposing the result. If we denote the adjoint of **A** by adj **A**, then we have

$$\text{(B.25)} \quad \text{adj}\,\mathbf{A} = \begin{bmatrix} A_{11} & A_{12} & \cdots & A_{1M} \\ A_{21} & A_{22} & \cdots & A_{2M} \\ \vdots & \vdots & & \vdots \\ A_{M1} & A_{M2} & \cdots & A_{MM} \end{bmatrix}' = \begin{bmatrix} A_{11} & A_{21} & \cdots & A_{M1} \\ A_{12} & A_{22} & \cdots & A_{M2} \\ \vdots & \vdots & & \vdots \\ A_{1M} & A_{2M} & \cdots & A_{MM} \end{bmatrix}.$$

The inverse of **A** is then obtained as follows:

$$\text{(B.26)} \quad \mathbf{A}^{-1} = \frac{1}{\det \mathbf{A}} \text{adj}\,\mathbf{A}.$$

It can be shown[1] that

$$\text{(B.27)} \quad (\mathbf{AB})^{-1} = \mathbf{B}^{-1}\mathbf{A}^{-1},$$

$$\text{(B.28)} \quad (\mathbf{A}^{-1})' = (\mathbf{A}')^{-1}.$$

Note that the result in (B.28) implies that if **A** is symmetric (and nonsingular), then $\mathbf{A}^{-1}$ is also symmetric.

[1] See, e.g., J. Johnston, *Econometric Methods* (New York: McGraw-Hill, 1963), pp. 85–86.

EXAMPLE 1 If

$$\mathbf{A} = \begin{bmatrix} a_{11} & a_{12} \\ a_{21} & a_{22} \end{bmatrix},$$

then

$$\mathbf{A}_{11} = a_{22},$$
$$\mathbf{A}_{12} = -a_{21},$$
$$\mathbf{A}_{21} = -a_{12},$$
$$\mathbf{A}_{22} = a_{11},$$

and

$$\text{adj } \mathbf{A} = \begin{bmatrix} a_{22} & -a_{21} \\ -a_{12} & a_{11} \end{bmatrix}' = \begin{bmatrix} a_{22} & -a_{12} \\ -a_{21} & a_{11} \end{bmatrix}.$$

Therefore,

$$\mathbf{A}^{-1} = \frac{1}{a_{11}a_{22} - a_{12}a_{21}} \begin{bmatrix} a_{22} & -a_{12} \\ -a_{21} & a_{11} \end{bmatrix}.$$

EXAMPLE 2 If

$$\mathbf{A} = \begin{bmatrix} 1 & 2 & 3 \\ 4 & 5 & 6 \\ 7 & 8 & 10 \end{bmatrix},$$

then

$$\mathbf{A}_{11} = 2, \quad \mathbf{A}_{21} = 4, \quad \mathbf{A}_{31} = -3,$$
$$\mathbf{A}_{12} = 2, \quad \mathbf{A}_{22} = -11, \quad \mathbf{A}_{32} = 6,$$
$$\mathbf{A}_{13} = -3, \quad \mathbf{A}_{23} = 6, \quad \mathbf{A}_{33} = -3,$$

and

$$\det \mathbf{A} = -3.$$

Therefore,

$$\text{adj } \mathbf{A} = \begin{bmatrix} 2 & 2 & -3 \\ 4 & -11 & 6 \\ -3 & 6 & -3 \end{bmatrix}' = \begin{bmatrix} 2 & 4 & -3 \\ 2 & -11 & 6 \\ -3 & 6 & -3 \end{bmatrix},$$

and

$$\mathbf{A}^{-1} = \frac{1}{-3} \begin{bmatrix} 2 & 4 & -3 \\ 2 & -11 & 6 \\ -3 & 6 & -3 \end{bmatrix} = \begin{bmatrix} -\frac{2}{3} & -\frac{4}{3} & 1 \\ -\frac{2}{3} & \frac{11}{3} & -2 \\ 1 & -2 & 1 \end{bmatrix}.$$

To check this result we multiply

$$\mathbf{A}^{-1}\mathbf{A} = \begin{bmatrix} -\frac{2}{3} & -\frac{4}{3} & 1 \\ -\frac{2}{3} & \frac{11}{3} & -2 \\ 1 & -2 & 1 \end{bmatrix} \begin{bmatrix} 1 & 2 & 3 \\ 4 & 5 & 6 \\ 7 & 8 & 10 \end{bmatrix}$$

$$= \begin{bmatrix} (-\frac{2}{3} - \frac{16}{3} + 7) & (-\frac{4}{3} - \frac{20}{3} + 8) & (-\frac{6}{3} - \frac{24}{3} + 10) \\ (-\frac{2}{3} + \frac{44}{3} - 14) & (-\frac{4}{3} + \frac{55}{3} - 16) & (-\frac{6}{3} + \frac{66}{3} + 20) \\ (1 - 8 + 7) & (2 - 10 + 8) & (3 - 12 + 10) \end{bmatrix} = \begin{bmatrix} 1 & 0 & 0 \\ 0 & 1 & 0 \\ 0 & 0 & 1 \end{bmatrix}.$$

Partitioned Inversion

Sometimes we may be interested in obtaining the inverse of a matrix in partitioned form. Suppose $\mathbf{A}$ is partitioned as

$$\mathbf{A} = \begin{bmatrix} \mathbf{P}_{11} & \mathbf{P}_{12} \\ \mathbf{P}_{21} & \mathbf{P}_{22} \end{bmatrix},$$

where the dimensions of the submatrices are

$$\mathbf{P}_{11} \rightarrow M_1 \times M_1,$$

$$\mathbf{P}_{12} \rightarrow M_1 \times M_2,$$

$$\mathbf{P}_{21} \rightarrow M_2 \times M_1,$$

$$\mathbf{P}_{22} \rightarrow M_2 \times M_2.$$

Then[2]

$$\mathbf{A}^{-1} = \begin{bmatrix} \mathbf{P}_{11}^{-1} + \mathbf{P}_{11}^{-1}\mathbf{P}_{12}\mathbf{Q}_{22}^{-1}\mathbf{P}_{21}\mathbf{P}_{11}^{-1} & -\mathbf{P}_{11}^{-1}\mathbf{P}_{12}\mathbf{Q}_{22}^{-1} \\ -\mathbf{Q}_{22}^{-1}\mathbf{P}_{21}\mathbf{P}_{11}^{-1} & \mathbf{Q}_{22}^{-1} \end{bmatrix}$$

where

$$\mathbf{Q}_{22} = \mathbf{P}_{22} - \mathbf{P}_{21}\mathbf{P}_{11}^{-1}\mathbf{P}_{12}.$$

Note that the inverse of a block-diagonal matrix is also block-diagonal. Specifically,

(B.29) If $\mathbf{A} = \begin{bmatrix} \mathbf{P}_{11} & 0 \\ 0 & \mathbf{P}_{22} \end{bmatrix}$, then $\mathbf{A}^{-1} = \begin{bmatrix} \mathbf{P}_{11}^{-1} & 0 \\ 0 & \mathbf{P}_{22}^{-1} \end{bmatrix}$.

Differentiation in Matrix Notation

Let $y = f(x_1, x_2, \ldots, x_M)$ be a scalar, and let $\mathbf{x}$ be a column vector defined as

$$\mathbf{x} = \begin{bmatrix} x_1 \\ x_2 \\ \vdots \\ x_M \end{bmatrix}.$$

Then, the first partial derivative of y with respect to each element of $\mathbf{x}$ is defined as

(B.30)
$$\frac{\partial y}{\partial \mathbf{x}} = \begin{bmatrix} \dfrac{\partial y}{\partial x_1} \\ \dfrac{\partial y}{\partial x_2} \\ \vdots \\ \dfrac{\partial y}{\partial x_M} \end{bmatrix},$$

[2] See A. S. Goldberger, *Econometric Theory* (New York: Wiley, 1964), p. 27.

and the second partial derivative as

$$\text{(B.31)} \qquad \frac{\partial^2 y}{\partial \mathbf{x}^2} = \begin{bmatrix} \frac{\partial^2 y}{\partial x_1^2} & \frac{\partial^2 y}{\partial x_1 \partial x_2} & \cdots & \frac{\partial^2 y}{\partial x_1 \partial x_M} \\ \frac{\partial^2 y}{\partial x_2 \partial x_1} & \frac{\partial^2 y}{\partial x_2^2} & \cdots & \frac{\partial^2 y}{\partial x_2 \partial x_M} \\ \vdots & \vdots & & \vdots \\ \frac{\partial^2 y}{\partial x_M \partial x_1} & \frac{\partial^2 y}{\partial x_M \partial x_2} & \cdots & \frac{\partial^2 y}{\partial x_M^2} \end{bmatrix}.$$

These basic rules can be applied to some frequently encountered cases. First, if

$$\mathbf{a} = \begin{bmatrix} a_1 \\ a_2 \\ \vdots \\ a_M \end{bmatrix}$$

where a_i $(i = 1, 2, \ldots, M)$ are constants, then

$$\text{(B.32)} \qquad \frac{\partial(\mathbf{a}'\mathbf{x})}{\partial \mathbf{x}} = \mathbf{a}.$$

This can be easily demonstrated by noting that

$$\mathbf{a}'\mathbf{x} = \sum_{i=1}^{M} a_i x_i,$$

and by using the rule (B.30). Second, if $\mathbf{A}$ is a symmetric matrix of order $M \times M$ whose typical element is a constant a_{ij}, then

$$\text{(B.33)} \qquad \frac{\partial(\mathbf{x}'\mathbf{A}\mathbf{x})}{\partial \mathbf{x}} = 2\mathbf{A}\mathbf{x}.$$

This follows from the fact that

$$\mathbf{x}'\mathbf{A}\mathbf{x} = \sum_{i=1}^{M} \sum_{j=1}^{M} a_{ij} x_i x_j,$$

and from the application of the rule of differentiation in (B.30). Finally, if $\mathbf{A}$ and $\mathbf{B}$ are two symmetric matrices whose elements are constants and whose order is $M \times M$, then

$$\text{(B.34)} \qquad \frac{\partial\left(\frac{\mathbf{x}'\mathbf{A}\mathbf{x}}{\mathbf{x}'\mathbf{B}\mathbf{x}}\right)}{\partial \mathbf{x}} = \frac{2(\mathbf{A}\mathbf{x})(\mathbf{x}'\mathbf{B}\mathbf{x}) - 2(\mathbf{x}'\mathbf{A}\mathbf{x})(\mathbf{B}\mathbf{x})}{(\mathbf{x}'\mathbf{B}\mathbf{x})^2}.$$

This can be proven in the same way as (B.33).

C. Computational Design for Least Squares Estimation

C–1 Simple Linear Regression Model

The following computational scheme is designed for obtaining simple least squares estimates of the regression parameters for the model,

$$Y_i = \alpha + \beta X_i + \varepsilon_i.$$

The procedure has been designed to achieve a high degree of computational accuracy.

Basic Calculations

First, we calculate the sums of squares and cross-products of X and Y. These are usually referred to as "sample moments about zero." A tabular presentation is

	1	X	Y
1	n	$\sum X_i$	$\sum Y_i$
X		$\sum X_i^2$	$\sum X_i Y_i$
Y			$\sum Y_i^2$

As a check, we construct n observations on an artificial variable S defined as

$$S_i = X_i + Y_i.$$

Then we must have

$$\sum S_i^2 = \sum X_i^2 + \sum Y_i^2 + 2 \sum X_i Y_i.$$

Next, we compute the values of the so-called "augmented sample moments about the means," which are defined as follows:

$$M_{XX} = n \sum X_i^2 - \left(\sum X_i\right)^2,$$

$$M_{XY} = n \sum X_i Y_i - \left(\sum X_i\right)\left(\sum Y_i\right),$$

$$M_{YY} = n \sum Y_i^2 - \left(\sum Y_i\right)^2,$$

$$M_{SS} = n \sum S_i^2 - \left(\sum S_i\right)^2.$$

These can be arranged as

	X	Y
X	M_{XX}	M_{XY}
Y		M_{YY}

To check our calculations, we note whether the following equality is preserved:

$$M_{SS} = M_{XX} + M_{YY} + 2M_{XY}.$$

Estimates of the Regression Coefficients

The least squares estimates of the regression coefficients are calculated as follows:

$$\hat{\beta} = \frac{M_{XY}}{M_{XX}},$$

$$\hat{\alpha} = \frac{(\sum Y_i - \hat{\beta} \sum X_i)}{n}.$$

Further,

$$n\text{SSR} = \hat{\beta} M_{XY},$$

$$n\text{SST} = M_{YY},$$

$$n\text{SSE} = n\text{SST} - n\text{SSR},$$

which leads to

$$R^2 = \frac{n\text{SSR}}{n\text{SST}},$$

$$ns^2 = \frac{n\text{SSE}}{n-2},$$

$$s_{\hat{\beta}}^2 = \frac{ns^2}{M_{XX}},$$

$$s_{\hat{\alpha}}^2 = \frac{(ns^2)(\sum X_i^2)}{nM_{XX}}.$$

The final result is

$$Y_i = \underset{(s_{\hat{\alpha}})}{\hat{\alpha}} + \underset{(s_{\hat{\beta}})}{\hat{\beta}} X_i + e_i, \qquad R^2 = \cdots.$$

C–2 Multiple Linear Regression Model

Here we present a computational scheme for the model

$$Y_i = \beta_1 + \beta_2 X_{i2} + \beta_3 X_{i3} + \beta_4 X_{i4} + \beta_5 X_{i5} + \varepsilon_i.$$

However, the procedure can be easily modified to apply to models with a smaller number of explanatory variables. The computational design is aimed at providing a reasonably high degree of accuracy combined with computational efficiency.

Computation of Augmented Moments

Let

$$M_{rs} = n \sum_i X_{ir} X_{is} - \Big(\sum_i X_{ir}\Big)\Big(\sum_i X_{is}\Big),$$

$$M_{rY} = n \sum_i X_{ir} Y_i - \Big(\sum_i X_{ir}\Big)\Big(\sum_i Y_i\Big),$$

$$M_{YY} = n \sum_i Y_i^2 - \Big(\sum_i Y_i\Big)^2,$$

$$M_{SS} = n \sum_i S_i^2 - \Big(\sum_i S_i\Big)^2,$$

$$r, s = 2, 3, 4, \text{ and } 5;$$

$$S_i = X_{i2} + X_{i3} + X_{i4} + X_{i5} + Y_i.$$

These moments may be presented as

	X_2	X_3	X_4	X_5	Y
X_2	M_{22}	M_{23}	M_{24}	M_{25}	M_{2Y}
X_3		M_{33}	M_{34}	M_{35}	M_{3Y}
X_4			M_{44}	M_{45}	M_{4Y}
X_5				M_{55}	M_{5Y}
Y					M_{YY}

If all calculations are correct, we must have

$$M_{SS} = M_{22} + M_{33} + M_{44} + M_{55} + M_{YY}$$
$$+ 2(M_{23} + M_{24} + M_{25} + M_{2Y} + M_{34} + M_{35} + M_{3Y} + M_{45} + M_{4Y} + M_{5Y}).$$

Scaling of Variables

It will contribute to the accuracy of the solution if all the moments are of approximately the same order of magnitude. Therefore, we change the units in which the variables are measured by multiplying each variable by an appropriate power of 10, so that the values of the diagonal moments lie between 0.1 and 10.0. Of course, this will lead to an adjustment of the off-diagonal moments, also. For many practical purposes it may be sufficient if all scaled moments are enumerated up to six decimal places. The scaled variables and their moments will be denoted by starred symbols.

EXAMPLE Suppose

$$M_{22} = 6560.3575, \qquad M_{YY} = 0.0604,$$
$$M_{33} = 320.12, \qquad M_{2Y} = 76.2344,$$
$$M_{23} = 21.066, \qquad M_{3Y} = 1.177.$$

Then, we adopt the following scaling:

$$X_{i2}^* = 10^{-2} X_{i2},$$
$$X_{i3}^* = 10^{-1} X_{i3},$$
$$Y_i^* = 10^1 Y_i.$$

Consequently,

$$M_{22}^* = 0.656036 \qquad M_{YY}^* = 6.040000$$
$$M_{33}^* = 3.201200 \qquad M_{2Y}^* = 7.623440$$
$$M_{23}^* = 0.021066 \qquad M_{3Y}^* = 1.177000$$

Basic Solution of Least Squares Normal Equations

To obtain the solution of the least squares normal equations, we use the Gauss-Doolittle method, which represents a systematic way of solving symmetric linear equations.[3] First, we present the augmented scaled moments in the following form:

		Column									
Row		(1)	(2)	(3)	(4)	(5)	(6)	(7)	(8)	(9)	(10)
(1)	R_1:	M_{22}^*	M_{23}^*	M_{24}^*	M_{25}^*	M_{2Y}^*	1	0	0	0	S_1
(2)	R_2:	M_{32}^*	M_{33}^*	M_{34}^*	M_{35}^*	M_{3Y}^*	0	1	0	0	S_2
(3)	R_3:	M_{42}^*	M_{43}^*	M_{44}^*	M_{45}^*	M_{4Y}^*	0	0	1	0	S_3
(4)	R_4:	M_{52}^*	M_{53}^*	M_{54}^*	M_{55}^*	M_{5Y}^*	0	0	0	1	S_4

[3] See P. S. Dwyer, *Linear Computations* (New York: Wiley, 1951).

Column (10) is a checking column and its elements are equal to row totals. The successive rows of the worksheet are obtained by the following rules:

(5) $A_{1j} = R_{1j}$ (i.e., reproduce row (1) here in the fifth row).

(6) $B_{1j} = A_{1j}/A_{11}$ (i.e., divide row (5) by its leading element).

(7) $A_{2j} = R_{2j} - A_{12}B_{1j}$.

(8) $B_{2j} = A_{2j}/A_{22}$.

(9) $A_{3j} = R_{3j} - A_{13}B_{1j} - A_{23}B_{2j}$.

(10) $B_{3j} = A_{3j}/A_{33}$.

(11) $A_{4j} = R_{4j} - A_{14}B_{1j} - A_{24}B_{2j} - A_{34}B_{3j}$.

(12) $B_{4j} = A_{4j}/A_{44}$.

The worksheet now includes the following entries below row (4):

Row		(1)	(2)	(3)	(4)	(5)	(6)	(7)	(8)	(9)	(10)
(5)	A_1:	A_{11}	A_{12}	A_{13}	A_{14}	A_{15}	1	0	0	0	S_4
(6)	B_1:	1	B_{12}	B_{13}	B_{14}	B_{15}	B_{16}	0	0	0	S_5
(7)	A_2:	0	A_{22}	A_{23}	A_{24}	A_{25}	A_{26}	1	0	0	S_6
(8)	B_2:	0	1	B_{23}	B_{24}	B_{25}	B_{26}	B_{27}	0	0	S_7
(9)	A_3:	0	0	A_{33}	A_{34}	A_{35}	A_{36}	A_{37}	1	0	S_8
(10)	B_3:	0	0	1	B_{34}	B_{35}	B_{36}	B_{37}	B_{38}	0	S_9
(11)	A_4:	0	0	0	A_{44}	A_{45}	A_{46}	A_{47}	A_{48}	1	S_{10}
(12)	B_4:	0	0	0	1	B_{45}	B_{46}	B_{47}	B_{48}	B_{49}	S_{11}

Continuing, the rules are

(13) $C_{4j} = B_{4j}$.

(14) $C_{3j} = B_{3j} - B_{34}C_{4j}$.

(15) $C_{2j} = B_{2j} - B_{23}C_{3j} - B_{24}C_{4j}$.

(16) $C_{1j} = B_{1j} - B_{12}C_{2j} - B_{13}C_{3j} - B_{14}C_{4j}$.

These rows are entered on the worksheet in *reverse order:*

Row		(1)	(2)	(3)	(4)	(5)	(6)	(7)	(8)	(9)	(10)
(16)	C_1:	1	0	0	0	C_{15}	C_{16}	C_{17}	C_{18}	C_{19}	S_{15}
(15)	C_2:	0	1	0	0	C_{25}	C_{26}	C_{27}	C_{28}	C_{29}	S_{14}
(14)	C_3:	0	0	1	0	C_{35}	C_{36}	C_{37}	C_{38}	C_{39}	S_{13}
(13)	C_4:	0	0	0	1	C_{45}	C_{46}	C_{47}	C_{48}	C_{49}	S_{12}

In completing the worksheet there is no need to calculate the entries that are shown to be equal to 0 or 1. Check each row *as it is produced* by using the check-sum column. That is, the entry in column (10) of each row should be equal to the sum of all the other entries in the row, or else an error has been made in computing that row. Of course, rounding errors (in sixth or fifth decimal place) may be tolerable. If the model includes only three, rather than four, explanatory variables, then columns (4) and (9) and rows (4), (11), (12), and (13) are not applicable, and rows (14), (15), and (16) have to be appropriately reduced.

Results

The least squares estimates of the regression coefficients appear in the last four rows of the worksheet. Specifically,

$$\hat{\beta}_2^* = C_{15},$$

$$\hat{\beta}_3^* = C_{25},$$

$$\hat{\beta}_4^* = C_{35},$$

$$\hat{\beta}_5^* = C_{45},$$

and

$$\hat{\beta}_1^* = \bar{Y} - \hat{\beta}_2^* \bar{X}_2^* - \hat{\beta}_3^* \bar{X}_3^* - \hat{\beta}_4^* \bar{X}_4^* - \hat{\beta}_5^* \bar{X}_5^*.$$

Furthermore,

$$n\text{SSR}^* = \sum_{r=2}^{5} \hat{\beta}_r^* M_{rY}^*,$$

$$n\text{SST}^* = M_{YY}^*,$$

$$n\text{SSE}^* = n\text{SST}^* - n\text{SSR}^*,$$

which leads to

$$R^2 = \frac{n\text{SSR}^*}{n\text{SST}^*}$$

and

$$ns^{*2} = \frac{n\text{SSE}^*}{n - 5}.$$

The estimated variances of the regression coefficients are obtained as follows:

$$s_{\hat{\beta}_2^*}^{*2} = (ns^{*2})C_{16},$$

$$s_{\hat{\beta}_3^*}^{*2} = (ns^{*2})C_{27},$$

$$s_{\hat{\beta}_4^*}^{*2} = (ns^{*2})C_{38},$$

$$s_{\hat{\beta}_5^*}^{*2} = (ns^{*2})C_{49}.$$

The estimated variance of $\hat{\beta}_1^*$ can be calculated by reference to formula (10.32) of the text. The F statistic for testing the hypothesis that no relationship exists can be calculated as

$$\frac{n\text{SSR}^*/4}{ns^{*2}} \sim F_{4, n-5}.$$

To return to the original, unstarred variables, we substitute for Y_i^* and for the X_i^*'s into

$$Y_i^* = \hat{\beta}_1^* + \hat{\beta}_2^* X_{i2}^* + \hat{\beta}_3^* X_{i3}^* + \hat{\beta}_4^* X_{i4}^* + \hat{\beta}_5^* X_{i5}^* + e_i^*$$

to get

$$(10^{a_Y}) Y_i = \hat{\beta}_1^* + \hat{\beta}_2^*(10^{a_2})X_{i2} + \hat{\beta}_3^*(10^{a_3})X_{i3} + \hat{\beta}_4^*(10^{a_4})X_{i4} + \hat{\beta}_5^*(10^{a_5})X_{i5} + e_i^*,$$

where $a_Y, a_2, \ldots, a_5$ represent the appropriate powers of 10 that were used for scaling the original variables. Then

$$\hat{\beta}_1 = (10^{-a_Y})\hat{\beta}_1^*,$$
$$\hat{\beta}_2 = (10^{a_2 - a_Y})\hat{\beta}_2^*,$$
$$\hat{\beta}_3 = (10^{a_3 - a_Y})\hat{\beta}_3^*,$$
$$\hat{\beta}_4 = (10^{a_4 - a_Y})\hat{\beta}_4^*,$$
$$\hat{\beta}_5 = (10^{a_5 - a_Y})\hat{\beta}_5^*.$$

Note that the estimated standard errors of the regression coefficients will be changed by the same factor as the regression coefficients themselves, and that R^2 and the F statistic remain unchanged.

D. Statistical Tables

Table D–1 Areas Under the Normal Distribution

z	.00	.01	.02	.03	.04	.05	.06	.07	.08	.09
0.0	.0000	.0040	.0080	.0120	.0160	.0199	.0239	.0279	.0319	.0359
0.1	.0398	.0438	.0478	.0517	.0557	.0596	.0636	.0675	.0714	.0753
0.2	.0793	.0832	.0871	.0910	.0948	.0987	.1026	.1064	.1103	.1141
0.3	.1179	.1217	.1255	.1293	.1331	.1368	.1406	.1443	.1480	.1517
0.4	.1554	.1591	.1628	.1664	.1700	.1736	.1772	.1808	.1844	.1879
0.5	.1915	.1950	.1985	.2019	.2054	.2088	.2123	.2157	.2190	.2224
0.6	.2257	.2291	.2324	.2357	.2389	.2422	.2454	.2486	.2517	.2549
0.7	.2580	.2611	.2642	.2673	.2704	.2734	.2764	.2794	.2823	.2852
0.8	.2881	.2910	.2939	.2967	.2995	.3023	.3051	.3078	.3106	.3133
0.9	.3159	.3186	.3212	.3238	.3264	.3289	.3315	.3340	.3365	.3389
1.0	.3413	.3438	.3461	.3485	.3508	.3531	.3554	.3577	.3599	.3621
1.1	.3643	.3665	.3686	.3708	.3729	.3749	.3770	.3790	.3810	.3830
1.2	.3849	.3869	.3888	.3907	.3925	.3944	.3962	.3980	.3997	.4015
1.3	.4032	.4049	.4066	.4082	.4099	.4115	.4131	.4147	.4162	.4177
1.4	.4192	.4207	.4222	.4236	.4251	.4265	.4279	.4292	.4306	.4319
1.5	.4332	.4345	.4357	.4370	.4382	.4394	.4406	.4418	.4429	.4441
1.6	.4452	.4463	.4474	.4484	.4495	.4505	.4515	.4525	.4535	.4545
1.7	.4554	.4564	.4573	.4582	.4591	.4599	.4608	.4616	.4625	.4633
1.8	.4641	.4649	.4656	.4664	.4671	.4678	.4686	.4693	.4699	.4706
1.9	.4713	.4719	.4726	.4732	.4738	.4744	.4750	.4756	.4761	.4767
2.0	.4772	.4778	.4783	.4788	.4793	.4798	.4803	.4808	.4812	.4817
2.1	.4821	.4826	.4830	.4834	.4838	.4842	.4846	.4850	.4854	.4857
2.2	.4861	.4864	.4868	.4871	.4875	.4878	.4881	.4884	.4887	.4890
2.3	.4893	.4896	.4898	.4901	.4904	.4906	.4909	.4911	.4913	.4916
2.4	.4918	.4920	.4922	.4925	.4927	.4929	.4931	.4932	.4934	.4936
2.5	.4938	.4940	.4941	.4943	.4945	.4946	.4948	.4949	.4951	.4952
2.6	.4953	.4955	.4956	.4957	.4959	.4960	.4961	.4962	.4963	.4964
2.7	.4965	.4966	.4967	.4968	.4969	.4970	.4971	.4972	.4973	.4974
2.8	.4974	.4975	.4976	.4977	.4977	.4978	.4979	.4979	.4980	.4981
2.9	.4981	.4982	.4982	.4983	.4984	.4984	.4985	.4985	.4986	.4986
3.0	.4987	.4987	.4987	.4988	.4988	.4989	.4989	.4989	.4990	.4990

Table D–2 Values of $t_{\alpha, \nu}$

ν	$\alpha = 0.10$	$\alpha = 0.05$	$\alpha = 0.025$	$\alpha = 0.01$	$\alpha = 0.005$	ν
1	3.078	6.314	12.706	31.821	63.657	1
2	1.886	2.920	4.303	6.965	9.925	2
3	1.638	2.353	3.182	4.541	5.841	3
4	1.533	2.132	2.776	3.747	4.604	4
5	1.476	2.015	2.571	3.365	4.032	5
6	1.440	1.943	2.447	3.143	3.707	6
7	1.415	1.895	2.365	2.998	3.499	7
8	1.397	1.860	2.306	2.896	3.355	8
9	1.383	1.833	2.262	2.821	3.250	9
10	1.372	1.812	2.228	2.764	3.169	10
11	1.363	1.796	2.201	2.718	3.106	11
12	1.356	1.782	2.179	2.681	3.055	12
13	1.350	1.771	2.160	2.650	3.012	13
14	1.345	1.761	2.145	2.624	2.977	14
15	1.341	1.753	2.131	2.602	2.947	15
16	1.337	1.746	2.120	2.583	2.921	16
17	1.333	1.740	2.110	2.567	2.898	17
18	1.330	1.734	2.101	2.552	2.878	18
19	1.328	1.729	2.093	2.539	2.861	19
20	1.325	1.725	2.086	2.528	2.845	20
21	1.323	1.721	2.080	2.518	2.831	21
22	1.321	1.717	2.074	2.508	2.819	22
23	1.319	1.714	2.069	2.500	2.807	23
24	1.318	1.711	2.064	2.492	2.797	24
25	1.316	1.708	2.060	2.485	2.787	25
26	1.315	1.706	2.056	2.479	2.779	26
27	1.314	1.703	2.052	2.473	2.771	27
28	1.313	1.701	2.048	2.467	2.763	28
29	1.311	1.699	2.045	2.462	2.756	29
inf.	1.282	1.645	1.960	2.326	2.576	inf.

This table is abridged from Table IV of R. A. Fisher, *Statistical Methods for Research Workers*, published by Oliver and Boyd Ltd., Edinburgh, by permission of the author and publishers.

Table D–3 Values of $\chi^2_{\alpha,\nu}$

ν	$\alpha = 0.995$	$\alpha = 0.99$	$\alpha = 0.975$	$\alpha = 0.95$	$\alpha = 0.05$	$\alpha = 0.025$	$\alpha = 0.01$	$\alpha = 0.005$	ν
1	0.0000393	0.000157	0.000982	0.00393	3.841	5.024	6.635	7.879	1
2	0.0100	0.0201	0.0506	0.103	5.991	7.378	9.210	10.597	2
3	0.0717	0.115	0.216	0.352	7.815	9.348	11.345	12.838	3
4	0.207	0.297	0.484	0.711	9.488	11.143	13.277	14.860	4
5	0.412	0.554	0.831	1.145	11.070	12.832	15.086	16.750	5
6	0.676	0.872	1.237	1.635	12.592	14.449	16.812	18.548	6
7	0.989	1.239	1.690	2.167	14.067	16.013	18.475	20.278	7
8	1.344	1.646	2.180	2.733	15.507	17.535	20.090	21.955	8
9	1.735	2.088	2.700	3.325	16.919	19.023	21.666	23.589	9
10	2.156	2.558	3.247	3.940	18.307	20.483	23.209	25.188	10
11	2.603	3.053	3.816	4.575	19.675	21.920	24.725	26.757	11
12	3.074	3.571	4.404	5.226	21.026	23.337	26.217	28.300	12
13	3.565	4.107	5.009	5.892	22.362	24.736	27.688	29.819	13
14	4.075	4.660	5.629	6.571	23.685	26.119	29.141	31.319	14
15	4.601	5.229	6.262	7.261	24.996	27.488	30.578	32.801	15
16	5.142	5.812	6.908	7.962	26.296	28.845	32.000	34.267	16
17	5.697	6.408	7.564	8.672	27.587	30.191	33.409	35.718	17
18	6.265	7.015	8.231	9.390	28.869	31.526	34.805	37.156	18
19	6.844	7.633	8.907	10.117	30.144	32.852	36.191	38.582	19
20	7.434	8.260	9.591	10.851	31.410	34.170	37.566	39.997	20
21	8.034	8.897	10.283	11.591	32.671	35.479	38.932	41.401	21
22	8.643	9.542	10.982	12.338	33.924	36.781	40.289	42.796	22
23	9.260	10.196	11.689	13.091	35.172	38.076	41.638	44.181	23
24	9.886	10.856	12.401	13.848	36.415	39.364	42.980	45.558	24
25	10.520	11.524	13.120	14.611	37.652	40.646	44.314	46.928	25
26	11.160	12.198	13.844	15.379	38.885	41.923	45.642	48.290	26
27	11.808	12.879	14.573	16.151	40.113	43.194	46.963	49.645	27
28	12.461	13.565	15.308	16.928	41.337	44.461	48.278	50.993	28
29	13.121	14.256	16.047	17.708	42.557	45.722	49.588	52.336	29
30	13.787	14.953	16.791	18.493	43.773	46.979	50.892	53.672	30

Based on Table 8 of *Biometrika Tables for Statisticians, Volume I.* By permission of the *Biometrika* trustees.

Table D–4A Values of $F_{0.05, \nu_1, \nu_2}$

ν_2 = degrees of freedom for denominator	ν_1 = degrees of freedom for numerator																		
	1	2	3	4	5	6	7	8	9	10	12	15	20	24	30	40	60	120	∞
1	161	200	216	225	230	234	237	239	241	242	244	246	248	249	250	251	252	253	254
2	18.5	19.0	19.2	19.2	19.3	19.3	19.4	19.4	19.4	19.4	19.4	19.4	19.4	19.5	19.5	19.5	19.5	19.5	19.5
3	10.1	9.55	9.28	9.12	9.01	8.94	8.89	8.85	8.81	8.79	8.74	8.70	8.66	8.64	8.62	8.59	8.57	8.55	8.53
4	7.71	6.94	6.59	6.39	6.26	6.16	6.09	6.04	6.00	5.96	5.91	5.86	5.80	5.77	5.75	5.72	5.69	5.66	5.63
5	6.61	5.79	5.41	5.19	5.05	4.95	4.88	4.82	4.77	4.74	4.68	4.62	4.56	4.53	4.50	4.46	4.43	4.40	4.37
6	5.99	5.14	4.76	4.53	4.39	4.28	4.21	4.15	4.10	4.06	4.00	3.94	3.87	3.84	3.81	3.77	3.74	3.70	3.67
7	5.59	4.74	4.35	4.12	3.97	3.87	3.79	3.73	3.68	3.64	3.57	3.51	3.44	3.41	3.38	3.34	3.30	3.27	3.23
8	5.32	4.46	4.07	3.84	3.69	3.58	3.50	3.44	3.39	3.35	3.28	3.22	3.15	3.12	3.08	3.04	3.01	2.97	2.93
9	5.12	4.26	3.86	3.63	3.48	3.37	3.29	3.23	3.18	3.14	3.07	3.01	2.94	2.90	2.86	2.83	2.79	2.75	2.71
10	4.96	4.10	3.71	3.48	3.33	3.22	3.14	3.07	3.02	2.98	2.91	2.85	2.77	2.74	2.70	2.66	2.62	2.58	2.54
11	4.84	3.98	3.59	3.36	3.20	3.09	3.01	2.95	2.90	2.85	2.79	2.72	2.65	2.61	2.57	2.53	2.49	2.45	2.40
12	4.75	3.89	3.49	3.26	3.11	3.00	2.91	2.85	2.80	2.75	2.69	2.62	2.54	2.51	2.47	2.43	2.38	2.34	2.30
13	4.67	3.81	3.41	3.18	3.03	2.92	2.83	2.77	2.71	2.67	2.60	2.53	2.46	2.42	2.38	2.34	2.30	2.25	2.21
14	4.60	3.74	3.34	3.11	2.96	2.85	2.76	2.70	2.65	2.60	2.53	2.46	2.39	2.35	2.31	2.27	2.22	2.18	2.13
15	4.54	3.68	3.29	3.06	2.90	2.79	2.71	2.64	2.59	2.54	2.48	2.40	2.33	2.29	2.25	2.20	2.16	2.11	2.07
16	4.49	3.63	3.24	3.01	2.85	2.74	2.66	2.59	2.54	2.49	2.42	2.35	2.28	2.24	2.19	2.15	2.11	2.06	2.01
17	4.45	3.59	3.20	2.96	2.81	2.70	2.61	2.55	2.49	2.45	2.38	2.31	2.23	2.19	2.15	2.10	2.06	2.01	1.96
18	4.41	3.55	3.16	2.93	2.77	2.66	2.58	2.51	2.46	2.41	2.34	2.27	2.19	2.15	2.11	2.06	2.02	1.97	1.92
19	4.38	3.52	3.13	2.90	2.74	2.63	2.54	2.48	2.42	2.38	2.31	2.23	2.16	2.11	2.07	2.03	1.98	1.93	1.88
20	4.35	3.49	3.10	2.87	2.71	2.60	2.51	2.45	2.39	2.35	2.28	2.20	2.12	2.08	2.04	1.99	1.95	1.90	1.84
21	4.32	3.47	3.07	2.84	2.68	2.57	2.49	2.42	2.37	2.32	2.25	2.18	2.10	2.05	2.01	1.96	1.92	1.87	1.81
22	4.30	3.44	3.05	2.82	2.66	2.55	2.46	2.40	2.34	2.30	2.23	2.15	2.07	2.03	1.98	1.94	1.89	1.84	1.78
23	4.28	3.42	3.03	2.80	2.64	2.53	2.44	2.37	2.32	2.27	2.20	2.13	2.05	2.01	1.96	1.91	1.86	1.81	1.76
24	4.26	3.40	3.01	2.78	2.62	2.51	2.42	2.36	2.30	2.25	2.18	2.11	2.03	1.98	1.94	1.89	1.84	1.79	1.73
25	4.24	3.39	2.99	2.76	2.60	2.49	2.40	2.34	2.28	2.24	2.16	2.09	2.01	1.96	1.92	1.87	1.82	1.77	1.71
30	4.17	3.32	2.92	2.69	2.53	2.42	2.33	2.27	2.21	2.16	2.09	2.01	1.93	1.89	1.84	1.79	1.74	1.68	1.62
40	4.08	3.23	2.84	2.61	2.45	2.34	2.25	2.18	2.12	2.08	2.00	1.92	1.84	1.79	1.74	1.69	1.64	1.58	1.51
60	4.00	3.15	2.76	2.53	2.37	2.25	2.17	2.10	2.04	1.99	1.92	1.84	1.75	1.70	1.65	1.59	1.53	1.47	1.39
120	3.92	3.07	2.68	2.45	2.29	2.18	2.09	2.02	1.96	1.91	1.83	1.75	1.66	1.61	1.55	1.50	1.43	1.35	1.25
∞	3.84	3.00	2.60	2.37	2.21	2.10	2.01	1.94	1.88	1.83	1.75	1.67	1.57	1.52	1.46	1.39	1.32	1.22	1.00

Abridged from M. Merrington and C. M. Thompson, "Tables of percentage points of the inverted beta (*F*) distribution," *Biometrika*, Vol. 33, 1943, p. 73. By permission of the *Biometrika* trustees.

Table D–4B Values of $F_{0.01, \nu_1, \nu_2}$

ν_2 = degrees of freedom for denominator	ν_1 = degrees of freedom for numerator																		
	1	2	3	4	5	6	7	8	9	10	12	15	20	24	30	40	60	120	∞
1	4052	5000	5403	5625	5764	5859	5928	5982	6023	6056	6106	6157	6209	6235	6261	6287	6313	6339	6366
2	98.5	99.0	99.2	99.2	99.3	99.3	99.4	99.4	99.4	99.4	99.4	99.4	99.4	99.5	99.5	99.5	99.5	99.5	99.5
3	34.1	30.8	29.5	28.7	28.2	27.9	27.7	27.5	27.3	27.2	27.1	26.9	26.7	26.6	26.5	26.4	26.3	26.2	26.1
4	21.2	18.0	16.7	16.0	15.5	15.2	15.0	14.8	14.7	14.5	14.4	14.2	14.0	13.9	13.8	13.7	13.7	13.6	13.5
5	16.3	13.3	12.1	11.4	11.0	10.7	10.5	10.3	10.2	10.1	9.89	9.72	9.55	9.47	9.38	9.29	9.20	9.11	9.02
6	13.7	10.9	9.78	9.15	8.75	8.47	8.26	8.10	7.98	7.87	7.72	7.56	7.40	7.31	7.23	7.14	7.06	6.97	6.88
7	12.2	9.55	8.45	7.85	7.46	7.19	6.99	6.84	6.72	6.62	6.47	6.31	6.16	6.07	5.99	5.91	5.82	5.74	5.65
8	11.3	8.65	7.59	7.01	6.63	6.37	6.18	6.03	5.91	5.81	5.67	5.52	5.36	5.28	5.20	5.12	5.03	4.95	4.86
9	10.6	8.02	6.99	6.42	6.06	5.80	5.61	5.47	5.35	5.26	5.11	4.96	4.81	4.73	4.65	4.57	4.48	4.40	4.31
10	10.0	7.56	6.55	5.99	5.64	5.39	5.20	5.06	4.94	4.85	4.71	4.56	4.41	4.33	4.25	4.17	4.08	4.00	3.91
11	9.65	7.21	6.22	5.67	5.32	5.07	4.89	4.74	4.63	4.54	4.40	4.25	4.10	4.02	3.94	3.86	3.78	3.69	3.60
12	9.33	6.93	5.95	5.41	5.06	4.82	4.64	4.50	4.39	4.30	4.16	4.01	3.86	3.78	3.70	3.62	3.54	3.45	3.36
13	9.07	6.70	5.74	5.21	4.86	4.62	4.44	4.30	4.19	4.10	3.96	3.82	3.66	3.59	3.51	3.43	3.34	3.25	3.17
14	8.86	6.51	5.56	5.04	4.70	4.46	4.28	4.14	4.03	3.94	3.80	3.66	3.51	3.43	3.35	3.27	3.18	3.09	3.00
15	8.68	6.36	5.42	4.89	4.56	4.32	4.14	4.00	3.89	3.80	3.67	3.52	3.37	3.29	3.21	3.13	3.05	2.96	2.87
16	8.53	6.23	5.29	4.77	4.44	4.20	4.03	3.89	3.78	3.69	3.55	3.41	3.26	3.18	3.10	3.02	2.93	2.84	2.75
17	8.40	6.11	5.19	4.67	4.34	4.10	3.93	3.79	3.68	3.59	3.46	3.31	3.16	3.08	3.00	2.92	2.83	2.75	2.65
18	8.29	6.01	5.09	4.58	4.25	4.01	3.84	3.71	3.60	3.51	3.37	3.23	3.08	3.00	2.92	2.84	2.75	2.66	2.57
19	8.19	5.93	5.01	4.50	4.17	3.94	3.77	3.63	3.52	3.43	3.30	3.15	3.00	2.92	2.84	2.76	2.67	2.58	2.49
20	8.10	5.85	4.94	4.43	4.10	3.87	3.70	3.56	3.46	3.37	3.23	3.09	2.94	2.86	2.78	2.69	2.61	2.52	2.42
21	8.02	5.78	4.87	4.37	4.04	3.81	3.64	3.51	3.40	3.31	3.17	3.03	2.88	2.80	2.72	2.64	2.55	2.46	2.36
22	7.95	5.72	4.82	4.31	3.99	3.76	3.59	3.45	3.35	3.26	3.12	2.98	2.83	2.75	2.67	2.58	2.50	2.40	2.31
23	7.88	5.66	4.76	4.26	3.94	3.71	3.54	3.41	3.30	3.21	3.07	2.93	2.78	2.70	2.62	2.54	2.45	2.35	2.26
24	7.82	5.61	4.72	4.22	3.90	3.67	3.50	3.36	3.26	3.17	3.03	2.89	2.74	2.66	2.58	2.49	2.40	2.31	2.21
25	7.77	5.57	4.68	4.18	3.86	3.63	3.46	3.32	3.22	3.13	2.99	2.85	2.70	2.62	2.53	2.45	2.36	2.27	2.17
30	7.56	5.39	4.51	4.02	3.70	3.47	3.30	3.17	3.07	2.98	2.84	2.70	2.55	2.47	2.39	2.30	2.21	2.11	2.01
40	7.31	5.18	4.31	3.83	3.51	3.29	3.12	2.99	2.89	2.80	2.66	2.52	2.37	2.29	2.20	2.11	2.02	1.92	1.80
60	7.08	4.98	4.13	3.65	3.34	3.12	2.95	2.82	2.72	2.63	2.50	2.35	2.20	2.12	2.03	1.94	1.84	1.73	1.60
120	6.85	4.79	3.95	3.48	3.17	2.96	2.79	2.66	2.56	2.47	2.34	2.19	2.03	1.95	1.86	1.76	1.66	1.53	1.38
∞	6.63	4.61	3.78	3.32	3.02	2.80	2.64	2.51	2.41	2.32	2.18	2.04	1.88	1.79	1.70	1.59	1.47	1.32	1.00

Abridged from M. Merrington and C. M. Thompson, "Tables of percentage points of the inverted beta (*F*) distribution," *Biometrika*, Vol. 33, 1943, p. 73. By permission of the *Biometrika* trustees.

Table D–5A Significance Points of d_L and d_U: 5%

n	$k' = 1$		$k' = 2$		$k' = 3$		$k' = 4$		$k' = 5$	
	d_L	d_U	d_L	d_U	d_L	d_U	d_L	d_U	d_L	d_U
15	1.08	1.36	0.95	1.54	0.82	1.75	0.69	1.97	0.56	2.21
16	1.10	1.37	0.98	1.54	0.86	1.73	0.74	1.93	0.62	2.15
17	1.13	1.38	1.02	1.54	0.90	1.71	0.78	1.90	0.67	2.10
18	1.16	1.39	1.05	1.53	0.93	1.69	0.82	1.87	0.71	2.06
19	1.18	1.40	1.08	1.53	0.97	1.68	0.86	1.85	0.75	2.02
20	1.20	1.41	1.10	1.54	1.00	1.68	0.90	1.83	0.79	1.99
21	1.22	1.42	1.13	1.54	1.03	1.67	0.93	1.81	0.83	1.96
22	1.24	1.43	1.15	1.54	1.05	1.66	0.96	1.80	0.86	1.94
23	1.26	1.44	1.17	1.54	1.08	1.66	0.99	1.79	0.90	1.92
24	1.27	1.45	1.19	1.55	1.10	1.66	1.01	1.78	0.93	1.90
25	1.29	1.45	1.21	1.55	1.12	1.66	1.04	1.77	0.95	1.89
26	1.30	1.46	1.22	1.55	1.14	1.65	1.06	1.76	0.98	1.88
27	1.32	1.47	1.24	1.56	1.16	1.65	1.08	1.76	1.01	1.86
28	1.33	1.48	1.26	1.56	1.18	1.65	1.10	1.75	1.03	1.85
29	1.34	1.48	1.27	1.56	1.20	1.65	1.12	1.74	1.05	1.84
30	1.35	1.49	1.28	1.57	1.21	1.65	1.14	1.74	1.07	1.83
31	1.36	1.50	1.30	1.57	1.23	1.65	1.16	1.74	1.09	1.83
32	1.37	1.50	1.31	1.57	1.24	1.65	1.18	1.73	1.11	1.82
33	1.38	1.51	1.32	1.58	1.26	1.65	1.19	1.73	1.13	1.81
34	1.39	1.51	1.33	1.58	1.27	1.65	1.21	1.73	1.15	1.81
35	1.40	1.52	1.34	1.58	1.28	1.65	1.22	1.73	1.16	1.80
36	1.41	1.52	1.35	1.59	1.29	1.65	1.24	1.73	1.18	1.80
37	1.42	1.53	1.36	1.59	1.31	1.66	1.25	1.72	1.19	1.80
38	1.43	1.54	1.37	1.59	1.32	1.66	1.26	1.72	1.21	1.79
39	1.43	1.54	1.38	1.60	1.33	1.66	1.27	1.72	1.22	1.79
40	1.44	1.54	1.39	1.60	1.34	1.66	1.29	1.72	1.23	1.79
45	1.48	1.57	1.43	1.62	1.38	1.67	1.34	1.72	1.29	1.78
50	1.50	1.59	1.46	1.63	1.42	1.67	1.38	1.72	1.34	1.77
55	1.53	1.60	1.49	1.64	1.45	1.68	1.41	1.72	1.38	1.77
60	1.55	1.62	1.51	1.65	1.48	1.69	1.44	1.73	1.41	1.77
65	1.57	1.63	1.54	1.66	1.50	1.70	1.47	1.73	1.44	1.77
70	1.58	1.64	1.55	1.67	1.52	1.70	1.49	1.74	1.46	1.77
75	1.60	1.65	1.57	1.68	1.54	1.71	1.51	1.74	1.49	1.77
80	1.61	1.66	1.59	1.69	1.56	1.72	1.53	1.74	1.51	1.77
85	1.62	1.67	1.60	1.70	1.57	1.72	1.55	1.75	1.52	1.77
90	1.63	1.68	1.61	1.70	1.59	1.73	1.57	1.75	1.54	1.78
95	1.64	1.69	1.62	1.71	1.60	1.73	1.58	1.75	1.56	1.78
100	1.65	1.69	1.63	1.72	1.61	1.74	1.59	1.76	1.57	1.78

Note: k' = number of explanatory variables excluding the constant term.

Source: J. Durbin and G. S. Watson, "Testing for Serial Correlation in Least Squares Regression," *Biometrika*, Vol. 38, 1951, pp. 159–177. Reprinted with the permission of the authors and the *Biometrika* trustees.

Table D–5B Significance Points of d_L and d_U: 2.5%

n	$k' = 1$		$k' = 2$		$k' = 3$		$k' = 4$		$k' = 5$	
	d_L	d_U	d_L	d_U	d_L	d_U	d_L	d_U	d_L	d_U
15	0.95	1.23	0.83	1.40	0.71	1.61	0.59	1.84	0.48	2.09
16	0.98	1.24	0.86	1.40	0.75	1.59	0.64	1.80	0.53	2.03
17	1.01	1.25	0.90	1.40	0.79	1.58	0.68	1.77	0.57	1.98
18	1.03	1.26	0.93	1.40	0.82	1.56	0.72	1.74	0.62	1.93
19	1.06	1.28	0.96	1.41	0.86	1.55	0.76	1.72	0.66	1.90
20	1.08	1.28	0.99	1.41	0.89	1.55	0.79	1.70	0.70	1.87
21	1.10	1.30	1.01	1.41	0.92	1.54	0.83	1.69	0.73	1.84
22	1.12	1.31	1.04	1.42	0.95	1.54	0.86	1.68	0.77	1.82
23	1.14	1.32	1.06	1.42	0.97	1.54	0.89	1.67	0.80	1.80
24	1.16	1.33	1.08	1.43	1.00	1.54	0.91	1.66	0.83	1.79
25	1.18	1.34	1.10	1.43	1.02	1.54	0.94	1.65	0.86	1.77
26	1.19	1.35	1.12	1.44	1.04	1.54	0.96	1.65	0.88	1.76
27	1.21	1.36	1.13	1.44	1.06	1.54	0.99	1.64	0.91	1.75
28	1.22	1.37	1.15	1.45	1.08	1.54	1.01	1.64	0.93	1.74
29	1.24	1.38	1.17	1.45	1.10	1.54	1.03	1.63	0.96	1.73
30	1.25	1.38	1.18	1.46	1.12	1.54	1.05	1.63	0.98	1.73
31	1.26	1.39	1.20	1.47	1.13	1.55	1.07	1.63	1.00	1.72
32	1.27	1.40	1.21	1.47	1.15	1.55	1.08	1.63	1.02	1.71
33	1.28	1.41	1.22	1.48	1.16	1.55	1.10	1.63	1.04	1.71
34	1.29	1.41	1.24	1.48	1.17	1.55	1.12	1.63	1.06	1.70
35	1.30	1.42	1.25	1.48	1.19	1.55	1.13	1.63	1.07	1.70
36	1.31	1.43	1.26	1.49	1.20	1.56	1.15	1.63	1.09	1.70
37	1.32	1.43	1.27	1.49	1.21	1.56	1.16	1.62	1.10	1.70
38	1.33	1.44	1.28	1.50	1.23	1.56	1.17	1.62	1.12	1.70
39	1.34	1.44	1.29	1.50	1.24	1.56	1.19	1.63	1.13	1.69
40	1.35	1.45	1.30	1.51	1.25	1.57	1.20	1.63	1.15	1.69
45	1.39	1.48	1.34	1.53	1.30	1.58	1.25	1.63	1.21	1.69
50	1.42	1.50	1.38	1.54	1.34	1.59	1.30	1.64	1.26	1.69
55	1.45	1.52	1.41	1.56	1.37	1.60	1.33	1.64	1.30	1.69
60	1.47	1.54	1.44	1.57	1.40	1.61	1.37	1.65	1.33	1.69
65	1.49	1.55	1.46	1.59	1.43	1.62	1.40	1.66	1.36	1.69
70	1.51	1.57	1.48	1.60	1.45	1.63	1.42	1.66	1.39	1.70
75	1.53	1.58	1.50	1.61	1.47	1.64	1.45	1.67	1.42	1.70
80	1.54	1.59	1.52	1.62	1.49	1.65	1.47	1.67	1.44	1.70
85	1.56	1.60	1.53	1.63	1.51	1.65	1.49	1.68	1.46	1.71
90	1.57	1.61	1.55	1.64	1.53	1.66	1.50	1.69	1.48	1.71
95	1.58	1.62	1.56	1.65	1.54	1.67	1.52	1.69	1.50	1.71
100	1.59	1.63	1.57	1.65	1.55	1.67	1.53	1.70	1.51	1.72

Note: k' = number of explanatory variables excluding the constant term.

Source: J. Durbin and G. S. Watson, "Testing for Serial Correlation in Least Squares Regression," *Biometrika*, Vol. 38, 1951, pp. 159–177. Reprinted with the permission of the authors and the *Biometrika* trustees.

Table D–5C Significance Points of d_L and d_U: 1%

n	k′ = 1		k′ = 2		k′ = 3		k′ = 4		k′ = 5	
	d_L	d_U	d_L	d_U	d_L	d_U	d_L	d_U	d_L	d_U
15	0.81	1.07	0.70	1.25	0.59	1.46	0.49	1.70	0.39	1.96
16	0.84	1.09	0.74	1.25	0.63	1.44	0.53	1.66	0.44	1.90
17	0.87	1.10	0.77	1.25	0.67	1.43	0.57	1.63	0.48	1.85
18	0.90	1.12	0.80	1.26	0.71	1.42	0.61	1.60	0.52	1.80
19	0.93	1.13	0.83	1.26	0.74	1.41	0.65	1.58	0.56	1.77
20	0.95	1.15	0.86	1.27	0.77	1.41	0.68	1.57	0.60	1.74
21	0.97	1.16	0.89	1.27	0.80	1.41	0.72	1.55	0.63	1.71
22	1.00	1.17	0.91	1.28	0.83	1.40	0.75	1.54	0.66	1.69
23	1.02	1.19	0.94	1.29	0.86	1.40	0.77	1.53	0.70	1.67
24	1.04	1.20	0.96	1.30	0.88	1.41	0.80	1.53	0.72	1.66
25	1.05	1.21	0.98	1.30	0.90	1.41	0.83	1.52	0.75	1.65
26	1.07	1.22	1.00	1.31	0.93	1.41	0.85	1.52	0.78	1.64
27	1.09	1.23	1.02	1.32	0.95	1.41	0.88	1.51	0.81	1.63
28	1.10	1.24	1.04	1.32	0.97	1.41	0.90	1.51	0.83	1.62
29	1.12	1.25	1.05	1.33	0.99	1.42	0.92	1.51	0.85	1.61
30	1.13	1.26	1.07	1.34	1.01	1.42	0.94	1.51	0.88	1.61
31	1.15	1.27	1.08	1.34	1.02	1.42	0.96	1.51	0.90	1.60
32	1.16	1.28	1.10	1.35	1.04	1.43	0.98	1.51	0.92	1.60
33	1.17	1.29	1.11	1.36	1.05	1.43	1.00	1.51	0.94	1.59
34	1.18	1.30	1.13	1.36	1.07	1.43	1.01	1.51	0.95	1.59
35	1.19	1.31	1.14	1.37	1.08	1.44	1.03	1.51	0.97	1.59
36	1.21	1.32	1.15	1.38	1.10	1.44	1.04	1.51	0.99	1.59
37	1.22	1.32	1.16	1.38	1.11	1.45	1.06	1.51	1.00	1.59
38	1.23	1.33	1.18	1.39	1.12	1.45	1.07	1.52	1.02	1.58
39	1.24	1.34	1.19	1.39	1.14	1.45	1.09	1.52	1.03	1.58
40	1.25	1.34	1.20	1.40	1.15	1.46	1.10	1.52	1.05	1.58
45	1.29	1.38	1.24	1.42	1.20	1.48	1.16	1.53	1.11	1.58
50	1.32	1.40	1.28	1.45	1.24	1.49	1.20	1.54	1.16	1.59
55	1.36	1.43	1.32	1.47	1.28	1.51	1.25	1.55	1.21	1.59
60	1.38	1.45	1.35	1.48	1.32	1.52	1.28	1.56	1.25	1.60
65	1.41	1.47	1.38	1.50	1.35	1.53	1.31	1.57	1.28	1.61
70	1.43	1.49	1.40	1.52	1.37	1.55	1.34	1.58	1.31	1.61
75	1.45	1.50	1.42	1.53	1.39	1.56	1.37	1.59	1.34	1.62
80	1.47	1.52	1.44	1.54	1.42	1.57	1.39	1.60	1.36	1.62
85	1.48	1.53	1.46	1.55	1.43	1.58	1.41	1.60	1.39	1.63
90	1.50	1.54	1.47	1.56	1.45	1.59	1.43	1.61	1.41	1.64
95	1.51	1.55	1.49	1.57	1.47	1.60	1.45	1.62	1.42	1.64
100	1.52	1.56	1.50	1.58	1.48	1.60	1.46	1.63	1.44	1.65

Note: k' = number of explanatory variables excluding the constant term.
Source: J. Durbin and G. S. Watson, "Testing for Serial Correlation in Least Squares Regression," *Biometrika*, Vol. 38, 1951, pp. 159–177. Reprinted with the permission of the authors and the *Biometrika* trustees.

Table D–6 Random Normal Numbers, $\mu = 0, \sigma = 1$

01	02	03	04	05	06	07	08	09	10
0.464	0.137	2.455	−0.323	−0.068	0.296	−0.288	1.298	0.241	−0.957
0.060	−2.526	−0.531	−0.194	−0.543	−1.558	0.187	−1.190	0.022	0.525
1.486	−0.354	−0.634	0.697	0.926	1.375	0.785	−0.963	−0.853	−1.865
1.022	−0.472	1.279	3.521	0.571	−1.851	0.194	1.192	−0.501	−0.273
1.394	−0.555	0.046	0.321	2.945	1.974	−0.258	0.412	0.439	−0.035
0.906	−0.513	−0.525	0.595	0.881	−0.934	1.579	0.161	−1.885	0.371
1.179	−1.055	0.007	0.769	0.971	0.712	1.090	−0.631	−0.255	−0.702
−1.501	−0.488	−0.162	−0.136	1.033	0.203	0.448	0.748	−0.423	−0.432
−0.690	0.756	−1.618	−0.345	−0.511	−2.051	−0.457	−0.218	0.857	−0.465
1.372	0.225	0.378	0.761	0.181	−0.736	0.960	−1.530	−0.260	0.120
−0.482	1.678	−0.057	−1.229	−0.486	0.856	−0.491	−1.983	−2.830	−0.238
−1.376	−0.150	1.356	−0.561	−0.256	−0.212	0.219	0.779	0.953	−0.869
−1.010	0.598	−0.918	1.598	0.065	0.415	−0.169	0.313	−0.973	−1.016
−0.005	−0.899	0.012	−0.725	1.147	−0.121	1.096	0.481	−1.691	0.417
1.393	−1.163	−0.911	1.231	−0.199	−0.246	1.239	−2.574	−0.558	0.056
−1.787	−0.261	1.237	1.046	−0.508	−1.630	−0.146	−0.392	−0.627	0.561
−0.105	−0.357	−1.384	0.360	−0.992	−0.116	−1.698	−2.832	−1.108	−2.357
−1.339	1.827	−0.959	0.424	0.969	−1.141	−1.041	0.362	−1.726	1.956
1.041	0.535	0.731	1.377	0.983	−1.330	1.620	−1.040	0.524	−0.281
0.279	−2.056	0.717	−0.873	−1.096	−1.396	1.047	0.089	−0.573	0.932
−1.805	−2.008	−1.633	0.542	0.250	−0.166	0.032	0.079	0.471	−1.029
−1.186	1.180	1.114	0.882	1.265	−0.202	0.151	−0.376	−0.310	0.479
0.658	−1.141	1.151	−1.210	−0.927	0.425	0.290	−0.902	0.610	2.709
−0.439	0.358	−1.939	0.891	−0.227	0.602	0.873	−0.437	−0.220	−0.057
−1.399	−0.230	0.385	−0.649	−0.577	0.237	−0.289	0.513	0.738	−0.300
0.199	0.208	−1.083	−0.219	−0.291	1.221	1.119	0.004	−2.015	−0.594
0.159	0.272	−0.313	0.084	−2.828	−0.439	−0.792	−1.275	−0.623	−1.047
2.273	0.606	0.606	−0.747	0.247	1.291	0.063	−1.793	−0.699	−1.347
0.041	−0.307	0.121	0.790	−0.584	0.541	0.484	−0.986	0.481	0.996
−1.132	−2.098	0.921	0.145	0.446	−1.661	1.045	−1.363	−0.586	−1.023
0.768	0.079	−1.473	0.034	−2.127	0.665	0.084	−0.880	−0.579	0.551
0.375	−1.658	−1.851	0.234	−0.656	0.340	−0.086	−0.158	−0.120	0.418
−0.513	−0.344	0.210	−0.736	1.041	0.008	0.427	−0.831	0.191	0.074
0.292	−0.521	1.266	−1.206	−0.899	0.110	−0.528	−0.813	0.071	0.524
1.026	2.990	−0.574	−0.491	−1.114	1.297	−1.433	−1.345	−3.001	0.479
−1.334	1.278	−0.568	−0.109	−0.515	−0.566	2.923	0.500	0.359	0.326
−0.287	−0.144	−0.254	0.574	−0.451	−1.181	−1.190	−0.318	−0.094	1.114
0.161	−0.886	−0.921	−0.509	1.410	−0.518	0.192	−0.432	1.501	1.068
−1.346	0.193	−1.202	0.394	−1.045	0.843	0.942	1.045	0.031	0.772
1.250	−0.199	−0.288	1.810	1.378	0.584	0.216	0.733	0.402	0.226
0.630	−0.537	0.782	0.060	0.499	−0.431	1.705	1.164	0.884	−0.298
0.375	−1.941	0.247	−0.491	0.665	−0.135	−0.145	−0.498	0.457	1.064
−1.420	0.489	−1.711	−1.186	0.754	−0.732	−0.066	1.006	−0.798	0.162
−0.151	−0.243	−0.430	−0.762	0.298	1.049	1.810	2.885	−0.768	−0.129
−0.309	0.531	0.416	−1.541	1.456	2.040	−0.124	0.196	0.023	−1.204
0.424	−0.444	0.593	0.993	−0.106	0.116	0.484	−1.272	1.066	1.097
0.593	0.658	−1.127	−1.407	−1.579	−1.616	1.458	1.262	0.736	−0.916
0.862	−0.885	−0.142	−0.504	0.532	1.381	0.022	−0.281	−0.342	1.222
0.235	−0.628	−0.023	−0.463	−0.899	−0.394	−0.538	1.707	−0.188	−1.153
−0.853	0.402	0.777	0.833	0.410	−0.349	−1.094	0.580	1.395	1.298

Source: *A Million Random Digits and One Hundred Thousand Deviates* (Santa Monica: Rand Corporation, 1950). Reproduced with the permission of the publishers.

Table D–6 (*cont.*) Random Normal Numbers, $\mu = 0, \sigma = 1$

11	12	13	14	15	16	17	18	19	20
−1.329	−0.238	−0.828	−0.988	−0.445	−0.964	−0.266	−0.322	−1.726	−2.252
1.284	−0.229	1.058	0.090	0.050	0.523	0.016	0.277	1.639	0.554
0.619	0.628	0.005	0.973	−0.058	0.150	−0.635	−0.917	0.313	−1.203
0.699	−0.269	0.722	−0.994	−0.807	−1.203	1.163	1.244	1.306	−1.210
0.101	0.202	−0.150	0.731	0.420	0.116	−0.496	−0.037	−2.466	0.794
−1.381	0.301	0.522	0.233	0.791	−1.017	−0.182	0.926	−1.096	1.001
−0.574	1.366	−1.843	0.746	0.890	0.824	−1.249	−0.806	−0.240	0.217
0.096	0.210	1.091	0.990	0.900	−0.837	−1.097	−1.238	0.030	−0.311
1.389	−0.236	0.094	3.282	0.295	−0.416	0.313	0.720	0.007	0.354
1.249	0.706	1.453	0.366	−2.654	−1.400	0.212	0.307	−1.145	0.639
0.756	−0.397	−1.772	−0.257	1.120	1.188	−0.527	0.709	0.479	0.317
−0.860	0.412	−0.327	0.178	0.524	−0.672	−0.831	0.758	0.131	0.771
−0.778	−0.979	0.236	−1.033	1.497	−0.661	0.906	1.169	−1.582	1.303
0.037	0.062	0.426	1.220	0.471	0.784	−0.719	0.465	1.559	−1.326
2.619	−0.440	0.477	1.063	0.320	1.406	0.701	−0.128	0.518	−0.676
−0.420	−0.287	−0.050	−0.481	1.521	−1.367	0.609	0.292	0.048	0.592
1.048	0.220	1.121	−1.789	−1.211	−0.871	−0.740	0.513	−0.558	−0.395
1.000	−0.638	1.261	0.510	−0.150	0.034	0.054	−0.055	0.639	−0.825
1.170	−1.131	−0.985	0.102	−0.939	−1.457	1.766	1.087	−1.275	2.362
0.389	−0.435	0.171	0.891	1.158	1.041	1.048	−0.324	−0.404	1.060
−0.305	0.838	−2.019	−0.540	0.905	1.195	−1.190	0.106	0.571	0.298
−0.321	−0.039	1.799	−1.032	−2.225	−0.148	0.758	−0.862	0.158	−0.726
1.900	1.572	−0.244	−1.721	1.130	0.495	0.484	0.014	−0.778	−1.483
−0.778	−0.288	−0.224	−1.324	−0.072	0.890	−0.410	0.752	0.376	−0.224
0.617	−1.718	−0.183	−0.100	1.719	0.696	−1.339	−0.614	1.071	−0.386
−1.430	−0.953	0.770	−0.007	−1.872	1.075	−0.913	−1.168	1.775	0.238
0.267	−0.048	0.972	0.734	−1.408	−1.955	−0.848	2.002	0.232	−1.273
0.978	−0.520	−0.368	1.690	−1.479	0.985	1.475	−0.098	−1.633	2.399
−1.235	−1.168	0.325	1.421	2.652	−0.486	−1.253	0.270	−1.103	0.118
−0.258	0.638	2.309	0.741	−0.161	−0.679	0.336	1.973	0.370	−2.277
0.243	0.629	−1.516	−0.157	0.693	1.710	0.800	−0.265	1.218	0.655
−0.292	−1.455	−1.451	1.492	−0.713	0.821	−0.031	−0.780	1.330	0.977
−0.505	0.389	0.544	−0.042	1.615	−1.440	−0.989	−0.580	0.156	0.052
0.397	−0.287	1.712	0.289	−0.904	0.259	−0.600	−1.635	−0.009	−0.799
−0.605	−0.470	0.007	0.721	−1.117	0.635	0.592	−1.362	−1.441	0.672
1.360	0.182	−1.476	−0.599	−0.875	0.292	−0.700	0.058	−0.340	−0.639
0.480	−0.699	1.615	−0.225	1.014	−1.370	−1.097	0.294	0.309	−1.389
−0.027	−0.487	−1.000	−0.015	0.119	−1.990	−0.687	−1.964	−0.366	1.759
−1.482	−0.815	−0.121	1.884	−0.185	0.601	0.793	0.430	−1.181	0.426
−1.256	−0.567	−0.994	1.011	−1.071	−0.623	−0.420	−0.309	1.362	0.863
−1.132	2.039	1.934	−0.222	0.386	1.100	0.284	1.597	−1.718	−0.560
−0.780	−0.239	−0.497	−0.434	−0.284	−0.241	−0.333	1.348	−0.478	−0.169
−0.859	−0.215	0.241	1.471	0.389	−0.952	0.245	0.781	1.093	−0.240
0.447	1.479	0.067	0.426	−0.370	−0.675	−0.972	0.225	0.815	0.389
0.269	0.735	−0.066	−0.271	−1.439	1.036	−0.306	−1.439	−0.122	−0.336
0.097	−1.883	−0.218	0.202	−0.357	0.019	1.631	1.400	0.223	−0.793
−0.686	1.596	−0.286	0.722	0.655	−0.275	1.245	−1.504	0.066	−1.280
0.957	0.057	−1.153	0.701	−0.280	1.747	−0.745	1.338	−1.421	0.386
−0.976	−1.789	−0.696	−1.799	−0.354	0.071	2.355	0.135	−0.598	1.883
0.274	0.226	−0.909	−0.572	0.181	1.115	0.406	0.453	−1.218	−0.115

Table D–6 (*cont.*) Random Normal Numbers, $\mu = 0$, $\sigma = 1$

21	22	23	24	25	26	27	28	29	30
−1.752	−0.329	−1.256	0.318	1.531	0.349	−0.958	−0.059	0.415	−1.084
−0.291	0.085	1.701	−1.087	−0.443	−0.292	0.248	−0.539	−1.382	0.318
−0.933	0.130	0.634	0.899	1.409	−0.883	−0.095	0.229	0.129	0.367
−0.450	−0.244	0.072	1.028	1.730	−0.056	−1.488	−0.078	−2.361	−0.992
0.512	−0.882	0.490	−1.304	−0.266	0.757	−0.361	0.194	−1.078	0.529
−0.702	0.472	0.429	−0.664	−0.592	1.443	−1.515	−1.209	−1.043	0.278
0.284	0.039	−0.518	1.351	1.473	0.889	0.300	0.339	−0.206	1.392
−0.509	1.420	−0.782	−0.429	−1.266	0.627	−1.165	0.819	−0.261	0.409
−1.776	−1.033	1.977	0.014	0.702	−0.435	−0.816	1.131	0.656	0.061
−0.044	1.807	0.342	−2.510	1.071	−1.220	−0.060	−0.764	0.079	−0.964
0.263	−0.578	1.612	−0.148	−0.383	−1.007	−0.414	0.638	−0.186	0.507
0.986	0.439	−0.192	−0.132	0.167	0.883	−0.400	−1.440	−0.385	−1.414
−0.441	−0.852	−1.446	−0.605	−0.348	1.018	0.963	−0.004	2.504	−0.847
−0.866	0.489	0.097	0.379	0.192	−0.842	0.065	1.420	0.426	−1.191
−1.215	0.675	1.621	0.394	−1.447	2.199	−0.321	−0.540	−0.037	0.185
−0.475	−1.210	0.183	0.526	0.495	1.297	−1.613	1.241	−1.016	−0.090
1.200	0.131	2.502	0.344	−1.060	−0.909	−1.695	−0.666	−0.838	−0.866
−0.498	−1.202	−0.057	−1.354	−1.441	−1.590	0.987	0.441	0.637	−1.116
−0.743	0.894	−0.028	1.119	−0.598	0.279	2.241	0.830	0.267	−0.156
0.779	−0.780	−0.954	0.705	−0.361	−0.734	1.365	1.297	−0.142	−1.387
−0.206	−0.195	1.017	−1.167	−0.079	−0.452	0.058	−1.068	−0.394	−0.406
−0.092	−0.927	−0.439	0.256	0.503	0.338	1.511	−0.465	−0.118	−0.454
−1.222	−1.582	1.786	−0.517	−1.080	−0.409	−0.474	−1.890	0.247	0.575
0.068	0.075	−1.383	−0.084	0.159	1.276	1.141	0.186	−0.973	−0.266
0.183	1.600	−0.335	1.553	0.889	0.896	−0.035	0.461	0.486	1.246
−0.811	−2.904	0.618	0.588	0.533	0.803	−0.696	0.690	0.820	0.557
−1.010	1.149	1.033	0.336	1.306	0.835	1.523	0.296	−0.426	0.004
1.453	1.210	−0.043	0.220	−0.256	−1.161	−2.030	−0.046	0.243	1.082
0.759	−0.838	−0.877	−0.177	1.183	−0.218	−3.154	−0.963	−0.822	−1.114
0.287	0.278	−0.454	0.897	−0.122	0.013	0.346	0.921	0.238	−0.586
−0.669	0.035	−2.077	1.077	0.525	−0.154	−1.036	0.015	−0.220	0.882
0.392	0.106	−1.430	−0.204	−0.326	0.825	−0.432	−0.094	−1.566	0.679
−0.337	0.199	−0.160	0.625	−0.891	−1.464	−0.318	1.297	0.932	−0.032
0.369	−1.990	−1.190	0.666	−1.614	0.082	0.922	−0.139	−0.833	0.091
−1.694	0.710	−0.655	−0.546	1.654	0.134	0.466	0.033	−0.039	0.838
0.985	0.340	0.276	0.911	−0.170	−0.551	1.000	−0.838	0.275	−0.304
−1.063	−0.594	−1.526	−0.787	0.873	−0.405	−1.324	0.162	−0.163	−2.716
0.033	−1.527	1.422	0.308	0.845	−0.151	0.741	0.064	1.212	0.823
0.597	0.362	−3.760	1.159	0.874	−0.794	−0.915	1.215	1.627	−1.248
−1.601	−0.570	0.133	−0.660	1.485	0.682	−0.898	0.686	0.658	0.346
−0.266	−1.309	0.597	0.989	0.934	1.079	−0.656	−0.999	−0.036	−0.537
0.901	1.531	−0.889	−1.019	0.084	1.531	−0.144	−1.920	0.678	−0.402
−1.433	−1.008	−0.990	0.090	0.940	0.207	−0.745	0.638	1.469	1.214
1.327	0.763	−1.724	−0.709	−1.100	−1.346	−0.946	−0.157	0.522	−1.264
−0.248	0.788	−0.577	0.122	−0.536	0.293	1.207	−2.243	1.642	1.353
−0.401	−0.679	0.921	0.476	1.121	−0.864	0.128	−0.551	−0.872	1.511
0.344	−0.324	0.686	−1.487	−0.126	0.803	−0.961	0.183	−0.358	−0.184
0.441	−0.372	−1.336	0.062	1.506	−0.315	−0.112	−0.452	1.594	−0.264
0.824	0.040	−1.734	0.251	0.054	−0.379	1.298	−0.126	0.104	−0.529
1.385	1.320	−0.509	−0.381	−1.671	−0.524	−0.805	1.348	0.676	0.799

Table D–6 (*cont.*) Random Normal Numbers, $\mu = 0, \sigma = 1$

31	32	33	34	35	36	37	38	39	40
1.556	0.119	−0.078	0.164	−0.455	0.077	−0.043	−0.299	0.249	−0.182
0.647	1.029	1.186	0.887	1.204	−0.657	0.644	−0.410	−0.652	−0.165
0.329	0.407	1.169	−2.072	1.661	0.891	0.233	−1.628	−0.762	−0.717
−1.188	1.171	−1.170	−0.291	0.863	−0.045	−0.205	0.574	−0.926	1.407
−0.917	−0.616	−1.589	1.184	0.266	0.559	−1.833	−0.572	−0.648	−1.090
0.414	0.469	−0.182	0.397	1.649	1.198	0.067	−1.526	−0.081	−0.192
0.107	−0.187	1.343	0.472	−0.112	1.182	0.548	2.748	0.249	0.154
−0.497	1.907	0.191	0.136	−0.475	0.458	0.183	−1.640	−0.058	1.278
0.501	0.083	−0.321	1.133	1.126	−0.299	1.299	1.617	1.581	2.455
−1.382	−0.738	1.225	1.564	−0.363	−0.548	1.070	0.390	−1.398	0.524
−0.590	0.699	−0.162	−0.011	1.049	−0.689	1.225	0.339	−0.539	−0.445
−1.125	1.111	−1.065	0.534	0.102	0.425	−1.026	0.695	−0.057	0.795
0.849	0.169	−0.351	0.584	2.177	0.009	−0.696	−0.426	−0.692	−1.638
−1.233	−0.585	0.306	0.773	1.304	−1.304	0.282	−1.705	0.187	−0.880
0.104	−0.468	0.185	0.498	−0.624	−0.322	−0.875	1.478	−0.691	−0.281
0.261	−1.883	−0.181	1.675	−0.324	−1.029	−0.185	0.004	−0.101	−1.187
−0.007	1.280	0.568	−1.270	1.405	1.731	2.072	1.686	0.728	−0.417
0.794	−0.111	0.040	−0.536	−0.976	2.192	1.609	−0.190	−0.279	−1.611
0.431	−2.300	−1.081	−1.370	2.943	0.653	−2.523	0.756	0.886	−0.983
−0.149	1.294	−0.580	0.482	−1.449	−1.067	1.996	−0.274	0.721	0.490
−0.216	−1.647	1.043	0.481	−0.011	−0.587	−0.916	−1.016	−1.040	−1.117
1.604	−0.851	−0.317	−0.686	−0.008	1.939	0.078	−0.465	0.533	0.652
−0.212	0.005	0.535	0.837	0.362	1.103	0.219	0.488	1.332	−0.200
0.007	−0.076	1.484	0.455	−0.207	−0.554	1.120	0.913	−0.681	1.751
−0.217	0.937	0.860	0.323	1.321	−0.492	−1.386	−0.003	−0.230	0.539
−0.649	0.300	−0.698	0.900	0.569	0.842	0.804	1.025	0.603	−1.546
−1.541	0.193	2.047	−0.552	1.190	−0.087	2.062	−2.173	−0.791	−0.520
0.274	−0.530	0.112	0.385	0.656	0.436	0.882	0.312	−2.265	−0.218
0.876	−1.498	−0.128	−0.387	−1.259	−0.856	−0.353	0.714	0.863	1.169
−0.859	−1.083	1.288	−0.078	−0.081	0.210	0.572	1.194	−1.118	−1.543
−0.015	−0.567	0.113	2.127	−0.719	3.256	−0.721	−0.663	−0.779	−0.930
−1.529	−0.231	1.223	0.300	−0.995	−0.651	0.504	0.138	−0.064	1.341
0.278	−0.058	−2.740	−0.296	−1.180	0.574	1.452	0.846	−0.243	−1.208
1.428	0.322	2.302	−0.852	0.782	−1.322	−0.092	−0.546	0.560	−1.430
0.770	−1.874	0.347	0.994	−0.485	−1.179	0.048	−1.324	1.061	0.449
−0.303	−0.629	0.764	0.013	−1.192	−0.475	−1.085	−0.880	1.738	−1.225
−0.263	−2.105	0.509	−0.645	1.362	1.504	−0.755	1.274	1.448	0.604
0.997	−1.187	−0.242	0.121	2.510	−1.935	0.350	0.073	0.458	−0.446
−0.063	−0.475	−1.802	−0.476	0.193	−1.199	0.339	0.364	−0.684	1.353
−0.168	1.904	−0.485	−0.032	−0.554	0.056	−0.710	−0.778	0.722	−0.024
0.366	−0.491	0.301	−0.008	−0.894	−0.945	0.384	−1.748	−1.118	0.394
0.436	−0.464	0.539	0.942	−0.458	0.445	−1.883	1.228	1.113	−0.218
0.597	−1.471	−0.434	0.705	−0.788	0.575	0.086	0.504	1.445	−0.513
−0.805	−0.624	1.344	0.649	−1.124	0.680	−0.986	1.845	−1.152	−0.393
1.681	−1.910	0.440	0.067	−1.502	−0.755	−0.989	−0.054	−2.320	0.474
−0.007	−0.459	1.940	0.220	−1.259	−1.729	0.137	−0.520	−0.412	2.847
0.209	−0.633	0.299	0.174	1.975	−0.271	0.119	−0.199	0.007	2.315
1.254	1.672	−1.186	−1.310	0.474	0.878	−0.725	−0.191	0.642	−1.212
−1.016	−0.697	0.017	−0.263	−0.047	−1.294	−0.339	2.257	−0.078	−0.049
−1.169	−0.355	1.086	−0.199	0.031	0.396	−0.143	1.572	0.276	0.027

Table D–6 (*cont.*) Random Normal Numbers, $\mu = 0, \sigma = 1$

41	42	43	44	45	46	47	48	49	50
−0.856	−0.063	0.787	−2.052	−1.192	−0.831	1.623	1.135	0.759	−0.189
−0.276	−1.110	0.752	−1.378	−0.583	0.360	0.365	1.587	0.621	1.344
0.379	−0.440	0.858	1.453	−1.356	0.503	−1.134	1.950	−1.816	−0.283
1.468	0.131	0.047	0.355	0.162	−1.491	−0.739	−1.182	−0.533	−0.497
−1.805	−0.772	1.286	−0.636	−1.312	−1.045	1.559	−0.871	−0.102	−0.123
2.285	0.554	0.418	−0.577	−1.489	−1.255	0.092	−0.597	−1.051	−0.980
−0.602	0.399	1.121	−1.026	0.087	1.018	−1.437	0.661	0.091	−0.637
0.229	−0.584	0.705	0.124	0.341	1.320	−0.824	−1.541	−0.163	2.329
1.382	−1.454	1.537	−1.299	0.363	−0.356	−0.025	0.294	2.194	−0.395
0.978	0.109	1.434	−1.094	−0.265	−0.857	−1.421	−1.773	0.570	−0.053
−0.678	−2.335	1.202	−1.697	0.547	−0.201	−0.373	−1.363	−0.081	0.958
−0.366	−1.084	−0.626	0.798	1.706	−1.160	−0.838	1.462	0.636	0.570
−1.074	−1.379	0.086	−0.331	−0.288	−0.309	−1.527	−0.408	0.183	0.856
−0.600	−0.096	0.696	0.446	1.417	−2.140	0.599	−0.157	1.485	1.387
0.918	1.163	−1.445	0.759	0.878	−1.781	−0.056	−2.141	−0.234	0.975
−0.791	−0.528	0.946	1.673	−0.680	−0.784	1.494	−0.086	−1.071	−1.196
0.598	−0.352	0.719	−0.341	0.056	−1.041	1.429	0.235	0.314	−1.693
0.567	−1.156	−0.125	−0.534	0.711	−0.511	0.187	−0.644	−1.090	−1.281
0.963	0.052	0.037	0.637	−1.335	0.055	0.010	−0.860	−0.621	0.713
0.489	−0.209	1.659	0.054	1.635	0.169	0.794	−1.550	1.845	−0.388
−1.627	−0.017	0.699	0.661	−0.073	0.188	1.183	−1.054	−1.615	−0.765
−1.096	1.215	0.320	0.738	1.865	−1.169	−0.667	−0.674	−0.062	1.378
−2.532	1.031	−0,799	1.665	−2.756	−0.151	−0.704	0.602	−0.672	1.264
0.024	−1.183	−0.927	−0.629	0.204	−0.825	0.496	2.543	0.262	−0.785
0.192	0.125	0.373	−0.931	−0.079	0.186	−0.306	0.621	−0.292	1.131
−1.324	−1.229	−0.648	−0.430	0.811	0.868	0.787	1.845	−0.374	−0.651
−0.726	−0.746	1.572	−1.420	1.509	−0.361	−0.310	−3.117	1.637	0.642
−1.618	1.082	−0.319	0.300	1.524	−0.418	−1.712	0.358	−1.032	0.537
1.695	0.843	2.049	0.388	−0.297	1.077	−0.462	0.655	0.940	−0.354
0.790	0.605	−3.077	1.009	−0.906	−1.004	0.693	−1.098	1.300	0.549
1.792	−0.895	−0.136	−1.765	1.077	0.418	−0.150	0.808	0.697	0.435
0.771	−0.741	−0.492	−0.770	−0.458	−0.021	1.385	−1.225	−0.066	−1.471
−1.438	0.423	−1.211	0.723	−0.731	0.883	−2.109	−2.455	−0.210	1.644
−0.294	1.266	−1.994	−0.730	0.545	0.397	1.069	−0.383	−0.097	−0.985
−1.966	0.909	0.400	0.685	−0.800	1.759	0.268	1.387	−0.414	1.615
−0.999	1.587	1.423	0.937	−0.943	0.090	1.185	−1.204	0.300	−1.354
0.581	0.481	−2.400	0.000	0.231	0.079	−2.842	−0.846	−0.508	−0.516
0.370	−1.452	−0.580	−1.462	−0.972	1.116	−0.994	0.374	−3.336	−0.058
0.834	−1.227	−0.709	−1.039	−0.014	−0.383	−0.512	−0.347	0.881	−0.638
−0.376	−0.813	0.660	−1.029	−0.137	0.371	0.376	0.968	1.338	−0.786
−1.621	0.815	−0.544	−0.376	−0.852	0.436	1.562	0.815	−1.048	0.188
0.163	−0.161	2.501	−0.265	−0.285	1.934	1.070	0.215	−0.876	0.073
1.786	−0.538	−0.437	0.324	0.105	−0.421	−0.410	−0.947	0.700	−1.006
2.140	1.218	−0.351	−0.068	0.254	0.448	−1.461	0.784	0.317	1.013
0.064	0.410	0.368	0.419	−0.982	1.371	0.100	−0.505	0.856	0.890
0.789	−0.131	1.330	0.506	−0.645	−1.414	2.426	1.389	−0.169	−0.194
−0.011	−0.372	−0.699	2.382	−1.395	−0.467	1.256	−0.585	−1.359	−1.804
−0.463	0.003	−1.470	−1.493	0.960	0.364	−1.267	−0.007	0.616	0.624
−1.210	−0.669	0.009	1.284	−0.617	0.355	−0.589	−0.243	−0.015	−0.712
−1.157	0.481	0.560	1.287	1.129	−0.126	0.006	1.532	1.328	0.980

Table D–6 (*cont.*) Random Normal Numbers, $\mu = 0, \sigma = 1$

51	52	53	54	55	56	57	58	59	60
0.240	1.774	0.210	−1.471	1.167	−1.114	0.182	−0.485	−0.318	1.156
0.627	−0.758	−0.930	1.641	0.162	−0.874	−0.235	0.203	−0.724	−0.155
−0.594	0.098	0.158	−0.722	1.385	−0.985	−1.707	0.175	0.449	0.654
1.082	−0.753	−1.944	−1.964	−2.131	−2.796	−1.286	0.807	−0.122	0.527
0.060	−0.014	1.577	−0.814	−0.633	0.275	−0.087	0.517	0.474	−1.432
−0.013	0.402	−0.086	−0.394	0.292	−2.862	−1.660	−1.658	1.610	−2.205
1.586	−0.833	1.444	−0.615	−1.157	−0.220	−0.517	−1.668	−2.036	−0.850
−0.405	−1.315	−1.355	−1.331	1.394	−0.381	−0.729	−0.447	−0.906	0.622
−0.329	1.701	0.427	0.627	−0.271	−0.971	−1.010	1.182	−0.143	0.844
0.992	0.708	−0.115	−1.630	0.596	0.499	−0.862	0.508	0.474	−0.974
0.296	−0.390	2.047	−0.363	0.724	0.788	−0.089	0.930	−0.497	0.058
−2.069	−1.422	−0.948	−1.742	−1.173	0.215	0.661	0.842	−0.984	−0.577
−0.211	−1.727	−0.277	1.592	−0.707	0.327	−0.527	0.912	0.571	−0.525
−0.467	1.848	−0.263	−0.862	0.706	−0.533	0.626	−0.200	−2.221	0.368
1.284	0.412	1.512	0.328	0.203	−1.231	−1.480	−0.400	−0.491	0.913
0.821	−1.503	−1.066	1.624	1.345	0.440	−1.416	0.301	−0.355	0.106
1.056	1.224	0.281	−0.098	1.868	−0.395	0.610	−1.173	−1.449	1.171
1.090	−0.790	0.882	1.687	−0.009	−2.053	−0.030	−0.421	1.253	−0.081
0.574	0.129	1.203	0.280	1.438	−2.052	−0.443	0.522	0.468	−1.211
−0.531	2.155	0.334	0.898	−1.114	0.243	1.026	0.391	−0.011	−0.024
0.896	0.181	−0.941	−0.511	0.648	−0.710	−0.181	−1.417	−0.585	0.087
0.042	0.579	−0.316	0.394	1.133	−0.305	−0.863	−1.318	−0.050	0.993
2.328	−0.243	0.534	0.241	0.275	0.060	0.727	−1.459	0.174	−1.072
0.486	−0.558	0.426	0.728	−0.360	−0.068	0.058	1.471	−0.051	0.337
−0.304	−0.309	0.646	0.309	−1.320	0.311	−1.407	−0.011	0.387	0.128
−2.319	−0.129	0.866	−0.424	−0.236	0.419	−1.359	−1.088	−0.045	1.096
1.098	−0.875	0.659	−1.086	−0.424	−1.462	0.743	−0.787	1.472	1.677
−0.038	−0.118	−1.285	−0.545	−0.140	1.244	−1.104	0.146	0.058	1.245
−0.207	−0.746	1.681	0.137	0.104	−0.491	−0.935	0.671	−0.448	−0.129
0.333	−1.386	1.840	1.089	0.837	−1.642	−0.273	−0.798	0.067	0.334
1.190	−0.547	−1.016	0.540	−0.993	0.443	−0.190	1.019	−1.021	−1.276
−1.416	−0.749	0.325	0.846	2.417	−0.479	−0.655	−1.326	−1.952	1.234
0.622	0.661	0.028	1.302	−0.032	−0.157	1.470	−0.766	0.697	−0.303
−1.134	0.499	0.538	0.564	−2.392	−1.398	0.010	1.874	1.386	0.000
0.725	−0.242	0.281	1.355	−0.036	0.204	−0.345	0.395	−0.753	1.645
−0.210	0.611	−0.219	0.450	0.308	0.993	−0.146	0.225	−1.496	0.246
0.219	0.302	0.000	−0.437	−2.127	0.883	−0.599	−1.516	0.826	1.242
−1.098	−0.252	−2.480	−0.973	0.712	−1.430	−0.167	−1.237	0.750	−0.763
0.144	0.489	−0.637	1.990	0.411	−0.563	0.027	1.278	2.105	−1.130
−1.738	−1.295	0.431	−0.503	2.327	−0.007	−1.293	−1.206	−0.066	1.370
−0.487	−0.097	−1.361	−0.340	0.204	0.938	−0.148	−1.099	−0.252	−0.384
−0.636	−0.626	1.967	1.677	−0.331	−0.440	−1.440	1.281	1.070	−1.167
−1.464	−1.493	0.945	0.180	−0.672	−0.035	−0.293	−0.905	0.196	−1.122
0.561	−0.375	−0.657	1.304	0.833	−1.159	1.501	1.265	0.438	−0.437
−0.525	−0.017	1.815	0.789	−1.908	−0.353	1.383	−1.208	−1.135	1.082
0.980	−0.111	−0.804	−1.078	−1.930	0.171	−1.318	2.377	−0.303	1.062
0.501	0.835	−0.518	−1.034	−1.493	0.712	0.421	−1.165	0.782	−1.484
1.081	−1.176	−0.542	0.321	0.688	0.670	−0.771	−0.090	−0.611	−0.813
−0.148	−1.203	−1.553	1.244	0.826	0.077	0.128	−0.772	1.683	0.318
0.096	−0.286	0.362	0.888	0.551	1.782	0.335	2.083	0.350	0.260

Table D–6 (*cont.*) Random Normal Numbers, $\mu = 0$, $\sigma = 1$

61	62	63	64	65	66	67	68	69	70
0.052	1.504	−1.350	−1.124	−0.521	0.515	0.839	0.778	0.438	−0.550
−0.315	−0.865	0.851	0.127	−0.379	1.640	−0.441	0.717	0.670	−0.301
0.938	−0.055	0.947	1.275	1.557	−1.484	−1.137	0.398	1.333	1.988
0.497	0.502	0.385	−0.467	2.468	−1.810	−1.438	0.283	1.740	0.420
2.308	−0.399	−1.798	0.018	0.780	1.030	0.806	−0.408	−0.547	−0.280
1.815	0.101	−0.561	0.236	0.166	0.227	−0.309	0.056	0.610	0.732
−0.421	0.432	0.586	1.059	0.278	−1.672	1.859	1.433	−0.919	−1.770
0.008	0.555	−1.310	−1.440	−0.142	−0.295	−0.630	−0.911	0.133	−0.308
1.191	−0.114	1.039	1.083	0.185	−0.492	0.419	−0.433	−1.019	−2.260
1.299	1.918	0.318	1.348	0.935	1.250	−0.175	−0.828	−0.336	0.726
0.012	−0.739	−1.181	−0.645	−0.736	1.801	−0.209	−0.389	0.867	−0.555
−0.586	−0.044	−0.983	0.332	0.371	−0.072	−1.212	1.047	−1.930	0.812
−0.122	1.515	0.338	−1.040	−0.008	0.467	−0.600	0.923	1.126	−0.752
0.879	0.516	−0.920	2.121	0.674	1.481	0.660	−0.986	1.644	−2.159
0.435	1.149	−0.065	1.391	0.707	0.548	−0.490	−1.139	0.249	−0.933
0.645	0.878	−0.904	0.896	−1.284	0.237	−0.378	−0.510	−1.123	−0.129
−0.514	−1.017	0.529	0.973	−1.202	0.005	−0.644	−0.167	−0.664	0.167
0.242	−0.427	−0.727	−1.150	−1.092	−0.736	0.925	−0.050	−0.200	−0.770
0.443	0.445	−1.287	−1.463	−0.650	−0.412	−2.714	−0.903	−0.341	0.957
0.273	0.203	0.423	1.423	0.508	1.058	−0.828	0.143	−1.059	0.345
0.255	1.036	1.471	0.476	0.592	−0.658	0.677	0.155	1.068	−0.759
0.858	−0.370	0.522	−1.890	−0.389	0.609	1.210	0.489	−0.006	0.834
0.097	−1.709	1.790	−0.929	0.405	0.024	−0.036	0.580	−0.642	−1.121
0.520	0.889	−0.540	0.266	−0.354	0.524	−0.788	−0.497	−0.973	1.481
−0.311	−1.772	−0.496	1.275	−0.904	0.147	1.497	0.657	−0.469	−0.783
−0.604	0.857	−0.695	0.397	0.296	−0.285	0.191	0.158	1.672	1.190
−0.001	0.287	−0.868	−0.013	−1.576	−0.168	0.047	0.159	0.086	−1.077
1.160	0.989	0.205	0.937	−0.099	−1.281	−0.276	0.845	0.752	0.663
1.579	−0.303	−1.174	−0.960	−0.470	−0.556	−0.689	1.535	−0.711	−0.743
−0.615	−0.154	0.008	1.353	−0.381	1.137	0.022	0.175	0.586	2.841
1.578	1.529	−0.294	−1.301	0.614	0.099	−0.700	−0.003	1.052	1.643
0.626	−0.447	−1.261	−2.029	0.182	−1.176	0.083	1.868	0.872	0.965
−0.493	−0.020	0.920	1.473	1.873	−0.289	0.410	0.394	0.881	0.054
−0.217	0.342	1.423	0.364	−0.119	0.509	−2.266	0.189	0.149	1.041
−0.792	0.347	−1.367	−0.632	−1.238	−0.136	−0.352	−0.157	−1.163	1.305
0.568	−0.226	0.391	−0.074	−0.312	0.400	1.583	0.481	−1.048	0.759
0.051	0.549	−2.192	1.257	−1.460	0.363	0.127	−1.020	−1.192	0.449
−0.891	0.490	0.279	0.372	−0.578	−0.836	2.285	−0.448	0.720	0.510
0.622	−0.126	−0.637	1.255	−0.354	0.032	−1.076	0.352	0.103	−0.496
0.623	0.819	−0.489	0.354	−0.943	−0.694	0.248	0.092	−0.673	−1.428
−1.208	−1.038	0.140	−0.762	−0.854	−0.249	2.431	0.067	−0.317	−0.874
−0.487	−2.117	0.195	2.154	1.041	−1.314	−0.785	−0.414	−0.695	2.310
0.522	0.314	−1.003	0.134	−1.748	−0.107	0.459	1.550	1.118	−1.004
0.838	0.613	0.227	0.308	−0.757	0.912	2.272	0.556	−0.041	0.008
−1.534	−0.407	1.202	1.251	−0.891	−1.588	−2.380	0.059	0.682	−0.878
−0.099	2.391	1.067	−2.060	−0.464	−0.103	3.486	1.121	0.632	−1.626
0.070	1.465	−0.080	−0.526	−1.090	−1.002	0.132	1.504	0.050	−0.393
0.115	−0.601	1.751	1.956	−0.196	0.400	−0.522	0.571	−0.101	−2.160
0.252	−0.329	−0.586	−0.118	−0.242	−0.521	0.818	−0.167	−0.469	0.430
0.017	0.185	0.377	1.883	−0.443	−0.039	−1.244	−0.820	−1.171	0.104

Table D–6 (*cont.*) Random Normal Numbers, $\mu = 0, \sigma = 1$

71	72	73	74	75	76	77	78	79	80
2.988	0.423	−1.261	−1.893	0.187	−0.412	−0.228	0.002	−1.384	−1.032
0.760	0.995	−0.256	−0.505	0.750	−0.654	0.647	0.613	0.086	−0.118
−0.650	−0.927	−1.071	−0.796	1.130	−1.042	−0.181	−1.020	1.648	−1.327
−0.394	−0.452	0.893	1.410	1.133	0.319	0.537	−0.789	0.078	−0.062
−1.168	1.902	0.206	0.303	1.413	2.012	0.278	−0.566	−0.900	0.200
1.343	−0.377	−0.131	−0.585	0.053	0.137	−1.371	−0.175	−0.878	0.118
−0.733	−1.921	0.471	−1.394	−0.885	−0.523	0.553	0.344	−0.775	1.545
−0.172	−0.575	0.066	−0.310	1.795	−1.148	0.772	−1.063	0.818	0.302
1.457	0.862	1.677	−0.507	−1.691	−0.034	0.270	0.075	−0.554	1.420
−0.087	0.744	1.829	1.203	−0.436	−0.618	−0.200	−1.134	−1.352	−0.098
−0.092	1.043	−0.255	0.189	0.270	−1.034	−0.571	−0.336	−0.742	2.141
0.441	−0.379	−1.757	0.608	0.527	−0.338	−1.995	0.573	−0.034	−0.056
0.073	−0.250	0.531	−0.695	1.402	−0.462	−0.938	1.130	1.453	−0.106
0.637	0.276	−0.013	1.968	−0.205	0.486	0.727	1.416	0.963	1.349
−0.792	−1.778	1.284	−0.452	0.602	0.668	0.516	−0.210	0.040	−0.103
−1.223	1.561	−2.099	1.419	0.223	−0.482	1.098	0.513	0.418	−1.686
−0.407	1.587	0.335	−2.475	−0.284	1.567	−0.248	−0.759	1.792	−2.319
−0.462	−0.193	−0.012	−1.208	2.151	1.336	−1.968	−1.767	−0.374	0.783
1.457	0.883	1.001	−0.169	0.836	−1.236	1.632	−0.142	−0.222	0.340
−1.918	−1.246	−0.209	0.780	−0.330	−2.953	−0.447	−0.094	1.344	−0.196
−0.126	1.094	−1.206	−1.426	1.474	−1.080	0.000	0.764	1.476	−0.016
−0.306	−0.847	0.639	−0.262	−0.427	0.391	−1.298	−1.013	2.024	−0.539
0.477	1.595	−0.762	0.424	0.799	0.312	1.151	−1.095	1.199	−0.765
0.369	−0.709	1.283	−0.007	−1.440	−0.782	0.061	1.427	1.656	0.974
−0.579	0.606	−0.866	−0.715	−0.301	−0.180	0.188	0.668	−1.091	1.476
−0.418	−0.588	0.919	−0.083	1.084	0.944	0.253	−1.833	1.305	0.171
0.128	−0.834	0.009	0.742	0.539	−0.948	−1.055	−0.689	−0.338	1.091
−0.291	0.235	−0.971	−1.696	1.119	0.272	0.635	−0.792	−1.355	1.291
−1.024	1.212	−1.100	−0.348	1.741	0.035	1.268	0.192	0.729	−0.467
−0.378	1.026	0.093	0.468	−0.967	0.675	0.807	−2.109	−1.214	0.559
1.232	−0.815	0.608	1.429	−0.748	0.201	0.400	−1.230	−0.398	−0.674
1.793	−0.581	−1.076	0.512	−0.442	−1.488	−0.580	0.172	−0.891	0.311
0.766	0.310	−0.070	0.624	−0.389	1.035	−0.101	−0.926	0.816	−1.048
−0.606	−1.224	1.465	0.012	1.061	0.491	−1.023	1.948	0.866	−0.737
0.106	−2.715	0.363	0.343	−0.159	2.672	1.119	0.731	−1.012	−0.889
−0.060	0.444	1.596	−0.630	0.362	−0.306	1.163	−0.974	0.486	−0.373
2.081	1.161	−1.167	0.021	0.053	−0.094	0.381	−0.628	−2.581	−1.243
−1.727	−1.266	0.088	0.936	0.368	0.648	−0.799	1.115	−0.968	−2.588
0.091	1.364	1.677	0.644	1.505	0.440	−0.329	0.498	0.869	−0.965
−1.114	−0.239	−0.409	−0.334	−0.605	0.501	−1.921	−0.470	2.354	−0.660
0.189	−0.547	−1.758	−0.295	−0.279	−0.515	−1.053	0.553	−0.297	0.496
−0.065	−0.023	−0.267	−0.247	1.318	0.904	−0.712	−1.152	−0.543	0.176
−1.742	−0.599	0.430	−0.615	1.165	0.084	2.017	−1.207	2.614	1.490
0.732	0.188	2.343	0.526	−0.812	0.389	1.036	−0.023	0.229	−2.262
−1.490	0.014	0.167	1.422	0.015	0.069	0.133	0.897	−1.678	0.323
1.507	−0.571	−0.724	1.741	−0.152	−0.147	−0.158	−0.076	0.652	0.447
0.513	0.168	−0.076	−0.171	0.428	0.205	−0.865	0.107	1.023	0.077
−0.834	−1.121	1.441	0.492	0.559	1.724	−1.659	0.245	1.354	−0.041
0.258	1.880	−0.536	1.246	−0.188	−0.746	1.097	0.258	1.547	1.238
−0.818	0.273	0.159	−0.765	0.526	1.281	1.154	−0.687	−0.793	0.795

Table D-6 (*cont.*) Random Normal Numbers, $\mu = 0$, $\sigma = 1$

81	82	83	84	85	86	87	88	89	90
−0.713	−0.541	−0.571	−0.807	−1.560	1.000	0.140	−0.549	0.887	2.237
−0.117	0.530	−1.599	−1.602	0.412	−1.450	−1.217	1.074	−1.021	−0.424
1.187	−1.523	1.437	0.051	1.237	−0.798	1.616	−0.823	−1.207	1.258
−0.182	−0.186	0.517	1.438	0.831	−1.319	−0.539	−0.192	0.150	2.127
1.964	−0.629	−0.944	−0.028	0.948	1.005	0.242	−0.432	−0.329	0.113
0.230	1.523	1.658	0.753	0.724	0.183	−0.147	0.505	0.448	−0.053
0.839	−0.849	−0.145	−1.843	−1.276	0.481	−0.142	−0.534	0.403	0.370
−0.801	0.343	−1.822	0.447	−0.931	−0.824	−0.484	0.864	−1.069	0.860
−0.124	0.727	1.654	−0.182	−1.381	−1.146	−0.572	0.159	0.186	1.221
−0.088	0.032	−0.564	0.654	1.141	−0.056	−0.343	0.067	−0.267	−0.219
0.912	−1.114	−1.035	−1.070	−0.297	1.195	0.030	0.022	0.406	−0.414
1.397	−0.473	0.433	0.023	−1.204	1.254	0.551	−1.012	−0.789	0.906
−0.652	−0.029	0.064	0.511	1.117	−0.465	0.523	−0.083	0.386	0.259
1.236	−0.457	−1.354	−0.898	−0.270	−1.837	1.641	−0.657	−0.753	−1.686
−0.498	1.302	0.816	−0.936	1.404	0.555	2.450	−0.789	−0.120	0.505
−0.005	2.174	1.893	−1.361	−0.991	0.508	−0.823	0.918	0.524	0.488
0.115	−1.373	−0.900	−1.010	0.624	0.946	0.312	−1.384	0.224	2.343
0.167	0.254	1.219	1.153	−0.510	−0.007	−0.285	−0.631	−0.356	0.254
0.976	1.158	−0.469	1.099	0.509	−1.324	−0.102	−0.296	−0.907	0.449
0.653	−0.366	0.450	−2.653	−0.592	−0.510	0.983	0.023	−0.881	0.876
−0.150	−0.088	0.457	−0.448	0.605	0.668	−0.613	0.261	0.023	−0.050
0.060	0.276	0.229	−1.527	−0.316	−0.834	−1.652	−0.387	0.632	0.895
−0.678	0.547	0.243	−2.183	−0.368	1.158	−0.996	−0.705	−0.314	1.464
2.139	0.395	−0.376	−0.175	0.406	0.309	−1.021	−0.460	−0.217	0.307
0.091	1.793	0.822	0.054	0.573	−0.729	−0.517	0.589	1.927	0.940
−0.003	0.344	1.242	−1.105	0.234	−1.222	−0.474	1.831	0.124	−0.840
−0.965	0.268	−1.543	0.690	0.917	2.017	−0.297	1.087	0.371	1.495
−0.076	−0.495	−0.103	0.646	2.427	−2.172	0.660	−1.541	−0.852	0.583
−0.365	−3.305	0.805	−0.418	−1.201	0.623	−0.223	0.109	0.205	−0.663
0.578	0.145	−1.438	1.122	−1.406	1.172	0.272	−2.245	1.207	1.227
−0.398	−0.304	0.529	−0.514	−0.681	−0.366	0.338	0.801	−0.301	−0.790
−0.951	−1.483	−0.613	−0.171	−0.459	1.231	−1.232	−0.497	−0.779	0.247
1.025	−0.039	−0.721	0.813	1.203	0.245	0.402	1.541	0.691	−1.420
−0.958	0.791	0.948	0.222	−0.704	−0.375	−0.246	−0.862	−0.871	0.056
1.097	−1.428	1.402	−1.425	−0.877	0.536	0.988	2.529	0.768	−1.321
0.377	2.240	0.854	−1.158	0.066	−1.222	0.821	−1.602	−0.760	−0.871
1.729	0.073	1.022	0.891	0.659	−1.040	0.251	−0.710	−1.734	−0.038
−1.329	−0.381	−0.515	1.484	−0.430	−0.466	−0.167	−0.788	−0.660	0.003
−0.132	0.391	2.205	−1.165	0.200	0.415	−0.765	0.239	−1.182	1.135
0.336	0.657	−0.805	0.150	−0.938	1.057	−1.090	1.604	−0.598	−0.760
0.124	−1.812	1.750	0.270	−0.114	0.517	−0.226	0.127	0.129	−0.751
−0.036	0.365	0.766	0.877	−0.804	−0.140	0.182	−0.483	−0.376	−0.564
−0.609	−0.019	−0.992	−1.193	−0.516	0.517	1.677	0.839	−1.134	0.675
−0.894	0.318	0.607	−0.865	0.526	−0.971	1.365	0.319	1.804	1.740
−0.357	−0.802	0.635	−0.491	−1.110	0.785	−0.042	−1.042	−0.572	0.243
−0.258	−0.383	−1.013	0.001	−1.673	0.561	−1.054	−0.106	−0.760	−1.009
2.245	−0.431	−0.496	0.796	0.193	1.202	−0.429	−0.217	0.333	−0.643
1.956	0.477	0.812	−0.117	0.606	−0.330	0.425	−0.232	0.802	0.656
1.358	0.139	0.199	−0.475	−0.120	0.184	−0.020	−1.326	0.517	−1.708
0.656	1.081	0.180	0.145	0.376	−1.363	−0.491	0.352	−1.477	1.280

Table D–6 (*cont.*) Random Normal Numbers, $\mu = 0, \sigma = 1$

91	92	93	94	95	96	97	98	99	100
−0.181	0.583	−1.478	−0.181	0.281	−0.559	1.985	−1.122	−1.106	1.441
1.549	−1.183	−2.089	−1.997	−0.343	1.275	0.676	−0.212	1.252	0.163
0.978	−1.067	−2.640	0.134	0.328	−0.052	−0.030	−0.273	−0.570	1.026
−0.596	−0.420	−0.318	−0.057	−0.695	−1.148	0.333	−0.531	−2.037	−1.587
−0.440	0.032	0.163	1.029	0.079	1.148	0.762	−1.961	−0.674	−0.486
0.443	−1.100	0.728	−2.397	−0.543	0.872	−0.568	0.980	−0.174	0.728
−2.401	−1.375	−1.332	−2.177	−2.064	−0.245	−0.039	0.585	1.344	1.386
0.311	0.322	−0.158	0.359	0.103	0.371	0.735	0.011	2.091	0.490
−1.209	0.241	−1.488	−0.667	−1.772	−0.197	0.741	−1.303	−1.149	2.251
0.575	−1.227	−1.674	1.400	0.289	0.005	0.185	−1.072	0.431	−1.096
−0.190	0.272	1.216	0.227	1.358	0.215	−2.306	−1.301	−0.597	−1.401
−0.817	−0.769	−0.470	−0.633	0.187	−0.517	−0.888	−1.712	1.774	−0.162
0.265	−0.676	0.244	1.897	−0.629	−0.206	−1.419	1.049	0.266	−0.438
−0.221	0.678	2.149	1.486	−1.361	1.402	−0.028	0.493	0.744	0.195
−0.436	0.358	−0.602	0.107	0.085	0.573	0.529	1.577	0.239	1.898
−0.010	0.475	0.655	0.659	−0.029	−0.029	0.126	−1.335	−1.261	2.036
−0.244	1.654	1.335	−0.610	0.617	0.642	0.371	0.241	0.001	−1.799
−0.932	−1.275	−1.134	−1.246	−1.508	0.949	1.743	−0.271	−1.333	−1.875
−0.199	−1.285	−0.387	0.191	0.726	−0.151	0.064	−0.803	−0.062	0.780
−0.251	−0.431	−0.831	0.036	−0.464	−1.089	−0.284	−0.451	1.693	1.004
1.074	−1.323	−1.659	−0.186	−0.612	1.612	−2.159	−1.210	0.596	−1.421
1.518	2.101	0.397	0.516	−1.169	−1.821	1.346	2.435	1.165	−0.428
0.935	−0.206	1.117	−0.241	−0.963	−0.099	0.412	−1.344	0.411	0.583
1.360	−0.380	0.031	1.066	0.893	0.431	−0.081	0.099	0.500	−2.441
0.115	−0.211	1.471	0.332	0.750	0.652	−0.812	1.383	−0.355	−0.638
0.082	−0.309	−0.355	−0.402	0.774	0.150	0.015	2.539	−0.756	−1.049
−1.492	0.259	0.323	0.697	−0.509	0.968	−0.053	1.033	−0.220	−2.322
−0.203	0.548	1.494	1.185	0.083	−1.196	−0.749	−1.105	1.324	0.689
1.857	−0.167	−1.531	1.551	0.848	0.120	0.415	−0.317	1.446	1.002
0.669	−1.017	−2.437	−0.558	−0.657	0.940	0.985	0.483	−0.361	0.095
0.128	1.463	−0.436	−0.239	−1.443	0.732	0.168	−0.144	−0.392	0.989
1.879	−2.456	0.029	0.429	0.618	−1.683	−2.262	0.034	−0.002	1.914
0.680	0.252	0.130	1.658	−1.023	0.407	−0.235	−0.224	−0.434	0.253
−0.631	0.225	−0.951	1.072	−0.285	−1.731	−0.427	−1.446	−0.873	0.619
−1.273	0.723	0.201	0.505	−0.370	−0.421	−0.015	−0.463	0.288	1.734
−0.643	−1.485	0.403	0.003	−0.243	0.000	0.964	−0.703	0.844	−0.686
−0.435	−2.162	−0.169	−1.311	−1.639	0.193	2.692	−1.994	0.326	0.562
−1.706	0.119	−1.566	0.637	−1.948	−1.068	0.935	0.738	0.650	0.491
−0.498	1.640	0.384	−0.945	−1.272	0.945	−1.013	−0.913	−0.469	2.250
−0.065	−0.005	0.618	−0.523	−0.055	1.071	0.758	−0.736	−0.959	0.598
0.190	−1.020	−1.104	0.936	−0.029	−1.004	−0.657	1.270	−0.060	−0.809
0.879	−0.642	1.155	−0.523	−0.757	−1.027	0.985	−1.222	1.078	0.163
0.559	1.094	1.587	−0.384	−1.701	0.418	0.327	0.669	0.019	0.782
−0.261	1.234	−0.505	−0.664	−0.446	−0.747	0.427	−0.369	0.089	−1.302
3.136	1.120	−0.591	2.515	−2.853	1.375	2.421	0.672	1.817	−0.067
−1.307	−0.586	−0.311	−0.026	1.633	−1.340	−1.209	0.110	−0.126	−0.288
1.455	1.099	−1.225	−0.817	0.667	−0.212	0.684	0.349	−1.161	−2.432
−0.443	−0.415	−0.660	0.098	0.435	−0.846	−0.375	−0.410	−1.747	−0.790
−0.326	0.798	0.349	0.524	0.690	−0.520	−0.522	0.602	−0.193	−0.535
−1.027	−1.459	−0.840	−1.637	−0.462	0.607	−0.760	1.342	−1.916	0.424

Suggested Further Readings

Entries are generally given in order of importance and relevance to the material presented in the text of each chapter.

Chapter 1 Introduction to Statistical Inference

W. A. WALLIS and H. V. ROBERTS, *The Nature of Statistics* (New York: The Free Press, 1956).

G. U. YULE and M. G. KENDALL, *An Introduction to the Theory of Statistics* (London: Charles Griffin, 1950), Chapter 16.

IAN HOCKING, *Logic of Statistical Inference* (New York: Cambridge University Press, 1965).

H. JEFFREYS, *Theory of Probability* (New York: Oxford University Press, 1961), Chapter 1.

C. L. LASTRUCCI, *The Scientific Approach* (Cambridge, Mass.: Schenkman, 1963).

Chapter 2 Experimental Derivation of Sampling Distributions

W. J. DIXON and F. J. MASSEY, *Introduction to Statistical Analysis* (New York: McGraw-Hill, 1957), Chapter 4.

J. M. HAMMERSLEY and D. C. HANDSCOMB, *Monte Carlo Methods* (New York: Wiley, 1964).

Chapter 3 Probability and Probability Distributions

S. H. HYMANS, *Probability Theory* (Englewood Cliffs, N.J.: Prentice-Hall, 1967), Chapters 1–4.

F. MOSTELLER, R. E. K. ROURKE, and G. B. THOMAS, *Probability with Statistical Applications* (Reading, Mass.: Addison-Wesley, 1961), Chapters 1–5.

J. E. FREUND, *Mathematical Statistics* (Englewood Cliffs, N.J.: Prentice-Hall, 1962), Chapters 1–6.

A. M. MOOD and F. A. GRAYBILL, *Introduction to the Theory of Statistics*, 2nd ed. (New York: McGraw-Hill, 1963), Chapters 1–5.

E. PARZEN, *Modern Probability Theory and Its Applications* (New York: Wiley, 1960).

Chapter 4 Theoretical Derivation of Sampling Distributions

S. S. WILKS, *Elementary Statistical Analysis* (Princeton, N.J.: Princeton University Press, 1958), Chapter 9.

S. H. HYMANS, *Probability Theory* (Englewood Cliffs, N.J.: Prentice-Hall, 1967), Chapters 5 and 6.

W. A. WALLIS and H. V. ROBERTS, *Statistics: A New Approach* (London: Methuen, 1957), Chapter 11.

C. R. RAO, *Linear Statistical Inference and Its Applications* (New York: Wiley, 1965), Chapter 3.

M. G. KENDALL and A. STUART, *The Advanced Theory of Statistics*, Vol. I, 2nd ed. (New York: Hafner, 1963), Chapters 11–13.

Chapter 5 Tests of Hypotheses

W. A. WALLIS, and H. V. ROBERTS, *Statistics: A New Approach* (London: Methuen, 1957), Chapters 12 and 13.

J. E. FREUND, *Mathematical Statistics* (Englewood Cliffs, N.J.: Prentice-Hall, 1962), Chapters 11 and 12.

A. M. MOOD and F. A. GRAYBILL, *Introduction to the Theory of Statistics*, 2nd ed. (New York: McGraw-Hill, 1963), Chapter 12.

R. L. ANDERSON and T. A. BANCROFT, *Statistical Theory in Research* (New York: McGraw-Hill, 1952), Chapters 11 and 12.

E. L. LEHMANN, *Testing Statistical Hypotheses* (New York: Wiley, 1959).

Chapter 6 Estimation

S. H. HYMANS, *Probability Theory* (Englewood Cliffs, N.J.: Prentice-Hall, 1967), Chapter 7.

B. W. LINDGREN, *Statistical Theory* (New York: Macmillan, 1968), Chapter 5.

A. S. GOLDBERGER, *Econometric Theory* (New York: Wiley, 1964), Chapter 3.

P. J. DHRYMES, *Econometrics*, (New York: Harper & Row, 1970), Chapter 3.

R. DEUTSCH, *Estimation Theory* (Englewood Cliffs, N.J.: Prentice-Hall, 1965).

Chapter 7 Simple Regression

J. JOHNSTON, *Econometric Methods* (New York: McGraw-Hill, 1963), Chapter 1.

A. S. GOLDBERGER, *Topics in Regression Analysis* (New York: Macmillan, 1968), Chapters 1 and 2.

R. L. ANDERSON and T. A. BANCROFT, *Statistical Theory in Research* (New York: McGraw-Hill, 1952), Chapter 13.

A. M. MOOD and F. A. GRAYBILL, *Introduction to the Theory of Statistics*, 2nd ed. (New York: McGraw-Hill, 1963), Chapter 13.

E. MALINVAUD, *Statistical Methods of Econometrics* (Chicago: Rand McNally, 1966), Chapter 3.

Chapter 8 Violations of Basic Assumptions

8–1 Heteroskedasticity

J. Johnston, *Econometric Methods* (New York: McGraw-Hill, 1963), Chapter 8, section 2.

E. J. Kane, *Economic Statistics and Econometrics* (New York: Harper & Row, 1968), Chapter 14.

H. C. Rutemiller and D. A. Bowers, "Estimation in a Heteroskedastic Regression Model," *Journal of the American Statistical Association*, Vol. 63, June 1968, pp. 552–557.

S. M. Goldfeld and R. F. Quandt, "Some Tests for Homoscedasticity," *Journal of the American Statistical Association*, Vol. 60, September 1965, pp. 539–547.

8–2 Autoregressive Disturbances

J. Johnston, *Econometric Methods* (New York: McGraw-Hill, 1963), Chapter 7.

E. Malinvaud, *Statistical Methods of Econometrics* (Chicago: Rand McNally, 1966), Chapter 13.

C. F. Christ, *Econometric Models and Methods* (New York: Wiley, 1966), Chapter 9, section 13, and Chapter 10, section 4.

8–3 Stochastic Explanatory Variable

A. S. Goldberger, *Econometric Theory* (New York: Wiley, 1964), Chapter 6.

Chapter 9 Estimation with Deficient Data

9–1 Errors of Measurement

J. Johnston, *Econometric Methods* (New York: McGraw-Hill, 1963), Chapter 6.

E. Malinvaud, *Statistical Methods of Econometrics* (Chicago: Rand McNally, 1966), Chapter 10.

M. G. Kendall and A. Stuart, *The Advanced Theory of Statistics*, Vol. II (London: Charles Griffin, 1961), Chapter 29.

M. Halperin, "Fitting of Straight Lines and Prediction When Both Variables Are Subject to Error," *Journal of the American Statistical Association*, Vol. 56, September 1961, pp. 657–669.

9–2 Estimation from Grouped Data

E. Malinvaud, *Statistical Methods of Econometrics* (Chicago: Rand McNally, 1966), Chapter 8, section 2.

J. S. Cramer, "Efficient Grouping, Regression and Correlation in Engel Curve Analysis," *Journal of the American Statistical Association*, Vol. 59, March 1964, pp. 233–250.

9–3 Estimation When Some Observations Are Missing

A. A. Afifi and R. M. Elashoff, "Missing Observations in Multivariate Statistics II. Point Estimation in Simple Linear Regression," *Journal of the American Statistical Association*, Vol. 62, March 1967, pp. 10–29.
A. A. Afifi and R. M. Elashoff, "Missing Observations in Multivariate Statistics III. Large Sample Analysis of Simple Linear Regression," *Journal of the American Statistical Association*, Vol. 64, March 1969, pp. 337–358.
A. A. Afifi and R. M. Elashoff, "Missing Observations in Multivariate Statistics IV. A Note on Simple Linear Regression," *Journal of the American Statistical Association*, Vol. 64, March 1969, pp. 359–365.

Chapter 10 Multiple Regression

J. Johnston, *Econometric Methods* (New York: McGraw-Hill, 1963), Chapters 2 and 4.
K. A. Fox, *Intermediate Economic Statistics* (New York: Wiley, 1968), Chapters 7 and 13.
A. S. Goldberger, *Econometric Theory* (New York: Wiley, 1964), Chapter 4.
E. Malinvaud, *Statistical Methods of Econometrics* (Chicago: Rand McNally, 1966), Chapter 6 and Chapter 8, section 5.
J. B. Ramsey, "Tests for Specification Errors in Classical Linear Least-squares Regresssion Analysis," *Journal of the Royal Statistical Society*, Series B, Vol. 31, 1969, pp. 350–371.

Chapter 11 Formulation and Estimation of Special Models

11–1 Models with Binary Variables

J. Johnston, *Econometric Methods* (New York: McGraw-Hill, 1963), Chapter 8, section 4.
A. S. Goldberger, *Econometric Theory* (New York: Wiley, 1964), Chapter 5, sections 2 and 3.
H. Scheffe, *The Analysis of Variance* (New York: Wiley, 1959).

11–2 Models with Restricted Coefficients

A. S. Goldberger, *Econometric Theory* (New York: Wiley, 1964), Chapter 5, section 6.
L. G. Judge and T. Takayama, "Inequality Restrictions in Regression Analysis," *Journal of the American Statistical Association*, Vol. 61, March 1966, pp. 166–181.
H. Theil and A. S. Goldberger, "On Pure and Mixed Statistical Estimation in Econometrics," *International Econometric Review*, Vol. 2, January 1961, pp. 65–78.

11–3 Nonlinear Models

E. Malinvaud, *Statistical Methods of Econometrics* (Chicago: Rand McNally, 1966), Chapter 9.

G. E. P. Box and D. R. Cox, "An Analysis of Transformations," *Journal of the Royal Statistical Society*, Series B, Vol. 26, 1964, pp. 211–243.

11–4 Distributed Lag Models

E. Malinvaud, *Statistical Methods of Econometrics* (Chicago: Rand McNally, 1966), Chapter 15.

Z. Griliches, "Distributed Lags: A Survey," *Econometrica*, Vol. 35, January 1967, pp. 16–49.

A. Zellner and M. S. Geisel, "Analysis of Distributed Lag Models with Applications to Consumption Function Estimation," paper presented to the European Meeting of the Econometric Society, Amsterdam, September 1968 (forthcoming in *Econometrica*).

Chapter 12 Generalized Linear Regression Model and Its Applications

12–1 Generalized Linear Regression Model

A. S. Goldberger, *Econometric Theory* (New York: Wiley, 1964), Chapter 5, section 4.

J. Johnston, *Econometric Methods* (New York: McGraw-Hill, 1963), Chapter 7, section 3.

12–2 Pooling of Cross-section and Time-Series Data

T. D. Wallace and A. Hussain, "The Use of Error Components Models in Combining Cross-Section with Time-Series Data," *Econometrica*, Vol. 37, January 1969, pp. 55–72.

P. Balestra and M. Nerlove, "Pooling Cross-Section and Time-Series Data in the Estimation of a Dynamic Model: The Demand for Natural Gas," *Econometrica*, Vol. 34, July 1966, pp. 585–612.

12–3 Seemingly Unrelated Regressions

A. Zellner, "An Efficient Method of Estimating Seemingly Unrelated Regressions and Tests for Aggregation Bias," *Journal of the American Statistical Association*, Vol. 57, June 1962, pp. 348–368.

L. G. Telser, "Iterative Estimation of a Set of Linear Regression Equations," *Journal of the American Statistical Association*, Vol. 59, September 1964, pp. 842–862.

J. Kmenta and R. F. Gilbert, "Small Sample Properties of Alternative Estimators of Seemingly Unrelated Regressions," *Journal of the American Statistical Association*, Vol. 63, December 1968, pp. 1180–1200.

R. W. Parks, "Efficient Estimation of a System of Regression Equations When Distributions Are Both Serially and Contemporaneously Correlated," *Journal of the American Statistical Association*, Vol. 62, June 1967, pp. 500–509.

Chapter 13 Simultaneous Equation Systems

E. Malinvaud, *Statistical Methods of Econometrics* (Chicago: Rand McNally, 1966), Chapters 16–18.
C. F. Christ, *Econometric Models and Methods* (New York: Wiley, 1966), Chapters 8 and 9.
F. M. Fisher, *The Identification Problem in Econometrics* (New York: McGraw-Hill, 1966).
A. S. Goldberger, *Econometric Theory* (New York: Wiley, 1964), Chapter 7.
J. Johnston, *Econometric Methods* (New York: McGraw-Hill, 1963), Chapters 9 and 10.
P. R. Fisk, *Stochastically Dependent Equations* (New York: Hafner, 1967).
P. J. Dhrymes, *Econometrics* (New York: Harper & Row, 1970), Chapters 4 and 6–8.

13–6 Analysis of Dynamic Econometric Models

A. S. Goldberger, *Impact Multipliers and Dynamic Properties of the Klein-Goldberger Model* (Amsterdam: North-Holland, 1959).
I. Adelman and F. L. Adelman, "The Dynamic Properties of the Klein-Goldberger Model," *Econometrica*, Vol. 27, October 1959, pp. 597–625.
L. R. Klein, M. K. Evans, and M. Hartley, *Econometric Gaming* (New York: Macmillan, 1969).
M. K. Evans and L. R. Klein, *The Wharton Econometric Forecasting Model* (Philadelphia: University of Pennsylvania Press, 1967).
G. Fromm and P. Taubman, *Policy Simulations with an Econometric Model* (Washington: The Brookings Institution, 1968).
H. Theil and J. C. G. Boot, "The Final Form of Econometric Equation Systems," *Review of the International Statistical Institute*, Vol. 30, 1962, pp. 136–152.

Appendix

B Elements of Matrix Algebra

J. Johnston, *Econometric Methods* (New York: McGraw-Hill, 1963), Chapter 3.
A. S. Goldberger, *Econometric Theory* (New York: Wiley, 1964), Chapter 2.
G. Hadley, *Linear Algebra* (Reading, Mass.: Addison-Wesley, 1961).

C Computational Design for Least Squares Estimation

R. L. Anderson and R. A. Bancroft, *Statistical Theory in Research* (New York: McGraw-Hill, 1952), Chapter 15.
L. R. Klein, *Textbook of Econometrics* (Evanston, Ill.: Row, Peterson, 1953), Chapter 4.
P. S. Dwyer, *Linear Computations* (New York: Wiley, 1951).

Index